POWER AND IDEOLOGY IN EDUCATION

Edited and with an Introduction by
JEROME KARABEL and A.H. HALSEY

NEW YORK   OXFORD UNIVERSITY PRESS   1977

14 15 16 17 18 19

Copyright © 1977 by Oxford University Press, Inc.
Library of Congress Catalogue Card Number: 76-56677
Printed in the United States of America
on acid free paper

Preface

This book is the outcome of a dialogue that began in October, 1972, at Nuffield College, Oxford. Every week through the following winter and spring we talked over our common interest in the sociology of education. Sociology, we agreed, had lost a dominant orthodoxy in the 1960s. Structural functionalism had never, of course, claimed universal adherence, but it had been a central focus around which controversy and innovation had proceeded in a reasonably orderly fashion. In the last decade, however, order had given way to evident disarray. Nevertheless, our conversations also led us to agree, the field of educational research had in recent years advanced in many ways on both sides of the Atlantic.

Accompanying this progress, however, was a bewildering proliferation of writing, made all the more unmanageable by the failure of the educational research community to communicate effectively across national and disciplinary boundaries. Could a coherent map of the theoretical questions and the positions of current schools of thought with respect to them now be drawn? We thought it could, but we saw the attempt as an unusually difficult one, most likely to succeed in the form of a critical introductory essay linked to a range of examples of significant recent writing from the competing schools and styles of study. The introductory essay below and the readings that follow constitute, we hope, a useful survey and criticism of the present state of social scientific knowledge in education.

We have brought contrasting academic and personal backgrounds to this enterprise. Many students of the sociology of education will know that Halsey engaged in a similar effort more than fifteen years ago; he and Jean Floud wrote a review of the sociology of education in Europe and America for *Current Sociology* 7, no. 3 (1958), on the basis of which, with C.A. Anderson, they put together *Education, Economy, and Society* (New York: Free Press, 1961). He has been active in the field for a quarter of a century. Karabel, a relative newcomer, had become interested in educational research as an undergraduate at Harvard in the late 1960s and made his first contribution to educational research in a study of the problems of open admissions at the City University of New York that was conducted by the American

Council on Education's Office of Research in 1971-72. Halsey, though he had lived in and frequently visited the United States and had continued to remain abreast of the research of his American colleagues, was deeply rooted in the British sociological tradition; Karabel, despite a year in Oxford and an active interest in British and continental educational research, was most familiar with developments in the United States. We were, then, both a generation and an ocean apart, but we looked upon our differences as complementary rather than contradictory.

What had brought us together was not only a common sociological interest in education, but also a shared political vision of a classless educational system dedicated to the pursuit of what Raymond Williams has called a common culture. There were, to be sure, important differences between us. Halsey seeks the Christian pragmatic, piecemeal, and democratic road to socialism, claiming descent from the British radical tradition of R.H. Tawney and Richard Titmuss. Karabel has been deeply influenced by both the American New Left and continental Marxism and is accordingly more inclined to look to C. Wright Mills and Antonio Gramsci for theoretical and political insight. Halsey came of age politically in the late 1940s at the London School of Economics during the first post-war Labour government. Karabel's transition to political adulthood took place twenty years later during the Vietnam War and the student unrest of the late 1960s.

We have included this brief autobiographical note because of our belief that personal background is an important factor in shaping an interpretation of a field, its significant theories, and relevant methods. More particularly, it was our belief that one could not fully understand what had happened in educational research in the last fifteen years without inquiring into the social origins of the main currents of thought. It was thus natural for us to turn to the sociology of sociology and the sociology of knowledge for assistance in our attempt to comprehend recent developments in the field. We recognize, of course, that questions of validity and origin are logically distinct, but we believe nonetheless that knowledge of the social and historical context in which research takes place is indispensable to the task of assessing it critically. In pursuing this task, we cannot claim neutrality, though we have struggled for objectivity.

The sheer volume of relevant literature has made the problem of selecting articles a particularly difficult one. It was, we felt, appropriate to confine our choices to work that had appeared since the Floud-Halsey review, that is, to the 1960s and 1970s; this we have done, with the exception of a recent translation of extracts from Durkheim's *L'évolution pédagogique en France*, which was not previously available in English. But this still left us with selections to be made from hundreds of possible sources. Inevitably, there are glaring omissions of authors and studies of the highest quality. Moreover, we were concerned to illustrate the strands of theory and substantive study that appear, in our view, to be particularly significant. It follows that we have not included the thirty-seven "best pieces" to appear since 1960, even in our own judgment. We have instead tried to present the various theories and methods that have been characteristic of the last ten to fifteen years.

The selections will, we hope, serve not only to reveal the diversity of competing approaches in contemporary educational research, but also to identify some of the substantive problems that remain to be solved. In our attempt to lend order to recent work, we have felt it necessary to criticize the contributions of a number of prominent researchers in the field, including some of those whose work is contained in this volume. This is in itself somewhat unusual in the context of a collection of readings. Our occasionally severe criticism of some of our contributors should not, however, be interpreted to mean that we do not take their work very seriously indeed. On the contrary, we feel that even the work of those of our colleagues with whom we disagree most strongly serves to raise important issues.

The bulk of our work on this book was carried out between September, 1974, and December, 1975. Karabel was, for the greater part of this period, affiliated with the École Pratique des Hautes Études in Paris, while Halsey remained in Oxford. Throughout these months, we were in constant contact with each other, both in person and by post. Karabel drew up the first list of suggestions for articles to be included, and in recognition of this work we have reversed the normal alphabetical order in the listing of our editorship of the book. We each wrote three of the introductions to the six parts into which the book is divided and revised them in the light of the other's comments. Of the general introductory essay it must be said that it would have been different had either of us written it individually. With a prolonged series of exchanges before and between drafts, Karabel wrote the first and third drafts, and Halsey the second and fourth. The fifth and final draft, which was written after an additional series of exchanges, draws on the thinking of both of us. We have had our differences but we nonetheless feel that the final version reflects a reasonable synthesis of our sociological positions.

We could not have finished the book without the assistance of our colleagues, friends, and students in several countries. We would like in particular to thank M. Heller and the staff of the Bibliothèque de la Maison des Sciences de l'Homme, the Centre National de Recherche Scientifique, Nuffield College, and the Department of Social and Administrative Studies at the University of Oxford. Mrs. Louise Keegan undertook not only the bulk of the typing but also the correspondence with authors and publishers to obtain permissions to reprint. Mrs. Schuster-Bruce and Mr. Kenneth Demsky also helped to prepare the manuscript. For their comments at various stages in the project we would also like to thank: Basil Bernstein, William Burke, Mohammed Cherkaoui, Randall Collins, Paul DiMaggio, Marco d'Eramo, Alan Fox, Herbert Gintis, Alvin Gouldner, Anthony Heath, David Istance, Christopher Jencks, Henry Karabel, Denise Murphy, Jagoda Pauković, Michael S. Schudson, David Swartz, Michael Useem, and Godfrey Williams. Above all, we would like to express our appreciation to Martha Browne, who meticulously copy-edited the entire manuscript. Responsibility for any errors contained herein remains, as authors and editors are unfortunately obliged to observe, ours alone.

January, 1976   JEROME KARABEL
                                                              Cambridge, Massachusetts
                                                                           A.H. HALSEY
                                                                        Oxford, England

Contents

II EDUCATION AND SOCIAL SELECTION 167

III EDUCATION, "HUMAN CAPITAL," AND THE LABOR MARKET 307

VI SOCIAL TRANSFORMATION AND EDUCATIONAL CHANGE   551

POWER AND IDEOLOGY
IN EDUCATION

1. Educational Research: A Review and an Interpretation

JEROME KARABEL AND A. H. HALSEY

Over the last generation educational research has come from the humblest margins of the social sciences to occupy a central position in sociology, as well as to receive considerable attention from economists, historians, and anthropologists. A parallel growth in the use of research for educational policy-making has been no less evident. To attempt a general appraisal of this branch of scholarship and its applications is to embark on a formidable task, not only because of the sheer volume of the relevant literature, but also because we write at a time when the relation between thought and political action is one of unusual if not unprecedented contention. We must therefore disclaim at the outset any pretension either to encyclopedic coverage or to cosmic objectivity. Nonetheless we have ventured to put forward a general view and to criticize, both broadly and in detail, the authors whose work we have chosen as illustrative of what we take to be the significant developments of research since 1960. Finally, we have examined, with special reference to the work of Durkheim and Bernstein, the potential for a new synthesis in educational research.

To classify schools and traditions of thought is inevitably to oversimplify a complex social reality, but it is also indispensable to coherent exposition. Our remarks on the outstanding trends, theories, and preoccupations of recent work are therefore grouped under the following headings:

(1) Functionalist theories of education
(2) The economic theory of human capital
(3) Methodological empiricism (within which we attach a special importance to empirical studies of educational inequality)
(4) Conflict theories of education
(5) The interactionist tradition in educational research and the challenge of the "new" sociology of education

These categories, however, are no more than flags of convenience; they do not represent mutually exclusive definitions of legitimate theories and methods, so that both particular studies and individual scholars may be discussed in more than one of them. Our purpose in identifying more or less distinct schools of thought is not to classify individuals but rather to throw into sharper relief the diverse theoretical and empirical developments of the last fifteen years.

An assessment of educational research is, in any case, overdue. It has not been attempted on a comprehensive scale since 1958, when Jean Floud and A.H. Halsey reviewed the literature in an issue of *Current Sociology*.[1] We shall not recapitulate the history of the sociology of education as outlined in this earlier work except to note that, despite the brilliant exposition of the subject by Émile Durkheim in the early years of the present century and the inspiration to be found in the works of Marx[2] and Weber,[3] the achievements of this branch of the discipline before the 1950s were meager.

When social scientists invaded the realm of educational research on a large scale during the 1950s, however, their characteristic tone was one of buoyant optimism. The study of education had, in their view, been dominated by unrigorous and mediocre "educationalists," but that period, which was already drawing to a close, would belong to the prehistory of the discipline once the superiority of the social scientific approach became widely recognized. And indeed, the optimism of those who advocated treating educational institutions with the scientific precision and detachment befitting the study of any social organization seemed well grounded, for by 1958 one well-known review of the field was able to assemble an impressive list of one hundred works.[4]

Of all the social sciences it was sociology that was at the forefront of the movement to make the study of education a scientific endeavor. The relationship between sociology and education did not, to be sure, date from the postwar period; the founding of the American *Journal of Educational Sociology* in 1927 is but one example of a long-standing interest in uniting the two disciplines. Yet the articles appearing in the *Journal of Educational Sociology* reflected less the application of general sociological principles than the concerns

1. Floud and Halsey (1958). The reader edited by Halsey, Floud, and Anderson, *Education, Economy, and Society* (New York: Free Press, 1961), was based on this review of previous work.
2. For a summary essay on Marx see Brian Simon (1971).
3. A sample of some of Weber's writings on education and social stratification is available in Cosin (1972: 211–241). For a brief summary of Weber's early formulation of a typology of educational systems in relation to the power structure of society, see Halsey (1968).
4. This review of the literature, conducted under the auspices of the Russell Sage Foundation, was carried out by Brim (1958). Halsey (1959), in a review of this work, challenged the omission of Veblen's classic essay on the higher learning and suggested that the omissions "stemmed in part from (Brim's) obvious affinity to functionalism, which in its modern Parsonian form, places socialization and values rather than interests or the 'substratum' in the center of sociological analysis."

of a subject that considered itself more a branch of education than one of sociology. The institutional correlate of this self-conception was the employment of most educational sociologists in schools of education rather than in university departments of sociology. The problem-oriented, applied sociological outlook that was predominant in the subject and the low esteem accorded to schools of education together constituted a serious barrier to scientific respectability. The founding of the American journal *Sociology of Education* in 1963 may be seen as an attempt both to integrate the subject with the larger concerns of sociology and to benefit from the growing prestige of the parent discipline.

By the 1950s the prevailing orthodoxy in American sociology of education was structural functionalism. As formulated by Talcott Parsons it offered an emerging subject both an all-encompassing theoretical framework and a valuable conceptual guide for setting research priorities. When these were combined with the canons of scientific procedure, which sociologists of education planned to follow with the utmost rigor, an approach of seemingly unlimited possibilities had been developed. It would hardly seem an exaggeration to say that researchers in the field, armed with the dual weapons of structural functionalist theory and scientific method, envisaged few problems that would ultimately prove intractable.

There were, of course, sociologists of education who worked in other traditions. In Britain, for example, socialist influence on the choice of problems was strong before the war, and continued after it, in the long tradition of empirical inquiry by royal commissions and private investigators of public issues. A Fabian social democratic use of data from such inquiries was concentrated characteristically on the analysis of social inequalities of educational opportunity. Floud and Halsey (1958:171), who worked in this tradition of "political arithmetic," had explicit reservations about functionalism: "The structural functionalist is preoccupied with social integration based on shared values—that is with consensus—and he conducts his analysis solely in terms of the motivated actions of individuals. For him, therefore, education is a means of motivating individuals to behave in ways appropriate to maintain the society in a state of equilibrium. But this is a difficult notion to apply to developed especially industrialized societies, even if the notion of equilibrium is interpreted dynamically. They are dominated by social change, and 'consensus' and 'integration' can only be very loosely conceived with regard to them."[5]

---

5. However, their own approach (see Halsey et al. [1961:1–13]), which stressed the emergence of technological society, converged with functionalism at many points, and the use of a structural functionalist framework, strongly influenced by the Weberian concept of "structures of domination," was the basis of Halsey's analysis (1961:456–465) of the changing functions of universities in industrial societies.

Nonetheless, functionalism, with its distinguished leadership from such men as Parsons, Shils, Merton, and Lazarsfeld, remained dominant in the 1950s not only in America but also in France, Germany, Scandinavia, and Japan. The sociology of education reflected the larger empire of theoretical sociology. A considerable number of empirically minded researchers did, to be sure, continue to gather and analyze data untroubled by the lack of any overarching theoretical scheme, but their inquiries posed no challenge to the hegemony of the functionalist framework.

During the 1960s, when the theory of structural functionalism found itself at the center of controversy in sociology at large, it became inevitable that the debate would ultimately penetrate the sociology of education itself. The overall effects of this debate, which has been stimulated by the resurgence of various forms of Marxism, phenomenology, and interactionist theory in Europe and America, have been liberating, for the consensual elements in functionalism had proved, despite Merton's (1968:92–96) demonstration of a certain logical neutrality in its analyses of social phenomena,[6] to inhibit the raising of a number of crucial questions more easily treated by other approaches, both Marxist and non-Marxist, which focus on conflict. Yet the acrimony of the debate is not without its dangers, including, as Basil Bernstein (1974:145–159) has suggested, a proliferation of *approaches* to problems rather than *explanations* of them.

Controversy, for example between Marxists and functionalists in the United States, or over the "old" and "new" sociology of education in Britain, is now sufficiently intense to have created something of a crisis in educational research. We propose to try to make sense of recent and current debates by placing them in their social and historical context.[7] We shall focus on a few salient problems in educational research with the object of showing how an awareness of the social settings from which they emerged can contribute to a deeper understanding of them. In this way we hope not only to offer a rough map on which to place the leading current schools of thought but also to provide an added dimension to the necessary task of critical assessment. We shall attend

---

6. Merton's *Social Theory and Social Structure* (1968) is a classic source on functionalist theory.
7. Alvin Gouldner (1971:490), one of the founders of the sociology of sociology perspective, captures the essence of our intent when he demands that "sociologists must—at the very least—acquire the ingrained *habit* of viewing (their) own beliefs as (they) now view those held by others." This perspective, which is derived from the sociology of knowledge, has gained momentum in recent years and would seem particularly well suited to offer insight into the work of educational researchers, for few areas of social scientific investigation are more profoundly marked by their social context. Apart from Gouldner's (1968; 1971) own contributions to the sociology of sociology, we have found particularly helpful the writings of C. Wright Mills (1963) collected under the heading of "knowledge" in *Power, Politics and People* (see especially "The Professional Ideology of Social Pathologists") and his classic, *The Sociological Imagination* (1959). We have also found useful the research of Mannheim (1936; 1952), Marx and Engels (1947), Merton (1968), Anderson (1968), Ringer (1969), Kuhn (1970), Shils (1970), Friedrichs (1970), Mullins (1973), and a number of the studies reported in Tiryakian (1971).

in particular to functionalism, human capital, methodological empiricism, conflict theory, and "interpretative" sociology.

THE SOCIOLOGY OF EDUCATIONAL RESEARCH

The influx of social scientific researchers into education coincided with a period of enormous growth of public expenditure on schools and universities. Between 1950 and the end of the 1960s, educational expenditure in the member countries of the Organization for Economic Cooperation and Development increased at an average rate of more than 10 percent a year, which was double the rate of increase of gross national product and one-and-a-half times the rate of growth of total public expenditure. Student numbers rose concurrently: over 30 percent in primary education, almost 100 percent in secondary education, and 200 percent in tertiary education (Emmerij, 1974:61). The magnitude of this expansion was unprecedented, and it brought with it a number of problems. At the same time, educational systems everywhere had become arenas of political and social conflict, and it is therefore hardly surprising that governments gave increased priority to the funding of educational research.

Particularly in those countries whose institutions embody planning and welfare ideologies, there is also a widespread tradition of eagerness to base institutional reform on prior empirical inquiry. At the same time, both the supporters and the critics of the status quo, and not least members of the social science community, have been anxious to gain access to relevant information and to use it in order to offer policy recommendations, whether critical of current policy or offering "scientific" legitimation for it. Thus the involvement of members of the academy, particularly of sociologists and economists, is a familiar feature of the academic-governmental landscape: royal and presidential commissions, consultations, and the execution of government-commissioned studies are but the most conspicuous examples of the intimate relation prevailing between state policy-makers and a segment of the educational research community.

Man's attempts at understanding the world through the social sciences are more than a century old, but if the point is to change the world through the systematic application of the findings of research to public decision-making processes, the social sciences are new. And what, specifically, is new is the existence of an identifiable and organized social science community whose members are in contact with the government. Keynes's aphorism about the academic scribbler of yesteryear who stands behind the current theories of the practical politician is well known. The academic scribbler has since become an available expert. But it is only in the last generation that connections between government and social science have been strongly institutionalized. The social sciences are, in other words, caught up in a process of incorporation into the state apparatus, partly through their dependence on state funding, partly in their own right as the disciplinary bases of economic and social planning, and—most recently—partly through the emergence of a new style of administration which is potentially of immense importance: experimental public policy formation. Since World War II, governments everywhere have increasingly and explicitly accepted responsibility for the management of economic growth. The assimilation of economists was brought about by their capacity to generate consensus as to the means to that end and the method of measurement of progress towards its attainment. The still more recent arrival of the sociologist reflects a shift in emphasis on the part of governments towards concern with distribution as well as production, with social order as well as economic progress, with the quality of social life as well as the quantity of economic resources.

There is, however, a serious underlying problem. It is in the interests of established government to define the social sciences as apolitical and organized social science as, in effect, an extension of the civil service. On such a view, problems are essentially technical and the role of the social scientist is that of a handmaiden. Research strategies and priorities, from this perspective, are finally left in the hands of the government. Within this framework, the social sciences can lay no claim to independence.

Theoretically informed exchanges between social scientists and governments may well reveal that there are "social problems" that cannot be formulated adequately in terms approximating those of medical problems and in which the social scientist is defined, by analogy, as a skilled diagnostician. Such a model, apart from assuming that there is a social science theory to be applied in the same way that doctors apply medical theory, also takes it for granted that there is agreement about social ends just as there is consensus about the nature and desirability of good health. If there were such agreement on all social problems, there would be no need for politicians. In fact, the language of "social problems" may all too often disguise an underlying conflict of political and social interests. The historic role of the social scientist as critic of the social order must set limits to his incorporation into administration just as the maintenance of political democracy must set strict limits to his participation in the making of decisions.[8]

Government influence on the scope and shape of social science research may be exercised through control of the bulk of research funding.[9] Private

8. For an elaborated exposition of this view, see Halsey (1970).
9. Useem (1976a) and McCartney (1971) provide useful studies of this topic. McCartney (1970:32–33) reports that, in thirteen of fifteen areas of sociology, articles acknowledging financial support were much more likely to use statistical methods. This is indirect evidence suggesting that sponsors are more likely to accept projects proposing quantitative analysis of data, but direct evidence requires study of the funding process itself. Such a study would ideally place particular emphasis on the characteristics of rejected proposals and would investigate the factors determining whether a researcher even attempts to obtain funds.
The decision to allocate state funds often makes or breaks a given research project. In the sample studied by

philanthropy plays a minor part even in non-communist countries. State financial support flows in two main forms—through research councils and the general funding of state institutions of higher education and through direct contracting by government departments and agencies. In the former type of financing social scientists are directly involved in determining the principles and practices of allocation.[10] The question of how far priorities, problems, and methods reflect governmental interest and how far they reflect a social science interest therefore becomes a subtle one. In the case of direct commissioning by government it is reasonable to suppose that the priorities will lie in the direction of policy-oriented studies. In the case of private philanthropy it may be that funding flows more easily for the support of what is fashionable and congruent with the interests of socially dominant groups and the mass media.

The interest of government in educational research is apparent, but the empirical evidence is too undifferentiated to determine with any precision what *type* of educational research the state tends to sponsor and what *consequences* this funding pattern has on the development of the field. Yet the findings of the available studies give us reason to suspect that in educational research, as in other domains, the government will favor policy-oriented, quantitative studies. Similarly, it seems reasonable to suppose that if government priorities can influence the distribution of research within a *discipline,* then it is equally likely that the allocation of funds can affect the distribution of funds within a *sub-discipline*—in this case, the sociology of education. There is, as we have already suggested, a multitudinous array of approaches vying for influence within educational research, and the absence of an intellectual orthodoxy or "paradigm" governing research priorities makes the field particularly vulnerable to external pressure. Among these pressures the role of government agencies obviously looms large.

State allocation of research monies does not, of course, exhaust the ways in which social context influences the development of educational research. From our own experiences as researchers, we would be among the first to admit that both our choice of problems and our manner of treating them have been influenced, independent of the question of funding, by our presence in a given social setting and in particular by our personal values. Yet to judge from that same experience, it would seem plausible to suggest that social factors are more relevant to questions of emphasis and neglect than to questions of validity and

---

Useem (1976a) nearly one-half of the social scientists whose proposals were rejected dropped their projects altogether.

10. Where social science applications are judged by social scientists an element of subtlety is introduced into the question of state allocation of research funds. Nevertheless, it remains possible that the scholars who serve on committees reviewing research proposals are themselves selected so as to distribute funds in a manner roughly corresponding to state priorities. There is little empirical evidence on the characteristics of such social scientists. One of the few available studies (Useem, 1976b) concludes that their own research is more quantitative and policy-oriented than that of their colleagues of similar professional standing.

error. It follows from this that social context perhaps exerts its most profound influence on the development of educational research in its capacity to lead us to be selectively inattentive to problems that are nonetheless real.

Alvin Gouldner, in his call for a reflexive sociology (1971:498), has asserted the paradox *"that those who supply the greatest resources for the institutional development of sociology are precisely those who most distort its quest for knowledge"* (italics his). Whether this proposition is true or false (and its exploration is one of the themes of this essay) we would not ourselves suggest that government funding in Western Europe or America is the sole, or even perhaps the most significant, external influence on educational research. Nor would we intend to imply that to place a school of thought socially is thereby to accomplish the task of substantive criticism. Assessment of the validity of ideas remains a vital enterprise independent of any attempt to trace their origins. An analysis of the social origins of the various approaches to education research, however, may direct our attention toward those elements of each perspective that are particularly susceptible to distortion from external sources. Further, if the fates of schools of thought are, as we believe, contingent not only upon their intellectual stature, but also upon the extent to which they correspond to changes in the surrounding political and cultural context, then an exploration of the social setting of educational research becomes indispensable to an understanding of recent developments in the field. As we keep these considerations in mind, the case of the functionalist theory of education offers a promising place to begin our analysis.

FUNCTIONALISM

After the Second World War, the United States and the Soviet Union became engaged in a "cold war," a crucial component of which was the "battle of production." Could the Western powers, emerging from the dislocations of depression and war, surpass the impressive material and technological progress of their Soviet rival? The development of nuclear weapons had provided dramatic evidence that technological superiority could be converted into military dominance. Both countries therefore looked to their systems of education to produce an adequate flow of scientists and engineers, and this added to the traditional concern with "human resources," which, at least in America, dated from the Depression. In 1949, the four major American national research councils appointed a Commission on Human Resources and Advanced Training. The Commission, directed by Dael Wolfle, sponsored a widely influential study, *America's Resources of Specialized Talent,* which appeared in 1954. In a statement characteristic of the period, Wolfle warned that "survival itself may depend on making the most effective use of the nation's intellectual resources" (quoted in Husén, 1974:40). Later but similarly in Britain, the Robbins Report on Higher Education, which appeared in 1963, was at pains to stress the importance of educating potential talent and to attack traditionally entrenched conceptions of a limited pool of educable ability.

This concern with the preservation of human resources marked the particular variety of functionalist theory that was most popular in educational research in the 1950s.[11] Thus Burton Clark, a prominent contributor to the sociology of education in America, in 1962 published a textbook under the title *Educating the Expert Society* in which he put forward a lucid version of what might be called technological functionalism. Emphasizing the rapidity of technological change, Clark declared that, "our age demands army upon army of skilled technicians and professional experts, and to the task of preparing these men the educational system is increasingly dedicated" (1962:3). Seen in this light, the expansion and the increasing differentiation of the educational system were inevitable outcomes of technologically determined changes in occupational structure requiring ever more intricate skills. At the same time, the drive for educational efficiency was congruent with the traditional socialist critique of inequality of educational opportunity between classes. At the level of policy Clark's functional analysis supported a program of transformation of the schools both to promote equal opportunity at home and to turn back "the expanding thrust of totalitarianism abroad" (1962:1).

Clark's formulation seems in retrospect to reflect some of the underlying ideological components of the technological functionalism which became fashionable after Russia launched Sputnik in 1957.

> Greater schooling for greater numbers also *has brought with it* and *evidently implies,* a greater practicality in what the schools teach and what they do for students. The existence of children of diverse ability *calls forth* the comprehensive school, or the multischool comprehensive structure, within which some students receive a broad general education but others take primarily a technical or commercial training. In short, increased quantity *means* greater vocationalism . . . Sorting *must* take place at some point in the education structure. If, at that level, it does not take place at the door, it *must* occur inside the doors, in the classroom and counseling office. . .
>
> Democracy encourages aspiration, and generous admission allows the student to carry his hopes into the school or now principally the college. But there his desires run into the standards *necessary* for the integrity of programs and the training of competent workers. The college offers the opportunity to try, but the student's own ability and his accumulative record of performance finally *insist* that he be sorted out . . .
> (1962:79–80; italics ours)

What is most striking about these passages is the necessitous implication of the italicized phrases. At the same time, since the description offered seemed to

---

11. For an introduction to functional analysis, see the articles by Marion J. Levy and Francesca M. Cancian in *The International Encyclopedia of the Social Sciences* (1968).

fit both modern America and modern Russia (Clark, 1962:45–57), it served to validate some general applicability of technological functionalism. But the differences between these countries in economics, politics, and education surely also reflect specifically different "structures of domination," as Weber would have put it. The use of the language of necessity implies that there are no alternatives to present structures and thus has the effect of legitimating the status quo and of diverting attention from the possibility at least of functional alternatives (see Merton, 1968:86–91).

In Britain in the 1950s a theory of "technological society" also provided the dominant framework for educational research. The essence of the theory was that technical change in the system of production provided the impetus for educational change, though there was also, as in the United States, some emphasis on the active role of education through its contribution to research and innovation. Where the characteristic outlooks of researchers in the two countries differed was mainly in the varying emphasis on "conflict and friction in the movement towards a technological society" (Halsey et al., 1961:2) and in the reluctance in Britain to embrace a functionalist theory of social change (Floud and Halsey, 1958:173). There was in any case an inherently reformist aspect of the theory of "technological society," which in the course of its natural development would eliminate onerous manual work while simultaneously establishing equal opportunity through the abolition of obsolete class-based ascription. The *locus classicus* of this kind of theory is in the work of the nineteenth-century Cambridge economist Alfred Marshall.[12] Marshall's theory of educational embourgeoisement, modified by T.H. Marshall's analysis (1965:71–134) of the rise of the welfare state as a principle of citizenship exercising increasing countervailing power against the force of class stratification, strongly supported the possibility of realizing a welfare society in which equality and liberty would be optimally balanced.

British researchers in education were as preoccupied with "wastage" and "dysfunctions" as their American colleagues but perhaps more animated by the egalitarian concerns of a country with a long-established and politically organized Labour movement. Nevertheless, these egalitarian sentiments were linked to concern for efficiency in education so as to preserve "human resources." The attack by British sociologists on inequality of educational opportunity was not only that it was unfair, but also that it was inefficient. And the historical context in which arguments about "matching ability and opportunity" (Floud and Halsey 1961:80) were put forward was one of political and ideological struggle over the structure of British education. As Bernstein put it in a recent essay on the history of the sociology of education in Britain, "*it is*

---

12. For a discussion of this element in Marshallian theory, see Halsey (1975).

important to realise that Floud and Halsey used the manpower and equality argument as a double-barrelled weapon to bring about change in the procedures of selection and the organizational structure of schools" (1974:152, italics his).

The characteristic methodology of the British school of sociology of education was "political arithmetic"—calculating the chances of reaching various stages in the educational process for children of different class origins. This approach derived from the mobility studies carried out under the direction of D.V. Glass at the London School of Economics and drew its larger framework from research in the area of social stratification. At the time when the studies were being carried out, the sociology of education was not a recognized subdiscipline in British universities, and it is likely that it was less the implicit structural-functionalist framework than the already-established respectability of the study of social stratification that served to legitimate the sociological study of educational institutions. In either case, however, given that education was held in poor repute as a field of research, the *institutionalization* of the sociological study of education was greatly facilitated by the prestige derived from borrowing theories, procedures, and substantive concerns from the larger and more respected fields of stratification and general sociology.[13]

Functionalist analysis is now in wide disrepute. In the educational field it has been criticized for exaggerating the role of technology and underestimating the importance of conflict and ideology (Collins, 1971, and Bowles and Gintis, 1972). The criticism has also been made that this framework, with its emphasis on selection and technical training, has led to a neglect of the *content* of the educational process (Young, 1971a). Yet during the period of its greatest influence functionalism undoubtedly advanced the sociological study of education by emphasizing connections between education and other major institutions such as the economy and the polity. A number of studies deriving from one form of functionalism or another (Parsons, 1959; Clark, 1960; Turner, 1960; Trow, 1961) are among the most respected achievements of educational research, and the attention given by functionalist analysis to the selective functions of educational institutions led to the accumulation of data that have proved extremely useful to researchers whether or not they adhere to a functionalist paradigm.

Reflecting the spirit of the period in which it came to prominence, functionalist theory, particularly as formulated by American scholars, placed undue emphasis on consensus and equilibrium in society. Technological functionalism also served to justify educational growth in the post-war period. Yet, if sociology provided a convincing theoretical rationale for the expansion and differentiation

---

13. The struggle to institutionalize a discipline will obviously influence its development, and the sociology of education deserves historical study from this point of view. For some interesting remarks on the British case in its formative period after World War II, see Bernstein (1974).

of education, it was unable to answer the economic question with which policy-makers were much concerned, namely, whether educational investment was worthwhile. This was a question for economists, and their response, which took the form of the theory of human capital, exerted a considerable influence not only in the academy but also on the development of educational systems throughout the world.

HUMAN CAPITAL THEORY

The rate of growth of educational systems after World War II dwarfed even the earlier lurch of European societies in the nineteenth century into universal primary education. In the United States, postwar expansion brought literally millions of students into higher education. Popular demand for expansion was in part motivated by the high rate of return to individuals who received extended schooling. But expansion was expensive and, to a variable but large degree, subsidized in most countries from the public purse. The question of the efficiency of these massive expenditures therefore arose and, at least in the United States, took on an added urgency in the context of international competition with the Soviet Union for military and economic supremacy.

Delivered in the context of public concern about the preservation of "human resources," Theodore W. Schultz's 1960 Presidential Address to the American Economic Association on the theme "Investment in Human Capital" not surprisingly evoked an enthusiastic response. His message was a simple one: the process of acquiring skills and knowledge through education was not to be viewed as a form of consumption, but rather as a productive investment. "By investing in themselves, people can enlarge the range of choice available to them. It is the one way free men can enhance their welfare" (1961:2). As Schultz made clear in the remainder of his address, investment in human capital not only increases individual productivity, but, in so doing, also lays the technical base of the type of labor force necessary for rapid economic growth.

These ideas were not new. We have already mentioned their place in the work of Alfred Marshall, and they can be traced to earlier nineteenth-century economists (if not to Adam Smith). They are, moreover, susceptible to a variety of political interpretations. But the tenor of Schultz's formulation was particularly apt for the social and political climate of the times, especially in the United States.[14] For the businessman there was the attractive appeal of

14. It is interesting to speculate why human capital theory flourished in the United States. The cultural setting, in which the utilitarian values of the bourgeoisie are uncontested either by the remains of an aristocratic ethos (as in England) or by the communitarian values of a mass working-class movement, is doubtless one factor. Another important element of any adequate explanation would be the scale of the American expansion of higher education as compared with that of Western Europe.

education as investment. For university teachers and researchers there was an apparently scientific justification for the expansion of their activity. For some politicians, at least, there was support for democratization of access to education, and for the "consumers" of education there was the prospect of widening opportunities for well-paid jobs. Yet because of the magnitude of finance involved and the suspicion that there might be more direct and hence more efficient ways of promoting economic growth, a clear-cut demonstration of the value of investment in education was needed.

The theory of human capital was consonant with the forms of technological functionalism which attracted many sociologists in the 1950s. Both theories stress the technical function of education and emphasize the efficient use of human resources. A concern with the elimination of waste also supports the liberal notion of equality of opportunity. For the technological functionalist there is the enemy of ascription and for the human capitalist the blight of under-investment. Both formulations justify the greater rewards accruing to the educated as incentives necessary to encourage extended study. Thus in their formulation of the functionalist theory of stratification Davis and Moore (1945:244) asserted that "a medical education is so burdensome and expensive that virtually none would undertake it if the M.D. did not carry a reward commensurate with the sacrifice"; for Schultz (1968:285), education can admittedly be considered a consumption good, but the benefit deriving therefrom is "undoubtedly small, for school days entail much hard work and long hours." But what must further be remarked about the theory of human capital is the direct appeal to pro-capitalist ideological sentiment that resides in its insistence that the worker is a *holder of capital* (as embodied in his skills and knowledge) and that he has the *capacity to invest* (in himself). Thus in a single bold conceptual stroke the *wage-earner,* who holds no property and controls neither the process nor the product of his labor, is transformed into a *capitalist.*

We cannot be surprised, then, that a doctrine reaffirming the American way of life and offering quantitative justification for vast public expenditure on education should receive generous sponsorship in the United States. Government agencies, private foundations, and such international organizations as the World Bank, the International Monetary Fund, and the Organization for Economic Cooperation and Development were actively involved in the promotion of the theory of human capital.[15] The compatibility of the theory with the ideology of liberal progressivism and its ability to align itself with the increasingly powerful

---

15. The role of financial support in the institutionalization of a discipline or a school of thought goes beyond the subsidizing of individual studies in universities. In the case of human capital, the theory was widely diffused through sponsored publications, international conferences, and consultations with leading educational policy-makers. The role of such sponsored support in the institutionalization of an approach in the social sciences is worthy of careful study.

interests of the higher education industry were doubtless factors in its attractiveness to the holders of research funds, quite apart from its intrinsic merits as an intellectual tool of analysis and its precise quantitative methods.

The scientific value of the theory of human capital is much disputed. Critics frequently point to one of its unrealistic assumptions—that the perfect competition prevailing in labor markets ensures that greater earnings reflect greater productivity.[16] Wages, they point out, are not so determined in the real world. This is not to say that the supply side of the wage and employment process is irrelevant; even an economist as critical of human capital as Bluestone (1972:46–47) admits that the characteristics of workers in a given industry affect that industry's wage scale. But many other factors besides worker characteristics determine wages: among them are unionization, the existence of a minimum wage, traditions of status, customary differentials, and "dual labor markets."[17] Furthermore, the wages of state employees are directly adminis-tered. Their market may be influenced by wages in the private sector, but they are not the outcome of perfect competition. Finally, it is essential not to lose sight of the fact that the degree of inequality of wages prevailing at any given historical moment is in part a result of struggles between social classes over the distribution of the national income.

Nevertheless, this does not undermine the proposition that an individual may find it advantageous to invest in an education for himself and that a society may also find it advantageous. It is true, of course, that the individual who profits from educational investment may do so in part because of selective mechanisms prevalent in his society, but a society may find that its rate of growth depends to some extent on the level of educational attainment of its workers. The actual level and type of educational investment that are optimal for economic growth is a matter of complex debate, but the idea that there is a social rate of return to education is not intrinsically unsound.

Despite its theoretical and empirical shortcomings, the influence of the human capital approach on social policy extended beyond the advanced capitalist countries into the nations of the Third World. The idea of using the theory of human capital in underdeveloped countries "to help them achieve economic growth" was adumbrated by Schultz's Presidential Address (1961:15). Struck by the rapid economic recovery of countries that had suffered massive destruction of physical capital during World War II, Schultz suggested that the "economic miracle" had been due, in no small part, to the reservoir of human capital that remained after the war. His conclusion was that underdeveloped countries,

16. Among the critical works are Bluestone (1972), Thurow (1972), Piore (1973), Taubman and Wales (1973), Carter and Carnoy (1974), and Bowles and Gintis (1975a).
17. See Doeringer and Piore (1971), Gordon (1971), and Reich et al. (1973) for detailed discussions of "dual labor markets." Some interesting empirical evidence is presented in Bluestone et al. (1975).

lacking in "the knowledge and skills required to take on and use efficiently the superior techniques of production," should be provided with aid designed to increase the quality of their human capital (1961:15–16).

Organizations such as the World Bank and the Ford Foundation responded to Schultz's appeal by providing funds for economists of education to spread the gospel of human capital among the nations of Asia, Africa, and Latin America. There was, to be sure, some truth in the theory, and the socialist countries of the Third World were equally concerned to organize their educational systems so as to promote economic growth (see Bastid, 1970, and Carnoy and Werthein, 1977). But the appeal of human capital theory to capitalist institutions such as the International Monetary Fund and the World Bank resided substantially in the comforting ideological character of its message. The nations of the Third World, the theory suggested, were poor not because of the structure of international economic relations, but because of internal characteristics—most notably their lack of human capital. As with the poor within the advanced countries, nothing in the situation of the Third World countries called for radical, structural change; development was possible if only they would improve the quality of their woefully inadequate human resources. Attention was thus deflected from structural variables onto individuals.[18] Application of this theoretical framework led to diverse and often unsuccessful results. For example, a study of Ghana by Philip Foster (1965) shows that the active sponsorship of technical and vocational education evoked little popular response because the populace, apparently more aware of the actual structure of job opportunities in Ghana than foreign economists, recognized that the exchange sector was simply too small to absorb very many graduates.

Virtually uncontested when it came into prominence in the early 1960s, the theory of human capital was under vigorous assault a decade later.[19] Discredited in the eyes of many by policy failures both in the American "war on poverty" and in the attempts to promote economic growth in the Third World, the human capital approach, though still retaining the loyalties of intelligent and articulate defenders,[20] no longer seemed to provide an adequate framework for understanding the relationship between education and the economy. And once

18. Bluestone (1972), in an analysis of the consequences of the theory of human capital on government strategies to fight poverty in the 1960s, points out that the manpower training approach favored by such economists as Schultz did not address itself to a crucial underlying problem—that the incomes attached to the low-paying jobs occupied by the substantial proportion of poor people who work full-time remain the same regardless of the human capital characteristics of the individuals holding them. Human capital theorists tend to ignore the structural sources of poverty. For a functionalist argument that the workings of the American economy depend on the existence of millions of people who, whether unemployed or working in low-wage jobs, are condemned to poverty, see Gans (1972).
19. See note 17 above.
20. See Blaug (1972) and Layard and Psacharopoulos (1974) for recent defenses of the human capital approach.

under attack, human capitalists found themselves in a difficult position, for their input-output models had never offered insight into what was going on in the "black box" of education that would explain its correlation with earnings. This inattention to the education *process* was not unique to human capitalists.[21] It was also characteristic of the approach favored by perhaps more educational researchers than any other: that of methodological empiricism. It is to this highly influential school of thought that we will now turn.

METHODOLOGICAL EMPIRICISM AND THE DEBATE OVER INEQUALITY

Although we now focus our attention on a branch of sociology that is defined in terms of its method, we are, at the same time, concerned substantively with the problem of inequality. While by no means identical, the method and the substance are closely linked in postwar educational research. In reviewing their development, we refer particularly to the works of Duncan, Coleman, Jencks, and their associates in America and to the "action-research" program in the British educational priority areas (Halsey, 1972). These authors and studies, however, are taken as illustrative of a larger body of work including that of Sewell in America, Boudon in France, Husén in Sweden, J.W.B. Douglas in Britain, and many others.

The debate over inequality has been at the center of political conflict in this century with respect to class and more recently with respect to race and sex. Particularly since World War II, with the spread of egalitarian ideologies, popular demand for equal educational opportunity has intensified. On the theoretical level, the debate has received new vigor from Marxist and other forms of conflict theory, to which we turn in the next section. Methodologically, research has developed in two directions. On the one hand, much energy and many of the significant results have taken the form of empirical, usually quantitative, studies of the role of education in reducing or maintaining structures of inequality that coexist with increasingly widespread egalitarian ideologies. On the other hand, there has been the development of action-research in the form of quasi-experiments, in most cases conducted under governmental auspices. This latter type of development raises in a sharp form the issue of the relation between government and social science to which we have referred. But much of the quantitative work has also been directly funded by government in the service of policy interests.

There are, of course, other forms of methodological empiricism, including the politically and morally committed work of such writers as D.V. Glass in Britain or Christopher Jencks in America and also including the high methodological sophistication of, for example, Keith Hope in Britain or O.D. Duncan in

21. The neglect of the content of education by sociologists was noticed and regretted in the 1961 reader by Halsey, Floud, and Anderson (1961:10).

America. Nevertheless, when the emphasis is on neutrality and the method is numerical, methodological empiricism is well adapted to the interests of administration, for it leaves *ends* in the hands of policy-makers and concentrates the efforts of the social scientist on the *means* by which these ends may be attained (Gouldner, 1971).[22]

We have earlier suggested that the influence of government funding on the character of educational research is likely to be in the direction of policy-oriented, quantitative studies.[23] Yet it is important not to overestimate the extent to which the high repute of methodological empiricism is a consequence of government funding. For one thing, mathematically informed analysis is in part an outcome of intellectual challenges intrinsic to the social sciences themselves. For another, a suspicion of theory as metaphysical and a preference for positivistic methodology is deeply rooted in Anglo-Saxon culture (Anderson, 1968) and pervades the history of the social sciences in Great Britain and the United States. For these reasons alone, therefore, the preeminence of methodological empiricism in educational research clearly has sources of social support that are quite independent of the source of research funds. At the same time, it would be naive not to recognize that state patronage has contributed to promoting atheoretical forms of methodological empiricism and has given less encouragement to other approaches.

The rise of methodological empiricism within the sociology of education may also be seen as a response to its simultaneous association with the poorly esteemed fields of education and sociology. A highly technical style of research was well suited to the needs of a discipline much concerned with showing that it, too, could be rigorous.[24] In their eagerness to establish their scientific

---

22. Despite our debt to Gouldner (1971:445), our use of the term "methodological empiricism" differs from his in that we do not wish to imply that in methodological empiricist studies there is typically "a neglect of *substantive* concepts and assumptions concerning specifically human behavior and social relations" (italics his). Nor do we wish to imply that government agencies are wholly dedicated to encouraging the social science community to produce work at the highest level of quantitative sophistication. Indeed, the "Royal Commission method" that is so quintessentially part of the welfare state tradition is often criticized by social scientists for its failure to use the most advanced methods of social science in assembling and analyzing evidence. In some ways, our concept of "methodological empiricism" borrows more from C. Wright Mills's (1959:50–75) critique of "abstracted empiricism" than from Gouldner. Within the framework of abstracted empiricism, writes Mills (1959:57), "the kinds of problems that will be taken up and the way in which they are formulated are quite severely limited by The Scientific Method."
23. Williamson (1974:6–7), in discussing the social democratic tradition of "political arithmetic" in the British sociology of education, points to its "pragmatism" as one of its distinctive features. He sees such writers as J.W.B. Douglas and A.H. Halsey as having had a close relationship with political decision-makers and as therefore having been pressed "to formulate their work and writing in such a way that some kind of political or policy action can flow from it." And, as Williamson notes, "a great deal of the work which makes up the old sociology has been to a greater or lesser degree sponsored" by official and semi-official agencies.
24. Another factor that contributed to the prominence of methodological empiricism was that it provided sociology with a standardized approach to social inquiry in a period in which sociological research was becoming a mass enterprise. In educational research, many sociologists of education had found the dominant functionalist theory of little assistance in guiding their own investigations; with the growth of the

credentials, methodological empiricists sometimes tended to confuse the empirical with the statistical, and frequently neglected those problems that did not readily lend themselves to quantification. Yet despite the narrowness of its approach, methodological empiricism has made a considerable contribution to the advancement of educational research, especially on the problem of schooling and social inequality.

(a) Blau and Duncan, *The American Occupational Structure*

One of the most influential studies carried out in the methodological empiricist tradition—and one that addressed itself to important substantive as well as methodological issues—was Blau and Duncan's book *The American Occupational Structure* (1967). Primarily concerned with the question of occupational mobility, the study included considerable material on the role of education in the intergenerational transmission of inequality. Its importance resided not only in its substantive findings but also in its methodological innovations. In particular, an imaginative use of path analysis, which Duncan had introduced to the sociological community in a famous 1966 article in the *American Journal of Sociology,* has powerfully influenced subsequent research in the sociology of education.

Blau and Duncan's statistical methods have been used within a wider theoretical framework of evolutionary functionalism. In its Parsonsian form this theory postulates a general movement in industrial societies from 'particularism' to 'universalism' with a correlative movement from 'ascription' to 'achievement'. In the final chapter of their book Blau and Duncan conclude that there is indeed "a fundamental trend towards expanding universalism (which) characterizes industrial society" (Blau and Duncan, 1967:429). A careful look at the data, however, brings this conclusion seriously into question. If the postulated movement were taking place there should be a diminishing correlation over time between parental and filial occupational status. Blau and Duncan's correlations with respect to total mobility and using four age cohorts were, however, .384, .388, .377, and .380, moving from the oldest to the youngest. Similarly, the correlation of the son's education with the status of his first job would be expected to increase over time with the waning of ascription and the waxing of achievement. These correlations in fact fluctuate between .557 and .554 for the

---

legitimacy of methodological empiricism, they could dispense with theory and get down to the serious business of "getting the facts." During this same period, what C. Wright Mills (1959:101–118) has called a "bureaucratic ethos" grew up in the sociological community; the state-sponsored research institutes that embodied it deeply troubled him, for "they provide employment for semi-skilled technicians on a scale and in a manner not known before; they offer to them careers having the security of the older academic life but not requiring the older sort of individual accomplishment" (1959:56). One may not fully subscribe to Mills's rather harsh assessment of the consequences of what he referred to as "abstracted empiricism," but the observation that the new research style served the needs of an expanding profession remains a perceptive one.

two oldest cohorts and .532 and .574 for the youngest (1967:178). The lack of any discernible pattern in these figures would seem to cast considerable doubt on the thesis of a trend toward universalism.

Another serious problem with Blau and Duncan's data, especially with respect to the Parsonsian theory of a movement from ascription to achievement, is that they do not permit us to measure how much occupational mobility occurs irrespective of changes in the occupational structure, i.e., to distinguish between total mobility and exchange mobility. The correlations presented above conflate exchange mobility with the consequences of a well-known movement in occupational structure that has replaced traditional manual with modern technical occupations. Unless and until a measure of exchange mobility is established we cannot be clear about trends towards 'achievement' as characteristics of modern society.[25]

Alternative evidence for the trend from ascription to achievement is provided by Blau and Duncan in their demonstration that family background has no significant effect on occupational status independent of educational attainment. On the basis of path analysis they conclude that "superior status cannot any more be directly inherited but must be legitimated by actual achievements that are socially acknowledged" (1967:430). This is an important finding, but it does not dispose of the problem. If, as Bourdieu (1973) and other writers suggest, the inheritance of status in modern societies takes place through the transmission of 'cultural capital', then the distinction between ascription and achievement becomes a misleading one. With the decline of the family firm, the privileged no longer reproduce their positions solely through property but also through the acquisition of superior education for their children. Rather than describing this process as heightened universalism it would seem more accurate to view it as a new mechanism performing the old function of social reproduction. Social inheritance, whether through the transmission of property or through the transmission of cultural capital, is still social inheritance.[26]

(b) The Coleman Report

Blau and Duncan's study represents the academic pole of educational research in the tradition of methodological empiricism. For an example of a more directly

25. In his forthcoming contribution to the volume reporting on the British social mobility study of 1972, Hope has produced a method of measuring exchange mobility on the basis of which he shows no trend towards greater fluidity or openness. His father-son correlations for different cohorts within the 1972 sample have no secular direction.
26. See Crowder (1974) for a general critique of Duncan's research on social stratification. Another group of researchers who have done important work on education in the tradition of methodological empiricism has been centered around William Sewell at the University of Wisconsin (see Sewell and Shah, 1967; Sewell, 1971; Sewell and Hauser, 1975). Haller and Portes (1973) provide a lucid discussion of the differences, which may look rather minor to an outsider, between the Duncan approach and the more social-psychological Sewell approach. For the major work of the Duncan school specifically concerned with education, see Duncan et al. (1975).

policy-oriented work we may turn to James Coleman's *Equality of Educational Opportunity* (1966).[27] This study was a response to Section 402 of the Civil Rights Act of 1964, which ordered the Commissioner for Education to "conduct a survey and make a report to the President and the Congress, within two years of the enactment of this title, concerning the lack of availability of equal educational opportunities for individuals by reasons of race, color, religion, or national origin in public educational institutions at all levels in the United States." It was widely expected that the study would show glaring inequalities between black and white schools and that differential scholastic achievement by race could be substantially explained by these differences. The Congressmen who sponsored the legislation hoped not only to document these differences in order to legitimate massive Federal intervention in ghetto schools, but also to determine which school characteristics could be most effectively changed in order to improve academic achievement. In a period in which riots in black ghettos threatened to unravel the social fabric of American life, continuing inequality of educational opportunity was widely held to be intolerable, and the Coleman study was designed to help bring it to an end.

Coleman's findings, most notably that black and white school characteristics were surprisingly equal and that school facilities seemed to have relatively little effect on student achievement, are now familiar and so, also, is the heated political and intellectual controversy that ensued.[28] Two features of the study and its aftermath are especially worth noting here. On the one hand, the survey was conducted in terms of an "official definition" of the problem of educational opportunity; on the other, a new academic definition of the problem was afterwards formulated by Coleman himself. The Congressmen who commissioned the survey suspected that ghetto schools had suffered from inadequate expenditures and their preoccupation with this issue meant that the survey design reflected the concerns of policy-makers rather than researchers. There were thus very little data either on the internal workings of schools or on the components of "family background." For this, the collection of qualitative data, preferably longitudinal, on interaction in the school and in the family would have been necessary. Given the unexpected result that the distribution of material resources in the education system itself was fairly equal, the structure of the survey did not permit adequate explanation of inequalities of performance between classes and races despite the imaginative analyses of those quantifiable variables that had been included.

27. The British equivalent of the Coleman study, and one that has a remarkably similar flavor, is the Plowden Report (Central Advisory Council for Education, 1967).
28. See, for example, *Harvard Educational Review*'s (Winter 1968) special issue on "Equal Educational Opportunity" and the re-analyses of the Coleman data reported in Mosteller and Moynihan (1972). Hodgson (1973) provides an illuminating journalistic account of the debate in the United States over schooling and inequality.

Before turning to Coleman's redefinition of the problem we must note that his data led him to the conclusion that family background was much more important than school characteristics in explaining differential achievement among school children. This finding permitted an interpretation in terms of the theory of cultural deprivation of ghetto families, a formulation that gave apparent scientific approval to widespread commonsensical belief and that was to guide Federal policy in later years.[29] Yet the conclusion that families rather than schools are responsible for relative failure does not necessarily follow from the data. For there may be something characteristic of *all* the schools that tends to inhibit the academic achievement of poor and black children; the fact that differences between schools fail to account for much variation would be decisive only if the schools did in fact differ significantly among themselves. That the workings of the schools themselves may be a source of inequality of educational opportunity is suggested by one of Coleman's findings: the difference between minority and majority children *increases* with time spent in school. It seems likely, then, that schools at least *reinforce* the inferior position of disadvantaged children with respect to educational opportunity. In any case, the core of what goes on in school can only be grasped by careful observation of the content and process of education, and about these Coleman had, of necessity, little to say.

Even within the constrictions of the "official definition" of the problem of educational inequality the findings of the Coleman Report constituted an important advance over previous research. They showed the inadequacy of attending to the most superficial and visible aspects of schools and therefore discredited some of the cruder strategies of educational reform. But what was more important was that Coleman's inquiry into the problem of inequality of educational opportunity led him to make a crucial distinction between the relatively passive notion of equality of opportunity and the more active one of equality of results (Coleman, 1968).[30] It no longer sufficed simply to offer individual children exposure to the schools; what was demanded was the active involvement of the school in the provision of equality of outcomes for identifiable social groups. This formulation of the question of equality of educational opportunity, with its insistence on the primacy of substance rather than procedure and of the group rather than the individual, marked a decisive advance in American thinking on the subject. At the same time, it should be noted, this radical conception of equality of results was in one sense consistent with the older liberal notion of equality of opportunity. The distinctive feature of the demand for equality of output, its emphasis on groups, meant that a proportionate share of blacks, women, and other subordinated groups was to

29. For critiques of the theory of the culture of poverty, see Valentine (1968) and Leacock (1971).
30. We regret, however, that Coleman (1975) has recently argued against the utility of this important distinction for policy purposes.

attain "success" in numbers commensurate with their proportions in the population. Such an eventuality would, to be sure, produce a dramatic change in the distribution of opportunity in America or in any other society, but it would not necessarily lead to a reduction in the underlying structure of inequality.

(c) Christopher Jencks and *Inequality*

The distinction between the ideals of mobility and social equality was clearly drawn by Michael Young in *The Rise of the Meritocracy* (1958), but it was not until the publication of Christopher Jencks's *Inequality* in 1972 that the distinction was made part of the conceptual framework of a major methodological empiricist study. Jencks's concern with the question was a long-standing one and was already evident four years earlier in his chapter on "Social Stratification and Mass Higher Education" in *The Academic Revolution*. In it he declared that "there seems to be something basically perverse and sadistic in trying to make society any more competitive and status conscious than it already is" and concluded that "America most needs . . . not more mobility but more equality" (Jencks and Riesman, 1968:150). This value position, rather unusual among American educational researchers, provided the underlying premise of *Inequality*.

Jencks himself (1973:138) explains that the origins of the study go back to his work in Washington from 1961 to 1967 and his disenchantment with the liberal social reform programs of the 1960s. An active participant in public policy-making, Jencks concluded that the reformist programs of the New Frontier and the Great Society would never be effective in confronting the problem of inequality. The reformists' obsession with education was, Jencks believed, ill-suited to the attainment even of the lesser goal of equality of opportunity. In 1966, at the Institute for Policy Studies, Jencks began work on a book designed to show the inadequacy of a reform strategy centered on education. Revealingly titled *The Limits of Schooling*, this was the beginning of a project that culminated in the publication of *Inequality*.[31]

An example of methodological empiricism at its best, *Inequality* merits careful attention for what it can reveal about both the contributions and the limitations of this approach. Essentially a continuation of the research by Blau and Duncan and by Coleman to which we have referred, the study offers a synthesis of existing sources of data on education and inequality. Perhaps its

---

31. Money for the project, an indispensable precondition for its realization considering the intricate and costly analyses of data carried out, came primarily from the Carnegie Corporation, but support was also provided by the Department of Health, Education, and Welfare, the Office of Economic Opportunity, the Ford and Guggenheim Foundations, and other private and governmental agencies (Jencks et al., 1972:vi).

most important contribution was the heavy blow it dealt to any strategy placing exclusive reliance on the equalization of education as a means of obtaining either equality of opportunity or equality. Scholars familiar with the research of Sewell, Blau and Duncan, and other major American contributors to the study of education and social stratification were, of course, already aware that schools are limited instruments of social reform, but there can be little doubt that Jencks's study did much to disabuse policy-makers and the larger public of the notion, recurrent in American history, that educational reform can serve as a substitute for more fundamental change. Further, as a description of the empirical relations prevailing in America among variables such as family background, education, and occupational attainment, *Inequality* provides a statistical portrait that will serve as a foundation for research on the subject for years to come.[32] Finally, in its explicit raising of the previously submerged issue of equality, Jencks's study has done much to advance the debate, in academic and policy circles alike, on education and social class.

There are, nonetheless, a number of serious problems in *Inequality*, many of them deriving from the book's polemical purpose. Intent on discrediting educational reform as a strategy for equality, Jencks was much concerned to show that schooling is a relatively modest determinant of adult success. His preferred technique of demonstrating the marginality of schooling in the process of social stratification—one that James Coleman (1973:1524) qualifies as the "skillful but highly motivated use of statistics"—is to compare the magnitude of the variance explained by education with all the unexplained variance. The resulting feebleness of education contrasted to the vast extent of the variance which remains unaccounted for must seem imposing to the lay reader, but to the researcher accustomed to the limited explanatory power of social science statistics, many of the relationships seem very substantial indeed. Education, for example, shows a correlation of .65 with occupational status (Jencks et al., 1972:181)—a remarkably high figure, which Jencks (1972:192) attempts to de-emphasize by noting that it leaves more than half of the variance unex- plained.[33] Jencks himself has, in public discussion of the book, referred to the problem of emphasis in interpreting the statistics reported in *Inequality* as the "half glass empty, half glass full" phenomenon, and it is by no means impossible

32. For technical critiques of *Inequality* and Jencks's response, see the symposiums in *Harvard Educational Review* (Fall 1973), *Sociology of Education* (Winter 1973), and *The American Educational Research Journal* (Spring 1974).
33. Sewell (1973), in a generally sympathetic review of Jencks, takes him to task for an "overconcern with R^2" (i.e., explained variance) that accounts for his "easy rejection of many relationships that by usual standards in quantitative social science would be considered quite important." Jencks, Sewell notes, "really comes down to setting a standard that says a causal variable (or set of causal variables) is unimportant if it does not explain most of the variance in the dependent variable of interest" (1973:1537).

to imagine that someone with a different polemical intention could have used the same statistics to put forward a powerful argument about the role of education as a determinant of inequality.

The obsession with "unexplained variance" in *Inequality* leads Jencks to conclude that "luck" is a major source of income inequality. Income, he suggests, depends on chance occurrences such as "whether bad weather destroys your strawberry crop, whether the new superhighway has an exit near your restaurant, and a hundred other unpredictable accidents" (Jencks et al., 1972:227). The identification of unexplained variance with "luck" seems a peculiar one for a sociologist, but it is a logical result of Jencks's decision to gather data only about individuals. Yet as Boudon (1974b) has argued in a review of Jencks, relationships that are objectively indeterminate for the individual may be anything but random when viewed from the perspective of social structure.[34] The limited but still high correlation of .65 between schooling and occupational status may, for example, be partially determined by changes in the occupational structure that create a disjuncture between the educational system and the world of work. *Inequality,* through its neglect of structural variables, adds the problems of *methodological individualism* to the limitations of methodological empiricism.[35]

One of the most interesting—but also one of the most problematic—aspects of *Inequality* is its effort to measure the magnitude of the effects that would result from the equalization of schooling. The characteristic procedure used by Jencks to measure the maximum potential effect of a given variable is to hold all other variables constant and then to determine how much effect the equalization of the variable in question would have on the dependent variable. The nature of this procedure is well illustrated by an example Jencks himself uses (1973:160): since the 1940 Census showed that schooling explained 21 per cent of the variance in income among men aged 35 to 44, "statistical logic therefore implies that reducing the variance in years of schooling could never reduce the variance

----

34. For examples of a type of methodological empiricist analysis of education and inequality that does not neglect the role of social structure, see Boudon (1973 and 1974a).
35. Even within the framework of methodological individualism, it is possible to criticize the measures of family socioeconomic status (generally a composite measure of parents' education and father's occupation) used in many of the studies (e.g., Blau and Duncan) upon which *Inequality* relies. Muller (1972), in a study in a medium-sized German town which includes direct data on brothers, finds that similarities in father's education and occupation explain 35 percent of the variance in son's occupational status, but that unmeasured "family residual" effects account for an additional 24 percent of the variance in the case of brothers (1972:242). What this finding strongly suggests is that there are elements in family background that, although they are important in the determination of adult status, are not captured by the usual techniques. Bowles (1972a), who also suspects that the usual methods of measuring the effects of socioeconomic status have the systematic consequence of underestimating them, suggests that the transmission of personality attributes, determined in part by parental position in the hierarchy of work relations, is an important component of family background.

in men's income more than 21 per cent." This statement, which on the face of it seems unimpeachable, actually conceals a number of important assumptions, the most crucial one of which is that it is actually possible to manipulate one variable without changing the ensemble of relations constituting the totality. Yet in the case cited here, it is highly questionable whether the absolute equalization of schooling would leave these relations untouched. Equalization of education might well upset the legitimating functions of schools and thereby set in motion a process that would change the values and relations among other variables, such as family background and income, that figure in the equation. At the very least, the notion that a change in one variable would leave all other variables except the selected "dependent" one unchanged cannot merely be asserted but rather needs to be argued on a theoretical level.

It is illuminating in this regard to examine in greater detail Jencks's example of the effect of absolute equalization of schooling on income. Schools, as Clark (1960), Rothbart (1970), and numerous other researchers have documented, play a crucial role in legitimating inequality by internalizing failure. The structure of the educational system upholds those meritocratic values that justify differential rewards, and the separation of the "successful" from the "failures" provides daily object lessons in inequality.[36] In view of the links between the hierarchical character of the educational system and the value system that underpins social inequality, is it realistic to assume that the absolute equalization of education would have no effects whatsoever on the American class structure? Yet that is precisely what is implied by the statistical operations in *Inequality,* which purport to show what effects would be produced by a system in which everyone had the same amount of education. Here, as in other areas, the absence of a theoretically informed analysis of what goes on in the "black box" of schooling is not merely an unfortunate omission, but rather one that casts serious doubts on the meaningfulness of many of the statistical calculations offered. The effect of an absolute equalization of schooling, predicted with quantitative precision by Jencks, is simply not susceptible to statistical calculation.

Jencks's conclusion that schools are "marginal institutions" in the quest for a more egalitarian society is a direct outgrowth of the "black box" view of schooling that runs through the pages of *Inequality.* Admitting that the study "ignored not only attitudes and values but the internal life of schools" (1972:13), Jencks points to precisely those aspects of the educational system

---

36. The finding by Esposito (1973) that placement in a low 'track' in school reduces self-esteem is but one example of how the operations of the educational system serve to teach the academically unsuccessful that they are deserving of less than a proportional share of society's rewards. For evidence that schools differentially socialize students by social origin in a manner that contributes to the reproduction of political and social inequality, see Litt (1963) and Steinitz et al. (1973).

that implicate it most deeply in the perpetuation of inequality.[37] The strategy
for equality proposed by Jencks, who rightfully points to the economy as a key
arena of struggle, is mechanistic rather than dialectical in its relegation of schools
to marginality; central to the socialization of each new generation, schools do
not turn 'inputs' into 'outputs' but shape the personalities of those who pass
through them. Though it brilliantly demolished the peculiarly American myth
that school reform can serve as a substitute for more fundamental social change,
Inequality may unfortunately have replaced it with another equally destructive
myth: that a viable strategy for social equality can afford to ignore the schools.

Inequality, which provided important but partial insights into the problem of
schooling and social inequality, reveals some of the limitations of methodological empiricism. Where it lacks theory and is unwilling to venture into "soft"
areas of social inquiry, methodological empiricism may permit a debatable
concept of rigor to determine not only the subjects of social science research,
but also the permissible ways of treating them. There is no harsher critic of this
point of view than Jencks himself, who wrote with David Riesman in the
introduction to *The Academic Revolution* (1968:xv) that "choosing one's
problems to fit the method and data that happen to be most satisfactory, strikes
us as an invitation to triviality and ultimately an abdication of social and
personal responsibility."

(d) Action-Research

Jencks's attack on liberal reformism, Coleman's delineation of the concept of
equality of results, and Blau and Duncan's emphasis on the distinction between
the description of mobility and the explanation of status attainment are all
works in the tradition of methodological empiricism that bear on the theoretical
and political debate over the liberal conception of equality of opportunity in
contrast to the socialist conception of equality. In Britain that debate was
already well advanced in the 1950s, and much if not most of the sociology of
education was devoted to it. Floud, Halsey, and Martin's *Social Class and
Educational Opportunity* (1956) and J.W.B. Douglas's *The Home and the School*
(1964) were widely read examples of the "political arithmetic" type of
methodological empiricism applied critically to one of the crucial features of a
class society. Similar work was undertaken in France by Girard, and in
Scandinavia, notably by Husén. In Western Europe as a whole this tradition of
research may be described politically as radically democratic. It owed little to

---

37. See, however, Astin (1970) for a resourceful attempt to provide an input-output model of higher
education that, despite its "black box" conceptualization of the educational institution, is expressly
designed to measure the effects of colleges and universities on student values. For a summary of studies of
college impact, many of which use an input-output model, see Feldman and Newcomb (1969).

Marxism, but—in contrast to its American equivalent—was not hostile to it. Its origins lay in liberal democratic thought and its commitment was towards making a reality of the idea of the Welfare State. Though it began as the mostly unaided work of individual scholars, it soon attracted the help of research councils, governments, and such international agencies as the Organization for Economic Co-operation and Development (O.E.C.D.). Its further development in the 1960s and 1970s has been accompanied by additional state support and by increasingly sharp radicalism, of which Byrne et al.'s (1975) work is an admirable example.

Another line of descent runs through Michael Young's hypothetical and ironical analysis of the meritocracy thesis and his influence on the British Plowden Report. It is developed further as a social science method in the action-research program carried out by Halsey and his associates in "educational priority areas."[38] This work is also an example of governmental sponsorship of educational research informed by the political principle of "positive discrimination" and by the method of action-research. In this case, methodological empiricism is carried into the realm of quasi-experiment. Even more noteworthy, however, is the explicit value commitment of this officially sponsored and published research. Halsey and his colleagues based their recommendations for policy on research experience over three years in four socially deprived districts. But they also relied on general political and social priorities, which they did not try to disguise. It follows, as they stated, that their "recommendations are neither the conclusive authority of social science nor beyond challenge on political and social grounds" (Halsey 1972:179).

Action in slum schools and their neighborhoods was undertaken with extra funds provided by the state, and research monitoring was built into the process. Under such circumstances the tension between government and social science interests is likely to become manifest. More particularly, the E.P.A. researchers concluded that the traditional separation of action and research into separate activities with separate ideologies is in part responsible for the widespread confusion over the nature of action-research. "Obviously there is no automatic identity of interest between the two spheres though it may be that the differences have been overemphasized. There has been a tendency to see facts and values as different social objects with different procedures of investigation necessary to each. This approach cannot be sustained: social science which is to be significant must be value-based. It cannot be a value-free collection of facts. The action-research context exposes this truth—perhaps unpleasantly. A realistic

38. These studies are reported generally in A.H. Halsey (1972). Further analyses and case studies are contained in John Payne, *E.P.A. Surveys and Statistics*, Vol. 2; J.A. Barnes, ed., *Curriculum Innovation in London's E.P.A.s*, Vol. 3; George Smith, ed., *E.P.A.: The West Riding Project*, Vol. 4; and Charles M. Morrison, *E.P.A.: A Scottish Study*, Vol. 5. All these volumes are published by H.M.S.O., London.

view of both action and research reduces the difference between them and casts doubt on the validity of the pure models of the planning or the research approach. Variables are difficult if not impossible to control fully in practice and results depend heavily on the particular local context of action. . . . The co-operation of research in policy formation has to develop 'organically' rather than 'mechanically'. Action-research is unlikely ever to yield neat and definite prescriptions from field-tested plans. What it offers is an aid to intelligent decision-making not a substitute for it. Research brings relevant information rather than uniquely exclusive conclusions" (Halsey, 1972:178).

Explicit recognition of the political character of social science research—as well as a clear awareness of the interest of state policy-makers in its findings—is, we suggest, a necessary development if social science is to retain its commitment to the quest for knowledge while at the same time continuing to negotiate public support. The difficulties of that negotiation, which have been raised with particular sharpness by the experience of action-research, become even more apparent when we now consider the conflict theories of education that have recently bid for attention.

CONFLICT THEORIES OF EDUCATION

The long roots of conflict theory lie in the works of Marx and Weber, but the contemporary branches are tangled. Thus Gouldner and Bowles are clearly influenced by Parsons, however much they disagree with him, while writers like Bernstein in England or Bourdieu in France draw from both Marxist and functionalist traditions, owing in both cases more to Durkheim than to Marx. In the 1950s conflict theory was relatively dormant outside orthodox Marxist circles, though the writings of C.Wright Mills (1956;1959) in America, Norman Birnbaum (1953) and David Lockwood (1956) in England, and Ralf Dahrendorf (1959) in Germany helped to keep it alive through criticism of both Parsonsian functionalism and Marx. Max Gluckman (1955), influenced by Georg Simmel among others, also contributed to conflict theory within the functionalist framework classically formulated by Radcliffe-Brown. Two of Gluckman's students, Hargreaves (1967) and Lacey (1970), were among the first to undertake studies of schools using a combined functionalist and conflict framework in the 1960s.

However, taking our view that sociology has been influenced more by its social context than by any "inner logic" of the development of the discipline, we would expect that, just as technological functionalism seems to fit the social conditions of the 1950s, conflict theory was likely to have come into greater prominence in the 1960s. For if social stability was the dominant mood of the 1950s, change and upheaval expressed the spirit of the 1960s. The political world of Eisenhower in America, Macmillan in England, and Adenauer in West Germany stands in marked contrast to that of the decade before the one in which we write. During the 1960s there was a sharpening of antagonism between classes, races, and nations that seems to have marked off a new generation with a dramatically different social and political outlook. We would expect, in particular, that the rise of a New Left movement that was disproportionately active in those universities that are preeminent in social scientific research would give added impetus to the development of conflict theory.[39]

The idea that social theories change in response to underlying social conditions would seem to be a reasonable—if not indeed a banal—assertion, but it has met with considerable resistance from social theorists themselves. The reason may be that an admission that external factors can influence the work of a social researcher would seem to bring into question the scientific character of his work. For science, after all, is governed by the canons of logic and evidence, and it is comforting for social scientists to believe that such factors as contradictions between new data and old theories are the motor force of progress. Such contradictions do obviously occur from time to time, and the changes that result take place on what Gouldner (1971:387) calls the "technical" level of social theory. This is the internal, scientific side of social research with which everyone is familiar, and it is the face that social scientists tend to put forward both to the public and to themselves. But there is also another level of social theory, one that is less known and less formal. This is what Gouldner calls the "infrastructure" of social theory, and it is composed of "the sentiments, the domain assumptions, the conceptions of reality accented by personal experience" that "constitute its individual and social grounding" (1971:29–49, 396–397).

It is a matter of debate which of these two levels predominates in explaining changes in social theory, but a strong case can be put forward that "infrastructure" is primary.[40] Friedrichs (1970:290–291), in a formulation similar to Gouldner's, argues that there are two paradigmatic levels in research in the social sciences, and that the paradigms characteristic of the conventionally scientific level emphasized by observers such as Kuhn are actually subordinate to a more primary level. This more fundamental level of social science paradigms includes the researcher, his activity, and his self-image as part of the subject matter of the

---

39. For a general discussion of the New Left and social theory, see Gouldner (1971:396–410).

40. Gouldner, after an intensive examination of functionalism, concludes that changes took place largely for reasons external to both the theory and the research of sociology (1971:370). In a more general formulation, Gouldner declares that "the most basic changes in any science commonly derive not so much from the invention of new research techniques but rather from new ways of looking at data that may have long existed" (1971:34). The core of the conflict theory of education, which has relied largely on data generated by technological functionalism and methodological empiricism while radically reinterpreting them, would tend to support Gouldner's hypothesis.

discipline. Seen in this light, functionalism grows out of a prior value commitment to the image of the social scientist as *value-free* while conflict theory emerges from a prior self-conception of the researcher as engagé.

The disproportionate acceptance of conflict theory by young researchers suggests that generational factors were at work in the undermining of functionalist theory. Mannheim (1952:291), in a classical essay on "The Sociological Problem of Generations," points out that individuals in the same age group share a "common location in the social and historical process," which limits them "to a specific range of potential experience" and predisposes them to a "certain characteristic type of historically relevant action." Their common location, socially and temporally, "excludes a large number of possible modes of thought, experience, feeling, and action" (the "negative delimitation"), but it also has the positive effect of "pointing towards certain definite modes of behavior, feeling, and thought." Without interpreting Mannheim's schema in an excessively deterministic fashion (which would, in any case, be contrary to the subtlety of his formulation), it would seem possible to view functionalist theory as among those characteristic patterns of thought more or less excluded by the generational experience of those researchers who came of age in the late 1960s and conflict theory as an alternative framework suggested by the experience of student radicalism.

If social theories do indeed change partially in response to contradictions between their technical level and their "infrastructure," it is appropriate here to attempt to identify those generationally linked factors that provided the social basis for the shift in educational research toward conflict theory. Prominent among these factors, at least in the United States, was surely the incompatibility of the New Left advocacy of active engagement with the traditional appeal to neutrality and detachment characteristic of much of the functionalist and methodological empiricist work of their elders. The version of "technological functionalism" that dominated theoretically informed educational research in the 1950s was particularly ill-suited to appeal to New Left sociologists whose anti-hierarchical impulse led them to doubt "technicist" explanations of the necessity of educational and social stratification. Further, the absence of conflict in functionalist theory corresponded neither to the personal lives of New Leftists nor to the events occurring in the society around them. And methodological empiricism, perceived as being intimately involved in the policy-making process of the Welfare State, could also be dismissed. The humanistic yearnings of the New Leftists could find little satisfaction by joining the quest for quantification. Finally, neither functionalism nor methodological empiricism seemed capable of explaining a subject of vital interest to radical researchers—why the New Left movement of which they themselves were a part had emerged in the 1960s.[41]

---

41. One of the earliest published works of Gintis (1970), a leading proponent of the conflict theory of education, was concerned with explaining the emergence of the New Left. Other analyses of the student

Among those who went on to careers in the teaching of sociology and research in education there was a renewed advocacy of active engagement against the traditional appeal to neutrality and detachment. An evil world needed change, not merely understanding. Second, there was a yearning for theory in the sense of powerful and holistic principles capable of interpreting the complexity of a world that seemed everywhere to fail to realize its declared ideals. The availability of Marx and Weber[42] provided a rich source of inspiration different from the technological functionalism and methodological empiricism that had previously established themselves in the professional mainstream of sociology.

(a) Neo-Weberian Conflict Theory

A researcher following the Weberian route to a conflict theory of education is Randall Collins (1971; 1974). In an explicit attack on the functionalist theory of educational stratification, he argues that the expansion of the American educational system reflects less the growing technical needs of the economy than the effects of competing "status groups" for wealth, power, and prestige. Collins's concept of status groups is, of course, derived from Max Weber's classical essay "Class, Status, and Party." "The main activity of schools," Collins writes, is "to teach particular status cultures, both in and outside the class-room." From this perspective, it is not important for schools to impart technical knowledge, but they must inculcate "vocabulary and inflection, styles of dress, aesthetic tastes, values and manners" (1971:1010).

Collins's view of the empirical literature bearing on the technical-function theory of education, though debatable,[43] clearly suggests that factors other than technological necessity have been at work in the rapid growth of school systems. To explore these other factors Collins looks to Weber and especially to his view that power is the crucial variable in the setting of educational requirements. In contrast to functionalists, Weber sees conflicting interests rather than "systemic needs" as shaping the educational system. His essay on "The Rationalization of

---

movement influenced by conflict theory, particularly in its neo-Marxist form, are offered by Touraine (1971), Flacks (1970; 1971), and Miles (1971; 1974). See Keniston (1968; 1971) for a liberal social psychological view and Aron (1969) and Shils (1969) for more conservative perspectives.

42. Another factor to be considered in the return to Marx and Weber is that the fragility of the intellectual and career position of non-orthodox students of education may have led them to look to the classical tradition in social theory as a source of legitimation for their own viewpoints.

43. Collins himself admits that evidence on the technical need for upgraded educational requirements *within* job categories is inadequate. Further, it is questionable whether the technical-function theory of education necessarily leads to the expectation that more educated workers will show greater productivity on a given job. It is entirely possible, for example, that "overeducated" workers in relatively low-status jobs are in those jobs precisely because they are uncharacteristically unproductive for workers of their educational attainment. More relevant to the technical-function theory is whether a certain educational level is a virtual precondition for the capacity to perform given jobs at all.

Education and Training" makes clear how *interests* penetrate the educational system, for even "educational ideals" as apparently detached as that of the "cultivated man" are "stamped by the structure of domination and by the social conditions for membership in the ruling stratum" (Weber, 1972:228). Similarly, in his essay on "The Chinese Literati" Weber noted that the nature of the "cultivated man" characteristic of Confucian education ultimately "depends on the decisive stratum's respective ideal of cultivation" (Weber, 1972:234). Thus the Weberian perspective emphasizes the power of dominant groups to shape the schools arbitrarily to their own purposes. Since group interests are at stake in the determination of the ideals that govern a school system, the process of imposing a given definition is inherently one of potential conflict.

To explain the rapid escalation of educational requirements, Collins (1974:421) draws from Weber the notion that education serves to reinforce "status cultures" by identifying "insiders" and posing barriers to "outsiders." The center of this status-based conflict over education lies in the labor market where organizations use educational requirements to allocate people to jobs with varying rewards. Seen in this light, struggles over educational requirements are often, in the end, conflicts between superordinate groups trying to monopolize positions of privilege and subordinate groups trying to gain access to them. As superior status groups raise educational requirements higher so as to reinforce their privileged position, groups of lower social status demand access to more education. There ensues an educational spiral that, rather than technical change, is most responsible for the rapidity of educational expansion.

Collins's theory of educational stratification inevitably directs him to examine the "black box" of schooling. For if schools teach not technical skills, but status cultures, it is important to identify the character of these cultures and the process by which they are transmitted. Unfortunately, however, Collins does not have direct empirical evidence on the internal workings of schools. But he does have data on the relationship between organizational characteristics and educational requirements. The general conclusion he draws from his analysis of 309 organizations in the San Francisco area is that those firms wishing to exercise a high degree of "normative control over their employees were the ones most likely to have high educational requirements" (Collins, 1974). What this implies is that organizations look to the schools to provide them with workers who have internalized the goals of the firm; technical training seems, in comparison, a relatively minor matter.[44] If true, this points to the educational system as a crucial agent in the differential socialization of school children by status groups of origin. This theory deserves empirical test.

---

44. Collins (1974:440) admits, however, that his measure of the effects of technological change on changes in the educational requirements of organizations is a rather weak one.

(b) Neo-Marxist Conflict Theory

Again following Weber, Collins places substantial emphasis on the autonomy of cultural and "life-style" factors in the development of group consciousness. The interpretation of Weberian stratification theory is, of course, an unsettled debate, especially with regard to the relation between class and status. Marxists heavily underline Weber's view of status as ultimately dependent on class. Bowles and Gintis are contemporary Marxists who begin from this standpoint in the elaboration of a conflict theory of education. They look first to the character of the forces and social relations of production for a key to the analysis of education systems. The social relations of production, which under capitalism are held to be based on the prevailing system of private property, are of particular interest to Bowles and Gintis for it is these social relations that are at the root of the "hierarchical division of labor." Much of their work is devoted to showing that the educational system is a crucial element in the reproduction of a division of labor that is itself largely a reflection of the hegemony of the capitalist class.[45] The dominance of the capitalist class is not, however, uncontested, and the centrality of the educational system in reproducing a system of inequality favorable to capitalist interests makes the schools an arena of class conflict. As Marxists, Bowles and Gintis believe that it is impossible to understand the workings of the educational system independently of an analysis of the class structure in which it is embedded.

The nexus linking the three institutions of family, work, and school provides the underlying framework of Bowles and Gintis's theory of the role of education in the reproduction of the social division of labor (Bowles, 1971a, and Bowles and Gintis, 1972). The workplace is considered to be the ultimately decisive member of this institutional triumvirate. Citing evidence from Melvin Kohn's (1969) research on social class and parental values, Bowles and Gintis point to position in the authority structure at the workplace as the source of differing values constitutive of class sub-cultures. Kohn describes this difference as one of middle-class "self-direction" and working-class "conformity," but Bowles and Gintis prefer to look at the values of the middle class as "internalized norms"

---

45. The role of the educational system in the reproduction of the division of labor is the subject of much discussion in France. Althusser (1972) provides a theoretical analysis of the role of schools as "ideological state apparatuses" in the perpetuation of capitalist hegemony. Baudelot and Estaplet's *L'école capitaliste en France* (1973) constitutes an important and empirically informed Marxist effort to understand the role of education as an agent of social reproduction, but it is somewhat marred by the crudeness of the dichotomous model of social class (the bourgeoisie vs. the proletariat) that is its theoretical base. Bourdieu and Passeron's *La reproduction* (1970), a widely discussed theoretical analysis of the reproductive function of schools, is not, properly speaking, a conflict theory of education at all, for its scheme leaves no room for working-class resistance to the cultural hegemony of the bourgeoisie. Often erroneously viewed as a Marxist in the Anglo-Saxon world, Bourdieu is better understood as a sociologist of philosophical formation deeply influenced by French structuralism and by the works of Max Weber and Émile Durkheim.

reflecting the demands of their positions in the hierarchy of production.[46] Membership in these sub-cultures serves to provide children of varying social class backgrounds with values and personality traits appropriate to future positions in the hierarchical division of labor roughly commensurate with their social origins. The educational system, both through class-linked inequality of academic success and through differential socialization by social class, reinforces inequalities based on the production process (Bowles, 1971a).

Bowles and Gintis have also carried conflict theory into an area of acute ideological controversy in education—the Intelligence Quotient (I.Q.) and the explanation of class and racial inequalities. In an attack on what they call the "technocratic-meritocratic" view of the hierarchical division of labor (1972), they argue that cognitive abilities as measured by I.Q. are not a crucial determinant of economic success. In opposition to genetic explanations of social inequality such as those of Jensen (1969), Herrnstein (1971), and Eysenck (1971), they present an analysis to show that the role of I.Q. in the intergenerational transmission of inequality is, at least in the United States, quite trivial.

If individual I.Q. scores do not explain social inequality, what does in fact explain the reproduction of hierarchical division of labor? Bowles and Gintis (1972), following the logic of a Marxist approach to the study of education, propose a "correspondence principle" between schooling and the social relations of production as a key element in the transmission of inequality. An example of "correspondence" between the character of the workplace and that of the school would be that pay is an incentive in the former and examination grades in the latter, the external character of both sets of rewards reflecting the absence of intrinsic satisfaction involved in work and study, respectively. There are many such parallels between school and work, but those that exist universally can obviously do little to explain the intergenerational reproduction of inequality. For this, it is necessary to analyze differential treatment of students by social class origin. Differential academic achievement is one element of class reproduction, but the thrust of Bowles and Gintis's argument is that cognitive factors play quite a minor role in the allocation of individuals to positions in the class structure. More important are the non-cognitive personality factors that are necessary for the proper performance of tasks at a given level in the hierarchy of the social relations of production (Gintis, 1971a). Schools, which treat students of varying social origins differently, reinforce those class-based personality traits that, much more than cognitive differences, explain why the children of the privileged tend to occupy the higher positions in the social division of labor.

The Marxist formulation of the problem of schooling and inequality differs radically from the functionalist theory of educational stratification. While some

---

46. See Bowles and Gintis's *Schooling in Capitalist America* (1976).

functionalists, for example, may take for granted that the superior technical knowledge of the highly schooled is responsible for their higher earnings, Marxist-oriented conflict theorists conclude that cognitive differences offer at best only a partial explanation for their visibly superior status, and point instead to personality factors. It is also possible to argue that where functionalists have provided a *description* of the relations existing between the educational system and other social institutions, conflict theorists have put forward an *explanation* of why these relations exist and how they change over time.[47] Moreover, where functionalists have tended to look at the socialization process as one of those common *values* that hold a society together, neo-Marxists and neo-Weberians have examined the *interests* that underlie these values and have noted that socialization differs systematically by social class. Finally, where functionalists have often viewed the educational system as offering opportunities for *mobility for individuals,* conflict theorists have generally stressed the role of education in *maintaining a system of structured social inequality.*

Despite the differences between functionalist and Marxist theories of education, these theories generally rely on the same empirical sources. Bowles (1971a), for example, in attempting to adduce evidence for his thesis that the educational system tends to reproduce inequality across generations, cites such staples of functionalism and methodological empiricism as the United States Bureau of the Census, Project TALENT, the Coleman Report, and Blau and Duncan. Gintis, himself a member of the team that produced *Inequality,* uses data gathered by the National Opinion Research Center as the basis for his joint attack with Bowles on "I.Q.-ism." Conflict theorists have, to be sure, also attempted to gather new data on such questions as the relationship between personality traits and productivity and the correspondence between class of origin and type of school socialization. But these bodies of data, which generally remain inadequate, were gathered after the foundations of the conflict approach had already been laid. The rise of the conflict theory of education may, in short, have provided a stimulus for the accumulation of new data, but both neo-Weberian and neo-Marxist approaches emerged as a result of new ways of looking at old data.

Conflict theory is extending its influence among educational researchers. A favorable social context encouraged the emergence of radical academic journals such as the *Review of Radical Political Economics, Politics and Society,* and *The Insurgent Sociologist,* which disseminated the views of conflict theorists as a recognizable school of thought. Partly through the accumulation of evidence and partly through mutual citation, conflict theorists have developed a view of

---

47. The attempt to explain the structural basis of educational inequality is common to all conflict theorists, from neo-Weberians such as Collins to neo-Marxists such as Bowles and Gintis, Karabel (1972), and Carnoy (1974).

education that constitutes a comprehensive alternative to both functionalism and methodological empiricism and that has made inroads into undergraduate curricula and doctoral programs in the economics and sociology of education. Conflict theory, to be sure, has hardly become the dominant approach to educational research, but the fact that articles expressing avowedly Marxist views now occasionally find their way into the pages of such traditional academic journals as the *American Economic Review* and the *Journal of Political Economy* shows its growing respectability. Though proponents of the more political versions of conflict theory may be at a disadvantage in the academic market place, a "critical mass" of teachers and researchers capable of assuring the future of neo-Marxist approaches to the study of education seems now to exist.

One rarely cited element in the rise of conflict theory is that its proponents too have benefited from the largesse of the funding agencies of the Welfare State. Collins's research, for example, was supported by grants from the Department of Labor and the Office of Education, and Bowles and Gintis's by the Ford Foundation. Such examples leave open the question whether radical social scientists face special problems in obtaining funds,[48] but they do dispose of the simplistic assumption that "establishment" sources are uniformly hostile to research proposals that do not reflect the preferences of state administrators for policy-oriented investigations. Moreover, the work of Bowles and Gintis in particular serves to guard against over-simple interpretation of the categories we have been employing in describing the different schools of thought. There are many elements of functionalism in their writing and, partly because of their origins as economists, they use sophisticated statistical techniques (for example, in their analysis of the relation between intelligence and occupational status).

The larger question raised by the resources which government agencies and private foundations provide for conflict theorists is whether, as suggested by Gouldner, such a funding pattern distorts the quest for knowledge. This is a difficult problem to resolve, but there is no prima facie reason to believe that conflict theorists would be immune to such distortion. And indeed there are grounds for suspecting that they too are susceptible to the subtle temptations involved in drawing up proposals designed to appeal to the preferences of those who control contested research funds.

Yet despite the dangers that government funding poses to the integrity of the research of conflict theorists, there are factors tending to mitigate the particular

48. Whether there is discrimination against radicals in the allocation of research monies is an empirical question. An ideal study would examine not only whether radical proposals were disproportionately rejected by funding agencies, but also whether left-wing researchers hesitate to apply for funds. It would further investigate whether dissenting social scientists subtly change their formulation of a particular problem so as to make it conform with the prevailing models of social science research.

distortions arising from "establishment" support. The first of these is that many scholars of diverse political persuasions pursue their research with no funding whatsoever. With a plethora of data already available, conflict theorists often have no need for new evidence. Instead, by relying on existing figures, they can often put forward radically new syntheses. Second, Weberian and Marxist versions of conflict theory provide researchers with important internal criteria of what constitutes priority in research. Third, the dissenting character of conflict theory is likely to make its adherents highly conscious of the distorting effects of state sponsorship on research. If an awareness of the impact of social context on the character of research is the mark of the discerning social scientist, then the Marxist, well attuned to the interests underlying various ideologies, should be (at least in a non-communist country) the very model of self-consciousness.

But however well-insulated he may be from the deformations induced by proximity to dominant social institutions, the Marxist, like other human agents, is not exempt from ideological distortions. If relatively deaf to the blandishments of the Welfare State, the Marxist listens attentively to what he takes to be the demands of the proletariat. From the Marxist perspective, there can be little doubt about the social character of educational research—it is, as Althusser (1972) would say, an element of an ideological battle, which is in turn part of the larger class struggle between the bourgeoisie and the proletariat. For the Marxist, then, research is a form of praxis.

If the socially-induced distortions of the conservative educational researcher derive from his nearness to the elite, the factor most threatening to the Marxist's quest for knowledge is his commitment to the working class.[49] Both commitments can be sources of insights, but subordinated social groups do not have the power to impose their version of educational research through control of purse strings. The distorting influence of social context on Marxist researchers in the West is thus typically of a different nature from that affecting functionalists or methodological empiricists.

Where Marxist formulations go beyond existing empirical evidence, we would expect them to put forward interpretations legitimating egalitarian claims. Even Bowles and Gintis, though among the more sophisticated of educational researchers, are not immune to the tendency to put forward as established scientific fact propositions that are only equivocally supported by available evidence. An example appears in their attempt to demonstrate that greater workers' control in industry leads to higher productivity—a proposition that, given their correspondence theory of the relationship between hierarchy in

---

49. The classical Marxist position is that commitment to the working class is illuminating rather than distorting because the proletariat is the universal class. For perhaps the most sophisticated presentation of this argument see Lukacs's *History and Class Consciousness* (1971).

schooling and hierarchy in the economy, is an important part of their argument for educational equality.

While Bowles and Gintis cite considerable evidence in support of their belief in workers' control, their insistence that hierarchy leads to inefficiency meets the difficult question of why, especially in the framework of their theory of an economy dominated by profit-maximizing, an enterprise obstinately insists on perpetuating a work organization that does not maximize output. Their answer is that capitalist firms recognize that greater worker participation, though more efficient, would inevitably lead to an assault on the control mechanisms of the capitalist system itself. But the problem with this answer is that a single capitalist who, behaving in accord with the self-interest attributed to him by Marxist theory, put his private interests above those of the capitalist class as a whole would thereby effectively undermine the united front against workers' control. If less hierarchy at the workplace did, indeed, lead to greater efficiency, the profit-maximizing capitalist would increase worker participation so as to raise productivity and thus gain a competitive edge over his rivals. Logically, only a remarkably class-conscious and monolithic capitalist class could prevent the emergence of such an *avant-garde* property owner who, in the pursuit of his individual interests, reduced hierarchy at the workplace. Bowles and Gintis do not, however, present any serious evidence that the capitalist class is either sufficiently class-conscious or sufficiently unified to prevent this outcome. If capitalists have not reduced the hierarchy of work organization in order to raise productivity, the reason may be less that they are fearful of their survival than that their time-and-motion studies tell them that greater worker participation has equivocal effects on productivity. It may be gratifying to the New Left Marxist to believe that workers' control would release the fettered "forces of production," but the behavior of capitalists suggests that the relationship between hierarchy and efficiency may be more complex than one would gather from Bowles and Gintis's review of the evidence.[50]

50. Gintis (1975), however, in an elaborate neo-Marxist analysis of the firm, maintains that workers' self-management is incompatible with the system of control in the *individual* enterprise, which, he argues, is designed to resolve the problem of extracting *labor* from *labor power* (see also Bowles and Gintis, 1975a). Bowles and Gintis's general argument that the hierarchical division of labor takes form within a given structure of class domination is doubtless correct, but this does not necessarily mean, as Marx points out in *Capital,* that all hierarchy at the workplace derives from the *social* rather than the *technical* division of labor. As for their emphasis on the primacy of non-cognitive traits, a careful examination of one of the key empirical studies upon which it is based, a doctoral thesis by Edwards (1972), reveals that the correlation between personality traits and position in the hierarchy of production is actually rather weak. Similarly, the centerpiece of their argument that position in the hierarchical division of labor determines family values, the study by Kohn (1969), shows quite modest correlations. Bowles and Gintis's theories of class reproduction and of the nature of the relationship between what is taught in school and what is useful in the production process are highly provocative, but an assessment of their validity would be premature. Their formulations are, however, susceptible to empirical test, and it is hoped that researchers will, over the next few years, conduct studies informed by Bowles and Gintis's larger theoretical concerns.

A theme that runs throughout Bowles and Gintis's work is the attribution of unequal education and the hierarchical division of labor to capitalism. Bowles (1971a) argues that educational inequalities are best seen as part of the web of capitalist society and therefore likely to persist as long as capitalism survives. Yet Bowles and Gintis are well aware of the hierarchical character of schooling and work in socialist societies such as the Soviet Union and often make passing remarks to that effect.[51] Their work is, to be sure, primarily concerned with the educational system of the United States, and it is impossible to understand the peculiar form that educational inequality takes in America without making repeated references to capitalist institutions. Yet the identification of hierarchy in school and work with capitalism is, even in the United States, a vast oversimplification, for the roots of inequality extend far beyond private ownership of the means of production to the division of labor itself.[52] This division of labor is, in the West, set within a capitalist framework, but an equally hierarchical organization of work is, as Bowles and Gintis know, perfectly compatible with Soviet-style socialism. Educational inequality may, as Bowles suggests, persist as long as capitalism survives, but the abolition of capitalism would hardly assure the emergence of a non-hierarchical school system. Bowles and Gintis are quite conscious of this possibility, but the rhetoric of their work, which is designed to de-legitimate the existing educational system, lends itself to crude equations of hierarchy with capitalism. Though there can be no question about Bowles and Gintis's position if they are read carefully, their manner of presenting their theory of correspondence between the economy and the educational system could mislead the reader into concluding that a hierarchical educational system could not survive the destruction of capitalism.

One of the strengths of the neo-Marxist analysis of education under capitalism

51. In "I.Q. in the Class Structure" (1972), for example, Bowles and Gintis observe in a footnote that state socialist countries have a "hierarchy of production" similar to the ones found under capitalism. In the final chapter of their recent book (1976:266), they advocate a form of "revolutionary socialism" that goes "far beyond the achievement of the Soviet Union and countries of Eastern Europe." "These countries have," in their view, "abolished private ownership of the means of production, while replicating the relations of control, dominance and subordination characteristic of capitalism." For an analysis of the problems that have been encountered in the attempt to construct a socialist educational system in Cuba, see Bowles (1971b).

52. The logic of Bowles and Gintis's approach, which emphasizes that different systems of *ownership* of the means of production can be characterized by similar *social relations* of production, leads to the conclusion that a hierarchical organization of the workplace can be a source of cultural and educational inequality under both capitalism and socialism. Bowles himself (1971a:30) comes to virtually the same position when he writes that educational inequality will be built into American society "as long as the social division of labor persists," but generally prefers to point to capitalism as the structural base of inequality. A theoretical formulation that unambiguously directs attention to the hierarchical division of labor itself, even in its socialist form, as the foundation of inequality is offered by the extreme left Il Manifesto group of Italy (see Rossanda et al., 1970). Deeply influenced by Maoist thought, members of Il Manifesto are highly critical of Soviet Marxism, which in their view emphasizes "expertise" at the expense of "redness" and reproduces essentially capitalistic forms of inequality.

is that its theoretical framework is quite applicable to the study of socialist educational systems. Some researchers may hesitate to engage in such studies, for they would present troubling political and intellectual difficulties, but a case could be made that Bowles's theory of "correspondence" and Bourdieu's theory of "cultural capital" are more suited to the Soviet Union than to the United States and France. Where, for example, is the relationship between the economy and the schools less mediated than in the U.S.S.R., which has an explicit policy of manpower planning? Similarly, where is the correspondence principle more clearly exemplified than in the changes of educational policy that follow from changes in production strategies in a revolutionary socialist society such as Cuba?[53] And where does cultural capital play a greater role in the transmission of inequality than in those societies that have abolished private ownership of the means of production?[54] In short, whether one refers to the subordination of schools to the economy or to the cultural reproduction function of the educational system, much of the analysis of radical educational researchers is at least as applicable to socialist societies as it is to the capitalist countries upon which they focus their attention.

(c) The Problem of Educational Change

In an effort to show the role of the educational system in the reproduction of social inequality, neo-Marxists propose a theoretical framework that suggests a virtually "perfect fit" between schooling and other major social institutions (Lopate, 1974).[55] There is a tidiness about the family-school-work triumvirate that in the neo-Marxist view serves to transmit inequality from generation to generation, but the process seems to work so smoothly and is based upon such an imposing system of domination that one must wonder how it is that

---

53. Carnoy and Werthein (1977) offer a detailed study of Cuban educational reform that shows how the theoretical framework of correspondence illuminates not only the changes deriving from the transition from capitalism to socialism, but also the reforms taking place *after* the introduction of socialism.

54. Yanowitch and Dodge (1968) and Dobson (1977) provide detailed empirical evidence showing considerable cultural reproduction through education in the Soviet Union via the superior opportunities for higher education enjoyed by the children of the intelligentsia. China, however, presents a strikingly different situation in that it is self-consciously trying to avoid establishing a Russian-style "bourgeois" educational system whose hierarchical character would lend itself to analysis based on the theoretical framework neo-Marxists use to criticize inegalitarian systems under capitalism. See Bastid (1970) and Nee (1969) for studies of educational reform during the Chinese Cultural Revolution.

55. In many ways, the intricate and harmonious relations obtaining between education and other social institutions in Bowles and Gintis's work recall some of the more elegant functionalist formulations. A major difference between the two theories is, however, that while the Marxist and the functionalist may agree on the "functions" performed by the educational system (e.g., Bowles and Gintis favorably cite Parsons), the functionalist tends to see them as serving the general interests of society as a whole whereas the Marxist views them as serving the particular interests of the capitalist class.

educational change ever takes place.[56] For if the educational system is not only a product of a structure of class domination, but also a vital component of the process by which that structure perpetuates itself, there would seem to be no way out of a ceaseless process of self-reproduction. Precisely such a vision of endless capitalist domination marked the work of the theoretical father of the New Left—Herbert Marcuse (1964). But since educational change obviously does, in fact, take place, the Marxist must provide an explanation of how the cycle of reproduction he has described is ever broken. Within the confines of the correspondence principle a revolutionary change in the economy would, of course, lead to a transformation of the educational system, but this way of posing the problem leads to the very general question of the conditions that lead to a revolutionary rupture.

A more concrete Marxist notion is that a given educational structure is the outcome of a political and ideological struggle between social classes, and this concept has been put to use by "revisionist" educational historians. Yet even this idea goes only part of the way to a Marxist theory of educational change, for it does not specify the conditions under which the educational system, usually considered "apolitical," becomes an arena of overt class conflict. In an attempt to resolve this difficulty and to confront the more general problem of educational change, some Marxists have recently added the concept of contradiction to that of correspondence in an effort to provide a comprehensive theory of educational reproduction and transformation.[57]

Like the functionalist concepts of ascription and achievement, the Marxist concepts of correspondence and contradiction are at once analytical and ideological. The notion of correspondence, for example, is an analytic device for understanding how the relation between the economy and the educational system serves to reproduce a given social structure, but it is also an ideological concept that can be used to attack capitalist schools by portraying them as subordinated to an unjust economic system that perpetuates glaring social inequalities. Similarly, the concept of contradiction can illuminate the process of change by pointing to disjunctures between the schools and the economy, but it can also be used to assure radicals that the ingenious process by which the system reproduces itself is not an unalterable one. Particularly in the United States, there is a deeply-felt need among Marxists to believe that the seemingly impregnable system may, after all, finally come tumbling down. Seen in this

---

56. The problem of the possibility of educational change is even more acute in the deterministic, structuralist theory that underlies Bourdieu and Passeron's *La reproduction* (1970).
57. See Carter (1974) for the most explicit formulation of the theory of correspondence and contradiction, and Bowles (1972b) for an early attempt to apply the concept of contradiction to the analysis of American higher education.

light, the search for contradictions is not merely an academic quest for knowledge, but also an ideologically charged effort to give sustenance to the politically engaged by showing the inherent vulnerability of the system and by pointing to those tensions that would, if properly exacerbated, bring into being a mass movement dedicated to the abolition of capitalism.

The discovery that education is an arena of political struggle can hardly be credited to Marxists, but it is probable that the emphasis on conflict intrinsic to Marxist theory pushed researchers working in that tradition towards a politics of education. In contrast to functionalists, for example, Marxists see class interests behind a given pattern of educational organization and wish to specify the social groups that support the relations prevailing between schools and other social institutions.[58] To the extent, however, that both Marxism and functionalism tend to see a harmonious fit between the educational system and the surrounding society, neither theory has much need for a politics of education. For if social formations tend to have educational systems that are "appropriate" to their needs, there would seem to be little reason to expect political struggle over the shape of the school system. If the functionalist is susceptible to a confusion of what is with what has to be, the Marxist may be inclined toward a form of hyper-functionalism that sees whatever educational system exists as a natural and essentially unavoidable reflection of the particular class structure in which it is embedded.

Many radical educational researchers (among them some Marxists), however, do not succumb to vulgar Marxist determinism of the kind that would negate the need for a politics of education. Katz (1968;1971), for example, focuses his innovative historical research on the process by which conflicting class interests shaped the structure of American education in the nineteenth century. Tyack (1974), a revisionist but non-Marxist educational historian, has investigated the class basis of the movement to "professionalize" control of educational institutions and has uncovered the political interests behind the ideology of "taking the school out of politics." Bowles and Gintis (1976), though relying mainly on secondary sources, have provided a stimulating, if at times quasi-conspiratorial, interpretation of the history of class conflict in American education.

The works of radical educational historians have tended to focus on conflicts over the *structure* of the educational system, for such conflicts have been typical of the struggles that have thrust the schools into political prominence. This is true not only in America, where the question of organization and control of the educational system has generally occupied the center of the stage, but also in

---

58. Further, the Marxist concept of contradiction pointed toward the idea that control of the educational system tends to become an overt political issue in those periods characterized by a lack of "correspondence" between the schools and the economy. For an interesting application of this scheme to the history of American education, see Bowles and Gintis (1975b).

Britain, where such issues as the school leaving age and the spread of comprehensive schools have dominated public debate. Less visible in many of these struggles has been the question of the *content* of education. The battle for comprehensive education in Britain, for example, has been fought over the structure of secondary education rather than over internal school organization and curriculum. Thus 'streaming' (or 'tracking') has established itself in many comprehensive schools with relatively little overt political conflict (Ford, 1969). Historians interested in the politics of education have accordingly looked more at the structure of schooling than at its content.[59]

For the further development of the politics of education it is necessary to go beyond the study of patterns of control and educational structure to an examination of the changes in the texture of daily life in educational institutions that follow from macrostructural transformations. Weber pointed researchers in the right direction when he suggested that a critical element of the power of dominant groups resides in their capacity to impose their own educational and cultural ideals on schools. These ideals are reflected both in what is taught and in how it is taught, for the goal of education is to form both the mind and the personality. Thus what is regarded as knowledge and the way it is transmitted are eminently political questions—and no less so in the absence of overt conflict. Indeed, as Bachrach and Baratz (1962) have argued, the capacity to keep an issue off the agenda of political debate may well be the ultimate form of power.[60]

If the absence in conflict theory of an analysis of the content of the educational system has proved damaging to the emergence of a radical theory of educational politics and hence to the development of a satisfactory theory of educational change, this same lack points to a weakness in conflict theory even with respect to the problem to which it has principally been addressed—that of class reproduction. Though ascriptive elements play a major role in educational and occupational attainment, few conflict theorists would deny that much of

---

59. This is not, however, meant to suggest that revisionist educational historians have totally ignored the question of the content of education; Lazerson, for example, has done research on the rise of the kindergarten and on the curricular changes accompanying the growth of tracking and vocational education (Lazerson, 1971; Cohen and Lazerson, 1972; Lazerson and Grubb, 1974).

60. The capacity to enforce non-decisions by keeping an issue from ever being raised (e.g., the ability of an economically powerful corporation in a company town to avoid anti-pollution legislation from being placed on the political agenda) is a profound, if largely invisible, form of political power. Surprisingly, the studies of radical educational researchers use a methodology that reflects less the viewpoints of Bachrach and Baratz than that of the behavioristic and generally conservative school of political science that considers it "unscientific" to study anything other than overt political issues (see Polsby, 1963). The preference shown by radicals for visible struggles as subjects of investigation is probably, however, a result less of direct influence from political science than of a stress on conflict inherent in neo-Marxist theory. Whatever its sources, the disproportionate emphasis placed by left-wing scholars on highly visible struggles and their concomitant neglect of the content of schooling has impeded the development of a radical politics of education. See Lukes (1974) for a further development of the view that the capacity to prevail over opponents in the decision-making process is only one element, albeit an important one, of political power.

class reproduction takes place through the differential levels of achievement of children from different social origins. Indeed, it is precisely this meritocratic feature of education to which radicals point as the key to its efficiency and legitimacy. How, then, is differential academic performance to be explained in conflict theory? Bowles's general answer (1971a) is that the "rules of the game" favor the affluent. This formulation might be thought to lead to an analysis of the social relations of pedagogy, showing how they reflect the cultural dominance of elites and thus handicap the learning of the children of the poor. Instead, however, Bowles offers two "prominent examples" of "rules of the game" that maintain the system of inequality—the principles of "rewarding excellence" and those of local school finance. Whatever the importance of these principles—and the findings of the Coleman Report suggest that local finance, at least, is rather insignificant—it would be difficult to argue that they illuminate the *process* leading to class differentials in academic achievement. The fact is that conflict theory, for all its concern with class reproduction via education, has virtually nothing to say about class-linked patterns of educational achievement.[61]

In rejecting genetic and cultural deprivation explanations of the correlation between scholastic achievement and social class, conflict theorists find themselves in the position of pointing to the schools as the source of the problem without being able to specify what it is about them that is responsible. Despite some insight into the non-cognitive aspects of the educational process, they have largely allowed the internal workings of schools to remain a black box. This relative neglect of the content of schooling is, we have suggested, also a feature of the functionalist and methodological empiricist approaches, and it has had similar consequences here—conflict theory, no less than its principal opponents, has been unable to resolve the perennial problem of working-class "educability."

THE "NEW" SOCIOLOGY OF EDUCATION

Political and ideological events, including the intensification of struggles for educational reform and the recrudescence of racially linked genetic theories of intelligence in the 1960s, added urgency to the problem of explaining differential academic achievement. By and large, the macrosociological approaches, whatever their political and ideological correlates, had proved inadequate to the task, and the time was thus opportune for analytical invention. In Europe, the major promise lay in the attempts of Bernstein in England and Bourdieu in France to relate the problem of educability to that of socially controlled cultural transmission. Bernstein's arrival in 1963 at the

---

61. See Rist (1973), however, for an attempt to integrate a microlevel analysis of a ghetto school with some of the more general concerns of conflict theory.

London Institute of Education, in particular, played an especially crucial role in stimulating the emergence of a new approach focusing directly on the content of education and the internal operation of schools, which has come to be called the "new" sociology of education.

At the end of the 1960s, Berger and Luckman (1967), whose theory of the "social construction of reality" was already exerting a widespread influence on the large discipline of sociology, seemed to offer promising lines of inquiry. Variously calling themselves ethnomethodologists, phenomenologists, and symbolic interactionists, a network of research workers sharing a common suspicion of macrosociological analysis and a diffuse commitment to studies of educational content appeared on the scene. Some heralds (Young, 1971a; Gorbutt, 1972) announced the beginning of a revolution and the birth of a new sociology of education. This is a claim worthy of serious attention, and we shall conclude our examination of competing perspectives in educational research with a discussion of it.

In 1965, in a critique of the educational policy of the British Labour Party, Quentin Hoare noted that the strategy for educational equality that had hitherto been followed put its main emphasis on structural reform but "never attacked the vital centre of the system, the curriculum, the *content* of what is taught" (Hoare, 1965:40). Failure to specify the content of a socialist education would, Hoare suggested, prove fatal to the realization of egalitarian aspirations, for the system of non-streamed comprehensive education desired by radicals would be impossible without transformed teaching methods and curricula. By 1969, a study by Julienne Ford had shown that comprehensive schools could reproduce old class differences in new ways, primarily through internal differentiation. And in 1972, looking back at British educational policy, Halsey commented that "the essential fact of twentieth century educational history is that egalitarian policies have failed" (Halsey, 1972:6).

If the failure of comprehensive schools to reduce educational inequality raised questions about the efficacy of structural reform, the organizational changes they brought with them raised problems that pointed to the need for curricular reform. Previously selective grammar schools were now faced with the influx of ordinary children whose backgrounds and interests clashed with traditional academic values. The raising of the school leaving age engendered a demand for new curricula that would be suited to the needs of pupils whose presence in school was, in many cases, involuntary. Finally, the abolition of the eleven-plus examination had freed teachers from the constraints inherent in the task of preparing pupils for it and had eased the way for curricular experiments in the primary schools.[62]

---

62. For discussion of the relationship between structural change in British education and the upsurge of interest in the curriculum, see Walker (1972:37–38), Young (1971b:20–22), Brown (1973:14), Silver (1973:xvi–xvii), Bernstein (1974:151), and Williamson (1974:8).

By the early 1970s, a school of thought stressing the significance of the content of education had formed, and one of its members (Gorbutt, 1972) was describing it as "the new sociology of education"—an emergent "alternative paradigm." Previous work was dismissed as a "positivistic" version of structural functionalism using "input-output models" and a "normative paradigm." The "old" sociology of education was soon to be transcended. Davies, in his critique of Hopper's (1968:29–44) typology of educational systems, dismissed research on educational selection with the cavalier remark that while it had been very important for collecting data, "one may wonder whether it has done much more than improve our knowledge of social stratification and raise uncomfortable questions about the consequences of public policy" (1971:117). Organizational studies, on the other hand, though "superior to what normally passes for the sociology of education," have the defect of not "necessarily contributing to a sociology of knowledge," and any comparative study which ignores the analysis of education as culture is "in danger of trivializing the entire subject" (1971:124). Davies goes on to state explicitly that "the management of knowledge" should be the central concern of the sociology of education (1971:133).

M.F.D. Young, the editor of the first reader in the sociology of education devoted to the 'interpretative paradigm', was also harshly critical of previous educational research. Even at its best, as in Westergaard and Little's study (1964) on educational opportunity and Lacey's (1970) investigation of grouping and selection procedures, the old sociology of education, "by treating as unproblematic what it is to be educated," does "little more than provide what is often a somewhat questionable legitimacy to the various pressures for administrative and curricular 'reform' " (Young, 1971a:2). In general, sociologists have taken educators' definitions of problems as given and have neglected the task of formulating their own problems. For the sociologist who undertakes this task, however, the "problems" identified by educators (e.g., the "below average child") are themselves phenomena to be explained. With "what counts as educational knowledge" highly problematic, the structural issues that dominated the normative paradigm recede into the background, and the microlevel problems of the "curricular, pedagogic and assessment categories held by school personnel," teacher-student interaction, and above all the curriculum become the dominant concerns of educational research. From this perspective, "the sociology of education is no longer conceived as an area of enquiry distinct from the sociology of knowledge" (Young, 1971a:3–5).

(a) The Social Origins of the Interpretative Critique

Without judging the accuracy of these pronouncements about the history of educational research, and before embarking on a critical assessment of the new approach, it may be helpful to examine the context in which they emerged. Perhaps the most striking feature of the "new" sociology of education is that it is almost entirely a British creation and has so far made few inroads into American educational research.[63] At first glance this is somewhat surprising, given the long and impressive tradition in the United States of classroom observation going back to Waller's 1932 classic, *The Sociology of Teaching,* and extending through Becker's (1952;1953) studies of the Chicago school teacher to Rist's (1970;1973) recent investigations of ghetto schools. Moreover, sociologists like Everett Hughes and others connected with the Chicago school of sociology have taught and written about phenomenology since before World War II. Nevertheless, the "new" sociology of education is a lively focus of debate in Britain and remains essentially unknown in the United States.

We cannot claim to offer more than tentative suggestions as to why the two countries should have developed so differently in this field. But our earlier remarks about comprehensive education and its curriculum perhaps point in the right direction. In comparative perspective there was no such problem in the United States, which had a long-established system of comprehensive secondary schools and a problem of structural reform that was different from the British and European problem of transforming a dual system into mass secondary education.[64]

Compared to Great Britain, America is a young, relatively populistic society, and there is nothing analogous either to the vigorous defense of high culture offered by T.S. Eliot or G.H. Bantock, or to the sheer weight of what Raymond Williams (1957) calls the Tradition. The elitist defense of the traditional grammar school curriculum to be found in such widely read documents as the Black Papers (Cox and Rhodes, 1975) has no American counterpart. Indeed, it may be that the saliency of the curriculum as a public issue in Great Britain reflects a historically rooted commitment to the preservation of socially hierarchical educational ideals that have no equivalent social base in a society like that of the United States, which the Polish sociologist Ossowski (1963) has described as one of "non-egalitarian classlessness."

63. This is not meant to imply that it has had no influence whatever. A number of social scientists grouped around Aaron Cicourel, one of the founders of ethnomethodology, have, for example, recently published a book (Cicourel et al., 1974), *Language Use and School Performance,* which expresses a set of concerns remarkably similar to those of the "new" sociology of education. Revealingly, however, its authors mention only one of the nine articles in Young's reader and show little familiarity with the work of British educational researchers working within the 'interpretative paradigm'.
64. The difficulties faced by British comprehensive schools in formulating a curriculum for students of diverse social backgrounds were compounded by particularly sharp cultural cleavages between social classes. Despite the lack of empirical data on the question, it would seem safe to say that there is a distinct working-class sub-culture in Great Britain that has no real counterpart in the United States. For a penetrating discussion of English working-class culture, see Hoggart (1959). See also Jackson and Marsden, *Education and the Working Class* (1963), and Jackson, *Working Class Community* (1968).

The intellectual context of specialist work on education within the wider discipline of sociology also differed between the two countries. In America, the main candidate for new leadership after the disarray of the 1960s was conflict theory (Friedrichs, 1970:45–61). In Britain, however, the challenge came much more from the new interpretative approaches.

However, to observe that the character of alternative approaches in the sociology of education in the two countries parallels general movements in sociology is not thereby to give an explanation.[65] Following the works of Gouldner (1971) and Friedrichs (1970), we might trace the more general movements to much the same set of factors. The relative stability of British society compared with American has remained striking in recent years. Great Britain did not experience radical student movements on anything resembling the scale of the American New Left. Nor, despite mounting social difficulties, were British social problems of the same order of magnitude as those in America occasioned by the Vietnam war and racial conflict. There may have been some intensification of traditional forms of class conflict in Britain in the early 1970s, but these industrial struggles had little impact on sociological theory and they raised few issues about education. In short, the British cultural and political context was much less conducive than its American counterpart to macro-sociological studies of social conflict.

Nevertheless, the question still remains why interpretative approaches were so warmly received in Britain. One factor, it may be suggested, was that the "new" sociology of education identified itself with the sociology of knowledge. Always considered a rather marginal, continental pursuit by American sociologists, the sociology of knowledge has roots in Britain at least as far back as the arrival of Karl Mannheim in the 1930s. The growing interest of recent years may also reflect the closer proximity of British sociologists to their German and French colleagues and in part their relatively greater philosophical sophistication in comparison to American sociologists. Although only vaguely familiar with continental philosophy, British sociologists tend to be aware of the epistemological problems raised by logical positivism. This greater familiarity with analytic philosophy makes them more receptive to approaches that raise questions about the social and philosophical basis of knowledge.

Though influenced by the phenomenological writings of Schutz (1962) and Berger and Luckman (1967), proponents of the new approaches in educational

---

65. The fact that ethnomethodology, which is a crucial component of the interpretative paradigm, is an essentially American invention does not negate our general proposition, for the ethnomethodological approach has been adopted by relatively few American sociologists and has never presented a serious challenge to either the functionalist or the conflict paradigms. Two of the founders of ethnomethodology, Cicourel (1964) and Garfinkel (1967), though both American, are perhaps more widely known in Great Britain than in the United States, and it would seem that their critique of the normative paradigm has had much more of an effect on mainstream British sociology than on its American counterpart.

research have also drawn heavily on the work of ethnomethodologists, especially Cicourel (1964) and Garfinkel (1967). The social setting most conducive to the growth and development of ethnomethodology is difficult to identify, but Gouldner (1971:390–395), in discussing Garfinkel, has made the suggestion that the hostility expressed by ethnomethodology towards the conventional character of the implicit rules that make stable social interaction possible appeals most strongly to the culturally alienated. What is being questioned by the ethnomethodologists in their demonstration of the fragility of tacit understandings underlying daily social interaction is not so much the legitimacy of existing social and political institutions as the accuracy of the common-sense view of reality itself. Though critical of the way things are, the ethnomethodologist directs his attention more to microlevel interactions than to larger social structures. His rebellion, though radical in its rejection of the routines of everyday life, avoids direct confrontation with the status quo.

What is perhaps most interesting about Gouldner's discussion of Garfinkel is the implication that ethnomethodology is most likely to prosper when dissent takes the form more of counter-cultural rebellion than of political radicalism. It would be inappropriate to press the point too insistently, but it may be that just such a situation has prevailed in many British universities. In the late 1960s cultural rather than political forms of radicalism influenced the values and life-styles of students. The depth and breadth of counter-cultural sentiment in British universities did not, in all likelihood, exceed the degree of cultural alienation present among American students, but the presence in America of a radical student movement tended to give dissent a more sharply political character. Accordingly, if young British researchers in the sociology of education were more attracted to interpretative approaches while their American colleagues preferred conflict theory, it may be that this was partly the outcome of different social and political conditions in the two countries.[66]

66. Despite our belief that there is a relationship between the rise of ethnomethodology and the growth of counter-cultural sentiments, we would stress that this is a highly tentative formulation that calls for careful empirical investigation. One piece of evidence that suggests that ethnomethodology prospers in a counter-cultural setting is that it emerged in southern California, perhaps the capital of youth culture (notably at the University of California at Los Angeles, Santa Barbara, and San Diego). As late as 1970, at least twenty-five of forty-eight American sociologists in the ethnomethodological "network" were still located in southern California (Mullins, 1973:200). That it has been well received in Great Britain, which has a strong counter-culture, fits well with our hypothesis, as does its failure to develop in France, where radicalism is almost exclusively political in character. The fact that ethnomethodology has had a relatively modest effect on American educational research conforms to our general explanation; especially in the research community, political radicalism has been more salient than cultural radicalism, and the predominance of conflict theory over ethnomethodology may well reflect that predominance. However, an analysis of many socio-historical factors other than the New Left and the counter-culture would be necessary to explain the divergent development of alternative approaches to the sociology of education in Great Britain and the United States.

In attempting to understand the origins and development of the "new" sociology of education, it is important to realize that it emerged less in university departments of sociology than in institutes and colleges of education. The University of London's Institute of Education, where in 1963 Basil Bernstein developed the first program to give higher degrees in the sociology of education, seems to have played a particularly important role in the development of the interpretative approach,[67] and the Open University, an institution that by its nature is much concerned with problems of pedagogy and curriculum, has been instrumental in disseminating its perspective to the academic public.[68] When one considers the substantive concerns of the "new" sociology of education, it seems quite fitting that its institutional incubator was the institute of education. For unlike the functionalist and conflict theories of education, both of which are essentially concerned with the macrosociological question of the structure of the relationships between schools and other social institutions, the interpretative approach focuses directly on the internal operations of the schools themselves. The preoccupations of the "new" sociology of education—above all, classroom interaction and the sociology of the curriculum—correspond quite strikingly to the professional interests of students in institutions primarily devoted to training school-teachers. Proponents of the interpretative approach (Esland, 1971:111; Gorbutt, 1972:9–10) have, indeed, explicitly cited its relevance to teacher training as one of its virtues, and the effort of the "new" sociology of education to illuminate what goes on in the classroom is doubtless one of the sources of its appeal not only to students in schools of education but also to those sociologists whose job it is to teach them.[69]

67. In his teaching at the London University Institute of Education, where many of the advocates of the interpretative approach studied with him, Bernstein gave as lectures to students the various papers on the organization and knowledge structures of schools that constitute Volume III of his *Class, Codes and Control.* At the same time, according to Bernstein (1975:1), the sociolinguistic thesis played little part in his teaching at the Institute. For a detailed discussion of Bernstein's unique contribution to the sociology of education—a contribution that cuts across the distinction between the 'interpretative' and 'normative' paradigms—see our remarks below, pp. 62-71.
68. M.F.D. Young holds a teaching position in the London Institute of Education, and two other leading proponents of the interpretative paradigm, Keddie (1971) and Esland (1971), were there as graduate students. Gorbutt, another advocate of the "new" sociology of education, teaches in the Department of Education at North-East London Polytechnic. The Open University has provided crucial institutional support for the "new" sociology of education by giving official "set book" status to two readers reflecting its viewpoint, *Knowledge and Control* (Young, 1971a) and *School and Society* (Cosin et al., 1971), and by making them part of the curriculum of its course on "School and Society."
69. The role of students in the formation of social theory is one of the most neglected areas in the sociology of sociology (see Gouldner, 1971:403). Faculty-student interaction is by no means a one-way process, and the case of the development of the "new" sociology of education suggests that the character of the student body is an important aspect of the institutional setting of academically-based social research. With respect to the popularity of the interpretative approach in institutes and colleges of education, an additional factor may have been lack of financial resources for research. According to Carter (1968), a heavily disproportionate number of sociologists in colleges of education complain of a lack of research funds. Their choice, therefore, of classroom observation as the basic research methodology is one

Having embarked upon their new course, advocates of the "new" sociology of education faced the formidable problem of legitimating their approach. Their difficulties resided not only in the newness of their formulation, but also in the fragility of the institutional base from which they operated. For if the sociology of education has relatively low status among the sub-disciplines of sociology, colleges and institutes of education also have low status as institutions for the aspiring sociologist. The "old" sociology of education dealt with the legitimation problem posed by the questionable character of its subject matter by attaching itself to the larger framework of the respected sub-discipline of social stratification. It was also assisted by its location within university departments of sociology. The new approach, with its main social base outside the universities, had no equally prestigious source of institutional support. Despite efforts to borrow status from the increasingly prominent but still marginal ethnomethodological and phenomenological approaches and from the rather esoteric sub-discipline of the sociology of knowledge, the "new" sociology of education still faced considerable legitimation problems.[70]

Foremost among the tactics of proponents of the 'interpretative paradigm' was the drawing of exceedingly sharp lines between "old" and "new" sociology of education. Through a series of bold attacks (Davies, 1969; Young, 1971b; Davies, 1971; Gorbutt, 1972) on the so-called normative (or "conventional") paradigm, the advocates of the interpretative approach offered an explicit challenge to the established sociology of education that could hardly be ignored.[71] If the loudness with which they announced an impending revolution in educational research caused skepticism in some quarters, the promise of "new directions for the sociology of education" (the subtitle of Young's reader) aroused eager anticipation in others. Throughout, they strongly emphasized the innova-

---

frequently made within severe financial constraints. The fact that the techniques called for by 'normative' sociology (e.g., survey research) would often be prohibitively expensive for the college of education sociologist is probably a rather minor source of his attraction to the 'interpretative paradigm', but it would be naive to suggest that the unpleasant realities of money play no role whatsoever in the determination of research styles.

70. The inherently "soft" character of the methodologies favored by the "new" sociology of education further compounded the legitimation problems of the 'interpretative paradigm'. In a discipline notably insecure about its scientific status, the non-quantitative and, in many cases, non-replicable and non-falsifiable propositions put forward by the "new" sociology of education were hardly likely to appeal to sociology's persistent quest for a positivistic type of "rigor." Young (1971b:26), in observing that sociologists in colleges, institutes, and departments of education tended for years to neglect the study of curriculum, has suggested that a fear of "boundary disputes" with philosophers of education and curriculum specialists led sociologists of education to shy away from an analysis of the content of schooling. There is doubtless an element of truth here, but a more crucial factor was probably the unwieldiness of studying in-school processes. If many sociologists of education for years avoided the study of curriculum, the reason they did so was probably the same one that led most of their colleagues to look askance at the sociology of knowledge—the ill-defined character of the available methodologies seemed incompatible with the development of a rigorously empirical, scientific discipline.

71. Halsey (1971), in the concluding essay to Hopper's *Readings in the Theory of Educational Systems,* offered a preliminary response.

tive character of the ethnomethodological approach and its incompatibility with the "old" sociology of education. Indeed, their criticisms of traditional educational research raised a number of important issues, and their own formulation was a strikingly novel one. Though holding only a tiny base in the universities and possessing no serious body of empirical research derived from its theoretical framework, the "new" sociology of education was, by 1972, able to present itself plausibly as an "emergent paradigm" constituting a comprehensive alternative to the approach that had dominated the discipline for two decades.[72]

(b) The "New" Sociology of Education: An Early Assessment

The interpretative approach has had a generally salutary effect on the sociology of education in Great Britain. Bernstein (1974:149) has recently noted that the traditional sociology of education in Great Britain "bore the hallmarks of British applied sociology; atheoretical, pragmatic, descriptive and policy focused." Primarily concerned with the structural problem of the relation between the educational system and the system of social stratification, research in the post-war years had had little to say about the content of education and had carried out few classroom studies.[73] Emerging within a discipline that despite impressive accomplishments had seemingly lost its forward momentum, the challenge raised by the interpretative school has infused new life into the sociology of education by pointing not only to crucial theoretical problems, but also to new areas of research.

The "new" sociology of education is too new to permit a confident assessment of its contribution. Its influence so far derives less from research findings than from the distinctively different research priorities it proposes. If the concerns of the traditional sociology of education, most notably selection and socialization, are not quite relegated to the historical dustbin, it is nevertheless

72. In launching a frontal attack on the established sociology of education, proponents of the interpretative paradigm were embarking upon a high-risk, but potentially high-return, strategy. Gouldner (1968:108), in his analysis of the "underdog" school in the sociology of deviance, notes that the adoption of an unorthodox position can evoke hostile criticism, but that "it may also bring higher and quicker returns than the adoption of an overdog standpoint which, being common, tends to glut the market and to depress the price paid per individual contribution." He then goes on to observe that the adoption of a dissenting position may "be thought of as a career strategy more appealing to high variance betters who, in turn, are more likely to be found among the ambitious young." It is worth noting in this regard that the two main alternative schools of thought in the sociology of sociology, the interpretative and conflict approaches, are disproportionately supported by young researchers.

73. As recently as 1972, a British sociologist was able to write that "observational research in the classroom is almost entirely an American tradition" (Walker, 1972:35). Young (1971b:26), however, makes clear that even the best of these studies, often conducted by symbolic interactionists, do not, despite their raising of important questions about "processes of interaction and the situational significance of beliefs and values," meet the requirements of the interpretative paradigm, for they do not "consider as problematic the knowledge that is made available in such interactions."

clear that they are now to be considered marginal to a discipline that looks upon the "management of knowledge" (Davies, 1971) as its central problem. With the 'interpretative paradigm', itself deeply influenced by the sociology of knowledge, providing the theoretical framework of the "new" sociology of education, three related problem areas emerge as the key concerns of the field: teacher-student interaction, the categories or concepts used by educators, and the curriculum.

The problem of classroom interaction, a subject already treated in some detail by American symbolic interactionists, has excited considerable interest among those British sociologists of education influenced by the work of the ethno-methodologists.[74] As yet, however, the excitement accompanying the identification of a neglected problem has not so far been followed by much empirical research. One notable exception is Keddie's (1971) article, "Classroom Knowledge." A study of the teaching of a course in the humanities at a large and heterogeneous comprehensive school, it is concerned with the knowledge teachers have of pupils and with what counts as knowledge suitable for discussion and evaluation in the classroom.

Keddie's study is an excellent expression of the interests of the "new" sociology of education, for in its search for the processes involved in the production of academic "failures" it looks simultaneously at teacher-student interaction, the categories used by educators, and the organization of the curriculum. Careful observation of teachers both inside and outside the classroom reveals that the concepts they hold, though often in contradiction with their aims as "educationalists," influence their relations with pupils in the classroom. The teacher will, for example, vigorously deny that ability is associated with social class and then proceed in concrete cases to suggest the most intimate relationship between social background and academic capacity. The concept of the "normal pupil" in a given ability category enables the teacher to categorize students about whom he has little direct knowledge and, accordingly, to treat identical student behavior in a radically different fashion, depending upon the category in which the student is placed. What counts as knowledge when suggested by an A (high ability) pupil may be dismissed as error or incomprehension in the case of a C (low ability) pupil. The differential treatment of pupils in different ability categories is, in turn, facilitated by a system of streaming that provides students with readily available labels. The internal structure of the school is thus shown to be closely related to a process of categorizing pupils that itself conditions interaction between student and teacher. Through the use of the interpretative approach, Keddie is able to show how the educators' socially constructed con-

---

74. The work of Hargreaves (1967) and Lacey (1970) shows, however, that interest among British sociologists of education in student-teacher interaction predates the emergence of the interpretative school.

cepts systematically influence their behavior in the classroom. The outcome is "the differentiation of an undifferentiated curriculum" (1971:143), and it is clear from Keddie's account that the nature of this differentiation impedes the academic achievement of lower-stream and lower-class students.

In an appeal for sociologists to look at the curriculum as an expression of the principles governing the organization and selection of knowledge, M.F.D. Young (1971b) points to an important subject that had been largely ignored by the traditional sociology of education and makes a number of suggestions about the relationship between the stratification of knowledge and the distribution of values and rewards in society. However, Young has not attempted to apply his suggestions to the analysis of a specific problem, and few followers of the interpretative approach have engaged in systematic studies of the curriculum.[75] Here, as in many other areas of educational research, the new sociology of education has identified an interesting problem and suggested a possible way of tackling it, but it has not yet produced either close ethnographic descriptions (Bernstein, 1974:152) or a serious body of empirical literature based on its theoretical framework. Unlike the conflict theory of education, which is well established in the United States, the 'interpretative paradigm' has produced many new departures but disturbingly few arrivals.

The reasons for this failure are not immediately apparent, but the reluctance of the critic to offer his own positive formulation of a problem, thereby putting forward propositions that would themselves be subject to refutation, is a well-known phenomenon. Ethnomethodologists may have felt particularly vulnerable on this issue, for it is in the nature of their approach to be acutely aware of the methodological difficulties involved in social research.

Two of the key research issues identified by the interpretative approach—the curriculum and the concepts of educators—posed particular problems for the prospective researcher, for the novelty of the subject matter called for the creation of new methods. Even the more familiar problem of student-teacher interaction, already treated by symbolic interactionists, posed at every turn the thorny question of what counts as valid knowledge. Clearly, empirical investigation of the problems raised by the interpretative approach could not proceed with the type of "rigor" demanded by a discipline that accords scientific status only to those propositions that are replicable and falsifiable. Equally clearly, the "new" sociology of education would never generate data as tidy as the quantitative figures on social stratification produced in the political arithmetic tradition. Furthermore, careful and long-term classroom observation called for an enor-

75. Eggleston, a proponent of the "new" sociology of education who nonetheless maintains a certain critical distance from some of its propositions (1973a, 1974:1–10), has put forward a model of the curriculum decision-making process based on some of the insights of both the interpretative paradigm and conflict theory (1973b).

mous investment of time and energy. Faced with these formidable obstacles, it is quite understandable that proponents of the "new" sociology of education should have been more successful in criticizing existing research than in producing their own body of substantive propositions.

It would be misleading, however, to convey the impression that supporters of an ethnomethodological approach to the sociology of education have undertaken no systematic empirical research. An ambitious field study in Southern California public schools, for example, has been led by one of the founders of ethnomethodology itself—Aaron V. Cicourel—and published as a series of articles under the title *Language Use and School Performance* (1974).

Sensitive, as ethnomethodologists are, to the fragility of "common-sense constructs," the authors investigate some of the assumptions implicit in the evaluation of the academic "performance" of school children. Their focus is on the test situation itself as a socially constructed phenomenon, and they pay particular attention to the interaction between the examiner and the examinee. They take nothing for granted—neither the concepts and procedures of the tester nor the linguistic comprehension and performance levels of the tested. The study is based on careful classroom observation, and its detailed analysis of the testing process constitutes a rebuke to those who would reify the results of ostensibly scientific scholastic examinations.

Yet despite the relative novelty of the ethnomethodological approach and the freshness of some of its insights, the most striking thing about the study led by Cicourel is its frequent banality. Roth (1974), for example, demonstrates in considerable detail that the cognitive operations leading to an answer marked as incorrect are often more complex than those which result in an acceptable response. Cicourel (1974:331) finds it necessary to reiterate the study's finding that bilingual children have particularly acute problems in understanding test instructions. In article after article, the authors advance the well-worn idea that the social setting in which a test takes place influences student performance. When one compares the self-consciously innovative work presented in *Language Use and School Performance* with the research of such representatives of the "traditional" sociology of education as Strodtbeck (1961) or Kahl (1961), it is hard to see how the interpretative approach has advanced understanding of a problem for which it seemed eminently apt—that of educability.[76]

76. Nor is it clear how the research of advocates of the "new" sociology of education has gone beyond the work of such symbolic interactionists as Waller and Becker. For a useful summary of the research of the "old" sociology of education on the problem of educability, see Chapters 4 and 5 of Banks (1971). Advocates of the interpretative paradigm often balk at the notion that the family factors cited by previous researchers play a role in differential scholastic performance, preferring instead to remain on the more familiar microsociological terrain of the school itself. This tendency to ignore the family in favor of the school in explaining racial and class differences in academic achievement doubtless reflects in part a feeling that any mention of factors external to the school would be ideologically unpalatable, but it also derives from the difficulty of explaining inter-institutional relations (e.g., between the family and the school)

Sociologists of diverse theoretical and methodological persuasions are vulnerable to the charge that they spend much of their time documenting the obvious. The ethnomethodologists, however, are distinctive in presenting their empirical analysis of the well-known distortions of test performance introduced by social context and linguistic misunderstanding within a framework of extreme relativism. Reading the studies reported in Cicourel (1974), for example, one is left with the impression that the tests used to measure reading comprehension are arbitrary human constructs laden with so many class-linked measurement problems that they are essentially unrelated to the student's actual capacity to understand written material.

There is an obvious egalitarian appeal in the notion that recorded differences in reading level between rich and poor children would disappear if one were able to measure their academic performance accurately, but such a formulation strains the limits of credibility. Yet the ideological impetus behind ultra-relativism is a powerful one, for if sociologists cannot eradicate glaring inequalities in the real world, they can perhaps do away with them on the conceptual level by denying that they are, appearances to the contrary notwithstanding, inequalities after all. What would seem to be racial and class differences in the distribution of knowledge are, instead, figments of a positivistic imagination.

This reluctance to recognize visible differences in knowledge is, in part, a product of ethnomethodological epistemology; Gorbutt (1972:7) states the position succinctly when he writes that "knowledge . . . becomes thoroughly relativized and the possibility of absolute knowledge is denied."[77] As a consequence of their belief that all knowledge is ideological (Gorbutt, 1972:7), ethnomethodologists find themselves in an awkward position when the subordinate social groups with whom they sympathize set out to diminish inequalities in the social distribution of knowledge which, were one to take seriously the semantic

---

within the framework of a paradigm based primarily on face-to-face "interactions," "definitions of the situation," and "constructions of reality." Floud and Halsey (1958:184) pointed out that educability studies tended to be one-sided in their emphasis on family environment over the "assumptions, values and aims embodied in the school," but there is no *a priori* reason to believe that family factors are not implicated in differential academic performance.

77. The problematic character of the extreme relativist position is vividly illustrated by Keddie's (1971) sophisticated empirical study of classroom knowledge. Stating that her approach "involves starting from the assumption that . . . we do not know what the knowledge to be got or the subject to be mastered properly is," Keddie (1971:144) goes on to declare that "subjects are what practitioners do with them." In analyzing classroom interaction between teacher and pupil, however, she is forced to attenuate her absolute relativism so as to be able to examine critically the negotiation occurring over what will count as legitimate knowledge. The arbitrariness of the teacher's attempt to impose his definition of the family on recalcitrant students, for example, is documented by an appeal to a higher form of knowledge—"the teacher (E)—*who is not a sociologist* and who has to rely on material on a pink card which includes a description of the joint family" is unaware of the concept of the "extended family as it is defined in Britain today" (Keddie, 1971:145, italics ours). That even someone as committed to extreme relativism as Keddie is forced to resort to external and hierarchical definition of what counts as valid knowledge is quite revealing, for it points to the virtual impossibility of making sense of competing definitions of knowledge if one believes, as does Gorbutt (1972:7), that all knowledge is colored by social bias and ideological distortion.

and conceptual acrobatics of the "new" sociology of education, do not exist. Ultra-relativism is a double-edged sword; while useful in denouncing such intellectually problematic and politically retrograde concepts as the "problem child," it can easily degenerate into what Goody and Watt (1963:344), referring to a similar tendency among their colleagues in anthropology, have called "sentimental egalitarianism." When it takes this form, relativism is of service neither to academic social science nor to the poor and minority groups it wishes to defend.

Perhaps the most powerful weapon wielded by ethnomethodologists in their assault on their archenemy—"positivistic" social science—is their critique of measurement techniques in conventional empirical research. The issues raised by Cicourel in *Method and Measurement in Sociology* (1964) have been familiar ones in sociology for over a decade, but only recently have they begun to penetrate educational research. Here the raising of basic problems about the collection and interpretation of data has proved extremely useful, for there has been a tendency over the years for sociologists of education to assume that evidence that is quantitative is automatically "scientific" in character. Ethnomethodologists have effectively deflated this myth, but their own criticism of measurement techniques often becomes a critique of the use of all statistical data.

Interpretative sociologists hold that social reality, which is "constantly in a state of becoming rather than being . . . is such as to preclude conventional social science approaches to data" (Gorbutt, 1972:6). In practice, this suspicion of quantitative evidence, coupled with a commitment to relativism, often leads ethnomethodologists to move from valid criticisms of measurement error to a wholesale dismissal of attempts to measure phenomena as diverse as academic performance and educational aspirations. If the ethnomethodologist's *bête noire,* the methodological empiricist, can be faulted for tending to believe that relationships that are not readily measurable are not quite real, the ethnomethodologist is guilty of concluding that relationships that *are* measurable, but imperfectly, are equally unreal. Opposites here converge. If the pure methodological empiricist characteristically avoids those phenomena that are difficult to quantify while the ethnomethodologist wages a relentless campaign of criticism against such efforts at measurement as have been made, there is a very real sense in which the one approach is the converse of the other. Their common coin is that of the obsessive search for rigor, and it is only an apparent paradox that they unite in their failure to observe C. Wright Mills's (1959) injunction against allowing the question of method to take precedence over the need to investigate pressing substantive problems.

The preferred method of the "new" sociology of education is that of participant observation (Gorbutt, 1972:7), though direct observation without participation is also looked upon with favor. These two research techniques require an intimate social setting, and they are well-suited to classroom investigations. Depending upon whether researchers draw their theoretical cues from ethnomethodology or from symbolic interactionism, they may speak of the "social construction of reality" or of the "definition of the situation," but their closely related concerns come together in sociological analysis of the process of "negotiation" over meanings. Above all, their careful observation of face-to-face relationships is designed to show that "everyday social interaction is a creative activity" (Cicourel, 1974:348) that enables man to make sense of his world.

Stress on the fact that relations in educational institutions are humanly constructed products is a welcome antidote to the deterministic and reifying tendencies of some of the "old" sociology of education. But emphasis on "man the creator" often fails to take adequate account of the social constraints on human actors in everyday life. There is, to be sure, a considerable latitude available to those engaged in struggles over the "definition of the situation," but the question of whose definition will ultimately prevail is preeminently one of *power.* Battles between students and teachers as to who will define the situation, for example, clearly illustrate this principle; teachers, by virtue of their powerful institutional positions, wield sanctions that not only delimit the boundaries of what may be "negotiated" but also give them a crucial advantage in determining whose "definitions" will prevail. The teachers themselves, however, also operate under external constraints; they may be prohibited by law from giving corporal punishment, and it is likely that they will lose their jobs if they do not follow prescribed evaluative procedures and curricular programs. There is, without doubt, an important element of creativity in student-teacher interaction; but there are also limits to the extent to which "definitions of the situation" may be negotiated.

The notion that "meanings" are created anew in every encounter in an educational institution contains an important element of truth, but it also diverts attention away from the tendency of interactions to occur in repetitive patterns. Teachers and children do not come together in a historical vacuum; the weight of precedent conditions the outcome of "negotiation" over meaning at every turn. If empirical work is confined to observation of classroom interaction, it may miss the process by which political and economic power sets sharp bounds to what is "negotiable." The classroom analyses of the "new" sociology of education are not, in short, related to *social structure,* and therefore tend to ignore the constraints under which human actors operate and so to exaggerate the fragility of the daily routine of school life.

Though a preference for microcosmic studies is at times elevated into a general principle, most proponents of the "new" sociology of education affirm the necessity of integrating structural and interactional levels of analysis. Keddie (1971:156), for example, points to a need to understand both "the linkages between schools and other institutions" and "the relationship between the social distribution of power and the distribution of knowledge." And M.F.D. Young (1971b:24) declares that "it is or should be the central task of the sociology of education to relate" the "principles of selection and organization that underlay curricula to their institutional and interactional setting in schools and classrooms to the wider social structure." To carry out such studies would be difficult, and the hostility of followers of the interpretative approach to structural analysis (extending, at times, to the suggestion that social structures exist only in the minds of human actors) suggests that the absence of serious attempts by them to articulate micro- and macrolevels of analysis is not purely a result of technical barriers. Indeed, acceptance of the idea that analyses of the structure and content of education must be integrated would give dramatic testimony to the complementarity of the methods and concerns of the "old" and "new" sociology of education.[78]

What, then, is one to make of the claim that the 'interpretative paradigm' marks the beginning of a "scientific revolution" in educational research? The careful reader of Kuhn (1970), from whom the model of a scientific revolution is derived, would be likely to react with skepticism, for one of the distinctive features of a true scientific revolution is its invisibility. When the transformation of a discipline is announced *before* the event, there is reason to suspect that one is witnessing not a scientific revolution but a more familiar phenomenon—an attempt by an emergent school of thought to legitimate its approach. According to Kuhn, scientific revolutions have historically entailed the restructuring of existing knowledge, *not,* as has been implied by proponents of the interpretative school, its dismissal (Eggleston, 1973a).[79] Only if the "new" sociology of education were able to incorporate into its framework the contribution of "traditional" educational research could it lay claim to scientific revolution. This it has been unable to do.

Instead of building incrementally on previous work, the "new" sociology of education has generally engaged in an adversary relationship to it.[80] Davies

---

78. A recent article by Erickson (1975), an American anthropologist who is not a partisan in the largely British battle between the "new" and "old" sociologies of education, demonstrates that researchers working primarily within an interpretative framework can nonetheless draw profitably upon normative studies. Erickson's own investigation, a careful observation-based analysis of counseling encounters in a community college, uses ethnomethodological techniques to study a question with important macrosociological implications: the role of counselors as gatekeepers in a racially and ethnically heterogeneous society. Though obviously indebted to Clark (1960), Erickson makes a distinctive contribution by showing how particularistic factors such as race and ethnicity affect the texture of interaction in counseling encounters and help predict the amount of special help students will receive.
79. See Eggleston (1973a; 1974:1–16) for two interesting discussions of the interpretative school and its relationship to the "old" sociology of education.
80. In manifesting a dismissive rather than incremental attitude toward previous educational research, interpretative sociologists have contradicted the Kuhnian model of scientific revolution that they purport to uphold (Eggleston, 1974:19).

(1971), for example, conveys the impression that those interested in the "management of knowledge" have little to learn from previous research, but loses sight of the fact that the studies of educational selection are, in a fundamental sense, about the distribution of knowledge (Smith, 1971:146). Eager to distance themselves from the "old" sociology of education, interpretative sociologists are slow to attend to the implications of the fact that much of the work of such researchers as Bernstein and Bourdieu, whose interests they cite as converging with their own, is rooted in the 'normative paradigm'. The research of Bernstein and Bourdieu, as well as that of Becker, Clark, and many others, suggests that the discontinuities between "old" and "new" sociology of education are not as dramatic as proponents of the 'interpretative paradigm' would like to believe.

The skepticism with which sociologists working within the interpretative framework treat administrative definitions of educational problems would seem to give them an important degree of intellectual autonomy not present among many "traditional" educational researchers, but a situation may well develop in which followers of the "new" sociology of education would have an even more intimate relationship with the state than their more "conventional" colleagues ever enjoyed.[81] The microcosmic analyses favored by interpretative sociologists are potentially more useful to educational policy-makers than any of the macrostructural research carried out by functionalists. Even methodological empiricism, said by Gouldner to be particularly well-suited to the research needs of the Welfare State, is only of limited usefulness to those who would solve the "official" educational problems of the day, for it, too, typically avoids the "black box" of schooling. Interpretative sociology, however, focuses precisely on those classroom processes that must be understood if there is to be any chance of reducing the class and racial differentials in academic achievement that concern the administrators of the Welfare State. The structural reforms of the educational system that were derived in part from macroscopic research have left behavior inside the schools substantially unchanged; even such apparently radical structural reforms as abolishing streaming and establishing a common curriculum would, as Keddie (1971:156,158) has pointed out, have little effect on the hierarchical categories of ability and knowledge that are so damaging to the scholastic performance of the "low-ability" working-class student.

---

81. Young (1971b:2), as previously noted, remarks that traditional studies of grouping and selection procedures treat as "unproblematic 'what it is to be educated'" and "do little more than provide what is often a somewhat questionable legitimacy to the various pressures for administrative and curricular 'reform'." This is an interesting remark in the context of the concerns of the sociology of sociology. Young is quick to observe how the "old" sociology of education serves "administrative" interests, but less eager to examine how the "new" sociology of education might itself be of use to the Welfare State. It is, in addition, quite striking that the examples cited by Young as serving a "legitimation" function, the studies by Westergaard and Little (1964) and Lacey (1970), actually serve to de-legitimate the existing educational system by providing important evidence of class inequalities in educational opportunity.

The possibility of an interpretative sociology of education aligned with the interests of educational policy-makers is thus apparent. Impelled by the problems raised by recent structural reforms in the educational system and by the intensity of debate, particularly in Great Britain, over what is to be learned in school, government administrators have recently developed a strong interest in the content of the educational process; for them, followers of the interpretative approach promise to deliver sociologically informed studies of the consequences of given types of curricular offerings. The continued existence of massive group differences in academic achievement is increasingly unacceptable both politically and ideologically. For officials in private and public bureaucracies who would like to see these inequalities diminished, the "new" sociology of education offers detailed investigations of student-teacher interaction that promise to identify the process by which such factors as the "self-fulfilling prophecy" (Rosenthal and Jacobson, 1968) influence student performance. If the sociology of education is ever to provide a basis for an applied sociology which effectively meets the needs of the Welfare State, it may come, paradoxically, neither from the functionalists nor from the conflict theorists, but from the "new" sociology of education whose point of departure was a criticism of the tendency of previous researchers to take the "official" educational problems of the day as their own.[82]

For the moment, however, the interpretative approach does not offer a viable alternative for either the policy concerns of the Welfare State or the research needs of the sociology of education. Yet even though the promise of a "scientific revolution" has been, and is likely to remain, unfulfilled, the interpretative perspective on educational research has stimulated controversy in the field and has generated a number of new ideas. What is now needed is a concerted effort by adherents of the interpretative school to carry out the program of empirical research it implies and to link its findings with the structural studies that have traditionally dominated the sociology of education and that continue to move the subject forward. For despite the existence of important differences between the interpretative and normative approaches to the sociology of education, it would be deplorable if the heat of polemic made it impossible for advocates of each of the two perspectives to recognize the light a considered appraisal of their opponents' position could shed on the problems that now face educational research.

82. Andreas M. Kazamias (1972), in a presidential address to the Comparative and International Education Society in March 1972 that contains an interesting substantive critique of the use of structural-functional theory in educational research, has pointed to the failure of functionalism to meet "what seem to be the demands of the market." Here, however, he is referring less to the struggle over research funds than to the battle for academic posts. An interest in questions of pedagogy will, it seems, yield not only intellectual dividends, but also jobs in a "rapidly shrinking market." Directing his remarks to his fellow comparative educationists, Kazamias counsels an intensified concern with the content of education "unless we want gradually to fade into oblivion." In addition to potentially serving the research needs of the Welfare-State, then, the "new" sociology of education may prove to be an impressively salable commodity.

THE FUTURE OF EDUCATIONAL RESEARCH

(a) Basil Bernstein: Harbinger of a New Synthesis?

Bernstein is an outstanding example of one who has made an original contribution to the sociology of education that does not hesitate to draw upon both the normative and the interpretative approaches. His early work, most elaborately expressed in his article "Social Class and Linguistic Development: A Theory of Social Learning" (1961), was a contribution to the debate over the problem of "educability" and was firmly anchored in the interest of "traditional" sociologists of education in finding ways to "prevent the wastage of working-class educational potential" (1961:308). 'Restricted' and 'elaborated' linguistic codes were never his only interest, however. The more general problem of cultural transmission and change led him to write, beginning in the early 1960s, four little-known papers on changes in the knowledge and organizational structures of schools (1975:36). This research adumbrated the emergence of the "new" sociology of education, which would place the problems of knowledge and educational processes at the center of its concerns.[83] When, in 1971, his article "On the Classification and Framing of Educational Knowledge" was first published, it was quickly apprehended as a crucial contribution by proponents of both "old" and "new" schools of thought in the sociology of education.

What is perhaps most distinctive about Bernstein's work is his persistent effort to integrate micro- and macrocosmic levels of analysis. Bernstein believes in the necessity of conducting educational research in such a way as to take account of both the 'structural' and the 'interactional' aspects of social life (1974:155; 1975:7), and a serious effort in this direction marks the two distinct but interrelated strands in his writing: the one concerned with sociolinguistics, "which focuses upon the reproduction of class relationships as these shape the structure of communication, and its social basis in the family," and the other concerned with cultural transmission, which attempts "to sketch the effect of class relationships upon the institutionalizing of elaborated codes in the school" (1975:1). No matter how intimate the phenomenon being examined, Bernstein believes that it should be possible to show how its form and development are influenced by the larger patterns of power and control.

His studies of social class and linguistic codes provide a concrete example of an integrated analysis of the *structure* and the *process* of class reproduction. "The genes of social class," he writes, "may well be carried less through a genetic

---

83. These four articles are published as the first four contributions to Volume III of Bernstein's *Class, Codes and Control* (1975). The other three selections in this volume, which is subtitled "Toward a Theory of Educational Transmissions," are "On the Classification and Framing of Educational Knowledge," "Class and Pedagogies–Visible and Invisible," and "The Sociology of Education: A Brief Account."

code but far more through a communication code that social class itself promotes" (1973a:165). The originality of his work lies not so much in its detailed descriptions of relationships between class and speech patterns as in its analyses of the ways in which social class *generates* distinct forms of communication. For Bernstein, "codes . . . are functions of a particular form of social relationship or, more generally, qualities of social structure" (1973a:93).

The search for the social conditions that give rise to linguistic codes leads Bernstein to attempt to link the macroinstitutional features of a given social formation with patterns of communication. Social structure is seen primarily as a system of class inequality, and the key mechanism by which its effects are transmitted linguistically is the family. Family class position is the fundamental determinant of linguistic code; the characteristic expressions of membership in working-class and middle-class families are, respectively, 'restricted' and 'elaborated' codes. Participation in working-class family and community life, in which social relations are based upon shared identifications, expectations, and assumptions, tends to generate a 'restricted code', for the speaker who is sure that the listener can take his intentions for granted has little incentive to elaborate his meanings and make them explicit and specific. Middle-class culture, in contrast, tends to place the "I" over the "we," and the resultant uncertainty that meanings will be intelligible to the listener forces the speaker to select among syntactic alternatives and to differentiate his vocabulary (1973a:169–170). The result is the development of an 'elaborated code' oriented to the communication of highly individuated meanings.[84]

The class structure also typically gives rise to different family role systems, which in turn encourage different modes of communication. In the traditional working-class family, in which decision-making is based upon formal status (often age and sex), authority derives from 'positional' rather than 'personal' qualities. The role system of such families, in which judgments are based on the status of the member rather than on individual qualities, is less likely than that of person-oriented families to facilitate the verbal exploration of individual

---

84. From Bernstein's descriptions of the texture of working-class and middle-class life, it is clear that the literature to which he refers (1973a:186) is primarily British. Since the class character of British society is particularly visible and since class-based differences in speech in Great Britain are unusually acute, it is an open question whether Bernstein's sociolinguistic thesis could be applied with the same force to other advanced industrial societies such as the United States or the Soviet Union. Indeed, it is difficult to imagine that a series of explorations as bold and innovative as Bernstein's studies in the sociology of language could have been developed in a society lacking the sharpness of British class relations and the overtness of the accompanying linguistic distinctions. That Bernstein himself originates from a poor neighborhood in the East End of London and taught in London City Day College, an institution dominated by working-class students, gives a personal dimension to the social context in which his research on sociolinguistics emerged and perhaps contributes toward an understanding of his unusual sensitivity to the social basis of language. Yet the rootedness of Bernstein's work in British life inevitably raises a troublesome question: to what extent are his general formulations on the problem of social class and linguistic codes products of the peculiarities of British society and to what extent are they universally applicable?

differences, intentions, and motives (1973a:178–179). As such, positional families are likely to promote a 'closed communication system', which is frequently associated with possession of a 'restricted code'.[85] This is not to say, however, that an exact fit is postulated among classes, family types, and linguistic usage. Positional and personal family types exist in both the middle and the working class, and elaborated codes differ from restricted codes within as well as between family types.

Bernstein's explorations of the social basis of language are imaginative and his formulations logically elegant, but they are also plagued by a certain empirical elusiveness. The concept of code, for example, is at the center of the sociolinguistic thesis, but since codes, as distinct from speech variants, are not themselves directly observable (1973:34), it is not clear how far the relationship between social class and linguistic code could ever be given any precision. Bernstein is well aware of this problem and has suggested that an analysis that attempts to identify the causal relationship between class and code should be "predictive" and should "give rise to measurable criteria for evaluating the interrelationships between role systems, forms of social control and linguistic orientations" (1973a:176). The effort by Bernstein and his collaborators to operationalize these concepts continues in an impressive if little-known body of empirical research.[86]

Despite the empirical difficulties of Bernstein's formulation of the problem of class, codes, and educability, his research on sociolinguistics has been widely cited to explain the relatively poor academic performance of working-class school children. This interpretation is not a misreading of Bernstein's thesis; there are repeated assertions in Volume I of *Class, Codes and Control* that the failure of working-class pupils to possess an elaborated code (called, in the earlier chapters, a "formal language") is intimately related to their low scholastic achievement (1973a:55–60, 159, 175, 221). Bernstein's model of the process that leads to differential academic performance emphasizes the distinction between working-class life, which often limits children who experience it to a restricted code, and the school, which demands a set of aptitudes embodied in an elaborated code. Restricted codes, which are embedded in a local context, encourage particularistic meanings; elaborated codes, less tied to a specific social context, tend to promote universalistic meanings (1973a:200). A consequence

85. For a detailed account of Bernstein's typology of positional and person-oriented families, which are by no means simply to be identified with restricted and elaborated codes, much less with the working class and the middle class, see his article, "A Sociolinguistic Approach to Socialization: With Some Reference to Educability" (1973a:165–192). This article attempts to identify not only the social origins of linguistic codes and family role systems, but also the structural factors that account for change.
86. Those interested in the empirical work of Bernstein and his collaborators should consult the series of books on "Primary Socialization, Language and Education" published by Routledge and Kegan Paul under the general editorship of Bernstein. For lucid discussions of Bernstein's work in general, see Lawton (1968) and Cherkaoui (1975).

of having one's experience mediated by a restricted rather than an elaborated code is orientation "to a less complex conceptual hierarchy and so to a lower order of causality." In Bernstein's view, "the relative backwardness of many working-class children . . . may well be culturally induced backwardness transmitted by the linguistic process" (1973a:175).

This sociolinguistic thesis would seem to have affinities with the theory of "cultural deprivation," even though any equation of the two formulations is denied by Bernstein. In a much-cited article entitled "Education Cannot Compensate for Society" (1970), he attacks the concepts of compensatory education, which, he argues, misleadingly direct attention away from the failings of schools onto the alleged deficiencies of children and their families. Instead of trying to "compensate" for something that is missing in the family, we should focus our energies on the internal organization of the school and on its educational context. If we fail to do so, we will inevitably be led to conceive of the problem in terms of linguistic and cultural deprivation—a formulation that, in its encouragement of the tendency to label working-class and minority children as deficient, is a part of the very problem it sets out to resolve.

Later in his critique of compensatory education, however, Bernstein puts forward an explanation of the problems faced by "disadvantaged" children in school that sounds strikingly similar to the thesis of cultural deprivation. After reiterating the contrast between a context-bound, particularistic, restricted code and a context-free, universalistic, elaborated code, Bernstein states that "the school is necessarily concerned with the transmission and development of universalistic orders of meaning." From this perspective, the "problem of educability . . . can be understood in terms of a confrontation between a) the school's universalistic orders of meaning and the social relationships which generate them, and b) the particularistic orders of meanings and the social relationships which generate them, which the child brings with him to the school" (1970:346). Bernstein then goes on to point to the form of transmission as a further handicap to working-class children. "Thus the working-class child may be placed at a considerable disadvantage in relation to the *total* culture of the school. It is not made for him: he may not answer to it."

But since the school is necessarily trying to convey "un-common sense," universalistic knowledge, it seems clear that pupils endowed with a code that orients them to particularistic meanings would be deficient compared to their middle-class counterparts. Unpalatable as it may be, the logic of Bernstein's sociolinguistic thesis leads inexorably to the conclusion that those whose experience is regulated by a restricted code are, in terms of the demands necessarily placed on them by the school, linguistically deprived.

Bernstein tries to soften the implications of working-class linguistic inferiority by stating that there "is nothing, but nothing, in the (working-class) dialect as such, which prevents a child from internalising and learning to use universalistic meanings" (1970:347). But while this may be true, it is neither documented nor demonstrated. In a postscript to *Class, Codes and Control* published in 1973, he again tries to deal with the problem of linguistic deprivation by reprinting a number of remarks from earlier papers that point to the force and beauty of a restricted code and to its rich communicative potential (1973a:272–275). Yet as Harold Rosen notes, "remarks of this sort are always essentially *parenthetic* in the sense that they are never explored and they are made in a context which explores tirelessly and intricately what the restricted code cannot do" (Rosen, 1974:78).[87] Finally, in the introduction to Volume III of *Class, Codes and Control,* Bernstein returns again to the specter of working-class linguistic inferiority. After reiterating his opposition to those who view working-class children, families, and communities "as so many pathological deficit systems," he admits that he finds himself "in the position of stating that working-class children, especially lower working-class children, relative to middle-class children, are crucially disadvantaged, given the way class relationships affect both the family and the school" (1975:27–28). Within the framework of the existing class system, then, it would seem to follow that working-class children lack something useful (an elaborated code made available to them "as an *essential* part of their socialization within the family") that most middle-class children possess.[88]

Thus Bernstein is in the anomalous position of attacking the theory of cultural deficit while at the same time providing meticulous descriptions of the ways in which the working-class sub-culture militates against the academic

87. Rosen's critique of Bernstein, which examines his work in painstaking detail, points out that the sociolinguistic thesis directs its attention to the home rather than to that "vast area of critical working-class experience, the encounter with exploitation at the place of work and the response to it" and thus ignores the potential effect of political struggle on the use of language (1974:68, 70). Rosen favorably cites Labov, whose article, "The Logic of Non-Standard English" (1970), provides a graphic textual analysis of Afro-American dialect that refutes the notion that the speech of ghetto blacks is a non-logical mode of communication reflecting failure to understand the tacit rules of the linguistic system. Unfortunately, however, Labov's illuminating exploration of black dialect contains an ill-advised attack on Bernstein, whom he associates with the view that "Negro children have no language at all" (Labov, 1970:156). This is clearly a distortion of Bernstein's work, which has in any case been concerned with the effects of class rather than race on language, but such a misunderstanding would probably not have occurred were there not some passages in Bernstein that express a sharply negative view of the language of the "lower working class."

88. In contrast to Bernstein, Marxists, whose commitment to the interests of the working class is inherent in their theory of society, are quite willing to recognize that it is preferable to possess an elaborated code. Levitas, an orthodox British Marxist, states that if "one type of linguistic equipment facilitates better performance than another in the school situation and prepares more successfully for a wider range of social probabilities, it is not merely different but better." In his view, Bernstein's "relativism" is misguided, for to "expose the various ways in which the proletariat is short-changed and kept subordinate is not to label it as inferior–it is to designate the modes of its oppression" (Levitas, 1974:144–149). In the Soviet Union itself, a theory indistinguishable from that of "cultural deprivation" has been developed to explain persistent class differentials in academic performance; like their counterparts in the capitalist world, Soviet sociologists point to "cultural level" and "family traditions" as determinants of scholastic achievement (Yanowitch and Dodge, 1968:252).

achievement of children who originate in it. Resolution of this dilemma is to be found, in our view, in the work of a great sociological theorist whose writings Bernstein has hitherto neglected—Max Weber. Weber has shown in his essay "The Chinese Literati" (1972:230–241) that the ideal of the cultivated man that is held up in a given society is an outcome of the power of the dominant social group to universalize its particular cultural ideal. There is an element of arbitrariness in the determination of which "ways of thought" and bodies of knowledge will determine educational prestige; depending, for example, on whether there is a rational bureaucratic or a patrimonial "structure of domination," the prevailing educational ideal will promote the ascent of "specialist" or "cultivated" types of man. Bernstein himself approaches this perspective when he writes that "the definition of 'educability' is itself at any one time, an attenuated consequence of . . . power relationships" (1970:347), but this abstract formulation lacks the vividness of Weber's historical writing. If dominant social groups have the power to determine what is valued in the educational system at a particular historical juncture, it would not be surprising to find that subordinate social groups are "deficient" in terms of criteria set by the powerful.[89] The children of the middle class may have more 'cultural capital' than the children of the working class, but Weber would have been quick to note that their "superiority" is ultimately based on power to determine what is admissible as 'cultural capital'.

If Bernstein's efforts to answer those who criticized him for implicitly supporting the theory of cultural deprivation have never produced a fully satisfactory response, they have nonetheless impelled him to engage in a critical reassessment of his work that has proved immensely fruitful. One of the consequences of this reexamination was already visible in his criticism of compensatory education (1970:347), for in it he noted the need to examine the social assumptions and power relationships "underlying the organization, distribution, and evaluation of knowledge." Bernstein had, of course, long been interested in the question of cultural and social transmission, but this was the first time that he had explicitly raised the issue of the social basis of knowledge. Scant attention, in his view, had been paid to this general problem compared to what had been paid to the applied problem of the factors affecting educability

---

89. To give this formulation greater concreteness, it would be illuminating to conduct a historical study of pre- and post-Revolutionary China. Now that proletarian and peasant cultural ideas hold sway in the Chinese educational system, bourgeois children, whose cultural background promotes neither ideological "redness" nor such valued personal traits as cooperativeness and eagerness to engage in manual labor, may be "culturally deficient" in terms of the values embodied in Chinese schools. In the United States, an interesting historical example of the capacity of a dominant social group to impose a set of educational ideals that served its own particular interests was the successful effort by Anglo-Saxon elites to limit the number of Jews in Ivy League institutions in the 1920s and 1930s by instituting a quota system that was justified on the grounds that academic performance, at which Jews excelled, must not lead admissions officers to ignore such important if intangible qualities as "character" (see Steinberg, 1971).

(1973a:37), and his own work has become increasingly concerned with the transmission of knowledge through formal education. His recent writings on this theme, though expressing interests similar to those of the "new" sociology of education, belong neither to the interpretative nor to the normative approach. Instead, Bernstein has, with characteristic originality, drawn on both schools in an attempt to integrate structural and interactional analysis. The result is a series of bold explorations into the content of the educational process that, in their effort to relate what goes on in school to larger structures of power and control, point the way toward a potential new synthesis in the sociology of education.

Bernstein's "On the Classification and Framing of Educational Knowledge" (1975:85–115) was a seminal contribution to the study of educational institutions as agents of cultural transmission. In it he considers the three major concerns of researchers working within the interpretative framework: curriculum, pedagogy, and evaluation. For Bernstein, as for the "new" sociologists of education, these three 'message systems' are inextricably intertwined with the problem of educational knowledge: "Curriculum defines what counts as valid knowledge, pedagogy defines what counts as a valid transmission of knowledge, and evaluation defines what counts as a valid realization of this knowledge on the part of the taught" (1975:85). Knowledge, however, is not passed on in a social vacuum; wider patterns of power and control penetrate the educational process at every turn. To discover these underlying principles of power and control Bernstein constructed two concepts: classification and framing.

Classification is concerned with the social organization of knowledge; its focus is the curriculum and it refers above all to the "degree of boundary maintenance between contents" (1975:83). Framing, on the other hand, is about the teacher-student relationship; its emphasis is on classroom interaction and it refers in particular "to the degree of control·teacher and pupil possess over the selection, organization, pacing and timing of the knowledge transmitted and received in the pedagogical relationship" (1975:89). Both concepts encompass elements of power and control. Strong classification, for example, implies the existence of social actors who have the power to enforce sharp boundaries between different contents and, at the same time, fosters a specialized and hierarchical conception of knowledge that leads to the formation of highly specific identities and hence to control from within (1975:90, 96).

Using the concepts of classification and framing as his point of departure, Bernstein (1975:90–111) postulates a broad historical trend from a "collection code" (in which contents are sharply insulated from one another) to an "integrated code" (in which contents stand in an open relationship to one another). The ideas of classification and framing are, he notes, *theoretical* concepts, and their application "requires at every point empirical evidence"

(1975:112). High among the empirical priorities of investigators working within this framework would be the analysis of the origins and consequences of specific combinations of classification and frames.

These theories of cultural transmission and change are illustrated empirically in a recent article, "Class and Pedagogies: Visible and Invisible" (1975:116–145)—a brilliant if untidy investigation of the social basis of British preschool (infant school) pedagogy. Bernstein shows that the open classroom, thought by its proponents to be universally progressive, actually reflects the life situation of a particular social group—the new middle class. The organizing concept of what Bernstein calls the "invisible pedagogy" is that of play; it is not only the basis of evaluation of the child's progress, but also the core of its learning theory. One of the distinguishing features of the invisible pedagogy is its refusal to distinguish work from play (i.e., these two phenomena are weakly classified and weakly framed). Since in the working class work and play are distinguished very sharply indeed, its children are at a disadvantage in the free atmosphere of the open classroom. For the children of the new middle class, however, the invisible pedagogy is a natural expression of the intermingling of work and play that characterizes both the work situation of their parents and the cultural style of their homes.

"Class and Pedagogies: Visible and Invisible" is not, however, most fundamentally about a conflict between the middle class and the working class, but rather about a struggle *within* the middle class. Drawing on the work of Bourdieu, Bernstein distinguishes between the property-owning middle class, whose reproduction depends upon the transmission of physical capital, and the non-property-owning new middle class, whose privileges depend upon the transmission of cultural capital. Earlier, Bernstein had referred to a shift from the production of goods to the production of services that has modified the structure of the middle class; more recently, he has referred to two fractions of the middle class—one that reproduces itself through ownership and control of capital and another that maintains its position by controlling the dominant forms of communication (1975:16–17). Because of their differing positions in the system of production, these two segments of the middle class have divergent ideologies of pedagogy, and a conflict over cultural transmission develops. At stake in this conflict, however, is not the system of class relationships itself, but the *form* of its reproduction (1975:121). Neither the visible nor the invisible pedagogy—both of which originate in the social situation of two fractions of the middle class—is likely to serve the interests of the lower working class (1975:191).

There is a Marxist element in Bernstein's analysis of the class basis of educational ideologies that is responsible for the unusual force of his most recent attempt to combine the analysis of educational transmission with that of power and control. The Marxist tradition, transmitted in part by the radical wing of the "old" sociology of education, has influenced Bernstein's belief in the primacy of the class structure in shaping social consciousness and in distributing knowledge within society (1973a:196–199). Nevertheless it would be misleading to describe Bernstein as a Marxist. He is aware of the far-reaching consequences of a system of structured inequality and he recognizes the existence of class conflict. But he has conducted his research, with the possible exception of his article on class and pedagogy, within the framework of an essentially functionalist theory of society.

In recent years, however, Bernstein has shown signs of moving toward a thoroughgoing confrontation with Marxism, and such an effort, which would entail an attempt to integrate his theory of education and cultural transmission with the Marxist analysis of the place of the educational system in the larger social structure, would be a highly productive enterprise. Bernstein's analysis of the class basis of the invisible pedagogy might, for example, be developed in relation to the Marxist theory of the correspondence between the social relations of production and the social relations of the classroom. As Bernstein himself observes, "a major defect of the class and pedagogies paper is the very imprecise specification of what is called the new middle class" (1975:16).[90] Similarly, Bernstein's provocative if loose use of the concept of contradiction could be analyzed in comparison with Marxist usage. If for Bernstein (1975:123) the contradictory position of the new middle class is exemplified by the tension between its search for variety and expression and the reality of a hierarchical division of labor, a Marxist would tend to see the contradiction as one stemming from its intermediate position between the ruling class and the working class. It is unlikely indeed that a Marxist would see the theories of members of the new class as being, in Bernstein's (1975:123) words, "at variance with their objective class relationship"; instead, he would seek the roots of the ambiguity of the theory of open schooling in the conflicting demands placed upon a social group that is at once relatively privileged and increasingly proletarianized (see Bowles and Gintis, 1976).

Yet if Bernstein's perspective differs at some points from the Marxist viewpoint, it is similar at many others, as for example in his recent remark that "work and education cannot be integrated at the level of social principles in class societies," but can only be separated or made to "*fit* with each other"[91]

90. For a neo-Marxist analysis of the structural position of the new middle class, see Miles (1974).
91. Further evidence that Bernstein's work, particularly in recent years, has come to converge with the Marxist perspective is provided by the striking similarity of his analysis of the invisible pedagogy with Gintis's analysis of the open classroom. In a review of Silberman's study, *Crisis in the Classroom*, Gintis (1971b) concludes that the model of open education that Silberman advocates is suited not to the interests of the working class, but rather to those of an expanding new middle class that wishes to give to its children the degree of autonomy and flexibility required for the occupation of relatively privileged positions in the hierarchical social division of labor. Gintis, it should be noted, not only comes to a conclusion essentially identical to Bernstein's; he also proceeds by the same method—class analysis of the social basis of educational ideologies.

(1975:135). What remains, however, is for him to go beyond convergence and to attempt a synthesis between his own work, which draws widely upon both the interpretative and the functionalist schools, and the research of the Marxist and Weberian conflict theorists.[92] A successful synthesis would not be a mere compromise among competing schools of thought, but an original and internally coherent formulation marking a decisive advance in the sociology of education. Marxists portray education as an arena of class struggle, and this perspective, which has already shed light on numerous historical conflicts over the structure of the educational system, may also be an appropriate framework for answering one of the main unresolved problems of Bernstein's work—how it is that "power relationships penetrate the organization, distribution and evaluation of knowledge through the social context" (Bernstein, 1970:347).

(b) The Contribution of Émile Durkheim: A Reassessment

The possibilities of theoretical and empirical advance through a synthesis of Marxist, Weberian, and Bernsteinian views of social and educational change are manifold. But there can be no denying that Bernstein's research on the sociology of linguistic codes and on the organization of educational knowledge has been informed by a powerful structural theory of society developed from Émile Durkheim, to whom Bernstein repeatedly acknowledges his debt (1973a:36, 194; 1975:7, 17—18).

Thus Durkheim's *The Division of Labor in Society* is taken as a point of departure by Bernstein for his theory that an increase in the complexity of the division of labor (i.e., a movement from mechanical to organic solidarity) is accompanied by a shift from restricted to elaborated codes. At the same time, the movement in economic production from goods to services will affect the type of elaborated code available by favoring the growth of the "person-oriented" mode over the "object-oriented" mode (1973a:169—173).[93] Again, in

92. One of the strengths of such a synthesis would be that it would bring together two highly complementary but mutually unaware schools of thought—the conflict and the interpretative approaches. Strangely enough, the two paradigms have waged war against common enemies—functionalist theory and methodological empiricism—without ever coordinating their critiques. The conflict theory of education is, of course, essentially a macrostructural approach, and this will doubtless displease some interpretative sociologists. But for most followers of the "new" sociology of education what is wrong with the normative paradigm is not so much that it is macrosociological as that it is basically conservative. Since the same can hardly be said of the conflict approach, whose radicalism resonates with the political sentiments of most interpretative sociologists, it seems likely that the neo-Marxist investigations of American researchers will be received sympathetically by the British apostles of a "new" sociology of education. The dialogue that will result from a confrontation of the two theories, one primarily macrosociological and the other essentially microsociological, may do much to promote the unification of the structural and interactional levels of analysis about which Bernstein is so concerned.

93. Were it possible to operationalize the concepts of 'restricted' and 'elaborated' codes, it would, in principle, be possible to provide empirical tests of the hypothesis that an increase in complexity of the division of labor is accompanied by (a) a shift from restricted to elaborated codes and (b) a shift from the object-oriented to the person-oriented mode of the elaborated code.

his "Open Schools—Open Society?" (1975:67–75), Bernstein links the ideological trend from "closed" to "open" schools to changing patterns of social integration and social control that are reflected in the historical movement from mechanical to organic forms of social solidarity. More recently, in his essay on class and pedagogies, Bernstein has yet again found conceptual inspiration in Durkheim's work on the division of labor, developing a distinction between *individualized* and *personalized* organic solidarity (1975:121). These two forms of organic solidarity correspond, respectively, to visible and invisible pedagogies.

Durkheim's ultimate contribution to the sociology of education, however, may reside less in *The Division of Labor in Society* than in his research on education itself, and, in particular, in a magnificent but neglected work— *L'évolution pédagogique en France* (1969).[94] This book, which was originally delivered as a series of lectures in 1904–1905 at the University of Paris, was not published until 1938. The analysis contained therein, while focusing on the content of the educational process, never loses sight of the social context in which a given educational system is situated. Durkheim looked at education in France from the period of the "primitive church" to that of the Third Republic, exploring the history of what the French call *les idées pédagogiques*—a concept that includes not only the formal curriculum, but also the way in which the knowledge it embodies is transmitted and evaluated. This interest is obviously close to that of the "new" sociology of education, but whereas interpretative sociologists have talked of showing how larger patterns of power and control penetrate the process of schooling and the structure of educational knowledge, Durkheim *demonstrated* it.[95] In so doing, he provided a unified analysis of the structure and process of educational transmission that may well serve as a model for future research in the sociology of education.

Durkheim's method in *L'évolution pédagogique en France* is historical; for him, "it is only in carefully studying the past that we will be able to predict the

---

94. Also worthy of attention are Durkheim's *Education and Sociology* (1956) and *Moral Education* (1961). These works, as Foster has noted (1973:92), have had little direct effect on the sociology of education, but their influence is clearly apparent on such figures as Parsons (1959) and Dreeben (1968). Durkheim (1956:98), in discussing the methodology of educational research, argued that the comparative approach should be one of the fundamental methods of the sociology of education. His advice has been generally ignored, and the resulting provincialism has had damaging consequences for the theoretical and empirical development of the discipline. For one of the few studies that successfully integrate the generally descriptive concerns of comparative education with the more theoretical interests of the sociology of education, see Foster's *Education and Social Change in Ghana* (1965). See also Dore's (1965) study of *Education in Tokugawa Japan*. Dore's study has the rare distinction since Durkheim of relating the content of education to social structure and social change.

95. Ironically, M.F.D. Young (1971b:31), in his article on curricula as socially-organized knowledge, writes that Durkheim's "specific works on education, apart from the emphasis on the social nature of curricula and pedagogy, are not very helpful." An intimate acquaintance with the intellectual heritage of their own discipline is relatively rare among the apostles of the new sociology of education, who, at times, seem to be suffering from a convenient form of historical amnesia.

future and to understand the present" (1969:16).[96] His insistence on the historical approach to sociology may come as a surprise to those who have been taught, as many in the Anglo-Saxon world are, that *Suicide* is his most representative work, but it is impossible to understand his evolutionism without appreciating that it derived in part from a historical analysis of human institutions. Despite what is often said about functionalist sociology, there is in Durkheim a theory of social change, a theory based on increases in the complexity of the division of labor. As for educational change, he saw the educational system as an essentially dependent set of social institutions that change when the social structure in which they are located changes.

There are a number of historical analyses of educational change in *L'évolution pédagogique en France,* but perhaps the most remarkable is Durkheim's examination of the social basis of pedagogical ideals during the Renaissance (1969:194–260). A generalization sets the stage for his analysis of educational change during the Renaissance: "a pedagogical transformation is always the result and the sign of a social transformation that explains it" (1969:194). The precipitating social change, according to Durkheim, was the rise of "polite society"—a phenomenon rooted in the economic growth of the late Middle Ages, which encouraged the development of a taste for a luxurious and elegant life not only among the aristocracy but also among the increasingly powerful bourgeoisie. Accordingly, the new educational ideals, which emphasized elegance in speech and writing, reflected a desire, especially common among a bourgeoisie whose social distance from the aristocracy was constantly diminishing, for "polish" and "refinement." The distinctive feature of the curriculum of Renaissance education was its almost exclusive reliance on the study of classical civilization. Through the study of ancient Greek and Roman literature, one was to develop the type of cultivated social personality suitable for taking one's place in polite society. Essentially aristocratic in spirit, the pedagogy of the Renaissance embodied a class ideology that did not and could not respond to the needs of the masses. Making rhetoric the foremost of its scholarly disciplines, it could only develop qualities geared to a life of luxury totally detached from the necessities of life that preoccupied the great majority of the population (Durkheim, 1969:238–239).

In studying the evolution of French education Durkheim was concerned with both the content of schooling and the methods by which it was to be transmitted. In an elaborate examination of the educational institutions run by the Jesuits, Durkheim (1969:260–303) uncovered the principles of social control implicit in their pedagogical system. Renowned for the rigorous discipline of

---

96. This translation and those that follow are ours. A complete English translation by Peter Collins of *L'évolution pédagogique en France* will soon be published by Routledge and Kegan Paul of London.

their schools, the Jesuits relied on two techniques for the maintenance of order in the classroom: constant and personal surveillance and the encouragement of emulation. The individual attention given to each student not only enabled the Jesuit priest to adapt his tutorial technique to diverse personal needs, but also, by providing him with an intimate knowledge of the student's personality, helped him to find effective ways of inculcating the teachings of the Church (1969:296–297). Promotion of the ethic of emulation, embodied in the structure of the classroom by its division into two hierarchical camps (modeled on the Roman Army and complete with consuls, praetors, tribunes, and senators), served to pit one student against another and thus to encourage individual striving for academic excellence.

The emphasis in both these principles of discipline on manipulation of the individual was not, in Durkheim's view, an arbitrary Jesuit invention, but rather an outgrowth of a historical trend in civil society toward individualization—a trend that could be traced to the humanism of the early Renaissance (1969:301–302). With the growth of self-conscious individualism in the sixteenth century, the group techniques of scholastic discipline that had been characteristic of the Middle Ages could no longer be maintained. In their place emerged the individualistic tutorial control of the Jesuits.

Whether he was examining the monastic schools of the Carolingian epoch or the secular lycées of the period immediately following the French Revolution, Durkheim pursued a method designed to show the connections between changes in pedagogical ideals and practices and changes in the larger society. Though occasionally somewhat crude and mechanistic, *L'évolution pédagogique en France* provides an unequalled example of the way in which it is possible, and indeed necessary, to integrate microcosmic and macrocosmic levels of sociological analysis. No sociologist of education has yet surpassed—in depth or in breadth—this investigation of the relationship between social structure and the process of educational transmission, written more than seventy years ago. This is a sobering commentary on the subsequent history of educational research; more than anything else, perhaps, it suggests that such inquiries, which Durkheim undertook as part and parcel of the sociological enterprise, are now widely considered scientifically illegitimate in the highly specialized and profes-sionalized community of sociological researchers.

(c) Dilemmas of Educational Research

What then are the contemporary substitutes for the bold investigations of a Durkheim? All too often they have been the careful but limited studies of abstracted empiricism—an approach that often allows methodology to determine its problems (Mills, 1959:57) while vainly hoping that the quest for statistical rigor can somehow substitute for a lack of theoretical imagination. Whether this approach, which now predominates in many professional journals of sociological and educational research, is likely to move the sociology of education forward is not at all evident; even researchers with empirical credentials as unimpeachable as those of Clark (1973) and Foster (1973) have begun to ask whether the proliferation of highly technical but atheoretical studies of schooling and social stratification will lead to significant advances in educational research. Yet small-scale empirical studies continue to pile up while questions of broader theoretical interest remain unexplored. In the face of a pervasive belief that it is impossible to examine admittedly important problems in a scientifically meaningful way, sociologists of education retreat into the study of "safe" if uninspired questions. Caution rather than curiosity is the order of the day, and expressions of intellectual initiative are dismissed as evidence of a lack of methodological realism. It is no wonder, then, that studies of the sweep of Durkheim's *L'évolution pédagogique en France* no longer appear. The timidity of the ambitions that we still dare to harbor is one measure of our distance from the promise of the classical tradition.

In a period in which educational researchers of sharply divergent perspectives rely increasingly on funds from government agencies, it is worthwhile to remember that the only facility upon which Durkheim was dependent was one which is available even to those unfortunate researchers who lack special funding—the library. As the number of sociologists of education who believe that it is impossible to conduct an investigation without access to expensive academic "hardware" (whether it be the video equipment favored by interpretative sociologists or the computers preferred by methodological empiricists) grows ever larger, one can envisage a possible state of affairs in which studies based on the use of existing materials will not be considered research at all.

Yet mountains of extraordinarily rich data remain unmined, even as ever more numerous investigators gather still more information. And there are many published studies—often of limited significance in themselves—that could, if scrutinized from a theoretical perspective, provide the basis for important advances in the sociology of education. Contemporary fashions in academic social science put "secondary analysis" low on their list of priorities. Yet, unfashionable as it may be to say so, an increase in the amount of time spent in the library by sociologists of education might be more profitable than the continued accumulation of studies with, in all too many cases, neither empirical nor theoretical significance.

Despite the trend toward ever larger and more expensive studies, some educational researchers have continued to follow the model of the individual craftsman and have accordingly been obstructed by little other than personal limitations in their effort to do work of the highest quality. But this model of research has less and less appeal in a period when quantitative studies conducted by renowned social scientists set standards that less well-known researchers wish to emulate. In educational research, this process is fairly well advanced, for government support has enhanced the already high status of the large-scale survey studies that have always been prominent in the field. As control of the process of social scientific research shifts from individual craftsmen to organized and more or less bureaucratized public and private agencies, educational researchers as well as other social scientists are in danger of being "expropriated" from their means of intellectual production (Mills, 1959:106). Sadly enough, the community of educational researchers, a substantial part of which has become convinced that it is impossible to conduct serious research in the absence of large sums of money, has itself been deeply involved in this process of expropriation.

On the other hand, a return to the ideal of intellectual craftsmanship, though possible for some, is not a viable solution to the problem of financial dependency on outside agencies. Such a movement would in any case deny to the discipline the fruits of recent developments in research technology, which, whatever their limitations, nonetheless enable empirical research to be carried out with a precision heretofore impossible. Nor is it possible to return to the traditional ideal of intellectual autonomy. This rather idealistic and unsociological view of the nature of the research enterprise with its image of the detached social scientist cannot be sustained. What is possible, however, is for educational researchers to show greater awareness of the inherently social character of their own work and of the distortions this inevitably imposes. A reflexive sociology cannot, as Gouldner has noted (1971:486), determine whether a given piece of research is true or false, but it can help us to understand its deeper character.

Ultimately, however, there can be no solution to the problem of socially induced distortions in the study of education, for to "resolve" the problem would be to wrench educational research from its social context—clearly an impossibility. Since the origins of truth as well as of error can be traced in considerable part to the social setting in which research takes place, it should be recognized that the effects of external influence on the sociology of education are by no means uniformly negative. Instead of formulating the problem in terms of a false dichotomy between "pure" and "contaminated" educational research, a more productive way of confronting the issue would be to attempt to identify the extent and direction of distortion by external influences.

We have tried to explore these influences in this essay. They are many and subtle and they emanate from within as well as from without the educational research community. Governmental finance provides crucial support, but may also bend the activities of scholars away from their own priorities and towards applied, atheoretical, quantitative studies in the service of the policy preoccupations of the ruling powers. To what extent we should think of such influences as distortions depends on our assessment of the governmental interest itself and its relation to whatever we deem to be the public interest. But that state patronage carries a threat to the integrity of social science cannot be denied. The traditional role of the social scientist as critic of the social order has always to be defended if it is to survive.

In attempting to identify the effects of social context on educational research, we have referred to bureaucratization within the organization of research, to biases growing out of the experience of particular generations, to the blandishments of service to dominant powers, and to the prejudices that come from commitment to particular ideologies or social groups. Perhaps we should have attended more to other influences—for example, the connection of so much teaching and research in the sociology of education to the institutions of teacher training and to the educational world itself, with its characteristic ideologies of reformist improvement.[97] Different groups of researchers and different theoretical approaches each have their peculiar weaknesses to sources of error, and no approach can hope to monopolize the pursuit of truth. The educational researcher, in short, cannot fully liberate himself from his social context. His realistic hope, and his duty to the best traditions of his calling, is to achieve greater awareness of the social character of his activity and thereby to attenuate the limitations of his social position.

97. See Bernbaum (1976) for an elaboration of this theme.

REFERENCES

Althusser, Louis. "Ideology and Ideological State Apparatuses." In *Education: Structure and Society,* edited by B. R. Cosin, pp. 242–280. Harmondsworth, Middlesex: Penguin Books, 1972.

Anderson, Perry. "Components of the National Culture." *New Left Review* 50 (July-August 1968): 3–57.

Anderson, C. Arnold, and Mary Jean Bowman, eds. *Education and Economic Development.* Chicago: Aldine, 1965.

Aron, Raymond. *The Elusive Revolution.* New York: Praeger, 1969.

Astin, Alexander W. "The Methodology of Research on College Impact," Part One and Part Two. *Sociology of Education* 43 (Summer and Fall 1970): 223–254 and 437–450.

Bachrach, Peter, and Morton S. Baratz. "The Two Faces of Power." *American Political Science Review* 56 (December 1962): 947–952.

Banks, Olive. *The Sociology of Education.* London: Batsford, 1971.

Bantock, G. H. *Education in an Industrial Society.* London: Faber and Faber, 1963.

Barbagli, Marzio. *Disoccupazione intellettuale e sistema scolastico in Italia (1859–1973).* Bologna: Il Mulino, 1974.

Barnes, J. A., ed. *Curriculum Innovation in London's E.P.A.s,* Volume Three. London: Her Majesty's Stationery Office, 1973.

Bastid, Marianne. "Economic Necessity and Political Ideals in Educational Reform during the Cultural Revolution." *China Quarterly* 42 (April-June 1970): 16–45. (Chapter 35 of this volume)

Baudelot, Christian, and Roger Establet. *L'école capitaliste en France.* Paris: François Maspéro, 1973.

Becker, Gary S. *Human Capital.* New York: National Bureau of Economic Research, 1964.

Becker, Howard S. "Social-Class Variations in the Teacher-Pupil Relationship." *Journal of Educational Sociology* 25 (April 1952): 451–465.

Becker, Howard S. "The Teacher in the Authority System of the Public School." *Journal of Educational Sociology* 26 (November 1953): 128–141.

Berger, Peter L., and Thomas Luckman. *The Social Construction of Reality.* Harmondsworth, Middlesex: Allen Lane, 1967.

Bernbaum, Gerald. *Knowledge and Ideology in the Sociology of Education.* London: Macmillan, 1976.

Bernstein, Basil. "Social Class and Linguistic Development: A Theory of Social Learning." In *Education, Economy, and Society,* edited by A. H. Halsey et al., pp. 288–314. New York: Free Press, 1961.

Bernstein, Basil. "Education Cannot Compensate for Society." *New Society* 387 (February 26, 1970): 344–347.

Bernstein, Basil. *Class, Codes and Control,* Volume One. London: Paladin, 1973a.

Bernstein, Basil, ed. *Class, Codes and Control,* Volume Two. London: Routledge and Kegan Paul, 1973b.

Bernstein, Basil. *Class, Codes and Control,* Volume Three. London: Routledge and Kegan Paul, 1975.

Bernstein, Basil. "Sociology and the Sociology of Education: A Brief Account." In *Approaches to Sociology,* edited by John Rex, pp. 145–159. London: Routledge and Kegan Paul, 1974.

Birnbaum, Norman. "Conflicting Interpretations of the Rise of Capitalism: Marx and Weber." *British Journal of Sociology* 4 (1953): 125–141.

Blau, Peter M., and Otis Dudley Duncan. *The American Occupational Structure.* New York: Wiley and Sons, 1967.

Blaug, Mark. "The Correlation Between Education and Earnings: What Does It Signify?" *Higher Education* 1 (1972): 53–77.

Bluestone, Barry. "Economic Theory and the Fate of the Poor." *Social Policy* 2 (January-February 1972): 30–31 and 46–48. (Chapter 18 of this volume)

Bluestone, Barry; William Murphy; and Mary Stevenson. "Education and Industry." In *Schooling in a Corporate Society,* 2nd ed., edited by Martin Carnoy, pp. 161–173. New York: David McKay and Company, 1975.

Boudon, Raymond. "Éducation et mobilité." *Sociologie et Société* 5 (1973): 111–124. (An English translation appears as Chapter 8 of this volume.)

Boudon, Raymond. *Education, Opportunity, and Social Inequality.* New York: John Wiley and Sons, 1974a.

Boudon, Raymond. "La sociologie des inégalités dans l'impasse?" *Analyse et Prévision,* no. 17 (1974b), pp. 83–95.

Bourdieu, Pierre. "Cultural Reproduction and Social Reproduction." In *Knowledge, Education, and Cultural Change,* edited by Richard Brown, pp. 71–112. London: Tavistock, 1973. (Chapter 29 of this volume)

Bourdieu, Pierre, and Jean-Claude Passeron. *La reproduction.* Paris: Les Éditions de Minuit, 1970.

Bowles, Samuel. "Unequal Education and the Reproduction of the Social Division of Labor." *Review of Radical Political Economics* 3 (Fall 1971a). (Chapter 5 of this volume)

Bowles, Samuel. "Cuban Education and the Revolutionary Ideology." *Harvard Educational Review* 41 (November 1971b): 472–500.

Bowles, Samuel. "Schooling and Inequality from Generation to Generation." *Journal of Political Economy* 80 (May-June 1972a): 219–251.

Bowles, Samuel. "Contradictions in Higher Education in the United States." In *The Capitalist System,* edited by Richard C. Edwards et al., pp. 491–503. Englewood Cliffs, N.J.: Prentice-Hall, 1972b.

Bowles, Samuel, and Herbert Gintis. "I.Q. in the U.S. Class Structure." *Social Policy* 3 (November-December 1972): 65–96. (Pp. 66–78 appear as Chapter 10 of this volume.)

Bowles, Samuel, and Herbert Gintis. "The

Problem with Human Capital—A Marxian Critique." *American Economic Review* 65 (May 1975a):74–82.

Bowles, Samuel, and Herbert Gintis. "Capitalism and Education in the United States." *Socialist Revolution* 5, no. 25 (1975b): 101–138.

Bowles, Samuel, and Herbert Gintis. *Schooling in Capitalist America: Educational Reform and the Contradictions of Economic Life.* New York: Basic Books, 1976.

Brim, Orville J. *Sociology and the Field of Education.* New York: Russell Sage Foundation, 1958.

Brown, Richard, ed. *Knowledge, Education, and Cultural Change.* London: Tavistock, 1973.

Byrne, David; Bill Williamson; and Barbara Fletcher. *The Poverty of Education: A Study in the Politics of Opportunity.* London: Martin Robertson, 1975.

Carnoy, Martin. *Education as Cultural Imperialism.* New York: David McKay, 1974.

Carnoy, Martin, ed. *Schooling in a Corporate Society: The Political Economy of Education in America.* 2nd ed. New York: David McKay, 1975.

Carnoy, Martin, and Jorge Werthein. "Socialist Ideology and the Transformation of Cuban Education." (Chapter 34 of this volume)

Carter, M. P. "Report on a Survey of Sociological Research in Britain." *Sociological Review* 16 (March 1968): 5–40.

Carter, Michael A. "Correspondence and Contradiction." Palo Alto, Cal.: Center for Economic Studies, 1974.

Carter, Michael A., and Martin Carnoy. "Theories of Labor Markets and Worker Productivity." Discussion Paper. Palo Alto, Cal.: Center for Economic Studies, August 1974.

Central Advisory Council for Education. *Children and their Primary Schools,* Volume One and Volume Two. The Plowden Report. London: Her Majesty's Stationery Office, 1967.

Cherkaoui, Mohammed. "Structure de classes, performance linguistique et types de socialisation: Bernstein et son école." *Revue Française de Sociologie* 15 (October-December 1975): 585–599.

Cicourel, Aaron V. *Method and Measurement in Sociology.* New York: The Free Press, 1964.

Cicourel, Aaron V., et al. *Language Use and School Performance.* New York: Academic Press, 1974.

Clark, Burton R. "The 'Cooling-Out' Function in Higher Education." *American Journal of Sociology* 65 (May 1960): 569–576.

Clark, Burton R. *Educating the Expert Society.* San Francisco: Chandler, 1962.

Clark, Burton R. "Development of the Sociology of Higher Education." *Sociology of Education* 46 (Winter 1973): 2–14.

Cohen, David K., and Marvin Lazerson. "Education and the Corporate Order." *Socialist Revolution* 2 (March-April 1972): 47–72. (Chapter 21 of this volume)

Coleman, James S., et al. *Equality of Educational Opportunity.* Washington, D.C.: U.S. Government Printing Office, 1966.

Coleman, James S. "The Concept of Equality of Educational Opportunity." *Harvard Educational Review* 38 (Winter 1968): 7–22.

Coleman, James S. "Review of Jencks's *Inequality.*" *American Journal of Sociology* 78 (May 1973): 1523–1527.

Coleman, James S. "Equal Educational Opportunity: A Definition." *Oxford Review of Education* 1, no. 1 (1975): 25–26.

Collins, Randall. "Functional and Conflict Theories of Educational Stratification." *American Sociological Review* 36 (December 1971): 1002–1019. (Chapter 4 of this volume)

Collins, Randall. "Where Are Educational Requirements for Employment Highest?" *Sociology of Education* 47 (Fall 1974): 419–442.

Cosin, B.R., et al. *School and Society: A Sociological Reader.* London: Routledge and Kegan Paul, in association with the Open University Press, 1972.

Cox, C.B., and Boyson Rhodes. *Black Paper 1975—The Fight for Education.* London: Dent, 1975.

Crowder, David N. "A Critique of Duncan's Stratification Research." *Sociology* 8 (January 1974): 19–45.

Dahrendorf, Ralph. *Class and Class Conflict in Industrial Society.* Stanford, Cal.: Stanford University Press, 1959.

Davies, Ioan. "Education and Social Science." *New Society* 345 (May 8, 1969): 710–711.

Davies, Ioan. "The Management of Knowledge: A Critique of the Use of Typologies in Educational Sociology." In *Readings in the Theory of Educational Systems,* edited by Earl Hopper, pp. 111–138. London: Hutchinson University Library, 1971.

Davis, Kingsley, and Wilbert E. Moore. "Some Principles of Stratification." *American Sociological Review* 10 (April 1945): 242–249.

Dobson, Richard B. "Social Status and Inequality of Access to Higher Education in the USSR." (Chapter 12 of this volume)

Doeringer, Peter B., and Michael J. Piore. *Internal Labor Markets and Manpower Analysis.* Lexington, Mass.: D.C. Heath, 1971.

Dore, Ronald P. *Education in Tokugawa Japan.* London: Routledge and Kegan Paul, 1965.

Douglas, J.W.B. *The Home and the School.* London: MacGibbon and Kee, 1964.

Dreeben, Robert. *On What is Learned in School.* Reading, Mass.: Addison-Wesley, 1968. (Pp. 66–73 appear as Chapter 32 of this volume.)

Duncan, Otis Dudley. "Path Analysis: Sociological Examples." *American Journal of Sociology* 72 (July 1966): 1–16.

Duncan, Otis Dudley; David L. Featherman; and Beverly Duncan. *Socioeconomic Background and Achievements.* New York: Academic Press, 1975.

Durkheim, Émile. *Education and Sociology.* Glencoe, Ill.: The Free Press, 1956.

Durkheim, Émile. *Moral Education.* Glencoe, Ill.: The Free Press, 1961.

Durkheim, Émile. *The Division of Labor in Society.* New York: Free Press, 1964.

Durkheim, Émile. *Suicide.* New York: Free Press, 1966.

Durkheim, Émile. *L'évolution pédagogique en France.* Paris: Presses universitaires de France, 1969. (Pp. 194–197, 198–201, 236–239, 266–269, 286–288, and 296–303 appear in English translation as Chapter 2 of this volume.)

Edwards, Richard C. "Alienation and Inequality: Capitalist Relations of Production in a Bureaucratic Enterprise." Ph.D. dissertation, Department of Economics, Harvard University, 1972.

Eggleston, John. "Knowledge and the School Curriculum." *Education for Teaching* 91 (Summer 1973a): 12–18.

Eggleston, John. "Decision-Making on the School Curriculum: A Conflict Model." *Sociology* 7 (September 1973b): 377–394.

Eggleston, John, ed. *Contemporary Research in the Sociology of Education.* London: Methuen, 1974.

Eliot, T.S. *Notes Towards the Definition of Culture.* London: Faber and Faber, 1948.

Emmerij, Louis. *Can the School Build a New Social Order?* New York: Elsevier Scientific Publishing Company, 1974.

Erickson, Frederick. "Gatekeeping and the Melting Pot." *Harvard Educational Review* 45 (February 1975): 44–70.

Esland, Geoffrey M. "Teaching and Learning as the Organization of Knowledge." In *Knowledge and Control,* edited by Michael F. D. Young, pp. 70–117. London: Collier-Macmillan, 1971.

Esposito, Dominick. "Homogeneous and Heterogeneous Grouping: Principal Findings and Implications for Evaluating and Designing Educational Environments." *Review of Educational Research* 43 (Spring 1973): 163–179.

Eysenck, Hans. *Race, Intelligence and Education.* London: Temple Smith, 1971.

Feldman, Kenneth A., and Theodore M. Newcomb. *The Impact of College on Students.* San Francisco: Jossey-Bass, 1969.

Flacks, Richard. "Young Intelligentsia in Revolt." *Transaction* 7 (June 1970): 47–55.

Flacks, Richard. *Youth and Social Change.* Chicago: Markham, 1971.

Floud, Jean, and A.H. Halsey. "English Secondary Schools and the Supply of Labour." In *Education, Economy, and*

Society, edited by A.H. Halsey et al., pp. 80–92. New York: Free Press, 1961.

Floud, Jean, and A.H. Halsey. "The Sociology of Education: A Trend Report and Bibliography." *Current Sociology* 7 (1958): 165–235.

Floud, Jean; A.H. Halsey; and F.M. Martin. *Social Class and Educational Opportunity*. London: Heineman, 1956.

Ford, Julienne. *Social Class and the Comprehensive School*. London: Routledge and Kegan Paul, 1969.

Foster, Philip J. *Education and Social Change in Ghana*. London: Routledge and Kegan Paul, 1965.

Foster, Philip J. "Discussion." *Sociology of Education* 46 (Winter 1973): 92–98.

Foster, Philip J. "The Vocational School Fallacy in Development Planning." In *Education and Economic Development*, edited by C.A. Anderson and M.J. Bowman, pp. 142–166. London: Frank Cass and Company, Ltd., 1966. (Pp. 142–153 appear as Chapter 20 of this volume.)

Friedrichs, Robert W. *A Sociology of Sociology*. New York: The Free Press, 1970.

Gans, Herbert. "The Positive Functions of Poverty." *American Journal of Sociology* 78 (September 1972): 275–289.

Garfinkel, Harold. *Studies in Ethnomethodology*. Englewood Cliffs, N.J.: Prentice-Hall, 1967.

Gintis, Herbert. "The New Working Class and Revolutionary Youth." *Socialist Revolution* 1 (May 1970).

Gintis, Herbert. "Education and the Characteristics of Worker Productivity." *American Economic Review* 61 (May 1971a): 266–279.

Gintis, Herbert. "The Politics of Education (Review of Charles Silberman's *Crisis in the Classroom*)." *Monthly Review* 23 (December 1971b): 40–51.

Gintis, Herbert. "The Nature of the Labor Exchange and the Theory of Capitalist Production." Unpublished manuscript. University of Massachusetts, March 1975.

Girard, Alain, et al. *Population et l'enseignement*. Paris: Presses universitaires de France, 1970.

Gluckman, Max. *Custom and Conflict in Africa*. London: Basil Blackwell, 1955.

Goody, Jack, and Ian Watt. "The Consequences of Literacy." *Comparative Studies in Society and History* 5 (July 1963): 304–345. (Pp. 304–326 and 344–345 appear as Chapter 27 of this volume.)

Gordon, David M. *Theories of Poverty and Underemployment*. Lexington, Mass.: D.C. Heath, 1971.

Gorbutt, David. "The New Sociology of Education." *Education for Teaching* 89 (Autumn 1972): 3–11.

Gouldner, Alvin W. "The Sociologist as Partisan: Sociology and the Welfare State." *American Sociologist* 3 (February 1968): 103–116.

Gouldner, Alvin W. *The Coming Crisis of Western Sociology*. New York: Avon Books, 1971.

Haller, Archibald O., and Alejandro Portes. "Status Attainment Processes." *Sociology of Education* 46 (Winter 1973): 51–91.

Halsey, A.H. "Review of Brim's *Sociology and the Field of Education*." *Harvard Educational Review* 29 (Summer 1959): 262–264.

Halsey, A.H. "The Changing Functions of Universities." In *Education, Economy, and Society*, edited by A.H. Halsey et al., pp. 456–465. New York: Free Press, 1961.

Halsey, A.H. "Educational Organization." In *International Encyclopedia of the Social Sciences*, Volume Four, pp. 525–532. New York: Crowell Collier Macmillan, 1968.

Halsey, A.H. "Social Science and Government." *Times Literary Supplement*, March 5, 1970.

Halsey, A.H. "Theoretical Advance and Empirical Challenge." In *Readings in the Theory of Educational Systems*, edited by Earl Hopper, pp. 262–281. London: Hutchinson University Library, 1971.

Halsey, A.H. *Educational Priority: EPA Problems and Policies*. London: Her Majesty's Stationery Office, 1972.

Halsey, A.H. "Sociology and the Equality Debate." *Oxford Review of Education* 1, no. 1 (1975): 9–23.

Halsey, A.H.; Jean Floud; and C. Arnold Anderson, eds. *Education, Economy, and Society*. New York: The Free Press, 1961.

Hargreaves, David H. *Social Relations in a Secondary School.* London: Routledge and Kegan Paul, 1967.

Herrnstein, Richard. "I.Q." *Atlantic Monthly,* September 1971, pp. 43–64.

Hoare, Quintin. "Education: Programmes and Men." *New Left Review* 32 (July-August 1965): 40–54.

Hodgson, Godfrey. "Do Schools Make a Difference?" *Atlantic Monthly,* March 1973, pp. 35–46.

Hoggart, Richard. *The Uses of Literacy.* London: Chatto and Windus, 1959.

Hopper, Earl. "A Typology for the Classification of Educational Systems." *Sociology* 2 (January 1968): 29–44. (Chapter 6 of this volume)

Husén, Torsten. *Talent, Equality and Meritocracy.* The Hague: Martinus Nijhoff, 1974. (Pp. 115–124 appear as Chapter 13 of this volume.)

Jackson, Brian. *Working Class Community.* Harmondsworth, Middlesex: Penguin Books, 1968.

Jackson, Brian, and Dennis Marsden. *Education and the Working Class.* London: Routledge and Kegan Paul, 1963.

Jencks, Christopher. "*Inequality* in Retrospect." *Harvard Educational Review* 43 (February 1973): 138–164.

Jencks, Christopher, and David Riesman. *The Academic Revolution.* New York: Doubleday, 1968.

Jencks, Christopher, et al. *Inequality: A Reassessment of the Effect of Family and Schooling in America.* New York: Basic Books, 1972.

Jensen, Arthur R. "How Much Can We Boost I.Q. and Scholastic Achievement?" *Harvard Educational Review* 39 (Winter 1969): 1–123.

Kahl, Joseph A. " 'Common Man' Boys." In *Education, Economy, and Society,* edited by A.H. Halsey et al., pp. 348–366. New York: Free Press, 1961.

Karabel, Jerome. "Community Colleges and Social Stratification." *Harvard Educational Review* 42 (November 1972): 521–562. (Chapter 11 of this volume)

Katz, Michael B. *The Irony of Early School Reform.* Cambridge, Mass.: Harvard University Press, 1968.

Katz, Michael B. *Class, Bureaucracy, and Schools.* New York: Praeger Publishers, 1971.

Kazamias, Andreas M. "Comparative Pedagogy: An Assignment for the '70s." *Comparative Education Review* 16 (October 1972): 406–411.

Keddie, Nell. "Classroom Knowledge." In *Knowledge and Control,* edited by Michael F. D. Young, pp. 133–160. London: Collier Macmillan, 1971.

Keniston, Kenneth. *Young Radicals.* New York: Harcourt, Brace and World, 1968.

Keniston, Kenneth. *Youth and Dissent.* New York: Harcourt, Brace, Jovanovich, 1971.

Kohn, Melvin L. *Class and Conformity: A Study in Values.* Homewood, Ill.: The Dorsey Press, 1969.

Kuhn, Thomas S. *The Structure of Scientific Revolutions,* 2nd ed. Chicago: The University of Chicago Press, 1970.

Labov, William. "The Logic of Nonstandard English." In *Language and Poverty,* edited by Frederick Williams, pp. 153–189. Chicago: Markham, 1970.

Lacey, Colin. *Hightown Grammar: The School as a Social System.* Manchester: Manchester University Press, 1970.

Lawton, Dennis. *Social Class, Language and Education.* London: Routledge and Kegan Paul, 1968.

Layard, Richard, and George Psacharopoulos. "The Screening Hypothesis and the Returns to Education." *Journal of Political Economy* 82 (September/October 1974): 985–999.

Lazerson, Marvin. *Origins of the Urban School.* Cambridge, Mass.: Harvard University Press, 1971.

Lazerson, Marvin, and W. Norton Grubb, eds. *American Education and Vocationalism.* New York: Teachers College Press, 1974.

Leacock, Eleanor Burke, ed. *The Culture of Poverty.* New York: Simon and Schuster, 1971.

Levitas, Maurice. *Marxist Perspectives in the Sociology of Education.* London: Routledge and Kegan Paul, 1974.

Levy, Marion J., and Francesca M. Cancian. "Functionalism." In *International Encyclopedia of the Social Sciences,* Volume Six, pp. 21–41. New York: Crowell Collier Macmillan, 1968.

Litt, Edgar. "Civic Education, Community Norms, and Political Indoctrination." *American Sociological Review* 28 (February 1963): 69–75.

Lockwood, David. "Some Remarks on 'The Social System.'" *British Journal of Sociology* 7 (June 1956): 134–146.

Lopate, Carol. "Approaches to Schools: The Perfect Fit." *Liberation*, September-October 1974, pp. 26–32.

Lukacs, Georg. *History and Class Consciousness*. Cambridge, Mass.: The M.I.T. Press, 1971.

Lukes, Steven. *Power: A Radical View*. London: Macmillan, 1974.

McCartney, James L. "On Being Scientific: Changing Styles of Presentation of Sociological Research." *American Sociologist* 5 (February 1970): 30–35.

McCartney, James L. "Effect of Financial Support on Growth of Sociological Specialties." In *The Phenomenon of Sociology*, edited by Edward A. Tiryakian, pp. 395–406. New York: Appleton-Century-Crofts, 1971.

Mannheim, Karl. *Ideology and Utopia*. New York: Harcourt, Brace and World, 1936.

Mannheim, Karl. *Essays on the Sociology of Knowledge*. London: Routledge and Kegan Paul, 1952.

Marcuse, Herbert. *One-Dimensional Man*. Boston: Beacon Press, 1964.

Marshall, T.H. *Class, Citizenship, and Social Development*. Garden City, N.Y.: Doubleday, 1965.

Marx, Karl, and Friedrich Engels. *The German Ideology*. New York: International Publishers, 1947.

Merton, Robert K. *Social Theory and Social Structure*. New York: Free Press, 1968.

Miles, Michael W. *The Radical Probe*. New York: Atheneum, 1971.

Miles, Michael W. "Student Alienation in the U.S. Higher Education Industry." *Politics and Society* 4 (1974): 311–341. (Pp. 311–322 and 330–341 appear as Chapter 26 of this volume, under the title "The Student Movement and the Industrialization of Higher Education.")

Mills, C. Wright. *The Power Elite*. New York: Oxford University Press, 1956.

Mills, C. Wright. *The Sociological Imagination*. New York: Oxford University Press, 1959.

Mills, C. Wright. *Power, Politics and People*. Edited by Irving Louis Horowitz. New York: Oxford University Press, 1963.

Morrison, Charles M. *E.P.A.: A Scottish Study*, Volume Five. London: Her Majesty's Stationery Office, 1973.

Mosteller, Frederick, and Daniel P. Moynihan, eds. *On Equality of Educational Opportunity*. New York: Random House, 1972.

Muller, Walter. "Family Background, Education and Career Mobility." *Social Science Information* 11 (October 1972): 223–255.

Mullins, Nicholas C. *Theories and Theory Groups in Contemporary American Sociology*. New York: Harper and Row, 1973.

Nee, Victor. *The Cultural Revolution at Peking University*. New York: Monthly Review Press, 1969.

Ossowski, Stanislaw. *Class Structure in the Social Consciousness*. London: Routledge and Kegan Paul, 1963.

Parsons, Talcott. "The School Class as a Social System: Some of its Functions in American Society." *Harvard Educational Review* 29 (Fall 1959): 297–318.

Payne, Joan. *E.P.A. Surveys and Statistics*, Volume Two. London: Her Majesty's Stationery Office, 1973.

Piore, Michael J. "Fragments of a Sociological Theory of Wages." *American Economic Review* 63 (May 1973): 377–384.

Polsby, Nelson W. *Community Power and Political Theory*. New Haven: Yale University Press, 1963.

Reich, Michael; David M. Gordon; and Richard C. Edwards. "A Theory of Labor Market Segmentation." *American Economic Review* 63 (May 1973): 359–365.

Ringer, Fritz K. "Higher Education in Germany in the Nineteenth Century." *Journal of Contemporary History* 2 (1967): 123–138. (Chapter 31 of this volume)

Rist, Ray C. "Student Social Class and Teacher Expectations: The Self-Fulfilling Prophecy in Ghetto Education." *Harvard Educational Review* 40 (August 1970): 411–450.

Rist, Ray C. *The Urban School: Factory for Failure.* Cambridge, Mass.: The M.I.T. Press, 1973.

Rosen, Harold. "Language and Class." In *Education or Domination?*, edited by Douglas Holly, pp. 58–87. London: Arrow Books, 1974.

Rosenthal, Robert, and Lenore Jacobson. *Pygmalion in the Classroom.* New York: Holt, Rinehart and Winston, 1968.

Rossanda, R.; M. Cini; and L. Berlinguer. "Tesi sulla scuola." *Il Manifesto,* February 1970. (Chapter 38 of this volume)

Roth, David R. "Intelligence Testing as a Social Activity." In *Language Use and School Performance,* edited by Aaron V. Cicourel et al., pp. 143–217. New York: Academic Press, 1974.

Rothbart, George S. "The Legitimation of Inequality: Objective Scholarship vs. Black Militance." *Sociology of Education* 43 (Spring 1970): 159–174.

Schultz, Theodore W. "Capital: Human." In *International Encyclopedia of the Social Sciences.* New York: Crowell Collier and Macmillan, 1968.

Schultz, Theodore W. "Investment in Human Capital." *American Economic Review* 51 (March 1961): 1–17. (Chapter 16 of this volume)

Schutz, Alfred. *Collected Papers I: The Problem of Social Reality.* The Hague: Martinus Nijhoff, 1962.

Sewell, William H. "Inequality of Opportunity for Higher Education." *American Sociological Review* 36 (October 1971): 793–809.

Sewell, William H. "Review of Jencks' *Inequality.*" *American Journal of Sociology* 78 (May 1973): 1532–1540.

Sewell, William H., and Robert M. Hauser. *Education, Occupation, and Earnings.* New York: Academic Press, 1975.

Sewell, William H., and Vimal P. Shah. "Socioeconomic Status, Intelligence, and the Attainment of Higher Education." *Sociology of Education* 40 (Winter 1967): 1–23. (Chapter 9 of this volume)

Shils, Edward. "Plenitude and Scarcity: The Anatomy of an International Culture Crisis." *Encounter* 32 (May 1969): 37–57.

Shils, Edward A. "Tradition, Ecology and Institution in the History of Sociology." *Daedalus,* Fall 1970, pp. 760–825.

Silberman, Charles. *Crisis in the Classroom.* New York: Random House, 1970.

Silver, Harold, ed. *Equal Opportunity in Education: A Reader in Social Class and Educational Opportunity.* London: Methuen, 1973.

Simon, Brian. "Karl Marx and Education." In Brian Simon, *Intelligence, Psychology and Education: A Marxist Critique.* London: Lawrence and Wishart, 1971.

Smith, Dennis. "Selection and Knowledge Management in Education Systems." In *Readings in the Theory of Educational Systems,* edited by Earl Hopper, pp. 139–158. London: Hutchinson University Library, 1971.

Smith, George, ed. *E.P.A.: The West Riding Project,* Volume Four. London: Her Majesty's Stationery Office, 1973.

Steinberg, Stephen. "How Jewish Quotas Began." *Commentary* 52 (September 1971): 67–76.

Steinitz, Victoria A.; Prudence King; Ellen R. Solomon; and Ellen Dean Shapiro. "Ideological Development in Working-Class Youth." *Harvard Educational Review* 43 (August 1973): 333–361.

Strodtbeck, Fred L. "Family Integration, Values, and Achievement." In *Education, Economy, and Society,* edited by A.H. Halsey et al., pp. 315–347. New York: Free Press, 1961.

Taubman, Paul J., and Terence J. Wales. "Higher Education, Mental Ability, and Screening." *Journal of Political Economy* 81 (January-February 1973): 28–55.

Thurow, Lester C. "Education and Economic Equality." *The Public Interest* 28 (Summer 1972): 66–81. (Chapter 17 of this volume)

Tiryakian, Edward A., ed. *The Phenomenon of Sociology.* New York: Appleton-Century-Crofts, 1971.

Touraine, Alain. *The May Movement: Revolt and Reform.* New York: Random House, 1971.

Trow, Martin. "The Second Transformation of American Secondary Education." *International Journal of Comparative*

Sociology 2 (September 1961): 144–166. (Pp. 144–155 and 162–166 appear as Chapter 3 of this volume.)

Turner, Ralph. "Sponsored and Contest Mobility and the School System." *American Sociological Review* 25 (October 1960): 855–867.

Tyack, David B. *The One Best System: A History of American Urban Education.* Cambridge, Mass.: Harvard University Press, 1974.

Useem, Michael. "State Production of Social Knowledge: Patterns in Government Financing of Academic Social Research." *American Sociological Review* 41 (August 1976a): 613–629.

Useem, Michael. "Government Influence on the Social Science Paradigm." *Sociological Quarterly* 17 (Spring 1976b): 146–161.

Valentine, Charles A. *Culture and Poverty: Critique and Counterproposals.* Chicago: University of Chicago Press, 1968.

Veblen, Thorstein. *The Higher Learning in America.* New York: Hill and Wang, 1957.

Walker, Rob. "The Sociology of Education and Life in School Classrooms." *International Review of Education* 18, special number (1972): 32–43.

Waller, Willard. *The Sociology of Teaching.* New York: John Wiley and Sons, 1967.

Weber, Max. "Selections on Education and Politics." In *Education: Structure and Society,* edited by B. R. Cosin, pp. 211–241. Harmondsworth, Middlesex: Penguin Books, 1972.

Westergaard, John, and Alan Little. "The Trend of Class Differentials in Educational Opportunity in England and Wales." *British Journal of Sociology* 15 (December 1964): 301–316.

Williams, Raymond. *Culture and Society.* London: Chatto and Windus, 1957.

Williamson, Bill. "Continuities and Discontinuities in the Sociology of Education." In *Educability, Schools and Ideology,* edited by Michael Flude and John Ahier, pp. 3–14. London: Croom Helm, 1974.

Wolfle, Dael. *America's Resources of Specialized Talent.* New York: Harper and Brothers, 1954.

Yanowitch, Murray, and Norton Dodge. "Social Class and Education: Soviet Findings and Reactions." *Comparative Education Review* 12 (October 1968): 248–267.

Young, Michael. *The Rise of the Meritocracy.* London: Thames and Hudson, 1958.

Young, Michael F.D., ed. *Knowledge and Control.* London: Collier-Macmillan, 1971a.

Young, Michael F.D. "An Approach to the Study of Curricula as Socially Organized Knowledge." In *Knowledge and Control,* edited by Michael F.D. Young, pp. 19–47. London: Collier-Macmillan, 1971b.

I

EDUCATION AND
SOCIAL STRUCTURE

Émile Durkheim (1858–1917), alone among the great figures of classical sociology, offered an analysis of the educational process as a crucial part of his general theory of society. He was concerned with the origins and consequences of those moral values that were, in his view, the foundation of social order, and he studied educational institutions in order to illuminate the process that held society together. Education was the means by which society perpetuated itself. But it also had a more complex role; an evolutionist both philosophically and politically, Durkheim believed that educational change was not only an important reflection of underlying structural and cultural change, but also an active agent in that process. From this perspective, no analysis of stability and change in a given society could be complete without a careful examination of its educational system.

It is little known that Durkheim, the first sociologist ever to hold a chair at the University of Paris, did not enter the Sorbonne as a sociologist at all. Sociology was struggling to establish itself at the turn of the century; it was not at first accepted at the Sorbonne, and indeed, according to Durkheim's student Maurice Halbwachs, Durkheim was able to introduce it only in his capacity as Professor of Pedagogy.[1] On taking his position at the University of Paris, Durkheim delivered several memorable series of lectures, which earned him his status as the founder of the sociology of education. Yet if Durkheim is, by common assent, the Founding Father of the effort to study educational institutions scientifically, his own writings on the subject have had peculiarly little influence on subsequent educational research. To be sure, a part of Durkheim's heritage has been transmitted indirectly—a reader of Parsons's now classic essay "The School Class as a Social System,"[2] for example, could hardly miss the enormous debt Parsons owes to Durkheim's *Education and Sociology*. But apart from a sprinkling of ritual references, the effects of this highly original work on later research in the sociology of education have been negligible.

Nor has Durkheim's *Moral Education,* which has been available in English translation since 1961, had much discernible impact on educational research. There are, indeed, a number of

---

1. Introduction to Émile Durkheim, *L'évolution pédagogique en France* (Paris: Presses universitaires de France, 1969), p. 1.
2. *Harvard Educational Review* 29 (Fall 1959): 297–318.

arguments in *Moral Education* that have a distinctly anachronistic ring, but beneath the book's relentless moralism and its rudimentary psychology lies a penetrating analysis of the school classroom as an agent of socialization. In a period in which research in the sociology of education is marked by a proliferation of studies of the school as a "social system,"[3] it would be unfortunate if the first sociological analysis of the classroom as a small society continued to be ignored.

Less well known in the Anglo-Saxon world than either *Education and Sociology* or *Moral Education* is the book that is by far Durkheim's greatest contribution to the sociology of education—*L'évolution pédagogique en France*. Not published in France until two decades after Durkheim's death, it is composed of a series of twenty-seven lectures given by Durkheim at the Sorbonne in 1904–1905 for a course on the history of French education. From this book, hitherto unavailable in English (except for a brief excerpt published in Anthony Giddens's collection of Durkheim's writings[4]), we have included a newly-translated selection on Renaissance and Jesuit education (Chapter 2). A complete translation of *L'évolution pédagogique en France* is now scheduled for publication, and its appearance in English should help to establish this long-neglected work as a classic contribution to the sociology of education.[5]

Perhaps the most remarkable aspect of the book is, as we suggested in our introduction, the exemplary way in which Durkheim combines his analysis of the content of the educational process with an examination of the place of the educational system in the larger social structure. For Durkheim, it is impossible to understand changes in curriculum and pedagogy without analyzing the broader social movements that generated them. This is seen clearly in his analysis of the pedagogical ideals of the Renaissance, which he traces to structural changes, particularly in class relations, occurring in late medieval society. Similarly, in his analysis of Jesuit education, he finds that the innovations the Jesuits introduced into the sphere of discipline derived their success from their compatibility with a growing trend toward individualism in seventeenth-century Europe.

Durkheim thus sees changes in educational ideals and practices as originating in the larger society, but this is in no way incompatible with the view that educational change has important social consequences. In a brilliant analysis of the effects of Jesuit education on French culture, Durkheim traces both the taste of seventeenth-century French literature for generalized and impersonal types (e.g., Célimène as the embodiment of flirtatiousness and Harpagon of avarice) and that of eighteenth-century politics for universal ideals (e.g., the rights not of Frenchmen but of man in general) to the abstract universalism of Jesuit education.[6] If educational change is ultimately rooted outside the educational system, its consequences also extend far beyond the school. But whether one is looking at the origin of changes in pedagogical ideals and practices or at their effects, a proper sociological analysis of the content of schooling, however detailed its attention to the texture of daily life in the classroom, must never lose sight of the social structure in which the school is located.

3. See, for example, the studies reprinted in Sam D. Sieber and David E. Wilder, eds., *The School in Society* (New York: Free Press, 1973).
4. Anthony Giddens, ed., *Émile Durkheim: Selected Writings* (London: Cambridge University Press, 1972). Giddens's introduction to this volume, which discusses some neglected aspects of Durkheim's work, is well worth reading.
5. The translation of *L'évolution pédagogique en France* will be published by Routledge and Kegan Paul.
6. Durkheim, *op. cit.,* pp. 309–317. For an interesting discussion that draws upon Durkheim's work, see Pierre Bourdieu, "Systems of Education and Systems of Thought," in *Knowledge and Control,* ed. Michael F. D. Young (London: Collier-Macmillan, 1971), pp. 189–207.

Martin Trow's study of stages in the historical development of American secondary education, reprinted here as Chapter 3, is in the modern tradition of evolutionary functionalism. An analysis of the transformation of the American high school from a mass terminal to a mass preparatory institution, it focuses on changes in the occupational structure in its effort to explain rapid increases in enrollment in American secondary and higher education. Its argument, though making reference to ideological and cultural factors, is in essence a technical-functional one; Trow sees a change in the division of labor from a relatively simple structure dominated by agricultural and industrial workers to an increasingly complex structure in which white-collar workers come to predominate as the driving force behind the expansion and differentiation of American secondary education.

Trow marshals impressive empirical evidence to support his thesis, but recent criticism has questioned the adequacy of his argument. Robert Dreeben, himself a functionalist (though of Parsonsian rather than technical-functional persuasion) and an admirer of Trow's work, surveys the evidence and finds that educational expansion far exceeds any conceivable growth in occupational requirements.[7] Changes in the technical requirements of jobs do, to be sure, explain part of the expansion in enrollments, but an analysis of historical data from the U.S. Bureau of the Census makes clear that Trow's article tells only part of the story. Furthermore, there is a certain theoretical looseness in Trow's argument, which, though generally stressing that changes in the "functions" of the educational system derive from changes in the division of labor, holds that curricular changes of the early twentieth century were engendered by the problems posed by the *personal* characteristics of culturally impoverished immigrant children rather than by *structural* changes in the emerging corporate economy that placed new demands on the educational system.[8] Underlying Trow's work is the assumption, present also in a more recent article on the transition from mass to universal higher education,[9] that educational expansion leads automatically to a hierarchy of colleges and schools. This assumption, which is a direct corollary of the functionalist theory of educational stratification, has been questioned by proponents of conflict theory.

Perhaps no article has raised the issues dividing the functionalist and conflict theories of education with greater clarity than Randall Collins's essay on educational stratification (Chapter 4). A vigorous critic of the technical-functional theory of education, Collins cites evidence that, though not conclusive, tends to support his view that competition between status groups for the educational qualifications necessary for employment is responsible for spiraling educational enrollments.[10] The concept of "status groups" is, of course, a Weberian notion, as is the belief that membership in a status group carries with it a more or less distinct sense of membership in a particular sub-culture.[11] Viewed from this perspective, the educational selection processes that functionalists like Trow consider inevitable outgrowths of the need to staff a highly technical division of labor may be seen as the outcome of a power

7. Robert Dreeben, "American Schooling: Patterns and Processes of Stability and Change," in *Stability and Social Change,* ed. Bernard Barber and Alex Inkeles (Boston: Little, Brown, 1971), pp. 82–119.
8. For an elaboration of the argument that the curricular changes occurring in early twentieth-century American secondary education derived from economically induced changes in class relations, see David K. Cohen and Marvin Lazerson, "Education and the Corporate Order," *Socialist Revolution,* March-April 1972, pp. 47–72 (Chapter 21 in this volume).
9. Martin Trow, "Reflections on the Transition from Mass to Universal Higher Education," *Daedalus,* Winter 1970, pp. 1–42.
10. Some of the empirical evidence to which Collins refers in Chapter 4 is presented in his article, "Where are Educational Requirements for Employment Highest?" *Sociology of Education,* Fall 1974, pp. 419–442.
11. See H. H. Gerth and C. Wright Mills, eds., *From Max Weber: Essays in Sociology* (New York: Oxford University Press, 1946).

struggle between groups competing for cultural dominion. Social class enters into Collins's theory of educational stratification as one of the three possible determinants of status group membership (along with power position and cultural conditions), but, following Weber, his theory gives primacy to cultural rather than economic conflict.

A conflict theory that places social class squarely at the center of its analysis of the educational system is offered in Chapter 5 by Samuel Bowles, a neo-Marxist economist who, with his colleague Herbert Gintis, has written a series of articles constituting a comprehensive critique of the functionalist view of the role of schooling in advanced capitalist society.[12] The article reprinted here, one of Bowles's earliest general formulations of the problem of education and class, is exploratory in character, but its influence on radical young researchers in America has nonetheless been considerable. One of the distinctive features of Bowles and Gintis's work—its broad theoretical sweep—is clearly visible in this article, which draws variously upon the literature of history, economics, and sociology to provide a structural analysis of the educational system in American society. The focus of this particular selection is on the role of schooling in the reproduction of the social division of labor, and in it Bowles argues that class inequality is perpetuated from generation to generation by class-linked differences in the family and the school that correspond to the hierarchical social relations at the workplace. Bowles and Gintis have been increasingly preoccupied by social change, and in trying to grapple with it they have given new emphasis to a very old Marxist idea—that of class conflict. Class divisions do, of course, underlie the argument of Chapter 5, but the relationship between the capitalist and the worker analyzed therein is viewed more in terms of class domination than in terms of class struggle. In their more recent work, however, Bowles and Gintis have stressed their view that the existing educational system is not simply a product of capitalist domination, but rather a compromise, albeit an unequal one, between the interests of dominant and subordinate social groups. The outcome of this compromise is substantially determined by conflict between social classes, and workers are active participants in the struggle. This concept of class conflict, hardly visible in "Unequal Education and the Reproduction of the Social Division of Labor," has come to be a vital component of Bowles and Gintis's later theory of educational reproduction and change.

A perspective used all too infrequently in both functionalist and conflict analyses of education and social structure is the comparative approach. One example, and perhaps the most widely cited article in the history of the sociology of education, is Ralph Turner's brilliant comparative analysis of the educational systems of Great Britain and the United States, "Sponsored and Contest Mobility and the School System."[13] Using Turner's scheme as his point of departure, Hopper (Chapter 6) develops a systematic typology of educational systems. His purpose is to provide a conceptual framework to encourage theoretically informed empirical research, and he suggests various ways in which the analysis of structural differences between educational systems might illuminate existing knowledge. The keystone of Hopper's framework is a typology of the various dimensions of the educational selection process, and a crucial element in it is the comparative analysis of educational ideology.

Hopper would seem to be on firm ground here, for the process of educational selection is among the most researched topics in the sociology of education, but it is precisely this stress on selection that comes under attack by Ioan Davies.[14] According to Davies, Hopper's

12. The final product of their collaboration, which extends back to the late 1960s, is their book, *Schooling in Capitalist America* (New York: Basic Books, 1976).

13. First published in *American Sociological Review,* October 1960, pp. 855–867.

14. Ioan Davies, "The Management of Knowledge: A Critique of the Use of Typologies in Educational Sociology," in *Readings in the Theory of Educational Systems,* ed. Earl Hopper (London: Hutchinson University Library, 1971), pp. 111–138.

typology has the unfortunate effect of directing educational research to the study of education's latent function of selecting people for jobs rather than to its manifest function of managing knowledge. The force of Davies's critique lies in its identification of a crucial problem that has generally been ignored by structurally oriented sociologists of education: that of the content of education. Yet the problem of the organization and transmission of knowledge in educational institutions is by no means unrelated to the question of educational selection; patterns of selection affect not only what is taught and how it is taught, but also who is taught, and in that sense they are important determinants of the distribution of knowledge. Davies does, however, insist that studies of educational knowledge, if they are to prove illuminating, must ultimately be linked to analyses of social structure. No one grasped this truth more clearly than the founder of the sociology of education, Émile Durkheim, and there is perhaps no better example of an investigation embodying it than the work with which we begin this section—*L'évolution pédagogique en France.*

SELECTIVE BIBLIOGRAPHY

Althusser, Louis. "Ideology and Ideological State Apparatuses." In *Education: Structure and Society,* edited by B. R. Cosin, pp. 242–280. Harmondsworth, Middlesex: Penguin Books, 1972.

Banks, Olive. *The Sociology of Education.* London: Batsford, 1971.

Bourdieu, Pierre, and Jean-Claude Passeron. "La comparabilité des systèmes d'enseignement." In *Éducation développement et démocratie,* edited by Pierre Bourdieu and Jean-Claude Passeron, pp. 21–48. Paris: Mouton, 1967.

Bowles, Samuel, and Herbert Gintis. *Schooling in Capitalist America.* New York: Basic Books, 1976.

Brookover, Wilbur B., and Edsel Erickson. *Sociology of Education.* Homewood, Ill.: The Dorsey Press, 1975.

Clark, Burton R. *Educating the Expert Society.* San Francisco: Chandler Publishing Company, 1962.

Collins, Randall. *Conflict Sociology: Towards an Explanatory Science.* New York: Academic Press, 1975.

Davies, Ioan. "The Management of Knowledge: A Critique of the Use of Typologies in Educational Sociology." In *Readings in the Theory of Educational Systems,* edited by Earl Hopper, pp. 111–139. London: Hutchinson University Library, 1971.

Durkheim, Émile. *Education and Sociology.* Glencoe, Ill.: The Free Press, 1956.

Durkheim, Émile. *Moral Education.* Glencoe, Ill.: The Free Press, 1961.

Floud, Jean, and A. H. Halsey. "The Sociology of Education: A Trend Report and Bibliography." *Current Sociology* 7 (1958): 165–235.

Foster, Philip. *Education and Social Change in Ghana.* London: Routledge and Kegan Paul, 1965.

Gerth, H. H., and C. Wright Mills. *From Max Weber: Essays in Sociology.* New York: Oxford University Press, 1946.

Gras, Alain, ed. *Sociologie de l'éducation: textes fondamentaux.* Paris: Librairie Larousse, 1971.

Hopper, Earl, ed. *Readings in the Theory of Educational Systems.* London: Hutchinson University Library, 1971.

Parsons, Talcott. "The School Class as a Social System: Some of its Functions in American Society." *Harvard Educational Review* 29 (Fall 1959): 297–318.

2. On Education and Society

ÉMILE DURKHEIM

Educational transformations are always the result and the symptom of the social transformations in terms of which they are to be explained. For a people to feel at any given moment the need to change its educational system, it is necessary that new ideas and needs have emerged for which the old system is no longer adequate. But these needs and ideas do not arise spontaneously; if they suddenly come to the forefront of human consciousness after having been ignored for centuries, it is necessarily the case that in the intervening period there has been a change and that it is this change of which they are an expression. Thus, in order to understand the educational achievement of the sixteenth century, we need as a preliminary to know in a general way what constituted the great social movement that historians call the Renaissance and of which a new educational theory was but one manifestation.

The essence of the Renaissance has often been identified with a return to the spirit of classical times; and indeed this is precisely the meaning of the word normally used to designate this period of European history. The sixteenth century is supposed to have been a period when man, abandoning the gloomy ideals of the Middle Ages, reverted to the gayer and more self-confident view of life which prevailed in the ancient pagan world. As to the cause of this change of direction, it allegedly consisted in the rediscovery of classical literature, the principal masterpieces of which were rescued during this period from the oblivion in which they had languished for centuries. On this view it was the discovery of the great works of classical literature that brought about this new change of outlook in the western European mind. But to speak of the Renaisssance in this way is only to point in the most

superficial way to its façade. If it were indeed true that the sixteenth century simply took up the classical tradition at the point it had reached when the Dark Ages arrived and temporarily blotted it out, the Renaissance would emerge as a movement of moral and intellectual reaction that would be hard to account for. We would have to assume that humanity had strayed from its natural path for fifteen centuries, since it had to retrace its steps back over a period of such length in order to embark upon a whole new stage in its career. Certainly progress does not proceed in a straight line; it makes turnings and detours; advances are followed by recessions; but that such an aberration should be prolonged over a period of fifteen hundred years is historically incredible. It is true that this view of the Renaissance accords with the way in which the eighteenth-century writers spoke of it. But just because they felt a kind of admiration for the simple life of primitive societies, are we to say that their social philosophy was an attempt to restore prehistoric civilization? Because the men of the Revolution thought that they were imitating the actions of the ancient Romans, are we to view the society that resulted from the Revolution as an imitation of the ancient city? People involved in action are the least well placed to see the causes that underlie their actions, and the way in which they represent to themselves the social movement of which they are a part should always be regarded as suspect and should by no means be thought of as having any special claim to credibility.

Besides, it is simply not true that classical literature was unknown during the centuries we have just been considering, that it was only discovered towards the beginning of the sixteenth century, and that it was this revela-

Excerpted from *L'évolution pédagogique en France* (Paris: Presses Universitaires de France, 1969), pp. 194–197, 198–201, 236–239, 266–269, 286–288, and 296–303. This translation was undertaken by Peter Collins. A translation of the full volume (under the title *The Evolution of Educational Thought*) is forthcoming from Routledge and Kegan Paul, Ltd.

tion that suddenly expanded the intellectual horizons of Europe. The fact is that there was not a single period during the whole of the Middle Ages when these literary masterpieces were not known; in every generation we find a few people sufficiently intelligent and sensitive to be able to appreciate their worth. Abélard, the hero of dialectic, was at the same time a literary scholar; Virgil, Seneca, Cicero, and Ovid were just as familiar to him as were Boethius and Augustine. During the twelfth century there was a famous school at Chartres which, inspired by its founder, Bernard de Chartres, offered a classical education similar to what would later be offered by the Jesuits. One could multiply examples of this type. It is true that these attempts to introduce classical literature into education remained isolated cases; they never succeeded in capturing the imagination of the Scholastics, who cast them back into obscurity. But they are nonetheless real, and they are sufficient to prove that if classical literature was not appreciated in the Middle Ages, if it played no part in education, this was not because people did not know of its existence. In short, the Middle Ages knew about all the main aspects of classical civilization, but it only retained what it regarded as important, what answered to its own needs. Its entire attention was caught by logic, and this eclipsed everything else. Thus, if everything changed in the sixteenth century, if suddenly Greek and Roman art and literature were recognized as being of incomparable educational value, this clearly must have been because at that moment in history, as a consequence of a change that had taken place in the public mind, logic lost its former prestige—while by contrast an urgent need was felt for the first time for a kind of culture that would be more refined, more elegant or literary. People did not acquire this taste because they had just discovered classical antiquity; rather, they demanded from the antiquity they already knew the means of satisfying the new taste they had just acquired. What we must seek, therefore, is an

account of this change of direction in the intellectual and moral outlook of the European peoples, if we wish to understand the nature of the Renaissance insofar as it affected educational thought no less than scientific and literary thought. A people only modifies its mental outlook to such an enormous extent when very fundamental features of social life have themselves been modified. We can therefore be certain in advance that the Renaissance derives, not, I repeat, from the fortuitous fact that certain classical works were exhumed at this time, but rather from profound changes in the organization of European societies. I cannot, of course, attempt here to paint a complete and detailed picture of these transformations, but I should like at least to point out the most important of them so as to be able to relate the educational movement we shall be exploring to its social roots.

In the first place, there was a group of interrelated changes in the economic sphere. People had finally got away from the paltry life-style of the Middle Ages, when the general insecurity of relations paralyzed the spirit of enterprise, when the limited number of markets stifled great ambition, when only the extreme simplicity of their tastes and needs enabled men to live in harmony with their environment. Gradually order had been established; better government and more efficient administration had rallied people's confidence. Towns had proliferated and become more populous. Most important of all, the discovery of America and the trade route via the Indies had galvanized economic activity by opening up new worlds in which it could operate. Consequently, the general welfare had been increased; vast fortunes had been amassed; and the acquisition of wealth stimulated and developed a taste for the easy, elegant life of luxury. . . .

However, if this transformation had been limited to the world of the aristocracy, it probably would not have had such extensive social consequences. But one of the effects of accrued wealth was to produce at the same time a narrowing of the gaps between social classes. Up till then the bourgeoisie had not even dared raise its eyes to look at the aristocracy across what it felt to be a great fixed gulf. And it found it natural to lead quite a different existence. But now that the bourgeoisie had become richer and consequently more powerful, it also became more ambitious and sought to narrow the gap. Its expectations had increased with its resources, making the life it had led up till then appear intolerable. It was no longer afraid to cast its gaze upwards and it wanted as well to live the life of the nobles, to imitate their style, their manners, their luxury. As one writer puts it: "Pride was reaching ever higher peaks in every section of the community. The bourgeoisie in the towns have started wanting to dress in the same way as the aristocracy . . . and the people from the villages in the same way as the bourgeoisie in the towns." According to another author, the bourgeois ladies grew bored with their life of obscurity; they now wanted to copy the great ladies. "One can scarcely distinguish any longer between a noble lady and a plebeian . . . one sees women who are worse than plebeian dressing in flowing robes embroidered in gold and silver . . . their fingers are loaded with emeralds and other precious stones . . . in the old days the practice of kissing a lady's hand in greeting was restricted to aristocrats, and noble ladies did not offer their hand to the first comer, let alone to anyone at all. Today men smelling of leather rush to kiss the hand of a woman whose escutcheon is exclusively aristocratic. Patrician ladies marry plebeian men, plebeian women marry patrician men; thus we are breeding hybrid creatures." It is easy to guess that so considerable a change in the way life was understood would inevitably be accompanied by a change in the way education was understood, and that instruction designed to produce a good bachelor of arts, versed in all the secrets of syllogism and argument, would be quite unsuited to the enterprise of producing an elegant and fluent nobleman

able to hold his own in a salon and possessing all the social graces.

However, in addition to this transformation, there was another one, no less important, which took place in the world of ideas.

By the sixteenth century, the great nation states of Europe had been in large measure established. Whereas in the Middle Ages there had been but one Europe, one Christendom, which was united and homogeneous, there now existed great individual collectivities with their own intellectual and moral characters. England found its identity and its unity with the Tudors, Spain with Ferdinand of Castile and his successors, Germany with the Hapsburgs (albeit more vaguely), and France did so before any of the others under the Capetians. The old unity of Christendom had thus been definitively shattered. However much people continued to profess respect for the fundamental doctrines, which still appeared highly abstract, each of the groups which had thus been formed had its own special mode of thought and feeling, its own national temperament whose particular emphasis tended to affect the systems of belief that had been accepted until that time by the vast majority of the faithful. And since the great moral figures that had arisen could only develop their individual natures, since they could not organize their thoughts and beliefs according to their own lights unless they were granted the right to deviate from accepted beliefs, they claimed this right and in claiming it they proclaimed it; that is to say they claimed the rights of schism and of free inquiry—albeit only to a limited extent, and not as absolute rights, since such a thing would have been inconceivable at the time. It is here that we find the root cause of the Reformation, that other aspect of the Renaissance that was the natural result of the movement towards individualization and differentiation taking place at that time within the homogeneous mass of Europe. In one sense, of course, Scholasticism had paved the way for it. Scholasticism had taught reason to be more self-confident by confronting it with monumental questions and equipping it with a rigorous logical training so that it might make fresh conquests. However, between the audacities of Scholasticism, especially at the end of the fifteenth century, which were always relatively moderate—between the more or less bold claims made by a few thinkers whose voices were scarcely heard outside the schools, and the sudden explosion that was the Reformation and that shook the whole of Europe, there is clearly a radical break, which bears witness to the fact that new forces had come into play.

Here we have a new causal factor, which was to bring about a change in the theory and practice of education. The Christian faith had played too large a part in medieval education for the educational system not to be affected by the upheavals that faith was undergoing. Moreover, there were other ways in which the economic factor exercised a parallel influence. It is clear, in fact, that the aesthetic ideal of the Middle Ages was quite unsuited for pupils who had acquired a taste for luxury and the life of leisure. And since this aesthetic ideal was the ideal of Christianity, Christianity itself was affected by the same phenomenon. For it was not possible that the aversion felt henceforth for the old view of life should not be extended to the whole system of beliefs upon which that view of life was grounded. If, as we have argued, Christianity was accepted so readily by the barbarians, this was precisely because of its starkness, its indifference towards the products of civilization, its disdain for the joys of existence. But the same reasons that accounted for its triumph then were now to diminish its authority over people's minds. Societies that had learned to savor the joy of living could no longer put up with a doctrine that rendered sacrifice, self-denial, abstinence, and suffering in general the supreme objects of desire.

Individuals, sensing that this system ran counter to their deepest feelings and op-posed the satisfaction of needs they regarded as quite natural, could only be disposed to cast doubt upon it, or at least to cast doubt upon the way it had been interpreted up to that time; for it is impossible to accept uncritically, unreservedly, and without sufficient reason a doctrine that in certain respects seems to go against nature. Without renouncing it completely, people came to feel the need to revise it, to interpret it afresh, in such a way that it would harmonize with the aspirations of the age. Now, any such revision and reinterpretation presuppose the right to revise, to inspect, and to interpret, in some sense the right to examine, which, however one looks at it, implies a diminution of faith. . . .

Now, it is clear that there is nothing in Scholasticism that could have satisfied these new tastes: on the contrary, it was bound to be hostile to them. Since it attached no importance to form, it did not hesitate to twist language savagely in order to satisfy all the needs of thought, without regard to considerations of purity or harmony. As a result of the very great place it accorded to debate, it developed a taste not for ideas that were delicate, subtle, measured, but rather for opinions that were dogmatic and clear-cut and whose features stood out in such a way that conflicting opinions could be clearly contrasted. Moreover, the violent arguments that were born of these contrasts could only encourage a coarseness in manners comparable to what had been upheld for so long by the noble knights in their tourneys and similar practices. The student of the Middle Ages was primarily concerned with crushing his opponent beneath the weight of his arguments and did not care in the least whether his presentation was attractive. His unkempt appearance and his rustic deportment and manners were expressions of this same state of mind.

Here we have the explanation of why the men of the new generation were quite literally horrified by Scholasticism and its methods. The extreme virulence of their polemics seems at first sight to be out of place in a purely educational quarrel. But the fact is that the issue was really more wide-ranging. The sixteenth century did not accuse Scholasticism simply of having engaged in certain debatable or regrettable academic practices but rather of having constituted a school of barbarousness and coarseness. Hence the frequency with which the words *barbarus, stoliditas, rusticitas* recur in the writings of Erasmus. To these refined minds a Scholastic is quite literally a barbarian (remember the title of Erasmus's book *Antibarbaros*), who speaks a language scarcely human, crude-sounding, formally inelegant; who delights only in arguments, in deafening yells, in verbal and other battles; who is ignorant, in sum, of all the benefits of civilization, of everything that contributes to the charm of life. We can readily conceive of the feeling such an educational system would be capable of arousing in men whose aim was to render humanity more tender, more elegant, more cultivated.

The only way to succeed in ridding the human intellect of its coarseness, to polish and refine it, was to introduce it to and make it intimate with an elegant and refined civilization, so that it might become imbued with its spirit. Now, the only civilization that could satisfy this condition at that time was that of the classical peoples as it had been expressed and preserved in the works of their great writers, poets, and orators. It was thus quite natural that these should be seen as providing the schoolteachers needed by the young. "What then," says Erasmus, "what then could have guided these coarse men of the Stone Age towards a more human life, towards being more gentle of character and more civilized in morals? Was it not literature? It is literature that molds the mind, that mollifies passions, that checks the untamed outbursts of natural temperament." For this purpose there existed no other established and developed literatures apart from those of Rome and Greece.

With this in view, the moral milieu in which the child was to be molded had to be made up of all the extant elements of these literatures. Hence the enormous attention accorded by the public at this time to the masterpieces of Greco-Roman civilization. If people esteemed and admired them, if they sought to imitate them, this is not because they were exhumed at this moment in history and, by being discovered, suddenly inculcated in people a taste for literature. Quite the reverse: it was because a taste for literature, a taste for a new kind of civilization, had just been acquired that they suddenly became objects of enthusiastic veneration; for they appeared, and quite rightly so, as the only means available of satisfying this new need. If this vast body of literature had hitherto been neglected, this was not because nothing was known of it (we have already seen that the major works were known); rather, its virtues were not appreciated because they did not meet any contemporary need. If, by contrast, they were then regarded in the eyes of public opinion, or at least of a certain section of it, as being of incomparable value, this was because a new attitude of mind was in the process of developing and could only be fully realized in the school of the classics. And one may even wonder whether the greater frequency of the finds and exhumations that occurred at this period was not a result of the fact that since, henceforth, the value of these discoveries was fully appreciated people devoted more of their ingenuity to making them. To find, one must seek, and one only seeks in earnest when one attaches importance to what one hopes to find.

Thus the educational ideas of the humanists were not the result of simple accidents. They derived, rather, from a fact whose influence on the moral history of our country it is difficult to exaggerate; I refer to the establishment of polite society. If France did indeed become from the sixteenth century onwards a center of literary life and intellectual activity, this was because, at this same period, there had developed among us a select society, a society of intellectually cultivated people to whom our writers addressed themselves. It was the ideas and the tastes of this society that they communicated; it was for this society that they wrote and for it that they thought. It was here in this particular environment that the driving force of our civilization from the sixteenth century to the middle of the eighteenth century arose. And the object of education as Erasmus conceived of it was to prepare man for this special and restricted society.

Here too we can see the essential character and at the same time the radical flaw of this educational theory. It is the fact that it is essentially aristocratic in nature. The kind of society that it seeks to fashion is always centered around a court, and its members are always drawn from the ranks of the aristocracy or at least from the leisured classes. And it was indeed here and here alone that that fine flowering of elegance and culture could take place, the nurturing and development of which were regarded as more important than anything else. Neither Erasmus nor Vivès had any awareness that beyond this small world, which for all its brilliance was very limited, there were vast masses who should not have been neglected and for whom education could have brought about higher intellectual and moral standards and an improved material condition.

When such a thought did occur to them it disappeared again very quickly without their thinking it necessary to examine it at length. Since he realizes that this expensive education is not suitable for everyone, Erasmus wonders what the poor will do; his answer to this objection is utterly simple. "You ask," he says, "what the poor will be able to do. How will those who can scarcely feed their children be able to give them over a sustained period of time the right kind of education? To this I can only reply by quoting the words of the comic writer: 'You can't ask that what we are capable of achieving should be as great as what we would like to achieve.' We are expounding the best way of bringing up a child, we cannot produce the

means of realizing this ideal." He restricts himself to expressing the wish that the rich will come to the help of those who are well-endowed intellectually but who would be prevented by poverty from developing their aptitudes. But he seems not to realize that even if this education were made available to everybody the difficulty would not be resolved, for this generalized education would not meet the needs of the majority. Indeed, for the majority the supreme need is survival, and what is needed in order to survive is not the art of subtle speech, it is the art of sound thinking, so that one knows how to act. In order to struggle effectively in the world of persons and the world of things more substantial weapons are needed than those glittering decorations with which the humanist educationalists were concerned to adorn the mind to the exclusion of anything else.

Think now how much Scholasticism, for all its abstractness, was imbued with a more practical, more realistic, and more social spirit. The fact is that dialectic answered real needs. Intellectual conflict, competition between ideas, constitutes a genuinely important part of life. Moreover, the strength and virility of thought which were acquired as a result of such arduous mental gymnastics could be used in the service of socially useful ends. Thus we must beware of thinking that the medieval schools served only to produce dreamers, seekers after quintessences, and useless pettifogging quibblers. The truth is quite the opposite. It was there that the statesmen, the ecclesiastical dignitaries, and the administrators of the day were brought up. This training, which has been so denigrated, created men of action. It was the education recommended by Erasmus that forms a totally inadequate preparation for life. In it rhetoric supplants dialectic. Now, if rhetoric had good reason for featuring in the education of the classical world, where the practice of eloquence constituted not only a career but the most important career, this was by no means the case in the sixteenth century, when it played only a very small part in the serious business of life. A theory of education that made rhetoric the principal academic discipline could thus only develop qualities related to the luxuries of existence and not at all to its necessities. . . .

In order to know what became of the educational theories of the Renaissance when they were translated into practice, it would thus seem that we have only to investigate how the University understood them and applied them. But what makes such a procedure impossible, what makes the whole question more complicated, is the great change that took place at this very moment in our academic organization. Up till that time the University had a complete monopoly on and sole responsibility for education, and consequently the future of any educational reforms was dependent upon the University and upon the University alone. However, towards the middle of the sixteenth century, over and against the University corporation there was established a new teaching corporation, which was to break the University's monopoly and which was even to achieve with quite remarkable rapidity a kind of hegemony in academic life. This was the corporation of the Jesuits.

The Jesuit order arose from the need felt by the Catholic Church to check the increasingly threatening progress of Protestantism. With extraordinary speed the doctrines of Luther and Calvin had won over England, almost the whole of Germany, Switzerland, the Low Countries, Sweden, and a considerable part of France. In spite of all the rigorous measures taken, the Church felt itself impotent and began to fear that its dominion in the world would collapse completely. It was then that Ignatius Loyola had the idea of raising a wholly new kind of religious militia the better to combat, and if possible to crush, heresy. He realized that the days were over when people's souls could be governed from the depths of a cloister. Now that people, carried by their own momentum, were tending to elude the Church, it was essential that the Church

move closer to them so as to be able to influence them. Now that particular personalities were beginning to stand out from the homogeneous moral and intellectual mass that had been the rule in preceding centuries, it was essential for the Church to be close to individuals, to accommodate its influence over them to intellectual and temperamental diversities. In short, the vast monastic masses familiar to the Middle Ages, which, stationary at their post, had restricted themselves to repulsing such attacks as occurred, without, however, knowing how to take the offensive themselves, had to be replaced. An army of light troops would be established that would be in constant contact with the enemy and consequently well-informed about all his movements, but at the same time sufficiently alert and mobile to be able to go at the slightest signal wherever there was danger, and yet sufficiently flexible to be able to vary its tactics in accordance with the diversity of people and circumstances; its troops would do all this while always and everywhere pursuing the same goal and cooperating in the same grand design. This army was the Company of Jesus.

What was distinctive about it was that it was able to contain within itself two characteristics, which the Middle Ages had adjudged irreconcilable and contradictory. On the one hand, the Jesuits belong to a religious order in the same way as the Dominicans or the Franciscans; they have a head, they are all subject to one and the same rule, to a communal discipline; indeed passive obedience and unity of thought and action have never been carried to such an extreme degree in any militia whether secular or religious. The Jesuit is thus a regular priest. But, on the other hand, he simultaneously possesses all the characteristics of the secular priest; he wears his habit; he fulfills his functions, he preaches, he hears confessions, he catechizes; he does not live in the shadow of a monastery, he rather mingles in the life of the world. For him duty consists not in the mortification of the flesh, in fasting, in abstinence, but in action, in the realization of the goal of the Society. "Let us leave the religious orders," Ignatius Loyola used to say, "to outdo us in fasts, in watches, in the austerity of the régime and habit that, out of piety, they impose upon themselves." "I believe that it is more valuable, for the glory of Our Lord, to preserve and to fortify the stomach and the other natural faculties rather than enfeebling them . . . you should not assault your own physical nature, because if you exhaust it your intellectual nature will no longer be able to act with the same energy."

Not only must the Jesuit mingle with the world, he must also open himself up to the ideas that are dominant within it. The better to guide his age he must speak its language, he must assimilate its spirit. Ignatius Loyola sensed that a profound change had taken place in manners and that there was no going back on this; that a taste for well-being, for a less harsh, easier, sunnier existence had been acquired that could not conceivably be stifled or fobbed off; that man had developed a greater degree of pity for his own sufferings and for those of his fellowmen, that he was more sparing of pain, and consequently that the old ideal of absolute renunciation was finished. To prevent the faithful from drifting away from religion the Jesuits devoted their ingenuity to divesting religion of its former austerity; they made it pleasant and devised all kinds of accommodating arrangements to make it easy to observe. It is true that in order to remain faithful to the mission they had assigned themselves, to avoid seeming to encourage the innovators against whom they were struggling by their own example, they had at the same time to stick to the letter of immutable dogma. It is well known how they extricated themselves from this difficulty and were able to reconcile these conflicting demands thanks to their casuistry, whose excessive flexibility and over-ingenious refinements have frequently been pointed out. While maintaining in their sacred form the traditional prescriptions of

Roman Catholicism, they were still able to place these within the scope not only of human weakness in general—there is no religion that has ever managed to escape this necessity—but of the elegant frivolousness of the leisured classes of the sixteenth century in particular; it was these leisured classes that it was so important to keep free from heresy and to preserve in the faith. And this is how, while they became essentially men of the past, defenders of the Catholic tradition, the Jesuits were able to exhibit towards the ideas, the tastes, and even the defects of the time an attitude of indulgence for which they have often, and not without reason, been reproached. They thus had a dual identity as conservatives, even as reactionaries, on the one hand, and as liberals on the other: a complex policy the nature and origins of which we needed to show here, for we shall encounter it again in the foundations of their educational theory.

But they very quickly came to realize that in order to achieve their end it was not enough to preach, to hear confession, to catechize: the really important instrument in the struggle for mastery of the human soul was the education of the young. Thus they resolved to seize hold of it. One fact in particular made them acutely aware of the urgent need for this; one would have had to be blind to all the evidence not to see that the new methods taking root in the schools could only have the effect of opening up the road to heresy. Indeed, the greatest minds of the time, the most illustrious of the humanists, had openly been converted to the new religion; this was the case with Dolet, with Ramus, with Mathurin Cordier, with the majority of the teachers in the Collège de France, recently founded by François I. Thus humanism by its very nature constituted a threat to the faith. And indeed it is clear that an inordinate taste for paganism was bound to cause people's minds to dwell in a moral environment with absolutely nothing Christian about it. Accordingly, if the evil was to be attacked at its source, it would be necessary, instead of abandoning the humanist movement to its own devices, to gain control of it and to direct it. . . .

The aim of the Jesuits thus had nothing to do with getting the pupil acquainted with and able to understand classical civilizations; it was exclusively concerned with teaching them to speak and write in Greek and Latin. This explains the importance attributed to written assignments and the nature of these assignments. This is why in the grammar classes prose composition prevailed and was far more important than translation from Latin, which was scarcely practiced at all. This is why stylistic exercises were so numerous and so varied. This attitude even influenced the way the expositions were carried out. Father Jouvency has left us model expositions of Latin authors; one has only to read them to see that their main aim is to get the pupils to appreciate the author's Latin and his literary style, and to encourage them to imitate these same qualities.

Far from seeking to get their pupils to think again the thoughts of antiquity, far from wishing to steep them in the spirit of classical times, the Jesuits had precisely the opposite aim. Indeed, this was because they could see no other way of extricating themselves from the contradictory situation in which they had quite deliberately placed themselves. Because the fashion was for humanism, because classical letters were the object of a veritable cult, the Jesuits, always sensitive to the spirit of their age, professed, as we have just seen, a form of humanism—even quite an uncompromising one, since Greek and Latin alone were permitted entry into their colleges. But from another point of view, as we have said, they realized full well that humanism constituted a threat, that there was a real danger in wishing to fashion Christian souls in the school of paganism. How could these two contradictory needs be reconciled? How could the faith be defended and safeguarded as was required by the self-imposed mission of the Jesuits, while they simultaneously made themselves the apologists and exegetes of pagan literature?

There was only one way of resolving this antinomy: this was, in the very words used by Father Jouvency, to expound the classical authors in such a way "that they became, although pagan and profane, the eulogists of the faith." To make paganism serve the glorification and the propagation of the Christian ethic was a daring undertaking and, it would appear, remarkably difficult; and yet, the Jesuits had enough confidence in their ability to attempt it and to succeed in it. But in order to do this they had deliberately to denature the ancient world; they had to show the authors of antiquity, the men they were and the men they portray for us, in such a way as to leave in the shadows everything that was genuinely pagan about them, everything that makes them men of a particular city at a particular time, in order to highlight only those respects in which they are simply men, men as they are at all times and in all places. All the legends, all the traditions, all the religious ideas of Rome and Greece were interpreted in this spirit so as to give them a meaning any good Christian could accept.

Thus the Greco-Roman environment in which they made their pupils live was emptied of everything specifically Greek or Roman, so that it became a kind of unreal, idealized environment peopled by personalities who had no doubt historically existed but who were presented in such a way that they had, so to speak, nothing historical about them. They were now simply figures betokening certain virtues and vices and all the great passions of humanity. Achilles is courage; Ulysses is wily prudence; Numa is the archetype of the pious king; Caesar, the man of ambition; Augustus, the powerful monarch and lover of learning; etc. Such general and unspecific types could easily be used to exemplify the precepts of Christian morality.

Such disinheriting of antiquity was made easier for the Jesuits by the fact that, at least for a long time, all teaching of history was almost completely absent from their colleges. Even literary history was unknown. A writer's works were expounded without any-one's bothering to notice the physiognomy of the author, his manner, the way he related it to his age, to his environment, to his predecessors. His historical personality mattered so little that it was normal to study not an author, not even a work, but selected passages and extracts. How was it possible to form a picture of a specific man out of such sparse and disjointed fragments, among which his individuality was dispersed and dissolved? Each of these pieces could scarcely appear to be anything other than an isolated model of literary style, a sort of fair copy of exceptional authoritativeness.

We can now understand better how it came about that the Jesuits, and perhaps to a lesser extent so many other educators, tended to attribute to the past and especially to the distant past an educational value greater than that which they attributed to the present. This was because the past, at least at a time when the historical sciences have not advanced sufficiently to render it almost as precise and specific as the present—the past, because we see it from afar, naturally appears to us in vague, fluid, unstable forms, which are consequently all the easier to mold according to our will. It constitutes a more malleable and plastic substance that we can transform and present according to our fancy. It is thus easier to bend it for educational purposes. These people, these things from former times, we embellish without realizing we are deceiving ourselves in order to turn them into models for youth to imitate. The present, because it is before our very eyes, forces itself upon our attention and does not lend itself to this kind of reworking; it is virtually impossible for us to see it other than as it is with its ugliness, its mediocrity, its vices, and its failings; and this is why it seems to us ill-adapted to serve our educational ends. It was in this way that antiquity in the hands of the Jesuits could become an instrument for Christian education, whereas they would not have been able to utilize literature of their own age in the same way, imbued as it was

with the spirit of rebellion against the church. In their desire to attain their goal, they had a powerful vested interest in fleeing from the moderns and taking refuge in antiquity....

But so far we have only studied the Jesuits' teaching. We must now consider their disciplinary structures. It is perhaps in this area that they showed the most art and originality and it is their superiority in this respect that best explains their success.

Their entire discipline was founded upon two principles.

The first was that there can be no good education without contact at once continuous and personal between the pupil and the educator—and this principle served a dual purpose. First, it ensured that the pupil was never left to his own devices. To be properly molded he had to be subjected to pressure that never let up or flagged; for the spirit of evil is constantly watchful. This is why the Jesuits' pupil was never alone. "A supervisor would follow him everywhere, to church, to class, to the refectory, to his recreation; in the living quarters and sleeping quarters he was always there examining everything." But this supervision was not intended only to prevent misconduct. It was also to enable the Jesuit to study at his ease "character and habits so that he might manage to discover the most suitable method of directing each individual child." In other words, this direct and constant intercourse was supposed not only to render the educational process more sustained in its effect but also to make it more personal and better suited to the personality of each pupil. Father Jouvency never stops recommending that a teacher not limit himself to exerting a general and impersonal influence on the anonymous crowd of pupils but rather graduate his influence and vary it according to age, intelligence, and situation. If he is conversing with a child in private, "let him examine the child's character so that he can mold what he says in accordance with it and, as they say, 'hook' his interlocutor with the appropriate bait." And the better to get the pupils to open their minds to him, he will need to make them open their hearts by endearing himself. Indeed there can be no doubt that in the course of the relationships thus cemented between teachers and pupils bonds of friendship were frequently formed that survived school life. Thus Descartes remained very sincerely attached to his former teachers at La Flèche.

One can readily imagine how effective this system of continuous immersion must have been. The child's moral environment followed him wherever he went; all around him he heard the same ideas and the same sentiments being expressed with the same authority. He could never lose sight of them. He knew of no others. And in addition to the fact that this influence never ceased to make itself felt, it was also all the more powerful because it knew how best to adapt to the diversity of individual personalities, because it was most familiar with the openings through which it could slip and insinuate itself in the pupil's heart. By comparison with the style of discipline that had been practiced in the Middle Ages this represented a major revolution. The medieval teacher addressed himself to large and impersonal audiences, among which each individual, that is to say each student, was lost, drowned, and consequently abandoned to his own devices. Now, education is essentially an individual matter, and as long as the medieval teacher was dealing with vast masses he could obtain only very crude results. Hence the rowdy indiscipline of the students of the Middle Ages, which the establishment of the fully residential colleges was an attempt—never fully successful—to counter. For the colleges did not have at their disposal a staff of teachers and supervisors sufficiently numerous or perhaps sufficiently committed to the task of supervision to be able to exercise the necessary control and influence over each individual.

But in order to train pupils in intensive formal work, which was moreover pretty lacking in substance, it was not enough to surround them, to envelop them at close

quarters with solicitude and vigilance; it was not enough to be constantly concerned to contain and sustain them; it was also necessary to stimulate them. The goad which the Jesuits employed consisted exclusively of competition. Not only were they the first to organize the competitive system in the colleges, they also developed it to a greater intensity than it has ever subsequently known.

Although today in our classrooms this system still has considerable importance, nevertheless it no longer functions without interruption. It is fair to say that with the Jesuits it was never suspended for a single moment. The entire class was organized to promote this end. The pupils were divided into two camps, the Romans on the one hand and the Carthaginians on the other, who lived, so to speak, on the brink of war, each striving to outstrip the other. Each camp had its own dignitaries. At the head of the camp there was an imperator, also known as dictator or consul, then came a praetor, a tribune, and some senators. These honors, which were naturally coveted and contested, were distributed as the outcome of a competition, which was held monthly. From another point of view, each camp was divided into groups consisting of ten pupils each ("decuries"), commanded by a captain (called the "decurion") who was selected from among the worthies we have just mentioned. These groups were not recruited at random. There was a hierarchy among them: the first groups were composed of the best pupils, the last groups of the weakest and least industrious of the scholars. Thus just as the camp as a whole was in competition with the opposite camp, so in each camp each group had its own immediate rival in the other camp at the equivalent level. Finally, individuals themselves were matched and each soldier in a group had his opposite number in the opposing group. Thus academic work involved a kind of perpetual hand-to-hand combat. Camp challenged camp; group struggled with group; pupils supervised one another, corrected one another, and took one another to task. On some occasions the teacher was not supposed to be afraid of pitting together two pupils of unequal ability. For example, an able pupil would have his work corrected by a less able pupil, says Father Jouvency, "so that those who have made mistakes may be the more ashamed and the more mortified by them." It was even possible for any pupil to do battle with a pupil from a higher group and, if victorious, to take his place.

It is interesting to note that these various ennoblements carried with them not only honorific titles but also active functions; and indeed it was these that constituted the prize. The captain enjoyed extensive powers. Seated opposite his group he was responsible for maintaining silence and attentiveness among his ten scholars, noting down absences, making the scholars recite their lessons, ensuring that assignments had been done with care and completed. The consuls exercised the same authority over the captains in their camp that these did over their own group members. Everyone was thus kept constantly in suspense. Never has the idea that the classroom is a small organized society been realized so systematically. It was a city-state where every pupil was a functionary. Moreover, it was thanks to this division of labor between the teacher and the pupils that one teacher was able without too much difficulty to run classes that sometimes numbered as many as two or three hundred pupils.

In addition to such regularly recurring competitions there were intermittent competitions too numerous to list. From time to time the best pieces of work were affixed to the classroom doors; the most noteworthy were read publicly in either the refectory or the Hall of Acts. Aside from the annual prize-giving, which took place solemnly to the sound of trumpets, prizes were given out spasmodically in the course of the year for a good piece of declamation, for a meritorious literary work, for a well executed dance, etc. From the second form onwards there was in each grade an Academy to which only the best pupils belonged. Then there were all kinds of public meetings in which the most brilliant pupils appeared and to which the families came to hear and applaud them. Thus an infinite wealth of devices maintained the self-esteem of the pupils in a constant state of extreme excitation.

Here again the Jesuits were effecting a revolution compared with what had gone before. We have seen that in the University and the colleges of the Middle Ages the system of competition was completely unknown; there were no rewards to recompense merit and induce effort, and exams were organized in such a way that for conscientious pupils they were little more than a formality. And here we have, quite suddenly, a totally different system, which not only establishes itself but which instantaneously develops to the point of superabundance. It is easier to understand now how the training given by the Jesuits managed to acquire the intensive character which we were recently remarking upon. Their entire system of discipline was organized towards this goal. The state of constant competition in which the pupils lived incited them to strain all the resources of their intelligence and will-power and indeed rendered this essential. At the same time the careful supervision to which they were subjected diminished the possibility of lapses. They felt themselves guided, sustained, encouraged. Thus everything induced them to exert themselves. As a result, within the colleges there was genuinely intense activity, no doubt flawed by being expended on the superficial rather than on the profound, but whose existence was incontestable.

However, now that we have noted the transformations that the Jesuits initiated in the realm of school discipline, we must seek their causes. Where did these two new principles come from? Did they derive exclusively from the particular aim the Jesuits were pursuing, from the very nature of their institution, from the mission they had assigned themselves, or were they not, by contrast, rather the effect of more general causes, were they not a response to some change that had occurred in public thought and ethics?

What must immediately rule out the first hypothesis is the fact that if the Jesuits were the first to realize these principles in academic practice, they had nevertheless been recognized and proclaimed already by the educational thinkers of the Renaissance. We remember Montaigne's protests against teachers unintelligent enough to wish to regiment the minds of all individuals in identical fashion. He too wants teachers to study the temperament of the pupil, to test him in order to understand him better, to make him, as he says, "run in front of himself" in order to be able to guide him in an enlightened way. And from another point of view, we have seen that the love of glory, the thirst for praise, and the sentiment of honor were for Rabelais and for Erasmus, as for the major thinkers of the sixteenth century, the essential motives for all intellectual activity and consequently for all academic activity. The Jesuits were thus on these two points, at least in principle, in agreement with their time. It is interesting to note that we know of at least one college where, before the time of the Jesuits, the competitive system was organized and practiced, moreover, in a form that in more than one respect resembled the one we have just described. This is the college at Guyenne, where Montaigne spent several years. The pupils in any one class were divided according to ability into sections that bore considerable resemblance to the Jesuits' groups of ten. Examinations took place frequently in which the pupils of one class were questioned by the pupils from a higher class or section. And here again we encounter competitions in public speaking, which took place before the assembly of all the classes.

It was the fact that a great change had taken place in the moral constitution of society that made this double change in the system of academic discipline necessary. In the seventeenth century the individual played a much greater part in social life than

that which had hitherto been accorded to him. If, in the Middle Ages, teaching was impersonal, if it could be addressed diffusely to the indistinct crowd of pupils without any disadvantage, this was because at that time the notion of individual personality was still relatively undeveloped. The movements that occurred in the Middle Ages were mass movements carrying along large groups of human beings in the same direction, in the midst of which individuals became lost. It was Europe in its entirety that rose up at the time of the Crusades; it was the whole of cultivated European society that soon afterwards, under the influence of a veritable collective urge, flooded towards Paris to receive instruction. The didactic style of the time was thus in accord with the moral condition of society.

With the Renaissance, by contrast, the individual began to acquire self-consciousness; he was no longer, at least in enlightened circles, merely an undifferentiated fraction of the whole; in a sense, he was himself already a whole, he was a person with his own physiognomy who had and who experienced at least the need to fashion for himself his own way of thinking and feeling. We know that at this period there occurred, as it were, a sudden blossoming of great personalities. Now, it is quite clear that in proportion as people's consciousness becomes individualized, education itself must become individualized. From the moment it is required to exert its influence on distinct and heterogeneous individuals it cannot continue to develop in blanket fashion, homogeneously and uniformly. Thus education had to be diversified, and this was only possible if the educator, instead of remaining distant from the pupil, came close to him to get to know him better and to be able to vary his actions according to his individual nature.

But from another point of view, it is equally clear that an individual possessed of self-awareness, with his own set of beliefs and interests, cannot be motivated or trained to act by the methods applicable to an amorphous crowd. For the latter methods mighty shakings of the foundations are needed, powerful collective impressions of a rather vague and general kind, like those that sent tremors through the multitudes gathered around Abélard on the Montagne Sainte-Geneviève. By contrast, in proportion as each individual has his own particular moral life he must be moved by considerations specifically appropriate to him. Thus one must indeed appeal to self-esteem, to the sense of personal dignity, to what the Germans call *Selbstgefühl*. It is no accident that competition becomes more lively and plays a more substantial role in society as the movement towards individualization becomes more advanced. And so, since the moral organization of the school must reflect that of civil society, since the methods that are applied to the child cannot differ in essence from those that later on will be applied to the man, it is clear that the processes of the medieval disciplinary system could not survive; it is clear that discipline had to become more personal, to take greater account of individual feelings, and consequently to allow for a degree of competitiveness.

There was thus nothing intrinsically arbitrary about the two innovations the Jesuits introduced into the disciplinary system: the principle underlying them, at least, was well-grounded in the nature of things, that is to say in the condition of society in the sixteenth century. But if the principle was right, if it was to be retained, if it deserved to survive, the Jesuits applied it in the spirit of extremism that is one feature of their academic policy and, simply by doing this, they denatured it. It was good to keep close to the child in order to be able to guide him confidently; the Jesuits came so close to him that they inhibited all his freedom of movement. And in this way the method worked against the end it was meant to serve. It was wise to get to know the child well in order to be able to help in the development of his nascent personality. The Jesuits, however, studied him in order to stifle more effectively his sense of self—and this was a potential source of schism. At least, once they had recognized the value of rivalry and competitiveness, they made such immoderate use of them that the pupils were virtually at war with one another. How can we fail to consider immoral an academic organization that appealed only to egotistical sentiments? Was there then no means of keeping the pupils active other than by tempting them with such paltry bait?

3. The Second Transformation of American Secondary Education

MARTIN TROW

The past few years have seen a very large amount of public controversy over education in America. The controversy has touched on every aspect and level of education, from nursery school to graduate education, and the spokesmen have represented many different interests and points of view. But the focus of the controversy has been the public high school, its organization and curriculum, and the philosophy of education that governs it. On one side, with many individual exceptions and variations in views, stand the professional educators and their organizations. As the creators and administrators of the existing system, American educators not surprisingly by and large

From *International Journal of Comparative Sociology* 2 (1961): 144–165. Reprinted by permission.

defend it, and while accepting and even initiating specific reforms, tend to justify existing practices, institutional arrangements,
and dominant philosophies of education. On
the other side, a more heterogeneous body
of laymen, college and university professors,
politicians and military men have attacked
fundamental aspects of secondary education
in America. The disputes extend over a
broad range of educational issues, but at the
heart of the argument is the charge by the
critics that the *quality* of American secondary education is poor, that the time and
energies of teachers and students are scattered and dispersed over a great variety of
activities and subjects, and that there ought
to be far greater emphasis on intellectual
training, academic subject matter, and the
acquisition of traditional skills and
knowledge.[1] Very often, the call for reform
is coupled with attacks on the policies and
philosophies of professional educators; the
critics claim that a watered-down progressive
education, doctrines of "life adjustment,"
the "child-centered school" and the "education of the whole person" have provided the
rationale for an indifference to the acquisition of knowledge and the development of
clarity of thought and expression which students gain when held to high standards of
achievement in course work centering on the
traditional "solid" subject matters of English, history, mathematics and the natural
sciences.

The public debate has largely restricted
itself to issues internal to education—to the
curriculum, to teacher training and certification, and the like. But the forces that most
heavily affect developments within education largely lie outside it, and are often not
reflected in the debates about it. It may be
useful to consider some of the historical
forces which give rise to the current controversies over secondary education.

THE TRANSFORMATION OF AMERICA

The Civil War is the great watershed of
American history. It stands midway between
the Revolution and ourselves, and symbolically, but not just symbolically, separates
the agrarian society of small farmers and
small businessmen of the first half of the
nineteenth century from the urbanized
industrial society with its salaried employees
that followed. And the mass public secondary school system as we know it has its
roots in the transformation of the economy
and society that took place after the Civil
War.

In 1820, at least 7 out of every 10 Americans in the labor force were farmers or farm
laborers. In 1870, farmers still comprised
about half the labor force. By 1960, that
figure was below 10 per cent. At the same
time, the proportion of salaried white collar
workers rose from less than 10 per cent in
1870 to nearly 40 per cent today.[2] The
proportion of non-farm manual workers in
the labor force rose until 1920, leveled off at
about 40 per cent since then and has shown
signs of falling over the past decade. Thus,
there has been a large and rapid growth of a
new salaried middle class, paralleled by a
large and rapid decline in the proportion of
the labor force in agriculture, with the proportions of manual workers rising till about
1920 but relatively constant over the past
forty years.

These changes in the occupational structure have reflected tremendous changes in
the economy and organization of work.
Since the Civil War, and especially in the
past fifty years, an economy based on thousands of small farms and businesses has been
transformed into one based on large bureaucratized organizations characterized by
centralized decision-making and administration carried out through coordinated managerial and clerical staffs.

When small organizations grow large,
papers replace verbal orders; papers replace
rule of thumb calculations of price and
profit; papers carry records of work flow
and inventory that in a small operation can
be seen at a glance on the shop floor and
materials shed. And as organizations grew,
people had to be trained to handle those

papers—to prepare them, to type them, to file them, to process them, to assess and use them. The growth of the secondary school system after 1870 was in large part a response to the pull of the economy for a mass of white collar employees with more than an elementary school education.

THE FIRST TRANSFORMATION OF AMERICAN SECONDARY EDUCATION

In 1870 there were roughly 80,000 students enrolled in high schools of all kinds in this country, and the bulk of these were in tuition academies. Public high schools were just beginning to grow in numbers—there were perhaps no more than 500 in the whole country, concentrated in the Northeast, and still greatly outnumbered by the tuition academies.[3] The 16,000 high school graduates in that year comprised only about 2 per cent of the seventeen year olds in the country.[4] Moreover, a very large proportion of those who went to secondary school went on to college.[5]

The American secondary school system of 1870 offered a classical liberal education to a small number of middle and upper middle class boys.[6] Very few students went to secondary school, most who went graduated, and many who graduated went on to college. By 1910, there were over 1,100,000 high school students, nearly 90 per cent of them enrolled in the over 10,000 public high schools, and they comprised about 15 per cent of the 14–17 year age group.[7] But for the bulk of these students, high school was as far as they were going. By 1957, 90 per cent of the 14–17 year age group were in school, while 62 per cent of the 17 year old cohort were gaining high school diplomas. Before 1870, the small secondary school system offered a curriculum and maintained standards of scholarship geared to the admissions requirements of the colleges.[8] After 1870, the growing mass secondary system was largely terminal, providing a useful and increasingly vocational education for the new body of white collar workers.

The evidence for the connection between education and occupation that developed after the Civil War is embedded in the census reports. In 1950, at the end of the fifty year period that might be called "the age of the terminal high school," the median years of schooling completed by men and women 25 years and older in various occupational groups were as follows:[9]

professionals:	16+
managers, officials, and proprietors:	11.3
clerical and kindred:	11.4
sales workers:	11.2
craftsmen, foremen, and kindred:	8.3
operatives and kindred:	7.7
laborers, except mine and farm:	7.0
service workers:	7.8

Of course, changes in the occupational structure do not provide the whole explanation of the extraordinary growth of secondary and higher education in the United States. The changes in the occupational structure have raised the educational aspirations of large parts of the American population, and the educational system has been responsive to these higher aspirations. The role of public education in American thought and popular sentiment, and its perceived connection with the national welfare and individual achievement, have, at least until recently, been greater in America than in any other country. Other countries, Great Britain to name one, have had comparable revolutions in their economic structure without comparable educational transformations. The commitment of America to equality of opportunity, the immense importance attached to education throughout American history, the very great role of education as an avenue of mobility in a society where status ascribed at birth is felt to be an illegitimate barrier to advancement—all of these historical and social psychological forces are involved in the extraordinary American commitment to mass secondary and higher education. Moreover, there were forces involved in the growth of the high school— such as large scale immigration and urbanization, and the movement to abolish child labor[10] —which are not present in the growth of mass higher education, whereas transformations of the occupational structure are common to both educational movements.

Now, the creation of a system of mass secondary education that accompanied the growth of mass organizations after 1870 could not be simply the extension of the old elite secondary system; it would be different in function (terminal rather than preparatory) and in organization (public locally controlled rather than private tuition and endowed schools). Moreover, it needed its own curriculum and its own teacher-training programs and institutions. It needed its own teacher-training programs first because the sheer number of secondary teachers required by mass secondary education was far beyond the capacities of the traditional colleges to supply, as they had supplied the older tuition academies.[11] In the old academies, the principals and masters were products of the colleges, and often went on to teach in the colleges; there was no sharp break between the academies and the colleges since they taught roughly the same subjects to the same kinds of students.[12] This was no longer possible with the new terminal public high school; the students were different, the curriculum was not preparation for college, by and large, and new Departments of Education and State Teachers Colleges were created at least in part to train the staffs of these new high schools.[13] These centers of professional education were not identified with the older, elite traditions of higher education, but created their own traditions of education for life, for citizenship, for useful tasks, the traditions, that is, of the mass democratic terminal secondary system that came to full flower between 1910 and 1940.[14]

By 1935, an observer sympathetic to these developments could write:

The twentieth century so far has witnessed a steady shifting of . . . control [over

secondary education] by college presidents and faculties to people more immediately concerned with the operation or professional study of secondary education . . . Not only are national committees dealing with the general aspects of secondary education becoming exclusively manned by secondary school leaders and specialists, but the whole process of curriculum making for high schools within states and within local school systems is rapidly becoming assumed by these professional categories. High school courses of study are less and less often handed down by college authorities even in the old academic fields. Secondary textbooks are more and more written by public school superintendents, high school principals, supervisors, teachers, and students of educational methods.

A further evidence of this general trend is the continuing introduction of new subjects and courses. Whereas in the past most new subjects appeared in the secondary school as reflections of the growing differentiation of the academic disciplines, most of the new subjects now appearing represent hitherto neglected aspects of social existence. As illustrations may be cited innumerable vocational courses, health courses, citizenship courses, and character courses.[15]

In the fifty years between 1880 and 1930, the numbers of students in public high schools in the United States roughly doubled every decade, rising from 110,000 to nearly four and a half million. And the new secondary education was shaped both by the enormous increase in numbers of students, and by their social characteristics. Many of the new students were in school unwillingly, in obedience to the new or more stringent state compulsory education laws; many came from poor, culturally impoverished homes and had modest vocational goals; many of these were the sons and daughters of recent immigrants, and seemed to observers very much in need of "Americanization."[16] These new students posed new problems for secondary education; and these problems, and the answers which they engendered, transformed public secondary education, its philosophy and its curriculum. Commenting on the influential National Education Association Report of 1918 entitled *Cardinal Principles of Secondary Education,* a report strongly influenced by the writings of John Dewey, and responsive to the new demands of mass secondary education, James Conant observes:

Confronted with a "heterogeneous high school population destined to enter all sorts of occupations," high school teachers and administrators and professors of education needed some justification for a complete overhauling of a high school curriculum originally designed for a homogeneous student body. The progressives with their emphasis on the child, "on learning by doing," on democracy and citizenship, and with their attack on the arguments used to support a classical curriculum were bringing up just the sort of *new* ideas that were sorely needed. After closing John Dewey's volume, *Democracy and Education,* I had the feeling that, like the Austro-Hungarian Empire of the nineteenth century, if John Dewey hadn't existed he would have had to be invented. In a sense perhaps he was, or at least his doctrines were shaped by school people with whom he talked and worked.[17]

The creation of a mass terminal system, with functions and orientations quite different from that of the traditional college preparatory system it succeeded, forced not merely certain changes in the curriculum, but a drastic shift in the basic assumptions underlying secondary education. Speaking of the writings of G. Stanley Hall in support of the "child-centered school," Lawrence Cremin notes that they

paved the way for a fundamental shift in the meaning of equal opportunity at the secondary level. Formerly, when the content and purpose of the secondary school had been fairly well defined, equal opportunity meant the right of all who might profit from secondary education as so defined to enjoy its benefits. Now, the "given" of the equation was no longer the school with its content and purposes, but the children with

their background and needs. Equal opportunity now meant simply the right of all who came to be offered something of value, and it was the school's obligation to offer it. The magnitude of this shift cannot be overestimated; it was truly Copernican in character. And tied as it was to the fortunes of the child-study movement, it gained vast popularity during the first decade of the twentieth century.[18]

The popularity of these new ideas and assumptions, and their impact on secondary education in the succeeding decades, suggests how educational doctrines are influenced by social trends.[19] With schools full of children for whom the traditional content and purpose of the secondary school curriculum were irrelevant, educators needed some rationale and justification for what they were doing. And what they were doing was trying to teach something that promised to be of some use for these terminal students, in ways that would hold, at least fleetingly, the interest of indifferent students whose basic interests lay outside the classroom. It was precisely the interest and motivation that one could no longer assume in the student, but had to engender in the school, that lay at the heart of W. H. Kilpatrick's influential *The Project Method,*[20] and before that, underlay the importance of motivation in Dewey's writings.

THE GROWTH OF MASS HIGHER EDUCATION IN AMERICA

During the decades when the institutions, the curriculum, and the philosophies of mass terminal education were being created, the college population was rising very slowly.[21] As recently as 1940 the total number of students enrolled in college comprised only 15 per cent of the college age group (the 18 to 21 year olds). By 1954, that proportion was up to 30 per cent, and by 1960 it was around 37½ per cent. Over both the longer 20 year period between 1940 and 1960 and the recent six year period, 1954–1960, the rate of increase in college enrollments as a proportion of the college age group has been about 1.3 per cent a year. If that rate of increase is maintained, and that is a conservative forecast, then by 1970 college enrollments will comprise about half of the college age group.[22] The rapid rate of increase since 1940 is in marked contrast with the average rate of increase of only 0.35 per cent per annum between 1920, when college enroll-

ments comprised 8 per cent of the college age group, and 1940, when that figure had risen to 15 per cent.

Figure I shows the phases in the parallel development of American secondary and higher education graphically. If we take, somewhat arbitrarily, an enrollment of 15 per cent of the age-grade as the beginning of the mass phase of an educational system, then secondary education passed this line around 1910, and higher education in 1940. The period 1870–1980 with which we are dealing falls naturally then into three phases. In Phase I secondary and higher education were by and large offering an academic education to an elite minority. Phase II, between roughly 1910 and 1940, saw the rapid growth of mass terminal education, with higher education still offered to a small but slowly growing minority.[23] Since 1940, or more precisely, since World War II, we are (in Phase III) seeing the rapid growth of mass higher education. With enrollments in higher education continuing to grow, and with secondary school enrollments (as a proportion of the 14–17 year old population) near saturation, the transformation of the terminal secondary system into a mass preparatory system is well under way.

It is interesting to compare rates of increase in college attendance during the first two decades of Phase III with the rate of increase in high school enrollments during the decades 1909–1939 (Phase II), the years of growth of the mass secondary system. In the last twenty years of Phase I, 1889–1909, the high school population (as a proportion of the 14–17 year olds) rose from 6.7 per cent to 15.4 per cent, an annual rate of increase of about 0.44 per cent. Over the next three decades (Phase II), the rate increased from 15.4 per cent to 73.3 per cent, an annual rate of increase of about 1.9 per cent. While this is somewhat higher than the rate of increase of about 1.3 per cent annually in college attendance (as a proportion of the 18–21 year olds) thus far in Phase III, there is in both cases a marked increase in the rate of

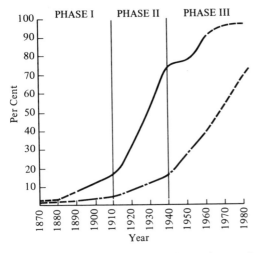

Figure I. Enrollment Rates in Secondary and Higher Education, United States, 1870–1980.

———— High school enrollments as a proportion of population 14–17 years of age.

—·— College and university enrollments as a proportion of population 18–21 years of age.

– – – Estimated.

Note: These curves are based on the figures at 10-year intervals, and do not show the enrollment rates during World War II and the Korean War.

Sources: *Progress of Public Education in the United States, 1959–1960 op. cit.*
Historical Statistics, op. cit.
Fact Book, op. cit.
Bogue, *The Population of the United States, op. cit.*

growth over the previous period. In the case of both secondary and higher education, the rate of increase has been about four times as great in the period of rapid growth as compared with the immediately preceding periods of slow growth. In both cases we see the rapid transformation of an education for a relatively small elite into a system of mass education. This process is about completed for the secondary education (in 1958 the high school population comprised nearly 90 per cent of the high school age group), while we are in the middle of the expansion of opportunities for higher education. And as with secondary education, there is no reason to believe that the United States will stop short of providing opportunities and facilities for nearly universal experience of some kind in higher education.

The immediate force behind these trends in both secondary and higher education are changes in public sentiment—in people's ideas of what they want and expect for their children in the way of formal education. Where most Americans have come to see a high school education as the ordinary, expected thing for their children, they are now coming to think of at least some time in college in the same way.[24] Behind these changes in sentiment are other social forces, not least among which is another change in our occupational structure, parallel to the massive growth in the white collar population which underlay the growth of the public secondary school system. The current change is the immense growth of demand for more highly trained and educated people of all kinds. Between 1940 and 1950, the number of engineers in the country doubled; the number of research workers increased by 50 per cent. Even more striking, between 1950 and 1960 the total labor force increased by only 8 per cent; but the number of professional, technical, and kindred workers grew by 68 per cent[25] —and these, of course, are the occupations that call for at least some part of a college education. Moreover, it is estimated that the period 1957–

1970 will see an increase of a further 60 per cent in this category of highly educated workers.[26] Where in the decades 1900–1930, clerical and kindred workers were the fastest growing occupational classification and by far, in the period 1950–1970 it has been and will be the professional and technical occupations.[27]

THE SECOND TRANSFORMATION OF AMERICAN SECONDARY EDUCATION

There are two major points to be made in summary here. First, much the same forces which made for the development of the mass secondary system in this country are now at work creating a system of mass higher education. And second, this development is rapidly changing the function of the secondary system. Secondary education in the United States began as an elite preparatory system; during its great years of growth it became a mass terminal system; and it is now having to make a second painful transition on its way to becoming a mass preparatory system. But this transition is a good deal more difficult than the first, because while the first involved the *creation* of the necessary institutions, the second is requiring the *transformation* of a huge existing institutional complex. It is almost always easier to create new institutions to perform a new function than it is to transform existing institutions to meet new functions. And as a further complication, during these long decades of transition, the secondary schools are going to have to continue to perform the old terminal education functions for very large if decreasing proportions of students who are not equipped, motivated, or oriented toward college. In the earlier transition, the old college preparatory schools continued to exist and to perform their preparatory functions, with much the same curriculum and kinds of personnel, thus permitting a rough division of function between the older and the newer schools. And where this was not possible, the number of preparatory students was shortly so small as compared with the terminal students that the schools did not have quite the same sense of equal but conflicting functions that secondary people are now coming to feel.[28]

By contrast, now and for the foreseeable future, both the preparatory and terminal functions will have to be performed by the same institutions and the same personnel. Of course, that has always been true to some extent—there have always been college-oriented students in our high schools, and provisions have been made for them. But by and large, they have been a minority in an institution created for the great mass of terminal students. The dominant philosophies and structure of the high school could be determined by its central function of providing a terminal secondary education for the mass of American youth. As preparatory students become an increasingly large proportion of all high school youth, and in more and more places a majority, they provide by their existence not just a demand for special provision, but a challenge to the basic structure and philosophy of the school. And this is the challenge that underlies the criticism of secondary education that flows from many sources.

The rough equality of the terminal and preparatory functions today may account for why the critics and the defenders of the schools largely talk past one another. The critics, who are often university professors, say, in effect, "We need not merely better provision for the preparatory student, but rather, a different guiding educational philosophy for a preparatory secondary system."[29] And the defenders, who are often professional educators, since it is they who created the educational system now under attack, reply, "We cannot ignore the needs and requirements of the great numbers of students who are not going on to college."[30] And when the numbers going on and the numbers not going on are approximately equal, as they are now in many places, neither side can point to numbers as simple justification for its argument. . . .

THE IMPACT OF THE TRANSFORMATION ON TERMINAL EDUCATION

The expansion of the college-going population fills the high schools with college preparatory students, and generates the pressures for a strengthening of the preparatory function that we have spoken of. But this development also affects the character of the terminal students, and of terminal education in high school, as well. When few students went on to college, there was no disgrace in not doing so; moreover, except for the professions, it was not so clear that occupational success was closely linked to academic achievement. The Horatio Alger myth, and the American folklore celebrating the successes of the self-made (and self-educated) man, served to define school achievement as only one among several legitimate avenues to success. But the rationalization of industry, and the increased importance of higher education for advancement beyond the lowest levels of the occupational structure, make educational achievement objectively more important for later success; the increased numbers of college-going students make this importance visible to high school students. The consequence of all this is to change the character of the students who do not go on to college when increasing majorities of students do so. Already in some localities, and increasingly in coming decades, the students not going on to college are being reduced to a hard core composed of two groups: children from ethnic and racial groups which do not place strong emphasis on high educational and occupational aspirations—for example, Negroes and Mexicans; and children of low intelligence who simply cannot handle college preparatory work.

The transformation of "not going to college" into "failure" has both social and psychological consequences. Among those who want to succeed in school but cannot, the effects of failure may be a loss of self-respect, with widespread if not highly visible and dramatic consequences for the social behaviors of those so affected. One English observer suggests that:

As a result of the close relationship between education and occupation a situation may soon be reached when the educational institutions legitimize social inequality by individualizing failure. Democratization of the means of education together with the internalizing of the achievement ethic by members of the working-class strata may lead to an individualizing of their failure, to a loss of self-respect which in turn modifies an individual's attitude both to his group and to the demands made upon him by his society.[31]

This problem of the motivated student of low ability may be more severe in England, and in other Western countries in the earlier stages of the democratization of education, than in the United States, where among our nearly 2,000 institutions of higher education there is a college somewhere for everybody.[32] Moreover, the elaborate student counselling programs in our mass public institutions are designed explicitly to help students of low academic ability accept their limitations, and direct their energies toward attainable educational and occupational goals without a sense of personal failure and resentment toward society.[33]

But while the emerging American educational system promises to make some provision for all those who accept its values, regardless of their academic ability, it is not so clear what it can do for those who deeply reject its values and purposes, along with many of the values and purposes of the larger society. The increasing extent and violence of juvenile delinquency in the United States may be closely linked to the extension of educational opportunities to the conforming majority. Where educational achievement (in terms at least of years completed) becomes more widespread and thus more visible, and more important to even modest success in the occupational world, then educational failure *pari passu* becomes more devastating to one's hopes of achieving the advertised "good life" through legitimate channels. Failure in school for many is part of a familiar vicious cycle. Absence of encouragement or concern with school performance in the home (especially marked in certain ethnic and racial groups) leads to failure to acquire basic skills, such as reading, in the early grades, which ensures academic failure in higher grades. These repeated failures make school seem a punishing prison, from which the boy escapes as early as the law allows. But lacking education or training, it is unlikely that he can get any but the poorest jobs. And the habits and resentments generated at home, on the street, and in school make it unlikely that such a boy can move into better jobs. After repeated failures in school and a succession of poorly paid odd jobs, the rewards of membership in a gang, and of participation in its delinquent subculture are considerable. And the more the high school is organized around the college preparatory programs, the more it stresses academic achievement, the more punishing it will be for the non-achievers.[34] The delinquent subculture is a way of dealing with deprivations of status, very largely experienced in the schools, and as a response to these deprivations, "the gang offers an heroic rather than an economic [or intellectual] basis of self-respect."[35]

Special school programs may help meet the complex problems of low aspirations and juvenile delinquency, though children growing up in disorganized families, or in cultures cut off from the dominant American value systems, or exposed to the corrosive effects of racial prejudice, present problems that cannot be wholly dealt with in and by the schools. The point here is that the growth of educational opportunity threatens to make the greater part of terminal education in high schools coincidental with the social problems of juvenile delinquency. This is not to say that every classroom full of non-college going students is or will be a "blackboard jungle." It does mean that the hostility toward the school characteristic of the juvenile gangs, but much more widespread than their membership, will be an increasing part of the educational problem faced by schools and teachers dealing with terminal students. The cluster of values which characterize juvenile delinquency— "the search for kicks, the disdain of work . . . and the acceptance of aggressive toughness as proof of masculinity"[36] —is incompatible with disciplined school work, either academic *or* vocational. Moreover, much of the serious vocational training the high schools have offered in the past is being increasingly shifted to higher education, especially to the junior colleges.[37]

The terminal education of the future will not simply be the terminal education of the past offered to a decreasing proportion of students. The growth of the college-going population changes the character of the remaining terminal students, it changes the meaning of their terminal work, and it will force changes in the organization and curriculum of terminal secondary education. It may also call for teachers with special skills and training in dealing with the problems of the minority or "hard-core" of terminal students. But if the increasingly important preparatory programs claim the best resources of secondary education and command the most able teachers, then terminal education will indeed be a second-class program for second-class students. And they will know it, and that knowledge will feed their bitterness and resentment. Neither the old terminal education for life, nor the strengthened academic programs will meet their needs. If the terminal education of the future is not to be an educational slum, it will demand large resources and much intelligence. But these are always in short supply, and terminal education will be competing for both with the more attractive programs of preparatory education.

CONCLUSION

Universal secondary education in the United States was achieved through a system of comprehensive high schools, devoted primar-ily to the education of the great mass of its students for work and life, and secondarily to the preparation of a small minority for higher education. The present concern with the reform of the high school curriculum and teacher training reflects the rapid growth of the college-going population, and the increased importance of the preparatory function.

Nevertheless, it may have been possible to combine terminal education for a majority and preparatory education for a minority more successfully than it will be to combine preparatory education for a majority and terminal education for a minority under one roof. Moreover, the shortage of highly qualified and motivated teachers of academic subjects may require that they be used where their talents and interests are most productive—that is, in teaching the academically most talented fraction of the student body. Secondary education in America may have to accept a higher measure of division of labor and differentiation of function than it has in the past. As a terminal system, it could in its comprehensiveness and emphasis on "education for life" simply carry further the basic education of the elementary school of which it was an outgrowth. As it becomes increasingly a preparatory system, it may be forced to take on some of the characteristics of higher education for which it is preparing, and place greater emphasis on differences among both teachers and students in academic ability and intellectual and occupational interests.

American higher education deals with the diversity of student abilities and talents largely through the great diversity of institutions which compose it, institutions which vary greatly in their selectivity, and in the academic abilities of their students.[38] American comprehensive high schools contain all this diversity within themselves, providing different streams or tracks for students with different educational or vocational intentions, or, as Conant has urged, grouping by ability, subject by subject.[39] But these arrangements ignore the effects of the students on one another, and of the student "mix" on the intellectual climate of the school. In a school where the academically motivated students are in a minority, they cannot help but be affected by the predominantly anti-intellectual values (and behaviors) of the majority;[40] similarly, where the low-achieving terminal students are in the minority, it is hard for them not to be defined as second-class students by other students and teachers, with the effects on them discussed earlier. It may be that the period we are entering will call for a critical evaluation of the comprehensive high school, the institution created by and for mass terminal secondary education.[41]

The current controversies in and about secondary education in America are a natural and healthy response to the transformation of the secondary education in this country. It can be expected that the discussion will grow in volume and scope as this transformation proceeds in the decades ahead. It can also be expected that the discussion ahead will be carried on largely between critics located outside the schools, and professional educators inside them. On one side there is a detached perspective but without first-hand knowledge of the schools; on the other, defensiveness, but also intimate experience with the problems under discussion. If the critics and the professional educators can sharpen and clarify the issues in the course of their discussion, and go on to learn from one another about the inconvenient facts that their respective positions do not adequately take into account, then the controversy may become a dialogue, and perhaps a fruitful one for American secondary education.

NOTES

1. For discussion and analysis of the controversy, and references to representative books and articles about the issues, see Paul Woodring, *A Fourth of a Nation* (New York: McGraw Hill, 1957), Chapters i–iii. For a very different view of the controversy and the issues, see Myron Lieberman, *The Future of Public Education* (Chicago: The University of Chicago Press, 1960), Chapters i and ii.

2. Sources: U.S. Bureau of the Census, *Statistical Abstract of the United States: 1960* (Eighty-first edition, Washington, D.C.: 1960), Table 279, p. 216. Donald J. Bogue, *The Population of the United States* (Glencoe, Illinois: The Free Press, 1959). Kurt Mayer, "Recent Changes in the Class Structure of the United States," *Transactions of the Third World Congress of Sociology* (Amsterdam: 1956), III, 66–80.

3. Ellwood P. Cubberley, *Public Education in the United States* (New York: Houghton-Mifflin Co., 1934), pp. 255, 627.

4. U.S. Bureau of the Census, *Historical Statistics of the United States, Colonial Times to 1957* (Washington, D.C.: 1960), p. 207.

5. Compare the annual output of the secondary schools in 1870 (16,000 graduates) with the total college enrollment of 52,000 in that year. *Ibid.*

6. On the academies in the nineteenth century, see E. E. Brown, *The Making of Our Middle Schools* (New York: Longmans, Green and Co., 1903). While the early academies were not intended as preparatory schools, "the idea of liberal culture (was) the dominant note of both academy and college education in the nineteenth century." (*Ibid.*, p. 229.)

7. U.S. Department of Health, Education, and Welfare, *Progress of Public Education in the United States, 1959–60* (Washington, D.C.: 1960), Table 2, p. 11. *Historical Statistics of the United States, Colonial Times to 1957*, p. 207.

8. Brown, *op. cit.*, p. 231.

9. Bogue, *op. cit.*, Table 17–11, p. 510. For over sixty years, the dominant stereotype of social class in America, based on solid reality but enshrined in folk-lore and mass fiction, has been that white collar people have been to high school, while manual workers by and large have not. These educational and class cleavages in America have also roughly coincided with religious and ethnic cleavages—between the older Protestant immigration from Northern and Western Europe and the later Catholic immigration from Southern and Eastern Europe. But the educational dimension of this cleavage is now changing. See below, footnote 23.

10. Although "the raising of the school-leaving age in many states followed the change in the pattern of school attendance of a majority of the youth." James Conant, *The Child, The Parent and The State* (Cambridge, Mass.: Harvard University Press, 1959), p. 95.

11. The number of public high school teachers increased from about 20,000 in 1900 to over 200,000 in 1930. U.S. Office of Education, *Biennial Survey of Education, 1928–1930, Bulletin*, No. 20, Vol. II (1931), pp. 8, 222.

12. "In 1872, 70 per cent of the students entering the eastern colleges were graduates of the academies." Cubberley, *op. cit.*, p. 260, footnote 1.

13. On the upgrading of Normal Schools to the status of four-year State Teachers Colleges, and the establishment of departments of education in other colleges and universities in the decades before 1920, see Benjamin W. Frazier, "History of the Professional Education of Teachers in the United States," and E. S. Evenden et al., "Summary and

Interpretations," U.S. Office of Education, *National Survey of Education, Bulletin 1933,* No. 10, Vols. V and VI (1935).

14. "During the first half of the present century, while many liberal arts colleges turned their backs on the problems of teacher education, legal requirements for certification were established in nearly all states. . . . [W]hile the liberal arts colleges were preoccupied with other things, while they ignored the problems of teacher education, a like-minded group of school administrators and other professional educators came to agreement among themselves on the necessity for professional preparation for teachers and transmitted their convictions into law. It was during this same period that the educators became imbued with a new philosophy of education, one far removed from the academic traditions of the liberal arts colleges." Paul Woodring, *New Directions in Teacher Education* (New York: The Fund for the Advancement of Education, 1957), p. 23. See also Merle L. Borrowman, *The Liberal and Technical in Teacher Education* (New York: Teachers College, Columbia University, 1956).

15. Matthew H. Willing, "Recent Trends in American Secondary Education," in William S. Gray, ed., *The Academic and Professional Preparation of Secondary-School Teachers* (Chicago: The University of Chicago Press, 1935), pp. 8—9, 12. See also Alfred L. Hall-Quest, *Professional Secondary Education in the Teachers Colleges,* "Contributions to Education," No. 169 (New York: Teachers College, Columbia University, 1925), pp. 20—27.

16. During the twelve years immediately preceding World War I, an average of almost one million new immigrants a year arrived in America; they were predominantly from Southern and Eastern Europe, and settled chiefly in the big cities of the Midwest and the Eastern seaboard.

17. Conant, *op. cit.,* pp. 93—94.

18. Lawrence A. Cremin, "The Revolution in American Secondary Education, 1893—1918," *Teachers College Record,* Vol. LVI (1955), No. 6, p. 303.

19. For a detailed account of the transformation of secondary education in Muncie, Indiana, during the twenties and early thirties, see Robert S. and Helen Merrell Lynd, *Middletown* (New York: Harcourt, Brace and Co., 1929), and *Middletown in Transition* (New York: Harcourt, Brace and Co., 1937). The Lynds make clear that in the middle twenties the Muncie high school offered a terminal, primarily vocational education, although the formal curriculum was still predominantly composed of the traditional academic courses. As the president of the School Board of Muncie said to them: "For a long time all boys were trained to be President. Then for a while we trained them all to be professional men. Now we are training boys to get jobs." (*Middletown,* p. 194.) The hollowness of the traditional course work under those circumstances is reflected in the remark of one high school English teacher: "Thank goodness, we've finished Chaucer's *Prologue*! I am thankful and the children are, too. They think of it almost as if it were in a foreign language, and they *hate* it."

(*Ibid.,* p. 193.) These sentiments, shared by both teachers and students in Muncie, were reflected in the quality of the academic preparation given those students who did go on to college; as the Lynds report, most of them dropped out or did poorly. (*Ibid.,* p. 195.)

20. *Teachers College Record,* Vol. XIX (1918), No. 4. Kilpatrick describes the "project" as "the hearty purposeful act" wherein the student pursues his own purposes wholeheartedly and with enthusiasm. And as "the purposeful act is . . . the typical unit of the worthy life in a democratic society, so also should it be made the typical unit of school procedure" (p. 323). The aim of this education would be "the man who is master of his fate, who with deliberate regard for a total situation forms clear and far-reaching purposes, who plans and executes with nice care the purposes so formed." (*Ibid.,* p. 322.) This is, of course, the ideal citizen of liberal democratic theory, a kind of man America had produced in larger numbers during the eighteenth and nineteenth centuries than any other society in history, and without benefit of the "project method." It was the decline of this liberal society, under the impact of industrialization and large organization, that led Kilpatrick and others to seek to achieve in and through education what one could no longer assume could be achieved through the economic and political life of the society.

21. Data on enrollments in both high school and college drawn from *Historical Statistics of the United States, Colonial Times to 1957; Progress of Public Education in the United States, 1959—60;* Bogue, *op. cit.;* American Council on Education, *Fact Book on Higher Education* (Washington, D.C.: n.d.).

22. Indeed, projections of the college age population of the United States reported in the *Fact Book (op. cit.),* coupled with U.S. Bureau of the Census estimates of college enrollments in 1970 (reported in Bogue, *op. cit.,* Table 26—10, p. 778),

By 1930 the new "scientific" educational philosophy had found expression in Muncie in a new curriculum "devoted to the principle that the schools should fit the needs of the individual pupil instead of forcing the child to fit himself to the standard curriculum, as has been the practice in the past." (*Middletown in Transition,* p. 221.) "With the high school and even the college no longer serving as a screen sifting out the 'scholars' from the 'non-scholars' even as roughly as they did before the World War, and with secondary education becoming a mass experience, the feeling has grown that education must not only be good but must be good for something—to the individual and to society." (*Ibid.,* p. 222.)

The new philosophy of education was a response not merely to a new kind of student but also to a new kind of society. An emphasis on the new students in the schools led to a new curriculum keyed to their vocational interests; an emphasis on the new society led to calls for the radical reconstruction of society through education. It was the first emphasis that found a response in Muncie and had by far the greater impact on the schools there and elsewhere.

give a figure of 55 per cent of the 18—21 age group. And a recent Roper study of parental expectations regarding their children's education suggests that even this figure may be considerably low. (See "Why College Enrollments May Triple by 1970," *College Board Review*, No. 40 (Winter, 1960), pp. 18—19.)

23. But the social composition of this minority was changing during this phase. Already in 1920, when college enrollments comprised only 8 per cent of the 18—21 year old population, some 40 per cent of the college population, by one estimate, came from lower-middle and working class backgrounds. By 1940, at the end of Phase II, 60 per cent of college students came out of those classes (R. J. Havighurst, *American Higher Education in the 1960s* (Columbus: Ohio State University Press, 1960), Table 7, p. 34).

24. Compare the recent Roper study done in 1959 (*Parents' College Plans Study*, The Ford Foundation, New York: mimeographed, n.d.), which shows that nearly 70 per cent of children under 12 are expected by their parents to go to college, with the Roper study of a decade earlier (*Higher Education*, a supplement to *Fortune*, September, 1949). The hopes of the earlier decade have become the expectations of today, and will probably be the enrollments of tomorrow. Of the latest Roper study, one observer noted that "it demonstrated that a college education has come to be widely regarded as the *sine qua non* of personal success, just as the high school diploma did earlier" (Philip Coombs, *College Board Review*, No. 40 (1960), p. 18).

25. *Statistical Abstract of the United States, 1960,* p. 216.

26. Bureau of Labor Statistics estimates, reported in Newell Brown, "The Manpower Outlook for the 1960's: Its Implications for Higher Education," Office of Education, U.S. Department of Education, *Higher Education* (December, 1959), pp. 3—6. It is also estimated that the number of engineers will double during this period.

27. Bogue, *op. cit.*, Table 17—2, p. 475, and *Fact Book, op. cit.*, p. 146.

28. For example, of those students entering high school in 1928, only 1 in 5 went on to college four years later, and only 2 in 5 of the high school graduates of 1932 went on to college. But in the coming decades the numbers of terminal and preparatory students in the high schools will be nearly equal. A third of the students entering high school in 1954 went on to college, and by 1958 half of the high school graduates in the United States were going on to some kind of higher education. (Computed from data in *Progress of Public Education, op. cit.*, Figure 1, p. 13.) And in some parts of the country that proportion is very much higher.

These transformations can be shown in another way. In 1880, there were roughly the same number of students in American colleges and universities as in our public high schools. By 1940 there were nearly five times as many students in the public high schools as in institutions of higher education. But by 1960, the ratio of high school to college

students had fallen to about three to one. (*Historical Statistics, op. cit.*, pp. 207 and 209, and for 1960, *Fact Book, op. cit.*, pp. 10 and 237.)

29. See for example the *Report of the San Francisco Curriculum Survey Committee* (April, 1960), prepared for the Board of Education, San Francisco Unified School District, by a committee of faculty members from various academic departments of the University of California, Berkeley, and Stanford University.

30. See *Judging and Improving the Schools: Current Issues,* California Teachers Association, 1960, prepared in answer to the San Francisco Curriculum Survey Committee Report cited above.

31. Basil Bernstein, "Some Sociological Determinants of Perception: An Enquiry Into Subcultural Differences," *The British Journal of Sociology,* I, 2 (June, 1958), p. 173.

32. See T. R. McConnell and Paul Heist, "The Diverse College Student Population," in N. Sanford, ed., *The American College* (New York: John Wiley and Sons, 1962).

33. See Burton R. Clark, "The Cooling-Out Function in Higher Education," *American Journal of Sociology,* LXV, 6 (May, 1960).

34. Speaking of this group "for whom adaptation to educational expectations at *any* level is difficult," Parsons notes: "As the acceptable minimum of educational qualifications rises, persons near and below the margin will tend to be pushed into an attitude of repudiation of these expectations. Truancy and delinquency are ways of expressing this repudiation. Thus the very *improvement* of educational standards in the society at large may well be a major factor in the failure of the educational process for a growing number at the lower end of the status and ability distribution." (Talcott Parsons, "The Social Class as a Social System: Some of its Functions in American Society," *Harvard Educational Review,* IV, 4 (Fall, 1959), p. 313.)

35. Jackson Toby, "Hoodlum or Business Man: An American Dilemma," in Marshall Sklare, *The Jews* (Glencoe, Illinois: The Free Press, 1958), p. 546. See also R. K. Merton, *Social Theory and Social Structure* (revised ed.; Glencoe, Illinois: The Free Press, 1957), Chapter iv, "Social Structure and Anomie"; and Albert K. Cohen, *Delinquent Boys: The Culture of the Gang* (Glencoe, Illinois: The Free Press, 1955), especially Chapter v, "A Delinquent Solution."

36. David Matza and Gresham Sykes, "Juvenile Delinquency and Subterranean Values," *American Sociological Review* (forthcoming).

37. See Burton R. Clark, *The Open Door College* (New York: McGraw-Hill Book Co., Inc., 1960).

38. McConnell and Heist, *op. cit.*

39. See his remarks on "ability grouping" in *The American High School Today* (NewYork: McGraw-Hill Book Co., Inc., 1959), pp. 49—50.

40. See James S. Coleman, "Academic Achievement and the Structure of Competition," *Harvard Educational Review,* XXIX, 4 (Fall, 1959), pp. 330—352. See also Alan B. Wilson, "Residential Segregation of Social Classes and Aspirations of

High School Boys," *American Sociological Review,* Vol. XXIV, No. 6 (December 1959), pp. 836–45. 41. One possibility, in the best experimental tradition of American education, would be to organize one or two academically selective high schools in each major city, where some of the gains and losses of institutional differentiation can be observed, and where experimental programs can be developed for later application in the comprehensive schools. The "hard-core" terminal students present a more difficult problem.

4. Functional and Conflict Theories of Educational Stratification *

RANDALL COLLINS

Education has become highly important in occupational attainment in modern America, and thus occupies a central place in the analysis of stratification and of social mobility. This paper attempts to assess the adequacy of two theories in accounting for available evidence on the link between education and stratification: a functional theory concerning trends in technical skill requirements in industrial societies; and a conflict theory derived from the approach of Max Weber, stating the determinants of various outcomes in the struggles among status groups. It will be argued that the evidence best supports the conflict theory, although technical requirements have important effects in particular contexts. It will be further argued that the construction of a general theory of the determinants of stratification in its varying forms is best advanced by incorporating elements of the functional analysis of technical requirements of specific jobs at appropriate points within the conflict model. The conclusion offers an interpretation of historical change in education and stratification in industrial America, and suggests where further evidence is required for more precise tests and for further development of a comprehensive explanatory theory.

THE IMPORTANCE OF EDUCATION

A number of studies have shown that the number of years of education is a strong determinant of occupational achievement in America with social origins constant. They also show that social origins affect educational attainment, and also occupational attainment after the completion of education (Blau and Duncan, 1967:163–205; Eckland, 1965; Sewell *et al.,* 1969; Duncan and Hodge, 1963; Lipset and Bendix, 1959: 189–192). There are differences in occupational attainment independent of social origins between the graduates of more prominent and less prominent secondary schools, colleges, graduate schools, and law schools (Smigel, 1964:39, 73–74, 117; Havemann and West, 1952:179–181; Ladinsky, 1967; Hargens and Hagstrom, 1967).

Educational requirements for employment have become increasingly widespread, not only in elite occupations but also at the bottom of the occupational hierarchy (see Table 1). In a 1967 survey of the San Francisco, Oakland, and San Jose areas (Collins, 1969), 17% of the employers surveyed re-

*I am indebted to Joseph Ben-David, Bennett Berger, Reinhard Bendix, Margaret S. Gordon, Joseph R. Gusfield, Stanford M. Lyman, Martin A. Trow, and Harold L. Wilensky for advice and comment; and to Margaret S. Gordon for making available data collected by the Institute of Industrial Relations of the University of California at Berkeley, under grants from the U. S. Office of Education and the U. S. Department of Labor. Their endorsement of the views expressed here is not implied.

From *American Sociological Review* 36 (1971): 1002–1019. Reprinted by permission.

Table 1. Percent of Employers Requiring Various Minimum Educational Levels of Employees, by Occupational Level.

	Unskilled	Semi-skilled	Skilled	Clerical	Managerial	Professional
National Survey, 1937–38						
Less than high school	99%	97%	89%	33%	32%	9%
High school diploma	1	3	11	63	54	16
Some college				1	2	23
College degree				3	12	52
	100%	100%	100%	100%	100%	100%
San Francisco Bay Area, 1967						
Less than high school	83%	76%	62%	29%	27%	10%
High school diploma	16	24	28	68	14	4
Vocational training beyond high school	1	1	10	2	2	4
Some college				2	12	7
College degree					41	70
Graduate degree					3	5
	100%	100%	100%	101%	99%	100%
	(244)	(237)	(245)	(306)	(288)	(240)

Sources: H.M. Bell, *Matching Youth and Jobs* (Washington: American Council on Education, 1940), p. 264, as analyzed in Lawrence Thomas, *The Occupational Structure and Education* (Englewood Cliffs: Prentice-Hall, 1956), p. 346; and Randall Collins, "Education and Employment," unpublished Ph.D. dissertation, University of California at Berkeley, 1969, Table III-1. Bell does not report the number of employers in the sample, but it was apparently large.

quired at least a high school diploma for employment in even unskilled positions;[1] a national survey (Bell, 1940) in 1937–1938 found a comparable figure of 1%. At the same time, educational requirements appear to have become more specialized, with 38% of the organizations in the 1967 survey which required college degrees of managers preferring business administration training, and an additional 15% preferring engineering training; such requirements appear to have been virtually unknown in the 1920s (Pierson, 1959:34–54). At the same time, the proportions of the American population attending schools through the completion of high school and advanced levels have risen sharply during the last century (Table 2). Careers are thus increasingly shaped within the educational system.

THE TECHNICAL-FUNCTION THEORY OF EDUCATION

A common explanation of the importance of education in modern society may be termed the technical-function theory. Its basic propositions, found in a number of sources (see, for example, B. Clark, 1962; Kerr *et al.*, 1960), may be stated as follows: (1) the skill requirements of jobs in industrial society constantly increase because of technological change. Two processes are involved: (a) the proportion of jobs requiring low skill decreases and the proportion requiring high skill increases; and (b) the same jobs are upgraded in skill requirements. (2) Formal education provides the training, either in specific skills or in general capacities, necessary for the more highly skilled jobs. (3) Therefore, educational requirements for employment constantly rise, and increasingly larger proportions of the population are required to spend longer and longer periods in school.

The technical-function theory of education may be seen as a particular application of a more general functional approach. The functional theory of stratification (Davis and Moore, 1945) rests on the premises (A) that occupational positions require particular

Table 2. Percentage Educational Attainment in the United States, 1869–1965.

ʿPeriod	High school graduates/ pop. 17 yrs. old	Resident college students/ pop. 18–21	B.A.'s or 1st prof. degrees/1/10 of pop. 15–24	M.A.'s or 2nd prof. degrees/1/10 of pop. 25–34	Ph.D.'s 1/10 of pop. 25–34
1869–1870	2.0	1.7			
1879–1880	2.5	2.7			
1889–1890	3.3	3.0			
1899–1900	6.4	4.0	1.66	0.12	0.03
1909–1910	8.8	5.1	1.85	0.13	0.02
1919–1920	16.8	8.9	2.33	0.24	0.03
1929–1930	29.0	12.4	4.90	0.78	0.12
1939–1940	50.8	15.6	7.05	1.24	0.15
1949–1950	59.0	29.6	17.66	2.43	0.27
1959–1960	65.1	34.9	17.72	3.25	0.42
1963	76.3	38.0			
1965			19.71	5.02	0.73

Sources: *Historical Statistics of the United States,* Series A-28-29, H 327-338; *Statistical Abstract of the United States* 1966, Tables 3 and 194; *Digest of Educational Statistics* (U. S. Office of Education, 1967), Tables 66 and 88.

kinds of skilled performance; and (B) that positions must be filled with persons who have either the native ability, or who have acquired the training, necessary for the performance of the given occupational role.[2] The technical-function theory of education may be viewed as a subtype of this form of analysis, since it shares the premises that the occupational structure creates demands for particular kinds of performance, and that training is one way of filling these demands. In addition, it includes the more restrictive premises (1 and 2 above) concerning the way in which skill requirements of jobs change with industrialization, and concerning the content of school experiences.

The technical-function theory of education may be tested by reviewing the evidence for each of its propositions (1a, 1b, and 2).[3] As will be seen, these propositions do not adequately account for the evidence. In order to generate a more complete explanation, it will be necessary to examine the evidence for the underlying functional propositions, (A) and (B). This analysis leads to a focus on the processes of stratification—notably group conflict—not expressed in the functional theory, and to the formalization of a conflict theory to account for the evidence.

Proposition (1a): *Educational requirements of jobs in industrial society increase because the proportion of jobs requiring low skill decreases and the proportion requiring high skill increases.* Available evidence suggests that this process accounts for only a minor part of educational upgrading, at least in a society that has passed the point of initial industrialization. Fifteen percent of the increase in education of the U. S. labor force during the twentieth century may be attributed to shifts in the occupational structure—a decrease in the proportion of jobs with low skill requirements and an increase in proportion of jobs with high skill requirements (Folger and Nam, 1964). The bulk of educational upgrading (85%) has occurred *within* job categories.

Proposition (1b): *Educational requirements of jobs in industrial society rise because the same jobs are upgraded in skill requirements.* The only available evidence on this point consists of data collected by the U. S. Department of Labor in 1950 and 1960, which indicate the amount of change in skill requirements of specific jobs. Under the most plausible assumptions as to the skills provided by various levels of education, it appears that the educational level of the U. S. labor force has changed in excess of that which is necessary to keep up with skill requirements of jobs (Berg, 1970:38–60). Over-education for available jobs is found particularly among males who have graduated from college and females with high school degrees or some college, and appears to have increased between 1950 and 1960.

Proposition (2): *Formal education provides required job skills.* This proposition may be tested in two ways: (a) Are better educated employees more productive than less educated employees? (b) Are vocational skills learned in schools, or elsewhere?

(a) *Are better educated employees more productive?* The evidence most often cited for the productive effects of education is indirect, consisting of relationships between *aggregate* levels of education in a society and its overall economic productivity. These are of three types:

(i) The national growth approach involves calculating the proportion of growth in the U. S. Gross National Product attributable to conventional inputs of capital and labor; these leave a large residual, which is attributed to improvements in skill of the labor force based on increased education (Schultz, 1961; Denison, 1965). This approach suffers from difficulty in clearly distinguishing among technological change affecting productive arrangements, changes in the abilities of workers acquired by experience at work with new technologies, and changes in skills due to formal education and motivational factors associated with a competitive or achievement-oriented society. The assignment of a large proportion of the residual category to education is arbitrary. Denison (1965) makes this attribution on the basis of the increased income to persons with higher levels of education inter-

preted as rewards for their contributions to productivity. Although it is a common assumption in economic argument that wage returns reflect output value, wage returns cannot be used to prove the productive contribution of education without circular reasoning.

(ii) Correlations of education and level of economic development for nations show that the higher the level of economic development of a country, the higher the proportion of its population in elementary, secondary, and higher education (Harbison and Myers, 1964). Such correlations beg the question of causality. There are considerable variations in school enrollments among countries at the same economic level, and many of these variations are explicable in terms of political demands for access to education (Ben-David, 1963–64). Also, the overproduction of educated personnel in countries whose level of economic development cannot absorb them suggests the demand for education need not come directly from the economy, and may run counter to economic needs (Hoselitz, 1965).

(iii) Time-lag correlations of education and economic development show that increases in the proportion of population in elementary school precede increases in economic development after a takeoff point at approximately 30–50% of the 7–14 years old age-group in school. Similar anticipations of economic development are suggested for increases in secondary and higher education enrollment, although the data do not clearly support this conclusion (Peaslee, 1969). A pattern of advances in secondary school enrollments preceding advances in economic development is found only in a small number of cases (12 of 37 examined in Peaslee, 1969). A pattern of growth of university enrollments and subsequent economic development is found in 21 of 37 cases, but the exceptions (including the United States, France, Sweden, Russia, and Japan) are of such importance as to throw serious doubt on any *necessary* contribution of higher education to economic development. The main contribution of education to economic productivity, then, appears to occur at the level of the transition to mass literacy, and not significantly beyond this level.

Direct evidence of the contribution of education to *individual* productivity is summarized by Berg (1970:85–104, 143–176). It indicates that the better educated employees are not generally more productive, and in some cases are less productive, among samples of factory workers, maintenance men, department store clerks, technicians, secretaries, bank tellers, engineers, industrial research scientists, military personnel, and federal civil service employees.

(b) *Are vocational skills learned in school, or elsewhere?* Specifically vocational education in the schools for manual positions is virtually independent of job fate, as graduates of vocational programs are not more likely to be employed than high school dropouts (Plunkett, 1960; Duncan, 1964). Most skilled manual workers acquire their skills on the job or casually (Clark and Sloan, 1966:73). Retraining for important technological changes in industry has been carried out largely informally on-the-job; in only a very small proportion of jobs affected by technological change is formal retraining in educational institutions used (Collins, 1969:147–158; Bright, 1958).

The relevance of education for nonmanual occupational skills is more difficult to evaluate. Training in specific professions, such as medicine, engineering, scientific or scholarly research, teaching, and law can plausibly be considered vocationally relevant, and possibly essential. Evidences comparing particular degrees of educational success with particular kinds of occupational performance or success are not available, except for a few occupations. For engineers,

high college grades and degree levels generally predict high levels of technical responsibility and high participation in professional activities, but not necessarily high salary or supervisory responsibility (Perrucci and Perrucci, 1970). At the same time, a number of practicing engineers lack college degrees (about 40% of engineers in the early 1950s; see Soderberg, 1963:213), suggesting that even such highly technical skills may be acquired on the job. For academic research scientists, educational quality has little effect on subsequent productivity (Hagstrom and Hargens, 1968). For other professions, evidence is not available on the degree to which actual skills are learned in school rather than in practice. In professions such as medicine and law, where education is a legal requirement for admission to practice, a comparison group of noneducated practitioners is not available, at least in the modern era.

Outside of the traditional learned professions, the plausibility of the vocational importance of education is more questionable. Comparisons of the efforts of different occupations to achieve "professionalization" suggest that setting educational requirements and bolstering them through licensing laws is a common tactic in raising an occupation's prestige and autonomy (Wilensky, 1964). The result has been the proliferation of numerous pseudo-professions in modern society; nevertheless these fail to achieve strong professional organization through lack of a monopolizable (and hence teachable) skill base. Business administration schools represent such an effort. (See Pierson, 1959:9, 55–95, 140; Gordon and Howell, 1959:1–18, 40, 324–337). Descriptions of general, nonvocational education do not support the image of schools as places where skills are widely learned. Scattered studies suggest that the knowledge imparted in particular courses is retained only in small part through the next few years (Learned and Wood, 1938:28), and indicate a dominant student culture concerned with nonacademic interests or with achieving grades with a minimum of learning (Coleman, 1961; Becker *et al.*, 1968).

The technical-function theory of education, then, does not give an adequate account of the evidence. Economic evidence indicates no clear contributions of education to economic development, beyond the provisions of mass literacy. Shifts in the proportions of more skilled and less skilled jobs do not account for the observed increase in education of the American labor force. Education is often irrelevant to on-the-job productivity and is sometimes counterproductive; specifically vocational training seems to be derived more from work experience than from formal school training. The quality of schools themselves, and the nature of dominant student cultures suggest that schooling is very inefficient as a means of training for work skills.

FUNCTIONAL AND CONFLICT PERSPECTIVES

It may be suggested that the inadequacies of the technical-function theory of education derive from a more basic source: the functional approach to stratification. A fundamental assumption is that there is a generally fixed set of positions, whose various requirements the labor force must satisfy. The fixed demand for skills of various types, at any given time, is the basic determinant of who will be selected for what positions. Social change may then be explained by specifying how these functional demands change with the process of modernization. In keeping with the functional perspective in general, the needs of society are seen as determining the behavior and the rewards of the individuals within it.

However, this premise may be questioned as an adequate picture of the fundamental processes of social organization. It may be suggested that the "demands" of any occupational position are not fixed, but represent whatever behavior is settled upon in bargaining between the persons who fill the positions and those who attempt to control them. Individuals want jobs primarily for the rewards to themselves in material goods, power, and prestige. The amount of productive skill they must demonstrate to hold their positions depends on how much clients, customers, or employers can successfully demand of them, and this in turn depends on the balance of power between workers and their employers.

Employers tend to have quite imprecise conceptions of the skill requirements of most jobs, and operate on a strategy of "satisficing" rather than optimizing—that is, setting average levels of performance as satisfactory, and making changes in procedures or personnel only when performance falls noticeably below minimum standards (Dill *et al.*, 1962; March and Simon, 1958:140–141). Efforts to predict work performance by objective tests have foundered due to difficulties in measuring performance (except on specific mechanical tasks) and the lack of control groups to validate the tests (Anastasi, 1967). Organizations do not force their employees to work at maximum efficiency; there is considerable insulation of workers at all levels from demands for full use of their skills and efforts. Informal controls over output are found not only among production workers in manufacturing but also among sales and clerical personnel (Roy, 1952; Blau, 1955; Lombard, 1955). The existence of informal organization at the managerial level, the widespread existence of bureaucratic pathologies such as evasion of responsibility, empire-building, and displacement of means by ends ("red tape"), and the fact that administrative work is only indirectly related to the output of the organization, suggest that managers, too, are insulated from strong technological pressures for use of technical skills. On all levels, wherever informal organization exists, it appears that standards of performance reflect the power of the groups involved.

In this light, it is possible to reinterpret the body of evidence that ascriptive factors continue to be important in occupational success even in advanced industrial society.

The social mobility data summarized at the onset of this paper show that social origins have a direct effect on occupational success, even after the completion of education. Both case studies and cross-sectional samples amply document widespread discrimination against Negroes. Case studies show that the operation of ethnic and class standards in employment based not merely on skin color but on name, accent, style of dress, manners, and conversational abilities (Noland and Bakke, 1949; Turner, 1952; Taeuber *et al.,* 1966; Nosow, 1956). Cross-sectional studies, based on both biographical and survey data, show that approximately 60 to 70% of the American business elite come from upper-class and upper-middle-class families, and fewer than 15% from working-class families (Taussig and Joselyn, 1932:97; Warner and Abegglen,1955:37—68;Newcomer,1955: 53; Bendix, 1956:198—253; Mills, 1963: 110—139). These proportions are fairly constant from the early 1800's through the 1950's. The business elite is overwhelmingly Protestant, male, and completely white, although there are some indications of a mild trend toward declining social origins and an increase of Catholics and Jews. Ethnic and class background have been found crucial for career advancement in the professions as well (Ladinsky, 1963; Hall, 1946). Sexual stereotyping of jobs is extremely widespread (Collins, 1969:234—238).

In the traditional functionalist approach, these forms of ascription are treated as residual categories: carry-overs from a less advanced period, or marks of the imperfections of the functional mechanism of placement. Yet available trend data suggest that the link between social class origins and occupational attainment has remained constant during the twentieth century in America (Blau and Duncan, 1967:81—113); the proportion of women in higher occupational levels has changed little since the late nineteenth century (Epstein, 1970:7); and the few available comparisons between elite groups in traditional and modern societies suggest comparable levels of mobility (Marsh, 1963). Declines in racial and ethnic discrimination that appear to have occurred at periods in twentieth-century America may be plausibly explained as results of political mobilization of particular minority groups rather than by an increased economic need to select by achievement criteria.

Goode (1967) has offered a modified functional model to account for these disparities: that work groups always organize to protect their inept members from being judged by outsiders' standards of productivity, and that this self-protection is functional to the organizations, preventing a Hobbesian competitiveness and distrust of all against all. This argument re-establishes a functional explanation, but only at the cost of undermining the technological view of functional requirements. Further, Goode's conclusions can be put in other terms: it is to the advantage of groups of employees to organize so that they will not be judged by strict performance standards; and it is at least minimally to the advantage of the employer to let them do so, for if he presses them harder he creates dissension and alienation. Just how hard an employer *can* press his employees is not given in Goode's functional model. That is, his model has the disadvantage, common to functional analysis in its most general form, of covering too many alternative possibilities to provide testable explanations of specific outcomes. Functional analysis too easily operates as a justification for whatever particular pattern exists, asserting in effect that there is a proper reason for it to be so, but failing to state the conditions under which a particular pattern will hold rather than another. The technical version of job requirements has the advantage of specifying patterns, but it is this specific form of functional explanation that is jettisoned by a return to a more abstract functional analysis.

A second hypothesis may be suggested: the power of "ascribed" groups may be the *prime* basis of selection in all organizations, and technical skills are secondary considerations depending on the balance of power. Education may thus be regarded as a mark of membership in a particular group (possibly at times its defining characteristic), not a mark of technical skills or achievement. Educational requirements may thus reflect the interests of whichever groups have power to set them. Weber (1968:1000) interpreted educational requirements in bureaucracies, drawing especially on the history of public administration in Prussia, as the result of efforts by university graduates to monopolize positions, raise their corporate status, and thereby increase their own security and power vis-à-vis both higher authorities and clients. Gusfield (1958) has shown that educational requirements in the British Civil Service were set as the result of a power struggle between a victorious educated upper-middle-class and the traditional aristocracy.

To summarize the argument to this point: available evidence suggests that the technical-functional view of educational requirements for jobs leaves a large number of facts unexplained. Functional analysis on the more abstract level does not provide a testable explanation of which ascribed groups will be able to dominate which positions. To answer this question, one must leave the functional frame of reference and examine the conditions of relative power of each group.

A CONFLICT THEORY OF STRATIFICATION

The conditions under which educational requirements will be set and changed may be stated more generally, on the basis of a conflict theory of stratification derived from Weber (1968:926–939; see also Collins, 1968), and from advances in modern organization theory fitting the spirit of this approach.

A. *Status groups.* The basic units of society are associational groups sharing common cultures (or "subcultures"). The core of such groups is families and friends, but they may be extended to religious, educational, or ethnic communities. In general, they comprise all persons who share a sense of status equality based on participation in a common culture: styles of language, tastes in clothing and decor, manners and other ritual observances, conversational topics and styles, opinions and values, and preferences in sports, arts, and media. Participation in such cultural groups gives individuals their fundamental sense of identity, especially in contrast with members of other associational groups in whose everyday culture they cannot participate comfortably. Subjectively, status groups distinguish themselves from others in terms of categories of *moral evaluation* such as "honor," "taste," "breeding," "respectability," "propriety," "cultivation," "good fellows," "plain folks," etc. Thus the exclusion of persons who lack the ingroup culture is felt to be normatively legitimated.

There is no *a priori* determination of the number of status groups in a particular society, nor can the degree to which there is consensus on a rank order among them be stated in advance. These are not matters of definition, but empirical variations, the causes of which are subjects of other developments of the conflict theory of stratification. Status groups should be regarded as ideal types, without implication of *necessarily distinct* boundaries; the concepts remain useful even in the case where associational groupings and their status cultures are fluid and overlapping, as hypotheses about the conflicts among status groups may remain fruitful even under these circumstances.

Status groups may be derived from a number of sources. Weber outlines three: (a) differences in life style based on economic situation (i.e., class); (b) differences in life situation based on power position; (c) differences in life situation deriving directly from cultural conditions or institutions, such as geographical origin, ethnicity, religion, education, or intellectual or aesthetic cultures.

B. *Struggle for Advantage.* There is a continual struggle in society for various "goods"–wealth, power, or prestige. We need make no assumption that every individual is motivated to maximize his rewards; however, since power and prestige are inherently scarce commodities, and wealth is often contingent upon them, the ambition of even a small proportion of persons for more than equal shares of these goods sets up an implicit counter-struggle on the part of others to avoid subjection and disesteem. Individuals may struggle with each other, but since individual identity is derived primarily from membership in a status group, and because the cohesion of status groups is a key resource in the struggle against others, the primary focus of struggle is between status groups rather than within them.

The struggle for wealth, power, and prestige is carried out primarily through organizations. There have been struggles throughout history among organizations controlled by different status groups, for military conquest, business advantage, or cultural (e.g., religious) hegemony, and intricate sorts of interorganizational alliances are possible. In the more complex societies, struggle between status groups is carried on in large part *within* organizations, as the status groups controlling an organization coerce, hire, or culturally manipulate others to carry out their wishes (as in, respectively, a conscript army, a business, or a church). Organizational research shows that the success of organizational elites in controlling their subordinates is quite variable. Under particular conditions, lower or middle members have considerable *de facto* power to avoid compliance, and even to change the course of the organizations (see Etzioni, 1961).

This opposing power from below is strengthened when subordinate members constitute a cohesive status group of their own; it is weakened when subordinates acquiesce in the values of the organization elite. Coincidence of ethnic and class boundaries produces the sharpest cultural distinctions. Thus, Catholics of immigrant origins have been the bulwarks of informal norms restricting work output in American firms run by WASPs, whereas Protestants of native rural backgrounds are the main "rate-busters" (O. Collins et al., 1946). Selection and manipulation of members in terms of status groups is thus a key weapon in intraorganizational struggles. In general, the organization elite selects its new members and key assistants from its own status group and makes an effort to secure lower-level employees who are at least indoctrinated to respect the cultural superiority of their status culture.[4]

Once groups of employees of different status groups are formed at various positions (middle, lower, or laterally differentiated) in the organization, each of these groups may be expected to launch efforts to recruit more members of their own status group. This process is illustrated by conflicts among whites and blacks, Protestants and Catholics and Jews, Yankee, Irish and Italian, etc. found in American occupational life (Hughes, 1949; Dalton, 1951). These conflicts are based on ethnically or religiously founded status cultures; their intensity rises and falls with processes increasing or decreasing the cultural distinctiveness of these groups, and with the succession of advantages and disadvantages set by previous outcomes of these struggles which determine the organizational resources available for further struggle. Parallel processes of cultural conflict may be based on distinctive class as well as ethnic cultures.

C. *Education As Status Culture.* The main activity of schools is to teach particular status cultures, both in and outside the classroom. In this light, any failure of schools to impart technical knowledge (although it may also be successful in this) is not important; schools primarily teach vocabulary and inflection, styles of dress, aesthetic tastes, values and manners. The emphasis on sociability and athletics found in many schools is not extraneous but may be at the core of the status culture propagated by the schools. Where schools have a more academic or vocational emphasis, this emphasis may itself be the content of a particular status culture, providing sets of values, materials for conversation, and shared activities for an associational group making claims to a particular basis for status.

Insofar as a particular status group controls education, it may use it to foster control within work organizations. Educational requirements for employment can serve both to select new members for elite positions who share the elite culture and, at a lower level of education, to hire lower and middle employees who have acquired a general respect for these elite values and styles.

TESTS OF THE CONFLICT THEORY OF EDUCATIONAL STRATIFICATION

The conflict theory in its general form is supported by evidence (1) that there are distinctions among status group cultures—based both on class and on ethnicity—in modern societies (Kahl, 1957:127–156, 184–220); (2) that status groups tend to occupy different occupational positions within organizations (see data on ascription cited above); and (3) that occupants of different organizational positions struggle over power (Dalton, 1959; Crozier, 1964). The more specific tests called for here, however, are of the adequacy of conflict theory to explain the link between education and occupational stratification. Such tests may focus either on the proposed mechanism of occupational placement, or on the conditions for strong or weak links between education and occupation.

Education As a Mechanism of Occupational Placement. The mechanism proposed is that employers use education to select persons who have been socialized into the dominant status culture: for entrants to their own managerial ranks, into elite culture; for lower-level employees, into an attitude of respect for the dominant culture and the elite which carries it. This requires evidence that: a) schools provide either training for the elite culture, or respect for it; and (b) employers use education as a means of selection for cultural attributes.

(a) Historical and descriptive studies of schools support the generalization that they are places where particular status cultures are acquired, either from the teachers, from other students, or both. Schools are usually founded by powerful or autonomous status groups, either to provide an exclusive education for their own children, or to propagate respect for their cultural values. Until recently most schools were founded by religions, often in opposition to those founded by rival religions; throughout the 19th century, this rivalry was an important basis for the founding of large numbers of colleges in the U. S., and of the Catholic and Lutheran school systems. The public school system in the U. S. was founded mainly under the impetus of WASP elites with the purpose of teaching respect for Protestant and middle-class standards of cultural and religious propriety, especially in the face of Catholic, working-class immigration from Europe (Cremin, 1961; Curti, 1935). The content of public school education has consisted especially of middle-class, WASP culture (Waller, 1932:15–131; Becker, 1961; Hess and Torney, 1967).

At the elite level, private secondary schools for children of the WASP upper class were founded from the 1880s, when the mass indoctrination function of the growing public schools made them unsuitable as means of maintaining cohesion of the elite culture itself (Baltzell, 1958:327–372). These elite schools produce a distinctive personality type, characterized by adherence to a distinctive set of upper-class values and manners (McArthur, 1955). The cultural role of schools has been more closely studied in Britain (Bernstein, 1961; Weinberg, 1967), and in France (Bourdieu and Passeron, 1964), although Riesman and his colleagues (Riesman, 1958; Jencks and Riesman, 1968) have shown some of the cultural differences among prestige levels of colleges and universities in the United States.

(b) Evidence that education has been used as a means of cultural selection may be found in several sources. Hollingshead's

(1949:360–388) study of Elmtown school children, school dropouts, and community attitudes toward them suggests that employers use education as a means of selecting employees with middle-class attributes. A 1945–1946 survey of 240 employers in New Haven and Charlotte, N. C., indicated that they regarded education as a screening device for employees with desirable (middle-class) character and demeanor; white-collar positions particularly emphasized educational selection because these employees were considered most visible to outsiders (Noland and Bakke, 1949:20–63).

A survey of employers in nationally prominent corporations indicated that they regarded college degrees as important in hiring potential managers, not because they were thought to ensure technical skills, but rather to indicate "motivation" and "social experience" (Gordon and Howell, 1959:121). Business school training is similarly regarded, less as evidence of necessary training (as employers have been widely skeptical of the utility of this curriculum for most positions) than as an indication that the college graduate is committed to business attitudes. Thus, employers are more likely to refuse to hire liberal arts graduates if they come from a college which has a business school than if their college is without a business school (Gordon and Howell, 1959:84–87; see also Pierson, 1959:90–99). In the latter case, the students could be said not to have had a choice; but when both business and liberal arts courses are offered and the student chooses liberal arts, employers appear to take this as a rejection of business values.

Finally, a 1967 survey of 309 California organizations (Collins, 1971) found that educational requirements for white-collar workers were highest in organizations which placed the strongest emphasis on normative control over their employees.[5] Normative control emphasis was indicated by (i) relative emphasis on the absence of police record for job applicants; (ii) relative emphasis on a record of job loyalty; (iii) Etzioni's

(1961) classification of organizations into those with high normative control emphasis (financial, professional services, government, and other public services organizations) and those with remunerative control emphasis (manufacturing, construction; and trade). These three indicators are highly interrelated, thus mutually validating their conceptualization as indicators of normative control emphasis. The relationship between normative control emphasis and educational requirements holds for managerial requirements and white-collar requirements generally, both including and excluding professional and technical positions. Normative control emphasis does not affect blue-collar education requirements.

VARIATIONS IN LINKAGE BETWEEN EDUCATION AND OCCUPATION

The conflict model may also be tested by examining the cases in which it predicts education will be relatively important or unimportant in occupational attainment. Education should be most important where two conditions hold simultaneously: (1) the type of education most closely reflects membership in a particular status group, and (2) that group controls employment in particular organizational contexts. Thus, education will be most important where the fit is greatest between the culture of the status groups emerging from schools, and the status group doing the hiring; it will be least important where there is the greatest disparity between the culture of the school and of the employers.

This fit between school-group culture and employer culture may be conceptualized as a continuum. The importance of elite education is highest where it is involved in selection of new members of organizational elites, and should fade off where jobs are less elite (either lower level jobs in these organizations, or jobs in other organizations not controlled by the cultural elite). Similarly, schools which produce the most elite graduates will be most closely linked to elite occupations; schools whose products are less well socialized into elite culture are selected for jobs correspondingly less close to elite organizational levels.

In the United States, the schools which produce culturally elite groups, either by virtue of explicit training or by selection of students from elite backgrounds, or both, are the private prep schools at the secondary level; at the higher level, the elite colleges (the Ivy league, and to a lesser degree the major state universities); at the professional training level, those professional schools attached to the elite colleges and universities. At the secondary level, schools which produce respectably socialized, non-elite persons are the public high schools (especially those in middle-class residential areas); from the point of view of the culture of WASP employers, Catholic schools (and all-black schools) are less acceptable. At the level of higher education, Catholic and black colleges and professional schools are less elite, and commercial training schools are the least elite form of education.

In the United States, the organizations most clearly dominated by the WASP upper class are large, nationally organized business corporations, and the largest law firms (Domhoff, 1967:38–62). Those organizations more likely to be dominated by members of minority ethnic cultures are the smaller and local businesses in manufacturing, construction, and retail trade; in legal practice, solo rather than firm employment. In government employment, local governments appear to be more heavily dominated by ethnic groups, whereas particular branches of the national government (notably the State Department and the Treasury) are dominated by WASP elites (Domhoff, 1967:84–114, 132–137).

Evidence on the fit between education and employment is available for only some of these organizations. In a broad sample of organizational types (Collins, 1971) educational requirements were higher in the bigger organizations, which also tended to be organized on a national scale, than in smaller

and more localistic organizations.[6] The finding of Perrucci and Perrucci (1970) that upper-class social origins were important in career success precisely within the group of engineers who graduated from the most prestigious engineering schools with the highest grades may also bear on this question; since the big national corporations are most likely to hire this academically elite group, the importance of social origins within this group tends to corroborate the interpretation of education as part of a process of elite cultural selection in those organizations.

Among lawyers, the predicted differences are clear: graduates of the law schools attached to elite colleges and universities are more likely to be employed in firms, whereas graduates of Catholic or commercial law schools are more likely to be found in solo practice (Ladinsky, 1967). The elite Wall Street law firms are most educationally selective in this regard, choosing not only from Ivy League law schools but from a group whose background includes attendance at elite prep schools and colleges (Smigel, 1964:39, 73–74, 117). There are also indications that graduates of ethnically-dominated professional schools are most likely to practice within the ethnic community; this is clearly the case among black professionals. In general, the evidence that graduates of black colleges (Sharp, 1970:64–67) and of Catholic colleges (Jencks and Riesman, 1968:357–366) have attained lower occupational positions in business than graduates of white Protestant schools (at least until recent years) also bolsters this interpretation.[7]

It is possible to interpret this evidence according to the technical-function theory of education, arguing that the elite schools provide the best technical training, and that the major national organizations require the greatest degree of technical talent. What is necessary is to test simultaneously for technical and status-conflict conditions. The most direct evidence on this point is the California employer study (Collins, 1971), which examined the effects of normative control emphasis and of organizational prominence, while holding constant the organization's technological modernity, as measured by the number of technological and organizational changes in the previous six years. Technological change was found to affect educational requirements at managerial and white-collar (but not blue-collar) levels, thus giving some support to the technical-function theory of education. The three variables—normative control emphasis, organizational prominence, and technological change—each independently affected educational requirements, in particular contexts. Technological change produced significantly higher educational requirements only in smaller, localistic organizations, and in organizational sectors not emphasizing normative control. Organizational prominence produced significantly higher educational requirements in organizations with low technological change, and in sectors de-emphasizing normative control. Normative control emphasis produced significantly higher educational requirements in organizations with low technological change, and in less prominent organizations. Thus, technical and normative status conditions all affect educational requirements; measures of association indicated that the latter conditions were stronger in this sample.

Other evidence bearing on this point concerns business executives only. A study of the top executives in nationally prominent businesses indicated that the most highly educated managers were not found in the most rapidly developing companies, but rather in the least economically vigorous ones, with highest education found in the traditionalistic financial and utility firms (Warner and Abegglen, 1955:141–143, 148). The business elite has always been highly educated in relation to the American populace, but education seems to be a correlate of their social origins rather than the determinant of their success (Mills, 1963:128; Taussig and Joslyn, 1932:200; Newcomer, 1955:76). Those members of the business elite who entered its ranks from lower social origins had less education than the businessmen of upper and upper-middle-class origins, and those businessmen who inherited their companies were much more likely to be college educated than those who achieved their positions by entrepreneurship (Bendix, 1956:230; Newcomer, 1955:80).

In general, the evidence indicates that educational requirements for employment reflect employers' concerns for acquiring respectable and well-socialized employees; their concern for the provision of technical skills through education enters to a lesser degree. The higher the normative control concerns of the employer, and the more elite the organization's status, the higher his educational requirements.

HISTORICAL CHANGE

The rise in educational requirements for employment throughout the last century may be explained using the conflict theory, and incorporating elements of the technical-functional theory into it at appropriate points. The principal dynamic has centered on changes in the supply of educated persons caused by the expansion of the school system, which was in turn shaped by three conditions:

(1) Education has been associated with high economic and status position from the colonial period on through the twentieth century. The result was a popular demand for education as mobility opportunity. This demand has not been for vocational education at a terminal or commercial level, short of full university certification; the demand has rather focused on education giving entry into the elite status culture, and usually only those technically-oriented schools have prospered which have most closely associated themselves with the sequence of education leading to (or from) the classical Bachelor's degree (Collins, 1969:68–70, 86–87, 89, 96–101).

(2) Political decentralization, separation of church and state, and competition among

religious denominations have made founding schools and colleges in America relatively easy, and provided initial motivations of competition among communities and religious groups that moved them to do so. As a result, education at all levels expanded faster in America than anywhere else in the world. At the time of the Revolution, there were nine colleges in the colonies; in all of Europe, with a population forty times that of America, there were approximately sixty colleges. By 1880 there were 811 American colleges and universities; by 1966, there were 2,337. The United States not only began with the highest ratio of institutions of higher education to population in the world, but increased this lead steadily, for the number of European universities was not much greater by the twentieth century than in the eighteenth (Ben-David and Zloczower, 1962).

(3) Technical changes also entered into the expansion of American education. As the evidence summarized above indicates: (a) mass literacy is crucial for beginnings of full-scale industrialization, although demand for literacy could not have been important in the expansion of education beyond elementary levels. More importantly, (b) there is a mild trend toward the reduction in the proportion of unskilled jobs and an increase in the promotion of highly skilled (professional and technical) jobs as industrialism proceeds, accounting for 15% of the shift in educational levels in the twentieth century (Folger and Nam, 1964). (c) Technological change also brings about some upgrading in skill requirements of some continuing job positions, although the available evidence (Berg, 1970:38–60) refers only to the decade 1950–1960. Nevertheless, as Wilensky (1964) points out, there is no "professionalization of everyone," as most jobs do not require considerable technical knowledge on the order of that required of the engineer or the research scientist.

The existence of a relatively small group of experts in high-status positions, however, can have important effects on the structure of competition for mobility chances. In the United States, where democratic decentralization favors the use of schools (as well as government employment) as a kind of patronage for voter interests, the existence of even a small number of elite jobs fosters a demand for *large-scale* opportunities to acquire these positions. We thus have a "contest mobility" school system (Turner, 1960); it produced a widely educated populace because of the many dropouts who never achieve the elite level of schooling at which expert skills and/or high cultural status are acquired. In the process, the status value of American education has become diluted. Standards of respectability are always relative to the existing range of cultural differences. Once higher levels of education become recognized as an objective mark of elite status, and a moderate level of education as a mark of respectable middle-level status, increases in the supply of educated persons at given levels result in yet higher levels becoming recognized as superior, and previously superior levels become only average.

Thus, before the end of the nineteenth century, an elementary school or home education was no longer satisfactory for a middle-class gentleman; by the 1930s, a college degree was displacing the high school degree as the minimal standard of respectability; in the late 1960s, graduate school or specialized professional degrees were becoming necessary for initial entry to many middle-class positions, and high school graduation was becoming a standard for entry to manual laboring positions. Education has thus gradually become part of the status culture of classes far below the level of the original business and professional elites.

The increasing supply of educated persons (Table 2) has made education a rising requirement of jobs (Table 1). Led by the biggest and most prestigious organizations, employers have raised their educational requirements to maintain both the relative prestige of their own managerial ranks and the relative respectability of middle ranks.[8] Education has become a legitimate standard in terms of which employers select employees, and employees compete with each other for promotion opportunities or for raised prestige in their continuing positions. With the attainment of a mass (now approaching universal) higher education system in modern America, the ideal or image of technical skill becomes the legitimating culture in terms of which the struggle for position goes on.

Higher educational requirements, and the higher level of educational credentials offered by individuals competing for position in organizations, have in turn increased the demand for education by the populace. The interaction between formal job requirements and informal status cultures has resulted in a spiral in which educational requirements and educational attainments become ever higher. As the struggle for mass educational opportunities enters new phases in the universities of today and perhaps in the graduate schools of the future, we may expect a further upgrading of educational requirements for employment. The mobilization of demands by minority groups for mobility opportunities through schooling can only contribute an extension of the prevailing pattern.

CONCLUSION

It has been argued that conflict theory provides an explanation of the principal dynamics of rising educational requirements for employment in America. Changes in the technical requirements of jobs have caused more limited changes in particular jobs. The conditions of the interaction of these two determinants may be more closely studied.

Precise measures of changes in the actual technical skill requirements of jobs are as yet available only in rudimentary form. Few systematic studies show how much of particular job skills may be learned in practice, and how much must be acquired through school background. Close studies of what is actually learned in school, and how long it is re-

tained, are rare. Organizational studies of how employers rate performance and decide upon promotions give a picture of relatively loose controls over the technical quality of employee performance, but this no doubt varies in particular types of jobs.

The most central line of analysis for assessing the joint effects of status group conflict and technical requirements are those which compare the relative importance of education in different contexts. One such approach may take organization as the unit of analysis, comparing the educational requirements of organizations both to organizational technologies and to the status (including educational) background of organizational elites. Such analysis may also be applied to surveys of individual mobility, comparing the effects of education on mobility in different employment contexts, where the status group (and educational) background of employers varies in its fit with the educational culture of prospective employees. Such analysis of "old school tie" networks may also simultaneously test for the independent effect of the technical requirements of different sorts of jobs on the importance of education. Inter-nation comparisons provide variations here in the fit between types of education and particular kinds of jobs which may not be available within any particular country.

The full elaboration of such analysis would give a more precise answer to the historical question of assigning weight to various factors in the changing place of education in the stratification of modern societies. At the same time, to state the conditions under which status groups vary in organizational power, including the power to emphasize or limit the importance of technical skills, would be to state the basic elements of a comprehensive explanatory theory of the forms of stratification.

NOTES

1. This survey covered 309 establishments with 100 or more employees, representing all major industry groups.
2. The concern here is with these basic premises

rather than with the theory elaborated by Davis and Moore to account for the universality of stratification. This theory involves a few further propositions: (C) in any particular form of society certain occupational positions are functionally most central to the operation of the social system; (D) the ability to fill these positions, and/or the motivation to acquire the necessary training, is unequally distributed in the population; (E) inequalities of rewards in wealth and prestige evolve to ensure that the supply of persons with the necessary ability or training meshes with the structure of demands for skilled performance. The problems of stating functional centrality in empirical terms have been subjects of much debate.

3. Proposition 3 is supported by Tables 1 and 2. The issue here is whether this can be explained by the previous propositions and premises.

4. It might be argued that the ethnic cultures may differ in their functionality: that middle-class Protestant culture provides the self-discipline and other attributes necessary for higher organizational positions in modern society. This version of functional theory is specific enough to be subject to empirical test: are middle-class WASPs in fact better businessmen or government administrators than Italians, Irishmen, or Jews of patrimonial or working class cultural backgrounds? Weber suggested that they were in the initial construction of the capitalist economy within the confines of traditional society; he also argued that once the new economic system was established, the original ethic was no longer necessary to run it (Weber, 1930:180–183). Moreover, the functional explanation also requires some feedback mechanism whereby organizations with more efficient managers are selected for survival. The oligopolistic situation in large-scale American business since the late 19th century does not seem to provide such a mechanism; nor does government employment. Schumpeter (1951), the leading expositor of the importance of managerial talent in business, confined his emphasis to the formative period of business expansion, and regarded the large, oligopolistic corporation as an arena where advancement came to be based on skills in organizational politics (1951:122–124); these personalistic skills are arguably more characteristic of the patrimonial cultures than of WASP culture.

5. Sample consisted of approximately one-third of all organizations with 100 or more employees in the San Francisco, Oakland, and San Jose metropolitan areas. See Gordon and Thal-Larsen (1969) for a description of procedures and other findings.

6. Again, these relationships held for managerial requirements and white-collar requirements generally, both including and excluding professional and technical positions, but not for blue-collar requirements. Noland and Bakke (1949:78) also report that larger organizations have higher educational requirements for administrative positions than smaller organizations.

7. Similar processes may be found in other societies, where the kinds of organizations linked to particular types of schools may differ. In England, the elite "public schools" are linked especially to the higher levels of the national civil service (Weinberg, 1967:139–143). In France, the elite École Polytechnique is linked to both government and industrial administrative positions (Crozier, 1964:238–244). In Germany, universities have been linked principally with government administration, and business executives are drawn from elsewhere (Ben-David and Zloczower, 1962). Comparative analysis of the kinds of education of government officials, business executives, and other groups in contexts where the status group links of schools differ is a promising area for further tests of conflict and technical-functional explanations.

8. It appears that employers may have raised their wage costs in the process. Their behavior is nevertheless plausible, in view of these considerations: (a) the thrust of organizational research since Mayo and Barnard has indicated that questions of internal organizational power and control, of which cultural dominance is a main feature, take precedence over purely economic considerations; (b) the large American corporations, which have led in educational requirements, have held positions of oligopolistic advantage since the late 19th century, and thus could afford a large internal "welfare" cost of maintaining a well-socialized work force; (c) there are inter-organizational wage differentials in local labor markets, corresponding to relative organizational prestige, and a "wage-escalator" process by which the wages of the leading organizations are gradually emulated by others according to their rank (Reynolds, 1951); a parallel structure of "educational status escalators" could plausibly be expected to operate.

REFERENCES

Anastasi, Anne
1967. "Psychology, psychologists, and psychological testing." American Psychologist 22 (April):297–306.

Baltzell, E. Digby
1958. An American Business Aristocracy. New York: Macmillan.

Becker, Howard S.
1961. "Schools and systems of stratification." Pp. 93–104 in A. H. Halsey, Jean Floud, and C. Arnold Anderson (eds.), Education, Economy, and Society. New York: Free Press.

Becker, Howard S., Blanche Geer, and Everett C. Hughes
1968. Making the Grade: The Academic Side of College Life. New York: Wiley.

Bell, H. M.
1940. Matching Youth and Jobs. Washington: American Council on Education.

Ben-David, Joseph
1963–64. "Professions in the class systems of present-day Societies." Current Sociology 12:247–330.

Ben-David, Joseph and Awraham Zloczower
1962. "Universities and academic systems in modern societies." European Journal of Sociology 31:45–85.

Bendix, Reinhard
1956. Work and Authority in Industry. New York: Wiley.

Berg, Ivar
1970. Education and Jobs. New York: Praeger.

Bernstein, Basil
1961. "Social class and linguistic development." Pp. 288–314 in A. H. Halsey, Jean Floud, and C. Arnold Anderson (eds.), Education, Economy, and Society. New York: Free Press.

Blau, Peter M.
1955. The Dynamics of Bureaucracy. Chicago: University of Chicago Press.

Blau, Peter M. and Otis Dudley Duncan
1967. The American Occupational Structure. New York: Wiley.

Bourdieu, Pierre and Jean-Claude Passeron
1964. Les Heritiers: Les Etudiants et la Culture. Paris: Les Editions de Minuit.

Bright, James R.
1958. "Does automation raise skill requirements?" Harvard Business Review 36 (July–August):85–97.

Clark, Burton R.
1962. Educating the Expert Society. San Francisco: Chandler.

Clark, Harold F. and Harold S. Sloan
1966. Classrooms on Main Street. New York: Teachers College Press.

Coleman, James S.
1961. The Adolescent Society. New York: Free Press.

Collins, Orvis, Melville Dalton, and Donald Roy
1946. "Restriction of output and social cleavage in industry." Applied Anthropology 5 (Summer):1–14.

Collins, Randall
1968. "A comparative approach to political sociology." Pp. 42–67 in Reinhard Bendix et al. (eds.), State and Society. Boston: Little, Brown.
1969. Education and Employment. Unpublished Ph.D. dissertation, University of California at Berkeley.
1971. "Educational requirements for employment: A comparative organizational study." Unpublished manuscript.

Cremin, Lawrence A.
1961. The Transformation of the School. New York: Knopf.

Crozier, Michel
1964. The Bureaucratic Phenomenon. Chicago: University of Chicago Press.

Curti, Merle
1935. The Social Ideas of American Educators. New York: Scribners.

Dalton, Melville
1951. "Informal factors in career achievement." American Journal of Sociology 56 (March):407–415.
1959. Men Who Manage. New York: Wiley.

Davis, Kingsley and Wilbert Moore
1945. "Some principles of stratification." American Sociological Review 10:242–249.

Denison, Edward F.
1965. "Education and economic productivity." Pp. 328–340 in Seymour Harris (ed.), Education and Public Policy. Berkeley: McCutchen.

Dill, William R., Thomas L. Hilton, and Walter R. Reitman
1962. The New Managers. Englewood Cliffs: Prentice-Hall.

Domhoff, G. William
1967. Who Rules America? Englewood Cliffs, New Jersey: Prentice-Hall.

Duncan, Beverly
1964. "Dropouts and the unemployed." Journal of Political Economy 73 (April):121–134.

Duncan, Otis Dudley and Robert W. Hodge
1963. "Education and occupational mobility: A regression analysis." American Journal of Sociology 68:629–644.

Eckland, Bruce K.
1965. "Academic ability, higher education, and occupational mobility." American Sociological Review 30:735–746.

Epstein, Cynthia Fuchs
1970. Woman's Place: Options and Limits in Professional Careers. Berkeley: University of California Press.

Etzioni, Amitai
1961. A Comparative Analysis of Complex Organizations. New York: Free Press.

Folger, John K. and Charles B. Nam
1964. "Trends in education in relation to

the occupational structure." Sociology of Education 38:19–33.

Goode, William J.
1967. "The protection of the inept." American Sociological Review 32:5–19.

Gordon, Margaret S. and Margaret Thal-Larsen
1969. Employer Policies in a Changing Labor Market. Berkeley: Institute of Industrial Relations, University of California.

Gordon, Robert A. and James E. Howell
1959. Higher Education for Business. New York: Columbia University Press.

Gusfield, Joseph R.
1958. "Equalitarianism and bureaucratic recruitment." Administrative Science Quarterly 2 (March):521–541.

Hagstrom, Warren O. and Lowell L. Hargens
1968. "Mobility theory in the sociology of science." Paper delivered at Cornell Conference on Human Mobility, Ithaca, N.Y. (October 31).

Hall, Oswald
1946. "The informal organization of the medical profession." Canadian Journal of Economic and Political Science 12 (February): 30–44.

Harbison, Frederick and Charles A. Myers
1964. Education, Manpower, and Economic Growth. New York: McGraw-Hill.

Hargens, Lowell and Warren O. Hagstrom
1967. "Sponsored and contest mobility of American academic scientists." Sociology of Education 40:24–38.

Havemann, Ernest and Patricia Salter West
1952. They Went to College. New York: Harcourt, Brace.

Hess, Robert D. and Judith V. Torney
1967. The Development of Political Attitudes in Children. Chicago: Aldine.

Hollingshead, August B.
1949. Elmtown's Youth. New York: Wiley.

Hoselitz, Bert F.
1965. "Investment in education and its political impact." Pp. 541–565 in James S. Coleman (ed.), Education and Political Development. Princeton: Princeton University Press.

Hughes, Everett C.
1949. "Queries concerning industry and society growing out of the study of

ethnic relations in industry." American Sociological Review 14:211–220.

Jencks, Christopher and David Riesman
1968. The Academic Revolution. New York: Doubleday.

Kahl, Joseph A.
1957. The American Class Structure. New York: Rinehart.

Kerr, Clark, John T. Dunlop, Frederick H. Harbison, and Charles A. Myers
1960. Industrialism and Industrial Man. Cambridge: Harvard University Press.

Ladinsky, Jack
1963. "Careers of lawyers, law practice, and legal institutions." American Sociological Review 28 (February):47–54.
1967. "Higher education and work achievement among lawyers." Sociological Quarterly 8 (Spring):222–232.

Learned, W. S. and B. D. Wood
1938. The Student and His Knowledge. New York: Carnegie Foundation for the Advancement of Teaching.

Lipset, Seymour Martin and Reinhard Bendix
1959. Social Mobility in Industrial Society. Berkeley: University of California Press.

Lombard, George F.
1955. Behavior in a Selling Group. Cambridge: Harvard University Press.

March, James G. and Herbert A. Simon
1958. Organizations. New York: Wiley.

Marsh, Robert M.
1963. "Values, demand, and social mobility." American Sociological Review 28 (August):567–575.

McArthur, C.
1955. "Personality differences between middle and upper classes." Journal of Abnormal and Social Psychology 50:247–254.

Mills, C. Wright
1963. Power, Politics, and People. New York: Oxford University Press.

Newcomer, Mabel
1955. The Big Business Executive. New York: Columbia University Press.

Noland, E. William and E. Wight Bakke
1949. Workers Wanted. New York: Harper.

Nosow, Sigmund
1956. "Labor distribution and the normative system." Social Forces 30:25–33.

Peaslee, Alexander L.
  1969. "Education's role in development."
  Economic Development and Cultural
  Change 17 (April):293–318.
Perrucci, Carolyn Cummings and Robert Perrucci
  1970. "Social origins, educational contexts, and career mobility." American
  Sociological Review 35 (June):451–463.
Pierson, Frank C.
  1959. The Education of American Businessmen. New York: McGraw-Hill.
Plunkett, M.
  1960. "School and early work experience
  of youth." Occupational Outlook Quarterly 4:22–27.
Reynolds, Lloyd
  1951. The Structure of Labor Markets.
  New York: Harper.
Riesman, David
  1958. Constraint and Variety in American Education. New York: Doubleday.
Roy, Donald
  1952. "Quota restriction and goldbricking in a machine shop." American Journal
  of Sociology 57 (March):427–442.
Schultz, Theodore W.
  1961. "Investment in human capital."
  American Economic Review 51 (March):
  1–16.
Schumpeter, Joseph
  1951. Imperialism and Social Classes.
  New York: Augustus M. Kelley.
Sewell, William H., Archibald O. Haller, and
  Alejandro Portes
  1969. "The educational and early occupational attainment process." American
  Sociological Review 34 (February):
  82–92.
Sharp, Laure M.
  1970. Education and Employment: The
  Early Careers of College Graduates. Baltimore: Johns Hopkins Press.

Smigel, Erwin O.
  1964. The Wall Street Lawyer. New
  York: Free Press.
Soderberg, C. Richard
  1963. "The American engineer." Pp.
  203–230 in Kenneth S. Lynn, The Professions in America. Boston: Beacon Press.
Taeuber, Alma F., Karl E. Taeuber, and Glen
  G. Cain
  1966. "Occupational assimilation and the
  competitive process: A reanalysis."
  American Journal of Sociology 72:278–
  285.
Taussig, Frank W. and C. S. Joslyn
  1932. American Business Leaders. New
  York: Macmillan.
Turner, Ralph H.
  1952. "Foci of discrimination in the employment of nonwhites." American
  Journal of Sociology 58:247–256.
  1960. "Sponsored and contest mobility
  and the school system." American Sociological Review 25 (October):855–867.
Waller, Willard
  1932. The Sociology of Teaching. New
  York: Russell and Russell.
Warner, W. Lloyd and James C. Abegglen
  1955. Occupational Mobility in American
  Business and Industry, 1928–1952. Minneapolis: University of Minnesota Press.
Weber, Max
  1930. The Protestant Ethic and the Spirit
  of Capitalism. New York: Scribner's.
  1968. Economy and Society. New York:
  Bedminster Press.
Weinberg, Ian
  1967. The English Public Schools: the
  Sociology of Elite Education. New York:
  Atherton Press.
Wilensky, Harold L.
  1964. "The professionalization of everyone?" American Journal of Sociology 70
  (September):137–158.

5. Unequal Education and the Reproduction of the Social Division of Labor

SAMUEL BOWLES

The ideological defense of modern capitalist society rests heavily on the assertion that the equalizing effects of education can counter the disequalizing forces inherent in the free market system. That educational systems in capitalist societies have been highly unequal is generally admitted and widely condemned. Yet educational inequalities are taken as passing phenomena, holdovers from an earlier, less enlightened era, which are rapidly being eliminated.

The record of educational history in the U.S., and scrutiny of the present state of our colleges and schools, lend little support to this comforting optimism. Rather, the available data suggest an alternative interpretation. In what follows I will argue 1) that schools have evolved in the U.S. not as part of a pursuit of equality, but rather to meet the needs of capitalist employers for a disciplined and skilled labor force, and to provide a mechanism for social control in the interests of political stability; 2) that as the economic importance of skilled and well educated labor has grown, inequalities in the school system have become increasingly important in reproducing the class structure from one generation to the next; 3) that the U.S. school system is pervaded by class inequalities, which have shown little sign of diminishing over the last half century; and 4) that the evidently unequal control over school boards and other decision-making bodies in education does not provide a sufficient explanation of the persistence and pervasiveness of inequalities in the school system. Although the unequal distribution of political power serves to maintain inequalities in education, their origins are to be found outside the political sphere, in the class structure itself and in the class subcultures typical of capitalist societies. Thus unequal education has its roots in the very class structure which it serves to legitimize and reproduce. Inequalities in education are thus seen as part of the web of capitalist society, and likely to persist as long as capitalism survives.

1. THE EVOLUTION OF CAPITALISM AND THE RISE OF MASS EDUCATION

In colonial America, and in most pre-capitalist societies of the past, the basic productive unit was the family. For the vast majority of male adults, work was self-directed, and was performed without direct supervision. Though constrained by poverty, ill health, the low level of technological development and occasional interferences by the political authorities, a man had considerable leeway in choosing his working hours, what to produce, and how to produce it. While great inequalities in wealth, political power, and other aspects of status normally existed, differences in the degree of autonomy in work were relatively minor, particularly when compared with what was to come.

Transmitting the necessary productive skills to the children as they grew up proved to be a simple task, not because the work was devoid of skill, but because the quite substantial skills required were virtually unchanging from generation to generation, and because the transition to the world of work did not require that the child adapt to a wholly new set of social relationships. The child learned the concrete skills and adapted to the social relations of production through learning by doing within the family. Preparation for life in the larger community was facilitated by the child's experience with the extended family, which shaded off without distinct boundaries, through uncles and fourth cousins, into the community. Chil-

From *Review of Radical Political Economics* 3 (Fall 1971). Reprinted by permission of the author.

dren learned early how to deal with complex relationships among adults other than their parents, and children other than their brothers and sisters.[1]

It was not required that children learn a complex set of political principles or ideologies, as political participation was limited and political authority unchallenged, at least in normal times. The only major socializing institution outside the family was the church, which sought to inculcate the accepted spiritual values and attitudes. In addition, a small number of children learned craft skills outside the family, as apprentices. The role of schools tended to be narrowly vocational, restricted to preparation of children for a career in the church or the still inconsequential state bureaucracy.[2] The curriculum of the few universities reflected the aristocratic penchant for conspicuous intellectual consumption.[3]

The extension of capitalist production, and particularly the factory system, undermined the role of the family as the major unit of both socialization and production. Small peasant farmers were driven off the land or competed out of business. Cottage industry was destroyed. Ownership of the means of production became heavily concentrated in the hands of landlords and capitalists. Workers relinquished control over their labor in return for wages or salaries. Increasingly, production was carried on in large organizations in which a small management group directed the work activities of the entire labor force. The social relations of production—the authority structure, the prescribed types of behavior and response characteristic of the work place—became increasingly distinct from those of the family.

The divorce of the worker from control over production—from control over his own labor—is particularly important in understanding the role of schooling in capitalist societies. The resulting social division of labor—between controllers and controlled—is a crucial aspect of the class structure of capitalist societies, and will be seen to be an important barrier to the achievement of social class equality in schooling.

Rapid economic change in the capitalist period led to frequent shifts in the occupational distribution of the labor force, and constant changes in the skill requirements for jobs. The productive skills of the father were no longer adequate for the needs of the son during his lifetime. Skill training within the family became increasingly inappropriate.

And the family itself was changing. Increased geographic mobility of labor and the necessity for children to work outside the family spelled the demise of the extended family and greatly weakened even the nuclear family.[4] Meanwhile, the authority of the church was questioned by the spread of secular rationalist thinking and the rise of powerful competing groups.

While undermining the main institutions of socialization, the development of the capitalist system created at the same time an environment—both social and intellectual—which would ultimately challenge the political order. Workers were thrown together in oppressive factories, and the isolation which had helped to maintain quiescence in earlier, widely dispersed peasant populations was broken down.[5] With an increasing number of families uprooted from the land, the workers' search for a living resulted in large-scale labor migrations. Transient—even foreign—elements came to constitute a major segment of the population, and began to pose seemingly insurmountable problems of assimilation, integration, and control.[6] Inequalities of wealth became more apparent, and were less easily justified and less readily accepted. The simple legitimizing ideologies of the earlier period—the divine right of kings and the divine origin of social rank, for example—fell under the capitalist attack on the royalty and the traditional landed interests. The broadening of the electorate of political participation generally—first sought by the capitalist class in the struggle against the entrenched interests of the pre-capitalist period—threatened soon to become an instrument for the growing power of the working class. Having risen to political power, the capitalist class sought a mechanism to insure social control and political stability.[7]

An institutional crisis was at hand. The outcome, in virtually all capitalist countries, was the rise of mass education. In the U.S., the many advantages of schooling as a socialization process were quickly perceived. The early proponents of the rapid expansion of schooling argued that education could perform many of the socialization functions which earlier had been centered in the family and to a lesser extent, in the church.[8]

An ideal preparation for factory work was found in the social relations of the school: specifically, in its emphasis on discipline, punctuality, acceptance of authority outside the family, and individual accountability for one's work.[9] The social relations of the school would replicate the social relations of the workplace, and thus help young people adapt to the social division of labor. Schools would further lead people to accept the authority of the state and its agents—the teachers—at a young age, in part by fostering the illusion of the benevolence of the government in its relations with citizens.[10] Moreover, because schooling would ostensibly be open to all, one's position in the social division of labor could be portrayed as the result not of birth, but of one's own efforts and talents.[11] And if the children's everyday experiences with the structure of schooling were insufficient to inculcate the correct views and attitudes, the curriculum itself would be made to embody the bourgeois ideology.[12] Where pre-capitalist social institutions—particularly the church— remained strong or threatened the capitalist hegemony, schools sometimes served as a modernizing counter-institution.[13]

The movement for public elementary and secondary education in the U.S. originated in the 19th century in states dominated by the burgeoning industrial capitalist class, most notably in Massachusetts. It spread rapidly to all parts of the country except the South.[14] In Massachusetts the extension of elementary education was in large measure a response to industrialization, and to the need for social control of the Irish and other non-Yankee workers recruited to work in the mills.[15] The fact that some working people's movements had demanded free instruction should not obscure the basically coercive nature of the extension of schooling. In many parts of the country, schools were literally imposed upon the workers.[16]

The evolution of the economy in the 19th century gave rise to new socialization needs and continued to spur the growth of education. Agriculture continued to lose ground to manufacturing; simple manufacturing gave way to production involving complex interrelated processes; an increasing fraction of the labor force was employed in producing services rather than goods. Employers in the most rapidly growing sectors of the economy began to require more than obedience and punctuality in their workers; a change in motivational outlook was required. The new structure of production provided little built-in motivation. There were fewer jobs like farming and piece-rate work in manufacturing in which material reward was tied directly to effort. As work roles became more complicated and interrelated, the evaluation of the individual worker's performance became increasingly difficult. Employers began to look for workers who had internalized the production-related values of the firm's managers.

The continued expansion of education was pressed by many who saw schooling as a means of producing these new forms of motivation and discipline. Others, frightened by the growing labor militancy after the Civil War, found new urgency in the social control arguments popular among the proponents of education in the antebellum period.

A system of class stratification developed within this rapidly expanding educational system. Children of the social elite normally attended private schools. Because working class children tended to leave school early, the class composition of the public high schools was distinctly more elite than the public primary schools.[17] And as a university education ceased to be merely training for teaching or the divinity and became important in gaining access to the pinnacles of the business world, upper class families used their money and influence to get their children into the best universities, often at the expense of the children of less elite families.

Around the turn of the present century, large numbers of working class and particularly immigrant children began attending high schools. At the same time, a system of class stratification developed within secondary education.[18] The older democratic ideology of the common school—that the same curriculum should be offered to all children—gave way to the "progressive" insistence that education should be tailored to the "needs of the child."[19] In the interests of providing an education relevant to the later life of the students, vocational schools and tracks were developed for the children of working families. The academic curriculum was preserved for those who would later have the opportunity to make use of book learning, either in college or in white-collar employment. This and other educational reforms of the progressive education movement reflected an implicit assumption of the immutability of the class structure.

The frankness with which students were channeled into curriculum tracks, on the basis of their social class background, raised serious doubts concerning the "openness" of the social class structure. The relation between social class and a child's chances of promotion or tracking assignments was disguised—though not mitigated much—by another "progressive" reform: "objective" educational testing. Particularly after World War I, the capitulation of the schools to business values and concepts of efficiency led to the increased use of intelligence and scholastic achievement testing as an ostensibly unbiased means of measuring the product of schooling and classifying students.[20] The complementary growth of the guidance counseling profession allowed much of the channeling to proceed from the students' own well-counseled choices, thus adding an apparent element of voluntarism to the system.

The legacy of the progressive education movement, like the earlier reforms of the mid-19th century, was a strengthened system of class stratification within schooling which continues to this day to play an important role in the reproduction and legitimation of the social division of labor.

The class stratification of education during this period had proceeded hand in hand with the stratification of the labor force. As large bureaucratic corporations and public agencies employed an increasing fraction of all workers, a complicated segmentation of the labor force evolved, reflecting the hierarchical structure of the social relations of production. A large middle group of employees evolved comprising the clerical, sales, bookkeeping, and low level supervisory workers.[21] People holding these occupations ordinarily had a modicum of control over their own work; in some cases they directed the work of others, while themselves being under the direction of higher management. The social division of labor had become a finely articulated system of work relations dominated at the top by a small group with control over work processes and a high degree of personal autonomy in their work activities, and proceeding by finely differentiated stages down the chain of bureaucratic command to workers who labored more as extensions of the machinery than as autonomous human beings.

One's status, income, and personal autonomy came to depend in great measure on one's place in the hierarchy of work relations. And in turn, positions in the social division of labor came to be associated with educational credentials reflecting the number of years of schooling and the quality of education received. The increasing importance of schooling as a mechanism for allocating children to positions in the class structure, played a major part in legitimizing the structure itself.[22] But at the same time, it undermined the simple processes which in the past had preserved the position and privilege of the upper class families from generation to generation. In short, it undermined the processes serving to reproduce the social division of labor.

In pre-capitalist societies, direct inheritance of occupational position is common. Even in the early capitalist economy, prior to the segmentation of the labor force on the basis of differential skills and education, the class structure was reproduced generation after generation simply through the inheritance of physical capital by the offspring of the capitalist class. Now that the social division of labor is differentiated by types of competence and educational credentials as well as by the ownership of capital, the problem of inheritance is not nearly as simple. The crucial complication arises because education and skills are embedded in human beings, and—unlike physical capital—these assets cannot be passed on to one's children at death. In an advanced capitalist society in which education and skills play an important role in the hierarchy of production, then, the absence of confiscatory inheritance laws is not enough to reproduce the social division of labor from generation to generation. Skills and educational credentials must somehow be passed on within the family. It is a fundamental theme of this paper that schools play an important part in reproducing and legitimizing this modern form of class structure.

2. CLASS INEQUALITIES IN U.S. SCHOOLS

Unequal schooling reproduces the social division of labor. Children whose parents occupy positions at the top of the occupational hierarchy receive more years of schooling than working class children. Both the amount and the content of their education greatly facilitates their movement into positions similar to their parents'.

Because of the relative ease of measurement, inequalities in years of schooling are particularly evident. If we define social class standing by the income, occupation, and educational level of the parents, a child from the 90th percentile in the class distribution may expect on the average to achieve over four and a half more years of schooling than a child from the 10th percentile.[23] As can be seen in Table 1, social class inequalities in the number of years of schooling received arise in part because a disproportionate number of children from poorer families do not complete high school.[24] Table 2 indicates that these inequalities are exacerbated by social class inequalities in college attendance among those children who did graduate from high school: even among those who had graduated from high school, children of families earning less than $3,000 per year were over six times as likely *not* to attend college as were the children of families earning over $15,000.[25]

Because schooling—especially at the college level—is heavily subsidized by the general taxpayer, those children who attend school longer have access—for this reason alone—to a far larger amount of public resources than those who are forced out or drop out early.[26] But social class inequalities in public expenditure on education are far more severe than the degree of inequality in years of schooling would suggest. In the first place, per-student public expenditure in four-year colleges greatly exceeds that in elementary schools; those who stay in school longer receive an increasingly large *annual* public subsidy.[27] Second, even at the elementary level, schools attended by children of the poor tend to be less well-endowed with equipment, books, teachers, and other inputs into the educational process. Evidence on the relationship between the level of school inputs and the income of the neighborhoods which the schools serve is presented in Table 3.[28] The data in this table indicate that both school expenditures and more direct measures of school quality vary directly with the income levels of the communities in which the school is located.

Table 1. Percentage of Male Children aged 16–17 Enrolled in Public School, and Percentage at Less than the Modal Grade Level, by Parent's Education and Income, 1960[a]

	% of male children aged 16–17 enrolled in public school	% of those enrolled who are below the modal level
1. Parent's education less than 8 years		
Family Income:		
less than $3,000	66.1	47.4
$3,000–4,999	71.3	35.7
$5,000–6,999	75.5	28.3
$7,000 and over	77.1	21.8
2. Parent's education 8–11 years		
Family income:		
less than $3,000	78.6	25.0
$3,000–4,999	82.9	20.9
$5,000–6,999	84.9	16.9
$7,000 and over	86.1	13.0
3. Parent's education 12 years or more		
Family income:		
less than $3,000	89.5	13.4
$3,000–4,999	90.7	12.4
$5,000–6,999	92.1	9.7
$7,000 and over	94.2	16.9

Source: Bureau of the Census, Census of Population, 1960, Vol. PC-(2)5A, Table 5.
a. According to Bureau of the Census definitions, for 16-year olds 9th grade or less and for 17-year olds 10th grade or less are below the modal level. Father's education is indicated if father is present; otherwise mother's education is indicated.

Table 2. College Attendance in 1967 among High School Graduates, by Family Income[a]

Family income[b]	Percent who did not attend college
Total	53.1
under $3,000	80.2
$3,000 to $3,999	67.7
$4,000 to $5,999	63.7
$6,000 to $7,499	58.9
$7,500 to $9,999	49.0
$10,000 to $14,999	38.7
$15,000 and over	13.3

a. Refers to individuals who were high school seniors in October 1965 and who subsequently graduated from high school. Source: U. S. Department of Commerce, Bureau of the Census, Current Population, Report, Series P-20, No. 185, July 11, 1969, p. 6. College attendance refers to both two- and four-year institutions.
b. Family income for 12 months preceding October 1965.

Inequalities in schooling are not simply a matter of differences in years of schooling attained or in resources devoted to each student per year of schooling. Differences in the internal structure of schools themselves and in the content of schooling reflect the differences in the social class compositions of the student bodies. The social relations of the educational process ordinarily mirror the social relations of the work roles into which most students are likely to move. Differences in rules, expected modes of behavior, and opportunities for choice are most glaring when we compare levels of schooling. Note the wide range of choice over curriculum, life style, and allocation of time afforded to college students, compared with the obedience and respect for authority expected in high school. Differentiation occurs also within each level of schooling. One needs only to compare the social relations of a

Table 3. Inequalities in Elementary School Resources: Percent Difference in Resource Availability Associated with a One Percent Difference in Mean Neighborhood Family Income

Resource	Within cities (1)	Between cities (2)
1. Current real education expenditure per student	n.a.	.73[b]
2. Average real elementary school teacher salary	.20[a]	.69[b]
3. Teacher-student ratio	.24[a]	n.a.
4. Real expenditure per pupil on teacher salary	.43[a]	n.a.
5. Verbal ability of teacher	.11[a]	1.20[a]

Sources:

a. John D. Owen, "An Empirical Analysis of Economic and Racial Bias in the Distribution of Educational Resources in Nine Large American Cities" (Center for the Study of Social Organization of Schools, Johns Hopkins University, 1969).

b. John D. Owen, "Towards a Public Employment Wage Theory: Some Econometric Evidence on Teacher Quality," *Industrial Labor Relations Review* (forthcoming, 1972).

junior college with those of an elite four-year college,[29] or those of a working class high school with those of a wealthy suburban high school, for verification of this point.[30]

The differential socialization patterns in schools attended by students of different social classes do not arise by accident. Rather, they stem from the fact that the educational objectives and expectations of both parents and teachers, and the responsiveness of students to various patterns of teaching and control, differ for students of different social classes.[31] Further, class inequalities in school socialization patterns are reinforced by the very inequalities in financial resources documented above. The paucity of financial support for the education of children from working class families not only leaves more resources to be devoted to the children of those with commanding roles in the economy; it forces upon the teachers and school administrators in the working class schools a type of social relations which fairly closely mirrors that of the factory. Thus financial considerations in poorly supported working class schools militate against small intimate classes, against a multiplicity of elective courses and specialized teachers (except disciplinary personnel), and preclude the amounts of free time for the teachers and free space required for a

more open, flexible educational environment. The lack of financial support all but requires that students be treated as raw materials on a production line; it places a high premium on obedience and punctuality; there are few opportunities for independent, creative work or individualized attention by teachers. The well-financed schools attended by the children of the rich can offer much greater opportunities for the development of the capacity for sustained independent work and the other characteristics required for adequate job performance in the upper levels of the occupational hierarchy.

While much of the inequality in U.S. education exists between schools, even within a given school different children receive different educations. Class stratification within schools is achieved through tracking, differential participation in extracurricular activities, and in the attitudes of teachers and particularly guidance personnel who expect working class children to do poorly, to terminate schooling early, and to end up in jobs similar to their parents.[32]

Not surprisingly, the results of schooling differ greatly for children of different social classes. The differing educational objectives implicit in the social relations of schools attended by children of different social classes has already been mentioned. Less important but more easily measured are differences in scholastic achievement. If we measure the output of schooling by scores on nationally standardized achievement tests, children whose parents were themselves highly educated outperform the children of parents with less education by a wide margin. A recent study revealed, for example, that among white high school seniors, those whose parents were in the top education decile were on the average well over three grade levels ahead of those whose parents were in the bottom decile.[33] While a good part of this discrepancy is the result of unequal treatment in school and unequal educational resources, it will be suggested below that much of it is related to differences in the early socialization and home environment of the children.

Given the great social class differences in scholastic achievement, class inequalities in college attendance are to be expected. Thus one might be tempted to argue that the data in Table 2 are simply a reflection of unequal scholastic achievement in high school and do not reflect any *additional* social class inequalities peculiar to the process of college admission. This view, so comforting to the admissions personnel in our elite universities,

is unsupported by the available data, some of which are presented in Table 4. Access to a college education is highly unequal, even for children of the same measured "academic ability."

The social class inequalities in our school system and the role they play in the reproduction of the social division of labor are too evident to be denied. Defenders of the educational system are forced back on the assertion that things are getting better; the inequalities of the past were far worse. And, indeed, there can be no doubt that some of the inequalities of the past have been mitigated. Yet new inequalities have apparently developed to take their place, for the available historical evidence lends little support to the idea that our schools are on the road to equality of educational opportunity. For example, data from a recent U.S. Census survey reported in Table 5 indicate that graduation from college has become increasingly dependent on one's class background. This is true despite the fact that the probability of high school graduation is becoming increasingly equal across social classes. On balance, the available data suggest that the number of years of schooling attained by a child depends upon the social class standing of the father at least as much in the recent period as it did fifty years ago.[34]

The argument that our "egalitarian" education compensates for inequalities generated elsewhere in the capitalist system is so patently fallacious that few will persist in maintaining it. But the discrepancy between the ideology and the reality of the U.S. school system is far greater than would appear from a passing glance at the above data. In the first place, if education is to compensate for the social class immobility due to the inheritance of wealth and privilege, education must be structured so as to yield a negative correlation between social class background of the child and the quantity and quality of her or his schooling. Thus the assertion that education compensates for inequalities in inherited wealth and privilege

Table 4. Probability of College Entry for a Male who has Reached Grade 11[a]

| | | Socioeconomic quartiles[b] | | | |
		Low 1	2	3	High 4
Ability	Low 1	.06	.12	.13	.26
Quartiles[b]	2	.13	.15	.29	.36
	3	.25	.34	.45	.65
	High 4	.48	.70	.73	.87

a. Based on a large sample of U.S. high school students as reported in John C. Flannagan and William W. Cooley, *Project TALENT, One-Year Follow-up Studies,* Cooperative Research Project Number 2333, School of Education, University of Pittsburgh, 1966.
b. The socioeconomic index is a composite measure including family income, father's occupation and education, mother's education, etc. The ability scale is a composite of tests measuring general academic aptitude.

Table 5. Among Sons who had Reached High School, Percentage who graduated from college, by Son's Age and Father's Level of Education

Son's age in 1962	Likely dates of college graduation[a]	<8 years	Father's education					
			Some high school		High school grad		Some college or more	
			% Graduating	Ratio to <8	% Grad	Ratio to <8	% Grad	Ratio to <8
25–34	1950–1959	07.6	17.4	2.29	25.6	3.37	51.9	6.83
35–44	1940–1949	08.6	11.9	1.38	25.3	2.94	53.9	6.27
45–54	1930–1939	07.7	09.8	1.27	15.1	1.96	36.9	4.79
55–64	1920–1929	08.9	09.8	1.10	19.2	2.16	29.8	3.35

a. Assuming college graduation at age 22.
Source: Based on U.S. Census data as reported in William G. Spady, "Educational Mobility and Access: Growth and Paradoxes," *American Journal of Sociology,* Vol. 73, No. 3 (November 1967).

is falsified not so much by the extent of the social class inequalities in the school system as by their very existence, or, more correctly, by the absence of compensatory inequalities.

Second, if we turn now from the problem of intergeneration immobility to the problem of inequality of income at a given moment, a similar argument applies. In a capitalist economy, the increasing importance of schooling in the economy will exercise a disequalizing tendency on the distribution of income even in the absence of social class inequalities in quality and quantity of schooling. To see why this is so, consider a simple capitalist economy in which only two factors are used in production: uneducated and undifferentiated labor, and capital, the ownership of which is unequally distributed among the population. The only source of income inequality in this society is the unequal distribution of capital. As the labor force becomes differentiated by type of skill or schooling, inequalities in labor earnings contribute to total income inequality, augmenting the inequalities due to the concentration of capital. This will be the case even if education and skills are distributed randomly among the population. The disequalizing tendency will of course be intensified if the owners of capital also ac-

quire a disproportionate amount of those types of education and training which confer access to high-paying jobs.[35] A substantial negative correlation between the ownership of capital and the quality and quantity of schooling received would have been required merely to neutralize the disequalizing effect of the rise of schooling as an economic phenomenon. And while some research has minimized the importance of social class biases in schooling,[36] nobody has yet suggested that class and schooling were inversely related!

3. CLASS CULTURE AND CLASS POWER

The pervasive and persistent inequalities in U.S. education would seem to refute an interpretation of education which asserts its egalitarian functions. But the facts of inequality do not by themselves suggest an alternate explanation. Indeed, they pose serious problems of interpretation. If the costs of education borne by students and their families were very high, or if nepotism were rampant, or if formal segregation of pupils by social class were practiced, or educational decisions were made by a select few whom we might call the power elite, it would not be difficult to explain the continued inequalities in U.S. education. The problem of interpretation, however, is to reconcile the above empirical findings with the facts of our society as we perceive them: public and virtually tuition-free education at all levels, few legal instruments for the direct implementation of class segregation, a limited role for "contacts" or nepotism in the achievement of high status or income, a commitment (at the rhetorical level at least) to equality of educational opportunity, and a system of control of education which if not particularly democratic, extends far beyond anything resembling a power elite. The attempt to reconcile these apparently discrepant facts leads us back to a consideration of the social division of labor, the associated class cultures, and the exercise of class power.

I will argue that the social division of labor—based on the hierarchical structure of production—gives rise to distinct class subcultures. The values, personality traits, and expectations characteristic of each subculture are transmitted from generation to generation through class differences in family socialization and complementary differences in the type and amount of schooling ordinarily attained by children of various class positions. These class differences in schooling are maintained in large measure through the capacity of the upper class to control the basic principles of school finance, pupil evaluation, and educational objectives.

This outline, and what follows, is put forward as an interpretation, consistent where testable with the available data, though lacking as yet in firm empirical support for some important links in the argument.

The social relations of production characteristic of advanced capitalist societies (and many socialist societies) are most clearly illustrated in the bureaucracy and hierarchy of the modern corporation.[37] Occupational roles in the capitalist economy may be grouped according to the degree of independence and control exercised by the person holding the job. There is some evidence that the personality attributes associated with the adequate performance of jobs in occupational categories defined in this broad way differ considerably, some apparently requiring independence and internal discipline, and others emphasizing such traits as obedience, predictability, and willingness to subject oneself to external controls.[38]

These personality attributes are developed primarily at a young age, both in the family and, to a lesser extent, in secondary socializing institutions such as schools.[39] Because people tend to marry within their own class (in part because spouses often meet in our class segregated schools), both parents are likely to have a similar set of these fundamental personality traits. Thus children of parents occupying a given position in the occupational hierarchy grow up in homes where child-rearing methods and perhaps even the physical surroundings tend to develop personality characteristics appropriate to adequate job performance in the occupational roles of the parents.[40] The children of managers and professionals are taught self-reliance within a broad set of constraints;[41] the children of production line workers are taught obedience.

While this relation between parents' class position and child's personality attributes operates primarily in the home, it is reinforced by schools and other social institutions. Thus, to take an example introduced earlier, the authoritarian social relations of working class high schools complement the discipline-oriented early socialization patterns experienced by working class children. The relatively greater freedom of wealthy suburban schools extends and formalizes the early independence training characteristic of upper class families.

Schools reinforce other aspects of family socialization as well. Students' and parents' aspirations and expectations concerning both the type and the amount of schooling are strongly related to social class.[42] The expectations of teachers, guidance counselors, and school administrators ordinarily reinforce those of the students and parents. Schools often encourage students to develop aspirations and expectations typical of their social class, even if the child tends to have "deviant" aspirations.

It is true that to some extent schools introduce common elements of socialization for all students regardless of social class. Discipline, respect for property, competition, and punctuality are part of the implicit curriculum of virtually all schools. Yet given the existing institutional arrangements, the ability of a school to change a child's personality, values, and expectations is severely limited. The responsiveness of children to different types of schooling seems to depend importantly upon the types of personality traits, values, and expectations which have been developed through the family. Furthermore, children spend a small amount of time in school—less than a quarter of their waking hours over the course of a year. Thus schools are probably more effective where they attempt to complement and reinforce rather than to oppose the socialization processes of the home and neighborhood. It is not surprising, then, that social class differences in scholastic achievement and other measures of school success are far greater than would be accounted for by differences in the measured school financial resources and other inputs (quality and quantity of teachers, etc.) alone.[43]

Class differences in the total effect of schooling are—in this interpretation—due primarily to differences in what I have called class subculture. The educational system serves less to change the results of the primary socialization in the home than to ratify them and render them in adult form. The complementary relationship between family socialization and schools serves to reproduce patterns of class culture from generation to generation.

The operation of the labor market translates differences in class culture into income inequalities and occupational hierarchies. The personality traits, values, and expectations characteristic of different class cultures play a major role in determining an individual's success in gaining a high income or prestigious occupation. The apparent contribution of schooling to occupational success and higher income seems to be explained primarily by the personality characteristics of those who have higher educational attainments.[44] Although the rewards to intellectual capacities are quite limited in the labor market (except for a small number of high level jobs), mental abilities are important in getting ahead in school. Grades, the probability of continuing to higher levels of schooling, and a host of other school success variables, are positively correlated with "objective" measures of intellectual capacities. Partly for this reason, one's experience in school reinforces the belief that promotion and rewards are distributed fairly. The close relationship between educational attainments and later occupational success thus provides a meritocratic appearance to mask the mechanisms which reproduce the class system from generation to generation.

So far, the perpetuation of inequality through the schooling system has been represented as an almost automatic, self-enforcing mechanism, operating only through the medium of class culture. An important further dimension of the interpretation is added if we note that positions of control in the productive hierarchy tend to be associated with positions of political influence. Given the disproportionate share of political power held by the upper class and their capacity to determine the accepted patterns of behavior and procedures, to define the national interest, and in general to control the ideological and institutional context in which educational decisions are made, it is not surprising to find that resources are allocated unequally among school tracks, between schools serving different classes, and between levels of schooling. The same configuration of power results in curricula, methods of instruction, and criteria of selection and promotion which confer benefits disproportionately on the children of the upper class.

It is not asserted here that the upper class

controls the main decision-making bodies in education, although a good case could probably be made that this is so. The power of the upper class is hypothesized as existing in its capacity to define and maintain a set of rules of operation or decision criteria—"rules of the game"—which, though often seemingly innocuous and sometimes even egalitarian in their ostensible intent, have the effect of maintaining the unequal system.

The operation of two prominent examples of these "rules of the game" will serve to illustrate the point. The first important principle is that excellence in schooling should be rewarded. Given the capacity of the upper class to define excellence in terms on which upper class children tend to excel (for example, scholastic achievement), adherence to this principle yields inegalitarian outcomes (for example, unequal access to higher education) while maintaining the appearance of fair treatment.[45] Thus the principle of rewarding excellence serves to legitimize the unequal consequences of schooling by associating success with competence. At the same time, the institution of objectively administered tests of performance serves to allow a limited amount of upward mobility among exceptional children of the lower class, thus providing further legitimation of the operations of the social system by giving some credence to the myth of widespread mobility.

The second example is the principle that elementary and secondary schooling should be financed in very large measure from local revenues. This principle is supported on the grounds that it is necessary to preserve political liberty. Given the degree of residential segregation by income level, the effect of this principle is to produce an unequal distribution of school resources among children of different classes. Towns with a large tax base can spend large sums for the education of their disproportionately upper class children even without suffering a higher than average tax rate.[46] Because the main resource inequalities in schooling thus exist between rather than within school districts,[47] and because there is no effective mechanism for redistribution of school funds among school districts, poor families lack a viable political strategy for correcting the inequality.[48]

The above rules of the game—rewarding "excellence" and financing schools locally—illustrate the complementarity between the political and economic power of the upper class. In each case, adherence to the rule has the effect of generating unequal consequences via a mechanism which operates largely outside the political system. As long as one adheres to the "reward excellence" principle, the responsibility for unequal results in schooling appears to lie outside the upper class, often in some fault of the poor—such as their class culture—which is viewed as lying beyond the reach of political action or criticism. Likewise, as long as the local financing of schools is maintained, the achievement of equality of resources among children of different social classes requires the class integration of school districts, an objective for which there are no effective political instruments as long as we allow a market in residential properties and an unequal distribution of income.

Thus it appears that the consequences of an unequal distribution of political power among classes complement the results of class culture in maintaining an educational system which has thus far been capable of transmitting status from generation to generation, and capable in addition of political survival in the formally democratic and egalitarian environment of the contemporary United States.

The role of the schools in reproducing and legitimizing the social division of labor has recently been challenged by popular egalitarian movements. At the same time, the educational system is showing signs of internal structural weakness.[49] These two developments suggest that fundamental change in the schooling process may soon be possible. Analysis of both the potential and the limits of educational change will be facilitated by drawing together and extending the strands of the above argument.

4. THE LIMITS OF EDUCATIONAL REFORM

If the above attempt to identify the roots of inequality in U.S. education is convincing, it has done more than reconcile apparent discrepancies between the democratic forms and unequal content of U.S. education. For it is precisely the sources of educational inequality which we must understand in order to develop successful political strategies in the pursuit of educational equality.

I have argued that the structure of education reflects the social relations of production. For at least the past century and a half, expansion of education and changes in the forms of schooling have been responses to needs generated by the economic system. The sources of present inequality in U.S. education were found in the mutual reinforcement of class subcultures and social class biases in the operations of the school system itself. The analysis strongly suggests that educational inequalities are rooted in the basic institutions of our economy. Reconsideration of some of the basic mechanisms of educational inequality lends support to this proposition. First, the principle of rewarding academic excellence in educational promotion and selection serves not only to legitimize the process by which the social division of labor is reproduced. It is also a basic part of the process which socializes young people to work for external rewards and encourages them to develop motivational structures fit for the alienating work of the capitalist economy.[50] Selecting students from the bottom or the middle of the achievement scale for promotion to higher levels of schooling would go a long way towards equalizing education, but it would also jeopardize the schools' capacity to train productive and well-adjusted work-

ers.[51] Second, the way in which local financing of schools operates to maintain educational inequality is also rooted in the capitalist economy, in this case in the existence of an unequal distribution of income, free markets in residential property, and the narrow limits of state power. However, it seems unwise to emphasize this aspect of the long run problem of equality in education, for the inequalities in school resources resulting from the localization of finance may not be of crucial importance in maintaining inequalities in the effects of education. Moreover, it seems that a significant undermining of the principle of local finance may already be under way in response to pressures from the poorer states and school districts.

Of greater importance in the perpetuation of educational inequality are differential class subcultures. These class-based differences in personality, values, and expectations, I have argued, represent an adaptation to the different requirements of adequate work performance at various levels in the hierarchical social relations of production. Class subcultures, then, stem from the everyday experiences of workers in the structure of production characteristic of capitalist societies.

It should be clear by this point that educational equality cannot be achieved through changes in the school system alone. Nonetheless, attempts at educational reform may move us closer to that objective if, in their failure, they lay bare the unequal nature of our school system and destroy the illusion of unimpeded mobility through education. Successful educational reforms—reducing racial or class disparities in schooling, for example—may also serve the cause of equality of education, for it seems likely that equalizing access to schooling will challenge the system either to make good its promise of rewarding educational attainment or find ways of coping with a mass disillusionment with the great panacea.[52]

Yet if the record of the last century and a half of educational reforms is any guide, we

should not expect radical change in education to result from the efforts of those con-
fining their attention to the schools. The
political victories of past reform movements
have apparently resulted in little if any effective equalization. My interpretation of the
educational consequences of class culture
and class power suggests that these educational reform movements failed because they
sought to eliminate educational inequalities
without challenging the basic institutions of
capitalism.

Efforts to equalize education through
changes in government policy will at best
scratch the surface of inequality. For much
of the inequality in U.S. education has its
origin outside the limited sphere of state
power, in the hierarchy of work relations
and the associated differences in class culture. As long as jobs are defined so that
some have power over many and others have
power over nothing—as long as the social
division of labor persists—educational inequality will be built into U.S. society.

NOTES

1. This account draws upon two important his-
torical studies: P. Aries, *Centuries of Childhood*
(New York, 1970); and B. Bailyn, *Education in the
Forming of American Society* (New York, 1960).
Also illuminating are anthropological studies of
education in contemporary pre-capitalist societies.
See, for example, J. Kenyatta, *Facing Mount
Kenya* (New York, 1962), pp. 95–124. See also
Edmund S. Morgan, *The Puritan Family: Religion
and Domestic Relations in Seventeenth Century
New England* (New York, 1944).
2. P. Aries, *Centuries of Childhood*. In a number
of places, Scotland and Massachusetts, for example, schools stressed literacy so as to make the
Bible more widely accessible. (See C. Cipolla,
Literacy and Economic Development (Baltimore,
1969); and E. Morgan, *The Puritan Family* (ch. 4).)
Morgan quotes a Massachusetts law of 1647 which
provided for the establishment of reading schools
because it was "one chief project of that old de-
luder, Satan, to keep men from knowledge of the
Scriptures."
3. H. F. Kearney, *Scholars and Gentlemen: Universities and Society in Pre-Industrial Britain*
(Ithaca, N.Y., 1971).
4. See B. Bailyn, *Education in the Forming of
American Society*, and N. Smelser, *Social Change
in the Industrial Revolution* (Chicago, 1959).
5. F. Engels and K. Marx, *The Communist Manifesto* (1848); K. Marx, *The 18th Brumaire of Louis
Bonaparte* (New York, 1852).
6. See, for example, S. Thernstrom, *Poverty and
Progress: Social Mobility in a 19th Century City*
(New York, 1969).
7. B. Simon, *Studies in the History of Education,
1780–1870*, Vol. I. (London, 1960).
8. Bailyn, *Education in the Forming of American
Society*.
9. A manufacturer, writing to the Massachusetts
State Board of Education from Lowell in 1841
commented:

> I have never considered mere knowledge . . . as
> the only advantage derived from a good Com-
> mon School education . . . (Workers with more
> education possess) a higher and better state of
> morals, are more orderly and respectful in their
> deportment, and more ready to comply with
> the wholesome and necessary regulations of an
> establishment . . . In times of agitation, on
> account of some change in regulations or
> wages, I have always looked to the most intelli-
> gent, best educated and the most moral for
> support. The ignorant and uneducated I have
> generally found the most turbulent and trouble-
> some, acting under the impulse of excited pas-
> sion and jealousy.

Quoted in Michael B. Katz, *The Irony of Early
School Reform* (Cambridge, Mass., 1968), p. 88.
See also David Isaac Bruck, *The Schools of Lowell,
1824–1861: A Case Study in the Origins of
Modern Public Education in America* (unpublished
senior thesis, Department of Social Studies, Harvard College, April 1971).
10. In 1846 the annual report of the Lowell,
Mass., School Committee concluded that universal
education was "the surest safety against internal
commotions." (*1846 School Committee Annual
Report*, pp. 17–18.) It seems more than coincidental that in England, public support for elementary education—a concept which had been
widely discussed and urged for at least half a century—was legislated almost immediately after the
enfranchisement of the working class by the electoral reform of 1867. See Simon, *Studies in the
History of Education, 1780–1870*. Mass public
education in Rhode Island came quickly on the
heels of an armed insurrection and a broadening of
the franchise. See F. T. Carlton, *Economic Influences upon Educational Progress in the United
States, 1820–1850* (Madison, Wisc., 1908).
11. Describing the expansion of education in the
19th century, Katz concludes:

> . . . a middle class attempt to secure advantage
> for their children as technological change
> heightened the importance of formal education
> assured the success and acceptance of universal
> elaborate graded school systems. The same re-
> sult emerged from the fear of a growing, un-
> schooled proletariat. Education substituted for
> deference as a source of social cement and
> social order in a society stratified by class
> rather than by rank.

(M. B. Katz, "From Voluntarism to Bureaucracy in
U.S. Education," mimeo, 1970.)

12. An American economist, writing just prior to the "common school revival," had this to say:

Education universally extended throughout the community will tend to disabuse the working class of people in respect of a notion that has crept into the minds of our mechanics and is gradually prevailing, that manual labor is at present very inadequately rewarded, owing to combinations of the rich against the poor; that mere mental labor is comparatively worthless; that property or wealth ought not to be accumulated or transmitted; that to take interest on money lent or profit on capital employed is unjust . . . The mistaken and ignorant people who entertain these fallacies as truths will learn, when they have the opportunity of learning, that the institution of political society originated in the protection of property.

(Thomas Cooper, *Elements of Political Economy* (1828), quoted on pp. 33–34 of Carlton, *Economic Influences upon Educational Progress in the United States, 1820–1850.*)

Political economy was made a required subject in Massachusetts high schools in 1857, along with moral science and civic polity. Cooper's advice was widely but not universally followed elsewhere. Friedrich Engels, commenting on the tardy growth of mass education in early 19th century England, remarked: "So shortsighted, so stupidly narrow-minded is the English bourgeoisie in its egotism, that it does not even take the trouble to impress upon the workers the morality of the day, which the bourgeoisie has patched together in its own interest for its own protection." (Engels, *The Condition of the Working Class in England* (Stanford, Calif., 1968).)

13. See Thernstrom, *Poverty and Progress.* Marx said this about mid-19th century France:

The modern and the traditional consciousness of the French peasant contended for mastery . . . in the form of an incessant struggle between the schoolmasters and the priests.

(Marx, *The 18th Brumaire of Louis Bonaparte,* p. 125.)

14. Janice Weiss and I are currently studying the rapid expansion of Southern elementary and secondary schooling which followed the demise of slavery and the establishment of capitalist economic institutions in the South.

15. Based on the preliminary results of a statistical analysis of education in 19th century Massachusetts being conducted jointly with Alexander Field.

16. Katz, *The Irony of Early School Reform* and "From Voluntarism to Bureaucracy in U.S. Education."

17. Katz, *The Irony of Early School Reform.*

18. Sol Cohen describes this process in his "The Industrial Education Movement, 1906–1917" (*American Quarterly,* Vol. 20, Spring 1968). Typical of the arguments then given for vocational education is the following, by the superintendent of schools in Cleveland:

It is obvious that the educational needs of children in a district where the streets are well paved and clean, where the homes are spacious and surrounded by lawns and trees, where the language of the child's playfellows is pure, and where life in general is permeated with the spirit and ideals of America—it is obvious that the educational needs of such a child are radically different from those of the child who lives in a foreign and tenement section.

(William H. Elson and Frank P. Bachman, "Different Course for Elementary School," *Educational Review,* XXXIX, April 1910; quoted in Cohen.)

See also L. Cremin, *The Transformation of the School* (New York, 1964), ch. 2, and David Cohen and Marvin Lazerson, "Education and the Industrial Order" (mimeo, 1970).

19. The superintendent of the Boston schools summed up the change in 1908:

Until very recently (the schools) have offered equal opportunity for all to receive *one kind* of education, but what will make them democratic is to provide opportunity for all to receive such education as will fit them *equally well* for their particular life work.

(Boston, *Documents of the School Committee,* 1908, #7, p. 53; quoted in Cohen and Lazerson, "Education and the Industrial Order.")

20. R. Callahan, *Education and the Cult of Efficiency* (Chicago, 1962); Cohen and Lazerson, "Education and the Industrial Order"; and Cremin, *The Transformation of the School.*

21. See M. Reich, "The Evolution of the U.S. Labor Force," in R. Edwards, M. Reich, and T. Weisskopf (eds.), *The Capitalist System* (Englewood Cliffs, N.J., 1971, forthcoming).

22. The role of schooling in legitimizing the class structure is spelled out in S. Bowles, "Contradictions in U.S. Higher Education" (mimeo, 1971).

23. The data for this calculation refer to white males who were aged 25–34 in 1962. See S. Bowles, "Schooling and Inequality from Generation to Generation," paper presented at the Far Eastern Meetings of the Econometric Society, Tokyo, 1970.

24. Table 1 understates the degree of social class inequality in school attendance in view of the fact that a substantial portion of the upper income children not enrolled in public schools attend private schools. Private schools provide a parallel educational system for the upper class. I have not given much attention to these institutions as they are not quantitatively very significant in the total picture. Moreover, to deal extensively with them might detract attention from the task of explaining class inequalities in the ostensibly egalitarian portion of our school system.

25. For recent evidence on these points, see U.S. Bureau of the Census, *Current Population Reports,* Series P-20, numbers 185 and 183.

26. W. L. Hansen and B. Weisbrod, "The Distribution of Costs and Direct Benefits of Public Higher Education: the Case of California," *Journal of Human Resources,* Vol. V, No. 3 (Summer 1970), pp. 361–370.

27. In the school year 1969–70, per pupil expenditures of federal, state, and local funds were

$1490 per colleges and universities and $747 for primary and secondary schools. (U.S. Office of Education, *Digest of Educational Statistics, 1969* (Washington: U.S. Government Printing Office, 1969).)

28. See also P. C. Sexton, *Education and Income* (New York, 1961).

29. See J. Binstock, *Survival in the American College Industry* (unpublished manuscript).

30. E. Z. Friedenberg, *Coming of Age in America* (New York, 1965). It is consistent with this pattern that the play-oriented, child-centered pedagogy of the progressive movement found little acceptance outside of private schools in wealthy communities. See Cohen and Lazerson, "Education and the Industrial Order."

31. That working class parents seem to favor more authoritarian educational methods is perhaps a reflection of their own work experiences which have demonstrated that submission to authority is an essential ingredient in one's ability to get and hold a steady, well-paying job.

32. See, for example, A. B. Hollingshead, *Elmtown's Youth* (New York, 1949); W. L. Warner and P. S. Lunt, *The Social Life of a Modern Community* (New Haven, 1949); R. Rosenthal and L. Jacobson, *Pygmalion in the Classroom* (New York, 1968); and W. E. Schafer, C. Olexa, and K. Polk, "Programmed for Social Class: Tracking in High School," *Trans-Action,* Vol. 7, No. 12 (October, 1970).

33. Calculation based on data in James S. Coleman, *et al., Equality of Educational Opportunity,* Vol. II (Washington, 1966), and methods described in S. Bowles, "Schooling and Inequality from Generation to Generation."

34. See P. M. Blau and O. D. Duncan, *The American Occupational Structure* (New York, 1967). More recent data do not contradict the evidence of no trend towards equality. A 1967 Census survey, the most recent available, shows that among high school graduates in 1965, the probability of college attendance for those whose parents had attended college has continued to rise relative to the probability of college attendance for those whose parents had attended less than eight years of school. See U.S. Bureau of the Census, *Current Population Reports,* Series P-20, No. 185, July 11, 1969.

35. A simple statistical model will elucidate the main relationships involved:

Let y (individual or family income) be the sum of w (earnings from labor, including embodied education and skills, L) and k (earnings from capital, K), related according to the equation $y = w + k = aK^A L^B$. The coefficients A and B represent the relative importance of capital and labor as sources of income. The variance of the logarithm of income (a common measure of inequality) can then be represented by the following expression:

var log $y = A^2$ var log $K + B^2$ var log L
$$+ 2AB \text{ covar } (\log L, \log K).$$

The first term on the right represents the contribution of inequalities in capital ownership to total inequality, the second measures that part of total income inequality due to inequalities of education

and skills embodied in labor, and the third represents the contribution to income inequality of social class inequalities in the supply of skills and schooling. Prior to the educational differentiation of the labor force, the variance of labor was zero. All workers were effectively equal. The variance of the logarithm of income would then be due entirely to capital inequality and would be exactly equal to A^2var log K. The rise of education as a source of income and labor differentiation will increase the variance of the logarithm of embodied labor unless all workers receive identical education and training. This is true even if the third term is zero, indicating no social class inequalities in the provision of skills and education.

To assert the conventional faith in the egalitarian influence of the rising economic importance of education, one would have to argue that the rise of education is likely to be associated with either a) a fall in A, the relative importance of capital as a source of earnings; b) a decrease in the size of the covariance of the logarithms of capital and labor; c) a decrease in the inequality of capital ownership; or d) an increase in equality in the supply of education. While each is possible, I see no compelling reason why education should *produce* these results.

36. See, for example, Robert Hauser, "Educational Stratification in the United States," *Sociological Inquiry,* Vol. 20, Spring, 1970.

37. Max Weber referred to bureaucracy as the "most rational offspring" of discipline, and remarked: ". . . military discipline is the ideal model for the modern capitalist factory . . ." ("The Meaning of Discipline," reprinted in H. H. Gerth and C. W. Mills, *From Max Weber: Essays in Sociology* (New York, 1958, p. 261).

38. For a survey of the literature see J. P. Robinson, R. Athanasiou, and K. Head, "Measures of Occupational Attitudes and Occupational Characteristics" (Survey Research Center, University of Michigan, February 1969).

39. See, for example, Benjamin Bloom, *Stability and Change in Human Characteristics* (New York, 1964).

40. Note, for example, the class differences in child-rearing with respect to the importance of obedience. See M. Kohn, "Social Class and Parental Values," in R. Coser (ed.), *The Family* (New York, 1964); and L. Dolger and J. Ginandes, "Children's Attitudes towards Discipline as Related to Socioeconomic Status," *Journal of Experimental Education,* Vol. 15 (1946), pp. 161–165. See also the study of differences in child-rearing practices in families headed by bureaucrats as opposed to entrepreneurs by D. Miller and G. Swanson, *The Changing American Parent* (New York, 1958). Also, E. E. Maccoby, P. K. Gibbs, *et al.,* "Methods of Child-Rearing in Two Social Classes," in W. E. Martin and C. B. Stendler (eds.), *Readings in Child Development* (New York, 1954). While the existence of class differences in child-rearing is supported by most of the available data (but see H. Lewis, "Child-Rearing Among Low-Income Families," in Ferman *et al.* (eds.), *Poverty in America* (New York, 1961)), the stability of these differences over time has been questioned by U. Bron-

fenbrenner ("Socialization and Social Class through Time and Space," in Kallenbach and Hodges (eds.), *Education and Society* (Columbus, 1963)).

41. See M. Winterbottom, "The Sources of Achievement Motivation in Mothers' Attitudes toward Independence Training," in D. C. McClelland *et al.*, *The Achievement Motive* (New York, 1953); and M. Kohn, "Social Class and Parent-Child Relationships: An Interpretation," *American Journal of Sociology*, 68, 1963, pp. 471–480.

42. See, for example, S. M. Lipset and R. Bendix, *Social Mobility in Industrial Society* (Berkeley, 1959); and T. Iwand and J. Stoyle, "Social Rigidity: Income and Occupational Choice in Rural Pennsylvania," *Economic and Business Bulletin*, Vol. 22 (Spring-Summer 1970), pp. 24–30.

43. S. Bowles, "Toward an Educational Production Function," in W. L. Hansen (ed.), *Education, Income, and Human Capital* (New York, 1970).

44. This view is elaborated in H. Gintis, "Education, Technology, and Worker Productivity," *American Economic Association Proceedings*, May 1971, pp. 266–279. For other studies stressing the non-cognitive dimensions of the schooling experience, see T. Parsons, "The School Class as a Social System: Some of its Functions in American Society," *Harvard Educational Review*, Vol. 29, No. 4 (Fall 1959), pp. 297–318; and R. Dreeben, *On What is Learned in School* (Reading, Mass., 1968).

45. Those who would defend the "reward excellence" principle on the grounds of efficient selection to ensure the most efficient use of educational resources might ask themselves this: why should colleges admit those with the highest college entrance examination board scores? Why not the lowest, or the middle? According to conventional standards of efficiency, the rational social objective of the college is to render the greatest *increment* in individual capacities ("value added," to the economist), not to produce the most illustrious graduat-

ing class ("gross output"). Yet if incremental gain is the objective, it is far from obvious that choosing from the top is the best policy.

46. Some dimensions of this problem are discussed in S. Weiss, "Existing Disparities in Public School Finance and Proposals for Reform" (research report to the Federal Reserve Bank of Boston, No. 46, February 1970).

47. Recall that Owen, whose data appear in Table 3, found that the relationship of various measures of teacher quality to the family income level of the area served by the schools was considerably higher between cities than within cities.

48. In 1969, federal funds constituted only 7 percent of the total financing of public elementary and secondary schooling. Moreover, current distribution formulae governing state and federal expenditures are only mildly egalitarian in their impact. See K. A. Simon and W. V. Grant, *Digest of Educational Statistics, 1969* (Washington: U.S. Dept. of Health, Education and Welfare, 1969).

49. See S. Bowles, "Contradictions in U.S. Higher Education" (mimeo, 1971).

50. Gintis, "Education, Technology, and Worker Productivity."

51. Consider what would happen to the internal discipline of schools if the students' objective were to end up at the bottom of the grade distribution!

52. The failure of the educational programs of the "war on poverty" to raise significantly the incomes of the poor is documented in T. I. Ribich, *Education and Poverty* (Washington, 1969). In the case of blacks, dramatic increases in the level of schooling relative to whites have scarcely affected the incomes of blacks relative to whites. (R. Weiss, "The effects of Education on the Earnings of Blacks and Whites," *Review of Economics and Statistics*, May 1970.) It is no wonder that Booker T. Washington's plea that blacks should educate themselves before demanding equality has lost most of its once widespread support.

6. A Typology for the Classification of Educational Systems

EARL I. HOPPER

Many sociologists agree that the most useful typology for the classification of educational systems is the one developed implicitly by Ralph H. Turner in "Contest and Sponsored Mobility and the School System."[1,2] A brief summary of his typology may be useful. Turner assumes that educational systems in industrial societies are the main "modes of upward social mobility," and he argues that the distinguishing characteristics of these modes are based on folk-norms which are pervasive throughout a given host society or type of host society. He distinguishes between a mode of "sponsorship mobility" based on "sponsorship folk-norms" and a mode of "contest mobility" based on "contest folk-norms." The former is defined as one in which

From *Sociology* 2 (1968):29–46. Reprinted by permission.

. . . elite recruits are chosen by the established elite or their agents, and elite status is given on the basis of some criterion of supposed merit and cannot be *taken* by any amount of effort or strategy. Upward mobility is like entry into a private club, where each candidate must be sponsored by one or more members. Ultimately, the members grant or deny upward mobility on the basis of whether they judge the candidate to have the qualities they wish to see in fellow members.

The latter, "contest mobility," is defined as

. . . a system in which elite status is the prize in an open contest by some rules of fair play, the contestants having wide latitude in the strategies they may employ. Since the "prize" of successful upward mobility is not in the hands of the established elite to give out, the latter are not in a position to determine who shall attain it and who shall not.

Since the folk-norms of mobility are said to ". . . shape the (educational system) directly through (their) effects on the values that implement social control . . ." of selection, a system based on a mode of sponsorship mobility is called a "sponsorship system" of education, and one based on a mode of contest mobility, a "contest system" of education.

Turner was primarily concerned with distinguishing between the educational systems of England and the United States, the former approximating to a sponsorship system and the latter to a contest system. But from his analysis an inference may erroneously be made that educational systems are likely to cluster around either the English or American pattern. Although some educational systems can be distinguished in this way, a large number of them cannot meaningfully be classified in terms of a "sponsorship-contest" dichotomy. For example, it does not allow one to distinguish between the systems of the U.S.S.R. and Sweden, France and England, Australia and the U.S.A. or Canada, Sweden and France, India and the U.S.A., etc. Although the dichot-

omy is sensitive to many of the ways in which the American and English educational systems differ, it also tends to over emphasize these differences, at least in comparison with other societies. However, by separating analytically the various dimensions which underlie this dichotomy it is possible to construct an expanded version of Turner's typology, and in this way to take account of the "deviant" systems. It is also possible to show that just as England and the United States represent only two special cases of a larger variety of societal types, so their educational systems represent only two special cases in an expanded typology.

THE EXPANDED TYPOLOGY

As societies industrialize they develop specialized and differentiated systems of education. Such systems have three primary manifest functions: the *selection* of children with different types and levels of ability; the provision of the appropriate type of *instruction* for the various categories of children created by the selection process; and the eventual *allocation* of trained personnel either directly to occupational roles or to agencies which specialize in occupational recruitment. Because the last two functions are closely linked to the first, the structure of educational systems, especially those within industrial societies, can be understood primarily in terms of the structure of their selection process.

Four questions may be asked about the selection process: *How* does educational selection occur? *When* are pupils initially selected? *Who* should be selected? and *Why* should they be selected? Four structural properties of an educational system are reflected in the answers to these questions. To a large extent, at least in the short run, these properties are independent with respect to one another. Consequently, with respect to these properties, one may conceptualize four dimensions along which educational systems may vary. A given educational system may be located at some point on each dimension.

It may also be classified according to its simultaneous positions on all four dimensions.

(i) The First Dimension: How Does Educational Selection Occur?

Two aspects of the answer to this question may be singled out for special attention: the degree to which an educational system has a centrally administered selection procedure; and the degree to which the provision of education, especially up to the point of initial selection, is standardized for the population as a whole. Although these two aspects of the total selection process are closely related, some systems have a centrally administered selection procedure and an unstandardized educational programme, and vice versa. Given centralized administration, however, standardization of the educational programme is likely to occur. It is reasonable, therefore, to think of two polar types: one in which the total selection process is centrally administered and standardized; and the other—its opposite—in which the total selection process is decentralized and unstandardized.

The position of an educational system on the continuum ranging between these two polar types is an indication of the degree to which the system in question is characterized by a combination of the following more specific properties: a specialized department within a national civil service or its equivalent which is concerned exclusively with problems of education; the inclusion of the entire population, or in the case of fairly rapid social change an entire cohort, within a nationally organized educational programme; and the absence of regional and local variations in the application of this programme, i.e., with respect to educational facilities, quality of instruction, stringency of selection procedures, and proportional opportunities for further training despite variations in population density and/or demand for further training. Again, each of these specific properties is closely inter-

related. But it should be stressed that a given system at a given time may be more centralized and standardized in some respects than in others.

Educational systems also vary with respect to the content of their "ideologies of implementation" concerning how selection *should* occur.[3] In this connection, at least two types of ideologies of implementation can be distinguished: a "sponsorship" ideology and a "contest" ideology. A sponsorship ideology specifies: that selection via sponsorship is necessary in order for the "best" people to be selected; that the sponsors are qualified "by right" for the task; and that they will exercise good judgement in making selections. A contest ideology specifies: that selection should not be determined through a centrally administered procedure but through the "natural laws" of a "free market," e.g., "survival of the fittest" and "supply and demand"; and that the only task of central administration is to keep the market "free."

Societies with a centralized and standardized selection process tend to have sponsorship ideologies, e.g., the U.S.S.R., and those with a decentralized and unstandardized selection process tend to have contest ideologies, e.g., the U.S.A.[4] At a given period of time, however, contest ideologies are found in societies with a relatively centralized and standardized selection process, as well as in those with a relatively decentralized and unstandardized process; similarly, sponsorship ideologies are found in societies of both types.[5] Although the evidence suggests that systems characterized by incongruence between their ideology and their patterns of organization are not rare, they tend to occur primarily during times of rapid social change. And when a "reasonably" long-term time perspective is taken, such systems can be seen to develop a congruent association between their ideologies and their patterns of organization.[6]

When the likely association between the ideology concerning how selection should occur and the organizational pattern of how it does occur is taken into account, the two polar types of systems, as outlined above, may be likened (for purposes of illustration) to different types of games. A system with a centralized and standardized selection process reinforced by a sponsorship ideology is similar to a "Talent Show" in which participants display their talent to a panel of judges who are assumed to have good judgement. A system with a decentralized and unstandardized selection process reinforced by a contest ideology is similar to a "Military Initiative Test" in which soldiers are expected to traverse a certain distance within a limited period of time by using only those means which they can acquire after the test begins. Both types of systems are designed to select winners and both demand that the contestants be motivated to win. But in the former the winners are likely to be selected formally, and *relatively* less importance is likely to be attached to their motivation; in the latter, a process analogous to natural selection is likely to occur, and a premium is likely to be attached to their motivation.

In sum, with respect to this first dimension, an approximate and tentative classification of a few educational systems is set out in the following table[7]:

Educational systems which are similar in the degree to which their total selection processes are centralized and standardized may, however, be different in other ways. Therefore, a second classificatory dimension must be introduced.

(ii) The Second Dimension: When Are Pupils Initially Selected?

Two aspects of the answer to this question may also be singled out for special attention: the degree to which an educational system is formally differentiated into specialized routes through which children are selected, trained, and guided to their future occupational roles; and the degree to which initial selection occurs early in the educational career.[8] Since people entering different types of occupations require, in part, different types of skills, and since educational systems are expected to play an important role in the development of such skills, almost all educational systems are likely to be characterized by some degree of internal differentiation and specialization, at least in those phases immediately prior to entry into the labour market. The crucial distinction is how long before the completion of education have children been formally segregated into specialized routes. In other words, only one variable need be considered: the degree to which an educational system is characterized by early formal differentiation and specialization of routes. And it is again reasonable to think of two polar types: one characterized by a high degree of early formal differentiation and specialization; and the other—its opposite—by a low degree.

The higher the degree of early formal differentiation and specialization, the greater the probability that a "suitable" person will be rejected because the selection procedures

Table 1

Dimension of the system	Degree	Classification*
	High	France Sweden U.S.S.R.
Centralization and Standardization of the Total Selection Process	Medium	W. Germany Australia England
	Low	U.S.A. Canada

*Intra-cell classifications may not be ranked.

which have been used are too "stringent"; the lower the degree, the greater the probability that an "unsuitable" person will be accepted because the selection procedures which have been used are too "lenient." Since the probability of the former type of error is inversely related to the probability of the latter type of error, no system can be structured in order to minimize both—at least not in the short run, and not with the conventional methods of teaching and classroom organization.[9] Of course this statement is based on two sets of related assumptions: that "suitability" is not fixed at birth and is subject to the constraints of experience; and that even if "suitability" were fixed at birth, the screening devices used at the initial selection would be imperfect, and the earlier they are used, the greater their imperfection.

Industrial societies and even those attempting to industrialize are quite similar with respect to the official versions of a second component of their ideologies of educational implementation, i.e., that concerning when initial selection *should* occur. In general, the official version is that within the confines of available economic and other resources, all people should have as much education as is possible.[10] Ordinarily, therefore, it is to be expected that the greater a society's available resources, the more it is likely that a society will have an educational system designed to minimize the probability of rejecting a "suitable" person, i.e., one characterized by a low degree of early formal differentiation and specialization of routes.[11] However, the evidence suggests three sets of exceptions to this general expectation: societies with approximately equal Gross National Products or, more importantly, *per capita* incomes vary with respect to the percentage of their available resources which they spend on education; even if the problem of investment priorities in government expenditure is disregarded, those societies which spend an approximately equal percentage of their resources on education vary in their degree of formal differentiation and specialization; and the degree to which societies have either increased or decreased the amount of differentiation and specialization in their educational systems is not strongly related to changes in either their *per capita* incomes or their expenditures on education.[12] It follows that variation in the organization of recruitment processes cannot be explained only or primarily in terms of available economic resources, and that many societies are characterized by incongruence between the official versions of their ideologies concerning when selection should occur and the actual organization of their recruitment processes. These cases are too numerous and have persisted for too long a time to be attributed to the effects of rapid social change. At least one additional variable must be considered.[13]

Although industrial societies are similar with respect to the official versions of their ideologies concerning when initial selection should occur, they vary with respect to the less official and more informal versions. With respect to the latter, it is possible to distinguish at least two further types of ideologies of implementation: an "elitist" ideology and an "egalitarian" ideology. An elitist ideology specifies, for example: that the maximum amount of education for each citizen should depend on his future ability to contribute to economic productivity; that "intelligence" and "educability" are determined primarily by hereditary factors such that some people could not possibly benefit from education above a given minimum; and that those who appear to be bound for elite positions should be separated at an early age from those who appear to be bound for lower positions so that the former gain in their confidence to lead and the latter in their willingness to follow. This ideology supports the view that initial selection should occur as early as possible, and that a relatively large number of routes should exist. An egalitarian ideology specifies, for example: that the maximum amount of education is the right of every citizen regardless of his future ability to contribute to economic productivity; that "intelligence" and "educability" are determined primarily by environmental factors such that with proper instruction all people could benefit from a maximum of education; and that those who appear to be bound for elite positions should work and play as long as possible with those who appear to be bound for lower positions so that the former will not lose touch with the "common man" and the latter will not become overly subordinate and lacking in initiative. This ideology supports the view that selection should occur as late as possible, and that a relatively small number of routes should exist.

Egalitarian ideologies are found in societies with relatively high *per capita* incomes, e.g., Sweden and the U.S.A., and in societies with relatively low ones, e.g., the U.S.S.R. prior to its more recent periods of rapid economic growth; similarly, elitist ideologies are found in societies of both types, e.g., England, France, Brazil, and Italy.[14] Because the content of such ideologies is buttressed by cultural folk norms, it changes very slowly, and industrialization processes do not have an overriding effect.[15] Although it is difficult to assign weights to each factor, it follows that the degree to which an educational system is characterized by early formal differentiation and specialization of routes is a function of both available resources and a less official but more pervasive version of its ideology concerning when educational selection should occur. Consequently, at least with respect to this aspect of the recruitment process, close congruence between the ideology of an educational system and its actual pattern of organization is not to be expected.

In sum, with respect to this dimension, an approximate and tentative classification of a few educational systems is set out in the following table:

Again, educational systems which are similar in the degree to which they are characterized by early formal differentiation and specialization of routes may be different, not only in the degree to which their total

Table 2[16]

Dimension of the system	Degree	Classification*
Early Formal Differentiation and Specialization of Educational Routes	High	France W. Germany England
	Medium	U.S.S.R.[17] Australia
	Low	U.S.A. Canada Sweden

*Intra-cell classifications are not ranked.

selection processes are administratively centralized and standardized, but in other important respects as well. Therefore, additional classificatory dimensions must be introduced.

(iii) The Third and Fourth Dimensions: Who Should be Selected? and Why Should They be Selected?

Stratified societies face, among others, the following three interrelated systemic problems: people in all positions in the various hierarchies of power must strive to justify their positions both to themselves and to others; in order to "rule" effectively and efficiently, the elite must strive to maintain at least a minimal semblance of allegiance and cooperation from less powerful groups; and, in order to prevent a successful challenge to their power, the elite must be flexible enough to assimilate potentially able leaders from subordinate and competing groups. Hence, competition over the distribution of power is inherent in stratified societies, and tension and conflict are inherent in competition for power. Neither the dilemmas themselves nor the resulting tension and conflict are ever handled by a society with complete success.

One way in which most stratified societies have attempted to cope with such dilemmas is to develop fairly explicit ideologies which define the types of people whom the society values most highly and which justify why more power is given to them than to others. These may be called "ideologies of legitimization." Since educational systems in stratified industrial societies are mechanisms of selection and allocation, such societies are likely to have explicit ideologies of legitimization concerning educational selection. These ideologies translate questions concerning the distribution of power into questions concerning the distribution of educational suitability. They define who should be selected for higher training and explain why some people should be rejected when others are selected.[18]

One way in which educational systems may be classified, therefore, is according to their ideologies of legitimization concerning educational selection. Two properties of these ideologies warrant special attention. In answer to the question "Who should be selected?" one can conceptualize a continuum ranging between two polar properties: the first representing a quality of complete *universalism;* and the second—its opposite—representing a quality of complete *particularism.* In answer to the question "Why should they be selected?" one can also conceptualize a continuum ranging between two polar types: the first representing a quality of complete *collectivism;* and the second—its opposite—representing a quality of complete *individualism.* Educational systems may be classified on each continuum.

The two continua can be combined, however, to produce four ideal types of ideologies of legitimization concerning educational selection: "aristocratic," "paternalistic," "meritocratic," and "communistic." Each ideal type may be defined as follows:

I. Particularistic

To the extent that pupils should be selected primarily on the basis of their diffuse skills and only secondarily on the basis of their technical skills, such that those with the most of the former need have least of the latter, the ideology has a "particularistic" quality. This assumes that the society has a system of ascribed statuses on the basis of which certain diffuse skills and ascribed characteristics are likely to become unequally distributed. It also assumes that the opportunity for learning such skills is strictly limited to particular groups and that substitutes for ascribed characteristics are unacceptable.[19]

(a) Aristocratic Ideology: An Individualistic Form of Particularism When particularistic selections are justified to the population in terms of the right of those selected to privilege on the basis of their diffuse skills and ascribed characteristics one may refer to the "aristocratic" quality of the ideology.

(b) Paternalistic Ideology: A Collectivistic Form of Particularism When particularistic selections are justified to the population in terms of the society's "need" for people with diffuse skills and certain ascribed characteristics in order that the society may be led by the most "suitable" people, one may refer to the "paternalistic" quality of the ideology.

2. Universalistic

To the extent that pupils should be selected primarily on the basis of their technical skills and only secondarily on the basis of their diffuse skills, such that those with the most of the former need have least of the latter, the ideology has a "universalistic" quality.[20] This assumes that the society does not have a system of ascribed statuses on the basis of which certain diffuse skills and ascribed characteristics are likely to become unequally distributed. It also assumes that maximum opportunity is available for such skills to be learned.[21]

(c) Meritocratic Ideology: An Individualistic Form of Universalism[22] When univer-

salistic selections are justified to the population in terms of the right of the selected to privilege as a reward for their talents, ambition, and technical skills, one may refer to the "meritocratic" quality of the ideology.

(d) Communistic Ideology: A Collectivist Form of Universalism When universalistic selections are justified to the population in terms of the society's need for the most talented, ambitious, and technically qualified men to be guided to positions of leadership and responsibility, and for those less qualified in these respects to be guided to appropriately subordinate positions, one may refer to the "communistic" quality of the ideology.

Most industrial societies contain several groups of elites with competing ideologies of legitimization of educational selection. Consequently, in order to represent the ideology of a given society as accurately as possible, the following technique was used: first, a paradigm was constructed by considering simultaneously the dimensions of universalism-particularism and individualism-collectivism, thereby producing four cells, indicating each of the four ideal types of ideologies; second, this paradigm was taken to be a "grid" on which the ideology of a given society could be located by means of a "topographical profile"; and, third, the cell of the paradigm containing the largest area of a profile was used to represent the dominant ideology of a given society. On this basis, an approximate and tentative classification of a few educational systems is set out in Figure I.

The societies classified as similar with respect to their ideologies of legitimization of educational selection are clearly different in many important respects, even aside from those already conceptualized as classifying dimensions. But these differences will not be considered here.

(iv) Summary

It is not necessary to integrate the four dimensions in terms of a table or figure in

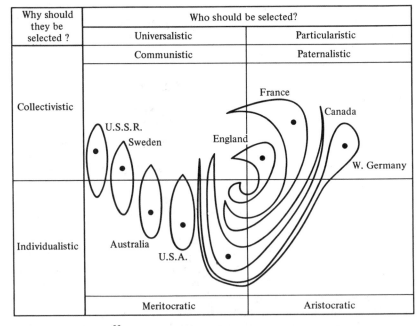

Figure 1[23] *Intra-cell classifications may not be ranked.

order to show that a general typology of educational systems can be constructed. By considering each of the dimensions simultaneously, it can be seen quite clearly that educational systems which are similar with respect to any one dimension may be different with respect to the other three; and those which are similar with respect to any two or even three dimensions may still be different with respect to the fourth. It should also be stressed that the educational system of the United States, what Turner called a "contest system," has been classified here as having a low degree of administrative centralization and standardization in its total selection process, a low degree of early formal differentiation and specialization of routes, and a "meritocratic" ideology of legitimization of selection; and the educational system of England, what Turner called a "sponsorship system," has been classified as having a medium degree of centralization and standardization, a high degree of differentiation and specialization, and primarily a "paternalistic" ideology. These two systems represent two special cases in the expanded typology outlined above.

A COMMENT ON THE EDUCATIONAL SYSTEM OF THE UNITED STATES

The evidence suggests that the actual pattern of educational selection in the United States is not congruent with its meritocratic ideology of legitimization of selection. Certain segments of the population are informally excluded from the "contest," or at least unable to participate on an equal basis. [24] Among the many factors responsible for their exclusion is that local, community-based components of the national educational system vary with respect to the quality of their educational programme, and in the degree to which they encourage students from all social backgrounds to attend university. It is likely that if a higher degree of administrative centralization and standardization were institutionalized in the United States, the educational system would become more effective and efficient in reaching the aims implied by its meritocratic ideology. [25]

Apparently it is difficult for many Americans to see this point. One reason for their difficulty may be that in the United States the ideological support for decentralization and grass roots control is based on folk-norms which define all centralized power as detrimental to freedom and universalistic practices. [26] In other words, the contest ideology in the United States (but not necessarily elsewhere) is associated with various cultural themes which are explicit in their disapproval of particularism in selection. And partly due to the constraints of a contest ideology in conjunction with these additional themes, Americans are led to emphasize only those aspects of their system which in fact do foster meritocratic selection patterns, e.g., "open-gate" colleges and universities, delayed career decisions, transfer to more advantageous routes as late as graduate school, etc., but to ignore those aspects which hinder such patterns, e.g., variations among locally based schools with respect to the quality of their educational programmes and the degree to which they encourage all students to aspire to higher education.

Of course this is not a static situation. One of the inherent contradictions of a contest ideology within an industrial society is that in order to maintain the desired "free market" for talent, a society is compelled to become more centralized in the administration of its total selection process. For example, it may have to accept the fact that in order to provide "equal educational opportunity for all" it must insure that the family environments of certain children do not retard their educability, or that those children whose educability has been retarded prior to their entering formal education will receive "positive discrimination." Since locally based administrations are unlikely to have the funds and the skills for such activities, the task tends to fall to the central agencies. In addition, the gradual emergence of a national elite in the United States favours the development of a sponsorship ideology of implementation. But some of the current patterns of conflict between local and national elites, and the current debates concerning Federal *vs.* State control suggest that these processes are neither rapid nor inevitable.[27]

SOME POSSIBLE APPLICATIONS OF THE EXPANDED TYPOLOGY

It may be possible to demonstrate that by classifying educational systems in the four dimensional typology one thereby acquires greater analytical power with respect to the understanding of how these systems work and of how they relate to their host societies. It is beyond the scope of this article to consider this task in detail. But several possible applications may be mentioned.

The comparative study of education has consisted, for the most part, of making detailed descriptions of educational systems in society after society. Although it is now clear that considerable variation exists in the structure of educational systems, even among societies at similar levels of industrial development, it is quite easy to become overwhelmed by this glut of "facts." This is especially so when a researcher begins to study a system for which there is abundant documentation. By highlighting some of the more important structural dimensions along which educational systems may vary, and, thereby, drawing attention to their more important similarities and differences, a typology for the classification of educational systems is a useful aid for the organization and interpretation of the wealth of available data.[28]

Secondly, it is often illuminating to analyse societies as though they were social systems, to conceptualize certain of their institutions as though they were sub-systems, and to treat these sub-systems as variables within the constructed social system. This enables a researcher to formulate propositions concerning relationships among the variables, e.g., the effects of variation in the structure of an economic sub-system on variation in the structure of an educational sub-system, with reference both to one society over time and to many societies at a given point in time or over time. This approach also draws attention to the fact that a society may not have a national educational system except in the most nominal sense, and that it may have several educational systems in a more concrete sense. To conceptualize educational institutions as a sub-system, however, demands that its defining dimensions be specified and, if at all possible, calibrated. Such a task is facilitated by thinking of educational systems in terms of their location in the above typology.[29]

Thirdly, the dimensions of the typology might be taken as guidelines for the study of the ways in which an educational system changes. Further, the dimensions can be treated as patterns towards which systems may be likely to converge as a result of industrialization processes. For example, a question which might be asked in this connection is "What is the relationship between the level and trajectory of industrial development and the degree of centralization and standardization of educational selection, or the content of ideologies of legitimization?"[30]

Fourthly, it would be of interest to study the effects of variations in the structure of educational systems on the structure of their educational routes. It would be helpful to know the pattern of interpersonal experiences and situations which are characteristic of each route within a given system, and how the structure of the system affects this pattern. For example, two questions which might be asked in this connection are as follows: "Are educational systems which share a given location in the typology similar with respect to the ways in which they cope with the problem of making ambition commensurate with assessed achievement potential?" and "How do educational systems use their formal routes to regulate the anticipatory socialization of different categories of students?"[31]

Finally, studies could be made of the effects of variation in the structure of educational systems and of the routes within any given system on a range of personality characteristics. For example, it is possible to reformulate for a wider variety of systems Turner's hypothesis that upward mobility through the English educational system has a lower propensity for creating anxiety among the upwardly mobile than does upward mobility through the American educational system.[32] A further question which might be asked in this connection is "What is the relationship between the educational route taken by parents and the level of ambition of their children, within various types of educational systems?"

In conclusion, a proviso must be entered. If more detailed knowledge indicates that the educational systems considered here have been classified incorrectly, then they should be reclassified. Indeed, classification as such is not the main point of this article. Rather, the typology has been presented as a heuristic device, and as a preliminary step to more narrowly focused research. If the typology fails to generate such research, then it should be altered or discarded.

NOTES

1. For their comments on earlier drafts of this article, I am indebted to: Eric G. Dunning (Department of Sociology, University of Leicester), John MacDonald (Department of Manpower, Canadian Government), R. L. Rowland (Peterhouse) and F. Birtek (St. Catherine's).

2. This article first appeared in *Amer. Sociol. R.*, 1960, 855–867; some of its themes were later developed in *The Social Context of Ambition*, San Francisco, Chandler Press, 1964. For an example of an overly simple typology, see Louis V. Bone, "Sociological Framework for a Comparative Study of Education Systems," *Education Review*, 1960, 121–126; for a lengthy list of imaginative questions and topics concerning education in any society, see Jules Henry, "Cross-cultural Outline of Education," *Current Anthropology*, 1960, 267–305.

3. This is only one component of an educational system's ideology of implementation. A second component will be considered in due course. Other researchers have preferred the term "method-ideology," e.g., see John W. Thompson, "Method Ideology and Educational Ideologies," *Educational Theory*, 1962, 110–117.

4. For evidence concerning these two examples, see the Unesco Series "The Development of Higher Education," especially *Access to Higher Education*, vol. II, 1965. See also I. N. Thut and Don Adams, *Educational Patterns in Contemporary Societies*, London, McGraw-Hill, 1964, especially the bibliographical references in the appropriate chapters.

5. Thut and Adams, *ibid.* They do not discuss this relationship explicitly, but they provide sufficient data to justify the inference. Further, and this is often overlooked by students of comparative education, contest ideologies are found in societies with a high degree of status rigidity in their stratification systems, e.g., possibly India, and in societies where stratification systems show a relatively low degree, e.g., the U.S.A.; similarly, sponsorship ideologies are found in societies of both types, e.g., France and the U.S.S.R. See W. D. Halls, *Society, Schools and Progress in France*, London, Pergamon Press, 1965, and Brian Holmes, *Problems in Education: A Comparative Approach*, London, Routledge and Kegan Paul, 1965.

6. This relationship reflects two constraints: the degree to which a society's total selection process is centralized and standardized, and the content of a society's ideology concerning how educational selection should occur are likely to be mutually reinforcing; and both properties are likely to be influenced in a mutually consistent way by industrialization processes, especially with respect to political and economic centralization. It is impossible to treat here the problems of why a system has a given degree of centralization and standardization and a given type of ideology. For a brief discussion of the effects of industrialization on each of these properties and on the association between them, see E. G. Dunning and E. I. Hopper, "Industrialization and the Problem of Convergence: A Critical Note," *Sociological Review*, 1966, 163–186.

7. It is impossible to provide here a complete bibliography of the material used to make these and later classifications. A cursory glance at any recent textbook in the comparative study of education will provide a useful starting point into the literature; especially useful in this connection is I. N. Thut and Don Adams, *Educational Patterns in Contemporary Societies, op. cit.* I have also found useful the bibliographical and statistical information on education provided by the London embassies of various countries. In addition, see Jean Floud and A. H. Halsey, "The Sociology of Education," *Current Sociology*, 7, 1958; Burton R. Clark, "The Sociology of Education," pp. 734–769, in R. E. L. Faris (ed.), *Handbook of Modern Sociology*, Chicago, Rand McNally and Co., 1964; A. H. Halsey, Jean Floud, and C. Arnold Anderson (eds.), *Education, Economy and Society*, New York, The Free Press of Glencoe, 1961; E. A. G. Robinson and J. E. Vaizey (eds.), *The Economics of Education*, London, Macmillan, 1966; and the Unesco Series, "The Development of Higher Education," 1965.

8. Educational routes are in fact likely to be ranked by prestige in terms of two criteria: the subsequent economic and prestige positions of those who use them; and the economic and prestige positions of the teachers and administrators associated with them. Because students are indeterminate with respect to stratification, it does not seem appropriate to speak of vertically ranked educational routes. Furthermore, since there is not a perfect association either between educational routes and subsequent adult statuses or between parental statuses and the child's educational route, it is misleading to think of educational routes as themselves being a vertical dimension of stratification. Of course some aspects of the routes may be considered in terms of their prestige connotations after a person takes his adult statuses, e.g., graduation from Cambridge rather than from London or Sheffield, and graduation from Harvard rather than from Missouri. For a slightly contrary view, see G. Elder, Jr., "Life Opportunities and Personality: Some Consequences of Stratified Secondary Education in Great Britain," *Sociology of Education*, 1965, 173–202.

9. It has often been suggested that, in part, so long as selection decisions are not completely determinate, this problem does not arise. However, in most societies where initial selection occurs formally at an early age, but where theoretically a person may switch at a later date from a less promising route to a more promising one, and vice versa, the evidence shows that although many initial selection errors are made, extremely few moves actually occur. This is one reason why the formality of differentiation and specialization of routes is so important, i.e., when the routes are informally structured, movement is more likely to occur. However, in the conceptualization of this dimension, there are insufficient data to determine the relative weight which should be given to "formality." For a discussion of some aspects of this problem with special reference to England, see J. W. B. Douglas, *The Home and the School*, London, MacGibbon and Kee, 1964.

10. For evidence to this effect see, for example, the Unesco Series, "The Development of Higher Education," 1965.

11. Many researchers have tried to explain the amount of differentiation and specialization of a given system in terms of the wealth of the host society. (For example, see Richard F. Tomasson, "From Elitism to Egalitarianism in Swedish education," *Sociology of Education*, 1965, 203–223.) Two sociologists have even drawn an analogy to the decision which a researcher must make in the selection of a probability level in order to test an hypothesis. In statistics, the rejection of a "true" hypothesis is called a Type I Error; and the acceptance of a "false" hypothesis, a Type II Error. The probability of making a Type I Error is inversely related to the probability of making a Type II Error. A researcher selects his probability level on the basis of the relative costs of making one type of error rather than the other. Similarly, an educational system may be classified in terms of the probability that it will make a Type I Error with respect to selection—rejecting a "suitable" person

by using overly "stringent" selection procedures—or that it will make a Type II Error with respect to selection—accepting an "unsuitable" person by using overly "lenient" selection procedures. The degree to which an educational system is characterized by early formal differentiation and specialization of routes reflects, in part, a society's decision on the relative costs of wasting "natural talent" and saving current resources as opposed to saving "natural talent" and wasting current resources. (See A. W. Cicourel and J. I. Kitsuse, *The Educational Decision Makers*, Indianapolis, Bobbs-Merrill, 1963.) Of course, in addition to the argument set out in the text of this article, it should be stressed that the evidence does not fully support their analogy. A low degree of early formal differentiation and specialization may be as effective and efficient in so far as those initially rejected are likely to be depreciated in value to the economy, and those initially selected may not be sufficiently appreciated to offset the loss.

12. John Vaizey, *The Economics of Education*, London, Faber and Faber, 1962; Vaizey and Robinson, *op. cit.;* and the Committee on Higher Education, *Higher Education*, Appendix Five, *Higher Education in Other Countries*, London, H.M.S.O., 1965. See also Thut and Adams, *op. cit.*

13. As mentioned previously, this article is not the place for a discussion of why any given system has a given set of properties. But blatant incongruence between ideology and pattern of organization is so interesting that it warrants a brief comment.

14. Of course the evidence concerning these points is not what one would wish. But reasonable inferences can be made from the following sources or from bibliographical material to which they refer. With respect to England and the United States, see: Douglas Pidgeon, "Education and the Concept of Intelligence," unpub. manuscript available from the National Foundation for Educational Research in England and Wales, 1966; Turner, *op. cit.;* J. Stuart Maclure (ed.), *Educational Documents: England and Wales* 1816–1963, London, Chapman and Hall, 1965; and Robert O. Hahn and David B. Bidna (eds.), *Secondary Education, Origins and Directions*, London, Collier-MacMillan, 1965. With respect to other countries which, by way of illustration, have been classified in the text: Tomasson, *op. cit.;* Marvin Farber (ed.), *The Philosophy of Education in France and the United States*, Buffalo, University of Buffalo Press; Halls, *op. cit.;* Grace Richards Conant, "West German Education in Transition; German Textbooks and the Nazi Past," *Saturday Review*, 20 July 1963, 52–53; Richard Plant, "West German Education in Transition," *Saturday Review*, 20 July 1963, 49–51 and 62–63; E. J. King (ed.), *Communist Education*, Indianapolis, Bobbs-Merrill, 1963; *Bringing Soviet Schools Still Closer to Life*, London, Soviet Booklets, 1958; James S. Coleman (ed.), *Education and Political Development*, Princeton University Press, 1965; John Porter, *The Vertical Mosaic: An Analysis of Social Class and Power in Canada*, Toronto, University of Toronto Press, 1965; Peter Coleman (ed.), *Australian Civilization*, Melbourne, F. W. Cheshire, 1962; and Vernon Mallinson, *An Introduction to the Study of Comparative Educa-*

tion, London, Heinemann Educational Books, Ltd., 1961.

15. For a discussion of folk-norms, see Turner, *op. cit.*

16. For evidence in support of these classifications, see references 5, 7, and 14, especially with respect to the bibliographies contained in the books and articles mentioned.

17. A difficult problem is illustrated by classifying the U.S.S.R. as "Medium" and, for example, England as "High." On the one hand, England is less differentiated and specialized than the U.S.S.R., but, on the other, the U.S.S.R. is thoroughly comprehensive up to the age of 15+. What are the relative weights to be assigned to the degree of formal differentiation and specialization of routes as opposed to the age at which these routes begin? In this case more weight has been assigned to age, but this should not be taken as a rule.

18. The greater the degree of status rigidity in the stratification system of a given society, the more is it likely that these systemic problems will be severe, and the society will have an *explicit* ideology with respect to the distribution of power; similarly, the more is it likely that the educational system in such a society will have an explicit ideology of legitimization of educational selection. However, it should be stressed that even though a society with a decentralized and unstandardized selection process is likely to have an ideology which specifies that selection should not be centrally administered, it still must define the types of people it values most highly and explain why these people are selected when others are rejected. Of course, it should also be stressed that the greater the status rigidity, the more likely that a society's ideology will have "paternalistic" and/or "aristocratic" qualities.

19. "Technical and diffuse skills" are discussed by D. Lockwood, "Social Mobility," pp. 501–520, in A. J. Welford, Michael Argyle, D. V. Glass, and J. N. Morris (eds.), *Society: Problems and Methods of Study,* London, Routledge and Kegan Paul Ltd., 1962. Although for some occupations a diffuse skill may actually be the main task requirement, e.g., salesmanship, and although most diffuse skills can be learned if the opportunity were available, e.g., table manners, the main point is that diffuse skills tend to be unequally distributed through the stratification system. To the extent that they have to be learned intentionally, for example, while on the job or after childhood has passed, the task becomes time consuming and arduous, and seldom completely successful.

20. Selection processes within complex educational systems are likely to have a partially informal character, no matter how centralized their administration. Particularism of sort is likely to be associated with informality. For example, when there are "ties" for a limited number of places in higher levels of training, those responsible for selection must often rely on such informal and particularistic devices as personal knowledge of a candidate's preparatory institution, his teachers, his family background, the amount of emotional support his family are likely to provide for higher

education, etc. In addition such factors as intelligence, motivation, and technical skills are never likely to be sufficient criteria for selection in any bureaucratically organized system. One must have the qualities of, for example, "psychological stability" and "good citizenship." Such qualities are difficult to assess, and they are impossible to assess in a value-free manner. Particularism in terms of middle class culture is almost certain to characterize such assessments. But these forms of particularism are likely to exist *even* in a society with meritocratic or communistic ideologies of selection. They should not be confused with the explicit ideology of particularistic selection as defined in the text.

21. For example, although compared to England, the United States has a less distinctive system of ascribed characteristics and a more equal distribution of diffuse skills, nonetheless, opportunities for acquiring such skills at a relatively early age, prior to initial selection, are being instituted in the United States, e.g., programmes for Negroes to learn to speak "middle class English"; programmes to teach working class boys various skills in order to free them from "production oriented" jobs; courses in "etiquette" and ballroom dancing in the schools, etc. Such programmes are also becoming available to adults (division of Adults and Vocational Research of the United States Office of Education, which administers the Vocational Education Act of 1963).

22. For a more detailed discussion of various aspects of meritocratic ideology, see Michael Young, *The Rise of Meritocracy,* Penguin, Harmondsworth, 1961.

23. Two problems in the identification of an ideology of legitimization of educational selection (as well as of the ideologies of implementation discussed above) demand arbitrary solutions: how to determine the content of the ideology, and how to determine the dominant ideology. Because there are no studies directly concerned with this type of ideology, one must depend on various kinds of public and official statements. Although they do not always indicate the ideologies of the majority, they are a reasonable indication of the ideologies of those with power. Some of the most useful statements are official legislation pertaining to education, speeches by government and civil service officials, government sponsored reports, the public statements by officials of such institutions as universities or well known secondary schools, statements by local interest groups, such as "Adults for . . . ," and newspaper editorials. When there is no *a priori* evidence for the existence of competing ideologies, the ideology of the dominant group is taken as the dominant ideology; when, as is usually the case, competing ideologies do exist, the ideology of the dominant group is again taken as dominant; but when there are competing ideologies within the dominant group itself, it is necessary to construct some sort of profile which represents the proportions of the group holding different ideologies and the relative distribution of power among the competing factions. Obviously, this is a very difficult problem, for which there is very little evidence. Therefore, I

have attempted to construct very approximate profiles on the basis of the kind of information mentioned above. These are admittedly preliminary and, in part, arbitrary. For further material concerning ideologies of legitimization of educational selection, see the literature listed in reference 14. For a general discussion of testing for "ability" and of ideology, see David A. Goslin, *The Search for Ability: Standardised Testing in Social Perspective*, New York, John Wiley and Sons, 1963; see also Thompson, *op. cit.*

24. For example, with respect to the Lower Social Class as opposed to the Middle Social Class, Negroes as opposed to Whites, the South as opposed to the North, and Rural areas as opposed to Urban areas, see Seymour Martin Lipset and Reinhard Bendix, *Social Mobility in Industrial Society*, London, William Heinemann, Ltd., 1959, and James B. Conant, *The American High School Today*, New York, McGraw-Hill, 1959, and *Slum and Suburbs*, New York, McGraw-Hill, 1964.

25. A similar point has been made by Cicourel and Kitsuse, *op. cit.*

26. This contrasts, for example, with the German philosophical traditions which define centralization as a possible, indeed, as a likely source of freedom for individuals against the whims of minority groups. Of course it is the structural dilemma of maintaining both freedom and equality which is at the root of these differences. And it is this dilemma which Turner overlooks when he implicitly equates a centralized and standardized selection process with a "paternalistic" ideology of legitimization, an "elitist" ideology of implementation, and a reduction of equality of educational opportunity; and a decentralized and unstandardized selection process with a "meritocratic" ideology of legitimization, an "egalitarian" ideology of implementation, and a maximization of equality of opportunity.

27. Dunning and Hopper, *op. cit.*

28. This point was made recently by A. Tropp, "The Social Functions of Educational Systems," *Social and Economic Studies*, 1966, 1–7; see also the remarks about "butterfly-collecting" in Edmund Leach, *Rethinking Anthropology*, London, London School of Economics Monographs on Social Anthropology, 1961.

29. For a further discussion of this approach, see E. I. Hopper and E. G. Dunning, "Some Preliminary Methodological and Conceptual Notes on Industrialization and the Problem of Convergence," unpub. manuscript, prepared for the Study Group on Economy and Sociology, 6th World Congress of Sociology, Evian, 1966.

30. See Dunning and Hopper, *op. cit.*, and Hopper and Dunning, *ibid*. With special reference to Japan see Herbert Passin, *Society and Education in Japan*, Bureau of Publications, Teachers College and East Asian Institute, Columbia University, 1965; and Marius B. Jansen and Lawrence Stone, "Education and Modernization in Japan and England," *Comparative Studies in Society and History*, 1967, No 2.

31. This problem is implied by Elder, *op. cit.* See also Burton R. Clark, "The 'Cooling-out' Function in Higher Education," *Amer. Journ. of Sociol.* 1960, 569–76.

32. Turner, *op. cit.*

II

EDUCATION AND
SOCIAL SELECTION

Educational institutions play an important part in most societies as agents of social control, cultural change, and, not least, social selection.[1] We turn in Part II to social selection and have chosen chapters that cover a series of problems overlapping with and intermediate between those covered in Part I, "Education and Social Structure," and those that appear in Part V, "Cultural Reproduction and the Transmission of Knowledge." Discussion of social structure in effect defines the aims and constraints that mold educational institutions. In Part V we are concerned with the aims and constraints at the cultural level and, as will be seen, we put special emphasis on the character of the social relationships through which cultural and symbolic capital is transmitted. In this section, however, our primary concern is to identify how social structure and, more particularly, the structure of class relations affect the role of educational institutions as agents of social selection.

One of the classics of the literature on the relation between education and stratification is Max Weber's typology of educational systems, which is based on the idea that the structure of domination defines the ends and therefore the criteria of selection.[2] The empirical discussion of trends toward meritocracy in Halsey's Chapter 7 (below) refers back to Weber's generalization that modern societies have conflicting definitions of education in terms of the "cultivated man" and the newer concept of the specialized "expert." Alternatively, social selection through education can be related to the trend towards increased universalism that Blau and Duncan postulate and from which they infer a trend from ascription to achievement in socially selective processes.[3] Here the underlying theoretical issues involve distinctions between the openness or fluidity of a society and what, in older literature, used to be called interchange between the classes. The former, experience suggests, may be realized through the relative expansion of professional and technical occupations accompanying economic growth. It may also, and often has in industrializing periods, come about through an inverse

1. Cf. Bill Williamson, "Continuities and Discontinuities in the Sociology of Education," in *Educability, Schools and Ideology* edited by Michael Flude and John Ahier (London: Croom Helm, 1974), p. 3.
2. Max Weber, "The Rationalization of Education and Training," in *From Max Weber: Essays in Sociology,* edited by Hans Gerth and C. Wright Mills (New York: Oxford University Press, 1946), pp. 240–244.
3. Peter M. Blau and Otis Dudley Duncan, *The American Occupational Structure* (New York: John Wiley and Sons, 1967).

correlation of fertility· with occupational status. But in the strictest sense fluidity may be held to refer to changes in the opportunity structure between children of different social origins independent of changes in the demographic and occupational structure of the society as a whole. It is logically possible for a society to display more upward mobility while at the same time class or racial inequalities of opportunity become more unequal.

The sociology of education has, during the past fifteen years, done much to advance understanding of the relationship between education and social mobility, but a number of critics have recently come forward to question whether a continuation of the discipline's traditional concern with this issue can be justified. One school of thought, that of the ethnomethodologically and phenomenologically oriented "new" sociology of education, argues that the problem of educational selection has already been over-studied and that researchers would more profitably expend their time and energy in examining the content of the educational process. This perspective has already been discussed in our Introduction. Another viewpoint, whose roots extend in America from George S. Counts[4] to New Left conflict theorists and in Britain from R.H. Tawney to the recent work of Byrne, Williamson, and Fletcher,[5] is marked by an increasing concern with equality rather than equality of opportunity and with substantive equality of outcomes rather than formal equality of access to privileged forms of education.

This radical strain of thought in educational research has subjected the liberal conception of equality of opportunity to sustained socialist criticism. The classic sources of this critique are R.H. Tawney's *Equality* and Michael Young's *The Rise of the Meritocracy*—two works that have exerted a wide influence on radical thinkers in the sociology of education.[6] Yet however critical egalitarians may be toward the traditional preoccupation of educational researchers with social mobility and educational selection, most of them nonetheless call for more rather than fewer studies of the connections between education and social class. Williamson, an articulate contemporary proponent of this view, argues that studies which recognize the "structural force" of class are needed "not only to understand inequality but also to cast some light on what in retrospect seems to be the rather affluent question of what it is which governs the selection and transmission of educational knowledge."[7]

An outstanding recent example of research focusing on the relationship between education and class structure is Williamson's own study, conducted in collaboration with Byrne and Fletcher, on the political economy of educational provision.[8] In the United States, Jencks's *Inequality,* though hardly a structural analysis of social class, provides systematic empirical evidence about individuals on the question of education and social stratification. Raymond Boudon, a French sociologist, is concerned with essentially the same analytic problem that interests Jencks—how it is that educational inequality can decline while opportunities for social

4. George S. Counts, *The Selective Character of American Secondary Education* (Chicago: University of Chicago Press, 1922); *The Social Composition of Boards of Education* (Chicago: University of Chicago Press, 1927); *School and Society in Chicago* (New York: Harcourt, Brace, 1928).
5. David Byrne, Bill Williamson, and Barbara Fletcher, *The Poverty of Education: A Study in the Politics of Opportunity* (London: Martin Robertson, 1975).
6. R.H. Tawney, *Equality* (London: Allen and Unwin, 1931; rev. ed., 1964); Michael Young, *The Rise of the Meritocracy* (London: Thames and Hudson, 1958).
7. Williamson, *op cit.,* pp. 11–12. In this same article, Williamson also recommends more historical studies of the nexus between education and social class so as to provide a means of assessing "the effect on education of different social groups with different degrees of effective social power" (p. 11). For Williamson, as for many other radical scholars, studies of educational provision are also inquiries into the *politics* of education.
8. Byrne et al., *op. cit.*

mobility remain stable. But Boudon's approach to the problem is quite different from Jencks's, for instead of relying on direct empirical evidence for individuals he constructs a formal model of education and mobility that incorporates structural elements (Chapter 8). The object of his argument is to explain how an increase in educational equality can bring about a decrease in what he calls social opportunity.[9] Despite the pessimism about educational reform that accompanies Boudon's argument, we would ourselves, while repeating our insistence on the limitations of educational reform as an instrument in the establishment of an egalitarian society, also repeat the warning proffered in our Introduction in reference to Jencks: that we must guard against the substitution of a myth of impotence for the previous prevailing belief in education as a cure for all social ills.

A more traditional approach to the problem of education and social stratification—and the one that has historically dominated research in this field—is visible in Sewell and Shah's careful empirical analysis of socioeconomic status (SES), measured ability, and the attainment of higher education (Chapter 9). This approach, which we referred to in our Introduction as "methodological empiricism," has made a vital contribution to the sociology of education and has advanced impressively in the last decade. These advances have consisted primarily in refinements in measurement techniques, and among the most significant of these new techniques has been the development of path analysis.[10] What path analysis does is provide a means of estimating the direct and indirect effects of independent variables in a causal sequence and of assessing their relative influence on dependent variables. In Chapter 9, Sewell and Shah use this technique with particular rigor and demonstrate that SES exerts an influence independent of measured intelligence on both college entrance and college graduation. For men, intelligence seems to be a more important influence than SES, while for women, social origins seem to play the larger role. But in either case, the empirical evidence shows that the meritocratic principles to which Sewell and Shah adhere are violated throughout the process of selection in higher education.[11]

The sophisticated statistical techniques with which methodological empiricism is generally associated are not, of course, its exclusive property. Radical researchers, many of them working within the framework of a conflict theory of educational stratification, have also used quantitative methods in their analyses of education and class structure. Bowles and Gintis, a pair of neo-Marxist economists whose research makes frequent use of mathematical techniques, use regression analysis in an attempt to cast light on a problem that has bedeviled social science in recent years—the role of I.Q. in the reproduction of social inequality. Their conclusion, following a series of analyses that control for social background and educational attainment, is that I.Q. has almost no independent effect on adult economic success. This argument, it should be noted, addresses itself not to the heredity-environment controversy, but rather to the role of I.Q. in the reproduction of the hierarchical division of

9. For an elaboration of Boudon's model that draws extensively upon OECD data for advanced capitalist countries, see Raymond Boudon, *Education, Opportunity, and Social Inequality* (New York: John Wiley and Sons, 1974).
10. For an especially lucid discussion of path analysis, see Otis Dudley Duncan, "Path Analysis: Sociological Examples," *American Journal of Sociology* 72 (July 1966):1–16.
11. The ideological impulse behind Sewell's research, evident in his presidential address to the American Sociological Association in 1971 (reprinted in *American Sociological Review* 36 (October 1971): 793–809), is that of a deep commitment to the liberal ideal of equality of opportunity. But there is nothing inherent in methodological empiricism that commits it to a particular set of political ideals. In Great Britain, the tradition of "political arithmetic" has been closely linked to a socialist critique of the existing educational inequality. For a discussion of British political arithmetic that attributes its "pragmatism" to a close relationship between sociologists and political decision-makers, see Williamson, *op. cit.,* p. 7.

labor.[12] In Bowles and Gintis's view, I.Q., far from being a shorthand for rare and sorely needed cognitive skills, is actually the cornerstone of a technocratic-meritocratic ideology that serves to legitimate glaring social inequalities.

Another conflict analysis of the role of educational institutions in reproducing social inequality from generation to generation is Karabel's investigation of submerged class conflict in American community colleges (Chapter 11). A revisionist account that brings into question the widespread belief that the expansion of community colleges has been a force for "democratization" of American higher education, Karabel's article argues that the growth of two-year public colleges has had the effect of extending a class-based tracking system. In addition to describing the position of community colleges within the structure of educational and social stratification, Karabel also attempts to analyze the social and political forces that have shaped them. One movement analyzed in particular in Chapter 11 is the effort by a national educational planning elite to expand tracking within two-year public colleges by expanding enrollment in vocational education.

Dobson's analysis of inequality of opportunity in Soviet higher education, published for the first time here (Chapter 12), makes clear that the role of educational institutions as agents of class reproduction is not limited to the capitalist countries of the West. Relying primarily on original data collected by Soviet sources, Dobson demonstrates that social background remains a significant independent factor in determining who will survive the rigorous process of educational selection in the Soviet Union. The data, though somewhat fragmentary, clearly show a pattern of class-linked tracking in Soviet higher education. Yet despite the numerous similarities between the Soviet system of higher education and its Western counterparts, the evidence seems to suggest that there is considerably less inequality of access to higher education in the U.S.S.R. than in the capitalist countries of Western Europe. The United States, however, seems to show a pattern of access quite similar to that of the Soviet Union.

Torsten Husén, a sociologist whose meticulous studies of education and social stratification are representative of the radical tradition in methodological empiricism, has for thirty years been intimately involved in the struggle for educational change in the showcase of social democracy—his native country of Sweden.[13] A long-time advocate of structural reforms designed to build a more egalitarian educational system, Husén argues in Chapter 13 that the replacement of traditional European selective secondary schools by comprehensive institutions does not threaten standards of academic performance. Citing data gathered by the International Association for the Evaluation of Educational Achievement, Husén shows that the standard of the elite in mathematics and science in comprehensive systems is comparable to that of the elite in selective systems. Whether this pattern would hold in areas other than mathematics and science cannot be determined on the basis of the evidence Husén presents.

12. See Arthur R. Jensen, *Educability and Group Differences* (London: Methuen, 1973); Richard J. Herrnstein, *I.Q. in the Meritocracy* (Boston: Atlantic Press, 1973); Christopher Jencks et al., *Inequality: A Reassessment of the Effect of Family and Schooling in America* (New York: Basic Books, 1972); Michael Young and J. Gibson, "In Search of an Explanation of Social Mobility," *British Journal of Statistical Psychology* 16 (1963): 27–36; Cyril Burt, "Intelligence and Social Mobility," *British Journal of Statistical Psychology* 14 (1961): 3–25; J. Gibson, "Biological Aspects of a High Socioeconomic Group: I.Q., Education and Social Mobility," *Journal of Biosocial Science* 2 (1970): 1–16; A.H. Halsey, "Genetic Social Structure and Intelligence," *British Journal of Sociology* 9 (1958): 15–28; Richard J. Light and Paul V. Smith, "Social Allocation Models of Intelligence: A Methodological Inquiry," *Harvard Educational Review* 39 (1969): 484–510. For a devastating attack on the quality of the data adduced to support the argument that I.Q. is inherited, see Leon J. Kamin, *The Science and Politics of I.Q.* (Potomac, Md.: Lawrence Erlbaum Associates, 1974).
13. See Torsten Husén and Gunnar Boalt, *Educational Research and Educational Change: The Case of Sweden* (Stockholm and New York: Almqvist and Wiksell and Wiley, 1968).

Husén has elsewhere[14] presented data showing that the movement toward comprehensive schools in European secondary education has been accompanied by an increase in equality of educational opportunity, but there is a growing body of evidence suggesting that class-linked patterns of educational selection can reproduce themselves within comprehensive schools. [15] In order to understand fully the actual *process* of educational selection and the class and racial differentials that are essential features of the process, it is necessary to depart somewhat from the macrosociological approaches that have traditionally dominated the sociology of education and to focus on the dynamics of interactions taking place within the school. Cicourel and Kitsuse, in a study of educational selection in a large American high school much cited by proponents of an ethnomethodological approach to educational research (Chapter 14), focus squarely on the process by which candidates for colleges are differentiated. Placing particular emphasis on the role of counselors within the organizational structure of the school, they show considerable departures from meritocratic norms in the classification of students. Rist, an American anthropologist who has conducted an important field study of classroom interaction in a ghetto school,[16] draws upon the perspectives of both symbolic interactionism and ethnomethodology to formulate his argument that labeling theory, which has previously been applied mainly in studies of deviance, offers a promising perspective for understanding the processes of schooling. Rist and Cicourel and Kitsuse have made an important contribution in drawing the attention of educational researchers interested in social selection and academic performance to interactions taking place inside the school; what remains to be done is to integrate their insights into in-school processes with the more structural concerns of scholars who have focused their research on the relationship between educational and social inequality.[17]

14. Torsten Husén, *Social Background and Educational Career: Research Perspectives on Equality of Educational Opportunity* (Paris: Organisation for Economic Co-operation and Development, 1972).
15. See especially Julienne Ford, *Social Class and the Comprehensive School* (London: Routledge and Kegan Paul, 1969).
16. Raymond Rist, "Student Social Class and Teacher Expectations: The Self-Fulfilling Prophecy in Ghetto Education," *Harvard Educational Review* 40 (August 1970): 411–450.
17. See Raymond Rist, *The Urban School: Factory for Failure* (Cambridge, Mass.: M.I.T. Press, 1973), and Frederick Erickson, "Gatekeeping and the Melting Pot," *Harvard Educational Review* 45 (February 1975): 44–70, for field-based investigations of in-school processes that attempt to address themselves to larger structural issues.

SELECTIVE BIBLIOGRAPHY

Baudelot, Christian, and Roger Establet. *L'école capitaliste en France*. Paris: François Maspéro, 1973.

Becker, Howard S.; Blanche Geer; and Everett C. Hughes. *Making the Grade: The Academic Side of College Life*. New York: John Wiley and Sons, 1968.

Boudon, Raymond. *Education, Opportunity, and Social Inequality*. New York: John Wiley and Sons, 1974.

Bourdieu, Pierre, and Jean-Claude Passeron. *Les héritiers*. Paris: Éditions de Minuit, 1964.

Byrne, David; Bill Williamson; and Barbara Fletcher. *The Poverty of Education: A Study in the Politics of Opportunity*. London: Martin Robertson, 1975.

Cicourel, Aaron V., et al. *Language Use and School Performance*. New York: Academic Press, 1974.

Coleman, James S., et al. *Equality of Educational Opportunity*. Washington: U.S. Government Printing Office, 1966.

Douglas, J.W.B. *The Home and the School*. London: MacGibbon and Kee, 1964.

Eckland, Bruce. "Academic Ability, Higher Education, and Occupational Mobility." *American Sociological Review* 30 (October 1965): 735–746.

Floud, Jean; A.H. Halsey; and F.M. Martin.

Social Class and Educational Opportunity. London: Heineman, 1956.

Folger, John K.; Helen S. Astin; and Alan E. Bayer. *Human Resources and Higher Education*. New York: Russell Sage, 1970.

Ford, Julienne. *Social Class and the Comprehensive School*. London: Routledge and Kegan Paul, 1969.

Girard, Alain, et al. *Population et l'enseignement*. Paris: Presses universitaires de France, 1970.

Hargreaves, David H. *Social Relations in a Secondary School*. London: Routledge and Kegan Paul, 1967.

Husén, Torsten. *Social Influences on Educational Attainment*. Paris: OECD, 1975.

Jencks, Christopher, et al. *Inequality: A Re-*assessment of the Effect of Family and Schooling in America*. New York: Basic Books, 1972.

Karabel, Jerome, and Alexander W. Astin. "Social Class, Academic Ability and College 'Quality'." *Social Forces* 53 (March 1975):381–398.

Lacey, Colin. *Hightown Grammar: The School as a Social System*. Manchester: Manchester University Press, 1970.

Sewell, William H., and Robert M. Hauser. *Education, Occupation, and Earnings*. New York: Academic Press, 1975.

Silver, Harold, ed. *Equal Opportunity in Education: A Reader in Social Class and Educational Opportunity*. London: Methuen, 1973.

7. Towards Meritocracy? The Case of Britain

A. H. HALSEY

Varying in their concrete forms and in their size, the channels of vertical circulation exist in any stratified society, and are as necessary as channels for blood circulation in the body. (Pitirim A. Sorokin, *Social Mobility*, 1927)

I. INTRODUCTION[1]

"Aristocracies," wrote Pareto, "do not last. Whatever the causes, it is an incontestable fact that after a certain length of time they pass away. History is a graveyard of aristocracies. . . . The genealogies of the English nobility have been very exactly kept; and they show that very few families still remain to claim descent from the comrades of William the Conqueror. The rest have vanished. . . . (Aristocracies) decay not in numbers only. They decay also in quality, in the sense that they lose their vigour. . . . The governing classes are restored in numbers . . . and quality by families rising from the lower classes and bringing with them the vigour . . . necessary for keeping themselves in power. They are also restored by the loss of their more degenerate members. . . . So the English aristocracy managed to prolong its terms of power in the second half of the nineteenth century down to the dawn of its decadence . . . in the first years of the twentieth."[2]

Pareto was referring here to mobility into and out of elite strata occasioned by accumulation of capital, marriage, and fortune. The twentieth-century story contains the hypothesis that education has superseded these more traditional "channels of vertical circulation," and this hypothesis was formulated in a highly original form by Michael Young.[3] Michael Young, for ironic and critical purposes, described a hypothetical Britain in which, in Linton's terminology, roles were allocated purely on the basis of achievement. Pareto, on the other hand, was asserting, as did Sorokin and as have most sociologists since, that in reality there have existed no pure "achievement" societies and equally no pure caste societies. In practice, analysis has always to be concerned with mixed determination of the distribution of individuals into social positions, and the task is to unravel the weight and process of the influence to be attributed to the diverse elements of both nature and nurture.

At the end of their magnificently meticulous book, Blau and Duncan give a different answer from Pareto's.[4] Their eyes were on modern industrial societies in general and America in particular. For them a trend from ascription to achievement is merely a corollary of the underlying evolution of industrial societies in terms of another two of Parsons's pattern variables—particularism and universalism. The role of education emerges from this interpretative framework.

Heightened universalism has profound implications for the stratification system. The achieved status of a man, what he has accomplished in terms of some objective criteria, becomes more important than his ascribed status, who he is in the sense of what family he comes from. This does not mean that family background no longer influences careers. What it does imply is that superior status cannot any more be directly inherited but must be legitimated by actual achievements that are socially acknowledged. Education assumes increasing significance for social status in general and for the transmission of social standing from fathers to sons in particular. Superior family origins increase a son's chances of attaining superior occupational status in the United States in large part because they help him to obtain a better education, whereas in less industrialized societies the influence of family origin on status does not seem to be primarily mediated by education.

This article appears here for the first time.

The functionalist inclinations of Blau and Duncan's approach may be remarked. Thus they also assert a connection between high rates of mobility (especially upward) and stable democracy. Marx would have agreed, though in a somewhat different spirit. His formulation was that "the more a ruling class is able to assimilate the foremost minds of a ruled class the more stable and dangerous becomes its rule."[5]

The older European tradition dominated by Marx was, in any case, more interested in the problem of the "interchange between the classes" than in the factors determining the occupational status of individuals. But even here twentieth-century writing has been interested less in the traditional Marxist theory of economic determinism, which confined mobility broadly to the precipitation of privileged feudal remnants and the unsuccessful bourgeoisie into the ranks of the proletariat, or even in the interpretation of occupational change and the proletarianization of white-collar work, than in the measurement of "social capillarity."

There are, of course, legitimate questions of class and class consciousness on the basis of which the study of social mobility is sometimes attacked as a disguised legitimation of liberal capitalist society. Discussion of the study of social mobility in the last decade has hinged in part on whether the conceptions used are ideologically biased. We cannot fully explore this question here. It must suffice to assert that, while ideology can shape sociological perception, it does not follow that a sociology is *necessarily* vitiated by its ideological derivation. Thus, for example, though it is not difficult to establish a connection between concern with social mobility and the advocacy of "consensual" as opposed to "class-conflict" conceptions of modern society, it does not follow that studies of mobility that use the idea of multiple status levels or even that of a status continuum cannot be used in the service of radical criticism of the social order. Indeed, the concept of an open society in the sense of random relation between

paternal and filial status has been used for that precise purpose in post-war mobility studies. Nor is it impossible to use mobility analysis to study movement between opposed classes or within the structure of what Ossowski has called "a state of classless inequality."[6] The methods of mobility analysis, in other words, are not themselves to be debunked by any demonstration that their author is committed to reform rather than revolution, or to socialism rather than capitalism. To ask how much movement takes place intergenerationally between different class or status groups may or may not imply a wish to attract attention towards or away from class struggle. The usefulness of the answer to such a question depends upon criteria other than the political motives of the questioner.

Current debate about the theory of social stratification and social change for the most part opposes deterministic and voluntaristic theories, though it should be noted that both types of theory are associated with the political left and the political right. The major works of Marx and Veblen may be associated with the one and those of Pareto, Weber, and Parsons with the other. But by no means can all contributors to the literature of social mobility be unequivocally labeled in this way, and even less is there a one-to-one correspondence between ideological inclinations and techniques of analysis.

The work of the Oxford sociologists on which this essay relies has been much influenced on the one hand by the pioneering work of D. V. Glass and his associates at L.S.E.,[7] and the studies inspired by their work under the auspices of the International Sociological Association,[8] and on the other by the work of Blau and Duncan and their followers in America in the 1960s.[9] The methods of neither of these two groups of our predecessors are unambiguously tied to any particular social or political position. The Glass study stands in the native British tradition of political arithmetic. It was strongly influenced politically by a radical stance towards the powers, privileges, and dubious efficiency of the elite professions, and expressed both a condemnation of waste and frustration through the neglect of ability among working-class children and a hope that expanded educational opportunity would produce a more efficient and socially sensitive elite. Its assumptions about stratification implied a greater interest in status than in class and conceived of the social structure in terms of a hierarchy of layers in which occupation was closely associated with distinct styles of life.

Blau and Duncan's conception of social stratification (which is descended from the work of W. L. Warner) entails the idea of a continuum of status, and, though making use of the conventional distinction between manual and non-manual work, rejects the notion of a dichotomous class structure. At the level of method of analysis, Glass's use of contingency tables and indices of association is essentially intermediate between an interest in interchange between classes or status groups and a concern with the determinants of occupational status to which Duncan's method of path analysis is appropriate.

My own basic interest in this work is to explore how far social policy in general and education in particular have succeeded in equalizing life-chances in Britain in the sense either of opportunity or of outcome: or, to use the Linton phraseology again, how far achievement has supplanted ascription in the creation of a new generation. Underlying this is a commitment similar to that which informed the study by Glass and his associates to the belief that higher rates of social mobility, particularly through education, would entail less waste of talent among working-class children and more efficiency in the direction of economic, social, and political affairs. This belief, again as with Glass, is coupled with an awareness of the dangers of meritocracy, which carries the possibility of sanctifying new and greater divisions between the powerful and the common man by what Bernstein has called "the individualization of failure."[10] To put the matter positively, equality rather than equality of opportunity is the aim and there is a belief in this tradition of political thought that a more equal distribution of power and advantage is not only desirable but also possible.

In the study of the 1972 British population conducted from Nuffield College we wanted to assess the impact of post-war reform and economic change on the degree of openness in British society.[11] But we were also aware that, in the meantime, new methods of analysis of mobility had been developed by O. D. Duncan and his colleagues and that, associated with these methods of multiple regression analysis, there had also been a shift away from the older conception of interchange towards the idea of hierarchical occupational differentiation in which the essential sociological task was to measure the determinants of individual occupational achievement. While wanting to leave open the question of the continuing validity of the concept of social class, or a hierarchy of layers of social status, used in the L.S.E. study, we decided also to take advantage of, and perhaps even to improve on, the methodological developments of our American colleagues.[12]

More particularly, we were anxious to discover the significance of the much-publicized developments in post-war educational policy, and the fluidity of movement between generations of members of the same family. Secondary education for all, free of financial handicaps, had been enshrined in the 1944 Act, the comprehensive movement in secondary education had gathered momentum in the 1950s, and the dramatic expansion of post-secondary education had occurred in the 1960s under the patronage of the State. Theories assuming a restricted pool of ability had been harried out of respectable belief through the efforts of social researchers.[13] Belief had been widespread that the maturing industrial societies were moving steadily towards meritocracy and certification as the principles of occupational placement in an ever more productive and efficient economic system of perpetual growth. Such societies would require greater rates of inter- and intragenerational mobility into an occupational structure gradually reducing its complement of unskilled, low-paid, and brutalizing labor while increasing its sector of professional, technical, and managerial occupations to serve an advanced technology and to deliver an ever higher per capita G.N.P.

Education, it seemed, was playing, and was destined still more to play, a crucial role in the formation of a more affluent and perhaps classless society. Education was perhaps the single most important determinant of a man's occupational destination. A new society involved a tightening bond between education and occupation; this might be so even if any overall increase in intergenerational mobility might be attributable to structural as distinct from exchange mobility.

In opposition to this line of reasoning are the views of such writers as Boudon and Thurow. Thurow concluded on the basis of American data that "our reliance on education as the ultimate public policy for curing all problems, economic and social, is unwarranted at best and in all probability ineffective."[14] Boudon, agreeing with Thurow, has argued that evidence from a wide range of industrial countries is consistent with the theory that educational expansion and even the reduction of inequality of educational opportunity do not lead to reduced dependence of a son's social status on that of his father.[15] These conflicting theories await conclusive empirical tests.

Education has been a possible avenue of occupational and social ascent in many if not most societies. Nevertheless, *la carrière ouverte aux talents* was a forlorn revolutionary slogan throughout the nineteenth century and demand for its realization continued as a standard element in the socialist critique of European capitalist society in the first half of the twentieth century. Education, and especially higher education, throughout this period was much more the

stamp put on the social character of individuals whose jobs and life-styles were predetermined by social origin than an institutional ladder for the talented of humble birth. We still do not know at all precisely how open a society Britain was in the nineteenth century. But that there was some mobility between the generations is beyond doubt, including leaps over the gulf which traditionally separated the manual class from the non-manual minority. But the more important ladders (and snakes) were capital accumulation, on-the-job promotion, and market acumen—not education.

The study led by Professor Glass was the major research achievement of empirical research at mid-century in British work on social mobility. It yielded an arithmetic picture of a stable hierarchy of occupational levels with, it was assumed, a linked hierarchy of status and styles of life. Between the generations there was relatively heavy self-recruitment at the top, a lesser rigidity at the bottom, and considerable fluidity in the middle. Thus the indices of association[16] (measures of intergenerational self-recruitment) were:

for status category 1
   (professional and high
   administrative)   13.158
for status category 2
   (managerial and executive)   5.865
for status category 5
   (skilled manual and routine
   grades of non-manual)   1.157
for status category 7
   (unskilled manual)   2.259

With respect to higher education the single most crucial figure was that 47 percent of the people at the top in the higher professional and managerial classes (i.e., the principal destination of those with higher education) were the sons of fathers who also held or had held these top positions. Radical criticism was directed at these rigidities on grounds both of social justice and of national economic efficiency.

But ever since Professor Glass published his study there have been argument and a conflict of views as to what was happening.[17] The L.S.E. picture was formed while the country was embarking, self-consciously and under a Labour government, on an ambitious program of social reform towards the Welfare State. In employment, income, social security, housing, and health as well as in education the declared intent was for a more equal and therefore a more just society. Can we say a generation later that social policy has made a difference in social reality? Has achievement gained at the expense of ascription? How far is occupation linked to education and how far is each tied to social origin? Is Britain moving towards meritocracy?

II: CLASS CHANCES FOR EDUCATION

The full picture of the class distribution of education is too complicated for our space here. We arrive at an economical indicator, however, if we consider the chances of proceeding from given class origins to a university degree for those educated before and after the 1944 Act. The analysis of our 1972 data in these terms is given in Table 1. First, the proportion of graduates is shown for the two age groups in each origin category. Three features emerge. All origin categories have increased their output of graduates; the proportions of graduates remain correlated with origin; and the differences between them have increased.

A more precise measure of trends in class differences of access to the universities is also included in Table 1. Each of the percentages is standardized by expressing it as a proportion of the percentage of the whole age group who obtained degrees. The resulting ratio (= 1.0 for the whole age group) shows no clear trend towards the elimination of class inequality in educational attainment. The top class has fallen from having 5.76 times the average chance to 4.50, but the bottom class has worsened its previously disadvantaged position from just over to just under one-third of the average chance. Moreover, it should be noted that whereas before the 1944 Act above-average chances were shared by sons from the top four classes

Table 1. Social Origin and University Degree

(A) Percent gaining university degree by class of origin									
Born	1	2	3	4	5	6	7	8	Total
1913–1931	15.0	7.4	3.8	3.0	1.5	1.3	0.9	0.9	2.6
1932–1947	27.0	17.6	5.8	5.1	3.6	2.3	2.4	1.8	6.0
(B) Relative class chances of university degree									
1913–1931	5.76	2.85	1.46	1.15	0.58	0.50	0.35	0.35	1.0
1932–1947	4.50	2.93	0.97	0.85	0.60	0.38	0.40	0.30	1.0

Source: Oxford Mobility Study National Male Sample 1972.
Population: Men in England and Wales aged 25–59 in 1972.
Sample: 6700.
Social Origin = Father's occupational class at respondent's age 14.
1 = Professional, high managerial, and large proprietors.
2 = Lower professional and managerial.
3 = White-collar.
4 = Self-employed (including farmers).
5 = Supervisors of manual work.
6 = Skilled manual workers.
7 = Semi-skilled and unskilled.
8 = Agricultural workers (including small holders without employees)
Relative class chances = percent from each origin gaining university degree divided by the total percent gaining a degree in that age cohort.

(amounting to nearly 30 percent of the population), superior chances in the more recent period have accrued only to the sons of classes 1 and 2 (amounting to rather less than 15 percent of the population). Admittedly, the chances of graduation have risen proportionately more for the sons of unskilled and semi-skilled workers (from 0.9 percent to 2.4 percent, i.e., by a factor of 2.7) than for sons of the professional and managerial class (from 15.0 percent to 27.0 percent, i.e., by a factor of 1.9). But the absolute percentage increases offer a more realistic appraisal of the trends. An extra 1.5 percent of working-class children found their way to the universities after the 1944 Act, compared with an extra 13 percent of upper-middle-class children. On this evidence, whatever we may mean by a trend from ascription to achievement, we must be more impressed by the persistence of influences which flow from class origin to educational attainment.

In order to explore this process further, it is convenient to turn to path analysis.

III: A PATH ANALYSIS

The techniques of path analysis begin with familial, educational, and occupational biographies. In the Oxford 1972 study we collected data on ten thousand adult males in England and Wales. The occupations and educational experience and qualifications are scaled, fathers and sons are located on the scales, and the correlations between pairs of scales (variables) are subjected to regression analysis (of which path analysis is a special form with regression equations that constitute a recursive set).[18] The scale positions are standardized (by subtracting the mean from each score and dividing by the standard deviation). Then the zero order correlation between any two variables may be calculated (r_{xy}), which gives the best estimate of the value of y linearly from x for a given individual. The coefficient of correlation, or standardized regression coefficient, is

$$r_{xy} = \sum_{i=1}^{N} \frac{x_i y_i}{N},$$

where x and y are the standardized forms of the original variables (i.e., $x_i = (X_i - \bar{X}) \div$ s.d. (X)).

In the L.S.E. 1949 study the correlation of father's present or last occupation to son's present occupation was 0.46; and in our Oxford 1972 study it is 0.36. In Blau and Duncan's American study (1962) it was 0.405.[19] This means that if one father is a standard deviation above another in occupational status we may predict that the son of the first father will be 0.46 (L.S.E. 1949), 0.36 (Oxford 1972), or 0.405 (U.S.A. 1962) s.d. units above the son of the second.

The same analysis also tells us that r_{xy}^2 of the variance of y is explained by x and $(1 - r_{xy}^2)$ is unexplained. Thus in the L.S.E. 1949 study $(0.46)^2 = 0.20$ of the variance of occupational status among sons is explained by paternal status. The Oxford 1972 study gives a comparable figure for explained variance of 0.126. This suggests that the determining strength of social origin as measured by father's occupation has declined in Britain in the post-war period. But this apparent inference cannot in fact be made because the two studies are not exactly comparable.[20] In order to derive inferences about trends in the absence of exactly replicated inquiries we have to rely on comparisons between age cohorts in the 1972 study.[21]

We can, however, be sure that there is a positive but less than perfect correlation between paternal and filial status and then take the next step—which is to ask which matters more in determining the occupational status of an individual, his father's occupational position or his own formal qualifications. The simplest possible path model will yield a first answer, as shown below for the Oxford 1972 data.

The elementary path analysis shown in Figure 1 takes us beyond zero order coefficients to give us an estimate of the direct

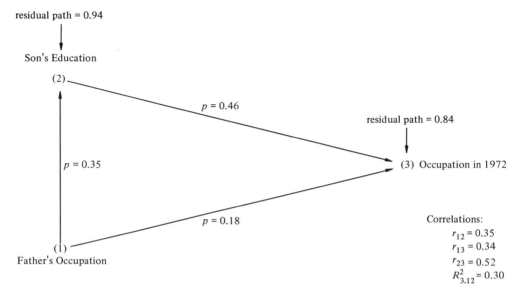

residual path = 0.94

Son's Education

(2)

p = 0.46

residual path = 0.84

p = 0.35

(3) Occupation in 1972

p = 0.18

Correlations:
$r_{12} = 0.35$
$r_{13} = 0.34$
$r_{23} = 0.52$
$R^2_{3.12} = 0.30$

(1)
Father's Occupation

Figure 1. A Simple Path Analysis of Origin, Education, and Destination: Britain 1972 Males

(1) = Father's occupation at respondent's age 14 scaled in Hope/Goldthorpe occupational categories 1–124
(2) = Respondent's education (all qualifications and examinations) scaled 0 (none) to 4 (degree level)
(3) = Respondent's occupation 1972 scaled as in (1)
Population: All men aged 20–64

effect (p) of paternal occupation and respondent's education on his occupational status in 1972. Whereas the simple correlations told us that education was only one and a half times as important as origin, the p values tell us that the direct effect of education is about two and one-half times as important as origin. To express this in another way: we start with the fact that the father/son status correlation is 0.34; of this the direct effect p_{31} = 0.18 or 53% and the indirect effect by education $(p_{32} \; r_{21})$ amounts to 0.16 or 47%.

We may conclude that the occupational positions of men in 1972 in Britain are de-

pendent more on qualifications than on origin as measured by father's occupational status. Indeed, the observed correlation of father's with son's status is in large part a transmission of status through formal qualifications.

We can go further, however, by complicating the model with respect to both social background and occupational career. For present purposes we proceed no further than the basic model used by Blau and Duncan in the American study as shown in Figure 2 below.[22]

The correlations between the variables in the model shown in Figure 2 are as follows:

	Father's education	Father's occupation	Respondent's education	Respondent's first job	Respondent's 1972 job
1. Father's education	1.0	0.385	0.345	0.251	0.224
2. Father's occupation	0.385	1.0	0.358	0.303	0.363
3. Respondent's education	0.345	0.358	1.0	0.555	0.530
4. Respondent's first job	0.251	0.303	0.555	1.0	0.487
5. Respondent's 1972 job	0.224	0.363	0.530	0.487	1.0

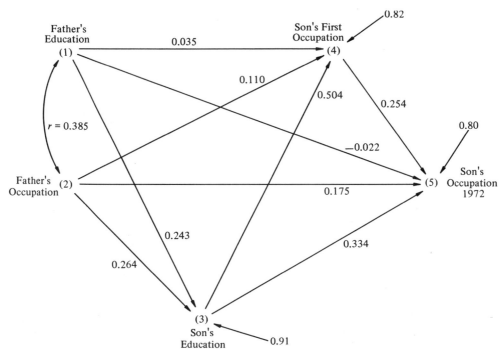

Figure 2. "Blau-Duncan" Path Analysis showing Path Coefficients (*P*): Britain 1972 Males

Variables

(1) Father's education: school examinations, professional/academic qualifications
(2) Father's occupation at respondent's age 14 [as for Fig. 1]
(3) Respondent's education as in (1)
(4) Respondent's first job as in (2)
(5) Respondent's 1972 job as in (2)

Population: Men aged 25–59 who were resident in England and Wales at age 14. Effective sample size 6,700.

Analyzing the correlations between respondent's education and the two measures of familial background into "direct" and "joint" components, we have $r_{31} = p_{31} + p_{32} r_{21}$ —i.e., the direct path accounts for 70% of the correlation of father's with son's education. Also, $r_{32} = p_{32} + p_{31} r_{12}$; since $r_{32} = 0.358$, p_{32} is 74% of the correlation; and again, most of the correlation of father's occupational status with son's education comes from the direct effect p_{32}. But perhaps most important to observe is that the residual path is very large. In other words, education acts as a means of introducing into the rest of the model influences which are uncorrelated with social background as measured by father's education and father's occupation. (The independence of the estimated residual is a necessary result of the technique we are using.)

Turning to the fourth variable, which is respondent's first job, we notice first that the variance explained by the preceding variables has risen sharply to 32% (i.e., the residual, $\sqrt{(1 - R^2)}$, has dropped to 0.82). Of this explained variance, as much as 65% can be assigned to the additional effect of respondent's education. This large proportion, it should be emphasized, operates over and above the effects of the correlation of education with the background variables of father's occupation and father's education. Thus it becomes increasingly clear that education is an extremely important variable in this model. It acts not only as a transmitter of the two specified background influences but also, and much more strikingly, as a transmitter of other residual effects. The expectation must therefore be that when we look at correlations involving the respondent's first job and the prior variables of the model we will see that respondent's education intervenes prominently as a transmitter of background, leaving the direct effects of variables (1) and (2) relatively small. We should also see that only a small part of these correlations can be attributed to the joint dependence on background of education and first job, because education is not very dependent in this sense. To put it another way, the correlation of respondent's education with first job will not turn out to be "spurious," in the classic sense; that is, it is not a correlation due to a common cause in the background, but rather reflects the "genuine" direct dependence of first job on education. A correlation can be spurious only if *both* variables are heavily dependent on some common, prior-causal factor.

If we consider the correlation between father's occupation and respondent's first job (r_{42}) we can break it down into $p_{42} + (p_{41} \ r_{12}) + (p_{43} \ p_{32}) + (p_{43} \ p_{31} \ r_{12}) = 0.303 \ (r_{42})$. These components can be expressed as percentages of the correlation, giving the following pattern: $p_{42} = 36\%$, $p_{41} \ r_{12} = 4\%$, $p_{43} \ p_{32} = 44\%$, and $p_{43} \ p_{31} \ r_{12} = 16\%$ (total, 100%). It emerges rather dramatically that the largest component of the correlation is contributed by the indirect path from father's occupation through education to first occupation $p_{43} \ p_{32}$. This represents the transmission of paternal status through education to first job; to this we can also add the further indirect effect that comes from the correlation of father's occupational status and education, given that father's education influences son's education

independently and thus transmits a further element of paternal status through the son's education to his first job, $p_{43} \ p_{31} \ r_{12}$. This influence amounts to 16%, so that about 60% of the correlation of father's status with son's first job status is transmitted via qualifications in one way or another. Correlatively this makes the direct and irreducible effect of father's job on son's first job relatively small $(p_{42} = 0.110)$, 36%.

A similar result emerges from the analysis of the paths from father's education to son's first job, though here the correlation (r_{41}) is smaller, 0.251. The direct path accounts for only 14% of the correlation. The main route via education $(p_{43} \ p_{31})$ accounts for almost 50%, and the indirect route via the correlation of father's education with father's occupation through education $(p_{43} \ p_{32} \ r_{21})$ adds another 20%.

By contrast, the correlation between son's education and his first job is, as we would expect, almost entirely a direct effect. Of the total correlation $(r_{43} = 0.555)$, p_{43} (0.504) represents over 90%. As predicted, this correlation is very far from spurious.

To sum up, then, with respect to the first four variables in the model, we can confirm that education is both an important independent influence on the distribution of men entering the labor market for the first time and a crucial transmitter of the prior influences of family background.

We turn now to the distribution of our respondents in their present (1972) jobs. This is the fifth variable, the variance of which is explained slightly more than that of first occupation and therefore much more than that of education (the residual, $\sqrt{(1 - R^2)}$, at 0.80 implies that about 36% of the variance is explained). If we follow the line of the analysis made with respect to the first four variables, it could be that the status of a respondent's first job takes over the role of transmission from qualifications and again makes correlations of the other variables with present job largely indirect. In fact, however, a much less clear pattern emerges.

When we consider, as before, the correlation of father's occupation with respondent's present occupation (r_{52} = 0.363, which is larger than r_{42} = 0.303), it turns out that almost 50% of the correlation is contributed by the direct effect of paternal status on son's present status, p_{52} = 0.175. Most of the remainder comes from transmission through education but not through first occupation. For example, the main indirect path through education from paternal status (p_{53} p_{32}) contributes 24% while the corresponding indirect path through first job (p_{54} p_{42}) contributes only 8%. A plausible interpretation of this pattern is that the increased explanation of variance which we find with respect to present as compared with first occupations reflects a qualitative change in the pattern of influences such that the distribution of occupational destinations is more cognate with that of social origin (i.e., paternal occupational status), so that the direct effect of father's occupation is increased. In other words, education, even in conjunction with the status of first job, does not act so efficiently as a transmitter of influence, and what was called occupational inheritance in the earlier literature operates more directly and visibly.

Of the reasonably high correlation between first and present jobs (r_{54} = 0.487), a rather high proportion is contributed by the joint dependence of present job and first job on respondent's education. The direct effect of first job amounts to 52%.

Finally, we can turn to the relation between education and present job. These two variables have a high correlation (r_{53} = 0.530). This correlation is in fact only slightly lower than that between first job and education. It might have been possible to attribute this correlation to transmission via first job, but in fact the direct effect (p_{53}) is by far the largest component, amounting to nearly two-thirds, with the route from education via first job (p_{54} p_{43}) adding another 24%. This pattern hardly differs from what we found in the correlation between first job and education (r_{43}), which was almost entirely a product of the

direct effect p_{43}. If we take these two elements in the correlation between present job and education together (p_{53} + p_{54} p_{43}), then there is roughly the same very small scope for the effects of joint dependence on background (father's job and father's education) as was the case with respect to the links between education and first job. In this sense, at least, the career is fairly self-contained.

To summarize, the effects of social origin as measured by paternal occupation are relatively small and appear to work in two main ways. First, these influences are transmitted (indirectly) through education. Second, status origin exercises a direct effect on present rather than first job; but this influence is small relative to that of either education or first job. The influence of father's education appears to drop out completely after contributing to a limited extent to the explanation of the pattern of education among sons.

We could at this point press the path analysis further by adding further scaled variables from our data. We shall not do this here[23] —nor shall we take the hazardous step of comparing the values derived from the application of the model for Britain in 1972 with those derived by Blau and Duncan for the U.S.A. in 1962.[24] Instead we shall take a step in another direction—to disaggregate the path analysis age cohorts in order to seek indications of trends in the strength of influence for each of the paths in the model. The results of dividing the sample between those aged 25–39 and those aged 40–59 in 1972, which means roughly between those educated before and those educated after the implementation of the Education Act of 1944, are shown in Figure 3 below.

On this analysis it appears that:

1. The correlation of paternal occupational status with paternal education is increasing (0.341 v. 0.422).
2. The direct effect of paternal status on respondent's first job is low and decreasing (0.137 v. 0.083), and the direct effect

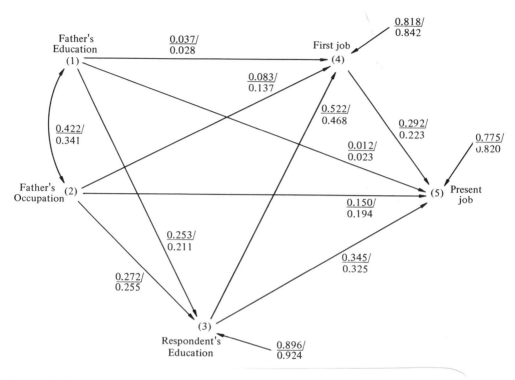

Figure 3. Path Analysis for Comparison of "Education and Mobility" Process before and after the 1944 Act

Basic model is "Blau and Duncan" type. *Population* (a) Men aged 25–39, educated in England and Wales, (b) Men aged 40–59, educated in England and Wales

Variables are as before: (1) Father's education, (2) Father's occupation, (3) Respondent's education, (4) Respondent's first job, (5) Respondent's present job.

Coefficients presented as (a)/(b)

Based on the correlations:

1. 1.00/1.00	0.422/0.341	0.368/0.298	0.264/0.214	0.255/0.188
2. 0.422/0.341	1.00/1.00	0.379/0.327	0.297/0.300	0.362/0.359
3. 0.368/0.298	0.379/0.327	1.00/1.00	0.567/0.521	0.563/0.498
4. 0.264/0.214	0.297/0.300	0.567/0.521	1.00/1.00	0.529/0.446
5. 0.255/0.188	0.362/0.359	0.563/0.498	0.529/0.446	1.00/1.00
(1)	(2)	(3)	(4)	(5)

of paternal education on first job is very low for both groups (0.028, 0.037); but

3. These two family background factors have increased their direct effect on the education of respondents: p_{32} rises from 0.255 to 0.272, and p_{31} from 0.211 to 0.253.

4. The direct effect of education on first job is high and getting higher (0.468 to 0.522).

5. The direct effect of education on present job is rising (0.325 to 0.345), subject to certain qualifications.[25]

6. The direct effect of father's job on pres-

ent job is decreasing (0.194 to 0.150), and the direct effect of paternal education on present job is negligible.

7. The direct effect of first job on present job is fairly high and rising.

IV: CONCLUSION

What then of meritocracy? Let us notice first that the "operationalizing" of Young's notion, which he defined in terms of "I.Q. plus effort" as the determinants of occupational attainment, is inadequately effected in the type of path analysis model we have used. To establish a trend towards Youngian meritocracy, it would be necessary to show first that the correlation between I.Q. and occupation had increased, and second that the correlation between effort and occupational status had also increased. Moreover, if income is substituted for status, third and fourth trends would similarly have to be established. Our data do not provide the relevant evidence, and there is no such evidence to my knowledge from any other source.[26]

If, however, we define meritocracy in terms of the distinction between ascription and achievement, using family background indicators for the former and educational qualifications for the latter, we can discern trends from the Nuffield evidence. Clearly there are both ascriptive and achievement forces at work in the passing of occupational status between generations. We live neither in a caste society nor in one in which the generations are severed from each other by random reallocation of status. We must also remember that a shift in the occupational structure over the past generation has produced more opportunities at the top and therefore net upward mobility in the society as a whole. Nevertheless, what has happened is the weighting of the dice of social opportunity according to class, and "the game" is increasingly played through strategies of child rearing refereed by schools through their certifying arrangements. The direct effect of the class hierarchy of families on educational opportunity and certification has *risen* since the war. And at the same time the articulation of education to the first entry into the labor market has been tightening. Thus education is increasingly the mediator of the transmission of status between generations. It commands the passage from school to work more completely now than it did a generation ago, and it is a mediator with power independent of the family. Institutionally, education is the principal agent of achievement. But at the same time the intergenerational process over which it exercises increasing sway is just as importantly one in which ascriptive forces find ways of expressing themselves as "achievement." Moreover, our path analysis has also shown that social origin or "ascription" has direct effects on the later career of a man, i.e., family influence does not cease after entry into the labor market.

Thus the old problem of equality as opposed to equality of opportunity still remains. Only its character and context change. Economic and technical changes since 1945 have enlarged occupational opportunities, but social and educational policy have not successfully seized on these circumstances in such a way as to realize either an egalitarian or a meritocratic society.

NOTES

1. I am much indebted to John Ridge for his calculations and guidance in the use of path analysis in this paper. More generally, the data reported here come from the labors of a team of sociologists at Oxford, including John Goldthorpe, Keith Hope, Phyllis Thorburn, Catriona Llewellyn, Anthony Heath, and Sara Graham. The results of the study as a whole will appear in four monographs to be published by Oxford University Press.
2. Vilfredo Pareto, *The Mind and Society* (New York: Harcourt, Brace, 1935), Vol. III, par. 20, 2053–4.
3. Michael Young, *The Rise of the Meritocracy 1870 to 2033* (London: Thames and Hudson, 1958).
4. Peter Blau and O. D. Duncan, *The American Occupational Structure* (New York: John Wiley, 1967).
5. Karl Marx, *Capital*, Vol. III (1926 edition), p. 586.

6. Stanislaw Ossowski, *Class Structure in the Social Consciousness* (London: Routledge & Kegan Paul, 1963).

7. D.V. Glass, *Social Mobility in Britain* (Routledge & Kegan Paul, 1954).

8. For example, K. Svalastoga, *Prestige, Class and Mobility* (Copenhagen: Gyldendal, 1959), and G. Carlsson, *Social Mobility and Class Structure* (Lund: C. W. Gleerup, 1958).

9. P. Blau and O. D. Duncan, *The American Occupational Structure* (New York: John Wiley, 1967).

10. Basil Bernstein, "Social Class and Linguistic Development: A Theory of Social Learning," in A. H. Halsey et al., *Education, Economy and Society* (New York: Free Press, 1961), p. 308.

11. Of course, since all mobility analysis essentially presents a historical picture, the full effects of post-war reform, especially the development of comprehensive secondary schools, will not appear before yet another generation has passed.

12. Keith Hope, ed., *The Analysis of Social Mobility* (London: Oxford University Press, 1972).

13. In this connection, Floud, Martin, and Halsey's *Social Class and Educational Opportunity* (London: Heinemann, 1957) was directly inspired by the Glass study. See also A. H. Halsey, ed., *Ability and Educational Opportunity* (Paris: O.E.C.D., 1961). Appendix 1 of the Robbins Report (Committee on Higher Education Report, London: H.M.S.O., 1963; Cmnd.2154) dealt an especially powerful blow to the pool-of-ability theories which had provided resistance to the expansion of higher education in Britain in the previous generation.

14. L. Thurow, "Education and Economic Equality," *The Public Interest*, Summer 1972, pp. 66–81.

15. Raymond Boudon, *Education, Opportunity and Social Inequality* (New York: John Wiley, 1973).

16. The index of association is the ratio of the actual proportion of sons who attained the same status as their fathers to the expected proportion which would obtain if there was a random relation between filial and paternal status. A ratio of unity denotes "perfect mobility"; ratios greater than unity indicate the extent of self-recruitment.

17. For example, A. Little and J. Westergaard produced some evidence to suggest that class chances in education were not being equalized by expansion. See their "Trend of Class Differentials in Educational Opportunity in England and Wales," *British Journal of Sociology* 15 (1969): 301–315.

18. For an explanation of path analysis see Blau and Duncan, *op. cit.*, chapters 4 and 5; O.D. Duncan, "Path Analysis," *American Journal of Sociology* 72 (1966): 1–16; Nathan Keyfitz, "Quality of Opportunity and Social Mobility: A Survey of Methods of Analysis" (paper presented to the O.E.C.D. seminar on Education, Inequality and Life Chances, 1975); and Keith Hope, "The Interpretation of Path Coefficients," *Sociology*, May 1974.

19. Blau and Duncan, *op.cit.*, p. 169. But note that Blau and Duncan took father's occupation at respondent's age 16.

20. Keith Hope's calculations suggest that the 1972 figure is likely to be more accurate.

21. See below, pp. 182–184.

22. Comparison of the British analysis shown in Figure 1 with the equivalent from the U.S.A. 1962 study (Blau and Duncan, *op.cit.*, p. 169) shows that the British correlation of father's to son's occupation is less (0.34 compared with 0.405), and that the education-occupation correlation is higher both in the case of fathers' occupations and in the case of sons'. This *suggests* that the model explains less variance in the British case, i.e., that the link of present occupation to education and origin is looser in Britain than in America.

23. A more comprehensive analysis of this type will appear in the forthcoming monograph my colleagues John Ridge and Anthony Heath are writing with me under the title of *Education and Mobility in Britain* (Oxford University Press, 1976).

24. Blau and Duncan, *op.cit.*, p. 170. It will be seen that the correlation of father's occupation with father's education in the U.S. is higher and that the path coefficients of father's education to son's education and father's occupation to first job are also higher, but that the path coefficients for father's occupation to present job and education to first job are lower.

25. A caveat must be introduced when comparing path (standardized) coefficients between models. There are two interestingly different sources of change in such cases. Path coefficients, and indeed correlations, may vary:

(a) because the slope, or "rate of exchange" of one variable into the other, has changed, or

(b) because the variance, or pattern of distribution, of one variable has changed compared with that of the other.

In the first case, we might say, from conclusion 4 above, that the "pay-off," in first-job status terms, of an extra level of qualification is greater for the younger age-group. The rate of exchange of qualifications into status has altered, such that a given qualification buys more status. This is really an assertion about the unstandardized regression coefficient b_{43}, *not* the path coefficient p_{43}. For b_{43} is not affected by any externally-produced changes in variances which might mislead us when we look at p_{43}. In fact, the relation between the quantities is, in general,

$$b_{yx} = p_{yx} \text{ (s.d.}_y/\text{s.d.}_x),$$

where s.d.$_y$, s.d.$_x$ are the relevant standard deviations. In the present case, where first job is y and qualifications x, it is clear that identical bs, but very different ps, would result if the variance of educational levels increased sharply, while the distribution of first-job status remained stable; analysis of the standardized coefficients alone (the ps) would suggest increased dependence of first job on education, while the change that actually occurred might have been quite a different one.

For this reason, the unstandardized b-coefficients have all been computed and compared with the path coefficients. It is necessary only to mention the cases in which the results entail a revision of the inferences drawn from the path coefficients. In fact, the only inference affected is 5, that the direct effect of education on present job is rising. It appears, instead, that it is the variance of education, or qualification-levels, that has increased sharply, while the variance of present-job status has hardly changed. The slope, or "exchange rate," has actually moved the other way: the older group get slightly more status for a given level than do the younger ones, at least for present job. The effect is almost certainly due to the artificial restriction of variance of present job among the young group, many of whom have not reached a "stable" career point. One should bear this in mind when interpreting any changes involving the variable of present job status, such as inference 7 above. For those who wish to work out the unstandardized coefficients themselves, the standard deviations are:

	Older men	Younger men
1.	0.425	0.589
2.	29.817	31.956
3.	0.861	1.107
4.	25.708	31.082
5.	36.298	37.193

26. Christopher Jencks has asserted the same conclusion with respect to American studies.

8. Education and Social Mobility: A Structural Model

RAYMOND BOUDON

One of the most difficult and controversial problems in sociology today concerns the consequences of the rapid growth in school enrollment rates that has characterized most countries over the last few decades. It is common knowledge that sociologists as well as politicians have long believed educational development to be the most important policy instrument for achieving social equality. Economists of education are still frequently attached to the idea that educational development will naturally lead to reduced inequality in income. Not so long ago, sociologists saw in growth in rates of school attendance a means for increasing social mobility.

Our purpose here, however, is not to deal with the problem of the consequences of overall increases in the rates of school attendance. Concerning the influence that this factor might have on income distribution, it suffices to refer the reader to a recent article by Thurow.[1] He shows that if we assume that the structure of employment is determined only to a slight extent by changes in educational stock, then the average increase in time spent in schooling does not lead to a reduction but rather to an actual increase in economic inequality. More precisely, if we consider only the three recognized levels of education (i.e., elementary, secondary, and college), we will observe (1) that the income *variance* for each of these three levels tends to decrease, and (2) that the differences in average salaries for the three levels tend to become greater.

It should be emphasized that this finding, derived from a seemingly quite reasonable hypothesis that posits that employment structure (i.e., income structure) changes more slowly than what we will call the educational structure (i.e., the distribution of individuals according to their level of schooling), contradicts some propositions frequently advanced by economists of education.[2]

The merit of Thurow's hypothesis is confirmed because the conclusions he draws correspond to empirical observation for the data he studies—data for the United States.

Between 1949 and 1969, we can observe two tendencies in the United States:

1. *Educational inequality decreased.* To measure this decrease, Thurow uses the Gini-Pareto method. Let n be the total years of schooling for a sample population at a given moment, and n_1, $n_2, \ldots, n_{10}$ the total years of schooling that correspond respectively to the least

This article first appeared in *Sociologie et Société* 5 (May 1973): 111—124. English translation by David Swartz.

educated 10% of the population, to the next 10% just above, and so on up to the most educated 10%. We can then observe that the part of the total educational *stock* belonging to the least educated 10% increased between 1949 and 1969 whereas the part for the best educated decreased.

2. *Economic inequality increased.* Between 1949 and 1969, the proportion of income going to the least privileged 10% tended to decrease whereas the proportion going to the most privileged increased. Thus, the increase in rates of school attendance was accompanied by both a decrease in educational inequality *and* an increase in economic inequality.[3]

On the other hand, American statistics show that in line with the consequences predicted by Thurow's hypothesis, there also occurred during the 1949–1969 period:

1. A reduction in the variance of income for each of the three levels of education; and
2. A divergence between the average incomes of the three levels.

I. EXPANSION IN RATES OF SCHOOL ATTENDANCE AND MOBILITY

In this article we are interested in the problem of how growth in rates of school attendance influences social mobility. If in the introduction we felt it useful to call attention to Thurow's study, it was first of all because the problem of the effect of expanded rates of school attendance on both social mobility and economic inequality has always given rise to similar controversies. And second, we can obtain in both cases much clearer results by integrating into our argument Thurow's hypothesis, which posits that income, or employment structure, or—for our particular case—the *social structure* (i.e., the distribution of social status), *is largely independent of the evolution of the educational structure.*

Let us simply add that the considerations

that follow summarize a part of the theory of social mobility formulated in my book *Inégalité des chances.*[4] My book was practically finished when my attention was drawn to Thurow's work,[5] and I am therefore using this article to relate my analysis and my conclusions to his work. Thurow's conclusion is that, contrary to general expectation, the development of the educational system does not necessarily reduce economic inequality; my own conclusion is that there is no reason to expect an increase in social mobility or equality *even if one assumes a decrease in inequality of education.*

The italicized portion of this last sentence calls for clarification. It is sometimes assumed in what is called "critical" sociology that the educational system reinforces rather than diminishes inequalities of social background. It follows that there is therefore no reason to expect that an expansion in rates of school enrollment will be accompanied by a democratization of education. It is true that we can produce certain statistics, referring to certain countries and concerning very short time periods, which indicate that inequalities of education do not seem to diminish. If we consider periods of twenty or ten years, or even shorter ones, however, and then try to observe the evolution of educational inequality in industrial societies as a whole, we cannot deny that Thurow's demonstration for the United States can justly be criticized, since he does not take into account the demographic structure of the American population between the two periods studied. But the impressive statistical documentation assembled by O.E.C.D. leaves no room for doubt: in industrial societies, and in particular in liberal industrial societies, *educational inequality shows a constant tendency to decrease.*[6]

The problem then becomes one of knowing to what extent both the expansion in rates of school attendance and the decrease in educational inequality bring about a decrease in inequality of *social opportunity,* or in somewhat more academic language, an increase in *social mobility.*

II. THE NECESSITY FOR A SYSTEMATIC THEORY OF SOCIAL MOBILITY

In order to answer this question it is necessary to resort to what could be called a systematic theory of mobility. It is, in other words, essential to consider the set of factors that affect mobility as a system of interdependent elements. A theory of this type has already been developed in detail in *Inégalité des chances.*[7] Since it is, of course, impossible to summarize fully that theory here, I will simply present in general outline form the model to which it leads. It is also impossible to present here empirical justifications for every hypothesis or consequence. Let us simply state that the axioms of the model as well as its consequences appear on the whole to conform to the existing body of data from industrial societies, whether based on school records or on sociological investigations. Without going into detail, the model is composed of three logical parts or, if one prefers, of three stages.

1. Assume first that for a population sample, the distribution of individuals according to educational attainment varies as a function of social class background. Assume further that each type of social class background has an associated decisional field that determines (according to social class and to degree of scholarly success) the probabilities that an individual will choose, at a given school level, to continue his education, and that he will choose to pursue a given kind of education. For example, he might choose to continue his schooling rather than to leave the educational system, or to follow a college preparatory curriculum rather than vocational training. Furthermore, we assume that the school levels and the branching points that demarcate the school program can vary from one school system to another and change over time. German statistics, for example, show that ten years ago the *mittlere Reife* (i.e., the intermediate high school certificate) was perceived as an important dividing point; middle and lower social class German families considered it as a sort of "natural" termination point for their children. Such a structure can be introduced into our model by assuming that the low survival probabilities for the average pupil in the educational system are determined by his level of educational attainment, his age, and other dimensions in the decisional field.

Without going into details, I will suggest that once these properties are formalized into a model, one can then reconstitute the distribution of a hypothetical cohort with regard to educational attainment. I will therefore suppose that in our model there exist three social classes (higher, middle, and lower), and that in a cohort of 100,000 pupils who finish their elementary education at a given moment, 10,000 have a higher, 30,000 a middle, and 60,000 a lower social class background. By correctly formalizing the preceding theoretical propositions and by choosing appropriate parameters, it will be possible to show how many pupils from each social background will reach each level of the school system.

Table 1 shows the results obtained from applying the model to one particularly simple case. Six levels of educational achievement are distinguished. Columns 1, 3, and 5 give the proportion of pupils who, in each social class, reach a given level of schooling; the other three columns show the accumulated proportions from the bottom to the top.

It is noteworthy that the results generated by the model are structurally consistent with findings provided by school statistics. The inequalities in secondary schooling that distinguish the three social classes are considerable; but the inequalities in college education are even more outstanding.

2. The second stage of the model-building process will permit us to move from a static to a dynamic hypothesis. We will suppose that the characteristics of the decisional fields change over time. In the simplest case, it can be assumed that the survival probabilities increase for pupils

Table 1. Educational attainment as a function of social class background.

| | *Social class background* | | | | | |
| | C_1 *(upper)* | | C_2 *(middle)* | | C_3 *(lower)* | |
Educational level	*(1)*	*(2)*	*(3)*	*(4)*	*(5)*	*(6)*
1. College graduation	0.1967	1.0000	0.0340	0.9999	0.0053	1.0000
2. Some college	0.0905	0.8033	0.0397	0.9659	0.0104	0.9947
3. High school graduation	0.0618	0.7128	0.0357	0.9262	0.0118	0.9843
4. More than three years of high school	0.1735	0.6510	0.1396	0.8905	0.0653	0.9725
5. Not more than three years of high school	0.2775	0.4775	0.3609	0.7509	0.3072	0.9072
6. Elementary school	0.2000	0.2000	0.3900	0.3900	0.6000	0.6000
Total	1.0000		0.9999		1.0000	

following a college preparatory curriculum. Furthermore, it can be assumed that the smaller the initial survival probability, the greater the increase. Therefore, let us suppose that p represents the survival probability beyond a given branching point, at a given time, for a given level of educational achievement, and at a given age. One can then suppose that p for the next period will equal $p + (1 - p)a$, where a is a positive coefficient less than 1. Tables 2a, 2b, and 2c give the principal results derived from the model when the hypotheses and parameters that lead to Table 1 are used, and when the foregoing dynamic hypothesis is introduced. The three parts of Table 2 correspond to the distributions that can be obtained for three successive time periods. Thus, it can be said that Table 1 corresponds to the time period t_0, and that Tables 2a, 2b, and 2c correspond respectively to the time periods t_1, t_2, and t_3.[8]

These tables reproduce the structural properties that can be observed from school records when these provide longitudinal data. Two observations are noteworthy:

(i)   From one period to another, the probability of attaining the higher levels in the educational system is multiplied by a coefficient that increases propor-

tionately with a decrease in social class background.

(ii)   However, for a thousand individuals, the increase from one period to another in the number of additional persons who are able to attend college is much lower for those of lower social class background than for those of higher social class background. These results are in accordance with the empirical data from school statistics.

We will not give further attention to these first two stages of the model. They concern the problem treated in this article only to the extent that they make it possible to determine:

(i)   the change over time in the total number of pupils attending school at the different educational levels; and

(ii)   the change over time in their social composition at each educational level.

These two points are naturally fundamental for analyzing social mobility in industrial societies, since the level of schooling certainly influences the individual's social status aspirations. This is why it has been necessary to present briefly the part of the model dealing with the changes over

Table 2. Educational attainment as a function of social class background for three successive periods: t_1, t_2, and t_3.

	Social class background					
	C_1 (upper)		C_2 (middle)		C_3 (lower)	
Educational level	(1)	(2)	(3)	(4)	(5)	(6)
(a) $t = t_1$						
1. College graduation	0.2319	1.0001	0.0491	0.9999	0.0092	1.0001
2. Some college	0.0947	0.7682	0.0490	0.9508	0.0153	0.9909
3. High school graduation	0.0629	0.6735	0.0418	0.9018	0.0164	0.9756
4. More than three years of high school	0.1707	0.6106	0.1526	0.8600	0.0832	0.9592
5. Not more than three years of high school	0.2599	0.4399	0.3564	0.7074	0.3360	0.8760
6. Elementary school	0.1800	0.1800	0.3510	0.3510	0.5400	0.5400
Total	1.0001		0.9999		1.0001	
(b) $t = t_2$						
1. College graduation	0.2689	1.0002	0.0680	1.0000	0.0151	1.0000
2. Some college	0.0977	0.7313	0.0584	0.9320	0.0215	0.9849
3. High school graduation	0.0631	0.6336	0.0474	0.8736	0.0217	0.9634
4. More than three years of high school	0.1662	0.5705	0.1629	0.8262	0.1018	0.9417
5. Not more than three years of high school	0.2423	0.4043	0.3474	0.6633	0.3539	0.8399
6. Elementary school	0.1620	0.1620	0.3159	0.3159	0.4860	0.4860
Total	1.0002		1.0000		1.0000	
(c) $t = t_3$						
1. College graduation	0.3069	1.0001	0.0904	1.0000	0.0233	1.0000
2. Some college	0.0993	0.6932	0.0676	0.9096	0.0288	0.9767
3. High school graduation	0.0626	0.5939	0.0524	0.8420	0.0277	0.9479
4. More than three years of high school	0.1604	0.5313	0.1703	0.7896	0.1197	0.9202
5. Not more than three years of high school	0.2250	0.3709	0.3350	0.6193	0.3629	0.8005
6. Elementary school	0.1459	0.1459	0.2843	0.2843	0.4376	0.4376
Total	1.0001		1.0000		1.0000	

time in unequal educational opportunity. Apart from its importance for analyzing social mobility, this part of the model can help clarify the theory of unequal educational opportunity. This point, however, is not treated here.

Let us take note of one final interesting structural characteristic of Tables 1 and 2:

the rate of growth in school attendance is greater, the higher the level of education. This result is also consistent with empirical data from educational statistics. For most of the industrially advanced countries, O.E.C.D. has been able to assemble appropriate statistics showing that the growth rate is higher in school enrollment for college level students than for high school. The growth rate of high school enrollment is in general also greater than for elementary school.

III. EDUCATION AND MOBILITY

We now take up the third stage of the model-building process, which deals directly with our problem: namely, the influence of growth in rates of school enrollment and reduced educational inequality on social mobility. In the first two stages of the model, the successive cohorts of pupils were distributed according to their level of educational attainment. The third stage will define the mechanism whereby an individual endowed with a given level of education is awarded a given social status.

With respect to this stage, what hypotheses must be introduced into the model? First of all, it can clearly be assumed that to some degree the industrial societies are all *meritocratic*. In other words, we will assume that, all other things being equal, those individuals of the highest level of educational attainment will tend to receive the highest social status. Later on we will see how this theoretical proposition can be given a precise form.

A second hypothesis suggests that, all other things being equal, individuals of the highest social class background will tend to obtain the highest social status. In particular, one can assume from the numerous findings of sociological investigation that individuals with the same level of educational attainment have a greater chance of achieving high social status if they are of high social background. In such a case, we will speak of an effect of *dominance*.

If our objective was to establish an exhaustive theory of social mobility, then yet other factors would have to be introduced. It is common knowledge, for example, that individuals of the same level of schooling aim for careers that vary in social status: thus, pupils of middle-class background who successfully complete high school aim less frequently for the prestigious careers, such

as medicine and law, than their classmates of higher social class background.

On the other hand, it is clear that ecological factors affect the mobility process; two persons with similar individual characteristics, such as social background, level of schooling, course of study, etc., have different chances of obtaining a given social status, depending on the type of environment to which they belong. The statistical data assembled by O.E.C.D. point to the existence of important regional variations in educational opportunity even when individual characteristics are held constant.

Let us begin then with the simplest case. Geographical mobility can be assumed to be sufficiently important that we may neglect these ecological factors. Moreover, since the question asked here seeks to determine to what extent social mobility is affected by the increase in rates of school attendance and by reduced educational inequality, the aforementioned effect of dominance can be neglected. We will therefore assume a *purely meritocratic structure*. If expansion in education and reduction in educational inequality are ever to have an effect on social mobility, then it certainly must be in this type of society.

How then can this meritocratic hypothesis be formalized so as to introduce it into the model? To simplify things, it can be assumed, as before, that three hierarchically ranked social strata can be distinguished: C_1 (higher), C_2 (middle), and C_3 (lower). Let us furthermore suppose that the social structure changes relatively little over time; that is, the distribution of individuals relative to the three types of social status is practically constant. In the first and second stages of the model, we supposed that a cohort of pupils finishing elementary school were distributed in the following manner: 10,000 at C_1, 30,000 at C_2, and 60,000 at C_3. To simplify things, we will assume that this cohort will have to fill 100,000 social positions, of which 10,000 will be at the C_1 level, 30,000 at C_2, and 60,000 at C_3.

Of course, it is hardly realistic to suppose

that pupils finishing elementary school will enter competition on the labor market at the same time; depending on their level of schooling, they will enter the job market at different times. Let us simply say that the model would quickly become complicated if it were assumed that the pupils entered the labor market at regular intervals, but that such an assumption would not modify the conclusions of this analysis.

In order then to give the meritocratic hypothesis operational form, it will suffice to consider that the pupils will receive their social status according to an inegalitarian process that will favor those having the highest level of schooling. Thus, at time t_0, 10,000 places are available in C_1, whereas 3,305 individuals from the initial cohort reach the highest level of education (see Table 1).

$$0.1967 \times 10,000 + 0.0340 \times 30,000 + 0.0053 \times 60,000 = 3,305$$

It will be assumed that a high proportion of these individuals, say 70%, will receive C_1-type social positions. Then, there will remain:

$$10,000 - 3,305 \times 0.70 = 7,686$$

available positions in C_1. Next we will assume that 70% of these positions will go to those individuals having achieved an educational level just below the highest one. We will continue in like manner, assigning the remaining social positions in C_1 to successive samples of candidates at lower levels of schooling.

Having completed this procedure for C_1, we can carry out the same operation for C_2 (middle level of social status) by first taking the candidates having the highest level of schooling, then those at the next lower level, and so on, down to the lowest. Of course, one will have to take into account that some of these candidates have already been located in C_1. But here again, it will be assumed that what could be called the *meritocratic parameter* is equal to 70%.

The distribution mechanism, as can be seen, is very simple, and therefore does not call for further presentation. Nevertheless, take note that in certain cases, it could happen that there are fewer social positions for a given type of social background than there are available candidates. With reference to Table 1, it is thus easy to see that for period t_0, the number of pupils leaving high school before graduation, that is,

$$0.2775 \times 10,000 + 0.3609 \times 30,000 + 0.3072 \times 60,000 = 32,035$$

is higher than the number of available social positions in C_2 after all of the candidates of higher educational level have been granted places. Let x be this number. We will suppose that in this case—for logical reasons which we cannot develop here—the meritocratic parameter applies to x. The number of C_2 positions left open for those individuals who have completed only high school will be equal to $0.70x$.

The application of the method just described leads to the results presented in Table 3. This table gives the number of individuals who, according to their level of schooling, reach each of the three types of social status for the four time periods considered. The meritocratic parameter is assumed to equal 70% for each of the four periods. The only element that varies from one period to another is therefore the *distribution of the levels of schooling* that characterizes each of the four cohorts.

The consequences of the general increase in levels of schooling on the relationship between the level of educational attainment and achieved social status are relatively complex. By examining Table 3, one observes the following:

1. The highest levels of educational achievement (i.e., S_1—college graduation—and S_2—some undergraduate study) are associated with a structure of social opportunity that remains stable over time.

2. The structure of social opportunity associated with the educational level S_3

(i.e., high school graduation) is initially constant and just as favorable as the one that characterizes the two higher levels. Nevertheless, in the last period, this level of social opportunity drops considerably: those who do not go beyond this educational level have a considerably lower probability of reaching the highest social status, whereas social opportunity at the middle and lower levels has grown as a consequence.

3. Social opportunity at the lower levels,

such as S_4 (i.e., more than three years of high school), S_5 (i.e., not more than three years of high school), and S_6 (i.e., elementary school), thus deteriorates continuously over time. It is noteworthy nevertheless that this deterioration is greater, the higher the relative level of schooling. Thus, for the first period, the S_4 level of schooling is associated with a reasonably high (0.2920) probability of attaining the high social status level C_1. For the fourth period, this probability is

Table 3. Number and proportion of pupils attaining each of the three levels of social status as a function of their educational achievement for the four periods ranging from t_0 to t_3.

Educational level		Social status						Total
		C_1		C_2		C_3		
t_0	S_1	2,313	(0.70000)	694	(0.2100)	298	(0.0900)	3,305
	S_2	1,904	(0.70000)	571	(0.2100)	245	(0.0900)	2,720
	S_3	1,678	(0.70000)	503	(2.2100)	216	(0.0900)	2,397
	S_4	2,874	(0.2920)	4,878	(0.4956)	2,090	(0.2124)	9,842
	S_5	862	(0.0269)	16,345	(0.5102)	14,828	(0.4629)	32,035
	S_6	369	(0.0074)	7,009	(0.1410)	42,323	(0.8516)	49,701
Total		10,000		30,000		60,000		100,000
t_1	S_1	3,041	(0.7000)	912	(0.2100)	391	(0.0900)	4,344
	S_2	2,334	(0.7000)	701	(0.2100)	300	(0.0900)	3,335
	S_3	2,007	(0.7000)	602	(0.2100)	258	(0.0900)	2,867
	S_4	1,833	(0.1625)	6,611	(0.5862)	2,833	(0.2512)	11,277
	S_5	550	(0.0164)	14,822	(0.4431)	18,077	(0.5404)	33,449
	S_6	235	(0.0053)	6,352	(0.1420)	38,141	(0.8527)	44,728
Total		10,000		30,000		60,000		100,000
t_2	S_1	3,944	(0.7000)	1,184	(0.2100)	507	(0.0900)	5,635
	S_2	2,813	(0.7000)	844	(0.2100)	362	(0.0900)	4,019
	S_3	2,348	(0.7000)	705	(0.2100)	302	(0.0900)	3,355
	S_4	627	(0.0495)	8,421	(0.6653)	3,609	(0.2851)	12,657
	S_5	188	(0.0055)	13,192	(0.3871)	20,698	(0.6074)	34,078
	S_6	80	(0.0020)	5,654	(0.1405)	34,522	(0.8576)	40,256
Total		10,000		30,000		60,000		100,000
t_3	S_1	5,025	(0.7000)	1,438	(0.2100)	716	(0.0900)	7,179
	S_2	3,324	(0.7000)	998	(0.2100)	427	(0.0900)	4,749
	S_3	1,156	(0.2995)	1,893	(0.4904)	811	(0.2101)	3,860
	S_4	346	(0.0249)	9,484	(0.6825)	4,065	(0.2926)	13,895
	S_5	104	(0.0031)	11,331	(0.3325)	22,639	(0.6644)	34,074
	S_6	45	(0.0012)	4,856	(0.1340)	31,342	(0.8648)	36,243
Total		10,000		30,000		60,000		100,000

more than ten times smaller (0.0249). On the other hand, however, deterioration in social opportunity for S_5, and above all for S_6, occurs more slowly.

It would, of course, be possible to obtain these results by an abstract analysis. We have preferred to utilize the simulation method (i.e., arithmetic analysis of the model) in order to make our demonstration more concrete. Intuitively, one can easily understand the reasons for the foregoing phenomenon: the social structure (i.e., distribution of available social positions) was assumed to be stable over time; however, the educational structure (i.e., distribution of individuals according to their level of schooling) tended to become clustered near the top; the growth in school attendance from one period to another is greater, the higher the level of schooling considered. It follows that the most prestigious social positions available are distributed at a rapidly growing rate to those individuals of a higher educational level. In time, this tendency brings about a sharp deterioration in the structure of social opportunity associated with the middle educational levels, and this deterioration is then slowly passed on to the lower levels.

An examination of the consequences of the model in terms of social mobility still remains to be carried out. Table 2 gives the proportion of individuals for each period who, according to their social background, reach a given educational level. Table 3, on the other hand, gives the proportion of individuals who, according to their level of educational attainment, reach each of the three levels of social status. Since it was assumed that achieved social status is determined solely by *merit,* and that the effects of dominance are negligible, it is possible to construct the matrices of intergenerational mobility corresponding to each of the four periods, by multiplying the matrices in Tables 2 and 3 for each of the four periods. The result is presented in Table 4. One can make the following comments about this table.

1. First, it can be seen, as we predicted,

Table 4. Tables of rates of social mobility generated by the model for the four periods from t_0 to t_3.

Social class background		*Achieved social status*			
		C_1	C_2	C_3	*Total*
t_0	C_1	0.3039	0.3290	0.3670	0.9999
	C_2	0.1299	0.3313	0.5387	0.9999
	C_3	0.0510	0.2795	0.6697	1.0002
t_1	C_1	0.3056	0.3226	0.3719	1.0001
	C_2	0.1304	0.3266	0.5428	0.9998
	C_3	0.0505	0.2829	0.6666	1.0000
t_2	C_1	0.3107	0.3174	0.3722	1.0003
	C_2	0.1323	0.3237	0.5440	1.0000
	C_3	0.0488	0.2852	0.6660	1.0000
t_3	C_1	0.3080	0.3198	0.3723	1.0001
	C_2	0.1319	0.3246	0.5435	1.0000
	C_3	0.0494	0.2855	0.6650	0.9999

that the structure of social mobility changes very little over time from the first period t_0, to the last t_3. The probabilities contained in each of the four tables are practically identical from one period to another. This result, which can be justified mathematically, has a paradoxical appearance. One will recall that the results presented in Table 4 are derived from the model in which we assumed:

(a) a rapid growth in school attendance between t_0 and t_3 at the highest educational levels;

(b) a significant reduction in unequal opportunity in education; and

(c) an important change over time of the educational structure as contrasted with the fixity of the social structure.

Intuitively, one would be tempted to conclude that these different factors would lead to change in the mobility structure. This analysis shows, however, that such is not the case. The model simultaneously generates important changes in the structure of educational achievement and educational opportunity, but these changes have no effect upon the structure of social mobility.

2. Let us now consider the slight changes that occur in the mobility structure between

t_0 and t_3. One can observe between t_0 and t_2 a slight tendency for increased self-recruitment at the C_1 level. At the same time, the downward mobility from C_1 (i.e., higher social class background) to C_3 (i.e., lower social class background) also increases slightly. Conversely, the self-recruitment characteristic of C_1 diminishes between t_2 and t_3. In glancing through the four tables it therefore becomes apparent that changes in the mobility structure both *are weak in amplitude* and *do not follow a definite pattern.*

Why is this? Without going into a mathematical analysis of this phenomenon, we can offer an intuitive explanation. Consider, for example, the individuals of a higher social background, and examine the effects that the structural changes postulated by the model between t_0 and t_3 have on their social opportunity. Between these two extreme periods, these individuals reach on an average the highest educational levels. Thus, in t_0, 1,967 of 10,000 pupils of higher social background reach the highest educational level (i.e., college graduation); in t_3, there are 2,689 (see Tables 1 and 2) who do so. It of course follows that the number of persons who do not graduate from college tends to *decrease.* But, at the same time, because of the effects of the generalized increase in educational demand, the structure of social opportunity for the lower, and especially for the middle, educational levels tends to deteriorate over time. Now the numbers of pupils of higher social background who reach only the middle educational levels is quite large between t_0 and t_3. A kind of *compensation effect* occurs that generates stability over time in the mobility structure characteristic of higher social background individuals. Of course, a similar type of analysis would also be possible for individuals of middle and lower social background. In all cases, the almost complete stability of the mobility structure results from the generalized increase in educational demand, which produces complex compensation effects.

3. Let us return now to Table 3, which presents the probabilities of social oppor-

tunity at $C_{1,2,3}$ as a function of educational attainment C_{1-6}. This table shows that the structures of social opportunity that characterize the educational levels tend to become increasingly differentiated over time. Thus, the social opportunity structure remains stable for the S_1 and S_2 levels; on the other hand, the structure associated with the S_5 and S_6 levels deteriorates. This result is consistent with the conclusions drawn by Thurow: the relationship between social aspirations and the level of educational attainment tends to be more and more clear. This factor is probably *in part* at the root of the generalized increase in educational demand which characterizes industrial societies. Nevertheless, the compensation effects released by this increase have not produced any appreciable change in the structure of social mobility.

CONCLUSION

It has not been possible in this article for us to develop in detail the logical consequences and presuppositions of the foregoing model. Let us simply say that the set of axioms and consequences that define the model appear to be consistent with the available empirical data for industrial societies.

The principal conclusion of this article is that there is no reason to expect that a considerable increase in educational demand, which is occurring in industrial societies, is connected to an increase in social mobility, even if accompanied, as it certainly is, by a reduction in unequal educational opportunity. The preceding model shows, on the contrary, that *under extremely general conditions,* the current expansion of education is generally consistent with a high level of stability in the mobility structure. This conclusion will hold unless unrealistic propositions are introduced: for example, that reduction of inequality in educational opportunity occurs much more rapidly than it in fact does; or that the changes in social structure, which are due to technological change in particular, are extremely rapid (at the same pace as those that characterize education).

Concerning this last point, it should be noted that in the presentation of the model we have assumed that the social structure is fixed in time. This assumption is obviously extreme. Technological change is clearly capable of bringing about modifications in the socio-professional structure by reducing, for example, the proportion of unskilled jobs. But the important point is that the conclusions of the foregoing model hold true even if one supposes that the social structure changes over time. Thus, one can introduce the hypothesis that, from one time period to another, the number of available positions of higher social status (C_1) increases whereas the number of positions of lower status (C_3) decreases. Unless, however, it is also to be assumed that changes in social structure are as rapid as those in the educational structure, one can conclude that the structure of mobility must remain practically stable over time.

In summary, then, it can be said that under extremely general conditions, expansion of educational opportunity does not bring about a reduction in that distinct and essential form of inequality which is the inequality of social opportunity (i.e., dependence of a son's social status upon his father's), even if it is accompanied by reduced inequality in educational opportunity. This result will perhaps explain the surprising conclusion of the well-known work on social mobility by Lipset and Bendix. When, near the end of the 1950s, these authors carried out a study comparing mobility in the different industrial societies, they concluded that there were similar rates of mobility in nations that nonetheless differed sharply in many ways, including their systems of stratification and education.[9] More than ten years later in a recent article in *The Public Interest,* Lipset confirmed this result.[10]

Finally, I would have to agree with Thurow's conclusions:

In any case, I would argue that our reliance on education as the ultimate public policy for curing all problems, economic and social, is unwarranted at best and in all probability ineffective.

The expansion of education, if one is to believe Thurow's analysis, has proved ineffective for reducing economic inequality, and it has probably not been any more successful in diminishing social immobility. In this respect, the principal effect of the increase in demand for education appears to be one of requiring the individual to spend more and more time to realize social aspirations which, themselves, have remained unchanged.

NOTES

1. Lester C. Thurow, "Education and Economic Equality," *The Public Interest,* Summer 1972, pp. 66–81.
2. It is impossible to give here a bibliography of the economics of education. For this, one should consult the very useful collection of texts assembled by UNESCO, *Textes choisis sur l'économie de l'éducation* (Paris: UNESCO, 1968).
3. Thurow shows that there is not only a correlation between these phenomena, but also a cause-effect relationship. The reader can refer to his text for this demonstration.
4. Raymond Boudon, *Inégalité des chances* (Paris: Librairie Armand Colin, 1973). English version: *Education, Opportunity, and Social Inequality* (New York: John Wiley & Sons, 1974).
5. I warmly thank Bernard Cazes for bringing this work to my attention.
6. *Conférence sur les politiques de développement de l'enseignement* (Paris: O.E.C.D., 1972).
7. See note 4.
8. The model applies to an ideal society rather than to a particular industrialized society, and it is difficult to synchronize the model time with real time. To facilitate understanding, one can assume that the time interval separating the two successive periods of the model equals approximately five years. One can then derive from the model a set of evolution curves close to those observed in school records.
9. R. Bendix and S.M. Lipset, *Social Mobility in Industrial Societies* (Berkeley: University of California Press, 1958).
10. S.M. Lipset, "Social Mobility and Educational Opportunity," *The Public Interest,* no. 29 (Fall 1972), pp. 99–108.

9. Socioeconomic Status, Intelligence, and the Attainment of Higher Education*

WILLIAM H. SEWELL and VIMAL P. SHAH

INTRODUCTION

The educational system plays an important role in the allocation of personnel to various occupational positions. It sorts people according to differences in valued abilities, channels them into streams of training which develop their capacities, and encourages them to aspire to adult roles that are in keeping with their talents.[1] However, many factors other than the ability of the student influence his eventual educational experiences and attainments. These include differences in the level and quality of education available in the country, region, or community in which he lives; differential access to educational facilities according to his social class status, religion, race, and ethnic origins; differences in his motivations, values, and attitudes; and differences in the willingness and ability of his parents and significant others to provide the financial and psychological supports necessary for the maximization of his talent potentials.[2]

Turner has distinguished two modes of social mobility which are reflected in contrasting strategies of educational selection.[3] Where aristocratic conditions underlie the contemporary class structure—as in Britain—mobility is sponsored and educational selection is overt, systematic, and prompt in the school career of an age group of children from which an able minority is chosen for higher education. In American society, on the other hand, an organizing norm of contest mobility is preserved with the aid of a tacit, belated, and prolonged selection through dropout from college rather than from elementary and secondary schools. Free education in public schools and the prescription of a legally permissible school-leaving age have brought about a nearly universal pattern of primary and secondary education. High school graduation has become the norm of the American population, and college education is increasingly common.

But, there is a point beyond which further education is a privilege of some rather than a right of all individuals whose intellectual capabilities qualify them for continued formal education. At the present time, for many Americans this point comes at graduation from high school. This is indicated by a number of studies that have reported that many students with high intelligence are unlikely to aspire to a college education or to go to college—especially if they come from families of low socioeconomic status, are females, are members of disadvantaged racial groups, or come from rural backgrounds.[4] However, the aspirations of many cross-pressured individuals (those who are low in status but high in ability, or vice versa) are encouraged by the ideology of equal opportunity and the existence of a great diversity of colleges and universities to fit the financial and intellectual capacities of most students. Consequently, studies of college plans and college attendance have tended to stress the influence of socioeconomic status, while those of college graduation have tended to emphasize the influence of ability.[5] This is best summarized by Wolfle who, after examining the evidence then available, reached the conclusion that

...the probability of enrolling in college decreases more sharply as one goes down the

*Paper prepared for the Research Group on the Sociology of Education at the Sixth World Congress of the International Sociological Association, Evian, France, September 1966. The research reported in this paper is financed by a grant from the National Institutes of Health, U.S. Public Health Service (M-6275). The writers acknowledge the services of the University of Wisconsin Computing Center and wish to thank Otis Dudley Duncan, Archibald O. Haller, and Bruce K. Eckland for their helpful comments on an earlier draft of this paper.

From *Sociology of Education* 40 (Winter 1967): 1–23. Reprinted by permission.

ability scale for children from economically and socially less favored homes than it does for children from more favored homes. After entering college, the situation changes. The student who gets into college has already overcome most of whatever handicaps his home environment offered; once there, his chances of graduating are much more dependent upon his ability and much less upon his family background than were his chances of getting into college in the first place.[6]

More recently Eckland, in his review of twenty-four studies published during the last fifteen years, observes that even when a positive relationship has been found between social class and college graduation, some researchers have tended to reach an interpretation similar to Wolfle's.[7] Eckland doubted the validity of this conclusion because most of these studies had been based on graduates from a single college and, consequently, did not include those students who entered the particular college, dropped out, enrolled in another college, and eventually graduated. In his follow-up study of male students in the freshman class of 1952 at the University of Illinois, over 70% of the dropouts had returned either to that university or had entered another college at some time during a ten-year period and about 55% of those who re-entered college eventually graduated. He found that social class was an important determinant of who will transfer or return to college and, consequently, of eventual college graduation. Scholastic ability, however, continued to play an important part in determining graduation from college.[8]

It seems that a student's persistence in his educational pursuit even in the face of academic failure plays an important part in the selective mechanism of the educational system. Up to high school graduation, persistence in educational pursuits may be merely an outcome of the legal structure as reflected in free and compulsory education up to a certain level and the prescription of a minimum school-leaving age. But at the college level, it may be greatly influenced by social origins because a determined student

of modest ability but high status may ultimately find an institution where he will not be weeded out; or a student of low socioeconomic status but superior ability may find an institution in which he will be given adequate opportunities and motivation to succeed in higher studies. Thus, the question of the relation of socioeconomic status and of ability to educational selection should be examined through time by following a cohort of students wherever they go for higher education, rather than by looking at the product of a single institution.

While there are local, statewide, and national studies that have attempted to examine the influences of socioeconomic status and ability on educational aspirations and achievements of students, past studies are deficient because of inadequate samples, failure to take account of those who dropped out, and insufficient follow-up to relate eventual educational attainment to either ability or status. Therefore, there is great need to determine the relative influences of socioeconomic status and ability at successive stages in the educational career of a large and representative cohort. Another advantage in studying the educational attainments of a cohort over time is that such a procedure provides an indirect control for those many events that influence in common the educational careers of all members of the cohort. The purpose of this study is to determine the relative influence of socioeconomic status and measured intelligence on the attainment of higher education for a randomly selected cohort of Wisconsin high school seniors during a seven-year period after their graduation from high school (1957–1964). A major advantage of this study over past research is that it presents a comparative picture of the influences of socioeconomic status and intelligence on the educational attainments of a large cohort of youth who pursued their higher education at diverse institutions over a period of years. Moreover, the statistical analysis followed in this paper permits not only the demarcation of certain subpopulations of socioeconomic status and intelligence which vary in educational plans and attainments, but also provides estimates of the direct and indirect effects of socioeconomic status and intelligence at successive stages in the educational careers of males and females separately.

The use of Wisconsin students for a study of this kind is, of course, less ideal than would be a large, randomly selected cohort of the nation's students chosen at some point earlier in the educational process than graduation from high school. Wisconsin, however, is in many ways a good state for a study of the educational attainment of high school youth. Its holding power over its school children is very high; more than 88% of its 16–17 year olds were in school in 1960.[9] Thus, the high school senior class retains a more representative body of students of all ability and socioeconomic levels than would be true in states where the dropout rate is higher. Moreover, Wisconsin provides greatly diversified opportunities for higher education with a large and prestigious state university, which includes not only its Madison and Milwaukee campuses but also a statewide network of university centers offering first- and second-year college level courses, a state college system consisting of nine four-year colleges offering a full range of curricula at low cost, a large urban Catholic university, and thirteen accredited private liberal arts colleges. It can be truly said that Wisconsin provides facilities of higher education suitable for most levels of ability if not for all levels of socioeconomic status.

PURPOSES AND STATISTICAL TECHNIQUES

The specific purposes of this paper are as follows:

(1) To examine the association of socioeconomic status with college plans, college attendance, and college graduation for a cohort of Wisconsin youth;

(2) To examine the association of measured intelligence with college plans, college attendance, and college graduation in this cohort;

(3) To examine the association of socioeconomic status with college plans, college attendance, and college graduation for various categories of measured intelligence in this cohort;

(4) To examine the association of measured intelligence with college plans, college attendance, and college graduation for various socioeconomic categories in this cohort;

(5) To obtain relative estimates of the magnitude of the direct and indirect effects of socioeconomic status and measured intelligence on college plans, college attendance, and college graduation for this cohort; and

(6) To examine the association of socioeconomic status and measured intelligence with college graduation for those members of the cohort who attended college.

The accomplishment of these purposes will require the use of several statistical procedures. For purposes (1) and (2), bivariate tables will be constructed showing the proportions with college plans, college attendance, and college graduation. For purposes (3) and (4), multiple cross-tabular analysis will be employed. This will result in tables that give the proportions with college plans and various levels of educational attainment for each combination of socioeconomic status and intelligence categories. The statistical significance of the associations will be determined by the chi-square test using the .05 probability level. To summarize the cross-tabular analysis, unweighted effect parameters will be computed. This statistic, developed by Coleman, provides a simple, convenient estimate of the effect of the independent variables on the dependent variable in a multivariate table and is based on percentage differences between ordered or continuous categories.[10] For purpose (5), the method of path analysis, developed by the geneticist Wright, and recently introduced into sociology by Boudon and by Duncan, will be used.[11] Path analysis provides a convenient and efficient method for determining the direct and indirect effects of each of the independent variables in a causal chain composed of standardized variables in a closed system. These effects are expressed in path coefficients which are the partial beta-weights of all of the preceding independent variables on the successive dependent variables in the system. For purpose (6), multiple cross-tabular analysis, effect parameters, and path coefficients will be employed.

Throughout the analysis, separate tabulations will be made for males and females because of known differences in their propensity to pursue higher education as well as likely differences in the influences of socioeconomic status and intelligence on their educational plans and attainments.

THE DATA

The data for the present study come from two sources: (1) a questionnaire survey of all high school seniors in Wisconsin public, private, and parochial schools in 1957[12] and (2) a follow-up study conducted in 1964–1965 of approximately a one-third sample of these students. The 1957 survey included information on a number of particulars including the student's educational and vocational plans, the socioeconomic status of his family, his high school record and course of study, educational attitudes of the student and his family, his parent's name and address, and similar matters. In the summer of 1964, seven years after the students were in the senior class of high school, a follow-up study was made of a random sample of 10,321 students. The purpose of the follow-up study was to obtain information on the educational and occupational attainments of the students since high school graduation.

The follow-up study was conducted by means of a mailed questionnaire and by telephone interviews. A postage-paid, double post-card questionnaire was sent to the parents of the students at their 1957 address. One side of the post card gave a brief explanation of the purposes of the study and asked the parents' cooperation in providing information on their child's educational and occupational activities since high school; the other side contained the questions the parents were to answer.[13] If the parents did not respond to the first questionnaire within a month after it was mailed out, a second post-card questionnaire stamped "Urgent Second Request" was sent. Nonrespondents to this second request were sent a third questionnaire marked "Urgent Third Request." Those who did not respond to the third request were written a personal letter on university stationery urging their participation, and were given another copy of the postage-paid questionnaire. Those who did not respond to this letter were interviewed by telephone, whenever a telephone number could be found. For the questionnaires returned by the post office because they were undeliverable for want of proper addresses, accurate up-to-date addresses were obtained, where possible, from Wisconsin tax rolls, and the process was begun over again. By these methods 91.1% of the parents were reached, and 95.8% of those reached furnished the information requested. Thus, responses were obtained for 9007 or 87.2% of the one-third sample used in the original survey. Various tabulations comparing known characteristics of the students indicate nonsignificant differences between those for whom responses were obtained and those for whom responses were lacking.[14]

The variables employed in this paper are sex of the student, the socioeconomic status of the student's family of origin, the student's measured intelligence, the student's college plans, the student's college attendance, the student's college graduation, and a summary measure of the student's educational attainment. Information for the first four variables came from the 1957 survey; the educational attainment information was based on the 1964 follow-up study.

The variable *socioeconomic status* (X_1) is based on a weighted combination of father's occupation, father's formal educational level, mother's formal educational level, an estimate of the funds the family could provide if the student were to attend college, the degree of sacrifice this would entail for the family, and the approximate wealth and income status of the student's family. The sample was divided into four roughly equal groups, labeled High, Upper Middle, Lower Middle, and Low in socioeconomic status.[15]

The variable *intelligence* (X_2) is based on scores on the Henmon-Nelson Test of Mental Maturity which is administered annually to all high school juniors in Wisconsin.[16] The categories used represent the division of the sample into approximately equal fourths in measured intelligence, according to established statewide norms, labeled High, Upper Middle, Lower Middle, and Low.

The variable *college plans* (X_3) is based on a statement by the student when he was a senior in high school that he definitely planned to enroll in a degree-granting college or university (or one whose credits are acceptable for advanced standing by the University of Wisconsin).

The variable *college attendance* (X_4) indicates that the student had enrolled in a degree-granting college or university (or one whose credits are acceptable for advanced standing by the University of Wisconsin) at some time between 1957 and 1964. It includes those who had graduated as well as those who had not yet received a bachelor's degree.

The variable *college graduation* (X_5) means that the student had obtained a bachelor's degree.[17]

The variable *educational attainment* (X_6), used only in the path analysis, indicates the level of higher education attained by the student. It is scored as follows: did not attend college (0), attended college, but did not graduate (1), and graduated from college (2).

RESULTS

Table 1 shows the percentage of Wisconsin male and female high school seniors who planned on college in 1957, the percentage who actually attended college, and the per-

Table 1. Percentage Who Planned on College, Attended College, and Graduated from College, by Socioeconomic Status and by Intelligence, Separately for Males and Females* (Total Cohort)

Socioeconomic status levels	Males				Females			
	Planned on college	Attended college	Graduated from college	N	Planned on college	Attended college	Graduated from college	N
Low	14.8	20.5	7.5	(972)	7.9	8.5	2.7	(1,101)
Lower Middle	26.8	33.8	14.2	(1,152)	20.4	21.2	7.9	(1,194)
Upper Middle	39.3	44.6	21.7	(1,155)	29.3	30.5	12.4	(1,195)
High	66.3	73.4	42.1	(1,107)	60.2	62.6	35.0	(1,131)
Total	37.4	43.7	21.8	(4,386)	29.5	30.7	14.5	(4,621)
Intelligence Levels								
Low	12.2	15.0	3.2	(1,070)	10.5	11.4	1.8	(1,122)
Lower Middle	25.4	33.5	11.5	(1,100)	20.9	22.5	7.1	(1,205)
Upper Middle	45.5	51.0	23.9	(1,083)	33.7	34.7	16.1	(1,183)
High	65.2	73.8	47.2	(1,133)	53.3	54.9	33.5	(1,111)
Total	37.4	43.7	21.8	(4,386)	29.5	30.7	14.5	(4,621)

*All χ^2's for each column in this table are significant beyond the 0.05 level.

centage who graduated from college for each of the categories of socioeconomic status and intelligence. Among males 37.4%, regardless of their socioeconomic status, planned to attend college at the time they were still seniors in high school, but only 14.8% of those of low socioeconomic status, in comparison with 66.3% of those with high socioeconomic status, indicated such plans. Likewise, 29.5% of all females planned on college but only 7.9% of those with low socioeconomic status, in comparison with 60.2% of those with high socioeconomic status, had such plans.

The picture is essentially the same when the students are classified by intelligence levels (Table 1). While only 12.2% of the males in the low quarter of the intelligence distribution planned to attend college, 65.2% of those in the high quarter had college plans. Of the girls in the low quarter of the intelligence distribution, 10.5% had planned on college, while 53.3% of those in the high quarter had college plans. As with socioeconomic status, for both males and females, there is not a single exception to the rule—the higher the intelligence level the higher the proportion who had planned on college.

Exactly the same relationship is found for both socioeconomic status and intelligence with college attendance and college graduation. Of the males in the low socioeconomic status category, 20.5% attended college and 7.5% graduated, while 73.4% of the high socioeconomic status males attended and 42.1% graduated. For females, in the low socioeconomic status category, 8.5% attended college and 2.7% graduated, while in the high socioeconomic status category, 62.6% attended and 35.0% graduated. In the low intelligence category, 15.0% of the males attended college and 3.2% graduated, in contrast to 73.8% and 47.2%, respectively, of the males in the high intelligence category. For females, 11.4% of the low intelligence category attended college and 1.8% graduated, while for the high intelli-

gence category 54.9% attended and 33.5% graduated.

Thus, when the educational progress of the whole cohort is examined through time, it is apparent that both socioeconomic origins and intelligence are significantly associated not only with plans for higher education but also with progress through the system of higher education.

Several other points should be made. The first is that progress through the system is by no means automatic. Whereas 43.7% of the total male cohort attended college, only 21.8% (less than half of those who had attended college) had graduated by 1964. For the females, the respective figures are 30.7% attended and 14.5% graduated.

Second, in all socioeconomic and intelligence categories females are less likely than males to have planned on college or to have attended college or to have completed college. This trend reflects the normative differentiation of male and female roles in American society. Although the proportion of women joining the labor force is higher now than ever in the past, there is still a prevalent norm that seems to lead many women to choose their household role as primary, and their occupational role as occasional, part-time and secondary. Unless women are strongly committed to a professional occupation as a full-time career, they are less likely than men to be oriented toward higher education. Also, it is apparent from the results already reported that socioeconomic status is of greater significance to the educational plans and attainments of females than of males, and that intelligence seems to be somewhat more decisive for males than for females.

Finally, perceptive readers will have noted some discrepancy between the plans and the actual college attendance of the students in the cohort. In general, a slightly larger proportion of both males and females in each category of socioeconomic status and intelligence actually attended college than had said in 1957 that they planned to go to college. This reflects the fact that the 1957 responses were to a question about definite plans to attend college. Doubtless some of the students who were still uncertain were reluctant to say that they had definite plans. Since there is less discrepancy in females' college plans and college attendance in each category of family socioeconomic status and intelligence than among the males in the respective categories, the plans of the female seniors were more realistic than those of the male seniors. This may in part have been due to the uncertainties that the males had about fulfilling their compulsory military obligations.

Since both socioeconomic status and intelligence are related to college plans, college attendance, and college graduation of both males and females, as shown by the analysis thus far, the influence of socioeconomic status on the educational attainments of the cohort at each of the successive stages should be examined while controlling for intelligence. Likewise, the influence of intelligence on educational attainment should be examined while controlling for socioeconomic status. The results of this analysis for college plans, college attendance, and college graduation are shown separately for males and females in Tables 2–4.

Table 2 presents the percentages of male and female students who planned on college by socioeconomic status and intelligence. The percentages shown in each cell of this and subsequent tables are based on the N's given in the parentheses in the respective cells. For example, among 363 low socioeconomic status males who are also low in intelligence, only 4.7% had planned on college, while 85.8% of the 442 high socioeconomic status males who are high in intelligence had college plans. Similarly, among the 411 females who are low in socioeconomic status and low in intelligence, 2.7% had planned on college, while among 458 high socioeconomic status females who are also high in intelligence, 72.7% had planned on college. Reading the table in this

way, it is observed that there is a positive, monotonic, and statistically significant relationship between socioeconomic status and college plans of males and females in each category of intelligence.

A similar relationship holds between intelligence and college plans of males and females in each category of socioeconomic status. Looking at the differences in the percentages of the lowest and the highest categories of socioeconomic status, it is found that the higher the level of intelligence, the greater the influence of socioeconomic status on college plans of both males and females. Similarly, looking at the difference in the percentages of the lowest and the highest categories of intelligence, it is apparent that the higher the level of socioeconomic status, the greater the influence of intelligence on college plans of males and females. The cross-pressured cells are particularly noteworthy in that high socioeconomic status males in the low intelligence category are a little less likely to plan on college (28.4%) than are highly intelligent males who are low in socioeconomic status (33.6%), while high socioeconomic status females who are low in intelligence (30.2%) are more likely to plan on college than are highly intelligent females who are low in socioeconomic status (26.1%).

From the cross-tabular analysis there is a monotonic relationship between the combined effects of socioeconomic status and intelligence on college plans of both males and females. The effect parameters given at the bottom of the table indicate that on the whole the plans of the male seniors are slightly more influenced by their intelligence than by their socioeconomic status (intelligence, .144; socioeconomic status, .131). On the other hand, the plans of the female seniors are more affected by their socioeconomic status than by their intelligence (intelligence, .105; socioeconomic status, .140).

From Table 3 it is observed that in each category of socioeconomic status and intelli-

Table 2. Percentage with College Plans, by Socioeconomic Status and Intelligence, Separately for Males and Females* (Total Cohort)

Socioeconomic status levels	Males Intelligence levels					Females Intelligence levels				
	Low	Lower middle	Upper middle	High	Total	Low	Lower middle	Upper middle	High	Total
Low	4.7 (363)	12.0 (267)	23.3 (193)	33.6 (149)	14.8 (972)	2.7 (411)	4.4 (316)	11.0 (236)	26.1 (138)	7.9 (1,101)
Lower Middle	9.3 (300)	19.8 (324)	33.5 (275)	49.4 (253)	26.8 (1,152)	10.2 (335)	17.3 (342)	24.4 (291)	35.0 (226)	20.4 (1,194)
Upper Middle	17.2 (273)	25.6 (277)	47.8 (316)	64.0 (289)	39.3 (1,155)	14.0 (250)	24.7 (324)	27.4 (332)	49.8 (289)	29.3 (1,195)
High	28.4 (134)	48.3 (232)	68.6 (299)	85.8 (442)	66.3 (1,107)	30.2 (126)	44.4 (223)	65.1 (324)	72.7 (458)	60.2 (1,131)
Total	12.2 (1,070)	25.4 (1,100)	45.5 (1,083)	65.2 (1,133)	37.4 (4,386)	10.5 (1,122)	20.9 (1,205)	33.7 (1,183)	53.3 (1,111)	29.5 (4,621)

*All χ^2's for each column and row in this table are significant beyond the 0.05 level.
Effect parameters: Males: Socioeconomic Status .131 Intelligence: .144
Females: Socioeconomic Status .140 Intelligence: .105

Table 3. Percentage Who Attended College, by Socioeconomic Status and Intelligence, Separately for Males and Females* (Total Cohort)

Socioeconomic status levels	Males Intelligence levels					Females Intelligence levels				
	Low	Lower middle	Upper middle	High	Total	Low	Lower middle	Upper middle	High	Total
Low	6.3 (363)	16.5 (267)	28.0 (193)	52.4 (149)	20.5 (972)	3.7 (411)	6.3 (316)	8.9 (236)	27.5 (138)	8.5 (1,101)
Lower Middle	11.7 (300)	27.2 (324)	42.6 (275)	58.9 (253)	33.8 (1,152)	9.3 (335)	20.2 (342)	24.1 (291)	36.7 (226)	21.2 (1,194)
Upper Middle	18.3 (273)	34.3 (277)	51.3 (316)	72.0 (289)	44.6 (1,155)	16.0 (250)	25.6 (324)	31.0 (332)	48.1 (289)	30.5 (1,195)
High	38.8 (134)	60.8 (232)	73.2 (299)	90.7 (442)	73.4 (1,107)	33.3 (126)	44.4 (223)	67.0 (324)	76.4 (458)	62.6 (1,131)
Total	15.0 (1,070)	33.5 (1,100)	51.0 (1,083)	73.8 (1,133)	43.7 (4,386)	11.4 (1,122)	22.5 (1,205)	34.7 (1,183)	54.9 (1,111)	30.7 (4,621)

*All χ^2's for each column and row in this table are significant beyond the 0.05 level.
Effect parameters: Males: Socioeconomic Status .134 Intelligence: .166
Females: Socioeconomic Status .146 Intelligence: .105

gence, more men than women actually attended college. The relationship of socioeconomic status to college attendance is positive, monotonic, and statistically significant for both males and females in each category of intelligence. Similarly, without any exception the relationship of intelligence to college attendance is positive, monotonic, and statistically significant for both males and females in each category of socioeconomic status. While only 6.3% of males with low intelligence and low socioeconomic status attended college, 90.7% of males with high intelligence and high socioeconomic status attended college. A similar trend holds for females: only 3.7% of females with low intelligence and low socioeconomic status attended college, but 76.4% of females with high intelligence and high socioeconomic status attended. The combined effect of socioeconomic status and intelligence on college attendance is monotonic for both males and females. However, the percentages in the cross-pressured cells— namely, the low socioeconomic status but high intelligence category and the low intelligence but high socioeconomic status category—are noteworthy. Of the males with high intelligence but low socioeconomic status, 52.4% attended college. The corresponding figure for males with high socioeconomic status but low intelligence is 38.8%. Of the females with high socioeconomic status but low intelligence, 33.3% attended college as compared with 27.5% of females with high intelligence but low socioeconomic status. Thus, the influence of intelligence on college attendance appears to be greater for males than for females, while the influence of socioeconomic status on college attendance is greater for females than for males. This is apparent also from the magnitudes of the effect parameters in this table. For males, the effect of intelligence (.166) is greater than the effect of socioeconomic status (.134) on college attendance. For females, the effect of family socioeconomic status (.146) is greater than

the effect of intelligence (.105) on college attendance.

From Table 4, it is observed that the association of socioeconomic status with college graduation continues to be positive, monotonic, and statistically significant for both males and females in each of the intelligence categories. Similarly, the association of intelligence with college graduation also continues to be positive, monotonic, and statistically significant for both males and females in each of the socioeconomic status categories. However, it seems that low level of intelligence rather than low level of socioeconomic status is the greater limitation in obtaining a college degree in the case of both males and females. This is evident in that only 10.5% of the males in the high socioeconomic status-low intelligence category graduated from college as against almost twice that proportion (20.1%) in the low socioeconomic status-high intelligence category. The same holds true for females; while 7.9% of females in the high socioeconomic status-low intelligence category graduated from college, 13.8% in the low socioeconomic status-high intelligence category graduated. Although the over-all effect of intelligence on college graduation is greater among males (.123) than among females (.083), the magnitude of the effect of socioeconomic status on graduation is almost the same for both males and females (.081 and .077, respectively). In terms of the relative influence of socioeconomic status and intelligence on college graduation, it seems that the males are somewhat more affected by intelligence than socioeconomic status, but the females are almost equally affected by intelligence and socioeconomic status.

The results of the cross-tabular analysis and the effect parameters presented in Tables 2–4 clearly indicate that both socioeconomic status and intelligence continue to be associated with the progress of the 1957 cohort of Wisconsin high school seniors through the educational system at every successive stage, beginning with plans for

Table 4. Percentage Who Graduated from College, by Socioeconomic Status and Intelligence, Separately for Males and Females* (Total Cohort)

Socioeconomic status levels	Males Intelligence levels					Females Intelligence levels				
	Low	Lower middle	Upper middle	High	Total	Low	Lower middle	Upper middle	High	Total
Low	0.3 (363)	7.9 (267)	10.9 (193)	20.1 (149)	7.5 (972)	0.2 (411)	1.3 (316)	2.5 (236)	13.8 (138)	2.7 (1,101)
Lower Middle	2.3 (300)	7.4 (324)	16.7 (275)	34.4 (253)	14.2 (1,152)	0.9 (335)	5.3 (342)	8.9 (291)	20.8 (226)	7.9 (1,194)
Upper Middle	4.4 (273)	9.8 (277)	24.4 (316)	46.7 (289)	21.7 (1,155)	2.4 (250)	9.3 (324)	12.1 (332)	24.9 (289)	12.4 (1,195)
High	10.5 (134)	23.3 (232)	38.5 (299)	64.0 (442)	42.1 (1,107)	7.9 (126)	15.3 (223)	36.4 (324)	51.1 (458)	35.0 (1,131)
Total	3.2 (1,070)	11.5 (1,100)	23.9 (1,083)	47.2 (1,133)	21.8 (4,386)	1.8 (1,122)	7.1 (1,205)	16.1 (1,183)	33.5 (1,111)	14.5 (4,621)

*All x^2's for each column and row in this table are significant beyond the 0.05 level.
Effect parameters: Males: Socioeconomic Status .081 Intelligence: .123
Females: Socioeconomic Status .077 Intelligence: .083

college, through college attendance, to college graduation. A comparison of the effect parameters reveals differences in the relative magnitude of the effects of socioeconomic status and intelligence on the various levels of educational attainment. There are also sex differences; the college plans of males are more influenced by their intelligence level than by their socioeconomic status, but the plans of females are more affected by their socioeconomic status than by their intelligence. This pattern continues for college attendance. But for college graduation the influence of intelligence is greater than that of socioeconomic status for males, while socioeconomic status and intelligence are about equally effective for females. On the basis of these findings, neither socioeconomic status nor intelligence can be discounted as influences on higher education at any stage in the process when the cohort is studied through time.

Although the results of the cross-tabular analysis are useful in mapping out the separate and joint effects of socioeconomic status and intelligence on college plans and various attainment levels in higher education, and although the effect parameters provide a summary picture of the cross-tabular analysis, there is still need for a more precise estimation of the relative influence of these variables in terms of a standardized measure that is strictly comparable from one stage to another and that takes into account the full range of the available data. As mentioned earlier, the path coefficients are appropriate measures for this purpose. The relative influence of socioeconomic status and intelligence on college plans at successive levels of higher education is examined in two separate path analyses—by first considering each stage separately, and then by considering stages in the educational pursuit of the total cohort. Figures 1 and 2 present this analysis.[18]

The simple path diagrams shown in Figure 1 indicate the influence of socioeconomic status and intelligence on each of the three dependent variables—college plans,

college attendance, and college graduation.[19] To illustrate, the first path diagram on the left side of the page shows that for males the influence of socioeconomic status on college plans, controlling for intelligence, is .32 while the influence of intelligence on college plans, controlling for socioeconomic status, is .34. Thus, each is about equally important as a determinant of college plans.[20]

Figure 1 shows that the independent influence of intelligence is greater than the independent influence of socioeconomic status on college plans, college attendance, and college graduation of males, but that the reverse is the pattern in the case of females; the independent influence of socioeconomic status is greater than the independent influence of intelligence on college plans, college attendance, and college graduation of females. The magnitude of the influence of intelligence increases slightly from college plans to college attendance, but the magnitude of the influence of socioeconomic status decreases at each successive stage in the educational pursuit of males. Although the magnitude of the influence of socioeconomic status is almost identical for college plans and college attendance and decreases for college graduation for females, the magnitude of the influence of intelligence on college plans, college attendance, and college graduation remains about the same. This is essentially what was found when the cross-classification tables and effect parameters were observed; path coefficients, however, give a more precise statement of the independent effects of the two variables at different points in the higher education process.

The path diagrams in Figure 2 give a comprehensive picture of the direct and indirect influences of socioeconomic status and intelligence on the attainment of higher education. Several points may be noted from Figure 2. First, the association between college plans and educational attainment is stronger than the association of either socioeconomic status or intelligence with college

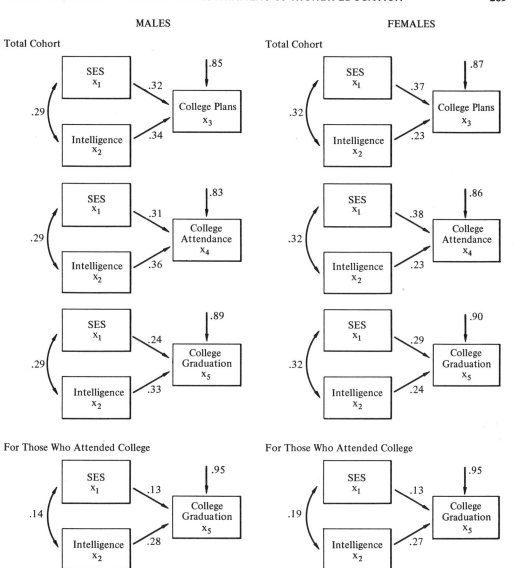

Figure 1. Path Diagrams Showing the Influence of Socioeconomic Status and Intelligence on College Plans, College Attendance, and College Graduation, for Males and Females.

plans or with educational attainment for both males and females. Second, there is a stronger net association between college plans and educational attainment for females (.67) than for males (.55). Third, for males the direct effect of socioeconomic status on the attainment of higher education is smaller than the direct effect of intelligence, although the indirect effects are approximately equal. But for females, both the direct and the indirect effects of socioeconomic status are larger than the direct and the indirect effects of intelligence on educational attainment. In summary, the

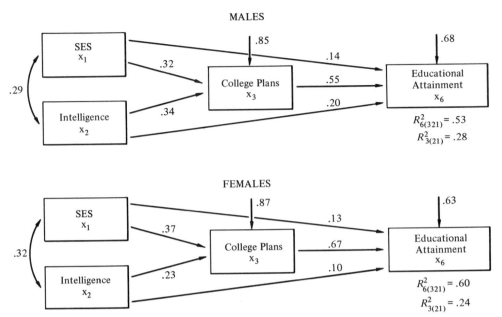

Figure 2. Path Diagrams Showing the Influence of Socioeconomic Status and Intelligence on the Attainment of Higher Education by Sex (Total Cohort).

preceding analysis suggests that both socioeconomic status and intelligence continue to influence the educational attainment of the 1957 cohort of Wisconsin high school seniors—through their direct effects on each step in the process of higher education and through indirect effects on college graduation via their effects on college plans and college attendance.

Although the results of all of the analysis thus far point unequivocally to the continuing influence of both socioeconomic status and intelligence on each stage in the higher education process through both direct and indirect causal paths, another question raised by the literature remains to be answered. This is Wolfle's observation that whereas socioeconomic status plays an important part in who goes to college, once one has cleared the hurdle of college entrance, socioeconomic status sharply declines as a factor in college graduation, and intelligence becomes the determining factor.[21] This idea, of course, is based on

the assumption that a good deal of socioeconomic selection has already taken place in determining who enters college, and that selection from this point on is largely based on performance, which presumably would be powerfully affected by intelligence. To test Wolfle's observation, a table has been prepared for both sexes showing college graduation by socioeconomic status and intelligence but based only on those students (1,916 males and 1,420 females) who actually entered college.

The relative influence of socioeconomic status and intelligence on college graduation for those who attended college is shown in Table 5, and is illustrated in the simple path diagrams at the bottom of Figure 1. From the table, it is seen that even for this group both socioeconomic status and intelligence continue to have considerable influence on college graduation. For example, only 4.4% of males in the low intelligence-low socioeconomic status category graduated from college, while 70.6% of males in the high

Table 5. Percentage Who Graduated from College, by Socioeconomic Status and Intelligence, Separately for Males and Females (Based on the number who attended college, not the total cohort)

Socioeconomic status levels	Males Intelligence levels					Females Intelligence levels				
	Low	Lower middle*	Upper middle	High*	Total*	Low	Lower middle	Upper middle*	High*	Total*
Low	4.4 (23)	47.7 (44)	38.9 (54)	38.5 (78)	36.7 (199)	6.7 (15)	20.0 (20)	28.6 (21)	50.0 (38)	31.9 (94)
Lower Middle	20.0 (35)	27.3 (88)	39.3 (117)	58.4 (149)	42.2 (389)	9.7 (31)	26.1 (69)	37.1 (70)	56.6 (83)	37.2 (253)
Upper Middle	24.0 (50)	28.4 (95)	47.5 (162)	64.9 (208)	48.7 (515)	15.0 (40)	36.1 (83)	38.8 (103)	51.8 (139)	40.5 (365)
High	26.9 (52)	38.3 (141)	52.5 (219)	70.6 (401)	57.3 (813)	23.8 (42)	34.3 (99)	54.4 (217)	66.9 (350)	55.9 (708)
Total	21.3 (160)	34.2 (368)	46.9 (552)	64.0 (836)	49.8 (1,916)	15.6 (128)	31.7 (271)	46.2 (411)	61.0 (610)	47.0 (1,420)

*χ^2's for each column designated and for all rows for both sexes are significant beyond the 0.05 level.
Effect parameters: Males: Socioeconomic Status .049 Intelligence: .131
Females: Socioeconomic Status .061 Intelligence: .142

intelligence-high socioeconomic status category graduated. Similarly, while only 6.7% of females in the low intelligence-low socioeconomic status category graduated from college, 66.9% of females in the high intelligence-high socioeconomic status category graduated. Except for three out of a total of thirty-two cells in this table, the pattern of relationship between socioeconomic status and college graduation is generally positive, monotonic, and statistically significant for both males and females in each category of intelligence. Likewise, except for males in the low socioeconomic status category, the relationship between intelligence and college graduation is positive, monotonic, and statistically significant for both males and females in each category of socioeconomic status. However, looking at the proportion of college graduates in the extremely cross-pressured cells, it becomes apparent that intelligence has a greater influence than socioeconomic status. Whereas 26.9% of males who are low in intelligence but high in socioeconomic status graduated from college, 38.5% of males who are low in socioeconomic status but high in intelligence graduated. Similarly, whereas 23.8% of females who are low in intelligence but high in socioeconomic status graduated from college, 50.0% of females who are low in socioeconomic status but high in intelligence graduated. The comparative magnitudes of the effect parameters indicate that the overall influence of intelligence is much greater than that of socioeconomic status for both males and females. The path coefficients indicate the same thing. Thus, these findings support the conclusion arrived at by Wolfle fifteen years ago. The fact that the magnitude of the effect of intelligence on college graduation among those who attended college is about the same as that for the total cohort suggests that Wolfle's statement regarding the increasing importance of ability on educational achievement among those who attend college may somewhat overstate the importance of intelligence. But the much smaller magnitude of the effect of socioeconomic status on college graduation

among those who attended college than for the total cohort is in agreement with his observation that the influence of socioeconomic status tends to decrease once college is entered. Nevertheless, it should be noted that along with intelligence, socioeconomic status continues to influence college graduation even after socioeconomic selection has taken place in the process of determining who will attend college.

Thus, all of the analysis reported in this paper points to the conclusion that one's socioeconomic origins exert a continuing influence on the process of educational selection beginning with planning to enter college, attending college, and, finally, graduation from college. Also, one's intelligence has a similar influence as one passes from one stage to the next in the process. Whereas males are more influenced by intelligence than by socioeconomic origins and females are more influenced by socioeconomic origins than by intelligence throughout the process of selection in higher education, both factors continue to operate on both sexes.[22]

Perhaps the most critical factor in the process of obtaining higher education is the decision to plan on and to enter college. At this point, over a fourth of the high ability males (those in the top quarter of the intelligence distribution) and almost half of the high ability females drop out of the process by not planning on or not entering college. Socioeconomic origins powerfully affect these decisions of high ability youth of both sexes; just over half (52.4%) of the high ability males of low socioeconomic status enroll in college in comparison with 90.7% of the high status males of equal ability; for females the corresponding percentages are 27.5 and 76.4 (Table 3). Moreover, the yield of college graduates from high ability males is only 20.1% for those with low socioeconomic status origins in comparison with 64.0% from those with high socioeconomic status backgrounds; for females the yields of college graduates are 13.8 and 51.1%, respectively (Table 4). Even if only those who enter college are considered, socioeconomic status exerts a powerful influence; only 38.5% of the high ability males who are low in socioeconomic status graduate in comparison with 70.6% of those of equal ability but high in socioeconomic status. For females the respective figures are 50.0 and 66.9% (Table 5). Similar trends hold for less able youth.

From all of this evidence it seems clear that although intelligence plays an important role in determining which students will be selected for higher education, socioeconomic status never ceases to be an important factor in determining who shall be eliminated from the contest for higher education in this cohort of Wisconsin youth.

SUMMARY AND CONCLUSIONS

This study of a randomly selected cohort of Wisconsin high school seniors over a seven-year period (1957–1964) shows that both socioeconomic status and intelligence are related to planning on college, college attendance, and college graduation for both sexes. When intelligence is controlled in multivariate tables, socioeconomic status is positively, monotonically, and significantly related to planning on college, college attendance, and college graduation for both sexes. Similarly, when socioeconomic status is controlled, intelligence is positively, monotonically, and significantly related to planning on college, college attendance, and college graduation for both sexes. On the whole, the relative effect of socioeconomic status is greater than is the effect of intelligence for females, while the relative effect of intelligence is greater than is the effect of socioeconomic status for males. This is true whether effect parameters or path coefficients are used to measure the effects.

When the whole process is studied by means of path analysis, both socioeconomic status and intelligence have direct effects on planning on college, college attendance, and college graduation, and considerable indirect effects on the level of educational attainment through their effects on college plans. Again this is true for both males and females

although there are differences in the magnitude of these effects by sex.

When only those who attended college are included in the analysis, it is clear that intelligence is much more important than socioeconomic status in determining who will eventually graduate. Prior socioeconomic selection has already exerted much of its influence on who attends college. After this point intelligence, probably as it is reflected in performance, is more important. However, even among this group socioeconomic status continues to exert an influence that is independent of intelligence in determining college graduation for both sexes. In general, these findings confirm and extend those of previous research by Wolfle, Eckland, and others, and should be of significance not only to those interested in higher education, but also to students of social mobility.

There are, of course, many other interesting ways in which socioeconomic status and intelligence may be examined in relation to the process of selection in higher education. For example, it would be most instructive to look at the differences in the quality of colleges that students with different backgrounds and abilities attend. It would also be useful to investigate the differences in the patterns by which the college degree is eventually obtained by students of different socioeconomic and intelligence levels—that is, whether they differ in the number of colleges they will attend or the length of time they will remain in college to obtain a degree. It would also be interesting to examine how factors other than socioeconomic status and intelligence may intervene and shape the educational progress of the student. These and other problems will be investigated in other papers based on the data of this research project.

NOTES

1. Pitirim A. Sorokin, *Social Mobility,* New York: Harper and Brothers, 1927, ch. 9, and Talcott Parsons, "The School Class As a Social System: Some of its Functions in American Society," *Harvard Educational Review,* 29 (1959), pp. 297–318.

2. There is a vast literature in this regard. References to these studies are given in: William H. Sewell, Archie O. Haller, and Murray A. Straus, "Social Status and Educational and Occupational Aspiration," *American Sociological Review,* 22 (February, 1957), pp. 67–73; William H. Sewell, "Community of Residence and College Plans," *American Sociological Review,* 29 (February, 1964), pp. 24–38; William H. Sewell and Alan M. Orenstein, "Community of Residence and Occupational Choice," *American Journal of Sociology,* 70 (March, 1965), pp. 551–563; William H. Sewell and Archie O. Haller, "Educational and Occupational Perspectives of Farm and Rural Youth," in Lee G. Burchinal (Ed.), *Rural Youth in Crisis,* U. S. Department of Health, Education, and Welfare, Washington, D.C.: Government Printing Office, 1965, pp. 149–169; and William H. Sewell and J. Michael Armer, "Neighborhood Context and College Plans," *American Sociological Review,* 31 (April, 1966), pp. 159–168.

3. Ralph H. Turner, "Sponsored and Contest Mobility and the School System," *American Sociological Review,* 25 (December, 1960), pp. 855–867. Also see Burton R. Clark, "The Cooling-Out Function in Higher Education," *American Journal of Sociology,* 65 (May 1960), pp. 569–576.

4. There have been numerous studies of college aspirations; many of the references are included in Sewell, *op. cit.,* pp. 24–25.

5. For references to the literature on college attendance see Bruce K. Eckland, "Social Class and College Graduation: Some Misconceptions Corrected," *American Journal of Sociology,* 70 (July, 1964), pp. 36–50.

6. Dael Wolfle, *America's Resources of Specialized Talent,* New York: Harper and Brothers, 1954, p. 163.

7. Eckland, *op. cit.,* pp. 44–49, found that the composite index of social class was a better predictor of college success than the separate indicators—education, income, and occupation—and also that a one-year measure of college performance was not significantly related to father's occupation and parents' education, but the four-year graduation rates differed significantly on these two variables. In his review, among the one-year studies, those using father's occupation or parents' education found college performance unrelated to social class, but three others using a composite index of social class found a positive relationship with college performance. Eleven of the seventeen two-to-four year studies reported positive correlations between social class indicators and college performance.

8. Eckland, *ibid.* See also his "Academic Ability, Higher Education, and Occupational Mobility," *American Sociological Review,* 30 (October, 1965), pp. 735–746. Although Eckland's research was a good step forward over most past studies, it too has certain limitations including the following: (i) since it deals only with college students, the effects of socioeconomic status and ability on the high school graduates who did not go to college are unknown, (ii) since his sample includes only full-time resident students at the Urbana campus of the University of Illinois, the effect due to the selective admission policy of the university is unknown, and the diversity among the institutions of higher education available to students in general is not taken into account, (iii) Eckland studied only the male students, and it is reasonable to hypothesize that the relative influences of family socioeconomic status and ability differ in magnitude at successive stages in the educational careers of males from that of females, and finally (iv) he lacked an adequate measure of ability with a single normative standard on which all members of his sample could be ranked.

9. In Wisconsin there is little variation in enrollment in this age group between major Census categories: urban, 89.2%; rural-nonfarm, 86.8%; and farm, 87.6%. See Douglas G. Marshall, *Wisconsin's Population: Changes and Prospects,* Madison: Wisconsin Agricultural Experiment Station Bulletin 241, 1963, p. 29.

10. James S. Coleman, *Introduction to Mathematical Sociology* (New York: Free Press of Glencoe, 1964), pp. 206–210.

11. The method of path analysis assumes a complete system including, if necessary, residual variables to represent unmeasured influences, which are assumed to be uncorrelated with the measured ones. See Raymond Boudon, "A Method of Linear Causal Analysis: Dependence Analysis," *American Sociological Review,* 30 (June, 1965), pp. 365–374. For a brief summary of the method of path analysis, see Otis Dudley Duncan, "Path Analysis: Sociological Examples," *American Journal of Sociology,* 72 (July, 1966), pp. 1–16; C. C. Li, *Population Genetics,* (Chicago: University of Chicago Press, 1955), ch. 12, and also C. C. Li, "The Concept of Path Coefficient and Its Impact on Population Genetics," *Biometrics,* 12 (June, 1956), pp. 190–210. For more details, see Sewall Wright, "The Method of Path Coefficients," *Annals of Mathematical Statistics,* 5 (September, 1934), pp. 161–215; Sewall Wright, "Path Coefficient and Path Regressions: Alternative or Complementary Concept?" *Biometrics,* 16 (June, 1960), pp. 189–202; and Sewall Wright, "The Treatment of Reciprocal Interaction With or Without Lag, in Path Analysis," *Biometrics,* 16 (September, 1960), pp. 423–445.

12. The results of this survey are given in J. Kenneth Little, *A Statewide Inquiry into Decisions of Youth about Education Beyond High School,* Madison: School of Education, University of Wisconsin, 1958.

13. Some readers will question the accuracy of the parents' responses to questions regarding the educational attainments of their children. A check is currently being made on all students in the sample whose parents reported that their child attended the University of Wisconsin. The final results are not yet available, but from the results obtained thus far, it seems that parents' reports on attendance and graduation are quite accurate.

14. The follow-up procedures and other details concerning the resulting sample are contained in a manuscript now being revised for publication as a journal article under the title "Characteristics of Willing and Reluctant Respondents."

15. The six indicators were factor-analyzed using

the principal-components method, and were orthogonally rotated according to the verimax criterion. This produced a three-factor structure composed of a factor on which the three economic items were most heavily loaded, a factor on which the two educational items were most heavily loaded, and a factor on which the occupational item was most heavily loaded. The composite socioeconomic status index was developed by squaring the loadings of the principal items on each factor as weights, then multiplying students' scores on the items by the respective weights, and finally summing the weighted scores of the principal items on each factor. The three factors were combined into a composite socioeconomic status score after multiplying the factor scores of all students by certain constants which would produce approximately equal variances for each status dimension. The resulting sum of the weighted scores was then multiplied by a constant to produce a theoretical range of scores between 0 and 99.

16. V. A. C. Henmon and M. J. Nelson, *The Henmon-Nelson Test of Mental Ability,* Boston: Houghton Mifflin Co., 1942.

17. Because the subsequent analysis deals only with higher education, a category is not included for those students who continued their education beyond high school in vocational and technical schools which do not offer college level curricula.

18. In these figures, the determination of the relationship between socioeconomic status and intelligence is not analyzed, and therefore only the zero-order correlation coefficient between socioeconomic status and intelligence is shown by two-headed arrows on a curved line. One-way arrows leading from each of the independent variables to the variables dependent on them are shown by straight lines to indicate that these relationships are analyzed assuming a recursive and closed system composed of all standardized variables. The quantities entered in the figure are the numerical values of path coefficients, or the beta-weights as they are commonly known. The residual paths are shown above each dependent variable.

19. The zero-order intercorrelation coefficients on which subsequent computations are based are given below, by sex:

Males

Variable		X_1	X_2	X_3	X_4	X_5	X_6
X_1	Socioeconomic status	...	.29	.42	.42	.34	.43
X_2	Intelligence	...	...	.43	.45	.40	.48
X_3	College Plans	...	...	...	.67	.56	.69
X_4	College Attendance	...	...	...	...	.60	.86
X_5	College Graduation	...	...	...	...	...	.82
X_6	Educational Attainment	...	...	...	...	...	...

Females

Variable		X_1	X_2	X_3	X_4	X_5	X_6
X_1	Socioeconomic Status	...	.32	.44	.45	.37	.45
X_2	Intelligence	...	...	.35	.35	.33	.37
X_3	College Plans	...	...	...	.78	.58	.76
X_4	College Attendance	...	...	...	...	.62	.87
X_5	College Graduation	...	...	...	...	...	.78
X_6	Educational Attainment	...	...	...	...	...	...

20. These quantities indicate only the direct effect of socioeconomic status and intelligence on college plans. Since no intervening variables are shown in the path diagram, there is no indirect influence of socioeconomic status or intelligence on college plans. Similarly in Figure 2 for males, the direct influences of socioeconomic status, intelligence, and college plans on educational attainment are .14, .20, and .55 respectively. The indirect effects of socioeconomic status and intelligence on educational attainment can be examined from their direct effects on college plans and the direct effect of college plans on educational attainment. Thus, any statement regarding the indirect effect is made only descriptively and it is not expressed in any quantitative terms.

21. Wolfle, *op. cit.,* p. 163.

22. Our results on the relative influence of socioeconomic status and intelligence on college graduation are also quite similar to those reported by Eckland for his sample of University of Illinois males, "Academic Ability, Higher Education, and Occupational Mobility," *op. cit.,* p. 470.

10. I.Q. in the U.S. Class Structure

SAMUEL BOWLES and HERBERT GINTIS

THE I.Q. CONTROVERSY

The argument that differences in genetic endowments are of central and increasing importance in the stratification systems of advanced technological societies has been advanced, in similar forms, by a number of contemporary researchers.[1] At the heart of this argument lies the venerable thesis that

From *Social Policy* 3 (November/December 1972, January/February 1973): 65–96. We have extracted pp. 66–78 for reproduction here. Copyright © 1972 by Samuel Bowles and Herbert Gintis. Reprinted by permission.

I.Q., as measured by tests such as the Stanford-Binet, is largely inherited via genetic transmission, rather than molded through environmental influences.*

This thesis bears a short elucidation. That I.Q. is highly heritable is merely to say that individuals with similar genes will exhibit similar I.Q.'s *independent* of differences in the social environments they might experience during their mental development. The main support of the genetic school is several studies of individuals with precisely the same genes (identical twins) raised in different environments (i.e., separated at birth and reared in families with different social statuses). Their I.Q.'s tend to be fairly similar.[2] In addition, there are studies of individuals with no common genes (unrelated individuals) raised in the same environment (e.g., the same family) as well as studies of individuals with varying genetic similarities (e.g., fraternal twins, siblings, fathers and sons, aunts and nieces) and varying environments (e.g., siblings raised apart, cousins raised in their respective homes). The difference in I.Q.'s for these groups is roughly conformable to the genetic inheritance model suggested by the identical twin and unrelated individual studies.[3]

As Eysenck suggests, while geneticists will quibble over the exact magnitude of heritability of I.Q., nearly all will agree heritability exists and is significant.[4] Environmentalists, while emphasizing the paucity and unrepresentativeness of the data, have presented rather weak evidence for their own position and have made little dent in the genetic position.[5] Unable to attack the central proposition of the genetic school, environmentalists have emphasized that it bears no important social implications. They have claimed that, although raised in the context of the economic and educational deprivation of Blacks in the United States,

the genetic theory says nothing about the "necessary" degree of racial inequality or the limits of compensatory education. First, environmentalists deny that there is any evidence that the I.Q. difference between Blacks and whites (amounting to about fifteen I.Q. points) is genetic in origin,† and second, they deny that any estimate of heritability tells us much about the capacity of "enriched environments" to lessen I.Q. differentials, either within or between racial groups.*

---

†Does the fact that a large component of the differences in I.Q. among whites is genetic mean that a similar component of the differences in I.Q. between Blacks and whites is determined by the former's inferior gene pool? Clearly not. First of all, the degree of heritability is an *average*, even among whites. For any two individuals, and *a fortiori*, any two groups of individuals, observed I.Q. differences may be due to any proportion of genes and environment—it is required only that heritability average properly over the entire population. For instance, *all* of the difference in I.Q. between identical twins is environmental, and presumably a great deal of the difference between adopted brothers is genetic. Similarly we cannot say whether the average difference in I.Q. between Irish and Puerto Ricans is genetic or environmental. In the case of Blacks, however, the genetic school's inference is even more tenuous. Richard J. Light and Paul V. Smith ("Social Allocation Models of Intelligence: A Methodological Inquiry," *Harvard Educational Review*, 39, No. 3 [August 1969]), have shown that even accepting Jensen's estimates of the heritability of I.Q., the Black-white I.Q. difference could easily be explained by the average environmental differences between the races. Recourse to further experimental investigations will not resolve this issue, for the "conceptual experiments" that would determine the genetic component of Black-white differences cannot be performed. Could we take a pair of Black identical twins and place them in random environments? Clearly not. Placing a Black child in a white home in an overtly racist society will not provide the same "environment" as placing a white child in that house. Similarly looking at the difference in I.Q.'s of unrelated Black and white children raised in the same home (whether Black or white, or mixed) will not tell us the extent of genetic differences, since such children cannot be treated equally, and environmental differences must continue to persist (of course, if in these cases, differences in I.Q. disappear, the environmentalist case would be supported. But if they do not, no inference can be made).

*Most environmentalists do not dispute Jensen's assertion that existing large-scale compensatory programs have produced dismal results. (See Jen-

---

*By I.Q. we mean—here and throughout this essay—those cognitive capacities that are measured on I.Q. tests. We have avoided the use of the word "intelligence" as in its common usage it ordinarily connotes a broader range of capacities.

But the environmentalists' defense strategy has been costly. First, plausible, if not logical, inference now lies on the side of the genetic school, and it's up to environmentalists to "put up or shut up" as to feasible environmental enrichment programs. Second, in their egalitarian zeal vis-à-vis racial differences, the environmentalists have sacrificed the modern liberal interpretation of social stratification. The modern liberal approach is to attribute social class differences to "unequal opportunity." That is, while the criteria for economic success are objective and achievement-oriented, the fail-

ures and successes of parents are passed onto their children via distinct learning and cultural environments. Thus the achievement of a more equal society merely requires that all youth be afforded the educational and other social conditions of the best and most successful.[6] But by focusing on the environmental differences *between* races, they implicitly accept that intelligence differences among whites of differing social class background are rooted in differences in genetic endowments. Indeed the genetic school's data comes precisely from observed differences in the I.Q. of whites across socioeconomic levels! The fundamental tenet of modern liberal social policy—that "progressive social welfare measures" can gradually reduce and eliminate social class differences, cultures of poverty and affluence, and inequalities of opportunity—seems to be undercut. Thus the "classical liberal" attitude[7] which emphasizes that social classes sort themselves out on the basis of innate individual capacity to cope successfully in the social environment, and hence tend to reproduce themselves from generation to generation, is restored.[8]

The vigor of reaction in face of Jensen's argument indicates the liberals' agreement that I.Q. is a basic social determinant (at least ideally) of occupational status and intergenerational mobility. In Jensen's words, "psychologists' concept of the 'intelligence demands' of an occupation . . . is very much like the general public's concept of the prestige or 'social standing' of an occupation, and both are closely related to an independent measure of . . . occupational status."[9] Jensen continues, quoting O. D. Duncan: ". . . 'intelligence' . . . is not essentially different from that of achievement or status in the occupational sphere . . . what we now *mean* by intelligence is something like the probability of acceptable performance (given the opportunity) in occupations varying in social status."[10] Moreover, Jensen argues that the purported trend toward intelligence's being an increasing requirement for occupational status will

---

sen, "How Much Can We Boost I.Q.," and, for example, Harvey Averch et al., *How Effective is Schooling? A Critical Review and Synthesis of Research Findings* (Santa Monica: The RAND Corporation, 1972). But this does not bear on the genetic hypothesis. As Jensen himself notes, the degree of genetic transmission of any trait depends on the various alternative environments that individuals experience. Jensen's estimates of heritability rest *squarely* on the existing array of educational processes and technologies. Any introduction of new social processes of mental development will change the average unstandardized level of I.Q., as well as its degree of heritability. For instance, the almost perfect heritability of height is well documented. Yet the average heights of Americans have risen dramatically over the years, due clearly to change in the overall environment. Similarly, whatever the heritability of I.Q., the average unstandardized test scores rose 83 percent between 1917 and 1943. See Jencks, *Inequality.*

But compensatory programs are obviously an attempt to change the total array of environments open to children through "educational innovation." While existing large-scale programs appear to have failed to produce significant gains in scholastic achievement, many more innovative small-scale programs have succeeded. See Carl Bereiter, "The Future of Individual Differences," *Harvard Educational Review,* Reprint Series no. 2, 1969, pp. 162–170; Charles E. Silberman, *Crisis in the Classroom* (New York: Random House, 1970); Averch, *How Effective Is Schooling?* Moreover, even accepting the genetic position should not hinder us from seeking new environmental innovation— indeed it should spur us to further creative activities in this direction. Thus the initial thrust of the genetic school can be at least partially repulsed: there is no reliable evidence either that long-term contact of Blacks with existing white environments would not close the Black-white I.Q. gap, or that innovative compensatory programs (i.e., programs unlike existing white childrearing or education environments) might not attenuate or eliminate I.Q. differences that are indeed genetic.

continue.[11] This emphasis on the role of intelligence in explaining social stratification is set even more clearly by Carl Bereiter in the same issue of the *Harvard Educational Review:* "The prospect is of a meritocratic caste system, based . . . on the natural consequences of inherited differences in intellectual potential. . . . It would tend to persist even though everyone at all levels of the hierarchy considered it a bad thing." [12] Something like death and taxes.

Jensen et al. cannot be accused of employing an overly complicated social theory. Jensen's reason for the "inevitable" association of status and intelligence is that society "rewards talent and merit," and Herrnstein adds that society recognizes "the importance and scarcity of intellectual ability." [13] Moreover, the association of intelligence and social class is due to the "screening process," [14] via education and occupation, whereby each generation is further refined into social strata on the basis of I.Q. Finally, adds Herrnstein, "new gains of wealth . . . will increase the I.Q. gap between upper and lower classes, making the social ladder even steeper for those left at the bottom." [15] Herrnstein celebrates the genetic school's crowning achievement by turning liberal social policy directly against itself, noting that the heritability of intelligence and hence the increasing pervasiveness of social stratification will increase, the more "progressive" our social policies: "the growth of a virtually hereditary meritocracy will arise out of the successful realization of contemporary political and social goals . . . as the environment becomes more favorable for the development of intelligence, its heritability will increase. . . . " [16] Similarly, the more we break down discriminatory and ascriptive criteria for hiring, the stronger will become the link between I.Q. and occupational success, and the development of modern technology can only quicken the process.[17]

Few will be surprised that such statements are made by the "conservative" genetic school. But why, amid a spirited liberal counterattack in which the minutest details of the genetic hypothesis are con-

tested and scathingly criticized, is the validity of the genetic school's description of the social function of intelligence blandly accepted? The widespread agreement among participants in the debate that I.Q. is an important determinant of economic success can hardly be explained by compelling empirical evidence adduced in support of the position. Quite the contrary. As we will show in the next section, the available data point strongly to the unimportance of I.Q. in getting ahead economically. In Section IV we shall argue that the actual function of I.Q. testing and its associated ideology is that of legitimizing the stratification system, rather than generating it. The treatment of I.Q. in many strands of liberal sociology and economics merely reflects its actual function in social life: the legitimization and rationalization of the existing social relations of production.

THE IMPORTANCE OF I.Q.

The most immediate support for the I.Q. theory of social stratification—which we will call I.Q.-ism—flows from the strong association of I.Q. and economic success. This is illustrated in Table 1, which exhibits the probability of achieving any particular decile in the economic success distribution for an individual whose adult I.Q. lies in a specified decile.*

*In Table 1, as throughout this paper, "adult I.Q." is measured by scores on a form of the Armed Forces Qualification Test. This measure is strongly affected both by early I.Q. (in this paper measured by Stanford-Binet or its equivalent at age six to eight) and years of schooling, and hence can be considered a measure of adult cognitive achievement. Economic success is measured throughout as the average of an individual's income and the social prestige of his occupation as measured on the Duncan occupational status index, each scaled to have standard deviation equal to one. See Duncan, "Properties and Characteristics of the Socioeconomic Index." For a description of the independent behavior of income and status, see Bowles, "The Genetic Inheritance of I.Q. and the Intergenerational Reproduction of Economic Inequality." We have chosen a weighted average for simplicity of exposition, and in recognition of their joint importance in a reasonable specification of economic success.

Table 1* Probability of Attainment of Different Levels of Economic Success for Individuals of Differing Levels of Adult I.Q., by Deciles

						Adult I.Q. by deciles					
y	x	10	9	8	7	6	5	4	3	2	1
10		30.9	19.8	14.4	10.9	8.2	6.1	4.4	3.0	1.7	0.6
9		19.2	16.9	14.5	12.4	10.5	8.7	7.0	5.4	3.6	1.7
8		13.8	14.5	13.7	12.6	11.4	10.1	8.7	7.1	5.3	2.8
7		10.3	12.4	12.6	12.3	11.7	11.0	10.0	8.7	7.0	4.1
6		7.7	10.4	11.4	11.7	11.8	11.5	11.0	10.1	8.7	5.7
5		5.7	8.7	10.1	11.0	11.5	11.8	11.7	11.4	10.4	7.7
4		4.1	7.0	8.7	10.0	11.0	11.7	12.3	12.6	12.4	10.3
3		2.8	5.3	7.1	8.7	10.1	11.4	12.6	13.7	14.5	13.8
2		1.7	3.6	5.4	7.0	8.7	10.5	12.4	14.5	16.9	19.2
1		0.6	1.7	3.0	4.4	6.1	8.2	10.9	14.4	19.8	30.9

Economic Success by Deciles (left axis label)

*Table 1 corresponds to a correlation coefficient r = .52.
Example of use: For an individual in the 85th percentile in Adult I.Q. (x = 9), the probability of attaining between the 20th and 30th percentile in Economic Success is 5.3 percent (the entry in column 9, row 3).

The data, most of which was collected by the U.S. Census Current Population Survey in 1962, refer to "non-Negro" males, aged 25 to 34, from nonfarm background in the experienced labor force. We have chosen this population because it represents the dominant labor force and the group into which minority groups and women would have to integrate to realize the liberal ideal of equal opportunity, and hence to whose statistical associations these groups would become subject. The data relating to childhood I.Q. and adult I.Q. are from a 1966 survey of veterans by the National Opinion Research Center and the California Guidance Study.[18] The quality of the data preclude any claims to absolute precision in our estimation. Yet our main propositions remain supported, even making allowance for substantive degrees of error. We must emphasize, however, that the validity of our basic propositions does not depend on our particular data set. While we believe our data base to be the most representative and careful construction from available sources, we have checked our results against several other data bases, including Jencks, Hauser, Lutterman, and Sewell, Conlisk, Griliches and Mason, and Duncan and Featherman.[19] When corrections are made for measurement

error and restriction of range (see Bowles[20] and Jencks), statistical analysis of each of these data bases strongly supports all of our major propositions.

The interpretation of Table 1 is straightforward.* The entries in the table are cal-

*A further word is in order on Tables 1 through 7. Most popular discussions of the relation of I.Q. and economic success (e.g., Jensen, *"How Much Can We Boost IQ"*; Herrnstein, "IQ"; Jencks, *Inequality*) present statistical material in terms of "correlation coefficients" and "contribution to explained variance." We believe that these technical expressions convey little information to the reader not thoroughly initiated in their use and interpretation. The concept of differential probability embodied in Tables 1 through 7, we feel, is operationally more accessible to the reader, and dramatically reveals the patterns of mobility and causality only implicit in summary statistics of the correlation variety.

Let us repeat, Tables 1 through 7 have *not* been constructed by directly observing the decile position of individuals on each of the various variables and recording the percentages in each cell of the relevant table. This approach is impossible for two reasons. First, such statistics are simply unavailable on the individual level. As we have noted, our statistical base embraces the findings of several distinct data sources, no single one of which includes all the variables used in our analysis. Second, for certain technical reasons (e.g., errors in variables and restrictions of range), correction factors must be applied to the raw data before they can be used for analysis. These general issues are discussed in Jencks, *Inequality*, and with respect to

culated directly from the simple correlation coefficient between our variables Adult I.Q. and Economic Success. In addition to reporting the correlation coefficient, we have described these data in tabular form as in Table 1 to illustrate the meaning of the correlation coefficient in terms of the differing probability of economic success for people at various positions in the distribution of I.Q.'s. We cannot stress too strongly that while the correlation coefficients in this and later tables are estimated from the indicated data, the entries in the table represent nothing more than a simple translation of their correlations, using assumptions that— though virtually universally employed in this kind of research—substantially simplify the complexity of the actual data. Now, turning to the table, we can see, for example, that a correlation between these two variables of .52 implies that an individual whose adult I.Q. lies in the top 10 percent of the population has a probability of 30.9 percent of ending up in the top tenth of the population in economic success, and a probability of 0.6 percent of ending up in the bottom tenth. Since an individual chosen at random will have a probability of 10 percent of ending up in any decile of economic success, we can conclude that being in the top decile in I.Q. renders an individual (white male) 3.09 times as likely to be in the top economic success decile, and .06 times as likely to end up in the bottom, as would be predicted by chance. Each of the remaining entries in Table 1 can be interpreted correspondingly.

our data, in Bowles, "The Genetic Inheritance of IQ and the Intergenerational Reproduction of Economic Inequality," and Gintis, "Education and the Characteristics of Worker Productivity."

Tables 1 through 7 are constructed by making explicit certain assumptions that are only implicit, but absolutely necessary to the correlational arguments of Jensen and others. These assumptions include the linearity of the relations among all variables and the approximate normality of their joint probability distribution. Our statistical technique, then, is standard linear regression analysis, with correlations, regression coefficients, and path coefficients represented in their (mathematically equivalent) tabular form.

Yet Tables 2 and 3, which exhibit the corresponding probabilities of economic success given number of years of schooling and level of socioeconomic background,† show that this statistical support is surely misleading: even stronger associations appear between years of schooling and economic success, as well as between social background and economic success. For example, being in the top decile in years of schooling renders an individual 3.76 times as likely to be at the top of the economic heap, and .01 times as likely to be at the bottom, while the corresponding ratios are 3.26 and .04 for social background. It is thus quite possible to draw from aggregate statistics, equally cogently, both an "educational attainment theory" of social stratification and a "socioeconomic background" theory. Clearly there are logical errors in all such facile inferences.

Of course, the I.Q. proponent will argue that there is no real problem here: the association of social class background and economic success follows from the importance of I.Q. to economic success, and the fact that individuals of higher class background have higher I.Q. Similarly one may argue that the association of education and economic success follows from the fact that education simply picks out and develops the talents of intelligent individuals. The problem is that equally cogent arguments can be given for the primacy of either education or social class, and the corresponding subordinateness of the others. The above figures are equally compatible with all three interpretations.

In this section we shall show that all three factors (I.Q., social class background, and education) contribute independently to economic success, but that I.Q. is by far the least important. Specifically we will demonstrate the truth of the following three pro-

†In Table 3, as throughout this paper, socioeconomic background is measured as a weighted sum of parental income, father's occupational status, and father's income, where the weights are chosen so as to produce the maximum multiple correlation with economic success.

Table 2* Probability of Attainment of Different Levels of Economic Success for Individuals of Different Levels of Education, by Deciles

| | | Years of schooling by deciles | | | | | | | | |
| | x | 10 | 9 | 8 | 7 | 6 | 5 | 4 | 3 | 2 | 1 |
y											
10		37.6	22.3	14.6	9.8	6.6	4.3	2.6	4.4	0.6	0.1
9		20.9	19.5	16.2	13.1	10.3	7.9	5.7	3.8	2.1	0.6
8		13.5	16.1	15.3	13.8	12.0	10.1	8.0	5.9	3.7	1.4
7		9.1	13.0	13.8	13.6	12.8	11.6	10.0	8.0	5.6	2.5
6		6.1	10.2	12.0	12.8	12.9	12.5	11.6	10.1	7.8	4.0
5		4.0	7.8	10.1	11.6	12.5	12.9	12.8	12.0	10.2	6.1
4		2.5	5.6	8.0	10.0	11.6	12.8	13.6	13.8	13.0	9.1
3		1.4	3.7	5.9	8.0	10.1	12.0	13.8	15.3	16.1	13.5
2		0.6	2.1	3.8	5.7	7.9	10.3	13.1	16.2	19.5	20.9
1		0.1	0.6	1.4	2.6	4.3	6.6	9.8	14.6	22.3	37.6

Economic Success by Deciles (row label, vertical)

*Table 2 corresponds to a correlation coefficient r = .63.
Example of use: For an individual in the 85th percentile in Education (x = 9), the probability of attaining between the 20th and 30th percentiles in Economic Success (y = 3) is 3.7 percent (the entry in column 9, row 3).

positions, which constitute the empirical basis of our thesis concerning the unimportance of I.Q. in generating the class structure.

First, although higher I.Q.'s and economic success tend to go together, higher I.Q.'s are not an important cause of economic success. The statistical association between adult I.Q. and economic success, while substantial, derives largely from the common association of both of these variables with social class background and level of schooling. Thus to appraise the economic importance of I.Q., we must focus attention on family and school.

Second, although higher levels of schooling and economic success likewise tend to go together, the intellectual abilities developed

Table 3* Probability of Attainment of Different Levels of Economic Success for Individuals of Differing Levels of Social Class Background

| | | Social class background by deciles | | | | | | | | |
| | x | 10 | 9 | 8 | 7 | 6 | 5 | 4 | 3 | 2 | 1 |
y											
10		32.6	20.4	14.5	10.7	7.8	5.7	3.9	2.5	1.4	0.4
9		19.7	17.5	14.9	12.6	10.5	8.5	6.7	5.0	3.2	1.3
8		13.8	14.9	14.1	12.9	11.6	10.1	8.6	6.9	4.9	2.4
7		10.0	12.5	12.9	12.6	12.0	11.1	10.0	8.5	6.7	3.7
6		7.3	10.4	11.5	12.0	12.0	11.7	11.1	10.1	8.5	5.3
5		5.3	8.5	10.1	11.1	11.7	12.0	12.0	11.5	10.4	7.3
4		3.7	6.7	8.5	10.0	11.1	12.0	12.6	12.9	12.5	10.0
3		2.4	4.9	6.9	8.6	10.1	11.6	12.9	14.1	14.9	13.8
2		1.3	3.2	5.0	6.7	8.5	10.5	12.6	14.9	17.5	19.7
1		0.4	1.4	2.5	3.9	5.7	7.8	10.7	14.5	20.4	32.6

Economic Success by Deciles (row label, vertical)

*Table 3 corresponds to a correlation coefficient r = .55.
Example of use: For an individual in the 85th percentile in Social Class (x = 9), the probability of attaining between the 20th and the 30th percentile in Economic Success (y = 3) is 4.9 percent (the entry in column 9, row 3).

or certified in school make little causal contribution to getting ahead economically. Thus only a minor portion of the substantial statistical association between schooling and economic success can be accounted for by the schools' role in producing or screening cognitive skills. The predominant economic function of schools must therefore involve the accreditation of individuals, as well as the production and selection of personality traits and other personal attributes rewarded by the economic system. Our third proposition asserts a parallel result with respect to the effect of social class background.

Third, the fact that economic success tends to run in the family arises almost completely independently from any genetic inheritance of I.Q. Thus, while one's economic status tends to resemble that of one's parents, only a minor portion of this association can be attributed to social class differences in childhood I.Q., and a virtually negligible portion to social class differences in genetic endowments, even accepting the Jensen estimates of heritability. Thus a perfect equalization of I.Q.'s across social classes would reduce the intergenerational

transmission of economic status by a negligible amount. We conclude that a family's position in the class structure is reproduced primarily by mechanisms operating independently of the inheritance, production, and certification of intellectual skills.

Our statistical technique for the demonstration of these propositions will be that of linear regression analysis. This technique allows us to derive numerical estimates of the independent contribution of each of the separate but correlated influences (social class background, childhood I.Q., years of schooling, adult I.Q.) on economic success, by answering the question: what is the magnitude of the association between any one of these influences among individuals who are equal on some or all the others? Equivalently it answers the question: what are the probabilities of attaining particular deciles in economic success among individuals who are in the same decile in some or all of the above influences but one, and in varying deciles in this one variable alone?

The I.Q. argument is based on the assumption that social background and education are related to economic success *because*

Table 4* Differential Probabilities of Attaining Economic Success for Individuals of Equal Levels of Education and Social Class Background, but Differing Levels of Adult I.Q.

		Adult I.Q. by deciles									
y	*x*	*10*	*9*	*8*	*7*	*6*	*5*	*4*	*3*	*2*	*1*
10		14.1	12.3	11.4	10.7	10.1	9.6	9.0	8.5	7.8	6.6
9		12.4	11.4	10.9	10.5	10.2	9.8	9.5	9.1	8.6	7.7
8		11.4	10.9	10.6	10.4	10.2	9.9	9.7	9.4	9.1	8.4
7		10.7	10.5	10.4	10.3	10.1	10.0	9.9	9.7	9.5	9.0
6		10.1	10.2	10.2	10.1	10.1	10.1	10.0	9.9	9.8	9.5
5		9.5	9.8	9.9	10.0	10.1	10.1	10.1	10.2	10.2	10.1
4		9.0	9.5	9.7	9.9	10.0	10.1	10.3	10.4	10.5	10.7
3		8.4	9.1	9.4	9.7	9.9	10.2	10.4	10.6	10.9	11.4
2		7.7	8.6	9.1	9.5	9.8	10.2	10.5	10.9	11.4	12.4
1		6.6	7.8	8.5	9.0	9.6	10.1	10.7	11.4	12.3	14.1

Economic Success by Deciles

Table 4 corresponds to a standardized regression coefficient $\beta = .13$.
Example of use: Suppose two individuals have the same levels of Education and Social Class Background, but one is in the 85th percentile in Adult I.Q. (x = 9), while the other is in the 15th decile in Adult I.Q. (x = 2). Then the first individual is 10.9/9.1 = 1.2 times as likely as the second to attain the 8th decile in Economic Success (column 9, row 8, divided by column 2, row 8).

they are associated with higher adult cognitive skills. Table 4 shows this to be essentially incorrect. This table, by exhibiting the relation between adult I.Q. and economic success among individuals with the same social class background and level of schooling, shows that the I.Q.-economic success association exhibited in Table 1 is largely a by-product of these more basic social influences. That is, for a given level of social background and schooling, differences in adult I.Q. add very little to our ability to predict eventual economic success. Thus, for example, an individual with an average number of years of schooling and an average socioeconomic family background, but with a level of cognitive skill to place him in the top decile of the I.Q. distribution, has a probability of 14.1 percent of attaining the highest economic success decile. This figure may be compared with 10 percent, the analogous probability for an individual with average levels of I.Q. as well as schooling and social background. Our first proposition—that the relation between I.Q. and economic success is not causal, but rather operates largely through the effects of the correlated variables, years of schooling and social class background—is thus strongly supported.* We are thus led to focus directly on the role of social class background and schooling in promoting economic success.

Turning first to schooling, the argument of the I.Q. proponents is that the strong association between level of schooling and economic success exhibited in Table 2 is due to the fact that economic success depends on cognitive capacities, and schooling both selects individuals with high intellectual ability for further training and then develops this ability into concrete adult cognitive

*This is not to say that I.Q. is never an important criteria of success. We do not contend that extremely low or high I.Q.'s are irrelevant to economic failure or success. Nor do we deny that for some individuals or for some jobs, cognitive skills are economically important. Rather, we assert that for the vast majority of workers and jobs, selection, assessed job adequacy, and promotion are based on attributes other than I.Q.

skills. Table 5 shows this view to be false. This table exhibits the effect of schooling on chances for economic success, for individuals who have the same adult I.Q. Comparing Table 5 with Table 2, we see that cognitive differences account for a negligible part of schooling's influence on economic success: individuals with similar levels of adult I.Q. but differing levels of schooling have substantially different chances of economic success. Indeed the similarity of Tables 2 and 5 demonstrates the validity of our second proposition—that schooling affects chances of economic success predominantly by the noncognitive traits which it generates, or on the basis of which it selects individuals for higher education.[21]

The next step in our argument is to show that the relationship between social background and economic success operates almost entirely independently of individual differences in I.Q. Whereas Table 3 exhibits the total effect of social class on an individual's economic success, Table 6 exhibits the same effect among individuals with the same childhood I.Q. Clearly these tables are nearly identical. That is, even were all social class differences in I.Q. eliminated, a similar pattern of social class intergenerational immobility would result.[22] Our third proposition is thus supported: the intergenerational transmission of social and economic status operates primarily via noncognitive mechanisms, despite the fact that the school system rewards higher I.Q.—an attribute significantly associated with higher social class background.

The unimportance of the specifically genetic mechanism operating via I.Q. in the intergenerational reproduction of economic inequality is even more striking. Table 7 exhibits the degree of association between social class background and economic success that can be attributed to the genetic inheritance of I.Q. alone. This table assumes that all direct influences of socio-economic background upon economic success have been eliminated, and that the noncognitive components of schooling's contribution to

Table 5* Differential Probabilities of Attaining Economic Success for Individuals of Equal Adult I.Q. but Differing Levels of Education

					Years of schooling by deciles					
Economic Success by Deciles — *y* \ *x*	*10*	*9*	*8*	*7*	*6*	*5*	*4*	*3*	*2*	*1*
10	33.2	20.6	14.6	10.6	7.7	5.5	3.8	2.4	1.3	0.4
9	19.9	17.8	15.1	12.7	10.5	8.5	6.6	4.8	3.1	1.2
8	13.8	15.0	14.2	13.0	11.6	10.1	8.5	6.8	4.8	2.3
7	9.9	12.6	13.0	12.7	12.1	11.2	10.0	8.5	6.6	3.5
6	7.2	10.4	11.6	12.1	12.1	11.8	11.2	10.1	8.4	5.1
5	5.1	8.4	10.1	11.2	11.8	12.1	12.1	11.6	10.4	7.2
4	3.5	6.6	8.5	10.0	11.2	12.1	12.7	13.0	12.6	9.9
3	2.3	4.8	6.8	8.5	10.1	11.6	13.0	14.2	15.0	13.8
2	1.2	3.1	4.8	6.6	8.5	10.5	12.7	15.1	17.8	19.9
1	0.4	1.3	2.4	3.8	5.5	7.7	10.6	14.6	20.6	33.2

*Table 5 corresponds to a standardized regression coefficient $\beta = .56$.
Example of use: Suppose two individuals have the same Adult I.Q., but one is in the 9th decile in Level of Education (x = 9), while the other is in the 2nd decile (x = 2). Then the first individual is 15.0/4.8 = 3.12 times as likely as the second to attain the 8th decile in Economic Success (column 9, row 8, divided by column 2, row 8).

economic success are eliminated as well (the perfect meritocracy based on intellectual ability). On the other hand, it assumes Jensen's estimate for the degree of heritability of I.Q. A glance at Table 7 shows that the resulting level of intergenerational inequality in this highly hypothetical example would be negligible.

The unimportance of I.Q. in explaining the relation between social class background and economic success, and the unimportance of cognitive achievement in explaining the contribution of schooling to economic success, together with our previously derived observation that most of the association between I.Q. and economic success can be ac-

Table 6* Differential Probabilities of Attaining Economic Success for Individuals of Equal Early I.Q. but Differing Levels of Social Class Background

					Social class background by deciles					
Economic Success by Deciles — *y* \ *x*	*10*	*9*	*8*	*7*	*6*	*5*	*4*	*3*	*2*	*1*
10	27.7	18.5	14.1	11.1	8.8	6.9	5.3	3.9	2.5	1.1
9	18.2	15.8	13.8	12.1	10.5	9.0	7.6	6.1	4.5	2.4
8	13.7	13.8	13.0	12.1	11.1	10.1	8.9	7.6	6.1	3.7
7	10.7	12.0	12.1	11.8	11.3	10.7	9.9	8.9	7.5	5.0
6	8.4	10.5	11.1	11.3	11.3	11.1	10.7	10.0	9.0	6.6
5	6.6	9.0	10.0	10.7	11.1	11.3	11.3	11.1	10.5	8.4
4	5.0	7.5	8.9	9.9	10.7	11.3	11.8	12.1	12.0	10.7
3	3.7	6.1	7.6	8.9	10.1	11.1	12.1	13.0	13.8	13.7
2	2.4	4.5	6.1	7.6	9.0	10.5	12.1	13.8	15.8	18.2
1	1.1	2.5	3.9	5.3	6.9	8.8	11.1	14.1	18.5	27.7

*Table 6 corresponds to a standardized regression coefficient $\beta = .46$.
Example of use: Suppose two individuals have the same Childhood I.Q., but one is in the 9th decile in Social Background, while the other is in the 2nd decile. Then the first is 18.5/2.5 = 7.4 times as likely as the second to attain the top decile in Economic Success (column 9, row 10, divided by column 2, row 10).

Table 7* The Genetic Component of Intergenerational Status Transmission, Assuming the Jensen Heritability Coefficient, and Assuming Education Operates Via Cognitive Mechanisms Alone

		Social class background by deciles									
y . x		10	9	8	7	6	5	4	3	2	1
	10	10.6	10.3	10.2	10.1	10.0	10.0	9.9	9.8	9.7	9.4
	9	10.4	10.2	10.1	10.1	10.0	10.0	9.9	9.9	9.8	9.6
	8	10.2	10.1	10.1	10.1	10.0	10.0	9.9	9.9	9.9	9.8
	7	10.1	10.1	10.1	10.0	10.0	10.0	10.0	9.9	9.9	9.9
	6	10.0	10.0	10.0	10.0	10.0	10.0	10.0	10.0	10.0	10.0
	5	10.0	10.0	10.0	10.0	10.0	10.0	10.0	10.0	10.0	10.0
	4	9.9	9.9	9.9	10.0	10.0	10.0	10.0	10.1	10.1	10.1
	3	9.8	9.9	9.9	9.9	10.0	10.0	10.1	10.1	10.1	10.2
	2	9.6	9.8	9.9	9.9	10.0	10.0	10.1	10.1	10.2	10.4
	1	9.4	9.7	9.8	9.9	10.0	10.0	10.1	10.2	10.3	10.6

Economic Success by Deciles (vertical axis label)

*Table 7 corresponds to .02 standard deviations difference in Economic Success per standard deviation difference in Social Class Background, in a causal model assuming Social Class Background affects Early I.Q. only via genetic transmission, and assuming Economic Success is directly affected only by cognitive variables.
Example of use: For an individual in the 85th percentile in Social Class Background (x = 9), the probability of attaining between the 20th and 30th percentiles in Economic Success (y = 3), assuming only genetic and cognitive mechanisms, is 10.1 percent (the entry in column 9, row 8).

counted for by the common association of these variables with education and social class, support our major assertion: I.Q. is not an important intrinsic criterion for economic success. Our data thus hardly lend credence to Duncan's assertion that "intelligence . . . is not essentially different from that of achievement or status in the occupational sphere,"[23] nor to Jensen's belief in the "inevitable" association of status and intelligence, based on society's "rewarding talent and merit,"[24] nor to Herrnstein's dismal prognostication of a "virtually hereditary meritocracy" as the fruit of successful liberal reform in an advanced industrial society.[25]

I.Q. AND THE LEGITIMATION OF THE HIERARCHICAL DIVISION OF LABOR

A Preview

We have disputed the view that I.Q. is an important causal antecedent of economic success. Yet I.Q. clearly plays an important role in the U.S. stratification system. In this section we shall argue that the set of beliefs surrounding I.Q. betrays its true function— that of legitimating the social institutions underpinning the stratification system itself.

Were the I.Q. ideology correct, understanding the ramifications of cognitive differences would require our focusing on the technical relations of production in an advanced technological economy. Its failure, however, bids us scrutinize a different aspect of production—its social relations. By the "social relations of production" we mean the system of rights and responsibilities, duties and rewards, that governs the interaction of all individuals involved in organized productive activity.[26] In the following section we shall argue that the social relations of production determine the major attributes of the U.S. stratification system.[27] Here, however, we shall confine ourselves to the proposition that the I.Q. ideology is a major factor in legitimating these social relations in the consciousness of workers.

The social relations of production in different societies are quite diverse; they lay the basis for such divergent stratification systems as communal-reciprocity, caste, feudal serf, slave, community-collective, and wage labor of capitalist and state socialist varieties. In advanced capitalist society the stratification system is based on what we term the hierarchical division of labor, characterized by power and control emanating from the top downward through a finely gradated bureaucratic order.[28] The distribution of economic reward and social privilege in the United States is an expression of the hierarchical division of labor within the enterprise.

In this section, then, we shall show that the I.Q. ideology serves to legitimate the hierarchical division of labor. First, we argue that such legitimation is necessary because capitalist production is "totalitarian" in a way only vaguely adumbrated in other social spheres—family, interpersonal relations, law, and politics. Indeed history exhibits periodic onslaughts upon the hierarchical division of labor and its acceptance is always problematic. Second, we argue that the I.Q. ideology is conducive to a general technocratic and meritocratic view of the stratification system that tends to legitimate these social relations, as well as its characteristic means of allocating individuals to various levels of the hierarchy. Third, we argue that the I.Q. ideology operates to reconcile workers to their eventual economic positions primarily via the schooling experience, with its putative objectivity, meritocratic orientation, and technical efficiency in supplying the cognitive needs of the labor force. Fourth, we shall argue that the use of both formal education and the I.Q. ideology was not merely a historical accident, but arose through the conscious policies of capitalists and their intellectual servants to perform the functions indicated above.

The Need for Legitimacy

If one takes for granted the basic economic organization of society, its members need only be equipped with adequate cognitive and operational skills to fulfill work requirements, and provided with a reward structure motivating individuals to acquire and supply these skills. U.S. capitalism accomplishes the first of these requirements through family, school, and on-the-job training, and the second through a wage structure patterned after the job hierarchy.

But the social relations of production cannot be taken for granted. The bedrock of the capitalist economy is the legally sanctioned power of the directors of an enterprise to organize production, to determine the rules that regulate workers' productive activities, and to hire and fire accordingly, with only moderate restriction by workers' organizations and government regulations. But this power cannot be taken for granted, and can be exercised forcefully against violent opposition only sporadically. Violence alone, observe Lassevell and Kaplan, is inadequate as a stable basis for the possession and exercise of power, and they appropriately quote Rousseau: "The strongest man is never strong enough to be always master, unless he transforms his power into right, and obedience into duty." Where the assent of the less favored cannot be secured by power alone, it must be part of a total process whereby the existing structure of work roles and their allocation among individuals are seen as ethically acceptable and even technically necessary.

In some social systems the norms that govern the economic system are quite similar to those governing other major social spheres. Thus in feudal society the authority of the lord of the manor is not essentially different from that of the political monarch, the church hierarchy, or the family patriarch, and the ideology of "natural estates" suffuses all social activity. No special normative order is required for the economic system. But in capitalist society, to make the hierarchical division of labor appear just is no easy task, for the totalitarian organization of the enterprise clashes sharply with the ideals of equality, democracy, and participation that pervade the political and legal spheres. Thus the economic enterprise as a political dictatorship and a social caste system requires special legitimation, and the mechanisms used to place individuals in unequal (and unequally rewarding) positions require special justification.

Indeed the history of U.S. labor is studded with revolts against the hierarchical division of labor, particularly prior to the full development of formal education and the I.Q. ideology in the early twentieth century.[29]

In 1844 the Lynn, Mass., shoe workers, losing control over their craft and their labor in the face of the rising factory system, wrote in their "Declaration of Independence":

Whereas, our employers have robbed us of certain rights ... we feel bound to rise unitedly in our strength and burst asunder as Freemen ought the shackles and fetters with which they have long been chaining and binding us, by an unjust and unchristian use of power ... which the possession of capital and superior knowledge furnishes.[30]

The ideology of the dispossessed farmer in the 1880s and 1890s or of the bankrupted small shopkeeper after the turn of the century is little different. That these radical thrusts against the hierarchical division of labor have by and large been deflected into more manageable wage or status demands bespeaks the power of the capitalist system to legitimize its changing structure, but in no way suggests that the perpetuation of the capitalist relations of production was ever a foregone conclusion.[31]

The Thrust of Legitimation: I.Q., Technocracy, and Meritocracy

We may isolate several related aspects of the social relations of production that are legitimized in part by the I.Q. ideology. To begin there are the overall characteristics of work in advanced U.S. capitalism: bureaucratic organization, hierarchical lines of authority, job fragmentation, and unequal reward. It is highly essential that the individual accept, and indeed come to see as natural, these undemocratic and unequal aspects of the workaday world.

Moreover, the mode of allocating individuals to these various positions in U.S. capitalism is characterized by intense competition in the educational system followed by individual assessment and choice by employers. Here again the major problem is that this "allocation mechanism" must appear egalitarian in process and just in outcome, parallel to the formal principle of "equality of all before the law" in a democratic juridical system based on freedom of contract.

While these two areas refer to the legitimation of capitalism as a social system, they have their counterpart in the individual's personal life. Thus, just as individuals must come to accept the overall social relations of production, workers must respect the authority and competence of their own "superiors" to direct their activities, and justify their own authority (however extensive) over others. Similarly, just as the overall system of role allocation must be legitimized, so individuals must assent to the justness of their own personal position, and the mechanisms through which this position has been attained. That workers be resigned to their position in production is perhaps adequate; that they be reconciled is even preferable.

The contribution of I.Q.-ism to the legitimation of these social relations is based on a view of society that asserts the efficiency and technological necessity of modern industrial organization, and is buttressed by evidence of the similarity of production and work in such otherwise divergent social systems as the United States and the Soviet Union. In this view large-scale production is a requirement of advanced technology, and the hierarchical division of labor is the only effective means of coordinating the highly complex and interdependent parts of the large-scale productive system. Thus bureaucratic order is awarded the status of an "evolutionary universal"; in the words of

Talcott Parsons: "Bureaucracy ... is the most effective large-scale administrative organization that man has invented, and there is no direct substitute for it."[32]

The 'hallmark of the "technocratic perspective" is its reduction of a complex web of social relations in production to a few rules of technological efficacy—whence its easy integration with the similarly technocratic view of social stratification inherent in the I.Q. ideology. In this view the hierarchical division of labor arises from its natural superiority in the coordination of collective activity and in the nurturing of expertise in the control of complex production processes. In order to motivate the most able individuals to undertake the necessary training and preparation for high level occupational roles, salaries and status must be closely associated with one's level in the work hierarchy. Thus Davis and Moore, in their highly influential "functional theory of stratification," locate the "determinants of differential reward" in "differential functional importance" and "differential scarcity of personnel." "Social inequality," they conclude, "is thus an unconsciously evolved device by which societies insure that the most important positions are conscientiously filled by the most qualified persons."[33] Herrnstein is a little more concrete: "If virtually anyone is smart enough to be a ditch digger, and only half the people are smart enough to be engineers, then society is, in effect, husbanding its intellectual resources by holding engineers in greater esteem and paying them more."[34]

This perspective, technocratic in its justification of the hierarchical division of labor, leads smoothly to a meritocratic view of the process of matching individuals to jobs. An efficient and impersonal bureaucracy assesses the individual purely in terms of his or her expected contribution to production. The main determinants of an individual's expected job fitness are seen as those cognitive and psycho-motor capacities relevant to the worker's technical ability to do the job. The technocratic view of production and the meritocratic view of job allocation yield an important corollary, to which we will later return. Namely, there is always a strong tendency in an efficient industrial order to abjure caste, class, sex, color, and ethnic origins in occupational placement. This tendency will be particularly strong in a capitalist economy, where competitive pressures constrain employers to hire on the basis of strict efficiency criteria.[35]

The technocratic view of production, along with the meritocratic view of hiring, provides the strongest form of legitimation of work organization and social stratification in capitalist society. Not only is the notion that the hierarchical division of labor is "technically necessary" (albeit politically totalitarian) strongly reinforced, but also the view that job allocation is just and egalitarian (albeit severely unequal) is ultimately justified as objective, efficient, and necessary. Moreover, the individual's reconciliation with his or her own position in the hierarchy of production appears all but complete; the legitimacy of the authority of superiors no less than that of the individual's own objective position flows not from social contrivance but from Science and Reason.

That this view does not strain the credulity of well-paid intellectuals is perhaps not surprising.[36] Nor would the technocratic/meritocratic perspective be of much use in legitimizing the hierarchical division of labor were its adherents to be counted only among the university elite and the technical and professional experts. But such is not the case. Despite the extensive evidence that I.Q. is not an important determinant of individual occupational achievement (Section II), and despite the fact that few occupations place cognitive requirements on job entry, the crucial importance of I.Q. in personal success has captured the public mind. Numerous attitude surveys exhibit this fact. In a national sample of high school students, for example, "intelligence" ranks second only to "good health" in importance as a desirable personal attribute.[37] Similarly a large majority chose "intelligence" along with "hard work" as the most important requirements of success in life. The public concern over the Coleman Report findings about scholastic achievement and the furor over the I.Q. debate are merely indications of the pervasiveness of the I.Q. ideology.

This popular acceptance, we shall argue, is due to the unique role of the educational system.

Education and Legitimation

To understand the widespread acceptance of the view that economic success is predicated on intellectual achievement we must look beyond the workplace, for the I.Q. ideology does not conform to most workers' everyday experience on the job. Rather, the strength of this view derives in large measure from the interaction between schooling, cognitive achievement, and economic success. I.Q.-ism legitimates the hierarchical division of labor not directly, but primarily through its relationship with the educational system.

We can summarize the relationship as follows. First, the distribution of rewards by the school is seen as being based on objectively measured cognitive achievement, and is therefore fair.* Second, schools are seen as being primarily oriented toward the production of cognitive skills. Third, higher levels of schooling are seen as a major, perhaps the strongest, determinant of economic success, and quite reasonably so, given the strong

*Recent studies, such as Hauser, Heyns, and Jencks, indeed indicate a lack of social class or racial bias in school grades; given a student's cognitive attainment, his or her grades seem not to be significantly affected by class or racial origins, at least on the high school level. See Robert Hauser, "Schools and the Stratification Process," *American Journal of Sociology*, 74 (May 1969): 587–611; Barbara Heyns, "Curriculum Assignment and Tracking Policies in Forty-Eight Urban Public High Schools," Ph.D. diss., University of Chicago, 1971; Jencks, *Inequality*. On the other hand, school grades are by no means based on cognitive achievement alone. An array of behavior and personality traits are rewarded as well—particularly those relevant to the student's future participation in the production system. For a statistical treatment of this question, see Gintis, "Education and the Characteristics of Worker Productivity."

association of these two variables exhibited in Table 2. It is concluded, thus, that high I.Q.'s are acquired in a fair and open competition in school and in addition are a major determinant of success. The conclusion is based on the belief that the relationship between level of schooling and degree of economic success derives largely from the contribution of school to an individual's cognitive skills. Given the organization and stated objectives of schools it is easy to see how people would come to accept this belief. We have shown in Tables 2 and 5 that it is largely without empirical support.

The linking of intelligence to economic success indirectly via the educational system strengthens rather than weakens the legitimation process. First, the day-to-day contact of parents and children with the competitive, cognitively oriented school environment, with clear connections to the economy, buttresses in a very immediate and concrete way the technocratic perspective on economic organization, to a degree that a sporadic and impersonal testing process divorced from the school environment could not aspire. Second, by rendering the outcome (educational attainment) dependent not only on ability but also on motivation, drive to achieve, perseverance, and sacrifice, the status allocation mechanism acquires heightened legitimacy. Moreover, personal attributes are tested and developed over a long period of time, thus enhancing the apparent objectivity and achievement orientation of the stratification system. Third, by gradually "cooling out" individuals at different educational levels, the student's aspirations are relatively painlessly brought into line with his probable occupational status. By the time most students terminate schooling they have validated for themselves their inability or unwillingness to be a success at the next highest level. Through competition, success, and defeat in the classroom, the individual is reconciled to his or her social position.[38]

The statistical results of the previous section fit in well with our description of the role of education in the legitimation process. The I.Q. ideology better legitimates the hierarchical division of labor the stronger are the statistical associations of I.Q. with level of schooling and economic success, and the weaker are the causal relations.† Weak causal relationships are also necessary for the efficient operation of the job allocation process. I.Q. is in fact *not* a crucial determinant of job adequacy; the placement of workers solely, or even largely, on the basis of cognitive abilities would seriously inhibit the efficient allocation of workers to occupational slots. Thus there must be a strong statistical association of I.Q. with economic success, but little economic reward for having a higher I.Q. in the absence of other traits normally associated with high I.Q.[39] Similarly there must be a strong statistical association between I.Q. and school success (grades), but enough individual variation to render "hard work" or good behavior important.[40] Again there must be a strong statistical association between school· success and final level of education attainment, but enough individual variation to allow any "sufficiently motivated" student to achieve higher educational levels. Lastly there must be a strong association between level of education and economic success, but enough individual variation to reward "achievement motivation" and· to allow for the multitude of personal attributes of differential value in educational and occupational performance.[41] All of these conditions appear to be satisfied. . . . .

Fifth, and cutting across all of the above, with the return to comparatively smooth capitalist development in the United States in the mid-1950s after the tumultuous decades of the 1930s and 1940s, the impact of far-reaching cumulative changes in the class structure is increasingly reflected in

---

†By "statistical association" we refer to the simple correlation coefficient between the two variables. By "causal relation" we mean the partial derivative of one variable with respect to another, namely, the effect of a change in one variable on another, holding constant all other relevant variables.

crises of public consciousness. The corporatization of agriculture and reduction of the farm population has particularly affected Blacks, who are subjected to the painful process of forceful integration into the urban wage labor system. The resulting political instabilities are not unlike those following the vast wave of immigrants in the early decades of the century. Changes in the technology of household production and the vast increase in female labor in the service industries also portend a radically altered economic position of women. Finally the large corporation and the state bureaucracies have replaced entrepreneurial, elite white-collar, and independent professional jobs as the locus of middle-class economic activity, and the effective proletarianization of white-collar labor marks the already advanced integration of these groups into the wage labor system. In each case contradictions have arisen between the traditional consciousness of these groups and their new objective economic situations. This has provided much of the impetus for radical movements among Blacks, women, students, and counter culture youth.

While searching for long-range structural accommodations to these contradictions, defenders of the capitalist order will likely be forced to place increasing reliance on the general legitimation mechanisms associated with the meritocratic-technocratic ideology. As a result it appears likely that the future will reveal increasing reliance on the "meritocratic" stratification mechanisms and the associated legitimating ideologies: I.Q.-ism and educational credentialism. Efforts and resources will doubtless multiply toward the "full equalization of opportunity," but the results, if our arguments are correct, will be limited as long as the hierarchical division of labor perpetuates itself.

The credentialist and I.Q. ideology upon which the "meritocratic" legitimation mechanisms depend is thus already under attack. Blacks reject the racism implicit in much of the recent work on I.Q.; they are not mystified by the elaborate empirical substantiation of the geneticist position, nor by the assertions of meritocracy by functionalist sociologists. Their daily experience gives them insights that seem to have escaped many social scientists. Likewise women—indeed many poor people of both sexes—know that their exclusion from jobs is not based on any deficiency of educational credentials.

We have here attempted to speed up the process of demystification by showing that the purportedly "scientific" empirical basis of credentialism and I.Q.-ism is false. In addition, we have attempted to facilitate linkages between these groups and workers' movements within the dominant white male labor force, by showing that the *same* mechanisms are used to divide strata against one another so as to maintain the inferior status of "minority" groups.

The assault on economic inequality and hierarchical control of work appears likely to intensify. Along with other social strains endemic to advanced capitalism, the growing tension between people's needs for self-realization in work and the needs of capitalists and managers for secure top-down control of economic activity opens up the possibility of powerful social movements dedicated to the elimination of the hierarchical division of labor. We hope our paper will contribute to this outcome.

NOTES

1. Jensen, "How Much Can We Boost IQ"; Carl Bereiter, "The Future of Individual Differences," *Harvard Educational Review*, Reprint Series no. 2, 1969, pp. 162–170; Herrnstein, "IQ"; Eysenck, *The IQ Argument*.
2. Arthur R. Jensen, "Estimation of the Limits of Heritability of Traits by Comparison of Monzygotic and Dizygotic Twins," *Proceedings of the National Academy of Science*, 58 (1967):149–157.
3. Jensen, "How Much Can We Boost IQ"; Christopher Jencks et al., *Inequality: A Reassessment of the Effects of Family and Schooling in America* (New York: Basic Books, 1972).
4. Eysenck, *The IQ Argument*, p. 9.
5. Jerome S. Kagan, "Inadequate Evidence and Illogical Conclusions," *Harvard Educational Review*, Reprint Series no. 2, 1969, pp. 126–134; J. McV. Hunt, "Has Compensatory Education Failed? Has It Been Attempted?" *Harvard Educational Review*, Reprint Series no. 2, 1969, pp. 130–152.
6. James S. Coleman et al., *Equality of Educa-*

tional Opportunity (Washington, D.C.: U.S. Government Printing Office, 1966).
7. For example, Edward A. Ross, *Social Control* (New York: Macmillan, 1924); Louis M. Terman, "The Conservation of Talent," *School and Society*, 19, no. 483 (March, 1924); Joseph Schumpeter, *Imperialism and Social Classes* (New York: Kelley, 1951).
8. This is not meant to imply that all liberal social theorists hold the I.Q. ideology. David McClelland, *The Achieving Society* (Princeton: Van Nostrand, 1967), and Oscar Lewis, "The Culture of Poverty," *Scientific American*, 215 (October 1966):16–25, among others, explicitly reject I.Q. as an important determinant of social stratification.
9. Jensen, "Estimation of the Limits of Heritability," p. 14.
10. Otis Dudley Duncan, "Properties and Characteristics of the Socioeconomic Index," in Albert J. Reiss, ed., *Occupations and Social Status* (New York: Free Press, 1961), p. 142.
11. Jensen, "Estimation of the Limits of Heritability," p. 19.
12. Bereiter, "The Future of Individual Differences," p. 166.
13. Herrnstein, "IQ," p. 51.
14. Jensen, "How Much Can We Boost IQ," p. 75.
15. Herrnstein, "IQ," p. 63.
16. *Ibid.*
17. *Ibid.*
18. See Peter Blau and Otis Dudley Duncan, *The American Occupational Structure* (New York: John Wiley, 1967); Otis Dudley Duncan, David L. Featherman, and Beverly Duncan, *Socioeconomic Background and Occupational Achievement: Extensions of a Basic Model*, Final Report Project No. 5-0074 (EO-191), Contract No. OE-5-85-072 (Washington, D.C.: U.S. Department of Health, Education, and Welfare, Office of Education, Bureau of Research, 1968); Bowles, "Schooling and Inequality from Generation to Generation"; and Bowles, "The Genetic Inheritance of IQ," for a more complete description. Similar calculations for other age groups yield results consistent with our three main empirical propositions.
19. Jencks, *Inequality;* Robert Hauser, Kenneth G. Lutterman, and William H. Sewell, "Socioeconomic Background and the Earnings of High School Graduates," unpublished manuscript, University of Wisconsin, August 1971; John Conlisk, "A Bit of Evidence on the Income-Education-Ability Interaction," *Journal of Human Resources*, 6 (Summer 1971):358–362; Zvi Griliches and William M. Mason, "Education, Income, and Ability," *Journal of Political Economy*, 80, no. 3 (May–June 1972); Otis Dudley Duncan and David L. Featherman, "Psychological and Cultural Factors in the Process of Occupational Achievement," Population Studies Center, University of Michigan, 1971.
20. Bowles, "The Genetic Inheritance of IQ."
21. For a more extensive treatment of this point, using data from nine independent samples, see Gintis, "Education and the Characteristics of Worker Productivity."
22. For a more extensive demonstration of this proposition, see Bowles, "The Genetic Inheritance of IQ."

23. Duncan, "Properties and Characteristics of the Socioeconomic Index."
24. Jensen, "Estimation of the Limits of Heritability," p. 73.
25. Herrnstein, "IQ," p. 63.
26. For an explication of the social relations of production, see Andre Gorz, "Capitalist Relations of Production and the Socially Necessary Labor Force," in Arthur Lothstein, ed., *All We Are Saying* . . . (New York: G. P. Putnam's, 1970), and Herbèrt Gintis, "Power and Alienation," in James Weaver, ed., *Readings in Political Economy* (Boston: Allyn and Bacon, forthcoming).
27. See Bowles, "Unequal Education and the Reproduction of the Social Division of Labor," *Review of Radical Political Economy,* 3 (Fall–Winter 1971); Bowles, "Contradictions in U.S. Higher Education," in James Weaver, ed., *Readings in Political Economy* (Boston: Allyn and Bacon, forthcoming), for an explanation of the connection between the social relations of production and the stratification system.
28. On the origins and functions of the hierarchical division of labor, see Stephen Marglin, "What Do Bosses Do?" unpublished manuscript, Department of Economics, Harvard University, 1971; Richard C. Edwards, "Alienation and Inequality: Capitalist Relations of Production in a Bureaucratic Enterprise," Ph.D. diss., Harvard University, July 1972; Max Weber, *From Max Weber: Essays in Sociology* (New York: Oxford University Press, 1946); Chester I. Barnard, *The Functions of the Executive* (Cambridge: Harvard University Press, 1938). A similar hierarchy in production occurs in state socialist countries.
29. We are presently witnessing a revival of such revolts with the partial breakdown of this ideology. See Judson Gooding, "Blue Collar Blues on the Assembly Line," *Fortune,* July 1970; Gooding, "The Fraying White Collar," *Fortune,* December 1970.
30. Quoted in Norman Ware, *The Industrial Worker: 1840–1860* (New York, 1964), p. 42.
31. For contemporary discussions of the feasibility of significant alternatives to the hierarchical division of labor, see Paul Blumberg, *Industrial Democracy* (New York: Schocken Books, 1969); Carole Pateman, *Participation and Democratic Theory* (Cambridge: Cambridge University Press, 1970); Murray Bookchin, *Post-Scarcity Anarchism* (Berkeley: Ramparts Press, 1971); Gintis, "Power and Alienation."
32. Talcott Parsons, "Evolutionary Universals in Society," *American Sociological Review,* 29, no. 3 (June 1964): 507.
33. K. Davis and W. E. Moore, "Some Principles of Stratification," in R. Bendix and S. M. Lipset, eds., *Class, Status and Power* (New York: Free Press, 1966).
34. Herrnstein, "IQ," p. 51.
35. For a statement of this position, see Milton Friedman, *Capitalism and Freedom* (Chicago: University of Chicago Press, 1962).
36. Jensen reports that a panel of "experts" determined that higher status jobs "require" higher I.Q. See Jensen, "How Much Can We Boost IQ."
37. O.G. Brim et al., *American Beliefs and Attitudes about Intelligence* (New York: Russell Sage Foundation, 1969).
38. See Burton R. Clark, "The 'Cooling Out' Function in Higher Education," *American Journal of Sociology,* 65, no. 6 (May 1960); Paul Lauter and Florence Howe, "The Schools are Rigged for Failure," *New York Review of Books,* June 20, 1970.
39. See Tables 1 and 4.
40. See Gintis, "Education and Characteristics of Worker Productivity"; Edwards, "Alienation and Inequality."
41. See Bowles, "Unequal Education and the Reproduction of the Social Division of Labor."

11. Community Colleges and Social Stratification: Submerged Class Conflict in American Higher Education

JEROME KARABEL

In recent years a remarkable transformation has occurred in American higher education, a change as far-ranging in its consequences as the earlier transformation of the American high school from an elite to a mass institution. At the forefront of this development has been the burgeoning two-year community college movement. Enrolling 153,970 students in 1948, two-year public colleges increased their enrollment by one million over the next twenty years to 1,169,635 in 1968 (Department of Health, Education, and Welfare, 1970, p. 75). This growth in enrollment has been accompanied by an increase in the number of institutions; during the 1960's, the number of com-

From *Harvard Educational Review* 42 (November 1972): 521–562. Copyright © 1972 by the President and Fellows of Harvard College. We have extracted pp. 521–530, 536–552, and 555–562 for reproduction here. Reprinted by permission.

munity colleges increased from 656 to 1,100. Nationally, one-third of all students who enter higher education today start in a community college. In California, the state with the most intricate network of community colleges, students who begin in a community college represent 80 per cent of all entering students (Medsker & Tillery, 1971, 16–17). In the future, the role of community colleges in the system of higher education promises to become even larger.

A complex set of forces underlies this extraordinary change in the structure of American higher education. One critical factor in the expansion and differentiation of the system of colleges and universities has been a change in the structure of the economy. Between 1950 and 1970, the proportion of technical and professional workers in the labor force rose from 7.1 per cent to 14.5 per cent (Bureau of the Census, 1971a, p. 225). Some of this increase took place among traditional professions, such as law and medicine, but much of it occurred among growth fields such as data processing and the health semi-professions which frequently require more than a high school education but less than a bachelor's degree. Community colleges have been important in providing the manpower for this growing middle-level stratum and, if current projections of occupational trends are correct, they are likely to become indispensable in filling labor force needs during the next few years. Openings for library technicians and dental hygienists, for example, jobs for which community colleges provide much of the training, will number 9,000 and 2,400 respectively per year for the next decade. Overall, the largest growth area until 1980 will be the technical and professional category with a projected increase of 50 per cent (Bushnell and Zagaris, 1972, p. 135). Without these major changes in the American economy, it is extremely unlikely that the community college movement would have attained its present dimensions.

Although a change in the nature of the labor force laid the groundwork for a system of two-year public colleges, the magnitude and shape of the community college movement owe much to American ideology about equal opportunity through education. Observers, both foreign and domestic, have long noted that Americans take pride in their country's openness—in its apparent capacity to let each person advance as far as his abilities can take him, regardless of social origins. This perceived freedom from caste and class is often contrasted to the aristocratic character of many European societies.[1] America, according to the ideology, is the land of opportunity, and the capstone of its open opportunity structure is its system of public education.

Americans have not only believed in the possibility of upward mobility through education, but have also become convinced that, in a society which places considerable emphasis on credentials, the lack of the proper degrees may well be fatal to the realization of their aspirations. In recent years higher education has obtained a virtual monopoly on entrance to middle and upper level positions in the class structure. Table 1 shows that the probability of holding a high status job, in this case defined as a professional or managerial position, increases sharply with the possession of a bachelor's degree. This stress on diplomas has led to a clamor for access to higher education, regardless of social background or past achievements. The American educational system keeps the mobility "contest"[2] open for as long as possible and has been willing and able to accommodate the demands of the populace for universal access to college.

Response to the pressure for entrance led to greater hierarchical differentiation within higher education.[3] Existing four-year colleges did not, for the most part, open up to the masses of students demanding higher education (indeed, selectivity at many of these institutions has increased in recent years); instead, separate two-year institutions stressing their open and democratic character were created for these new students. Herein lies the genius of the com-

Table 1. Percentage of U. S. Younger Employed Males in Professional and Managerial Occupations, by Level of Educational Attainment, Latter 1960's

Level of educational attainment	Percentage, professional and managerial
High school graduation only	7
One or two terms of college	13
Three or four terms of college	28
Five to seven terms of college	32
Eight or more terms of college	82

Source: Unpublished tabulations of the October 1967, 1968, and 1969 Current Population Surveys of the Bureau of the Census, in which the occupations of younger persons, and the imputed earnings for the various occupations, were related to levels of educational attainment. (Jaffe and Adams, 1972, p. 249)

munity college movement: it seemingly fulfills the traditional American quest for *equality of opportunity* without sacrificing the principle of *achievement.* On the one hand, the openness of the community college[4] gives testimony to the American commitment to equality of opportunity through education; an empirical study by Medsker and Trent (1965) shows that, among students of high ability and low social status, the rate of college attendance varies from 22 per cent in a community with no colleges to 53 per cent in a community with a junior college. On the other hand, the community colleges leave the principle of achievement intact by enabling the state colleges and universities to deny access to those citizens who do not meet their qualifications. The latent ideology of the community college movement thus suggests that everyone should have an opportunity to attain elite status, but that once they have had a chance to prove themselves, an unequal distribution of rewards is acceptable. By their ideology, by their position in the implicit tracking system of higher education—indeed, by their very relationship to the larger class structure—the community colleges lend affirmation to the merit principle which, while facilitating individual upward mobility, diverts attention from underlying questions of distributive justice.

The community college movement is part of a larger historical process of educational expansion. In the early twentieth century, the key point of expansion was at the secondary level as the high school underwent a transition from an elite to a mass institution. Then, as now, access to education was markedly influenced by socioeconomic status.[5]

As the high school became a mass institution, it underwent an internal transformation (Trow, 1966). Formerly providing uniform training to a small group of relatively homogeneous students in order to enable them to fill new white-collar jobs, the high school responded to the massive influx of students by developing a differentiated curriculum. The main thrust of this new curriculum was to provide terminal rather than college preparatory education.

Martin Trow places this "first transformation of American secondary education" between 1910 and 1940. During this period, the proportion of the 14 to 17 age group attending rose from about 15 per cent to over 70 per cent. Since World War II, a similar transformation has been taking place in American higher education: in 1945, 16.3 per cent of the 18 to 21 age group was enrolled in college; by 1968, the proportion had grown to 40.8 per cent (Department of Health, Education, and Welfare, 1970, p. 67). This growth has been accompanied by increasing differentiation in higher education, with the community colleges playing a pivotal role in this new division of labor. In short, educational expansion seems to lead to some form of tracking which, in turn, distributes people in a manner which is roughly commensurate with both their class origins and their occupational destination.

The process by which the educational system expands without narrowing relative differences between groups or changing the underlying opportunity structure may be referred to as "educational inflation" (cf. Milner, 1972). Like economic inflation, educational inflation means that what used to be quite valuable (e.g., a high school diploma) is worth less than it once was. As lower socioeconomic groups attain access to a specific level of education, educational escalation is pushed one step higher. When the high school was democratized, sorting continued to take place through the mechanism of tracking, with higher status children taking college preparatory programs and lower status children enrolling in terminal vocational courses; similarly as access to college was universalized, the allocative function continued to occur through the provision of separate schools, two-year community colleges which would provide an education for most students that would not only be different from a bachelor's degree program, but also shorter. The net effect of educational inflation is thus to vitiate the social impact of extending educational opportunity to a higher level.

If the theory of educational inflation is correct, we would expect that the tremendous expansion of the educational system in the twentieth century has been accompanied by minimal changes in the system of social stratification. Indeed, various studies indicate that the rate of social mobility has remained fairly constant in the last half-century (Lipset and Bendix, 1959; Blau and Duncan, 1967) as has the distribution of wealth and income (Kolko, 1962; Miller, 1971; Jencks, 1972). Apparently, the extension of educational opportunity, however much it may have contributed to other spheres such as economic productivity and the general cultural level of the society, has resulted in little or no change in the overall extent of social mobility and economic inequality.

To observe that educational expansion has not resulted in fundamental changes in the American class structure is in no way to deny that it *has* been critical in providing upward mobility for many individuals. Nor is the assertion that patterns of mobility and inequality have been fairly stable over time meant to reflect upon the intentions of those who were instrumental in changing the shape of the educational system; at work have been underlying social processes, particularly economic and ideological ones, which have helped give shape to the community college.

The thesis of this paper is that the community college, generally viewed as the leading edge of an open and egalitarian system of higher education, is in reality a prime contemporary expression of the dual historical patterns of class-based tracking and of educational inflation. The paper will examine data on the social composition of the community college student body, the flow of community college students through the system of higher education, and the distributive effects of public higher education. Throughout, the emphasis will be on social class and tracking. An analysis of existing evidence will show that the community college is itself the bottom track of the system of higher education in both class origins and occupational destinations of its students. Further, tracking takes place *within* the community college in the form of vocational education. The existence of submerged class conflicts, inherent in a class-based tracking system, will receive considerable attention, with special emphasis on the processes which contribute to these conflicts remaining latent. The paper will conclude with a discussion of the implications of its findings on class and the community college.

THE COMPOSITION OF THE COMMUNITY COLLEGE STUDENT BODY

If community colleges occupy the bottom of a tracking system within higher education that is closely linked to the external class

Table 2. Father's Occupational Classification by Type of College
Entered (percentages)

| Type of college | Father's occupational classification | | | |
	Skilled, semi-skilled, unskilled	Semi-professional, small business, sales and clerical	Professional and managerial	Total
Public two-year	55	29	16	100
Public four-year	49	32	19	100
Private four-year	38	30	32	100
Public university	32	33	35	100
Private university	20	31	49	100

Source: Medsker and Trent (1965)

structure, the social composition of the two-year public college should be proportionately lower in status than that of more prestigious four-year institutions. Christopher Jencks and David Riesman, in *The Academic Revolution* (1968, p. 485), however, citing 1966 American Council on Education data, suggest that the "parents of students who enroll at community colleges are slightly *richer* than the parents of students at four-year institutions." This conclusion is derived from the small income superiority students at two-year public colleges had over students at four-year public colleges in 1966; it ignores public universities and all private institutions. Several other studies, most of them more recent, show that community college students *do* come from lower class backgrounds, as measured by income, occupation, and education, than do their counterparts at four-year colleges and universities (Medsker and Trent, 1965; Schoenfeldt, 1968; American Council on

Education, 1971; Medsker and Tillery, 1971; Bureau of the Census, 1972).

Table 2 presents data showing the distribution of fathers' occupations at various types of colleges. Community colleges are lowest in terms of social class; they have the fewest children of professionals and managers (16 per cent) and the most of blue-collar workers (55 per cent). Private universities, the most prestigious of the categories and the one linked most closely to graduate and professional schools, have the highest social composition: 49 per cent professional and managerial and only 20 per cent blue-collar. Interestingly, the proportion of middle-level occupations shows little variation among the various types of colleges.

Now that the lower-middle and working-class character of community colleges has been demonstrated, it would seem to follow that college type is also related to family income. Table 3, based on nationally representative American Council on Education

Table 3. Family Income by Type of College Entered (percentages)

| Type of college | Family income | | | | |
	Under $8,000	$8,000–12,499	$12,500–20,000	Over $20,000	Total
Public two-year	27.2	34.8	26.4	11.5	100
Public four-year	25.4	31.7	28.3	14.7	100
Public university	15.1	29.7	32.8	22.3	100
Private university	10.6	20.4	27.3	41.8	100

Source: American Council on Education (1971, p. 39)

Table 4. Father's Education by Type of College Entered (percentages)

	Father's education						
Type of college	Grammar school or less	Some high school	High school graduate	Some college	College graduate	Post-graduate degree	Total
Public two-year	12.7	21.3	31.7	19.1	11.5	3.8	100
Public four-year	12.1	19.4	34.7	17.9	11.1	4.8	100
Public university	8.0	13.9	29.0	20.3	19.0	9.8	100
Private university	4.6	9.6	21.9	18.9	24.4	20.5	100
Elite[a]	1.2	3.5	10.6	13.1	31.3	40.5	100

Source: American Council on Education (1966, p. 22)

[a]Elite colleges are defined as institutions having average freshman SAT's over 650. For more data on elite colleges see Karabel and Astin (1975).

data for 1971, reveals systematic income differences among the student bodies at various types of colleges. Over one-quarter of all community college students are from relatively low income families (under $8000) compared with about 11 per cent at private universities. Affluent students (over $20,000) comprise 12 per cent of the student body at community colleges but over 40 per cent at private institutions. The four-year public colleges show income distributions between community colleges and private universities.

Prestige differences among colleges also correspond to differences in fathers' educational attainment. In Table 4, American Council on Education data for 1966 show that the proportion of students whose fathers graduated from college ranges from 15.3 per cent at community colleges to 71.8 per cent at elite institutions (colleges with average Scholastic Aptitude Tests over 650). Over one third of public two-year college students have fathers who did not graduate from high school compared with less than 5 per cent at elite colleges.

The data on occupation, income, and education all run in the same direction and testify to an increase in social class position as one ascends the prestige hierarchy of colleges and universities. Community colleges, at the bottom of the tracking system in higher education, are also lowest in student body class composition. That college pres-

tige is a rough indicator of factors leading to adult occupational attainment and of adult socioeconomic status itself is borne out by a number of studies (Havemann and West, 1952; Reed and Miller, 1970; Wolfle, 1971; Pierson, 1969; Collins, 1971; Spaeth, 1968; Sharp, 1970; Folger et al., 1970). Thus, the current tracking system in higher education may help transmit inequality intergenerationally. Lower class students disproportionately attend community colleges which, in turn, channel them into relatively low status jobs.

However related attendance at a community college may be to social origins, students are not explicitly sorted into the hierarchically differentiated system of higher education on the basis of social class. More important than class background in predicting where one goes to college is measured academic ability (Folger et al., 1970, pp. 166–167; Karabel and Astin, forthcoming). Schoenfeldt (1968), using Project TALENT data, reports that junior college students are more like non-college students in terms of academic ability and more like four-year college students in terms of socioeconomic status. A review of research on the ability of junior college students by Cross (1968) concludes that they show substantially less measured academic ability than their four-year counterparts although there is a great diversity in academic ability *among* junior college students. In a sample of 1966 high school graduates in four states who entered community colleges, 19 per cent were in the highest quartile of academic ability (Medsker & Tillery, 1971, p. 38). As is common with aggregate data, generalizations obscure important variations among individuals. In California, where admission to the state colleges and university is limited to the top 33 1/3 and 12 1/2 per cent in ability respectively, approximately 26 and 6 per cent of students who choose a junior college would have been eligible for a state college or university (Coordinating Council, 1969, p. 79).

There is evidence that many high ability students who attend community colleges are of modest social origins. In California, for example, the proportion of eligible students who choose to attend the state colleges or university varies from 22.5 per cent among students from families with incomes of under $4,000 to over 50 per cent in the $20,000–25,000 category (Hansen and Weisbrod, 1969, p. 74). It is assumed that many of these low-income students attend a nearby two-year college. Table 5 estimates the probability of a male student entering a junior college (public and private). The likeliest entrant at a two-year college is the person of high academic ability and low social status followed by the high status student of less than average ability. These data, however, cannot be construed as providing the relative proportion of intelligent, poor students as opposed to mediocre, rich students in the community college; instead, they merely show the probability of attending a two-year college *if* someone falls into a particular category. Table 5 also illustrates that there is a diversity of both social class and academic ability in the community college. Internal diversity notwithstanding, the community college does indeed stand at the bottom of the tracking system in higher education not only from the perspective of social class, but also from that of academic ability. . . .

Cooling Out: Process and Functions

The preceding section on patterns of attendance among community college students showed large discrepancies between aspirations and their realization. Unrealized educational aspirations, almost always linked to a desire for upward mobility, reach genuinely massive proportions among community college students. Clearly, the social process which enables those who entered the junior college with high hopes never to be realized to adjust to their situation bears close investigation.

The key to this process is what Burton Clark (1960), in a classic case study of San José City College (a two-year institution), referred to as "cooling out." The community college, according to Clark, has three types of students; pure terminal (usually occupational), pure transfer, and latent terminal. The latent terminal student, the one who would like to transfer but who is not likely to meet the qualifications, poses a serious problem for the junior college. The crux of the dilemma is how to gently convince the latent terminal student that a transfer program is inappropriate for him without seeming to deny him the equal educational opportunity that Americans value so highly. Clark does not specify the class origins of these students, but since the modal community college student is of relatively low social status (Cross, 1971) and since SES is itself related both to academic ability and to the probability of dropping out of college, it seems fair to assume that many of them are working class or lower

Table 5. Probability of a Male Entering a Two-Year College

		Ability quarter			
Socioeconomic quarter		Low 1	2	3	High 4
Low	1	.04	.07	.06	.16
	2	.03	.07	.10	.08
	3	.07	.11	.10	.08
High	4	.11	.12	.11	.05

Source: Schoenfeldt (1968, p. 357)

middle class. A great deal is thus at stake here: failure to give these students a "fair shake" would undermine American confidence in the democratic character of the educational system and, very possibly, of the larger society.

"Cooling out," the process described by Clark (pp. 71–76) of handling latent terminal students, begins even before the student arrives as a freshman. A battery of pre-entrance tests are given, and low scores lead to remedial classes which not only cast doubt on the student's promise, but which also slow his movement toward courses for credit. The second step is a meeting with a counselor to arrange the student's class schedule. In view of test scores, high school record, and the student's objectives, the counselor tries to assist the student in choosing a realistic program.[6]

The next step of the process Clark describes in his case study of San José is a specially devised course called "Psychology 5, Orientation to College." A one-unit mandatory course, it is designed to assist the student in selecting a program and places special emphasis on the problem of "unrealistic aspirations." Counselors report that the course provides an ideal opportunity "to talk tough" in an impersonal way to latent terminal students.

The cooling out process has, until this point, been gentle, and the latent-terminal student can refuse to heed the subtle and not-so-subtle hints he has been given. The fourth step of the process, however—dissemination of "need for improvement notices," given to students in courses where they are getting low grades—is impossible to ignore. If the student does not seek guidance, the counselor, with the authority of the disciplinary apparatus behind him, requests to see the student. All of this goes into the student's permanent record.

The fifth and possibly most decisive step of the process is the placing of a student on probation. This is to pressure him into a realistic program. "The real meaning of probation," says Clark, "lies in its killing off

the hope of some of the latent terminal students" (p. 75).

The purpose of the drawn-out counseling procedure is not to bludgeon the student into dropping out, but rather to have the student himself decide to switch out of the transfer program. If the student can be persuaded to take himself out of the competition without being forced out of it (through being flunked out), he is much more likely to retain a benign view of the sorting process.

The opaqueness of the cooling out function is indispensable to its successful performance. In a revealing passage, Clark describes the nature of the problem:

A dilemma of this role, however, is that it needs to remain reasonably latent, not clearly perceived and understood by prospective clientele. Should the function become obvious, the ability of the junior college to perform it would be impaired. The realization that the junior college is a place where students reach undesired destinations would turn the pressure for college admission back on the "protected" colleges. The widespread identification of the junior college as principally a transfer station, aided by the ambiguity of the "community college" label, helps keep this role reasonably opaque to public scrutiny. (p. 165)

The implication of this passage, of course, is that the community college would be unable to perform its task of allowing high aspirations to gently subside if its social function were understood by those most directly affected by it. Clark considers "the student who filters out of education while in the junior college . . . to be very much what such a college is about" (p. 84), and refers to the "transforming of transfer students into terminal students" as the community college's "operational specialty" (p. 146).

One problem with Clark's analysis of the community college is that he perceives the "situation of structured failure" to emerge out of a conflict between the rigorous academic standards of higher education and the non-selective open door. What Clark has failed to do here is to take his analysis a step further to analyze the social function of standards. Rothbart (1970) notes that "objective" academic standards also serve to exclude the poor and minorities from the university. The even-handed application of these standards to all groups gives each individual the feeling that he "had his chance." Academic standards, far from being the quintessential expression of an objective ivory tower concept, justify the university as a means of distributing privilege and of legitimating inequality. This is not to deny that academic standards have important intellectual substance, but it is to say that standards do have a class function. Indeed, what appears to Clark to be a conflict between professors committed to standards and students who do not "measure up" is, in a wider sense, a conflict between low-status students demanding upward mobility and a system unable to fully respond to their aspirations because it is too narrow at the top. Academic standards are located in the midst of this conflict and serve as a "covert mechanism" which, according to Rothbart, enables the university to "do the dirty work for the rest of the society" (p. 174). The cooling out process, the opaqueness of which Clark himself stresses, is thus the expression not only of an academic conflict, but also of a submerged class conflict.

Community colleges, which are located at the very point in the structure of educational and social stratification where cultural aspirations clash head on with the realities of the class system, developed cooling out as a means not only of allocating people to slots in the occupational structure, but also of legitimating the process by which people are sorted. One of its main features is that it causes people to blame themselves rather than the system for their "failure." This process was an organic rather than a conscious one; cooling out was not designed by anyone but rather grew out of the conflict between cultural aspirations and economic reality. Commitment to standards, sincerely held by many academics, may have played a small part in this process, but professorial devotion to academic rigor could disappear and the underlying cultural and structural conflict would remain. Cooling out, or something very much like it, was and is inevitable given this conflict.

The cooling out process not only allows the junior college to perform its sorting and legitimation functions; given the class composition of the community college and the data on attrition, it also enables the two-year college to contribute to the intergenerational transmission of privilege (Bowles, 1971 and 1972). At the bottom of an increasingly formalized tracking system in higher education, community colleges channel working-class students away from four-year colleges and into middle level technical occupations. Having gained access to higher education, the low status student is often cooled out and made to internalize his structurally induced failure. The tremendous disjunction between aspirations and their realization, a potentially troublesome political problem, is thus mitigated and the ideology of equal opportunity is sustained. That community colleges have a *negative* impact on persistence, that they do *not* increase the number of bachelor's degrees, that they seem to provide the greatest opportunity for transfer (and hence mobility) to *middle* class students—these are all facts which are unknown to their clientele. The community college movement, seemingly a promising extension of equal educational opportunity, in reality marks the extension of a class-based tracking system into higher education and the continuation of a long historical process of educational escalation without real change.

TRACKING WITHIN THE COMMUNITY COLLEGE—VOCATIONAL EDUCATION

The subordinate position of the community college within the tracking system of higher education has often been noted. What has been less frequently noted is that tracking also takes place *within* the community college. Two-year public colleges are almost always open door institutions, but admission to programs within them is often on a selective basis. What this generally means in practice is that students who are not "transfer material" are either tracked into vocational programs or cooled out altogether.

Class-based tracking, whether between schools, within schools, or both, is not new in American education. This pattern extends back into the early twentieth century, the period during which the American high school became a mass institution.[7] If the theory of class-based hierarchical differentiation in education is applied to the question of tracking within the community college, it would lead us to expect a relatively low class composition among students in vocational programs.

Data presented in Table 6 show a pronounced class bias in the composition of community college students enrolled in vocational programs. Compared with students in transfer programs, vocational students are markedly lower in family income, father's education, and father's occupation. While almost half of community college students in the transfer curriculum are from white-collar families, only one-fourth of the students in vocational programs are from such backgrounds. Students enrolled in technical programs fall in between vocational and transfer students along various measures of socioeconomic status. Black students show themselves to be considerably more likely than white students to enroll in community college vocational programs.[8]

The relatively low social origins of vocational and technical students are likely to be reflected in their adult occupations. Community college occupational programs are broadly designed to prepare people for entrance into the growing technical and semi-professional stratum. Estimates as to the size of this expanding class suggest that it may comprise one-third of the labor force by 1975 (Harris, 1971, p. 254). This stratum occupies the lower-middle levels of the system of social stratification, but it creates a sensation of upward mobility among its members because it is representative of the change from a blue-collar (or secondary) to a white-collar (or tertiary) economy. Since many members of this "new working class" originate from blue-collar backgrounds, their movement into this stratum does in fact represent mobility. Yet it may be conjec-

Table 6. Selected Characteristics of Students Enrolled in Three Curriculums in 63 Comprehensive Community Colleges (percentages)

Characteristics	College parallel	Technical	Vocational
Father's occupation			
Unskilled or semiskilled	18	26	35
White collar	46	35	25
Parental income			
Less than $6,000	14	14	24
More than $10,000	36	28	21
Father's formal education			
Less than high school graduation	27	34	50
Some college or more	31	20	14
Race			
Caucasian	91	79	70
Negro	5	7	14
Oriental	1	7	7
Other	1	4	6

Source: Comparative Guidance and Placement Program, 1969. (Cross, 1970, p. 191)

Table 7. Yearly Income of U. S. Younger Employed Males, by Level of Educational Attainment, Late 1960s (Base: High school graduation income = 100)

Level of educational attainment	Income	Percentage of all college dropouts
High school graduation	100	–
One or two terms of college	110	40
Three or four terms of college	119	37
Five to seven terms of college	121	23
Eight or more terms of college	150	–

Source: Unpublished tabulations of the October 1967, 1968, and 1969 Current Population Surveys of the Bureau of the Census, in which the occupations of younger persons, and the imputed earnings for the various occupations, were related to levels of educational attainment. (Jaffe and Adams, 1972, p. 249)

tured that this perception of mobility is only temporary; as more and more people move into these jobs, the prestige of a white-collar position may undergo a corresponding decline in status.[9]

Evidence on the economic returns of these vocational programs is, at best, indirect, and empirical studies on this topic would be extremely useful. Yet it is apparent that, in general, having two years of college is not half as good as having four years (Bowles, 1972, Jaffe & Adams, 1972). Table 7, based on recent Census Bureau data, indicates that the recipient of five to seven terms of college is closer in income to a high school graduate than to a college graduate. Possibly, there is some sort of "sheepskin effect" associated with the attainment of a bachelor's degree. But whatever the reasons, having part of a college education seems to be of limited economic value. Whether this is also true for community college students in programs specially designed to prepare them for an occupation remains to be seen.[10]

The Sponsors of the Vocational Movement

Unlike the movement for open admissions to college, which received much of its impetus from mass pressure, there has been little popular clamor for community college vocational programs. Indeed, most junior college entrants see the two-year college as a way-station to a four-year college and shun occupational programs (see the next section). Despite this, there has been an enormous push to increase enrollment in community college occupational programs. This push from the top for more career education marks one of the major developments in the evolution of the community college movement.

The interest of the business community in encouraging occupational training at public expense is manifest. With a changing labor force which requires ever-increasing amounts of skill to perform its tasks and with manpower shortages in certain critical areas, private industry is anxious to use the community college as a training ground for its employees. An associate of the Space Division of the North American Rockwell Corporation makes the corporate viewpoint clear: "industry . . . must recognize that junior colleges are indispensable to the fulfillment of its needs for technical manpower" (Ryan, 1971, p. 71). In the Los Angeles area, Space Division personnel and junior college faculty work together to set up curricular requirements, frame course content, determine student competence, and formulate "on-the-job performance objectives."

The influence of the business community on the junior college is exerted in part through membership of local industrial notables on community college boards of trustees. Hartnett (1969, p. 28) reports that

33 per cent of public junior college trustees are business executives and that over half of all community college trustees agree that "running a college is basically like running a business." Overt business interference in the affairs of the community college is, however, probably rare; the ideological influence of the business community, with its emphasis on pragmatism and economic efficiency, is so pervasive in the two-year college that conflicts between the industrial and educational communities would not normally arise. One imagines that Arthur M. Cohen (1971b, p. 6), Director of the ERIC Clearinghouse for Junior Colleges, is hardly exaggerating when he says that when "corporate managers ... announce a need for skilled workers, ... college administrators trip over each other in their haste to organize a new technical curriculum."

Foundations have also shown an intense interest in junior college vocational programs, an interest which is somewhat more difficult to explain than that of business and industry. The Kellogg Foundation, which over a period of years has made grants to the community college movement totaling several million dollars (Gleazer, 1969, p. 38), has a long-standing interest in career training. In 1959, the general director of the Kellogg Foundation noted approvingly that the "community college movement can do much to supply the sub-professionals, the technicians so necessary to the professions and industry in the years ahead" (Powell, 1965, p. 17). Kellogg followed up on this interest in career education with grants to Chicago City Junior College in 1963 and 1964 for associate degree programs in nursing and business which came to $312,440 and $112,493 respectively (Sunko, 1965, p. 42). In addition, in the late 1950's, Kellogg made a several hundred thousand dollar commitment to support the American Association of Junior Colleges, the national organization of the two-year college movement which has itself been a long-time advocate of vocational programs (Brick, 1964).

The Carnegie Commission on Higher Education, financially sponsored by, but independent of, the Carnegie Corporation of New York, has also been active in sponsoring career education. In its widely read pamphlet, *The Open-Door Colleges,* the Carnegie Commission (1970) made explicit policy proposals for community colleges. Members of the Commission came out strongly for occupational programs, and stated that they "should be given the fullest support and status within community colleges" and should be "flexibly geared to the changing requirements of society" (1970, p. 1). Later in the report (pp. 15–16) the Commission recommended that community colleges remain two-year institutions lest they "place less emphasis on occupational programs." Community colleges, the Commission said, "should follow an open-enrollment policy, whereas access to four-year institutions should generally be more selective." The net impact of these recommendations is to leave the tracking system of higher education intact. Considering the class composition of the community college, to maintain the status quo in higher education tracking is, in essence, to perpetuate privilege (see Wolfe, 1971).

The influence of foundations in fostering vocational education in community colleges is difficult to measure precisely, but it is clear that they have been among its leading sponsors.[11] State master plans (see Hurlburt, 1969; Cross, 1970) have also done much to formalize the subordinate status of the community college within higher education and to encourage the growth of their vocational curricula. The federal government, too, has promoted vocational training in the two-year institutions. Federal involvement dates back at least to 1963. At that time, Congress authorized the spending of several hundred million dollars to encourage post-secondary technical education. More recently, the Higher Education Act of 1972 (pp. 77–78) authorized $850,000,000 over the next three years for post-secondary occupational education. In comparison, the entire sum authorized for the establishment of new community colleges and the expansion of old ones is less than one-third as much—$275,000,000.

The language of the Higher Education Act of 1972 makes clear just what is meant by vocational education:

The term 'postsecondary occupational education' means education, training, or retraining . . . conducted by an institution . . . which is designed to prepare individuals for gainful employment as semi-skilled or skilled workers or technicians or sub-professionals in recognized occupations (including new and emerging occupations) . . . but excluding any program to prepare individuals for employment in occupations . . . to be generally considered professional or which require a baccalaureate or advanced degree. (p. 87)

The import of this definition of occupational education is to exclude four-year programs leading to a B.A. from funding. The intent of this legislation, which provides enormous sums of money for community college career education, is obvious: it is designed to fill current manpower shortage in the middle and lower-middle levels of the occupational structure.

The idea of career education which the U.S. Office of Education is "working to spread throughout elementary, secondary and at least community college circles" (Marland, 1972, p. 217) is that the student, regardless of when he leaves the educational system, should have sufficient skills to enable him to be gainfully employed. The idea is a worthy one, but it implicitly accepts the existing system of social stratification. The philosophy of career education is that the proper function of the educational system is to respond to current manpower needs and to allocate people to positions characterized by large disparities in rewards. Commissioner of Education Sidney Marland observes that no more than 20 per cent of all jobs in the 1970's will require a bachelor's degree; apparently, this is supposed to provide a rough index as to how many people

should attend college for four years. Further, it is worth noting that career education does not seem to extend above the community college level. An idea whose "time has come," it somehow does not seem applicable to the sons and daughters of the middle and upper classes who attend four-year colleges and universities.

Federal sponsorship of vocational programs in the community college may have contributed to the development of a rigid track system (Cohen, 1971a, p. 152). By prohibiting the allocation of funds to non-vocational programs, federal laws have deepened the division between transfer and occupational programs. This division fosters separate facilities, separate brochures, and separate administrations. The result is a magnification of the differences between transfer and vocational programs leading to a decline in the desirability of occupational training.

Also at the forefront of the movement to expand vocational programs in community colleges have been various national higher education organizations. The American Association of Junior Colleges (AAJC), almost since its founding in 1920, has exerted its influence to encourage the growth of vocational education. Faced with the initial problem of establishing an identity for two-year colleges, the AAJC set out to describe the unique functions of the junior college. Prominent among these was the provision of two-year occupational training at the post-secondary level. In 1940 and 1941 the AAJC sponsored a Commission on Junior College Terminal Education. According to Ralph Fields (1962), a long-time observer of the junior college, this commission was instrumental in lending legitimacy to vocational training in the community college.

In recent years, the AAJC has continued its active encouragement of occupational programs in the community college. Numerous pamphlets, training programs, and conferences on vocational training in the two-year college have been sponsored by

AAJC. In that the AAJC, the leading national association of junior colleges, has probably done more than any other single organization to give definition to the community college movement, its enthusiasm for vocational training takes on particular importance.

The American Council on Education, the umbrella organization for the various associations of higher education, is considered by many to be the leading spokesman for American higher education. It, too, has given major support to post-secondary technical education. In 1963, the Council sponsored a study of the place of technical and vocational training in higher education. One of the conclusions of the report was that "two-year colleges, if they are to assume their proper and effective role in the educational system of the nation, should make vocational and technical education programs a major part of their mission and a fundamental institutional objective" (Venn, 1964, p. 165). Edmund Gleazer, Jr. (1968, p. 139), Executive Director of AAJC, points to this report as critical in gaining acceptance for vocational training within the higher education community.

Finally, many American universities have looked with favor on the development of the community college into a "comprehensive" institution with occupational programs in addition to its more traditional transfer programs. From the origins of the junior college in the late nineteenth and early twentieth centuries as an institution designed to extend secondary education for two years in order to keep the university pure, there has been a recognition among many university academics that it is in their interest to have a diversity of institutions in higher education (Thornton, 1960, pp. 46–50). A number of observers have noted that the community colleges serve as a safety valve, diverting students clamoring for access to college away from more selective institutions (Clark, 1960; Jencks and Riesman, 1968; Cohen, 1971b). Elite colleges neither want nor need these students; if separate institutions, or,

for that matter, vocational programs within these institutions help keep the masses out of their colleges, then they are to be given full support.[12] Paradoxically, the elite sector of the academic community, much of it liberal to radical, finds itself in a peculiar alliance with industry, foundations, government, and established higher education associations to vocationalize the community college.[13]

The Response to Vocational Education: Submerged Class Conflict

Despite the massive effort by leading national educational policy-makers to encourage the development of occupational education in the community college, student response to vocational programs has been limited. Estimates vary as to how many community college students are enrolled in career education programs, but the figures seem to range from 25 to 33 per cent (Cross, 1970; Ogilvie, 1971; Medsker and Tillery, 1971). Over two-thirds of two-year college entrants aspire to a bachelor's degree, and a similar proportion enroll, at least initially, in college-parallel or transfer programs. Many of these students, of course, are subsequently cooled out, but few of them seem to prefer a vocational program to leaving the community college altogether.

Leaders of the occupational education movement have constantly bemoaned the lack of student enthusiasm for vocational education (Venn, 1964; Gleazer, 1968; Carnegie, 1970; Medsker and Tillery, 1971; Cross, 1971). The problem, they believe, is the low status of career training in a society that worships the bachelor's degree. Medsker and Tillery (p. 140), for example, argue that "negative attitudes toward vocational education . . . are by-products of the academic syndrome in American higher education." Marland (1972, p. 218) refers to the difficulty as "degree fixation." The problem, then, since it is one of an irrational preoccupation with obtaining a traditional four-year education, leads to an obvious solution:

raising the status of vocational education. This proposed solution has been suggested by the Carnegie Commission on Higher Education, the Office of Education, the American Association of Junior Colleges, the American Council on Education, leaders of industry, and scholars in the field of community colleges.

Despite the apparent logic and simplicity of raising the status of vocational education, the task presents enormous difficulties. Minority students, though more likely to be enrolled in occupational programs than white students, seem especially sensitive to being channeled into vocational tracks. Overall, students are voting with their feet against community college vocational programs.

This is not an irrational obsession with four-year diplomas on the part of the students. It is not just snobbish prejudice; there are sound structural reasons for the low status of career education in the community college. At the base of an educational institution's prestige is its relationship to the occupational and class structure of the society in which it operates (Clark, 1962, pp. 80–83). The community college lies at the base of the stratification structure of higher education both in the class origins of its students and in their occupational destinations. Within the community college, the vocational curriculum is at the bottom of the prestige hierarchy—again, in terms of both social composition and likely adult status.

It is unrealistic, then, to expect that community college vocational programs, the bottom track of higher education's bottom track, will have much status. It is worth noting that the British, generally more hardheaded about matters of social class than Americans, faced the matter of educational status directly some years ago. In the 1950's in Great Britain, there was a great deal of talk about "parity of esteem" in English secondary education. The problem was to give equal status to grammar schools (college preparatory), technical schools (middle level managerial and technical), and secondary modern schools (terminal). After considerable debate, the British realized that "parity

of esteem" was an impossible ideal given the encompassing class structure (Banks, 1955; Marshall, 1965).

The educational establishment's concern with the low status of occupational programs in the community colleges reveals much more about its own ideology than it does about the allegedly irrational behavior of students resistant to vocational education. A great deal of emphasis is placed on improving the public image of vocational education, but little attention is paid to the substantive matter of class differences in income, occupational prestige, power, and opportunities for autonomy and expression at the workplace. The Carnegie Commission, whose ideology is probably representative of the higher education establishment, blurs the distinction between *equality* and *equality of opportunity* (Karabel, 1972a, p. 42). Discussing its vision of the day when minority persons will be proportionately represented in higher occupational levels, the Commission hails this as an "important signal that society was meeting its commitment to equality." The conception of equality conveyed in this passage is really one of equality of opportunity; the Commission seems less interested in reducing gross differences in rewards than in giving everyone a chance to get ahead of everyone else. The Carnegie Commission, reflecting the values not only of the national educational leadership but also of the wider society, shows concern about opportunities for mobility, but little concern about a reduction in inequality.

The submerged class conflict that exists between the sponsors of vocational education in the junior college, who represent the interests and outlook of the more privileged sectors of society, and community college students, many of them working class, occasionally becomes overt. At Seattle Community College in 1968–1969, the Black Student Union vigorously opposed a recommendation to concentrate trade and technical programs in the central (Black) campus while the "higher" semiprofessional programs were allocated to the northern and southern (white) campuses (Cohen, 1971a:

142). Rutgers (Newark) was the scene in 1969 of extensive demonstrations to gain open admissions to a branch of the state university. The import of the case of Rutgers (Newark) was that the protests took place in a city where students already had access to an open-door community college (Essex) and a mildly selective state college (Newark State). What the students were resisting here was not being tracked within the community college, but rather being channeled into the community college itself.[14] The well-known struggle for open admissions at CUNY in the spring of 1969 was not primarily for access per se, but for access to the more prestigious four-year institutions: City, Brooklyn, Queens, and Hunter.

The pattern in these isolated cases of manifest resistance to tracking within or between colleges is one of minority student leadership. In the United States, where race is a much more visible social cleavage than class, it is not surprising that Black students have shown the most sensitivity to tracking in higher education. Channeling of Black students to community colleges and to vocational programs within them is, after all, fairly visible; in contrast, the *class* character of the tracking system is much less perceptible. Were it not for the militancy of some minority students, it is likely that the conflict over vocational education would have long continued to manifest itself in enrollment patterns without becoming overt.

The class nature of the conflict over tracking has, however, not always been invisible. In Illinois in 1913, there was a battle over a bill in the state legislature to establish a separate system of vocational schools above the sixth grade. Business strongly backed the bill, sponsored by Chicago School Superintendent Edwin G. Cooley. The Chicago Federation of Labor, lobbying against the bill, expressed fear that it reflected

an effort on the part of large employers to turn the public schools into an agency for supplying them with an adequate supply of docile, well-trained, and capable workers [which] . . . aimed to bring Illinois a caste

system of education which would shunt the children of the laboring classes at an early age first into vocational courses and then into the factories (Counts, 1928, p. 167).

After a bitter fight, the bill was defeated in the legislature.

The tracking which takes place in the community college is, however, much more invisible than that proposed in the Cooley Bill. For one thing, the community college, by the very use of the word "college" in its title, locates itself squarely within the system of higher education and gives it at least the minimal status which comes from being a college rather than a technical school. For another, the apparent emphasis of the junior college on the transfer function leads to a perception of it as a way station on the road to a four-year college. This view of the community college as a place of transfer rather than a track is strengthened by the subtlety and smoothness of the cooling out process. The community college is a "comprehensive" institution; like the high school before it, it provides preparatory and terminal education in the same building and offers sufficient opportunities for movement between programs to obscure the larger pattern of tracking. Finally, the very age at which students enter the community college makes tracking a less serious issue; there *is* a difference between channeling an eleven-year-old child and channeling a young adult of eighteen.

Whatever the differences between high school and college tracking, there is a marked similarity in the rationales given in each case for curricular differentiation. The argument is that a common curriculum denies equality of opportunity by restricting educational achievement to a single mode which will inevitably lead to some form of hierarchy. In 1908, the Boston school superintendent argued:

Until very recently [the schools] have offered equal opportunity to receive *one kind* of education, but what will make them democratic is to provide opportunity for all to receive such an education as will fit them *equally well* for their particular life work. (Cohen and Lazerson, 1972: 69)

Similarly, K. Patricia Cross (1971: 162), a leading researcher on the junior college, argues more than 60 years later:

Surely quality education consists not in offering the same thing to all people in a token gesture toward equality but in maximizing the match between the talents of the individual and the teaching resources of the institution. Educational quality is not unidimensional. Colleges can be *different* and excellent too.

In principle, colleges can be different and excellent, too. But in a stratified society, what this diversity of educational experiences is likely to mean is that people will, at best, have an equal opportunity to obtain an education that will fit them into their appropriate position in the class structure. More often than not, those of lower class origins will, under the new definition of equality of educational opportunity, find themselves in schools or curricula which train them for positions roughly commensurate with their social origins.

The current movement to vocationalize the community college is a logical outgrowth of the dual historical patterns of class-based hierarchical differentiation in education and of educational inflation. The system of higher education, forced to respond to pressure for access arising from mobility aspirations endemic in an affluent society which stresses individual success and the democratic character of its opportunity structure, has let people in and has then proceeded to track them into community colleges and, more particularly, into occupational programs within these two-year colleges. This push toward vocational training in the community college has been sponsored by a national educational planning elite whose social composition, outlook, and policy proposals are reflective of the interests of the more privileged strata of our society. Notably absent among those pressuring for more occupational training in the junior college have been the students themselves. . . .

DISCUSSION

The recent Newman Report on Higher Education (1971: 57) noted that "the public, and especially the four-year colleges and universities, are shifting more and more responsibility onto the community colleges for undertaking the toughest tasks of higher education." One of the most difficult of these tasks has been to educate hundreds of thousands of students, many of them of modest social origins, in whom more selective colleges and universities showed no interest. Community colleges have given these students access to higher education and have provided some of them a chance to advance their class position.

Despite the idealism and vigor of the community college movement, there has been a sharp contradiction between official rhetoric and social reality. Hailed as the "democratizers of higher education," community colleges are, in reality, a vital component of the class-based tracking system. The modal junior college student, though aspiring to a four-year diploma upon entrance, receives neither an associate nor a bachelor's degree. The likelihood of his persisting in higher education is *negatively* influenced by attending a community college. Since a disproportionate number of two-year college students are of working-class origins, low status students are most likely to attend those institutions which increase the likelihood that they will drop out of college. Having increased access to higher education, community colleges are notably unsuccessful in retaining their students and in reducing class differentials in educational opportunity.

If current trends continue, the tracking system of higher education may well become more rigid. The community college, as the bottom track, is likely to absorb the vast majority of students who are the first generation in their families to enter higher education. Since most of these students are from relatively low status backgrounds, an increase in the already significant correlation between social class and position in the tracking system of higher education is likely to occur. As more and more people enter post-secondary education, the community college will probably become more distinct from the rest of higher education both in class composition and in curriculum. With the push of the policy-planning elite for more career education, vocational training may well become more pervasive, and the community college will become even more a terminal rather than a transfer institution. These trends, often referred to as expressions of higher education's "diversity" and of the community college's "special and unique role," are the very processes which place the community college at the bottom of the class-based tracking system. The system of higher education's much-touted "diversity" is, for the most part, hierarchy rather than genuine variety (see Karabel, 1972a and 1972b), a form of hierarchy which has more to do with social class than educational philosophy.

The high rate of attrition at community colleges may well be functional for the existing social system. The cooling out function of the junior college, as Clark puts it, is what "such a college is about." Community colleges exist in part to reconcile students' culturally induced hopes for mobility with their eventual destinations, transforming structurally induced failure into individual failure. This serves to legitimize the myth of an equal opportunity structure; it shifts attention to questions of individual mobility rather than distributive justice. Cooling out, then, can be seen as conflict between working class students and standards that legitimize the position of the privileged—a veiled class conflict. Similarly, there is class conflict implicit in the differences over vocational education between the aspirations of students and the objectives of policy-makers. This has occasionally become overt, but the community colleges seem to serve their legitimizing function best when the conflict remains submerged.

Can the inability of the community college movement to modify the American class structure be overcome? An assessment of some specific reforms that have been proposed may yield some insight. One obvious reform would be to reverse the pattern that Hansen and Weisbrod (1969) document—simply to invest more money in the community colleges than in the four-year public institutions. The idea of this reform would be both to provide the highest quality education to those who have socioeconomic and cognitive disadvantages to overcome and to put an end to the pattern of poor people subsidizing relatively affluent people through public systems of higher education. This proposal, which may be justified on grounds of equity, is unlikely to make much difference in terms of either education or social class. A repeated finding in social science research, confirmed by both the Coleman Report (1966) and the recent Jencks (1972) study, is that educational expenditures seem to be virtually unrelated to cognitive development at the elementary and secondary levels, and there is no reason to believe that money is any more effective in colleges. However desirable a shift in resources from four-year colleges to community colleges might be on other grounds, it is unlikely to seriously affect the larger pattern of class-based tracking in higher education.

Another possibility would be to transform the community college into a four-year institution—the very proposal that the Carnegie Commission on Higher Education strongly opposes. The purpose of this reform would be to upgrade the status of the community college and to diminish the rigidity of the tracking system. Yet it is highly questionable whether making the junior college into a senior college would have any such effect; there are marked status distinctions among four-year colleges and, in all likelihood, the new four-year institutions would be at the bottom of the prestige hierarchy. Further, the creation of more four-year colleges would probably accelerate the process of educational inflation.

The proposal to vocationalize the community college exemplifies the dilemma faced by those who would reform the public two-year college. Noting that many community college students neither transfer nor get an associate degree, proponents of vocational education argue that the students should stop engaging in a uni-dimensional academic competition which they cannot win and should instead obtain a marketable skill before leaving the educational system. If one accepts the existing system of social stratification, there is an almost irresistible logic to the vocational training argument; there are, after all, manpower shortages to be filled and it *is* true that not everyone can be a member of the elite.

In a sense, the community colleges are "damned if they do and damned if they don't." The vocational educational reform provides a striking example of their dilemma, for the question of whether community colleges should become predominantly vocational institutions may well be the most critical policy issue facing the two-year institutions in the years ahead. If they move toward more career education, they will tend to accentuate class-based tracking. If they continue as "comprehensive institutions" they will continue to be plagued by the enormous attrition in their transfer curricula. Either way, the primary role of the colleges derives from their relation to the class structure and feasible reforms will, at best, result in minor changes in their channeling function. . . .

As for educational reform making this a more egalitarian society, we cannot be sanguine. Jencks (1972) has shown that the effects of schooling on ultimate income and occupation are relatively small. Even if the community colleges were to undergo a major transformation, little change in the system of social stratification would be likely to take place. If we are genuinely concerned about creating a more egalitarian society, it will be necessary to change our economic institutions. The problems of inequality and inequality of opportunity are, in short, best dealt with not through educational reform but rather by the wider changes in economic and political life that would help build a socialist society.

Writing in favor of secondary education

for everybody many years ago, R. H. Tawney, the British social historian, remarked that the "intrusion into educational organization of the vulgarities of the class system is an irrelevance as mischievous in effect as it is odious in conception." That matters of social class have intruded into the community college is beyond dispute; whether the influence of class can be diminished not only in the community college but also in the larger society remains to be seen.

NOTES

1. Contrary to popular perceptions, American and European rates of social mobility, at least as measured by mobility from manual to non-manual occupations, are very similar. For data on this point see Lipset and Bendix (1959).
2. See Ralph Turner's "Modes of Social Ascent through Education" (1966) for a discussion of how differing norms in the United States and England lead to patterns of "contest" and "sponsored" mobility.
3. For an empirical study of hierarchical differentiation within higher education, see "Social Class, Academic Ability, and College 'Quality'" by Jerome Karabel and Alexander W. Astin (1975).
4. The term "community college" is used in this study to refer to all *public two-year colleges*. Excluded from this definition are private two-year colleges and all four-year colleges and universities. In the text, the terms "junior college" and "two-year college" are used interchangeably with community college though they are not, strictly speaking, synonyms. The name community college has become the more frequently used because of the increasing emphasis of two-year public institutions on fulfilling local needs. Further, as the community college struggled to obtain a distinct identity and as greater stress was placed on two-year programs, the junior college label, which seemingly describes a lesser version of the four-year college geared almost exclusively to transfer, became increasingly inappropriate.
5. Two of the most comprehensive recent studies of the influence of social class and ability on access to higher education are Sewell and Shah (1967) and Folger et al. (1970). George Counts (1922: 149), in a classical empirical study of the American high school of a half century ago, concluded that "in very large measure participation in the privilege of a secondary education is contingent on social and economic status." Similarly, Michael Katz (1968), in a study of public education reform in nineteenth century Massachusetts, found that the early high school was overwhelmingly a middle class institution.
6. In discussing the role of guidance in the junior college, it is interesting to observe the connection between the growth of the school counseling pro-

fession and educational tracking. As long as the curriculum at a particular level of schooling remains unified, there is relatively little need for guidance. However, when a number of curricula leading to occupations of varying prestige come into being, counseling becomes a virtual necessity. It is worth noting in this connection the long-standing enthusiasm of the business community for guidance programs. George S. Counts, in a study entitled *School and Society in Chicago* (1928), noted the fervor with which the Chicago Association of Commerce, the city's dominant business association, supported the establishment of a program of vocational guidance in the public schools in the early twentieth century.

7. When George L. Counts examined class differences in secondary schools in the early twenties, he wrote:

These differences in the extent of educational opportunity are further accentuated through the choice of curricula. As a rule, those groups which are poorly represented in the high school patronize the more narrow and practical curricula, the curricula which stand as terminal points in the educational system and which prepare for wage-earning. And the poorer their representation in high school, the greater is the probability that they will enter these curricula. The one- and two-year vocational courses, wherever offered, draw their registration particularly, from the ranks of labor (Counts, 1922, p. 143).

See also Trow, 1966; Cohen and Lazerson, 1972; Greer, 1972.

8. Minority students are also disproportionately enrolled in two of the lower rungs of the higher education tracking system—community colleges and unselective black colleges. Patterns of enrollment, of course, vary from region to region with community colleges dominant in the West and black institutions more prominent in the South. For data showing that the proportion of minority students decreases as one progresses up the three-track California system see Coordinating Council (1969: 23) and Jaffe and Adams (1972: 232).

9. At the same time, however, it is easy to forget that *absolute* changes in occupation, income, and educational attainment can have important consequences in everyday life and may raise general levels of satisfaction. Having more people attend college, while not narrowing the educational gap in relative terms, may lead to a more enlightened populace. Keniston and Gerzon (1972) attack the narrowly economic view of higher education and argue that important non-pecuniary benefits accrue from college attendance. Similarly, a change from a blue-collar to a white-collar economy may eliminate many menial tasks and hence lead to greater job satisfaction. Finally, an absolute increase in the standard of living, while not necessarily abolishing poverty (which, as Jencks argues, is primarily a relative phenomenon), may result in a higher quality of life than was possible under conditions of greater scarcity.

10. Grubb and Lazerson (in press, 1972) report that economic returns to vocational education are almost uniformly low, but their review does not include studies of programs at community colleges. Some skepticism as to the allegedly high incomes of graduates of occupational programs for blue-collar jobs may, however, be expressed. Contrary to popular mythology about the affluent worker, the proportion of male blue-collar workers earning more than $15,000 in 1970 was a minuscule 4 percent (Bureau of the Census, 1971b: 30). Only 3 out of 10 blue-collar workers earned more than $10,000 in 1970.

We do not know what economic rewards accrue to graduates of community college vocational programs, nor do we know much about the occupational and economic status of the community college drop-out. This is fertile ground for empirical inquiry. A longitudinal study of three groups of high school graduates—students who do not enter college, community college drop-outs, and community college entrants who obtain a degree (A.A. or B.A.)—matching students with similar personal characteristics, would do much to illuminate the effects of attending a community college.

11. Karier (1972) has written a provocative essay on the role of foundations in sponsoring educational testing. The role of far-sighted foundations in fostering educational reform, possibly as a means of rationalizing the social order, is a topic worthy of careful investigation.

12. Amitai Etzioni (1970), chairman of the Department of Sociology at Columbia University, expresses this point of view well: "If we can no longer keep the floodgates closed at the admissions office, it at least seems wise to channel the general flow away from four-year colleges and toward two-year extensions of high school in the junior and community colleges." Vice President Agnew (1970), in a speech attacking open admissions, approvingly cited this quotation.

13. See Riessman's "The 'Vocationalization' of Higher Education: Duping the Poor" for an analysis of the movement to turn the community college into a technical institution. For a brilliant article on the elitism of leftist academics toward working-class students see McDermott (1969).

14. I am indebted to Russell Thackrey for pointing out the implications of the interesting case of Rutgers (Newark).

REFERENCES

Agnew, S. Toward a middle way in college admissions. *Educational Record* 51 (Spring, 1970), pp. 106–111.

American Council on Education, Office of Research. National norms for entering college freshmen—Fall 1966. ACE Research Reports, Vol. 6, No. 6. Washington, D.C.: 1966.

American Council on Education, Office of Research. The American freshman: National norms for Fall 1971. ACE Research Reports, Vol. 6, No. 6. Washington, D.C.: 1971.

Banks, O. *Parity and prestige in English*

secondary education. London: Routledge and Kegan Paul, Ltd., 1955.

Blau, P. M. & Duncan, O. D. *The American occupational structure.* New York: Wiley, 1967.

Bowles, S. Contradictions in U. S. higher education. James Weaver (Ed.) *Political economy: radical vs. orthodox approaches.* Boston: Allyn & Bacon, 1972.

Bowles, S. Unequal education and the reproduction of the social division of labor. *Review of radical political economics,* 3 (Fall), 1971.

Brick, M. *Forum and focus for the junior college movement.* New York: Bureau of Publications, Teachers College, Columbia University, 1964.

Bureau of the Census. *The American almanac.* New York: Grosset & Dunlap, 1971a.

Bureau of the Census. Educational attainment: March 1971. Series P20, No. 229. Washington, D.C.: U. S. Government Printing Office, 1971b.

Bureau of the Census. Undergraduate enrollment in two-year and four-year colleges: October 1971. Series P20, No. 236. Washington, D.C.: U. S. Government Printing Office, 1972.

Bushnell, D. S. & Zagaris, I. *Report from Project FOCUS: Strategies for change.* Washington, D.C.: American Association of Junior Colleges, 1972.

Carnegie Commission on Higher Education. *The open-door colleges.* New York: McGraw-Hill, 1970.

Clark, B. R. *The open door college.* New York: McGraw-Hill, 1960.

Clark, B. R. *Educating the expert society.* San Francisco: Chandler, 1962.

Cohen, A. M. *et al. A constant variable.* San Francisco: Jossey-Bass, 1971a.

Cohen, A. M. Stretching pre-college education. *Social Policy* (May/June, 1971b), pp. 5–9.

Cohen, D. K. & Lazerson, M. Education and the corporate order. *Socialist Revolution,* 2 (March/April, 1972), pp. 47–72.

Coleman, J. S., *et al. Equality of educational opportunity.* Washington, D. C.: U. S. Government Printing Office, 1966.

Collins, R. Functional and conflict theories of stratification. *American Sociological Review* 36 (December, 1971), pp. 1002–19.

Coordinating Council for Higher Education. *The undergraduate student and his higher education: Policies of California colleges and universities in the next decade.* Sacramento, Cal. 1969.

Counts, G. S. *School and society in Chicago.* New York: Harcourt, Brace, 1928.

Counts, G. S. *The selective character of American secondary education.* Chicago: University of Chicago Press, 1922.

Cross, K. P. The junior college student: A research description. Princeton, N. J.: Educational Testing Service, 1968.

Cross, K. P. The role of the junior college in providing postsecondary education for all. In *Trends in postsecondary education.* Washington, D. C.: U. S. Government Printing Office, 1970.

Cross, K. P. *Beyond the open door.* San Francisco: Jossey-Bass, 1971.

Department of Health, Education, and Welfare. *Digest of educational statistics.* Washington, D. C.: U. S. Government Printing Office, 1970.

Etzioni, A. The high schoolization of college. *Wall Street Journal,* March 17, 1970.

Fields, R. R. *The community college movement.* New York: McGraw-Hill, 1962.

Folger, J. K., Astin, H. S., & Bayer, A. E. *Human resources and higher education.* New York: Russell Sage, 1970.

Gleazer, E. J., Jr. *This is the community college.* Boston: Houghton Mifflin, 1968.

Greer, C. *The great school legend.* New York: Basic Books, 1972.

Grubb, W. N. & Lazerson, M. *Education and industrialism: Documents in vocational education.* New York: Teachers College, Columbia University, in press.

Hansen, W. L. & Weisbrod, B. A. *Benefits, costs, and finance of public higher education.* Chicago: Markham, 1969.

Harris, N. C. The middle manpower job spectrum. In W. K. Ogilvie, and M. R. Raines (Eds.), *Perspectives on the Community-Junior College.* New York: Appleton-Century-Crofts, 1971.

Hartnett, R. T. College and university trustees: Their backgrounds, roles, and educational attitudes. Princeton, N. J.: Educational Testing Service, 1969.

Havemann, E. & West, P. *They went to college.* New York: Harcourt, Brace, 1952.

Higher Education Act of 1972. Public Law 92-318. 92nd Congress, 659, June 23, 1972.

Hurlburt, A. L. *State master plans for community colleges.* Washington, D. C.: American Association of Junior Colleges, 1969.

Jaffe, A. J. & Adams, W. Two models of open enrollment. In L. Wilson and O. Mills (Eds.), *Universal higher education.* Washington: American Council on Education, 1972.

Jencks, C. & Riesman, D. *The academic revolution.* Garden City, N. Y.: Doubleday, 1968.

Jencks, C. *et al. Inequality: a reassessment of the effect of family and schooling in America.* New York: Basic Books, 1972.

Karabel, J. Perspectives on open admissions. *Educational Record,* 53 (Winter, 1972a), pp. 30–44.

Karabel, J. Open admissions: Toward meritocracy or equality? *Change,* 4 (May, 1972b), pp. 38–43.

Karabel, J. & Astin, A. W. Social class, academic ability, and college 'quality.' *Social Forces,* 53 (March 1975), pp. 381–398.

Karier, C. J. Testing for order and control in the corporate liberal state. *Educational Theory,* 22 (Spring, 1972), pp. 154–180.

Katz, M. B. *The irony of early school reform.* Boston: Beacon Press, 1968.

Keniston, K. & Gerzon, M. Human and social benefits. In L. Wilson and O. Mills, *Universal Higher Education.* Washington, D. C.: American Council on Education, 1972.

Kolko, G. *Wealth and power in America.* New York: Praeger, 1962.

Lipset, S. M. & Bendix, R. *Social mobility in industrial society.* Berkeley: University of California Press, 1959.

Marland, S. P., Jr. A strengthening alliance. In L. Wilson and O. Mills (Eds.), *Universal higher education.* Washington, D. C.: American Council on Education, 1972.

Marshall, T. H. *Class, citizenship, and social development.* Garden City, N.Y.: Anchor, 1965.

McDermott, J. The laying on of culture. *The Nation,* March 10, 1969.

Medsker, L. L. & Trent, J. W. The influence of different types of public higher institutions on college attendance from varying socioeconomic and ability levels. Berkeley: Center for Research and Development in Higher Education, 1965.

Medsker, L. L. & Tillery, D. *Breaking the access barriers.* New York: McGraw-Hill, 1971.

Miller, H. *Rich man, poor man.* New York: Thomas Y. Crowell, 1971.

Milner, M., Jr. *The illusion of equality.* San Francisco: Jossey-Bass, 1972.

Morsch, W. O. *Costs analysis of occupational training programs in community colleges and vocational training centers.* Washington, D. C.: Bureau of Social Science Research, 1971.

Newman, F., *et al. Report on higher education.* Reports to the U. S. Department of Health, Education, and Welfare. Washington, D. C.: U. S. Government Printing Office, 1971.

Ogilvie, W. K. Occupational education and the community college. In W. K. Ogilvie & M. R. Raines (Eds.), *Perspectives on the Community-Junior College.* New York: Appleton-Century-Crofts, 1971.

Pierson, G. W. *The education of American leaders.* New York: Praeger, 1969.

Powell, H. B. The foundation and the future of the junior college. In *The foundation and the junior colleges.* Washington, D.C.: American Association of Junior Colleges, 1965.

Reed, R. & Miller, H. Some determinants of the variation in earnings for college men. *Journal of Human Resources,* 5 (Spring, 1970), pp. 177–190.

Riessman, F. The 'vocationalization' of higher education: Duping the poor. *Social Policy,* 2 (May/June, 1971), pp. 3–4.

Rothbart, G. S. The legitimation of inequality: objective scholarship vs. black militance. *Sociology of Education,* 43 (Spring, 1970), pp. 159–174.

Ryan, P. B. Why industry needs the junior college. In W. K. Ogilvie & M. R. Raines (Eds.), *Perspectives on the Community-Junior College.* New York: Appleton-Century-Crofts, 1971.

Schoenfeldt, L. F. Education after high school. *Sociology of Education,* 41 (Fall 1968), pp. 350–369.

Sewell, W. H. and Shah, V. P. Socioeconomic status, intelligence, and the attainment of higher education. *Sociology of Education,* 40 (Winter, 1967), pp. 1–23.

Sharp, L. M. *Education and employment.* Baltimore, Johns Hopkins, 1970.

Spaeth, J. L. The allocation of college graduates to graduate and professional schools. *Sociology of Education,* 41 (Fall, 1968), pp. 342–349.

Sunko, Theodore S. Making the case for junior college foundation support. In *The Foundation and the junior college.* Washington, D. C.: American Association of Junior Colleges, 1965.

Thornton, J. W., Jr. *The community junior college.* New York: John Wiley, 1960.

Trent, J. W., & Medsker, L. L. *Beyond high school.* San Francisco: Jossey-Bass, 1968.

Trow, M. The second transformation of American secondary education. In R.

Bendix and S. Lipset (Eds.), *Class, status and power.* New York: Free Press, 1966.

Turner, R. Modes of social ascent through education. In R. Bendix and S. Lipset (Eds.), *Class, status and power.* New York: Free Press, 1966.

Venn, G. *Man, education and work.* Washington, D. C.: American Council on Education, 1964.

Watson, N. Corporations and the community colleges: a growing liaison? *Technical Education News,* Vol. 29, No. 2 (April/May 1970), pp. 3–6.

Wegner, E. L. & Sewell, W. H. Selection and context as factors affecting the probability of graduation from college. *American Journal of Sociology,* 75 (January, 1970), pp. 665–679.

Wolfe, A. Reform without reform: the Carnegie Commission on Higher Education. *Social Policy,* 2 (May/June, 1971), pp. 18–27.

Wolfle, D. *The uses of talent.* Princeton, N.J.: Princeton University Press, 1971.

12. Social Status and Inequality of Access to Higher Education in the USSR

RICHARD B. DOBSON

Since its inception, the Soviet government has committed itself to the democratization of higher education. After coming to power, the Bolshevik Party set out to use education as a tool to reshape the social order—to provide the necessary ideological tempering, transmit the technical skills required for the building of a modern industrial economy, and obliterate distinctions between social groups and classes. Policies ensuring workers and peasants access to the higher schools, in particular, were designed to bring talent to the top, to break the "ruling classes" ' monopoly of education, "culture," and privilege, and to create a new "socialist intelligentsia" devoted to the Soviet regime.[1]

The drive to industrialize in the thirties coupled with a rapid expansion of the specialized secondary and higher educational institutions, made possible an extraordinary degree of upward mobility. Access to higher education was by no means afforded by merit alone—social and political considerations were no less important. Preparatory programs called "workers' faculties" (*rabfaky*) fed thousands of recruits from the working class into the higher schools. The graduates of the "proletarianized" *vuzy* (higher educational institutions*) in turn swelled the ranks of the intelligentsia.[2]

Vuz is an often used acronym for the Russian *vysshee uchebnoe zavedenie,* meaning "higher educational institution." *Vuzy* is the plural of *vuz.*

In the latter half of the thirties, pressure to enroll great numbers of workers and peasants was relaxed. Restrictions on access to higher education for "alien social elements" were removed, and academic standards were raised. By 1936, achievement tests were instituted in order to allow the selection of the best qualified. The proportion of students classified as "workers" or "peasants" declined from 72 percent in 1932 to 56 percent in 1938. From that year until recently, figures on the social composition of students in higher education were not published. It is very likely that working-class and peasantry representation declined further in subsequent years as a result of other changes. Not only were the workers' faculties phased out, but modest tuition fees were introduced in 1940 (and continued until 1956) for students in the upper grades of the secondary school and in *vuzy*.[3]

In the course of the thirties, while crushing real and imagined opposition within the society, the Stalinist dictatorship was concentrating in its hands information on political and social matters. In 1936, "pedology"—the social-psychological study of the learning process—was authoritatively denounced as a "bourgeois" pseudo-science and was suppressed.[4] Independent research by social scientists was ruled out; valuable studies of the factors affecting educational performance which had begun in the twenties ceased. The question of the extent to which differences in status affected educational opportunity, occupational attainment, and the distribution of rewards in society became shrouded in official secrecy. Certainly no Soviet sociological research explored this problem.[5]

The issue of how privilege may be transmitted through the educational system was revived in the late fifties. Expressing both practical and ideological concerns, Premier Khrushchev spoke bluntly about the shortcomings of the educational system which was to serve the building of communism. As more and more young people went on not only to complete the mandatory seven years

of schooling, but to graduate from secondary school, not every graduate could count on getting a higher education. The secondary school, which traditionally served as a springboard to higher education, was said to foster a disdainful attitude toward manual work. It was "divorced from life"—at variance both with the economy's needs for skilled workers and with the values of the new communist man.

Access to higher education had become restricted for those of lower status. Khrushchev disclosed that only 30 to 40 percent of the students in Moscow's higher educational institutions came from working-class or collective-farm families, although the latter comprised the great bulk of the population.[6] Sometimes, he asserted, admittance to *vuzy* was the result less of the student's motivation and ability than of "a competition of parents" who would not only push their children along the path toward a high-status position, but who, by influencing or even bribing admissions officials, would pave their way.[7]

The antedote for these social ills, in Khrushchev's view, was a solid dose of labor training in secondary school, followed by practical work "in production." Regulations governing admission to *vuzy* were to be changed, as well. Recommendations of Party, Komsomol, and union organizations were to weigh more heavily, and "production candidates" (those with a secondary education who had worked for at least two years) were to comprise up to four-fifths of the entering classes. In this way, youth would be taught to respect labor, and the work period would weed out the less motivated and less able and thus equalize to some degree working-class and intelligentsia youth's chances for higher education.[8]

The sweeping reforms carried out at the end of the fifties gave rise to additional problems. Although pupils learned trades in secondary school, and most *vuz* students acquired work experience, they regarded work in a factory, shop, or farm as an unfortunate detour from their main objectives—higher education, then work as a "specialist." In the course of working, trigonometry theorems and chemistry formulae were forgotten. Upon entering the higher school, many found themselves unprepared for serious study. An increasing number failed their courses and dropped out before graduating. The rate of attrition was particularly high among working-class and peasant youth.[9]

Even before Khrushchev's removal from power, a reversal of the reforms began. In 1964, the eleventh year which had been added to the ten-year program in order to provide extra time for vocational training was dropped. In the following year, the regulations governing *vuz* admissions were changed so that secondary school graduates could apply to *vuzy* right after graduation. Although some preference has continued to be given to those with two or more years' work experience, a renewed stress has been placed on academic performance in school and on the entrance examinations in determining who should be admitted.[10] Concurrently, the number of students enrolled in higher education has continued to grow. By 1970, there were four and a half million students in the USSR, approximately twice as many as in 1960. Half of these were full-time students; the remainder were enrolled in evening or correspondence programs.[11]

Although neither Khrushchev's reforms nor their reversal solved the problems which he had publicized, other changes wrought under his leadership laid the ground for a fuller discussion and more able study of these problems. Having been broached and then openly debated at high levels, questions concerning privilege and the purpose of education in Soviet society became more or less legitimate subjects of discussion for the leadership, the press, and even the larger, amorphous "public" (*obshchestvennost'*). Also, in the wake of de-Stalinization, sociology as an empirical science had been revived. Whereas previously it had been branded as a "bourgeois pseudo-science" antithetical to Marxism, now it came to be

regarded as a method which, as long as it remained firmly grounded in "dialectical materialism" and did not challenge official Party ideology and policy, would be a useful tool for social engineering.[12]

The numerous studies conducted by Soviet sociologists since the end of the fifties have greatly increased our understanding of the socio-occupational stratification of Soviet society and have shed new light on the educational attainment process.[13] Recent research provides a contradictory picture of the extent to which children's educational attainment is related to their parents' educational level or occupational status. For example, in an attempt at multivariate analysis of survey data pertaining to the rural population of the Tatar Autonomous Republic, Iu. V. Arutiunian reports that mother's and father's educational level together account for 54 percent of the variance in the children's educational attainment.[14] With data from a 1965 survey of some three thousand workers and employees in the towns of Ufa and Orenburg, N. A. Aitov found an extremely strong correlation ($r = .8$) between parents' and children's educational level; in contrast, on the basis of a 1967 survey of more than four thousand residents of the city of Kazan, O. I. Shkaratan and V. O. Rukavishnikov report a low correlation ($r = .18$) between father's educational level and the children's educational attainment at the start of their work career.[15]

While stressing the high rate of upward social mobility in the USSR, Aitov states

the basic reason why, all the same, the majority of individuals remain in their parents' social group is the level of their education. Thus, as of 1965 [according to these survey data], individuals who had been born in workers' families had an average level of education of 7.66 grades, those [urban residents] born in peasants' families had 7.31 grades, and those from white-collar workers' families 12.22 grades.[16]

At the same time, he argues that the status-attainment process in socialist society is radically different from that in capitalist societies:

Under capitalism, the basic thing determining the position of man in society—capital—is transmitted through inheritance. Under socialism, that means—education—is not received as an inheritance; rather, each should attain it for himself. Under capitalism, [the gaining of] "a place in the sun" depends principally on the parents, and there it is easier to make one's way up the ladder of the social hierarchy for those whose father holds that ladder in his hands.[17]

In a similar vein, F. R. Filippov argues that the "external resemblance of the school's and teacher's functions under capitalism and socialism cannot conceal the fundamentally different purpose of these functions, for in opposition to capitalism, the school in a socialist society solves the problem of the gradual overcoming of social-class differences based on differences in educational and cultural levels and brings about a high degree of social mobility for youth who graduate from school."[18]

SOCIAL SELECTION IN THE SOVIET EDUCATIONAL SYSTEM

Notwithstanding Aitov's and Filippov's insistence on these basic differences, the studies conducted by Soviet sociologists demonstrate that the educational attainment process in the USSR is in many ways similar to that observed in Western countries. A young person's educational attainment is largely a function of parents' socio-occupational status and educational level, family per capita income, and place of residence (e.g., village, small town, or large urban area).[19] Much of the influence of these background variables on attainment is exerted through several intervening variables—most notably, parental encouragement, the child's academic performance, the type of school attended, and the subject's educational and occupational aspirations.

Because of the combined influence of material and cultural factors, children of more humble origins are less likely to perform well in school and tend to set their sights lower than those from higher-status families. In comparison to offspring of the intelligentsia,* children of workers, peasants, or low-skill white-collar workers are more likely to repeat grades or to drop out of school at an early age. After completing eight years of mandatory schooling, they are more likely to go to work, enroll in vocational schools, or study in technicums which train lower-level "specialists" (technicians, accountants, nurses, etc.). Thus, a smaller proportion of lower-status youth continue in the upper grades of the general educational school, which serve as the main "college track." Among secondary school graduates, fewer from the lower-status groups apply to *vuzy* or pass the entrance examinations. Those who do succeed in passing are more likely to be enrolled in lower or middle-level institutions than in the more prestigious ones. As a result, the chances of lower-status children's joining the ranks of the professional workers are considerably lower than higher-status children's chances of maintaining or improving upon their initial status.

Children who grow up in higher-status families are more likely to have their interests aroused and their abilities developed than their less fortunate age-mates. Table 1 presents data from three separate surveys conducted in and around the town of Ufa in the Russian Republic. The first two columns show the extent of certain disparities in cultural consumption according to educational level: in comparison with adults having four grades of schooling or less, roughly three times as many of those with higher education make use of a public library and six times as many have their own library at home. As the right-hand columns demonstrate, children from culturally more well-endowed families are more likely to get good grades in school, while being less likely to repeat grades because of poor performance.

*As commonly defined by contemporary Soviet sociologists, the intelligentsia is a group comprising all "specialists"—skilled white-collar workers possessing either a higher or a specialized secondary education. The latter are the approximate equivalents of "professionals" and "semi-professionals."

Table 1. Indices of the Family's Cultural Level, Number of Children Receiving High Marks in School, and Number of Grade-Repeaters among School Children, According to the Parents' Educational Level

| | UFA and Environs, 1966, 1967 | | | |
| | Survey of adult population (1) | | | |
Educational level (of adult respondent or of parent)	Percentage making use of public libraries	Percentage having a library at home[a]	Children receiving "excellent" and "good" marks (2)	Parents reporting that children repeated a grade (3)
Higher	90%	86% (378)	51%[b]	3%[b]
Incomplete Higher	89%	69% (125)	45%	7%
Specialized Secondary	83%	60% (300)	43%	5%
Secondary (10 Grades)	78%	49% (333)	29%	7%
8–9 Grades	63%	35% (285)	28%	10%
5–7 Grades	48%	23% (346)	24%	12%
1–4 Grades	31%	14% (158)	18%	16%
Total Number of Respondents		1,925	2,417	1,086

Sources: (1) Data from a survey of adults conducted in Ufa in 1966. P.A. Zlotnikov, "Svobodnoe vremia i samoobrazovanie molodezhi" [Youth's free-time and self-education], in Molodezh', ee interesy, stremleniia, idealy [Youth: Its interests, aspirations, ideals] (Moscow: Molodaia gvardiia, 1969), p. 319. (2) Results of a 1967 survey of pupils in grades 7 through 10 in twenty schools in the towns of Ufa and Beloretska and in three neighboring rural districts. Pupils earning grades of "5" only or of "4" and "5" only fall within this category. L.G. Zemtsov, Sotsial'nye problemy obshcheobrazovatel'noi shkoly na sovremennom etape [Social problems of the general-education school at the present stage], unpublished dissertation for the degree of Candidate of Sciences (Ufa, 1971), p. 115, Table 15 (adapted). (3) Results of a 1967 survey of parents of pupils in grades 1–10 in ten schools in the town of Beloretska and three rural districts. Ibid., p. 116, Table 16 (adapted).
[a]Definition of "home library" not given.
[b]Percentage bases not given.

When broken down by socio-occupational group, these survey data reveal marked variations in school performance. Whereas one out of five of the children of industrial or agricultural workers receives only "good" and "excellent" grades, the proportion rises to 30 percent among low-level white-collar workers' offspring and reaches 46 percent among children of semi-professional and professional workers.[20] Thirteen to 18 percent of the parents in the manual occupational groups reported that their children had had to repeat a grade in school as compared with

4 percent of the specialists.[21] In studying this relationship, L. G. Zemtsov also analyzed data collected by the administration of several schools in Ufa. Whereas among students with "good" and "excellent" grades specialists' and workers' children were represented almost equally, workers' children accounted for three-quarters of the failing pupils, being ten times as numerous as specialists' offspring.[22]

Children from better educated, more well-to-do, or higher status families not only tend to get higher grades, but are more likely to aspire to higher education than children from the lower strata. Analyzing data on eighth-grade pupils gathered in the medium-size town of Syzran' in 1968, V. G. Gendel' found that 47 percent of the pupils from specialists' families, 26 percent of the white-collar workers' children, and 16 percent of the workers' offspring expressed the desire to become specialists with a higher education.[23] In Table 2, we see the relationship between father's education and the pupils' grades and plans. The percentage of eighth graders planning to enroll in the ninth grade and then attend a *vuz* after graduating from the tenth grade rises from 11 percent among those whose father had completed no more than six grades of schooling to 59 percent among those whose father had completed

higher education. It is equally obvious that the pupils' aspirations are strongly associated with their academic achievement. Scarcely any of the students with low marks plan to pursue a higher education. Yet, among those with high grades, there are still pronounced differences in aspiration according to the father's education. In short, much, but not all, of the influence of father's educational level on the children's aspirations is mediated by the pupils' own performance.

The way in which social origins and school performance combine in determining the likelihood of a child's entering the ninth grade of the general-education school is well demonstrated by data from a large sample of Leningrad school children in 1968 (see Table 3). The children's chances of entering the

Table 2. Eighth Graders' Academic Performance and Educational Aspirations, as Related to Father's Education and Own Grades

	Syzran', 1968			
	Percent planning to enter 9th grade and then pursue a higher education[a]			
Father's education	High grades[b]	Low grades[b]	All	Percent with high grades[b]
Higher	91% (22)	13% (15)	59% (37)	59%
Incomplete Higher or Specialized Secondary	75% (28)	4% (24)	42% (52)	54%
Tenth Grade	76% (41)	5% (43)	39% (84)	49%
7–9 Grades	54% (41)	3% (91)	19% (132)	31%
5–6 Grades	39% (23)	0% (57)	11% (80)	29%
4 Grades or Less	42% (19)	2% (64)	11% (83)	23%
Not Indicated	(2)	(8)	(10)	
Total	64% (176)	3% (302)	25% (478)	37% (478)

Source: V.G. Gendel', *Problemy sotsial'noi podvizhnosti molodezhi pri sotsializme,* unpublished dissertation for the degree of Candidate of Sciences (Leningrad, 1971), p. 156, Table 3 (adapted).
[a]A higher proportion of the eighth graders plan to continue in the ninth grade of the general-education school (39 percent). Shown here are those who intend to enter the ninth grade *and also* plan to enroll in a higher educational institution after graduation.
[b]Grades "5" (excellent) and "4" (good) are coded as "high grades"; grades "2" (unsatisfactory) and "3" (average), as "low grades."

Table 3. Percentage of Eighth-Grade Pupils Continuing in the Ninth Grade of the General-Education School, According to Grade-Point Average and Parents' Social-Occupational Status

	Leningrad, 1968		
	Grade average[d]		
Parents' status[a]	Under 3.5	3.5 and over	All
Professionals[b]	77	89	86
Semi-professionals[c]	50	80	70
Skilled Workers	38	69	52
Semiskilled and Unskilled Manual and Non-Manual Workers	19	41	25

Source: E.K. Vasil'eva, Sotsial'no-professional'nyi uroven' gorodskoi molodezhi (Leningrad: Leningrad State University Press, 1973), p. 41 (Tables 15 and 16, adapted).
[a]In cases where parents belonged to different social-occupational groups, the children were classified according to the one with higher status.
[b]"Specialists" with a higher education.
[c]"Specialists" with a specialized secondary education.
[d]Grades run from "2" (unsatisfactory) to "5" (excellent). "3" is "average".

ninth grade increase as the parents' social status rises, while at every socio-occupational level, the chances of those with high grades exceed those with lower grades. As a result of this selection process, the social composition of the ninth grade class typically differs appreciably from that of the eighth grade. From the eighth to ninth grade, according to this Leningrad study, the share of professionals' children grew by 46 percent, and that of semi-professionals' offspring increased by 24 percent. But the proportion coming from skilled manual workers' families declined by 10 percent, while the share of children of semi-skilled and unskilled manual and non-manual personnel fell by 54 percent.[24]

Although children with low grades and low status are more prone than others to leave the general-education school before finishing the tenth grade, background factors continue to influence the academic performance and aspirations of those who graduate. "As among the eighth graders," G. V. Gendel' observes in his study of school children in Syzran', "as size of income increases, its role as a hindrance decreases and the influence of academic performance [on the

determination of plans] grows."[25] In comparison with the eighth graders, more of the tenth-grade pupils receive high grades and aspire to higher education, a fact mainly explained by the selection which has occurred. Nonetheless, as Table 4 shows, tenth graders whose father has a higher education are about twice as likely to get high marks as their classmates whose father has not completed secondary education (i.e., ten years of schooling). Among both the high-achieving and the low-achieving pupils, the children's aspirations are positively associated with the father's educational level. Yet, the differences in aspiration within each of these two groups are modest compared with the differences at each level according to the student's performance. Thus, the higher aspirations of the culturally advantaged youth are largely derived from their ability to earn high grades.

COMPETITION FOR ADMISSION TO HIGHER EDUCATIONAL INSTITUTIONS

With a few exceptions discussed below, admission to vuzy is determined primarily according to results on competitive examina-

Table 4. Tenth Graders' Academic Performance and Educational Aspirations, as Related to Father's Education and Own Grades

	Syzran', 1968			
	Percent planning to enroll in a higher educational institution			
Father's education	High grades[a]	Low grades[a]	All	Percent with high grades[a]
Higher	96%	30%	83%	80%
	(92)	(23)	(115)	
Incomplete Higher or	95%	33%	81%	77%
Specialized Secondary	(88)	(27)	(115)	
Tenth Grade	91%	16%	58%	55%
	(77)	(62)	(139)	
7–9 Grades	80%	16%	43%	42%
	(101)	(141)	(242)	
5–6 Grades	76%	17%	41%	40%
	(46)	(70)	(116)	
4 Grades or Less	69%	8%	32%	40%
	(56)	(85)	(141)	
Not Indicated	(2)	(8)	(10)	
Total	86%	16%	53%	53%
	(462)	(416)	(878)	(878)

Source: Gendel', Problemy sotsial'noi podvizhnosti, p. 198, Table 15 (adapted).
[a]Grades are coded as in Table 2.

tions. Since 1972, secondary school grades have been deemed equally important.[26] The admission criteria naturally affect the social composition of the students. Although children from higher-status families make up a disproportionately large share of the applicants to vuzy, they increase their share in the entering class because they are more successful in passing the entrance examinations.[27] Data from the 1968 Leningrad study (presented in Table 5) show that the selection process for higher education following the tenth grade is much like that at the eighth grade level: the chances of being admitted to a vuz are a function both of parents' social status and of school performance. Thus, secondary school graduates with high grades and favorable family circumstances (high status) are most likely to attend higher educational institutions.[28]

Table 5. Percentage of Tenth-Grade Graduates Enrolled in Higher Education (All Divisions[a]) in the Fall Following Graduation, by Grade-Point Average and Parents' Social-Occupational Status

	Leningrad, 1968	
	Grade average	
Parents' status[b]	Under 3.5	3.5 and over
Professionals	40	73
Semi-professionals	34	61
Skilled Workers	16	44
Semiskilled and Unskilled Manual and Non-Manual Workers	7	21

Source: Vasil'eva, Sotsial'no-professional'nyi uroven', p. 42 (Table 17, adapted).
[a]Day, evening, and correspondence programs.
[b]Groups defined as in Table 3.

The results of the entrance competition in 1966 at Rostov State University, one of the better provincial schools in the Russian Republic, illustrate this selection process. Whereas children of workers and non-specialist white-collar workers made up 58 percent of the applicants, they comprised 47 percent of the entering class. Children of collective farmers constituted 15 percent of the applicants, but less than 3 percent of those admitted. In contrast, specialists' children increased their representation from 27 to 50 percent.[29] Altogether, children of non-manual origin made up 75 percent of the first-year class.[30]

Privileged youth's advantage in securing admission to higher educational institutions is not simply a consequence of their more affluent home environment and cultural advantages which enable them to achieve better secondary-school records and to excel in examinations. Since 1966–67, more and more schools have begun to offer elective courses suited to the students' interests, while increasing numbers of specialized schools offering intensive training in science, languages, or the arts have been established.[31] Although "tracking" had previously been proscribed, now it is sometimes practiced.[32] The increasing differentiation of study programs may give added advantages to intelligentsia children, since they are the ones most likely to be enrolled in the special classes.[33]

The relatively small number of special general-education schools are designed for children with aptitude for mathematics, physics, chemistry, foreign languages, and other disciplines corresponding to the particular school's specialization.

These children [in Leningrad] take an intensified program, and they are taught by the best teachers, not only secondary school teachers but higher school teachers as well. The graduates of these schools pass the competitive examinations, as a rule (98% to 99% pass), and they not only enter the higher schools but, more important, graduate from them with high marks. ... Even now the

alumni of the specialized schools make up one-third of all students in Leningrad State University's physics and mathematical engineering divisions.[34]

Because of the special training which such schools provide and the high representation of intelligentsia children in them, some have criticized them for "social elitism" contrary to the democratic principles of education in the USSR. "The selection of children for special schools is, more often than not, based not on their gifts, but on the ambition of some parents," writes Georgi Kulagin, the director of a machine-construction combine in Leningrad. "Even if we were to admit that the general program in the mass schools retards the development of the really gifted child, this circumstance is much less detrimental to society than instilling from childhood the idea that a chosen person is set apart."[35]

Parents also vie with one another in trying to get their children enrolled in a university or institute. As *Komsomol'skaia pravda* reported,

Strange transformations occur in August and at the beginning of September. Reliable and respected engineers and teachers, intelligent people who have been through the war and the period of reconstruction, suddenly lose their human dignity and become pitiable supplicants, blocking the doorways of rectors' offices and ministries, bombarding prominent friends with telephone calls and imploring almost on their knees: 'Get my daughter (or son) into an institute.'

"No stone is left unturned," the writer observes, "from the exploitation of the names and the reputation of forebears to gambling with what are the most sacred values for us all."[36]

More significant than "pull" or bribery is the ability of the privileged to use their income to provide special tutoring for their children or to keep them off the labor market while preparing for the next year's entrance exams. In 1969, the Rector of Moscow University, in discussing the advantages which some had in gaining admission, pointed out that many children make use of the services of private coaches. In that year, 85 percent of those admitted to the Faculty of Mechanics and Mathematics had received private instruction before taking the entrance examinations.[37] Another survey was conducted at one of the leading technical institutes in Moscow. "The results were shocking, though not unexpected," a teacher disclosed that same year. "About 90 percent of the [successful] applicants, it turned out, had resorted to tutors."[38] A more recent article in *Komsomol'skaia pravda* underscores the social implications of this common practice:

"The contest of tutors"—do you remember how at first this sounded like a joke? But only at first. Just listen to your acquaintances, sit in on the entrance examinations for the higher schools, where the parents of secondary school graduates nervously await the results—it is a surprising fact that people are no longer ashamed of having tutors, they are proud of them. They call them by their titles and, among circles of friends, by the posts they hold. The costlier the tutor, the more prestige he has. This means that our system of free education, equally available to everyone and based on competition in knowledge, has been invaded by the ruble.[39]

The intensive study programs and widespread use of tutors not only enhance intelligentsia children's chances of gaining entrance to a *vuz*, but work to the disadvantage of rural youth. Sometimes outright resentment and indignation is expressed at these inequities:

What should we do, the villagers? Young men and women who grow up here also dream about one or another institute and also deserve to receive a higher education. Where are they to find coaches? We have no professors or Ph.D. candidates in our villages. Here it is difficult just to find good teachers. Who will prepare our children for entrance to the institute?

Even without this [coaching], the village school is behind the city schools. Here the people often complain: the teacher is not as good, and the equipment is not the same, and the libraries do not compare at all with those in the city. The village children, especially those who live far away from the regional roads, are deprived of museums, theaters, lectures. Consequently their preparation is already worse. But in addition to all these other things, one must add "the competition of the purse. . . ."[40]

Soviet scholars may acknowledge the "bias" in favor of those from higher-status families under the present admission requirements. For instance, M. N. Rutkevich and F. R. Filippov take note of this fact, but find the requirements necessary for the selection of those who will be able to make the greatest contribution to social and economic development:

Socialist society is interested in selecting those individuals who will yield maximum benefits in the future as skilled specialists. Competitive examinations for higher educational institutions, generally speaking, enable us to choose those who are best prepared to master a given specialty. But it is well known that the degree of preparation of an applicant depends not only on his natural abilities, but also on the material and cultural level of the family in which he was raised, on the quality of teaching in the secondary school that he attended, and on many other factors that promote the early development of abilities and the acquisition of greater knowledge by the time of the examination. . . . In ignoring the conditions under which applicants are trained, and in making judgments based only on the applicants' knowledge, admissions committees in effect sanction inequality of opportunity.[41]

In spite of a good deal of contrary evidence, they argue that competitive selection for Soviet *vuzy* is a "special form of socialist competition" which has nothing in common with selection procedures in the West. "In capitalist countries, competition for admission to higher educational institutions does not exist in our sense of the word. Everything depends on the ability to pay for one's studies. . . . Competition in knowledge is replaced by the 'competition' of the purse."[42]

THE SOCIAL COMPOSITION OF STUDENTS IN *VUZY*

"It must be particularly emphasized," sociologist V. N. Shubkin stated in 1965, "that the increased competition for admission to higher educational institutions, combined with the rise in the number of secondary-school graduates, may lead to a diminution in the percentage of children of workers and peasants entering higher educational institutions."[43] A cursory glance at some official statistics would suggest that this apprehension was confirmed in the second half of the sixties. Unpublished aggregate data gathered by the Central Statistical Administration show an unmistakable trend toward lessened working-class and peasant representation among full-time students in the RSFSR. In 1963–64, "white-collar workers and their children" accounted for 44.4 percent of all the students, "workers and their children" made up 41.8 percent, and "collective farmers and their children" comprised 13.8 percent.[44] In each of the next six years, the non-manual group's share increased, so that by 1969–70, the social composition was as follows: "white-collar workers and their children," 52.6 percent; "workers and their children," 37.7 percent; and "collective farmers and their children," 9.7 percent.[45]

However, it is not clear that these figures can be taken at face value. Students who have worked for two or more years are supposed to be classified according to their acquired social status rather than their social origins. This procedure probably results in a net increase in the number placed in the "workers and their children" category. Some knowledgeable Soviet citizens believe that students are classified as "workers" if *either* their father *or* their mother is a worker, thereby also increasing the proportion of "workers' children" among the students. The same procedure may be followed with collective farmers' children. Changes in the

students' social composition during the sixties may therefore be an artifact of the method of classification (particularly since in the first half of the sixties a much larger share of the entering students had worked for two years before enrolling). It is also possible that the apparent increase in "white-collar workers and their children" reflects the growth of this group in the population in the course of the decade.[46]

Is access to higher education more egalitarian than it is in western countries? Peculiarities in various countries' educational systems, variations in their occupational distributions, and differences in the way social origins are determined all make it difficult to provide a simple and straightforward answer to this question on the basis of available information. Among the western countries themselves there appear to be differences in the degree of educational inequality. Judging simply by working-class children's representation in higher educational institutions, Frank Parkin infers that higher education is more accessible to working-class youth in Great Britain and Scandinavia than in other West European countries.[47] Raymond Poignant notes that the United States has lower social-occupational differentials in enrollment rates than the West European countries and suggests that the Soviet Union probably resembles the United States in this regard.[48] Similarly, Raymond Boudon hazards the judgment that the degree of inequality in opportunity for higher education in East European countries is closer to that of the United States or the Scandinavian countries than to that of the West European continental nations.[49] *If* the figures cited above reflect more or less accurately the social origins of students in Russia, it would indeed appear that access to higher education has been considerably more egalitarian than in the West European countries and thus more similar to the United States.[50]

Notwithstanding manifest differences between the United States and the Soviet Union, there are certain structural similarities which account, in some measure, for the greater egalitarianism in access to higher education. Owing in part to the absence of "aristocratic survivals," the United States and the Soviet Union appear to have less well-defined "status groups" than the more traditional European societies. Both societies are characterized by a widespread belief in opportunities for achievement through the educational system and by high levels of aspiration. These beliefs and the perception of an "open class structure" are no doubt reinforced by high rates of upward mobility into the elite occupational groups, which probably have exceeded those of the West European countries.[51] Furthermore, the educational systems differ from those of West Europe in their degree of differentiation, content, and extent of coverage. Although there may be "tracking" within schools, the Soviet and American educational systems are still less differentiated than their West European counterparts.[52] In American and Soviet schools decidedly less attention is devoted to the study of the Classics, which is associated with traditional European upper-class culture and has been an important basis for differentiation among study programs in the European systems.[53] Finally, a higher percentage of the youth cohort finishes secondary education, a necessary condition for proceeding to the higher level.[54] These two systems therefore place fewer obstacles in the path of lower-class children's completing secondary education, and so a greater proportion of low-status children acquire the certification and maintain the level of motivation and aspiration required for higher education.

In part because the higher educational system in the United States and the USSR has been less closely linked with established social elites, it has been expanded to a greater extent, has been more responsive to changing economic needs and opportunities, and has trained a larger share of the students in fields other than the traditional learned professions.[55] The fact that American colleges and universities take in a much greater share of the youth cohort than either their Soviet or their European counterparts increases the relative chances for admission of American children from lower-status families.[56] (Working-class children, however, are most strongly represented in the two-year community colleges which represent the lower "track" of the American system.)[57] In the Soviet Union, social differences giving rise to inequality in access to higher education are lessened by the provision of tuition-free education, state-subsidized food and housing, and stipends for three-quarters of the full-time students.[58] These measures may be more effective in facilitating lower-class children's access to the higher schools than maintenance grants in such countries as Great Britain, where proportionately more lower-class children leave the "college track" at an early age.

While providing rough indices of various social groups' participation in higher education, the aggregate data presented above obscure differences in social composition according to field of study, type of academic institution, and geographic location. As in other countries, the Soviet system of higher education is hierarchically differentiated in terms of "quality," prestige, and the social origins of the student bodies.[59] Typically, the higher the prestige of an occupation, the higher the prestige of a *vuz* providing training for that specialty, and the higher the representation of non-manual (especially intelligentsia) offspring in its student body.[60] The nature of the town in which the *vuz* is located, the school's "quality," and its general "profile" (i.e., whether it is more "applied" and technical or more strictly "academic") all affect a specific institution's relative standing. "As a rule," Moscow sociologist F. R. Filippov notes, "capital city *vuzy, vuzy* which are close to major academic and scientific centers, and so on, enjoy the greatest prestige."[61] He continues,

Fundamentally, these differences [in the attractiveness of higher educational institutions] reside in the actual objectiv~ variations in the level of preparation of specialists, which depends on the academic and material basis of the *vuz,* the composition of the teaching staff, the specific social and cultural environs, etc. This is one of the specific manifestations of the actual social differences inherent in a socialist society. At the present stage of development of Soviet society, a formally identical level of higher education which was obtained in any of the country's *vuzy* presupposes and by no means excludes actual differences in the quality of the training of specialists, and for that reason, the 'worth' [*tsena*] of a diploma received in different *vuzy* is not the same.[62]

Some appreciation of the differences between capital city and provincial town *vuzy* may be gained from a comparison of the social composition of day-students in Moscow, capital of the Soviet Union and the Russian Republic, and Kostroma, a medium-size industrial town to the north-east of Moscow. E. S. Samoilova, who carried out a survey of every fifth applicant to five Moscow *vuzy* and three *vuzy* in Kostroma in 1968, found sharp differences between the two towns in the social characteristics of applicants and entering students.[63] Whereas only 24 percent of the parents of the first-year Moscow students performed physical labor, 40 percent of the Kostroma parents did. Conversely, 57 percent of the Moscow students' parents, but only 29 percent of the Kostroma students' parents were specialists.[64] Of all students enrolled in *vuzy* in Moscow in 1969–70, 92 percent were of urban origin, and only 8 percent came from the countryside. In Kostroma, the corresponding figures were 54 and 46 percent.[65] To some degree, these disparities stem from differences in the composition of the work force in the two towns and the surrounding areas.

Among the institutions in each town, as Table 6 demonstrates, there were clear variations in the social composition of the student body. These are suggestive of the stratification of Soviet higher education and of the different patterns of recruitment of various types of *vuzy.* In 1968, for instance,

"collective farmers and their children" made up 44 percent of the students in agricultural institutes in the USSR, 14 percent of those in pedagogical institutes in the Russian Republic, and just 9 percent of Russia's medical students. Conversely, "white-collar workers and their children" constituted a fifth of the students in the low-status agricultural institutes, nearly half of the students in the pedagogical institutes, and three-fifths of those in the medical institutes.[66]

PROBLEMS AND PROSPECTS

Given the ideological insistence upon egalitarianism and the superiority of socialism over capitalism, the pattern of inequality in access to higher education continues to be a politically sensitive subject in the USSR. Regarding future trends and government policy, there have been divergent points of view. M. N. Rutkevich stated in 1967, "The basic objective tendency consists in the social composition of those accepted by *vuzy* steadily approaching the population's social composition, since the reduction in differences in material and cultural conditions leads to an equalization of the conditions for the preparation of the young recruits entering *vuzy.*"[67] This "objective tendency" may be strengthened by policies for the improvement of low-quality schools, especially in rural areas, and the achievement of universal secondary education in the foreseeable future. As a result of the latter, not only will a greater share of the youth cohort have formal access to higher education, but children of successive generations will be less likely to suffer disadvantages because of their parents' low educational achievement.

Others have seen the prospects in a less sanguine fashion. The advantages held by privileged youth have been shown at all stages, and as several Soviet scholars have stressed, their advantages are more pronounced when the competition for admission to *vuzy* is more intense. As the number

Table 6. Social Composition of Students in Higher Educational Institutions in Moscow and Kostroma, Russian Republic, 1968–69

	Percentage in each social group		
	White-collar state employees	State employed workers[b]	Collective-farm peasants
Distribution of Employed Population, 1970 (1)			
Russian Republic (RSFSR)	28	62	10
Moscow Province	33	66	1
Kostroma Province	25	64	11
Distribution of All Day Students Enrolled in Higher Educational Institutions, 1968–69 (2)			
RSFSR[a]	51	38	11
Moscow City[a]	68	28	4
Kostroma Town[a]	40	41	19
Distribution of Entering Class in Selected Institutions, Day Division, 1968–69 (3)			
Moscow			
State University[a]	73	23	3
Petrochemical and Gas Industry Institute	69	30	1
Engineering and Construction Institute	60	33	6
Machine-Tool Instrument Institute	58	41	1
Chemical Technology Institute	58	41	1
Institute of Engineers of Agricultural Production	43	40	17
Kostroma			
Technological Institute	51	43	6
Pedagogical Institute	49	42	9
Agricultural Institute	19	36	45

Sources: (1) USSR, Tsentral'noe Statisticheskoe Upravlenie, *Itogi Vsesoiuznoi perepisi naseleniia 1970,* 5 (Moscow: Statistika, 1973): 34–35. (2) Data gathered by the Central Statistical Administration on all day students enrolled in higher educational institutions in these areas, cited in E.S. Samoilova, *Sotsial'nye aspekty formirovaniia kontingentov sovetskikh studentov v period stroitel'stva kommunizma (1961–1971 g.),* unpublished dissertation for the degree of Candidate of Sciences (Moscow, 1973), pp. 119 (Table 22), 123 (Table 24), 131 (Table 28). (3) These data, with the exception of those for Moscow State University, are derived from a 20 percent random sample of all applicants to these institutions in 1968 and reflect *social origins.* Shown here is the distribution of accepted applicants. Ibid., pp. 236 and 243. Data for first-year students at Moscow University are taken from materials in the university's archives and from records of the Moscow City Statistical Division, as reported ibid., p. 129 (Table 27).
[a]Students who had been working for two or more years prior to entrance were classified according to their *acquired* social status. Otherwise, social origin (presumably the social status of the head of the household, usually the father) was used.
[b]Industrial and agricultural workers in state enterprises.

of young people receiving a secondary education continues to grow, the chances of disadvantaged youth may worsen. In view of the persuasive evidence of the sociological studies, many leading policy makers and sociologists have become convinced that the government should take positive measures to "regulate" the social composition of the student body.[68]

In 1969, the government adopted measures to establish preparatory divisions (reminiscent of the "workers' faculties" of an earlier period) at higher educational institutions. Working youth, collective farm youth, and demobilized servicemen are eligible for admission. The heads of enterprises in which the young people have worked for at least a year decide, on the recommendations of Party, Komsomol, and union organizations, who should be sent to these programs. "Auditors" who successfully complete a year's study are then enrolled in the regular first-year class. In addition, preference in admission to certain fields linked with agriculture or the development of the countryside is given to rural youth. [69] Between 1969–70 and 1973–74, the number entering *vuzy* directly from the preparatory programs increased fourfold to 60,000, and it is expected that by 1975, one out of five new *vuz* students will have passed through the programs. [70]

It is still difficult to ascertain to what degree these remedial measures have improved the chances of disadvantaged youth. Iu. N. Kozyrev, a sociologist at the Institute of Sociological Research in Moscow, maintains that their position has substantially improved, in part because of an actual decline in competition:

The system of advantages in the entrance competition [*konkursnykh l'got*] for these groups of applicants [viz., workers and peasants], the work of the preparatory divisions, acting in the same direction with the decrease in competition, has fundamentally altered the social composition of the student body today as compared with that which occurred six or seven years ago: the share of workers and workers' children in the composition of the studentry is steadily growing. In the *vuzy* in the city of Gorkii in 1966, for instance, workers and peasants accounted altogether for about 40 percent of the entering class. In 1970 these groups' share exceeded 60 percent. [71]

Recent data on the social composition of the entering class at Leningrad State University and of all day-students enrolled in *vuzy* in Sverdlovsk Province show an increase in the representation of "workers and their children" in the early seventies. [72]

According to other reports, the preparatory faculties are not doing effectively what they were designed to do—help the disadvantaged. Because of insufficient publicity, many workers are not aware of the opportunities open to them, and factory managers are reluctant to release able workers. In some higher schools, only one-half of the graduates of the "workers' faculties" get as far as the second or third year, and in the Russian Republic as a whole, just over a third of the first class which graduated from these programs in 1970 reached the fifth year in the regular program. [73] On the average, one-third of the "production workers" have had a single year's work experience. Most of them are secondary-school graduates who have already tried to pass the entrance exams, and failed.

For them, the most important thing is the opportunity to get into a higher school without taking the competitive examination (to be accepted as a student, it's enough to receive a three [average grade] on examinations taken following studies in a workers' faculty). So, instead of feeding mature and independent young people to the higher schools, as was intended, the workers' faculties send them youths who have served out a year in production. [74]

Since admission to the programs is determined by "social position," rather than origins, there is nothing to prevent privileged youth's entering *vuzy* through the back door, so to speak. Even worse, a sizeable number gain admission with forged documents testifying to their exemplary (but fictitious) work career. In 1975 alone, 17 percent of the students whose documents were checked in the Armenian Republic had presented fake work-records and recommendations. [75] Thus, writes a correspondent for *Komsomol'skaia pravda*, "with the help of parental connections and forged documents, young idlers take the places in the preparatory divisions and workers' faculties which rightfully belong to young workers and collective farmers." [76]

The problem of inequality of access to higher education obviously continues to be a matter of much concern in the Soviet Union. The evidence which we have reviewed demonstrates that the process of social selection performed by the educational system in the USSR is in many ways similar to that observed in other industrial countries and that a child's social status determines, to a considerable extent, his chances to attend a *vuz* and thereby enter the intelligentsia. Yet, consideration of the social composition of students in *vuzy* leads to the conclusion that the selection process does not work as rigorously to limit lower-class children's access to higher education as it has in West European countries. In the Soviet Union, secondary and higher education have been rapidly expanded. Whereas lower-status offspring are much less likely to reach higher education than children of higher-status families, they make up a very substantial part of those enrolled in *vuzy* because of their social groups' preponderance in the population at large.

These findings are symptomatic of the contradictory forces which will affect access to education in coming years. While the continuing expansion of secondary education will serve to equalize access to higher institutions by increasing the number of potential entrants, differentiation and specialization of study programs at the secondary level may increase the advantages of those from better-educated, higher-status families whose relative weight in the population has been growing rapidly. Since the mid-sixties, the greater emphasis upon academic performance, the increased competition for admission, and the widespread use of tutors have worked to the disadvantage of workers' and collective farmers' children. Although preparatory divisions have been established to offset these trends, it remains to be seen to what extent they will accomplish this objective.

ACKNOWLEDGEMENTS

This article is a revised version of a paper presented at the 70th Annual Meeting of the American Sociological Association in August, 1975. My research was supported by a U. S. Government Fulbright-Hays Fellowship and an International Research and Exchange Board Fellowship while I was in the Soviet Union on the officially sponsored exchange program, February to August, 1974. I further wish to express my gratitude to the Soviet scholars and librarians who assisted me in my work, to Michael Swafford of Vanderbilt University who was in the USSR at the same time, to the staff of the Russian Research Center at Harvard University, and to Christopher Jencks of Harvard University for his critical comments on an earlier draft of this article.

NOTES

1. On early Soviet policy, see Nicholas Hans and Sergius Hessen, *Educational Policy in Soviet Russia* (London: P.S. King and Son, 1930); Sheila Fitzpatrick, *The Commissariat of Enlightenment: Soviet Organization of Education and the Arts Under Lunacharsky, October 1917–1919* (Cambridge: Cambridge University Press, 1970); Frederic Lilge, "Lenin and the Politics of Education," *Slavic Review* 27 (June 1968): 230–57; and James C. McClelland, "Bolshevik Approaches to Higher Education, 1917–1921," *Slavic Review* 30 (December 1971): 818–31.

2. One of the best discussions of Bolshevik policy designed to bring working-class and peasant youth into the higher schools is found in Robert A. Feldmesser, *Aspects of Social Mobility in the Soviet Union*, Ph.D. dissertation, Harvard University, 1955. Feldmesser estimates that from 1928 to the end of the first Five-Year Plan (1932), the proportion of former workers among all specialists with a higher education rose from 7.8 percent to 22.1 percent, and of former peasants from 17.8 percent to 20.9 percent. Correspondingly, the share of former non-manual workers fell from 74.4 percent to 57.1 percent. He notes that in the course of the thirties, as a result of changes in educational policy "stressing lengthy preparation and academic performance, the workers and peasants never again came even as close to equality of opportunity with employees as they did at this time" (p. 167). See also David Lane, "The Impact of Revolution: The Case of Selection of Students for Higher Education in Soviet Russia, 1917–1928," *Sociology* 7 (May 1973): 241–52, and Nicholas DeWitt, *Education and Professional Employment in the USSR* (Washington, D.C.: United States Government Printing Office, 1961), pp. 246–48, 655.

3. DeWitt, *op. cit.*, and Alex Inkeles, "Social Stratification and Mobility in the Soviet Union," in his *Social Change in Soviet Russia* (Cambridge,

Mass.: Harvard University Press, 1968), pp. 162–67.

4. Resolution of the Central Committee of the VKP(b), "O pedologicheskikh izvrashcheniiakh v sisteme Narkomprosov" [On pedological distortions in the system of the People's Commissariats of Education], in A.A. Abakumov, N.P. Kuzin, F.I. Puzyrev, and L.F. Litvinov, comps., *Narodnoe obrazovanie v SSSR: Obshcheobrazovatel'naia shkola, Sbornik dokumentov 1917–1973* [Public education in the USSR: The general-education school, a collection of documents, 1917–1973] (Moscow: Pedagogika, 1974), pp. 172–75. On the circumstances surrounding the resolution, see Raymond A. Bauer, *The New Man in Soviet Psychology* (Cambridge, Mass.: Harvard University Press, 1952), pp. 116–27.

5. However, in the early fifties, American social scientists participating in the Harvard Project on the Soviet Social System carried out extensive research on Soviet citizens who had become "displaced persons" as a result of the Second World War. Findings on the pre-war situation with respect to educational opportunity and social mobility are reported in Alex Inkeles and Raymond A. Bauer, *The Soviet Citizen: Daily Life in a Totalitarian Society* (Cambridge, Mass.: Harvard University Press, 1959).

6. N.S. Khrushchev, memorandum, "On Strengthening the Ties Between School and Life and on Further Developing the System of Public Education in the Country," *Pravda*, Sept. 21, 1958, trans. in *The Current Digest of the Soviet Press* (CDSP) 10, 38: 3–7. Moscow was evidently not atypical in this respect. M.N. Rutkevich and F.R. Filippov note that "in the mid-1950s in a number of higher schools (particularly in regional capitals)" there was "an uncontrolled increase in the proportion of children of intelligentsia families among the student body." M.N. Rutkevich and F.R. Filippov, "Social Sources of Recruitment of the Intelligentsia," in Murray Yanowitch and Wesley A. Fisher, eds., *Social Stratification and Mobility in the Soviet Union* (White Plains, N.Y.: International Arts and Sciences Press, 1973), p. 255.

7. N.S. Khrushchev, speech to the Thirteenth Komsomol Congress, "Gain Active and Conscious Builders of Communist Society," *Pravda*, April 19, 1958, pp. 1–3, condensed in *CDSP* 10, 17: 17.

8. For further details on the reforms, see DeWitt, *Education and Professional Employment in the USSR*, and Nigel Grant, *Soviet Education* (Baltimore: Penguin Books, 1964).

9. M.N. Rutkevich, "Why a Student Does Not Arrive at the 'Finish'," *Vestnik vysshei shkoly* 7 (1965), trans. in *Soviet Education* 8 (Jan. 1966): 28–37. See also M.N. Rutkevich, ed., *The Career Plans of Youth*, ed. and trans. Murray Yanowitch (White Plains, N.Y.: International Arts and Sciences Press, 1969), pp. 1–27, and on the politics of implementing the reforms, see Joel J. Schwartz and William R. Keech, "Group Influence and the Policy Process in the USSR," *American Political Science Review* 62 (Sept. 1968): 840–51.

10. Rectors of higher educational institutions were instructed to select students from two pools of applicants—those who had been working and those who were applying directly from secondary school—in proportion to the number in each. Although results on competitive entrance examinations provide the main criteria for the selection, the fact that applicants are divided into two groups improves the chances of the "production candidates," since the latter tend to get lower average grades on the exams. V.P. Yelyutin, "Higher Educational Institutions Await Good Entering Class," *Pravda*, March 20, 1965, p. 6, trans. in *CDSP* 17, 10: 9–10.

11. USSR, Tsentral'noe Statisticheskoe Upravlenie, *Narodnoe obrazovanie, nauka i kul'tura v SSSR* [Public education, science and culture in the USSR] (Moscow: Statistika, 1971), p. 152.

12. On the revival and development of sociology, see George Fisher, *Science and Ideology in Soviet Society* (New York: Atherton Press, 1967); Alex Simirenko, ed., *Soviet Sociology: Historical Antecedents and Current Appraisals* (London: Routledge and Kegan Paul, 1967); Elizabeth Ann Weinberg, *The Development of Sociology in the Soviet Union* (Boston: Routledge and Keagan Paul, 1974); and Zev Katz, "Sociology in the Soviet Union," *Problems of Communism* 20 (May-June 1971): 22–40.

13. See Murray Yanowitch and Norton T. Dodge, "Social Class and Education: Soviet Findings and Reactions," *Comparative Education Review* 12 (Oct. 1968): 248–67; Murray Yanowitch and Norton T. Dodge, "The Social Evaluation of Occupations in the Soviet Union," *Slavic Review* 28 (Dec. 1969): 619–43; Janina Markiewicz-Lagneau, *Éducation, égalité et socialisme: théorie et practique de la différenciation sociale en pays socialistes* (Paris: Anthropos, 1969); David Lane, *The End of Inequality? Stratification Under State Socialism* (Baltimore: Penguin Books, 1971); Zev Katz, *Patterns of Social Stratification in the USSR* (Cambridge, Mass.: Center for International Studies, MIT, 1972); Zev Katz, *Patterns of Social Mobility in the USSR* (Cambridge, Mass.: Center for International Studies, MIT, 1972); Mervin Matthews, *Class and Society in Soviet Russia* (New York: Walker, 1972); and Seymour Martin Lipset and Richard B. Dobson, "Social Stratification and Sociology in the Soviet Union," *Survey* 19 (Summer 1973); 114–85. An excellent collection of recent Soviet research is found in Yanowitch and Fisher, eds., *Social Stratification and Mobility in the Soviet Union*.

14. According to the regression equation, an increase of one year in the father's educational level is associated with a rise of .47 years in the respondent's educational level, while an additional year of schooling for the mother raises the respondent's attainment by .58 years. This survey of more than two thousand individuals in the Tatar Republic was carried out in the late sixties. Iu.V. Arutiunian, *Sotsial'naia struktura sel'skogo naseleniia SSSR* [The social structure of the rural population of the USSR] (Moscow: Mysl', 1971), pp. 322, 355–57.

15. N.A. Aitov, "Obrazovanie i sotsial'nye peremeshcheniia" [Education and social interchanges], in *Stroitel'stvo kommunizma i izmeneniia sotsial'noi struktury sovetskogo obshchestva (Materialy ko Vtoroi Vsesoiuznoi kon-*

ferentsii po probleme "Izmenenie sotsial'noi struktury sovetskogo obshchestva") [The building of communism and changes in the social structure of Soviet society (Materials for the Second All-Union Conference on the Problem "Change of the Social Structure of Soviet Society")] 3: *Sotsial'naia struktura i problema obrazovaniia* [Social structure and the problem of education] (Moscow: Znanie, 1971), p. 51. O. I. Shkaratan and V. O. Rukavishnikov, "The Impact of the STR on Social Differentiation and Integration in the Soviet City," presented at the VIII World Congress of Sociology, Toronto, 1974, p. 12.

16. Aitov, *op. cit.*, p. 49.

17. Ibid., pp. 51–52. A similar point about the importance of education in the determination of social status is, of course, often made by western sociologists. The latter are more inclined to see it as a consequence of the heightened "universalism" of industrial societies in general, rather than as a distinctive feature of socialist societies in particular. Compare, e.g., Peter M. Blau and Otis Dudley Duncan, *The American Occupational Structure* (New York: John Wiley & Sons, 1967), p. 430.

18. F.R. Filippov, "K voprosu o sotsial'noi roli sovetskoi shkoly" [With respect to the social role of the Soviet school], in *Sotsiologicheskie problemy narodnogo obrazovaniia* [Sociological problems of public education], Uchenye zapiski Sverdlovskogo gosudarstvennogo pedagogicheskogo instituta, 56 (Sverdlovsk, 1967), p. 20.

19. The fact that most of the published Soviet data is presented as percentages in cross-tabulations of two (or sometimes three) variables obviously makes multivariate analysis difficult, if not impossible. In addition, some variables which one would wish to have for purposes of comparison with western research—especially, measures of intelligence—are not included in *any* of the studies. Among the variables affecting educational aspirations and attainment, sex, national identity, and other family characteristics—e.g., absence of one of the parents—are also important, though beyond the scope of this paper. On sex differences, see Richard B. Dobson, "The Education of Russian Women: Educational Policies and Occupational Achievement," in Dorothy Atkinson, Alexander Dallin, and Gail Lapidus, eds., *Women in Russia* (Stanford: Stanford University Press, forthcoming).

20. L. G. Zemtsov, *Sotsial'nye problemy obshcheobrazovatel'noi shkoly na sovremennom etape* [Social problems of the general-education school at the present stage], unpublished dissertation for the degree of Candidate of Sciences (Ufa, 1971), p. 106, Table 11.

21. Ibid., p. 107, Table 12.

22. Ibid., p. 108, Table 13.

23. V.G. Gendel', *Problemy sotsial'noi podvizhnosti molodezhi pri sotsializme* [Problems of youth's social mobility under socialism], unpublished dissertation for the degree of Candidate of Sciences (Leningrad, 1971), p. 175, Table 2-z. The parents' aspirations for their children closely paralleled the pupils' plans. Fifty-two percent of the specialist parents, 28 percent of the white-collar workers, and 18 percent of the workers favored their children's entering the ninth grade in the fall

with the aim of pursuing a higher education after graduation (p. 168, Table 6-b).

24. E. K. Vasil'eva, *Sotsial'no-professional'nyi uroven' gorodskoi molodezhi* [The social-occupational level of urban youth] (Leningrad: Leningrad State University Press, 1973), p. 42. (A translation of this volume is scheduled for publication in 1976 by the International Arts & Sciences Press, White Plains, N.Y.)

25. Gendel', *Problemy*, p. 205. Gendel' arrives at this conclusion after testing the strength of association between "grades" and "plans" with the Tchuprov coefficient, while controlling for family per capita monthly income. With an increase in income, the strength of association increases: 30 roubles or less, T = .36; 31–50 r., T = .52; 51–70 r., T = .53; more than 70 roubles, T = .74. At the tenth-grade level, 76 percent of the pupils from specialists' families, 50 percent of the white-collar workers' offspring, and 37 percent of the working-class children plan to attend *vuz* immediately after graduation from secondary school (Table 14-e, p. 220).

26. "School Grades To Figure in Admissions: New Rules for Admission to Higher Educational Institutions," *Pravda*, March 15, 1972, p. 6, cond. in *CDSP* 24, 11: 29.

27. For instance, whereas children from specialists' families made up 50 percent of the applicants to the prestigious Physics Faculty at Novosibirsk State University in 1968, they comprised 55 percent of those who passed the entrance examinations and 60 percent of those getting high grades (18 to 20 points). A high success rate was particularly marked among those from families the head of which had a higher education. This group constituted 28 percent of the applicants, but 35 percent of those passing the physics examination and 46 percent of those getting top grades. L.F. Liss, *Sotsial'nye faktory, vliiaiushchie na protsess vybora professii (Opyt konkretno-sotsiologicheskikh issledovanii)* [Social factors affecting the process of selection of an occupation: results of concrete-sociological studies], unpublished dissertation for the degree of Candidate of Sciences (Novosibirsk, 1969), p. 263, Table 32. The same pattern is seen at Moscow State University. In 1969, the proportion of applicants receiving "good" and "excellent" grades (4 and 5 points) on the written examination in mathematics for the Natural Science Faculties (day division) was 18 percent for those of non-manual origin, 10 percent for workers' children, and 8 percent for children of collective-farm peasants. At the other extreme, the percentage failing the examination was, respectively, 46, 60, and 70 percent. E.S. Samoilova, *Sotsial'nye aspekty formirovaniia kontingentov sovetskikh studentov v period stroitel'stva kommunizma (1961–1971 g.)* [Social aspects of the formation of contingents of Soviet students in the period of the building of communism, 1961–1971], unpublished dissertation for the degree of Candidate of Sciences (Moscow, 1973), p. 157.

28. Vasil'eva, *Sotsial'no-professional'noi uroven'*, p. 43. Vasil'eva found that tenth-grade graduates who went to work right after graduation or entered vocational schools had quite the opposite charac-

teristics—unfavorable family circumstances (low status) and low grades. Among those entering technicums, graduates with relatively low grades coming from the middle social strata (i.e., families of specialists with specialized secondary education and of skilled workers) predominated.

29. These are the findings of a survey conducted by sociologists at Rostov State University in 1966, as reported in B. Rubin and Iu. Kolesnikov, *Student glazami sotsiologa (Sotsiologicheskie problemy vosproizvodstva rabochei sily vysshei kvalifikatsii)* [The student through the eyes of the sociologist: sociological problems of the reproduction of the high-skill work force] (Rostov-on-the-Don: Rostov University Press, 1968), p. 70.

30. A.V. Isaiko, "Nekotorye sotsial'nye problemy vysshego zaochnego i vechernego obrazovaniia" [Some social problems of higher correspondence and evening education], in Iu. Leonavichius, ed., *Effektivnost' podgotovki spetsialistov: Materialy mezhrespublikanskogo simpoziuma, Kaunas 28–31 ianvaria 1969* [The effectiveness of undergraduate training: Materials from an inter-republic symposium held in Kaunas, Jan. 28–31, 1969] (Kaunas: Kaunas Polytechnical Institute Press, 1969), p. 224. Moscow sociologist Iu.N. Kozyrev observes that "the number of white-collar personnel and their children among those enrolled in *vuzy* is greater when the competition is more intense, and vice versa. In 1966 when there was a "dual" graduation from the tenth and eleventh grades of the general-education school, the ratio of applicants to those accepted was the highest it has ever been in the history of our higher school. Correspondingly, the representation of white-collar workers and their children among those enrolled was the highest." Iu.N. Kozyrev, "Formirovanie studenchestva v usloviiakh sotsializma" [Formation of the student body under conditions of socialism], in *Vsesoiuznaia nauchnaia konferentsiia "Lenin i molodezh'," posviashchennaia 50-letiu prisvoeniia komsomoly imeni V.I. Lenina: Tezisy dokladov i soobshchenii* [All-Union scholarly conference "Lenin and Youth," dedicated to the 50th anniversary of the conferring of the name of V.I. Lenin on the Komsomol: Paper abstracts and communications], 1: *Sotsial'naia struktura razvitogo sotsialisticheskogo obshchestva i molodezh'* [The social structure of developed socialist society and youth], ed. N.M. Blinov and G.A. Slesarev (Moscow: Institute of Sociological Research of the Academy of Sciences of the USSR, 1974), pp. 42–43.

31. Matthews, *Class and Society*, pp. 270–73.

32. One journalist describes the "tracking" system which has been adopted at School No. 214 in Leningrad: "True, the words 'specialized' and 'intensified study' are missing on the school's signboard . . . [but] this school is not so ordinary. It turned out that out of two graduating classes totaling 76 students, 72 entered higher schools, while only 30 members of [the] two other graduating classes entered higher schools. It also turned out, that the first two classes were specialized! . . . After soberly evaluating its possibilities, the school had adopted a policy of selecting for special ninth-

grade classes pupils who had done especially well in mathematics and physics." I. Kossakovsky, "There Is Such a School," *Izvestia*, March 23, 1972, p. 5, cond. in *CDSP* 24, 12: 17.

33. Sociologists studied the social origins of students in School No. 114 in Ufa, which offers in-depth study programs in literature and mathematics in the upper grades. Whereas workers' children predominated in the standard program, they were slightly outnumbered by white-collar workers' and specialists' children in the intensive literature program. In the in-depth mathematics program, specialists' children alone made up nearly three-fourths of the pupils. In a special foreign-language school in the same town, three-quarters of the pupils came from specialists' families. Zemtsov, *Sotsial'nye problemy*, p. 64.

34. Kossakovsky, "There Is Such a School," p. 17.

35. G. Kulagin, "Problems and Judgements: The School of Labor," *Pravda*, June 19, 1971, p. 3, cond. in *CDSP* 23, 24: 20. However, sociologist M.N. Rutkevich contends that special schools and study programs are essential for improving the academic preparation of *vuz* applicants. M.N. Rutkevich, "Taking the Best as Our Model: Problems of the Five-Year Plan," *Izvestia*, March 16, 1971, p. 3, abstracted in *CDSP* 23, 11: 13.

36. *Komsomol'skaia pravda*, Sept. 19, 1970, cited in Susan Jacoby, *Inside Soviet Schools* (New York: Hill and Wang, 1974), p. 141.

37. Cited in S.S. Voronitsyn, "Class Distinction in Soviet Higher Education," *Bulletin of the Institute for the Study of the USSR* [Munich] 17 (Nov. 1970): 42–43.

38. B. Eppel', "O fakul'tativakh, repitatorakh i abiturientakh" [On electives, tutors, and applicants], *Uchitel'skaia gazeta*, May 13, 1969, p. 3.

39. Z. Vasiltsova, "Tutor of Success?" *Komsomol'skaia pravda*, Jan. 17, 1975, p. 2, cond. in *CDSP* 27, 4: 5.

40. *Literaturnaia gazeta*, March 8, 1972, cited in Jacoby, *Inside Soviet Schools*, p. 140.

41. Rutkevich and Filippov, "Social Sources," pp. 256–57. These Soviet scholars stop short of drawing a more general inference—that there may be a conflict of interests between social groups over the norms governing access to higher education, because different admissions policies benefit some strata at the expense of others. This is recognized, however, by the Polish sociologist Wlodzimierz Wesolowski: "The culturally differentiated conditions of individual homes account for differences in the initial levels of children of different social strata. Hence, workers and peasants accept the preferential system of access to schools, a system in which supplementary points are awarded to their children to compensate for their social milieu. This system acts against the chances of admission of the children of the intelligentsia. This is why the culturally privileged prefer a system of selection based exclusively on the results of examinations testing pure ability. The latter system tends naturally to reduce the chances of workers and peasants." W. Wesolowski, "The Notion of Strata and Class in a Socialist Society," in André Béteille, ed., *Social Inequality* (Baltimore: Penguin Books,

1969), p. 143. See also in this volume, Randall Collins, "Functional and Conflict Theories of Educational Stratification."

42. Rutkevich and Filippov, "Social Sources," p. 257.

43. V.N. Shubkin, "Youth Starts Out in Life," *Voprosy filosofii* 5 (1961), trans. in Stephen P. Dunn, ed., *Sociology in the USSR* (White Plains, N.Y.: International Arts and Sciences Press, 1969), p. 26.

44. E.S. Samoilova, *Sotsial'nye aspekty*, p. 119, Table 22.

45. Ibid.

46. In 1960–61, "white-collar workers and their children" accounted for 49.8 percent of all day students in the Russian Republic, "workers and their children" constituted 37.2 percent, and "collective farmers and their children" made up 13 percent (ibid.). In 1959, the total population of the Russian Republic was distributed as follows among the social groups: white-collar workers (state employees) 20.2 percent, state workers (industrial and agricultural) 55.4 percent, and collective-farm peasants 24.2 percent. In 1970, the corresponding figures for the total population were 24.3, 61.3, and 14.3 percent. USSR, Tsentral'noe Statisticheskoe Upravlenie, *Itogi Vsesoiuznoi perepisi naseleniia 1970 goda* [Results of the All-Union census of the population in 1970], 5 (Moscow: Statistika, 1973): 9.

47. Frank Parkin, *Class Inequality and Political Order: Social Stratification in Capitalist and Communist Societies* (New York: Praeger, 1971), pp. 109–11.

48. Raymond Poignant, *Education and Development in Western Europe, the United States, and the U.S.S.R.: A Comparative Study* (New York: Teachers College Press, 1969), pp. 170–73.

49. Raymond Boudon, *Education, Opportunity, and Social Inequality: Changing Prospects in Western Society* (New York: John Wiley & Sons, 1974), pp. 43–48.

50. It should be emphasized, however, that the situation in Western Europe appears to be changing rapidly. Recent data indicate that many of the West European countries have become considerably more egalitarian with respect to access to higher education in the past decade. See, for instance, Georg Busch, "Inequality of Educational Opportunity by Social Origin in Higher Education," in *Education, Inequality and Life Chances* 1 (Paris: O.E.C.D., 1975): 159–81.

51. Comparative analyses of social mobility suggest that both the United States and the USSR have had exceptionally high rates of movement from the working class into "elite" occupational strata. Using the only available data for the USSR (data on displaced persons collected by American sociologists as part of the Harvard Project on the Soviet Social System), S.M. Miller concluded that the Soviet Union had the highest rates of mobility from the working class into the nonmanual strata and from the manual strata into the "elite" occupations. The United States had a high rate of mobility from the manual strata into nonmanual occupations, but not one that was distinctively

higher than that of France or the USSR. On the other hand, the American mobility rate from the manual groups into the elite strata was higher than in all nations except the Soviet Union. S.M. Miller, "Comparative Social Mobility: A Trend Report," *Current Sociology* 9, 1 (1960): 58. Using more recent and reliable data for the United States, Peter Blau and Otis Duncan provide further substantiation for the thesis that there is a higher rate of movement from the working class into elite strata in the USA than in seven West European countries and Japan. "It is the underprivileged class of manual sons," they conclude, "that has exceptional chances for mobility into the elite in this country.... The high level of popular education in the United States, perhaps reinforced by the lesser emphasis on formal distinctions of social status, has provided the disadvantaged lower strata with outstanding opportunities for long-distance upward mobility." Blau and Duncan, *The American Occupational Structure*, p. 435. These American data are not taken into account by Frank Parkin, who argues that working-class youth in socialist societies are more likely to have high educational and occupational aspirations and to achieve upward mobility into the elite strata than their counterparts in capitalist societies. Parkin, *Class Inequality and Political Order*, pp. 155–57.

52. Poignant, *Education and Development*, p. 26.

53. Ibid., pp. 38–39, 80.

54. Ibid., pp. 60–61, 79. Between 1960–61 and 1969–70, the percentage of the 17–18 year-old age-group completing secondary education through the regular (day) program rose from 20 to 45 percent in the Soviet Union. If graduates of evening and correspondence secondary-education programs are added, the 1969–70 figure reaches 58 percent. These rates of secondary-education completion are somewhat higher than in the West European countries, though substantially below the level in the United States (75 percent in 1965). T. Revenko, *L'enseignement supérieur en l'Union soviétique* (Paris: O.E.C.D., 1973), pp. 152 (Table 33), 154, 214. Of course, reforms have been undertaken in various European countries to "democratize" secondary education.

55. Joseph Ben-David, "The Growth of the Professions and the Class System," in Reinhard Bendix and Seymour Martin Lipset, eds., *Class, Status, and Power*, 2nd ed. (New York: The Free Press, 1966), p. 469.

56. Poignant, *Education and Development*, pp. 271–72. According to a report prepared for the OECD, enrollment rates for college-age youth in the USSR more than tripled in the case of full-time students between 1950 and 1968. By 1968, however, only 13 percent of the 20–24 year-old age-group were enrolled as full-time *vuz* students. If evening and correspondence students are added, the proportion rises to 30 percent. This rate was substantially below that for full-time students in the United States (43 percent in 1968). In France and Great Britain, the corresponding rates of enrollment for full-time students in higher education were, respectively, 19 and 13 percent. Revenko, *L'enseignement supérieur*, pp. 115–16, 211.

57. See in this volume, Jerome Karabel, "Community Colleges and Social Stratification."

58. On the other hand, the argument may be made that the better educated, more well-to-do stratum receives a disproportionately large share of these subsidies because its children are more likely to get good grades, to pursue a higher education, etc. Compare in this volume, Samuel Bowles, "Unequal Education and the Reproduction of the Social Division of Labor."

59. On differentiation of the French and American systems, see in this volume Pierre Bourdieu, "Cultural Reproduction and Social Reproduction," and Karabel, "Community Colleges." See also Jerome Karabel and Alexander W. Astin, "Social Class, Academic Ability, and College 'Quality,' " *Social Forces* 53 (March 1975): 381—98.

60. On the relative "attractiveness" or prestige of "specialist" occupations, see Yanowitch and Dodge, "The Social Evaluation of Occupations"; V.V. Vodzinskaia, "Orientations Toward Occupations," in Yanowitch and Fisher, eds., *Social Stratification and Mobility*, pp. 153—86; and Lipset and Dobson, "Social Stratification and Sociology," pp. 141—47.

61. F.R. Filippov, "Sotsial'naia orientatsiia i sotsial'nye peremeshcheniia molodezhi" [Youth's social orientation and social interchanges], in *Molodezh' kak obshchestvennaia gruppa: Tezisy dokladov ko vtoroi Vsesoiuznoi nauchnoi konferentsii po probleme "Izmenenie sotsial'noi struktury sovetskogo obshchestva" 22 fevralia 1972* [Youth as a social group: Abstracts of papers for the Second All-Union Scholarly Conference on the Problem "Change of the Social Structure of Soviet Society," Feb. 22, 1972], ed. Iu.E. Volkov, F.R. Filippov, and N.D. Bondarenko (Moscow: USSR Academy of Sciences' Academic Council for the Study of the Complex Problem "Regularities in the Development of Social Relations and Cultural Life in Soviet Society" and the Higher Komsomol School, 1972), p. 145.

62. Ibid., pp. 145—46.

63. Out of the total number of respondents (3,217), 2,138 were applicants to Moscow *vuzy*, and 1,079 to *vuzy* in Kostroma. Twice as many applicants to the Moscow *vuzy* were children of non-manual fathers with a higher education (42 vs. 22 percent) and of working-class fathers with a secondary education (21 vs. 11 percent). Samoilova, *Sotsial'nye aspekty*, pp. 92—93.

64. Ibid., p. 98. If to this group of intelligentsia children are added those whose parents do not have specialized education, but work in the service sector, then the group of white-collar children increases to 62 percent in Moscow and 40 percent in Kostroma (p. 104).

65. Data of the Central Statistical Administration cited ibid., p. 73.

66. Ibid., pp. 131—32; A.K. Iurenko, "K voprosu ob izmenenii sotsial'nogo sostava sovetskogo studenchestva (na materialakh pedagogicheskikh institutov RSFSR) [Regarding the question of change in the social composition of the Soviet student body based on data pertaining to the pedagogical institutes of the RSFSR], in V.F. Generalov, ed., *Voprosy nauchnogo kommunizma: sbornik statei* [Questions of scientific communism: a collection of articles] (Moscow: Moscow State University Press, 1971), pp. 80—81; B.M. Cheknev, V.S. Nekhoroshev, and L.A. Blinov, "Pervye itogi raboty podgotovitel'nykh otdelenii meditsinskikh institutov Rossiiskoi federatsii" [Initial results of the work of the preparatory divisions of medical institutes of the Russian Federation], *Sovetskoe zdravookhranenie* 10 (1971): 42, Table 2.

67. M.N. Rutkevich, "Sotsial'nye istochniki popolneniia sovetskoi intelligentsii" [The social sources of replenishment of the Soviet intelligentsia], *Voprosy filosofii* 6 (1967): 19.

68. Some Soviet citizens and émigrés with whom the author has spoken in the USSR and abroad have an interpretation quite different from that publicly expressed by the Soviet officials. These individuals believe that the reasons for the establishment of the preparatory programs lie less in the government's commitment to equal opportunity than in the regime's desire to quell dissident thought among the students and to prevent the formation of a critical intelligentsia which would challenge its prerogatives. Working-class and peasant youth are thought to be more conservative and docile, more concerned with achieving vocational goals, and generally more supportive of the regime than some youth from families of the intelligentsia. These critics point out that the decision to introduce the preparatory programs on a large scale followed in the wake of student disturbances not only in the West, but in Czechoslovakia, Poland, and other East European countries. In view of the Party's consistent effort to maintain its monopoly of power and its use of educational policy toward that end, it is plausible that such considerations entered into the decision to increase low-status youth's representation in the higher schools. Under the regular admissions procedure, "political reliability" is taken into account in the selection of students, and students who engage in political activity of an "oppositionalist" nature are liable to expulsion and other sanctions. See also Robert J. Kaiser, "Soviet Education a Misnomer, For Loyal Only," *The Boston Globe*, Aug. 3, 1975, pp. 48, 50.

69. "On the Organization of Preparatory Departments at Higher Educational Institutions," *Pravda*, Sept. 6, 1969, and Rutkevich and Filippov, "Social Sources," pp. 160—61.

70. V.T. Lisovskii and A.V. Dmitriev, *Lichnost' studenta* [The personality of the student] (Leningrad: Leningrad State University Press, 1974), pp. 46—47.

71. Kozyrev, "Formirovanie studenchestva," p. 43.

72. Lisovskii and Dmitriev, *Lichnost' studenta*, p. 48, Table 6; F.R. Filippov, *Obrazovanie v usloviiakh razvitogo sotsializma* [Education under the conditions of developed socialism] (Moscow: Znanie, 1976), p. 42. These figures suggest that the preparatory divisions and the advantages given to working youth have substantially increased the flow of lower-status youth into these *vuzy*. As in most such tabulations, however, there is no way of ascertaining from these data how many are in fact working-class by social origin, as opposed to chil-

dren of white-collar workers who have worked for a short time.
73. E. Maksimova and I. Ovchinnikova, "Whom Does the Workers' Faculty Need?" *Izvestia*, April 5, 1975, p. 5, cond. in *CDSP* 27, 14: 12.

74. Ibid.
75. A. Sarkisian, "V teni pod lipoi" [In the shade of the linden tree], *Komsomol'skaia pravda*, Sept. 11, 1974, p. 4.
76. Ibid.

13. Academic Performance in Selective and Comprehensive Schools

TORSTEN HUSÉN

TWO TYPES OF SCHOOL STRUCTURE— TWO EDUCATIONAL PHILOSOPHIES

The "enrollment explosion" at the secondary school level and the expanded admission to the university-preparing school as well as to the university itself has given rise to questions about the "standard" of the students processed through a system of mass education as compared to an élitist one. The present author has dealt with the problem of comprehensiveness versus élitism in other connections (Husén, 1962 and 1973). Suffice it to indicate here that the criteria of "standards" are not as self-evident as they might seem *prima facie*, simply because the comprehensive system is based partly on other values than the élitist and therefore cannot be evaluated according to identical criteria. The very term "standard" has had a time-honoured place in educational folklore. The danger of "lowered standards" has often been pointed out by those who oppose broadening access to advanced education.

One of the problems singled out for particular analysis in the survey research conducted by the International Association for the Evaluation of Educational Achievement (IEA) has for a long time been a central policy issue in Europe, namely whether and the extent to which a comprehensive school system should replace the prevailing selective one. The IEA Project provided an unprece-

dented opportunity to compare what happens to the superior students when upper secondary school enrollment is broadened. The reason for the passion that often has gone into the debate on the comprehensive versus the selective school is that it is not merely didactic principles or methods of organizing the curriculum that are at issue. At the heart of the matter we find two opposing educational philosophies reflecting strong vested interests. On one hand we have the egalitarian and reconstructivist view, and on the other, the by and large conservative and élitist view of the educational system.

A comprehensive system provides a publicly supported school education for all children of mandatory school age in a given catchment area. This means that all programs or curricular offerings are provided in the same school unit. Another essential feature of comprehensiveness is that no differentiation or grouping practices that definitively determine the ensuing educational and occupational careers are employed. Children from all walks of life are taken care of.

In a selective system children are by means of organizational differentiation at an early age allocated to different types of school, and, also at an early stage of their school career, grouping practices are employed aiming at spotting those who are supposed to be particularly academically-

This article first appeared under the title "Standard of the Elite in Selective and Comprehensive Systems" in *Talent, Equality and Meritocracy* (The Hague: Martinus Nijhoff, 1974), pp. 115–124. Reprinted by permission.

oriented. Apart from selective admission and grouping, the system is as a rule also characterizęd by a high attrition rate in terms of grade-repeating ąnd drop-out.

In the debate on the relative merits and drawbacks of the two systems it has been maintained, on the one hand, that the top pupils in a comprehensive system will suffer by having to be taught together with their more slow-learning peers. This will impair their standard of achievement in comparison with pupils of equal intellectual standing in systems where an organizational differentiation in terms of selection for separate academically oriented schools takes place at an early age or where strict homogeneous grouping within the school is employed.

The adherents of comprehensive education, on the other hand, maintain that the top pupils will not suffer as much in their system as the great mass of the less academically-oriented students in a selective system, particularly those who rather early are left in the elementary school after the "book-oriented" have been selected for the university-preparing secondary schools.

The élitists maintain that a system of selection based on fair and equally employed criteria of excellence will open the avenues to high-status occupation to those from all walks of life who deserve it by possessing the necessary (mainly inherited) talent. The comprehensivists counter by claiming that a selective system is beset with a greater social bias than the comprehensive one. As one moves up the ladder of the formal educational system the proportion of lower-class pupils is much lower in a selective than in a comprehensive system, which is interpreted as evidence for biàs.

The two propositions, both the one on the standard of the élite and the one on social bias, were tested on national systems of education in the first two large-scale surveys conducted by IEA (Husén, 1967; Postlethwaite, 1967; Comber and Keeves, 1973). The national systems of education differ tremendously with regard to the size of the pre-university group (in per cent of the relevant age groups). In the mathematics study this group varied from less than 10 per cent in some European countries to more than 70 per cent in the United States. In the Science study (stage 2) the variation was by and large of the same order of magnitude. The variability in Europe had, however, decreased somewhat. Evidently, there is no point in making comparisons between mean performances behind which there are school populations representing such variations in terms of the proportion of the relevant age group. Thus, it was decided to take advantage of the IEA survey data for Population 4, that is to say, pupils who are in the terminal grade of the pre-university school. Typical national illustrations of this population are for instance the *Oberprimaner* in Germany, the pupils who are about to sit for the GCE A-level in England, and for the *baccalauréat* in France.

The problem of "comparing" the terminal pupils is not as simple as it might appear from the popular debate on the relative "standard" of secondary systems with a rather strict selection versus those with an open door policy. The problem of whether the one or the other system is to be preferred is a matter of what criteria one wants to employ in evaluating them, and therefore in the last run a question of political preferences. Even if the evaluators can agree upon what criteria should be employed, they will certainly put them in different orders of priority. The adherent of an élitist system tends to. evaluate the schools in terms of the quality of their *end-products,* either leaving out those who are lost in the selection and/ or attrition process or attaching a lower priority to their educational fate. The comprehensivist prefers to look at what happens to the great mass of students. His overriding question is: How many are brought how far?

STANDARD OF THE ELITE IN MATHEMATICS

In what follows we shall focus on the standard of the élite in the industrialized IEA countries, using as our criteria achievements in mathematics and science at the pre-university level. The national systems which have been studied vary considerably with regard to retention rate or "holding power" at the upper secondary level. The high school seniors consist of some 75 per cent of the relevant age group in the United States, those who finish *gymnasium* and continuation school in Sweden (grades 11 and 12) are some 45 per cent of the age group, the *Oberprimaner* (grade 13) in the Federal Republic of Germany are some 10 per cent etc. It is rather pointless to limit a comparison of student achievements in these and other countries to mean performances, simply because of the highly variable portion of the relevant age group we are dealing with. It is more nearly fair to compare *equal portions* of the age cohorts.

But such comparisons are conducted under the assumption that those who are *not* in school at that age level have not, either by previous schooling or other learning opportunities, reached the level of competence achieved by the élite still in school. On the basis of analysis of the distributions of achievements, both at the beginning and at the end of secondary school, we concluded that had the ideal conditions of being able to test the entire age group existed those who were not in school would not have scored high enough to affect the means for the top 5 per cent of the age group.

The objection has been raised that the method of comparing equal portions of the age group is unfair to national systems with a low retention rate (or high selectivity). The validity of such an objection can be questioned on pure logical grounds, simply because it is not consistent with the élitist philosophy. In systems where until recently only some 5–15 per cent of the entire age group is retained up to the pre-university grade, the prevailing educational philosophy has been that such a system rather efficiently takes care of most of the able pupils and does not bias against any category of

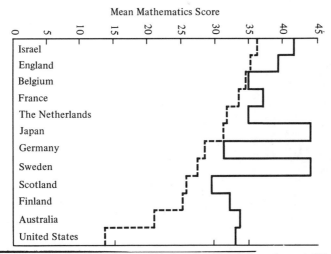

Figure 1. *Mean Mathematics Test Scores* (1) *for the Total S mple and* (2) *for Equal Proportions of Age Group in Each Country for Terminal Mathemat s Populations*

——————Average mathematics test score for equal proportions of age roups
— — — —Average mathematics test score for country

Source: T. Husén (Ed.): International Study of Achievement n Mathematics: A Comparison Between Twelve Countries. New York: Wiley, 1967.

them. Thus, those who favour an élitist system cannot reasonably object to a comparison between equal proportions of the age group by maintaining that the comparison is unfair to the selective system because it does not retain the able pupils. There is, however, a valid statistical objection. Härnqvist (1974) in reviewing the IEA surveys in science, reading and literature points out that the errors of measurement contribute to an overestimation of the size standard of the élite in comprehensive systems and conversely to an underestimation in selective systems.

When in the IEA mathematics study (Husén, 1967) the average performance in different countries of terminal students taking mathematics was compared, we found that the US high school graduates were far below the other countries. However, in the US 18 per cent of the age group of 17–18 year olds took mathematics as compared to

4–5 per cent in some European countries. In order to arrive at an answer to the question to what extent it is possible to produce an élite in a comprehensive system, one has to compare equal proportions of the relevant age group in the respective countries. The dotted line in Figure 1 gives the average performance of the terminal mathematics student in the twelve countries. The solid line gives the averages for the top four percent of the total age group. This percentage was selected because it represented the lowest proportion in any one country taking mathematics. As can be seen, the range between countries is more narrow than for the entire group of terminal mathematics pupils. The United States' top four percent score at about the same level as the corresponding group in other countries.

On the basis of the distribution of total score of the terminal pupils in all countries, international percentile norms were ob-

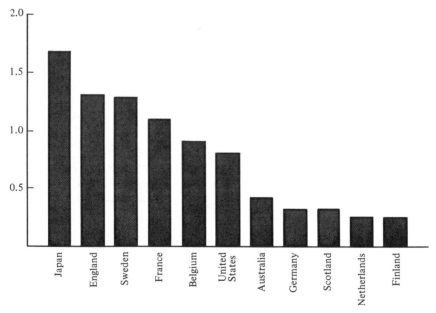

Figure 2. *Percent of Age Group Reaching Upper Tenth of Terminal Mathematics Pupils by International Standards*

Source: T. Husén (Ed.): International Study of Achievement in Mathematics: A Comparison Between Twelve Countries. New York: Wiley, 1967.

tained. In Figure 2 we have given the percentage of the total age group within each country which has reached the standard of the upper tenth of the terminal mathematics pupils. As can be seen, none of the systems with high retention rates and/or a comprehensive structure are among the five systems at the bottom.

STANDARD OF THE ELITE IN SCIENCE

Similar comparisons were conducted with terminal students in science (Comber and Keeves, 1973). In this case all the Population 4 pupils were included in the comparisons, irrespective of whether they were or were not taking science in the grade when testing took place. It was decided to compare the top 9 per cent of Population 4 in the industrialized countries. This percentage was chosen because it represented the lowest proportion in Population 4 of the relevant age group in any of the countries. In order to arrive at measures of two more limited élites, the top 5 and 1 per cent were also

chosen. Table 1 and Figure 3 present the outcomes of the comparisons for the three élite groups. The mean score for the entire graduate population ranges from 30.8 for New Zealand to only 14.2 for the United States. As can be seen in Table 1, the Population 4 pupils represent 13 per cent of the entire age group in the former country as compared to 75 in the latter. When the mean scores for the top 9 per cent were compared, it was found that countries with a high retention rate got sharply increased means. The United States doubled its mean and scored higher than, for instance, Germany and France. By and large the same picture emerged when countries were compared with regard to the top 5 and 1 per cent of the students.

The assessment of the standard of élite pupils at the pre-university level does not support the contention that systems with broader or more open access and with relative high retention rate until the end of upper secondary school do not succeed in "producing" élite pupils. An élite can be

Table 1. Means and Standard Deviations for Science Test Scores for Total Sample and Equivalent Proportions of an Age Group

	% at		Full sample		Top 1%		Top 5%		Top 9%	
Country	School	N	Mean	SD	Mean	SD	Mean	SD	Mean	SD
New Zealand	13	1,676	30.8	12.6	52.8	2.8	43.5	5.9	36.8	9.0
England	20	2,181	24.4	12.4	51.6	3.2	41.6	6.5	35.5	8.5
Australia	29	4,194	26.1	11.5	51.5	3.2	44.0	4.7	39.9	5.9
Scotland	17	1,321	24.4	12.9	50.7	3.8	40.6	6.4	34.4	8.7
Sweden	45	2,754	20.1	10.9	49.5	3.4	41.2	5.3	37.0	6.2
Hungary	28	2,828	24.0	9.6	48.0	3.8	39.0	5.4	35.0	6.1
Netherlands	13	1,138	24.4	12.0	47.1	3.6	37.2	6.5	30.3	9.4
Finland	21	1,725	20.8	10.5	46.0	4.1	35.7	6.4	30.7	7.4
USA	75	2,514	14.2	9.9	45.8	2.8	36.8	5.5	33.1	5.9
FRG	9	1,989	28.4	9.6	45.0	4.1	35.3	6.2	28.4	9.6
France	29	3,523	19.1	9.1	40.5	3.5	33.3	4.4	29.9	5.1
Belgium (Fl)	47	467	18.1	8.5	39.8	3.7	33.0	4.0	30.5	4.2
Italy	16	15,719	16.5	9.2	38.2	4.7	27.4	6.5	22.7	7.3
Belgium (Fr)	47	941	16.0	8.3	36.2	2.0	30.9	3.1	28.4	3.7
Average			22.0		45.9		37.1		32.3	
Range			16.6		16.6		16.6		17.2	
Chile	16	1,947	9.3	6.3	23.5	3.8	16.8	4.3	13.6	4.8
India	14	3,040	6.3	6.1	20.8	3.7	12.8	4.8	9.5	5.2
Iran	9	1,051	10.8	5.9	21.9	3.6	14.8	4.4	10.8	5.9
Thailand	10	724	12.5	6.1	23.2	2.4	17.4	3.6	13.6	5.3

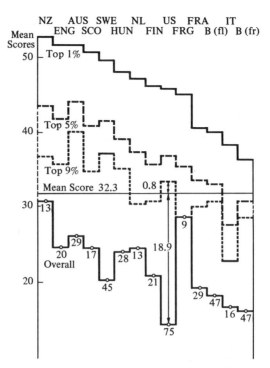

Figure 3. *Science Mean Scores of Top 1%, Top 5%, Top 9% of an Age-Group and of Overall Group*

Source: L. C. Comber and John P. Keeves: Science Education in Nineteen Countries. Stockholm and New York: Almqvist & Wiksell and Wiley-Halsted Press, 1973.

cultivated within a comprehensive educational system. Whether or not an élite produced in the latter system is worth its price is another question.

In selective systems the high standard of the élite is often bought at the price of limiting opportunities of the mass of the pupils. By comparing the distribution of father's occuption at the 14-year-old level with the one at the pre-university level, it is possible within each country to arrive at an estimation of the amount of social selection that operates between the two levels. An index of social disproportion was derived from the proportion of pupils with fathers who belonged to the professional and managerial category on one hand and the semi-skilled or unskilled category on the other. The index was unity when the upper and lower strata

have the same representation at the pre-university level as at the 14-year-old level. The index was 1.3 and 2.4 respectively for the United States and Sweden, two countries with relatively comprehensive and retentive systems; whereas it was 7.9 for England and as high as 37.7 for the Federal Republic of Germany, where the systems are much more selective and less retentive. An index of dissimilarity between socio-economic strata developed by Anderson (1967) gives by and large the same results. Table 2 gives the percentages for the two contrasted status categories. Since the categorization has not been consistent over countries, comparisons should be made *between* levels *within* countries. One should notice the low representation in England and the Federal Republic of Germany of pupils with working class back-

Table 2. Percentage of Pupils Within Each Population From Selected Categories of Parental Occupation

	Population I (10-year-olds)		Population II (14-year-olds)		Population IV (17–19 year-olds)	
	Professional & managerial	Unskilled & semi-skilled workers	Professional & managerial	Unskilled & semi-skilled workers	Professional & managerial	Unskilled & semi-skilled workers
England	16	21	14	14	38	5
Fed. Rep. of Germany	13	7	14	8	49	1
Finland	9	35	10	34	20	15
Hungary	15	43	20	36	38	18
Netherlands	26	12	20	12	55	5
Sweden	23	31	26	27	35	15
USA	24	18	31	16	34	14

Source: L. C. Comber and John P. Keeves: Science Education in Nineteen Countries. Stockholm and New York: Almqvist & Wiksell and Wiley-Halsted Press, 1973.

ground at the pre-university level. The overall conclusion from the comparisons is that the comprehensive system, by its openness, lack of selective examinations during the primary and initial secondary school period and its high retention rate, is a more effective strategy in taking care of all the talent of a nation. By casting a net as widely as possible an attempt is made to "catch" an optimum number of fish. A selective system with early separation of pupils who are rated to have academic potential is destined to produce good end products. But this advantage is bought at the high price of excluding a sizeable number of pupils from lower class homes from further education and of limiting the opportunities for the great mass of pupils to get access to quality education.

REFERENCES

Comber, L.C., and John P. Keeves (1973) *Science Education in Nineteen Countries:* *An Empirical Study,* with a Foreword by Torsten Husén, Stockholm: Almqvist & Wiksell; New York: Wiley.

Husén, Torsten (1962) *Problems of Differentiation in Swedish Compulsory Schooling,* Stockholm: Svenska Bokförlaget-Scandinavian University Books.

Husén, Torsten (Ed.) (1967) *International Study of Achievement in Mathematics: A Comparison of Twelve Countries,* Stockholm and New York: Almqvist & Wiksell, and Wiley.

Husén, Torsten (1973) Implications of the IEA Findings for the Philosophy of Comprehensive Education, Paper presented at the Harvard Conference on Educational Achievement, Harvard Graduate School of Education, November 1973 (mimeo).

Postlethwaite, T. Neville (1967) *School Organization and Student Achievement: A Study Based on Achievement in Mathematics in Twelve Countries,* Stockholm and New York: Almqvist & Wiksell, and Wiley.

14. The School as a Mechanism of Social Differentiation

AARON V. CICOUREL AND JOHN I. KITSUSE

The standard approach to the study of students who are and are not admitted to college begins with examination of the characteristics of college-qualified graduates to determine how they differ from those of nonqualified students. The findings of investigations oriented by this approach suggest that the more "obvious" explanations, such as that the college-qualified students have higher I.Q. scores, higher grade records, greater financial support from their parents, etc., than their non-college-qualified peers, are inadequate to account for students who are qualified but do not get to college. For example, a recent volume[1] reports a finding by Stouffer that many students with high I.Q. scores did not go to college. He reports also that of the high I.Q. students who did not go to college, many had consistently good academic records during their high school careers.

In view of such findings, social scientists have increasingly directed their attention to "non-intellective" determinants of educational, occupational, and general life aspirations. Among students whose tested capabilities and course grades are high, the determinants of college-going aspirations and actual college enrollment have been sought in cultural, social, and motivational factors. Performance and achievement are conceived to be products of ability and motivation when talent is above a minimum level considered necessary for success in college. Thus, Turner,[2] using a sample of male college students, has investigated the motivational significance of the standards of reference groups used by future-oriented students to evaluate the relative success of their own performance. Strodtbeck[3] has also emphasized the social and cultural motivational sources of academic achievement in his study of Jewish and Italian high school students. His findings suggest the motivational significance of group differences in family interaction, particularly power relations in the socialization process and value orientations toward achievement. Similarly, Parsons,[4] Kahl,[5] and others have underlined the importance of social class membership as a major determinant of the occupational aspirations and achievement of youth. They have emphasized class-related differentials in the socialization of children and the consequences of such differences for the attitudes of youth toward academic achievement, occupational aspirations, and plans for college education.

Hollingshead's study of adolescence in Elmtown[6] presents a somewhat different perspective on the relation between social class and the social as well as academic status of students within the school system. His concern with the organization of adolescent activities among the youth in Elmtown directed him to investigate the influences of social class membership upon clique formation and the effects of such cliques upon the treatment and evaluation of students by administrative and teaching personnel within the school. Since the publication of Hollingshead's book, peer groups and related peer cultures and their influences upon the organization of adolescent attitudes, activities, and achievement have been subjects of sociological investigation, both theoretical and empirical.[7] In his recent study, Coleman[8] specifically examined these influences by investigating the normative effects of peer group climates upon the relative valuation of peer achievement in academic, athletic, and social activities among the student populations of ten high schools varying in size and organization.

In the following pages we present an alternative formulation that conceives of the differentiation of students as a consequence of the administrative organization and decisions of personnel in the high school. We shall contend that the distribution of students in such categories as college-qualified and non-college-qualified is to a large extent characteristic of the administrative organization of the high school and therefore can be explained in terms of that organization. We shall be concerned primarily with the relation between the administrative organization of the high school and the ways in which the students are processed through it. More specifically, we wish to investigate how the routine decisions of the guidance and counseling personnel within the high school are related to the college/non-college decisions and, by implication, to the occupational choices made by students.

Our more general concern with the allocation of personnel within the occupational structure of the larger society is similar to that of Parsons. We view as problematic, however, his assumption that the "virtually ascribed" college-going expectation among the middle- and upper-class segments of the population *accounts for* the higher rate of students from those social classes who do in fact go to college.[9] Although he identifies the school and prior academic achievement as the institutional setting within which the college-going expectation is expressed, he does not systematically consider how the formal organization of the school affects the realization of those expectations. In stressing the class-ascribed character of the college aspiration, he assumes that the organizational processing of the aspiration is routine and non-problematic. We wish to question this assumption in our study.

Although heightened competition for college facilities has stimulated the growth and development of colleges throughout the nation, it has also given impetus to a policy of restricted enrollment for "quality" education and raised the entrance requirements among the "better" colleges to which students of the middle and upper social classes aspire. In view of the changing ratios of supply and demand in college facilities, it should also be noted that the theoretically significant distribution of high school seniors is not the gross college/non-college dichotomy, but the distribution of students according to their admission into colleges ranging from those having the highest applicant/enrollment ratio and admission requirements to those accepting any high school graduate. Class-ascribed college-going expectations might be considered an adequate explanation of the gross college/non-college distribution, but it cannot explain how students are distributed among hierarchically ranked (prestige) colleges. An explanation of such a distribution requires an investigation of the ways in which admission to various colleges is subject to specifically *organizational* contingencies.

Assuming that parents have college aspirations, to whatever quality of college, for their children, and assuming that their children have internalized those aspirations, whether or not such students do in fact become eligible for college entrance depends upon: (1) the communication by parents and/or the student to the school of the student's intention to prepare for college admission; (2) the enrollment of the student in high school courses that will qualify him for college—i.e., courses that will meet college entrance requirements; (3) the satisfactory completion of such courses;[10] and (4), in some instances, the recommendation of high school authorities in support of the student's college applications, particularly in the case of applications to the "better" colleges. Organizational decisions and actions that affect these preconditions may occur at any point in the student's transition through the school system and may be quite independent of either his or his parents' aspirations.[11]

In stressing the significance of such organizational contingencies for the explanation of college/non-college or "good"/"better"/"best" college distributions of the student population, we do not deny that the formal organization of the high school progressively implements the college and occupational goals of the majority of students. Such student goals, however, are processed and actualized through a system subject to the contingencies of organizational processes. Indeed, it is precisely the routine aspects of the organizational processing activity that are of interest and are revealed by the variety of "problems" that attend the movement of a cohort of students through the high school system. . . .

In order to obtain information concerning the process of student evaluation as practiced by the counseling personnel, we systematically questioned the counselor to whom the students in our sample were assigned. We were particularly interested in the criteria used in categorizing student achievement and in how the achievement-type classification compares with the "objective" measures of student ability (SCAT) and performance (grade-point average in the freshman year). The materials obtained in our interviews with this counselor are presented below.

The counselor's achievement types. When we asked the counselor how she would classify each of the students in our sample, [12] she employed the following categories (which were widely used by the teaching as well as the counseling personnel at Lakeshore High) of classification: (1) "Excellent student," (2) "Average achiever," (3) "Underachiever," (4) "Overachiever," (5) "Opportunity student." Asked what she considered the most stable basis for her judgment of a student, she replied:

"Probably ability—that's the most specific and measurable."

Interviewer: "And how do you determine ability?"

Counselor: "By tests and performance, generally."

If we assume that the counselor's evaluation of student performance is to assess the

Table 1. Counselor's Achievement Types by SCAT Scores and Ninth-grade Point Average

Achievement types	Ninth-grade point average					
	1.00–1.50	1.75–2.00	2.25–3.00	3.25–4.00	4.25–5.00	N
Opportunity student			(15)	(06)(10) (12)(16)	(01)(02) (02)(13)	9
Overachiever		(42)	(27)	(16)		3
Underachiever		(68)	(68)(68) (73)(80)(84) (87)(90)(96)	(17)(39) (58)(75)(78) (80)(93)	(10)(39)	18
Average achiever		(47)(64) (64)(75)	(27)(32)(35) (39)(50)(64) (64)(68)(68) (68)(68)(73) (73)(78)(84) (87)(90)	(15)(20)(20) (35)(42)(42) (50)(52)(54) (75)	(28) (39)	33
Excellent student	(73)(73)(80) (84)(85)(94) (95)(97)	(75)(78) (84)(84) (90)(93) (95)(96)	(94)	(90)		18
N	8	14	28	23	9	81*

*No information for 8 cases.

students' progress in the courses to which they have been assigned, we would expect a systematic relationship between the achievement-type classification and the distribution of SCAT/grade-point discrepancies. In Table 1 we have included the SCAT scores and grade-point averages of each of the students classified by the counselor in order to show the relation between discrepancies and achievement types. An examination of the table will show the range of discrepancies classified in the five achievement types by the counselor. (The range of discrepancies for each category of achievement types is summarized in Table 2.) For example, the

"excellent student" category includes 9 students with SCAT scores of 90–95 and with grade-point averages ranging from 1.00 to 3.25. On the other hand, the 2.25–3.00 grade point column shows that there are 4 students with SCAT scores of 90–95, but 2 are classified as "underachievers," another as an "average achiever," and the fourth as an "excellent student." These classifications are not a strict application of the SCAT/grade-point discrepancy criterion. The classification of other students (e.g., the SCAT 68/1.75–2.00 "underachiever," the SCAT 17/3.25–4.00 "underachiever," the SCAT 47/1.75–2.00 "average achiever," etc.) pro-

Table 2. Range of SCAT and Ninth-grade Point Average by Counselor's Classification of Achievement Types

Achievement types	SCAT range	Grade-point range	N
Excellent student	73–97	1.00–3.25	18
Average achiever	15–90	1.75–4.25	33
Underachiever	10–96	2.00–4.66	18
Overachiever	16–42	2.00–3.75	3
Opportunity student	01–16	3.00–5.00	9
			81*

*No information for 8 cases.

vides added evidence that the criterion is not consistently applied and does not account for the distribution of achievement types. The table shows that neither SCAT nor grade point alone accounts for the achievement-type classifications.

The inconsistencies revealed in this classification of students are of more than passing interest, for the achievement types are not merely descriptive categories to the personnel who use them. The classification of students as achievement types in effect produces a distribution of students who are conceived by the organizational personnel to have "problems." With the exception of students classified, by whatever criteria, as "average achiever" and "excellent student," the achievement-type classification identifies those students who are performing below the level of their ability ("underachiever") or above it ("overachiever"), or who are lacking in both ability and performance ("opportunity student"). In the following chapter we shall discuss how these "problems" are articulated with the organizational activities of counselors at Lakeshore High and 19 other high schools. We wish here to pursue further the criteria applied in the process of evaluating student performance.

If the more or less "rational criterion" of SCAT/grade-point discrepancy does not account for the counselor's achievement-type classification of students, what are the bases of her judgments? What are the variables that might operate to produce the variations in the distribution discussed above? Social-class characteristics of the student population, commonly found by social researchers to influence the evaluations of students by school personnel, are variables that deserve examination. In our investigation of this possibility we were directed by our theoretical orientation, which emphasizes the vocabulary and syntax used by the organizational personnel, to obtain the social-class categories that *the counselor* used to differentiate the student population.

The counselor's social types. To explore the relation between the stratification system as perceived by the counselor and her classification of achievement types, we questioned her as follows:

a: How many social statuses, that is, social-class groups, would you say there are here at Lakeshore High School?
b: How would you describe, in general, each of the groups you mentioned?
c: How would you place each of the students named on these cards (handing her a set of cards with the names of all the students in our sample) into each of the groups you mentioned?

The phrasing of the questions assumes that social-status categories are recognized, if not employed, by the counselor as one dimension of her classification of students. The questions, however, allow the counselor to interpret "social status, that is, social-class groups" in her own terms. We would expect the counselor to base her evaluations on the same kind of common-sense criteria one would expect from persons in the general population—i.e., the categories and criteria should be characteristically general, vaguely defined, and perhaps inconsistently applied.

When the counselor was asked question *a*, she offered without prompting from the interviewer a description of each group as she identified them. That is, the interviewer found it unnecessary to ask question *b*. The counselor's categories and comments were as follows:

1. First there's the main group—the in-group. This is the group that belongs to the "Y." They head this group, they're at the forefront of the activities in the school, they're the leaders. Most of them live in Lakeshore. They belong to the Presbyterian Church there, or is it a Methodist Church?
2. Then there's the group just below this group. They're trying to attain the [main] group. They're sometimes included in the activities of the first group, but they don't really belong. They might be the campaign managers for members of the first group if they're running for an

office. This group will do almost anything to get into the other group.

3.. There's the other element. These students would not at all consider getting into the first group. They get into a lot of trouble, they have difficulties with their studies. Most of the drop-outs are from this group—they drop out at 16 or 17.

4. We can't deny that there's a Negro group here at Lakeshore. They have their own group, their own identification. In some instances there are those who cut across the line, but they don't participate in their "Y" activities. The "Y" seems to be the center of activities, and the "Y" is a segregated group.

5. Then there's the group that's left [not politically left, but left by subtraction]. This is not really a group. They don't have a group of their own. There are some strong individualists in this group.

6. We should make some note of those other students who are not in a group. They are noteworthy individuals. Because they are outstanding they are known to everybody. But they don't belong to any group. They're the kind that might wear black leotards or carry a guitar. They're a group, but not a group. They come to our attention in some way—they're outstanding scholastically, or they're extremely sensitive, [the counselor smiled here, which was interpreted to mean that she did not want to be more explicit] or intelligent. Some of them are referred for psychiatric care. [The counselor cited the case of a student in our sample who would fit this group. She called this group "loners."]

7. [The counselor then mentioned another group who were "like loners" but she said they were "rebelling." This group dressed, she said, in extreme fashion.] They wear their skirts too short. [In our sample, this group consists of four or five girls who are described as being tightly banded together, but who are not thought to have the "nerve" to do anything as individuals.] They find it difficult to fit into things at Lakeshore High. Anything typical of teen-agers here is ridiculous for them. [The counselor stated that the "loner" described in the last group might wear leotards or braids or carry a guitar even if no one else were doing so.]

The counselor's response to question *a* indicates that she interpreted "social status, that is, social class" to mean different *social types* of students within the stratification system of the high school, and we shall refer to them hereafter by that term. With the exception of Social Types *1* and *2,* and perhaps the "Negro group" (Social Type *4*), her descriptions do not necessarily imply a strict hierarchical ranking in the conventional terms of social class. The pluralistic classification appears to be based on some combination of aspiration, rejection, or withdrawal of students from participation in school and out-of-school social activities.

Table 3. Counselor's Social Types by Counselor's Classification of Achievement Designations

| Social types | Achievement types | | | | | N |
	Excel.	Aver.	Under	Over	Oppor.	
7	0	1	0	1	1	3
6	1	0	0	0	0	1
5	0	10	7	1	4	22
4	0	1	0	0	2	3
3	0	2	4	0	1	7
2	4	16	6	1	2	29
1	12	2	1	0	0	15
N	17	32	18	3	10	80*

*No information on 9 cases.

In response to question *c,* the counselor classified the students in our sample into the categories that she enumerated and described. Table 3 shows the relation between her social-type and achievement-type classifications of students. Twelve of the 17 students classified as "excellent students" were also classified as Social Type *1.* Conversely, all but 3 of the 15 Social Type *1* students were classified as "excellent students." In none of the remaining categories in which the frequencies are large enough to warrant consideration (i.e., Social Types 2 and 5, and the achievement types of "average achiever" and "underachiever") is there a suggested relationship which approaches that between the "excellent student"—Social Type *1* classification.

It would appear that there is a fusion of academic and social-type criteria in the counselor's classification of the "excellent" Social Type *1* student. Table 4, which presents the distribution of social types with reference to the students' SCAT scores and grade-point averages, provides a clue to the

nature of the academic criteria that may have been applied by the counselor in the social-type classification. With one exception (one student with SCAT of 68), all students in Social Type *1* have SCAT scores of 73 or higher, but their grade-point averages range from 1.00 to 4.00. The classification of the 94/2.25–3.00 student and the 90/3.25–4.00 student in Social Type *1* shows that these relatively large SCAT/grade-point discrepancies (indicating underachievement) did not disqualify them from inclusion in this category. We note, however, that although high SCAT appears to be a characteristic of Social Type *1* students, there is an equal number of students with scores of 73 or higher who were classified in other social-type categories.

The characterization of the "excellent" Social Type *1* student that may be made from Tables 3 and 4 is that of a student whom the counselor considers to be a "leader," who is in the "main group," and who has a relatively high SCAT score even if he does not have a high grade-point average.

Table 4. Counselor's Social Types by SCAT Scores and Ninth-grade Point Average

Social type	Ninth-grade point average					N
	1.00–1.50	1.75–2.00	2.25–3.00	3.25–4.00	4.25–5.00	
7				(15)	(13)	2
6	(97)					1
5		(47)	(15)(27)(32)(39)(64)(68)(68)(73)(80)	(17)(20)(35)(52)(58)	(02)(07)(10)	18
4			(78)	(06)(50)(10)(12)	(01)	4
3				(39)(42)(54)(78)	(39)	7
2	(85)	(42)(64)(64)(75)(90)(93)	(27)(35)(50)(64)(68)(68)(84)(84)(87)(87)(90)(90)(96)	(16)(20)(42)(75)(93)	(02)	26
1	(73)(73)(80)(84)(94)(95)	(68)(75)(78)(84)(84)(95)(96)	(73)(73)(94)	(75)(90)		18
N	8	14	27	21	7	76*

*No information for 13 cases.

Table 4 also indicates that neither SCAT nor grade-point average separately nor the discrepancy between them is systematically related to the classification of social types. Our materials suggest that the counselor's social-type classification does not account for the majority of her achievement-type classification of students.

The counselor's social-class ratings. The counselor's response to question *a* raised the question of whether or not she differentiated students by social-class categories in the conventional sense. If so, would her classification of students in those terms better account for the achievement types than the social types? To obtain this information, we explained to the counselor that we would like her to classify our student sample into five strata of social classes. Using a fivefold classification, we presented these strata to her as: Class I, Upper; Class II, Lower Upper; Class III, Upper Middle; Class IV, Lower Middle; and Class V, Lower. No further criteria for the classification of students, except as indicated immediately below, were given to the counselor. When she was presented with these strata, the counselor asked:

What do you mean by "upper"? In Lakeshore that would have to be old-guard Lakeshore. There may be some with more money, but they wouldn't be old guard. For example, the ――― boy's family has lots of money, but they don't make it on the old guard.
Interviewer: So, the ――― boy would not be placed in the "upper" class if that's true.

Table 5 shows the social-class distribution that resulted from the counselor's classification of students by achievement-type categories. It should be noted that although the counselor indicated by her remark about the "old-guard Lakeshore" that she recognized the existence of an "upper" class, she did not assign any of the students in our sample to that social class. As in the case of Social Type *1*, "excellent students" are predominantly from one category—all but one

Table 5. Distribution of Achievement Types by Counselor's Social-class Ratings

Achievement types	Counselor's social-class ratings					N
	I	II	III	IV	V	
Opportunity		2	1	4	2	9
Overachiever		2	1			3
Underachiever		10	5	4		19
Average achiever		12	13	5	1	31
Excellent		17	1			18
N		42	21	13	3	80*

*No information on 9 cases.

in Social Class II. The converse relationship, however, does not obtain: i.e., only 40 per cent (17 out of 42) Class II students are classified as "excellent students." Thus, although the social-class category adds the characteristic of Social Class II to the description of the "excellent student," it does no better than the social-type classification in suggesting the basis for the over-all distribution of achievement types. . . .

INDIVIDUAL EFFORT AND ORGANIZATIONAL SPONSORSHIP

Our study provides illustrative data that are relevant for an examination of Turner's analysis of the two educational systems. His analysis proceeds on the assumption that

. . . within a formally open class system that provides for mass education the organizing folk norm which defines the accepted mode of upward mobility is a crucial factor in shaping the school system, and may be even more crucial than the extent of upward mobility.[13]

He proposes that the organizing folk norm in the United States differs from that in England and as a consequence the relation of the two systems of education to the processes of social mobility are characteristically different. The American and British educational systems are characterized in the following ideal typical terms:

Contest mobility is a system in which elite status is the prize in an open contest and is taken by the aspirants' own efforts. While the "contest" is governed by some rules of fair play, the contestants have wide latitude in the strategies they may employ. Since the "prize" of successful upward mobility is not in the hands of an established elite to give out the latter can not determine who shall attain it and who shall not. Under *sponsored* mobility elite recruits are chosen by the established elite or their agents, and elite status is *given* on the basis of some criterion of supposed merit and cannot be *taken* by any amount of effort or strategy. Upward mobility is like entry into a private club where each candidate must be "sponsored" by one or more of the members. Ultimately the members grant or deny upward mobility on the basis of whether they judge the candidate to have those qualities they wish to see in fellow members.[14]

Turner's characterization of the American educational system as one that promotes a contest among individuals who "have wide latitude in the strategies they may employ" to facilitate their mobility must be modified if our illustrative materials are indicative of a trend in American high schools. Our materials indicate first of all that in the bureaucratically organized high school the day-to-day activities of the school personnel effectively control the access of students to the limited number of curriculums available, particularly their access to the curriculum most instrumental for upward mobility, i.e., the college preparatory curriculum. Our case study suggests that through their control over the student's course programs, the school personnel may include or exclude students from the "contest" and that the "aspirants' own efforts" are neither the only nor the critical determinant of their qualification as "contestants."

This is not to say that the aspirants' efforts are irrelevant to qualifying them for the "contest" or advancing their position within it, but rather that their efforts are not necessarily evaluated, as might be assumed, by academic standards alone. If the SCAT

scores and grade-point averages of students may be considered indicative of their efforts, our materials suggest that, in a number of cases, students who show such effort may be handicapped or even excluded from the "contest."

It should be noted that the educational system in the United States does manifest all the formal characteristics that Turner attributes to contest mobility. There is an emphasis upon periodic examinations; formalized criteria govern the progress of students in the hierarchy of grade levels; college entrance requirements are not automatically achieved by virtue of enrollment in high school; and college admission is an outcome of a competitive process. Our research, however, supports the view that the student's progress in this sequence of transitions is contingent upon the interpretations, judgments, and action of school personnel vis-à-vis the student's biography, social and personal "adjustment," appearance and demeanor, social class, and "social type," as well as his demonstrated ability and performance. In this respect, mobility in the highly bureaucratized high school bears a striking resemblance to the sponsorship found in graduate departments of universities, in which judgments about the student's maturity, emotional stability, character, and personal appearance are often important determinants of his social mobility.

Secondly, although Turner assumes that the folk norm of contest mobility is "present at least implicitly in people's thinking, guiding their judgments of what is appropriate in many specific matters,"[15] the degree to which such thinking is articulated in the organizational judgments and actions of the school personnel must be viewed as problematic. This is particularly true in an educational system in which school policies are increasingly professionalized and bureaucratically implemented. The advances and setbacks in the process of mobility in such a system are governed less by the folk norms of the larger society than by the doctrines and practices of a professionalized bureaucracy. Insofar as the rationalization and bureaucratization of procedures imply greater "objectivity" in the evaluation of performance and distribution of rewards, it might be argued that the application of such organizational techniques represents an institutionalization of the folk norm of contest mobility. Our materials do not support such an argument. Examination of how students are assigned to college and non-college curriculums, distributed among different ability-grouped courses, and identified as various "problems" suggests that the professed ideal of equal access to educational opportunities for those of equal ability is not necessarily served by such procedures.

Indeed, our materials on the differential interpretation of test scores and grade-point averages by school personnel, the definitions and treatment of student "problems," and the organizational activities directed toward facilitating the processing of low performance students toward college entrance indicate that the patterned deviations from bureaucratic procedures amounts to a form of sponsorship. The differentiation of students by objective criteria obviously is not *the* rational basis for the allocation of educational opportunities, for the bureaucracy permits considerable discretion in decision-making. The views of professional educators concerning "adjustment," "motivation," "realistic goals," "overachievers," "participation," and the like are accommodated in the bureaucratic setting, and they constitute significant qualifications of the folk norm of contest mobility. The accommodation of such conceptions has created a complicated system of organizational sponsorship in which discrepancies of ability and performance, aspirations, and realistic possibilities are adjusted, modified, or created in some instances, ignored in others. Decisions for such actions are made by professionals who are guided not by folk norms but by explicit and implicit educational doctrines and practices.

The organizational sponsorship that occurs in American schools may not be as obvious or as explicitly acknowledged as the form of sponsorship that Turner attributes to the British schools. It is quite clear that even in Hollingshead's class-conscious Elmtown the differential treatment and sponsorship of students by school personnel were covertly practiced. Although the bureaucratic organization of the modern comprehensive high school is undoubtedly less vulnerable to the inequities of the social-class pressures documented by Hollingshead, the distribution of educational opportunities is conditioned by decisions and actions that effectively accommodate social-class as well as other information about students.

The rationalization of the school system through the incorporation of the concepts and methods of psychiatry, psychology, and the social sciences has legitimized the relevance of personal and social factors for the interpretation of the "objective" measures of the student's ability and performance. Such factors are explicitly acknowledged as educationally relevant and incorporated into a complex system of organizational policies and procedures. Thus, although testing procedures are extensively employed and course grades are routinely reviewed, the information they provide are in some instances the sole basis for organizational decisions, but in other instances their significance is qualified by considerations of personal and social factors. In such a system, a student's mobility may be more than incidentally contingent upon the sponsorship of organizational personnel who certify him to be a "serious, personable, well-rounded student with leadership potential."

In presenting these objections to Turner's thesis we stress once again the importance of investigating the processes of social mobility at the level of the day-to-day organizational activities in which often unstated rules of mobility are defined and the direction and rate of progress through the system are controlled. Insofar as contest and sponsored mobility are characterizations of organizations, investigation should be directed to the organizationally defined activities of school personnel as well as to the characteristics of individuals who are upwardly or downwardly mobile. One of the critical problems we face in theorizing about comparative differences in the organization and control of social mobility is that the studies utilizing the techniques of large scale survey research are not articulated with the more focused organizational analyses. Generalizing from the findings of either the survey studies, which do not provide data concerning the organizational processes of mobility, or of the limited organizational studies, which cannot claim to be representative or to produce data on a large enough sample, is hazardous.

NOTES

1. David C. McClelland et al., Talent and Society. New York: Van Nostrand, 1958. The paper by Samuel A. Stouffer, "Social Mobility of Boys in the Boston Metropolitan Area," delivered at the SSRC Conference on "Non-intellective Determinants of Achievement," Princeton, New Jersey, 1953, is cited on page 16.
2. Ralph H. Turner, "Reference Groups of Future-Oriented Men," Social Forces, 34 (December 1955), pp. 130–136.
3. Fred L. Strodtbeck, "Family Interaction, Values and Achievement," in David C. McClelland et al., Talent and Society. New York: Van Nostrand, 1958, pp. 135–191.
4. Talcott Parsons, "General Theory in Sociology," in R. K. Merton et al., Sociology Today. New York: Basic Books, 1958, pp. 3–38.
5. Joseph A. Kahl, "Educational and Occupational Aspirations of 'Common Man' Boys," Harvard Educational Review, 23 (Summer 1953), pp. 186–203.
6. August B. Hollingshead, Elmtown's Youth. New York: Wiley, 1949.
7. See David Riesman et al., The Lonely Crowd. New Haven: Yale University Press, 1949, esp. Chapter 3; Carolyn Tryon, "The Adolescent Peer Group," 43rd Yearbook of the National Society for the Study of Education. Chicago: The University of Chicago Press, 1944, Part I, "Adolescence"; James S. Coleman, The Adolescent Society. Glencoe: Free Press, 1961; Talcott Parsons, "Age and Sex in the Social Structure of the United States," American Sociological Review, 7 (October 1942), pp. 604–616; C. W. Gordon, The Social System of the High School. Glencoe: Free Press, 1957; Frederick Elkin and William A. Westley, "The Myth of Adolescent Culture," American Sociological Review, 20 (December 1955), pp. 680–684.
8. James S. Coleman, op. cit.; also "The Adolescent Sub-Culture and Academic Achievement," American Journal of Sociology, 65 (January 1960), pp. 337–347.
9. Talcott Parsons, op. cit., p. 27.
10. "Satisfactory" in this context means that the student earned grades that were adequate for admission to the college of his choice.
11. The consequences of such organizational activity may be unknown to the student or his parents until he seeks admission to a college, or indeed, they may never become known to him. The articulation of parental and/or student aspirations with the organizational processes that differentiate and channel students through the school system cannot, therefore, be assumed, for it requires a flow of information to, from, and within the family and school organizations.
12. The counselor did not classify 7 students for various reasons, such as drop-outs, transfers to another division, and no information.
13. Ralph H. Turner, "Sponsored and Contest Mobility and the School System," Amer. Sociological Rev., 25 (December 1960), p. 856.
14. Ibid., p. 856.
15. Ibid., p. 856.

15. On Understanding the Processes of Schooling: The Contributions of Labeling Theory

RAY C. RIST

There have been few debates within American education which have been argued with such passion and intensity as that of positing causal explanations of success or failure in schools.[1] One explanation which has had

This article appears here for the first time.

considerable support in the past few years, particularly since the publication of Pygmalion in the Classroom by Rosenthal and Jacobson (1968), has been that of the "self-fulfilling prophecy." Numerous studies have appeared seeking to explicate the mechanisms by which the teacher comes to hold certain expectations of the students and how these are then operationalized within the classroom so as to produce what the teacher had initially assumed. The origins of teacher expectations have been attributed to such diverse variables as social class, physical appearance, contrived test scores, sex, race, language patterns, and school records. But in the flurry of recent research endeavors, there has emerged a hiatus between this growing body of data and any larger theoretical framework. The concept of the self-fulfilling prophecy has remained simply that—a concept. The lack of a broader conceptual scheme has meant that research in this area has become theoretically stymied. Consequently, there has evolved instead a growing concern over the refinement of minute methodological nuances.

The thrust of this paper is to argue that there is a theoretical perspective developing in the social sciences which can break the conceptual and methodological logjam building up on the self-fulfilling prophecy. Specifically, the emergence of *labeling theory* as an explanatory framework for the study of social deviance appears to be applicable to the study of education as well. Among the major contributions to the development of labeling theory are Becker, 1963, 1964; Broadhead, 1974; Lemert, 1951, 1972, 1974; Douglas, 1971, 1972; Kitsuse, 1964; Lofland, 1969; Matza, 1964, 1969; Scheff, 1966; Schur, 1971; Scott and Douglas, 1972; and Rubington and Weinberg, 1973.

If the labeling perspective can be shown to be a legitimate framework from which to analyze social processes influencing the educational experience and the contributions of such processes to success or failure in school, there would then be a viable *interactionist* perspective to counter both biological and cultural determinists' theories of educational outcomes. While the latter two positions both place ultimate causality for success or failure *outside* the school, the labeling approach allows for an examination of what, in fact, is happening *within* schools. Thus, labeling theory would call our atten-

tion, for example, to the various evaluative mechanisms (both formal and informal) operant in schools, the ways in which schools nurture and support such mechanisms, how students react, what the outcomes are for interpersonal interaction based on how these mechanisms have evaluated individual students, and how, *over time,* the consequences of having a certain evaluative tag influence the options available to a student within a school. What follows first is a summary of a number of the key aspects of labeling theory as it has been most fully developed in the sociological literature; second is an attempt to integrate the research on the self-fulfilling prophecy with the conceptual framework of labeling theory. Finally, the implications of this synthesis are explored for both future research and theoretical development.

I. BECOMING DEVIANT: THE LABELING PERSPECTIVE

Those who have used labeling theory have been concerned with the study of *why* people are labeled, and *who* it is that labels them as someone who has committed one form or another of deviant behavior. In sharp contrast to the predominant approaches for the study of deviance, there is little concern in labeling theory with the motivational and characterological nature of the person who committed the act.

Deviance is understood, not as a quality of the person or as created by his actions, but instead as created by group definitions and reactions. It is a social judgment imposed by a social audience. As Becker (1963:9) has argued:

The central fact of deviance is that it is created by society. I do not mean this in the way it is ordinarily understood, in which the causes of deviance are located in the social situation of the deviant, or the social factors, which prompted his action. I mean, rather, that social groups create deviants by making the rules whose infraction constitute deviance, and by applying those rules to particular people and labeling them as outsiders. From this point of view, *deviance is not the quality of the act the person commits, but rather a consequence of the application by others of rules and sanctions to an "offender." The deviant is one to whom the label has been successfully applied. Deviant behavior is behavior that people so label.* (emphasis added)

The labeling approach is insistent on the need for a shift in attention from an exclusive concern with the deviant individual to a major concern with the *process* by which the deviant label is applied. Again citing Becker (1964:2):

The labeling approach sees deviance always and everywhere as a process and interaction between at least two kinds of people: those who commit (or who are said to have committed) a deviant act, and the rest of the society, perhaps divided into several groups itself. . . . One consequence is that we become much more interested in the process by which deviants are defined by the rest of the society, than in the nature of the deviant act itself.

The important questions, then, for Becker and others, are not of the genre to include, for example: Why do some individuals come to act out norm-violating behavior? Rather, the questions are of the following sort: Who applied the deviant label to whom? Whose rules shall prevail and be enforced? Under what circumstances is the deviant label successfully and unsuccessfully applied? How does a community decide what forms of conduct should be singled out for this kind of attention? What forms of behavior do persons in the social system consider deviant, how do they interpret such behavior, and what are the consequences of these interpretations for their reactions to individuals who are seen as manifesting such behavior? (See Akers, 1973.)

The labeling perspective rejects any assumption that a clear consensus exists as to what constitutes a norm violation—or for that matter, what constitutes a norm—within a complex and highly heterogeneous society. What comes to be determined as deviance

and who comes to be determined as a deviant is the result of a variety of social contingencies influenced by who has the power to enforce such determinations. Deviance is thus problematic and subjectively given. The case for making the societal reaction to rule-breaking a major independent variable in studies of deviant behavior has been succinctly stated by Kitsuse (1964:101):

A sociological theory of deviance must focus specifically upon the interactions which not only define behaviors as deviant, but also organize and activate the application of sanctions by individuals, groups, or agencies. For in modern society, the socially significant differentiation of deviants from the nondeviant population is increasingly contingent upon circumstances of situation, place, social and personal biography, and the bureaucratically organized activities of agencies of social control.

Traditional notions of who is a deviant and what are the causes for such deviance are necessarily reworked. By emphasizing the processual nature of deviance, any particular deviant is seen to be a product of being caught, defined, segregated, labeled, and stigmatized. *This is one of the major thrusts of the labeling perspective—that forces of social control often produce the unintended consequence of making some persons defined as deviant even more confirmed as deviant because of the stigmatization of labeling. Thus, social reactions to deviance further deviant careers.* Erikson (1966) has even gone so far as to argue that a society will strive to maintain a certain level of deviance within itself as deviance is functional to clarifying group boundaries, providing scapegoats, creating out-groups who can be the source of furthering in-group solidarity, and the like.

The idea that social control may have the paradoxical effect of generating more of the very behavior it is designed to eradicate was first elaborated upon by Tannenbaum. He noted (1938:21):

The first dramatization of the "evil" which separates the child out of his group . . . plays a greater role in making the criminal than perhaps any other experience. . . . He now lives in a different world. He has been tagged. . . . The person becomes the thing he is described as being.

Likewise, Schur (1965:4) writes:

The societal reaction to the deviant, then, is vital to an understanding of the deviance itself and a major element in—if not the cause of—the deviant behavior.

The focus on outcomes of social control mechanisms has led labeling theorists to devote considerable attention to the workings of organizations and agencies which function ostensibly to rehabilitate the violator or in other ways draw him back into conformity. Their critiques of prisons, mental hospitals, training schools, and other people-changing institutions suggest that the results of such institutions are frequently nearly the opposite of what they were theoretically designed to produce. These institutions are seen as mechanisms by which opportunities to withdraw from deviance are sealed off from the deviant, stigmatization occurs, and a new identity as a social "outsider" is generated. There thus emerges on the part of the person so labeled a new view of himself which is one of being irrevocably deviant.

This movement from one who has violated a norm to one who sees himself as a habitual norm violator is what Lemert (1972:62) terms the transition from a primary to a secondary deviant. A primary deviant is one who holds to socially accepted roles, views himself as a nondeviant, and believes himself to be an insider. A primary deviant does not deny that he has violated some norm, and claims only that it is not characteristic of him as a person. A secondary deviant, on the other hand, is one who has reorganized his social-psychological characteristics around the deviant role. Lemert (1972:62) writes:

Secondary deviation refers to a special class of socially defined responses which people make to problems created by the societal reaction to their deviance. These problems . . . become central facts of existence for those experiencing them. . . . Actions, which have these roles and self-attitudes as their referents make up secondary deviance. The secondary deviant . . . is a person whose life and identity are organized around the facts of deviance.

A person can commit repeated acts of primary deviation and never come to view himself or have others come to view him as a secondary deviant. Secondary deviation arises from the feedback whereby misconduct or deviation initiates social reaction to the behavior which then triggers further misconduct. Lemert (1951:77) first described this process as follows:

The sequence of interaction leading to secondary deviation is roughly as follows: 1) primary deviation; 2) societal penalties; 3) further primary deviation; 4) stronger penalties and rejections; 5) further deviations, perhaps with hostilities and resentments beginning to focus upon those doing the penalizing; 6) crisis reached in the tolerance quotient, expressed in formal action by the community stigmatizing of the deviant; 7) strengthening of the deviant conduct as a reaction to the stigmatizing and penalties; and 8) ultimate acceptance of deviant social status and efforts at adjustment on the basis of the associated role.

Thus, when persons engage in deviant behavior they would not otherwise participate in and when they develop social roles they would not have developed save for the application of social control measures, the outcome is the emergence of secondary deviance. The fact of having been apprehended and labeled is the critical element in the subsequent construction of a deviant identity and pursuit of a deviant career.

II. THE ORIGINS OF LABELING: TEACHER EXPECTATIONS

Labeling theory has significantly enhanced our understanding of the process of becoming deviant by shifting our attention from the deviant to the judges of deviance and the forces that affect their judgment. Such judgments are critical, for a recurrent decision made in all societies, and particularly frequent in advanced industrial societies, is that an individual has or has not mastered some body of information, or perhaps more basically, has or has not the capacity to master that information. These evaluations are made periodically as one moves through the institution of school and the consequences directly affect the opportunities to remain for an additional period. To be able to remain provides an option for mastering yet another body of information, and to be certified as having done so. As Ivan Illich (1971) has noted, it is in industrial societies that being perceived as a legitimate judge of such mastery has become restricted to those who carry the occupational role of "teacher." A major consequence of the professionalization of the role of teacher has been the ability to claim as a near exclusive decision whether mastery of material has occurred. Such exclusionary decision-making enhances those in the role of "teacher" as they alone come to possess the authority to provide certification for credentials (Edgar, 1974).

Labeling theorists report that in making judgments of deviance, persons may employ information drawn from a variety of sources. Further, even persons within the same profession (therapists, for example) may make divergent use of the same material in arriving at an evaluative decision on the behavior of an individual. Among the sources of information available to labelers, two appear primary: first-hand information obtained from face-to-face interaction with the person they may ultimately label, and second-hand information obtained from other than direct interaction.

The corollary here to the activities of teachers should be apparent. Oftentimes, the evaluation by teachers (which may lead to the label of "bright," "slow," etc.) is based on first-hand information gained through face-to-face interaction during the course of the time the teacher and student spent together in the classroom. But a goodly amount of information about the student which informs the teacher's evaluation is second-hand information. For instance, comments from other teachers, test scores, prior report cards, permanent records, meetings with the parents, or evaluations from welfare agencies and psychological clinics are all potential informational sources. In a variation of the division between first-hand and second-hand sources of information, Johnson (1973) has suggested that there are three key determinants of teacher evaluations: student's prior performance, social status characteristics, and present performance. Prior performance would include information from cumulative records (grades, test scores, notes from past teachers or counselors, and outside evaluators) while social status and performance would be inferred and observed in the on-going context of the classroom.

What has been particularly captivating about the work of Rosenthal and Jacobson (1968) in this regard is their attempt to provide empirical justification for a truism considered self-evident by many in education: School achievement is not simply a matter of a child's native ability, but involves directly and inextricably the teacher as well. Described succinctly, their research involved a situation where, at the end of a school year, more than 500 students in a single elementary school were administered the "Harvard Test of Inflected Acquisition." In actuality this test was a standardized, relatively nonverbal test of intelligence, Flanagan's (1960) Test of General Ability (TOGA). The teachers were told that such a test would, with high predictive reliability, sort out those students who gave strong indication of being intellectual "spurters" or "bloomers" during the following academic year. Just before the beginning of school the following fall, the teachers were given lists with the names of between one and nine of their students. They were told that these students scored in the top twenty percent of the school on the test, though, of course, no factual basis for such determinations existed. A twenty percent subsample of the "special" students was selected for intensive analysis. Testing of the students at the end of the school year offered some evidence that these selected children did perform better than the nonselected. The ensuing debate as to the validity and implications of the findings from the study will be discussed in the next section.

The findings of Deutsch, Fishman, Kogan, North, and Whiteman (1964); Gibson (1965); Goslin and Glass (1967); McPherson (1966); and Pequignot (1966) all demonstrate the influence of standardized tests of intelligence and achievement on teacher's expectations. Goaldman (1971), in a review of the literature on the use of tests as a second-hand source of information for teachers, noted: "Although some of the research has been challenged, there is a basis for the belief that teachers at all levels are prejudiced by information they receive about a student's ability or character." Mehan (1971, 1974) has been concerned with the interaction between children who take tests and the teachers who administer them. He posits that testing is not the objective use of a measurement instrument, but the outcome of a set of interactional activities which are influenced by a variety of contingencies which ultimately manifest themselves in a reified "test score." Mehan suggests (1971):

Standardized test performances are taken as an unquestioned, non-problematic reflection of the child's underlying ability. The authority of the test to measure the child's real ability is accepted by both teachers and other school officials. Test results are accepted without doubt as the correct and valid document of the child's ability.

Characteristics of children such as sex and race are immediately apparent to teachers. Likewise, indications of status can be quickly inferred from grooming, style of dress, need for free lunches, information on enrollment cards, discussion of family activities by children, and visits to the school by parents. One intriguing study recently reported in this area is that by two sociologists, Clifford and Walster (1973:249). The substance of their study was described as follows:

Our experiment was designed to determine what effect a student's physical attractiveness has on a teacher's expectations of the child's intellectual and social behavior. Our hypothesis was that a child's attractiveness strongly influences his teachers' judgments; the more attractive the child, the more biased in his favor we expect the teachers to be. The design required to test this hypothesis is a simple one: Teachers are given a standardized report card and an attached photograph. The report card includes an assessment of the child's academic performance as well as of his general social behavior. The attractiveness of the photos is experimentally varied. On the basis of this information, teachers are asked to state their expectations of the child's educational and social potential.

Based on the responses of 404 fifth grade teachers within the state of Missouri, Clifford and Walster concluded (1973:255):

There is little question but that the physical appearance of a student affected the expectations of the teachers we studied. Regardless of whether the pupil is a boy or girl, the child's physical attractiveness has an equally strong association with his teacher's reactions to him.

The variables of race and ethnicity have been documented, by Brown (1968), Davidson and Lang (1960), Jackson and Cosca (1974), and Rubovits and Maehr (1973), among others, as powerful factors in generating the expectations teachers hold of children. It has also been documented that teachers expect less of lower-class children than they do of middle-class children (cf. Becker, 1952; Deutsch, 1963; Leacock, 1969; Rist, 1970, 1973; Stein, 1971; Warner, Havighurst, and Loeb, 1944; and

Wilson, 1963). Douglas (1964), in a large scale study of the tracking system used in British schools, found that children who were clean and neatly dressed in nice clothing, and who came from what the teachers perceived as "better" homes, tended to be placed in higher tracks than their measured ability would predict. Further, when placed there they tended to stay and perform acceptably. Mackler (1969) studied schools in Harlem and found that children tended to stay in the tracks in which they were initially placed and that such placement was based on a variety of social considerations independent of measured ability. Doyle, Hancock, and Kifer (1971) and Palardy (1969) have shown teacher expectations for high performance in elementary grades to be stronger for girls than boys.

The on-going academic and interpersonal performance of the children may also serve as a potent source of expectations for teachers. Rowe (1969) found that teachers would wait longer for an answer from a student they believed to be a high achiever than for one from a student they believed to be a low achiever. Brophy and Good (1970) found that teachers were more likely to give perceived high achieving students a second chance to respond to an initial incorrect answer, and further, that high achievers were praised more frequently for success and criticized less for failure.

There is evidence that the expectations teachers hold for their students can be generated as early as the first few days of the school year and then remain stable over the months to follow (Rist, 1970, 1972, 1973; Willis, 1972). For example, I found during my three-year longitudinal and ethnographic study of a single, *de facto* segregated elementary school in the black community of St. Louis, that after only eight days of kindergarten, the teacher made permanent seating arrangements based on what she assumed were variations in academic capability. But no formal evaluation of the children had

taken place. Instead, the assignments to the three tables were based on a number of socio-economic criteria as well as on early interaction patterns in the classroom. Thus, the placement of the children came to reflect the social class distinctions in the room—the poor children from public welfare families all sat at one table, the working class children sat at another and the middle class at the third. I demonstrated how the teacher operationalized her expectations of these different groups of children in terms of her differentials of teaching time, her use of praise and control, and the extent of autonomy within the classroom. By following the same children through first and second grade as well, I was able to show that the initial patterns established by the kindergarten teacher came to be perpetuated year after year. By second grade, labels given by another teacher clearly reflected the reality each of the three groups experienced in the school. The top group was called the "Tigers," the middle group the "Cardinals," and the lowest group, the "Clowns." What had begun as a subjective evaluation and labeling by the teacher took on objective dimensions as the school proceeded to process the children on the basis of the distinctions made when they first began.

Taken together, these studies strongly imply that the notion of "teacher expectations" is multi-faceted and multi-dimensional. It appears that when teachers generate expectations about their students, they do so not only for reasons of academic or cognitive performance, but for their classroom interactional patterns as well. Furthermore, not only ascribed characteristics such as race, sex, class, or ethnicity are highly salient, interpersonal traits are also. Thus, the interrelatedness of the various attributes which ultimately blend together to generate the evaluation a teacher makes as to what can be expected from a particular student suggests the strength and tenacity of such subsequent labels as "bright" or "slow" or "trouble-maker" or "teacher's little helper."

It is to the outcomes of the student's having one or another of these labels that we now turn.

III. AN OUTCOME OF LABELING: THE SELF-FULFILLING PROPHECY

W. I. Thomas, many years ago, set forth what has become a basic dictum of the social sciences when he observed, "If men define situations as real, they are real in their consequences." This is at the core of the self-fulfilling prophecy. An expectation which defines a situation comes to influence the actual behavior within the situation so as to produce what was initially assumed to be there. Merton (1968:477) has elaborated on this concept and noted: "The self-fulfilling prophecy is, in the beginning, a *false* definition of the situation evoking a new behavior which makes the originally false conception come true." (emphasis in the original)

Here it is important to recall a basic tenet of labeling theory—that an individual does not become deviant simply by the commission of some act. As Becker (1963) stressed, deviance is not inherent in behavior *per se*, but in the application by others of rules and sanctions against one perceived as being an "offender." Thus, the only time one can accurately be termed a "deviant" is after the successful application of a label by a social audience. Thus, though many persons may commit norm violations, only select ones are subsequently labeled. The contingencies of race, class, sex, visibility of behavior, age, occupation, and who one's friends are all influence the outcome as to whether one is or is not labeled. Scheff (1966), for example, demonstrated the impact of these contingencies upon the diagnosis as to the severity of a patient's mental illness. The higher one's social status, the less the willingness to diagnose the same behavioral traits as indicative of serious illness in comparison to the diagnosis given to low status persons.

The crux of the labeling perspective lies not in whether one's norm violating behavior is known, but in whether others decide to do something about it. Further, if a label is applied to the individual, it is posited that this in fact causes the individual to become that which he is labeled as being. Due to the reaction of society, the change in the individual involves the development of a new socialized self-concept and social career centered around the deviant behavior. As Rubington and Weinberg (1973:7) have written:

The person who has been typed, in turn, becomes aware of the new definition that has been placed upon him by members of his groups. He, too, takes this new understanding of himself into account when dealing with them. . . . When this happens, a social type has been ratified, and a person has been socially reconstructed.

As noted, Rosenthal and Jacobson's *Pygmalion in the Classroom* (1968) created wide interest in the notion of the self-fulfilling prophecy as a concept to explain differential performance by children in classrooms. Their findings suggested that the expectations teachers created about the children randomly selected as "intellectual bloomers" somehow caused the teachers to treat them differently, with the result that the children really did perform better by the end of the year. Though the critics of this particular research (Snow, 1969; Taylor, 1970; Thorndike, 1968, 1969) and those who have been unsuccessful in replicating the findings (Claiborn, 1969) have leveled strong challenges to Rosenthal and Jacobson, the disagreements are typically related to methodology, procedure, and analysis rather than to the proposition that relations exist between expectations and behavior.

The current status of the debate and the evidence accumulated in relation to it imply that teacher expectations are *sometimes* self-fulfilling. The early and, I think, over-enthusiastic accounts of Rosenthal and Jacobson have obscured the issue. The gist of such accounts have left the impression, as

Good and Brophy (1973:73) have noted, that the mere existence of an expectation will automatically guarantee its fulfillment. Rather, as they suggest:

The fact that teachers' expectations can be self-fulfilling is simply a special case of the principle that any expectations can be self-fulfilling. This process is not confined to classrooms. Although it is not true that "wishing can make it so," our expectations do affect the way we behave in situations, and the way we behave affects how other people respond. In some instances, our expectations about people cause us to treat them in a way that makes them respond just as we expect they would.

Such a position would be borne out by social psychologists who have demonstrated that an individual's first impressions of another person do influence subsequent interactions (Dailey, 1952; Newcomb, 1947) and that one's self-expectations influence one's subsequent behavior (Aronson and Carlsmith, 1962; Brock and Edelman, 1965; and Zajonc and Brinkman, 1969).

The conditionality of expectations related to their fulfillment is strongly emphasized by labeling theorists as well. Their emphasis upon the influence of social contingencies on whether one is labeled, how strong the label, and if it can be made to stick at all, points to a recognition that there is a social process involved where individuals are negotiating, rejecting, accepting, modifying, and reinterpreting the attempts at labeling. Such interaction is apparent in the eight stages of the development of secondary deviance outlined above by Lemert. Likewise, Erikson (1964:17), in his comments on the act of labeling as a rite of passage from one side of the group boundary to the other, has noted:

The common assumption that deviants are not often cured or reformed, then, may be based on a faulty premise, but this assumption is stated so frequently and with such conviction that it often creates the facts which later "prove" it to be correct. If the returning deviant has to face the commu-

nity's apprehensions often enough, it is understandable that he, too, may begin to wonder whether he has graduated from the deviant role—and *so respond to the uncertainty by resuming deviant activity.* In some respects, this may be the only way for the individual and his community to agree as to what kind of person he really is, for it often happens that the community is only able to perceive his "true colors" when he lapses momentarily into some form of deviant performance. (emphasis added)

Explicit in Erikson's quote is the fact of the individual's being in interaction with the "community" to achieve some sort of agreement on what the person is "really" like. Though Erikson did not, in this instance, elaborate upon what he meant by "community," it can be inferred from elsewhere in his work that he sees "community" as manifesting itself in the institutions persons create in order to help organize and structure their lives. Such a perspective is clearly within the framework of labeling theory, where a major emphasis has been placed upon the role of institutions in sorting, labeling, tracking, and channeling persons along various routes depending upon the assessment the institution has made of the individual.

One pertinent example of the manner in which labeling theory has been applied to the study of social institutions and their impact upon participants has been in an analysis of the relation of schooling to juvenile delinquency. There have been several works which suggest as a major line of argument that schools, through and because of the manner in which they label students, serve as a chief instrument in the creation of delinquency (Hirschi, 1969; Noblit and Polk, 1975; Polk, 1969; Polk and Schafer, 1972; Schafer and Olexa, 1971). For example, Noblit and Polk (1975:3) have noted:

In as much as the school is the primary institution in the adolescent experience—one that promises not only the future status available to the adolescent, but also that gives or denies status in adolescence itself—it can be expected that its definitions are of particular significance for the actions of youth. That is, the student who has been sorted from success via the school has little reason to conform to the often arbitrary and paternalistic regulations and rules of the school. In a very real sense, this student has no "rational constraints" against deviance. It is through the sorting mechanisms of the school, which are demanded by institutions of higher education and the world of work, that youth are labeled and thus sorted into the situation where deviant behavior threatens little while providing some alternative forms of status.

It is well to reiterate the point—interaction implies behavior and choices being made by both parties. The person facing the prospect of receiving a new label imputing a systemic change in the definition of his selfhood may respond in any of a myriad number of ways to this situation. Likewise, the institutional definition of the person is neither finalized nor solidified until the end of the negotiation as to what precisely that label should be. But, in the context of a single student facing the authority and vested interests of a school administration and staff, the most likely outcome is that over time, the student will increasingly move towards conformity with the label the institution seeks to establish. Good and Brophy (1973:75) have elaborated upon this process within the classroom as follows:

1. The teacher expects specific behavior and achievement from particular students.
2. Because of these different expectations, the teacher behaves differently toward the different students.
3. This teacher treatment tells each student what behavior and achievement the teacher expects from him and affects his self-concept, achievement motivation, and level of aspiration.
4. If this teacher treatment is consistent over time, and if the student does not actively resist or change it in some way, it will tend to shape his achievement and behavior. High-expectation students will be led to achieve at high levels, while the achievement of low-expectations students will decline.
5. With time, the student's achievement and behavior will conform more and more closely to that originally expected of him.

The fourth point in this sequence makes the crucial observation that teacher expectations are not automatically self-fulfilling. For the expectations of the teacher to become realized, both the teacher and the student must move towards a pattern of interaction where expectations are clearly communicated and the behavioral response is consonant with the expected patterns. But as Good and Brophy (1973:75) also note:

This does not always happen. The teacher may not have clear-cut expectations about a particular student, or his expectations may continually change. Even when he has consistent expectations, he may not necessarily communicate them to the student through consistent behavior. In this case, the expectation would not be self-fulfilling even if it turned out to be correct. Finally, the student himself might prevent expectations from becoming self-fulfilling by overcoming them or by resisting them in a way that makes the teacher change them.

Yet, the critique of American education offered by such scholars as Henry (1963), Katz (1971), Goodman (1964), or Reimer (1971), suggests the struggle is unequal between the teacher (and the institution a teacher represents) and the student. The vulnerability of children to the dictates of adults in positions of power over them leaves the negotiations as to what evaluative definition will be tagged on the children more often than not in the hands of the powerful. As Max Weber himself stated, to have power is to be able to achieve one's ends, even in the face of resistance from others. When that resistance is manifested in school by children and is defined by teachers and administrators as truancy, recalcitrance, unruliness, and hostility, or conversely defined as a lack of motivation, intellectual apathy, sullenness, passivity, or withdrawal, the process is ready to be repeated and the options to escape further teacher definitions are increasingly removed.

POSTSCRIPT: BEYOND THE LOGJAM

This paper has argued that a fruitful convergence can be effected between the research being conducted on the self-fulfilling prophecy as a consequence of teacher expectations and the conceptual framework of labeling theory. The analysis of the outcomes of teacher expectations produces results highly similar to those found in the study of social deviance. Labels are applied to individuals which fundamentally shift their definitions of self and which further reinforce the behavior which had initially prompted the social reaction. The impact of the self-fulfilling prophecy in educational research is comparable to that found in the analysis of mental health clinics, asylums, prisons, juvenile homes, and other people-changing organizations. What the labeling perspective can provide to the study of educational outcomes as a result of the operationalization of teacher expectations is a model for the study of the *processes* by which the outcomes are produced. The detailing over time of the interactional patterns which lead to changes in self-definition and behavior within classrooms is sadly lacking in almost all of the expectation research to date. A most glaring example of this omission is the study by Rosenthal and Jacobson themselves. Their conclusions are based only on the analysis of a pre- and post-test. To posit that teacher expectations were the causal variable that produced changes in student performances was a leap from the data to speculation. They could offer only suggestions as to how the measured changes in the children's performance came about, since they were not in the classrooms to observe how assumed teacher attitudes were translated into subsequent actual student behavior.

To extend the research on the educational experiences of those students who are differentially labeled by teachers, what is needed is a theoretical framework which can clearly isolate the influences and effects of certain kinds of teacher reactions on certain types of students, producing certain typical outcomes. The labeling perspective appears particularly well-suited for this expansion of both research and theoretical development on teacher expectations by offering the basis for analysis at either a specific or a more general level. With the former, for example, there are areas of investigation related to 1) types of students perceived by teachers as prone to success or failure; 2) the kinds of reactions, based on their expectations, teachers have to different students; and 3) the effects of specific teacher reactions on specific student outcomes. At a more general level, fruitful lines of inquiry might include 1) the outcomes in the post-school world of having received a negative vs. a positive label within the school; 2) the influences of factors such as social class and race on the categories of expectations teachers hold; 3) how and why labels do emerge in schools as well as the phenomenological and structural meanings that are attached to them; and 4) whether there are means by which to modify or minimize the effects of school labeling processes on students.

Labeling theory provides a conceptual framework by which to understand the processes of transforming attitudes into behavior and the outcomes of having done so. To be able to detail the dynamics and influences within schools by which some children come to see themselves as successful and act as though they were, and to detail how others come to see themselves as failures and act accordingly, provides in the final analysis an opportunity to intervene so as to expand the numbers of winners and diminish the numbers of losers. For that reason above all others, labeling theory merits our attention.

NOTE

1. The preparation of this paper has been aided by a grant (GS-41522) from the National Science Foundation—Sociology Program. The views expressed here are solely those of the author and no

official endorsement by either the National Science Foundation or the National Institute of Education is to be inferred.

REFERENCES

Akers, R. L. *Deviant Behavior: A Social Learning Approach.* Belmont, Cal.: Wadsworth, 1973.

Aronson, E., and Carlsmith, J. M. "Performance Expectancy as a Determinant of Actual Performance." *Journal of Abnormal and Social Psychology* 65 (1962): 179–182.

Becker, H. S. "Social Class Variations in the Teacher-Pupil Relationship." *Journal of Educational Sociology* 25 (1952):451–465.

Becker, H. S. *Outsiders.* New York: The Free Press, 1963.

Becker, H. S. *The Other Side.* New York: The Free Press, 1964.

Broadhead, R. S. "A Theoretical Critique of the Societal Reaction Approach to Deviance." *Pacific Sociological Review* 17 (1974):287–312.

Brock, T. C., and Edelman, H. "Seven Studies of Performance Expectancy as a Determinant of Actual Performance." *Journal of Experimental Social Psychology* 1 (1965):295–310.

Brophy, J., and Good, T. "Teachers' Communications of Differential Expectations for Children's Classroom Performance: Some Behavioral Data." *Journal of Educational Psychology* 61 (1970):365–374.

Brown, B. *The Assessment of Self-Concept among Four Year Old Negro and White Children: A Comparative Study Using the Brown IDS Self-Concept Reference Test.* New York: Institute for Developmental Studies, 1968.

Claiborn, W. L. "Expectancy Effects in the Classroom: A Failure to Replicate." *Journal of Educational Psychology* 60 (1969):377–383.

Clifford, M. M., and Walster, E. "The Effect of Physical Attractiveness on Teacher Expectations." *Sociology of Education* 46 (1973):248–258.

Dailey, C. A. "The Effects of Premature Conclusion upon the Acquisition of Understanding of a Person." *Journal of Psychology* 33 (1952):133–152.

Davidson, H. H., and Lang, G. "Children's Perceptions of Teachers' Feelings toward Them." *Journal of Experimental Education* 29 (1960):107–118.

Deutsch, M. "The Disadvantaged Child and the Learning Process," in *Education in Depressed Areas,* edited by H. Passow. New York: Teachers College Press, 1963.

Deutsch, M.; Fishman, J. A.; Kogan, L.; North, R.; and Whiteman, M. "Guidelines for Testing Minority Group Children." *Journal of Social Issues* 20 (1964):129–145.

Douglas, J. *The Home and the School.* London: MacGibbon and Kee, 1964.

Douglas, J. *The American Social Order.* New York: The Free Press, 1971.

Douglas, J. (ed.). *Deviance and Respectability.* New York: Basic Books, 1972.

Doyle, W.; Hancock, G.; and Kifer, E. "Teachers' Perceptions: Do They Make a Difference?" Paper presented at the meeting of the American Educational Research Association, 1971.

Edgar, D. E. *The Competent Teacher.* Sydney, Australia: Angus & Robertson, 1974.

Erikson, K. T. "Note on the Sociology of Deviance," in *The Other Side,* edited by H. S. Becker. New York: The Free Press, 1964.

Erikson, K. T. *Wayward Puritans.* New York: Wiley, 1966.

Flanagan, J. C. *Test of General Ability: Technical Report.* Chicago: Science Research Associates, 1960.

Gibson, G. "Aptitude Tests." *Science* 149 (1965):583.

Goaldman, L. "Counseling Methods and Techniques: The Use of Tests," in *The Encyclopedia of Education,* edited by L. C. Deighton. New York: MacMillan, 1971.

Good, T., and Brophy, J. *Looking in Classrooms.* New York: Harper and Row, 1973.

Goodman, P. *Compulsory Mis-Education.* New York: Random House, 1964.

Goslin, D. A., and Glass, D. C. "The Social Effects of Standardized Testing on American Elementary Schools." *Sociology of Education* 40 (1967):115–131.

Henry, J. *Culture Against Man.* New York: Random House, 1963.

Hirschi, T. *Causes of Delinquency.* Berkeley: University of California Press, 1969.

Illich, I. *Deschooling Society.* New York: Harper & Row, 1971.

Jackson, G., and Cosca, C. "The Inequality of Educational Opportunity in the Southwest: An Observational Study of Ethnically Mixed Classrooms." *American Educational Research Journal* 11 (1974): 219–229.

Johnson, J. *On the Interface between Low-income Urban Black Children and Their Teachers during the Early School Years: A Position Paper.* San Francisco: Far West Laboratory for Educational Research and Development, 1973.

Katz, M. *Class, Bureaucracy and Schools.* New York: Praeger, 1971.

Kitsuse, J. "Societal Reaction to Deviant Behavior: Problems of Theory and Method," in *The Other Side,* edited by H. S. Becker. New York: The Free Press, 1964.

Leacock, E. *Teaching and Learning in City Schools.* New York: Basic Books, 1969.

Lemert, E. *Social Pathology.* New York: McGraw-Hill, 1951.

Lemert, E. *Human Deviance, Social Problems and Social Control.* Englewood Cliffs, N.J.: Prentice-Hall, 1972.

Lemert, E. "Beyond Mead: The Societal Reaction to Deviance." *Social Problems* 21 (1974):457–468.

Lofland, J. *Deviance and Identity.* Englewood Cliffs, N.J.: Prentice-Hall, 1969.

Mackler, B. "Grouping in the Ghetto." *Education and Urban Society* 2 (1969): 80–95.

Matza, D. *Delinquency and Drift.* New York: Wiley, 1964.

Matza, D. *Becoming Deviant.* Englewood Cliffs, N.J.: Prentice-Hall, 1969.

McPherson, G.H. *The Role-set of the Elementary School Teacher: A case study.* Unpublished Ph.D. dissertation, Columbia University, New York, 1966.

Mehan, H. B. *Accomplishing Understanding in Educational Settings.* Unpublished Ph.D. dissertation, University of California, Santa Barbara, 1971.

Mehan, H. B. *Ethnomethodology and Education.* Paper presented to the Sociology of Education Association conference, Pacific Grove, California, 1974.

Merton, R. K. "Social Problems and Social Theory," in *Contemporary Social Problems,* edited by R. Merton and R. Nisbet. New York: Harcourt, Brace and World, 1968.

Newcomb, T. M. "Autistic Hostility and Social Reality." *Human Relations* 1 (1947):69–86.

Noblit, G. W., and Polk, K. *Institutional Constraints and Labeling.* Paper presented to the Southern Sociological Association meetings, Washington, D.C., 1975.

Palardy, J. M. "What Teachers Believe–What Children Achieve." *Elementary School Journal,* 1969, pp. 168–169 and 370–374.

Pequignot, H. "L'équation personnelle du juge." In *Semaine des Hopitaux* (Paris), 1966.

Polk, K. "Class, Strain, and Rebellion and Adolescents." *Social Problems* 17 (1969):214–224.

Polk, K., and Schafer, W. E. *Schools and Delinquency.* Englewood Cliffs, N.J.: Prentice-Hall, 1972.

Reimer, E. *School is Dead.* New York: Doubleday, 1971.

Rist, R. C. "Student Social Class and Teachers' Expectations: The Self-fulfilling Prophecy in Ghetto Education." *Harvard Educational Review* 40 (1970):411–450.

Rist, R. C. "Social Distance and Social Inequality in a Kindergarten Classroom: An Examination of the 'Cultural Gap' Hypothesis." *Urban Education* 7 (1972): 241–260.

Rist, R. C. *The Urban School: A Factory for Failure.* Cambridge, Mass.: The M. I. T. Press, 1973.

Rosenthal, R., and Jacobson, L. "Teachers' Expectancies: Determinants of Pupils' IQ Gains." *Psychology Reports* 19 (1966): 115–118.

Rosenthal, R., and Jacobson, L. *Pygmalion in the Classroom.* New York: Holt, Rinehart, and Winston, 1968.

Rowe, M. "Science, Silence and Sanctions." *Science and Children* 6 (1969):11–13.

Rubington, E., and Weinberg, M. S. *Deviance: The Interactionist Perspective.* New York: MacMillan, 1973.

Rubovits, P., and Maehr, M. L. "Pygmalion Black and white." *Journal of Personality and Social Psychology* 2 (1973): 210–218.

Schafer, W. E., and Olexa, C. *Tracking and*

Opportunity. Scranton, Pa.: Chandler, 1971.

Scheff, T. *Being Mentally Ill.* Chicago: Aldine, 1966.

Schur, E. *Crimes without Victims.* Englewood Cliffs, N.J.: Prentice-Hall, 1965.

Schur, E. *Labeling Deviant Behavior.* New York: Harper and Row, 1971.

Scott, R. A., and Douglas, J. C. (eds.). *Theoretical Perspectives on Deviance.* New York: Basic Books, 1972.

Snow, R. E. "Unfinished Pygmalion." *Contemporary Psychology* 14 (1969):197–199.

Stein, A. "Strategies for Failure." *Harvard Educational Review* 41 (1971):158–204.

Tannenbaum, F. *Crime and the Community.* New York: Columbia University Press, 1938.

Taylor, C. "The Expectations of Pygmalion's Creators." *Educational Leadership* 28 (1970):161–164.

Thorndike, R. L. "Review of *Pygmalion in the Classroom.*" *Educational Research Journal* 5 (1968):708–711.

Thorndike, R. L. "But Do You Have to Know How to Tell Time?" *Educational Research Journal* 6 (1969):692.

Warner, W. L.; Havighurst, R.; and Loeb, M. B. *Who Shall be Educated?* New York: Harper & Row, 1944.

Willis, S. *Formation of Teachers' Expectations of Student Academic Performance.* Unpublished Ph.D. dissertation, University of Texas, Austin, Texas, 1972.

Wilson, A. B. "Social Stratification and Academic Achievement," in *Education in Depressed Areas,* edited by H. Passow. New York: Teachers College Press, 1963.

Zajonc, R. B., and Brinkman, P. "Expectancy and Feedback as Independent Factors in Task Performance." *Journal of Personality and Social Psychology* 11 (1969):148–150.

EDUCATION, "HUMAN CAPITAL," AND THE LABOR MARKET

Advanced economies, whatever their political structures and cultural traditions, all seem to have been characterized in recent years both by increasing capital/labor ratios and by a relative increase in the number of professional and technical occupations accompanied by a relative decrease in unskilled labor. At the same time, though not to be exaggerated, the link between education and occupational status has shown a trend towards tightening, especially at the point of entry of young people into the labor market. Human capital theory, which views education as a form of investment, offers an explanation of this phenomenon. But the wider problem of the historical and developmental relation between education and labor markets remains highly contentious, as does the more limited problem of explaining the well-known positive correlation between education and earnings.

A classical formulation of the theory of human capital, which according to Mark Blaug[1] marks "the 'birth' of the economics of education," is contained in Theodore W. Schultz's presidential address to the Annual Meeting of the American Economic Association in December 1960 (Chapter 16). The thrust of Schultz's argument is that education, in addition to being a form of consumption, is also an individually and socially productive investment. From this perspective, laborers can be considered capitalists, for their investment in the acquisition of knowledge and skill has given them ownership of economically valuable capacities. Low earnings, especially those of members of minority groups, reflect, according to Schultz, inadequate investment in their health and education.

In the early 1960s the theory of human capital was, for reasons we have discussed in the Introduction to this volume, clearly ascendant in academic and policy circles, especially in the United States. The Organization for Economic Cooperation and Development, a Paris-based organization of advanced capitalist countries dedicated to the encouragement of economic growth, played a particularly important role in disseminating the ideas of human capital theorists. At a 1961 OECD conference held in Washington, D.C., which brought together academics and government policy-makers, it was argued that investment in education facilitated economic growth in two ways: by fostering technological innovation and by

---

1. Mark Blaug, ed., *Economics of Education*, Volume 1 (Baltimore, Md.: Penguin Books, 1968), p. 11.

307

increasing the productivity of labor.[2] In 1964, the OECD published Edward F. Denison's widely influential *Measuring the Contribution of Education (and the Residual) to Economic Growth*. Denison argues that investment in education brings higher returns than investment in physical capital and that an increase in educational expenditures is accordingly a highly effective means of increasing the Gross National Product.[3]

Throughout the 1960s the theory of human capital continued to serve as both a guideline and a justification for rising educational expenditures, but by the end of the decade doubts began to arise about a number of its assumptions—particularly that higher earnings reflect greater marginal productivity and that national differences in rates of economic growth can be causally attributed to varying degrees of educational investment. Further, critics began to question the assumption of human capital theorists that labor markets actually conform to the classical model of perfect competition. By 1975, proponents of human capital theory were on the defensive; a conference held in January of that year at OECD, which had only fourteen years earlier given impetus to the idea of greater investment in education at its Washington meeting, sharply questioned whether increased expenditures on education were an effective means of achieving either economic growth or social equality.[4]

As formulated by Schultz, Denison, Becker,[5] and others, the theory of human capital was replete with policy implications. Prominent among these was the suggestion that greater investment in the human capital characteristics of low-income individuals would be an effective strategy for abolishing poverty. The results of this strategy are examined in Chapter 18 by Barry Bluestone. According to him, the anti-poverty policies inspired by the theory of human capital—primarily manpower training and human-resources development—yielded meager results because they neglected the *structure* of the economy and deflected attention toward the characteristics of individuals. Poor people, Bluestone argues, often do possess a considerable amount of human capital, but suffer from low wages because they occupy job slots in low-wage industries or are unable to find any work at all.[6] Resolution of the problem of poverty, he suggests, depends less upon greater investment in human capital than upon the creation of an adequate supply of good jobs.

The debate over human capital theory raises the question whether the strategy of educational expansion has had any effect at all on income distribution. Lester Thurow shows in Chapter 17 that, in the case of the United States, educational attainment (as measured by years of schooling completed) has become more equal over the last quarter of a century while income inequality has remained much the same. Although it remains possible that the distribution of income might have become more unequal in the absence of an equalization of educational attainment, this apparent paradox nonetheless requires an explanation. Thurow's own analysis suggests that the assumptions made by human capital theorists about the way that labor markets work may be at fault.

2. The proceedings of this conference are reported in OECD, *Policy Conference on Economic Growth and Investment in Education* (Paris, 1962).
3. Edward F. Denison, *Measuring the Contribution of Education (and the Residual) to Economic Growth* (Paris: OECD, 1964). See also Denison's "The Sources of Economic Growth in the United States and the Alternatives Before Us," Supplementary Paper Number 13 (New York: Committee for Economic Development, 1962), and his study (with J.P. Poullier), *Why Growth Rates Differ* (Washington: The Brookings Institution, 1967).
4. The proceedings of this conference are reported in OECD, *Education, Inequality and Life Chances* (Paris, 1975).
5. Gary S. Becker, *Human Capital* (New York: National Bureau of Economic Research, 1964).
6. For empirical evidence on the relative effects of educational level and industry type on wages, see Barry Bluestone, William Murphy, and Mary Stevenson, "Education and Industry," in *Schooling in a Corporate Society*, ed. Martin Carnoy (New York: David McKay, 1975), pp. 161–173.

In place of the traditional wage competition approach, Thurow offers a job competition view of labor markets. In this model the employer is assumed to choose among applicants with a view towards minimizing the cost of training within the enterprise. Workers are thought of as forming a queue, those at the head of the queue requiring lower training costs. Thus, if the supply of highly educated labor increases, highly qualified workers do not compete exclusively with one another for jobs that are held to require a given level of training. Instead, some are forced back in the queue and have to take jobs that otherwise would have gone to less qualified people. In this way graduates may receive lower wages, but this is also true for those with less education as they too are pushed further back in the queue. Meanwhile, the differentials between educational groups may remain the same.[7]

A positive correlation between education and income has been demonstrated in more than thirty countries.[8] Yet if this correlation is a widely documented fact, the issue remains as to how to explain it. For human capital theory, the key to an explanation resides in the contribution that the content of education, particularly in its creation of cognitive skills, makes to marginal productivity. But there are alternative explanations for the greater earning power of educated laborers. A hypothesis put forward by Gintis[9] is that educational qualifications reflect personality characteristics that employers seek in their employees. He suggests that what is important to employers about education is not so much that it provides technical training as that it socializes for docile and efficient adaptation to work in bureaucratic and industrial hierarchies. Education does, in his view, make a contribution to productivity, but this contribution is primarily indirect. In a more recent formulation of this argument, Bowles and Gintis stress the role of education in fragmenting the labor force and in legitimating and reproducing the power structure of the firm.[10]

Other writers, however, challenge the thesis that education is related to productivity either directly or indirectly. Ivar Berg, for example, in *Education and Jobs: The Great Training Robbery,* has put forward a theory of credentialism. In his view, educational expansion adds little to worker productivity. Oversupply of the educated merely leads to upgrading of the qualifications required for entry to an increasing range of professional and technical occupations. But, as Angus Maddison has commented, "even if we accept Berg's hypothesis that there is a tendency to upgrade paper qualifications demanded for particular jobs in conditions of excess supply, this does not mean that the process of educational expansion will snowball indefinitely. If this did occur on a large scale, relative earnings of the more highly educated would decline, for Berg does not suggest that employers upgrade pay to match increased paper qualifications. The fall in earnings would presumably act as a signal and deter some entrants to the higher levels of education. The recent falling off in the growth rate for

7. For an elaboration of Thurow's model see Lester C. Thurow and Robert E.B. Lucas, *The American Distribution of Income: A Structural Problem,* Hearings before the Joint Economic Committee of the Congress of the United States (Washington: U.S. Government Printing Office, March 1972). For a critique of Thurow's model that argues that it fails to explain why labor supply plays no role in wage determination or why, within the framework of queuing theory, eager workers do not bid down wages, see Michael A. Carter and Martin Carnoy, "Theories of Labor Markets and Worker Productivity" (Palo Alto, Cal.: Center for Economic Studies, August 1974), pp. 18–20.
8. George Psacharopoulos, *Returns to Education: An International Comparison* (Amsterdam: Elsevier, 1973). Most economists dismiss Jencks's estimation of the correlation between education and earnings as too low because it does not standardize for such variables as age and region. See Psacharopoulos, "Review of *Inequality,*" *Comparative Education Review* 18 (October 1974): 446–450.
9. Herbert Gintis, "Education, Technology, and the Characteristics of Worker Productivity," *American Economic Review* 61 (May 1971): 266–279.
10. Samuel Bowles and Herbert Gintis, "The Problem with Human Capital Theory—A Marxian Critique," *American Economic Review* 65 (May 1975): 74–82.

new entrants to universities shows that there are some self adjusting mechanisms which make the snowball view unrealistic in its extreme forms."[11]

In an alternative model of "screening," education is also assumed to make no contribution to productivity.[12] Here the idea is that the character qualities required for success in education are also those that produce good workers. Thus employers can use educational credentials as screening devices to identify the most productive workers and to save themselves the cost of inventing and applying their own tests.[13] Hence if income differentials between different educational groups do not equalize when the supply of education is expanded, this might be due to increases by employers in the level of educational credentials demanded for a particular type of job.

Another model of the relation between education and earnings posits a threshold notion of education—often the statutory compulsory schooling that every future citizen is expected to attain and that accordingly has little market value. According to this model, the spread of schooling in African countries during the 1960s robbed literacy of the great bulk of its market value. Whatever the level of the threshold, those who do not attain it are typically regarded as unemployable or only marginally employable. Earnings differentials, insofar as they are determined by education, derive from the differentiation of educational groups beyond the minimum school leaving age. It would seem to follow from this that, as Ockner and Rivlin have suggested, the human capital model may apply best at the higher end of the educational scale, where stretching out rather than equalization has occurred, and that the alternative models may fit better at the lower end.[14] If this is indeed the case, the emerging theory of "dual labor markets" may do much to explain a pattern of relations between education and earnings that differs according to one's position in the structure of class, sexual, and racial stratification.[15]

11. Angus Maddison, "What is Education For?" *Lloyd's Bank Review,* no. 112, April 1974, p. 29.
12. Some important formulations of the screening hypothesis are Kenneth Arrow, "Higher Education as a Filter," *Journal of Public Economics* 2 (July 1973): 193–216; Michael Spence, "Job Market Signaling," *Quarterly Journal of Economics* 87 (August 1973): 355–374; Peter Wiles, "The Correlation between Education and Earnings: The External-Test-Not-Content Hypothesis (ETNC)," *Higher Education* 3 (1974): 43–58; Paul J. Taubman and Terence J. Wales, "Higher Education, Mental Ability, and Screening," *Journal of Political Economy* 81 (January-February 1973): 28–55. A critique of the screening hypothesis in general and of the Taubman-Wales article in particular is presented in Richard Layard and George Psacharopoulos, "The Screening Hypothesis and the Returns to Education," *Journal of Political Economy* 82 (September-October 1974): 985–998. We have not included Thurow's article (Chapter 17 below) as a formulation of the screening hypothesis, because it suggests that education may lower the cost of producing a given output by lowering training costs.
13. The logic of the screening hypothesis was well captured by Macaulay more than a century ago when he wrote: "If the Ptolemaic system were taught at Cambridge, instead of the Newtonian, the senior wrangler would nevertheless be in general a superior man to the wooden spoon. If instead of learning Greek, we learned the Cherokee, the man who understood the Cherokee best, who made the most correct and melodious Cherokee verses, who comprehended most accurately the effect of the Cherokee particles, would generally be a superior man to him who was destitute of these accomplishments." Quoted in Wiles, *op. cit.,* p. 44.
14. Benjamin A. Ockner and Alice M. Rivlin, "Income Distribution Policy in the United States," in *Education, Inequality and Life Chances,* Volume 2 (Paris: OECD, 1975), pp. 182–219.
15. For a presentation of the theory of dual labor markets, see Peter B. Doeringer and Michael J. Piore, *Internal Labor Markets and Manpower Analysis* (Lexington, Mass.: D.C. Heath, 1971). The inability of the human capital model to explain income differentials by race and sex among individuals who have made the same investment in education is often cited by critics as pointing to its theoretical and empirical shortcomings. A large number of empirical studies of the earnings of blacks and whites show lower returns for blacks at every level of education; see David M. Gordon, *Theories of Poverty and Unemployment* (Lexington, Mass.: D.C. Heath, 1972), p. 118. Randall Weiss (see "The Effect of Education on the Earnings

Massimo Paci, an Italian economist, offers a perspective that has been much neglected in the economics of education—that of historical analysis of the relationship between schooling and structures of employment (Chapter 19). While not disputing the demonstrated connection between the diffusion of secondary and higher education and economic development, Paci reinterprets Marx to offer a theory of stages of development of, on the one hand, educational systems and, on the other, labor markets. He rejects the liberal thesis that economic development is dependent on educational expansion and addresses himself to what he regards as a more convincing interpretation—that the determinants of educational expansion are independent of market demand and indeed lead to potential "contradictoriness between scholarization and the requirements of the economic system." In this way he emphasizes the potential of education as both an instrument for integrating subordinate classes into the social and economic system and as a factor of "contradiction and excess" in relation to the labor market.

It should be noted that Paci differs from Bowles in that he does not use a correspondence theory in his explanatory description of stages in the development of capitalist labor markets. He identifies three phases. In the first phase the demand for manpower is principally directed towards unskilled labor required for the expansion of new markets and for work in new branches of production. Overpopulation is held to supply this type of labor and to create a "reserve army." The second phase consists of the growth of large scale industry. In this phase relatively more skilled labor is required, and this encourages the expansion of secondary and higher education. Overpopulation disappears and qualifications have market value. Nevertheless, at the same time what Paci calls "stagnant overpopulation" continues to exist alongside the more technologically advanced forms of industry in a capitalist society. In the main, in this second phase, the function of the school is held to be that of integrating the working class into the capitalist system. The third phase is monopoly capitalism, and here the development of mass systems of education leads to "imbalance" in the labor market and tension and conflict in society. Mass higher education produces an excess supply of educated labor that cannot be absorbed into the productive system.[16]

The problem of a disjunction between the educational system and employment opportunities, as Philip Foster's analysis of educational development planning in Ghana (Chapter 20) makes clear, is not confined to advanced economies. Discussing the widespread view that investment in education can serve as a motor of economic development—a perspective made explicit by Schultz in Chapter 16—Foster argues that the expansion of education can be useful only to the extent that there is an expansion of opportunities in the exchange sector of the economy. In Ghana, creation of jobs has lagged behind the production of graduates, with mass unemployment among school leavers as a result. African students do, to be sure, favor academic-type schools over the vocational institutions preferred by development planners, but this is because they recognize that academic education *is* vocational education and provides access to the most prestigious and lucrative occupations in the Ghanaian economy. No amount of investment in education, Foster concludes, can serve as a substitute for the development of real and perceived opportunities in the economy.

---

of Blacks and Whites," *Review of Economics and Statistics* 52 (May 1970): 150–159) reports that blacks in three of four age groups realized *no* significant returns to their investment in education. In general such variables as education and age can explain only about half of the earnings gap between black and white earnings and even less of the differential between males and females (see Gordon, *op. cit.,* p. 39).

16. For a detailed historical analysis of the recurrent problem of intellectual unemployment in Italy, see Marzio Barbagli, *Disoccupazione intellettuale e sistema scolastico in Italia (1859–1973)* (Bologna: Il Mulino, 1974).

Foster's analysis of the failure in Ghana of economic development strategies based on the expansion of vocational education and Bluestone's critique of American anti-poverty programs based on manpower and investment in human resources underline the inability of human capital theory to explain some important aspects of the relationship between education and occupational structure. Yet despite important contributions to the economics of education by proponents of screening, dual labor market, job queuing, and personality formation hypotheses, no comprehensive theory of education and labor markets has yet been formulated. The construction of such a theory, which must draw upon the concept of human capital while transcending its limitations, remains a vital task in the years ahead.

SELECTIVE BIBLIOGRAPHY

Anderson, C. Arnold, and Mary Jean Bowman, eds. *Education and Economic Development.* Chicago: Aldine, 1965.

Arrow, Kenneth. "Higher Education as a Filter." *Journal of Public Economics* 2 (July 1973):193–216.

Barbagli, Marzio. *Disoccupazione intellettuale e sistema scolastico in Italia (1859–1973).* Bologna: Il Mulino, 1974.

Becker, Gary S. *Human Capital.* New York: National Bureau of Economic Research, 1964.

Blaug, Mark. "The Correlation Between Education and Earnings: What Does It Signify?" *Higher Education* 1 (1972): 53–77.

Blaug, Mark. *An Introduction to the Economics of Education.* London: Allen Lane, 1970.

Bourdieu, Pierre; Luc Boltanski; and Monique de Saint Martin. "Les stratégies de reconversion." *Social Science Information* 12 (1973): 61–113.

Bowles, Samuel, and Herbert Gintis. "The Problem with Human Capital–A Marxian Critique." *American Economic Review* 65 (May 1975): 74–82.

Carnoy, Martin, ed. *Schooling in a Corporate Society: The Political Economy of Education in America,* 2nd. ed. New York: David McKay, 1975.

Carter, Michael, and Martin Carnoy. "Theories of Labor Markets and Worker Productivity." Discussion paper. Palo Alto, Cal.: Center for Economic Studies, August 1974.

Doeringer, Peter B., and Michael J. Piore. *Internal Labor Markets and Manpower Analysis.* Lexington, Mass.: D.C. Heath, 1971.

Gintis, Herbert. "Education and the Characteristics of Worker Productivity." *American Economic Review* 61 (May 1971): 266–279.

Gordon, David M. *Theories of Poverty and Unemployment.* Lexington, Mass.: D.C. Heath, 1972.

Moock, Peter R. "Economic Aspects of the Family as Educator." *Teachers College Record* 76 (December 1974): 266–278.

Piore, Michael J. "Fragments of a Sociological Theory of Wages." *American Economic Review* 63 (May 1973): 377–384.

Psacharopoulos, George. *Returns to Education: An International Comparison.* Amsterdam: Elsevier, 1973.

Reich, Michael; David M. Gordon; and Richard C. Edwards. "A Theory of Labor Market Segmentation." *American Economic Review* 63 (May 1973): 359–365.

Segré, Monique; Lucie Tanguy; and Marie-France Lortic. "A New Ideology of Education." *Social Forces* 50 (March 1972): 313–332.

16. Investment in Human Capital

THEODORE W. SCHULTZ

Although it is obvious that people acquire useful skills and knowledge, it is not obvious that these skills and knowledge are a form of capital, that this capital is in substantial part a product of deliberate investment, that it has grown in Western societies at a much faster rate than conventional (nonhuman) capital, and that its growth may well be the most distinctive feature of the economic system. It has been widely observed that increases in national output have been large compared with the increases of land, man-hours, and physical reproducible capital. Investment in human capital is probably the major explanation for this difference.

Much of what we call consumption constitutes investment in human capital. Direct expenditures on education, health, and internal migration to take advantage of better job opportunities are clear examples. Earnings foregone by mature students attending school and by workers acquiring on-the-job training are equally clear examples. Yet nowhere do these enter into our national accounts. The use of leisure time to improve skills and knowledge is widespread and it too is unrecorded. In these and similar ways the *quality* of human effort can be greatly improved and its productivity enhanced. I shall contend that such investment in human capital accounts for most of the impressive rise in the real earnings per worker.

I shall comment, first, on the reasons why economists have shied away from the explicit analysis of investment in human capital, and then, on the capacity of such investment to explain many a puzzle about economic growth. Mainly, however, I shall concentrate on the scope and substance of human capital and its formation. In closing I shall consider some social and policy implications.

I. SHYING AWAY FROM INVESTMENT IN MAN

Economists have long known that people are an important part of the wealth of nations. Measured by what labor contributes to output, the productive capacity of human beings is now vastly larger than all other forms of wealth taken together. What economists have not stressed is the simple truth that people invest in themselves and that these investments are very large. Although economists are seldom timid in entering on abstract analysis and are often proud of being impractical, they have not been bold in coming to grips with this form of investment. Whenever they come even close, they proceed gingerly as if they were stepping into deep water. No doubt there are reasons for being wary. Deep-seated moral and philosophical issues are ever present. Free men are first and foremost the end to be served by economic endeavor; they are not property or marketable assets. And not least, it has been all too convenient in marginal productivity analysis to treat labor as if it were a unique bundle of innate abilities that are wholly free of capital.

The mere thought of investment in human beings is offensive to some among us.[1] Our values and beliefs inhibit us from looking upon human beings as capital goods, except in slavery, and this we abhor. We are not unaffected by the long struggle to rid society of indentured service and to evolve political and legal institutions to keep men free from bondage. These are achievements that we prize highly. Hence, to treat human beings as wealth that can be augmented by investment runs counter to deeply held

Presidential Address delivered at the Seventy-Third Annual Meeting of the American Economic Association, Saint Louis, December 28, 1960. The author is indebted to his colleagues Milton Friedman, for his very helpful suggestions to gain clarity and cogency, and Harry G. Johnson for pointing out a number of ambiguities.

From *American Economic Review* 51 (March 1961): 1–17. Reprinted by permission of author and publisher.

values. It seems to reduce man once again to a mere material component, to something akin to property. And for man to look upon himself as a capital good, even if it did not impair his freedom, may seem to debase him. No less a person than J. S. Mill at one time insisted that the people of a country should not be looked upon as wealth because wealth existed only for the sake of people [15]. But surely Mill was wrong; there is nothing in the concept of human wealth contrary to his idea that it exists only for the advantage of people. By investing in themselves, people can enlarge the range of choice available to them. It is one way free men can enhance their welfare.

Among the few who have looked upon human beings as capital, there are three distinguished names. The philosopher-economist Adam Smith boldly included all of the acquired and useful abilities of all of the inhabitants of a country as a part of capital. So did H. von Thünen, who then went on to argue that the concept of capital applied to man did not degrade him or impair his freedom and dignity, but on the contrary that the failure to apply the concept was especially pernicious in wars; ". . . for here . . . one will sacrifice in a battle a hundred human beings in the prime of their lives without a thought in order to save one gun." The reason is that, ". . . the purchase of a cannon causes an outlay of public funds, whereas human beings are to be had for nothing by means of a mere conscription decree" [20]. Irving Fisher also clearly and cogently presented an all-inclusive concept of capital [6]. Yet the main stream of thought has held that it is neither appropriate nor practical to apply the concept of capital to human beings. Marshall [11], whose great prestige goes far to explain why this view was accepted, held that while human beings are incontestably capital from an abstract and mathematical point of view, it would be out of touch with the market place to treat them as capital in practical analyses. Investment in human beings has accordingly seldom been incorporated in the

formal core of economics, even though many economists, including Marshall, have seen its relevance at one point or another in what they have written.

The failure to treat human resources explicitly as a form of capital, as a produced means of production, as the product of investment, has fostered the retention of the classical notion of labor as a capacity to do manual work requiring little knowledge and skill, a capacity with which, according to this notion, laborers are endowed about equally. This notion of labor was wrong in the classical period and it is patently wrong now. Counting individuals who can and want to work and treating such a count as a measure of the quantity of an economic factor is no more meaningful than it would be to count the number of all manner of machines to determine their economic importance either as a stock of capital or as a flow of productive services.

Laborers have become capitalists not from a diffusion of the ownership of corporation stocks, as folklore would have it, but from the acquisition of knowledge and skill that have economic value [9]. This knowledge and skill are in great part the product of investment and, combined with other human investment, predominantly account for the productive superiority of the technically advanced countries. To omit them in studying economic growth is like trying to explain Soviet ideology without Marx.

II. ECONOMIC GROWTH FROM HUMAN CAPITAL

Many paradoxes and puzzles about our dynamic, growing economy can be resolved once human investment is taken into account. Let me begin by sketching some that are minor though not trivial.

When farm people take nonfarm jobs they earn substantially less than industrial workers of the same race, age, and sex. Similarly nonwhite urban males earn much less than white males even after allowance is made for the effects of differences in unemployment, age, city size and region [21]. Because these differentials in earnings correspond closely to corresponding differentials in education, they strongly suggest that the one is a consequence of the other. Negroes who operate farms, whether as tenants or as owners, earn much less than whites on comparable farms.[2] Fortunately, crops and livestock are not vulnerable to the blight of discrimination. The large differences in earnings seem rather to reflect mainly the differences in health and education. Workers in the South on the average earn appreciably less than in the North or West and they also have on the average less education. Most migratory farm workers earn very little indeed by comparison with other workers. Many of them have virtually no schooling, are in poor health, are unskilled, and have little ability to do useful work. To urge that the differences in the amount of human investment may explain these differences in earnings seems elementary. Of more recent vintage are observations showing younger workers at a competitive advantage; for example, young men entering the labor force are said to have an advantage over unemployed older workers in obtaining satisfactory jobs. Most of these young people possess twelve years of school, most of the older workers six years or less. The observed advantage of these younger workers may therefore result not from inflexibilities in social security or in retirement programs, or from sociological preference of employers, but from real differences in productivity connected with one form of human investment, i.e., education. And yet another example, the curve relating income to age tends to be steeper for skilled than for unskilled persons. Investment in on-the-job training seems a likely explanation, as I shall note later.

Economic growth requires much internal migration of workers to adjust to changing job opportunities [10]. Young men and women move more readily than older workers. Surely this makes economic sense when one recognizes that the costs of such migration are a form of human investment. Young people have more years ahead of them than older workers during which they can realize on such an investment. Hence it takes less of a wage differential to make it economically advantageous for them to move, or, to put it differently, young people can expect a higher return on their investment in migration than older people. This differential may explain selective migration without requiring an appeal to sociological differences between young and old people.

The examples so far given are for investment in human beings that yield a return over a long period. This is true equally of investment in education, training, and migration of young people. Not all investments in human beings are of this kind; some are more nearly akin to current inputs as for example expenditures on food and shelter in some countries where work is mainly the application of brute human force, calling for energy and stamina, and where the intake of food is far from enough to do a full day's work. On the "hungry" steppes and in the teeming valleys of Asia, millions of adult males have so meager a diet that they cannot do more than a few hours of hard work. To call them underemployed does not seem pertinent. Under such circumstances it is certainly meaningful to treat food partly as consumption and partly as a current "producer good," as some Indian economists have done [3]. Let us not forget that Western economists during the early decades of industrialization and even in the time of Marshall and Pigou often connected additional food for workers with increases in labor productivity.

Let me now pass on to three major perplexing questions closely connected with the riddle of economic growth. First, consider the long-period behavior of the capital-income ratio. We were taught that a country which amassed more reproducible capital relative to its land and labor would employ such capital in greater "depth" because of its growing abundance and cheapness. But apparently this is not what happens. On the contrary, the estimates now available show that less of such capital tends to be employed relative to income as economic growth proceeds. Are we to infer that the ratio of capital to income has no relevance in explaining either poverty or opulence? Or that a rise of this ratio is not a prerequisite to economic growth? These questions raise fundamental issues bearing on motives and preferences for holding wealth as well as on the motives for particular investments and the stock of capital thereby accumulated. For my purpose all that needs to be said is that these estimates of capital-income ratios refer to only a part of all capital. They exclude in particular, and most unfortunately, any human capital. Yet human capital has surely been increasing at a rate substantially greater than reproducible (nonhuman) capital. We cannot, therefore, infer from these estimates that the stock of *all* capital has been decreasing relative to income. On the contrary, if we accept the not implausible assumption that the motives and preferences of people, the technical opportunities open to them, and the uncertainty associated with economic growth during particular periods were leading people to maintain roughly a constant ratio between *all* capital and income, the decline in the estimated capital-income ratio[3] is simply a signal that human capital has been increasing relatively not only to conventional capital but also to income.

The bumper crop of estimates that show national income increasing faster than national resources raises a second and not unrelated puzzle. The income of the United States has been increasing at a much higher rate than the combined amount of land, man-hours worked and the stock of reproducible capital used to produce the income. Moreover, the discrepancy between the two rates has become larger from one business cycle to the next during recent decades [5]. To call this discrepancy a measure of "resource productivity" gives a name to our ignorance but does not dispel it. If we accept

these estimates, the connections between national resources and national income have become loose and tenuous over time. Unless this discrepancy can be resolved, received theory of production applied to inputs and outputs as currently measured is a toy and not a tool for studying economic growth.

Two sets of forces probably account for the discrepancy, if we neglect entirely the index number and aggregation problems that bedevil all estimates of such global aggregates as total output and total input. One is returns to scale; the second, the large improvements in the quality of inputs that have occurred but have been omitted from the input estimates. Our economy has undoubtedly been experiencing increasing returns to scale at some points offset by decreasing returns at others. If we can succeed in identifying and measuring the net gains, they may turn out to have been substantial. The improvements in the quality of inputs that have not been adequately allowed for are no doubt partly in material (nonhuman) capital. My own conception, however, is that both this defect and the omission of economies of scale are minor sources of discrepancy between the rates of growth of inputs and outputs compared to the improvements in human capacity that have been omitted.

A small step takes us from these two puzzles raised by existing estimates to a third which brings us to the heart of the matter, namely the essentially unexplained large increase in real earnings of workers. Can this be a windfall? Or a quasirent pending the adjustment in the supply of labor? Or, a pure rent reflecting the fixed amount of labor? It seems far more reasonable that it represents rather a return to the investment that has been made in human beings. The observed growth in productivity per unit of labor is simply a consequence of holding the unit of labor constant over time although in fact this unit of labor has been increasing as a result of a steadily growing amount of human capital per worker. As I read our record, the human capital component has become very large as a consequence of human investment.

Another aspect of the same basic question, which admits of the same resolution, is the rapid postwar recovery of countries that had suffered severe destruction of plant and equipment during the war. The toll from bombing was all too visible in the factories laid flat, the railroad yards, bridges, and harbors wrecked, and the cities in ruin. Structures, equipment and inventories were all heaps of rubble. Not so visible, yet large, was the toll from the wartime depletion of the physical plant that escaped destruction by bombs. Economists were called upon to assess the implications of these wartime losses for recovery. In retrospect, it is clear that they overestimated the prospective retarding effects of these losses. Having had a small hand in this effort, I have had a special reason for looking back and wondering why the judgments that we formed soon after the war proved to be so far from the mark. The explanation that now is clear is that we gave altogether too much weight to nonhuman capital in making these assessments. We fell into this error, I am convinced, because we did not have a concept of *all* capital and, therefore, failed to take account of human capital and the important part that it plays in production in a modern economy.

Let me close this section with a comment on poor countries, for which there are virtually no solid estimates. I have been impressed by repeatedly expressed judgments, especially by those who have a responsibility in making capital available to poor countries, about the low rate at which these countries can absorb additional capital. New capital from outside can be put to good use, it is said, only when it is added "slowly and gradually." But this experience is at variance with the widely held impression that countries are poor fundamentally because they are starved for capital and that additional capital is truly the key to their more rapid economic growth. The reconciliation is again, I believe, to be found in

emphasis on particular forms of capital. The new capital available to these countries from outside as a rule goes into the formation of structures, equipment and sometimes also into inventories. But it is generally not available for additional investment in man. Consequently, human capabilities do not stay abreast of physical capital, and they do become limiting factors in economic growth. It should come as no surprise, therefore, that the absorption rate of capital to augment only particular nonhuman resources is necessarily low. The Horvat [8] formulation of the optimum rate of investment which treats knowledge and skill as a critical investment variable in determining the rate of economic growth is both relevant and important.

III. SCOPE AND SUBSTANCE OF THESE INVESTMENTS

What are human investments? Can they be distinguished from consumption? Is it at all feasible to identify and measure them? What do they contribute to income? Granted that they seem amorphous compared to brick and mortar, and hard to get at compared to the investment accounts of corporations, they assuredly are not a fragment; they are rather like the contents of Pandora's box, full of difficulties and hope.

Human resources obviously have both quantitative and qualitative dimensions. The number of people, the proportion who enter upon useful work, and hours worked are essentially quantitative characteristics. To make my task tolerably manageable, I shall neglect these and consider only such quality components as skill, knowledge, and similar attributes that affect particular human capabilities to do productive work. In so far as expenditures to enhance such capabilities also increase the value productivity of human effort (labor), they will yield a positive rate of return.[4]

How can we estimate the magnitude of human investment? The practice followed in connection with physical capital goods is to estimate the magnitude of capital formation by expenditures made to produce the capital goods. This practice would suffice also for the formation of human capital. However, for human capital there is an additional problem that is less pressing for physical capital goods: how to distinguish between expenditures for consumption and for investment. This distinction bristles with both conceptual and practical difficulties. We can think of three classes of expenditures: expenditures that satisfy consumer preferences and in no way enhance the capabilities under discussion—these represent pure consumption; expenditures that enhance capabilities and do not satisfy any preferences underlying consumption—these represent pure investment; and expenditures that have both effects. Most relevant activities clearly are in the third class, partly consumption and partly investment, which is why the task of identifying each component is so formidable and why the measurement of capital formation by expenditures is less useful for human investment than for investment in physical goods. In principle there is an alternative method for estimating human investment, namely by its yield rather than by its cost. While any capability produced by human investment becomes a part of the human agent and hence cannot be sold; it is nevertheless "in touch with the market place" by affecting the wages and salaries the human agent can earn. The resulting increase in earnings is the yield on the investment.[5]

Despite the difficulty of exact measurement at this stage of our understanding of human investment, many insights can be gained by examining some of the more important activities that improve human capabilities. I shall concentrate on five major categories: (1) health facilities and services, broadly conceived to include all expenditures that affect the life expectancy, strength and stamina, and the vigor and vitality of a people; (2) on-the-job training, including old-style apprenticeship organized by firms; (3) formally organized education at the elementary, secondary, and higher levels; (4) study programs for adults that are not organized by firms, including extension programs notably in agriculture; (5) migration of individuals and families to adjust to changing job opportunities. Except for education, not much is known about these activities that is germane here. I shall refrain from commenting on study programs for adults, although in agriculture the extension services of the several states play an important role in transmitting new knowledge and in developing skills of farmers [17]. Nor shall I elaborate further on internal migration related to economic growth.

Health activities have both quantity and quality implications. Such speculation as economists have engaged in about the effects of improvements in health,[6] has been predominantly in connection with population growth, which is to say with quantity. But surely health measures also enhance the quality of human resources. So also may additional food and better shelter, especially in underdeveloped countries.

The change in the role of food as people become richer sheds light on one of the conceptual problems already referred to. I have pointed out that extra food in some poor countries has the attribute of a "producer good." This attribute of food, however, diminishes as the consumption of food rises, and there comes a point at which any further increase in food becomes pure consumption.[7] Clothing, housing and perhaps medical services may be similar.

My comment about on-the-job training will consist of a conjecture on the amount of such training, a note on the decline of apprenticeship, and then a useful economic theorem on who bears the costs of such training. Surprisingly little is known about on-the-job training in modern industry. About all that can be said is that the expansion of education has not eliminated it. It seems likely, however, that some of the training formerly undertaken by firms has been discontinued and other training programs have been instituted to adjust both to the rise in the education of workers and to changes in the demands for new skills. The amount invested annually in such training can only be a guess. H. F. Clark places it near to equal to the amount spent on formal education.[8] Even if it were only one-half as large, it would represent currently an annual gross investment of about $15 billion. Elsewhere, too, it is thought to be important. For example, some observers have been impressed by the amount of such training under way in plants in the Soviet Union.[9] Meanwhile, apprenticeship has all but disappeared, partly because it is now inefficient and partly because schools now perform many of its functions. Its disappearance has been hastened no doubt by the difficulty of enforcing apprenticeship agreements. Legally they have come to smack of indentured service. The underlying economic factors and behavior are clear enough. The apprentice is prepared to serve during the initial period when his productivity is less than the cost of his keep and of his training. Later, however, unless he is legally restrained, he will seek other employment when his productivity begins to exceed the cost of keep and training, which is the period during which a master would expect to recoup on his earlier outlay.

To study on-the-job training Gary Becker [1] advances the theorem that in competitive markets employees pay all the costs of their training and none of these costs are ultimately borne by the firm. Becker points out several implications. The notion that expenditures on training by a firm generate external economies for other firms is not consistent with this theorem. The theorem also indicates one force favoring the transfer from on-the-job training to attending school. Since on-the-job training reduces the net earnings of workers at the beginning and raises them later on, this theorem also provides an explanation for the "steeper slope of the curve relating income to age," for skilled than unskilled workers, referred to earlier.[10] What all this adds up to is that the stage is set to undertake meaningful economic studies of on-the-job training.

Happily we reach firmer ground in regard to education. Investment in education has risen at a rapid rate and by itself may well account for a substantial part of the otherwise unexplained rise in earnings. I shall do no more than summarize some preliminary results about the total costs of education including income foregone by students, the apparent relation of these costs to consumer income and to alternative investments, the rise of the stock of education in the labor force, returns to education, and the contribution that the increase in the stock of education may have made to earnings and to national income.

It is not difficult to estimate the conventional costs of education consisting of the costs of the services of teachers, librarians, administrators, of maintaining and operating the educational plant, and interest on the capital embodied in the educational plant. It is far more difficult to estimate another component of total cost, the income foregone by students. Yet this component should be included and it is far from negligible. In the United States, for example, well over half of the costs of higher education consists of income foregone by students. As early as 1900, this income foregone accounted for about one-fourth of the total costs of elementary, secondary and higher education. By 1956, it represented over two-fifths of all costs. The rising significance of foregone income has been a major factor in the marked upward trend in the total real costs of education which, measured in current prices, increased from $400 million in 1900 to $28.7 billion in 1956 [18]. The percentage rise in educational costs was about three and a half times as large as in consumer income, which would imply a high income elasticity of the demand for education, if education were regarded as pure consumption.[11] Educational costs also rose about three and a half times as rapidly as did the gross formation of physical capital in dollars. If we were to treat education as pure investment this result would suggest that the returns to education were relatively more attractive than those to nonhuman capital.[12]

Much schooling is acquired by persons who are not treated as income earners in most economic analysis, particularly, of course, women. To analyze the effect of growth in schooling on earnings, it is therefore necessary to distinguish between the stock of education in the population and the amount in the labor force. Years of school completed are far from satisfactory as a measure because of the marked increases that have taken place in the number of days of school attendance of enrolled students and because much more of the education of workers consists of high school and higher education than formerly. My preliminary estimates suggest that the stock of education in the labor force rose about eight and a half times between 1900 and 1956, whereas the stock of reproducible capital rose four and a half times, both in 1956 prices. These estimates are, of course, subject to many qualifications.[13] Nevertheless, both the magnitude and the rate of increase of this form of human capital have been such that they could be an important key to the riddle of economic growth.[14]

The exciting work under way is on the return to education. In spite of the flood of high school and college graduates, the return has not become trivial. Even the lower limits of the estimates show that the return to such education has been in the neighborhood of the return to nonhuman capital. This is what most of these estimates show when they treat as costs all of the public and private expenditures on education and also the income foregone while attending school, and when they treat all of these costs as investment, allocating none to consumption.[15] But surely a part of these costs are consumption in the sense that education creates a form of consumer capital[16] which has the attribute of improving the taste and the quality of consumption of students throughout the rest of their lives. If one were to allocate a substantial fraction of the total costs of this education to consumption, say one-half, this would, of course, double the observed rate of return to what would then become the investment component in education that enhances the productivity of man.

Fortunately, the problem of allocating the costs of education in the labor force between consumption and investment does not arise to plague us when we turn to the contribution that education makes to earnings and to national income because a change in allocation only alters the rate of return, not the total return. I noted at the outset that the unexplained increases in U.S. national income have been especially large in recent decades. On one set of assumptions, the unexplained part amounts to nearly three-fifths of the total increase between 1929 and 1956.[17] How much of this unexplained increase in income represents a return to education in the labor force? A lower limit suggests that about three-tenths of it, and an upper limit does not rule out that more than one-half of it came from this source.[18] These estimates also imply that between 36 and 70 per cent of the hitherto unexplained rise in the earnings of labor is explained by returns to the additional education of workers.

IV. A CONCLUDING NOTE ON POLICY

One proceeds at his own peril in discussing social implications and policy. The conventional hedge is to camouflage one's values and to wear the mantle of academic innocence. Let me proceed unprotected!

1. Our tax laws everywhere discriminate against human capital. Although the stock of such capital has become large and even though it is obvious that human capital, like other forms of reproducible capital, depreciates, becomes obsolete, and entails maintenance, our tax laws are all but blind on these matters.

2. Human capital deteriorates when it is idle because unemployment impairs the skills that workers have acquired. Losses in

earnings can be cushioned by appropriate payments but these do not keep idleness from taking its toll from human capital.

3. There are many hindrances to the free choice of professions. Racial discrimination and religious discrimination are still widespread. Professional associations and governmental bodies also hinder entry; for example, into medicine. Such purposeful interference keeps the investment in this form of human capital substantially below its optimum [7].

4. It is indeed elementary to stress the greater imperfections of the capital market in providing funds for investment in human beings than for investment in physical goods. Much could be done to reduce these imperfections by reforms in tax and banking laws and by changes in banking practices. Long-term private and public loans to students are warranted.

5. Internal migration, notably the movement of farm people into industry, made necessary by the dynamics of our economic progress, requires substantial investments. In general, families in which the husbands and wives are already in the late thirties cannot afford to make these investments because the remaining payoff period for them is too short. Yet society would gain if more of them would pull stakes and move because, in addition to the increase in productivity currently, the children of these families would be better located for employment when they were ready to enter the labor market. The case for making some of these investments on public account is by no means weak. Our farm programs have failed miserably these many years in not coming to grips with the costs and returns from off-farm migration.

6. The low earnings of particular people have long been a matter of public concern. Policy all too frequently concentrates only on the effects, ignoring the causes. No small part of the low earnings of many Negroes, Puerto Ricans, Mexican nationals, indigenous migratory farm workers, poor farm people and some of our older workers, re-

flects the failure to have invested in their health and education. Past mistakes are, of course, bygones, but for the sake of the next generation we can ill afford to continue making the same mistakes over again.

7. Is there a substantial underinvestment in human beings other than in these depressed groups? [2] This is an important question for economists. The evidence at hand is fragmentary. Nor will the answer be easily won. There undoubtedly have been overinvestments in some skills, for example, too many locomotive firemen and engineers, too many people trained to be farmers, and too many agricultural economists! Our schools are not free of loafers and some students lack the necessary talents. Nevertheless, underinvestment in knowledge and skill, relative to the amounts invested in nonhuman capital would appear to be the rule and not the exception for a number of reasons. The strong and increasing demands for this knowledge and skill in laborers are of fairly recent origin and it takes time to respond to them. In responding to these demands, we are heavily dependent upon cultural and political processes, and these are slow and the lags are long compared to the behavior of markets serving the formation of nonhuman capital. Where the capital market does serve human investments, it is subject to more imperfections than in financing physical capital. I have already stressed the fact that our tax laws discriminate in favor of nonhuman capital. Then, too, many individuals face serious uncertainty in assessing their innate talents when it comes to investing in themselves, especially through higher education. Nor is it easy either for public decisions or private behavior to untangle and properly assess the consumption and the investment components. The fact that the return to high school and to higher education has been about as large as the return to conventional forms of capital when all of the costs of such education including income foregone by students are allocated to the investment component, creates a strong

presumption that there has been under-investment since, surely, much education is cultural and in that sense it is consumption. It is no wonder, in view of these circumstances, that there should be substantial underinvestment in human beings, even though we take pride, and properly so, in the support that we have given to education and to other activities that contribute to such investments.

8. Should the returns from public investment in human capital accrue to the individuals in whom it is made?[19] The policy issues implicit in this question run deep and they are full of perplexities pertaining both to resource allocation and to welfare. Physical capital that is formed by public investment is not transferred as a rule to particular individuals as a gift. It would greatly simplify the allocative process if public investment in human capital were placed on the same footing. What then is the logical basis for treating public investment in human capital differently? Presumably it turns on ideas about welfare. A strong welfare goal of our community is to reduce the unequal distribution of personal income among individuals and families. Our community has relied heavily on progressive income and inheritance taxation. Given public revenue from these sources, it may well be true that public investment in human capital, notably that entering into general education, is an effective and efficient set of expenditures for attaining this goal. Let me stress, however, that the state of knowledge about these issues is woefully meager.

9. My last policy comment is on assistance to underdeveloped countries to help them achieve economic growth. Here, even more than in domestic affairs, investment in human beings is likely to be underrated and neglected. It is inherent in the intellectual climate in which leaders and spokesmen of many of these countries find themselves. Our export of growth doctrines has contributed. These typically assign the stellar role to the formation of nonhuman capital, and take as an obvious fact the super-abundance of human resources. Steel mills are the real symbol of industrialization. After all, the early industrialization of England did not depend on investments in the labor force. New funds and agencies are being authorized to transfer capital for physical goods to these countries. The World Bank and our Export-Import Bank have already had much experience. Then, too, measures have been taken to pave the way for the investment of more private (non-human) capital abroad. This one-sided effort is under way in spite of the fact that the knowledge and skills required to take on and use efficiently the superior techniques of production, the most valuable resource that we could make available to them, is in very short supply in these underdeveloped countries. Some growth of course can be had from the increase in more conventional capital even though the labor that is available is lacking both in skill and knowledge. But the rate of growth will be seriously limited. It simply is not possible to have the fruits of a modern agriculture and the abundance of modern industry without making large investments in human beings.

Truly, the most distinctive feature of our economic system is the growth in human capital. Without it there would be only hard, manual work and poverty except for those who have income from property. There is an early morning scene in Faulkner's *Intruder in the Dust,* of a poor, solitary cultivator at work in a field. Let me paraphrase that line, "The man without skills and knowledge leaning terrifically against nothing."

NOTES

1. This paragraph draws on the introduction to my Teller Lecture [16].
2. Based on unpublished preliminary results obtained by Joseph Willett in his Ph.D. research at the University of Chicago.
3. I leave aside here the difficulties inherent in identifying and measuring both the nonhuman capital and the income entering into estimates of this ratio. There are index number and aggregation problems aplenty, and not all improvements in the

quality of this capital have been accounted for, as I shall note later.

4. Even so, our *observed* return can be either negative, zero or positive because our observations are drawn from a world where there is uncertainty and imperfect knowledge and where there are windfall gains and losses and mistakes aplenty.

5. In principle, the value of the investment can be determined by discounting the additional future earnings it yields just as the value of a physical capital good can be determined by discounting its income stream.

6. Health economics is in its infancy; there are two medical journals with "economics" in their titles, two bureaus for economic research in private associations (one in the American Medical and the other in the American Dental Association), and not a few studies and papers by outside scholars. Selma Mushkin's survey is very useful with its pertinent economic insights, though she may have underestimated somewhat the influence of the economic behavior of people in striving for health [14].

7. For instance, the income elasticity of the demand for food continues to be positive even after the point is reached where additional food no longer has the attribute of a "producer good."

8. Based on comments made by Harold F. Clark at the Merrill Center for Economics, summer 1959; also, see [4].

9. Based on observations made by a team of U. S. economists of which I was a member, see *Saturday Rev.*, Jan. 21, 1961.

10. Becker has also noted still another implication arising out of the fact that the income and capital investment aspects of on-the-job training are tied together, which gives rise to "permanent" and "transitory" income effects that may have substantial explanatory value.

11. Had other things stayed constant this suggests an income elasticity of 3.5. Among the things that did change, the prices of educational services rose relative to other consumer prices, perhaps offset in part by improvements in the quality of educational services.

12. This of course assumes among other things that the relationship between gross and net have not changed or have changed in the same proportion. Estimates are from my essay, "Education and Economic Growth" [19].

13. From [19, Sec. 4]. These estimates of the stock of education are tentative and incomplete. They are incomplete in that they do not take into account fully the increases in the average life of this form of human capital arising out of the fact that relatively more of this education is held by younger people in the labor force than was true in earlier years; and, they are incomplete because no adjustment has been made for the improvements in education over time, increasing the quality of a year of school in ways other than those related to changes in the proportions represented by elementary, high school and higher education. Even so the stock of this form of human capital rose 8.5 times between 1900 and 1956 while the stock of reproducible nonhuman capital increased only 4.5 times, both in constant 1956 prices.

14. In value terms this stock of education was only 22 per cent as large as the stock of reproducible physical capital in 1900, whereas in 1956 it already had become 42 per cent as large.

15. Several comments are called for here. (1) The return to high school education appears to have declined substantially between the late 'thirties and early 'fifties and since then has leveled off, perhaps even risen somewhat, indicating a rate of return toward the end of the 'fifties about as high as that to higher education. (2) The return to college education in the case of nonwhite urban males, of late 'thirties in spite of the rapid influx of college-trained individuals into the labor force. (3) Becker's estimates based on the difference in income between high school and college graduates based on urban males adjusted for ability, race, unemployment and mortality show a return of 9 per cent to total college costs including both earnings foregone and conventional college costs, public and private and with none of these costs allocated to consumption (see his paper given at the American Economic Association meeting, December 1959 [2]). (4) The returns to this education in the case of nonwhite urban males, or rural males, and of females in the labor force have been somewhat lower (see Becker [2]). (5) My own estimates, admittedly less complete than those of Becker and thus subject to additional qualifications, based mainly on lifetime income estimates of Herman P. Miller [12], lead to a return of about 11 per cent to both high school and college education as of 1958. See [19, Sec. 5].

Whether the consumption component in education will ultimately dominate, in the sense that the investment component in education will diminish as these expenditures increase and a point will be reached where additional expenditures for education will be pure consumption (a zero return on however small a part one might treat as an investment), is an interesting speculation. This may come to pass, as it has in the case of food and shelter, but that eventuality appears very remote presently in view of the prevailing investment value of education and the new demands for knowledge and skill inherent in the nature of our technical and economic progress.

16. The returns on this consumer capital will not appear in the wages and salaries that people earn.

17. Real income doubled, rising from $150 to $302 billion in 1956 prices. Eighty-nine billions of the increase in real income is taken to be unexplained, or about 59 per cent of the total increase. The stock of education in the labor force rose by $355 billion of which $69 billion is here allocated to the growth in the labor force to keep the per-worker stock of education constant, and $286 billion represents the increase in the level of this stock. See [19, Sec. 6] for an elaboration of the method and the relevant estimates.

18. In per cent, the lower estimate came out to 29 per cent and the upper estimate to 56 per cent.

19. I am indebted to Milton Friedman for bringing this issue to the fore in his comments on an early draft of this paper. See preface of [7] and also Jacob Mincer's pioneering paper [13].

REFERENCES

1. G. S. Becker, preliminary draft of study undertaken for Nat. Bur. Econ. Research. New York 1960.
2. ____, "Underinvestment in College Education?," *Proc., Am. Econ. Rev.*, May 1960, *50*, 346–54.
3. P. R. Brahmanand and C. N. Vakil, *Planning for an Expanding Economy.* Bombay 1956.
4. H. F. Clark, "Potentialities of Educational Establishments Outside the Conventional Structure of Higher Education," *Financing Higher Education, 1960–70*, D.M. Keezer, ed. New York 1959.
5. Solomon Fabricant, *Basic Facts on Productivity Change*, Nat. Bur. Econ. Research, Occas. Paper 63. New York 1959. Table 5.
6. Irving Fisher, *The Nature of Capital and Income.* New York 1906.
7. Milton Friedman and Simon Kuznets, *Income from Independent Professional Practice*, Nat. Bur. Econ. Research. New York 1945.
8. B. Horvat, "The Optimum Rate of Investment," *Econ. Jour.*, Dec. 1958, *68*, 747–67.
9. H. G. Johnson, "The Political Economy of Opulence," *Can. Jour. Econ. and Pol. Sci.*, Nov. 1960, *26*, 552–64.
10. Simon Kuznets, *Income and Wealth in the United States.* Cambridge, England 1952. Sec. IV, Distribution by Industrial Origin.
11. Alfred Marshall, *Principles of Economics*, 8th ed. London 1930. App. E, pp. 787–88.
12. H. P. Miller, "Annual and Lifetime Income in Relation to Education: 1939–1959," *Am. Econ. Rev.*, Dec. 1960, *50*, 962–86.
13. Jacob Mincer, "Investment in Human Capital and Personal Income Distribution," *Jour. Pol. Econ.*, Aug. 1958, *66*, 281–302.
14. S. J. Mushkin, "Toward a Definition of Health Economics," *Public Health Reports*, U. S. Dept. of Health, Educ. and Welfare, Sept. 1958, *73*, 785–93.
15. J. S. Nicholson, "The Living Capital of the United Kingdom," *Econ. Jour.*, Mar. 1891, *1*, 95; see J. S. Mill, *Principles of Political Economy*, ed. W. J. Ashley, London 1909, p. 8.
16. T. W. Schultz, "Investment in Man: An Economist's View," *Soc. Serv. Rev.*, June 1959, *33*, 109–17.
17. ____, "Agriculture and the Application of Knowledge," *A Look to the Future*, W. K. Kellogg Foundation, Battle Creek, 1956, 54–78.
18. ____, "Capital Formation by Education," *Jour. Pol. Econ.*, Dec. 1960, *68*, Tables 3 through 7.
19. ____, "Education and Economic Growth," *Social Forces Influencing American Education*, H. G. Richey, ed. Chicago 1961.
20. H. von Thünen, *Der isolierte Staat*, 3rd ed., Vol. 2, Pt. 2, 1875, transl. by B. F. Hoselitz, reproduced by the Comp. Educ. Center, Univ. Chicago, pp. 140–52.
21. Morton Zeman, *A Quantitative Analysis of White-Nonwhite Income Differentials in the United States.* Unpublished doctoral dissertation, Univ. Chicago, 1955.

17. Education and Economic Equality

LESTER C. THUROW

However much they may differ on other matters, the left, the center, and the right all affirm the central importance of education as a means of solving our social problems, especially poverty. To be sure, they see the education system in starkly contrasting terms. The left argues that the inferior education of the poor and of the minorities reflects a discriminatory effort to prevent them from competing with better-educated groups, to force them into menial, low-income jobs. The right argues that the poor are poor because they have failed to work hard and get the education which is open to them. Moderates usually subscribe to some mixture of these arguments: The poor are poor because they have gotten bad educations, partly as a result of inadequately funded and therefore inferior school systems, but partly also as a result of sociological factors (e.g., disrupted families) that prevent poor children from absorbing the education that is available. Yet despite these differences, people at all points of the political spectrum agree that, if they were running the country, education policy would be the cornerstone of their effort to improve the condition of the poor and the minorities: If the poor or the minorities were better educated, they could get better jobs and higher income. This idea has had a profound influence on public policy in the last decade.

This acceptance of the efficacy of education is itself derived from a belief in the standard economic theory of the labor market. According to this theory, the labor market exists to match labor demand with labor supply. At any given time, the pattern of matching and mismatching gives off various signals: Businesses are "told" to raise wages or redesign jobs in skill-shortage sectors, or to lower wages in skill-surplus sectors; individuals are "told" to acquire skills in high-wage sectors and are discouraged from seeking skills and jobs in sectors where wages are low and skills are in surplus. Each skill market is "cleared," in the short run, by increases or reductions in wages, and by a combination of wage changes, skill changes, and production-technique changes over the long run. The result, according to the theory, is that each person in the labor market is paid at the level of his marginal productivity. If he adds $3,000 to total economic output, he is paid $3,000; if he adds $8,000, he is paid $8,000.

This theory posits *wage competition* as the driving force of the labor market. It assumes that people come into the labor market with a definite, pre-existing set of skills (or lack of skills), and that they then compete against one another on the basis of wages. According to this theory, education is crucial because it creates the skills which people bring into the market. This implies that any increase in the educational level of low-income workers will have three powerful—and beneficial—effects. First, an educational program that transforms a low-skill person into a high-skill person raises his productivity and therefore his earnings. Second, it reduces the total supply of low-skill workers, which leads in turn to an increase in *their* wages. Third, it increases the supply of high-skill workers, and this lowers their wages. The net result is that total output rises (because of the increase in productivity among formerly uneducated workers), the distribution of earnings becomes more equal, and each individual is still rewarded according to merit. What could be more ideal?

Empirical studies seemingly have confirmed this theory. The economic literature on "human capital" is full of articles that estimate the economic rate of return for different levels of education; while the results differ slightly depending on the data

From *The Public Interest* 28 (Summer 1972): 66–81. Copyright © 1972 by National Affairs, Inc. Reprinted by permission.

and methods used, most studies find a rate of return on higher education slightly above 10 per cent per year for white males. This rate of return, as it happens, is approximately the same as that of investments in "physical capital" (e.g., new machines). From these findings, two conclusions seem to follow. First, educational investment produces just as much additional output as physical investments in plant and capital; and second, education is a powerful tool for altering the distribution of income in society. Such calculations are in common use in discussions of public education policy, and they form a major justification for heavy public investment in education.

Yet, despite this seeming confirmation, there is reason to doubt the validity of this view of the labor market and the importance of the economic role it assigns to education. As we shall see, a large body of evidence indicates that the American labor market is characterized less by wage competition than by *job competition.* That is to say, instead of people looking for jobs, there are jobs looking for people—for "suitable" people. In a labor market based on job competition, the function of education is not to confer skill and therefore increased productivity and higher wages on the worker; it is rather to certify his "trainability" and to confer upon him a certain status by virtue of this certification. Jobs and higher incomes are then distributed on the basis of this certified status. To the extent that job competition rather than wage competition prevails in the American economy, our long-standing beliefs about both the economic benefits of education and the efficacy of education as a social policy which makes for greater equality may have to be altered.

DEFECTS OF THE "WAGE COMPETITION" THEORY

While it is possible to raise a number of theoretical objections against the "human capital" calculations which seem to confirm the wage competition theory, it is more instructive to see if in our actual post-war experience, existing educational programs have had the effects that the wage competition theory would predict. In fact, there are a number of important discrepancies. The first arises from the fact that, in the real world, the distributions of education and IQ are more equal than the distribution of income, as Figure I indicates. The usual explanation for this disparity is that income is disproportionately affected by the *combination* of education and intelligence. This would explain the wider *dispersion* of income than of education or intelligence—but it cannot explain the markedly different *shapes* of the distributions. Clearly, other factors are at work.

A second discrepancy is revealed by the fact that, while the distribution of education has moved in the direction of greater equality over the post-war period, the distribution of income has not. In 1950, the bottom fifth of the white male population had 8.6 per cent of the total number of years of education, while the top fifth had 31.1 per cent (See Table 1). By 1970, the share of the bottom fifth had risen to 10.7 per cent and that of the top fifth had dropped to 29.3 per cent. According to the wage competition theory, this should have led to a more equal distribution of earnings, whereas in fact the distribution of income among white males has become more *un*equal, as Table 2 indicates. From 1949 to 1969, the share of total income going to the lowest fifth has dropped from 3.2 per cent to 2.6 per cent while the share going to the highest fifth rose from 44.8 per cent to 46.3 per cent. Empirically, education has not been having the equalizing impact that the rate-of-return calculations would have led one to expect.

Black/white income gaps reveal the same discrepancies. From 1952 to 1968, the mean education of black male workers rose from 67 per cent to 87 per cent of that of white male workers—yet median wage and salary incomes rose only from 58 per cent to 66 per cent. Most of this increase, moreover,

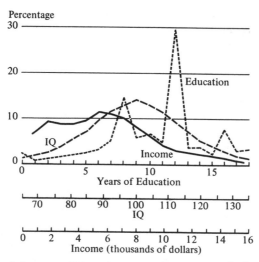

Figure 1. Distribution of Income, Education, and Intelligence (IQ) of Males Twenty-five Years of Age and Over in 1965.

Sources: Income data from U.S. Bureau of the Census, *Current Population Reports,* Series P-60, No. 51 "Income in 1965 of Families and Persons in the United States" (1967), p. 34; education data estimated from U.S. Bureau of the Census, *Statistical Abstract of the United States; 1967,* p. 113; IQ data from David Wechsler, *Wechsler Adult Intelligence Scale Manual* (Psychological Corp., 1955), p. 20.

can be traced to black emigration from the South, with its lower relative incomes for blacks. As a result, education does not seem to have equalized black and white incomes in the manner that the rate-of-return calculations would indicate.

Similarly, a more rapid rate of growth of education should have led to a more rapid growth of the economy. In the early 1950's, the college-educated labor force was growing at a rate of 3 per cent per year. In the late 1960's, it was growing at a 6 per cent rate.

Yet there does not seem to be any evidence that the rate of growth of productivity of the economy as a whole has accelerated correspondingly. If anything, the opposite has happened. Productivity today may be increasing more slowly than its historic rate of growth of 2.9 per cent per year.

Moreover, the entire theory assumes a labor market where wage competition is the most important short-run method for equilibrating the supplies and demands for different types of labor. Yet the real world

Table 1. Distribution of Education Among Adult White Males

	Percentage share of years of educational attainment	
	1950	1970
Lowest Fifth	8.6	10.7
Second Fifth	16.4	16.4
Middle Fifth	19.0	21.3
Fourth Fifth	24.9	22.3
Highest Fifth	31.1	29.3

Table 2. Distribution of Income Among Adult White Males

	Percentage shares of total money income	
	1949	1969
Lowest Fifth	3.2	2.6
Second Fifth	10.9	9.4
Middle Fifth	17.5	16.7
Fourth Fifth	23.7	25.0
Highest Fifth	44.8	46.3

reveals very sluggish wage adjustments in most sectors of the economy. Not only is there considerable variance in wages for different individuals with the same skills; there is also little tendency for the existence of unemployment to lower wages. There may be many unemployed airline pilots or engineers today, but their joblessness does not lead to lower wages for those lucky enough to remain employed. In fact, wage competition simply is not the all-pervasive force that economic theory supposes it to be.

Perhaps the most devastating problem with the simple wage competition view is that it cannot explain the existence of unemployment. When the demand for labor falls, wages are supposed to fall until enough jobs have been generated to keep everyone fully employed at the new lower wages. Yet the real world is full of unemployed workers whose presence does not seem to have led to falling wages for those who are employed.

The absence of wage competition is also indicated by employers' lack of interest in relative wage differentials when designing new plants. In the several cases investigated by Piore and Doeringer, plant designers typically did not take account of (or even know) the relative prices of different types of labor when designing new plants. They could not economize on expensive skills since they did not know which skills were expensive and which cheap. They simply used an average wage rate in making their calculations.

Now there are plausible *ad hoc* explanations for all of these aberrant observations—but the necessity for so many *ad hoc* explanations is itself suspicious. Our experience with large investments in higher education entitles us to have doubts about the value of education as a means of altering the distribution of income. In the post-war years, this experience has not been encouraging. Large investments have been made. What little has happened to the post-war distribution of adult white male incomes has been contrary to expectation. Before

further investments are made for such purposes, we should first get clear on why past investments have not had the expected and desired results.

THE "JOB COMPETITION" MODEL

Governmental education and training policies have not had the predicted impact because they have ignored the "job competition" elements in the labor market. In a labor market based on job competition, an individual's income is determined by (a) his relative position in the labor queue and (b) the distribution of job opportunities in the economy. Wages are based on the characteristics of the job, and workers are distributed across job opportunities on the basis of their relative position in the labor queue. The most preferred workers get the best (highest-income) jobs. According to this model, labor skills do not exist in the labor market; on the contrary, most actual job skills are acquired informally through on-the-job training *after* a worker finds an entry job and a position on the associated promotional ladder.

As a matter of fact, such a training process is clearly observable in the American economy. A survey of how American workers acquired their actual job skills found that only 40 per cent were using skills that they had acquired in formal training programs or in specialized education—and, of these, most reported that some of the skills they were currently using had been acquired through informal on-the-job training. The remaining 60 per cent acquired all of their job skills through such informal on-the-job training. More than two-thirds of the college graduates reported that they had acquired job skills through such informal processes. When asked to list the form of training that had been most helpful in acquiring their current job skills, only 12 per cent listed formal training and specialized education.

Thus the labor market is primarily a market, not for matching the demands for and supplies of different job skills, but for matching trainable individuals with training ladders. *Because most skills are acquired on the job, it is the demand for job skills which creates the supply of job skills.* The operative problem in a job competition economy is to pick and train workers to generate the desired productivity with the least investment in training costs. For new workers and for entry-level jobs, it is the "background characteristics" of the workers that form the basis of selection. Those workers whose backgrounds promise the lowest training costs will be hired. For workers with previous job experience, existing job skills (including skills like reliability and punctuality) are relevant to the selection process to the extent that they might lead to lower training costs.

In such a system, depending as it does on informal on-the-job transmission of knowledge and skills, the absence of direct wage competition and the restriction of any job competition to entry-level jobs are absolutely necessary. If workers feel that they are training a potential wage or job competitor every time they show another worker how to do their job, they have every incentive to stop giving such informal training. Each man, under the circumstances, would try to build his own little monopoly by hoarding skills and information and by resisting any technical improvements that would reduce the number of job opportunities in his occupation. But in a training system where no one is trained unless a job is available (which is what on-the-job training means), where strong seniority provisions exist, and where there is no danger of some competitor bidding down your wages, employees can freely transmit information to new workers and more readily accept new techniques. If anyone is made redundant by such techniques, it will be a clearly defined minority—new workers.

In a labor market governed by job competition, employers rank workers on a continuum from the best potential worker (trainee) to the worst potential worker (trainee) on the basis of estimated potential training costs. (Such costs certainly include the costs of inculcating norms of industrial discipline and good work habits.) But because employers rarely have direct and unambiguous evidence of the specific training costs for specific workers, they end up ranking workers according to their background characteristics—age, sex, educational attainment, previous skills, performance on psychological tests, etc. Each of these is used as an indirect measure of the costs necessary to produce some standard of work performance.

Entirely subjective and arbitrary elements may also affect the labor queue. If employers discriminate against blacks, blacks will find themselves lower in the labor market queue than their training costs would warrant. To some extent, the smaller the actual differences in training costs, the more such subjective preferences can determine the final ordering. If every individual had identical training costs, blacks could be placed at the bottom of the labor queue with no loss in efficiency.

The national labor queue depends upon the distribution of these background characteristics and upon employers' ranking of different background characteristics. While no two workers may be exactly alike, the costs of discovering small differences are so large that individuals are ranked on a finite number of background characteristics. This means that there are a finite number of rankings in the labor queue and that many individuals have identical rankings.

Jobs and their corresponding training ladders are distributed to individuals in order of their rank, working from those at the top of the queue down to those at the bottom. The best jobs go to the best workers and the worst jobs to the worst workers. Given a need for untrained labor, some workers at the bottom of the queue will receive little or no training on their jobs. In periods of labor scarcity, training will extend farther and farther down the queue as employers are forced to train more costly workers to fill job vacancies. In periods of labor surplus, it is those at the bottom of the labor queue who will be unemployed.

To the extent that education and formal training are an important background characteristic used for screening individuals, alterations in the distribution of education can have an important impact on the shape of the labor queue. This queue can be skinnier at the top, at the bottom, or in the middle. The relevant empirical question is the weight that is attached to education in screening, relative to the weight that is attached to other factors. Although this obviously differs from job to job, educational screening tests are in fact ubiquitous. But although education can affect the shape of the labor queue, this does not necessarily mean that it can change the actual distribution of income. This is a function, not only of the labor queue, but also of the distribution of job opportunities. An equal group of laborers (with respect to potential training costs) might be distributed across a relatively unequal distribution of job opportunities. After receiving the resultant on-the-job training, the initially equal workers would have unequal productivities since they would now have unequal skills. As a result, the distribution of incomes is determined by the distribution of job opportunities and not by the distribution of the labor queue, which only determines the order of access—and the distribution of access—to job opportunities.

THE DISTRIBUTION OF JOB OPPORTUNITIES

The shape of the job distribution (and hence of the income distribution) across which individual laborers will be spread is governed by three sets of factors: (1) the character of technical progress, which generates certain kinds of jobs in certain proportions; (2) the sociology of wage determination—trade unions, traditions of wage differentials, etc.; and (3) the distribution of training costs

between employees and employers, which will influence the wage that is associated with each job. The interaction among these factors is exceedingly complicated—and little studied.[1] The outcome of such studies would tell us with some assurance where exactly the American economy is to be located on a continuum between a wage competition economy and a job competition economy. Let me point out, however, that observed changes over the post-war period are in accordance with a job competition model.

If, at the beginning of the post-war period, an observer had been told that the composition of the adult white male labor force was going to change from 47 per cent with a grade school education, 38 per cent with a high school education, and 15 per cent with a college education, to 20 per cent with a grade school education, 51 per cent with a high school education, and 28 per cent with a college education (the actual 1949 to 1969 changes), expectations about the distribution of income would have been very different depending upon whether the observer subscribed to a job competition model or a wage competition model. Assuming there were no offsetting changes on the demand side of the market, the observer subscribing to a wage competition model of the economy would have predicted a substantial equalization of earnings. But the observer subscribing to the job competition model would have predicted something quite different. He would have expected an equalization of income within the most preferred group (college-educated workers), a rise in its incomes relative to other groups, and a decrease relative to the national average. He would have reasoned as follows: As the most preferred group expanded, it would filter down the job distribution into lower-paying jobs. This would lead to a fall in wages relative to the national average. As it moved into a denser portion of the national job (income) distribution, it would, however, experience within-group equalization of income. By taking what had previously been the best high school jobs, college incomes would rise relative to high school incomes.

Such a prediction would have been correct. The proportion of college incomes going to the poorest 25 per cent of white male college-educated workers rose from 6.3 to 9.0 per cent from 1949 to 1969, while the proportion going to the richest 25 per cent fell from 53.9 per cent to 46.0 per cent. While the median income of college-educated workers was rising from 198 per cent to 254 per cent of the median for grade-school-educated workers and from 124 per cent to 137 per cent of the median for high-school-educated workers, it was falling from 148 per cent to 144 per cent of the national median.

As the least preferred group (those with a grade school education) contracted in size, a job competition observer would have expected it to be moving out of the denser regions of the income distribution and becoming more and more concentrated on the lower tail of the income distribution. Given the shape of the lower tail of the American income distribution, such a movement would have led to falling relative incomes and increasing income equality. In fact, the incomes of grade school laborers have fallen from 50 per cent to 39 per cent of college incomes and from 63 per cent to 54 per cent of high school incomes. The income going to the poorest 25 per cent of all grade school laborers has risen from 2.9 per cent to 6.6 per cent of the group's total, and the income going to the richest 25 per cent has fallen from 53.5 per cent to 49.4 per cent.

Predictions of the position of the middle group (the high-school-educated) would have depended upon an analysis of the relative densities of the income distribution at its margin with the college-educated and the grade-school-educated. Since the American income distribution is denser on the margin with the grade-school-educated than on the margin with the college-educated, an expansion in the size of the middle group should have led to more within-group equality, an income rise relative to the grade-school-ed-

ucated, and an income fall relative to the college-educated. In fact, the proportion of income going to the poorest 25 per cent of all the high-school-educated has risen from 8.2 per cent to 10.2 per cent, while the proportion going to the highest 25 per cent has fallen from 46.0 per cent to 41.6 per cent. High school incomes have risen relative to grade school incomes (from 160 per cent to 185 per cent) and fallen relative to college incomes (from 81 per cent to 73 per cent).

An alternative method for viewing the same changes is to look at the probability each of these educational groups has of holding a job at different levels in the American job hierarchy. The increasing economic segregation based on education can be seen in Table 3, where each cell has been adjusted for changes in the proportions of those with college, high school, and grade school educations. (The table is constructed so that each cell would have the number 1.000 if incomes were randomly drawn with respect to education.) In 1949, a college graduate was six times as likely to hold a job in the top tenth of jobs as a grade school graduate, but by 1969 he was 15 times as likely to hold a job in the top tenth. Conversely, the probability of a grade school graduate holding a job in the lowest tenth has risen from three to six times that of a college graduate. Similarly, probabilities of holding the best job have risen for college graduates relative to high school graduates (from 2.5 to 4 times those of high school graduates), while there has been a rise in relative probabilities of holding the worst jobs for high school graduates (from 1.2 to 1.5 times those of college graduates). Extrapolation of these trends for another 20 years would lead to a world where income was almost perfectly segregated according to education.

Although the job competition model seems to "post-cast" accurately what happened to the American distribution of income in the post-war period, post-casting is not a definitive test, and there are other possible explanations for what happened in the post-war period. One explanation would

Table 3. Normalized Probabilities (Adult White Males).[1]

	Per cent of total males in each job class, in 1950 & 1970, by educational attainment (divided by per cent of total males with that educational attainment that year)					
	Elementary		High school		College	
Quality of jobs (determined by income of total males with income, 25 yrs. & older)	(1950)	(1970)	(1950)	(1970)	(1950)	(1970)
10% Best Jobs—1950: $5,239.3 & up 1970: $15,000 & up	.436	.1714	1.066	.648	2.715	2.549
2nd Best 10%—1950: $4,028.84–$5,239.2 1970: $12,506.26–$14,999	.599	.3535	1.337	1.130	1.523	1.468
3rd 10%—1950: $3,519.7–$4,028.83 1970: $10,012.9–$12,506.25	.772	.3535	1.354	1.130	.940	1.468
4th 10%—1950: $3,025.2–$3,519.6 1970: $8,752–$10,012.8	.776	.621	1.354	1.248	.927	.960
5th 10%—1950: $2,553.6–$3,025.1 1970: $7,573.9–$8,751	.952	.692	1.221	1.251	.649	.881
6th 10%—1950: $2,101–$2,553.5 1970: $6,449.6–$7,573.8	1.079	.871	1.069	1.238	.5695	.704
7th 10%—1950: $1,530–$2,100 1970: $5,148.3–$6,449.5	1.193	1.128	.910	1.148	.5629	.586
8th 10%—1950: $706–$1,529 1970: $3,576.6–$5,148.2	1.328	1.564	.708	.933	.5827	.500
9th 10%—1950: $270.6–$705 1970: $2,008.2–$3,576.5	1.500	1.960	.527	.712	.4304	.468
10% Worst Jobs—1950: $0–$270.5 1970: $0–$2008.1	1.458	2.303	.564	.552	.4768	.3818

[1] Figures for: 1950—Money Income in 1949, Population in 1950; 1970—Money Income in 1969, Population in 1970.

be that increasing technical progress has simply made education more necessary for acquiring income-producing skills. Training costs differentials have risen, and this could explain the increasing economic segregation based on education. Another explanation would be that higher education has become more meritocratic in the post-war period (i.e., it is becoming more perfectly correlated with other income-producing factors), which would create the appearance of more economic segregation based on education. Still another explanation would be that the American economy has become more of a "credential society," in which education is used as a cheap (or defensible) screening device even though it is not very closely related to training costs.

ECONOMIC IMPLICATIONS

While education has many non-economic benefits, its strictly economic benefits may be of three types: First, education directly increases the productivity of a country's labor force and indirectly increases the productivity of its physical capital. The result is more output and a higher real living standard. Second, by altering the distribution of individual productivities, education can lead to changes in the distribution of earned income between rich and poor. It can help the poor to catch up with the rich. Third, education can lead to economic mobility. Black earnings may catch up with white earnings, and the children of low-productivity parents need not themselves be low-productivity individuals. It is important to recognize, however, that each of these three impacts is merely possible. They may or may not occur. Whether they do or do not is an empirical question.

Even on the wage competition view of the labor market, education can be expanded to the point where it no longer increases a country's productivity. Nevertheless, large observed earnings differentials between the high-school-educated and the college-educated (after standardization for other factors such as IQ) have been taken as evidence to substantiate the fact that there are actual gains to be made. But if there is a substantial element of job competition in the economy, education's impact on individual productivity cannot be determined simply with rate-of-return calculations based on normalized income differentials. The exact impact on productivity of an alteration in the distribution of education depends upon a set of factors beyond the scope of this essay, but large observed income differentials could persist after the productivity impact of education was exhausted. An increasing supply of the college-educated would lead them to accept jobs farther down the job opportunities distribution. In the process, they would take the best high school jobs and thus bring down average high school incomes. This would preserve the observed wage differential between college and high school labor, but the differential would not indicate potential productivity gains or opportunities to equalize incomes between rich and poor.

There is, then, a need to be much more agnostic about the productivity impacts of education than public rhetoric would indicate to be our present inclination. In the wage competition view of education, additional education for someone with more education than I can never hurt my prospects. If anything, it must raise my potential earnings. From the job competition point of view, however, education may become a defensive necessity. As the supply of edu-

cated labor increases, individuals find that they must improve their educational level simply to defend their current income positions. If they don't, others will, and they will find their current job no longer open to them. Education becomes a good investment, not because it would raise people's incomes above what they would have been if no one had increased his education, but rather because it raises their income above what it will be if others acquire an education and they do not. *In effect, education becomes a defensive expenditure necessary to protect one's "market share."* The larger the class of educated labor and the more rapidly it grows, the more such defensive expenditures become imperative. Interestingly, many students currently object to the defensive aspects of acquiring a college education. This complaint makes no sense from a wage competition point of view, but it makes good sense from a job competition point of view.

While the current public policy emphasis on on-the-job training programs seems to fit in with the job competition view of the world, on-the-job training programs can have an impact only if they really lead to the training of a different class of workers than would ordinarily have been trained through the job market. Unfortunately, many government training programs have simply led to the training of the groups that would have been trained in any case; the only operative difference is that government foots the training bills.

Based on a wage competition view of the labor market, government programs to equalize incomes and to raise the productivity of low-income individuals have been almost entirely devoted to changing the labor characteristics that an individual brings into the labor market. This is done in spite of the fact that individual labor characteristics typically do not explain more than half of the observed income differences between black and white, rich and poor, or male and female. Thus the emphasis has been entirely on changing the supplies of different types of workers rather than the demands for different types of workers.

In addition to being uncalled for by economic theory, this emphasis on altering labor supplies is at variance with our own history. To find a period of increasing income equality it is necessary to go back to the Great Depression and World War II. From 1929 to 1941 the share of total income going to the bottom 40 per cent of the population rose from 12.5 per cent to 13.6 per cent, while the share of income going to the top 5 per cent fell from 30.0 per cent to 24.0 per cent and the share of income going to the top 20 per cent fell from 54.4 per cent to 48.8 per cent. From 1941 to 1947 the share going to the bottom 40 per cent rose to 16.0 per cent, while the share going to the top 5 per cent fell to 20.9 per cent and the share going to the top 20 per cent fell to 46.0 per cent. In both cases alterations in the demand side, rather than the supply side, of the market seem to have provided the mechanism for equalizing incomes.

In the Great Depression an economic collapse was the mechanism for changes. Individual fortunes were lost, firms collapsed, and a wage structure emerged that was noticeably more equal than before the collapse. While interesting, the deliberate collapsing of an economy in order to equalize the distribution of income is not a policy that commends itself.

The World War II period is more interesting from this vantage point. As a result of an overwhelming consensus that the economic burdens of the war should be shared equally, the federal government undertook two major actions. First, it instituted a very progressive income tax (more progressive than the current federal income tax) that converted a regressive tax system into a mildly progressive tax system. Second, it used a combination of wage controls and labor controls to equalize market wages. This was accompanied by a conscious policy of restructuring jobs to reduce skill requirements

and to make use of the existing skills of the labor force. To some extent, old skill differences were simply cloaked with a new set of relative wages and, to some extent, skill differentials were actually collapsed. Together the two factors led to an equalization of market incomes that was not dissipated after the war ended.

To some extent the wage policies of World War II were a deliberate—and successful—attempt to change the sociology of what constitutes "fair" wage differentials. As a result of the war, our judgments as to what constituted fair differentials changed, and this was reflected in wage patterns. As a consequence of the widespread consensus that wage differentials should be reduced, it was possible to make a deliberate attempt to reduce wage differentials. After they had been embedded in the labor market for a number of years, these new differentials came to be regarded as the "just" differentials and stuck after the egalitarian pressures of World War II disappeared.

From this experience, I would suggest that any time a consensus emerges on the need for more equality, it can be at least partly achieved by making a frontal attack on wage differentials. Elaborate educational programs are not necessary. Without such a consensus, I would suggest, massive educational investments are apt to be wasted. They simply will not bring about the desired equalization.

In addition to a frontal attack on wage differentials, programs to alter the demands for different types of employees would include research and development efforts to alter the skill-mix generated by technical progress; guaranteed government jobs; fiscal and monetary policies designed to create labor shortages; public wage scales designed to pressure low-wage employers; and incentives to encourage private employers to compress their wage differentials. If quick results are desired, quotas must seriously be considered since they are the only technique for quickly altering the types of laborers demanded.

In any case, I would argue that our reliance on education as the ultimate public policy for curing all problems, economic and social, is unwarranted at best and in all probability ineffective.

NOTE

1. Further discussion of this matter may be found in Lester C. Thurow, "The American Distribution of Income: A Structural Problem," Committee Print, U.S. Congress Joint Economic Committee, 1972.

18. Economic Theory and the Fate of the Poor

BARRY BLUESTONE

Economists often work with abstract models of "perfect" economies that obey strict mathematical laws. In some cases this serves to sharpen the focus of empirical research. Yet when the abstractions neglect reality and play on minutiae, the theory can make for disastrous practice. Such is the case with modern labor theory and manpower policy.

"Bourgeois" economics assumes that people try to maximize their "utility" within the framework of economic constraints. Applied to labor, the assumption is that workers make the most of their condition by investing in themselves and making choices between work and leisure according to limitations of time and the costs of schooling and training. Though the theory may be logically correct, it often leads economists to propose the wrong policies for the wrong people. The trouble lies not in the theory, but in the emphasis given its separate parts. Economists tend to focus attention on the maximizing behavior of individuals and to neglect the real economic constraints before them. This is especially true with regard to the poor.

Traditional economic theory assumes the existence of competitive product markets, adequately mobile labor, and sufficient labor-market information; it fails to acknowledge certain realities such as barriers between labor markets, the inadequacy of labor-market information, and unequal opportunities among different groups in society. Competition among firms and individuals supposedly distributes workers so that the more skilled earn higher wages; therefore, those who earn less *must* be less skilled, since each worker is paid only what he is "worth." It then follows that the poor must be unskilled, unhealthy, or lack the proper work attitudes, and that the only way to improve their standard of living is to change *them*. Society may actually be responsible for the poor's lack of education, training, and a healthful environment; but most analyses of their situation lead to policies based on the assumption that the fault lies with the poor themselves—they are blamed for their poverty. Policy-makers then prescribe a multitude of manpower programs designed to overcome one or another personal trait in the poor that presumably contributes to unemployment or low wages.

What economists overlook is the glaring fact that the economy does not create enough good jobs and that consequently many people with adequate skills are denied adequate employment. Because of racism, sexism, regional limitations, and the risk attached to geographic and employment mobility, millions of workers have no jobs. Millions more are trapped in jobs that fail to pay a living wage. The basic structure of the economy is such that it creates good jobs and bad ones and then parcels them out on the basis of race, sex, and luck.

More often than not, the economist's role

From *Social Policy* 2 (January/February 1972): 30–31 and 46–48. Copyright © 1972 by the Social Policy Corporation. Reprinted by permission.

has been to justify this distribution of opportunities, not change it. Rarely is the structure of the economy considered at fault for the poverty of the poor. And even less frequently do economists propose solutions aimed at the structure of the labor market instead of the behavior and characteristics of its victims.

A HISTORICAL REVIEW OF LABOR ECONOMICS

Although it is true that economists seldom defend the economically disadvantaged, it is not true that economists have always ignored the structural characteristics of individual labor markets. The currently accepted view of labor economics, that associated with the "human-capital" school, is not the only view of labor-market dynamics. It presently holds sway among academicians and policy-makers, but other labor-market paradigms do exist, and new ones are being developed. The policy implications of the conflicting paradigms are at such variance that they deserve more attention.

In the 1940s and 1950s, labor economists recognized the importance of barriers to mobility and the inadequacy of labor-market information. Many institutional factors were observed to impinge on the wage-determination process—e.g., government regulation, minimum wage legislation, unionization. Even the founders of the neoclassical analysis were

troubled by the "peculiarities" of the labor market—the fact that the worker sells himself with his services, that his immediate financial need may place him at a disadvantage in negotiating with employers, that he is influenced by nonpecuniary motives, that he has limited knowledge of alternative opportunities, and that there are numerous objective barriers to free movement of labor.[1]

During the 1950s, labor economists, including Harold Levinson, Arthur Ross, Clark Kerr, Sumner Slichter, and Lloyd Reynolds, pursued research that asked, "What is it about *different industries, different regions* of the nation, and *different labor markets* that accounts for the wide variance in employment and wage rates?"[1] Others wondered why individual labor markets make for great differences in unemployment and underemployment. These economists were studying the differences in industrial structure that were correlated with wage differentials, asking questions about the effect of unionization and minimum wages, and indirectly posing some of the right questions about the determinants of income distribution.

The critical variables were on the demand or industry side of the wage and employment equation: unionization, profitability, government attitude toward collective bargaining, the firm's ability to pay, the capital intensity of production, and the racial and sexual composition of the work force. It was assumed, more or less correctly, that the skills required for most production jobs and many white-collar clerical occupations did not vary greatly *between* industries, firms, and regions.

The conclusion of much of this early research has been summed up in Sumner Slichter's "Notes on the Structure of Wages."[2] His research and that of others led him to conclude ". . . that wages, within a considerable range, reflect managerial discretion, that where managements can easily pay high wages they tend to do so, and that where managements are barely breaking even they tend to keep wages down." The important differences in wages paid to individuals, and indeed the differences in the labor-force status of working-class employees, were shown to be related to the type and place of industrial employment. Whether a person lived in Appalachia or Chicago was seen to have a great deal to do with the probability of locating employment; working in the steel industry versus a dry-cleaning establishment seemed pretty much to determine income.

Differences in education, training, skills, and "discipline" were considered to have some effect on labor-force status, but were by no means the only variables, or even the most critical ones.

Although much of the early research failed to focus on *who* got into *what* industry and who lived *where,* it was assumed that economic minorities—Blacks, Chicanos, Indians, teenagers, and women—would be restricted to the less skilled occupations *regardless* of the skill level of the worker.

Much of this research was related to the key question of the day: "What is the effect of unions on the efficiency of labor markets?" Consequently, some of the more far-reaching implications for public policy were ignored even though it seemed clear that social policy was needed to deal with market barriers and industry structure. The creation of job opportunities as alternatives to both unemployment and low-wage employment was certainly implied in this research. But the 1950s came to an end, and a new development in labor economics began to purge much of such research from the leading economic journals.

In 1960, T. W. Schultz, Edward Denison, and Gary Becker were beginning to develop a coherent "human-capital" economics to replace the fragmented institutional and neoclassical theories that had prevailed up to that point. By calling nearly everything that comprises worker productivity "human capital," these theorists were able, with a single semantic stroke, to explain all variance in employment status and wage rates in terms of the one parameter.[3]

Correctly enough, the human-capital theorists observed the strong correlation between education, training, skills, and competencies of the work force and the incomes individuals and families receive. They noted that physicians have more education (human capital) than janitors and that doctors are better paid. Based on so simple an observation, the "human capitalists" extrapolated their finding to cover all labor-force research. Treating labor as shells into which human capital was poured, in greater or lesser amounts, they were able to "explain" the wages and employment of all individuals. Those who invested more in themselves would (almost automatically) find employment more often, reap higher wages, and benefit from greater economic security.

But the extrapolation of the global finding to each and every segment of the labor force inevitably led to critical errors and misconceptions, and to dangerously mistaken policy implications as well. On the basis of their reasoning and the assumption that labor markets were workably competitive, the human-capital theorists concluded, in essence, that those who earned little, those who were involuntarily employed part time, and those who ended up with no employment at all were unskilled and unproductive by *definition.* The responsibility of the economic structure itself for low wages and unemployment was rarely considered.[4] The labor market was assumed to be perfect, so that once the human capital of an individual was raised, he or she would be able to rise above low-wage employment, underemployment, or joblessness. *The solution to the poverty problem thus resolved into a technical exercise of finding the right combination of manpower programs or human-resource-development schemes to lift each individual from personal disadvantage.*

But many of those who suffer from low wages and unemployment *have* a considerable amount of human capital. They fail to find jobs that pay a living wage because of racism, sexism, economic depression, and uneven economic development of industries and regions. Compared with some workers who have found steady employment in the high-wage industries, these workers have, in many cases, even more human capital, but happen to be the wrong color or sex, to be too young or too old, or to live on the wrong side of town or in the wrong part of the country. The inadequacy of the economic system is a more important cause of poverty than the inadequacy of people. Yet the human-capital school has attempted to immunize the patient when it should have been eradicating the disease.

Admittedly, the labor-market theorists of the 1950s underestimated important elements on the supply or human-capital side of the wage and employment process. But the disregard of the demand side by the human-capital school is also in error, and dangerously so, since it puts the onus of poverty reduction on those who suffer it rather than on the economic system that promulgates it. A labor-market paradigm is needed that takes into consideration the strengths and weaknesses of both positions and begins to analyze both sides of the labor-market process. This new paradigm is now being developed, some of the preliminary results are in, and more definitive conclusions will soon be forthcoming.[5]

Glimpses of the initial results confirm the suspicion that both sides of the labor-force equation are important. Both human-capital and economic-structure variables are critical in understanding wage determination and differential unemployment rates. It is becoming clear that industry structural variables such as unionization, region, and city size are still highly significant in explaining the wage rates of full-time workers even if human-capital variables such as education and job experience are taken into account. My own research reveals that workers who obtain employment in an industry that is highly profitable, unionized, capital intensive, and supported by government purchases will receive higher wages even if their training, education, health, and discipline are average or below average. Workers who are trapped (primarily because of sex and race discrimination) in unorganized, less profitable industries, operating with little capital per worker and gaining little support from government or foreign purchases, will be low paid even if they are well educated and have an adequate supply of human capital.

An extremely extensive multivariate analysis is now under way, using a massive set of data compiled on individuals, their occupations, and the industries in which they work.[6] Furthermore, after extensive research, my colleagues and I have found that within education groups, and with race and sex taken into consideration, there is great variance in wage rates across industries.[7]

LOW WAGES AND THE WORKING POOR

A good deal of current economic research grows out of the recent awareness that the majority of the poor in America work for their poverty. The evidence indicates that over 50 percent of the very poorest families have household heads and often additional family members who work. Sometimes this work is only part time and interrupted by periods of involuntary unemployment. Yet in at least *one poor family in four,* the head of the household is employed full time throughout the year. In a significant number of additional families, the head of the household may not be employed full time, but someone else is, and the family still remains poor. In millions of other families not counted in the official poverty statistics, at least one person is working full time at extremely low pay.

Full-time wages are low enough in some occupations and industries that an individual with a moderate-sized family can work 40 hours a week, 52 weeks a year, and still face the bleakest poverty. In New York City alone there are approximately a quarter of a million families whose breadwinners are working at full-time jobs for wages so low that their families are eligible for Public Assistance Income Supplements under New York State's Home Relief Program. Throughout the United States this unfortunate situation is repeated over and over. In 1968 there were 2.25 million families, with nearly 10 million individuals, living below the low-income cutoff who had family heads working full time all year.

Moreover, special tabulations from the 1967 Survey of Economic Opportunity clearly indicate that the low-paid are not necessarily uneducated or unskilled. Over 17 percent of all white males with full-time regular jobs earn $2.25 or less an hour; even one in eight of those who have some college education earn this little. For minorities the figures are much higher. Two of five Black male high-school graduates earn below this low-wage figure, and nearly six of ten white women and seven of ten Black women with the same amount of education fall into the same wage category. Even one-quarter of all white female college graduates working full time all through the year earn less than this wage. At the other extreme, a significant number of white males without a high-school education earn adequate incomes because they have landed in profitable industries.

For many of the low-paid, low wages are not due to lack of education or human capital. Low wages are mainly the result of entrapment in low-wage, nondurable, manufacturing firms, retail-trade establishments, service industries, and, to some extent, wholesale trade. Being black, brown, or female is often sufficient to narrow occupational choice to a low-wage clerical, operator, laborer, or service position in one of these industries. Few alternative job opportunities are available, especially for those living in depressed regions of the country. Since these workers are crowded into industries that already have a reduced *ability* to pay, wages are forced even lower by the sheer "oversupply" of labor.

Given the opportunity to escape to the high-wage sector, many low-wage workers would perform admirably. Without years of extra education, without massive doses of institutional and on-the-job training, without learning a new "industrial discipline," many low-wage workers could fit into a unionized, profitable, capital-intensive industry and begin to earn a living wage. High-wage firms that have waived credentials in order to hire high-school dropouts and even the hard-core unemployed report that with little special training, these new workers assume a productivity and an industrial discipline charac-

teristic of their normal employees.[8] Nevertheless, until very recently, the core of antipoverty strategy consisted of manpower training and human-resource development rather than job development. The human-capital school dominated in the choice of social policy.

At best, the results from following this policy direction have been mixed. For those who completed training under the Manpower Development and Training Act (MDTA), only three of five advanced in pay during the middle 1960s, and the increased earnings were quite small. According to the largest study of MDTA, involving over 100,000 institutional training graduates, the average wage for males *after* training was only $2.06 per hour, 27 percent higher than the average pretraining wage rate. For females the post-training wage was boosted to $1.53, less than 20 percent above pretraining average earnings. These results are for people who actually finished the program *and* found jobs. Thousands of others failed to complete programs, and still others finished training but were unable to find suitable employment. Another of the federal manpower programs, On-the-Job Training (OJT), has provided more people directly with jobs; but the training component appears to be a subsidy for specific job training that the employer would normally have provided.[9]

The important point is not that manpower training is irrelevant in improving the condition of the economically disadvantaged, but that for many workers, the major problem is the total lack of good jobs. The major policy thrust must be in the direction of creating adequate jobs for people to fill, not training people for nonexistent jobs.

NOTES

1. Lloyd G. Reynolds, *The Structure of Labor Markets* (New York: Harper and Brothers, 1951), p. 2.
2. Sumner Slichter, "Notes on the Structure of Wages," *Review of Economics and Statistics,* 1950, *32,* 80–91.
3. For an extension of this concept, see the excellent monograph, by David M. Gordon, *Economic*

Theories of Poverty and Underemployment (New York: National Bureau of Economic Research, January 1971).

4. This criticism, of course, does not apply to all labor economists of the "human-capital" school. Some economists, including Lester Thurow, who embrace this approach are not blind to the extensive economic, political, and social barriers that limit the extent of correlation between human capital and economic status.

5. See Howard Wachtel and Charles Betsey, "Employment at Low Wages" (Institute of Labor and Industrial Relations, University of Michigan-Wayne State University, 1971), unpublished manuscript; Lester Thurow, *Poverty and Discrimination* (Washington, D.C.: The Brookings Institution, 1969); Albert Rees and George P. Shultz, *Workers and Wages in an Urban Labor Market* (Chicago: University of Chicago Press, 1970); Barry Bluestone, Mary H. Stevenson, and William M. Murphy, "Low Wages and the Working Poor" (Institute of Labor and Industrial Relations, University of Michigan-Wayne State University, 1971), unpublished manuscript.

6. Wachtel and Betsey, *op. cit.* For more detail, see my forthcoming dissertation, "The Personal Distribution of Earnings: Individual and Institutional Determinants" (Ann Arbor, Mich.: Department of Economics, University of Michigan, Ph.D. dissertation).

7. Bluestone, Stevenson, and Murphy, *op. cit.*

8. The Ford Motor Company, following the 1967 Detroit rebellion, waived normal credentials and hired more than 5,000 poor workers for regular employment. In a sample of 2,000 of these workers, 75 percent were high-school dropouts. These new workers were evaluated by Ford at the end of their first year with the company. They were found to meet previously set standards in terms of retention, absenteeism, and capacity to adjust. Similar results were found in the special program developed by IBM in New York City's Bedford-Stuyvesant area. See Bennett Harrison, "Manpower Policy and Public Service Employment," *New Generation*, 1971, *53* (1), 6.

9. The federal government's General Accounting Office (GAO) found that: "OJT contracts had served primarily to reimburse employers for OJT which they would have conducted even without the government's financial assistance. These contracts were awarded even though the intent of the program was to induce new or additional training efforts beyond those usually carried out." U.S. General Accounting Office, *Improvements Needed in Contracting for On-the-Job Training Under the Manpower Development and Training Act of 1962* (Washington: General Accounting Office, 1968).

19. Education and the Capitalist Labor Market

MASSIMO PACI

A certain bewilderment can be noticed today, both among those responsible for the national educational policies and among scholars of educational economy. This is a result of the collapse of those predictions, formulated not long ago, that forecast that with the development of the economy there would be an increase in the need for skilled personnel, that is, for those with secondary or higher education. In Italy, for example, the same sources that at the beginning of the sixties predicted a dramatic lack of skilled manpower, and therefore pressed for a rapid increase in scholarization at all levels, today write, in a self-critical key:

The quantitative increase in education has also coincided with an "enlightened" philo-sophy of development that ascribes to education too many chances for social and economic evolution. In reality, numerous problems are left open. . . . But the most significant point lies not so much in the disillusionment about certain enlightened hopes as in the fact that the growth of education is a source of new problems. The key problem concerns the *imbalance, by now structural, between the scholastic yield and the possibilities of introducing this flux into working activity.* (emphasis in the original)[1]

In fact, we do not today possess a satisfactory theory on the relationships between the development of education and the evolution of the economic system's labor demand. Is mass scholarization to the level of second-

This article first appeared as "Istruzione e mercato capitalistico del laboro" in *Scuola e mercato del lavoro* (Bologna: Il Mulino, 1973), pp. 42–49. English translation by Hugh Ward-Perkins.

ary or high school in the more advanced capitalist countries useful to the labor market, or does it represent a factor of imbalance, and in the long run of overflow, in the market? This is the question that is to be found at the heart of the theoretical and political debate on schools, both in Italy and elsewhere.

In these pages we certainly do not intend to provide an exhaustive answer to this question. Our aim, which is much more modest, is to demonstrate how a "rereading" of Marx, and in particular of certain passages in *Das Kapital* devoted to the subject of the "large-scale industry" and the reconstitution of a "relative overpopulation," can help us considerably in establishing a correct approach to the problem.

Certainly, the studies recently carried out in the field of "human capital" show that there is quite a close connection between the diffusion of higher secondary education and economic development. Harbison and Myers, for example, found, for seventy-five countries at different levels of economic development, significant correlations between the national income per capita and a series of indices concerning the level of education among the population and the labor forces. The most significant correlations are those between the national income per capita and: attendance of elementary school (0.67); attendance of the lower secondary school (0.82); attendance of the higher secondary school (0.82); number of physicists per 10,000 inhabitants (0.70); and number of scientists and engineers per 10,000 inhabitants (0.83).[2] Similarly Denison, who is, as is well known, analyzing the contribution of a variety of factors to the growth of real income in America between 1929 and 1957, estimates the contribution of the qualitative variations in the labor factor as being approximately one-quarter of the average annual rate of real growth in the income itself (and it must be noted that education emerges as the element by far the most responsible for the qualitative variations in the labor factor).[3]

The connection that has been observed between education and economic development, however, does not necessarily mean that the raising of the standard of education for the labor forces is a requisite of economic development. It could also mean that, following an increase in income, the inclination on the part of the population to receive a secondary and higher education, and the objective possibility of their attaining it, also increase. The same Harbison and Myers also observe in their conclusions:

Except in the case of a few professions, there is no precise relationship between occupations and educational background. One cannot be sure whether an administrator or manager must have a university education. In many African countries elementary school teachers have only a primary education, whereas in the advanced countries they require completion of some form of higher education. Presumably, skilled craftsmen need a second-level education, yet petroleum companies have demonstrated that men who are hardly literate can be trained as painters, carpenters or welders in less than a year. As we have indicated already the supply of educated manpower determines in part the demand also. In similar activities, an advanced country will absorb many more highly educated persons than a less developed country. And in less developed countries, certain production processes can be designed to utilize effectively persons with very limited education.[4]

On the other hand we have seen that in particular situations of social mobilization, as for example during the war effort in the United States in the years 1940–1945, large quotas of manpower lacking any kind of secondary education or professional qualification (such as women, colored people, and young men) showed themselves to be perfectly capable of performing those functions of skilled labor left vacant by the men called to the front.[5] Finally and more generally, various inquiries have shown that often for the same type of work the formal educational qualifications required of the new work recruits are far higher than those required of the preceding generation.[6]

From this point of view, we are far from being able to recognize the existence of a cause-and-effect relationship between economic development and the diffusion of scholarity. The examples mentioned above suggest, rather, that the employment of more educated manpower depends on the characteristics of the market, that is, on the greater availability of educated manpower. Against the "enlightened" hypothesis of the economic system's growing "need for education," one might set up a hypothesis that reverses the relationship between the demand and the supply of labor: in this case, scholarization would seem to respond to an independent mechanism of "pressure from below" on the part of increasing quotas of the population, to which the economic system would be compelled, in the long run, to conform.

It is clear, however, that this second hypothesis, if fully analyzed, presents a prospect of substantial incompatibility, if not of contradictoriness, between the development of education and the functioning of the labor market. In fact, how can the economic system manage to absorb indefinitely the growing quotas of increasingly more educated manpower when it plainly has no need for them?

Would one, therefore, inevitably arrive at a systematic under-use of human resources, through the exclusion from productive life of those who plainly have the skill yet lack the formal educational requirements, and above all through the allocation of educated personnel to unskilled jobs? The hypothesis of a process of scholarization independent of the requirements of economic development results, therefore, in a prospect of *endemic excess* or *waste* as far as qualified manpower is concerned, and, for that very reason, of imbalance and overflow in the labor market.

On the other hand, one would arrive at the same conclusions if one examined the problem from the point of view of the evolution of the content of education, which appears to become more and more separated from the training requirements of specific professional duties. As, in fact, has recently been observed:

Its formative autonomy implies that the school assumes the task of imparting a sum of knowledge and practical skills that cannot in any way be associated with what today one understands as manpower. Indeed, today schools do not produce, or form, manpower, but instead a mass that is far more articulate and developed in its skills than that which the economic apparatus directly uses. There is, it is true, a tendency to improve, by means of education, the utility value of labor, but one cannot say that the schools form just this utility value or, in other words, purely that knowledge that the productive process will use. It is, in fact, a characteristic of more mature capitalism to find itself in a situation of growing discrepancy between potential skills (either diffuse or produced through the schools) and the skills that are actually employed.... The separation of the values that regulate the allocation of labor roles from the values imparted by the schools has the result of emphasizing the derivative and transitory character of the values of the labor market. The transformation of the school ... thus becomes an essential part of a project for exceeding the labor market.[7]

Certainly the interpretation is in substance correct. There is no doubt that at this level of generalization the hypothesis of independence, and in fact of a tendential contradictoriness, between scholarization and the requirements of the economic system seems more comprehensive than the alternative hypothesis of a growing need for education being stimulated by technical and economic progress. Nevertheless, we must analyze the problem in more detail. In order to ascertain the validity of the hypothesis, we must consider how, in given historical situations in particular countries, certain advances in scholarization and certain changes in the educational system have functioned, with respect to the changes in the labor market and with respect to the mechanism of economic development.

There is no need to mention that there is an almost complete lack of analyses at this level. (A consequence of this has been the weakness of many of the political interpretations of the role of the school that have had currency in the last few years in the student movement and in those political forces that have been strongly committed to the world of the school.) In fact, even if the general hypothesis is completely valid as an indication of a trend, it cannot necessarily be turned into an explanatory key that may be used to interpret any given historical situation. The "growth on itself" mechanism of scholarization represents, certainly, an element of imbalance and, in the long run, of contradiction in relation to the labor market, but the imbalance can reveal itself to be more or less intense and the contradiction more or less decisive, depending on the presence (or absence) of a series of circumstances connected with the particular structure of the economic development and the political forces in each country. For example (to anticipate a point that we will discuss further on), it is possible that a particular type of progress in scholarization, such as the birth and development of the mass secondary school, can in certain cases (such as the United States) be completely in harmony with the logic and requirements of the national economic development, whereas in other cases (such as Italy), it becomes an element of social and economic imbalance, to counteract which there have been feverish *ex post facto* attempts to reform the schools.

While we may accept, then, as a general hypothesis the tendential contradictoriness between scholarization and the requirements of the economic system, it is clear that in examining the phenomenon in its concrete form, and with reference to specific levels of scholarity (for example, the development of the mass secondary school), one must be aware of its double potentiality, both as an instrument for integrating the subordinate classes into the social and economic system and as a factor of contradiction and excess in relation to the labor market. This is, in fact, the idea that Marx gives, so at this point it would perhaps be helpful to reread the well-known passage in *Das Kapital* devoted to the relationship between education and the development of large-scale industry:

... Large-scale industry, on the other hand, through its catastrophes imposes the necessity of recognising, as a fundamental law of production, variation of work, consequently fitness of the labourer for varied work, consequently the greatest possible development of his varied aptitudes. It also becomes a question of life and death that the monstrosity of an unhappy reserve army of labour kept at the disposal of capital for its varying needs in the way of exploitation shall be replaced by the perfect adaptability of the individual human being to the changing demands of human labour; and to replace the detail worker by the fully developed individual, fit for a variety of labours and free to adapt himself to different social functions. One step already spontaneously taken towards effecting this revolution is the establishment of technological and agricultural schools, and of "écoles d'enseignement professionel," in which the children of the working-men receive some little instruction in technology and in the practical handling of the various implements of labour. Though the Factory Act, that first and meagre concession coming from capital, is limited to combining elementary education with work in the factory, there can be no doubt that when the working-class comes into power, as inevitably it must, technological instruction, both theoretical and practical, will take its place in the working-class schools. There is also no doubt that such revolutionary ferments, the final result of which is the abolition of the old division of labour, are diametrically opposed to the capitalistic form of production, and to the economic status of the labourer corresponding to that form. But the historical development of the antagonisms is the only way in which that form of production can be dissolved and a new form established.[8]

In this passage it is clear that in Marx's opinion the mass diffusion of higher education ("technological, ... theoretical and practical") is, at one and the same time, a requirement of the large-scale industry (for which it is a "question of life and death" to have at its disposal a versatile and "fully developed" labor force) and a contradiction of the system, "revolutionary ferments" destined in the long run to dissolve both the old division of labor and the historical capitalistic form of production itself. On the one hand, therefore, Marx describes the diffusion of education within the context of a reformist initiative led by large-scale industry, which in this manner manages to eliminate the "monstrosity of an unhappy reserve army of labour kept at the disposal of capital for its varying needs in the way of exploitation" (education, in fact, permits the creation of a labor force so mobile and versatile that it overcomes, at least in part as we shall see further on, the mechanism for fluidifying the supply of labor based on the permanence of a "reserve army of labour").

On the other hand, however, the diffusion of education to ever-increasing population quotas creates the background for an inevitable rupture in the capitalistic division of labor. Even if Marx does not elaborate further on this point, it seems possible to believe that this process occurs on account of the excess in the educated population that naturally follows the growth "on itself" of scholarization; that is, we would be witnessing the formation of an "educated relative overpopulation," which, even if during a preliminary period it appears to be functioning in accordance with the requirements of large-scale industry, subsequently grows to become an element of imbalance and rupture in the capitalistic organization of labor.

The point that Marx makes, then, is that in order to understand how far the process of scholarization responds to a requirement of development on the part of capitalism, and how far, on the other hand, it comes into contradiction with it, one must analyze historically how this process stands in relation to the observable changes in the importance and type of "relative overpopulation." It is in this direction, therefore, that analysis must be directed. With this object in mind, the "rereading" of Marx can be aided by the introduction of a convenient schematization that divides the evolution of the capitalistic labor market into three phases.

In the initial phase of capitalistic development, the need for manpower has essentially two characteristics: on the one hand, it is concerned with unskilled manpower (largely made up of women and children); on the other hand, it is concerned with the great masses of workers that are suddenly required by the expansion of new markets and the opening of whole new branches of production. "The mass of social wealth"—writes Marx—"which becomes superabundant owing to the advance of accumulation and transformable into additional capital, urgently seeks investment, either in old branches of production for whose products the market has suddenly expanded, or else in newly formed branches (such as railways, etc.), the need for which has grown out of the development of the old ones. In all such cases, it is essential that there should be a possibility of providing great masses of workers whose activities can be engaged at the decisive points without any interruption in the work of production in other spheres. Overpopulation supplies these masses."[9]

There are, above all, two mechanisms that ensure the continual availability of manpower during this phase: first, the capitalistic penetration into precapitalistic sectors and areas (agriculture, artisan work, etc.), thereby requiring the proletarianization of a large number of independent workers, and second, the reinvestment of capital in more modern machinery and techniques, which continually "liberate" labor. To these two principal mechanisms can be made to correspond the two chief types of overpopulation singled out by Marx, namely, the "latent" overpopulation of the precapitalistic sectors and areas, which is made available by the penetration of capitalistic production, and the "fluid" or "fluctuating" overpopulation that moves from one sector to another and from one factory to another under the pressure of technical progress.

Immediately beside these two types Marx places a third: the "stagnant" overpopulation, which is composed of the quota of manpower that has been expelled from production and that remains permanently on the margins of working activity, or at least on the margins of the more stable activity assured by the more advanced industrial sectors. (The "principal form" of the stagnant overpopulation is, in fact, constituted by work at home.)[10]

It is not possible here to examine in any detail those pages in which Marx describes the modes of functioning of the relative overpopulation. Nevertheless, it is important to emphasize one point: the typology, mentioned above, of latent, fluid, and stagnant overpopulation is not just descriptive. Its importance as an explanatory instrument becomes clear only when we take into account its dynamic aspect. As the process of capitalistic penetration into traditional areas and sectors is completed, so will the latent overpopulation be destined to lose its importance; the investment of capital in new machines and techniques therefore acquires an increasingly important role in the reconstitution of the "reserve army of labour." On the other hand, the formation of a stagnant overpopulation made up of manpower that has been expelled, either from traditional sectors gradually subjected to capitalistic production or from modern sectors undergoing further technological improvement of production itself, ensures the survival and the reproduction of "backward" productive forms (such as, for example, work at home) and the creation of "marginal" sectors and areas within the national economic system.

The second identifiable phase of capital-istic development is that coinciding with the advent and growth of the "large-scale industry." The type of manpower most in demand, at this stage, no longer consists of barely skilled or totally unskilled women and children, but is made up of workers and technicians in possession of a "generic" or basic qualification on which, in the case of a significant quota of manpower, are grafted specific professional specializations. It is in this phase, as we have already seen, that the diffusion of secondary and higher education becomes a requirement of capitalistic development in general, and of large-scale industry in particular. On the other hand, the quota of latent overpopulation is by this time heavily diminished, following the almost complete submission of the traditional sectors and areas to capitalistic production. Nor is it possible for the stagnant overpopulation, which does not possess the required qualifications, to replace the latent overpopulation in its role as supplier of manpower to large-scale industry. This always drives large-scale industry to resort to the instrument of reinvesting in labor-saving machinery and techniques in order to maintain and increase the "fluctuating" quota of the relative overpopulation. Hence the crucial role, as instrument for fluidifying the supply of labor, that is conferred on the diffusion of education: in fact, it is only through an adequate education that the worker can gain the "generic qualification," the ability to adapt himself to change, and versatility, which are precisely those qualities necessary to make him "fluctuate" according to the changeable requirements of large-scale industry. From this point of view, therefore, the increase of scholarization appears to be useful to capitalistic development.

One must not forget, however, that the diffusion of large-scale industry does not imply the elimination of the stagnant overpopulation (consisting of work at home and other forms of similar under-employment); alongside the advanced capitalistic sectors, in which large-scale industry is dominant, remain large zones of production, also capitalistic, naturally, but employing "second class" manpower. Even if, from the point of view of the total requirements of the capitalistic system, the diffusion of education has to be stimulated to a certain extent to guarantee the necessary quantity of educated manpower required by large-scale industry, it need not, however, be complete, because the market for precarious and marginal labor always needs to be supplied. Hence the maintenance, in the schools, of certain selective mechanisms and of an ideology of competition and mobility.

In the main, however, the function of the school, in this phase, seems to be that of integrating the working class into the capitalistic system: a function that is the more easily carried out, the more effectively the labor market produces a rupture between an urban-industrial working-class, which is educated and reformistically privileged, and a marginal proletariat, which has been expelled from school prematurely and which is, for that very reason, banished to the less stable and remunerative occupations and sectors, if not even compelled to join the unemployed and officially inactive population.

The third phase, that of "monopolistic capitalism" or "late capitalism," illustrates the transition of mass education from the moment when it is useful to the development requirements of the economic system (and when it acts as an instrument for integrating the subordinate classes into the social system) to the moment when it becomes an element of imbalance in the labor market and of tension and conflict in society. In fact, once the mechanism of scholarization has been started up, it ends by producing a quantity of intellectual resources clearly exceeding the needs of the productive system.

The fact that the economies of the more developed capitalistic countries are displaying difficulty in absorbing the ranks of young men coming out of school shows that we are now entering this phase; in the United States in 1965, for example (and we will return to this question further on), more than half (52.1 percent) of the young men between the ages of eighteen and twenty-four were either students, soldiers, or unemployed.[11] A new form of "stagnant overpopulation" is being added to the old form; it consists of the intellectual or skilled labor force that does not find employment in productive activity. In this way, it goes to supply a labor market distinct from the directly productive market dominated by the large-scale industry of the more advanced sectors: the intellectual labor market. This latter market is supplied, as is the marginal work market, by the stagnant overpopulation of the old type. It seems to be the expression of the distorted or "dualist" development of capitalism, which, while it increases exploitation in certain sectors and areas, generates in others waste and under-utilization of human resources. There is, however, a fundamental point on which the two types of stagnant overpopulation differ: while the old type of stagnant overpopulation consists of skilled manpower prematurely expelled from school, so that its banishment from the more profitable productive sectors seems, in some way, justified, the stagnant overpopulation of the new type consists essentially of educated manpower for which the banishment from production and the degraded productive utilization are sources of tension and social conflict.

In order to avoid the tensions and conflicts, the economic system attempts to absorb the intellectual labor force within the sectors of the "unproductive tertiary," which in this phase undergoes considerable expansion. In particular, the welfare sector is constantly developing, making it possible, at one and the same time, to cope with the increase in the stagnant overpopulation of the old type and to employ, in the administration of welfare, considerable quotas of intellectual overpopulation. More generally, all the apparatuses of the state, and in particular the military and educational apparatuses, are developing. However, the point that one must emphasize with regard to this trend is that this development of the "unproductive tertiary" depends on the success of the operation of integrating the subordinate classes, and in particular the working class, during the preceding phase; it is only on this basis, in fact, that the accumulation of capital necessary to support the swelling of the unproductive sectors and the absorption of the educated relative overpopulation can continue in the directly productive sector.

As a whole, therefore, the school is burdened with a delicate task that is crucial for the equilibrium of the labor market and the very stability of the capitalistic economic and social system. It must carry out different functions simultaneously, proportioning them in the correct measure and gradually stressing some, while paying careful attention not to make errors of emphasis; in fact, heaven help it if certain mechanisms of selection or development in scholarization are anticipated or delayed too much. A timely transformation of the secondary school is necessary in order that the expansion of scholarization not start up at this level the processes of imbalance and crisis in the labor market (processes that are, however, merely put off till the next phase, in which mass scholarization will involve higher education).

The secondary school, in particular, must transform itself from an elite preparatory school into a mass terminal school *in time* to absorb the pressure from below towards scholarization on the part of large quotas of the working class. Only in this way does it become possible to supply large-scale industry with the highly mobile and versatile labor force it needs without relinquishing the "banishment" of a consistent class of proletariat.

Above all, only in this way can one stop the irruption of the masses within the old structures of the elite secondary school from prematurely starting up the mechanism of development in the educated relative overpopulation and from putting into a state of crisis the balance of the labor market, at a time when the integration of the working class into the productive sector has not yet been completed, and when as a result it is not at all certain that the system will have at its disposal sufficient economic means to finance those reforms of the "unproductive tertiary" that are necessary to absorb, at least for a certain period, the growing educated relative overpopulation.

The success of the secondary school in carrying out these tasks is not, therefore, assured; it depends on numerous conditions that in specific historical situations in various countries do not always obtain. Without attempting to go far beyond the mere singling out of some explanatory points, it is possible, perhaps, to give examples of a few of these conditions with reference to the role carried out by the secondary school in the United States.

The construction of a mass secondary school in the United States seems to be a process that has weakened in the course of half a century, but one that is still timely and useful as regards the requirements of balance in the labor market and of stability in the social system. Already in 1910 there could be counted over a million students attending high school, that is, 15 percent of young men and women between the ages of fourteen and seventeen. By 1957 the percentage had risen to over 90 percent.[12]

It is important to emphasize that, in the first decades of the century, this process, far from expressing "social pressure from below," was provoked and administered by legislation that introduced and extended compulsory schooling in the various States of the Union:

Many of the new students were in school unwillingly, in obedience to the new or more stringent state compulsory education laws; many came from poor, culturally impoverished homes and had modest vocational goals; many of these were the sons and daughters of recent immigrants, and seemed to observers very much in need of "Americanization."[13]

For a long time (practically until a decade ago), however, attendance for a few years and, at most, the diploma were the most that the high school offered to the majority of students; in fact, only a small percentage of students went on to college. In the previous century, the functioning of the secondary school was quite different: in those days the great majority of high school students entered the university as soon as they had obtained their diploma. In this sense, one can describe the transformation of the American secondary school in terms of a transition from elite preparatory school to mass terminal school.[14]

A characteristic of the terminal secondary school, therefore, is to impinge directly on the labor market. In the United States, the principal organizations operating in the world of the school, such as, for example, the National Education Association, were well aware of this right from the start. In its 1918 Report the NEA warned teachers to bear in mind that they are dealing with "a 'heterogeneous' high school population destined to enter all sorts of occupation."[15] A large part of these occupations are the skilled manual occupations supplied by the development of large-scale industry and of the more advanced capitalistic sectors. In this way, at the end of the American secondary school's period of expansion, a solid belt of the working class seems substantially similar to the middle classes as far as education is concerned; in fact, in 1950 the skilled American workers between the ages of twenty-five and twenty-nine boasted an average scholarity of twelve years, that is, only a year less than that of the clerical employees of the same age group.[16]

And it is on the basis of this high level of education for skilled workers that the working conditions, hierarchical organization, and career chances of these same workers have changed. We witness what was even in the early fifties being called the "professionalization" of skilled manual labor, that is, its inclusion within the bureaucratic organizational schemes (similar in all respects to those for clerical work), which carry with

them, in particular, the introduction of the "business career" based no longer on the accumulation of experience on the job, but precisely on the interiorization of the new technological culture through formal educational processes.[17]

In this way a privileged band of the American working class ends up by being allocated levels of income that are equal, or even superior, to those of the clerical middle classes: in 1959, for example, the average annual income for "skilled workers and foremen" ($5,444) was higher than that for the "clerical and kindred workers" ($5,216).[18] Therefore in America the modification of the retributive system and the business organizations designed to favor the integration of a solid stratum of the working class within the middle class is complementary to the homogenizing role of the terminal secondary school.

What has been said so far, however, must not make us forget that, especially during the first decades of this century, the majority of students leaving high school went to occupy the unskilled and therefore less remunerative and more unstable manual jobs. This was made possible by the assurance, made at the same moment as the open secondary school was set up, that there would be a high level of early leaving and of non-fulfillment of the academic requirements. Again in 1959, 40 percent of the males and 36 percent of the females aged seventeen had not completed their secondary studies.[19] It is, above all, these students who will go to constitute the bands of the stagnant overpopulation; also, if we were to refer to the figures on official unemployment, which is only one component of the stagnant overpopulation, we would discover the significant fact that, in 1960, while on the national level 5.6 percent of the labor force remained unemployed, this percentage rose to 27 percent for the labor force that had not fulfilled its scholastic requirements.[20]

Though it may seem paradoxical, this selective work performed by the American school was assisted by the democratizing transformation of the structures, methods, and contents of teaching that accompanied the birth of the mass terminal secondary school. The transformation of the school "centered on the curriculum" into the school "centered on the pupil" is accompanied by a great deal of democratic rhetoric, which emphasizes the abandonment of the contents and obligations in the curriculum that were characteristic of the old elite secondary school. But precisely insofar as the transformation conditions the work of the teacher to the "background" and "needs" of the pupil, it provides only an "egalitarian" ideological veil on the class selection that in fact takes place (and who does not know that a boy's aspirations are merely a function of the class to which he belongs?).[21]

In this way the American secondary school, in the compass of fifty years, has succeeded in carrying out two important functions: on the one hand, it forms the homogeneous, mobile, and versatile labor force required by "large-scale industry"; on the other hand, it keeps in circulation a substantial flux of "second class" manpower that is destined to supply the market for marginal work and the stagnant overpopulation. On the one hand, it creates the indispensable foundations for the formation of an undifferentiated "middle mass" into which flows the skilled stratum of the working class; on the other hand, it offers a formal and "universalistic" sanction for the class discrimination of a large band of the proletariat. On the one hand, finally, it deceptively expresses in terms of increasing social mobility the fluctuation between jobs to which the labor force on the urban-industrial market is subjected; on the other hand, it rationalizes in terms of individual failure the decline it provokes in the market for marginal work and in the stagnant overpopulation.[22]

Thus, without shocks, the United States arrives at the present phase, in which mass scholarization reaches the level of the high school and the university.[23] The problems, avoided for many years, relative to the sur-plus of intellectual resources leaving school arise again with new intensity. However, the American economy, by virtue also of the high rate of profit assured by the integration of the working class into the directly productive sector (which occurred in the preceding phase), can now permit itself to devote considerable resources to the expansion of the "unproductive tertiary," which consists of the educational, welfare, and military sectors and which is capable of absorbing large quotas of intellectual manpower. The labor forces directly or indirectly employed by virtue of military expenditure, for example, were over 22 million in 1970, that is, 14.2 percent of the total American labor forces.[24] Equally impressive is the growth of employment in the educational sector: between 1950 and 1965, for example, while the total employment grew by 21 percent, that of the educational sector increased by 130 percent, so that in effect one out of every six jobs created in this period belonged to the sector of education.[25]

These developments of the "unproductive tertiary," however, do not seem sufficient to contain the rate of unemployment in America, which in 1970 officially rose to 6.2 percent of the labor forces, and which, according to some commentators, would rise to 10 percent if one included "inactive" adults.[26] As a whole, therefore, American capitalism seems fully to have entered the phase in which the waste of intellectual resources, considered in connection with the waste contained in the stagnant overpopulation of the old type, becomes a contradiction of the system. Until today, however, the conflicts that have arisen on the basis of the contradiction and that have involved the bands of marginal manpower (students, women, and colored population) have not constituted a grave threat to the stability of the American social system, since there has been no accord with the working class of the directly productive sector.

We can now seek to examine briefly the connections between the expansion of scholarity at the level of the Italian secondary school and the evolution of the labor market, in order to prove how, unlike what happened in the United States, the mass secondary school here succeeds in creating many more problems than it solves, as far as both the equilibrium of the labor market and the stability of the political and social systems are concerned.[27]

During the fifties Italy stood as a typical example of economic development based on the abundance of work supply.[28] A consequence of this has been an "extensive" increase in dependent industrial employment; the low cost of labor has, in fact, for many years produced an incentive to resort to additional units of labor, even if of low productivity, thereby allowing a broadening of the basis of exploitation, rather than to resort to new machinery and techniques that are designed to increase and intensify the exploitation itself. The latent overpopulation in the precapitalistic or "backward" capitalistic areas and sectors, such as the agriculture of the fifties, was the natural source of this cheap labor. So here one is witnessing the introduction into working activity of large quotas of manpower from the rural population, young men, and women, which go to enlarge the base of the structure of qualifications for working employment.[29]

Until 1963 the number of those employed in industry with academic qualifications equivalent to, or lower than, the elementary school certificate *continued to increase each year* (in this year they constituted over 7 million out of the total 8 million—or a little more—who were employed in industry). For much of the fifties, on the other hand, a *de facto* wage freeze took place that left unchanged, or perhaps even aggravated, the considerable distance on the social and economic plane, existing between the working class as a whole and the middle classes.[30] There is, therefore, no visible evidence in the Italian situation of the timely reformist approach displayed by American capitalism: the remunerative structure and the business organizations remained

heavily differentiated as far as the workers and staff were concerned, and secondary education remained a characteristic (and privilege) of the middle classes. When confronted with the possibility of extensively exploiting a superabundant generic labor force, Italian capitalism renounced, right from the start, the possibility of undertaking an entrepreneurial and reformist initiative in the area of schools and union-company negotiations.

On the other hand the abundance of generic labor did not fully correspond to the need of large-scale industry to make manual labor "fluid" at all levels, in particular at the level of skilled and specialized workers. The great mobility of the unskilled labor force, though extremely useful for the capitalistic development of these years, principally consisted in a fluctuation—of entering and leaving work, and of horizontal mobility between sectors—involving almost exclusively the bottom of the hierarchy and of the working units of the companies. As a matter of fact the mobility of the specialized and skilled nuclei of the working class, traditionally employed in the industries of northern Italy, appears to be extremely scarce.[31]

This explains why, on the market for skilled manual work, even in a situation of abundant labor supply, tensions and rigidity occur to which can be attributed in part the origins of the phenomenon of "wage-drift" (which can be observed in a few sectors) and of the "dualism" of Italian industry—as it is described by various authors when referring to the situation in these years.[32] Therefore, the absence of a stratum of skilled workers who possess a secondary education, and who for that very reason are sufficiently versatile to adapt themselves to the numerous requirements of large-scale industry, made itself felt, at least at the times of greatest economic expansion and at the highest points of capitalistic expansion.

Hence the various attempts, and even proposals of an innovative and reformist character, that came (and not by chance) from the more advanced capitalistic sectors and that were intentionally aimed at modifying the structures of the schools, on the one hand, and the traditional professional classification of dependent labor, on the other.[33] These proposals, later criticized as being "utopian" and "enlightened," instead seem extremely interesting if regarded as an unsuccessful attempt, on the part of a certain more advanced capital, to formulate a timely reformist initiative similar to the one described earlier in reference to the American situation.

In Italy, therefore, the same lower secondary school remained an elite school, at least in the sense that it was socially exploited as an instrument of flight from the workers' condition, and of ascent to the middle classes. The expansion of scholarization, which began well before the introduction of the *media unica* in 1963, expressed the response of the subordinate classes to the wage freeze and to the maintenance, throughout the fifties, of a high social and economic differential between the working class and the ranks of clerical employees. The subsequent development of scholarization, attaining higher and higher levels, would clearly show these signs of its origins. No longer would it be possible, in the sixties, to use it to form versatile working manpower, for the very reason that it now functioned as an instrument of flight from the workers' condition.

Hence the Italian secondary school, in becoming a mass institution, did not transform itself into a terminal school like its American counterpart, but remained, in its structures and—what was more important—in the goals of those who attended it, an elite preparatory institution.

So the sixties started without the creation by Italian capitalism of any instrument at the scholastic level, let alone at the level of union-company negotiations, that would be capable of effecting a division within the working class between a reformistically privileged stratum integrated (or integrable) to the level of the clerical employee ranks and a stratum destined to occupy the less remuner-ative and more unstable jobs. The arrival at a situation of full (or almost full) employment thus caught Italian capitalism unawares. The workers' struggles of 1961–63, the achievement of equal salaries for women and young men over eighteen years, the reduction and control of apprenticeship, etc., all made for a strong consolidation and homogenization within the working class. All workers, both young and old, men and women, southern immigrants and northerners, found themselves closer to each other and more united than ever. The absence in the Italian situation of a colored proletariat, or of foreign immigration on the workers' level, has certainly helped this process of unification. It is clear, however, that the principal cause is to be found in the policy, pursued by Italian industry in the preceding decades, of extensive exploitation and repression of the workers in the areas of salaries and professional status.

Italian capitalism's reply to this new force in the working class was, as is well known, the recession of the years 1963–66 and the restructuring of workers' employment that went with it. It was following this restructuring that the banishment from employment, or at least from the more remunerative industrial sectors, came of the "weak quotas" of the labor force, consisting of young men, women, old people, and immigrants from the country.[34] Officially these quotas go to enlarge the inactive population, which reaches very high levels, levels that are without comparison in any other capitalist country. More precisely, perhaps, we should say that in these years the stagnant overpopulation, which supplies the market of marginal labor and unemployment, was continuously increasing.

In effect one witnessed, from then on, a progressive increase in such kinds of work as work at home, juvenile work, part-time work for peasant workers and student laborers, temporary or seasonal work abroad, subcontracted work, etc.

In the meantime, within the industrial sector (in the strict sense of the word) one might observe vigorous activity in organizational and financial concentration, sectorial restructuring and reconversion, etc., which provoked a noticeable intensification in the work tempo and the exploitation of labor. In parallel fashion, the industrial sector's demand became more selective and concentrated on the request for predominantly male manpower, neither too old nor too young and already socialized into the industrial environment, "stable in character," and above all (as far as we are concerned) in possession of an education that is higher on the average.[35]

From 1964 onwards, therefore, one may notice, on the one hand, a progressive decrease in the number of those employed in industry who are in possession of the elementary school leaving certificate and, on the other hand, a corresponding increase in the number of those in possession of the lower secondary school leaving certificate.[36]

The Italian large-scale industry now realized that it needed a mobile and versatile labor force sufficiently flexible to be capable of adapting itself to the reconversions and restructurings in progress. On the other hand, only a reasonably prolonged education can guarantee these qualities in the labor force, and it is in the light of this requirement that the reform of the lower secondary school in 1963 must be considered (a somewhat similar remark could be made about the launching of the union negotiation that also happened in these years, on the initiative of the more advanced "public" industrial sectors).

Italian capitalism, therefore, attempted—though a little late in the day—to put into effect, on the question of the structure of employment, a political operation almost like the one that was successfully carried out by American capitalism. Important mechanisms for dividing the working class were put into motion, thereby banishing a part of this class from the principal productive sector and directing it to the peripheral sectors and areas, which are less stable and less remunerative. This stage of the operation had a certain success: despite the absence of a colored proletariat in the Italian situation, the processes of banishment were based on the equally "natural" and "objective" criteria of age, sex, and, not least, the level of education attained by the labor force. The boosting of the stagnant overpopulation, in this way, provided the material basis for renewed exploitation of the workers in the peripheral sectors and areas; this frequently occurred under new guises, which would merit examination were there a sufficient amount of relevant information at our disposal.[37]

The second part of the operation, however, the part designed to guarantee a sufficiently mobile and versatile labor force within the principal productive sector, did not take place.

The supply of manual labor in possession of the required qualifications remained scarce, at least on the urban industrial labor market of northern Italy. In particular, there was a scarcity in the supply of manual labor in possession of the lower secondary school leaving certificate, which, as we have seen, is what was chiefly required in these years. If we consider as an indicator of the type of supply of manual labor the extent of school leaving following the lower secondary school leaving certificate, and if we compare the year 1960—a year of considerable expansion in workers' employment, preceding the reform of the secondary school—to the year 1968—also a year of economic recovery before the trade union struggles of the "Hot Autumn"—we do not observe any perceptible change in the extent of this "potential supply of manual labour with a secondary education," despite the strong increase in scholarization at this level: the amount of school leaving after the attainment of the secondary school leaving certificate in fact changed from 82,000 in 1960 to 91,700 in 1968, despite the fact that at the same time the number of those attending the third grade changed from 311,700 to 507,500.[38]

That means, in effect, that at least for the whole of the sixties, the Italian secondary school functioned not as a "terminal" school, that is, in a manner designed to direct students, once they have attained their diplomas, towards the labor market, but instead as an elite preparatory school, providing the incentive for students to flee from the working condition towards higher levels of scholarization.

This is one of the factors that explain the situation of rigidity in the supply of manual labor on the urban-industrial market. (Another important factor is that the "weak quotas" of the labor force, that is, those that supply the seasonal migration and swell the national market for marginal labor, are plainly not in competition with the manual labor force, since they do not possess the qualifications required by large-scale industry.)

An analysis for separate geographical areas, in particular an analysis carried out on the big metropolitan industrial areas of northern Italy, could only confirm, and indeed emphasize, the trends we have described on the national level.

Once the mechanism of secondary scholarization has been started up, however, it grows on itself and in the space of a few years doubles the attendance at the higher secondary school, even tripling that at the university. Therefore one soon arrives at the formation of a supply of intellectual labor that exceeds the requirements. For example, in 1970 over 10 percent of the labor forces in possession of the secondary school leaving certificate were either unemployed or else looking for their first job.[39] It is to this structural situation that one must attribute the origins of the student movement and on this basis that one can interpret its recurrent falls in corporatist directions. And it is on the structural basis of the particularly favorable labor-market relations that one must interpret the resumption and spreading of the workers' struggles in 1968–69. From this point of view, therefore, one must reevaluate

a lot of the interpretations (all "political" or "superstructural") that were made concerning the workers' and students' struggles in the years of the "French May" or the "Hot Autumn."

In this way, Italy comes to experience a situation in the labor market that is characterized by an abundance in the supply both of marginal labor and, at the other extreme, of intellectual labor, and (at the same time) by a scarcity in the supply of manual labor in possession of the qualifications required by large-scale industry. It reaches the situation, peculiar to mature capitalism, of waste in working resources, in which there is added to the stagnant overpopulation of the old type (concentrated in the marginal sectors and areas) the new "educated relative overpopulation," but without there being any success in the completion of the integration of the working class of the principal productive sector. That is the consequence of—among other factors peculiar to the Italian situation—both the absence of a timely reformist initiative on the level of the scholastic structures and the nature of the union-company negotiations.

Secondary and higher scholarization, in particular, occurs on the basis of "social pressure from below," which imposes on the whole process rhythms and tempi that are independent of the attempts at reform and control made by political powers. It has created an expansion in intellectual resources that has been premature, as regards the possibility of absorbing them: the failed social integration of the working classes of the directly productive sector has, in fact, blocked (or at least almost blocked) the mechanism of capitalistic accumulation, thereby reducing considerably the margins available for a policy for reform and for relaunching the "unproductive tertiary"—the only outlet for the abundant intellectual manpower leaving school.

In practice, Italian capitalism is already living the contradictions typical of mature capitalism (banishment of entire productive sectors and areas; endemic excess of intellectual resources), while the principal contradictions, portrayed in the struggles of the working class of the directly productive sector, are anything but solved.[40]

NOTES

1. Censis, "Sviluppo economico e istruzione," in *Quindicinale di note e commenti* VIII, June 1972, n. 164, pp. 627–628.
2. F. Harbison and C.A. Myers, *Education, Manpower and Economic Growth* (New York, 1964).
3. E.F. Denison, *The Source of Economic Growth and the Alternative Before Us*, Supplementary Paper no. 13, Committee for Economic Development, New York, January 1962.
4. Harbison and Myers, *op. cit.*, pp. 205–206.
5. See H. Parnes, *Forecasting Educational Needs for Economic and Social Development* (Paris: OECD, 1962), p. 19.
6. This also emerged from our investigation carried out on the labor forces of Lombardy. See ILSES, *La qualificazione delle forze di lavoro nella industria lombarda*, edited by G. Barile and M. Paci (Milan, 1969), pp. 64–82.
7. R. Stefanelli, *Le leve del sistema*, in *Il Capitale istruzione* (Bari, 1971), part III, ch. 5, p. 304.
8. K. Marx, *Das Kapital*, Book I, part IV: *Machinery and Large-Scale Industry*.
9. Marx, *op. cit.*, Book I, part VII: *General Law of Capitalistic Accumulation*.
10. The category of "stagnant overpopulation" should, in our opinion, attract the greatest attention in any analysis of the Marxian "model" for the functioning of the labor market with regard to capitalistic development. Many passages in *Das Kapital*, in fact, permit an interpretation (the one we make our own in the text) that sees in the stagnant overpopulation a contradiction of capitalistic development. In fact, unlike the latent and fluctuating overpopulation, the stagnant overpopulation does not seem, in the strict sense, to form a part of the "reserve army of labour"; that is to say, it does not form a part of that quota of manpower that is plainly available for the development of "large-scale industry." Instead, it is available for forms of capitalistic exploitation in marginal and seemingly "backward" sectors and areas, as for instance work at home. (For this point of view see what is said below in note 37.) The stagnant overpopulation, from this point of view, would at the level of the labor market represent the moment of *underdevelopment*, intrinsic to capitalistic development because it is necessarily produced by the latter. In this sense, therefore, the Marxian "model" for the functioning of the labor market anticipates recent contributions to Marxist theory regarding the intrinsically "dualist" nature of capitalistic development.
11. John and Margaret Rowntree, "I giovani come classe," in *Problemi del Socialismo* X, March-April 1968, no. 28–29, p. 418.
12. We take these figures from Martin Trow, "The Second Transformation of American Secondary Education," in R. Bendix and S.M. Lipset, *Class, Status and Power*, second ed. (New York, 1966), pp. 436–449. We will frequently refer to this text in the present article.
13. Trow, *op. cit.*, p. 440.
14. Ibid., p. 443.
15. National Education Association, *Cardinal Principles of Secondary Education*, 1918 (cited in Trow, *op. cit.*, p. 440).
16. K. Mayer, "Recent Changes in the Class Structure of the United States," in *Transactions of the Third World Congress of Sociology*, III (Amsterdam, 1956), p. 70. By this author see also: "The Changing Shape of American Class Structure," in *Social Research*, winter 1963, in particular p. 464.
17. N. Foote, "The Professionalization of Labor in Detroit," in *American Journal of Sociology*, January 1953, pp. 371–380; by the same author see also: "The Movement from Jobs to Careers in American Industry," in *Transactions of the Third World Congress of Sociology*, II, pp. 99–107.
18. U.S. Bureau of the Census, *Final Report, Occupation by Earnings and Education* in *Census of Population 1960* (Washington, 1964).
19. Harbison and Myers, *op. cit.*, p. 142.
20. Ibid., p. 167.
21. For a description of the transition from the school "centered on the curriculum" to that "centered on the pupil" and for a further bibliography, see Trow, *op. cit.*, pp. 440–441.
22. Naturally, we do not wish to assert here that the school was the only instrument in this big reformist operation on the part of American capitalism. One need only consider (to give a couple of examples) the role carried out by the reform of trade-union relations or the importance that the presence of socially discriminated colored proletariat had in the United States. However, a not inconsiderable role was carried out by the school, above all in relation to the *timeliness* with which it was transformed.
23. The student population attending the colleges today constitutes over 50 percent of young men and women between the ages of 18 and 21. See M. Trow, *op. cit.*, p. 441.
24. Paul M. Sweezy, "A proposito della teoria del capitalismo monopolistico," in *Monthly Review* (Italian edition) V, July-August 1972, no. 7–8, pp. 7–8.
25. J. and M. Rowntree, *op. cit.*, p. 416.
26. Sweezy, *op. cit.*, p. 7.
27. It is hardly necessary to remind ourselves that our treatment of the Italian situation, like that of the American situation (discussed above), must be understood as essentially introductory; we are merely trying here to sketch out an interpretation without subtleties, emphasizing perhaps too strongly the role of the school (among other things), while awaiting further detailed research.
28. For a similar opinion see C. Kindleberger, *Lo sviluppo economico europeo*, Italian translation (Milan, 1969).
29. Elsewhere we have described these processes in detail. See M. Paci, "Qualifiche e mercato del

lavoro," in *Quaderni di Rassegna Sindacale* IX, 1971, no. 30, pp. 84–97, and "Le contraddizioni del mercato del lavoro," in *Inchiesta* II, spring 1972, no. 6, pp. 3–19.

30. See the phased periodization of the Italian salary structure contained in AA. VV., *Movimento Sindacale e contrattazione collettiva 1945–1970*, p. 21 ff.

31. For the differences that have been observed between the mobility of skilled workers and that of unskilled workers, see M. Paci, *L'evoluzione dell'occupazione in Lombardia e la mobilità delle forze di lavoro* (Milan: ILSES, 1968).

32. For the fifties see Vera Lutz, *Italy, A Study in Economic Development* (London, 1962). For the tensions created on the labor market during the years of the "economic miracle," see S. Lombardini, *La Programmazione: Idee, esperienze, problemi* (Turin, 1967), pp. 113–114, and F. Caffè, *Teorie e problemi di politica sociale* (Bari, 1970), p. 135. As regards the phenomenon of "wage-drift," it is interesting to note that on the basis of data collected by L. Pallagrosi, in 1962, the category of workers in the sector of the automobile that experienced the greatest wage-drift was constituted by ordinary workmen: this is a sign that the tensions of the labor market in those years had come to involve even the principal backbone of the working-class of the big factories. See L. Pallagrosi, "L'evoluzione dei differenziali salariali di fatto," in *Quaderni di Rassegna Sindacale* IX, no. 30, p. 45.

33. We refer, essentially, to the suggestions that Gino Martinole put forward in those years, both on his own and in collaboration with other scholars and experts, in particular with Svimez. These were later collected in the volume by Martinoli, *Tecnica, sviluppo, economico e scuola* (Milan, 1962).

34. On this point, taken up later in many studies and analyses (even recent ones), let us refer to our research reports, ILSES, and in particular to that cited in note 31, which were later collected in M. Paci, "Migrazioni interne e mercato capitalistico del lavoro," in *Problemi del Socialismo* XII (1970): 671–687.

35. On this increased selectivity of the labor demand, see the recent work of M. De Cecco, "Una interpretazione ricardiana della dinamica della forza lavoro in Italia nel decennio 1959–69," in *Note Economiche*, 1972, no. 1, pp. 76–77. This author, however, does not examine the phenomenon from the point of view of the level of education of the labor force.

36. Taking as a base (=100) those employed in industry according to the educational qualification of 1959, we have the following values for the years 1963 and 1969: for the elementary certificate, 112 and 99 respectively; for the lower secondary school certificate, 134 and 202; for the higher secondary school diploma, 132 and 165; and for the university, 115 and 110 (from our processing of ISTAT data).

37. See, for example, the recovery of the phenomenon of work at home in Lombardy, as it appears in the inquiry carried out by L. Frey, "Il lavoro a domicilio in Lombardia," in *Relazioni Sociali*, no. 10–11, 1971. It is interesting to remember, on this question, what Marx observes when he deals with the reconstitution of work at home in capitalistic development: "This so-called modern domestic industry has nothing to do with the old type (with which it only has the name in common) since the latter presupposes an independent urban craft industry, an autonomous agriculture and, in particular, a *house of the working family*. Today domestic industry has become an *external division of the factory, of the manufacture or of the goods shed*. Capital, together with the workers of the factories and of the manufacturers, and together with the artisans whom it assembles in a particular place over which it exercises its direct control, ties to itself another army which is scattered in the big cities and in the countryside—that of the workers at home." In K. Marx, *op. cit.* (the emphasis is by Marx).

38. Our processing of ISTAT data.

39. See CNEL: *IV Rapporto sulla situazione sociale del paese* (Milan, 1971), p. 66. On the function of "parking" unemployed manpower practiced by the schools, see the recent work of R. Emma and M. Rostan, *Scuola e mercato del lavoro* (Bari, 1971).

40. For an early exposition of this interpretation, carried out by reviewing a few of the principal contributions that have recently appeared on these themes, see M. Paci, "Le Contraddizioni del mercato del lavoro," in *Inchiesta* (cited in note 29).

20. The Vocational School Fallacy in Development Planning

PHILIP J. FOSTER

In current controversies regarding the relationship between the provision of formal education and the economic growth of underdeveloped areas, few issues have been debated with more vehemence than the question of the desirability of providing technical, vocational, and agricultural instruction within the schools. So far as Africa is concerned, the controversy has been sharpened by the recent publication of a series of observations by the British economist, Thomas Balogh, on the conclusions of the 1961 Conference of African Ministers of Education at Addis Ababa.[1]

Briefly put, Balogh's views may be stated in the following manner: Since between 80 and 95 per cent of Africans are dependent upon agriculture, the essential need in African education is the development of large scale technical and agricultural programs within the schools at all levels: "The school must provide the nucleus of modern agriculture within the villages" and play a central role in the general raising of standards of living within the subsistence sector. Present educational facilities constitute an obstacle to rural progress because people are not trained for agriculture, and academic systems of formal education are the chief determinant of attitudes hostile to the practice of rural agriculture. Schools are regarded as primarily responsible for the flight from the rural areas to the towns. Balogh's views, stated in perhaps more measured terms, are paralleled in a recent United Nations publication in which it is observed that one of the chief educational priorities in economically developing areas is "the creation of a fully integrated system of agricultural education within the general framework of technical and vocational education."[2]

Although only two examples of this trend of thought are given here, it is possible to indicate numerous current publications dealing with education and economic development that accord high priority to schemes for agricultural, vocational, and technical education as against the provision of substantially more "academic" types of instruction. In the following pages I hope to show that these views are generally fallacious and ignore a series of crucial variables that must be taken into account if any realistic proposals for stimulating economic growth are to emerge. In developing the discussion I shall use examples from Ghana, which is not altogether unique among African territories in spite of the relatively high level of per capita income that it enjoys.

It should be said at the outset that there is no disagreement with two of Balogh's contentions. First, it seems clear that agricultural development and a rapid rise in rural incomes must definitely be accorded priority in all development schemes. Apart from the probability that such growth must precede even limited industrial development, there is the immediate question of raising the bare subsistence basis upon which many African cultivators are obliged to exist. Second, it is likely that such programs must depend in part .upon the provision of technical and agricultural education as a necessary but by no means sufficient condition of growth.

However, in spite of vague general agreement on the desirability of such programs, there is a virtual absence of explicit dicta regarding their nature. For example, what would an educational scheme adjusted to developmental needs look like? What role would the schools themselves play in such a program? At what stage in formal education should specifically vocational subjects be begun, and how would technical and agricul-

From *Education and Economic Development*, ed. C. Arnold Anderson and Mary Jean Bowman (Chicago: Aldine Publishing Company, 1965), pp. 142–166. We have extracted pp. 142–153 for reproduction here. Copyright © 1965 by the Aldine Publishing Company. Reprinted by permission.

tural schools be integrated with the general system? Then there is the problem of the content of studies; frequently vocational curricula are ill designed to serve the needs of developing economies. Agreeing on the need for agricultural development does not lead us directly to any particular specifications for educational content or organization. Even assuming that well-validated prescriptions existed, it is equally apparent that these would vary considerably with the degree of effective centralized control exerted by governments. This latter factor seems to be rarely considered by educational planners, yet it is probably the single most crucial variable in determining the effectiveness of an agricultural or a technical program.

Having entered these caveats, our major disagreement with Balogh lies in the "strategy" that he proposes and the degree to which he places reliance upon *formal* educational institutions in instituting change. Secondly, Balogh tends to view vocational and general education as substitutes for each other rather than to see them as essentially complementary and hardly substitutable.

There is, perhaps, a general tendency to accord to the schools a "central" position in strategies designed to facilitate economic development. To some extent this reflects an appreciation of the relative lack of alternative institutions that can be utilized, but it stems partially from the notion that schools are particularly manipulable institutions. It is widely believed that schools can readily be modified to meet new economic needs and, more particularly, to accord with the intentions of social and economic planners. I shall argue, on the contrary, that schools are remarkably clumsy instruments for inducing prompt large-scale changes in underdeveloped areas. To be sure, formal education has had immense impact in Africa, but its consequences have rarely been those anticipated, and the schools have not often functioned in the manner intended by educational planners.

I. THE COLONIAL EXPERIENCE IN GHANA

If there is anything surprising in Balogh's views it lies not in their originality but in the degree to which they reproduce with virtually no modification a series of arguments that were first stated in equally cogent fashion by the Education Committee of the Privy Council in 1847.[3] So far as Ghana, in particular, is concerned, the viewpoint was forcefully advanced in the Appendix to the Report of the Commission on the West Coast of Africa in 1842 and by a succession of colonial governors and educators thereafter.[4] Indeed, stress on the provision of vocational and agricultural education was included *without exception* in every major document related to educational development in the Gold Coast up till the grant of independence in 1957.

In spite of this, by 1959 the structure of the Ghanaian educational system was essentially that prevailing in most of British Africa: an expanding base of primary and middle school education of a predominantly academic variety capped by a group of highly selective grammar schools and a university college modeled closely upon British prototypes.[5] In that year only about 1 per cent of all persons enrolled in formal educational institutions were receiving instruction in vocational, technical, or agricultural subjects. The paradox in Ghanaian education has been the emphasis placed on vocational and agricultural training in all documentary sources and the relative absence of it within the actual system of education.[6]

A priori, it might be suspected that no serious attempt was ever made to implement schemes for agricultural and vocational training in the schools or that such proposals remained stillborn as the result of disinterest in them by the colonial rulers. In the case of Ghana this argument can be totally dismissed. There is ample documentary evidence throughout the latter half of the nineteenth century and the early twentieth that strenuous efforts were being made by both government and missions to establish agricultural schools, devise special agricultural curricula, and provide technical and vocational education. The development of academic secondary schools upon the British model was regarded with disfavor, as being inappropriate for the economic needs of the Gold Coast. Agricultural education was regarded as the key to economic development in that area. Particularly in the case of the activities of the Basel Mission, a system of schools based on agricultural and technical education was attempted which was probably unrivaled in any other territory in Africa.[7] Yet all of these earlier experiments were unsuccessful, and the educational history of the Gold Coast is strewn with the wreckage of schemes corresponding to Balogh's proposals.

In practice, the demand by Africans for western education was and is predominantly oriented towards the provision of more academic-type schools. This preference springs, I contend, from a remarkably realistic appraisal of occupational opportunities generated within the exchange sector of the economy as a result of European overrule. So far as the clientele of the schools was concerned, the primary function of formal education was to enable individuals to move from subsistence activities to occupations within the European-dominated sector. An examination of opportunities within that sector throughout the colonial period reveals that *relatively* there was a greater demand for clerical and commercial employees than for technically trained individuals. Opportunities certainly existed in technical fields and in agriculture, but they were inferior to the other alternatives. Access to most of the highly paid occupations was, therefore, achieved through academic-type institutions. Those who criticize the "irrational" nature of African demand for "academic" as opposed to "vocational" education fail to recognize that the strength of academic education has lain precisely in the fact that

it is preeminently a *vocational* education providing access to those occupations with the most prestige and, most important, the highest pay within the Ghanaian economy. The financial rewards and the employment opportunities for technically trained individuals were never commensurate with opportunities in the clerical field. Since the graduates of the academic school were manifestly more advantageously placed,[8] the pressure for "academic" education reflected fairly accurately the demands for alternative types of skill within the exchange sector of the economy. One of the major ironies of the situation is that while proponents of technical education were criticizing the neglect of technical provision in the schools, the products of such technical institutions as existed were often experiencing difficulties in obtaining employment. Frequently those persons entered occupations unrelated to the training they had undergone.[9]

This form of "wastage" among trained manpower is endemic in underdeveloped countries.

1. Initially, trained individuals may be produced for whom there is no actual demand so far as the market is concerned. There may be a considerable "surplus" of these trained men where "new nations," in their desire to emulate more economically developed areas, invest considerable sums in the training of technicians before they can be utilized in the existing economy.

2. Second, a real demand may exist for trained personnel, but at the same time scarce personnel are not utilized and skilled workers are involved in tasks not directly relevant to their professional accomplishments. This would appear to occur more commonly in government service and we shall draw attention to it specifically in later pages.

3. Third, skilled personnel may not enter the type of job for which they have been trained because opportunities seem so much greater in alternative occupations. Thus, for example, many graduates of the Basel Mission schools who received agricultural

and industrial training entered clerical employment. Here the most saleable component of their education experience was literacy, not trade training, and the former was thus utilized in the job market.[10] Wastage of skills must always be considered in assessing programs of vocational training.

To be sure, such wastage has also been characteristic of developed countries, but in the case of many of the "new nations" such a phenomenon is particularly undesirable in view of the limited resources available.

We do not intend here to underestimate non-economic factors that contributed to African demand for academic schools though these, in fact, reinforced the pattern we have described above. The European colonial elite itself acted as a reference group for African aspirations; emulation of that elite led to a pressure for "parity" between metropolitan and colonial institutions. Since the colonial elite provided only a partial image of western society and was composed overwhelmingly of administrators and government servants educated primarily in academic institutions, African demand for education was understandably oriented to the acquisition of that kind of education that was perceived to be the key to European-type occupational roles. In this the Africans were acting astutely. One of the striking features of most post-colonial economies is the domination by government agencies of well-paid and high-status employment opportunities. Since such institutions, through recruiting primarily upon the basis of "universalistic" criteria, stress the possession of an academic formal education, a higher premium is placed upon such schooling than occurred in early stages of development in most western societies.

In this context, one of the most striking differences between many of the new nations and the western world at earlier periods of its development is their lack of mobility opportunities lying outside the formal educational structure. Systems of apprenticeship, opportunities to open small enterprises, etc., all provided institu-tionalized modes of social and economic ascent in western society. The relative absence of those sorts of alternatives to formal education in many new nations sometimes produces the paradoxical result, as in Ghana, that educational requirements for obtaining employment are now as high, if not higher, than in the former metropole itself, notwithstanding a very low level of diffusion of formal education in the population as a whole.

Thus when colonial peoples were involved in unequal competition with resident Europeans for a limited number of high-status jobs, it was considered imperative to obtain qualifications virtually identical to those prevalent in the metropole. This was a perfectly rational estimate of the relative advantages of alternative types of education; in the competition for scarce job opportunities nonmetropolitan curricula were by definition inferior.

It is important to note, however, that the termination of colonial overrule has made virtually no difference to the over-all structure of occupational opportunities within the exchange sector. To be sure, Ghanaians are less involved in direct competition with Europeans for high-ranking posts within the administration. However, in the nongovernmental sector there has been little change in the premium placed on academic training; indeed, there has been an intensification of certain features apparent in the colonial period. At present, out of a total employed labor force of 2.56 million not more than 13.7 per cent (or 350,000) are employed full-time in the "modern" sector of the economy. It has been calculated that the rate of growth in wage employment opportunities amounts to just over 4 per cent per annum; though this estimate is probably too low, a rather generous estimate of employment growth would be 20 to 25 thousand per annum.[11] On the other hand, the annual output of the middle schools alone has now risen to over 30 thousand per annum.

Parallel with this, however, has been the fact that government employment has absorbed an increasing proportion of the labor force: 42 per cent in 1951 and 51 per cent in 1957. The progressive enlargement of existing government agencies and the creation of new public corporations has, if anything, tended to favor employment for clerical and administrative workers. Since, relatively speaking, the balance of job opportunities has shifted even more in favor of clerical employment, there is a mounting demand for the academic secondary school education that provides access to such positions.[12]

What is implied here is that although considerable attention has always been paid to the so-called problem of "white-collar" unemployment in West Africa, there has been little realization that opportunities for technical employment have been even more limited and certainly more poorly paid. In virtually every African territory there appears to be a current stress upon the need for the provision of technical education upon a massive scale to meet the "needs" of the economy. Sometimes such demands are based upon the conclusions of manpower surveys, the source of whose projections may not be too clear. Yet a sober inspection of the actual structure of job opportunities within an economy such as that of Ghana gives no reason to suppose that the products of technical schools can be absorbed soon on a large scale.[13] In actuality, we are not faced by the problem of white-collar unemployment at all but by a far more serious form of generalized unemployment.

II. THE "WHITE-COLLAR" MYTH AND VOCATIONAL ASPIRATIONS

There is no doubt that unemployment among school-leavers has reached alarming proportions in West Africa. Investigations by Callaway in Nigeria and by the present writer in Ghana confirm its extent and incidence and give no reason to suppose that it is likely to diminish in the near future.[14] However, the crucial question is not the amount of such unemployment but the

delineation of significant factors determining its incidence. It has been frequently asserted that the problem has its source in the reluctance of literate individuals and school graduates to enter manual occupations and in their unrealistic search for white-collar employment, which they believe to be commensurate with their status as "educated men."[15] In this interpretation unemployment is conceived to be "frictional" in nature, and the schools are perceived to be the villains of the piece; it is inferred that the type of education to which students are exposed (specifically, the curriculum of the schools) largely determines their vocational aspirations and operates as an independent variable in setting the level of vocational choice. This has been a favorite theme for well nigh a century. Balogh, for example, specifically attributes the present employment crisis in Nigeria to the provision of a particular form of academic elementary education that has generated unrealistic employment expectations for clerical work, caused a flight from the rural areas, and fostered a disdain for manual occupations.[16] If this diagnosis of the problem were correct, the solution would be simple: change the curricula to provide instruction based upon agriculture and technical subjects, and the aspirations of young people will, in consequence, be directed towards agricultural activities; the flight from the land will be checked and the volume of "frictional" unemployment will correspondingly diminish.

This reasoning is largely fallacious.[17] It has already been pointed out by others that the idea that children's vocational aspirations can be altered by massive changes in curriculum is no more than a piece of folklore with little empirical justification.[18] In Nigeria and Ghana the graduates of the primary and middle schools do work with their hands and they often seek employment as general laborers. Conversely, it is possible to show that even where students have been educated in agricultural or technical schools, a high proportion of them have never en-

Table 1. Occupational Choices of Form IV Children in Ghana Middle Schools (N = 210)

Occupational category*	(1) Free choices		(2) Job expectations		Difference between (1) and (2)	
	Percentage	Number	Percentage	Number	Percentage	Number
I Higher professional	11.0	23	5.2	11	-5.8	-12
II Lower professional	10.0	21	1.9	4	-8.1	-17
III Teacher	0.9	2	3.8	8	+2.9	+6
IV Clerical and allied	8.1	17	10.0	21	+1.9	+4
V Artisans and skilled workers	51.0	107	22.4	47	-27.6	-60
VI Commercial	1.9	4	9.5	20	+7.6	+16
VII Semiskilled and unskilled	3.3	7	35.2	74	+31.9	+67
VIII Uniformed services	2.4	5	4.3	10	+2.4	+5
IX Fishermen and farmers	10.5	22	6.7	14	-3.8	-8
X Miscellaneous and unclassified	0.9	2	0.0	0	-0.9	-2
No Answer	0.0	0	0.5	1	+0.5	+1
Total	100.0	210	100.0	210	—	—

*The occupational categories were:

Higher professional: Doctor, lawyer, minister of religion, etc.

Lower professional: Nurse, dispenser, draughtsman, journalist, agricultural officer, surveyor, etc.

Teacher: All teaching roles within the primary, middle, secondary or technical institutions.

Clerical and allied: Clerk (unspecified), cashier, bookkeeper, typist, bank clerk, librarian, letter writer, etc.

Artisans and skilled workers: Electrician, motor mechanic, plumber, carpenter, mason, printer, painter, shoemaker, locomotive engineer, tailor, etc.

Commercial: Petty trades and small-scale shopkeepers.

Semiskilled or unskilled workers: Laborer (various), messenger, bus conductor, watchman, steward, quarry-man, miner, cook, etc.

Uniformed services: Police, army, Builders Brigade.

Fishermen and farmers

Miscellaneous and unclassifiable: Musician, boxer, artist, jockey, etc.

tered those occupations for which they were trained but have gravitated to alternative employments offering greater opportunities. These observations would tend to throw some doubt on programs whose efficacy depends on the notion that the schools exercise a decisive influence upon vocational aspirations of students. However, more definite empirical evidence is available to suggest that in Ghana, at least, the disdain for manual labor believed to be so typical of the products of formal education is not at all in accord with fact.

In December 1959 the author drew a sample of 210 boys from the fourth forms of nine academic-type middle schools in Accra. These students were in their final month of studies preparatory to seeking employment or, in a few cases, continuing their education in other schools. They were asked, first, what kind of employment they would most like to obtain if they were *completely free* to choose. This enabled children to fantasy as much as they wished regarding their careers. Then they were asked what type of employment they actually *expected* to be able to obtain.

The findings in no sense indicate a predisposition to favor professional and white-collar employment (Table 1). Even where children were free to respond as they wished, no fewer than 62 per cent favored artisan employment or farming (even in an urban center such as Accra). Only 30 per cent favored employment in varying levels of white-collar activity (categories I–III). The most instructive section of the table, however, concerns job expectations. The pupils displayed a remarkable level of realism. Although 51 per cent expressed the hope of ultimately becoming skilled artisans, only 22 per cent *expected* to be able to do so, and 35 per cent were fully reconciled to entering semiskilled or unskilled occupations. These observations (which confirm an earlier study by Barnard) would seem to indicate that there is little foundation to theories attributing to the curriculum a major influence on vocational aspirations.[19]

It seems clear that mass unemployment among school-leavers in many new African nations is due to dysfunctions existing between the gross rate of school output and the slow expansion of occupational opportunities of all types within the exchange sector. It may be easy enough to increase the output of the schools but it is far more difficult to expand employment opportunities. The operative fact here is not that graduates will not accept certain types of employment but rather that the schools (irrespective of what they teach) have been shrewdly used as the gateway into the "emergent" sector of the economy. The schools themselves can do little about this. So long as parents and students perceive the function of education in this manner, agricultural education and vocational instruction *in the schools* is not likely to have a determinative influence on the occupational aspirations and destinations of students. Aspirations are determined largely by the individual's perception of opportunities within the exchange sector of the economy, destinations by the *actual* structure of opportunities in that sector. The nature of educational instruction has little to do with the process, and the schools are unfairly criticized for creating a condition for which they have not been responsible—except insofar as they turn out too many graduates.

The reasons why graduates do not return to subsistence or quasi-subsistence agriculture has, of course, little to do with a disdain for farming that is created by an academic education. In 1961, a questionnaire was administered by the present writer to more than 700 Ghanaian male students in 20 highly selective academic secondary schools. The students were asked to rate 25 diverse occupations in terms of two criteria, occupational prestige and perceived income (Table 2). In practice, farming was rated 16th in prestige rankings (above middle and primary school teaching and office work, for example) and 10th in perceived income. Even among these advanced students farming is still rated moderately high. However,

Table 2. Secondary Student Perceptions of the Occupational Hierarchy (N = 775)

Occupation	(1) Prestige rankings			(2) Income rankings		
	Mean score	S.D.	Rank	Mean score	S.D.	Rank
Medical doctor	1.12	0.31	1	1.24	0.47	1
University teacher	1.16	0.38	2	1.28	0.51	2
Lawyer	1.45	0.64	3	1.40	0.55	3
Chief	1.89	0.78	4	2.47	0.80	8.5
Author	1.97	0.80	5	2.25	0.86	6
Secondary school teacher	2.05	0.51	6	2.23	0.58	5
Clergyman	2.96	0.84	7	3.10	0.95	15
Merchant or businessman	2.50	0.73	8	1.92	0.79	4
Nurse	2.60	0.64	9	3.01	0.57	13
Political party worker	2.70	0.93	10	2.38	0.90	7
Government clerk	2.71	0.59	11	2.78	0.58	11
Soldier	2.78	0.81	12	3.00	0.64	12
Actor	2.81	0.90	13	2.47	0.94	8.5
Chief's counsellor	2.82	0.74	14	3.21	0.79	17
Policeman	2.94	0.73	15	3.21	0.55	17
Farmer	2.95	0.96	16	2.75	1.06	10
Office worker	2.96	0.60	17	3.03	0.56	14
Middle school teacher	3.00	0.50	18	3.21	0.51	17
Primary school teacher	3.25	0.67	19	3.53	0.65	21
Motorcar fitter	3.59	0.73	20	3.35	0.77	19
Petty trader	3.62	0.75	21	3.36	0.82	20
Shop assistant	3.80	0.66	22	3.84	0.64	23
Carpenter	3.84	0.73	23	3.73	0.75	22
Farm laborer	4.47	0.70	24	4.51	0.63	24
Streetcleaner	4.74	0.56	25	4.73	0.53	25

only one per cent of the students wished to become farmers in spite of the fact that it was rated higher in terms of both prestige and income than was primary or middle school teaching, which no less than 34 per cent of the students expected to enter.

It would seem that the factors inhibiting the "return to the land" lie primarily in the institutional milieu of farming. Initially, of course, in certain areas of Ghana (such as Ewe territory) acute population pressure and land fragmentation pose the problem of getting people away from the villages and into alternative employment, or at least into areas where land is available. In other localities suitable cash crops that might provide the basis for reasonable cash incomes to supplement subsistence activities have not yet been discovered. However, even in areas where cash crop farming can be moderately profitable, it takes place within a neotradi-

tional framework. The farmer is not only obliged to reside in areas whose amenities are demonstrably inferior to those of the urban areas, but he is necessarily involved in the obligations and constraints of traditional rural structure. The demands of kin and the constrictions of traditional land tenure with its usual concomitant of endless litigation combine to make "progressive" farming a hazardous endeavour. In effect, if we are to really appreciate the factors that militate against individuals entering agriculture, we must examine the neotraditional institutional complex in which agricultural activities take place. It is probably in this complex and in the structure of accompanying incentives that the primary variables lie—not in the deficiencies of agricultural instruction in the schools nor in the "academically" oriented values of students. Young people do not object to farming per se or to the desirability of entering "modern" farming. [20] They are perfectly aware, however, that this is precisely what the institutional framework does not offer. Vocational instruction in agriculture by itself cannot induce youth to take up farming until an institutional complex exists which makes the utilization of new techniques profitable and meaningful. This reluctance would still prevail even if it were evident that such instruction was the principal mode of raising agricultural production. A high priority for research is indeed the delineation of those disincentives which spring from the neotraditional complex of institutions surrounding agriculture.

We have argued so far that the vocational aspirations of children and the occupations which they enter are almost exclusively determined by factors which lie outside the schools. Indeed, in terms of the actual opportunities open to them, the students' perceptions are remarkably realistic. It follows, therefore, that no amount of formal technical, vocational or agricultural instruction alone is going to check the movement from the rural areas, reduce the volume of unemployment, or indeed necessarily have any effect on the rate of economic development. Those factors which really give the impetus to early economic growth are far more subtle than the proponents of vocational education suppose. We would suggest that the crucial variables lie, instead, in the structure of incentives within the economic system and in the degree to which the institutional milieu is supportive of entrepreneurial activity. Without such a milieu no amount of vocational instruction can be effective since the skills acquired will not be utilized. To put the issue more colloquially, in the initial stages technical and vocational instruction is the cart rather than the horse in economic growth, and its development depends upon real and perceived opportunities in the economy. The provision of vocational education must be directly related to those points at which some development is already apparent and where demand for skills is beginning to manifest itself....

NOTES

1. UNESCO, United National Economic Commission for Africa, *Conference of African States on the Development of Education in Africa*, UNESCO/ED/181 (Addis Ababa, 1961). Balogh's observations are to be found in "Catastrophe in Africa," *Times Educational Supplement*, Jan. 5th, 1962, p. 8; and Feb. 9, 1962, p. 241. Also in "What Schools for Africa?" *New Statesman and Nation* (March 23, 1962), p. 412.

2. United Nations, Committee on Information from Non-Self Governing Territories, *Special Study on Educational Conditions in Non-Self Governing Territories* (New York, 1960), p. 8.

3. The text of this early document is to be found in H. S. Scott, "The Development of the Education of the African in Relation to Western Contact," *The Yearbook of Education* (London: Evans Bros., 1938), pp. 693–739.

4. There is considerable literature on this point but a few major examples may be cited. See the report of the Commissioner in the Appendix to the "Report of the Committee on the West Coast of Africa," *Parliamentary Papers*, Vol. XI, 1852. Also Gold Coast, *Report of the Committee of Educationalists* (Accra: Government Printer, 1920); Jesse Jones, *Education in Africa: A Study of West, South, and Equatorial Africa by the African Education Commission* (New York: Phelps Stokes Fund, 1922); Gold Coast, *Report of the Education Committee, 1937–1941* (Accra: Government Printer, 1942). This list cannot present numerous additional statements of this nature and there should be no need to refer the reader to the famous policy statements of the Advisory Committee on Education in the Colonies. However, in Appendix I to this paper we have included a selection of statements from these earlier documents.

5. Ghana, Statistical Reports Series I, No. 6, *Education Statistics 1959* (Accra: Office of the Government Statistician, 1959).

6. The Ghanaian Ministry of Education, like most African Ministries, does not include in its reports technical and vocational training being undertaken in special schools connected with Railways and Harbors, the Public Works Department, etc.

7. For a succinct account of the activities of the Basel Mission see W. J. Rottman, "The Educational Work of the Basel Mission," Appendix A.I to *Special Reports on Educational Subjects*, Vol. XIII, Part II. (London: H.M.S.O., 1905), pp. 307–318.

8. See also I. M. Wallerstein, *The Emergence of Two West African Nations: Ghana and the Ivory Coast* (New York: Columbia University Press, 1959), p. 241.

9. See Gold Coast, *Report of the Education Department*, 1935, para. 332; also Gold Coast, *Legislative Council Debates*, 1933, pp. 5, 94; and 1935, p. 5.

10. Rottman, *op. cit.*, p. 300.

11. These estimates have been computed from the 1960 *Population Census of Ghana*, Advance Report of Vols. III and IV; Ghana, *Quarterly Digest of Statistics* (Accra: Office of the Government Statistician, 1959); and Ghana, *Economic Surveys, 1955–1958* (Accra: Government Printer, 1959).

12. This trend in demand for academic secondary is, of course, indicated most sharply by the growth of private and proprietary secondary schools in Ghana which by 1961 numbered no less than 52 schools.

13. No data exist on the occupational destinations of the products of technical institutes, but in 1961 there was some concern that the products of Junior Technical Institutes, in particular, were experiencing difficulty in finding adequate employment.

14. Arch C. Callaway, "School Leavers in Nigeria: 1," *West Africa,* No. 2286 (March 25, 1961), p. 325.

15. This view is to be found throughout the literature. For a recent example see Ghana, *Economic Survey 1958,* p. 24.

16. Balogh, *op. cit., Times Educational Supplement,* Feb. 9, 1962, p. 241.

17. We do not wish to imply here that the problem of the "unemployed intellectual" who refuses to accept a type of employment "below his status" is a myth in all areas. There is little doubt that this phenomenon was clear enough in India. However, this is a very different thing from saying that such attitudes were a result of the kind of formal western schooling undergone by students. They probably stemmed from a much older tradition of Brahmanic intellectualism. However, in the case of West Africa, this would not appear to be the case, and there is a very high correlation between perceived prestige and perceived income variables.

18. Callaway, "School Leavers in Nigeria: 3," *West Africa,* Vol. 2288 (April 8, 1962), p. 371.

19. G. L. Barnard, "Gold Coast Children out of School," *Oversea Education,* Vol. XXIII, No. 4 (January 1957), pp. 163–172.

20. See also Callaway, *loc. cit.*

IV

THE POLITICS OF EDUCATION

Of the major social science disciplines, perhaps none has devoted less of its resources to the study of education than political science. In contrast to sociologists, whose investigations of education and social background have illuminated the relationship between schools and the class structure (see Part II), and economists, whose inquiries into schooling and the labor market have done much to reveal the complex connections between the educational system and the economy (see Part III), political scientists have failed to produce a serious body of research in the politics of education. Michael W. Kirst, one of the few political scientists whose work focuses on schools, has described the politics of education as a "new and still largely uncharted area of research concentration."[1] Despite its obvious importance for a general theory of educational change, we know surprisingly little about the process by which the structure of power influences the shape of educational systems. Even the decision-making approach, a staple of conventional political science, has been rarely applied to the study of the educational system.[2] The recent appearance of Maurice Kogan's study of educational policy-making in Britain (Kogan, 1975) may, we hope, signal increasing interest in a crucial but neglected field of study. Given the large and growing state spending on education and the concern of political scientists with the politics of the budgetary process, the shortage of educational decision-making studies seems curious indeed.

The political scientists' lack of interest in education may be attributed in part to their susceptibility to a myth that appeals to scholars and laymen alike: that schools are not political institutions. The idea that education should be kept out of politics and politics out of the schools, a notion that has been particularly widespread in the United States since the late nineteenth century,[3] may have little analytical value, but it has served as a powerful brake on

---

1. Michael W. Kirst, ed., *State, School and Politics* (Lexington, Mass.: D. C. Heath, 1972), p. xvii.
2. Andre Benoit notes the absence of studies of educational decision-making in "A Note on Decision-Making Processes in the Politics of Education," *Comparative Educational Review* 19 (February 1975): 155–168.
3. See David B. Tyack, *The One Best System* (Cambridge, Mass.: Harvard University Press, 1974), and Chapter 23 of this volume, for an analysis of the origins of the view that schools should be controlled by "disinterested" professionals.

those who have wished to make the control of the schools an overt political issue. There have been relatively few dramatic political conflicts over education in the United States, and those that have occurred have tended, because of the lack of centralized control, to play themselves out at the local level, and have therefore failed to capture the attention of political scientists who prefer to focus their energies on the workings of the federal government.

Fortunately for the development of the politics of education, however, a group of sophisticated educational historians have stepped into the void left by political scientists. Part of a broader "revisionist" movement among American historians that came into prominence in the 1960s, their work brings into question the rather benign view of American institutions that dominated previous research, particularly in education. David Cohen and Marvin Lazerson, in a provocative reinterpretation of the history of early twentieth-century American education (Chapter 21), draw upon a key work of revisionist history—James Weinstein's study of corporate liberalism[4]—to reorganize evidence in support of their thesis that the educational history of this period can best be understood as an adaptation of the schools to large-scale corporate capitalism. Another leading revisionist historian, Michael B. Katz, best known for his study of class conflict in education in nineteenth-century Massachusetts,[5] offers a penetrating analysis of the social basis of conflicts over forms of organizational control of education—conflicts that reflect, in his view, fundamental value differences (Chapter 22). And David B. Tyack, in an essay that owes much to Samuel P. Hays's pioneering reinterpretation of the Progressive movement,[6] shows that the movement to centralize city school systems at the turn of the century, ostensibly devoted to the objective of giving power to non-political professional experts, actually established dominance by a social elite over urban education (Chapter 23). The success of progressive educational reformers derived in part from their ability to present their particular values as universal ones, and Tyack's analysis of the movement to bureaucratize city schools is, in that sense, a case study of the role of ideology in the exercise of political power.

Patterns of control over the educational system vary, of course, from one society to another, and the comparative approach can do much to clarify the ways in which education, political power, and social structure may be interrelated. Rolland Paulston applies this perspective to the Peruvian school system in search of the factors that obstruct educational change and finds that the highly hierarchical character of Peru's social structure is itself the main impediment to rationalization (Chapter 24). Though control of the educational system is only a minor theme of Paulston's article, his study is nonetheless a contribution to the politics of education, for it shows how power *inheres* in Peru's complex system of overlapping class and cultural inequalities. Unlike some advocates of the decision-making approach, who do not see power except in those cases where there is overt conflict, Paulston is well aware that there is a "mobilization of bias" in a given institutional structure, which reflects the power of some groups over others.[7]

In many ways, Paulston's formulation of the problem of power in education is similar to that of Max Weber, who held that the educational ideals and practices of a particular society

---

4. James Weinstein, *The Corporate Ideal in the Liberal State, 1900–1919* (Boston: Beacon Press, 1968).
5. Michael B. Katz, *The Irony of Early School Reform* (Cambridge, Mass.: Harvard University Press, 1968).
6. Samuel P. Hays, "The Politics of Reform in Municipal Government in the Progressive Era," *Pacific Northwest Quarterly*, October 1964, pp. 157–169.
7. See Steven Lukes, *Power: A Radical View* (London: Macmillan, 1974), for a critique of the decision-making approach to politics. For studies that focus, as Lukes advocates, on "non-decisions" and on control over the political agenda, the comparative perspective would seem likely to prove helpful in providing the needed empirical controls.

should be viewed in terms of its "structure of domination."[8] Where Weber focuses on the way in which the cultural ideals of the dominant stratum penetrate the *content* of schooling, Paulston emphasizes their effects on the *structure* of the educational system. Both these problems are crucial for the development of a comprehensive theory of the politics of education, and both are amenable to empirical exploration. In order to investigate them adequately, however, educational researchers will have to go beyond the behaviorist techniques favored by political scientists. The writings of Weber and Durkheim (see Chapter 2) provide a useful beginning here, but a politics of education deriving from their analyses of the cultural and structural bases of educational power has yet to be constructed.[9]

One aspect of the relationship between the educational system and the political system that has been explored in some detail by political scientists is the role of schooling in developing political awareness. Hess and Torney, in one of the best-known studies on this subject, have declared, though without direct empirical evidence, that the school is the "most important and effective institution of political socialization in the United States."[10] Relying upon the standard research instrument used by students of political learning—the question-naire administered to a captive audience of schoolchildren—they conclude that "children in working-class areas of the city are less completely socialized (in the sense of being prepared for political participation) than children from middle-class homes."[11] Viewed from this perspective, the process of political learning among working-class schoolchildren is not merely different from that occurring among their middle-class counterparts, but inferior; the political attitudes of children from working-class homes with respect to "efficacy" are, for example, viewed as being "behind" those of middle-class children.

A careful examination of Hess and Torney's "index of efficacy" reveals that one's level of political development increases in direct proportion to one's willingness to respond negatively to such statements as, "I don't think people in the government care much about what people like my family think."[12] Those poor and minority children who, drawing on their own experience, express agreement with such assertions are, as a consequence, labeled as "deficient" by political scientists whose own views of the realities of power are, to say the least, peculiarly benign. The incompletely socialized should not lose hope, however, for effective state intervention may reduce their deficit; as one leading researcher puts it, "quality education can produce not only compensatory intellectual training, but also compensatory political socialization."[13] With proper instruction, then, working-class children and blacks can

8. See Weber's "The Rationalization of Education and Training" and "The Chinese Literati" in *From Max Weber: Essays in Sociology,* edited by H. H. Gerth and C. Wright Mills (New York: Oxford University Press, 1946), pp. 240–244, 416–444.
9. As a Marxist approach to the problem of the exertion of power in education in the absence of observable conflict, Gramsci's concept of ideological hegemony would seem to open up a particularly promising avenue of thought. See Antonio Gramsci, *Selections from the Prison Notebooks* (New York: International Publishers, 1971).
10. Robert D. Hess and Judith V. Torney, *The Development of Political Attitudes in Children* (Chicago: Aldine, 1969), p. 101.
11. *Ibid.,* p. 225.
12. *Ibid.,* p. 256.
13. Richard M. Merelman, *Political Socialization and Educational Climates* (New York: Holt, Rinehart, and Winston, 1971), p. 111. Despite its use of the value-laden concept of "compensatory political socialization," Merelman's study shows a degree of theoretical and methodological sophistication rare among political scientists using the survey approach. Other important studies of political socialization conducted within the mainstream of political science are David Easton and Jack Dennis, *Children in the Political System: A History of American Urban Education* (New York: Oxford University Press, 1969), and M. Kent Jennings and Richard G. Niemi, *The Political Character of Adolescence* (Princeton, N.J.: Princeton University Press, 1974).

overcome "deficiencies" in their political socialization and develop a commitment to those middle-class values and beliefs that contribute to the maintenance of a democratic regime based on consensus.[14]

An approach to the problem of political socialization that differs radically from the perspective of mainstream American political science is offered by two Italian sociologists, Marzio Barbagli and Marcello Dei (Chapter 25). While Americans tend to look upon the process of value transmission as a source of *consensus,* Barbagli and Dei, working within a Marxist framework, view it as a crucial support for a system of *class domination.* The values transmitted by the school are, they argue, the dominant values of the society and as such reflect the power of ruling groups to impose them on the rest of society. Thus the apparently neutral injunction against classroom discussion of "partisan" values (i.e., those that are in conflict with dominant values) is seen as part of a subtly conservative ideology of educational autonomy that serves to promote either depoliticization or a constricted political consensus.

Perhaps even more important to the process of political socialization than the role of schooling in the direct transmission of political values is its indirect effect on the development of a political personality. Barbagli and Dei, whose study, *Le vestali della classe media,* actually focuses less upon the process of political socialization among students than upon the social position of Italian schoolteachers,[15] nonetheless make a provocative suggestion about the indirect contribution of schooling to political socialization: that the degree of hierarchy in the teacher-pupil relationship is likely to affect the student's attitudes toward authority not only in the school, but also in the larger society. Attitudes towards authority are, of course, profoundly political and would seem likely to make themselves felt with particular force in authority relations at the workplace, but the relationship between hierarchy in the school and hierarchy in the office and factory has been little explored, especially by political scientists, who generally do not look upon power relationships in the process of production as political at all. Instead, they focus their attention on what is overtly political in the educational process, thereby neglecting the implications of the "hidden curriculum" of schooling. For example, the ostensibly meritocratic selection procedures embodied in the workings of the educational system might be thought to provide important legitimation for social inequality,[16] but the formulation of such a hypothesis is outside the range of a framework that ignores ideologies implicit in the structure and process of education. Until serious attention is paid to the indirect as well as the direct effects of schooling, our knowledge of the role of the educational system in the development of the adult political actor is likely to remain superficial.

That schools do not always incline students towards support for the status quo is suggested by the fact that the New Left, a movement that radically questioned the values and

14. For a comprehensive critique of conventional studies of political socialization, see R. W. Connell and Murray Goot, "Science and Ideology in American 'Political Socialization' Research," *Berkeley Journal of Sociology,* 1972–1973, pp. 165–193. Other interesting critiques include David Marsh, "Political Socialization: The Implicit Assumptions Questioned," *British Journal of Political Science* 1 (October 1971): 453–465, and Kenneth Prewitt, "Some Doubts About Political Socialization Research," *Comparative Education Review* 19 (February 1975): 105–114. For a discussion of possible new directions in research on schooling and political socialization, see Michael W. Kirst, ed., *op. cit.,* pp. 231–237.
15. Indeed, Barbagli and Dei's study (Bologna: Il Mulino, 1969), only a small portion of which is reproduced in this volume, is one of the most impressive sociological investigations of the schoolteacher to appear in recent years. For other studies of teachers that contain information on their political attitudes, see Harmon Zeigler, *The Political Life of American Teachers* (Englewood Cliffs, N.J.: Prentice-Hall, 1967), and A. H. Halsey and Martin Trow, *The British Academics* (London: Faber and Faber, 1971).
16. See, for example, George S. Rothbart, "The Legitimation of Inequality: Objective Scholarship vs. Black Militance," *Sociology of Education* 43 (Spring 1970): 159–174.

practices of the existing social order, emerged within the university itself. Few social phenomena have been as carefully investigated as the student movement; American student radicalism, in particular, has been the subject of literally hundreds of empirical studies. Most of them, however, concentrate upon individual differences between activists and non-activists; a few go on to examine institutional differences in the incidence of radical activity.[17] Yet despite the imposing body of empirical data these investigations have produced, the great majority of them, possessing neither a theoretical nor a historical framework, have contributed little toward an understanding of the student movement.

One notable exception is the analysis offered by Michael W. Miles (Chapter 26), who not only places student radicalism in its historical context, but also links it to parallel changes occurring in the American class structure and in the "higher education industry."[18] The key to the student movement, Miles argues, lies in its origins in the new middle class—a group whose awareness of the precarious character of its social position, almost constantly threatened by the possibility of proletarianization, was made more acute by the process of industrialization taking place in American higher education. Miles's analysis is a controversial one, for it attempts to explain both the rise and the fall of student radicalism in terms of a neo-Marxist theory of student alienation. His interpretation leads him, in the end, to suggest the possible emergence of a student movement based in the new working-class sector of higher education; that this form of student radicalism will, in fact, ever become a mass phenomenon seems unlikely at the present moment, but it is worth remembering that the social scientists of the late 1950s did not predict the rise of a student movement that would engulf their own universities just a few years later.

17. A detailed list of these studies is contained in Kenneth Keniston, *Radicals and Militants: An Annotated Bibliography of Empirical Research on Campus Unrest* (Lexington, Mass.: D. C. Heath, 1973).
18. For a more elaborated analysis of the student movement, see Miles's *The Radical Probe* (New York: Atheneum, 1971). Other important studies of student radicalism include Richard Flacks, *Youth and Social Change* (Chicago: Markham, 1971); Kenneth Keniston, *Youth and Dissent* (New York: Harcourt Brace Jovanovich, 1971); Seymour Martin Lipset, *Rebellion in the University* (Boston: Little, Brown, 1971); and Alain Touraine, *The May Movement: Revolt and Reform* (New York: Random House, 1971).

SELECTIVE BIBLIOGRAPHY

Bilski, Raphaela. "Ideology and the Comprehensive Schools." *Political Quarterly*, April–June, 1973, pp. 197–211.

Callahan, Raymond E. *Education and the Cult of Efficiency*. Chicago: University of Chicago Press, 1962.

Coleman, James S., ed. *Education and Political Development*. Princeton, N.J.: Princeton University Press, 1965.

Connell, R. W. *The Child's Construction of Politics*. Melbourne: Melbourne University Press, 1971.

Cremin, Lawrence A. *The Transformation of the School: Progressivism in American Education, 1876–1957*. New York: Alfred A. Knopf, 1961.

Karier, Clarence T. "Testing for Order and Control in the Corporate Liberal State." *Education Theory* 22 (Spring 1972): 154–180.

Katz, Michael B. *The Irony of Early School Reform*. Cambridge, Mass.: Harvard University Press, 1968.

Kogan, Maurice. *Educational Policy Making: A Study of Interest Groups and Parliament*. London: George Allen and Unwin, 1975.

Merelman, Richard M. "Social Stratification and Political Socialization in Mature Industrial Societies." *Comparative Education Review* 19 (February 1975): 13–30.

Ravitch, Diane. *The Great School Wars: New York City 1805–1972*. New York: Basic Books, 1974.

Rubin, Lillian B. *Busing and Backlash*. Berkeley: University of California Press, 1972.

Schudson, Michael S. "Organizing the

'Meritocracy': A History of the College Entrance Examination Board." *Harvard Educational Review* 42 (February 1972): 34–69.

Simon, Brian. *Education and the Labour Movement, 1870–1920.* London: Lawrence and Wishart, 1965.

Smith, David. *Who Rules the Universities?* New York: Monthly Review Press, 1974.

Tyack, David B. *The One Best System: A History of American Urban Education.* Cambridge, Mass.: Harvard University Press, 1974.

Useem, Elisabeth L., and Michael Useem, eds. *The Education Establishment.* Englewood Cliffs, N.J.: Prentice-Hall, 1974.

Vaughan, Michelina, and Margaret Scotford-Archer. *Social Conflict and Educational Change in England and France, 1789–1848.* Cambridge: Cambridge University Press, 1971.

Wirt, Frederick M., and Michael W. Kirst. *The Political Web of American Schools.* Boston: Little, Brown, 1972.

Ziegler, Harmon, and Wayne Peak. "The Political Functions of the Educational System." *Sociology of Education* 43 (Spring 1970): 115–142.

21. Education and the Corporate Order

DAVID K. COHEN and MARVIN LAZERSON

During the last fifteen years mounting conflict over the nature and function of schools has generated heightened concern over education and an unprecedented awareness of school failure. Few would now proclaim, as Angelo Patri did in 1927, that "the schools of America are the temples of a living democracy."[1] A new history of American education reflecting these social conflicts has emerged. It focuses on the development of city school bureaucracy and professionalism, the education of European immigrant and black children, and inequality of educational opportunity.[2] Yet, despite the broadened scope of historical research on education, the new work remains disparate. In this paper we try to take the next step by suggesting several unifying themes and outlining a framework for understanding the development of education in the United States in this century.[3]

In our view this history has to be understood in the framework of the schools' adaptation to large-scale corporate capitalism and the conflicts this engendered. Infusing the schools with corporate values and reorganizing them in ways seen as consistent with this new economic order has been the dominant motif. Education has been closely tied to production—schooling has been justified as a way of increasing wealth, of improving industrial output, and of making management more effective. The schools' role has been to socialize economically desirable values and behavior, teach vocational skills, and provide education consistent with students' expected occupational attainment. As a result, the schools' culture became closely identified with the ethos of the corporate workplace. Schooling came to be seen as work or the preparation for work;

schools were pictured as factories, educators as industrial managers, and students as the raw materials to be inducted into the production process. The ideology of school management was recast in the mold of the business corporation, and the character of education was shaped after the image of industrial production.[4]

But the schools' adaptation to advanced corporate capitalism has not been accomplished without conflict. While the corporate society seemed to require schools that socialized students for work and evaluated their success in economic terms, the counter-argument that education should be playful and evaluated only on intrinsic and non-economic criteria has grown progressively more insistent. Industrialization drew and held a multitude of immigrants to the cities, but the public schools promulgated an essentially native version of American culture. From the outset, some newcomers reacted against schooling which barely recognized them, and sought alternative schools to legitimize and preserve their cultures. The corporate society required an academic meritocracy that selected students on the basis of ability and educated them accordingly. The great inequities in this selection system were a function of the students' presumed occupational destination and could not be squared with prevailing ideas of equality.

These conflicts still pervade the school system: schooling as work against education as play; cultural diversity against assimilation and non-recognition; academic merit against equality. These tensions are a product of the schools' adaptation to large-scale corporate capitalism, and cannot be understood apart from its evolution.[5]

From *Socialist Revolution* 2 (March/April 1972): 47–72. Reprinted by permission.

This essay is a revised version of a paper entitled "Education and the Industrial Order" presented to the meetings of the American Educational Research Association, 1970. Copyright 1970 by David K. Cohen and Marvin Lazerson.

THE INDUSTRIAL SYSTEM OF SCHOOLING

The leading idea of the corporate capitalist system of schooling was that education was an economic activity. Schooling was justified as a way to expand wealth by improving production. Skill and behavior training were stressed; students were selected for occupation strata based on ability, and matched to occupations through counseling and training. *Education was fashioned into an increasingly refined training and selection mechanism for the labor force.* These ideas were reflected in the formulation of a Michigan educator in 1921:

We can picture the educational system as having a very important function as a selecting agency, a means of selecting the men of best intelligence from the deficient and mediocre. All are poured into the system at the bottom; the incapable are soon rejected or drop out after repeating various grades and pass into the ranks of unskilled labor. . . . The more intelligent who are to be clerical workers pass into the high school; the most intelligent enter the universities, whence they are selected for the professions.[6]

Such ideas had important implications for the conception and organization of schooling. If schools were the primary occupational training and selection mechanism, then the criteria of merit within schools had to conform to the criteria of ranking in the occupational structure. *The schools' effectiveness then could be judged by how well success in school predicted success at work.* The criteria for these predictions were work behavior and academic ability.

From the late nineteenth century onward, educators' concern with student behavior was justified in terms of training for work. In 1909 the Boston School Committee described the program of instruction in an elementary school given over to "prevocational" classes—a school for children expected to become factory workers:

Everything must conform as closely as possible to actual industrial work in real life. The product must be not only useful, but must be needed, and must be put to actual use. It must be something which may be produced in quantities. The method must be practical, and both product and method must be subjected to the same commercial tests, as far as possible, as apply to actual industry.[7]

Typically, school officials stressed that classroom activities should inculcate the values thought to make good industrial workers—respect for authority, discipline, order, cleanliness and punctuality—and the schools developed elaborate schemes for grading, reporting, and rewarding student behavior. "One great benefit of going to school, especially of attending regularly for eight or ten months each year for nine years or more," argued A. E. Winship, editor of the *Journal of Education* in 1900, "is that it establishes a habit of regularity and persistency in effort." "Indeed," Winship claimed, "the boy who leaves school and goes to work does not necessarily learn to work steadily, but often quite the reverse."[8] Going to school was better preparation for becoming a good worker than work itself!

If schooling was conceived as a preparation for work, it was only natural to organize it on the model of the factory. School superintendents saw themselves as plant managers, and proposed to treat education as a production process in which children were the raw materials.[9] It was equally natural to evaluate schooling in terms of economic productivity. If education was work then its success or failure could be measured by income returns to schooling. This tendency to use market criteria in evaluating education flowered around the turn of the century: between 1880 and 1910 scores of studies of income returns to education appeared.[10] Superintendents, plant managers, and teachers' associations published reports that sought to show that the more education students received, the greater their later earnings would be. This was reflected in the schools' internal evaluation systems, as grades and school retention were justified as strategies for raising later earnings.

The ability criterion was no less important. The notion that adult success depended on school achievement came to have the status of religious dogma. As Ellwood Cubberley revealed in 1909, this idea is closely linked to the view that as the level of technology in production rises, workers require more education:

Along with these changes there has come not only a tremendous increase in the quantity of our knowledge, but also a demand for a large increase in the amount of knowledge necessary to enable one to meet the changed conditions of modern life. The kind of knowledge needed, too, has fundamentally changed. The ability to read and write and cipher no longer distinguishes the educated from the uneducated man. A man must have better, broader, and a different kind of knowledge than did his parents if he is to succeed under modern conditions.[11]

The idea that knowledge is power dates back to the scientific revolution, but here Cubberley was articulating a new version. It was not simply that knowledge was power, but that technological training was the key to personal success.

These ideas were powerfully reinforced by the results of early testing research. The U.S. Army World War I tests, for example, showed a clear correlation between measured intelligence and occupational attainment.[12] This was generally presumed to prove that the occupational structure was meritocratic, allocating people to occupations on the basis of innate intelligence. Early test results also showed that people who completed more years of school had higher IQs—from which it was inferred that "on the average, the stage in the school system attained by the average individual corresponds roughly with his capacity ... the amount of education is pretty closely related to the degree of natural intel-

ligence."[13] These results gave an enormous boost to the notion that students who ranked high in school would later have high-ranking jobs. If people were poor, these tests seemed to prove that it was because they were stupid. It occurred to few (least of all the pioneers in testing) that people might test "stupid" because they were poor—that the tests might be biased to favor certain classes and social strata.

Whatever the merit of these inferences, they did provide a powerful thrust for educational testing. If smarter people got better jobs, then it was essential to make the ability criterion in IQ and achievement tests operational. Armed with such instruments, educators could separate students on the basis of a projection to adult status and thus tailor educational offerings to occupational expectations. The tests quickly came to be seen as the surest way to classify students and to organize schools for their work in occupational pre-selection. Cubberley maintained in his introduction to Lewis Terman's *The Measurement of Intelligence* that "the educational significance of the results to be obtained from careful measurements of intelligence of children can hardly be over-estimated. Questions relating to the choice of studies, vocational guidance, schoolroom procedures, the grading of pupils, [and] promotional schemes ... all alike acquire new meaning and significance when viewed in the light of the measurement of intelligence."[14]

Educational testing grew rapidly during the two decades after World War I. Between 1921 and 1936 more than five thousand articles on testing appeared in print; a 1939 list of mental tests reported 4,279, and six printed pages of bibliographies on testing.[15] By then almost every major school system had a full program of achievement and IQ testing and a research bureau to administer the tests and interpret the results. A new sub-profession, educational psychology, had been established, complete with separate graduate training programs, distinct departments with education schools, different degrees, and professional journals. School psychology had become a quasi-independent career line within the schools, integrated into the administrative structure from local schools to the central research bureaus. Of one hundred fifty large cities surveyed in connection with a White House Conference on vocational education, called by President Hoover in 1932, three-quarters were using intelligence tests to classify and assign their students for instruction.[16]

Occupationally diversified curriculum was the corollary of testing. Curricular differentiation began before the testing movement, but testing provided a powerful reinforcement and rationale for it. The increasing differentiation of work in an urban corporate economy, the demand of business and industrial leaders for appropriately trained and disciplined workers—and at the same time the desire to protect educational standards for non-working-class children—gave rise to diverse curricula before the theory of meritocracy was developed. Under the pressure of these forces the older curriculum had begun to give way at the turn of the century—years before the testing movement emerged—and was being replaced by a multiplicity of course offerings geared to the major strata of job categories. The National Education Association's 1910 *Report of the Committee on the Place of Industries in Public Education* summarized the rationale for educational differentiation:

1. Industry, as a controlling factor in social progress, has for education a fundamental and permanent significance.
2. Educational standards, applicable in an age of handicraft, presumably need radical change in the present day of complex and highly specialized industrial development.
3. The social aims of education and the psychological needs of childhood alike require that industrial (manual-constructive) activities form an important part of school occupations. . . .

4. The differences among children as to aptitudes, interests, economic resources, and prospective careers furnish the basis for a rational as opposed to a merely formal distinction between elementary, secondary, and higher education.[17]

The last point is important, for the inventory of differences among children clearly reveals the class character of educational differentiation. Working-class children should not only get a different sort of schooling, but also should get less. Industrial elementary schools, prevocational programs, and junior high schools all were offered as ways of assuring that working-class children would stay in school and receive appropriate training.[18] At the same time, Cleveland's school superintendent, for example, argued that working-class children would neither continue their education beyond the compulsory minimum, nor learn very much if they did stay. He proposed that their schooling be limited to the elementary years, with a curriculum that imparted basic literacy, good behavior, and rudimentary vocational skills.[19]

Later, as the high schools became less and less the preserves of children from advantaged families, curricular differentiation was necessary to maintain differences in educational opportunity within the same period of schooling. Differentiation centered more and more on curricular differences within secondary schools. At the turn of the century special business and commercial courses already had been established in the high schools; by the second decade many cities had created vocational, business, and academic curricula. The school board president in the Lynds' *Middletown* summarized the change succinctly, in the mid-1920s: "For a long time all boys were trained to be President. Then for a while we trained them all to be professional men. Now we are training boys to get jobs."[20]

The differentiation of educational offerings ran across the grain of established ideas about equality in education. As in so many things, Cubberley characterized the situation bluntly in 1909:

Our city schools will soon be forced to give up the exceedingly democratic idea that all are equal, and our society devoid of classes . . . and to begin a specialization of educational effort along many lines in an attempt to adapt the school to the needs of these many classes. . . . Industrial and vocational training is especially significant of the changing conception of the school and the classes in society which the school is in the future expected to serve.[21]

Some educators insisted that differentiation implied no change in the reigning ideas of equal opportunity, but a greater number tried to reconcile differentiation and its implications for equality. The NEA juxtaposed "equality of opportunity as an abstraction" to the idea that education should be based on "the reality of opportunity as measured by varying needs, tastes, and abilities."[22] Although such formulations were offered to support differentiation of educational offerings along class lines, this was rarely seen as inconsistent with the idea that "education should give to all an equal chance to attain any distinction in life."[23] The reconciliation lay in the ready identification of ability with inherited social and economic status, an idea which the early testing movement reinforced. In theory, at least, there was no tension between the differentiation of school offerings and the academic meritocracy.

The appeal of the meritocratic idea extended far beyond a rationale for curricular differentiation. Educators and social reformers at the turn of the century were disturbed by the accumulation of a large, heavily immigrant industrial proletariat in the cities; they feared the prospect of class warfare, and found in educational opportunity a ready formula for remedy. Schools would provide a mechanism whereby those who were qualified could rise on the basis of ability. Even the greatest skeptics about the influence of environment on ability—E. L.

Thorndike, for example—agreed that the schools should provide avenues for mobility based on selection of talent.[24] And liberals maintained that schools ought to remedy deficiencies that the environment inflicted upon children. Frank Carleton, for example, wrote in 1907 that the schools should reduce crime and dependency by providing special education for disadvantaged children. If schools compensated for environmental deficiencies, they would improve children's chances for success in later life.[25]

This faith in the transforming power of education has been the basis for compensatory education and social welfare programs since the late nineteenth century. Schooling was conceived as an engine of social reform, a mechanism whereby injustice could be remedied by distributing rewards on the basis of talent rather than inheritance. It was an idea peculiarly suited to corporate liberalism. The redistribution of social and economic status promised through schooling was neither an attack on property nor an effort to weaken the class structure. Rather than eliminating inequalities in social status or wealth, schooling would insure that these were consistent with qualification instead of birth. *The great appeal of social reform through education was that all issues of distributive social justice were translated into matters of individual ability and effort in school and marketplace.*

These developments did not occur all at once, nor was the new system of schooling monolithic. As Michael Katz has pointed out, many educators who sought to model their schools on industrial lines seemed to have little idea of how industrial corporations worked.[26] And efforts to make the curriculum correspond to the occupational structure did not mean that educators knew, or tried to find out, what labor skills were actually needed. As production utilized increasingly advanced technology, the schools slowly followed suit—just as now the old model of the schools as factories is beginning to change, as manpower needs change. But the commitment to the ability criterion, testing, guidance, and differentiated schooling has only been accentuated. While the character of work is changing, the schools' role as the primary labor training and selection mechanism continues.

TENSIONS IN THE NEW ORDER

In the course of the schools' adaptation to large-scale corporate capitalism, conflicts emerged in three areas. One centered on the system's essential educational values—extrinsically rewarded work—and the school culture this encouraged. Although the ethos of work has been dominant, the notion that education should involve play and intrinsic rewards has become increasingly prominent. A second involved the schools' role in political and cultural socialization, and the conflicts this provoked between successive groups of urban immigrants and the schools. These have been manifest in struggles over school governance and curriculum, and in the rejection of public education in favor of alternative educational institutions. Finally, tension occurred between the ideology of class structure—academic meritocracy—and the ideas of equality presumed to govern public education.

Work and Play. The tension between these two conceptions of social activity increasingly permeates advanced industrial societies; it extends from the character of productive activity to the quality of pedagogy. In education, the notion of play contains several elements. It suggests a learning environment and process that in its pure form stresses self-expression, independence, and spontaneity. Several ideas underlie this. One is the view that learning is best if it is not compelled, but occurs freely through "natural" interactions—in games, in social intercourse among children and adults, and in the reach of intermittent curiosity. Another is the assumption that the ethos of education should be arranged so as to protect children from the rigors of work—

instead of instilling the disciplines of the workplace, schools should avoid routine, compelled, and occupationally oriented learning. The advocates of play in education have reflected diverse political and pedagogical viewpoints, sometimes stressing academic learning and in other cases emphasizing affective education or socialization. Some have justified play as an initial and more efficient method for producing good workers, but usually there has been hostility to extrinsic, market-oriented criteria of educational merit. Typically, the advocates of play in schooling are found in the "child-centered" wing of American education.[27]

The idea of education as play received its first major institutional expression in the kindergarten movement at the turn of the century, and later in the nursery school movement. Upper-middle- and upper-class advocates of early childhood education opposed their notion of school as play to the more disciplined forms of schooling then current. Their young charges were to learn through games, songs, stories, and other forms of casual interaction; direct compulsion and outright discipline were to be avoided. Although they sought to harmonize this with the work ethic by claiming that play was a better preparation for work than rigid discipline and by asserting that play was the child's natural work, the advocates of kindergarten education were unable to avoid conflict with the established public schools. The kindergartens were often considered undisciplined: some educators argued that kindergarten children came to school poorly prepared, either to learn or to behave properly. While the notion that preschool education should be playful gradually became accepted by early childhood educators, it continued to find itself in conflict with public school personnel.[28]

With the Progressive movement in education the idea of schooling as play was more widely diffused, and attempts were made to bridge the work-play conflict. Rejecting dualism in any form, John Dewey believed that work and play were part of a continuum, differing only in terms of "time-span" and the rigor of commitment to a specified goal. "In play," he argued, the "activity is its own end, instead of having an ulterior result." Play was "free, plastic," it meant keeping "alive a creative and constructive attitude." Yet Dewey could harmonize work and play only by rejecting prevailing notions of work. He contended that work in an industrial society, "especially in cities," was "anti-educational," because it took its definition from the needs of the economy, rather than individual or social needs. To offset this, schools should function with an "absence of economic pressure," allowing students to build upon individual and social experience. In school, activities "are not carried on for pecuniary gain but for their own content. Freed from extraneous associations and the pressure of wage-earning, they supply modes of experience which are intrinsically valuable; they are truly liberalizing in quality." Though Dewey would oppose the child-centeredness of later play advocates, his call for a learning process which began with the experience of the learner gave an added emphasis to intrinsic learning.[29]

Other educational reformers also juxtaposed learning from experience to learning by rote or from books. They sought to infuse the curriculum and pedagogy with spontaneity and free expression. The extreme incarnation of playful education was the child-centered school. In these schools, two commentators on the child-centered movement wrote in 1928, children "dance . . . sing . . . play house and build villages; they keep store and take care of pets; they model in clay and sand; they draw and paint, read and write, make up stories and dramatize them." Education in the child-centered classroom was designed to produce "individuality through the integration of experience." The ideal was expressed by one five-year-old who said of her painting, "It looks the way you feel inside." To the traditional notions of order, regimentation, and vocationalism, the child-centered

school opposed spontaneity, freedom and self-expression.[30]

It would be wrong, however, to counterpose the movement to bring "warmth" and spontaneity into the classroom to the process of the schools' adaptation to corporate capitalism. The educational reformers often had little impact on public education. The best examples of reform were usually found in private schools for middle-class children. This more "natural" schooling process fits in nicely with the trend in middle-class child-rearing ideas, away from repression and externally imposed discipline, toward greater freedom, and happiness in learning seemed to be linked with higher levels of achievement.[31] It also fit in with the decline in the ethic of asceticism, the increase in leisure time that followed rising productivity in industry, and the promotion of a new ethic of consumption during the 1920s. Later, particularly in the period after World War II, with the growth of a large labor force engaged in social control and services, the playful style has begun to find its way into public education.

The urban school reform movement has increasingly gravitated in this direction, as Leicestershire styles of schooling emphasizing naturalness, freedom, and experiential learning, have grown in influence. Educational theoreticians have for the first time adopted a stance of conscious opposition to the notion of school as externally disciplined work. Holt, Denison, Leonard, Illich, and Friedenberg attack not only the discipline and work ethos of the public schools, but also the extrinsic rewards to which schooling is presumed to lead. They distinguish education from schooling, identifying education with freedom, natural authority, and learning-on-the-hoof; any discipline that does not arise immediately from the subject matter or the student-teacher relationship is rejected as illegitimate. They have called the entire authority structure of public education into question by rejecting the market values on which it rests. This is precisely the major change of the last decade: the polarity between work and play in education has become an overt issue of policy rather than a persistent conflict of pedagogical styles.

The source of the conflict between work and play lies in the changing character of productive activity. The increasingly technological nature of production has created a demand for a more highly trained and differentiated labor force, engaged not only in goods production, but also in the production of culture, socialization, and welfare. Among the new strata of workers, labor has become more technological, cerebral, and mobile, and has created more room for leisure. Not only must the training period of such a labor force be extended, but the kind of training must be changed. An emphasis on "creativity" replaces a pure emphasis on discipline. Play as an educational ideal becomes opposed to work, insofar as it encourages creativity.

Play is, then, closely linked to the changes in the character of urban middle- and upper-middle-income groups and the emergence of these new occupational strata as a cultural aristocracy. Schools organized to satisfy the educational values of these strata also have distinct "class" character: they often are exclusive, and more important, they represent an effort to escape or deny the ethos of the industrial system and its traditional asceticism. The free schools— like the styles of their pupils' parents— reflect not only differences in taste, but a freedom and a leisure that the distribution of wealth denies to the lower- and lower-middle-income groups.[32] Nonetheless, these new groups have become important agents of political and social change.

The development of corporate capitalism toward increasingly technological forms of production carries with it vast changes in the life styles and occupational needs of middle-income groups. If our analysis is correct, these developments carry with them values antithetical to earlier conceptions of education. The educational style of the urban upper-middle-income groups stands in increasing opposition to the central values of the established system of schooling. While the discipline of that system is still dominant, there have been enough changes to achieve an irretrievable legitimacy for play. The continued growth of the welfare-socialization-culture industries and the development of technological industrialism will only increase the pressure to treat schooling as a form of play and pleasure.

Cultural and Political Tensions. Cultural differences between urban immigrants and the schools were a second point of conflict. Industrialization attracted immigrants to the cities and held them there, producing a deluge of non-English-speaking families at the turn of the century, especially in the East. The response was twofold: efforts were made to use the schools as vehicles of intensive and rapid socialization—preparation for citizenship and work—and the movement to centralize urban school government was accelerated.

American educators had always assumed that the public school was essential to cultural unity, but at the turn of the century that idea received intensive application. Immigrants were inculcated with the values of the dominant culture through evening schools—often compulsory for the non-English-speaking—language instruction, civics, and American history, the celebration of patriotic holidays, and countless informal ways. ·Specially designed textbooks taught immigrants cleanliness, hard work, and how to apply for a job and naturalization papers, and informed them that rural, Protestant America epitomized the best in American life. Evening school teachers in Lawrence, Massachusetts, were told to convince the foreign-born of the efficacy of schooling: "Try to make them feel that they are coming to school not because they are obliged to, but because they wish to, because they know America means Opportunity ... and the Opportunity now knocks at their door. . . ."[33]

Americanization programs were also established outside the schools. In the International Harvester Company plants, immigrants learned English through such lessons as:

I hear the whistle. I must hurry.
I hear the five minute whistle.
It is time to go into the shop. . . .
I change my clothes and get ready to work. . . .
I work until the whistle blows to quit.
I leave my place nice and clean.[34]

Yet if a variety of institutions sought to integrate the newcomer, the public school was almost universally considered the primary agency of assimilation. "The American school," educators and public agreed, "is the salvation of the American republic."[35]

How immigrants responded to this Americanization process is unclear. Were language instruction and the curriculum's social content points of tension? Did immigrants go to evening schools? Did particular immigrant groups relate to the public schools in different ways? The evidence is mixed. Some historians and contemporary writers report great enthusiasm for public education as a vehicle of assimilation and social mobility. Mary Antin found her first day at school "the apex of my civic pride and contentment": "To most people their first day at school is a memorable occasion. In my case the importance of the day was a hundred times magnified, on account of the years I had waited, the road I had come, and the conscious ambitions I had entertained."[36] On the other hand, there was substantial conflict at both the state and municipal levels and between immigrant nationalities over foreign language teaching in the public schools.[37] Some immigrant groups established educational institutions of their own—among Catholics usually in the form of parochial schools,[38] and among Jews as part-time educational alternatives. In the larger cities there were numerous afternoon and weekend Jewish schools—many of them apparently in wretched condition—designed to transmit religious and cultural traditions.[39]

Another source of conflict seems to have been the public schools' staff, though evidence on this is hard to come by. Teachers in immigrant neighborhoods often were antagonistic to the newcomers, and there is some evidence of resistance to accepting teaching positions in immigrant neighborhoods. Michael Gold, in his autobiographical novel *Jews without Money*, records the hostility of his teacher in a Lower East Side elementary school, calling her a "Ku Kluxer before [her] time," a woman tortured by having to teach in a predominantly Jewish school.[40] And even those teachers not explicitly hostile to immigrants rejected their unfamiliar behavior and values. Rarely were pleas for pluralism in the schools heard from professional educators.[41]

These conflicts were partly resolved by the process of ethnic succession to bureaucratic power in city school systems. Although the process occurred at different times, even by 1909 it was fairly well advanced in some of the larger cities.[42] At least in the large eastern cities, the Jews and the Irish were solidly entrenched in the teaching force by the 1920s. In addition, conflict was muted by the second-generation immigrant identification with the dominant culture; as the children of immigrants entered urban school bureaucracies they may often have rejected demands for ethnic pluralism.

The political response to the immigrants involved changes in the organization and control of urban school systems. As the Europeans inundated the cities, local schools were removed from ward and neighborhood control, and given over into the hands of central boards controlled by the established city elites. This shift away from district control and ward-oriented politicians to centralized agencies was central to the Progressive movement in politics, and it drew heavily on the Progressive ideology of reform: efficiency, expertise, and nonpartisanship. But these ideas were also linked to bigotry and explicit class biases. School centralization in the interests of efficiency had the effect—and in at least some cases the intent—of removing power and influence over schooling from the hands of the poor and the culturally different.[43]

Cubberley made this explicit, in his rationale for replacing the ward system of school government with centralized school committees:

The tendency of people of the same class or degree of success to settle in the same part of the city is a matter of common knowledge. . . .

One of the important results of the change from ward representation to election from the city at large, in any city of average decency and intelligence, is that the inevitable representation from these "poor wards" is eliminated, and the board comes to partake of the best characteristics of the city as a whole.[44]

Cubberley gave the example of a city in which the board was divided between working-class and professional members, and argued that this pointed up the "constant danger" in the ward system: "The less intelligent and progressive element would wear out the better elements and come to rule the board."[45] When he came to suggesting the sort of people who might best serve on the new citywide boards, Cubberley was no less forthright:

To render such intelligent service to the school system of a city as has been indicated requires the selection of a peculiar type of citizen for school board member. . . . Men who are successful in the handling of large business undertakings—manufacturers, merchants, bankers, contractors, and professional men of large practice—would perhaps come first. . . . College graduates who are successful in their business or professional affairs, whatever may be their profession or occupation, also usually make good board members. . . .[46]

Opportunities for schooling were extended to immigrant children partly to transform them into a stable, quiescent labor force. The school demanded cultural homogeneity and extolled the virtues of work; work was viewed not as a way of staying alive, but as a pattern of behavior. *Placing people in an industrial complex and making them dependent upon it—economically and psychologically—forged a link between them and the system's prosperity.* It was toward this end that the cultural and political activities of public education worked.

The parallels to the recent black struggle for control of education are striking. In part the current conflict represents an effort to establish a legitimate black culture and control the instruments of its diffusion, but it is also an effort to reconstitute more particularism in school government. Although there are many important distinctions, because of the very different historical experiences of European immigrants and Negro Americans, the structural features of conflict in education are strikingly similar. The schools are still essentially WASP in their values—even with ethnic succession to teaching and administration—and they have conceded little to racial, national, or class cultures. *Cultural diversity is still a matter of basic struggle in education,* and groups seeking it have had to adopt alternatives outside the public system.

Merit and Equality. In theory, the schools' relation to the social structure has been egalitarian and reformist—to allocate status on the basis of achievement rather than inheritance, thereby providing a remedy for injustice. Historically, however, the extent to which the meritocracy actually worked, and the value of merit selection and its implications for equality, have been in dispute.

At the turn of the century, the issue centered on differentiating educational opportunities. Tension arose between the egalitarian principle that the state should treat all citizens equally, and the meritocratic notion that equality meant status allocated by achievement. The first implied exposure of all students to a common curriculum, while the second involved allocating educational resources based on expectations of students' adult status. The established egalitarian ideology of public schooling seemed to demand the inculcation of common values, absorption of a common heritage, and exposure to the same school experiences. The notion of schools as an industrial meritocracy implied diversification, discrimination, and hierarchy.[47] As the differentiation of school offerings spread, a new notion of equality emerged—equal school achievement for equal ability. Differentiation was justified as a way of organizing education to conform with social and economic realities, and this in turn was presented as a way of providing meaningful equality of educational opportunity. As the Boston school superintendent argued in 1908:

Until very recently [the schools] have offered equal opportunity for all to receive *one kind* of education, but what will make them democratic is to provide opportunity for all to receive such education as will fit them *equally well* for their particular life work.[48]

The idea was difficult to oppose, for the advocates of equality—the unified curriculum—were identified with tradition during a ferment of progressive reform. Their defense of common learning asserted the need for broad "mental training" at a time when influential psychologists like E. L. Thorndike were calling for training for specific ends. But most important, the traditionalists seemed hostile to the educational needs of working-class and immigrant children entering the schools in large numbers.[49] The diversifiers needed only to point to evidence of massive school retardation and dropouts to make their case; the choice was diversification and vocational orientation or continued inefficiency.[50] As long as the alternatives were so limited, it is hardly surprising that differentiated educational "equality" met with such rapid acceptance.

For those who accepted this notion of equality, the success of the new system was measured by the extent to which students were actually afforded education on the basis of the announced merit criteria. From the outset critics argued that the academic meritocracy involved considerable discrimination. George Counts, for example, argued in 1922 that the differentiation of secondary educational offerings selected students on the basis of race, nationality, and class.[51] His research showed that the inherited indicia of social status played an enormous role in determining entrance to secondary school, the likelihood of remaining in school, and the curricula pursued within schools. Counts concluded that:

. . . the inequalities among individuals and classes are still perpetuated to a considerable degree in the social inheritance. While the establishment of free public high schools marked an extraordinary educational advance, it did not by any means equalize educational opportunity. Education means leisure, and leisure is an expensive luxury. In most cases today this leisure must be guaranteed the individual by the family. Thus, secondary education remains largely a matter for family initiative and concern, and reflects the inequalities of family means and ambition.[52]

He maintained that public support for secondary education could not be justified as long as the selectivity was so badly biased by students' background. Either selection should be absolutely rigorous and objective, scientifically selecting an educated elite from all classes, or the same education should be made available to all without any selection. Counts maintained that the measurement technology was inadequate to support a really scientific system, although his opposition to selectivity was political, not technological. He favored the absolute universalization of secondary education.[53]

The problem was that while Counts got his wish—secondary education rapidly became virtually universal—this was accompanied by selectivity based on the measurement technology he regarded as inadequate.

Although an impressive literature grew up which raised questions about the class and ethnic bias of the tests,[54] their use to group and assign students increased. Although scores of studies of ability grouping failed to reveal any clear advantage for students in the practice, ability grouping became widespread.[55] Although—as Counts pointed out in 1922, and critics of vocational education have pointed out since—curricular differentiation really helped little in job training or placement, the spread of differentiation continued.[56] Since the 1920s evidence has accumulated that children of the poor and the working class, and those from immigrant groups, were disadvantaged by grouping, differentiation and intelligence testing. Whether educational progress was measured by curricular placement, school completion, or the tests themselves, those who were economically disadvantaged or culturally different usually came out at the bottom of the heap.[57]

The chief implication of all this was reasonably clear: the schools' methods for measuring merit—especially the tests—were seriously biased by inherited status and culture. Evenhandedness and the application of "objective measures" could not provide equal chances for school success among groups of children who arrived in school with differing class and cultural backgrounds. But educators, researchers, and reformers have generally taken different views.

Most reformers have accepted the principle of merit selection because they saw education as a vehicle for promoting social reform through individual mobility. The notion that education was a means for deferring direct (redistributive) social change by displacing it onto individual achievement has been a central element in modern American liberalism. It rests on a desire to promote social justice without attacking the distribution or ownership of property. The consequence for education has been curious—the more evidence has accumulated that school success depended upon inherited economic and social status, the more the liberal reformers insisted that the schools should compensate for environmental differences among children. Such efforts have been tried increasingly over the past four or five decades, but there is scant evidence that they work any particular advantage for the children concerned. Nonetheless, every evidence of failure seems only to reinforce the idea that more compensation is required. Because of the liberal commitment to social reform through individual achievement, the development of school reform has been perversely related to the evidence: *the more it shows that school performance is profoundly conditioned by inherited status, the more insistent the demands for compensatory schooling have grown; there never has been much mention of directly reducing the underlying status inequalities.* It is testimony to the power of liberal ideology—and the class character of school reform efforts—that evidence on the educational consequences of inequality produces efforts to improve the meritocracy, rather than efforts to reduce the inequality.

The reason for this is apparent: since the underlying function of the school system is not challenged by the educational reformers, the only thing that can be done to make it more democratic is to eliminate the barriers facing the "brighter," or more ambitious, children of minority or low-income parents. The attempt has been made over the last several decades, and especially in the 1960s, to apply the principle of merit as fairly as possible (given the class purpose of public education) so that an occupational elite can be chosen from all groups in American society while class and social stratification remains intact. Equality in education will require the elimination of the meritocratic structure, but that reform cannot take place in an educational system whose purpose is to socialize children into a stratified class society.

NOTES

1. Angelo Patri, *The Problems of Childhood* (New York, 1927), p. 10.

2. Among the recent studies are Michael Katz, *The Irony of Early School Reform: Educational Innovation in Mid-Nineteenth Century Massachusetts* (Cambridge, 1968); Marvin Lazerson, *Origins of the Urban School: Public Education in Massachusetts, 1870–1915* (Cambridge, 1971); Katz, "The Emergence of Bureaucracy in Urban Education: The Boston Case, 1850–1884," *History of Education Quarterly* 8: Summer-Fall 1968, pp. 155–88, 319–57; David Tyack, "Bureaucracy and the Common School: The Example of Portland, Oregon, 1851–1913," *American Quarterly* 19: Fall 1967, pp. 475–98; Tyack, "City Schools at the Turn of the Century: Centralization and Social Control," unpublished ms. in authors' possession; Berenice Fisher, *Industrial Education: American Ideals and Institutions* (Madison, 1967); Sol Cohen, "The Industrial Education Movement, 1906–17," *American Quarterly* 20: Spring 1968, pp. 95–110; Tyack, "Onward Christian Soldiers: Religion in the American Common School," in Paul Nash, ed., *History and Education* (New York, 1970); Timothy Smith, "Immigrant Social Aspirations and American Education, 1880–1930," *American Quarterly* 21: Fall 1969, pp. 523–43; Colin Greer, "Immigrants, Negroes, and the Public Schools," *Urban Review*, January 1969, pp. 9–12; Greer, "Public Schools: Myth of the Melting-Pot," *Saturday Review*, 15 November 1961; and the articles by David K. Cohen, Tyack, S. Cohen, Neil Sutherland, Daniel Calhoun, and Katz in *History of Education Quarterly* 9: Fall 1969.
3. For other attempts at such a framework, see Lawrence Cremin, *The Genius of American Education* (New York, 1965); Henry Perkinson, *The Imperfect Panacea* (New York, 1968); and Robert Wiebe, "The Social Functions of Public Education," *American Quarterly* 21: Summer 1969, pp. 147–64. For attempts to explain the more general revolution in organizational values in which the transformation of the schools occurred see Robert Wiebe, *The Search for Order, 1877–1920* (New York, 1967); and James Weinstein, *The Corporate Ideal in the Liberal State, 1900–1918* (Boston, 1968).
4. Raymond Callahan, *Education and the Cult of Efficiency* (Chicago, 1962).
5. Various aspects of the industrial system of schooling are discussed in Callahan, S. Cohen, and Fisher. See also Edward A. Krug, *The Shaping of the American High School* (New York, 1964), chs. 8–11; Marvin Lazerson, *Origins of the Urban School*, chs. 5–7; and Thomas Green, *Work, Leisure, and the American Schools* (New York, 1968).
6. W. B. Pillsbury, "Selection—An Unnoticed Function of Education," *Scientific Monthly* 12: January 1921, p. 71.
7. Boston, *Documents of the School Committee*, 1908, no. 7, pp. 48–53.
8. A. E. Winship, *Jukes-Edwards* (Harrisburg, Pennsylvania, 1900), p. 13.
9. Callahan, *Cult of Efficiency*.
10. A. C. Ellis, *The Money Value of Education*, Bulletin no. 22, U.S. Bureau of Education (Washington, 1917).
11. Ellwood Cubberley, *Changing Conceptions of Education* (Cambridge, 1909), pp. 18–19.

12. Robert Yerkes and C. S. Yoakum, *Army Mental Tests* (1920).
13. Pillsbury, "Selection," p. 64.
14. Cubberley in Lewis Terman, *The Measurement of Intelligence* (Boston, 1916), pp. vii–viii.
15. Florence Goodenough, *Mental Testing* (New York, 1949), pp. 89–90.
16. White House Conference on Child Health and Protection, *Vocational Guidance* (New York, 1932), pp. 25–27.
17. National Education Association, *Report of the Committee on the Place of Industries in Public Education*, 1910, pp. 6–7.
18. Frank M. Leavitt and Edith Brown, *Prevocational Education in the Public Schools* (Boston, 1915).
19. S. Cohen, "Industrial Education," pp. 105–6.
20. Robert and Helen Lynd, *Middletown* (New York, 1956 ed.), p. 194.
21. Cubberley, *Changing Conceptions*, pp. 53–57.
22. Ibid., pp. 21–22.
23. National Education Association, *Place of Industries*, p. 7.
24. E. L. Thorndike, *Educational Psychology* (New York, 1903), pp. 44–46.
25. Frank Carleton, "The School as a Factor in Industrial and Social Problems," *Education* 28: October 1907, pp. 77–79.
26. Katz, "Bureaucracy," pp. 167–68.
27. Various aspects of education as play are discussed in Cremin, *The Transformation of the School* (New York, 1961), pp. 201–24, 276–91, 309–13. On playfulness as an intellectual attribute, see Richard Hofstadter, *Anti-Intellectualism in America* (New York, 1962), pp. 29–33. The conflict between work and play is also discussed in Green, *Work, Leisure, and the American Schools*.
28. Lazerson, *Origins of the Urban School*, ch. 2; and Lazerson, "Social Reform and Early Childhood Education: Some Historical Perspectives," *Urban Education* 5: April 1970.
29. John Dewey, *Democracy and Education* (New York, 1966 edition), ch. 15. John and Evelyn Dewey, *Schools of Tomorrow* (New York, 1962 edition), details Dewey's attempt to harmonize the work–play tension.
30. Harold Rugg and Ann Shumaker, *The Child-Centered School* (Yonkers-on-the-Hudson, 1928), pp. 3, 5–6, and passim; Agnes DeLima, *Our Enemy the Child* (New York, 1926). Contrast the classrooms in Rugg and Shumaker and DeLima with Lynd, *Middletown*, pp. 188–205.
31. Bernard Wishy, *The Child and the Republic* (Philadelphia, 1968), is suggestive on nineteenth-century changes in child-rearing.
32. Education-as-play is not simply an American phenomenon. The playful style gained popular currency among the bourgeoisie in eighteenth-century Europe, and in many respects is simply the natural consequence of the emphasis on individuality and liberation common to the Enlightenment and the Romantic movement. But the idea that play is a legitimate form of activity and a suitable medium for cultural expression has its roots in the society and chivalric culture of the high Middle Ages, and in the Renaissance cult of individuality. Historically, at least, the cultivation of play is profoundly aristocratic. And in fact, striving for

aristocratic culture and values always has been an important activity in the upper middle class, no less in America than in Europe.

33. Lawrence, Massachusetts, *A Syllabus for the Instruction of Non-English-Speaking Pupils in the Evening Schools* (Lawrence, 1908); Sara O'Brien, *English for Foreigners* (Boston, 1909).

34. Quoted in Gerd Korman, *Industrialization, Immigrants, and Americanizers* (Madison, 1967), pp. 144–45.

35. E. O. Vaile, "Teaching Current Events in School," National Education Association, *Proceedings and Addresses*, 1892, p. 142. See also Oscar Handlin, *John Dewey's Challenge to Education* (New York, 1959); Edward Hartmann, *The Movement to Americanize the Immigrant* (New York, 1948); Lazerson, *Origins of the Urban School*, ch. 8.

36. Mary Antin, *The Promised Land* (Boston, 1912), p. 198; Smith, "Immigrant Social Aspirations."

37. J. Fishman, *Language Loyalty in the United States* (New York, 1966), pp. 206–52; Leonard Covello, *The Heart Is the Teacher* (New York, 1958); Rudolph Vecoli, "Prelates and Peasants," *Journal of Social History*, Spring 1969, pp. 217–68.

38. Robert Cross, "Origins of Catholic Parochial Schools in America," *American Benedictine Review* 16, June 1965, pp. 194–209; Alice Masaryk, "The Bohemians in Chicago," *Charities* 13:3 December 1904.

39. Leo Honor, "Jewish Elementary Education in the United States, 1901–1950," American Jewish Historical Society, *Publications* 42: September 1952, pp. 1–42; Leibush Lehrer, "The Jewish Secular School," *Jewish Education* 7, January-March 1935, pp. 33–43; Lloyd Gartner, *Jewish Education in the United States* (New York, 1969). There are a number of autobiographical and fictional accounts of part-time Jewish schools; see, e.g., Henry Roth, *Call It Sleep* (New York, 1962 edition), pp. 211–25.

40. Michael Gold, *Jews without Money* (New York, 1965 edition), p. 22.

41. Tyack, "Onward Christian Soldiers"; and Tyack, "The Perils of Pluralism: Oregon's Compulsory Public School Bill of 1922," unpublished ms. in authors' possession.

42. U.S. Immigration Commission, "The Children of Immigrants in the Schools," *Reports* (Washington, 1911), vols. 29–35.

43. Tyack, "City Schools at the Turn of the Century."

44. Cubberley, *Public School Administration* (Cambridge, 1916), p. 93.

45. Ibid., p. 93.

46. Ibid., pp. 124–25.

47. Lazerson, *Origins of the Urban School*, ch. 7.

48. Boston, *Documents of the School Committee*, 1908, no. 7, p. 53.

49. Krug, *Shaping of the American High School*, chs. 8–9.

50. Leonard Ayres, *Laggards in Our Schools* (New York, 1909); D. Cohen, "Immigrants and the Schools," *Review of Educational Research* 40: February 1970, pp. 13–27.

51. George Counts, *The Selective Character of American Education* (Chicago, 1922).

52. Ibid., p. 148.

53. Ibid., pp. 149–56.

54. C. Brigham, "Intelligence Tests of Immigrant Groups," *Psychological Review* 37 (1930), pp. 158–65; National Society for the Study of Education, *Twenty-Seventh Yearbook* (Bloomington, Indiana, 1928).

55. U.S. Office of Education, *Cities Reporting the Use of Homogeneous Grouping and of the Winnetka Technique and the Dalton Plan*, city school leaflet 22, December 1926; see the discussion of ability grouping in National Society for the Study of Education, *Thirty-Fifth Yearbook* (Bloomington, Indiana, 1936), part 2.

56. Counts, *Selective Character*.

57. D. Cohen, "Immigrants and the Schools."

22. From Voluntarism to Bureaucracy in American Education

MICHAEL B. KATZ

The creation of institutions preoccupied early-nineteenth-century Americans. Whether they were building banks or railroads, political parties or factories, hospitals or schools, Americans confronted the inappropriateness of traditional organizational arrangements, and their attempts to find a suitable fit between the form and context of social life stimulated a prolonged national debate. For the most part, the public record of the controversy rests in massively tedious proposals for the introduction or alteration of particular organizational details; it appears to be the prosaic and even trivial

From *Education in American History*, edited by Michael B. Katz (New York: Praeger, 1973), pp. 38–50. Copyright © 1973 by Praeger Publishers, Inc. Reprinted by permission. An elaborated and more fully documented version may be found in *Sociology of Education* 44 (Summer 1971): 297–332.

record of practical men solving everyday problems. Yet, the arguments of these practical men over the external features of institutions frequently represented a fundamental clash of social values. For the task of appropriately arranging public activities formed an intimate part of the problem of building a nation, and alternative proposals embodied different priorities and dissimilar aspirations for the shape of American society.

It is my hypothesis that four major models of organization conflicted in the first half of the nineteenth century. The four models I shall term paternalistic voluntarism, corporate voluntarism, democratic localism, and incipient bureaucracy.

For the most part, the debate centered on objective questions—that is, definite structural characteristics on which organizations may be said to differ. The primary dimensions in the controversy were: scale (or size), control, professionalism, and finance. Each proposal concerning one of these organizational characteristics rested on social values, which, though often remaining implicit, had enormous emotional significance. (We have only to recall the decentralization controversy in New York City today to realize the emotion-laden value content of issues of control and professionalism in education.) At the same time, issues of value often explicitly enveloped the debate, especially when proponents raised questions of organizational purpose. And here the issue most frequently at odds became the degree of standardization desirable in American institutional forms, behavior, and cultural values.

I

The New York Public School Society, established as the New York Free School Society in 1805, represents the paradigm case of paternalistic voluntarism in educational organization. Its purpose was to provide rudimentary training in literacy and morals for lower-class children not catered to by existing denominational schools. However, the Society expanded its scope and ambition until, in the early 1820's, it became the agency that dispersed virtually the entire public grant for elementary education in the city of New York. By its use of the term "free school," it should be noted, the Society did not advocate free, tax-supported education in our contemporary sense. Rather, it promoted free schooling only for the very poor. In fact, voluntarism underlay the organization of the Society, which was administered by an unpaid, self-perpetuating board of first citizens. It was precisely this fact—the unrewarded and disinterested dedication of able men, the enlistment of the energy of that class of distinguished citizens who would not stoop to practice democratic politics—that gave this form of organization its distinctive virtues in the view of its champions. In this conception, voluntarism was a variety of *noblesse oblige;* it rested on faith in the individual talented amateur and, at an over-all administrative level, scorned the need for elaborate organization, state control, or professional staff. From one perspective, paternalistic voluntarism worked extremely well. With a minimum of administrative expense and scrupulous financial integrity, with commendable efficiency and unpaid administrators, the Society maintained an extensive network of schools that for decades taught thousands of children annually.

But have no doubt about it: This was a class system of education. It provided a vehicle for the efforts of one class to civilize another and thereby ensure that society would remain tolerable, orderly, and safe. The Society offered mass education on the cheapest possible plan—the monitorial, or Lancasterian, system, which counterbalanced the lack of central organization with rigid internal arrangements for each school. Aside from its minuscule per pupil cost, this mechanistic form of pedagogy, which reduced education to drill, seemed appropriate because the schools served lower-class children who were likened to unfinished products needing efficient inculcation with norms of docility, cleanliness, sobriety, and obedience. The zealous amateurs of the New York Public School Society did not design their system for their own children or for the children of their friends. Rather, they attempted to ensure social order through the socialization of the poor in cheap, mass schooling factories.

Critics of paternalistic voluntarism stressed three defects. First, it was undemocratic. Under this system, education remained a monopoly of self-perpetuating trustees unresponsive and unaccountable to the public. As such, it violated the basis of the democratic theory of public organizations and perverted the notion of voluntarism, which had shifted its meaning and by then, in the American context, found expression most favorably through willingly offered participation in the conduct of institutions owned and managed by elected public representatives. In one sense, the repudiation of paternalistic voluntarism participated in the general attack on monopolies that characterized public discourse in Jacksonian America.

To its critics, paternalistic voluntarism ignored the variety of American life and reflected an unacceptable cultural bias by imposing uniform services upon a diverse clientele. Though often couched in religious terms, this criticism revealed a perception of important cultural differences, of which religious doctrines served as symptoms. An educational system that ignored, or tried to stamp out, these variations clearly appeared to violate the criteria for free and democratic institutions.

Animosity to upper-class benevolence underscored both religious and political denunciations of paternalistic voluntarism. A Catholic spokesman, Bishop Hughes, argued that the class bias inherent in the schools of the New York Public School Society alienated poor Catholic children and their parents. In this view, irregular attendance—a problem of which the society complained—reflected the insensitivity of the schools to working-class children, not an ignorant lower-class rejection of education as the Society's sponsors maintained. Bourgeois hostility to paternalistic voluntarism forms a related theme. Through the existence of organizations like the Public School Society, free education, public education, and the monitorial system had all become identified with lower-class education. Only a radical reorganization, a rejection of paternalistic voluntarism, could divorce the concepts of public and pauper and thereby provide institutions acceptable to proud and enterprising parents of limited means.

The first alternative proposed was democratic localism. Its sponsors sought to adapt to the city an organizational form current in rural areas, the district or community school. They asked for an absolute minimum of state or city supervision and the conduct of schools through elected neighborhood boards, which would permit local variation. They assumed that emulation between schools and local pride would promote educational progress more effectively than any central body. Democratic localism subordinated considerations of efficiency and organizational rationality to an emphasis on responsiveness, close public control, and local involvement.

Democratic localists fought, actually, on two fronts, against paternalistic voluntarism and against bureaucracy or centralization as well. Their stress on variety, local adaptability, and the symbiotic relation of school and community permeated both conflicts. In the latter, however, the resistance to bureaucracy, two other aspects of their attitude emerged most strongly. One was antiprofessionalism. They were not, as had been the sponsors of the New York Public Society, vaguely indifferent to the concept of the professional educator; they were, instead, hostile and suspicious. They saw little reason why school teaching should become a career or profession, or why, even more, it required special training centers or, above all, a special administrative class and state apparatus. The state apparatus, represented to the democrats the essence of the centralizing viewpoint: the imposition of social change and the attempt to force attitudes on the people. Neither of these, argued the democratic localists, would work; changes in society, in habits, and in attitudes came only from within a people themselves as they slowly, haltingly, but surely exercised their innate common sense and intelligence. By leaving them to their own devices, by perhaps encouraging, cajoling, and softly educating, but not by forcing, one would rouse the people to the importance of universal education and of the regular school attendance of their children.

As a proposal for the organization of urban education (for instance, the scheme put forward by the New York Secretary of State to replace the Public School Society), democratic localism flourished for only a short time. Its failure was predictable from the start, for it rested on a distinctively rural point of view. The propounders of democratic localism did not adapt their viewpoint to the city, and hence ignored critical differences between rural and urban contexts and the particular problems that the latter posed for the conduct of education. Nor did its sponsors—for instance, Berkshire Congregationalists in Massachusetts—see the ironically undemocratic possibilities inherent in giving free rein to local majorities.

Indeed, at its worst, democratic localism was the expression of tyrannical local majorities whose ambition was control and the dominance of their own narrow sectarianism or political bias in the schoolroom. But, at its best, democratic localism embraced a broad and humanistic conception of education as uncharacteristic of nineteenth- as of twentieth-century schools and schoolmen. Consider, for example, the exhortation of one democratic localist (probably Orestes Brownson) who eschewed the specially utilitarian in education in terms of a distinctively American social structure:

Here professions and pursuits are merely the accidents of individual life. Behind them we recognize Humanity, as paramount to them all. Here man, in theory at least, is professor. Professions and pursuits may be changed according to judgment, will, or caprice, as circumstances permit, or render necessary or advisable. Consequently, here we want an education for that which is permanent in man, which contemplates him as back of all the accidents of life, and which shall be equally valuable to him whatever be the mutations which go on around him, the means he may choose or be compelled to adopt to obtain a livelihood.

The education of importance thus was "general education," or the "education of Humanity," the education that "fits us for our destiny, to attain our end as simple human beings."

A third model coexisted with paternalistic voluntarism and democratic localism. This was corporate voluntarism, the conduct of *single* institutions as individual corporations operated by self-perpetuating boards of trustees and financed through endowment and tuition. Corporate voluntarism characterized primarily secondary and higher education, academies and colleges. Because it would place each institution under a different administrative authority, corporate voluntarism seemed to combine the virtues of the other two models: Without the stigma of lower-class affiliation, it offered disinterested, enlightened, and continuous management that kept the operation of education out of the rough and unpredictable field of politics. At the same time, it retained the limited scope essential to institutional variety, flexibility, and adaptation to local circumstances. Moreover, this corporate mode of control was congruent with contemporary arrangements for managing other forms of public business. As states turned from mercantilist regulation of the economy, they adopted a liberal stance that identified public interest with unrestricted privileges of incorporation and the removal of regulations governing economic activity. The argument that autonomous, competing corporations, aided but not controlled by the state, best served the public interest extended easily from finance, transportation, and manufacturing to education. Academies, for instance, were educational corporations.

In the late eighteenth and early nineteenth centuries, states promoted corporate voluntarism as public policy by giving legislative and financial assistance to academies, which were supposed to fulfill an evident need for institutions of secondary education. Academies represented the quintessence of voluntarism as *noblesse oblige* because they rapidly diffused throughout the country a combination of public goals and private control wrapped in the mantle of disinterested service. Academies shared a fate similar to that of the New York Public School Society when popular attitudes began to exclude from the public domain institutions managed and owned by self-perpetuating boards of trustees. As it became apparent that only institutions financed by the community or state and directly controlled by its officers merited definition as public, both paternalistic and corporate voluntarism were doomed.

Among the competing organizational models, incipient bureaucracy triumphed. The promoters of bureaucracy, including the great figures of the "educational revival," concentrated on attacking democratic localism, which was the chief hindrance to their schemes. They struck first at the notion that democratic localism was, in fact, democratic, by pointing out that it would permit 51 per cent of local parents to dictate the religious, moral, or political ideas taught to the children of the remainder. The proponents of democratic localism erred by assuming the widespread existence of homogeneous potential units of school administration. In actuality, the variety within most communities, city wards, or neighborhoods would foster intensely political competition for control of the local school in order to ensure the propagation of particular points of view or, at the least, the exclusion of rival ones.

Aside from the debilitating effect of political struggle upon education, the result could easily abridge the liberties of parents by forcing them to choose between submitting their children to alien points of view and expensive private schooling.

The second defect of democratic localism was its rural bias, which overlooked the special educational problems posed by cities. Population growth and heterogeneity made extremely decentralized administration inefficient in an urban setting, because it permitted duplication of facilities and the maintenance of uneconomical units that squandered financial resources. As well, democratic localism within a city encouraged an inequitable situation, for it allowed a lack of parity in educational facilities and standards within a relatively small geographical area. Nor did democratic localism permit the schools to undertake the distinctive tasks assigned them in urban settings. For a complex set of reasons that we cannot consider here, schools came to be perceived as key agencies for uplifting the quality of city life by stemming the diffusion of poverty, crime, and immorality, which were thought to accompany urban and industrial development. A demand for the regular attendance of all children upon a prolonged, systematic, and carefully structured formal education followed obviously from the heightened conception of the importance of schooling to urban social order. This demand, in turn, required capacities for coordination and supervision lacking in democratic localism.

Thus, the first generation of professional urban schoolmen rejected democratic localism. Fully developed plans for systems of schools and elaborate architecture, curricula, and pedagogy mark the reports and appeals of Mann, Barnard, and their counterparts. Their goal was to uplift the quality of public education by standardizing and systematizing its structure and content. All their plans had certain characteristics in common, most importantly centralization. Centralization had two principal components: first, the modification and eventual elimination of the bastion of democratic localism, the district system, whereby each section of a town or city managed its own schools with a great deal of autonomy. Public high schools were to reduce the powers and scope of the district committees by siphoning off the older scholars into central institutions. Revitalized central school committees or boards were to manage the high schools and encroach gradually upon the prerogatives of the districts, thus preparing the way for their abolition. The second and related component of centralization was the grading of schools. Careful gradation between and within schools was to provide the hallmark of a properly centralized system.

An emphasis on supervision accompanied centralization. The opponents of democratic localism argued eloquently for state boards of education with paid secretaries and, at the local level, for superintendents of schools. The stress on paid, full-time supervision spilled over into arguments for professional expertise. Arguments both for the appointment of superintendents and for upgrading teaching through the creation of normal schools shared an important assumption: Education had become a difficult and complex undertaking whose conduct and administration demanded the attention of individuals with specialized talents, knowledge, and experience.

The content of education presented a twofold problem: honoring minority sensibilities while inculcating the norms requisite for upright and orderly urban social living. The official response to the problem of minority sensibility was to proclaim the schools religiously and politically neutral, though, in practice, they represented a chauvinistic, pan-Protestant point of view that remained particularly offensive to Catholics. The class bias of educational content was even more pervasive than its tepid Protestant tone. A configuration of moral and cultural values best described as mid-Victorian permeated school textbooks and statements of educational objectives. It was apparent that the traits of character deemed necessary to fit the working class for upright urban living represented a Victorian middle-class portrait of itself.

Herein lies an irony: Schoolmen who thought they were promoting a neutral and classless, indeed a *common*, school education remained unwilling to perceive the extent of cultural bias and imposition inherent in their own writing and activity. However, the bias was central and not incidental to the standardization and administrative rationalization of public education. For, in the last analysis, the rejection of democratic localism rested only partly on inefficiency and violation of parental prerogative. It stemmed equally from a gut fear of the cultural divisiveness inherent in the increasing religious and ethnic variety of American life. Cultural homogenization played counterpoint to administrative rationality. Bureaucracy was intended to standardize far more than the conduct of public business.

Yet, the movement of the bureaucrats was not entirely toward order and rigid system. Their proposals for the actual conduct of the classroom and the reform of pedagogy moved in precisely the opposite direction. In this, they represented the reverse of the paternalistic voluntarists, who accompanied a relative lack of external order with a rigid internal system of teaching. To the common-school revivalists, "mechanical," as applied to pedagogy, was a thoroughly pejorative term. As they systematized the administration and grading of schools, these schoolmen, for a very complex variety of reasons, argued for a softening of pedagogy, marked by an emphasis on the motivating of students through the arousal of interest, the abandonment of interpersonal competition, and the virtual elimination of corporal punishment. The model for the teacher-pupil relation became the relation of parent and child at its finest, firm and affectionate.

In one other crucial way the leading figures of the educational revival did not behave like traditional bureaucrats: They did not adopt the bureaucratic ideal of personality. Neither their ideal teacher nor their ideal administrator was to be a colorless public servant efficiently and quietly executing the public will. Quite to the contrary: The model for the educational administrator came from neither business nor the military, but, instead, from evangelical religion. It was not by accident that the period of mid-century reform was called, even at the time, the educational revival. It was to be a secular evangelicalism. Often reared in religious orthodoxy, from which they had fled, as in Mann's case, to Unitarianism, these schoolmen retained the evangelical ideal of a moral and spiritual regeneration of American society through the moral and spiritual regeneration of individual personalities. It is this goal that lay at the center of the new, soft, child-centered pedagogy. It was to be a pedagogy that recognized the sterility and even danger of purely cold and intellectual education. Education had, as well, to be moral, which meant that schools had to awaken and shape the affective side of personality by delicately stimulating and cultivating the emotions. Evangelical models inspired, as well, the campaigns of these educational promoters, who saw their mission as converting the populace—if need be, town by town—to the cause of salvation through the common school.

Compulsory education followed inexorably upon the demise of democratic localism. Abridgement of the freedom of property owners by compulsory taxation for school support forecast the elimination of the freedom to be unschooled. Proponents of bureaucracy argued that the heightened importance of education in urban society required a vast increase in the proportion of community resources devoted to schooling. Furthermore, part of the price of removing the stigma of pauperism from free schooling became the universal distribution of the burden of school finance through general property taxation. Clearly, for the schools to work, everyone had to attend, but schoolmen did not anticipate that this would pose a problem. Educational promoters expected an overwhelming voluntary response, even from the working class, to the excellence and transparent utility of their new institutions. But only the middle classes responded with enthusiasm and regularity. At first, school promoters tried a number of expedients to improve attendance, the most notable of which was the creation of reform schools, special compulsory institutions to mop up the residue left by the regular public schools. But the residue proved larger and more intractable than anyone had anticipated. Thus, a number of strands came together and pointed in only one direction. If everyone was taxed for school support, if this was justified by the necessity of schooling for the preservation of urban social order, if the beneficial impact of schooling required the regular and prolonged attendance of *all* children, and, finally, if persuasion and a variety of experiments had failed to bring all the children into school, then, clearly, education had to be compulsory. In the crunch, social change would be imposed.

Bureaucracy retained a legacy from the organizational models that it superseded. It bowed in the direction of the democrats by accepting their redefinition of voluntarism and consequently placing educational institutions under boards that were publicly elected rather than self-perpetuating. It innovated in its rejection of a loose, personalistic style of operation for organizational rationality, impersonality, and professionalism. Nevertheless, in two respects the path from paternalistic voluntarism to bureaucracy is direct. First, bureaucracy retained the notion of a central monopoly and systematized its operation through the creation of elaborately structured schools and school systems. Second, bureaucracy continued, and even strengthened, the notion that education was something the better part of the community did to the others to make them orderly, moral, and tractable. Unfortunately, the embodiment of that idea in compulsory, bureaucratic monopolies has continued to characterize American education.

II

One can make the precise differences between models emerge more distinctly by focusing on the four objective dimensions—scale, control, professionalism, and finance—and comparing the positions of the models on each. As for scale, both the democrats and the corporate voluntarists advocated smallness and viewed the proper administrative unit as the individual institution or, at most, a section of a town. Both of the others, of course, stressed size in their definition of administrative area, and recommended the entire town or city at the least, the whole state desirably, and, in some cases, the nation. On the other hand, the two varieties of voluntarists united on the question of control and sponsored essentially amateur self-management by boards removed from direct public control. Here, at one level, the democrats and bureaucrats united in stressing the importance of management assigned to bodies directly responsible to, and representative of, the public. However, the bureaucrats extended this position to advocate the delegation by these public bodies of executive responsibility to public professionals—a proposal the democrats treated with horror.

Neither variety of voluntarist was particularly concerned with the question of professionalism. Both assumed that, as talented, educated amateurs, they were fit to manage educational institutions. Thus, when they were in control, the question of professionalism simply did not arise. Where the democrats were indifferent, interestingly, was on the question of finance. They did not especially care whether schools were absolutely free and tax-supported or whether they were partly supported by rates. In fact, if free schools meant the imposition of state authority against community will, they were

positively opposed. The point is that free schools, while ultimately desirable, remained subordinate on their scale of priorities to community self-determination. The bureaucrats, with a few notable exceptions, most ardently championed free schools, which were logically necessary to their ideal of universal education. The voluntarists supported tuition for those who could pay, free education for the poor, and endowment wherever possible.

On the question of the social role of education, the corporate voluntarists and democrats retained a pluralistic and libertarian vision. As one democrat put the matter, government had as a "right no control over our opinions, literary, moral, political, philosophical, or religious." To the contrary, its task was "to reflect, not to lead, nor to create the general will." Government thus "must not be installed as the educator of the people." The democrats could see no particular virtue in uniformity. It was, after all, the same writer who said that it was the idiosyncratic character of community schools, shaped by local parents, that gave the common school its "charm."

The paternalistic voluntarists and the bureaucrats, of course, saw education precisely *as* the educator of the people, leading, not reflecting, the general will and, at the least, shaping moral opinions. The "charm" of the common school did not especially concern them, if, indeed, they ever noticed it. They hoped for, basically, an increasing standardization of institutions, practices, and culture in American society. Safety of property, upright behavior, a reduction in crime and welfare expense—these values marked both as the advocates of law and order of their day. As an acute critic of the Massachusetts Board of Education pointed out, with unmerciful clarity, the Board viewed education as "merely a branch of general police" and "schoolmasters" as only a "better sort of constables." The "respectable" members of the Board promoted universal education "because they esteem it the most effectual means possible of checking pauperism and crime, and making the rich secure in their possession." Education thus had "a certain utility," whose measure was "solid cash saved to the Commonwealth."

III

With the exception of the bureaucrats, whose love for system led them to expound their point of view repeatedly and at the slightest excuse, the best source for highlighting the difference between models is the analysis of moments of conflict. The controversy between the New York Public School Society and its antagonists—first, the Catholic Church and, later, the State of New York—brings dramatically into play the confrontation between paternalistic voluntarism and democratic localism, and highlights the poignancy of the paternalists, men of good will who worked hard and honestly only to find themselves suddenly rejected and condemned. The same note of poignancy permeates another classic, and even more complex, controversy, namely, that over the abolition of the Boston Primary School Committee, which could not understand why, suddenly, it had become to all the world (and this is the word used by one of its apologists) an "anachronism."

The literature of the academy-high school controversy throughout the United States reveals the conflict between corporate voluntarists and centralizers, for the high school was the favorite institutional innovation of the latter. Of all the controversial literature that I have seen on this issue, by far the most interesting involves the Norwich Free Grammar School, an endowed secondary school founded in the early 1850's to serve as the high school for Norwich, Connecticut, but owned and managed by a board of trustees in the same manner as the academies. The proponents of the school clearly saw in it a desirable alternative to the public high school, and their controversy with the public school men of Massachusetts over this

point is an important document in educational history.

The conflicts between the democratic localists and the bureaucrats often assumed the atmosphere of an undeclared guerrilla war of sabotage and resistance, as local school districts refused to comply with state regulations and parents refused to cooperate with the state's representative, the teacher. Insofar as most of this resistance came from inarticulate people, it is the hardest and most maddening aspect of nineteenth-century educational history to document. That it existed is, however, beyond doubt, as the frustrated testimony of local and state reformers testifies in almost every document they wrote.

Still, excellent examples of democratic localism can be found. The proposals of New York State Secretary John C. Spencer have already been mentioned. Excellent, too, on this score is the controversy over free schools in both New York and Pennsylvania, instance, problems of devising or revising institutions to cope with poverty, ignorance, and other forms of social distress enlisted enormous amounts of thought and energy in precisely the same period. The explanation of that fact requires the formulation of relationships between organizations and other key aspects of nineteenth-century society—a task clearly outside my scope here in any detailed sense. However, it is important to speculate, even briefly, on the nature of that relationship and hence the direction the inquiry into its delineation might assume. Tentatively, therefore, I should like to advance the proposition that the importance of organization derived from its mediating position between social structure and social change.

The mediating position of organizations becomes evident from a consideration of the three broad areas that must be included in any comprehensive analysis of the nineteenth century: First is social change, perhaps best described as industrialization and urbanization. Of the three areas, this is the one about which we know most. Second are changes in social structure and demographic characteristics. We have some idea of the change in the ethnic composition of the population, of its physical distribution, of the white birth rate. We know very little, in an empirical sense, about changes in structure, particularly the family or patterns of stratification and mobility, though a number of scholars are working on these topics. However, we can be generally certain that there were some changes of a fairly substantial nature, whatever they may turn out to be precisely. The third area of the change is organizational, which I have sketched here with regard to education.

We can observe some relations between these major areas of change already. Paternalistic voluntarism was the form of organization characteristic of education in the pre-industrial, mercantile city. Corporate voluntarism and democratic localism characterized rural areas and were proposed for urban places precisely at times of transition between mercantile and industrial stages of development. Incipient bureaucracy spread with incipient industrialization. In terms of social structure, one might suggest that paternalistic voluntarism characterized a society in which stratification was based on traditional notions of rank and deference, rather than class in the more modern sense. Some evidence indicates that the poor and the working classes, threatened by industrialization, supported democratic localism in times of technological transition. However, a middle-class attempt to secure advantage for their children as technological change heightened the importance of formal education ensured the success and acceptance of universal, elaborate, graded school systems. The same result emerged from the fear of a growing, unschooled proletariat. Education substituted for deference as a source of social cement and social order in a society stratified by class rather than by rank.

In each instance, the organization was in the middle. It was the medium through which groups or classes organized their response to social imperatives. In short, to repeat my hypothesis, organization mediated between social change and social structure. Hence, men brought to the design of their organizations, their values, their ambivalences, their fears, and, above all, their aspirations for the shape of American particularly the extensive debates on education in the latter during the constitutional convention of 1837–38. There, most explicitly, the democrats and centralizers confronted each other and, using the issue of language, debated the problem of cultural uniformity; then, turning to free schools, they explicitly clashed over the source and pace of social change. The other major collision between democrats and centralizers happened in Massachusetts, when the former mounted a concerted attack on the newly formed Massachusetts Board of Education. The statement of the committee of the legislature that advocated the abolition of the Board is in many ways the classic statement of the democrats. More reflective, more philosophical, and one of the finest educational statements of the mid-nineteenth century is the attack on the Board in the *Boston Quarterly Review,* from which the earlier quotations have been taken. For the viewpoint of the bureaucrats, in addition to their replies in conflict, the standard sources of educational history suffice: state and local school reports; Henry Barnard on school attendance, linking up the various strands in the argument I have described; George Boutwell putting the case for the high school with devastating directness; Horace Mann rhetorically linking crime, poverty, disorder, and education; and so it goes. For these were the most articulate of the proponents. They were also victorious.

IV

Even if the specific models proposed in this paper are rejected, it is my hope that the underlying argument has been persuasive. That argument is that the analysis of organizational models provides direct insight into the key value conflicts within nineteenth-century society. In their arguments over the details of organizations, nineteenth-century Americans revealed most clearly their aspirations and, as well, their anxieties concerning the society they would build and bequeath. However, if we accept the centrality of organizational form to nineteenth-century people, we are left with an important general question: Why has the nature of organization been of such primary importance? From one direction, the question points to a comparative inquiry. Was the nature of organization as passionate and value-laden a subject of controversy in other countries during the same period? I suspect the answer, at least insofar as England and Canada are concerned (although I may well be wrong), is no; Americans made organization uniquely their own national problem. And they did so precisely because they lacked fixed traditions and the security of ancient forms. The search for the distinctively American in art, architecture, and government, to name but three aspects of American culture, is too well known a subject to belabor. This nervous self-consciousness knew few boundaries; it made the creation of organizations—their forms and characteristics—an intellectual and even nationalistic issue. It thus assumed special importance in the American context.

But the question of the centrality of organization can be put in a more general context as well. Even if not quite so emotionally charged, it nevertheless was important elsewhere during the nineteenth century. In both England and Canada, for instance, problems of devising or revising institutions to cope with poverty, ignorance, and other forms of social distress enlisted enormous amounts of thought and energy in precisely the same period. The explanation of that fact requires the formulation of relationships between organizations and other key aspects of nineteenth-century society—a task clearly outside my scope here in any detailed sense. However, it is important to speculate, even briefly, on the nature of that relationship and hence the direction the inquiry into its delineation might assume. Tentatively, therefore, I should like to advance the proposition that the importance of organization derived from its mediating position between social structure and social change.

The mediating position of organizations becomes evident from a consideration of the three broad areas that must be included in any comprehensive analysis of the nineteenth century: First is social change, perhaps best described as industrialization and urbanization. Of the three areas, this is the one about which we know most. Second are changes in social structure and demographic characteristics. We have some idea of the change in the ethnic composition of the population, of its physical distribution, of the white birth rate. We know very little, in an empirical sense, about changes in structure, particularly the family or patterns of stratification and mobility, though a number of scholars are working on these topics. However, we can be generally certain that there were some changes of a fairly substantial nature, whatever they may turn out to be precisely. The third area of the change is organizational, which I have sketched here with regard to education.

We can observe some relations between these major areas of change already. Paternalistic voluntarism was the form of organization characteristic of education in the pre-industrial, mercantile city. Corporate voluntarism and democratic localism characterized rural areas and were proposed for urban places precisely at times of transition between mercantile and industrial stages of development. Incipient bureaucracy spread with incipient industrialization. In terms of social structure, one might suggest that paternalistic voluntarism characterized a society in which stratification was based on traditional notions of rank and deference, rather than class in the more modern sense. Some evidence indicates that the poor and the working classes, threatened by industrialization, supported democratic localism in times of technological transition. However, a middle-class attempt to secure advantage for their children as technological change heightened the importance of formal education ensured the success and acceptance of universal, elaborate, graded school systems. The same result emerged from the fear of a growing, unschooled proletariat. Education substituted for deference as a source of social cement and social order in a society stratified by class rather than by rank.

In each instance, the organization was in the middle. It was the medium through which groups or classes organized their response to social imperatives. In short, to repeat my hypothesis, organization mediated between social change and social structure. Hence, men brought to the design of their organizations, their values, their ambivalences, their fears, and, above all, their aspirations for the shape of American society.

V

Two general points about the significance of the organizational debate remain to be made. First of all, it refocuses the issue in the decreasingly profitable debate between proponents of consensus and controversy as keys to the American past. If my underlying contention is valid, men did argue over fundamental value differences, which they articulated in reference to the practical problem of organization building. Their interchange, the competition among organizational forms and the visions they expressed, did provide a dynamic of controversy to nineteenth-century history. But it is a dynamic that implies no lack of faith in Lockean liberalism, no desire to subvert the existing social order, and no lack of commitment to America. The politics of organization building *were* politics of value clash, but the nature of that clash is not described by conventional categories of economic or class division. Determination of just what those categories are—how to go beyond the empirical facts of organizational form to organized systems of values and their relationship to social structure—should be, I would argue, the major goal of American social historians.

The other point of significance regards alternatives. Men did see alternatives in the American past. Those whose vision embraced a path other than bureaucracy lost. But, if the present was inevitable, it did not seem so to men at the time. Perhaps, if they had been that much wiser—who can say? Their failure and their vision provide, respectively and at once, enduring notes of pessimism and hope, to which we cannot afford not to listen today.

23. City Schools: Centralization of Control at the Turn of the Century

DAVID B. TYACK

DIAGNOSIS AND PRESCRIPTION

The imperatives have a familiar ring in the 1970s:

Make schoolmen strictly accountable for the quality of education.

The author is deeply indebted to the Carnegie Corporation for a grant which supported this and related research and to several colleagues who criticized an earlier draft of this essay.

Adapt the structures and processes of schooling to new social conditions.

Cut the red tape that constricts reform.

Develop national networks to share innovative ideas and to generate political support for change.

Face the realities of class and power in American urban society.

Create new local political leadership to re-

From *Building the Organizational Society*, edited by Jerry Israel (New York: Free Press, 1972), pp. 57–72 and 257–263. Reprinted by permission of the Macmillan Publishing Co., Inc. Copyright © 1972 by The Free Press, a Division of the Macmillan Publishing Co., Inc.

place the vested interests controlling city schools.

In the period from 1890 to 1920, both the context and the implications of these statements were quite different from their meaning to school reformers today. The chief problem in city schools, said an early spokesman for change in 1885, was "excessive decentralization of administration."[1] "The only real progress in . . . municipal reform has been made through the imposition of limitations upon the common suffrage," said a leading advocate of centralization, "through taking away authority from the representatives of the people [and] through the centralization of power and responsibility in fewer individuals. . . ."[2] "Bureaucracy and red-tape are the meat upon which corruption feeds," argued a school board member in St. Louis; his cure was an apolitical meritocracy.[3] A prominent professor of school administration urged educational officials to "give up the exceedingly democratic idea that all are equal, and that our society is devoid of classes," and told them to adapt the schools to the classes.[4]

There emerged a nationwide interlocking directorate of university presidents and professors, a new group of "progressive" school superintendents, and lay allies from the business and professional elites in the cities. Their purpose: to vest control of urban schools in boards which were small rather than large, elected from the city as a whole rather than by wards, and absolutely emancipated from partisan politics. They believed that these reformed boards should delegate full authority and responsibility for running the schools to the superintendent and his staff, who would be held strictly accountable for results. Take power from the people who hold it; give it to a few responsible citizens on "non-political" school boards; delegate it to professionals who will then have a free hand to shape the schools to the needs of an industrial, complex urban society—thus did the reformers translate the imperatives.[5]

Though differing over minor details in both their diagnoses and prescriptions, the centralizers agreed that corruption sabotaged the efficiency of urban schools. They claimed that all across the nation, politicians regarded schools as part of the spoils system and awarded jobs and contracts not on the basis of competence or competition but as political favors. The superintendent of the Cleveland schools declared that "the unscrupulous politician is the greatest enemy we have to contend with in public education," echoing similar anonymous "confessions" of teachers and administrators published in the *Atlantic Monthly* in 1896.[6] Lincoln Steffens and other muckrakers revealed how textbook publishers and contractors allied with corrupt school trustees for common boodle in the common school.[7]

But dishonesty and graft were only part of the problem as the reformers saw it. The governance of schools was archaic and inept, boards too large and members too narrow in outlook. As cities mushroomed, new school board members from outlying wards swelled the size of governing bodies. Often elected by wards, school trustees represented parochial rather than citywide interests and constituencies. Hartford, Connecticut, posed an extreme example of decentralization, for there each school had its own autonomous committee. In 1905 Philadelphia had 43 elected district school boards consisting of 559 members. In Pittsburgh, Philadelphia, and New York, the central boards of education shared with local boards the responsibility for hiring staff, building and maintaining schools, and other related functions. In 1892, 16 of 28 cities of more than 100,000 population had boards of 20 members or more, a majority of them elected by ward.[8]

Even where school boards were small and the members honest, they commonly meddled far too much, said the reformers, in matters properly left to the professional staff. In many cities, "the superintendent is a superintendent in name only" since boards refused to relinquish control over the everyday operations of the district. Instead of granting authority to the administrators, they delegated tasks to subcommittees of the board.[9] Such subcommittees dealt with the ventilation of buildings, ways of teaching reading, examining teachers, choice of textbooks, printing, and the purchase of doorknobs—no topic was too trivial or exalted. At one time, Chicago had 79 subcommittees, Cincinnati, 74.[10] In Boston, subcommittees administered different districts of the school system (*e.g.,* Charlestown), thereby in effect decentralizing the schools into wards even though the members of the central committee were officially elected at large. In Philadelphia, Scott Nearing found that the board of 21 members conducted almost all its business through its ten standing subcommittees (1323 of 1386 resolutions passed by the board stemmed from these subcommittees).[11] Indeed, granted the size of most big city boards and the mass of administrivia they handled, subcommittees were the only feasible means of conducting business. A member of the Boston board, however, spoke for the reformers when he said that these functions were illegitimate:

The feeling that I should be called upon to formulate a course of study for a primary class, or a Latin school, or a manual training school, became oppressive when I realized that I was not what is called "equipped" for such a service; nor did I hanker for the opportunity to designate what textbooks should be used in the schools; a task which, in fact, amounts to nothing more than choosing between text-book publishing houses.[12]

Publishers recognized that administrators and teachers often had nothing to do with the selection of books. "If we can't have Frye's *Geography,* they shan't have Metcalf's *Grammar,*" said one bitter Boston school board member to another.[13]

But corruption, lay meddling, and inefficiency were not all that bothered the reformers. They worried also about something they called "bureaucracy," a negative label they pinned on the internal functioning of the schools. B. A. Hinsdale, former Superintendent of the Cleveland Public Schools, warned in 1894 that "in all cities, and most of all in large ones, the tendency toward machinery and bureaucracy is very strong in all kinds of work. It is hard for the individual to assert his personal force."[14] Charles William Eliot, President of Harvard, had long criticized the machinery created by urban schools to educate thousands of children uniformly and simultaneously: "it almost inevitably adopts military or mechanical methods, and these methods tend to produce a lock-step and a uniform speed." In his survey of the New York schools in 1911, Paul Hanus recommended abolishing the Board of Superintendents:

We find that the Board of Superintendents has become bureaucratic, and hence non-progressive. When it was first constituted, it may have been the best instrumentality available to bring about homogeneity and coherence—unity of aim and effort—within the school system. But it does not now represent either as to constitution, organization, or function a really serviceable agency for the initiation or development of educational policies; or for professional growth on the part of supervisors, principals, or teachers.[15]

In short, by "bureaucracy" the centralizers meant a system bound by obsolete rules and regulations, rigid and uniform in dealing with students and staff, ill-adapted to changing conditions, and stifling to men of initiative and imagination.

This sort of "bureaucracy" in urban schools was an exaggerated expression of certain aims of the common school reformers of the mid-19th century. In place of a chaos of different types of schools with different clienteles and purposes they sought to substitute a common school, standardized by such devices as the age-grading of students, the use of uniform textbooks, and routine procedures and rules. The crusade had evangelical roots: The primary rhetoric had been ethical, the purpose to create a moral and civic consensus amid the dangers threatening the Republic. As Robert Wiebe has observed, mid-19th century cities tended to be "island communities," isolated from each other, while educators were provincial in orientation and hired "to construct a model environment around the child" during his impressionable early years.[16] As the sense of moral strategy waned during the later years of the century, the quest for standardization turned into unexamined routine and "trained incapacity." Cities became more heterogeneous in population, their leaders more cosmopolitan in outlook, their social and economic life more complex, yet the schools persisted in their search for homogeneity.

What the centralizers wished to do was to substitute a more modern and specialized form of "bureaucracy" (in roughly Max Weber's sense of the word) for the older model based on a military or simple factory system.[17] They wanted the board to grant autonomy to the superintendent so that he could innovate freely without regard to obsolete rules, meddling by subcommittees of the board, or accumulated red tape. They wanted greater specialization of function within the hierarchy and administration by experts appointed purely on the basis of merit. They sought a diverse rather than uniform curriculum. Their organizational models were the complex corporate structures emerging at the turn of the century, their cynosure, the captain of industry whose vision was national as well as local.

In short, they believed that the keys to success in urban education were centralization of control, expert and flexible leadership, functional specialization, and professional accountability. The trouble with the present system, said Andrew Draper, is that no one is clearly responsible: What does the parent do who thinks the schools are failing his child?

You seek redress. Going to the teacher you see that she is not disposed, or is not allowed, to hold much converse with you. She refers you to the principal. He means rightly but does not view things through your end of the telescope. He resents your imputations and is powerless to give you relief. . . . You go to the superintendent. At times he can help you, and if he can he will; but again, he would have to walk right into the jaws of official death to redress your wrongs. . . . You go to the members of the board of education only to find that they . . . shuffle out the responsibility. . . . [18]

Accountability, a war on "bureaucracy"—these would become watchwords of change a half-century later. In the meantime, the centralizers went to work at the turn of the century, confident that they knew what was wrong with American urban education and how to repair it.[19]

ACTORS AND ACTIONS

In 1908 President Charles W. Eliot spoke about realism in adapting the schools to the new "social and industrial conditions in our democracy." We must face the fact, he said, that the "democratic society is divided, and is going to be divided into layers. . . . The upper one is very thin; it consists of the managing, leading, guiding class—the intellectual discoverers, the inventors, the organizers, and the managers and their chief assistants." He liked to reassure his audiences that this small elite could, in fact, secure important changes in urban education:

It was an extraordinarily small group of men acting under a single leader that obtained from the Massachusetts legislature the act which established the Boston School Committee of five members. The name of that leader was James J. Storrow. I am happy to believe that the group were all Harvard men. . . . We used to have twenty-four men, most of whom were not good. Now we have five men, all of whom are good. . . . I have been much interested during the last year in studying both municipal evils and the chances of municipal reform; and I find the greatest encouragement for the ultimate success of that cause in the fact that many school committees in American cities have been redeemed, and made efficient, far-seeing, and thoroughly trustworthy.[20]

A large proportion of the architects of centralized control of urban education came from Eliot's "thin layer." The most prominent spokesmen were university presidents and professors of educational administration, superintendents of city schools, and leading lawyers and businessmen. As men who had perfected large organizations, they had national reference groups and were cosmopolitan rather than local in outlook. Successful in their own careers, they assumed that what was good for their class and private institutions was good public policy as well.[21] They developed inter-city networks of influence through the National Education Association, through newspapers, general magazines, and professional journals like *School Board Journal* and *Educational Review,* through sharing ideas in their elite Public Education Associations and businessmen's clubs (including Chambers of Commerce), and through service on commissions of school reorganization and school boards.[22] They were convinced that the way to improve urban education was to place on school boards a few "Americans of good quality—that is, honest men who have proved their capacity in their private business" and to turn the schools over to the progressive expert—"a man who, knowing the shortcomings and defects in his business, is eager to try experiments in overcoming them."[23] They regarded themselves both as progressives in municipal political reform and as progressives in education. They shaped structural changes which affected children in classrooms at least as much as the more individualized and philosophical programs which have been traditionally defined as "progressive education."[24]

University presidents spearheaded the reform movement. Some of them saw a close analogy between the role of college trustees and the proper function of urban school boards. The jobs of superintendent and college president demanded similar expertise, they thought.[25] It was common for presidents to become superintendents and vice-versa: Andrew Draper left the Cleveland superintendency to become president of the

University of Illinois; E. Benjamin Andrews headed the Chicago schools after service as president at Brown University; Daniel Coit Gilman at Johns Hopkins University was a prominent candidate for the New York superintendency (Nicholas Murray Butler said that had Gilman served "for two or three years," he would have reorganized "the New York school system and put it on its feet"[26]). At Columbia, Butler masterminded the reforms of 1896 in New York which destroyed the powers of the ward school trustees. He orchestrated publicity in the newspapers and printed muckraking articles and reformist tracts in his *Educational Review.*[27] For three decades Eliot spoke, wrote and agitated for centralization of power. His successor at Harvard, Abbott Lawrence Lowell, served on the Boston school board and was a key reformer.[28] William Rainey Harper, president of the University of Chicago, chaired the Educational Commission of Chicago, whose report in 1899 was a compendium of reform views on structural defects and remedies in city schools (he had consulted Eliot, Draper, Gilman, Butler, and David Starr Jordan of Stanford, as well as several other university presidents).[29] Eliot, Butler, and Jordan were presidents of the N.E.A., while Draper and Gilman were presidents of departments of the N.E.A. Through these professional organizations and periodicals, they had ample opportunity to spread their ideas on educational reform. And if the reforms created a demand for experts, the universities stood to gain, for their new departments and schools of education would train those experts.

Superintendents and professors of educational administration often exchanged jobs during their careers, as in the case of the college presidents. They had special reasons for favoring "nonpolitical" elite boards and the elevation of the expert. A civil service system based on merit lessened the danger of being fired for political reasons.[30] In addition, a hierarchy of specialized administrative offices built a ladder of success for the ambitious schoolman, while the demand for expertise sent him to the university for credentials. With but few exceptions, superintendents and professors of administration at the turn of the century admired businessmen and saw in the specialized forms of corporate bureaucracy new models for the control and organization of urban schools. Increasingly, school administrators turned for guidance to their national professional associations.[31]

There are three cities in which lay participation in school centralization has been carefully studied—New York, Philadelphia, and St. Louis. In each case, it is clear that the key individuals belonged mostly to Eliot's "upper layer." David Hammack's analysis of the members of the "Committee of One Hundred," which advocated centralization in New York in 1896, supplements Sol Cohen's study of the membership of the Public Education Association in that city. Clearly the bulk of these citizens were members of the city's social and power elite. Ninety-two members of the 104 people in the Committee of One Hundred appeared in the *Social Register* in 1896; 49 were lawyers, frequently partners of prominent legal firms (most of these also served as officers or directors of business corporations); 18 were bankers; and several were leading merchants and professional men. Hammack points out that these men had participated "in the reorganization of American business and the development of the professions in the decades following the Civil War," a process which had reinforced their desire to rationalize organizations, to employ experts, and to take a national or even international perspective.[32] In Philadelphia, likewise, upper class leaders took the forefront in the campaign to abolish the ward school boards, as William Issel has shown. Seventy-five per cent of the officers of the Public Education Association from 1882–1912 were listed either in the *Social Register* or the *Blue Book,* while 100 per cent of the officers of the Civic Club, another reform organization, were so listed in 1904. Issel concludes that:

Modernization stripped the ward school boards of power, left them intact only as

boards of visitors, and placed control of the schools in the hands of cosmopolitan and efficiency minded upper class businessmen and professionals, whose legislative decisions would be carried out by dispassionate, university trained, educational experts according to the impersonal criteria of bureaucratic social organization.[33]

Elinor Gersman has analyzed the occupations of St. Louis school board members before the reorganization in 1896 and after the centralization reforms in 1897. Professional men on the board jumped from 4.8 per cent to 58.3 per cent, and big businessmen, from 9.5 per cent to 25 per cent; while small businessmen dropped from 47.6 per cent to 16.7 per cent, and wage-earning employees, from 28.6 per cent to none.[34]

Other cities showed similar patterns. Andrew Draper said that the Cleveland school bill, which became law in 1892, was written by four men: three lawyers (one a judge) and a bank president.[35] In Los Angeles, when a new charter reduced the board to seven elected from the city at large, the municipal league selected 100 leading citizens who in turn nominated "seven of the most prominent and busiest men of the city." The result, said a resident, was "a non-partisan Board of Education . . . and we are getting toward the next step in the development; that is, what is better than non-partisan,—a non-personal administration of public school affairs."[36] After the reform charter of 1899 in Baltimore, the mayor appointed nine board members from the local elite, including Daniel Coit Gilman and eminent lawyers. One of the first things they did was to ask Butler and Eliot to recommend an expert superintendent.[37] A study of city school boards by Scott Nearing in 1916 showed that more than three fifths of the members were merchants, manufacturers, bankers, brokers and real estate men, and doctors and lawyers.[38] Subsequent studies by George Struble and George Counts confirmed the fact that wage-earners were grossly underrepresented on urban school boards, while Eliot's "upper layer" controlled them.[39]

This dominance by business and professional men was, of course, what the reformers had desired all along: They wanted power to *their* people. In 1892 the United States Commissioner of Education, William T. Harris, stated what would become the conventional wisdom in writings on school administration. There are three common types of school board members, he said:

First, the business men chosen from the class of merchants, bankers, manufacturers, or professional men who have no personal ends to serve and no special cause to foster. . . . Second, there are the men representing the element of reform or change . . . honest and well-meaning, but . . . prone to . . . an unbalanced judgment. . . . A third class of men . . . is the self-seeking or selfish man. . . .

The first, of course, were the superintendent's natural allies; the second group he must "educate into broader views" (possibly he might accept some of their suggestions "after freeing them from all features of danger to the established order").[40] The ideal board was gentlemanly and business-like—qualities most likely to be found in gentlemen of business. "The work of the board," wrote the Boston superintendent after the reforms of 1905, "is conducted in a conversational tone; speeches made for political effect that were common in the larger board no longer are delivered. The deliberations of the board are not essentially different from those of a board of directors."[41] Ellwood Cubberley agreed: "If the board confines itself to its proper work, an hour a week will transact all of the school business which the board should handle. There is no more need for oratory in the conduct of a school system than there would be in the conduct of a national bank."[42]

The drive toward centralization in urban education at the turn of the century largely succeeded in reshaping the formal structure of control of the schools. In the cities with over 100,000 population in 1910, the average size of the school board dropped approximately from 16 in 1895 to 9 in 1915. The changes were greatest in the largest cities. In 1892 Cleveland changed from a board of 26 to a 7-man "school council." In 1896 a bill destroyed most of the power of New York's ward committees. Under the consolidation of the New York boroughs, however, the central board of education retained "delegates" until 1917, when the board was reduced to 7 persons. The St. Louis reorganization in 1897 cut the board from 21 elected by wards to 12 elected at large from the city. Milwaukee that year changed its board from 42 members—in effect chosen by the ward aldermen—to 21 members chosen by four "citizens of suitable character and education" appointed by the mayor. In 1907 this was changed to 15 elected at large. The Baltimore Charter of 1898 changed the selection procedure in that city: Instead of each councilman nominating one of the 22 school commissioners, the mayor appointed all 9 members. In 1905 Philadelphia's board dropped from 42 to 21, appointed at large rather than by wards. The local boards lost most of the powers that had made them keystones of the spoils system. That year, the Massachusetts Federal Court sliced the Boston board from 24 to 5. In 1911, the Pennsylvania legislature cut the size of the Pittsburgh and Philadelphia boards to 15 members, and changed the ward committees into investigative "school visitors." Detroit eliminated representation by wards and reduced its board from 18 to 7 in 1916. After two decades of attempted reforms, Chicago finally diminished its board in 1917 from 21 to 11 members, appointed by the mayor. Accompanying these changes in the structure of the school boards in most cases were substantial enlargements of the power of the superintendents in hiring and firing of staff, determining curriculum, and deciding other professional and fiscal matters.[43]

Only careful study, city by city, will reveal the exact alignments of power, class, ethnicity, race, religion, and ideology involved in the struggles for centralization of control. The specific political strategies differed locally as well, for in some cities reformers had to turn to the state legislatures for redress, while in others, they enacted new laws within city boundaries. In a number of cases one political party dominated the state legislature, another the city. Neither party enjoyed a monopoly of urban school reform. As Samuel Hays has observed, reformers wanted "not simply to replace bad men with good; they proposed to change the occupational and class origins of decision-makers."[44] Beneath the symbolic crusades lay differing conceptions of private interest and public good, and it is to this struggle we now turn.

CONFLICTS OF VALUE

"No one thing is more needed in American life today than frank admission of inequality, with all that implies." So responded Professor Albion Small to the Harper Committee when it sought advice in 1898 about how the schools should train citizens.

In this connection I assert that our schools have been delinquent, equivocal and sometimes cowardly.... Wherever politics has laid its hand on the schools there has persistently appeared a tendency to truckle to mob demand for artificial leveling .... our schools of today are playing into the hands of that despicable demagoguery which holds back the realization of the only rational democracy by catering to the popular conceit of indiscriminate equality.

Children must be taught that "personal merit is the only valid title to civic rank and social consideration," said Small. Only that school system which contains "strong features of authoritative discipline which the pupils must observe with military promptness and precision" would actually teach the essential lesson of "straight-out-obedience."[45] You should no more democratize the schools than democratize appendicitis, Nicholas Murray Butler told the Merchants Club in Chicago in a speech directed against teachers' unions.[46] Reformers thought that schools existed to socialize ill-prepared children to their roles in a complex corporate world and that education should therefore reflect the changing nature of that society.

"The elementary school should facilitate and simplify the process of economic selection," said members of a committee recommending changes in the New York Schools, "and should act as a transmitter between human supply and industrial demand."[47]

Many of the men who advocated centralization clearly saw schools as a means of social control. Undoubtedly a large percentage of the reformers were moved by humane concern for children as well. In many cities, school buildings were dank, dark, unsafe and crowded; thousands of pupils could not find even a seat; frequently teachers were grotesquely unprepared for their work; the old curriculum was often hopelessly rigid and out of touch with current reality; graft and inefficiency siphoned off funds needed to build classrooms and hire teachers.[48] And it is clear that urban education faced staggering tasks of preparing hundreds of thousands of poor children from dozens of ethnic groups to survive and advance in American society. But the rhetoric of concern sometimes contained disdain and fear directed towards the dispossessed, nor could the claim to be "nonpolitical" or "nonpersonal" mask the ways in which the centralizers wished to favor their own interests. Social control for whose benefit? Economy and efficiency for what purpose? A buffer zone of "professionalism" to protect whom from whom? Underlying the debates over the organizational forms of American education lay conflicting concerns and convictions about the nature of American society.[49]

The question of motives and interests of elite reformers and school board members is highly complex. As W. W. Charters, Jr., has observed, studies like Counts', which showed that the majority of school board members came from "the dominant class," generally did not prove that boards did in fact act in the interests of that class. Furthermore, such "status studies" tend to ignore the semiautonomous norms of behavior which have attended professionalization and bureaucratization of school administration and teaching. Hence empirical investigation must provide links between the social characteristics of those who in formal terms "control" education and the real or alleged interests served in the actual operation of schools. Of course, it would be equally a form of *a priori* reasoning to argue that socio-economic status of board members did *not* influence their educational policy decisions, since such class membership has been shown to shape many other kinds of behavior.[50]

We also need to know more about how diverse kinds of school board members have become socialized to their roles as committeemen. If school boards tended to approximate the model of a corporate board of directors as urged by the reformers, then role prescriptions would hardly favor the give-and-take of pluralistic politics. If interaction among social unequals results in disproportionate influence by persons of higher status—as predicted in status interaction theory and confirmed in a study by Alexander Proudfoot in Alberta, Canada—then elite members would generally predominate even where there were committeemen of humbler rank.[51] For better or worse, the ideal of nonpartisanship has fostered the norm of nonrepresentativeness; that is, a Catholic factory worker from the west side on a school board is expected to speak for all the children of the city, not to represent chiefly those people he knows best. School board manuals have usually stressed members should take this universalistic view. Of course, informal checks and balances of power and interests frequently appeared on urban school boards, but in ideal type the reformers' goal was a closed system of politics.[52]

There are, of course, many possible ways to approach the question of the motives of the centralizers. I shall briefly discuss three as illustrations.

The first is to explore ways in which the elite gained direct economic benefits from school politics. An obvious opportunity was to keep school taxes low by lowering costs; this was a major concern of the reform board in St. Louis.[53] In Chicago several large corporations actually evaded paying school taxes entirely until feisty Margaret Haley of the Chicago Teachers' Federation brought suit against them. In another notorious case, the president of the Chicago board, who was an attorney employed by the *Chicago Tribune,* joined the majority of businessmen who voted to grant the *Tribune* a 99 year lease on land owned by the schools, thereby resulting in the loss of hundreds of thousands of dollars of school revenue, since prior to that time the property had been revalued upwards each ten years.[54] In his swashbuckling book, *The Goslings,* Upton Sinclair gave a socialist analysis of the "Black Hand's" stranglehold on American education and detailed case after case of business graft in the construction of buildings, the sale of land and supplies, and the purchase of textbooks. As a number of muckrakers discovered, businessmen were adept at school graft or tax evasion, but usually operated on a bigger scale and in a somewhat more legal manner than the immigrant political machines.[55] William Maxwell, superintendent of schools in New York, accused industrialists of forcing the schools to underwrite apprenticeship programs which the factories themselves should have provided.[56]

For the most part, though, the elite did not seek crude private benefit. A second and more important way to examine motives is to explore the larger strategy of using schools to make the society more stable, efficient, and rational. Here the elite might well identify its own interests with those of the larger community. Those who sought to reform urban education from the top down—to create small elite boards and to grant experts autonomy in running the schools—had an understandable faith in their own values (after all, these beliefs and practices had worked for them). Deviations from the American norm were to be eradicated by educational intervention. To be sure, the task was difficult, especially in the case of Southeastern European immigrants, who were, thought Cubberley, "illiterate, docile, lacking in self-reliance and initiative, and not possessing the Anglo-Saxon conceptions of law, order, and government. . . ."[57] Few of the reformers believed that different social values and patterns might be equally valid or that the schools should reflect the pluralism of the society. Intervention must start early: An adviser to the Harper Commission urged that kindergarten teachers inculcate "honesty, sobriety, habits of attention and observation." Children are "wards of the state," he said, and "careful educational training is the best possible . . . safeguard against all sorts of fanatical schemes and social vagaries."[58]

Norms in the school could provide socialization required for the complex urban world: punctuality, respect for authority, competition for rewards according to institutionally fixed criteria, and acceptance of standardized work routines. Thus employers benefitted from an elementary school which served "as a transmitter between human supply and industrial demand." The explicit lesson of the school taught the doctrine of self-help and equality of opportunity, so that a well-socialized child blamed himself and not the social order if he did not succeed in life. The implicit lessons were perhaps even more important: the requirements of obedience, punctuality, silence, cleanliness, and ritualistic acceptance of the unreality portrayed in textbooks.

But general socialization was not enough. The schools also needed to prepare youth for diverse vocations in a technological society. As more and more working-class children entered secondary schools, businessmen and educators developed vocational training programs in which largely working class children were enrolled. The academic tracks led to the best jobs and remained largely the preserve of the middle and upper classes.[59]

In seeking to modify education in these ways, employers might well have assumed that what was good for their company was good for the child and good for the nation. Any class interest or motive, they might have argued, was subsumed in an enlightened and rational adaptation of the schools to a changed economy and social order.

In the third approach to motivation of the school reformers, one might claim that neither the elite nor the followers really had control over the processes of technology and modernization, but that both were swept up in changes which they neither understood nor directed. Under such a vision, comparable to Jacques Ellul's picture of *The Technological Society,* the centralizers were neither the villainous "Black Hand" of Sinclair's devil theory, nor the architects and mollifiers of social change, but unwitting agents of unavoidable human transformation.[60]

From whatever approach one analyzes the work of the school centralizers—and it seems clear that many angles of vision are needed—a number of basic social developments confronted the schools at the turn of the century:

A rapid and vast surge in the numbers of school-age children;

An ethnically diverse population;

Staggering changes in the technology of production, transportation, and communication;

Corresponding transformations in the forms of human organization to cope with this new technology and the challenge of great concentrations of people.

Fresh from traditional communities where the sun was their clock, the seasons their calendar, masses of rural folk entered factories and tenements. Immigrants speaking dozens of languages met bureaucracies that knew ethnic peculiarities only as inefficient aberrations. The city itself—technology itself—became teachers of families, while schoolmen reminded each other that the tasks of the schoolhouse in the city were expanding beyond familiar comprehension. A sense of institutional crisis pervaded the urban climate; in responding to the challenge the centralizers followed those patterns of values and organization which had worked for them.

Whatever the motives of the centralizers or the relative benefits of centralization of control, many urban dwellers opposed the process. Some teachers feared the concentration of power in the superintendent's office. Margaret Haley's strong Chicago Teachers' Federation consistently fought the elite reformers and "one-man rule."[61] The great mass of schoolmen in New York wished to retain the ward committee system and attacked Butler and his allies in the 1896 "school war."[62] In Baltimore, a majority of teachers resisted the reform superintendent and collaborated with politicians who sought to remove him.[63] When Superintendent Frederick of the Cleveland schools black-listed six elementary teachers who were organizing a union in 1914, they sought an injunction against him. "You are out of harmony with the public, your real employer," said the judge to the superintendent:

You are not employed by the board of education, but by the public. In your loyal service to your nominal master, the board, you have drifted away from your real master. . . . The system is sick, very sick. Two things only will cure it: Light and air, agitation and ventilation. 'Pull down the blinds! Turn out the lights!' says Mr. Frederick. 'Then we shall have harmony in the schools! Well, to be in harmony with such a system is to be out of harmony with everything else that is good and commendable.'[64]

In a number of cities, teachers feared the autocracy possible in such a hermetic system quite as much as the hazard of "politics" under the old system of ward trustees.

Predictably, many of the district committeemen and state and city politicians regarded the reformers as rival operators with covert interests of their own.[65] A number of the local leaders in the cities saw educational reform not as a "battle against the slum" (Jacob Riis' view) but as an attack on their group identity, assaulting the innovators as "anglomaniacs," aristocrats, and anti-Catholics.[66] If local boards retained power to select teachers and adapt the schools to the community, they might settle such touchy questions as religion in the schools or the teaching of foreign languages.

This would increase public support for the schools, they argued, and resolve conflicts at the local level. An opponent of centralization in New York wrote in 1896 that:

The varied character of our population, and the concentration of special classes of our people in certain districts, makes it desirable that these people be represented in school matters, and this will be possible only by the appointment of local officials with necessary powers of action, who are acquainted with the distinctive characteristics (national, racial, and religious) of the several neighborhoods.[67]

To these groups, ethnic or religious differences were not to be homogenized in a universalistic school bureaucracy, but values to be accommodated within urban diversity.

Political, ethnic, and religious differences were, of course, too crucial in urban society to disappear from school politics even in those cities where the centralizers had temporarily won their way. In Baltimore, Democratic Mayor Preston vowed that he would "popularize the schools" after a decade of elite rule and appointed a board willing to remove Superintendent Van Sickle.[68] Shortly after the Chicago board was reduced in size, Mayor Thompson sallied into school politics. When the New York Board of Education was reorganized in 1917 to seven members and gained real power for the first time, it ceased to be an "enclave of gentlemen." Subsequent mayors were careful to maintain a balance of ethnic and religious groups in their appointments.[69] Successive ethnic groups in various cities managed to penetrate the supposedly impersonal civil service systems of the schools, making them in some cases more "patrinomial" than bureaucratic.[70]

The centralist reforms at the turn of the century, however, left legacies and unintended consequences which still deeply influence urban education. One of these legacies is what Wallace Sayre has called a "self-serving doctrine and myth" that "education must be 'taken out of politics.' " The centralizers argued that educational government should be "above politics" and that the notions of a "loyal opposition" or partisan representation were out of place on school boards. To a large degree this has become a standard profession of belief if not an actuality. As Sayre observes, "this myth is not reserved for bureaucratic strategy only; it is taught to the children too. Thus the children of democracy are taught to distrust one of the basic institutions of democracy."[71] Lawrence Iannaccone has maintained that this closed system of school governance tends to stifle lay demands for educational change until they become explosive. A corollary of the myth of "nonpartisanship" is that education should be entrusted to the professional experts. One consequence has been a general naiveté—and sometimes obscurantism—about the actual forces that shape education in this country.[72]

Another heritage of the reform movement has been an enormous expansion of central administrative bureaucracies in the large cities. These are clothed with such great influence—to obstruct change if not to induce it—that school boards have increasingly become legitimizing bodies rather than real sources of authority. While originally the reformers thought that this delegation of power would render the superintendent and his staff strictly accountable to the public, it has largely had the opposite effect. The growth of layers of officials has often enabled schoolmen to evade responsibility and to strangle innovation in a tangle of red tape. Far from believing that they can demand accountability from school leaders, many parents and children feel like subjects, not citizens, of their educational system.[73]

Lastly, the destruction of the local ward or district committees, once possessing real power and responsibility, has dissolved political subsystems which formerly kept educational control closer to the people. If decentralization is to be tried as a remedy for the failures of urban education, these political structures and constituencies will need to be created anew.[74]

Now, as then, conflicts of value in the politics and operation of schools reflect deep cleavages in the aims of Americans as well as differing perceptions of means. But in some respects, the myth that the school was "above politics" served not only schoolmen but the children also. If schools had taught only the narrow and parochial set of beliefs and values dictated by their immediate patrons and parents, they might have perpetuated antagonistic subcultures and they might have circumscribed the choices available to the young in careers, life-styles, and convictions. One need only examine Mayor Thompson's campaigns against "pro-British" textbooks in Chicago or the state anti-evolution laws to see the threat to freedom of learning implicit when politics did invade the specific content of schooling.[75] The school, with all its shortcomings, served to bridge the constraints of the private world of family, church, and clan across to the broader public world in which citizens spent an increasing part of their time. And there is considerable evidence that most professionals have been more interested than most laymen in innovative school programs in human relations, in new areas of knowledge, and in new methods of teaching. Hence some autonomy for the "expert" seems more than a "self-serving" device.[76]

If the imperatives which began this essay have a different meaning today in educational reform, it is in part because substantial segments of this society no longer believe in centralism as an effective response to human needs, no longer trust in an enlightened paternalism of elites, no longer accept the justice of the distribution of power along existing racial and class lines, and no longer think that technological change implies progress. To whom, and for what purposes, the schools should be accountable today remains the sharpest issue.

NOTES

1. John D. Philbrick, *City School Systems in the United States* (U. S. Bureau of Education, Circular of Information No. 1. 1885; Washington: U. S. Government Printing Office, 1885), p. 19.

2. Andrew S. Draper, "Plans of Organization for School Purposes in Large Cities," *Educational Review,* VII (June, 1893), 1. For an insightful study of Draper's thought and work, see Ronald M. Johnson, "Captain of Education: An Intellectual Biography of Andrew S. Draper, 1848–1913" (Ph.D. Dissertation, University of Illinois, 1970).

3. Edward C. Eliot, "A Nonpartisan School Law," National Educational Association (hereafter cited as NEA), *Addresses and Proceedings,* 1905, p. 229.

4. Ellwood P. Cubberley, *Changing Conceptions of Education* (Boston: Houghton Mifflin Company, 1909), pp. 56–57.

5. Two representative NEA committee reports advancing such ideas are the following: Committee on City School Systems, "School Superintendence in Cities," *NEA Proceedings and Addresses,* 1890, pp. 309–17; Committee of Fifteen, "Report of the Sub-Committee on the Organization of City School Systems," *Educational Review,* IX (March, 1895), 304–22. Of course there were some observers who warned against this centralization of power. Frank Wiley, secretary to the St. Louis superintendent of schools, said that some "students of administrative problems feel that a number of evil consequences will inevitably come from placing the control of our schools in the hands of a body of specialized administrators and thus excluding the people from that participation which they have formerly enjoyed. In such a system they see the growth of a bureaucracy with all of its attendant evils, such as the continental countries of Europe have had to contend with. In the provision for uniformity of standards and attainments they see ultimately a suppression of that local initiative to which so much of our educational advance must be ascribed." ["The Layman in School Administration," *Teachers College Record,* XI (November, 1910), 310]. The best general account of the centralization movement is by Joseph M. Cronin, "The Board of Education in the 'Great Cities,' 1890–1964," (Ed.D. dissertation, Stanford University, 1965).

6. L. H. Jones, "The Politician and the Public School: Indianapolis and Cleveland," *Atlantic Monthly,* LXXVII (June, 1896), 810; G. Stanley Hall, "The Case of the Public Schools: The Witness of the Teachers," *Atlantic Monthly,* LXXVII (March, 1896), 402–13; Ellwood P. Cubberley, "The School Situation in San Francisco," *Educational Review,* XXI (April, 1901), 368–69.

7. One of the most openly corrupt cities was Philadelphia—see Adele M. Shaw, "The Public Schools of a Boss-Ridden City," *World's Work,* VII (Feb. 1904), 4460–64; in his survey of city schools—*The Public School System of the United States* (New York: Century, 1893)—Joseph M. Rice found that urban politicians commonly treated the schools as part of the patronage system.

8. Draper, "Plans of Organization," p. 7; Philbrick, *City School Systems,* pp. 15–19.

9. Thomas M. Gilland, *The Origins and Development of the Powers and Duties of the City-School Superintendent* (Chicago: University of Chicago Press, 1935), ch. 6.

10. Theodore Reller, *The Development of the City Superintendency of Schools in the United States* (Philadelphia: Published by the author, 1935), ch. 8.

11. Scott Nearing, "The Workings of a Large Board of Education," *Educational Review,* XXXVIII (June, 1909), 44–46.

12. S. A. Wetmore, "Boston School Administration," *Educational Review,* XIV (September, 1897), 107.

13. *Ibid.,* 112.

14. B. A. Hinsdale, "The American School Superintendent," *Educational Review* V (January, 1894), 50.

15. Charles W. Eliot, "Undesirable and Desirable Uniformity in Schools," *NEA Addresses and Proceedings,* 1893, p. 82; Paul Hanus, in survey Committee on School Inquiry, Board of Estimate and Apportionment, City of New York, *Report* (New York: City of New York, 1911–13), I, p. 183.

16. Robert Wiebe, "The Social Functions of Public Education," *American Quarterly,* XXI (Summer, 1969), 150. For studies of the growth of school bureaucracies in the 19th century, see Michael Katz, "The Emergence of Bureaucracy in Urban Education: The Boston Case, 1850–1884," *History of Education Quarterly,* VIII (Summer and Fall, 1968), 155–88, 319–57; David Tyack, "Bureaucracy and the Common School: The Example of Portland, Oregon, 1851–1913," *American Quarterly,* XIX (Fall, 1967), 475–98. My interpretation here represents a slight revision of the views Michael Katz and I expressed in these articles. I now see less continuity in "bureaucracy" and in the politics of urban schools from the middle 19th century to the present.

17. For a recent survey on bureaucracy in schools, see James G. Anderson, *Bureaucracy in Education* (Baltimore: Johns Hopkins Press, 1968).

18. Andrew S. Draper, *The Crucial Test of the Public School System* (Urbana, Ill.: Published by the author, 1898), pp. 4–5.

19. *Cf.* Roy Lubove's discussion of "the Progressive infatuation with the expert" in "The Twentieth Century City: The Progressive as Municipal Reformer," *Mid-America,* XLI (October, 1959), 195–209.

20. Charles W. Eliot, "Educational Reform and the Social Order," *The School Review,* XVII (April, 1909), 217–20.

21. Harvey Hubbert, "What Kind of Centralization, If Any, Will Strengthen Our Local School System?" *NEA Addresses and Proceedings,* 1898, pp. 986–88.

22. David Ricker reported that in Chicago the militant teachers opposed centralization as a notion advanced by Eastern university men: "The School Teacher Unionized," *Educational Review,* XXX (November, 1905), 348.

23. Charles W. Eliot, "School Board Reform," *School Board Journal* XXXIX (July, 1909), 3.

24. Most interpreters of "progressive education" have focused on the philosophical-psychological-individualistic stream of the "new education" rather than looking at the sophisticated sociological strategies of the "administrative progressives" like Cubberley. In his provocative and useful book *Education and the Cult of Efficiency* (Chicago: University of Chicago Press, 1962), Raymond Callahan does call attention to the work of the institution-builders, but his preoccupation with the single notion of business efficiency tends to obscure other elements of their strategy. In *Education and*

the New America (New York: Vintage, 1962), Solon T. Kimball and James E. McClellan offer fascinating leads for historians interested in tracing the genesis and impact of a non-child-centered "progressivism." Samuel Hays and Robert Wiebe suggest insightful ways to link educational and political-social history in the Progressive period in the following essays: Hays, "The Politics of Reform in Municipal Government in the Progressive Era," *Pacific Northwest Quarterly*, LV (October, 1964), 157–69; Wiebe, "Social Functions." "But educational historians might do well to follow the lead of Peter F. Filene in political history and question the very existence of a coherent "Progressive movement"—"An Obituary for 'The Progressive Movement,' " *American Quarterly*, XXII (Spring, 1970), 20–34.

25. See, for example, the correspondence between Mayor William Gaynor of New York and President Nicholas Murray Butler of Columbia on the subject of a paid board of education: *Educational Review*, XLII (September, 1911), 204–10.

26. Editorial by Butler, *Educational Review*, XII (September, 1896), 201; for a sample of Andrews' cast of mind, see "The Public School System of Chicago," *Education*, XX (December, 1899; January, 1900), 201–07, 264–69.

27. David C. Hammack, "The Centralization of New York City's Public School System, 1896: A Social Analysis of a Decision" (M.A. Dissertation, Columbia University, 1969), ch. 1.

28. A. Lawrence Lowell, "The Professional and the Non-professional Bodies in Our School System, and the Proper Function of Each," *NEA Addresses and Proceedings*, 1895, pp. 999–1004; George A. O. Ernst, "The Movement for School Reform in Boston," *Educational Review*, XXVIII (December, 1904), 438–40.

29. *Report of the Educational Commission of the City of Chicago* (Chicago: Lakeside Press, 1899).

30. Anon., "Why Superintendents Lose Their Jobs," *American School Board Journal*, LII (May, 1916), 18–19.

31. While superintendents often became "professional gypsies," going from city to city, deeply rooted in none, gaining a sense of identity and direction from their professional reference groups, there were, of course, many others who were "local" in orientation rather than cosmopolitan. For an excellent study of one relatively provincial system, see Peter Schrag, *Village School Downtown* (Boston: Beacon Press, 1967).

32. Sol Cohen, *Progressives and Urban School Reform* (New York: Bureau of Publications, Teachers College, 1964), ch. 2; Hammack, "Centralization," p. 56, ch. 2; Stephen Olin, "Public School Reform in New York," *Educational Review*, VIII (June, 1894), 1–6. In his work as publicist, N. M. Butler tried to make it appear that there was a mass movement against the decentralized system, but Cohen and Hammack cast doubt on this.

33. William Issel, "Modernization in Philadelphia School Reform, 1882–1905," *Pennsylvania Magazine of History and Biography*, XCIV (July 1970), 358–83.

34. Elinor M. Gersman, "Progressive Reform of the St. Louis School Board, 1897," *History of Education Quarterly*, X (Spring, 1970), 8, 15, and Table 1 of original MS of published essay.

35. Draper, "Plan of Organization," 9–10.

36. M. C. Bettinger, "Twenty-five Years in the Schools of Los Angeles," Historical Society of California, *Publications*, VIII (1910), 70–71; *cf.* pattern in Pittsburgh cited by Hays, "Politics of Reform," 161–63.

37. George Strayer, "The Baltimore School Situation," *Educational Review*, XLII (November, 1911), 328.

38. Scott Nearing, "Who's Who in Our Boards of Education?" *School and Society*, V (January 20, 1917), 89–90.

39. George Struble, "A Study of School Board Personnel," *American School Board Journal*, LXV (October, 1922), 48–49, 137–38; George Counts, *The Social Composition of Boards of Education: A Study in the Social Control of Public Education* (Chicago: University of Chicago Press, 1927). For some cautions in the use of such data see W. W. Charters, Jr., "Social Class Analysis and the Control of Public Education," *Harvard Educational Review*, XXIII (Fall, 1953), 268–83.

40. William T. Harris, "City School Supervision," *Educational Review*, III (February, 1892), 168–69; as an illustration of how completely Harris's assumptions had been accepted, see Cubberley, *Public School Administration*, 109–15.

41. Arthur H. Chamberlain, "The Growth and Enlargement of the Power of the City School Superintendent," University of California, *Publications*, III (May 15, 1913), 401; also see William S. Mack, "The Relation of a Board to Its Superintendent," *NEA Addresses and Proceedings*, 1896, pp. 980–87.

42. Cubberley, *Public School Administration*, p. 92, footnote 1.

43. Cronin, "Board of Education," ch. 4–5, provides the most complete analysis of these changes; see also: Frank Rollins, "School Administration in Municipal Government" (Ph.D. dissertation, Columbia University, New York, 1902), pp. 24–31 for useful statistical charts; Cubberley, *Public School Administration*, ch. VIII; Duane Mowry, "The Milwaukee School System," *Educational Review*, XX (September, 1900), 141–51; Arthur B. Moelman, *Public Education in Detroit* (Bloomington, Ill.: Public School Publishing Company, 1925), pp. 173–80.

44. Hays, "Politics of Reform," 163.

45. *Report of Educational Commission of Chicago*. pp. 174–75, 178; *cf.* the remark of Superintendent William Maxwell of New York ("Good and Bad in New York Schools," *Educational Review*, XLVII [January, 1914], 77) that "the first duty of every child in every school is to obey."

46. On the Chicago Teachers Federation, see the excellent study Robert Reid, "The Professionalization of Public School Teachers: The Chicago Experience" (Ph.D. Dissertation, Northwestern University, 1968), p. 130 on Butler's visit. Also see Wilbur S. Jackman, "The School Problem in Chicago," *Elementary School Teacher*, VII (February, 1907), 361–67.

47. New York, Committee on Inquiry, *Report*, p. 56.

48. Selma Berrol, "The Schools of New York in Transition, 1898–1914," *The Urban Review*, I (December, 1966), 15–20.

49. In "Education in the Turn-of-the-Century School," *Urban Education*, I (Spring, 1969), 169–82, Dana F. White discusses the quest for "social sanitation" through education; David K. Cohen and Marvin Lazerson have treated some of the questions listed above in their unpublished paper delivered at the 1970 AERA conference, "Education and the Industrial Order"; also see the articles on urban education by Daniel Calhoun, David Cohen, Sol Cohen, Michael Katz, Neill Sutherland, and David Tyack in *History of Education Quarterly*, IX (Fall, 1969).

50. W. W. Charters, Jr., "Social Class Analysis"; and his "Research on School Board Personnel: Critique and Prospectus," *Journal of Educational Research*, XLVII (January, 1954), 321–35.

51. Alexander Proudfoot, "A Study of the Socio-Economic Status of School Board Members in Alberta as Related to their Attitudes toward Certain Common Problems Confronting School Boards" (Ed.D. Dissertation, University of Oregon, 1962).

52. For a perceptive discussion of school politics as a "closed system" see Lawrence Iannaccone, *Politics in Education* (New York: Center for Applied Research in Education, 1967). H. Thomas James and the staff of the school board studies project compiled an excellent "School Board Bibliography" (mimeographed, School of Education, Stanford University).

53. Gersman, "St. Louis," 16–18.

54. Reid, "Chicago," 125–27.

55. Upton Sinclair, *The Goslings* (Pasadena, Cal.: the Author, 1922); George Counts, *School and Society in Chicago* (New York: Harcourt, Brace & Company, 1928), esp. ch. 9.

56. William H. Maxwell, "On a Certain Arrogance in Educational Theorists," *Educational Review*, XLVII (January–May, 1914), 175–76.

57. Cubberley, *Changing Conceptions;* for a survey of the 20th-century literature on the academic achievement of immigrant children, see David K. Cohen, "Immigrants and the Schools," *Review of Educational Research*, XL (February, 1970), 13–28.

58. Educational Commission of Chicago, *Report*, p. 175.

59. Sol Cohen, "The Industrial Education Movement, 1906–17," *American Quarterly*, XX (Spring, 1968), 95–110; Robert Dreeben, *On What Is Learned in School* (Reading, Mass.: Addison-Wesley, 1968).

60. Jacques Ellul, *The Technological Society* (John Wilkinson, trans., New York: Vintage Books, 1964), esp. ch. 5; for contrasting radical interpretations, see James Weinstein, *The Corporate Ideal in the Liberal State*, 1900–1918 (Boston: Beacon Press, 1968) and Gabriel Kolko, *The Triumph of Conservatism: A Reinterpretation of American History*, 1900–1916 (New York: The Free Press, 1963).

61. Reid, "Chicago"; Edward C. Eliot, "School Administration: The St. Louis Method," *Educational Review*, XXVI (December, 1903), 475; Margaret Haley, "Why Teachers Organize," *NEA Addresses and Proceedings*, 1904, 146–52.

62. Hammack, "Centralization," ch. 3.

63. Strayer, "Baltimore."

64. Samuel Gompers, "Teachers' Right to Organize," *American Federationist*, XXI (December, 1914), 1083–84.

65. Hammack, "Centralization," 124; Reid, "Professionalization," 86–87; N. M. Butler, editorial on New York Schools in *Educational Review*, XII (September, 1896), 196–205; Gersman, "Progressive Reform" 8–10.

66. Hammack, "Centralization," 105–8; Gersman, MS draft of "Progressive Reform," 10–15.

67. Hammack, "Centralization," 114, *cf.* Ernst, "Boston," 434.

68. Strayer, "Baltimore," 338–41.

69. Theodore J. Lowi, *At the Pleasure of the Mayor: Patronage and Politics in New York City*, 1898–1958 (Glencoe, Ill.: Free Press, 1964), 29–39; Counts, Chicago.

70. For illuminating statistics on the percentages of first and second generation immigrant teachers in urban schools in 1908, see Immigration Commission, *Abstracts of Reports* (Senate Document No. 747, 61st Congress, 3d session, Washington, D. C.: U. S. Government Printing Office, 1911), II, 48–62. Schrag, Village School; Berrol, "Transition." I am indebted to my colleague H. Thomas James for the designation "patrinomial."

71. Wallace Sayre, "Additional Observations on the Study of Administration," *Teachers College Record*, LX (October, 1958), 75; in an unpublished manuscript, Robert Hess and Michael Kirst of Stanford University have investigated the connection between the characteristic political posture of teachers and the nature of political socialization within the classroom.

72. Iannaccone, *Politics*.

73. David Rogers, *110 Livingston Street: Politics and Bureaucracy in the New York City School System* (New York: Random House, 1968); Marilyn Gittell, *Participants and Participation* (New York: Center for Urban Education, 1967).

74. On the political ramifications of decentralization, see Henry Levin, ed., *Community Control of Schools* (Washington, D. C.: The Brookings Institution, 1969); Joe L. Rempson, "Community Control of Local School Boards," *Teachers College Record*, LXVIII (April, 1967), 572–75.

75. Walter Lippmann, *American Inquisitors* (New York, 1928).

76. I am especially indebted to Joseph Cronin and Lawrence Veysey for suggestions on this point, as well as to Harold W. Pfautz' and Leonard J. Fein's essays in Levin, ed., *Community Control*, pp. 13–39, 76–99.

24. Educational Stratification and Cultural Hegemony in Peru*

ROLLAND G. PAULSTON

One of the most durable educational beliefs, especially among North Americans, is that free universal public education is one of the fastest routes to increased social mobility, to cultural integration, to modernization, and to nationhood. This article examines some of the consequences of attempts to develop universal schooling in Peru, an Andean country where over half of the population is Indian or recently Indian, and where colonial social patterns and power relationships are perhaps as enduring as in any South American country. Peru, unlike Mexico and Bolivia, has not experienced a social revolution. The Indian remains totally outside the national Hispanic culture and can become a Peruvian citizen only if he rejects his indigenous culture and enters into a long apprenticeship of learning to be a *cholo* (or partially Westernized Indian). Perhaps after a generation or two, his children will be accepted as mestizos. Then it will be their turn to abuse and deprecate the "loathsome Indian," and complain about the "pushy, upstart cholos aping their betters."

In large measure, because of Peru's enduring colonial patterns on the one hand and rapid, if highly uneven, modernization on the other, many social scientists have examined attempts by the 2-class superordinate Hispanicized minority (the mestizos and *blancos*) to modernize while at the same time trying to perpetuate their dominance of the non-Hispanicized indigenous and cholo majority. This article seeks to build upon and add to this body of research by examining how the recent nationwide provision of universal primary and secondary education in Peru has come to function as an additional mechanism in part supporting social disintegration while maintaining the privileged status of the superordinate groups.[1]

During the 3 centuries of colonial rule, education in the viceroyalty of Peru was mostly private and for the small creole class. With independence from Spain, a public educational system of inferior quality was created during the nineteenth century to serve the educational demands of the expanding mestizo class. In the decades following World War II, the public school system has, with considerable U.S. encouragement and assistance, been extended and structurally differentiated to include children from the 2 lowest sociocultural groups, the cholos and the Indians, who collectively comprise over 75 percent of the total population (see table 1).

If we are to understand properly how formal schooling serves to help maintain the highly hierarchical Peruvian social system and concurrently seeks to acculturate subordinate groups, it will be necessary first to review a number of relevant research studies that pertain to the political, economic, and sociocultural dimensions of internal dominance. Then, against this backdrop, an exploratory stratification model will be presented to describe educational functions vis-à-vis social and cultural organization and to suggest, at least in part, why the attainment of substantive qualitative change in Peru's rapidly expanding schools, both at the primary and secondary levels, is an unrealistic goal under existing conditions of cultural conflict, educational stratification, and sweeping demographic change.

*An earlier draft of this topic was presented at the Interdisciplinary Conference on Power, Policy, and Education: Studies in Development, held at the State University of New York at Albany, on 16 November 1968. Fieldwork for this study took place in Peru during 1966–68 when the author served as Advisor in Educational Research and Planning to the Peruvian Ministry of Education as a member of the Teachers College, Columbia University, USAID Contract Team. All views, interpretations, conclusions, and recommendations in this article are those of the author and not necessarily those of the supporting and cooperating organizations.

From *Journal of Developing Areas* 5 (April 1971): 401–415. Reprinted by permission.

Table 1. Distribution of Income by Major Social Groups in 1963

Social group	Percentage of total population	Percentage of total national income received
Blancos: large landowners, industrialists, capitalists, some professionals	0.1	19.9
Mestizos: bureaucrats, businessmen, professionals and subprofessionals, employees, skilled workers, military officers	20.4	53.0
Cholos: unskilled workers, peddlers, domestics, drivers, clerks, enlisted men	22.8	14.2
Indians: mountain-dwelling farmers, herders, hacienda laborers, army draftees	56.7	12.9

Source: Edgardo Seoana, *Surcos de Paz* (Lima, 1963), p. 33. It should be noted that rapid demographic and social changes are occurring, with heavy Indian migration to urban areas and cholo return migration. Relatively and absolutely, Indian population is shrinking as the cholo group grows proportionately. The blanco and mestizo groups are much more resistant to mobility and tend to maintain their respective size.

MECHANISMS OF INTERNAL DOMINATION AND COLONIZATION

Superordinate political domination has been firmly maintained since the early 1500s when Spaniards conquered and Hispanicized the narrow strip of coastal Peru and subjugated the Andean highlands where the subordinate indigenous population remains concentrated in the cold, windswept *mancha india* ("Indian heartland") with its capital at Cuzco. Independence and the growth of a large mestizo class only served to heighten the dependence and exploitation of the subordinate groups. Power formerly held by Spain and administered by the colonial bureaucracies was usurped by the minuscule creole landowning elite and their mestizo administrators, and coastal Peru rapidly assumed the metropolitan functions previously held by Spain. Lima, the seat of the civil, religious, commercial, and military bureaucracies during the colonial period, has continued to maintain these functions and in nearly every sphere dominates the country. With intensified industrialization, most of which is located in and about Lima, and with heavy internal migration, mostly to Lima, the capital is continuously growing in both relative and absolute size, power, and importance.

This entrenched pattern of internal colonization, with Lima dominating the coastal region which in turn dominates the highland area, is reflected in the highlands where mestizo towns socially, economically, and politically control the frequently impoverished surrounding rural areas. Stavenhagen has pointed out that in Latin America, underdeveloped regions within a country perform the role of internal colonies. Local populations do not control their economic life, and most income is drained off with little being returned for local development. Not only is capital transferred from the periphery to the metropolis, but the fortunes of the periphery—be it a nation, a region, or a sector—are determined almost exclusively by, and to the advantage of, the metropolis. Thus, instead of stating the problem in terms of cultural dualism (i.e., Hispanic vs. indigenous), it might be more accurate to speak of internal colonialism.[2] Something of the relative advantage maintained by the creole coast is indicated by the following percentages for the coast and highlands respectively: national population (47, 46), national income (67, 24), urban (69, 29), literacy of those over 15 years of age (79, 47), and national electorate (69, 26).[3] Data for Peru's third region, the tropical *selva,* is not included, although this area is clearly another region dominated by the superordinate Hispanic minority on the coast.

As nonspeakers of Spanish, over 80 percent of the adult Indian population were, before the 1968 military coup, excluded from participation in the national political system and had no true representation. Indians were, however, counted when apportioning representatives, mostly mestizos, to Congress in Lima. With some 78 percent of the total rural population illiterate, this electoral mechanism discriminated markedly against the total peasant population in all regions. Colter, for example, found a positive rank correlation of 0.83 between the economically active population in agriculture and the illiterate population, and a negative correlation of 0.87 between the agricultural labor population, and the national electorate population.[4]

Although Peruvian social organization is undergoing rapid change that is only partially and imperfectly understood, it has most frequently been described as dualistic with the blancos and the mestizos comprising the upper and middle strata of the upper level. The lower level is also composed of 2 distinct groups: the Indians, a marginal and "floating" group cut off from the institutions and resources of the national society, and the cholos, a rapidly growing class.[5] Members of this transitional group have, to various degrees, rejected the Indian subculture and are moving by way of assimilation toward the mestizo class, which carries the *criollo* national culture.[6] Using the metropolitan-colonial analogy, it would seem to be more accurate to view Peru as a society integrated in such a way as to perpetuate the relative inferiority of the indigenous culture vis-à-vis the Hispanic culture and of the rural areas vis-à-vis the urban centers.

It will not be possible within the limits of this article to analyze in detail all of the many control mechanisms used until recently to maintain the mestizo-Indian relationship. Suffice it to say that they included the currently much weakened hacienda with its semifeudal *colonato* system (somewhat akin to sharecropping in the United States), the privatization of power by mestizo families and individuals (especially in the Sierra), the neutralization of integrated sectors of the national society through segmental incorporation (as has often occurred in the "aristocratization" of labor unions), and the perpetuation of an "ideal value" construct in education and in the mass media that channels aspirations of the masses toward the usually unattainable life styles exhibited by the higher classes.[7]

The distribution of income in Peru, as reported in 1963 (see table 1), clearly reflects the consequences of internal colonization and the economic advantages of the superordinate group. Not unnaturally, members of this group, having once inherited or won their rewards, use their vastly superior power, prestige, and wealth to widen still further the existing inequalities in their favor.[8]

More recent data confirms the highly skewed distribution of wealth and income. A 1965 report from the National Planning Institute states that 60 percent of all disposable income goes to the top 10 percent of the population. Moreover, 35 percent of all income goes to a mere 8,760 spending units, or some 0.25 percent of the Peruvian population.[9] In brief, the range of wealth and income distribution in Peru is extreme. It is more unequal than in any other underdeveloped country for which comparative data is available.[10]

In sum, using a wide variety of control mechanisms, the superordinate group has both consciously and otherwise successfully maintained their power, prestige, and dominance.

Because of their knowledge of the Spanish language, their Hispanic culture and their education, and through restriction of these resources to Indian and cholo groups, the mestizos—along with the smaller, foreign-oriented *blanco* elite—are able to control economic, political, judicial, repressive, and cultural resources: they are the representa-

Table 2. Peruvian Sociocultural and Educational Stratification

| | General Attributes | | | | | |
Subculture	Location in social hierarchy	Location	Languages spoken	Occupation	Schools usually attended	Usual length of schooling
Blanco: entrance highly restricted, using socio-economic, cultural, and genetic criteria	Upper	Urban (Lima and abroad)	Spanish and other European	Owners	Elite private schools (Lima and abroad)	University-level study in Lima and abroad
Mestizo: access open but contested, using largely cultural criteria	Middle	Urban (provincial and Lima)	Mostly Spanish	Managers, professionals, bureaucrats, and skilled workers	Lesser private schools and better public schools in larger cities	High school and study at university level in national schools in Lima or in provincial cities
Cholo: acculturation encouraged and rewarded in urban settings, restricted in rural	Lower	Urban and rural, and urban-rural (migratory)	Indigenous (Quechua or Aymara) and Spanish	Unskilled workers, menials, vendors, soldiers, and domestics	Public schools	Primary and some secondary in larger cities
Indian: social mobility blocked	Marginal	Rural-indigenous communities or haciendas	Indigenous (Quechua or Aymara) and males some Spanish	Agricultural laborers, small farmers, and herders	Nuclear (Indian schools of the Sierra) and bilingual "jungle" schools	Males: several years of primary or unschooled; females: largely unschooled

tives and senators, the hacienda owners or administrators, the departmental prefects, subprefects and governors: they are also the judges and teachers dominating all authority spheres. . . . [11]

We should take note, however, that with rapid if uneven change in Peru, traditional control mechanisms, although still operative, are becoming less effective. Industrialization, land reform, improved communications and transportation, and the cholofication process are all modifying traditional relationships between social groups, and new patterns are beginning to emerge. Formal education plays 2 important roles in this regard: one is its integrative function as a socializing agent; the second is its disintegrative function. The remainder of this paper will be devoted to this second function, especially with regard to schooling's lack of relevance to developmental values.

EDUCATIONAL CONSEQUENCES OF SOCIOCULTURAL STRATIFICATION

Mestizo control of the public education system might best be likened to part of a total-dominance model where, following differentiation, each new social stratum has historically come to be linked with a distinct educational subsystem. These subsystems are closely tied to each of the 4 social groups: the blancos, the mestizos, the cholos, and the Indians. Table 2 presents a social and educational stratification model that also includes typical attributes of members in each sociocultural stratum.

This model, it should be noted, has limitations. It is largely hypothetical and has yet to be empirically tested. It is intended solely as an exploratory device to further description, explanation, and prediction at a national level, and to suggest possible fruitful lines for further research. All social sectors do not fit neatly into the model, nor was this my intent. Mestizo farmers found largely in the northern highlands and on the coast are a case in point.[12] The near absence of blanco and Indian groups in north-central Peru is another limitation. Moreover, with growing pockets of industrialization and modernization, the Peruvian social structure—especially at the lower levels—is undergoing marked if exceedingly uneven change.

The criteria used for social classification, as well as the classes themselves, are therefore slowly changing. These criteria, moreover, have always varied considerably in different regions, and neither social classes nor subcultures can be defined with precision.

My objective here is to suggest that the social class-linked educational structure reflects and helps to perpetuate the hierarchical social system and, in so doing, is influential in obstructing educational rationalization and development.[13] This is as true for the seemingly democratic public primary schools as for the highly selective and expensive elite private primary schools. Although there is some overlap because of the limited upward and downward social mobility, the class-linked school subsystems are in all cases attended by the vast majority of school-aged children in each social stratum. (The degree to which Peruvian adults and school children are aware of the rewards and punishments implicit in the model and the extent to which such understanding influences their actions and perceptions will be investigated at a later date.)

Indian children did not begin attending schools, aside from a few scattered religious efforts, in appreciable numbers until after World War II when the nuclear schools of the Sierra and the bilingual "jungle" schools were begun and supported substantially by monetary, skill, and motivation inputs from North American government agencies (ICA, AID, etc.) and non-Peruvian missionary groups (Summer Institute of Linguistics, etc.). Although increasing numbers of Indians now attend these schools, most students drop out after a year or two and few complete primary school.

Obstacles to improving Indian education are overwhelming. Schools are few, isolated, and impoverished; moreover, rural education usually lacks supporting institutions to give it meaning. It is, in addition, under the direct supervision of the highly inefficient and political Ministry of Education in Lima.[14] Other equally debilitative factors have been: (1) the gradual withdrawal of USAID support and the failure of Peruvians to assume additional responsibilities; (2) the desperate poverty, the occasional starvation, and the need for child labor in rural areas of the Sierra; (3) the use of Spanish as the exclusive language of instruction, even in non-Spanish speaking areas; and (4) a totally irrelevant national curriculum based on an idealized version of coastal urban high culture. All these factors restrict and limit schooling for most Indian children to a maximum of a few years at best.[15] Moreover, for an Indian to attend school is to begin the rejection of his culture, his community, his family, his friends. Many Indian parents, especially in the southern Sierra, cling persistently to what they commonly refer to as the *patria chica,* or Indian national community, and seek to prevent the acculturation of their children by avoiding schools in particular and mestizos in general. Acculturation is not altogether voluntary, however. There is compulsory military service in Peru, supposedly for all, but mostly for Indians, which has been very effective in drafting Indian boys and teaching them in a tightly controlled situation to be ashamed of indigenous culture and, thus, to reject it.[16]

Cholos, in contrast, avidly seek public schooling, preferably of the humanistic type, and the explosive expansion of public education during the recently deposed government of Fernando Belaunde (1963–68) is in large part a direct consequence of increased cholo and Indian migration to the coast and to the cities of the Sierra.[17] Both the absence and provision of schooling in the Sierra has stimulated migration to the urban areas where most public schooling is located. In much of the Sierra those seeking schooling could only find it in urban, or mestizo, settings. Where schools for Indians have been established, the educational experience, as is true of military service, socializes the participants and greatly facilitates their recruitment into the national economy and political culture.[18]

That internal migration both from rural to urban areas and from urban slums to shantytowns (*barriadas*) has been primarily a phenomenon of youth migration can be seen in the following data. Of Lima's 1970 population of some 2,500,000 inhabitants, over one-third (some 800,000) live in shantytowns, now euphemistically called *pueblos jovenes* by decree of the Revolutionary Junta. Shantytown dwellers are indeed young; 75 percent are under 25 years of age, while 50 percent are less than 15 years old.[19]

Public education is now truly mass education and not as formerly almost exclusively for the superordinate groups. Nearly 80 percent of all children now register for the first year of school (*transición*). Almost one-half do not return the following year, however, and only about one-third complete the sixth and final year of primary schooling.[20]

With the ever larger wave of cholos enrolling in urban public schools formerly occupied by mestizos, this latter group has increasingly placed its children in the many new and usually inferior private schools that have sprung up in all of the larger urban centers. Mestizo parents frequently make great financial sacrifices to place their children in private schools attended by other mestizos, even though many will acknowledge that free public primary and secondary schools, especially in the larger urban centers, occasionally offer better instruction and facilities.

Children of the blanco upper class usually attend the several dozen highly selective and expensive private schools in Greater Lima operated for the most part by foreign nationals and religious orders, or they study abroad. Not surprisingly, with the universalization of public schooling, the number of private schools has skyrocketed. These institutions in 1968 enrolled about 10 percent of all primary students, over 28 percent of all secondary students, and approximately 35 percent of all normal school pupils.[21]

Although Peru's educational hierarchy differs only in degree from those found in many plural societies where subcultures are organized into superordinate and subordinate groups, there is one characteristic of most Latin American societies that is crucial for understanding the resistance to qualitative change at the subsystem level, especially in the critical sector of public education.[22] That characteristic is race (*raza*), and it is largely defined in social and cultural terms. An Indian could conceivably be accepted as a blanco if he had the requisite economic means and background of European culture. As nearly all Indians and cholos, and most mestizos (and even many blancos) are predominantly Amerindian racially, there is a great resistance among members of these groups (or "social races") to behave in a manner that might lead to identifying them with the Indian culture or with the growing number of culturally mobile ex-Indians who have opted for cholofication.[23]

With open, if restricted, channels for upward social and cultural mobility, there is a strong tendency for the successfully mobile at all levels to reject their subculture of origin and to identify with the cultural behavior and values of the next higher stratum.[24] It may well be that much of the rigidity and resistance to educational planning and to qualitative change in the national education system stems from this fact, that each group in large measure draws its teachers and administrators from the next higher subculture in the hierarchy, i.e., each social level tends to control the next lower educational subsystem.[25] Thus, the elite private schools are dominated by the next higher group in the social hierarchy, the Europeans and North Americans. Downwardly mobile blancos operate, for financial reasons, the lesser private schools for aspiring mestizo children whom they commonly regard as parvenu or *huachafo*. Mestizos, for the most part, staff and operate the public schools attended by cholo children. Their mobility aspirations are frequently openly derided by the members of the mestizo bureaucracy which tightly controls the highly centralized, if poorly coordinated, public school system. And because mestizo teachers seek to avoid "contaminating" contacts with Indians, whom they commonly describe as "the animal most similar to man," teachers in the Indian schools of the Sierra and Selva (or forest) are most frequently the lowliest of public school teachers, i.e., cholos who seek to hide their recent "evolution" from indigenous to Hispanic culture.[26]

Dysfunctional consequences of this control pattern are not difficult to find. Teachers and administrators tend to place their children in one class-linked educational system and to work with children in schools of the next lower level. Needless to say, within this type of relationship, teachers et al. are usually more concerned with matters of personal gain than with improved instruction and student achievement.[27] The educational bureaucracy that operates the public schools, for example, receives in wages over 95 percent of the educational budget that annually totals nearly one-third of the national budget.[28] Moreover, a considerable part of the remaining 5 percent is paid to landlords who rent private homes and buildings to the Ministry of Education for use as classrooms. More than one-third of all public school classes are held in rented facilities, many of which are owned by relatives of school administrators, and many of which are in decrepit and unsanitary conditions. Textbooks and school uniforms must be purchased by all students—many of whom come from families living at or near the starvation level—while instructional materials, supplies, audiovisual aids, and the like, are virtually nonexistent in public schools and found only in the better private schools.

Aspects of the educational process associated with the superordinate groups (i.e., humanistic studies, gentlemanly leisure, intellectual speculation, and "beautiful words") are seen as rewarding; while aspects associated with the subordinate groups (i.e., agricultural and vocational studies, rural situations, practicality, and physical work) are commonly perceived as more or less threatening and undesirable. The failure of periodic attempts to plan and reform public education to meet better the manpower needs in the agricultural, technical, and scientific sectors can largely be explained by considerations of cultural self-identification. Most students study in agricultural and technical schools only because they are unable, for one reason or another, to enter the academic secondary stream. William F. Whyte and others have found that the majority of technical students reject the idea of future technical employment and instead seek university entrance for professional studies.

Due to the inability of many primary graduates to get into the preferred secondary academic school, the technical school becomes an alternative for university preparation. As a result, many technical-school students will not accept jobs and go to work. They try to go to the university; some succeed, but most are frustrated and unemployed.[29]

Schools are generally not maintained, classes are usually grossly overcrowded, and more than half of all students do not have proper school desks. In sum, the Peruvian public school student is the neglected man in the educational system. His well-being, growth, and development are consistently subordinated to the vested interests of the mestizo teachers and administrators who seek his acculturation and indoctrination with the least possible expenditure directly benefiting the student population. Despite an impressive expenditure of nearly 6 percent of the G.N.P. on formal education, benefits to students are declining.[30]

Rote learning of an inflexible nationwide curriculum stresses the cultural superiority of the superordinate groups, respect for authority, and the legitimacy of the existing institutions (the military, the church, the civil bureaucracy). Both the content of the curriculum and the thought-inhibiting instructional methods help to perpetuate the practice of internal colonization used by the superordinate groups to help maintain their privileged positions.[31]

Primary schooling, aside from its "cooling down" and "selecting out" functions, also serves as a first hurdle in the route to the university and the professions where, for the successful few, mestizo status is assured. In December 1968, 53,586 students graduated from the fifth year of secondary school; of these, some 46,000 took university entrance examinations but only some 5,000 candidates, less than 10 percent, secured admission.[32] Thus, schooling both facilitates limited upward mobility, reinforces existing class divisions, and provides a means by which the masses of cholo children are taught an idealized version of the rewards of national Hispanic culture. Even the vast majority of cholo students who drop out learn the rudiments of literacy and arithmetic, the inferiority of their cholo status and Indian origins, and the superiority of the superordinate groups who enjoy rewards "appropriate" to their high status. Public school children are, in short, taught "their place."[33]

The need for Indian and cholo students to disassociate entirely from their Indianness, to identify with the national Hispanic culture, and to accept the doctrine of social evolution from *Indio puro* to *Indio civilizado* to non-Indian is, of course, crucial to the continuation of existing patterns of social organization, domination, and power. The marked contrast between Mexico and Peru in this regard might be noted. Mexican school children since the Revolution of 1910 have been taught to glory in their mixture of Indian and Hispanic culture (or *raza*) since Indians *are* Mexicans. The Museum of Anthropology in Mexico City where thousands of school children daily view displays of pre-Hispanic and contemporary indigenous achievements and culture is a monumental commitment to this symbolic value. Peruvian school children, in painful contrast, are taught to be ashamed of their Indian origins

and culture and to deny them, at what price we cannot yet say.[34]

SUMMARY AND CONCLUSIONS

This paper has considered some of the functional relationships between Peruvian sociocultural organization and the structure and content of the educational system. Public education has been characterized, especially at the lower levels, as essentially colonializing rather than rational. Primary functions of formal schooling continue to stress: (1) the acculturation but limited assimilation of non-Hispanic elements, (2) the legitimization of superordinate cultural, economic, and political dominance, and (3) the certification, on the basis of length and type of education, of where individuals should be placed in the sociocultural hierarchy.[35]

We have noted that a number of factors, such as relatively recent extension of public education to the subordinate groups, improved transportation and extended mass media, economic development, and population pressure have converged to stimulate heavy internal migration. With nearly 30 percent of the total population migrating (mostly to or within urban areas), the national school system has come under increasing pressure from the cholo element to consolidate their recent upward social and cultural mobility and to facilitate continued social evolution. At the same time, elements of the superordinate groups seeking to modernize and develop the national economy have been relatively unsuccessful in occasional attempts to rationalize public education. Their concern to create a more development-oriented school system has, in large measure, been opposed by the majority of public school pupils, by their parents, and by their teachers. The first 2 groups are more concerned with continuing to improve their status (from *Indio puro* to *Indio civilizado* to non-Indian) in the evolutionary continuum. The teachers, as with most mestizos, are primarily concerned with maintaining the existing social and cultural organization and the formal, articulated educational organization that serves as one of the primary mechanisms for acculturation without'integration.

Although Peru is currently experiencing renewed attempts to alter the country's institutional structure, it appears unlikely that these efforts stand much chance of success without corresponding changes in the existing ideology of sociocultural evolution, an underlying rationale that has been used to justify the privileges and institutions of the superordinate groups since the Conquest.[36] Until Peru begins to experience a *poder indigena* movement and responds with attempts to develop a new national culture that, as in Bolivia and Mexico, seeks to combine in some greater degree both the Hispanic and indigenous elements in a new cholo national culture, efforts at educational modernization will quite likely continue to be both acclaimed and subverted.

It may well be that in highly pluralistic societies, such as Peru, where formal schooling is preoccupied with conferring status, the nonformal educational systems—the "shadow education systems" including training programs in industry, in unions, in cooperatives, in agricultural extension programs, and in a wide variety of voluntary organizations—offer (short of violent social and educational revolution) the best opportunities to compensate for and to circumvent the elite-dominated and increasingly dysfunctional articulated school system. In this way, confrontation with superordinate groups might be avoided while new educational institutions and organizations better able to mobilize and prepare the human resources required for national development could be created and nurtured.

NOTES

1. Joseph Fisher has pointed out the critical need for this type of study in "Social and Cultural Aspects of Educational Development," Southeast Asia Development Advisory Group, Paper no. 10 (New York: Asia Society, 1967). He calls for intensive case histories of (1) how educational systems actually socialize, enculturate, and serve as channels of social mobility and (2) how educational structures and functions relate to social, cultural, and economic organization.

2. Rodolfo Stavenhagen, "Seven Fallacies about Latin America," in *Latin America: Reform or Revolution*, ed. James Petras and Maurice Zeitlin (New York: Fawcett, 1968), pp. 16–18.

3. The 1961 national census and Banco Central de Reserve del Perú, *Renta Nacional del Perú, 1942–1956* (Lima, 1958), p. 67. Percentages for urbanization and literacy are by region. A considerable amount of economic activity in the Sierra is outside the cash economy and not included in the highland's share of national income.

4. Julio Colter, "The Mechanics of Internal Domination and Social Change in Peru," *Studies in Comparative International Development* 3, no. 12 (1967–68): 236. See also the sections "Who Votes" and "Electoral Representation" in Institute for the Comparative Study of Political Systems, *Peru Election Memoranda* (Washington, D.C.: The Institute, n.d.), pp. 22–27. The electoral population was about 2.2 million out of a voting-age population of some 7 million in 1968.

5. The cholofication process is characterized by rural urbanization, urban ruralization, the mixing of Indian and mestizo cultural traits, the learning of new occupations, and a break with mestizo patronage. The process has been seen by some as the formation of a new social type capable of evolving a new, more inclusive "national" culture. See especially the work of Francois Bourricand, *Changements à Puno: Etude de Sociologie Andine* (Paris: Institute des Hautes Etudes de l'Amérique Latine, 1962) and his *Poder y Sociedad en el Perú Contemporaneo* (Buenos Aires: Sur, 1967). *Blanco* control of power and wealth is analyzed and discussed by Carlos Malpica in *Los Dueños del Perú* (Lima: Ediciones Ensayos Sociales, 1968) and *Hambre en el Perú* (Lima: F. Moncloa, 1966). See also William F. Whyte and Lawrence K. Williams, *Towards an Integrated Theory of Development* (Ithaca, N.Y.: Cornell University, 1968).

6. Mestizo culture is described by Ozzie G. Simmons in "The Criollo Outlook in the Mestizo Culture of Coastal Peru," *American Anthropologist* 62 (1955): 107–17. Although mestizo culture varies considerably between the coast and the Sierra, it is generally characterized by lack of trust, by nationalistic fervor, and by stress on *Peruanidad*, or national culture. The ideal criollo personality is quick, brilliant, skilled at *viveza, ingenio, picardía*, and verbal suasion (*palabrear*). The quintessence of Lima criolloism is to gain some desirable objectives through the absolute minimum of effort, or to overcome an opponent through astute trickery. Simmons notes that where high valuation is placed on "getting away" with something or turning an adverse situation to one's advantage—be it in play or in earnest—there can be little confidence and mutual trust.

7. Colter, "The Mechanics of Internal Domination," p. 237.

8. The ultimately incommensurable nature of power, justice, and social necessity is discussed in

Dennis H. Wrong, "The Functional Theory of Stratification: Some Neglected Considerations," *American Sociological Review* 24 (1959): 772—82. Social and economic power of the superordinate blanco and mestizo cultural groups is described in Gabriel Escobar, *Organización Social y Cultural del Sur del Perú* (Mexico, D. F.: Instituto Ingenista Interamericano, 1967), and Edward Dew, *Politics in the Altiplano* (Austin: University of Texas Press, 1969), p. 62 ff.

9. Eugene A. Brady, "La Distribución de la Penta Monetaria Agregada en el Perú" (Lima: Instituto Nacional de Planificación, 1965).

10. See Milton C. Taylor, "Problems of Development in Peru," *Journal of Inter-American Studies* 9 (January 1967): 85, and E. A. Brady, "The Distribution of Total Personal Income in Peru," *International Studies in Economics* (January 1968).

11. Colter, "The Mechanics of Internal Domination." Given the mestizo-controlled dominance patterns between the coast and the highlands, between urban and rural areas, and between the mestizos and Indians, it becomes something less of a puzzle as to why public school administrators and teachers have, in the main, been less than enthusiastic for interventionist-sponsored reform programs calling for administrative decentralization of the school system, for schools for Indians, for vocational training, and for the "democratization" of the system through curriculum and related reforms. U.S. educational assistance teams have operated in Peru during 4 periods: 1909—14, 1918—22, 1944—62, and 1963—69. All of these missions have repeatedly attempted the aforementioned basic reforms of public schooling.

12. See Paul L. Doughty, *Huaylas: An Andean District in Search of Progress* (Ithaca, N.Y.: Cornell University Press, 1968), pp. 57—87 on "The Elements of Cultural and Social Stratification."

13. The Peruvian press carries numerous articles concerning the need to reform public instruction and the Ministry of Education. Results of periodic attempts to improve education, however, have been negligible. The director of educational planning for 1964—68 has observed, "It is a well-known aphorism that any educational reform in Peru ends in failure." Carlos Salazar Romero, *Educación* (October 1966), p. 39.

14. See, for example, Jack W. Hopkins, *The Government Executive of Modern Peru* (Gainesville: University of Florida Press, 1967), p. 11 ff.

15. See Miguel A. Arestegui Moras, *Sistema de Nucleos Escolares Campesinos* (Cuzco: H. G. Rozas, 1966), and the study by John Baum, *Estudio sobre la Educación Rural en el Perú: Los Nucleos Escolares Campesinos* (Mexico, D. F.: Regional Technical Aids Center, 1967). The Peruvian government has now and then promoted rural community-development programs in the *mancha india,* as with the current $20-million International Bank for Reconstruction and Development loan program. These reform attempts have been at best superficial and at worst merely bureaucratic operations offering mestizo administrators, etc., jobs, increased salaries, commercial transactions, graft, etc. In contrast, several university programs, as

Cornell University at Vicos and Cuzco University at Cuyo Chico have had notable if limited success in directed change. A variety of these programs are described in Roiland G. Paulston, *Educación y el Cambio Dirigido de la Comunidad: Una Bibliografía Anotada con Referencia Especial al Perú,* Center for Studies in Education and Development Occasional Paper no. 3 (Cambridge, Mass.: Harvard University, Graduate School of Education, 1969). See especially chaps. 4 and 5 on empirical studies and specific programs.

16. See David F. Gates et al., *An Exploratory Study of the Role of Armed Forces in Education: Iran, Israel, Peru, Turkey* (McLean, Va.: Research Analysis Corporation, 1968), p. 39.

17. From 1958 to 1968, the following growth occurred in Peruvian primary and secondary public education: (1) public school students increased from 1.47 to 3.15 million (113.7 percent) and (2) teachers increased from 64 to 118.4 thousand (84.9 percent), while the total population was increasing from 9.11 to an estimated 12.8 million (40.4 percent). See Fernando Belaúnde Terry, *Mensaje Presidencial, 1968* (Lima: Minerva, 1968), p. 478 ff.

18. See for example Ira Silverman, "Rural Education for Peruvian Political Development" (Lima: Princeton University in Peru Program, December 1967), mimeographed, for a case study of the Quinua *nucleo* located between Ayachucho and Huancayo.

19. Roger S. Sattler, "Lima's Pueblos Jovenes," *Peruvian Times,* 16 January 1970, pp. 6—8. See also Centro de Investigaciones Sociales por Muestreo, *Barriadas de Lima* (Lima: Ministerio de Trabajo y Comunidades, 1967), p. 4; and the works of William Mangen, "Squatter Settlements," *Scientific American* 217 (October 1967) and "Latin American Squatter Settlements: A Problem and a Solution," *Latin American Research Review* 2, no. 3 (1967).

20. See "En 1970 se quedará sin estudiar solo 21 porciento de población escolar," *El Comercio* (Lima), 17 June 1968.

21. Ministerio de Educación Pública, *La Educación en Gráficos* (Lima: Centro de Investigaciones Pedagogicas, 1968).

22. The complacent North American belief that free universal public education does in fact provide "equal educational opportunity" and unrestricted mobility to all able students has been shattered by several recent studies, most notably the massive Coleman Report. These studies leave little doubt that in the United States, as in Peru, there is extreme inequality of achievement along social class and racial lines and that public schools are increasingly reinforcing social inequalities rather than alleviating them. In Peru, because of its more rigid social hierarchy, the structured educational inequality is merely more visible and restrictive.

23. Problems of applying the concepts of "social race," "ethnic class," and "socioeconomic class" are discussed in Richard W. Patch, "La Parada," *American University Field Service Reports,* West Coast South America Series, vol. 14, no. 2 (February 1967); Charles W. Wagley, "On the Concept

of Social Race in the Americas," *Actas del 33 Congreso Internacional de Americanistas* 1 (San José: Lehman, 1959): 403–17; and Julian Pitt-Rivers, "Race, Color, and Class in Central America and the Andes," *Daedalus* (Spring 1967). Pitt-Rivers notes that while race is a matter of culture and community, not genes, social class status is in various ways connected with genes.

24. Beals claims that an "almost completely impermeable" mobility barrier exists between the blanco and mestizo groups, but this has been sharply challenged by Chaplin's recent study on changes in the distribution of wealth and income. He concludes that there has been a "high level of social mobility among the traditional landed aristocracy, contrary to a mistaken picture of rigid stability among such groups." See Ralph L. Beals, "Social Stratification in Latin America," *American Journal of Sociology* 58 (1963): 334, and David Chaplin, "Industrialization and the Distribution of Wealth in Peru," *Studies in Comparative International Development* 3, no. 3 (1967–68): 61. Chaplin also notes, however, that most commonly the blanco group recruits new members from abroad—usually Europe–rather than from the mestizo class. Blanco *indigenistas* have romanticized Peru's Indians, but always at a distance; and they tend to blame their country's many ills on the mestizos. The mestizo has been described as a psychic and spiritual hybrid who has inherited the defects of his Indian and Spanish ancestors without being able to conserve the remains of the gentlemanly life of the conquerors. See for example Alejandro O. Duestua, *Ante el Conflicto: Problemas economico-sociales y morales del Perú* (Lima, 1931), p. 11.

25. See M. Telleria S., "El Maestro Actual," *Expreso*, 20 May 1968.

26. For a discussion of the mutual distrust between mestizos and Indians of the Peruvian Sierra, and the control practices of the former contrasted to the survival patterns of the latter, see Jacob Fried, "The Indian and Mestizaje in Peru," *Human Organization* (Spring 1961), p. 24. For an example of the widespread idea that *cultura* is the critical element in social evolution from the lowest (Indian) to the highest (blanco) social levels, see William C. Sayres, "Social Evolution in Mestizo Philosophy," *Social Forces* 35 (1957): 370–73. Evidence supporting the suggestion that educational professionals are drawn mainly from the next higher subculture is presented in M. T. Marcés P., *La educación en la comunidad de Sacara* (Cuzco: University of Cuzco, 1966); Mark C. Connelly, "Puno" (Lima: Peruvian American Fulbright Commission, 1967), pp. 108–9; and unpublished socioeconomic status data from the first national teacher census completed in 1968 by the Ministry of Education.

27. The indifference of the public school system to the needs of pupils, the inefficiency of the system, and the financial greed of school teachers and administrators have been constant complaints of the Peruvian popular press in demanding educational reform. Law 15215 of 1964, which greatly increased school employees' salaries, intensified these complaints. See, for example, the critique of

Fernando Romero, "Un grave problema educativo," *La Prensa*, 23 November 1968, p. 22.

28. See the educational budgets (1966–68) for the Ministry of Education, and Belaúnde, *Mensaje Presidencial 1968*.

29. Whyte, "Culture, Industrial Relations, and Industrial Development: The Case of Peru," *Industrial and Labor Relations Review* (July 1963), pp. 583–94. Quote from R. L. Garrison, "End-of-Tour Report" (Lima: Teachers College, Columbia University Contract Team, September 1968), pp. 2–3.

30. Evidence on the declining student services and overall quality of public schooling is analyzed in Maurico San Martín, "El Futuro de la universidad peruana" (Paper delivered at the Primer Seminario Nacional de Planificación Educativa, Lima, 31 August 1968), p. 2, mimeographed, and in the highly critical Ministry of Education, *Diagnóstico* (August 1969), p. 3 ff. See also Luís Alberto Sánchez et al., *Informe sobre el estado de la educación pública* (Lima: Comisión Bicameral del Congreso del Perú, 1967). Sections on "Agitación en el campo educacional" and "Anarquía administrativa" in part 2, pp. 148–85, are especially informative.

31. See the content analysis of Peruvian school texts, *Planes y Programas*, in Thomas P. Carter, "An Analysis of Some Aspects of Culture and the School in Peru" (Ph.D. diss., University of Texas, 1965), p. 231 ff., and the study by R. M. Sparks Miro Quesada, *Actitudes y Valores en un grupo de adolescentes peruanos* (Lima: Universidad Catolica, 1968). For a more general treatment of the problem in Latin America, see Seymour M. Lipset, "Values, Education and Entrepreneurship," in *Elites in Latin America*, ed. Lipset and Aldo Solari (New York: Oxford University Press, 1967), pp. 3–60.

32. *El Comercio*, 21 May 1969.

33. Ivan Illich, "The Futility of Schooling in Latin America," *Saturday Review* (20 April 1968), pp. 57–59 ff., concludes that schooling does not and cannot realize the development objectives set by Latin American governments, AID, UNESCO et al. It has not led to significant reduction of rural marginality, of social distance between "The closed, feudal, hereditary elite" and the "landless rural masses." Schooling has not led to greater social integration. It "is a narrow bridge across a widening social gap. As the only legitimate passage to the middle class, the school restricts all unconventional crossings and leaves the underachiever to bear the blame for his marginality."

34. Frederick B. Pike has noted a shift in Peruvian prejudices from primarily racial to cultural considerations. "The discriminated-against Indian can look forward to acceptance and fair treatment in society if he ceases to be an Indian, and adopts the cultural outlooks, values, habits, and the white, or *mestizo*, Westernized way of life. Cultural prejudice is less vicious and permanent than racial, for people can, and in Peru increasingly do, change their cultures." See his "Mestizaje and the Future," in *The History of Modern Peru*, ed. Pike (London: Werdenfeld and Nicolson, 1967), pp. 21–23. Educational programs at the National Museum of

Anthropology in Mexico City are described in Aaron Sheon, "Museums and Cultural Resources Utilization," *Journal of Developing Areas* 3 (July 1969): 546.
35. These conclusions are to a considerable degree corroborated by David Chaplin, "Peruvian Stratification and Mobility: Revolutionary and Developmental Potential," in *Structured Social Inequality*, ed. Celia S. Heller (New York: Macmillan, 1969), pp. 427–38.

36. For a recent treatment of other restraints on the Junta's attempts to induce revolutionary and nonrevolutionary change from the top down, see James Petras and Nelson Rimensnyder, "What Is Happening in Peru?" *Monthly Review* 21 (February 1970): 15–28, and Rolland G. Paulston, "Education, Nationalism and Revolution in Peru," *School and Society* (April 1971), pp. 35–38.

25. Socialization into Apathy and Political Subordination
MARZIO BARBAGLI and MARCELLO DEI

. . . We have discussed the second conservative role played by teachers, that is, the transmission of dominant values in the formation of the model citizen, and in this connection we examined the problem of sexual socialization. The case of political socialization offers us another example of how this second role can function.

As a preliminary observation we may say that "political socialization, in other words, is essentially a conservative process facilitating the maintenance of the 'status quo' by making people accept the system under which they are born."[1] This observation must not, however, lead us to think that the only characteristic of this process is that it perpetuates the existing political system by reproducing it entirely unchanged. Even if it is true that every political system, just like every individual, has within itself strong survival instincts, nevertheless we know that in addition it has to reckon with a series of relationships and stresses (both external and internal) that force it to change in order to survive. We get nearer to the truth, perhaps, if we say that the process of socialization is a mechanism through which the political system tries to confront the stresses that threaten it.[2] It is through this mechanism that the system reduces both the volume and the range of political demands that might be placed upon it. Furthermore, it accustoms

its own members to accept the decisions of the authorities, and arouses in them a certain level of "diffuse support" towards it.[3]

Empirical research carried out so far on this question has sought to throw light on the period of an individual's life in which this process mainly takes place.[4] This research has arrived at the conclusion that political socialization is already present at the pre-school age (that is, between four and five) and—what is particularly important for our purposes—that its most important phase of development occurs between the ages of eleven and thirteen, that is, precisely in the period that in Italy corresponds to the lower-middle school, the *scuola media inferiore.*[5]

As far as the agents of socialization are concerned, the research carried out has concentrated its attention on the family, since, in the light of the data collected so far, it has until recently been considered the most important agent. As a result, the roles of the school and the teachers have been insufficiently examined. However, the most recent inquiries have questioned these results and have redimensioned and limited the importance of the family,[6] concluding that the school is "the most important and effective instrument of political socialization in the United States."[7]

In the school we may distinguish two

This article first appeared as Chapter IV, Section 6, of *Le vestali della classe media: Ricerca sociologica sugli insegnanti* (Bologna: Il Mulino, 1969), pp. 278–289. English translation by Hugh Ward-Perkins.

Table 1. Headmasters: Role Norms of the Teachers as Regards Sex Education and Political Socialization (Number of cases = 328)

Attitudes / Sanctions	He definitely must do it and it would be better if he did			Behavior not sanctioned	He definitely must not do it and it would be better if he did not			No reply	Total
	Censure	Written warning	Friendly reproach		Friendly reproach	Written warning	Censure		
Talking in class about sexual problems	–	–	2	57	24	11	2	4	100
Talking in class about political problems (e.g., about the center-left government or the Vietnam war)	–	–	3	53	23	15	4	2	100
Revealing in class his own opinion on these political problems (e.g., declaring himself to be favorable or otherwise to the center-left government)	–	–	–	17	46	28	7	2	100
Criticizing the authorities severely in class	–	–	–	7	26	50	15	2	100

Table 2. Attitudes and Conceptions of the Role of the Teacher in the Transmission of Political Information (the Proposition: "Speaking in Class on Political Problems, for Example, the Center-left Government or the Vietnam War")

	He definitely must do it	It would be better if he did do it	He may or may not (as he chooses)	It would be better if he did not do it	He definitely must not do it	No reply	Total	Number of cases
Teachers	3	19	29	17	31	1	100	374
Parents	1	4	12	30	53	–	100	200
Headmasters	2	17	31	26	22	2	100	328

different forms of political socialization: direct and indirect.[8] The indirect form consists of the transmission and acquisition of values and information that are not in themselves political but that impinge, or at least may impinge, on the development of the political personality of an individual. This is so, above all, for the acquisition of one's basic attitudes towards authority. The social climate that is created in a class depends substantially on the kind of existing teacher-pupil relationship. The more hierarchical and autocratic these relationships are, and the more they are characterized by the concentration of decisions in the hands of the teacher and by a rigid control on the behavior of the pupils, the more easily will the latter acquire attitudes of docility and submission to authority.[9] It is very likely that with the passing of time this general attitude towards authority, which the pupils acquire in their relationship with the teacher, will end up by being transformed, especially if strengthened by similar relationships with other agents of socialization (such as the family or the peer group), into a true political orientation, that is, an attitude of complete subordination to the political authorities.

As far as Italian teachers are concerned, we have had occasion in the preceding pages to speak of the authoritarianism in their attitudes and ideologies. We think it is fair to state, on the basis of the results we have outlined, that most of them fully carry out in class the role of socializers into docility and consequently that of socializers into subordination in the sphere of politics. However, to give a more precise judgment on the existing social climate in Italian schools it is necessary to have terms of comparison. Fortunately, a well-known comparative survey carried out a few years ago in five different countries gives us some information on the matter.[10] From it, in fact, it appears that of the five countries taken into consideration as many as three (in increasing order of authoritarianism: the United States, Great Britain,

Germany) presented a social climate less authoritarian than that in Italy (which was less authoritarian only than Mexico).[11]

The second form of political socialization—direct political socialization—consists, on the other hand, of the process of transmission and acquisition of information and values that are specifically political. As far as the transmission of information is concerned, it must be said that the Italian middle school still adheres to a large extent to the old motto, "here you work, you don't discuss politics." In fact, the data we have collected clearly show that the majority of the teachers do not believe that the transmission of political information forms a part of their responsibilities. Forty-eight percent reject such a view of their role, while 29 percent are indifferent. A similar distribution is observable in the attitudes of the headmasters (48 percent and 31 percent respectively). Towards this aspect of political socialization there is, therefore, among both teachers and headmasters the same degree of hostility (or indifference) we saw when we discussed the transmission of information on sexual matters. In the case of both the teachers and the headmasters the distribution of attitudes and views on their roles is very similar for the two types of behavior (see Table 2). Furthermore, it is generally the same teachers and headmasters who are against information on sexual matters that are opposed to political information. The correlation here is 0.37 for teachers and 0.33 for headmasters.

The matter is rather different where the parents are concerned. As has often been said, they are very willing to delegate to the teachers the task of transmitting to their own children the most important elements of sex education. We cannot, however, say the same for their attitudes on the teachers' role in the transmission of political information. In fact, both Table 2 and Table 3 show us that the parents are even more against allowing the schools to perform this task than are the teachers and headmasters.

Table 3. Percentages of the Subjects of the Three Samples Who Think That the Teacher "Definitely Must Not," or That "It Would Be Better if He Did Not," Speak on Political Matters in Class; Classified According to Ages.*

	Teachers		Parents		Headmasters	
	%	N.	%	N.	%	N.
24–35 years	35	(126)				
36–45 years	51	(130)	52	(114)	44	(104)
46–55 years	51	(76)	63	(63)	45	(139)
56 or over	69	(42)			60	(73)

*In this, as in other tables of this type, we have not reported the data for the first age-class in the case of the headmasters or for the first and last age-classes in the case of the parents, because for these the number of cases at our disposal was too small to make possible a calculation of percentages.

But those teachers who (leaving aside for a moment the question of the greatness of the Roman Empire) dare to inform their pupils that in Italy there is a center-left government and that the United States is conducting a war in Vietnam have to fear not so much the wrath of the parents (for only 25 percent of these would complain to the headmaster) as the reactions of their own headmasters, who would, according to our data, resort in 42 percent of the cases to some kind of sanction (see Table 1).

Nevertheless, it is clear in spite of this that even in the case of political information there is a crisis in the old, yet still dominant, ideas of roles. This crisis was first formally acknowledged by the introduction into the Italian schools in 1958 of the teaching of civic education, even if the syllabus provided for the transmission only of formal legal concepts and not of contemporary political information.[12] Two facts bear witness to this crisis: in the first place, in the three samples studied, the behavior we are here examining is that on which the level of agreement about roles is lowest; in the second place, as we realized when controlling the variable of age, the headmasters, who (as we have said) are the first to adhere to new norms, are in general more favorable to the teaching of political information than are the teachers (see Table 3).

But let us now see what happens in the other type of political socialization, that is, in the transmission of values. The great majority of the subjects of the three samples are opposed to any teacher's taking a particular position on current affairs in class: that is, 82 percent of the teachers, 59 percent of the parents, and 90 percent of the headmasters (see Table 4).[13]

So, should the deviant teacher, after having first challenged the role norms (by informing the pupils of the existence of a war in Vietnam), then dare to go as far as to criticize the United States, by perhaps describing this war as "imperialist" or simply "unjust," he would find himself faced with the hostility of his colleagues (who have a completely different conception of their own role), with the protests of the parents (35 percent of those interviewed would go to the headmaster) and, above all, with the sanctions of the headmaster (and as many as 81 percent would resort to some form of sanction). (See Table 1.)

The teacher cannot, therefore, discuss questions of current political affairs and he above all cannot take a position on them. He must ignore the present and only discuss the

Table 4. Attitudes and Conceptions of the Role of the Teacher in the Transmission of Political Values (the Proposition: "Revealing in Class His Own Opinions on These Problems, 'for Example, by Declaring Himself Favorable or Otherwise to the Center-left Government, etc.' ")

	He definitely must do it	It would be better if he did do it	He may or may not (as he chooses)	It would be better if he did not do it	He definitely must not do it	No reply	Total	Number of cases
Teachers	1	3	13	33	49	1	100	374
Parents	3	23	15	21	38	–	100	200
Headmasters	–	1	7	30	60	2	100	328

Table 5. Percentage of the Subjects of the Three Samples Who Think That the Teacher "Definitely Must Not," or That "It Would Be Better if He Did Not," Express His Opinion in Class on Current Affairs; Classified According to Ages.

	Teachers		Parents		Headmasters	
	%	N.	%	N.	%	N.
24–35 years	74	(126)				
36–45 years	85	(130)	80	(114)	87	(104)
46–55 years	85	(76)	89	(63)	90	(139)
56 or over	90	(42)			92	(73)

past. It is expected of him (and there will be consequences if he refuses to comply) that when he enters the class, he leaves outside everything that is controversial or that could in any way recall the existence of struggles and conflicts in the political sphere.[14] As the *Premessa* to the *Decreto per l'insegnamento dell'educazione civica in Italia* states, "bringing into the schools in a crude state the forms in which life is articulated," to translate literally "i moduli in cui la vita si articola," "cannot but be sterile and even deviant."[15]

The role norms that regulate this aspect of political socialization are institutionalized extremely securely in the Italian schools. The level of agreement as to roles in this case is very high in all three samples. Furthermore, even controlling the variable of age, we observed that, unlike what we had seen concerning the norms that regulate sexual and political information, the headmasters adhere even more strongly to the dominant norms than do the teachers (see Table 5).

The meaning of this request for neutrality is clear. There is no need to reassert here that in dealing with political questions (and not only political questions, for that matter) neutrality is impossible to attain, because it is already abandoned in the choosing of the subject under discussion. As a result, the only guarantee a teacher can give his pupils is that of making explicit his views and

political opinions. Here we need merely remind ourselves that a recent piece of empirical research has shown that precisely in the field of politics teachers are not able to distinguish facts from values.[16] The neutrality demanded of the teacher, to which indeed he adheres with such conviction, is in reality a partial neutrality. It is not expected of the teacher that he not transmit political values in his teaching,[17] only that he not be "unilateral" or "partisan,"[18] –that is, in effect, that he not transmit values contrary to the dominant values. As has been observed, "by and large affirmations can be described as unilateral if they conflict

Table 6. Percentage of Teachers who Think That "They Definitely Must Not," or That "It Would Be Better if They Did Not," Express Their Own Opinion in Class on Current Affairs; Classified According to Degree of Political Conservatism.

	Teachers	
	%	N.
Political conservatism		
Points 0–1	51	(49)
Points 2–3	80	(124)
Points 4	89	(95)
Points 5	94	(90)

Table 7. Attitudes and Conceptions of the Role of the Teacher as Regards Criticism of the Authorities in Class (the Proposition: "Severely Criticizing the Authorities in Class").

	He definitely must do it	It would be better if he did do it	He may or may not (as he chooses)	It would be better if he did not do it	He definitely must not do it	No reply	Total	Number of cases
Teachers	—	1	6	21	71	1	100	374
Parents	—	1	6	25	68	—	100	200
Headmasters	—	—	2	10	86	2	100	328

with the dominant climate of opinion. But the ideas and norms that dominate society are, as a rule, the ideas and norms of the social groups with the greatest power. Consequently, he who ingenuously accepts criticism of 'unilaterality' and is not aware of the implications and political consequences of this acceptance effectively renounces his freedom to think. This mechanism operates in such a way that precisely those areas of social mechanism that are, from the point of view of democratization, the most critical are excluded. Practiced in this way, political neutrality leads either to a depoliticalization of consciousness or to more or less blind acceptance of the existing power relationships in society."[19] It is not, therefore, by chance that a connection exists between the teachers' conception of their own role in the transmission of political values and their own political values and political ideologies. As Table 6 shows, compliance on the part of the teachers with the request for political neutrality in class is much more frequent where the level of political conservatism is greater.

There is, furthermore, another fact that, as well as shedding light on the indirect form of political socialization, clarifies the meaning of this demand for neutrality. Ninety-two percent of the teachers, 93 percent of the parents, and 96 percent of the headmasters do not accept the idea that teachers should be permitted to criticize the authorities severely in front of the pupils (see Table 7). If this were to happen, 35 percent of the parents and as many as 91 percent of the headmasters would be ready to resort to sanctions against the deviant teacher.

It is unnecessary to add that even this norm, like the preceding one, is firmly rooted and institutionalized in Italian schools. Of the eighteen types of behavior examined in our three samples, this one registered one of the highest levels of agreement on role. Furthermore, after controlling the variable of age, we noted that even in this case the greatest hostility is among the

headmasters, that is, among those who have the very task of ensuring that the dominant norms are respected.

NOTES

1. R. Sigel, "Assumptions about the Learning of Political Values," in *The Annals*, 361 (1965), p. 7.
2. For this definition, see D. Easton and J. Dennis, *Children in the Political System* (New York: McGraw-Hill, 1969), p. 51.
3. These defensive mechanisms against the stresses, here only briefly touched upon, are described in detail in Easton and Dennis, *op. cit.*, pp. 52–69. By "diffuse support," understand "the generalized trust and confidence that members give to the various objects of the system and see as ends in themselves," a confidence that "is not contingent on any quid pro quo," but that is "offered unconditionally" (p. 63).
4. The best known review of the studies, though now decidedly out of date, is H. Hyman, *Political Socialization* (New York: Free Press, 1959; a new edition came out in 1969). Of the more recent reviews the following are useful: R. E. Dawson, "Political Socialization," in J. A. Robinson (ed.), *Political Science Annual* (Indianapolis: Bobbs-Merrill, 1966), pp. 1–84; and R. E. Dawson and K. Prewitt, *Political Socialization* (Boston: Little, Brown, 1969).
5. See in particular J. Adelson and R. P. O'Neil, "Growth of Political Ideas in Adolescence: The Sense of Community," in *Journal of Personality and Social Psychology* 4 (1966): 304–305.
6. M. K. Jennings and R. G. Niemi, "The Transmission of Political Values from Parent to Child," in *American Political Science Review* 62 (1968): 169–184.
7. R. D. Hess and J. V. Torney, *The Development of Political Attitudes in Children* (Chicago: Aldine, 1967), p. 101. We do not feel, however, that the present degree of knowledge on this question can fully justify the statement made by Hess and Torney. As far as we understand, the only inquiry conducted on this question in Italy is that by T. M. Hennessey, *The Political Socialization of Italian Youth: The Case of Pistoia and Arezzo* (unpublished doctoral dissertation, The University of North Carolina at Chapel Hill, 1968). Some of the results of this research can be seen in his article, "Democratic Attitudinal Configurations Among Italian Youth," published in *Mid-West Journal of Political Science* 12 (1969): 167–193. However, at the time of writing, an extensive inquiry is being carried out by the Instituto C. Cattaneo under the direction of Anna Oppo. In France, the only research that has so far been published is that by C. Roig and F. Bollon-Grand, *La socialisation politique des enfants* (Paris: A. Colin, 1968). As far as Germany is concerned, see: J. Habermas, L. von Friedeburg, C. Oehler, and F. Weltz, *Student und Politik* (Neuwied: H. Luchterhand Verlag, 1961); M. Teschner, *Politik und Gesellschaft im Unter-*

richt (Frankfurt am Main: Europäische Verlags-anstalt, 1967); E. Becker, S. Herkommer, and J. Bergmann, *Erziehung zur Anpassung?* (Frankfurt am Main: Wochenschau Verlag, 1967); and L. von Friedeburg and P. Hubner, *Das Geschichtsbild der Jugend* (Munich: Juventa Verlag, 1964), which is above all a review of German studies on the influence of the teaching of history and civic education on the political formation of the young.

8. For this distinction see Dawson and Prewitt, *op. cit.,* pp. 63–80.

9. For a review of some of the empirical research that justifies this assertion, see R. Tausch, "Soziale Interaktion Lehrer-Schüler und Sozialklima in Schülen: Erziehungsfaktoren für Diktatur und Demokratie," in K. Aurin *et al., Politische Erziehung als psychologisches Problem* (Frankfurt am Main: Europäische Verlagsanstalt, 1966), pp. 107–116. For an acute analysis of the process of the acquisition of "docility" in school, see J. Henry, "Docility or Giving Teacher What She Wants," in *Journal of Social Issues* 11: 33–41.

10. G. Almond and S. Verba, *The Civic Culture* (Princeton, N.J.: Princeton University Press, 1963), pp. 352–363.

11. For an idea of what this means, one need only read the description made by Tausch (*op. cit.*), on the basis of the results of several inquiries, of the profoundly authoritarian climate that dominates in the German schools.

12. See the text of the *Premessa* of the *Decreto per l'insegnamento dell'educazione civica in Italia* (13 June 1958), in A. Capitini (ed.), *L'educazione civica nella scuola e nella vita sociale* (Bari: Laterza, 1967), pp. 127–132.

13. J. M. Foskett, in *The Normative World of the Elementary School Teacher* (Eugene, Ore.: CASEA Publications, 1967; see p. 26), came to similar conclusions in an inquiry conducted on a sample of over 300 American elementary school teachers.

14. A. Klönne and A. Tschoepe also came to the same conclusion after analyzing the contents of some of the textbooks adopted in Germany for the teaching of civic education. See their article, "Sozialkundliche Unterrichtsbücher," in *Soziale*

Welt 15 (1964): 347–350. On this question see also R. Schmiederer, "Zur Problematik der politischen Bildung in der Schule," in *Das Argument* 8 (1966): 386–397.

15. Capitini, *op. cit.,* p. 128.

16. We are referring to the study by H. Zeigler, *The Political Life of American Teachers* (Englewood Cliffs, N. J.: Prentice-Hall, 1967). The author observes that "it is difficult for a teacher to hide his own values. For high school teachers the distinction between facts and values is very obscure" (p. 116). And in fact, 42 percent of the teachers interviewed in his survey said that the statement "the American form of government may not be perfect, but it is still the best form of government invented by man" was a fact and not an opinion, and that it could therefore be expressed freely in class.

17. On this point the above-mentioned *Premessa* to the *Decreto per l'insegnamento dell'educazione civica in Italia* says: "to go from *fact* to *value* is the methodological journey that must be undertaken" (p. 131); the italics are in the text. The same *Premessa* clarifies perfectly, though in a generic fashion, what kind of values are being alluded to: "the educational action, in this phase of psychic development, will be aimed at forming a secure and harmonious spiritual balance, by overcoming uncertainties and hesitations, and using and channeling the vigor, generosity, and intransigence of the youthful personality" (p. 130).

18. Dawson and Prewitt remark: "It is expected of teachers—and they do not disappoint these expectations—that they propagate the points of view and political beliefs properly described as 'consensus values.' Teachers must not make the class a place for the discussion of 'partisan values' and of controversial opinions, and in general they do not. Democracy, the two-party system, free enterprise, fundamental liberties, etc., . . . are not only topics permitted in class: it is expected of the teacher that he impresses them on his pupils" (*op. cit.,* p. 160).

19. Teschner, *op. cit.,* p. 118.

26. The Student Movement and the Industrialization of Higher Education

MICHAEL W. MILES

The American student movement rose . . . and it fell. For a few years, it carried all before it, mobilizing millions, overthrowing the mighty, spinning off ideologies, ignoring its critics, dominating the scene by its ubiquitous, self-centered, and invincible *presence.* The movement reached high tide with the May 1970 strike in protest of the

This article first appeared in *Politics and Society* 4 (1974): 311–341, under the title "Student Alienation in the U.S. Higher Education Industry." We have extracted pp. 311–322 and 330–341 for reproduction here. Reprinted by permission.

invasion of Cambodia and the killing of students at Kent State and Jackson State. Thereafter, it began to decline, slowly at first and then ever more rapidly, until time actually seemed to reverse itself.

The problem is to explain *both* the rise and fall of the student movement. If the movement's decline cannot be understood by the logic of the hypothesis accounting for its rise, then we are dealing with *ad hoc* rationalization. The key to the rise and fall of the student movement lies in the post-war development of a "higher education industry." "Youth culture," which is regarded by many social analysts as the fundamental structural cause of student rebellion, is actually only a function of this "industry," which extends the "role moratorium" to millions of people and further intensifies the trend to generational stratification in industrial societies. The industrialization of higher education promotes student rebellion by its direct educational effects, primarily the steady deterioration of undergraduate education, and by its disintegration of traditional college communities and "urbanization" of the educational enterprise. The concentration of student masses in youth ghettoes and the diversification of subcultures within educational institutions are products of what Clark Kerr called the "educational city" in *The Uses of the University.*

I propose to call the impact of educational industrialization on students, *alienation.* Student alienation is continuous with the Marxist concept of alienated labor to the extent that student labor time must be considered a resource input in the calculation of "educational output," whether consumer services or "human capital." As an educational cost, student labor time is negatively calculated as "opportunity costs" or foregone income, which some economists put at more than half of all educational costs while others prefer to minimize it in the context of inelastic labor markets and an economy at considerably less than full employment. The point is that students cannot be considered simply as "consumers" of educational services even though they pay for a share of the costs or as investors in themselves since most will ultimately have as little control over the disposition of their own human capital as over any other. Nevertheless, students also cannot be regarded as a "proletariat" because their time, like that of housewives, is uncompensated, and the educational product to which they contribute—knowledge, skills, research, and productive attitudes toward work and organization—does not so much increase economic growth directly within higher education as at a latter stage in other industries. The ambiguous status of student labor is best conveyed by considering students as *trainees.* To the extent that the industrialization of higher education involves an increasing division of labor, loss of control over the educational process, and atomization of the social environment and that students contribute to educational production with their labor, students are alienated in the classical Marxist sense. In fact, human capital theory implies that students are themselves the product since human capital is embodied capital. I will argue that the alienation of students through the industrialization of higher education is a prime structural cause of student rebellion. Institutional size, a rough indicator of the progress of industrialization within an institution, strongly correlates with the probability of student protest.

Still, students as unpaid trainees are outside the labor force in the strict sense and their studies are largely subsidized by their families and the state. To this degree, they are divorced from the "real world" of earned income. It is an exaggeration to consider this aspect of student status as a "role moratorium" but there is a "prolongation of adolescence" if adulthood is defined as financial self-support and usually family responsibilities. The psychological frustrations of reaching mental and physical maturity without adult status undoubtedly contributed to student rebellion. More importantly, the prolongation of adolescence helps to account for the strong influence on the student movement of "youth culture" with its denial of the "work ethic," and this influence was a major factor in the failure of the movement. Thus the ambiguities of student consciousness reflect a tension in the objective status of students as trainees. I will refer to the political manifestation of student consciousness as *student idealism.*

If there were a simple linear relationship between student protest and educational industrialization, one might argue that student protest should have been most severe in the community colleges. This was, of course, not the case. Instead, there is a strong correlation between student protest and selectivity in admissions. These facts do not require a rejection of the industrialization thesis but an examination of the relationship between the industrializing process and the social origins and social destination of students. Direct surveys of the social background of student radicals found that they tended to be the children of liberal, urban professionals of Jewish or Protestant religious affiliation. It is not true that there was a direct relationship between protest and "affluence," much less bourgeois origins in the strict sense of propertied wealth. It is also stretching a point to claim that the family background of student radicals was "new working class." To the degree that these professional families were self-employed they may be considered bourgeois or petit-bourgeois, but it is more often true that they were salaried personnel working in large organizations. C. Wright Mills called salaried managers, officials, and higher-level professional and technical personnel a "new middle class," as distinct from the "old middle class" or petit-bourgeoisie. I will follow this usage and offer possession of at least three of the following criteria as qualification for new middle class position:

1. Income derived primarily from wages and salaries rather than from wealth and business enterprise;

2. Group control over the job: As distinct from wage labor, professional work involves definition by the professional membership of the nature of, and requirements for entrance into, an occupation. It may also involve collective control over hiring and firing in a certain job category within a firm or organization. Through this control, professional groups are often able to create artificial scarcities which increase the average income of the membership. Trade unions with restrictive practices often achieve the same objective and qualify their membership for the same social class position.

3. High income relative to the average income of the working class: Besides the above means, high relative income may reflect a tradition of paying certain occupations more than their real contribution to production, or conversely, the major contribution to production made by certain scarce, usually highly specialized, skills. Other occupations offer the opportunity of supplemental income through petit-bourgeois private enterprise. The professional faculties of universities, for example, supplement their income through writing, grants, consultancies, and the lecture and conference circuit.

4. Command functions: These are routinely exercised by management and officialdom. Professionals usually do not exercise command but normally escape close surveillance by those outside the profession.

5. Bourgeois prospects: A major attraction of this class position is that it can serve as a platform for mobility into the bourgeoisie. The main avenue is through top-level managerial or official positions which offer investment perquisites or opportunities. Less often, members of the middle class have personal entrepreneurial opportunities. Almost universally, they are petty investors and rentiers.

These criteria offer grounds for clearly distinguishing the new middle class from the other Marxist class categories and situate it as a satellite class of the bourgeoisie, intermediate between it and the proletariat. But it is far from clear why this class or its offspring should be a source of rebellion. In his *History of the Russian Revolution,* Trotsky already speaks of a "new middle caste" but as a source of revisionism, not revolt.

If the student movement had evolved within the parameters of liberal ideology, the leading role of students of new middle class background would be less of a problem. But it did spill over into open rebellion, a vague "radicalism." Yet it is also clear, or should be clear, that the body of the movement never developed a socialist orientation or indicated a proletarian character. On the face of it, this fact would seem to preclude the relevance of a concept of student alienation. Here again, we are dealing with the fundamental ambiguity of student status. I would argue that the impact of industrialization and alienation would be greatest on those students for whom the experience was a shock. For working class students, industrialized education and their subordinate relationship to it would be continuous with past experience in other contexts. For bourgeois and new middle class students, the experience of industrialized education would be discontinuous. The initial shock of alienated conditions would provoke rebellion. There is evidence supporting this thesis. The family socialization of student rebels tended to be "permissive," that is, to stress autonomy and competitive mettle in a manner typical of new middle class families. Those analysts emphasizing this point as a factor in student rebellion have noted the discontinuity between family socialization and the educational environment. In his studies, Keniston noted that the political activist, as distinct from the cultural drop-out, tended to have a rather well-integrated childhood and adolescence.

This argument assumes that students from these class backgrounds actually do encounter industrialized education. This assumption would seem to be contradicted by the abundant sociological evidence indicating relatively close correlations between the class background of students and differing types of institutions. I will attempt to demonstrate later that the rapid expansion of higher education since World War II and the qualitative changes in its character and function have affected the vast majority of students in the United States, including those attending elite institutions. What is striking is not the elegance with which the higher educational system has reproduced the class structure and appropriate types of class consciousness but the inefficiency with which it has pursued these objectives. The "elite" education meted out to undergraduates in "multiversities" is one example of this inefficiency. Student rebellion is another. Current trends in national education policy are aimed at correcting many of these "dysfunctions."

For most students of bourgeois background and many of new middle class background, the alienation experienced in the higher education system is temporary. They are not destined for the proletariat and their indignation at the "system" is ephemeral. This anticipation accounts for the survival of bourgeois ideology within the movement, often given an anarchist twist. Thus the doctrine of the "post-industrial society" emerges re-packaged as "post-scarcity anarchism." However, except for bourgeois students whose status is passed on to them directly through the transmission of wealth, student anticipations of their future status are cloaked in uncertainty. Although investigations of social mobility show no tendency for a higher rate in recent decades, they agree in finding a fairly high absolute rate of upward and downward mobility. And although there is no evidence that education plays a greater part now than earlier, its role in determining social mobility is substantial. As the independent role of educational credentials is more critical for new middle class than for bourgeois students, the possibility of *downward* mobility weighs more heavily upon them than for students from any other class background. For new middle class students, downward mobility spells proletarianization.

Downward mobility and proletarianization are only *possibilities*. Many new middle class students will maintain or improve their position, and *this* possibility tends to erode the formation of an unambiguous class consciousness. Similar dynamics with similar results also operate in later life, but they are especially critical in the higher education system, a main function of which is to allocate manpower and thus determine the life chances of the population. Students may attempt to relieve their anxieties by gauging their progress in the ferocious competition for "meritocratic" success. These calculations are undermined by the dynamics of economic development in the post-war period, which have witnessed a rapid expansion of the "knowledge industry" and the "service sector." These employ a large number of "professional and technical" personnel, an occupational category which has more than doubled as a percentage of the labor force. Since the second and third tenths of the income distribution have slightly increased their share of national income in the post-war period, the new middle class, as defined above, may have grown slightly as a percentage of the population. But this class is by no means identical with the occupational category of professional and technical personnel and does not begin to match its expansion. Yet this occupational category includes many positions which would have conferred new middle class status at an earlier period. As the percentage of "professionals" in the labor force increases, their actual status declines and they are drafted into the "new working class." Concretely, this means that their relative income shares decrease and their control of their working conditions and membership is eliminated. In higher education, for instance, management finds it increasingly necessary to break the professional faculty.

In this situation, students will find it difficult to gauge their class prospects because they must run up a downward-moving escalator. "Success" may prove quite illusory; witness the current condition of the academic PhD. Two factors raise the prospect of proletarianization: social mobility in and out of the new middle class and the derogation of occupations, formerly of the middle class, to the new working class (strictly speaking, a new *stratum of* the working class). The conditions of industrialized education lead students to expect the worst. Students of new middle class background played a leading role in student revolt because of the initial shock of alienation within the higher education system and because of the prospect, quite justified, of proletarianization which this alienation raised. Their role was a function of *anticipatory proletarianization*. Working on an "anticipation," not fully confirmed in fact, students of new middle class background were inhibited in the development of a movement based on a working class consciousness. Like the status of students as trainees, the anticipation of proletarianization by students of the new middle class both produced student rebellion and limited its development.

Student rebellion, then, can be seen as a function of the *interaction* of the closely-linked elements of educational industrialization and new middle class student constituencies. The incidence of student protest was highest where both factors were strongly in evidence, as in the elite state universities. Where one factor was strong and the other weak, the probability of protest was lower, but still significant. In the elite, private liberal arts colleges, new middle class students were relatively insulated from industrializing trends, but still subject to competitive pressure to maintain or improve their class position. In the state colleges and community colleges, there were fewer middle class students but a heavy industrial harness. Where both factors were absent, as in the religious denominational schools, the probability of student protest was very low.

Finally, the national political crisis of the 1960s activated the student movement. The main elements of this crisis were racial conflict, the Indo-China War, and the decomposition of the Cold War structure of international politics. The movement required "activation" because of the limits, already discussed, of a student consciousness grounded in trainee status and an uncertain class character. Student idealism needed to fix upon an object beyond the limits of its own sources in order to become politically operative. The images of peace and racial justice were the catalysts. Once under way, the movement addressed itself to its own situation—contrary to some claims—as much as to the "issues" of war and race, and there is statistical evidence to prove it.

I. THE HIGHER EDUCATION INDUSTRY

Since World War II, the system of higher education has grown as part of the general expansion of the "knowledge industry," estimated by Fritz Machlup to constitute as much as 30 per cent of the gross national product and which includes such undertakings as science, research and development, communications, information, and professional services. In turn, the knowledge industry largely overlaps with the "service sector," the expanding tertiary sector (more than 50 per cent of GNP) of the economy growing up on the foundations of the primary and secondary sectors of agriculture and manufacture. Even after the huge influx of veterans attending school under the GI Bill, approximately $1 billion was devoted in 1947 to the higher education of 2.2 million students, some 16 per cent of the college-age population at any one moment. By the early 1970s, $25 billion (2½ per cent of the GNP) was spent on 8 million students, some 40 per cent of the college-age population.[1]

This development is generally known as "mass higher education." Why call it an industry? Higher educational services are, after all, bought and sold on the market only to a limited degree; for the most part, the system is subsidized by tax monies. Since students are both input and output, its inputs, processes, and outputs are not easily separable and quantifiable. Its "productivity" has been retarded by its reliance upon labor-intensive processes. By fiat, one might declare most any segment of public expenditures an "industry" producing consumer services. A view of higher education as consumption expenditures would be a convenience for economic analysis and could be made compatible with any vision of its role, even the most cultural and utopian.

The decisive question is whether higher educational expenditures represent an *investment*. If so, there is a calculable "rate of return" to higher educational expenditures which should determine, if marginalist analysis is strictly applied, the allocation of resources to higher education as a whole and to various undertakings within the system. This approach is no mere convenience and would determine the whole character of the system. The allocation of resources according to criteria of economic utility is not compatible with the traditional view of higher education as a "community of scholars" which transmits culture from generation to generation and advances knowledge "for its own sake." The maximization of the rate of return is not compatible with the provision of "equal educational opportunity" for all who are willing and able to take advantage of it. It is not even compatible with the vision of higher education as indoctrinating the population in the values of liberal democracy. All of these things might go on to some degree within the parameters of efficiency but, were the investment orientation taken seriously, would be discouraged from proceeding to the point of inefficiency.

The human capital school of thought, originated in the late 1950s by Theodore Schultz, calculates the rate of return as the lifetime earnings added by years of schooling against the total costs of higher education, including opportunity costs. Using a different approach, Edward F. Denison has estimated that improvements in the quality of labor, attributed to education, and advances in knowledge have accounted for 23 percent and 15 per cent respectively of economic growth in the United States in the post-war period. There are, it must be said, many objections to both these approaches. Employing neo-classical marginalist analysis, the human capital school assumes that differences in income reflect real differences in productivity rather than market imperfections. Using an "aggregate production function," Denison finds that there is a large "residual" output which the inputs of capital and labor, conventionally figured, cannot explain, but he appears to underestimate qualitative changes in the productivity of capital and rather arbitrarily throws education and knowledge into the unexplained breech. Other economists prefer to call the "residual factor" the "coefficient of ignorance."

Clearly, there has been "conspicuous production" of higher education which now exceeds the actual requirements of the occupational structure, and there is not much evidence that education beyond job requirements increases productivity. There is also some doubt how necessary the "requirements" themselves are. Industry appears to have indulged in a penchant for "credentialling" jobs beyond their real requirements as a means of simplifying its personnel tasks. The human capital economists are unperturbed by all of these criticisms. For them, it is simply a matter of distinguishing between consumption and investment expenditures on higher education, and of estimating market imperfections in determining income derived from years of schooling. All of the objections raise for them a problem of accurate calculation, not of principle. Although most of these economists have generally claimed that the rate of return from higher education is high, they are not committed to any figure, but only to the principle that a rate of return is calculable. They are not even committed to the proposition that the rate should be made the basis of policy.

An apparent paradox is the "low productivity" of higher education. Even adjusting for inflation, educational costs per unit of output are rising, not falling as in manufacturing industry. This fact is a function of the limited application, as yet, of labor-saving technology in higher education, while labor costs tend to rise at a rate comparable to that of the labor force as a whole. This characteristic is typical of many service industries and does not mean that every effort is not made to use capital efficiently and to hold down labor costs. In higher education, rising labor costs also reflect labor shortages during the period of the industry's most rapid expansion. Some economists have argued that improvements in the quality of the output—namely, students, particularly scientific manpower making a major contribution to production in the general economy—might compensate for the apparent increase in costs per unit of output. This may or may not be true. What is more likely is that the rate of return from higher education has tended to decline over time. This tendency could actually be expected in an industry which has grown as enormous as higher education.

When all objections have been lodged, the economic value of higher education has not been disproved. Even Christopher Jencks, who is to educational sociology what William of Occam was to philosophy, grants an annual rate of return from higher education of from 4 to 7 per cent.[2] The community college "movement" is clearly an effort to improve the productivity of the labor force and to transfer on-the-job training costs onto the public weal.[3] The "over-production" of degrees would disprove the economic orientation of higher education only if the authorities took this "crisis" in their stride and continued to blithely expand the system for other reasons. In fact, they are busy rationalizing the system to cope with the crisis of overproduction.

What appears to be true is that human investment analysis is the theoretical rationalization of a hunch. The controllers of higher education have not actually employed human capital analysis to determine expenditures, but have worked on the assumption that higher education pays, which economists then justified. "Manpower forecasting," which estimates specific manpower needs in various job categories, has had much more direct influence. There are quarrels between the manpower forecasters and human capital economists because the former do not employ rates of return but estimate manpower needs directly, and assume inelastic labor markets and the nonsubstitutibility of skills rather than classical markets. Ultimately, the two approaches come to the same thing. If a technologically-developing economy requires specifically-trained manpower, then higher education certainly contributes to economic growth and has a calculable rate of return. Even the manpower approach has far from completely determined the allocation of resources in higher education in any precise fashion, and the "state of the art" is not highly advanced. The point is that the *trend* is toward increasing determination of educational priorities by economic criteria, not the opposite.

This trend does not mean that higher education serves only economic purposes. *As* the system fulfills its economic purposes or fails to fulfill them, it also accomplishes, or fails to accomplish, social and cultural objectives. As Herbert Gintis has noted, the "structure of social relations in schools reproduces rather faithfully the capitalist work-environment."[4] However, Gintis' argument that the reproduction of this work environment and the "inculcation of personality characteristics" are themselves the contribution of higher education to productivity is unconvincing. It would seem odd to expend $25 billion simply to "reproduce" a social environment, which already exists everywhere else at no additional cost and to "socialize" students in values which are rarely contradicted in any other context. The real training and manpower development functions of higher education, however inefficiently pursued, are critical. As these objectives are pursued, capitalist social relations are reproduced. These social relations

involve not only subordination and alienation but "liberal" cultural attitudes and "democratic values."

Besides manpower development, the higher education industry is engaged in another major economic activity: research and development. By 1970, over $3 billion, some 15 percent of higher educational expenditures, was devoted to organized research. By and large, this research was utilitarian, serving economic, military, and less often, social purposes but rarely representing the pursuit of knowledge for its own sake. At least half of all R&D monies are not expended on "basic research" but on applied research and development. Two-thirds of organized research, including most basic research, is funded by the Federal Government, and of the Federal monies, most originate with the "mission-oriented" agencies, particularly the "defense-space group" (Department of Defense, Atomic Energy Commission, National Aeronautics and Space Administration). If the crucial Federally-Funded Research and Development Centers (Los Alamos, Brookhaven, Argonne, etc.), which are university-managed and usually conveniently forgotten in the accounting of the universities and their apologists, are included in the grand total, half of all Federal research money is allocated by the military/aerospace group.[5] In this context, it is fatuous to regard research and development as a purely cultural activity or to identify basic research with the pursuit of knowledge for its own sake. Some "pure" research does go on, of course, just as pilot fish follow white sharks.

The pursuit of culture for its own sake also survives as a remnant of the liberal arts tradition. Since this tradition is under attack everywhere, the prospects of culture as a self-justifying activity are none too good. Except for the interstices of the research establishment and for the dying enclaves of the liberal arts, the ideals of the community of scholars and the pursuit of knowledge for its own sake mainly serve an *ideological* function of disguising what does exist with the illusion of what does not exist. Much the same can be said for the ideal of "equal educational opportunity." Higher education continues to make a certain contribution to social mobility. But the system is highly stratified, and the correlation between education and social mobility shows no tendency to improve. There has been "educational inflation" as the general level of educational attainment has increased rapidly, while relative social prospects remain much the same. Educational inflation serves the important ideological functions of providing the illusion of upward social mobility and of "cooling out" students with meritocratic grounds for failure. To the extent, then, that higher education provides real opportunities for social mobility, it preserves the class system through acting as an objective safety valve, and to the extent that it does not provide social mobility, it still perpetuates class distinctions as an ideological safety valve. This role has had, however, the important effect of pressing the expansion of the higher educational system beyond the limits of marginal utility and, thus, of disrupting the economic rationality of the system. On the other hand, enclaves representing the ideal of pure culture—principally the liberal arts faculties, sometimes joined by students—have had the opposite effect of retarding the progress of industrialization by the resistance they put up to managerial innovation. In this connection, it should also be said that culture for its own sake is, and always has been, only an ideal. Its roots are in an earlier period when higher education served principally the ruling class and the higher intelligentsia for whom a generalist education under human conditions was an essential privilege. The education of these groups remains *one* of the functions of higher education, and there is a growing consensus in the higher educational establishment that the demolition of liberal arts education may have been pressed too far.

The economic utility of limitless higher education was an unquestioned axiom of educational thinking in the 1960s. The economic stagnation of the late '60s and early '70s has revealed some weaknesses in these claims. It has turned out higher education is less functional than most people had presumed. There has been a vast over-production of higher degrees, particularly PhDs in liberal arts fields. The BA degree does not always appear to improve the potential productivity of its holders. The United States has found itself under intense competitive pressure in high-technology markets from countries, such as Japan, whose labor force has a much lower degree of educational attainment. This crisis has only lent momentum to the economic rationalization of higher education. The herculean efforts of the Carnegie Commission on Higher Education point to the emerging official conclusions:

1. Higher education has been too *academic;*
2. "Universal access" to higher education must replace the "goal" of "universal higher education," i.e., higher education must cease to expand at a high rate and its enrollments be stabilized by 1980;
3. A vigorous cost reduction program must be implemented;
4. The manpower development and research and development functions must be separated so that both may be undertaken more efficiently;
5. Tuition rates in the public sector should be allowed to rise drastically to promote market-enforced efficiency, to maintain the competitive position of the private sector, and ease the burden of public subsidy. Basic Educational Opportunity Grants according to financial need can compensate for any problem of educational opportunity. . . .

II. THE ORIGINS OF STUDENT REBELLION

The industrialization of higher education has affected students in three fundamental ways.

First, there are the direct educational effects, which manifest themselves in the decline of general education and the low priority of undergraduate teaching. Administration and faculty are equally responsible for these. The priority of research, the public service functions of universities, the relative decline of the liberal arts colleges, and the specialization of the faculty guarantee the decline of general education and the failure to transmit an integrated culture. The same factors, plus the priority of graduate education and the substitution of technology and less qualified labor for faculty, produce a decline in undergraduate teaching. In the universities, graduate education absorbs an increasing percentage of faculty time: there are 1 million graduate students in the United States, 12 per cent of total enrollment. Student-faculty ratios move up inexorably. Weighting graduate enrollment by a factor of three, the general ratio from 1955 to 1967 increased from approximately 16, to 20 to 1 in public four-year institutions and from 14, to 16 to 1 in private four-year schools, while remaining stable in the two-year institutions at 20 to 1.[6]

Combined with declining teaching loads, these ratios spelled increasing class sizes in American higher education. Educational economists have pointed out that the results of empirical studies of the relationship of class size to learning have been ambiguous at best. This is not necessarily the point. Industrialized education can certainly outproduce traditional education on a per-unit cost basis, and large classes may even match the learning of smaller ones. But large classes are *alienating*; so are the minute division of labor in learning, the regimentation of the institutions, the anomie of the environment, and the lack of control over the process.

The second effect of educational industrialization on students is the decline of the "educational community" and the rise of the "educational city." This development is not entirely negative. In the universities, the urbanized environment par excellence, the student has more personal and educational "options," a wider range of potential experience, and more exposure to people of differing ethnic and social backgrounds. The negative side of the educational city is the mass character of student life. Concentrated by the thousands in single locations, students are housed in barracks-like dormitories and deal with the institution through impersonal bureaucracies. In a crucial stage in the formation of personal identity, students are left without guidance among a cacophony of possibilities. In *Education and Identity,* Arthur Chickering argues that "clarity and consistency of objectives" are crucial to effective education and notes of the multiversities: "Although many small colleges are indistinguishable from each other and from their university counterparts and have failed to develop a coherent integration of purposes and practices, the diversity of persons and the diversity of functions that come to characterize the 'multiversity' make such development nearly impossible, even when the undergraduate liberal arts college itself has considerable autonomy and freedom of movement."[7] In the universities, there is some recognition of this problem to which "cluster colleges" and other models of decentralization have been offered as a solution. Although these concepts have been implemented in some schools with a degree of success, they hardly characterize the national situation as a whole. For many students, the variety of options is merely a source of confusion and demoralization. In *Big School, Small School*, Barker and Gump found that students in small schools held an average of 3.5 responsible positions per student (athletics, arts, organizations, etc.) against .5 positions in large schools. Further, they found that students in small schools received twice as many pressures to participate and academically marginal students five times the pressure to participate as in large schools.[8]

The third effect of educational industrialization on students is the expansion of "youth culture." Youth culture is the product of stages of life known as "adolescence" and "post-adolescence" (or "youth"). These stages of life are intervening periods between childhood as such and adulthood. If we define adulthood as self-support through fulltime employment and as normally marriage as well, we have a negative definition of adolescence and youth. These stages of life are the results of industrialization which requires a larger number of people with literacy and training before entrance into the labor force. There is a progressive "prolongation of adolescence" as industrialization proceeds and occupational requirements become more elaborate. Thus the high schools and colleges are the social base for youth culture, although analogous situations, such as military service or lower-class unemployment among the young, also generate youth cultures. The expansion of higher education since World War II has prolonged youth into the early twenties, and with the expansion of graduate education (1 million students) up to age thirty and beyond. This stage of life produces a "culture" which reflects a special situation and its problems, especially its lacks. As youth is regimented by educational and military bureaucracies, its culture stresses personal expression and feeling. Since the student living situation is socially atomized, the culture celebrates community. Because youth are searching for personal identity in ambiguous circumstances, the culture generates grandiose, usually fictional world views.

The political definition of youth culture is low. It is not inherently leftist but becomes an "adversary culture" on the basis of generational stratification. Furthermore, it is not a "culture" but a subculture. The effort in the 1960s to portray youth culture as a "new culture" expressing the supersession of the "work ethic" in a "post-scarcity" golden age was misbegotten. Youth under conditions of extended education is inherently a kind of limbo and youth culture cannot really provide permanent personal identities based upon it. The subculture provides a common symbolism and a "life style" to

share, but it does not solve the fundamental problems of impersonality and anomie. Although the youth movement made noble attempts to organize itself, it was ultimately based in atomized youth ghettoes. In its expressive strength (rock music, drugs, hair) and social weakness, the youth subculture resembles the black subculture with which it identifies. The youth culture is a "community" of the nameless.

My thesis is that the interaction of educational industrialization with new middle class students explains the incidence of student rebellion. Empirical studies have established the social characteristics of students who are most "protest-prone." They tend to major in the humanities or the more theoretically-oriented areas of the sciences. By social background, they come from the families of educated professionals of Jewish or liberal Protestant religious affiliation, usually of an urban and liberal bent. Their family socialization is not "permissive" per se but stresses independence and competitive mettle without undue parental intervention. Politically, these students do not rebel against their parents' values but extend and apply them. In its early years, a significant proportion of the movement's activists, perhaps one sixth, was descended from left-wing parents.[9] I have argued that these characteristics add up to new middle class background.

What evidence supports the industrialization theses? First, institutional size strongly correlates with student protest. Kenneth Keniston and others have discounted this fact and argued that a certain institutional size is only necessary for a "critical mass" of "protest-prone" students to form. This critical mass is supposed to set the stage for a self-reinforcing activist subculture which is the base for student protests. If the critical mass theory were correct, one would expect the correlation between size and protest to level off once the size necessary for a critical mass were reached. This is not the case. In their 1968 survey, Foster and Long found a direct correlation between size and protest with no tendency toward a levelling off. The incidence of protest, which was 21 per cent for schools of 500 enrollment or less, climbed steadily as size increased until it reached 100 per cent for institutions of 20,000 or more. In its survey of student protests in 1969, the Urban Research Corporation discovered an even steeper increase in protest as size grew: 1 per cent for schools of less than 500 students, 3 per cent for schools of less than 1000 students, 8 per cent for schools of less than 5000, 27 per cent of those under 10,000, and 54 per cent of those over 10,000. In his survey undertaken in the 1968–69 school year, Harold Hodgkinson obtained similar results and concluded: "With regard to student protest, the data do not seem to reveal any kind of 'critical mass' beyond which size the institution is more likely to have increased protest. . . . There seems to be no single point at which the curve jumps toward increased protest; rather it is a steady increase in protest as enrollment increases."[10]

On the other hand, there is a difference in the incidence of protest among *types* of institutions. In my judgment, this difference reflects the degree of industrialization and the "quality" of the student body—namely, the concentration of new middle class students in the school. In his 1967–68 survey, Richard Peterson found a large increase in the probability of protest in the large public universities compared to the national sample. In their study of protest in 1968–69, Astin and Bayer discovered the highest incidence of protest in the medium and large universities and in the large community colleges. Hodgkinson found a steep increase in the probability of protest according to highest degree awarded: 24.8 per cent for less-than-BA-awarding institutions, 33.5 per cent for BA-awarding schools, 50.0 per cent for MA-awarding, and 67.1 per cent for PhD-granting institutions. Controlling for highest degree awarded, Hodgkinson also found that the larger institutions *within* types had a higher probability of protest. The PhD-granting and less-than-BA-awarding institu-

tions which reported an increase in protest over the previous ten years were approximately twice as large as those which reported no change, while the MA-awarding schools were 50 per cent larger. The BA-awarding schools which reported an increase in protest were only slightly larger than those which did not, reflecting the relative insulation of liberal arts colleges from the industrializing process and the importance of student body characteristics for the occurrence of protests at those schools.

The incidence of protest during the May 1970 student strike also indicates the crucial role of size and selectivity. In his study for the Carnegie Commission, Richard Peterson found a range of protest of 40 per cent for institutions of less than 1000 enrollment up to 90 per cent for those with enrollment of 12,000 or more. The studies of the Urban Research Corporation and the Urban Institute also uncovered a correlation between size and protest in the May strike. In the case of "destructive demonstrations," Peterson discovered an even sharper relationship with size: 6.5 per cent for institutions of less than 12,000 enrollment, 29.7 per cent for those with more. By selectivity, he found that schools with more or less open admissions experienced significant protest in 59.6 per cent of the cases against 88.9 per cent for schools drawing students from the upper 10 per cent of high school graduating classes. "Federal Grant Universities" had the highest incidence of protest of all: 95.9 per cent had significant protest of some kind, 30.6 per cent "destructive demonstrations."[11]

In their survey comparing the results of the 1968–69 and 1970–71 school years, Astin and Bayer found that private universities were more likely to have protests than public universities as a group, and consequently that the correlation of size and protest was not strong for universities although it was very marked for other four-year and two-year institutions. Among universities, the correlation between selectivity and protest was very strong. In my judgment, these results reflect the importance of the interaction of the industrializing process with the characteristics of "protest-prone" students. Private universities as a group have a higher proportion of these students than public institutions as a group, though the largest public universities are often elite schools and enroll a high percentage of these students. This factor would explain Peterson's results finding the largest public universities to have a higher incidence of protest than other types—thus the centrality of the elite public multiversities of Berkeley, Wisconsin, and Michigan to the movement. Astin and Bayer find a strong correlation between selectivity and protest among universities and other four-year institutions, though not among the two-year schools where one, however, would not expect it to be decisive or even measurable. Taking the interaction of size and selectivity as critical, one would expect a rank order of the incidence of protest as follows:

selective public universities (often large)
private universities (often selective)
other public universities
nonsectarian private colleges (often selective)
public colleges (often large)
large two-year colleges
other two-year colleges
sectarian colleges

Surveys generally confirm this order, although no studies have specifically controlled by both size and selectivity. By 1970–71, the public colleges had overtaken the nonsectarian private colleges in the incidence of protest. Except for very large institutions, the community colleges have lagged behind. Partly, this fact reflects the low proportion of new middle class students which community colleges enroll. More importantly, as commuter schools enrolling a high percentage of part-time students who are employed, community colleges tend to dissolve student status as a total social role and to operate as adjuncts to employer organizations.

There are also correlations between other aspects of educational industrialization and student protest. Hodgkinson found correlations between student protest and trimester systems and between protest and increased proportions of the institutional budget deriving from Federal support. His survey also uncovered a relationship between student protest and increased hours of faculty time spent in research, as well as decreased hours spent on teaching. Hodgkinson found correlations between the educational city and student protest. Thus schools with a greater heterogeneity of the student body in terms of age, socioeconomic background, transfers, out-of-state students, and ethnic composition had a higher incidence of protest. Taking into account such factors as the ratio of out-of-state to in-state students and the ratio of foreign-born to native-born students, Joseph Scott and Mohamed el-Assal discovered that 87 per cent of the "complex" institutions in their sample reported protests in 1964 and 1965, compared to 43 per cent of the "simple" institutions. Protest was also more likely to occur in institutions located in large cities rather than small towns. In classifying institutions as complex or simple, Scott and El-Assal also attempted to judge the effect of the bureaucratization and functional diversity of multiversities by calculating in their measure of complexity such factors as the number of departments and degrees, the student/faculty ratio, the ratio of undergraduate to graduate students, and the ratio of dormitory to non-dormitory students. They found that *100 per cent* of the complex, large, high-quality institutions in their sample had protests, compared to 34 per cent of the simple, small, low-quality schools.[12]

In a subsequent issue of the *American Sociological Review,* Scott and El-Assal were criticized on the grounds that students did not seem to protest *against* any of these institutional characteristics. In his reply, Scott correctly noted that the criticism was neither here nor there because the *correlation* between these characteristics and protest remained. The criticism was in any case ill-founded. In its survey of 1969 protests, the Urban Research Corporation discovered that student power issues were raised in 44 per cent of the cases of student protest, *ahead* of war protests and second only to issues of "black recognition." The third major category of protest issues related to "quality of student life" which also ranked ahead of war-related protest. In their study for the American Council on Education, Astin and Bayer also found that "instructional procedures" relating to class size, quality of instruction, the grading system, and student evaluations constituted an important protest category. Classifying six sets of issues as "student power issues," they found these to be more prominent than other sets of questions including both war- and race-related issues. In their follow-up survey of 1970–71 protests, Astin and Bayer discovered that student power issues continued to be the leading demands, followed by a set of eight issues classified as "services to students."

Up to this point, the trajectory of the student movement has been sketched against the background of the general expansion of higher education in the post-war period. A more specific breakdown strengthens the case. Immediately after World War II, the influx of war veterans doubled enrollments from 1 to 2 million from 1945 to 1946. There was no student rebellion but one was not in prospect because of the political climate and the nature of the veteran clientele. After this initial growth, enrollments levelled off and actually declined in the early 1950s. From 1955 to 1960, enrollments resumed their growth: 2.6 to 3.6 million or approximately 35 per cent. With the maturation of the war baby generation, the rate of growth reached its peak: 55 per cent between 1960 and 1965, continuing at a high level of 30 per cent between 1965 and 1970. The highest percentage growth in enrollments was 1964, the year of the Free Speech Movement at Berkeley. The potential for rebellion was released by the political crisis of the 1960s. Because of the uncer-

tainty built into trainee status without clear class moorings, the student movement required external stimuli which were "real" and "objective." These objective realities arrived in the form of the black movement and the Indo-China War. Many New Left cadres worked in the civil rights movement, particularly the student sit-in movement of 1960, and were drawn to the left by the urban rebellions of the 1964–68 period. This was also the period of the "escalation" of the Vietnam War, which the U.S. Government attempted to wage while it undermined the domestic anti-Communist consensus of the 1950s with its policy of *detente* with the Soviet Union. The left saw its opportunity and reemerged to lead a militant student rebellion.

III. DECLINE OF THE MOVEMENT

Hardly had the Columbia rebellion occurred in the spring of 1968, followed by a wave of protest at more than 500 schools, before observers began to search for signs of the movement's demise. When the campuses were quiet in the fall of 1969, commentators stated categorically that the movement was "dead." This impression was dispelled by the national student strike against the invasion of Cambodia in May 1970. Thereafter, the coroners were not contradicted, particularly when students failed to respond to the invasion of Laos the following year.

Certainly, the national strike of 1970 was the apogee of the movement, but its decline was not sudden and complete. The movement both first started and first subsided in the elite universities which were "visible" to the national press. Thus Bayer and Astin found that in 1970–71, the year following the Cambodia strike, 43 per cent, or more than 1000, of all institutions experienced some form of student protest. The incidence of protest represented only a very slight decline from 1968–69 when the movement first became a national phenomenon, although it was down from 1969–70. However, as student protest became old news, national press coverage declined drastically from 40 per cent of the institutions experiencing "severe protest" in 1968–69 to 10 per cent in 1970–71. *None* of the institutions of lower selectivity which experienced severe protest received national coverage, while 20 per cent of the institutions of medium or high selectivity received coverage from the national media.

The trend was toward a diffusion of student protest throughout the higher educational system and throughout all regions of the country, while protest simultaneously declined gradually in the elite schools. "With the exception of the universities and the private nonsectarian colleges," Bayer and Astin reported, "higher educational institutions have generally been experiencing severe protest incidents at the same or higher levels than in 1968–1969."[13] The correlation between size and protest held up, with the qualifications that have been mentioned, although the relationship "flattened out" somewhat as the student movement began to lap the shores of unlikely places such as Catholic colleges and sectarian Protestant institutions. As protest actually increased in the public colleges and community colleges in 1970–71 over 1968–69, the student movement began to reach into the "new working class" sector of the student population. Flacks and Mankoff also report a broadening of the social base of student protest in the universities.[14]

It is certain that the student movement declined more sharply after 1970–71, although in the absence of empirical surveys the degree of its decline is unclear. Just how unclear was demonstrated by the killing of two black students by state police and National Guardsmen in a student demonstration at Southern University in Baton Rouge, Louisiana, in November 1972. The decline of the movement parallels a decline in the rate of expansion of higher education and a constriction in the job market for educated labor. Since financial stringency in the higher educational system actually forced the pace of industrialization, this factor was probably not decisive in itself although it certainly weakened the strategic position of student rebels. For similar reasons, industrial strikes are more prevalent in periods of prosperity than of recession.

Equally important was that the "causes" which were objects of student idealism began to fade. There were no major black uprisings after 1968 and the "Vietnamization" of the war by the Nixon Administration served its purpose. The Laos invasion, which did not involve American troops, did not provoke a significant student response. Political repression took its toll. The killing of four Kent State students, not to mention the death of 10 other students in the movement, sapped student morale and demonstrated the limits of moral protest based on direct action. The movement gradually exhausted its political possibilities and lost faith in its guiding myths that students were leading the "people" and that "revolution" was nigh. Instead, a reactionary coalition with majority potential began to develop in opposition to the student movement, the counter-culture, the anti-war movement, and the racial minorities. In the wake of the Free Speech Movement and black militancy, Ronald Reagan won the governorship of California by a million-vote majority in 1966. From the Presidential primaries of 1964, the "movement" of George Wallace grew into a national political force. With Spiro Agnew as his hit man, Richard Nixon won the Presidency in 1968 and 1972 and pursued his plans, based on a "Southern strategy," of making the Republican Party the dominant political force. Although the "left-wing" campaign of Senator McGovern in 1972 should not be abruptly dismissed, his crushing defeat was conclusive evidence of the limited potential of "new politics" and its liberal middle class and non-white constituencies. In the face of these events, the student movement lost its *élan* and even its nerve. Students eagerly seized the one gift which the Nixon Administration offered them: lost innocence.

In this climate, campus administrations

worked hard to protect themselves against future assaults. Their strategy of containment was not based on unlimited repression but on an effort to split the coalition of liberals and radicals which was crucial to the early success of the movement. To this end, they implemented reform programs and due process procedures to win over liberal and moderate elements, while taking advantage of the demobilization of the movement to launch a national purge of student and faculty radicals from the campuses. Since their policy was generally enacted after the decline of the movement was well under way, it was a prophylactic. Its efficacy has not been tested.[15]

Finally, there was the political failure of the movement itself, which had a structural basis in the dualistic character of student status. From the beginning, the student movement was torn between political alternatives based on the role of student as a trainee for the labor force and those based on the youth culture arising out of the encapsulation of student life. The movement followed the latter course with disastrous results. The New Left capitulated to the capture of the student movement by anarchist youth culture ideology because the subculture, hyped by the media, spread New Left notions to millions of young people. Eventually, the New Left was swallowed by it. The gains of the exposure of liberal ideology and politics in the 1960s were lost, and liberalism returned in a "cultural" guise. To some extent, this fate was unavoidable. As the student movement began to exhaust its political possibilities, utopian anarchism seemed to offer routes of escape, whether through communes or terrorism. Suspended in educational bureaucracies, uncertain of their social role and class destinations, students inclined to a peculiar form of idealism, which, though not strictly bourgeois in character, drew on its tradition. In the Romantic tradition, most of the basic themes of the American youth culture are anticipated. Against the mechanization of the social order, the romantics of the early 19th cen-

tury asserted the "revolution for life." In desperate defense as industrial rationalization encroached on their own domain, artists evolved the doctrine that they were the "unacknowledged legislators of the world" as the custodians of "culture" and the "creative imagination." Against the transformation of nature by the industrial system, the romantics instituted a cult of nature. Against the rationalism and materialism of a secular order, the romantics celebrated a variety of mysticisms. Against the class conflict of capitalist society, the romantics looked back to the Middle Ages for the model of class harmony in an "organic society." Student idealism, rooted in the objective circumstances of student status, blinded students to their real situation, obstructed the development of a long-term political struggle based on a viable social program, and ultimately exposed the movement to an epithet of its own devising: *irrelevance.*

Is the student movement, then, dead and gone forever? Not necessarily. The industrialization of higher education proceeds. If current projections hold up, student enrollment will rise from 8 to over 13 million between 1970 and 1980, an increase of more than 50 per cent. Expenditures are projected to increase from $24 billion to $44 billion. The Carnegie Commission has estimated that $50 billion would be required to meet 1980 costs, given present assumptions and procedures, and has recommended ways and means to reduce expenditures to $40 billion. This cost reduction program of 20 per cent gives a rough idea of the intensification of the industrializing process which is in store. After 1980, enrollments are expected to stabilize and the pace of industrialization may well level off.

What will be more important is the character of this industrialization. If current trends and the recommendations of the Carnegie Commission are any indication, these are the prospects: 1.) a rapid expansion of the community college systems and, to a lesser degree, the public sector as a whole; 2.) rising tuition rates in the public sector, as well as in the private sector, and the accentuation of class-based tracking systems; 3.) "educational innovations," such as external degree programs, open universities, and the like, which serve to integrate education more closely with the general economy; 4.) a decline of "academic" education and more emphasis on vocational and professional education; 5.) increasing proletarianization of the instructional staff; 6.) the continuation of current industrializing trends, such as increasing institutional size, concentration of authority, and alienation of students.

These trends entail a further economic rationalization of higher education and an increasing degree of functional integration of education and manpower requirements. These trends also contain the seeds of a solution to the impasse of the student movement. As the encapsulation of student life is progressively eliminated, so will be eliminated the distortions in student consciousness based upon it. Certain advantages will also be lost. Part-time, continuing, and commuter education break up the youth ghettoes and reintegrate the generations. As youth culture withers, some of the impetus of student rebellion will be lost. Its passing should not be mourned, however, because its political orientation has led nowhere and its possibilities have been exhausted. On the other hand, the integration of students with the labor force, the loss of the professional illusions of the instructional staff, the clarification of the class character of the higher educational system raise *new* possibilities. This is not a speculation. We have seen that student protest in the state colleges and the community colleges was rising in 1969–71, while it declined in the elite schools. The forces moving higher education create the possibility of a student movement which is a new working class movement with staying power and a socialist program. Such a movement would have realistic opportunities for alliances with the American working class. The potential militancy of the latter is at this moment a speculation, but the social and economic conditions of the 1970s do not make it an idle speculation. Most importantly, this is the *only* avenue which can generate new political possibilities and raise realistic hopes for political victory on a national level, and without these there will not be another student movement.

NOTES

1. Higher educational statistics in this article are drawn from the U.S. National Center for Educational Statistics, *Digest of Educational Statistics*, published annually, and *Projections of Educational Statistics to 1979–80* (Washington, D.C., 1971); see also Harold Hodgkinson, *Institutions in Transition* (New York, 1971).
2. Christopher Jencks *et al.*, *Inequality* (New York, 1972), p. 224.
3. See Jerome Karabel, "Community Colleges and Social Stratification," *Harvard Educational Review*, November, 1972.
4. Herbert Gintis, "Education, Technology, and the Characteristics of Worker Productivity," *American Economic Review*, May 1971, p. 276.
5. See National Science Foundation, *Federal Support to Colleges and Universities* (Washington, D.C., published annually).
6. Carnegie Commission on Higher Education, *The More Effective Use of Resources* (New York: McGraw-Hill, 1972), p. 65.
7. Arthur Chickering, *Education and Identity* (San Francisco, 1969) p. 185.
8. See R. G. Barker and P. V. Gump, *Big School, Small School* (Stanford, Calif., 1964).
9. See the studies of Somers, Selvin and Hagstrom, and Lyonns in Seymour Martin Lipset and Sheldon S. Wolin, eds., *The Berkeley Student Revolt* (New York, 1965); Richard Flacks in *Journal of Social Issues*, July 1967; Watts and Whittaker in *Journal of Applied Behavioral Science*, 1966,2; Block, Haan, and Smith in James F. Adams, ed., *Contributions to an Understanding of Adolescence* (Boston, 1968); Paul Heist, O.A. Knorr and W.V. Mintner, eds., *Order and Freedom on the Campus* (Boulder, Colo., 1965); Braungart and Lubell results reported in Lipset and Altbach survey in S.M. Lipset, *Student Politics* (New York, 1967); Block, Haan, and Smith in *Journal of Social Issues*, Fall 1969; Kenneth Keniston, *Young Radicals* (New York, 1968).
10. Hodgkinson, pp. 255–56. The other surveys are Richard Peterson, *The Scope of Organized Protest in 1964–65* (Princeton, N.J., 1966) and *The Scope of Organized Student Protest in 1967–68* (Princeton, N.J., 1968); Foster and Long, "Levels of Protest," in Julian Foster and Durwood Long, *Protest! Student Activism in America* (New York, 1970); Alexander Astin and Alan E. Bayer, *Campus Disruption During 1968–69* (Washington, D.C., 1969) and "Campus Unrest, 1970–71: Was It Really All That Quiet?," *Educational Record* (Fall 1971) Urban Research Corporation, *Student Protests 1969* (Chicago, 1970).
11. Richard Peterson and John Bilorusky, *May 1970: the Campus Aftermath of Cambodia and*

Kent State (Berkeley, 1971); Urban Research Corporation, *On Strike . . . Shut It Down* (Chicago, 1970); Garth Buchanan and Joan Brackett, *Survey of Campus Incidents as Interpreted by College Presidents, Faculty Chairmen, and Student Body Presidents,* Urban Institute (Washington, D.C., 1970); Alexander Astin, *Educational Record* winter, 1971.
12. Joseph W. Scott and Mohamed el-Assal, "Multiversity, University Size, University Quality, and Student Protest: An Empirical Study," *American Sociological Review,* Oct. 1969.
13. Astin and Bayer, Fall 1971, pp. 304–305.
14. Milton Mankoff and Richard Flacks, "The Changing Base of the American Student Movement," *The Annals* of the American Academy of Political and Social Science, May 1971, pp. 54–68.
15. See Michael Miles, "The Triumph of Reaction," *Change,* winter 1972–73.

V

CULTURAL REPRODUCTION
AND THE TRANSMISSION
OF KNOWLEDGE

Behind the study of politics, which we treated in its relation to education in the last section, there has always lain the most fundamental problem in sociology—the explanation of social order and conflict. We move to this level of analysis in the present section, but in a new context. It is familiar and conventional, especially in the Anglo-Saxon world, to begin the discussion of order and continuity with the problem as formulated by Hobbes, who made the analytical distinction between the state of nature and the state of civil society. Much modern philosophical, sociological, and political writing attempts to analyze the transition Hobbes described: a fragmented, individualized, and endemic conflict over the distribution of scarce means to desired ends is transformed into an ordered system of both ends and the means of their attainment. Discussion since Hobbes follows two main lines. One is the liberal tradition, which, as formulated by Talcott Parsons, emphasizes the passing on of culture and the development of consensus through various social institutions. The other is the Marxist tradition, in which the central concept of class conflict replaces that of socialization.[1] For Marxists, the process that Parsons calls "socialization"·is actually the subjection of subordinate classes to the ideological hegemony of the bourgeoisie.[2]

Cultural reproduction and the transmission of knowledge, therefore, are processes that may be interpreted from these two contrasted perspectives. Consensus theory puts its emphasis on a common value system imparted to children through their relations with adults. Conflict theory puts its emphasis on the control over the content of socialization that is exercised by a dominant class. Thus the transmission of knowledge is, as has been noted by the "new" sociology of education,[3] mediated through the power structure of a society; what counts as knowledge, who has access to it, and how it is measured and certified involve processes derived from social structure. It is to these structures and processes that this part of the book is addressed.

---

1. For a discussion of these two traditions in sociological thought, see John Horton, "Order and Conflict Theories as Competing Ideologies," *American Sociological Review* 71 (May 1966): 701–713.
2. See Louis Althusser, "Ideology and Ideological State Apparatuses," *Education: Structure and Society,* ed. B. R. Cosin (Harmondsworth, Middlesex: Penguin Books, 1972), pp. 242–280.
3. See our discussion of the "new" sociology of education in the Introduction.

In this section, Robert Dreeben (Chapter 32) discusses the role played by schools in socialization, concentrating particularly on the way children learn certain values. Following Talcott Parsons[4] he argues that, by virtue of the nature and sequence of the structural arrangement of schools, pupils are exposed to social experiences and opportunities to learn norms in anticipation of adult public life. His stress here, in the analysis of complex societies, is on the possibilities offered by formal schooling for children to learn the social norms of independence, achievement, universalism, and specificity more fully than they could within the kinship system. Formal schooling is seen as an intermediary socializing process, and the underlying approach follows that of the first line of descent from the Hobbesian problem, to which we have referred.

In the work of Bowles and Gintis we have seen an example of the Marxist approach to the same problems, which advances a correspondence theory and interprets education as a means of reproducing the social relations of the workplace. The essays by Bernstein and Bourdieu in this section have added interest in that they attempt to combine "order" and "conflict" perspectives in their analyses of the process of cultural transmission. Both writers try to clarify the nature of class reproduction and to relate it to the passing on of economic and cultural wealth. We have discussed Bernstein's continuing studies of the relation between the content of knowledge and the structure of power at some length in our Introduction, and we noted there the two interrelated strands in Bernstein's research: his studies of the social basis of language and his analyses of education as an agency of social control. In the two essays that appear below he presents an exploration of the relation between class and language (Chapter 28) and a more recent analysis of the cultural content of the teaching of very young children (Chapter 30). This involves an explanation of the idea of "invisible pedagogy," which is realized through what Bernstein describes as weak classifications and weak frames.[5] What emerges is a study of the subtlety of social control in modern forms of infant education, which are linked by Bernstein to an empirical distinction within the middle class between the traditional bourgeoisie and the new middle class that fills the expanding major and minor professions concerned with personal services.[6]

Bourdieu's work on similar problems in France is presented in Chapter 29. In advanced industrial societies, cultural capital is an increasingly important component of the perpetuation of classes through generations. But Bourdieu recognizes that the two processes of cultural reproduction and social reproduction are not in exact correspondence. As he sees it, the evolution of power relationships between classes in such societies "tends more completely to exclude the imposition of a hierarchy based upon the crude and ruthless affirmation of the power relationship." To the extent that social hierarchies are transformed into academic hierarchies, modern educational systems fulfill a function of legitimation that is more and more necessary to the perpetuation of the social order in societies with a complex division of labor. Education can play this role in that the placing of individuals in social and occupational hierarchies can be based on academic achievement as demonstrated and certified through educational processes.

4. Talcott Parsons, "The School Class as a Social System," *Harvard Educational Review* 29 (Fall 1959): 297–318.
5. For an elaboration of the concepts of classification and framing and an exploration of their relevance to the sociological analysis of curriculum, see Basil Bernstein, "On the Classification and Framing of Educational Knowledge," in *Knowledge and Control: New Directions in the Sociology of Education*, ed. Michael F. D. Young (London: Collier-Macmillan, 1971).
6. The distinction between "old" and "new" middle class is discussed further in Basil Bernstein, *Class, Codes and Control*, Volume Three: *Towards a Theory of Educational Transmissions* (London: Routledge and Kegan Paul, 1975).

Bourdieu asks whether the transmission of cultural capital is replacing the passing on of economic capital; he concludes that it is not, stating that qualifications, "intelligence," and certification represent "but one particular form of capital which comes to be added, in most cases, to the possession of economic capital and the correlative capital of power and social relationships," and that "the holders of economic power have more chances than those who are deprived of it also to possess cultural capital and, in any case, to be able to do without it since academic qualifications are a weak currency and possess all their value only within the limits of the academic market." In a more recent formulation by Bourdieu the educational system becomes an arena of class conflict in which the structure of educational expansion reflects the dynamics of a struggle for social position whose particular form is imposed upon subordinate classes by the dominant class.[7]

Thus the theories formulated by Bernstein and Bourdieu go beyond the concepts of ascription and achievement to throw light on the processes that link social reproduction to the transmission of knowledge. Fritz Ringer in Chapter 31 draws upon Max Weber's distinction between "class" and "status" with respect to higher education in Germany in the nineteenth century and has, in effect, used the concept of cultural capital to describe the distinctive social status of the educated group of higher officials, secondary school teachers, judges and lawyers, doctors, and university professors that was "perhaps the most important and influential social group in Germany until late in the nineteenth century." Preservation of this elite came about, as Ringer shows, predominantly through self-recruitment. Between 1860 and 1889 no less than 65 percent of those who were *habilitiert* to lecture at German universities were the sons of higher officials, professors, and academically educated professionals. Of course, as Max Weber pointed out in contrasting the German and American systems of his day, "the career of the academic man in Germany is generally based upon plutocratic prerequisites." Habilitation as a *privatdozent* was a long process in which the aspiring scholar had largely to support himself. Nevertheless the continuance of a unique social group with a characteristic set of values that controlled the admission of new members also depended on the passing on of a particular culture through the generations. It was an illuminating example of the process of transmission and reproduction of cultural capital.[8]

In order to place the chapters by Bernstein, Bourdieu, Dreeben, and Ringer in the larger context of the evolution of literacy and its consequences for the social structure of complex societies, we have included an extract from an essay on this topic by two anthropologists, Jack Goody and Ian Watt (Chapter 27). These authors argue that it was through language that man achieved forms of social organization with a range and complexity that made them different in kind from those of animals. They identify the basic elements of cultural transmission in non-literate societies and then go on to distinguish the important intellectual differences in the cultural traditions of complex societies. In particular, they stress the invention of writing associated with the urban revolution of the ancient Near East and show how this transformed the handing on of culture. "Potentially, human intercourse was now no longer restricted to the impermanency of oral converse. But since the first methods of writing employed were difficult to master, their effects were relatively limited, and it was only when

7. Pierre Bourdieu, Luc Boltanski, and Monique de Saint Martin, "Les stratégies de reconversion: les classes sociales et le système d'enseignement," *Social Science Information* 12, no. 5 (1973): 61–113.

8. Ringer's analysis of nineteenth-century German higher education is part of a larger study of German academics, which draws upon the sociology of knowledge to illuminate their characteristic cultural concerns. Through an analysis of the social position of the "Mandarin," Ringer is able to link features of German social structure to the content of German higher education. See Fritz Ringer, *The Decline of the German Mandarins: The German Academic Community, 1890–1933* (Cambridge, Mass.: Harvard University Press, 1969).

the simplicity and flexibility of later alphabetic writing made widespread literacy possible that for the first time there began to take concrete shape in the Greek world of the 7th century B.C. a society that was essentially literate and that soon established many of the institutions that became characteristic of all later literate societies." Goody and Watt conclude that the rejection of a simple dichotomy between "primitive" and "civilized" modes of thought has gone too far and has degenerated into what they term "diffuse relativism and sentimental egalitarianism."[9]

It is a distinguishing mark of the "new" sociology of education to give research priority to the problem of what constitutes valid knowledge in a society. The work of Bernstein and Bourdieu attempts to relate this question to the structure of society and to analyze the processes of cultural transmission, linking the strategies adopted by families, including the use of schools and public cultural resources, to efforts to maintain or improve children's opportunities to inherit the status and privileges possessed by their parents. Yet a number of problems remain unresolved—among them the effects of a given form of the organization of knowledge on the experience of formal education among schoolchildren of different social backgrounds and the *process* by which the power structure of a society penetrates the content of education. The contributions of Weber and Durkheim, who insist that analyses of educational ideals must be linked to analyses of the larger society, point us in the right direction, but much hard, theoretically informed empirical work remains to be done if we are to understand the connections between social structure and the process of education.

9. For a collection of empirical studies based on Goody and Watt's seminal article on the consequences of literacy, see Jack Goody, ed., *Literacy in Traditional Societies* (Cambridge: Cambridge University Press, 1968).

SELECTIVE BIBLIOGRAPHY

Aries, Philippe. *Centuries of Childhood: A Social History of Family Life.* New York: Alfred A. Knopf, 1962.

Ben-David, Joseph, and Awraham Zloczower. "Universities and Academic Systems in Modern Societies." *European Journal of Sociology* 3 (1962): 45–84.

Bernstein, Basil. *Class, Codes and Control, Volume Three: Towards a Theory of Educational Transmissions.* London: Routledge and Kegan Paul, 1975.

Bourdieu, Pierre, and Jean-Claude Passeron. *La reproduction.* Paris: Les Éditions de Minuit, 1970.

Cohen, Rosalie A. "Conceptual Styles, Culture Conflict, and Nonverbal Tests of Intelligence." *American Anthropologist* 71 (October 1969): 828–856.

Cole, Michael J., et al. *The Cultural Context of Learning and Thinking.* New York: Basic Books, 1971.

Henry, Jules. "A Cross-Cultural Outline of Education." *Current Anthropology* 1, no. 4: 267–305.

Holly, Douglas. *Society, Schools and Humanity.* London: MacGibbon and Kee, 1971.

Kohn, Melvin L. *Class and Conformity: A Study in Values.* Homewood, Ill.: The Dorsey Press, 1969.

McDermott, John. "The Laying On of Culture." *The Nation,* 10 March 1969.

Mannheim, Karl. *Ideology and Utopia.* New York: Harcourt, Brace and World, 1936.

Ringer, Fritz K. *The Decline of the German Mandarins: The German Academic Community, 1890–1933.* Cambridge, Mass.: Harvard University Press, 1969.

Shils, Edward. "The Intellectual Between Tradition and Modernity: The Indian Situation." *Comparative Studies in Society and History,* Supp. 1 (1961), pp. 8–87.

Spindler, George Dearborn, ed. *Education and Cultural Process.* New York: Holt, Rinehart and Winston, 1974.

Squibb, P.G. "The Concept of Intelligence— A Sociological Perspective." *The Sociological Review* 21 (February 1973): 57–75.

Thabault, R. *L'ascension d'une peuple 1848–1914. Mon village—ses hommes, ses routes, son école.* Paris: Librairie Dela-grave, 1945.

Wax, Murray, et al., eds. *Anthropological Perspectives on Education.* New York: Basic Books, 1971.

Wilkinson, Rupert H. "The Gentleman Ideal and the Maintenance of a Political Elite." *Sociology of Education* 37 (Fall 1963): 9–26.

Williams, Raymond. *Culture and Society.* London: Chatto and Windus, 1957.

Young, Michael F.D., ed. *Knowledge and Control.* London: Collier-Macmillan, 1971.

27. The Consequences of Literacy

JACK GOODY AND IAN WATT

The accepted tripartite divisions of the formal study both of mankind's past and present are to a considerable extent based on man's development first of language and later of writing. Looked at in the perspective of time, man's biological evolution shades into prehistory when he becomes a language-using animal; add writing, and history proper begins. Looked at in a temporal perspective, man as animal is studied primarily by the zoologist, man as talking animal primarily by the anthropologist, and man as talking and writing animal primarily by the sociologist.

That the differentiation between these categories should be founded on different modes of communication is clearly appropriate; it was language that enabled man to achieve a form of social organisation whose range and complexity was different in kind from that of animals: whereas the social organisation of animals was mainly instinctive and genetically transmitted, that of man was largely learned and transmitted verbally through the cultural heritage. The basis for the last two distinctions, those based on the development of writing, is equally clear: to the extent that a significant quantity of written records are available the pre-historian yields to the historian; and to the extent that alphabetical writing and popular literacy imply new modes of social organisation and transmission, the anthropologist tends to yield to the sociologist.

But why? And how? There is no agreement about this question, nor even about what the actual boundary lines between non-literate and literate cultures are. At what point in the formalisation of pictographs or other graphic signs can we talk of "letters," of literacy? And what proportion of the society has to write and read before the culture as a whole can be described as literate?

These are some of the many reasons why the extent to which there is any distinction between the areas and methods peculiar to anthropology and sociology must be regarded as problematic; and the difficulty affects not only the boundaries of the two disciplines but also the nature of the intrinsic differences in their subject matter.[1] The recent trend has been for anthropologists to spread their net more widely and engage in the study of industrial societies side by side with their sociological colleagues. We can no longer accept the view that anthropologists have as their objective the study of primitive man, who is characterised by a "primitive mind," while sociologists, on the other hand, concern themselves with civilised man, whose activities are guided by "rational thought" and tested by "logico-empirical procedures." The reaction against such ethnocentric views, however, has now gone to the point of denying that the distinction between non-literate and literate society has any significant validity. This position seems contrary to our personal observation; and so it has seemed worthwhile to enquire whether there may not be, even from the most empirical and relativist standpoint, genuine illumination to be derived from a further consideration of some of the historical and analytic problems connected with the traditional dichotomy between non-literate and literate societies.

I. THE CULTURAL TRADITION IN NON-LITERATE SOCIETIES

For reasons which will become clear it seems best to begin with a generalised description of the ways in which the cultural heritage is transmitted in non-literate societies, and then to see how these ways are changed by the widespread adoption of an easy and effective means of written communication.

From *Comparative Studies in Society and History* 5 (July 1963): 304–345. We have extracted pp. 304–326 and 344–345 for reproduction here. Reprinted by permission.

When one generation hands on its cultural heritage to the next, three fairly separate items are involved. First, the society passes on its material plant, including the natural resources available to its members. Secondly, it transmits standardised ways of acting. These customary ways of behaving are only partly communicated by verbal means; ways of cooking food, of growing crops, of handling children may be transmitted by direct imitation. But the most significant elements of any human culture are undoubtedly channelled through words, and reside in the particular range of meanings and attitudes which members of any society attach to their verbal symbols. These elements include not only what we habitually think of as customary behavior but also such items as ideas of space and time, generalised goals and aspirations, in short the *weltanschauung* of every social group. In Durkheim's words, these categories of the understanding are "priceless instruments of thought which the human groups have laboriously forged through the centuries and where they have accumulated the best of their intellectual capital."[2] The relative continuity of these categories of understanding from one generation to another is primarily ensured by language, which is the most direct and comprehensive expression of the social experience of the group.

The transmission of the verbal elements of culture by oral means can be visualised as a long chain of interlocking conversations between members of the group. Thus all beliefs and values, all forms of knowledge, are communicated between individuals in face-to-face contact; and, as distinct from the material content of the cultural tradition, whether it be cave-paintings or hand-axes, they are stored only in human memory.

The intrinsic nature of oral communication has a considerable effect upon both the content and the transmission of the cultural repertoire. In the first place it makes for a directness of relationship between symbol and referent. There can be no reference to "dictionary definitions," nor can words accumulate the successive layers of historically validated meanings which they acquire in a literate culture. Instead the meaning of each word is ratified in a succession of concrete situations, accompanied by vocal inflexions and physical gestures, all of which combine to particularize both its specific denotation and its accepted connotative usages. This process of direct semantic ratification, of course, operates cumulatively; and as a result the totality of symbol-referent relationships is more immediately experienced by the individual in an exclusively oral culture, and is thus more deeply socialised.

One way of illustrating this is to consider how the range of vocabulary in a non-literate society reflects this mode of semantic ratification. It has often been observed how the elaboration of the vocabulary of such a society reflects the particular interests of the people concerned. The inhabitants of the Pacific island of Lesu have not one, but a dozen or so, words for pigs,[3] according to sex, color, and where they come from—a prolixity which mirrors the importance of pigs in a domestic economy that otherwise includes few sources of protein. The corollary of this prolixity is that where common emphases and interests, whether material or otherwise, are not specifically involved, there is little verbal development. Malinowski reported that in the Trobriands the outer world was only named insofar as it yielded useful things, useful, that is, in the very broadest sense;[4] and there is much other testimony to support the view that there is an intimate functional adaptation of language in non-literate societies, which obtains not only for the relatively simple and concrete symbol-referents involved above, but also for the more generalized "categories of understanding" and for the cultural tradition as a whole.

In an essay he wrote in collaboration with Mauss, "De quelques formes primitives de classification,"[5] Durkheim traces the interconnections between the ideas of space and the territorial distribution of the Australian aborigines, the Zuni of the Pueblo area and the Sioux of the Great Plains. This inter-meshing of what he called the collective representations with the social morphology of a particular society is clearly another aspect of the same directness of relationship between symbol and referent. Just as the more concrete part of a vocabulary reflects the dominant interests of the society, so the more abstract categories are often closely linked to the accepted terminology for prag-matic pursuits. Among the LoDagaa of Northern Ghana, days are reckoned accord-ing to the incidence of neighboring markets; the very word for day and market is the same, and the "weekly" cycle is a six-day revolution of the most important markets in the vicinity, a cycle which also defines the spatial range of everyday activities.[6]

The way in which these various institu-tions in an oral culture are kept in relatively close accommodation one to another surely bears directly on the question of the central difference between literate and non-literate societies. As we have remarked, the whole content of the social tradition, apart from the material inheritances, is held in memory. The social aspects of remembering have been emphasised by sociologists and psycholo-gists, in particular Maurice Halbwachs.[7] What the individual remembers tends to be what is of critical importance in his experi-ence of the main social relationships. In each generation, therefore, the individual memory will mediate the cultural heritage in such a way that its new constituents will adjust to the old by the process of interpretation that Bartlett calls "rationalizing" or the "effort after meaning"; and whatever parts of it have ceased to be of contemporary relevance are likely to be eliminated by the process of forgetting.

The social function of memory—and of forgetting—can thus be seen as the final stage of what may be called the homeostatic organisation of the cultural tradition in non-literate society. The language is developed in intimate association with the experience of the community, and it is learned by the

individual in face-to-face contact with the other members. What continues to be of social relevance is stored in the memory while the rest is usually forgotten: and language—primarily vocabulary—is the effective medium of this crucial process of social digestion and elimination which may be regarded as analogous to the homeostatic organisation of the human body by means of which it attempts to maintain its present condition of life.

In drawing attention to the importance of these assimilating mechanisms in non-literate societies, we are denying neither the occur-rence of social change, nor yet the "survi-vals" which it leaves in its wake. Nor do we overlook the existence of mnemonic devices in oral cultures which offer some resistance to the interpretative process. Formalised patterns of speech, recital under ritual condi-tions, the use of drums and other musical instruments, the employment of professional remembrancers—all such factors may shield at least part of the content of memory from the transmuting influence of the immediate pressures of the present. The Homeric epics, for instance, seem to have been written down during the first century of Greek literature between 750 and 650 B.C., but "they look to a departed era, and their sub-stance is unmistakably old."[8]

With these qualifications, however, it seems correct to characterize the transmis-sion of the cultural tradition in oral societies as homeostatic in view of the way in which its emphasis differs from that in literate societies. The description offered has, of course, been extremely abstract; but a few illustrative examples in one important area—that of how the tribal past is digested into the communal orientation of the present—may serve to make it clearer.

Like the Bedouin Arabs and the Hebrews of the Old Testament, the Tiv people of Nigeria give long genealogies of their fore-bears which in this case stretch some twelve generations in depth back to an eponymous founding ancestor.[9] Neither these geneal-ogies, nor the Biblical lists of the descendants of Adam, were remembered purely as feats of memory. They served as mnemonics for systems of social relations. When on his deathbed Jacob delivered prophecies about the future of his twelve sons, he spoke of them as the twelve tribes or nations of Israel. It would seem from the account in Genesis that the genealogical tables here refer to contemporary groups rather than to dead individuals;[10] the tables presumably serve to regulate social relations among the twelve tribes of Israel in a manner similar to that which has been well analysed in Evans-Pritchard's work on the Nuer of the Southern Sudan and in Fortes' account of the Tallensi of Northern Ghana.[11]

Early British administrators among the Tiv of Nigeria were aware of the great importance attached to these genealogies, which were continually discussed in court cases where the rights and duties of one man towards another were in dispute. Consequently they took the trouble to write down the long lists of names and preserve them for posterity, so that future administrators might refer to them in giving judgment. Forty years later, when the Bohannans carried out anthropological field work in the area, their successors were still using the same genealogies.[12] However, these written pedigrees now gave rise to many disagreements; the Tiv maintained that they were incorrect, while the officials regarded them as statements of fact, as records of what had actually happened, and could not agree that the unlettered indigenes could be better informed about the past than their own literate predecessors. What neither party realised was that in any society of this kind changes take place which require a constant readjustment in the genealogies if they are to continue to carry out their function as mnemonics of social relationships.

These changes are of several kinds: those arising from the turnover in personnel, from the process of "birth and copulation and death"; those connected with the rearrangement of the constituent units of the society, with the migration of one group and the fission of another; and lastly those resulting from the effects of changes in the social system itself, whether generated from within or initiated from without. Each of these three processes (which we may refer to for convenience as the processes of generational, organisational and structural change) could lead to alterations of the kind to which the administration objected.

It is obvious that the process of generation leads in itself to a constant lengthening of the genealogy; on the other hand, the population to which it is linked may in fact be growing at quite a different rate, perhaps simply replacing itself. So despite its increasing length the genealogy may have to refer to just as many people at the present time as it did fifty, a hundred, or perhaps two hundred years ago. Consequently the added depth of lineages caused by new births needs to be accompanied by a process of genealogical shrinkage; the occurrence of this telescoping process, a common example of the general social phenomenon which J. A. Barnes has felicitously termed "structural amnesia," has been attested in many societies, including all those mentioned above.[13]

Organisational changes lead to similar adjustments. The state of Gonja in Northern Ghana is divided into a number of divisional chiefdoms, certain of which are recognised as providing in turn the ruler of the whole nation. When asked to explain their system the Gonja recount how the founder of the state, Ndewura Jakpa, came down from the Niger Bend in search of gold, conquered the indigenous inhabitants of the area and enthroned himself as chief of the state and his sons as rulers of its territorial divisions. At his death the divisional chiefs succeeded to the paramountcy in turn. When the details of this story were first recorded at the turn of the present century, at the time the British were extending their control over the area, Jakpa was said to have begotten seven sons, this corresponding to the number of divisions whose heads were eligible for the supreme office by virtue of their descent from the founder of the particular chiefdom.

But at the same time as the British had arrived, two of the seven divisions disappeared, one being deliberately incorporated in a neighboring division because its rulers had supported a Mandingo invader, Samori, and another because of some boundary changes introduced by the British administration. Sixty years later, when the myths of state were again recorded, Jakpa was credited with only five sons and no mention was made of the founders of the two divisions which had since disappeared from the political map.[14]

These two instances from the Tiv and the Gonja emphasise that genealogies often serve the same function that Malinowski claimed for myth; they act as "charters" of present social institutions rather than as faithful historical records of times past.[15] They can do this more consistently because they operate within an oral rather than a written tradition and thus tend to be automatically adjusted to existing social relations as they are passed by word of mouth from one member of the society to another. The social element in remembering results in the genealogies being transmuted in the course of being transmitted; and a similar process takes place with regard to other cultural elements as well, to myths, for example, and to sacred lore in general. Deities and other supernatural agencies which have served their purpose can be quietly dropped from the contemporary pantheon; and as the society changes, myths too are forgotten, attributed to other personages, or transformed in their meaning.

One of the most important results of this homeostatic tendency is that the individual has little perception of the past except in terms of the present; whereas the annals of a literate society cannot but enforce a more objective recognition of the distinction between what was and what is. Franz Boas wrote that for the Eskimo the world has always been as it is now:[16] it seems probable, at least, that the form in which non-literate societies conceive the world of the past is itself influenced by the process of transmission described. The Tiv have their genealogies, others their sacred tales about the origin of the world and the way in which man acquired his culture. But all their conceptualisations of the past cannot help being governed by the concerns of the present, merely because there is no body of chronologically ordered statements to which reference can be made. The Tiv do not recognise any contradiction between what they say now and what they said fifty years ago, since no enduring records exist for them to set beside their present views. Myth and history merge into one: the elements in the cultural heritage which cease to have a contemporary relevance tend to be soon forgotten or transformed; and as the individuals of each generation acquire their vocabulary, their genealogies, and their myths, they are unaware that various words, proper-names and stories have dropped out, or that others have changed their meanings or been replaced.

II. KINDS OF WRITING AND THEIR SOCIAL EFFECTS

The pastness of the past, then, depends upon a historical sensibility which can hardly begin to operate without permanent written records; and writing introduces similar changes in the transmission of other items of the cultural repertoire. But the extent of these changes varies with the nature and social distribution of the writing system; varies, that is, according to the system's intrinsic efficacy as a means of communication, and according to the social constraints placed upon it, that is, the degree to which use of the system is diffused through the society.

Early in prehistory, man began to express himself in graphic form; and his cave paintings, rock engravings and wood carvings are morphologically, and presumably sequentially, the forerunners of writing. By some process of simplification and stylisation they appear to have led to the various kinds of pictographs found in simple societies.[17]

While pictographs themselves are almost universal, their development into a self-sufficient system capable of extended discourse occurs only among the Plains Indians.[18]

Pictographs have obvious disadvantages as means of communication. For one thing a vast number of signs is needed to represent all the important objects in the culture. For another, since the signs are concrete, the simplest sentence requires an extremely elaborate series of signs: many stylised representations of wigwams, footprints, totemic animals and so on are required just to convey the information that a particular man left there a few days ago. Finally, however elaborately the system is developed, only a limited number of things can be said.

The end of the fourth millennium saw the early stages of the development of more complex forms of writing, which seem to be an essential factor in the rise of the urban cultures of the Orient. The majority of signs in these systems were simply pictures of the outside world, standardised representations of the object signified by a particular word; to these were added other devices for creating word signs or logograms, which permitted the expression of wider ranges of meaning. Thus in Egyptian hieroglyphics, the picture of a beetle was a code sign not only for that insect but also for a discontinuous and more abstract referent "became."[19]

The basic invention used to supplement the logograms was the phonetic principle, which for the first time permitted the written expression of all the words of a language. For example, by the device of phonetic transfer the Sumerians could use the sign for *ti*, an arrow, to stand for *ti*, life, a concept not easy to express in pictographic form. In particular, the need to record personal names and foreign words encouraged the development of phonetic elements in writing.

But while these true writing systems all used phonetic devices for the construction of logograms (and have consequently been spoken of as word-syllabic systems of writing), they failed to carry through the application of the phonetic principle exclusively and systematically.[20] The achievement of a system completely based upon the representation of phonemes (the basic units of meaningful sound) was left to the Near Eastern syllabaries, which developed between 1500–1000 B.C., and finally to the introduction of the alphabet proper in Greece. Meanwhile these incompletely phonetic systems were too clumsy and complicated to foster widespread literacy, if only because the number of signs was very large; at least six hundred would have to be learned even for the simplified cuneiform developed in Assyria, and about the same for Egyptian hieroglyphs.[21] All these ancient civilisations, the Sumerian, Egyptian, Hittite and Chinese, were literate in one sense and their great advances in administration and technology were undoubtedly connected with the invention of a writing system; but when we think of the limitations of their systems of communication as compared with ours, the term "protoliterate," or even "oligoliterate," might be more descriptive in suggesting the restriction of literacy to a relatively small proportion of the total population.[22]

Any system of writing which makes the sign stand directly for the object must be extremely complex. It can extend its vocabulary by generalisation or association of ideas, that is, by making the sign stand either for a more general class of objects, or for other referents connected with the original picture by an association of meanings which may be related to one another either in a continuous or in a discontinuous manner. Either process of semantic extension is to some extent arbitrary or esoteric; and as a result the interpretation of these signs is neither easy nor explicit. One might perhaps guess that the Chinese sign for a man carries the general meaning of maleness; it would be more difficult to see that a conventionalised picture of a man and a broom is the sign for a woman; it's a pleasing fancy, no doubt, but not one which communicates very readily until it has been learned as a new character, as a separate sign for a separate word, as a logogram. In Chinese writing a minimum of 3000 such characters have to be learned before one can be reasonably literate;[23] and with a total repertoire of some 50,000 characters to be mastered, it normally takes about twenty years to reach full literate proficiency. China, therefore, stands as an extreme example of how, when a virtually non-phonetic system of writing becomes sufficiently developed to express a large number of meanings explicitly, only a small and specially trained professional group in the total society can master it, and partake of the literate culture.

Although systems of word signs are certainly easier to learn, many difficulties remain, even when these signs are supplemented by phonemic devices of a syllabic sort. Other features of the social system are no doubt responsible for the way that the writing systems developed as they did: but it is a striking fact that—for whatever ultimate causes—in Egypt and Mesopotamia, as in China, a literate elite of religious, administrative and commercial experts emerged and maintained itself as a centralised governing bureaucracy on rather similar lines. Their various social and intellectual achievements were, of course, enormous; but as regards the participation of the society as a whole in the written culture, a wide gap existed between the esoteric literate culture and the exoteric oral one, a gap which the literate were interested in maintaining. Among the Sumerians and Akkadians writing was the pursuit of scribes and preserved as a "mystery," a "secret treasure." Royalty were themselves illiterate; Ashurbanipal (668–626 B.C.) records that he was the first Babylonian king to master the "clerkly skill."[24] "Put writing in your heart that you may protect yourself from hard labour of any kind," writes an Egyptian of the New Kingdom: "The scribe is released from manual tasks; it is he who commands."[25] Significantly, the classical age of Babylonian culture, beginning under Hammurabi in the late

eighteenth century B.C., appears to have coincided with a period when the reading and writing of Akkadian cuneiform was not confined to a small group, nor to one nation; it was then that nearly all the extant literature was written down, and that the active state of commerce and administration produced a vast quantity of public and private correspondence, of which much has survived.

These imperfectly phonetic methods of writing survived with little change for many centuries;[26] so too did the cultures of which they were part.[27] The existence of an elite group, which followed from the difficulty of the writing system, and whose continued influence depended on the maintenance of the present social order, must have been a powerfully conservative force, especially when it consisted of ritual specialists;[28] and so, it may be surmised, was the nature of the writing system itself. For pictographic and logographic systems are alike in their tendency to reify the objects of the natural and social order; by so doing they register, record, make permanent the existing social and ideological picture. Such, for example, was the tendency of the most highly developed and longest-lived ancient writing system, that of Egypt, whose society has been described with picturesque exaggeration as "a nation of fellahin ruled with a rod of iron by a Society of Antiquaries."

This conservative or antiquarian bias can perhaps be best appreciated by contrasting it with fully phonetic writing; for phonetic writing, by imitating human discourse, is in fact symbolising, not the objects of the social and natural order, but the very process of human interaction in speech: the verb is as easy to express as the noun; and the written vocabulary can be easily and unambiguously expanded. Phonetic systems are therefore adapted to expressing every nuance of individual thought, to recording personal reactions as well as items of major social importance. Non-phonetic writing, on the other hand, tends rather to record and reify only those items in the cultural reper-toire which the literate specialists have selected for written expression; and it tends to express the collective attitude towards them.

The notion of representing a sound by a graphic symbol is itself so stupefying a leap of the imagination that what is remarkable is not so much that it happened relatively late in human history, but rather that it ever happened at all. For a long time, however, these phonetic inventions had a limited effect because they were only partially exploited: not only were logograms and pictograms retained, but a variety of phono-grams were used to express the same sound. The full explicitness and economy of a phonetic writing system "as easy as A B C" was therefore likely to arise only in less advanced societies on the fringes of Egypt or Mesopotamia, societies which were starting their writing system more or less from scratch, and which took over the idea of phonetic signs from adjoining countries, and used them exclusively to fit their own lan-guage.[29] These phonetic signs could, of course, be used to stand for any unit of speech, and thus developed either into syllabaries or into alphabets. In a few cases, such as Japanese, the particular nature of the language made it possible to construct a rela-tively simple and efficient syllabary; but as regards the great majority of languages the alphabet, with its signs for individual conso-nants and vowels, proved a much more economical and convenient instrument for representing sounds. For the syllabaries, while making writing easier, were still far from simple;[30] they were often combined with logograms and pictographs.[31] And whether by necessity or tradition or both, pre-alphabetic writing was still mainly restricted to elite groups. The Mycenean script disappeared completely after the 12th century B.C., a fact which was possible because of the very restricted uses of literacy and the close connection between writing and palace administration.[32] It is doubtful

whether any such loss could have occurred in Greece after the introduction of a com-plete alphabetic script, probably in the eighth century B.C.

The alphabet is almost certainly the supreme example of cultural diffusion:[33] all existing or recorded alphabets derive from Semitic syllabaries developed during the second millennium. Eventually there arose the enormous simplification of the Semitic writing system, with its mere twenty-two letters; and then only one further step re-mained: the Greek script, which is, of course, much closer than the Semitic to the Roman alphabet, took certain of the Semitic signs for consonants which the Greek lan-guage didn't need, and used them for vowels, which the Semitic syllabary did not repre-sent.[34] The directness of our inheritance from these two sources is suggested by the fact that our word "alphabet" is the latin-ized form of the first two letters of the Greek alphabet, "alpha," derived from the Semitic "aleph," and "beta," from the Semi-tic "beth."

The reason for the success of the alpha-bet, which David Diringer calls a "demo-cratic" script as opposed to the "theocratic" scripts of Egypt, is itself based on the fact that, uniquely among writing systems, its graphic signs are representations of the most extreme and most universal example of cul-tural selection—the basic phonemic system. The number of sounds which the human breath stream can produce is vast; but nearly all languages are based on the formal recog-nition by the society of only forty or so of these sounds. The success of the alphabet (as well as some of its incidental difficulties) comes from the fact that its system of graphic representation takes advantage of this socially-conventionalized pattern of sound in all language systems; by symboliz-ing in letters these selected phonemic units the alphabet makes it possible to write easily and read unambiguously about anything which the society can talk about.

The historical picture of the cultural

impact of the new alphabetic writing is not altogether clear. As regards the Semitic system, which was widely adopted elsewhere, the evidence suggests that—in part perhaps because of the intrinsic difficulties of the system, but mainly because of the established cultural features of the societies which adopted it—the social diffusion of writing was slow. There was, for one thing, a strong tendency for writing to be used as a help to memory rather than as an autonomous and independent mode of communication; and under such conditions its influence tended towards the consolidation of the existing cultural tradition. This certainly appears to be true of India and Palestine.[35] Gandz notes, for example, that Hebrew culture continued to be transmitted orally long after the Old Testament had begun to be written down. As he puts it, the introduction of writing:

did not at once change the habits of the people and displace the old method of oral tradition. We must always distinguish between the *first introduction* of writing and its *general diffusion*. It often takes several centuries, and sometimes even a millennium or more, until this invention becomes the common property of the people at large. In the beginning, the written book is not intended for practical use at all. It is a divine instrument, placed in the temple "by the side of the ark of the covenant that it may be there for a witness" (Deuteronomy, xxxi, 26), and remains there as a holy relic. For the people at large, oral instruction still remained the only way of learning, and the memory—the only means of preservation. Writing was practiced, if at all, only as an additional support for the memory . . .

It was not, in fact, until some six centuries after the original Hebrew adoption of the Semitic writing system that, at the time of Ezra (*ca.* 444 B.C.), an official "generally recognized text" of the Torah was published, and the body of the religious tradition ceased to be "practically . . . a sealed book" and became accessible to anyone who chose to study it.[36]

Even so, of course, as the frequent diatribes against the scribes in the Gospels remind us,[37] there remained a considerable gap between the literati and the laymen; the professionals who plied their trade in the market-place belonged to "families of scribes," perhaps organized as guilds, within which the mystery was handed down from father to son.[38]

Anything like popular literacy, or the use of writing as an autonomous mode of communication by the majority of the members of society, is not found in the earliest societies which used the Semitic writing system; it was, rather, in the sixth and fifth centuries B.C. in the city states of Greece and Ionia that there first arose a society which as a whole could justly be characterized as literate. Many of the reasons why literacy became widespread in Greece, but not in other societies which had Semitic, or indeed any other, simple and explicit writing systems, necessarily lie outside the scope of this essay; yet considerable importance must surely be attributed to the intrinsic advantages of the Greek adaptation of the Semitic alphabet, an adaptation which made it the first comprehensively and exclusively phonetic system for transcribing human speech.[39] The system was easy, explicit and unambiguous—more so than the Semitic where the lack of vowels is responsible for many of the cruxes in the Bible: for instance, since the consonant in the Hebrew words is the same, Elijah may have been fed by "Ravens" or "Arabs."[40] Its great advantage over the syllabaries lay in the reduction of the number of signs and in the ability to specify consonant and vowel clusters. The system was easy to learn: Plato sets aside three years for the process in the *Laws*,[41] about the time taken in our schools today; and the much greater speed with which alphabetic writing can be learned is shown, not only by such reports as those of the International Institute of Intellectual Cooperation in 1934,[42] but also by the increasing adoption of the Roman script, and even more widely of alphabetic systems of writing, throughout the world.

The extensive diffusion of the alphabet in Greece was also materially assisted by various social, economic and technological factors. In the first place the 8th century saw a great burst of economic activity following the revival of the eastern trade which had declined after the Mycenean collapse in the 12th century.[43] Secondly, while the Greek society of the period had, of course, its various social strata, the political system was not strongly centralized; especially in the Ionic settlements there appears to have been a good deal of flexibility and in them we discern the beginnings of the Greek city state. Thirdly, the increased contact with the East brought material prosperity and technological advance. The wider use of iron, the advent of the true Iron Age, was perhaps one of the results.[44] More closely connected with literacy was the fact that trade with Egypt led to the importation of papyrus; and this made writing itself easier and less expensive, both for the individual writer and for the reader who wanted to buy books: papyrus was obviously much cheaper than parchment made from skins, more permanent than wax tablets, easier to handle than the stone or clay of Mesopotamia and Mycenae.

The chronology and extent of the diffusion of literacy in Greece remains a matter of debate. With the Mycenean collapse in the 12th century, writing disappeared; the earliest Greek inscriptions in the modified Semitic alphabet occur in the last two decades of the 8th century.[45] Recent authorities suggest the new script was adopted and transformed about the middle of the 8th century in Northern Syria.[46] The extensive use of writing probably came only slowly in the 7th century, but when it eventually came it seems to have been used in a very wide range of activities, intellectual as well as economic, and by a wide range of people.[47]

It must be remembered, of course, that Greek writing throughout the classical period was still relatively difficult to decipher, as words were not regularly separated;[48] that the copying of manuscripts was a long and laborious process; and that silent reading as we know it was very rare until the advent of printing—in the ancient world books were used mainly for reading aloud, often by a slave. Nevertheless, from the sixth century onwards literacy seems to be increasingly presumed in the public life of Greece and Ionia. In Athens, for example, the first laws for the general public to read were set up by Solon in 593–4 B.C.; the institution of ostracism early in the fifth century assumes a literate citizen body— 6,000 citizens had to write the name of the person on their potsherds before he could be banished;[49] there is abundant evidence in the fifth century of a system of schools teaching reading and writing[50] and of a book-reading public—satirized already by Aristophanes in *The Frogs*;[51] while the final form of the Greek alphabet, which was established fairly late in the fifth century, was finally adopted for use in the official records of Athens by decree of the Archon Eucleides in 403 B.C.

III. ALPHABETIC CULTURE AND GREEK THOUGHT

The rise of Greek civilization, then, is the prime historical example of the transition to a really literate society. In all subsequent cases where a widespread introduction of an alphabetic script occurred, as in Rome, for example, other cultural features were inevitably imported from the loan country along with the writing system; Greece thus offers not only the first example of this change, but also the essential one for any attempt to isolate the cultural consequences of alphabetic literacy.

The fragmentary and ambiguous nature of our direct evidence about this historical transformation in Greek civilization means that any generalizations must be extremely tentative and hypothetical; but the fact that the essential basis both of the writing systems and of many characteristic cultural institutions of the Western tradition as a whole are derived from Greece, and that they both arose there simultaneously, would seem to justify the present attempt to outline the possible relationships between the writing system and those cultural innovations of early Greece which are common to all alphabetically-literate societies.

The early development of the distinctive features of Western thought is usually traced back to the radical innovations of the pre-Socratic philosophers of the sixth century B.C. The essence of their intellectual revolution is seen as a change from mythical to logico-empirical modes of thought. Such, broadly speaking, is Werner Jaeger's view; and Ernst Cassirer writes that "the history of philosophy as a scientific discipline may be regarded as a single continuous struggle to effect a separation and liberation from myth."[52]

To this general picture there are two kinds of theoretical objection. First, that the crucial intellectual innovations—in Cassirer as in Werner Jaeger—are in the last analysis attributed to the special mental endowments of the Greek people; and insofar as such terms as "the Greek Mind" or "genius" are not simply descriptive, they are logically dependent upon extremely questionable theories of man's nature and culture. Secondly, such a version of the transformation from "unphilosophical" to "philosophical" thought assumes an absolute—and untenable—dichotomy between the "mythical" thought of primitives and the "logico-empirical" thought of civilized man.

The dichotomy, of course, is itself very similar to Lévy-Bruhl's earlier theory of the "prelogical" mentality of primitive peoples, which has been widely criticised. Malinowski and many others have demonstrated the empirical elements in non-literate cultures,[53] and Evans-Pritchard has carefully analyzed the "logical" nature of the belief systems of the Azande of the Sudan;[54]

while on the other hand the illogical and mythical nature of much Western thought and behavior is evident to anyone contemplating either our past or our present.

Nevertheless, although we must reject any dichotomy based upon the assumption of radical differences between the mental attributes of literate and non-literate peoples, and accept the view that previous formulations of the distinction were based on faulty premises and inadequate evidence, there may still exist general differences between literate and non-literate societies somewhat along the lines suggested by Lévy-Bruhl. One reason for their existence, for instance, may be what has been described above: the fact that writing establishes a different kind of relationship between the word and its referent, a relationship that is more general and more abstract, and less closely connected with the particularities of person, place and time, than obtains in oral communication. There is certainly a good deal to substantiate this distinction in what we know of early Greek thought. To take, for instance, the categories of Cassirer and Werner Jaeger, it is surely significant that it was only in the days of the first widespread alphabetic culture that the idea of "logic"—of an immutable and impersonal mode of discourse—appears to have arisen; and it was also only then that the sense of the human past as an objective reality was formally developed, a process in which the distinction between "myth" and "history" took on decisive importance.

a. Myth and History

Non-literate peoples, of course, often make a distinction between the lighter folk-tale, the graver myth, and the quasi-historical legend.[55] But not so insistently, and for an obvious reason. As long as the legendary and doctrinal aspects of the cultural tradition are mediated orally, they are kept in relative harmony with each other and with the present needs of society in two ways; through the unconscious operations of memory, and through the adjustment of the reciter's terms and attitudes to those of the audience before him. There is evidence, for example, that such adaptations and omissions occurred in the oral transmission of the Greek cultural tradition. But once the poems of Homer and Hesiod, which contained much of the earlier history, religion and cosmology of the Greeks, had been written down, succeeding generations were faced with old distinctions in sharply aggravated form: how far was the information about their Gods and heroes literally true? how could its patent inconsistencies be explained? and how could the beliefs and attitudes implied be brought into line with those of the present?

The disappearance of so many early Greek writings, and the difficulties of dating and composition in many that survive, make anything like a clear reconstruction impossible. Greek had of course been written, in a very limited way, during Mycenean times. At about 1200 writing disappeared and the alphabet was not developed until some four hundred years later. Most scholars agree that in the middle or late eighth century the Greeks adapted the purely consonantal system of Phoenicia, possibly at the trading port of al Mina (Poseidon?). Much of the early writing consisted of "explanatory inscriptions on existing objects—dedications on offerings, personal names on property, epitaphs on tombs, names of figures in drawings."[56] The Homeric poems were written down between 750 and 650 B.C., and the seventh century saw first the recording of lyric verse and then (at the end) the emergence of the great Ionian school of scientist philosophers.[57] Thus within a century or two of the writing down of the Homeric poems, many groups of writers and teachers appeared, first in Ionia and later in Greece, who took as their point of departure the belief that much of what Homer had apparently said was inconsistent and unsatisfactory in many respects. The logographers, who set themselves to record the genealogies, chronologies and cosmologies which had been handed down orally from the past,

soon found that the task led them to use their critical and rational powers to create a new individual synthesis. In non-literate society, of course, there are usually some individuals whose interests lead them to collect, analyse and interpret the cultural tradition in a personal way; and the written records suggest that this process went considerably further among the literate elites of Egypt, Babylon and China, for example. But perhaps because in Greece reading and writing were less restricted to any particular priestly or administrative groups, there seems to have been a more thorough-going individual challenge to the orthodox cultural tradition in sixth-century Greece than occurred elsewhere. Hecataeus, for example, proclaimed at about the turn of the century, "What I write is the account I believe to be true. For the stories the Greeks tell are many and in my opinion ridiculous,"[58] and offered his own rationalizations of the data on family traditions and lineages which he had collected. Already the mythological mode of using the past, the mode which, in Sorel's words, makes it "a means of acting on the present,"[59] has begun to disappear.

That this trend of thought had much larger implications can be seen from the fact that the beginnings of religious and natural philosophy are connected with similar critical departures from the inherited traditions of the past; as W.B. Yeats wrote, with another tradition in mind, "Science is the critique of myths, there would be no Darwin had there been no *Book* of Genesis." [60] Among the early pre-Socratics there is much evidence of the close connection between new ideas and the criticism of the old. Thus Xenophanes of Colophon (*fl. ca.* 540 B.C.) rejected the "fables of men of old," and replaced the anthropomorphic gods of Homer and Hesiod who did "everything that is disgraceful and blameworthy among men" with a supreme god, "not at all like mortals in body and mind";[61] while Heraclitus of Ephesus (*fl. ca.* 500 B.C.), the first great philosopher of the problems of knowledge, whose system is based on the unity of oppo-

sites expressed in the *Logos* or structural plan of things, also ridiculed the anthropomorphism and idolatry of the Olympian religion.[62]

The critical and sceptical process continued, and according to Cornford, "a great part of the supreme god's biography had to be frankly rejected as false, or reinterpreted as allegory, or contemplated with reserve as mysterious myth too dark for human understanding."[63] On the one hand the poets continued to use the traditional legends for their poems and plays; on the other the prose writers attempted to wrestle with the problems with which the changes in the cultural tradition had faced them. Even the poets, however, had a different attitude to their material. Pindar, for example, used *mythos* in the sense of traditional stories, with the implication that they were not literally true; but claimed that his own poems had nothing in common with the fables of the past.[64] As for the prose writers, and indeed some of the poets, they had set out to replace myth with something else more consistent, with their sense of the *logos,* of the common and all-encompassing truth which reconciles apparent contradictions.

From the point of view of the transmission of the cultural tradition, the categories of understanding connected with the dimensions of time and space have a particular importance. As regards an objective description of space, Anaximander (b. 610 B.C.) and Hecataeus (*fl. ca.* 510–490), making use of Babylonian and Egyptian techniques, drew the first maps of the world.[65] Then their crude beginnings were subject to a long process of criticism and correction—by Herodotus[66] and others; and from this emerged the more scientific cartography of Aristotle, Eratosthenes and their successors.[67]

The development of history appears to have followed a rather similar course, although the actual details of the process are subject to much controversy. The traditional view gave priority to local histories which were followed by the more universal accounts of Herodotus and Thucydides. Dionysius of Halicarnasus writes of the predecessors of these historians who "instead of co-ordinating their accounts with each other . . . treated of individual peoples and cities separately . . . They all had the one same object, to bring to the general knowledge of the public the written records that they found preserved in temples or in secular buildings in the form in which they found them, neither adding nor taking away anything; among these records were to be found legends hallowed by the passage of time . . ."[68]

Jacoby however has insisted "the whole idea is wrong that Greek historiography began with local history."[69] As far as Athens is concerned, history begins with the foreigner Herodotus who, not long after the middle of the fifth century, incorporated parts of the story of the town in his work because he wanted to explain the role it played in the great conflict between East and West, between Europe and Asia. The aim of Herodotus' *History* was to discover what the Greeks and Persians "fought each other for";[70] and his method was *historia—*personal inquiry or research into the most probable versions of events as they were to be found in various sources. His work rested on oral tradition and consequently his writings retained many mythological elements. So too did the work of the logographer, Hellanicus of Lesbos, who at the end of the fifth century wrote the first history of Attica from 683 to the end of the Peloponnesian war in 404. Hellanicus also tried to reconstruct the genealogies of the Homeric heroes, both backwards to the Gods and forwards to the Greece of his own time; and this inevitably involved chronology, the objective measurement of time. All he could do, however, was to rationalize and systematize largely legendary materials.[71] The development of history as a documented and analytic account of the past and present of the society in permanent written form took an important step forward with Thucydides, who made a decisive distinction between myth and history, a distinction to which little attention is paid in non-literate society.[72] Thucydides wanted to give a wholly reliable account of the wars between Athens and Sparta; and this meant that unverified assumptions about the past had to be excluded. So Thucydides rejected, for example, the chronology that Hellanicus had worked out for the prehistory of Athens, and confined himself very largely to his own notes of the events and speeches he related, or to the information he sought out from eye-witnesses and other reliable sources.[73]

And so, not long after the widespread diffusion of writing throughout the Greek world, and the recording of the previously oral cultural tradition, there arose an attitude to the past very different from that common in non-literate societies. Instead of the unobtrusive adaptation of past tradition to present needs, a great many individuals found in the written records, where much of their traditional cultural repertoire had been given permanent form, so many inconsistencies in the beliefs and categories of understanding handed down to them that they were impelled to a much more conscious, comparative and critical, attitude to the accepted world picture, and notably to the notions of God, the universe and the past. Many individual solutions to these problems were themselves written down, and these versions formed the basis for further investigations.[74]

In non-literate society, it was suggested, the cultural tradition functions as a series of interlocking face-to-face conversations in which the very conditions of transmission operate to favor consistency between past and present, and to make criticism—the articulation of inconsistency—less likely to occur; and if it does, the inconsistency makes a less permanent impact, and is more easily adjusted or forgotten. While scepticism may be present in such societies, it takes a personal, non-cumulative form; it does not lead to a deliberate rejection and reinterpretation of social dogma so much as

to a semi-automatic readjustment of belief.[75]

In literate society, these interlocking conversations go on; but they are no longer man's only dialogue; and insofar as writing provides an alternative source for the transmission of cultural orientations it favors awareness of inconsistency. One aspect of this is a sense of change and of cultural lag; another is the notion that the cultural inheritance as a whole is composed of two very different kinds of material; fiction, error and superstition on the one hand; and on the other, elements of truth which can provide the basis for some more reliable and coherent explanation of the gods, the human past and the physical world. . . .

SUMMARY

Recent anthropology has rightly rejected the categorical distinctions between the thinking of "primitive" and "civilized" peoples, between "mythopoeic" and "logico-empirical" modes of thought. But the reaction has been pushed too far: diffuse relativism and sentimental egalitarianism combine to turn a blind eye on some of the most basic problems of human history. Where the intellectual differences in the cultural traditions of complex and simple societies are given adequate recognition, the explanations offered are unsatisfactory. In the case of Western civilization, for example, the origins are sought in the nature of the Greek genius, in the grammatical structure of the Indo-European languages, or, somewhat more plausibly, in the technological advances of the Bronze Age and the associated developments in the division of labor.

In our view, however, insufficient attention has been paid to the fact that the urban revolution of the Ancient Near East produced one invention, the invention of writing, which changed the whole structure of the cultural tradition. Potentially, human intercourse was now no longer restricted to the impermanency of oral converse. But since the first methods of writing employed were difficult to master, their effects were relatively limited, and it was only when the simplicity and flexibility of later alphabetic writing made widespread literacy possible that for the first time there began to take concrete shape in the Greek world of the 7th century B.C. a society that was essentially literate and that soon established many of the institutions that became characteristic of all later literate societies.

The development of an easy system of writing (easy both in terms of the materials employed and the signs used) was more than a mere pre-condition of the Greek achievement; it influenced its whole nature and development in fundamental ways. In oral societies the cultural tradition is transmitted almost entirely by face-to-face communication; and changes in its content are accompanied by the homeostatic process of forgetting or transforming those parts of the tradition that cease to be either necessary or relevant. Literate societies, on the other hand, cannot discard, absorb, or transmute the past in the same way. Instead, their members are faced with permanently recorded versions of the past and its beliefs; and because the past is thus set apart from the present, historical enquiry becomes possible. This in turn encourages scepticism; and scepticism, not only about the legendary past, but about received ideas about the universe as a whole. From here the next step is to see how to build up and to test alternative explanations: and out of this there arose the kind of logical, specialized, and cumulative intellectual tradition of sixth-century Ionia. The kinds of analysis involved in the syllogism, and in the other forms of logical procedure, are clearly dependent upon writing, indeed upon a form of writing sufficiently simple and cursive to make possible widespread and habitual recourse both to the recording of verbal statements and then to the dissecting of them. It is probable that it is only the analytic process that writing itself entails, the written formalization of sounds and syntax, which make possible the habitual separating out into formally distinct units of the various cultural elements whose indivisible wholeness is the essential basis of the "mystical participation" which Lévy-Bruhl regards as characteristic of the thinking of non-literate peoples.

One of the problems which neither Lévy-Bruhl nor any other advocate of a radical dichotomy between "primitive" and "civilized" thought has been able to resolve is the persistence of "non-logical thinking" in modern literate societies. But, of course, we must reckon with the fact that in our civilization, writing is clearly an addition, not an alternative, to oral transmission. Even in our *buch und lesen* culture, childrearing and a multitude of other forms of activity both within and outside the family depend upon speech: and the relationship between the written and the oral traditions must be regarded as a major problem in Western cultures.

A consideration of the consequences of literacy in these terms, then, throws some light not only upon the nature of the Greek achievement but also upon the intellectual differences between simple and complex societies. There are, of course, many other consequences we have not discussed—for instance, the role of writing in the running of centralized states and other bureaucratic organizations; our aim has only been to discuss in very general terms some of the more significant historical and functional consequences of literacy.

NOTES

1. Some writers distinguish the field of Social Anthropology from that of Sociology on the basis of its subject matter (i.e. the study of non-literate or non-European peoples), others on the basis of its techniques (e.g. that of participant observation). For a discussion of these points, see Siegfried F. Nadel, *The Foundations of Social Anthropology* (London, 1951), p. 2.
2. Emile Durkheim, *The Elementary Forms of the Religious Life*, trans. Joseph W. Swain (London, 1915), p. 19.
3. Hortense Powdermaker, *Life in Lesu* (New York, 1933), p. 292. See also *Language, Thought, and Culture*, ed. Paul Henle (Ann Arbor, 1958), pp. 5–18.
4. Bronislaw Malinowski, "The Problem of Mean-

ing in Primitive Languages," in C. K. Ogden and I. A. Richards, *The Meaning of Meaning* (London, 1936), pp. 296–336, esp. p. 331. But see also the critical comments by Claude Lévi-Strauss, *La Pensée Sauvage* (Paris, 1962), pp. 6, 15–16.

5. *L'Année sociologique*, 7 (1902–3), pp. 1–72. See also S. Czarnowski, "Le morcellement de l'étendue et sa limitation dans la religion et la magie," *Actes du congrès international d'histoire des religions* (Paris, 1925), I, pp. 339–359.

6. Jack Goody, unpublished field notes, 1950–52. See also E. E. Evans-Pritchard, *The Nuer* (Oxford, 1940), chapter 3, "Time and Space," and David Tait, *The Konkomba of Northern Ghana* (London, 1961), pp. 17 ff. For a general treatment of the subject, see A. Irving Hallowell, "Temporal Orientations in Western Civilisation and in a Preliterate Society," *American Anthropologist*, 39 (1937), pp. 647–670.

7. *Les Cadres sociaux de la mémoire* (Paris, 1925); "Mémoire et sociéte," *L'Année sociologique*, 3e série, 1 (1940–8), pp. 11–177; *La Mémoire collective*, Paris, 1950. See also Frederic C. Bartlett on the tendency of oral discourse to become an expression of ideas and attitudes of the group rather than the individual speaker, in *Remembering* (Cambridge, 1932), pp. 265–7, and *Psychology and Primitive Culture* (Cambridge, 1923), pp. 42–3, 62–3, 256.

8. M. I. Finley, *The World of Odysseus* (New York, 1954), p. 26.

9. Laura Bohannan, "A Genealogical Charter," *Africa*, 22 (1952), pp. 301–15; Emrys Peters, "The Proliferation of Segments in the Lineage of the Bedouin of Cyrenaica," *Journal of the Royal Anthropological Institute*, 90 (1960), pp. 29–53. See also Godfrey and Monica Wilson, *The Analysis of Social Change* (Cambridge, 1945), p. 27.

10. Ch. 49; further evidence supporting this assumption is found in the etymology of the Hebrew term *Toledot*, which originally denoted "genealogies," and assumed also the meaning of "stories and accounts" about the origin of a nation. "In this sense the term was also applied to the account of the creation of heaven and earth" [Solomon Gandz, "Oral Tradition in the Bible" in *Jewish Studies in Memory of George A. Kohut*, ed. Salo W. Baron and Alexander Marx (New York, 1935), p. 269].

11. *The Nuer* (Oxford, 1940); "The Nuer of the Southern Sudan" in *African Political Systems*, ed. Meyer Fortes and Edward Evan Evans-Pritchard (London, 1940); Meyer Fortes, *The Dynamics of Clanship among the Tallensi* (London, 1945).

12. "A Genealogical Charter," p. 314.

13. John A. Barnes, "The Collection of Genealogies," *Rhodes-Livingstone Journal: Human Problems in British Central Africa*, 5 (1947), pp. 48–56, esp. p. 52; Meyer Fortes, "The Significance of Descent in Tale Social Structure," *Africa*, 14 (1944), p. 370; Evans-Pritchard, *The Nuer*, pp. 199–200; Peters, "The Proliferation of Segments," p. 32. See also I. G. Cunnison, *The Luapula Peoples of Northern Rhodesia* (Manchester, 1959), pp. 108–14.

14. Jack Goody, unpublished field notes, 1956–7; the heads of the divisions who could not succeed to the paramountcy also claimed descent from sons of the founding ancestor, Jakpa, but this was not an intrinsic part of the myth as usually told, and in any case their number remained constant during the period in question.

15. *Myth in Primitive Psychology* (London, 1926), pp. 23, 43.

16. Franz Boas, "The Folklore of the Eskimo," *Journal of American Folklore*, 64 (1904), p. 2. Lévi-Strauss treats the absence of historical knowledge as one of the distinctive features of *la pensée sauvage* in contrast to *la pensée domestiquée* (*La Pensée sauvage*, p. 349).

17. Ignace J. Gelb, *A Study of Writing* (Chicago, 1952), pp. 24ff.

18. C. F. and F. M. Voegelin, "Typological Classification of Systems with Included, Excluded and Self-sufficient Alphabets," *Anthropological Linguistics*, 3 (1961), pp. 84, 91.

19. Voegelin, "Typological Classification," pp. 75–76.

20. C. F. and F. M. Voegelin classify all these systems (Chinese, Egyptian, Hittite, Mayan and Sumerian-Akkadian) as "alphabet included logographic systems": because they make use of phonetic devices, they include, under the heading "self-sufficient alphabets," systems which have signs for consonant-vowel sequences (i.e. syllabaries), for independent consonants (IC), e.g. Phoenician, or for independent consonants plus independent vowels (IC + IV), e.g. Greek. In this paper we employ "alphabet" in the narrower, more usual, sense of a phonemic system with independent signs for consonants and vowels (IC + IV).

21. Gelb, *Study of Writing*, p. 115; David Diringer, *The Alphabet: A Key to the History of Mankind* (New York, 1948), pp. 48, 196.

22. "Protoliterate" is often employed in a rather different sense, as when S. N. Kramer ["New Light on the Early History of the Ancient Near East," *American Journal of Archaeology*, 52 (1948), p. 161] uses the term to designate the Sumerian phase in Lower Mesopotamia when writing was first invented. There seems to be no generally accepted usage for societies where there is a fully developed but socially restricted phonetic writing system. Sterling Dow ["Minoan Writing," *American Journal of Archaeology*, 58 (1954), pp. 77–129] characterises two stages of Minoan society: one of "stunted literacy," where little use was made of writing at all (Linear A); and one of "special literacy" where writing was used regularly but only for limited purposes (Linear B). Stuart Piggott refers to both these conditions under the name of "conditional literacy" [*Approach to Archaeology* (London, 1959), p. 104].

23. Alfred C. Moorhouse, *The Triumph of the Alphabet* (New York, 1953), pp. 90, 163.

24. G. R. Driver, *Semitic Writing* (London, 1954, rev. ed.), pp. 62, 72.

25. *cit.* V. Gordon Childe, *Man Makes Himself* (London, 1941), pp. 187–8; see also *What Happened in History* (London, 1942), pp. 105, 118.

26. "Egyptian hieroglyphic writing remained fundamentally unchanged for a period of three thousand years," according to David Diringer [*Writing* (London, 1962), p. 48]. He attributes the

fact that it never lost its cumbrousness and elaboration to "its unique sacredness" (p. 50).

27. Many authorities have commented upon the lack of development in Egypt after the initial achievements of the Old Kingdom: for a discussion (and a contrary view), see John A. Wilson in *Before Philosophy*, ed. H. Frankfort and others (London, 1949), pp. 115–16 [pub. in U.S.A. as *The Intellectual Adventure of Ancient Man* (Chicago, 1946)].

28. "The world view of the Egyptians and Babylonians was conditioned by the teaching of sacred books; it thus constituted an orthodoxy, the maintenance of which was in the charge of colleges of priests" [Benjamin Farrington, *Science in Antiquity* (London, 1936), p. 37]. See also Gordon Childe, *What Happened in History*, p. 121.

29. Gelb, *Study of Writing*, p. 196, maintains that all the main types of syllabary developed in just this way. Driver rejects the possibility that the Phoenician alphabet was invented on Egyptian soil, as it would have been "stifled at birth" by the "deadweight of Egyptian tradition, already of hoary antiquity and in the hands of a powerful priesthood" (*Semitic Writing*, p. 187).

30. "Immensely complicated," Driver calls the pre-alphabetic forms of writing Semitic (*Semitic Writing*, p. 67).

31. For Hittite, see O. R. Gurney, *The Hittites* (London, 1952), pp. 120–21. For Mycenean, see John Chadwick, *The Decipherment of Linear B* (Cambridge, 1958).

32. Chadwick, *The Decipherment of Linear B*, p. 130; see also "A Prehistoric Bureaucracy," *Diogenes*, 26 (1959), pp. 7–18.

33. As is exhaustively documented in David Diringer, *The Alphabet, A Key to the History of Mankind* (New York, 1948).

34. *The Alphabet*, pp. 214–218. On the "accidental" nature of this change see C. F. and F. M. Voegelin, "Typological Classification," pp. 63–4.

35. According to Ralph E. Turner, *The Great Cultural Traditions* (New York, 1941), I, pp. 346, 391, the Hebrews took over the Semitic system in the eleventh century B.C., and the Indians a good deal later, probably in the eighth century B.C.

36. Gandz, "Oral Tradition in the Bible," pp. 253–4.

37. e.g. Luke, 20; Matthew, 23; in the 7th century B.C., even kings and prophets employed scribes, Jer. xxxvi, 4, 18.

38. Driver, *Semitic Writing*, pp. 87–90, where he instances the case of one scribe who having no son "taught his wisdom to his sister's son."

39. "If the alphabet is defined as a system of signs expressing single sounds of speech, then the first alphabet which can justifiably be so called is the Greek alphabet." Gelb, *Study of Writing*, p. 166.

40. I. Kings 17, iv–vi; see *A Dictionary of the Bible* . . . ed. James Hastings (New York, 1898–1904), *s.v.* "Elijah."

41. 810 a. From the ages 10 to 13.

42. *L'Adoption universelle des caractères latins* (Paris, 1934); for more recent developments and documentation, see William S. Gray, *The Teaching of Reading and Writing: An International Survey*, Unesco Monographs on Fundamental Education X (Paris, 1956), especially pp. 31–60.

43. Chester G. Starr, *The Origins of Greek Civilization* (New York, 1961), pp. 189–190, 349 ff.

44. Starr, *The Origins of Greek Civilization*, pp. 87–88, 357.

45. Starr, *The Origins of Greek Civilization*, p. 169.

46. L. H. Jeffery, *The Local Scripts of Archaic Greece* (Oxford, 1961), p. 21; R. M. Cook and A. G. Woodhead, "The Diffusion of the Greek Alphabet," *American Journal of Archaeology*, 63 (1959), pp. 175–78. For North Syria, see Sir Leonard Woolley, *A Forgotten Kingdom* (London, 1953).

47. Chester Starr speaks of its use by "a relatively large aristocratic class" (p. 171) and Miss Jeffery notes that "writing was never regarded as an esoteric craft in early Greece. Ordinary people could and did learn to write, for many of the earliest inscriptions which we possess are casual graffiti" (p. 63).

48. Frederic G. Kenyon, *Books and Readers in Ancient Greece and Rome* (2nd ed., Oxford, 1951), p. 67.

49. Jérôme Carcopino, *L'Ostracisme athénien* (Paris, 1935), pp. 72–110.

50. *Protagoras*, 325 d.

51. 1. 1114; in 414 B.C. See also Plato, *Apology*, 26 d, and the general survey of Kenyon, *Books and Readers in Ancient Greece and Rome*.

52. *The Philosophy of Symbolic Forms* (New Haven, 1955), II, p. xiii; and *An Essay on Man* (New York, 1953), especially pp. 106–130, 281–3. For Werner Jaeger, see especially *The Theology of The Early Greek Philosophers* (Oxford, 1947).

53. "Magic, Science and Religion" in *Science, Religion and Reality*, ed. Joseph Needham (New York, 1925), reprinted *Magic, Science and Religion* (New York, 1954), p. 27. For an appreciation of Lévy-Bruhl's positive achievement, see Evans-Pritchard, "Lévy-Bruhl's Theory of Primitive Mentality," *Bulletin of the Faculty of Arts, University of Egypt*, 2 (1934), pp. 1–36. In his later work, Lévy-Bruhl modified the rigidity of his earlier dichotomy.

54. *Witchcraft, Oracles and Magic Among the Azande* (Oxford, 1937). See also Max Gluckman's essay, "Social Beliefs and Individual Thinking in Primitive Society," *Memoirs and Proceedings of the Manchester Literary and Philosophical Society*, 91 (1949–50), pp. 73–98. From a rather different standpoint, Lévi-Strauss has analysed "the logic of totemic classifications" (*La Pensée sauvage*, p. 48 ff.) and speaks of two distinct modes of scientific thought; the first (or "primitive") variety consists in "the science of the concrete," the practical knowledge of the handy man (*bricoleur*), which is the technical counterpart of mythical thought (p. 26).

55. e.g. the Trobriands (Malinowski, *Myth in Primitive Psychology*, pp. 33ff).

56. Jeffery, *The Local Scripts of Archaic Greece*, p. 46.

57. "It was in Ionia that the first completely rationalistic attempts to describe the nature of the world took place" [G. S. Kirk and J. E. Raven, *The Presocratic Philosophers* (Cambridge, 1957), p. 73]. The work of the Milesian philosophers,

Thales, Anaximander and Anaximenes, is described by the authors as "clearly a development of the genetic or genealogical approach to nature exemplified by the Hesiodic *Theogony*" (p. 73).

58. F. Jacoby, *Die Fragmente der Griechischen Historiker*, Vol. I, *Genealogie und Mythographie* (Berlin, 1923), fr. 1.a.

59. *Reflections on Violence*, trans. T. E. Hulme (New York, 1941), p. 136; *cit.* Robert Redfield, *The Primitive World and its Transformations* (Ithaca, New York, 1953), p. 125.

60. *cit.* Joseph Hone, *W. B. Yeats* (London, 1942), p. 405 (our italics).

61. Hermann Diels, *Die Fragmente der Vorsokratiker* (Berlin, 1951), fr. 11, 23; see also John Burnet, *Early Greek Philosophy* (2nd ed. London, 1908), pp. 131, 140–141, and Werner Jaeger, *The Theology of the Early Greek Philosophers* (Oxford, 1947), pp. 42–7; Kirk and Raven, *The Presocratic Philosophers*, pp. 163 ff.

62. Diels, *Fragmente der Vorsokratiker*, fr. 40, 42, 56, 57, 106; see also Francis M. Cornford, *Principium Sapientiae: The Origins of Greek Philosophical Thought* (Cambridge, 1952), pp. 112 ff.; Kirk and Raven, *The Presocratic Philosophers*, pp. 182 ff.

63. Francis M. Cornford, *Greek Religious Thought from Homer to the Age of Alexander* (London, 1923), xv–xvi. See also Burnet, *Early Greek Philosophy*, p. 1.

64. 1st Olympian Ode.

65. See Eric H. Warmington, *Greek Geography* (London, 1934), pp. xiv, xxxviii.

66. *History*, 4, 36–40.

67. Warmington, *Greek Geography*, pp. xvii–xviii, xli ff.

68. *Cit.* Lionel Pearson, *Early Ionian Historians* (Oxford, 1939), p. 3.

69. Felix Jacoby, *Atthis* (Oxford, 1949), p. 354.

70. *History*, I, 1. See also Moses I. Finley (ed.), *The Greek Historians* (New York, 1959), pp. 4 ff.

71. See Pearson, *Early Ionian Historians*, pp. 152–233, especially pp. 193, 232–33.

72. See, for instance, Bronislaw Malinowski, *Argonauts of the Western Pacific* (London, 1922), pp. 290–333.

73. Thucydides, *History*, I, 20–22, 97. For a picture of note-taking (*hypomnemata*) among Athenians, see *Theaetetus*, 142 c-143 c.

74. Felix Jacoby notes that "fixation in writing, once achieved, primarily had a preserving effect upon the oral tradition, because it put an end to the involuntary shiftings of the *mnemai* (remembrances), and drew limits to the arbitrary creation of new *logoi* (stories)" (*Atthis*, 1949, p. 217). He points out that this created difficulties for the early literate recorders of the past which the previous oral *mnemones* or professional "remembrancers" did not have to face: whatever his own personal view of the matter, "no true Atthidographer could remove Kekrops from his position as the first Attic king ... Nobody could take away from Solon the legislation which founded *in nuce* the first Attic constitution of historical times." Such things could no longer be silently forgotten, as in an oral tradition.
The general conclusion of Jacoby's polemic against Wilamowitz's hypothesis of a "pre-literary chronicle" is that "historical consciousness ... is not older than historical literature" (p. 201).

75. As writers on the indigenous political systems of Africa have insisted, changes generally take the form of rebellion rather than revolution; subjects reject the King, but not the kingship. See Evans-Pritchard, *The Divine Kingship of the Shilluk of the Nilotic Sudan* (The Frazer lecture, Cambridge, 1948), pp. 35ff; Max Gluckman, *Rituals of Rebellion in South-East Africa* (The Frazer lecture, 1952), Manchester, 1954.

28. Social Class, Language and Socialisation

BASIL BERNSTEIN

INTRODUCTION[1]

It may be helpful to make explicit the theoretical origins of the thesis I have been developing over the past decade. Although, initially, the thesis appeared to be concerned with the problem of educability, this problem was imbedded in and was stimulated by the wider question of the relationships between symbolic orders and social struc-

ture. The basic theoretical question, which dictated the approach to the initially narrow but important empirical problem, was concerned with the fundamental structure and changes in the structure of cultural transmission. Indeed, any detailed examination of what superficially may seem to be a string of somewhat repetitive papers, I think would show three things:

From *Current Trends in Linguistics*, Volume 12, ed. A. S. Abramson et al. (Mouton, 1973). Reprinted by permission.

1. The gradual emergence of the dominance of the major theoretical problem from the local, empirical problem of the social antecedents of the educability of different groups of children.

2. Attempts to develop both the generality of the thesis and to develop increasing specificity at the contextual level.

3. Entailed in (2) were attempts to clarify both the logical and empirical status of the basic organising concept, code. Unfortunately, until recently these attempts were more readily seen in the *planning* and *analysis* of the empirical research than available as formal statements.

Looking back with hindsight, I think I would have created less misunderstanding if I had written about sociolinguistic codes rather than linguistic codes. Through using only the latter concept it gave the impression that I was reifying syntax and at the cost of semantics. Or worse, suggesting that there was a one to one relation between meaning and a given syntax. Also, by defining the codes in a context free fashion, I robbed myself of properly understanding, at a theoretical level, their significance. *I should point out that nearly all the empirical planning was directed to trying to find out the code realisations in different contexts.*

The concept of sociolinguistic code points to the social structuring of meanings *and* to their diverse but *related* contextual linguistic realisations. A careful reading of the papers always shows the emphasis given to the form of the social relationship, that is, the structuring of relevant meanings. Indeed, role is defined as a complex coding activity controlling the creation and organisation of specific meanings and the conditions for their transmission and reception. The general sociolinguistic thesis attempts to explore how symbolic systems are both realisations and regulators of the structure of social relationships. The particular symbolic system is that of speech, *not* language.

It is pertinent, at this point, to make explicit earlier work in the social sciences which formed the implicit starting point of the thesis. It will then be seen, I hope, that the thesis is an integration of different streams of thought. The major starting points are Durkheim and Marx, and a small number of other thinkers have been drawn into the basic matrix. I shall very briefly, and so selectively, outline this matrix and some of the problems to which it gave rise.

Durkheim's work is a truly magnificent insight into the relationships between symbolic orders, social relationships and the structuring of experience. In a sense, if Marx turned Hegel on his head, then Durkheim attempted to turn Kant on his head. For in *Primitive classification* and in *The elementary forms of the religious life,* Durkheim attempted to derive the basic categories of thought from the structuring of the social relation. It is beside the point as to his success. He raised the whole question of the relation between the classifications and frames of the symbolic order *and* the structuring of experience. In his study of different forms of social integration he pointed to the implicit, condensed, symbolic structure of mechanical solidarity and the more explicit and differentiated symbolic structures of organic solidarity. Cassirer, the early cultural anthropologists, and in particular Sapir (I was not aware of von Humboldt until much later) sensitised me to the cultural properties of speech. Whorf, particularly where he refers to the fashions of speaking, frames of consistency, alerted me to the selective effect of the culture (acting through its patterning of social relationships) upon the *patterning* of grammar *together* with the pattern's semantic and thus cognitive significance. Whorf more than anyone, I think, opened up, at least for me, the question of the deep structure of linguistically regulated communication.

In all the above work I found two difficulties. If we grant the fundamental linkage of symbolic systems, social structure and the shaping of experience, it is still unclear *how* such shaping takes place. The *processes* underlying the social structuring of experience are not explicit. The second difficulty is in dealing with the question of change of symbolic systems. George Herbert Mead is of central importance in the solution of the first difficulty, the HOW. Mead outlined in general terms the relationships between role, reflexiveness and speech, and in so doing provided the basis of the solution to the HOW. It is still the case that the Meadian solution does not allow us to deal with the problem of change. For the concept, which enables role to be related to a higher order concept, "the generalised other" is, itself, not subject to systematic enquiry. Even if "the generalised other" is placed within a Durkheimian framework, we are still left with the problem of change. Indeed, in Mead change is introduced only at the cost of the re-emergence of a traditional Western dichotomy in the concepts of the "I" and the "me." The "I" is both the indeterminate response to the "me" and yet at the same time shapes it. The Meadian "I" points to the voluntarism in the affairs of men, the fundamental creativity of man, made possible by speech; a little before Chomsky.

Thus Meadian thought helps to solve the puzzle of the HOW but it does not help with the question of change in the structuring of experience; although both Mead implicitly and Durkheim explicitly pointed to the conditions which bring about pathological structuring of experience.

One major theory of the development of and change in symbolic structures is, of course, that of Marx. Although Marx is less concerned with the internal structure and the process of transmission of symbolic systems he does give us a key to their institutionalisation and change. The key is given in terms of the social significance of society's productive system and the power relationships to which the productive system gives rise. Further, access to, control over, orientation of and *change* in critical symbolic systems, according to the theory, are governed by these power relationships as these are embodied in the class structure. It is not only capital, in the strict economic sense, which is subject to appropriation, manipulation and exploitation, but also *cultural* capital in the form of the symbolic systems through which man can extend and change the boundaries of his experience.

I am not putting forward a matrix of thought necessary for the study of the basic structure and change in the structure of cultural transmission, *only* the specific matrix which underlies my own approach. Essentially and briefly I have used Durkheim and Marx at the macro level and Mead at the micro level, to realise a sociolinguistic thesis which could meet with a range of work in anthropology, linguistics, sociology and psychology.

OTHER VIEWS OF THE RELATION OF LINGUISTIC AND CULTURAL SYSTEMS

I want also to make clear two views I am not concerned with. Chomsky in *Aspects of the theory of syntax* neatly severs the study of the rule system of language from the study of the social rules which determine their contextual use. He does this by making a distinction between competence and performance. Competence refers to the child's tacit understanding of the rule system, performance relates to the essentially social use to which the rule system is put. Competence refers to man abstracted from contextual constraints. Performance refers to man in the grip of the contextual constraints which determine his speech acts. Competence refers to the Ideal, performance refers to the Fall. In this sense Chomsky's notion of competence is Platonic. Competence has its source in the very biology of man. There is no difference between men in terms of their access to the linguistic rule system. Here Chomsky, like many other linguists before him, announces the communality of man, all men have equal access to the creative act which is language. On the other hand, performance is under the control of the social—performances are culturally specific acts, they refer to the choices which are made in specific speech encounters. Thus from one point of view, Chomsky indicates the tragedy of man, the potentiality of competence and the degeneration of performance (this view explicitly derives from Hymes 1966).

Clearly, much is to be gained in rigour and explanatory power through the severing of the relationship between the formal properties of the grammar and the meanings which are realised in its use. But if we are to study speech, *la parole*, we are inevitably involved in a study of a rather different rule system, we are involved in a study of rules, formal and informal, which regulate the options we take up in various contexts in which we find ourselves. This second rule system is the cultural system.

This raises immediately the question of the causal relationship between the linguistic rule system and the cultural system. Clearly, specific linguistic rule systems are part of the cultural system, but it has been argued that the linguistic rule system in various ways shapes the cultural system. This very briefly is the view of those who hold a narrow form of the linguistic relativity hypothesis. I do not intend to get involved in that particular quagmire. Instead, I shall take the view that the code which the linguist invents to explain the formal properties of the grammar is capable of generating any number of speech codes, and there is no reason for believing that any one language code is better than another in this respect. On this argument, language is a set of rules to which all speech codes must comply, but which speech codes are realised is a function of the culture acting through social relationship in specific contexts. Different speech forms or codes symbolize the form of the social relationship, regulate the nature of the speech encounters, and create for the speakers different orders of relevance and relation. The experience of the speakers is then transformed by what is made significant or relevant by the speech form.

This is a sociological argument because the speech form is taken as a consequence of the form of the social relation or, put more generally, as a quality of a social structure.

Let me qualify this immediately. Because the speech form is initially a function of a given social arrangement, it does not mean that the speech form does not in turn modify or even change that social structure which initially evolved the speech form. This formulation, indeed, invites the question: under what conditions does a given speech form free itself sufficiently from its embodiment in the social structure so that the system of meanings it realises points to alternative realities, alternative arrangements in the affairs of men? Here we become concerned immediately with the antecedents and consequences of the boundary maintaining principles of a culture or sub-culture. I am here suggesting a relationship between forms of boundary maintenance at the cultural level and forms of speech.

LANGUAGE, SOCIALISATION AND CLASS

I am required to consider the relationship between language and socialisation. It should be clear that I am not concerned with language, but with speech, and concerned more specifically with the contextual constraints upon speech. Now what about socialisation? I shall take the term to refer to the process whereby a child acquires a specific cultural identity, *and* to his responses to such an identity. Socialisation refers to the process whereby the biological is transformed into a specific cultural being. It follows from this that the process of socialisation is a complex process of control, whereby a particular moral, cognitive and affective awareness is evoked in the child and given a specific form and content. Socialisation sensitizes the child to various orderings of society as these are made substantive in the various roles he is expected to play. In a sense then socialisation is a process for making people safe. The process acts selectively on the possibilities of man by creating through time a sense of the inevitability of a given social arrangement, and through limiting the areas of permitted change. The basic agencies of socialisation in contemporary societies are the family, the peer group, school and work. It is through these agencies, and in particular through their relationship to each other, that the various orderings of society are made manifest.

Now it is quite clear that given this view of socialisation it is necessary to limit the discussion. I shall limit our discussion to socialisation within the family, but it should be obvious that the focussing and filtering of the child's experience within the family in a large measure is a microcosm of the macroscopic orderings of society. Our question now becomes: what are the sociological factors which affect linguistic performances within the family critical to the process of socialisation?

Without a shadow of doubt the most formative influence upon the procedures of socialisation, from a sociological viewpoint, is social class. The class structure influences work and educational roles and brings families into a special relationship with each other and deeply penetrates the structure of life experiences within the family. The class system has deeply marked the distribution of knowledge within society. It has given differential access to the sense that the world is permeable. It has sealed off communities from each other and has ranked these communities on a scale of individuous worth. We have three components, knowledge, possibility, invidious insulation. It would be a little naive to believe that differences in knowledge, differences in the sense of the possible, combined with invidious insulation, rooted in differential *material* well-being would not affect the forms of control and innovation in the socialising procedures of different social classes. I shall go on to argue that the deep structure of communication itself is affected, but not in any final or irrevocable way.

As an approach to my argument, let me glance at the social distribution of knowledge. We can see that the class system has affected the distribution of knowledge. Historically and now, only a tiny percentage of the population has been socialised into knowledge at the level of the meta-languages of control and innovation, whereas the mass of the population has been socialised into knowledge at the level of context-tied operations.

A tiny percentage of the population has been given access to the principles of intellectual change whereas the rest have been denied such access. This suggests that we might be able to distinguish between two orders of meaning. One we could call universalistic, the other particularistic. Universalistic meanings are those in which principles and operations are made linguistically explicit whereas particularistic orders of meaning are meanings in which principles and operations are relatively linguistically implicit. If orders of meaning are universalistic, then the meanings are less tied to a given context. The meta-languages of public forms of thought as these apply to objects and persons realise meanings of a universalistic type. Where meanings have this characteristic then individuals may have access to the grounds of their experience and can change the grounds. Where orders of meaning are particularistic, where principles are linguistically implicit, then such meanings are less context independent and *more* context bound; that is, tied to a local relationship and to a local social structure. Where the meaning system is particularistic, much of the meaning is imbedded in the context and may be restricted to those who share a similar contextual history. Where meanings are universalistic, they are in principle available to all because the principles and operations have been made explicit and so public.

I shall argue that forms of socialisation orient the child towards speech codes which control access to relatively context-tied or relatively context-independent meanings. Thus I shall argue that elaborated codes orient their users towards universalistic meanings, whereas restricted codes orient, sensitize, their users to particularistic meanings: that the linguistic realisations of the two orders are different, and so are the social relationships which realise them. Elaborated codes are less tied to a given or local structure and thus contain the potentiality of change in principles. In the case of elaborated codes the speech is freed from its evoking social structure and takes on an autonomy. A university is a place organised around talk. Restricted codes are more tied to a local social structure and have a reduced potential for change in principles. Where codes are elaborated, the socialised has more access to the grounds of his own socialisation, and so can enter into a reflexive relationship to the social order he has taken over. Where codes are restricted, the socialised has less access to the grounds of his socialisation, and thus reflexiveness may be limited in range. *One of the effects of the class system is to limit access to elaborated codes.*

I shall go on to suggest that restricted codes have their basis in condensed symbols whereas elaborated codes have their basis in articulated symbols. That restricted codes draw upon metaphor whereas elaborated codes draw upon rationality. That these codes constrain the contextual use of language in critical socialising contexts and in this way regulate the orders of relevance and relation which the socialised takes over. From this point of view, change in habitual speech codes involves changes in the means by which object and person relationships are realised.

ELABORATED AND RESTRICTED SPEECH VARIANTS

I want first to start with the notions of elaborated and restricted speech variants. A variant can be considered as the contextual constraints upon grammatical-lexical choices.

Sapir, Malinowski, Firth, Vygotsky, Luria have all pointed out from different points of view that the closer the identification of speakers, the greater the range of shared interests, the more probable that the speech will take a specific form. The range of syntactic alternatives is likely to be reduced and the lexis to be drawn from a narrow range. Thus, the form of these social relations is acting selectively on the meanings to be verbally realised. In these relationships the intent of the other person can be taken for granted as the speech is played out against a back-drop of common assumptions, common history, common interests. As a result, there is less need to raise meanings to the level of explicitness or elaboration. There is a reduced need to make explicit through syntactic choices the logical structure of the communication. Further, if the speaker wishes to individualise his communication, he is likely to do this by varying the expressive associates of the speech. Under these conditions, the speech is likely to have a strong metaphoric element. In these situations the speaker may be more concerned with how something is said, when it is said; silence takes on a variety of meanings. Often in these encounters the speech cannot be understood apart from the context, and the context cannot be read by those who do not share the history of the relationship. Thus the form of the social relationship acts selectively on the meanings to be verbalised, which in turn affect the syntactic and lexical choices. The unspoken assumptions underlying the relationship are not available to those who are outside the relationship. For these are limited, and restricted to the speakers. The symbolic form of the communication is condensed yet the specific cultural history of the relationship is alive in its form. We can say that the roles of the speakers are communalised roles. Thus, we can make a relationship between restricted social relationships based upon communalised roles and the verbal realisation of their meaning. In the language of the earlier part of this paper, restricted social relationships based upon communalised role evoke particularistic, that is, context-tied meanings, realised through a restricted speech variant.

Imagine a husband and wife have just come out of the cinema, and are talking about the film: "What do you think?" "It had a lot to say." "Yes, I thought so too— let's go to the Millers, there may be something· going there." They arrive at the Millers, who ask about the film. An hour is spent in the complex, moral, political, aesthetic subtleties of the film and its place in the contemporary scene. Here we have an elaborated variant, the meanings now have to be made public to others who have not seen the film. The speech shows careful editing, at both the grammatical and lexical levels, it is no longer context tied. The meanings are explicit, elaborated and individualised. Whilst expressive channels are clearly relevant, the burden of meaning inheres predominantly in the verbal channel. The experience of the listeners cannot be taken for granted. Thus each member of the group is on his own as he offers his interpretation. Elaborated variants of this kind involve the speakers in particular role relationship, and *if you cannot manage the role, you can't produce the appropriate speech.* For as the speaker proceeds to individualise his meanings, he is differentiated from others like a figure from its ground.

The roles receive less support from each other. There is a measure of isolation. *Difference* lies at the basis of the social relationship, and is made verbally active, whereas in the other context it is *consensus.* The insides of the speaker have become psychologically active through the verbal aspect of the communication. Various defensive strategies may be used to decrease potential vulnerability of self and to increase the vulnerability of others. The verbal aspect of the communication becomes a vehicle for the transmission of individuated symbols. The "I" stands over the "We." Meanings which are discrete to the speaker must be offered so that they are intelligible to the listener. Communalised roles have given way to individualised roles, condensed symbols to articulated symbols. Elaborated speech variants of this type realise universalistic meanings in the sense that they are less context-tied. Thus individualised roles are realised through elaborated speech variants which involve complex

editing at the grammatical and lexical levels and which point to universalistic meanings.

Let me give another example. Consider the two following stories which Peter Hawkins, Assistant Research Officer in the Sociological Research Unit, University of London Institute of Education, constructed as a result of his analysis of the speech of middle-class and working-class five-year-old children. The children were given a series of four pictures which told a story and they were invited to tell the story. The first picture showed some boys playing football, in the second the ball goes through the window of a house, the third shows a woman looking out of the window and a man making an ominous gesture, and in the fourth the children are moving away.

Here are the two stories:

(1) Three boys are playing football and one boy kicks the ball and it goes through the window the ball breaks the window and the boys are looking at it and a man comes out and shouts at them because they've broken the window so they run away and then that lady looks out of her window and she tells the boys off.

(2) They're playing football and he kicks it and it goes through there it breaks the window and they're looking at it and he comes out and shouts at them because they've broken it so they run away and then she looks out and she tells them off.

With the first story the reader does not have to have the four pictures which were used as the basis for the story, whereas in the case of the second story the reader would require the initial pictures in order to make sense of the story. The first story is free of the context which generated it, whereas the second story is much more closely tied to its context. As a result the meanings of the second story are implicit, whereas the meanings of the first story are explicit. It is not that the working-class children do not have in their passive vocabulary the vocabulary used by the middle-class children. Nor is it the case that the children differ in their tacit understanding of the linguistic rule system. Rather, what we have here are differences in the use of language arising out of a specific context. One child makes explicit the meanings which he is realising through language for the person he is telling the story to, whereas the second child does not to the same extent. The first child takes very little for granted, whereas the second child takes a great deal for granted. Thus for the first child the task was seen as a context in which his meanings were required to be made explicit, whereas the task for the second child was not seen as a task which required such explication of meaning. It would not be difficult to imagine a context where the first child would produce speech rather like the second. What we are dealing with here are differences between the children in the way they realise in language use apparently the same context. We could say that the speech of the first child generated universalistic meanings in the sense that the meanings are freed from the context and so understandable by all. Whereas the speech of the second child generated particularistic meanings, in the sense that the meanings are closely tied to the context and would be only fully understood by others if they had access to the context which originally generated the speech.

It is again important to stress that the second child has access to a more differentiated noun phrase, but there is a restriction on its *use*. Geoffrey Turner, Linguist in the Sociological Research Unit, shows that working-class, five-year-old children in the same contexts examined by Hawkins, use fewer linguistic expressions of uncertainty when compared with the middle-class children. This does not mean that working-class children do *not* have access to such expressions, but that the eliciting speech context did not provoke them. Telling a story from pictures, talking about scenes on cards, *for-mally framed* contexts may not encourage working-class children to consider the possibilities of alternate meanings and so there is a reduction in the linguistic expressions of uncertainty. Again, working-class children have access to a wide range of syntactic choices which involve the use of logical operators, "because," "but," "either," "or," "only." The constraints exist on the conditions for their *use*. Formally framed contexts used for eliciting context independent universalistic meanings may evoke in the working-class child, relative to the middle-class child, restricted speech variants, because the working-class child has difficulty in managing the role relationships which such contexts require. This problem is further complicated when such contexts carry meanings very much removed from the child's cultural experience. In the same way we can show that there are constraints upon the middle-class child's use of language. Turner found that when middle-class children were asked to role play in the picture story series, a higher percentage of these children, when compared with working-class children, initially refused. When the middle-class children were asked "What is the man saying?" or linguistically equivalent questions, a relatively higher percentage said "I don't know." When this question was followed by the hypothetical question "What do you think the man might be saying?" they offered their interpretations. The working-class children role played without difficulty. It seems then that middle-class children at five need to have a very precise instruction to *hypothesise in that particular context*. This may be because they are more concerned here with getting their answers right or correct. When the children were invited to tell a story about some doll-like figures (a little boy, a little girl, a sailor and a dog), the working-class children's stories were freer, longer, more imaginative than the stories of the middle-class children. The latter children's stories were tighter, constrained within a strong narrative frame. It was as if these children were dominated by what they took to be the *form* of a narrative and the content was secondary. This is an example of the concern of the middle-class child with the structure of the contextual frame.

It may be worthwhile to amplify this further. A number of studies have shown that when working-class black children are asked to associate to a series of words, their responses show considerable diversity, both from the meaning and form-class of the stimulus word. In the analysis offered in the text this may be because the children for the following reasons are less constrained. The form-class of the stimulus word may have reduced associative significance and so would less constrain the selection of potential words *or* phrases. With such a weakening of the grammatical frame a greater range of alternatives are possible candidates for selection. Further, the closely controlled middle-class linguistic socialisation of the young child may point the child towards both the grammatical significance of the stimulus word and towards a tight logical ordering of semantic space. Middle-class children may well have access to deep interpretive rules which regulate their linguistic responses in certain formalised contexts. The consequences may limit their imagination through the tightness of the frame which these interpretive rules create. It may even be that with *five*-year-old children, the middle-class child will innovate *more* with the arrangements of objects (i.e. bricks) than in his linguistic usage. His linguistic usage is under close supervision by adults. He has more *autonomy* in his play.

To return to our previous discussion, we can say briefly that as we move from communalised to individualised roles, so speech takes on an increasingly reflexive function. The unique selves of others become palpable through speech and enter into our own self, the grounds of our experience are made verbally explicit; the security of the condensed symbol is gone. It has been replaced

by rationality. There is a change in the basis of our vulnerability.

FOUR CONTEXTS

So far, then, I have discussed certain types of speech variants and the role relationships which occasion them. I am now going to raise the generality of the discussion and focus upon the title of the paper. The socialisation of the young in the family proceeds within a critical set of inter-related contexts. Analytically, we may distinguish four contexts.

1. The regulative context—these are authority relationships where the child is made aware of the rules of the moral order and their various backings.

2. The instructional context, where the child learns about the objective nature of objects and persons, and acquires skills of various kinds.

3. The imaginative or innovating contexts, where the child is encouraged to experiment and re-create his world on his own terms, and in his own way.

4. The interpersonal context, where the child is made aware of affective states—his own, and others.

I am suggesting that the critical orderings of a culture or subculture are made substantive—are made palpable—through the forms of its linguistic realisations of these four contexts—initially in the family and kin.

Now if the linguistic realisation of these four contexts involves the predominant use of restricted speech variants, I shall postulate that the deep structure of the communication is a restricted code having its basis in communalised roles, realising context bound meanings, i.e., particularistic meaning orders. Clearly the specific grammatical and lexical choices will vary from one context to another.

If the linguistic realisation of these four contexts involves the predominant usage of elaborated speech variants, I shall postulate that the deep structure of the communication is an elaborated code having its basis in individualised roles realising context free, universalistic, meanings.

In order to prevent misunderstanding some expansion of this point is necessary. It is likely that where the code is restricted, the speech in the regulative context may well be limited to command and simple rule announcing statements. The latter statements are not context dependent in the sense previously given for they announce general rules. We need to supplement the context independent (universalistic) and context dependent (particularistic) criteria with criteria which refer to the extent to which the speech in the regulative context varies in terms of its *contextual specificity*. If the speech is context-specific then the socialiser cuts his meanings to the *specific* attributes/intentions of the socialised, the specific characteristics of the problem, the specific requirements of the context. Thus the general rule may be transmitted with degrees of *contextual specificity*. When this occurs the rule is individualised (fitted to the local circumstances) in the process of its transmission. Thus with code elaboration we should expect:

1. Some developed grounds for the rule.
2. Some qualification of it in the light of the particular issue.
3. Considerable *specificity* in terms of the socialised, the context and the issue.

This does *not* mean that there would be an *absence* of command statements. It is also likely that with code elaboration the socialised would be *given* opportunities (role options) to question.

Bernstein and Cook (1965) and Cook (1970) have developed a semantic coding grid which sets out with considerable delicacy a general category system which has been applied to a limited regulative context. G. Turner, linguist to the Sociological Research Unit, is attempting a linguistic realisation of the same grid.

We can express the two sets of criteria diagrammatically. A limited application is given by Henderson (1970):

Realisation of the Regulative Context

Universalistic

Specific   Non-specific

Particularistic

It may be necessary to utilise the two sets of criteria for *all* four socialising contexts. Bernstein (1967, published 1972) suggested that code realisation would vary with context.

If we look at the linguistic realisation of the regulative context in greater detail we may be able to clear up another source of possible misunderstanding. In this context it is very likely that syntactic markers of the logical distribution of meaning will be extensively used.

"If you do that, then. . . ."
"Either you . . . or. . . ."
"You can do that but if. . . ."
"You do that and you'll pay for it"

Thus it is very likely that young children may well in the *regulative* context have access to a range of syntactic markers which express the logical/hypothetical irrespective of code restriction or elaboration. However, where the code is restricted it is expected that there will be reduced specificity in the sense outlined earlier. Further, the speech in the control situation is likely to be well-organised in the sense that the sentences come as wholes. The child responds to the total *frame*. However, I would suggest that the informal *instructional* contexts within the family may well be limited in range and frequency. Thus the child, of course, would have access to and so have *available*, the hypotheticals, conditionals, disjunctives etc. but these might be rarely used in *instructional* contexts. In the same way, as we have suggested earlier, all children have access to linguistic expressions of uncertainty but they may differ in the context in which they receive and realise such expressions.

I must emphasise that because the code is restricted it does not mean that speakers at

no time will use elaborated speech variants. Only that the use of such variants will be infrequent in the socialisation of the child in his family.

Now, all children have access to restricted codes and their various systems of condensed meaning, because the roles the code pre-supposes are universal. But there may well be selective access to elaborated codes because there is selective access to the role system which evokes its use. Society is likely to evaluate differently the experiences realised through these two codes. I cannot here go into details, but the different focussing of experience through a restricted code creates a major problem of educability only where the school produces discontinuity between its symbolic orders and those of the child. Our schools are not made for these children; why should the children respond? To ask the child to switch to an elaborated code which presupposes different role relationships and systems of meaning without a sensitive understanding of the required contexts may create for the child a bewildering and potentially damaging experience.

FAMILY TYPES AND COMMUNICATION STRUCTURES

So far, then, I have sketched out a relationship between speech codes and socialisation through the organisation of roles through which the culture is made psychologically active in persons. I have indicated that access to the roles and thus to the codes is broadly related to social class. However, it is clearly the case that social class groups today are by no means homogeneous groups. Further, the division between elaborated and restricted codes is too simple. Finally, I have not indicated in any detail how these codes are evoked by families, and how the family types may shape their focus.

What I shall do now is to introduce a distinction between family types and their communication structures. These family types can be found empirically within each social class, although any one type may be rather more modal at any given historical period.

I shall distinguish between families according to the strength of their boundary maintaining procedures. Let me first give some idea of what I mean by boundary maintaining procedures. I shall first look at boundary maintenance as it is revealed in the symbolic ordering of space. Consider the lavatory. In one house, the room is pristine, bare and sharp, containing only the necessities for which the room is dedicated. In another there is a picture on the wall, in the third there are books, in the fourth all surfaces are covered with curious postcards. We have a continuum from a room celebrating the purity of categories to one celebrating the mixture of categories, from strong to weak boundary maintenance. Consider the kitchen. In one kitchen, shoes may not be placed on the table, nor the child's chamber pot—all objects and utensils have an assigned place. In another kitchen the boundaries separating the different classes of objects are weak. The symbolic ordering of space can give us indications of the relative strength of boundary maintaining procedures. Let us now look at the relationship between family members. Where boundary procedures are strong, the differentiation of members and the authority structure is based upon clear-cut, unambiguous definitions of the status of the member of the family. The boundaries between the statuses are strong and the social identities of the members very much a function of their age, sex and age-relation status. As a shorthand, we can characterise the family as *positional.*

On the other hand, where boundary procedures are weak or flexible, the differentiation between members and the authority relationships are less on the basis of position, because here the status boundaries are blurred. Where boundary procedures are weak, the differentiation between members is based more upon *differences between persons.* In such families the relationships become more egocentric and the unique attributes of family members more and more are made substantive in the communication structure. We will call these *person-centred* families. Such families do not reduce but increase the substantive expression of ambiguity and ambivalence. In person-centred families, the role system would be continuously evoking, accommodating and assimilating the different interests, attributes of its members. In such families, unlike positional families, the members would be making their roles, rather than stepping into them. In a person-centred family, the child's developing self is differentiated by continuous adjustment to the verbally realised and elaborated intentions, qualifications and motives of others. The boundary between self and other is blurred. In positional families, the child takes over and responds to the formal pattern of obligation and privilege. It should be possible to see, without going into details, that the communication structure within these two types of family are somewhat differently focussed. We might then expect that the reflexiveness induced by positional families is sensitized to the general attributes of persons, whereas the reflexiveness produced by person-centred families is more sensitive towards the particular aspects of persons. Think of the difference between Dartington Hall or Gordonstoun Public Schools in England, or the difference between West Point and a progressive school in the USA. Thus, in person-centred families, the insides of the members are made public through the communication structure, and thus more of the person has been invaded and subject to control. Speech in such families is a major media of control. In positional families of course, speech is relevant but it symbolizes the boundaries given by the formal structure of the relationships. So far as the child is concerned, in positional families he attains a strong sense of social identity at the cost of autonomy; in person-centred families, the child attains a strong sense of autonomy but his social identity may be weak. Such ambiguity in the sense of identity, the lack of boundary, may move

such children towards a radically closed value system.

If we now place these family types in the framework of the previous discussion, we can see that although the code may be elaborated, it may be differently focussed according to the family type. Thus, we can have an elaborate code focussing upon persons or an elaborated code in a positional family may focus more upon objects. We can expect the same with a restricted code. Normally, with code restriction we should expect a positional family, however, if it showed signs of being person-centred, then we might expect the children to be in a situation of potential code switch.

Where the code is elaborated, and focussed by a person-centred family, then these children may well develop acute identity problems, concerned with authenticity, of limiting responsibility—they may come to see language as phony, a system of counterfeit masking the absence of belief. They may move towards the restricted codes of the various peer group sub-cultures, or seek the condensed symbols of affective experience, or both.

One of the difficulties of this approach is to avoid implicit value judgements about the relative worth of speech systems and the cultures which they symbolize. Let it be said immediately that a restricted code gives access to a vast potential of meanings, of delicacy, subtlety and diversity of cultural forms, to a unique aesthetic whose basis in condensed symbols may influence the form of the imagining. Yet, in complex industrialized societies, its differently focussed experience may be disvalued, and humiliated within schools or seen, at best, to be irrelevant to the educational endeavour. For the schools are predicated upon elaborated code and its system of social relationships. Although an elaborated code does not entail any specific value system, the value system of the middle class penetrates the texture of the very learning context itself.

Elaborated codes give access to alternative realities yet they carry the potential of alienation, of feeling from thought, of self from other, of private belief *from role obligation.*

SOURCES OF CHANGE

Finally I should like to consider briefly the source of change of linguistic codes. The first major source of change I suggest is to be located in the division of labour. As the division of labour changes from simple to complex, then this changes the social and knowledge characteristics of occupational roles. In this process there is an extension of access, through education, to elaborated codes, but access is controlled by the class system. The focussing of the codes I have suggested is brought about by the boundary maintaining procedures within the family. However, we can generalise and say that the focussing of the codes is related to the boundary maintaining procedures as these affect the major socialising agencies, family, age group, education and work. We need, therefore, to consider together with the question of the degree and type of complexity of the division of labour the value orientations of society which it is hypothesized affect the boundary maintaining procedures. It is the case that we can have societies with a similar complexity in their division of labour but which differ in their boundary maintaining procedures.

I suggest then that it is important to make a distinction between societies in terms of their boundary maintaining procedures if we are to deal with this question of the focussing of codes. One possible way of examining the relative strength of boundary maintenance, at a somewhat high level of abstraction, is to consider the strength of the *constraints* upon the choice of values which legitimize authority/power relationships. Thus in societies where there is weak constraint upon such legitimising values, that is, where there are a variety of formally permitted legitimising values, we might expect a

marked shift towards person type control. Whereas in societies with strong constraints upon legitimising values, where there is a severe *restriction* upon the choice, we might expect a marked shift towards positional control.

I shall illustrate these relationships with reference to the family:

Division of labour	Constraints upon legitimising values (Boundary Maintenance)	
Simple→Complex	Strong	Weak
↓	↓	↓
Speech Codes	*Positional*	*Personal*
Restricted Code	Working-Class	Working-Class
↓		
Elaborated Code	Middle-Class	Middle-Class

Thus the division of labour influences the availability of elaborated codes; the class system affects their distribution; the focussing of codes can be related to the boundary maintaining procedures, i.e. the value system. I must point out that this is only a coarse interpretive framework.

CONCLUSION

I have tried to show how the class system acts upon the deep structure of communication in the process of socialisation. I refined the crudity of this analysis by showing how speech codes may be differently focussed through family types. Finally, it is conceivable that there are general aspects of the analysis which might provide a starting point for the consideration of symbolic orders other than languages (see Douglas 1970). I must point out that there is more to socialisation than the forms of its linguistic realisation.

NOTE

1. This work was supported by grants from the Department of Education and Science, the Ford Foundation and the Nuffield Foundation, to whom grateful acknowledgement is made. I would also like to take the opportunity of acknowledging my debt to Professor Courtney Cazden, Dr. Mary

Douglas, Professor John Gumperz, Professor Dell Hymes, and in particular to Professor Michael Halliday. I am also grateful for the constant constructive criticism I have received from members of the Sociological Research Unit, University of London Institute of Education.

BIBLIOGRAPHY

Bernstein, B. 1970a. Education cannot compensate for society. New Society No. 387, February, 1970.

_____. 1972. Family role systems, socialisation and communication. Directions in sociolinguistics, ed. by D. Hymes and J. J. Gumperz. New York, Holt, Rinehart and Winston. Also appeared as Manuscript, Sociological Research Unit, University of London Institute of Education (1967).

Bernstein, B., and J. Cook. 1965. Coding grid for maternal control. Available from Department of Sociology, University of London Institute of Education.

Bernstein, B., and D. Henderson. 1969. Social class differences in the relevance of language to socialisation. Sociology 3/1.

Bright, W., ed. 1966. Sociolinguistics. The Hague, Mouton.

Carroll, J.B., ed. 1956. Language, thought and reality: Selected writings of Benjamin Lee Whorf. New York, John Wiley & Sons, Inc.

Cazden, C.B. 1969. Sub-cultural differences in child language: An interdisciplinary review. Merrill-Palmer Quarterly 12.

Chomsky, N. 1965. Aspects of the theory of syntax. Cambridge, M.I.T. Press.

Cook, J. 1970. An enquiry into patterns of communication and control between mothers and their children in different social classes. Ph.D. Thesis, awaiting submission to the University of London (1970).

Coulthard, M. 1969. A discussion of restricted and elaborated codes. Educational Review 22/1.

Douglas, M. 1970. Natural symbols. London, Barrie & Rockliff, The Cresset Press/New York, Pantheon.

Fishman, J.A. 1960. A systematisation of the Whorfian hypothesis. BS 5.

Halliday, M.A.K. 1969. Relevant models of language. Educational Review 22/1.

Hawkins, P.R. 1969. Social class, the nominal group and reference. L & S 12/2.125−35.

Henderson, D. 1970. Contextual specificity, discretion and cognitive socialisation: With special reference to language. Sociology 4/3.

Hoijer, H., ed. 1954. Language in culture. American Anthropological Association Memoir No. 79−also published by the University of Chicago Press.

Hymes, D. 1966. On communicative competence. Research Planning Conference on Language Development among Disadvantaged Children. Ferkauf Graduate School, Yeshiva University. Also in Hymes and Gumperz, 1972.

_____. 1967. Models of the interaction of language and social setting. Journal of Social Issues 23.

Hymes, D., and J. J. Gumperz, eds. 1972. Directions in sociolinguistics. New York, Holt, Rinehart and Winston.

Labov, W. 1965. Stages in the acquisition of standard English. Social dialects and language learning, ed. by W. Shuy. Champaign, Illinois, National Council of Teachers of English.

_____. 1966. The social stratification of English in New York City. Washington, D.C., Center for Applied Linguistics.

Mandelbaum, D., ed. 1949. Selected writings of Edward Sapir. University of California Press.

Parsons, T., and E. A. Shils, eds. 1951. Toward a general theory of action. Cambridge, Mass.; Harvard University Press. Also Harper Torchbooks TB1083N. [Chapter 1, especially]

Schatzman, L., and A.L. Strauss. 1955. Social class and modes of communication. American Journal of Sociology 60.328−38.

Turner, G., and R.E. Pickvance. 1970. Social class differences in the expression of uncertainty in five-year-old children. L & S 13.

Williams, F., and R.C. Naremore. 1969. On the functional analysis of social class differences in modes of speech. Speech Monographs 36/2.

29. Cultural Reproduction and Social Reproduction

PIERRE BOURDIEU

The specific role of the sociology of education is assumed once it has established itself as the science of the relations between cultural reproduction and social reproduction. This occurs when it endeavours to determine the contribution made by the educational system to the reproduction of the structure of power relationships and symbolic relationships between classes, by contributing to the reproduction of the structure of the distribution of cultural capital among these classes. The science of the reproduction of structures, understood as a system of objective relations which impart their relational properties to individuals whom they preexist and survive, has nothing in common with the analytical recording of relations existing within a given population, be it a question of the relations between the academic success of children and the social position of their family or of the relations between the positions filled by children and their parents. The substantialist mode of thought which stops short at directly accessible elements, that is to say individuals, claims a certain fidelity to reality by disregarding the structure of relations whence these elements derive all their sociologically relevant determinations, and thus finds itself having to analyse intra- or inter-generational mobility processes to the detriment of the study of mechanisms which tend to ensure the reproduction of the structure of relations between classes; it is unaware that the controlled mobility of a limited category of individuals, carefully selected and modified by and for individual ascent, is not incompatible with the permanence of structures, and that it is even capable of contributing to

social stability in the only way conceivable in societies based upon democratic ideals and thereby may help to perpetuate the structure of class relations.

Any break with substantialist atomism, even if it does not mean going as far as certain structuralists and seeing agents as the simple "supports" of structures invested with the mysterious power of determining other structures, implies taking as our theme the process of education. This means that our object becomes the production of the habitus, that system of dispositions which acts as a mediation between structures and practice; more specifically, it becomes necessary to study the laws that determine the tendency of structures to reproduce themselves by producing agents endowed with the system of predispositions which is capable of engendering practices adapted to the structures and thereby contributing to the reproduction of the structures. If it is conceived within a theoretical framework such as this, the sociology of educational institutions and, in particular, of institutions of higher education, is capable of making a decisive contribution to the science of the structural dynamics of class relations, which is an often neglected aspect of the sociology of power. Indeed, among all the solutions put forward throughout history to the problem of the transmission of power and privileges, there surely does not exist one that is better concealed, and therefore better adapted to societies which tend to refuse the most patent forms of the hereditary transmission of power and privileges, than that solution which the educational system provides by contributing to the reproduction of the

From *Knowledge, Education, and Cultural Change,* ed. Richard Brown (London: Tavistock, 1973), pp. 71–112. In this reprinting we have omitted the tables and figures of its Appendix (pp. 100–104). This article © Pierre Bourdieu 1973.

structure of class relations and by concealing, by an apparently neutral attitude, the fact that it fills this function.

THE ROLE OF THE EDUCATIONAL SYSTEM IN THE REPRODUCTION OF THE STRUCTURE OF THE DISTRIBUTION OF CULTURAL CAPITAL

By traditionally defining the educational system as the group of institutional or routine mechanisms by means of which is operated what Durkheim calls "the conservation of a culture inherited from the past," i.e. the transmission from generation to generation of accumulated information, classical theories tend to dissociate the function of cultural reproduction proper to all educational systems from their function of social reproduction. Transposing, as they do, the representation of culture and of cultural transmission, commonly accepted by the ethnologists, to the case of societies divided into classes, these theories are based upon the implicit assumption that the different pedagogic actions which are carried out within the framework of the social structure, that is to say, those which are carried out by families from the different social classes as well as that which is practised by the school, work together in a harmonious way to transmit a cultural heritage which is considered as being the undivided property of the whole society.

In fact the statistics of theatre, concert, and, above all, museum attendance (since, in the last case, the effect of economic obstacles is more or less nil) are sufficient reminder that the inheritance of cultural wealth which has been accumulated and bequeathed by previous generations only really belongs (although it is *theoretically* offered to everyone) to those endowed with the means of appropriating it for themselves. In view of the fact that the apprehension and possession of cultural goods as symbolic goods (along with the symbolic satisfactions which accompany an appropriation of this kind) are possible only for those who hold

the code making it possible to decipher them or, in other words, that the appropriation of symbolic goods presupposes the possession of the instruments of appropriation, it is sufficient to give free play to the laws of cultural transmission for cultural capital to be added to cultural capital and for the structure of the distribution of cultural capital between social classes to be thereby reproduced. By this is meant the structure of the distribution of instruments for the appropriation of symbolic wealth socially designated as worthy of being sought and possessed.

In order to be persuaded of the truth of this, it must first be seen that the structure of the distribution of classes or sections ("fractions") of a class according to the extent to which they are consumers of culture corresponds, with a few slight differences such as the fact that heads of industry and commerce occupy a lower position than do higher office staff, professionals, and even intermediate office staff, to the structure of distribution according to the hierarchy of economic capital and power (see *Table I*).[1]

The different classes or sections of a class are organized around three major positions: the lower position, occupied by the agricultural professions, workers, and small tradespeople, which are, in fact, categories excluded from participation in "high" culture; the intermediate position, occupied on the one hand by the heads and employees of industry and business and, on the other hand, by the intermediate office staff (who are just about as removed from the two other categories as these categories are from the lower categories); and, lastly, the higher position, which is occupied by higher office staff and professionals.

The same structure is to be seen each time an assessment is made of cultural habits and, in particular, of those that demand a cultured disposition, such as reading, and theatre, concert, art-cinema, and museum attendance. In such cases, the only distortions are those that introduce the use of

Table 1. Expenditure on Culture[2]

Annual budget coefficients	Agricultural workers	Farmers	Workers	Small tradespeople	White-collar workers	Intermediate office staff	Heads of industry and commerce	Professionals and higher office staff
Durable goods	0.6	0.5	0.8	0.8	1.4	2.8	1.5	3.6
Other expenditure	1.6	1.9	2.2	2.2	3.2	3.6	3.3	6.2

Table 2. Cultural Activities of Different Occupational Categories

Purchasers of books during last month[3]		Readers of books[4]		Regular theatre, concert, cinema attendance in the Parisian region[5]			Have been to the theatre at least once in year 1964[6] (all of France)
Farmers	14	Farmers, agricultural workers	15.5	Farmers			18
Workers	22	Workers	33	Workers	21	8	70	17
Heads of industry & commerce	31	White-collar workers	53.5	Tradespeople & craftsmen	46	14	71	22
White-collar workers, intermediate office staff	39	Craftsmen & tradespeople, intermediate office staff	51.5	White-collar workers, intermediate office staff	47	22	80	32
Professionals, higher office staff	50	Heads of industry, professionals, higher office staff	72	Heads of industry, professionals, higher office staff	65	33	81	63

different principles of classification (*Table 2*).

Although statistics based like these upon the statements of those being questioned and not upon direct observation tend to overestimate the extent to which an activity is practised by reason of the propensity of the persons questioned to align themselves, at least when talking, to the activity that is recognized as legitimate, they do make it possible to make out the real structure of the distribution of cultural capital. In order to achieve this, it is sufficient to note that the statistics for the purchase of books omit all distinction between small self-employed craftsmen and tradespeople, whose activities are known to be very similar to those of the workers, and industrial and business management, whose cultural consumption is close to that of intermediate office staff; it is also to be noticed that the statistics for the readers of books (books which have been purchased, but doubtless also books which have been borrowed or read in libraries, which explains the movement of the structure towards the upper part) group together small self-employed craftsmen and tradespeople, who seldom practise a cultural activity, and intermediate office staff, who

practise cultural activities to a greater extent than do white-collar workers.

Although they remain relatively disparate, the categories made use of in terms of level of education make possible a more direct comparison, and all throw light upon the existence of an extremely pronounced relationship between the different "legitimate" activities and the level of education (*Table 3*).

If, of all cultural activities, cinema attendance in its common form is the one that is least closely linked to level of education, as opposed to concert-going, which is a rarer activity than reading or theatre-going, the fact remains that, as is shown by the statistics for art-cinema attendance, the cinema has a tendency to acquire the power of *social distinction* that belongs to traditionally approved arts.

The greater reliability of the survey carried out by the Centre of European Sociology (Centre de Sociologie Européenne) of the European museum public is due to the fact that it was based upon the degree of effective practice and not on the statements of those being questioned. It makes it possible, moreover, to construct the system of social conditions for the production of the

Table 3. Cultural Activities and Level of Education

	Have purchased a book in the last month[3]	Readers of books[4]	Regular attendance at:				Have been to the theatre:	
			Theatre[5]	Concert[5]	Cinema[5]	Art cinema	at least once in 1964	4 times or more
Primary	15	28	18	7	62	3	15	2
Primary, Higher, Commercial & technical		60	41	15	76		24	5
Secondary	44	Secondary & Higher 80	57	25	79	15	38	12
Higher	64		69	43	88	32	49	21

"consumers" of cultural goods considered as the most worthy of being consumed, i.e. the mechanisms of reproduction of the structure of the distribution of cultural capital which is seen in the structure of the distribution of the consumers of the museum, the theatre, the concert, the art cinema, and, more generally, of all the symbolic wealth that constitutes "legitimate" culture. Museum attendance, which increases to a large extent as the level of education rises, is almost exclusively to be found among the privileged classes. The proportions of the different socio-professional categories figuring in the public of the French museums are almost exactly the inverse ratio of their proportions in the overall population. Given that the typical visitor to French museums holds academic qualifications (since 55 per cent of visitors have at least the *baccalauréat,* the French school-leaving certificate), it is not surprising that the structure of the public distributed according to social category is very similar to the structure of the population of the students of the French faculties distributed according to social origin: the proportion of farmers is 1 per cent, that of

workers 4 per cent, that of skilled workers and tradesmen is 5 per cent, that of white-collar workers and intermediate office staff is 23 per cent (of whom 5 per cent are primary-school teachers), and the proportion of the upper classes is 45 per cent. If, for the rate of attendance of the different categories of visitors in the whole of the museum public, we substitute the probability of their going into a museum, it will be seen (in *Table 4*) that, once the level of education is established, knowledge of the sex or socio-professional category of the visitors generally provides only a small amount of additional information (although it may be noted in passing that, when the level of education is the same, teachers and art specialists practise this activity to a distinctly greater extent than do other categories and, particularly, other sections of the dominant classes).

In short, all of the relations observed between museum attendance and such variables as class or section of a class, age, income, or residence come down, more or less, to the relation between the level of education and attendance. The existence of

Table 4. Annual Attendance Rates for the French Museums According to Occupational Categories[7]

(mathematical expectation of visits over a period of a year expressed as a percentage)

	Without diploma	Certificate of primary studies	Certificate of secondary studies	Baccalaureat	Licence (=BA, BSc) and beyond	Total
Farmers	0.2	0.4	20.4			0.5
Workers	0.3	1.3	21.3			1
Craftsmen & tradespeople	1.9	2.8	30.7	59.4		4.9
White-collar workers, intermediate office staff		2.8	19.9	73.6		9.8
Higher office staff, heads of industry, professionals		2.0	12.3	64.4	77.6	43.3
Teachers, art specialists			(68.1)	153.7	(163.8)	151.5
Total	1	2.3	24	70.1	80.1	6.2
Men	1	2.3	24.4	64.5	65.1	6.1
Women	1.1	2.3	23.2	87.9	122.8	6.3

such a powerful and exclusive relationship between the level of education and cultural practice should not conceal the fact that, in view of the implicit presuppositions that govern it, the action of the educational system can attain full effectiveness only to the extent that it bears upon individuals who have been previously granted a certain familiarity with the world of art by their family upbringing. Indeed, it would seem that the action of the school, whose effect is unequal (if only from the point of view of duration) among children from different social classes, and whose success varies considerably among those upon whom it has an effect, tends to reinforce and to consecrate by its sanctions the initial inequalities. As may be seen in the fact that the proportion of those who have received from their families an early initiation into art increases to a very marked extent along with the level of education, what is measured by means of the level of education is nothing other than the accumulation of the effects of training acquired within the family and the academic apprenticeships which themselves presupposed this previous training.

If this is the case, the main reasons are, first, that the appropriation of works of art depends in its intensity, its modality, and its very existence upon the mastery that the spectator has of the available instruments of appropriation and, more specifically, of the generic and particular code of the work or, if it is preferred, of the peculiarly artistic lines of interpretation that are directly appropriate to each particular work and are the necessary condition for the deciphering of the work;[8] second, that, in the specific case of works of "high" culture, mastery of the code cannot be totally acquired by means of the simple and diffuse apprenticeships provided by daily existence but presupposes an education methodically organized by an institution specially equipped for this purpose. It is to be noted, however, that the yield of pedagogic communication, entrusted, among other functions, with the responsibility of transmitting the code of

works of "high" culture, along with the code according to which this transmission is carried out, is itself a function of the cultural competence that the receiver owes to his family upbringing, which is more or less close to the "high" culture transmitted by the colleges and to the linguistic and cultural models according to which this transmission is carried out. In view of the fact that reception of the pictorial message and the institutionally organized acquisition of cultural competence, which is the condition for the reception of this message, are subject to the same laws, it is not surprising that it is difficult to break the circle in which cultural capital is added to cultural capital. The museum that demarcates its public and legitimizes its social quality by the mere effect of its "level of emission,"[9] i.e. by the simple fact that it presupposes the possession of the fairly complex, and therefore fairly rare, cultural code which is necessary in order to decipher the works exhibited, may be seen as the limit towards which an educational action is directed (it might be possible to use the words "pedagogic action" here were it not for the fact that it is rather, in this case, a non-pedagogic action), implicitly requiring of those on whom it bears that they possess the conditions necessary to its full productivity.

The educational system reproduces all the more perfectly the structure of the distribution of cultural capital among classes (and sections of a class) in that the culture which it transmits is closer to the dominant culture and that the mode of inculcation to which it has recourse is less removed from the mode of inculcation practised by the family. Inasmuch as it operates in and through a relationship of communication, pedagogic action directed at inculcating the dominant culture can in fact escape (even if it is only in part) the general laws of cultural transmission, according to which the appropriation of the proposed culture (and, consequently, the success of the apprenticeship which is crowned by academic qualifications) depends upon the previous possession of the instruments of appropriation, to the extent and only to the extent that it explicitly and deliberately hands over, in the pedagogic communication itself, those instruments which are indispensable to the success of the communication and which, in a society divided into classes, are very unequally distributed among children from the different social classes. An educational system which puts into practice an implicit pedagogic action, requiring initial familiarity with the dominant culture, and which proceeds by imperceptible familiarization, offers information and training which can be received and acquired only by subjects endowed with the system of predispositions that is the condition for the success of the transmission and of the inculcation of the culture. By doing away with giving explicitly to everyone what it implicitly demands of everyone, the educational system demands of everyone alike that they have what it does not give. This consists mainly of linguistic and cultural competence and that relationship of familiarity with culture which can only be produced by family upbringing when it transmits the dominant culture.

In short, an institution officially entrusted with the transmission of the instruments of appropriation of the dominant culture which neglects methodically to transmit the instruments indispensable to the success of its undertaking is bound to become the monopoly of those social classes capable of transmitting by their own means, that is to say by that diffuse and implicit continuous educational action which operates within cultured families (often unknown to those responsible for it and to those who are subjected to it), the instruments necessary for the reception of its message, and thereby to confirm their monopoly of the instruments of appropriation of the dominant culture and thus their monopoly of that culture.[10] The closer that educational action gets to that limit, the more the value that the educational system attributes to the products of the educational work carried out by families of the different

social classes is directly a function of the value as cultural capital which is attributed, on a market dominated by the products of the educational work of the families of the dominant classes, to the linguistic and cultural competence which the different classes or sections of a class are in a position to transmit, mainly in terms of the culture that they possess and of the time that they are able to devote to its explicit or implicit transmission. That is to say that the transmission of this competence is in direct relation to the distance between the linguistic and cultural competence implicitly demanded by the educational transmission of educational culture (which is itself quite unevenly removed from the dominant culture) and the linguistic and cultural competence inculcated by primary education in the different social classes.

The laws of the educational market may be read in the statistics which establish that, from the moment of entering into secondary education right up to the *grandes écoles*, the hierarchy of the educational establishments and even, within these establishments, the hierarchy of the sections and of the fields of study arranged according to their prestige and to the educational value they impart to their public, correspond exactly to the hierarchy of the institutions according to the social structure of their public, on account of the fact that those classes or sections of a class which are richest in cultural capital become more and more over-represented as there is an increase in the rarity and hence in the educational value and social yield of academic qualifications. If such is the case, the reason is that, by virtue of the small real autonomy of an educational system which is incapable of affirming the specificity of its principles of evaluation and of its own mode of production of cultured dispositions, the relationship between the pedagogic actions carried out by the dominated classes and by the dominant classes may be understood by analogy with the relationship which is set up, in the economic field, between modes of production of different epochs when for example, in a dualist economy, the products of a traditional local craft industry are submitted to the laws of a market dominated by the chain-produced products of a highly developed industry: the symbolic products of the educational work of the different social classes, i.e. apart from knowledge and know-how, styles of being, of speaking, or of doing, have less value on the educational market and, more widely, on the symbolic market (in matrimonial exchanges, for instance) and on the economic market (at least to the extent that its sanctions depend upon academic ratification) in that the mode of symbolic production of which they are the product is more removed from the dominant mode of production or, in other words, from the educational norms of those social classes capable of imposing the domination of criteria of evaluation which are the most favourable to their products. It is in terms of this logic that must be understood the prominent value accorded by the French educational system to such subtle modalities in the relationship to culture and language as affluence, elegance, naturalness, or distinction, all of which are ways of making use of the symbolic products whose role of representing excellence in the field of culture (to the detriment of the dispositions produced by the school and paradoxically devalued, by the school itself, as being "academic") is due to the fact that they belong only to those who have acquired culture or, at least, the dispositions necessary for the acquisition of academic culture, by means of familiarization, i.e. imperceptible apprenticeships from the family upbringing, which is the mode of acquisition of the instruments of appropriation of the dominant culture of which the dominant classes hold the monopoly.

The sanctions of the academic market owe their specific effectiveness to the fact that they are brought to bear with every appearance of legitimacy: it is, in fact, as though the agents proportioned the investments that are placed in production for the academic market—investments of time and enthusiasm for education on the part of the pupils, investments of time, effort, and money on the part of families—to the profits which they may hope to obtain, over a more or less long term, on this market, as though the price that they attribute to the sanctions of the academic market were in direct relation to the price attributed to them by the sanctions of this market and to the extent to which their economic and symbolic value depends on the value which they are recognized to possess by the academic market. It follows from this that the negative predispositions towards the school which result in the self-elimination of most children from the most culturally unfavoured classes and sections of a class—such as self-depreciation, devaluation of the school and its sanctions, or a resigned attitude to failure and exclusion—must be understood as an anticipation, based upon the unconscious estimation of the objective probabilities of success possessed by the whole category, of the sanctions objectively reserved by the school for those classes or sections of a class deprived of cultural capital. Owing to the fact that it is the product of the internalization of value that the academic market (anticipating by its formally neutral sanctions the sanctions of the symbolic or economic market) confers upon the products of the family upbringing of the different social classes, and of the value which, by their objective sanctions, the economic and symbolic markets confer upon the products of educational action according to the social class from which they originate, the system of dispositions towards the school, understood as a propensity to consent to the investments in time, effort, and money necessary to conserve or increase cultural capital, tends to redouble the symbolic and economic effects of the uneven distribution of cultural capital, all the while concealing it and, at the same time, legitimating it. The functionalist sociologists who announce the brave new world when, at the conclusion of a longitudinal study of academic and social careers, they discover that, as though by a pre-established harmony, individuals have hoped for nothing that they have not obtained and obtained nothing that they have not hoped for, are simply the least forgivable victims of the ideological effect which is produced by the school when it cuts off from their social conditions of production all predispositions regarding the school such as "expectations," "aspirations," "inclinations," or "desire," and thus tends to cover up the fact that objective conditions—and in the individual case, the laws of the academic market—determine aspirations by determining the extent to which they can be satisfied.

This is only one of the mechanisms by which the academic market succeeds in imposing upon those very persons who are its victims recognition of the existence of its sanctions by concealing from them the objective truth of the mechanisms and social motives that determine them. To the extent to which it is enough for it to be allowed to run its own course, that is to say to give free play to the laws of cultural transmission, in order to ensure the reproduction of the structure of distribution of cultural capital, the educational system which merely records immediate or deferred self-elimination (in the form of the self-relegation of children from the underprivileged classes to the lower educational streams) or encourages elimination simply by the effectiveness of a nonexistent pedagogical practice (able to conceal behind patently obvious procedures of selection the action of mechanisms tending to ensure in an almost automatic way—that is to say, in a way which conforms to the laws governing all forms of cultural transmission—the exclusion of certain categories of recipients of the pedagogic message), this educational system masks more thoroughly than any other legitimation mechanism (imagine for example what would be the social effects of an arbitrary limitation of the public carried out in the name of ethnic or social criteria) the arbitrary nature of the actual demarcation of its public, thereby imposing more subtly the legitimacy of its products and of its hierarchies.

CULTURAL REPRODUCTION AND SOCIAL REPRODUCTION

By making social hierarchies and the reproduction of these hierarchies appear to be based upon the hierarchy of "gifts," merits, or skills established and ratified by its sanctions, or, in a word, by converting social hierarchies into academic hierarchies, the educational system fulfils a function of legitimation which is more and more necessary to the perpetuation of the "social order" as the evolution of the power relationship between classes tends more completely to exclude the imposition of a hierarchy based upon the crude and ruthless affirmation of the power relationship. But does the continual increase, in most highly industrialized societies, in the proportion of the members of the ruling classes who have passed through the university system and the best universities lead one to conclude that the transmission of cultural capital is tending to be substituted purely and simply for the transmission of economic capital and ownership of the means of production in the system of mechanisms of reproduction of the structure of class relationships?

Apart from the fact that the increase in the proportion of holders of the most prestigious academic qualifications among the members of the ruling classes may mean only that the need to call upon academic approval in order to legitimate the transmission of power and of privileges is being more and more felt, the effect is as though the cultural and educational mechanisms of transmission had merely strengthened or taken over from the traditional mechanisms such as the hereditary transmissions of economic capital, of a name, or of capital in terms of social relations; it is, in fact, as if the investments placed in the academic career of children had been integrated into *the system of strategies of reproduction,* which strategies are more or less compatible and more or less profitable depending on the type of capital to be transmitted, and by which each generation endeavours to transmit to the following generation the advantages it holds. Considering that, on the one hand, the ruling classes have at their disposal a much larger cultural capital than the other classes, even among those who constitute what are, relatively, the least well-off sections of the ruling classes and who, as has been seen, still practise cultural activities to at least as great an extent as the most favoured sections of the middle class, and considering that, on the other hand, they also have at their disposal the means of ensuring for this capital the best academic placing for its investment (that is to say the best establishments and the best departments), their academic investments cannot fail to be extremely profitable, and the segregation that is established right at the beginning of secondary education among students from different establishments and different departments cannot help but be reinforced the further one gets into the academic course by reason of the continual increase in the differences resulting from the fact that the most culturally privileged find their way into institutions capable of reinforcing their advantage. Institutions of higher education which ensure or legitimate access to the ruling classes, and, in particular, the *grandes écoles* (among which must be counted the *internat de médecine*) are therefore to all intents and purposes the monopoly of the ruling classes. The objective mechanisms which enable the ruling classes to keep the monopoly of the most prestigious educational establishments, while continually appearing at least to put the chance of possessing that monopoly into the hands of every generation, are concealed beneath the cloak of a perfectly democratic method of selection which takes into account only merit and talent, and these mechanisms are of a kind which converts to the virtues of the system the members of the dominated classes whom they eliminate in the same way as they convert those whom they elect, and which ensures that those who are "miraculously elected" may experience as "miraculous" an exceptional destiny which

is the best testimony of academic democracy.

Owing to the fact, first, that the academic market tends to sanction and to reproduce the distribution of cultural capital by proportioning academic success to the amount of cultural capital bequeathed by the family (as is shown, for example, by the fact that, among the pupils of the *grandes écoles*, a very pronounced correlation may be observed between academic success and the family's cultural capital measured by the academic level of the forbears over two generations on both sides of the family), and, second, because the most privileged sections of the dominant classes from the point of view of economic capital and power are not necessarily the most well-off in terms of cultural capital, it may be expected that the hierarchy of values attributed by the academic market to the products of the educational work of the families of the different sections will not correspond very closely to the hierarchy of these sections with regard to economic capital and power. Should it be concluded from this that the relative autonomy of the mechanisms of reproduction of the structure of cultural capital in relation to the mechanisms ensuring the reproduction of economic capital is of a kind to cause a profound transformation, if not in the structure of class relationships (despite the fact that the most culturally privileged sections of the middle class such as the sons of primary school and secondary school teachers are able triumphantly to hold their own on the academic market against the least culturally privileged sections of the upper class), at least in the structure of relationships between the sections of the dominant classes?

The structure of the distribution of cultural capital among the different sections of the dominant classes may be constructed on the basis of the collection of convergent indices brought together in the following conspectus (see *Table 5*).[11]

With the exception of a few inversions in which is expressed the action of secondary

Table 5. The Distribution of Cultural Capital among Different Sections of the Dominant Classes

	1 Teachers	2 Public admin.	3 Professionals	4 Engineers	5 Managers	6 Heads of industry	7 Heads of commerce
Readers of *Le Monde* (penetration index per 1000)	410	235	210	145	151	82	49
Readers of *Le Figaro Littéraire* (ditto)	168	132	131	68	100	64	24
Readers of non-professional books 15 hrs and more per week	21	18	18	16	16	10	10
Theatre-goers (at least once every 2 or 3 months)	38	29	29	28	34	16	20
Listeners to classical music	83	89	86	89	89	75	73
Visitors to museums and exhibitions	75	66	68	58	69	47	52
Visitors to art galleries	58	54	57	45	47	37	34
Possessors of FM radio	59	54	57	56	53	48	48
Non-possessors of television	46	30	28	33	28	14	24

variables such as place of residence, along with the objective possibilities of cultural practice which are closely linked to it, and income,[12] along with the possibilities which it offers, it can be seen that the different sections are organized according to a single hierarchy with the differentiation of the cultural capital possessed in terms of the kind of training received being shown above all in the fact that engineers give proof of a greater interest in music (and in other leisure activities demanding the application of logical skills, such as bridge and chess) than in literary activities (reading of *Le Figaro Littéraire* or theatre-going). If the proportion of individuals who do not possess television (and who are distinguished from the possessors of that instrument by the fact that they go in more often for activities commonly held to be the expression of an authentically "cultured" or refined disposition)[13] varies according to the same law, it is because a refusal to indulge in this activity, which is suspected of being "vulgar" by reasons of its wide availability (*divulgation*), is one of the least expensive ways of expressing cultural pretensions (see *Table 6*).[14]

These indicators probably tend to minimize to a large extent the divergences between the different sections of the dominant classes. Indeed, most cultural consumer goods also imply an economic cost, theatregoing, for instance, depending not only on the level of education (in a population of executive personnel it ranges from 41 per cent to 59 and 68 per cent between the primary, secondary, and higher levels) but also on income (i.e. 46 per cent for incomes less than 20,000 francs per year against 72 per cent for incomes more than 75,000 francs); furthermore, equipment such as FM radio or hi-fi sets may be used in very different ways (e.g. to listen to modern music or dance music), and the value accorded to these different utilizations may be just as disparate, by reference to the dominant hier-

Table 6. Reading Habits, Occupational Categories, and Levels of Education[15]

	Teachers	Top civil servants	Professionals	Engineers	Managers	Heads of industry	Heads of commerce
Detective novels	25 (6)	29 (1)	27 (4)	28 (3)	29 (1)	27 (4)	25 (6)
Adventure stories	16 (7)	20 (3)	18 (6)	24 (1)	22 (2)	19 (4)	19 (4)
Historical accounts	44 (4)	47 (2)	49 (1)	47 (2)	44 (4)	36 (6)	27 (7)
Art books	28 (2)	20 (3)	31 (1)	19 (5)	20 (3)	17 (6)	14 (7)
Novels	64 (2)	68 (1)	59 (5)	62 (3)	63 (3)	45 (6)	42 (7)
Philosophy	20 (1)	13 (3)	12 (5)	13 (3)	15 (2)	10 (7)	12 (5)
Political essays	15 (1)	12 (2)	9 (4)	7 (5)	10 (3)	5 (6)	4 (7)
Economics	10 (1)	8 (3)	5 (6)	7 (5)	9 (2)	8 (3)	5 (6)
Sciences	15 (3)	14 (4)	18 (2)	21 (1)	9 (7)	10 (6)	11 (5)

	University	Grande école	Secondary	Technical	Primary
Detective novels	28	27	27	32	24
Adventure stories	17	14	22	27	17
Historical accounts	47	49	42	41	25
Art books	25	24	22	18	10
Novels	65	54	62	60	35
Philosophy	19	13	15	11	7
Political essays	16	14	6	6	3
Economics	12	19	5	3	4
Sciences	18	27	11	10	6

Table 7. Theatre-going and Occupational Categories

Theatre	Play	Workers	Tradespeople, craftsmen	White-collar workers	Intermediate office staff	Students, pupils	Teachers	Heads of firms, higher office staff, professionals	Without profession	Others	
Odéon	La remise	4	1	11	12	28	26	9	4	4	100
Montparnasse	Sainte-Jeanne	4	2	7	14	24	18	17	13	3	100
Vieux-Colombier	Noces de sang	3	1	4	16	39	15	10	11	1	100
TEP	La locandiera	6	3	13	11	33	13	10	8	2	100
TNP	Romulus le Grand	7	1	13	14	27	12	12	11	2	100
Athénée	Le vicaire	9	4	10	12	28	8	11	11	5	100
Odéon	Tartuffe	3	2	2	9	41	12	20	9	3	100
Comédie-Française	Cinna	4	2	13	11	43	6	12	9	3	100
Comédie-Française	Cyrano	2	2	8	12	29	7	25	13	3	100
Théâtre de Paris	Comment réussir dans les affaires	3	1	5	14	11	12	23	26	7	100
Ambigu	Charmante soirée	3	1	9	11	6	7	22	34	6	100
Antoine	Mary-Mary	8	4	13	16	7	4	26	31	2	100
Michodière	La preuve par quatre	4	9	7	14	8	4	31	18	3	100
Ambassadeurs	Photo-finish	4	5	5	10	13	6	35	24	—	100
Variétés	Un homme comblé	5	6	5	17	7	3	33	22	3	100
Total		4	3	8	14	23	13	19	14	3	100

archy of possible uses, as the different kinds of reading or theatre; thus, as is shown in *Table 6,* the position of the different sections, arranged in a hierarchy in terms of the interest they place in the different kinds of reading, tends to draw nearer to their position in the hierarchy set up in terms of wealth in cultural capital the more that it is a question of reading-matter which depends more upon level of education and which is placed higher in the hierarchy of degrees of cultural legitimacy.

Everything seems to indicate that the choices concerning the theatre follow the same principle. Thus, what emerges from *Table 7,* which deserves much more extensive commentary, is that the overrepresentation of teachers (and of students)—which is shown by the divergence between their rate of attendance at each theatre and their average rate of attendance at theatres as a whole—in the public of different theatres is continually on the decrease, whereas the overrepresentation of the other sections (heads of firms, higher office staff, and professionals, unfortunately all mixed up together in the statistics) undergoes a parallel increase, when one passes from the avant-garde theatre, or theatre considered as such, to the classical theatre and, particularly, from the latter to the *théâtre de boulevard* which recruits between a third and a quarter of its public from among the least

"intellectual" sections of the dominant classes.[16]

With the exception of the liberal professions, who occupy, in this field too, a high position, the structure of the distribution of economic capital is symmetric and opposite to the structure of the distribution of cultural capital—that is to say, in order, heads of industry and of commerce, professionals, managers, engineers, and, lastly, civil servants and teachers (see *Table 8*).[17]

Analysis of the mobility between sections tends to show that the dominant principle of the hierarchy formed by the sections is the possession of economic capital—to the extent, at least, that it is very closely linked to the possession of power. Thus, examination of the intra-generational mobility of the individuals from the different sections who are part of the *Who's Who* census reveals that the proportion of individuals who have moved towards the bottom of the hierarchy during their career, which is more or less nil among business and industrial management, increases more and more as one descends the hierarchy of the sections as it is formed according to the economic criterion. Another index which is just as significant is the fact that the relationship between the proportion of individuals from the dominant section of the dominant classes (the heads of industry) and the proportion of individuals from other social classes in the different

Table 8. Distribution of Economic Capital

	Heads of industry	Heads of commerce	Professionals	Managers	Engineers	Civil servants	Teachers
Own their own residence[18]	70	70	54	40	44	38	51
Upper-category automobile	33	34	28	22	21	20	12
Holidays in hotel	32	26	23	21	17	17	15
Boat	13	14	14	12	10	8	8
Average income in thousands of francs	33	36	41	37	36	32	33
(Rate of nondeclaration)	(24)	(28)	(27)	(13)	(9)	(8)	(6)

Table 9. An Index of Mobility

	Proportion of sons of heads of industry	Proportion of individuals from other classes	Relationship
Heads of industry	42.6	20.5	2.0
Heads of commerce	35.0	19.2	1.8
Professionals	20.5	16.1	1.2
Civil servants	11.9	28.0	0.4
Teachers	15.0	31.0	0.4

sections decreases steadily as one descends the hierarchy (*Table 9*).

Secondary analysis of the national survey carried out by the INSEE on inter-generational professional mobility makes it possible to check that the proportion in each section of individuals from the ruling classes and the proportion of individuals coming from the same section decrease together as one descends the hierarchy of the sections, with a pronounced division between the three sections of the upper position and the three sections of the lower position (*Table 10*).

If such is indeed the structure of relationships between the structure of the distribution of cultural capital and the structure of the distribution of economic capital among the different sections of the ruling classes, it may be expected that, to the extent that the educational system proportions success to cultural capital, the products of the pedagogic work of the different sections receive, on the academic market, values which are organized along the lines of a hierarchy which reproduces the hierarchy of the sec-

tions arranged in terms of their amount of cultural capital.[19] And the fact that this occurs is all the more certain in that, obeying a mechanism already analysed, the different sections must tend to invest the capital which they may transmit in the market that is capable of guaranteeing for it the best yield, and they must therefore invest all the more in the education of their children in that their social success, that is to say, at least, their being able to maintain themselves in the dominant classes, depends all the more completely upon it.

Those sections which are richest in cultural capital are more inclined to invest in their children's education at the same time as in cultural practices liable to maintain and increase their specific rarity; those sections which are richest in economic capital set aside cultural and educational investments to the benefit of economic investments: it is to be noted, however, that heads of industry and commerce tend to do this much more than do the new "bourgeoisie" of the managers who reveal the same concern for rational investment both in the economic

Table 10. Inter-generational Mobility

Father	Heads of industry	Heads of commerce	Professionals	Engineers	Civil servants	Teachers
Heads of industry	33.5	2.8	2.3	6.1	4.4	1.5
Heads of commerce	1.9	31.0	–	1.8	5.0	0.8
Professionals	0.6	0.9	20.0	0.9	2.4	7.6
Engineers	–	–	6.4	6.7	2.3	4.6
Civil servants	1.9	3.3	9.9	13.2	14.3	7.6
Teachers	0.6	–	2.9	2.7	0.3	6.1
Total ruling class	38.5	38.0	41.5	31.4	28.7	28.2

sphere and in the educational sphere.[20] Relatively well provided for with both forms of capital, but not sufficiently integrated into economic life to put their capital to work within it, the professionals (and especially lawyers and doctors) invest in their children's education but also and above all in consumer goods capable of symbolizing the possession of the material and cultural means of conforming to the rules governing the bourgeois style of life and thereby guaranteeing a social capital or capital of social relationships which will provide, if necessary, useful "supports": a capital of honourability and respectability which is often indispensable if one desires to attract clients in socially important positions, and which may serve as currency, for instance, in a political career.[21]

In fact those sections which are richest in cultural capital have a larger proportion in an educational institution to the extent that the institution is highly placed in the specifically academic hierarchy of educational institutions (measured, for instance, by the index of previous academic success); and this proportion attains its maximum in the institution responsible for ensuring the reproduction of the academic body (École Normale Supérieure) (*Table 11*).[22]

Owing to the fact that the different institutions may be distinguished from each other not only in terms of the different training that they grant, and, therefore, in terms of the type of capital that they demand (the proportion of engineers' sons being particularly high in the various scientific institutions—science faculties, 8.1 per cent; preparatory classes for the scientific *grandes écoles*, 15.1 per cent; École Polytechnique, 19.7 per cent; and the science section of the École Normale Supérieure, 14.5 per cent), but also in terms of the careers to which they provide access, the specifically academic hierarchy is imposed in such a thorough way only upon the children of teachers who have been led by their family upbringing to identify success with academic success. To the extent that it records and ratifies the differences separating the different sections from the point of view of cultural capital (and, secondarily, of the type of capital) and of the propensity to invest this capital in the academic market and in the most favourable sector of this market, the educational system tends to reproduce (in the double sense of the word) the structure of relations between the structure of the distribution of cultural capital and the structure of the distribution of economic capital among the sections both in and by the relations of opposition and complementarity which define the system of institutions of higher education. In fact, to

Table 11. Cultural Capital and Educational Investment

	Faculty				Prep. class for polytech.	ENA	Polytech.	Ulm arts	Ulm sc.
	Law	Medicine	Science	Arts					
Proportion of teachers' children	3.2	4.5	4.5	5.2	5.4	9.0	9.9	19.4	17.7
Index of previous academic success	0.4		0.3	0.5	1.2	2.0	2.9	3.1	3.6

ENA: École Nationale d'Administration
Ulm Arts: École Normale Supérieure d'Ulm (Arts)
Ulm Sc.: École Normale Supérieure d'Ulm (Science)

the extent that it is the product of the application of two opposed principles of hierarchical ordering, the structure of the system of institutions of higher education may be interpreted in a twofold way: *the dominant hierarchy within the educational institution,* i.e. the hierarchy which orders the institutions in terms of specifically academic criteria and, correlatively, in terms of the proportion of those sections richest in cultural capital figuring in their public, is opposed diametrically to *the dominant hierarchy outside the educational institution,* i.e. the hierarchy which orders the institutions in terms of the proportion in their public of those sections richest in economic capital (and in power) and according to the position in the hierarchy of the economic capital and power of the professions to which they lead.[23] The *grandes écoles* range, therefore, in a more or less continuous way, between the two extreme poles marked on the one hand by the colleges leading to economic and politico-administrative power (Polytechnique, ENA) and on the other hand by the colleges leading to teaching and, more generally, to the intellectual professions (École Normale Supérieure littéraire et scientifique), with the indices corresponding to one of the principles of hierarchization tending steadily to diminish as the indices corresponding to the other principle increase (see *Table 12*).

Analysis of the specifically academic mechanisms according to which apportionment is effected between the different institutions makes it possible to understand one of the most subtle forms of the trick (*ruse*) of social reason according to which the academic system works objectively towards *the reproduction of the structure of relations between the sections of the dominant classes* when it appears to make full use of its own principles of hierarchical ordering.[24] Knowing, first, that academic success is directly dependent on cultural capital and on the inclination to invest in the academic market (which is itself, as is known, dependent on the objective chances of academic success)

and, consequently, that the different sections are recognized and approved by the school system the richer they are in cultural capital and are also, therefore, all the more disposed to invest in work and academic prowess,[25] and knowing, second, that the support accorded by a category to academic sanctions and hierarchies depends not only on the rank the school system grants to it in its hierarchies but also on the extent to which its interests are linked to the school system, or, in other words, on the extent to which its commercial value and its social position depend (in the past as in the future) on academic approval, it is possible to understand why the educational system never succeeds quite so completely in imposing recognition of its value and of the value of its classifications as when its sanctions are brought to bear upon classes or sections of a class which are unable to set against it any rival principle of hierarchical ordering. While those sections which are richest in economic capital authorize and encourage a life-style whose seductions are sufficient to rival the ascetic demands of the academic system and while they ensure or promise guarantees beside which the college's guarantees can only appear both costly and of little value ("academic qualifications don't give you everything"), those sections which are richest in cultural capital have nothing to set against the attraction exercised by the signs of academic approval which make their academic prowess worthwhile to them.[26] In short, the effectiveness of the mechanisms by means of which the educational system ensures its own reproduction encloses within itself its own limitation: although the educational system may make use of its relative autonomy to propose and impose its own hierarchies and the university career which serves as its topmost point, it obtains complete adherence only when it preaches to the converted or to lay brethren, to teachers' sons or children from the working or middle classes who owe everything to it and expect everything of it. Far from diverting for its own profit children from the dominant sec-

Table 12. Proportions of Students from the Upper Classes of the Different "Grandes Écoles" Possessing One or Other of These Characteristics

	Ulm lettres	Ulm sciences	Sèvres lettres	Sèvres sciences	Polytechnique	Mines Paris	ENA 1er concours	HEC	Centrale
Father's diploma *licence* or higher	*85.8*	**88.8**	73.1	84.9	76	68.3	85.4	74.1	71.9
Mother's diploma *licence* or higher	38.3	**44.1**	39.2	*42.7*	30.8	29.8	36.5	22.1	26.2
Proportion of teachers	29.5	26.2	*31.2*	**33**	15	4.6	15.2	4.2	7.9
Section "A" in *première*	*29.9*	**44.3**	29.6	23.8	24.4	24.3	18.7	14.9	18.3
Index of previous academic success	**3.6**	*3.5*	3.2	2.7	3.1	3.1	2	1.1	2.3
Marxism	**51.1**	30.4	31.4	*35*	12.2	19	1.8	7.2	7.7
Concerts: average number	1.8	**2.4**	*2.2*	1.3	1.2	1.6	1.1	1.1	1.1
Theatre: average number of plays	3.8	3.4	**4.7**	4	3.6	*4.6*	2.5	2.3	2.3
Size of family 4 children or more	40.3	**50.9**	34.9	39.2	44	42.2	36.9	43.4	*47.6*
Practising Catholics	29.7	31.6	39.1	38.8	*41.6*	39.1	39.8	—	**48.9**
Private teaching college in secondary school	14.6	17.8	*19.4*	9.5	17.9	18.7	24.9	**23.9**	13.5
Right of centre, right wing, extreme right	3.8	7.2	3.2	12.6	—	12.5	*19.9*	**27.9**	16.9
Higher office staff	41.3	23.2	44.1	32.6	36.2	53.2	30.9	**57.4**	*55.7*
Paternal grandfather upper classes	56.6	41.7	44	31.3	48	*62.6*	61.6	**63**	47.5
Maternal grandfather upper classes	37.3	51.2	55.7	34.1	54.8	*60*	53.6	**62**	48.6
Resident in Paris	32.4	41.3	41.4	32.6	45.6	53.9	**66.6**	*55.3*	46.5

Source: CSE *grandes écoles* survey.
The most marked trend in each row is shown in bold type and the second most pronounced trend in italic.

tions of the dominant classes (as one may be led to believe by a few striking examples which authorize the most conservative sections of the bourgeoisie to denounce the corruption of youth and teachers or the intellectuals to believe in the omnipotence of their ideas), it puts off children from the other sections and classes from claiming the value of their academic investments and from drawing the economic and symbolic profit which the sons of the dominant section of the ruling classes know how to obtain, if necessary, better situated as they are to understand the relative value of academic verdicts.

But would the school system succeed so completely in diverting for its own profit those categories which it recognizes as possessing the greatest value (as is shown, for instance, by the difference in academic quality between students from the ENS and those from the ENA) if the diplomas that it awards were convertible at par on the market of money and power? The limits of the autonomy allowed to the school system in the production of its hierarchies coincide exactly with the limits objectively assigned to its power of guaranteeing outside the academic market the economic and symbolic value of the diplomas it awards. The same academic qualifications receive very variable values and functions according to the economic and social capital (particularly the capital of relationships inherited from the family) which those who hold these qualifications have at their disposal and according to the markets in which they use them: it is known, for instance, that the professional success of the former students of the École des hautes études commerciales (recruited, for the most part, among the Parisian business section) varies far more in relation to the way in which they obtained their first professional post (i.e. through family relations or by other ways) than in relation to their position in the college-leaving examination; it is also known that civil servants whose fathers were white-collar workers received in 1962 an average yearly salary of

18,027 francs as against 29,470 francs for civil servants whose fathers were industrialists or wealthy tradespeople (Praderie 1966: 346-7). And if, as has been shown by the survey carried out by the Boulloche commission over 600 firms, only 2.4 per cent of the 17,000 administrative personnel employed by these firms have degrees or are doctors of science as against 37 per cent who have diplomas from an engineering *grande école,* it is because those who possess the most prestigious qualifications also have at their disposal an inherited capital of relationships and skills which enable them to obtain such qualifications; this capital is made up of such things as the practice of the games and sports of high society or the manners and tastes resulting from good breeding, which, in certain careers (not to mention matrimonial exchanges which are opportunities for increasing the social capital of honourability and relationships), constitute the condition, if not the principal factor, of success.[27] The habitus inculcated by upper-class families gives rise to practices which, even if they are without selfish motives, such as cultural activities, are extremely profitable to the extent that they make possible the acquisition of the maximum yield of academic qualifications whenever recruitment or advancement is based upon co-optation or on such diffuse and total criteria as "the right presentation," "general culture," etc.[28]

What this amounts to is that, as in a pre-capitalist economy in which a guarantee is worth as much as the guarantor, the value of the diploma, outside the specifically academic market, depends on the economic and social values of the person who possesses it, inasmuch as the yield of academic capital (which is a converted form of cultural capital) depends upon the economic and social capital which can be put to its valorization: for the industrialist's son who comes out of HEC, the diploma is only an additional qualification to his legitimately succeeding his father or to his occupying the director's post guaranteed for him by his network of family relations, whereas the white-collar worker's son, whose only way of obtaining the same diploma was by means of academic success, cannot be sure of obtaining a post of commercial attaché in the same firm. [29] In a word, if, as is shown by the analysis of the social and academic characteristics of the individuals mentioned in *Who's Who,* the diploma is all the more indispensable for those from families less favoured in economic and social capital, the fact remains that the educational system is less and less in a position to guarantee the value of the qualifications that it awards the further one goes away from the domain that it controls completely, namely, that of its own reproduction; and the reason for this is that the possession of a diploma, as prestigious as it may be, is in any case less and less capable of guaranteeing access to the highest positions and is never sufficient to guarantee in itself access to economic power. Inversely, as is shown by the diagram of correlation, access to the dominant classes and, *a fortiori,* to the dominant sections of the dominant classes, is relatively independent of the chances of gaining access to higher education for those individuals from sections closest to economic and politico-administrative power, i.e. top civil servants and heads of industry and commerce. [30] It would appear, therefore, that the further one goes away from the jurisdiction of the school system the more the diploma loses its particular effectiveness as a guarantee of a specific qualification opening into a specific career according to formalized and homogeneous rules, and becomes a simple condition of authorization and a right of access which can be given full value only by the holders of a large capital of social relationships (particularly in the liberal professions) and is, at its extreme limit, when all it does is legitimate heritage, but a kind of optional guarantee.

Thus the relative autonomy enjoyed by the academic market on account of the fact that the structure of distribution of cultural capital is not exactly the same as the structure of economic capital and of power gives the appearance of a justification for meritocratic ideology, according to which academic justice provides a kind of resort or revenge for those who have no other resources than their "intelligence" or their "merit," only if one chooses to ignore, first, that "intelligence" or academic goodwill represents but one particular form of capital which comes to be added, in most cases, to the possession of economic capital and the correlative capital of power and social relationships, and, second, that the holders of economic power have more chances than those who are deprived of it also to possess cultural capital and, in any case, to be able to do without it since academic qualifications are a weak currency and possess all their value only within the limits of the academic market.

NOTES

1. We have translated approximately as follows: *salarié agricole,* agricultural worker; *agriculteur,* farmer; *ouvrier,* worker; *employé,* white-collar worker; *artisan-commerçant,* craftsman and tradesman; *cadre moyen,* intermediate office staff; *cadre supérieur,* higher office staff; *profession libérale,* professional; *patrons de l'industrie et du commerce,* heads of industry and commerce.
2. Household consumption, INSEE–CREDOC survey carried out in 1956 of 20,000 households—tables of household consumption by socio-professional categories.
3. Syndicat national des éditeurs (National Union of Publishers), "La clientèle du livre," July 1967, survey carried out by the IFOP.
4. Syndicat national des éditeurs, "La lecture et le livre en France," January-April 1960, survey carried out by the IFOP.
5. Survey of theatre attendance in the Parisian region carried out by the IFOP, 1964.
6. Survey of theatre attendance, SOFRES, June 1964. The rates established by the SOFRES survey are distinctly lower, especially as far as the middle classes are concerned, than those that emerge from the IFOP surveys. The probable reason for this is partly to be found in the fact that the SOFRES survey was based on a national sample whereas the IFOP survey covered only the Parisian region, and the structure of class relations is decidedly different in Paris and in the provinces, particularly in the field of culture, since the gap between the upper classes and the middle classes is much less pronounced in Paris. The reason is also to be found in the fact that the SOFRES based its inquiries not on "normal" attendance rhythms but on real theatre attendance during the past year (theatre used in the restrictive sense, i.e. as opposed to

opera, musical comedy, and music hall, concerning which questions were also asked). In spite of this the SOFRES report quite rightly observes that the attendance rates were probably overestimated, first, because the question made no distinction between professional theatre and amateur theatre (and yet in 1963 there were, in the provinces, 19,000 amateur performances as opposed to 13,000 professional performances) and, second, because it may be assumed that refusals to reply were more numerous among those whose attendance rates were low and that those who replied to the questions exaggerated the extent to which they practised such a prestigious activity.

7. Cf. P. Bourdieu & A. Darbel (1969: 40).

8. In order to realize that specific rarity in the field of culture is not connected to the goods but to the instruments of appropriation of those goods, it is sufficient to consider those statistics wherein it may be seen that the possession of the material instruments of appropriation of music (which, as is known, increases in proportion to income and level of education) is not enough to ensure symbolic appropriation; the extent to which the reception of France-Musique (which broadcasts classical music almost exclusively, that is to say 96.6 hours a week) varies is still very large among possessors of FM radio.

9. Concerning this concept, see Bourdieu & Darbel (1969: 104–10).

10. The extremely close relationship that may be observed between museum attendance and level of education, on the one hand, and early attendance at museums, on the other hand, follows the same logic.

11. SOFRES (1964), *Le Marché des cadres supérieurs français*, Paris.

12. The heads of industry questioned more often live in small towns than do the heads of commerce—40 per cent against 33 per cent, of whom 27 per cent against 15 per cent live in rural communities; members of public or private administration and engineers reside more often than teachers and professionals (a large proportion of whom—28 per cent—live in small towns) in towns with more than 100,000 inhabitants, that is to say, 66 per cent for the first two categories, 65 per cent for the third, and 60 per cent for the last two, which doubtless explains the inversions as far as the theatre is concerned. Apart from place of residence, the effect of income, which is easily higher in the liberal professions than in the public services, doubtless explains the other inversions observed, particularly as far as the possession of FM radio sets or exhibition attendance are concerned.

13. Here are some indicators of the opposition between the two systems of dispositions, an element of which is the refusal of television:

14. A number of indicators suggest that the different sections of the dominant classes can also be distinguished according to the amount of free time at their disposal. Thus, for example, the proportion of individuals who go on holiday varies from 95 per cent for teachers, to 92 per cent for engineers, 91 per cent for civil servants, 89 per cent for professionals, 87 per cent for managers, and 81 and 80 per cent for heads of industry and of commerce. The effect of this principle of differentiation is to be seen in a number of activities possessed of a cultural dimension, such as the use of radio or television.

15. The figures in parentheses represent the positions of each section. The readership of economic and scientific works has been given separately inasmuch as interest in these kinds of literature depends on secondary factors, namely the kind of professional activity for some (hence the positions of managers, heads of industry and of commerce) and the kind of intellectual training for others (hence the positions of the engineers).

16. Based on SEMA, *Le Théâtre et son public*, Vol. 2, Table 215a.

17. None of the indices of consumption (automobile, boat, hotel) is perfectly univocal (to the extent that the first also depends on the type of professional activity and the other two on the capital in free time, which is very unevenly spread between the sections; possession of a residence depends, further, on there being a stable residence (and this is less likely as far as civil servants, engineers, and teachers are concerned). Lastly, the incomes of the different categories have been very unevenly minimized (the rate of non-declaration may be seen as an indicator of the tendency to under-declare). A strict evaluation of the incomes of the different sections would presuppose the inventory of the secondary profits connected with the different professions. It is known, for instance, that managers and some engineers often have a car (and sometimes a chauffeur) at their disposal, provided by the firm which sometimes puts the general maid or the cleaning woman on a salaried basis. The survey quoted makes it possible to form an idea of the secondary profits, which are easily concealed, obtained by the different professions, such as business meals (26 per cent for heads of industry and for managers, 22 per cent for engineers, 17 per cent for heads of commerce, 14 per cent for civil servants, against only 10 per cent for professionals and 4 per cent for teachers) or business trips (41 per cent for heads of industry, 36 per cent for managers, 35 per cent for engineers, 31 per cent for heads of commerce, against 19 per cent for civil servants, 16 per cent for professionals, and 4 per cent for teachers).

18. Among the personalities mentioned in *Who's*

	Listen to classical music	Play a musical instrument	Visit museums or exhibitions	Visit art galleries	Play bridge	Go to the theatre
Possess television	82	12	60	45	19	55
Do not possess television	91	15	70	53	28	70

Who, the following proportions in the following occupational categories reside in the districts which contain the highest proportion of families of executives in relation to the total number of households (7th, 8th, and 16th *arrondissements*): 39.7 per cent of the heads of industry and commerce, 40 per cent of those in senior administration, 31 per cent of those in the liberal professions, and 22 per cent of the teachers.

19. The opposition that is set up, within the middle class, between intermediate office staff (and in particular primary-school teachers) and medium-sized industrial and business management is the homologue of the opposition, within the upper class, between secondary-school teachers and the heads of industry and commerce. It is not by chance that the ideology of the academic meritocracy is particularly deep-rooted in those sections of the middle class which are richest in cultural capital and that ascent through two generations (from peasant to primary-school teacher to secondary-school teacher) is so often invoked by champions of "the liberating effect of the school." Indeed, primary-school teachers (along with subordinate categories in secondary education) and, more generally, members of the public administrative sector of intermediate rank occupy a very strange position, on the hinge of the middle classes and the dominant classes. Owing to the privileged position that they occupy in terms of the educational system, they can triumphantly hold their own in academic competition with the other sections, which are richer in economic capital, and even with those sections of the dominant classes which are least prosperous in cultural capital. Since the logic that governs the relationship between secondary-school teachers and the other members of the dominant classes is *a fortiori* applicable to primary-school teachers, their children must pay for their being allowed into the dominant classes (where they form about 25 per cent) by being relegated to the positions of teaching, or industrial or administrative technicians.

20. Managers have a much more "modernistic" style of life than do the traditional "bourgeoisie"— the heads of industry and commerce: they attain positions of power at a younger age; they more often possess university qualifications; they more often belong to larger and more modern businesses; they are the largest group to read the financial newspaper *Les Échos* (penetration index of 126 as opposed to 91 for heads of industry) and weeklies dealing with economics and finance (penetration index of 224 as against 190 for heads of industry); they seem less inclined to invest their capital in real estate; they indulge more often in "modern" leisure activities such as ski-ing, yachting, etc. Above all, they more completely identify themselves with the role of the modern executive who looks towards foreign countries (along with members of the civil servants and engineers, they make the highest rate of journeys abroad) and who is open to modern ideas (as is shown by their very active participation in professional symposia or seminars, with 30 per cent of them taking part in such activities at least three or four times a year, as against 26 per cent for civil servants and heads of

commerce, 25 per cent for engineers, and 17 per cent for heads of industry). A final, apparently minor, but in fact very significant, sign of this opposition can be seen in the varying proportions of members of the different sections who state that they have a permanent supply of whisky or champagne in their homes: for whisky, the figures are 81 per cent for managers, 80 per cent for engineers, 74 per cent for professionals, 69 per cent for civil servants, 62 per cent for heads of commerce, and 58 per cent for teachers; and for champagne, 80 per cent for heads of industry, 75 per cent for heads of commerce and professionals, 73 per cent for managers, 72 per cent for top civil servants and engineers, and 49 per cent for teachers.

21. Only a survey such as the one that is being carried out at the present time at the Centre de Sociologie Européenne, whose object is to grasp the systems of the reproduction strategies of the different sections and to determine, in particular, the place of educational investment within each one of these systems, could make it possible to validate these hypotheses and render them more subtle. We shall content ourselves, therefore, with provisionally reporting some indices which seem to confirm the propositions put forward above, particularly in relation to the liberal professions. According to the SOFRES survey already quoted, the hierarchy of the sections in terms of an index of status (based on possession of goods such as a drier, a freezer, a dish-washer, a record-player, high-fidelity equipment, FM radio, tape-recorder, camera and slide-projection equipment, cine-camera, caravan, boat, high-category car, second residence) is found to be: professionals (5.1), engineers (4.8), managers (4.7), heads of industry (4.6), heads of commerce (4.4), top civil servants (4.4), teachers (4.2). In the most highly selected population of *Who's Who,* membership of clubs and inscription in *le Bottin Mondain* are distributed as follows: heads of industry and commerce (49.5 and 32.6), law (38.1 and 36.5), medicine (30.1 and 28.9), top civil servants (25.7 and 24.4), university (24.3 and 22). Readership of the newspaper *Les Échos,* which is an index of participation in the economy and of information concerning finance, is distributed as follows (SOFRES): managers (126), heads of industry (91), top civil servants (68), engineers (66), professionals and heads of commerce (15), teachers (0). In the same way, the penetration index of the economic and financial weeklies is only 124 for the liberal professions as against 190 for heads of industry, 224 for managers, and 250 for engineers. The final revealing index of the particular position of the professionals and, more specifically, of the doctors, is the fact that 30 per cent of the doctors registered in *Who's Who* belong to the local political circle.

22. The analyses proposed below are based upon a systematic group of surveys, carried out over the last few years by the Centre de Sociologie Européenne, of the faculties of arts, sciences, law, and medicine, and of all the literary and scientific *grandes écoles* and of the preparatory classes for these colleges. The guiding idea behind this research was that of treating the institutions of

higher education as a *system*, and of building the structure of the relationships which unite them. In short, the intention was to break with the (consciously or unconsciously) monographic approach of most research work dealing with higher education—research which is bent on ignoring the most specific properties of the different institutions, namely, those they owe to their position in the system of institutions and to the effects of structural distinction which that position allows. Thus studies centred on the arts or science faculties which omit to situate these institutions in relation to the preparatory classes for the *grandes écoles* and to the *grandes écoles* themselves do not make it possible to understand or explain what is owed by the social and academic recruitment of the public of these institutions, by the pedagogy which they put into practice, or by the careers to which they give access, to the fact that these are second-class establishments to which are relegated children from the middle and working classes who manage to get into higher education or else a form of refuge for the children from the dominant classes whose academic results have not allowed them into the most prestigious institutions. Likewise, most studies devoted to any of the *grandes écoles* are not different in any clear-cut way from studies carried out for practical or justificatory ends by old boys' and teachers' associations in that they reveal, more often than not, the survival of a relationship of enchantment to the school which may be concealed just as well by the false distance of objectivity as in the resounding break or disenchanted reversal of a first relationship of enchantment. The supposition underlying such a methodological project was that, at the risk of showing a loss in the specific information relating to each institution, the technical operations—starting with the construction of questionnaires or of analysis grids—should be subordinated to the imperatives of comparability: that which, at the beginning, might appear as a rather crippling abstraction appeared as the condition of the emergence of the most specific characteristics whereas certain concessions which were made with an eye to taking into account particularities (and especially the most apparent features by means of which each *grande école* is endowed with a set idiosyncrasy) prevented, in the last analysis, the making of comparisons capable of resulting in the principle of really pertinent differences.

23. The discordance between the two hierarchies and the predominance, within the institution, of the specifically academic hierarchy is at the basis of the meritocratic illusion whose most typical form is the ideology of the "liberating effects of the school" along with the indignation aroused among teaching staff, who are the first victims of this kind of academic ethnocentrism, at the discordance between the social hierarchies and the academic hierarchies.

24. If the role of the system of institutions of higher education in the reproduction of the relations between the sections of the dominant classes often goes unnoticed, it is because surveys of mobility accord more attention to mobility between classes than to mobility within the differ-

ent classes and, in particular, within the dominant classes. Another reason is that the analytic and atomistic mode of thought which governs research into mobility does not allow the classical surveys of "elites" to go beyond the apprehension of phenomena such as simple professional heredity. In fact, the structure of relations between the sections may remain unaltered while the population that forms them undergoes a profound change: thus, to take but one example, the structure of relations between the intellectual and artistic sections and the other sections of the dominant classes has remained more or less unchanged in France since the middle of the nineteenth century, whereas the social recruitment of artists and intellectuals has varied considerably according to the period.

25. For an analysis of the dialectic of approval and recognition at the final stage of which the school recognizes its members, or, in other words, those who recognize the school, see P. Bourdieu & M. de Saint-Martin (1970).

26. Adherence to values conveyed by catholic tradition doubtless contributes to a certain extent to the turning away of children of the dominant sections of the dominant classes from academic careers in university or intellectual posts, and it does this both directly, by provoking a certain suspicion towards learning and its values, and indirectly, by promoting (with an eye to ensuring for the children that they "mix with the right people," that is, by ensuring the social homogeneity of the peer group and the guarantee of "morality") the choice of private educational establishments whose educational yield is known to be lower, all other things being equal. Among the individuals mentioned in *Who's Who*, the rates of former students of private colleges are 55.3 per cent, 36.2 per cent, 18.5 per cent, and 16 per cent, respectively, for business, law, top-level administration and medicine, and the university.

27. The proportion of students who play bridge or practise the "smart" sports increases the nearer one approaches the pole of economic power.

28. Any analysis which tends to consider cultural consumption as simple "conspicuous consumption," neglecting the directly palpable gratifications which always supplement symbolic gratifications, may well cause this fact to be forgotten. The simple ostentation of material prosperity, although it may not have such an obvious legitimating function as cultural ostentation, has at least the effect, in certain sections of the dominant classes, of vouching for success and of attracting confidence, esteem, and respect which, in certain professions, particularly the liberal ones, may serve as an important factor of success.

29. Secondary analysis of the survey carried out by the INSEE on professional mobility also allows it to be established that the positions occupied in firms by engineers, higher office staff, and technicians are closely linked to social origin, with the sons of primary and secondary teachers and of professionals, for instance, being the most represented sections in management positions whereas the qualified sons of labourers, foremen, and technicians are the most represented sections in production, manufacture, and maintenance.

30. The fact that entrance into the liberal professions presupposes the possession of high academic qualifications should not conceal the fact that access to the highest positions in these professions doubtless depends scarcely any less than it does in the industrial and commercial sector on the possession of economic and social capital, as is shown by the presence of a very high rate of professional heredity, particularly in the elite of the medical profession where can be found veritable dynasties of chief doctors.

REFERENCES

Bourdieu, P. & Darbel, A. 1969. *L'Amour de l'art: les musées d'art européens et leur public*. Paris: Les Éditions de Minuit.
Bourdieu, P. & De Saint-Martin, M. 1970. L'excellence scolaire et les valeurs du système d'enseignement français. *Annales* I, January-February.
Praderie, M. 1966. Héritage social et chances d'ascension. In Darras, *Le Partage des bénéfices*. Paris: Les Éditions de Minuit.
SEMA. n.d. *Le Théâtre et son public*.
SOFRES. 1964. *Le Marché des cadres supérieurs français*. Paris.
Syndicat national des éditeurs (National Union of Publishers). 1960. La lecture et le livre en France (January-April 1960, survey carried out by the IFOP).
Syndicat national des éditeurs. 1967. La clientèle du livre (July 1967, survey carried out by the IFOP).

30. Class and Pedagogies: Visible and Invisible
BASIL BERNSTEIN

I shall examine some of the assumptions and the cultural context of a particular form of preschool/infant school pedagogy. A form which has at least the following characteristics:

(1) Where the control of the teacher over the child is implicit rather than explicit.

(2) Where, ideally, the teacher arranges the *context* which the child is expected to re-arrange and explore.

(3) Where within this arranged context, the child apparently has wide powers over what he selects, over how he structures, and over the time scale of his activities.

(4) Where the child apparently regulates his own movements and social relationships.

(5) Where there is a reduced emphasis upon the transmission and acquisition of specific skills (see Note I).

(6) Where the criteria for evaluating the pedagogy are multiple and diffuse and so not easily measured.

INVISIBLE PEDAGOGY AND INFANT EDUCATION

One can characterise this pedagogy as an invisible pedagogy. In terms of the concepts of classification and frame, the pedagogy is realised through weak classification and weak frames. Visible pedagogies are realised through strong classification and strong frames. The basic difference between visible and invisible pedagogies is in the *manner* in which criteria are transmitted and in the degree of specificity of the criteria. The more implicit the manner of transmission and the more diffuse the criteria the more invisible the pedagogy; the more specific the criteria, the more explicit the manner of their transmission, the more visible the pedagogy. These definitions will be extended later in the paper. If the pedagogy is invisible, what aspects of the child have high visibility for the teacher? I suggest two aspects. The first arises out of an inference

From *Studies in the Learning Sciences* (Paris: O.E.C.D., 1975). Reprinted with revisions and additions by the author by permission of the O.E.C.D.

the teacher makes from the child's ongoing behaviour about the *developmental* stage of the child. This inference is then referred to a concept of *readiness.* The second aspect of the child refers to his external behaviour and is conceptualised by the teacher as busyness. The child should be busy doing things. These inner (readiness) and outer (busyness) aspects of the child can be transformed into one concept of "ready to do." The teacher infers from the "doing" the state of "readiness" of the child as it is revealed in his present activity and as this state adumbrates future "doing."

We can briefly note in passing a point which will be developed later. In the same way as the child's reading releases the child from the teacher and socialises him into the privatised solitary learning of an explicit anonymous past (i.e. the textbook), so busy children (children doing) release the child from the teacher but socialise him into an ongoing inter-actional present in which the past is invisible and so implicit (i.e. the teachers' pedagogical theory). Thus a non-doing child in the invisible pedagogy is the equivalent of a non-reading child in the visible pedagogy. (However, a non-reading child may be at a greater disadvantage and experience greater difficulty than a "non-doing" child.)

The concept basic to the invisible pedagogy is that of play. This is not the place to submit this concept to logical analysis, but a few points may be noted.

(1) Play is the means by which the child exteriorises himself to the teacher. Thus the more he plays and the greater the range of his activities, the more of the child is made available to the teacher's screening. Thus, play is the fundamental concept with "readiness" and "doing" as subordinate concepts. Although not all forms of doing are considered as play (hitting another child, for example) most forms can be so characterised.

(2) Play does not merely describe an activity, it also contains an evaluation of that activity. Thus, there is productive and

less productive play, obsessional and free-ranging play, solitary and social play. Play is not only an activity, it entails a theory from which interpretation, evaluation and diagnosis are derived and which also indicates a progression. A theory which the child can never know in the way a child can know the criteria which are realised in visible pedagogy. Play implies a potentially all-embracing theory, for it covers nearly all if not all the child's doing and not doing. As a consequence, a very long chain of inference has to be set up to connect the theory with any one exemplar ("a doing" or a "not doing"). The theory gives rise to a total—but invisible—surveillance of the child, because it relates his inner dispositions to all his external acts. The "spontaneity" of the child is filtered through this surveillance and then implicitly shaped according to interpretation, evaluation and diagnosis.

(3) Both the means and ends of play are multiple and change with time. Because of this, the stimuli must be, on the whole, highly abstract, available to be contextualised by the child, and so the unique doing of each child is facilitated. Indeed, play encourages each child to make his own mark. Sometimes however, the stimulus may be very palpable when the child is invited to feel a leaf, or piece of velour, but what is *expected* is a *unique* response of the child to his own sensation. What is the code for reading the marks; a code the child can never know, but implicitly acquires. How does he do this?

(4) The social basis of this theory of play is not an individualised act, but a personalised act; not strongly framed, but weakly framed encounters. Its social structure may be characterised as one of *overt* personalised organic solidarity, but covert mechanical solidarity. Visible pedagogies create social structures which may be characterised as *covert* individualised organic solidarity and *overt* mechanical solidarity.[1] (See later discussion.)

(5) In essence, play is work and work is play. We can begin to see here the class

origins of the theory. For the working class, work and play are very strongly classified and framed; for certain sub-groups of the middle class, work and play are weakly classified and weakly framed. For these sub-groups, no strict line may be drawn between work and play. Work carries what is often called "intrinsic" satisfactions, and therefore is not confined to *one* context. However, from another point of view, work offers the opportunity of symbolic narcissism which combines inner pleasure and outer prestige. Work for certain sub-groups of the middle class is a personalised act in a privatised social structure. These points will be developed later.

THEORIES OF LEARNING AND INVISIBLE PEDAGOGY

We are now in a position to analyse the principles underlying the selection of theories of learning which invisible pre-school infant school pedagogies will adopt. Such pedagogies will adopt any theory of learning which has the following characteristics.

(1) The theories in general will be seeking universals and thus are likely to be developmental and concerned with sequence. A particular context of learning is only of interest in as much as it throws light on a sequence. Such theories are likely to have a strong biological bias.

(2) Learning is a tacit, invisible act, its progression is not facilitated by explicit public control.

(3) The theories will tend to abstract the child's personal biography and local context from his cultural biography and institutional context.

(4) In a sense, the theories see socialisers as potentially, if not actually, dangerous, as they embody an adult focused, therefore reified concept of the socialised. Exemplary models are relatively unimportant and so the various theories in different ways point towards *implicit* rather than explicit hierarchical social relationships. Indeed, the

imposing exemplar is transformed into a *facilitator*.

(5) Thus the theories can be seen as interrupters of cultural reproduction and therefore have been considered by some as progressive or even revolutionary. Notions of child's time replace notions of adult's time, notions of child's space replace notions of adult's space; facilitation replaces imposition and accommodation replaces domination.

We now give a group of theories, which despite many differences fulfil at a most abstract level all or nearly all of the five conditions given previously:

Piaget	1	2	3	4	5
Freud	1	2	3	4	5
Chomsky	1	2	3	4	5
Ethological theories of critical learning	1	2	3		
Gestalt		2	3	4	5

What is of interest is that these theories form rather a strange, if not contradictory group. They are often selected to justify a specific element of the pedagogy. They form in a way the theology of the infant school. We can see how the crucial concept of play and the subordinate concepts of readiness and doing fit well with the above theories. We can also note how the invisibility of the pedagogy fits with the invisible tacit act of learning. We can also see that the pre-school/infant school movement from one point of view is a progressive, revolutionary, colonising movement in its relationships to parents, and in its relationship to educational levels above itself. It is antagonistic for different reasons to middle class (m.c.) and working class (w.c.) families, for both create a deformation of the child. It is antagonistic to educational levels above itself, because of its fundamental opposition to their concepts of learning and social relationships. We can note here that as a result the child is abstracted from his family and his future educational contexts.

Of central importance is that this pedagogy brings together two groups of educationists who are at the extremes of the educational hierarchy, infant school teachers and University teachers and researchers. The consequence has been to professionalise and raise the status of the pre-school/infant school teacher; a status not based upon a specific competence, a status based upon a weak educational identity (no subject). The status of the teachers from this point of view is based upon a diffuse, tacit, symbolic control which is legitimised by a closed explicit ideology, the essence of weak classification and weak frames.

CLASS AND THE INVISIBLE PEDAGOGY

From our previous discussion, we can abstract the following:

(1) The invisible pedagogy is an interrupter system, both in relation to the family and in its relation to other levels of the educational heriarchy.

(2) It transforms the privatised social structures and cultural contexts of visible pedagogies into a personalised social structure and personalised cultural contexts.

(3) Implicit nurture reveals unique nature.

The question is what is it interrupting? The invisible pedagogy was first institutionalised in the private sector for a fraction of the m.c.—the new m.c. If the ideologies of the old m.c. were institutionalised in the public schools and through them into the grammar schools, so the ideology of the new m.c. was first institutionalised in private pre-schools, then private/public secondary schools, and finally into the state system, at the level of the infant school. Thus the conflict between visible and invisible pedagogies, from this point of view, between strong and weak classification and frames, is an ideological conflict with the m.c. The ideologies of education are still the ideologies of class. The old m.c. were domesticated through the strong classification and frames of the family and public schools, which attempted, often very successfully, cultural reproduction. But what social type was reproduced?

We know that every industrialised society produces organic solidarity. Now Durkheim, it seems to me, was concerned with only *one* form of such solidarity—the form which created individualism. Durkheim was interested in the vicissitudes of the types as their classification and framing were no longer, or only weakly, morally integrated, or when the individual's relation to the classification and frames underwent a change. His analysis is based upon the old m.c. He did not foresee, although his conceptual procedures make this possible, a form of organic solidarity based upon weak classification and weak frames; that is, a form of solidarity developed by the new m.c. Durkheim's organic solidarity refers to *individuals* in privatised class relationships; the second form of organic solidarity refers to persons in privatised class relationships. The second form of organic solidarity celebrates the apparent release, not of the individual, but of the persons and *new* forms of social control (see Note II). Thus, we can distinguish *individualised* and *personalised* forms of organic solidarity *within* the m.c., each with their own distinctive and conflicting ideologies and each with their own distinctive and conflicting forms of socialisation and symbolic reality.[2] These two forms arise out of developments of the division of labour within class societies. Durkheim's individualised organic solidarity developed out of the increasing complexity of the economic division of labour; personalised organic solidarity, it is suggested, develops out of increases in the complexity of the division of labour of cultural or symbolic control which the new m.c. have appropriated. The new m.c. is an interrupter system, clearly not of class relationships, but of the *form* of their reproduction. In Bourdieu's terms, there has been a change in habitus, but not in function. This change in habitus has had far reaching effects on the selective institutionalisation of symbolic codes and codings in the areas of sex, aesthetics, and upon preparing and repairing agencies, such as the family, school, and mental hospitals. In all these areas there has been a shift towards weak classification and frames (see Note III).

This conflict within the m.c. is realised sharply in different patterns of the socialisation of the young. In the old m.c., socialisation is into strong classification and strong framing, where the boundaries convey tacitly critical condensed messages. In the new m.c., socialisation is into weak classification and weak frames, which promote, through the explicitness of the communication code, far greater ambiguity and drive this class to make visible the ideology of its socialisation; crucial to this ideology is the concept of the *person* not of the *individual.* Whereas the concept of the *individual* leads to specific, unambiguous role identities and relatively inflexible role performances, the concept of the *person* leads to ambiguous personal identity and flexible role performances. Both the old and the new m.c. draw upon biological theories, but of very different types. The old m.c. held theories which generated biologically fixed types, where variety of the type constituted a threat to cultural reproduction. The new m.c. also hold theories which emphasise a fixed biological type, but they also hold that the type is capable of great variety. This, in essence, is a theory which points towards social mobility—towards a meritocracy. For the old m.c., variety must be severely reduced in order to ensure cultural reproduction; for the new m.c., the variety must be encouraged in order to ensure interruption. Reproduction and interruption are created by variations in the strength of classifications and frames (see Note IV). As these weaken, so the socialisation encourages more of the socialised to become visible, his uniqueness to be made manifest. Such socialisation is deeply penetrating, more total as the surveillance becomes more invisible. This is the basis of control which creates personalised organic solidarity. Thus the forms of socialisation within these two conflicting fractions of the m.c. are the origins of the visible and invisible pedagogies of the school. We have a homologue between the interruption of the new m.c. of the reproduction of the old and the interruption of the new educational pedagogy of the reproduction of the old; between the conflict within the m.c. and the conflict between the two pedagogies: yet it is the conflict between and interruption of *forms* of transmission of class relationships. This point we will now develop. The new m.c. like the proponents of the invisible pedagogy are caught in a contradiction; for their theories are at variance with their objective class relationship. A deep rooted ambivalence is the ambience of this group. On the one hand, they stand for variety against inflexibility, expression against repression, the inter-personal against the inter-positional; on the other hand, there is the grim obduracy of the division of labour and of the narrow pathways to its positions of power and prestige. Under individualised organic solidarity, property has an essentially physical nature, however, with the development of personalised organic solidarity, although property in the physical sense remains crucial, it has been partly psychologised and appears in the form of ownership of valued skills made available in educational institutions. Thus, if the new m.c. is to repeat its position in the class structure, then appropriate secondary socialisation into privileged education becomes crucial. But as the relation between education and occupation becomes more direct and closer in time then the classifications and frames increase in strength. Thus the new m.c. take up some ambivalent enthusiasm for the invisible pedagogy for the early socialisation of the child, but settle for the *visible* pedagogy of the secondary school. And it will continue to do this until the University moves to a weaker classification and a weaker framing of its principles of transmission and selection. On the other hand, they are among the leaders of the movement to institutionalise the invisible pedagogy in State pre-schools and often for its colonisation of the primary school and further extension into the secondary school. And this can be done with confidence for the secondary school is likely to provide both visible and invisible pedagogies.[3] The former for the m.c. and the latter for the w.c.

SYMBOLIC CONTROL[4] AND THE IDENTIFICATION OF THE NEW MIDDLE CLASS

However a ruling class is defined, it has a relatively direct relationship to the means and forms of production, but a relatively *indirect* relationship to the means and forms of cultural reproduction. It is the various strata of the middle class which have a direct relationship to the means and forms of cultural reproduction, but only an indirect relationship to the means and forms of production. What we call here the old middle class, essentially nineteenth-century, based itself on the ideology of radical individualism (a form of integration referred to as individualised organic solidarity), whether its functions were entrepreneurial or professional. The ideology of radical individualism presupposes explicit and unambiguous values. It is this clarity in values which is fundamental to the transmission and reproduction of visible pedagogies. The explicit hierarchies of visible pedagogies require legitimation based upon explicit and unambiguous values. The new middle class as a structure is a middle-late twentieth century formation, arising out of the scientific organisation of work. The new middle class is both a product and sponsor of the related expansion of education and fields of symbolic control. It is ambiguously located in the class structure.[5] The ambiguity of the location is probably related to an ambiguity in its values and purpose. Such ambiguity shifts the modality of social control. Invisible pedagogies rest upon implicit hierarchies, which do not require legitimation by explicit and unambiguous values. The form of integration of this fraction shifts to personalised organic solidarity. This fraction of the middle class can be regarded as the *disseminators* of new forms of social control. The opposition between fractions of the middle class is not an opposition about radical change in class structure, but an opposition based upon conflicting forms of social control. We shall offer a classification of the agencies/agents of symbolic control.

(1) Regulators: Members of the legal system, Police, Prison Service, Church.
(2) Repairers: Members of the medical/psychiatric services and their derivatives; social services.
(3) Diffusers: Teachers at all levels and in all areas. Mass and specialised media.
(4) Shapers: Creators of what counts as developments within or change of symbolic forms, in the arts and sciences, including their agents of distribution, e.g. musicians, actors, producers, etc.
(5) Executors: Civil Service—Bureaucrats.

Whilst it is true that category (1)—Regulators—might well be classified as *maintainers,* we want to emphasise that they play an important legal role in regulating flow of people, acts, ideas. In the same way, some repairers may well have more of the function of regulators (in the above sense) than repairers. Further, each category has both its own hierarchy and its own internal ideological conflicts. In the same way, there may well be ideological conflicts *between* the categories which unite agents occupying dissimilar or similar positions in the respective hierarchies. Whilst we can distinguish the structure of integration, social control and processes of transmission which characterise the new middle class, the *agents* will be found in different proportions in different levels of the hierarchy in each category. This is a matter of continuing research. It is a matter of some importance (following Bourdieu) to consider the underlying structure of the cultural field of reproduction constituted by the agents and agencies of symbolic control, the underlying structure of the interrelationships of agents and agencies and the *forms* of symbolic control. Agents may be strongly or weakly classified in terms of the extent of their activity in more than one category and they may employ strong or weak framing procedures. The classification and framing analysis may be applied *within* a category *or* between categories. *The analysis in this paper is focussing upon changes in the form of transmission.*

Brief Discussion of the Classification

(1) Regulators: These are the agencies and agents whose function is to define, monitor and maintain the limits of persons and activities. Why place the official religious agencies with regulators? These agencies at one time both informed and legitimised the features of the legal system. Today the relationship between official religious agencies and the legal system is more complex. The role of official religious agencies as moral regulators has been considerably weakened, although in certain societies, official religious agencies have been active in supporting those who wish to change the system of regulation (e.g. the Roman Catholic Church in Latin America). Official religious agencies have been grouped with the structure of legal agencies because of their *function* as regulating agencies of symbolic control.

(2) Repairers: These are the agencies and agents whose function is to prevent, or repair, or isolate what counts as breakdowns in the body, mind, social relationships. As we have mentioned in the text, at different times and in different societies some repairers may well act as regulators, at other times sub-groups may well be in conflict with regulators.

(3) Diffusers: These are the agencies and agents whose *function* is to disseminate certain principles, practices, activities, symbolic forms, or to appropriate principles and practices, symbolic forms for the purpose of inducing consumption of symbolic forms, goods, services or activities.

(4) Shapers: These are the agencies and agents whose *function* is the developing of what counts as changing, crucial symbolic codes in the arts or sciences. The problem here is that at certain levels there is an overlap with diffusers. We would argue that film producers, gallery owners, theatre owners, publishers, are an *important sub-set* of diffusers on the grounds that they operate specialised media. However, what do we do with performers (actors, musicians, dancers) and specialised critics? I think we would argue that performers should be classified as diffusers and specialised critics should be classified as shapers.

(5) Executors: These are the agencies and agents whose function is administrative. The crucial agency here is the Civil Service and Local Government, although it is important to point out that they exist as agents in the above agencies.

We have left out the whole area of sport, which is undoubtedly a crucial agency in its own right, for the following reason. The classification has been set up in order to examine changes in the *form* of symbolic control *crucial* to the problem of the relationship between class and cultural reproduction. From this point of view, and *only* from this point of view, sport is not a crucial agency.

THE CLASS ASSUMPTIONS OF PEDAGOGIES

Women as Crucial Preparing Agents of Cultural Reproduction within the Middle Class (see Note V)

The shift from individualised to personalised organic solidarity in the m.c. changes the structure of family relationships and in particular the role of the woman in socialising the child. Historically, under individualised organic solidarity the mother is not important as a transmitter of physical or symbolic property. She is almost totally abstracted from the means of reproduction of either physical or symbolic property. The caring for and preparation of the children is delegated to others—nanny, governess, tutor. She is essentially a domestic administrator and it follows she can only be a model for her daughter. The woman was capable of cultural reproduction for often she possessed a more sensitive awareness and understanding of the general literature of the period than her husband. This concept of the abstracted maternal function perhaps reappears in the concept of the pre-school assistant as a baby-minder and the governess as the teacher of elementary competences. Thus individualised organic solidarity might generate two models for the early education by women of the child:

The Abstracted Mother

Child Minder (Nanny)   Teacher of Elementary Competences (Governess)

Visible Pedagogies (Infant School)

Initially, with individualised organic solidarity, property has a physical basis, existing in forms of capital where ownership and control are combined. Access to, and reproduction of class position here is related to access to and ownership of capital. Although there is clearly a link between class and forms of education, education in itself plays a relatively minor role in creating access to and reproduction of class position. However, with developed forms of capitalism, not only do management functions become divorced from ownership, but there is an expansion of social control positions which have their basis in specialised forms of communication, more and more available from the expanding system of education. With this extension and differentiation of control functions the basis of property becomes partly psychologised, and its basis is located in ownership of specialised forms of communication. These in turn have their origin in specialised *forms of interaction* initiated, developed and focussed very early in the child's life. The role of the mother in

the rearing of her children undergoes a qualitative change. The mother is transformed into a crucial preparing agent of cultural reproduction who provides access to symbolic forms and shapes the dispositions of her children so that they are better able to exploit the possibilities of public education. We can see an integration of maternal functions as the basis of class position becomes psychologised. *Delegated* maternal caring and preparation *becomes* maternal caring and preparation. What is of interest here is the *form* of the caring and the form of the preparation. According to the thesis, the form may be constituted by either a visible or an invisible pedagogy. The old middle class perpetuated itself through a visible pedagogy whereas the new middle class, the bearers of the structures of personalised organic solidarity, developed invisible pedagogies.

With the shift from individualised to personalised organic solidarity within fractions of the middle class, the woman is transformed into a crucial preparing agent of cultural reproduction. There is, however, a contradiction in her structural relationships. Unlike the mother in a context of individualised solidarity (visible pedagogy) she is unable to get away from her child. The weak classification and framing of her child rearing firmly anchor her to her child (see 3 below). For such a mother, interaction and surveillance are totally demanding, whilst at the same time her own socialisation into both a personal and an occupational identity points her away from the family. These tensions may be partly resolved by placing the child early in a pre-school, which faithfully reproduces the ambience of her own child rearing. The infant school, however, may amplify the messages, and wish to extend them into the junior school. Here we can see a second contradiction for such an amplification brings the middle class mother and the school into conflict. The public examination system is based upon a visible pedagogy realised through strong classification and relatively stronger framing. It is this pedagogy which generates symbolic property, the means whereby class position is reproduced. If access to a visible pedagogy is delayed too long, then examination success may be in danger.

The argument here is that an invisible pedagogy is based upon a concept of the woman as a *particular* preparing agent of cultural reproduction. An agent having its origins in a particular fraction of the middle class.

We will now turn to more specific class assumptions of invisible pedagogy.

1. Concept of Time

In the first place, invisible pedagogies are based upon a middle class concept of time because they pre-suppose a long educational life. If all children left school at fourteen, there would be no invisible pedagogies. Visible pedagogies are regulated by *explicit* sequencing rules; that is the progression of the transmission is ordered in time by explicit rules. In a school the syllabus regulates the progression of a subject and the curriculum regulates the relationships between subjects *and* those selected as appropriate for given ages. The sequencing rules, when they are explicit, define the future expected states of the child's consciousness and behaviours. However, in the case of invisible pedagogies the sequencing rules are not explicit, they are *implicit*. The progression of the transmission is based upon theories of the child's inner development (cognitive, moral, emotional, etc.). The sequencing rules are derived from particular theories of child development. In the case of invisible pedagogies are regulated by differ- for the child to know or be aware of the principles of the progression. He/she cannot know the principles of his/her own development as these are expressed in the regulating theories. Only the transmitter knows the principle, the sequencing rules. The sequencing rules are *implicit* in the transmission rather than explicit. We can generalise and say that the sequencing rules of a transmis-

sion define its time dimension. However, they do more than this. In as much as they regulate future expected states of consciousness and behaviours they define what the child is expected *to be* at different points of time. In which case they define the concept of child. It follows that because visible and invisible pedagogies are regulated by different, indeed from one point of view, opposing sequencing rules, then they entail different concepts of time and they also are based upon different concepts of child. Visible and invisible pedagogies are based upon different concepts of childhood and its progressive transformation, which have their origin in different fractions of the middle class.

2. Concepts of Space

In the first place, invisible pedagogies require for their transmission a different material structure from the material structure upon which a visible pedagogy is based. A visible pedagogy requires only a very small fixed space; essentially a table, a book and a chair. Its material structure is remarkably cheap. However, in order for the material base to be exploited, it still requires a form of acquisition regulated by an elaborated code. However, in the case of an invisible pedagogy, its material basis is a very much larger surface. Consider the large sheets of paper, the space demands of its technology, bricks, kits for doing the creativity thing, an assembly of media whereby the child's consciousness may be uniquely revealed. The technology requires a relatively large space for the child. In this sense the production of an invisible pedagogy in the home cannot be effected in an overcrowded, materially inadequate home. However, invisible pedagogies are based upon a concept of space which is more fundamental. Visible pedagogies are realised through strongly classified space, that is, there are very strong boundaries between one space and another *and* the control of the spaces are equally strongly classified. Rooms in the house have specialised functions, seating arrangements for example at meals are specific to classes of person—mother, father, children, there are explicit, strongly marked boundaries regulating the movement in space of persons at different times. Further, the contents of different spaces are not interchangeable, e.g. dining spaces are dining spaces, children's areas and contents are children's areas and contents, the kitchen is the kitchen, etc. The explicit hierarchy of a visible pedagogy creates spaces and relationships between spaces which carry a specific set of symbolic messages—all illustrating the principle—things must be kept apart.

However, in the case of invisible pedagogies space has a different symbolic significance, for here spaces and their contents are relatively weakly classified. The controls over flow of persons and objects between spaces are much weaker. This means that the *potential space available to the child is very much greater.* The privacy embodied in space regulated by visible pedagogies is considerably reduced. Architects tend to call the spatial organisation of invisible pedagogies "open-plan living." *The child learns to understand the possibilities of such weakly classified spaces and the rules upon which such learning is based.* We can point out in passing the irony of, on the one hand, an invisible pedagogy, but on the other the fact of the continuous *visibility* of persons and their behaviour: the possibility of continuous surveillance. Invisible pedagogies are based upon concepts of space derived from a fraction of the middle class.

3. Concept of Social Control

Where the pedagogy is visible the hierarchy is explicit, space and time are regulated by explicit principles, there are strong boundaries between spaces, times, acts, communications. The power realised by the hierarchy maintains the strong boundaries, the apartness of things. As the child learns these rules, he acquires the classification. An infringement of the classification is immediately visible, for any infringement signals *something is out of place,* communication, act, person or object. The task is to get the child to accept (not necessarily to understand) the ordering principles. This can be accomplished (not always necessarily) by linking infringements with an explicit calculus of punishment and relatively simple announcements of proscribing and prescribing rules. Motivation is increased by a gradual widening of privileges through age. The hierarchy is manifest in the classifications, in the strong boundaries, within the insulations. *The language of social control is relatively restricted and the relationships of control, explicitly hierarchical.*[6]

However, where the pedagogy is invisible, the hierarchy is *implicit,* space and time are weakly classified. This social structure does not create in its symbolic arrangements strong boundaries which carry critical messages of control. Because the hierarchy is implicit *(which does not mean it is not there, only that the form of its realisation is different)* there is a relative absence of *strongly marked* regulation of the child's acts, communication, objects, spaces, times and progression. In what lies the control? We will suggest that control inheres in *elaborated inter-personal communication* in a context where maximum surveillance is possible. *In other words, control is vested in the process of inter-personal communication.* A particular function of language is of special significance and its realisation is of an elaborated form in contrast to the more restricted form of communication where the pedagogy is visible. The form of transmission of an invisible pedagogy encourages more of the child to be made public and so more of the child is available for direct and indirect surveillance and control. Thus invisible pedagogies realise specific modalities of social control which have their origins in a particular fraction of the middle class.

We have attempted to make explicit four class assumptions underlying the transmission of an invisible pedagogy.

(1) It pre-supposes a particular concept of the mother as a crucial preparing agent of cultural reproduction.

(2) It pre-supposes a particular concept of time.

(3) It pre-supposes a particular concept of space.

(4) It pre-supposes a particular form of social control—which inheres in interpersonal communication (elaborated code—person focussed).

The educational consequences of an invisible pedagogy will be, according to this thesis, crucially different depending upon the social class position of the child.

We started this section by abstracting the following points from our initial discussion of the invisible pedagogy.

(1) The invisible pedagogy is an interrupter system, both in relation to the home and in relation to other levels of the educational hierarchy.

(2) It transforms the privatised social structure and cultural contents of visible pedagogies into a personalised social structure and personalised cultural contents.

(3) It believes that implicit nurture reveals unique nature.

We have argued that this pedagogy is one of the realisations of the conflict between the old and the new middle class, which in turn has its social basis in the two different forms of organic solidarity, individualised and personalised; that these two forms of solidarity arise out of differences in the relation to and the expansion of the division of labour within the middle class; that the movement from individualised to personalised interrupts the *form* of the reproduction of class relationships; that such an interruption gives rise to different forms of *primary* socialisation within the middle class; that the form of primary socialisation within the middle class is the model for primary socialisation into the school; that there are contradictions within personalised organic solidarity which create deeply felt ambiguities; as a consequence, the outcomes of the

form of the socialisation are less certain. The contemporary new middle class are unique for in the socialisation of their young is a sharp and penetrating contradiction between a subjective personal identity and an objective privatised identity; between the release of the person and the hierarchy of class. The above can be represented diagrammatically:

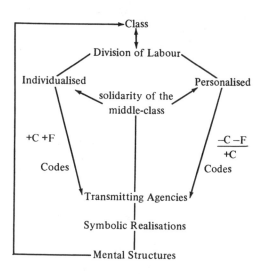

Whereas it is possible for school and University to change the basis of its solidarity from individualistic to personalised, i.e. to relax its classification and frames, it is more difficult for those agencies to change their privatising function, i.e. the creation of knowledge as private property. It by no means follows that a shift to personalised organic solidarity will change the privatising function. Indeed, even the shift in the form of solidarity is more likely to occur in that part of the educational system which creates no private property, as in the case of the education of the lower working class, or in the education of the very young. We are then left with the conclusion that the major effects of this change in solidarity will be in the areas of condensed communication (sex, art, style) and in the form of social control (from explicit to implicit).

TRANSITION TO SCHOOL

Class Culture Power and Conflict

This shift from visible to invisible pedagogies at the pre- and primary levels of education changes the relationships between the family and the school. We have already noted the ambiguous attitude of the m.c. to such a shift. In the case of the w.c., the change is more radical. The weak classification and weak framing of the invisible pedagogy potentially make possible the inclusion of the culture of the family and the community. Thus the experience of the child and his everyday world could be psychologically active in the classroom and if this were to be the case, then the school would legitimise rather than reject the class-culture of the family. In as much as the pacing of the knowledge to be transmitted is relaxed and the emphasis upon early attainment of specific competencies is reduced, then the progression is less marked by m.c. assumptions. In the case of visible pedagogies early reading and especially writing are essential. Once the child can read and write such acts free the teacher but of more importance, once the child can read he can be given a book, and once he is given a book he is well on the way to managing the role of the solitary privatised educational relationship. The book is the preparation for receiving the past realised in the text book. And the text book in turn tacitly transmits the ideology of the collection code: for it epitomises strong classification and strong frames. The text book orders knowledge according to an explicit progression, it provides explicit criteria, it removes uncertainties and announces hierarchy. It gives the child an immediate index of where he stands in relation to others in the progression. It is therefore a silent medium for creating competitive relationships. Thus socialisation into the textbook is a critical step towards socialisation into the collection code. The stronger the collection code, that is the stronger clas-

sification and frames, the greater the emphasis on early reading and writing. The m.c. child is prepared for this emphasis, but not so in the case of the w.c. child. The weakening of classification and frames reduces the significance of the textbook and transforms the impersonal past into a personalised present. It would appear that the invisible pedagogy carries a beneficial potential for w.c. children. However, because the form we are discussing has its origins in a fraction of the m.c., this potential may not be actualised.

This point we will now develop. From the point of view of w.c. parents, the visible pedagogy of the collection code at the primary level is immediately understandable. The basic competencies which it is transmitting of reading, writing, and counting, in an ordered explicit sequence, make sense. The failures of the children are the children's failures not the school's for the school is apparently carrying out impersonally its function. The school's form of social control does not interfere with the social control of the family. The infant school teacher will not necessarily have high status as the competencies she is transmitting are, in principle, possible also for the mother. In this sense, there is symbolic continuity (or rather extension) between the w.c. home and the school. However, in the case of the invisible pedagogy, there is possibly a sharp discontinuity. The competencies and their progression disappear, the form of social control may well be at variance with the home. The theory of the invisible pedagogy may not be known by the mother or may be imperfectly understood. The lack of stress on competencies may render the child a less effective (useful) member of the family, e.g. running errands, etc. However, there is a more fundamental source of tension. The invisible pedagogy contains a different theory of transmission and a new technology, which views the mother's own informal teaching, where it occurs, or the mother's pedagogical values, as irrelevant if not downright harmful. There are new reading schemes, new mathematics replace arithmetic, an expressive aesthetic style replaces one which aims at facsimile. If the mother is to be helpful, she must be re-socialized or kept out of the way. If it is the former or the latter, then the power relationships have changed between home and school: for the teacher has the power and the mother is as much a pupil as the pupil. This in turn may disturb the authority relationships within the home: this disturbance is further facilitated by the use of implicit forms of social control of the school. Even if the pedagogy draws its contents from the class culture, basic forms of discontinuity still exist. If the mother wishes to understand the theory of the invisible pedagogy, then she may well find herself at the mercy of complex theories of child development. Indeed, whichever way the w.c. mother turns, the teacher has the power: although the mother may well be deeply suspicious of the whole ambiance.[7]

Where, as in the case of the visible pedagogy there are, for the w.c.. relative to the m.c., implicit forms of discontinuity and explicit forms of inequality in the shape of the holding power of the school over its teachers, the size of class and possibly streaming: in the case of the invisible pedagogy, there is also an *explicit* symbolic discontinuity which may well go with inequalities in provision and quality of teaching staff. The teacher also has difficulties, because the invisible pedagogy presupposes a particular form of maternal primary socialisation *and* a small class of pupils *and* a particular architecture. Where these are absent, the teacher may well find great difficulty. Ideally, the invisible pedagogy frees the teacher so that time is available for ameliorating the difficulties of any one child, but if the class is large, the socialisation, from the point of view of the school, inadequate, the architecture inappropriate, then such individual assistance becomes infrequent and problematic. Here again we can

see that such a pedagogy, if it is to be successfully implemented in its own terms, necessarily requires minimally the same physical conditions of the middle class school. It is an *expensive* pedagogy because it is derived from an expensive class: the middle class.

From the point of view of the middle class, there is at least an intellectual understanding of the invisible pedagogy, if not always an acceptance of its values and practice. Further, if the middle class child is not obtaining the basic competencies at the rate the mother expects, an educational support system can be organized through private coaching or through the mother's own efforts. The power relationships between the middle class mother and the teacher are less tipped in favour of the teacher. Finally, the middle class mother always has the choice of the private school or of moving near a state school of her choice. However, because of the middle class mother's concept of the function of secondary education, she is likely to be anxious about the acquisition of basic competencies and this will bring her into conflict with the school at some point.

Finally, in as much as age and sex statuses within the family are strongly classified and ritualised, then it is likely that the acquisition, progression and evaluation of competencies obtained within the school will become part of the markers of age and sex status within the family. For example, there is a radical change in the status and concept of the child when he is transformed into a pupil. Now to the extent that the infant/primary school fails to utilise age and sex as allocating categories *either* for the acquisition and progression of competencies *or* for the allocation of pupils to groups and spaces, then the school is weakening the function of these categories in the family and community. Visible pedagogies not only reinforce age and sex classification, they also provide markers for progression within them. Invisible pedagogies are likely to weaken such classifications and in as much as they do this they transform the concept of the child and the concepts of age and sex status.

Class, Pedagogy and Evaluation

Interesting questions arise over the system of evaluating the pupils. Where the pedagogy is visible an "objective" grid exists for the evaluation of the pupils in the form of (a) clear criteria and (b) a delicate measurement procedure. The child receives a grade or its equivalent for any valued performance. Further, where the pedagogy is visible, it is likely to be standardized and so schools are directly comparable as to their successes and failures. The profile of the pupil may be obtained by looking across his grades. The pupil knows where he is, the teacher knows where he is and so do the parents. The parents have a yardstick for comparing schools. When children change schools they can be slotted into place according to their academic profile. Further, it is difficult for the parent to argue about the profile for it is "objective." Clearly, there are subjective elements in the grading of the children, but these are masked by the apparent objectivity of the grid. In the case of invisible pedagogies, no such grid exists. The evaluation procedures are multiple, diffuse and not easily subject to apparently precise measurement. This makes comparison between pupils complex and also comparisons between schools.[8] Firstly, the invisible pedagogy does not give rise to progression of a *group*, but is based upon progression of a person. Secondly, there is likely to be considerable variation between infant/pre-school groups *within* the general form of the pedagogy. There is less difficulty in slotting a child into a new school because there is no explicit slot for him. Thus the mother is less able to diagnose the child's progress and as a consequence she cannot *provide specific educational support.* She would be forced into providing a general educational milieu in the home and this she may only be able to do if she had fully internalised the invisible

pedagogy's theoretical basis. As we have previously argued, this is less likely to be the case where the parents are working class. Thus these parents are cut off from the evaluation of the child's progress. More, they are forced to accept what the teacher counts as progress.

Because an apparently objective grid exists for the evaluation of the visible pedagogies, then this grid acts selectively on those dispositions of the child which become candidates for labelling by the teacher. Clearly motivation and interest are probably relevant to any pedagogy, but their significance will vary with the pedagogy, and certainly their consequences. In the case of visible pedagogies, the behaviour of the child is focused on the teacher so that, in this case, attentiveness to, co-operation with, the teacher become relevant: persistence and carefulness are also valued by the teacher. Further, it is possible for there to be a conflict between the child's academic profile *and* the teacher's evaluation of his attitudes and motivation. These objective and subjective criteria may have different consequences for different class groups of pupils. Either criteria, irrespective of their validity, are likely to be *understood* by working class parents. In the case of invisible pedagogy, as more of the child is made available, and, because of the theory which guides interpretation, diagnosis and evaluation, a different class of acts and dispositions of the child become relevant. In the case of visible pedagogies we have argued that the attention of the child is focused on the teacher, however, in the case of invisible pedagogies the attention of the teacher is focused on the *whole* child: in its total doing and "not doing." This can lead to discrepancies between the teacher's and parents' views of the child unless the parents share the teacher's theory. Indeed it is possible that the dispositions and acts which are subject to evaluation by the teacher may be considered by some parents as irrelevant or intrusive or inaccurate or all three. Where this occurs the child's behaviour is being shaped by conflicting criteria.

From the point of view of the teacher, the child becomes an *innovating* message to the home. The invisible pedagogy is not only an interrupter system in the context of educational practice, but it also transforms the child under certain conditions, into an innovating message to the family.

This pedagogy is likely to lead to a change in the school's procedures of evaluation, both objective and subjective. Where the pedagogy is visible, there is a profile which consists of the grading of specific competencies and a profile which consists of the grading of the child's motivation and work attitudes. It is likely that the latter will consist of rather short, somewhat stereotyped unexplicated judgements. In the case of invisible pedagogies, these highly condensed, unexplicated but *public* judgements, are likely to be replaced by something resembling a dossier which will range across a wide variety of the child's internal processes and states *and* his external acts. Further, the connection between inner and outer is likely to be made *explicit*. In other words, there is likely to be an explicit elaborated account of the relationships between the child's internal states and his acts. It is now possible that the school will have a problem of secrecy. How much is to go into the dossier, where is it to be kept, how much of and in what way are its contents to be made available to parents or to others in the school and outside of it? Thus invisible pedagogies may also generate *covert* and *overt* forms and contents of evaluation. Such a system of evaluation increases the power of the teacher to the extent that its underlying theory is not shared by parents *and* even when it is shared.

Finally, the major analysis in this section has been of idealised pedagogies. If, however, the argument is correct, that there may be a disjunction in the forms of socialisation between primary and secondary stages, *or* between secondary and tertiary stages, then behind weak classification and weak frames may well be strong classification and strong frames. Thus we can have a situation where strong Cs and Fs follow weak Cs and Fs, *or* where weak Cs and Fs follow strong Cs and Fs, as, possibly, in the case of the training of infant school teachers in England. It is important not only to understand continuity in the strength of classification and frames, but also *disjunction* and *when* the disjunction occurs. It is more than likely that if we examine empirically invisible pedagogies we shall find to different degrees a stress on the transmission of *specific* isolated competencies. Thus the " hidden curriculum" of invisible pedagogies may well be, embryonically, strong classification, albeit with relatively weak frames. It becomes a matter of some importance to find out which children or groups of children are particularly responsive to this "hidden curriculum." For some children may come to see or be led to see that there are two transmissions, one overt, the other covert, which stand in a figure-ground relation to each other. We need to know for which teachers, and for which children, what is the figure and what is the ground. Specifically, will middle class children respond to the latent visible pedagogy, or are they more likely to be selected as receivers? Will lower working class children respond more to the invisible pedagogy or receive a weaker form of the transmission of visible pedagogy? The "hidden curriculum" of invisible pedagogies may well be a visible pedagogy. However, the outcomes of the imbedding of one pedagogy in the other are likely to be different than in the case of the transmission of any *one* pedagogy. From a more theoretical standpoint, the crucial component of visible pedagogy is the strength of its *classification,* for in the last analysis, it is this which creates what counts as valued property, and also in so doing regulates mental structures. Frame strength regulates the modality of the socialisation into the classification. In the microcosm of the nursery or infant class, we can see embryonically the new forms of transmission of class relationships.

Let us take a concrete example to illustrate the above speculation. An infant school teacher in England may experience the following conjunctions or disjunctions in her socialisation:

(1) Between socialisation in the family and between primary and secondary school.

(2) Between secondary school and teacher training. The higher the qualifications required by the college of education, the more likely that the socialisation in the later years of the secondary school will be through strong classification and frames. On the other hand, the socialisation into the college of education may well be into classification and frames of varying strengths.

TRANSITION BETWEEN STAGES OF EDUCATION

We have examined aspects of the transition to school; there is also the question of transition between stages of education, from preschool to primary, from primary to secondary. These transitions between stages are marked by three inter-related features:

(1) An increase in the strength of classification and frames (initiation into the collective code).

(2) An increase in the range of different teachers; that is, the pupil is made aware of the insulations within the division of labour. He also learns that the principle of authority transcends the individuals who hold it, for as teachers/subjects change his role remains the same.

(3) The weak classification and frames of the invisible pedagogy emphasise the importance of *ways* of knowing, of constructing problems, whereas the strong classification and frames of visible pedagogies emphasise states of knowledge and received problems. Thus there is a crucial change in what counts as having knowledge, in what counts as a legitimate realisation of that knowledge *and* in the social context.

Thus the shift from invisible to visible pedagogies in one phrase is a change in code; a change in the principles of relation and evaluation whether these are principles of knowledge, of social relationships, of practices, of property, of identity.

It is likely that this change of code will be more effectively made (despite the difficulties) by the new middle-class children as their own socialisation within the family contains *both* codes—the code which creates the manifestation of the person and the code which creates private property. Further, as we have argued elsewhere, it is more likely that the working class children will experience continuity in code between stages of education. The class bias of the collection code (which creates a visible pedagogy) may make such a transmission difficult for them to receive and exploit. As a consequence, the continuation of the invisible pedagogy in the form of an integrated code is likely for working class children, and its later institutionalisation for the same children at the secondary level.

We can now begin to see that the condition for continuity of educational code for *all* children, irrespective of class, is the type of code transmitted by the University. Simply expanding the University, increasing differentiation within the tertiary level, equalising opportunity of access and outcome will not fundamentally change the situation at levels below. We will only have expanded the size of the cohort at the tertiary level. From another point of view, although we may have changed the organisational structure we have *not* changed the code controlling transmission; the process of reproduction will not be fundamentally affected. To change the code controlling transmission involves changing the culture and its basis in privatised class relationships. Thus if we accept, for the sake of argument, the greater educational value of invisible pedagogies, of weak classification and frames, the condition for their effective and total institutionalism at the secondary level is a fundamental change of code at the tertiary level. If this does not occur then codes and class will remain firmly linked in schools.

Finally, we can raise a basic question. The movement to invisible pedagogies realised through integrated codes may be seen as a superficial solution to a more obdurate problem. Integraded codes are integrated at the level of ideas, they do *not* involve integration at the level of institutions, i.e. between school and work. Yet the crucial integration is precisely between the principles of education and the principles of work. There can be no such integration in western societies (to mention only one group) because the work epitomises class relationships. Work can only be brought into the school in terms of the function of the school as a selective mechanism or in terms of social/psychological adjustment to work. Indeed, the abstracting of education from work, the hallmark of the liberal tradition, or the linkage of education to leisure, masks the brutal fact that work and education cannot be integrated at the level of social principles in class societies. They can either be separated or they can *fit* with each other. Durkheim wrote that changes in pedagogy were indicators of a moral crisis; they can also disguise it and change its form. However, in as much as the move to weak classification and frames has the *potential* of reducing insulations in mental structures and social structures, has the potential of making explicit the implicit and so creating *greater* ambiguity but less disguise, then such a code has the potential of making visible fundamental social contradictions.

NOTE I

This raises a number of questions. We cannot consider skills abstracted from the context of their transmission, from their relationships to each other and their function in creating, maintaining, modifying or changing a culture. Skills and their relationship to each other are culturally specific competences. The manner of their transmission and acquisition socialises the child into their contextual usages. Thus, the unit of analysis cannot simply be an abstracted specific competence like reading, writing, counting but the *structure* of social relationships which produces these specialised competences. The formulation "where there is a reduced emphasis upon transmission and acquisition of specific skills" could be misleading, as it suggests that in the context under discussion there are few specialised repertoires of the culture. It may be better to interpret the formulation as indicating an emphasis upon the inter-relationships between skills which are relatively weakly classified and weakly framed. In this way any skill or sets of skills are referred to the *general features of the socialisation*.

NOTE II

It is a matter of some interest to consider changes in emphasis of research methodologies over recent decades. There has been a shift from the standardised closed questionnaire or experimental context to more unstructured contexts and relationships. It is argued that the former methodology renders irrelevant the subjective meanings of those who are the object of study. In so doing, the researched offer their experience through the media of the researchers' imposed strong classification and strong frames. Further, it is argued that such a method of studying people is derived from a method for the study of objects and therefore it is an outrage to the subjectivity of man for him to be transformed into an object. These arguments go on to link positivist methods with the political control of man through the use of the technology of social science. The new methodology employs apparently weak classification and weak frames, but it uses techniques (participant observation, tape-recordings, video tapes, etc.) which enable more of the researched to be visible, and its techniques allow a range of others to witness the spontaneous behaviour of the observed. Even if these public records of natural behaviour are treated as a means of dialogue between the recorded and the recorder, this dialogue is, itself, subject to the disjunction

between intellectual perspectives which will
shape the communication. The self-editing
of·the researcher's communication is different from that of the researched, and this is
the *invisible* control. On the other hand,
paradoxically, in the case of a closed questionnaire the privacy of the subject is safeguarded, for all that can be made public is a
pencil mark which is transformed into an
impersonal score. Further, the methods of
this transformation must be made public so
that its assumptions may be criticised. In the
case of the new methodology, the principles
used to restrict the vast amount of information and the number of channels are often
implicit. One might say that we could distinguish research methodologies in terms of
whether they created invisible or visible
pedagogies. Thus the former give rise to a
total surveillance of the person who, relative
to the latter, makes public more of his inside
(e.g. his subjectivity) which is evaluated
through the use of diffuse, implicit criteria.
We are suggesting that the structural origins
of changes in the classification and framing
of forms of socialisation may perhaps also
influence the selection of research methodologies. The morality of the research relationships transcends the dilemmas of a
particular researcher. Research methodologies in social science are themselves elements
of culture.

NOTE III

It is interesting to see, for example, where
the invisible pedagogy first entered the
secondary school curriculum. In England we
would suggest that it first penetrated the
non-verbal area of *unselective* secondary
schools. The area which is considered to be
the least relevant (in the sense of not producing symbolic property) and the most
strongly classified: the area of the art room.
Indeed, it might be said that until very
recently, the greatest symbolic continuity of
pedagogies between primary and secondary
stages lay in the non-verbal areas of the
curriculum. The art room is often viewed by
the rest of the staff as an area of relaxation

or even therapy, rather than a space of
crucial production. Because of its strong
classification and irrelevance (except at
school "show-off" periods) this space is
potentially open to change. Art teachers are
trained in institutions (at least in recent
times) which are very sensitive to innovation
and therefore new styles are likely to be
rapidly institutionalised in schools, given the
strong classification of art in the secondary
school curriculum, and also the belief that
the less able child can at least do something
with his hands even if he finds difficulty
with a pen. We might also anticipate that
with the interest in such musical forms as
pop on the one hand and Cage and Stock-
hausen on the other, music departments
might move towards the invisible pedagogy.
To complete the direction in the non-verbal
area, it is possible that the transformation of
physical training into physical education
might also extend to movement. If this
development took place, then the non-verbal
areas would be realised through the invisible
pedagogy. We might then expect a drive to
integrate the three areas of sight, sound and
movement; *three* modalities would then be
linked through a common code. In summary
this movement is from reproduction to production.

NOTE IV

We can clarify the issues raised in this paper
in the following way. Any socialising context must consist of a transmitter and an
acquirer. These two form a matrix in the
sense that the communication is regulated
by a structural principle. We have suggested
that the underlying principle of a socialising
matrix is realised in classification and
frames. The relationship between the two
and the strengths show us the structure of
the control and the form of communication.
We can, of course, analyse this matrix in a
number of ways:

(1) We can focus upon the transmitter.
(2) We can focus upon the acquirer.
(3) We can focus upon the principles
underlying the matrix.

(4) We can focus upon a given matrix and ignore its relationship to other matrices.

(5) We can consider the relationships between critical matrices, e.g. family, peer group, school, work.

We can go on to ask questions about the function of a matrix and questions about the change in the form of its realisation, i.e. changes in the strength of its classification and frames. We believe that the unit of analysis must always be the matrix and the matrix will always include the theories and methods of its analysis (see Note II on research methodology). Now any one matrix can be regarded as a reproducer, an interrupter, or a change matrix. A reproduction matrix will attempt to create strong classification and strong frames. An interrupter matrix changes the *form* of transmission, but not the critical relationship *between* matrices. A change matrix leads to a fundamental change in the structural relationship *between* matrices. This will require a major change in the institutional structure. For example, we have argued that within the middle class there is a conflict which has generated two distinct socialising matrices, one a reproducer, the other an interrupter. And these matrices are at work within education for similar groups of children up to possibly the primary stage, and different groups of pupils at the secondary stage. However, in as much as the structural relationship between school and work is unchanged (i.e. there has been no change in the basic principles of their relationship) then we cannot by this argument see current differences in educational pedagogy as representing a change matrix. In other words, the form of the reproduction of class relationships in education has been *interrupted* but not changed. We might speculate that ideological conflict within the middle class takes the form of a conflict between the symbolic outcomes of reproduction and interruption matrices. If one takes the argument one stage further, we have to consider the reproduction of the *change* in the form of class relationships. In this case, the reproduction of an interrupter matrix is through weak classification and weak frames. However, it is possible that such a form of reproduction may at some point evoke its own interrupter i.e. an increase in either classification or frame strength, or both.

NOTE V

Women played an active role in initiating (Montessori), shaping and disseminating invisible pedagogies. Consider:

(1) The application of Freudian theory by Anna Freud to child analysis; the modification of Freudian theory by Melanie Klein and her followers, Hanna Segal, Joan Riviere, Marion Milner; and the development of the interpretation of play as phantasy content in child analysis.

(2) The extension of psycho-analytic theory into education and the training of teachers (post 1945) through Susan Isaacs at the University of London Institute of Education, and its further development by Dolly Garner. Parallel work with a Piagetian basis was carried out by Molly Brierley, Principal of the Froebel College of Education.

(3) A number of women in a much earlier period were active in the education and training of teachers, e.g. Philippa Fawcett, Rachel McMillan.

It is possible that women were crucial agents in the last quarter of the nineteenth century (and perhaps even before). For in as much as the concept of the child was changed, so was the hierarchy, to which women were subordinate. At the same time, the pedagogy provided the basis of a professional identity. From this point of view, women transformed maternal caring and preparing into a *scientific* activity.

A NOTE ON THE CODING OF OBJECTS AND MODALITIES OF CONTROL

The Coding of Objects

The concepts of classification and frame can be used to interpret communication between objects. In other words, objects and their relationships to each other constitute a message system whose code can be stated in terms of the relationship between classification and frames of different strengths.

We can consider:

(1) The strength of the rules of exclusion which control the array of objects in a space. Thus the stronger the rules of exclusion the more distinctive the array of objects in the space; that is, the greater the difference between object arrays in different spaces.

(2) The extent to which objects in the array can enter into different relationships to each other.

Now the stronger the rules of exclusion the stronger the *classification* of objects in that space and the greater the difference between object arrays in different spaces. In the same way in which we discussed relationships between subjects we can discuss the relationships between object arrays in different spaces. Thus the stronger the classification the more the object arrays resemble a collection code, the weaker the classification the more the object arrays resemble an integrated code. The greater the number of different relationships objects in the array can enter into with each other the weaker their framing. The fewer the number of different relationships objects in the array can enter into with each other the stronger their framing.[9]

We would expect that the social distribution of power and the principles of control to be reflected in the coding of objects. This code may be made more delicate if we take into account:

(1) The number of objects in the array.
(2) The rate of change of the array.

We can have strong classification with a large *or* a small number of objects. We can have strong classification of large or small arrays where the array is fixed across time *or* where the array varies across time. Consider, for example, two arrays which are strongly classified; a late Victorian middle-class living-room and a middle 20th century trendy middle-class "space" in Hampstead. The Victorian room is likely to contain a very large number of objects whereas the middle-class room is likely to contain a small number of objects. In one case the object array is foreground and the space background, whereas in the second case the space is a vital component of the array. The Victorian room represents both strong classification and strong framing. Further, whilst objects may be added to the array, its fundamental characteristics would remain constant over a relatively long time period. The Hampstead room is likely to contain a small array which would indicate strong classification (strong rules of exclusion) but the objects are likely to enter into a variety of relationships with each other; this would indicate weak framing. Further, it is possible that the array would be changed across time according to fashion.

We can now see that if we are to consider classification (C) we need to know:

(1) Whether it is strong or weak.
(2) Whether the array is small or large (x).
(3) Whether the array is fixed or variable (y).

At the level of frame (F) we need to know:
Whether it is strong or weak (p); that is, whether the coding is restricted or elaborated.

It is also important to indicate in the specification of the code the context (c) to which it applies. We should also indicate the nature of the array by adding the concept realisation (r). Thus, the most abstract formulation of the object code would be as follows:

$$f(c, r, C(x,y), F(p))$$

The code is some unspecified function of the variables enclosed in the brackets.

It is important to note that because the classification is weak it does not mean that there is less control. Indeed, from this point of view it is not possible to talk about amount of control only of its modality. This point we will now develop.

Classification, Frames and Modalities of Control

Imagine four lavatories. The first is stark, bare, pristine, the walls are painted a sharp white; the washbowl is like the apparatus, a gleaming white. A square block of soap sits cleanly in an indentation in the sink. A white towel (or perhaps pink) is folded neatly on a chrome rail or hangs from a chrome ring. The lavatory paper is hidden in a cover and peeps through its slit. In the second lavatory there are books on a shelf and some relaxing of the rigours of the first. In the third there are books on the shelf, pictures on the wall and perhaps a scattering of tiny objects. In the fourth lavatory the rigour is *totally relaxed*. The walls are covered with a motley array of postcards, there is a various assortment of reading matter and curio. The lavatory roll is likely to be uncovered and the holder may well fall apart in use.

We can say that as we move from the first to the fourth lavatory we are moving from a strongly classified to a weakly classified space: from a space regulated by strong rules of exclusion to a space regulated by weak rules of exclusion. Now if the rules of exclusion are strong then the space is strongly marked off from other spaces in the house or flat. The *boundary* between the spaces or rooms is sharp. If the rules of exclusion are strong, the boundaries well marked, then it follows that there must be some strong boundary maintainers (authority). If things are to be kept apart then there must be some strong hierarchy to ensure the apartness of things. Further, the first lavatory constructs a space where pollution is highly visible. In as much as a user leaves a personal mark (a failure to replace the towel in its original position, a messy bar of soap, scum in the washbowl, lavatory paper floating in the bowl, etc.) this constitutes pollution and such pollution is quickly perceived. Thus the

criteria for competent usage of the space are both *explicit* and *specific*. So far we have been discussing aspects of classification; we shall now consider framing.

Whereas classification tells us about the structure of relationships in *space,* framing tells us about the structure of relationships in *time.* Framing refers us to interaction, to the power relationships of interaction; that is, framing refers us to communication. Now in the case of our lavatories, framing *here* would refer to the communication between the occupants of the space and those outside of the space. Such communication is normally strongly framed by a door usually equipped with a lock. We suggest that as we move from the strongly classified to the weakly classified lavatory, despite the potential insulation between inside and outside, there will occur a reduction in frame strength. In the case of the first lavatory we suggest that the door will always be closed and after entry will be locked. Ideally no effects on the inside should be heard on the outside. Indeed, a practised user of this lavatory will acquire certain competencies in order to meet this requirement. However, in the case of the most weakly classified lavatory, we suggest that the door will normally be open; it may even be that the lock will not function. It would not be considered untoward for a conversation to develop or even be continued either side of the door. A practised user of this most weakly classified and weakly framed lavatory will acquire certain communicative competencies rather different from those required for correct use of the strongly classified one.

We have already noted that lavatory one creates a space where pollution is highly visible, where criteria for behaviour are explicit and specific, where the social basis of the authority maintaining the strong classification and frames is hierarchical. Yet it is also the case that such classification and frames create a *private* although impersonal space. *For providing that the classification and framing are not violated the user of the space is beyond surveillance.*

However, when we consider lavatory four which has the weakest classification and weakest frames it seems at first sight that such a structure celebrates weak control. There appear to be few rules regulating what goes into a space and few rules regulating communication between spaces. Therefore it is difficult to consider what counts as a violation or pollution. Indeed, it would appear that such a classification and framing relationship facilitates the development of spontaneous behaviour. Let us consider this possibility.

Lavatory one is predicated on the rule "things must be kept apart" be they persons, acts, objects, communication, and the stronger the classification and frames the greater the insulation, the stronger the boundaries between classes of persons, acts, objects, communications. Lavatory four is predicated on the rule that approximates to "things must be put together." As a consequence, we would find objects in the space that could be found in other spaces. Further, there is a more relaxed marking off of the space and communication is possible between inside and outside. We have as yet not discovered the fundamental principles of violation.

Imagine one user, who seeing the motley array and being sensitive to what he or she takes to be a potential of the space decides to add to the array and places an additional postcard on the wall. It is possible that a little later a significant adult might say "Darling, that's beautiful but it doesn't quite fit" or "How lovely but wouldn't it be better a little higher up?" In other words, we are suggesting that the array has a principle, that the apparently motley collection is ordered but that the principle is implicit and although it is not easily discoverable it is capable of being violated. Indeed, it might take our user a very long time to infer the *tacit* principle and generate choices in accordance with it. Without knowledge of the principle our user is unlikely to make appropriate choices and such choices may require a long period of socialisation. In the case of

lavatory one no principle is required; all that is needed is the following of the command "Leave the space as you found it."[10]

Now let us examine the weak framing in more detail. We suggest that locking the door, avoiding or ignoring communication, would count as violation; indeed anything which would offend the principle of *things must be put together*. However, in as much as the framing between inside and outside is weak then it is also the case that the user is potentially or indirectly under continuous surveillance, in which case there is no privacy. Here we have a social context which at first sight appears to be very relaxed, which promotes and provokes the expression of the person, "a do your own thing" space where highly personal choices may be offered, where hierarchy is not explicit yet on analysis we find that it is based upon a form of implicit control which carries the potential of total surveillance. Such a form of implicit control encourages more of the person to be made manifest yet such manifestations are subject to continuous screening and general rather than specific criteria. *At the level of classification the pollution is "keeping things apart"; at the level of framing the violation is "withholding"; that is, not offering, not making visible the self.*

If things are to be put together which were once set apart, then there must be some principle of the new relationships, but this principle cannot be mechanically applied and therefore cannot be mechanically learned. In the case of the rule "things must be kept apart," then the apartness of things is something which is clearly marked and taken for granted in the process of initial socialisation. The social basis of the categories of apartness is implicit but the social basis of the authority is explicit. In the process of such socialisation the insulation between things is a condensed message about the all-pervasiveness of the authority. It may require many years before the social basis of the principles underlying the category system is made fully explicit and by that time the mental structure is well-initiated into the classification and frames. Strong classification and frames celebrate the *reproduction* of the past.

When the rule is "things must be put together" we have an *interruption* of a previous order, and what is of issue is the authority (power relationships) which underpin it. Therefore the rule "things must be put together" celebrates the present over the past, the subjective over the objective, the personal over the positional. Indeed when everything is put together we have a total organic principle which covers all aspects of life *but* which admits of a vast range of combinations and re-combinations. This points to a very abstract or general principle from which a vast range of possibilities may be derived so that individuals can both register personal choices *and* have knowledge when a combination is not in accordance with the principle. What is taken for granted when the rule is "things must be kept apart" is *relationships* which themselves are made explicit when the rule is "things must be put together." They are made explicit by the weak classification and frames. But the latter create a form of implicit but potentially continuous surveillance and at the same time promote the making public of the self in a variety of ways. We arrive finally at the conclusion that the conditions for the release of the person are the absence of explicit hierarchy but the presence of a more intensified form of social interaction which creates continuous but invisible screening. From the point of view of the socialised they would be offering novel, spontaneous combinations.

Empirical Note

It is possible to examine the coding of objects from two perspectives. We can analyse the coding of overt or visible arrays and we can compare the code with the codings of covert or invisible arrays (e.g. drawers, cupboards, refrigerators, basements, closets, handbags, etc.). We can also compare the coding of verbal messages with the coding of non-verbal messages. It would be interesting to carry out an empirical study of standardised spaces, e.g. L.E.A. housing estate, M.C. suburban "town" house estate, modern blocks of flats, formal educational spaces which vary in their architecture and in the pedagogy.

I am well aware that the lavatory may not be seen as a space to be *specially contrived* and so subject to *special regulation* in the sense discussed. Some lavatories are not subject to the principles I have outlined. Indeed some may be casually treated spaces where pieces of newspaper may be stuffed behind a convenient pipe, where the door does not close or lock, where apparatus has low efficiency and where sound effects are taken for granted events.

ACKNOWLEDGEMENTS

This paper was written on the suggestion of Henri Nathan for a Meeting on the effects of scholarisation, itself, a part of the International Learning Sciences Programme, C.E.R.I., O.E.C.D. I am grateful to Henri Nathan for his insistence on the need to understand the artefacts of learning.

The basis of this paper was written whilst I was a visitor to the Ecole Practique des Hautes Etudes (Centre de Sociologie Europeenne under the direction of Pierre Bourdieu). I am very grateful to Peter Corbishley, graduate student in the Department of the Sociology of Education for his help in the explication of the concept of an "interrupter system." The definition used in this paper owes much to his clarification. Finally I would like to thank Gerald Elliot, Professor of Physics (Open University) who whilst in no way ultimately responsible assisted in the formal expression of an "object code."

NOTES

1. This can be seen if we examine a school class; visible pedagogies create *homogenous* learning contexts, invisible pedagogies create *differentiated* learning contexts.

2. From the production of types of discrete individuals to the production of a type of person.
3. At the secondary level invisible pedagogies are transformed into integrated codes.
4. Symbolic control is the means of cultural reproduction, in the terms of Bourdieu. What is reproduced is a function of the degree of integration within *or* conflict between the transmitting agents *and* the response of those who are subject to the transmission. What must be explored is the complex relationship between changes in the forms of production and changes in the forms of symbolic control.
5. See Samuel Bowles and Herbert Gintis, *Schooling in Capitalist America* (New York: Basic Books, 1976).
6. The basic code is elaborated. We are suggesting here that the control of the child is realised through a restricted *variant*.
7. This does *not* mean that *all* teachers wish to have the power or use it.
8. Paradoxically, this situation carries a potential for increasing competitiveness.
9. If the objects in the array can be called lexical items, then the syntax is their relationships to each other. A restricted code is a syntax with few choices: an elaborated code a syntax which generates a large number of choices.
10. The rules of reproduction of lavatory one are explicit and simple but the rules for lavatory four are more implicit and complex. Its apparent casualness is more *difficult* to reproduce.

REFERENCES

Bernstein, B., Peters, R. & Elvin, L. (1966), Ritual in Education. *Philosophical Transactions of the Royal Society,* Series B, 251, No. 772.

Bernstein, B. (1967), Open Schools, Open Society? *New Society,* Sept. 14.

Bernstein, B. (1971), *Class, Codes and Control,* Vol. I, Part III. (London, Routledge & Kegan Paul).

Bernstein, B. (1975), *Class, Codes and Control,* Vol. III (London, Routledge & Kegan Paul).

Boltanski, L. (1969), *Prime Éducation et Morale de Classe* (Paris, The Hague, Mouton).

Blyth, W. A. L. (1965), *English Primary Education,* Vol. I & II (London, Routledge & Kegan Paul).

Bourdieu, P. & Passeron, J. C. (1970), *La Reproduction; eléments pour une théorie du système d'enseignement* (Paris, Les Éditions de Minuit).

Brandis, W. & Bernstein, B. (1973), *Selection and Control: a study of teachers' ratings of infant school children* (appendix) (London, Routledge & Kegan Paul).

Cremin, L. (1961), *The Transformation of the School* (New York, Knopf).

Chamboredon, J-C. & Prevot, J. Y. (1973), Le métier d'enfant: définition sociale de la prime enfance et fonctions differentielles de l'école maternelle. Centre de Sociologie Européenne (Basic paper).

Douglas, M. (1973), *Natural Symbols,* Revised edition (London, Allan Lane).

Durkheim, E. (1933), *The Division of Labour in Society,* Transl. George Simpson (New York, Macmillan Publishing Co.).

Durkheim, E. (1938), *L'Évolution Pedagogique en France* (Paris, Alcan).

Durkheim, E. (1956), *Education and Sociology,* Transl. D. F. Pocock, chapters 2 & 3 (London, Cohen & West).

Gardner, B. (1973), *The Public Schools* (London, Hamish Hamilton).

Goldthorpe, J. & Lockwood, D. (1963), Affluence and the class structure. *Sociological Review,* vol. XI.

Green, A. G. (1972), *Theory and Practice in Infant Education, a sociological approach and case study.* M.Sc. dissertation Un. of London. Institute of Education Library (for discussion of "busyness").

Halliday, M. A. K. (1973), *Exploration in the Function of Language* (London, Edward Arnold).

Houdle, L. (1968), *An Enquiry into the Social Factors affecting the Orientation of English Infant Education since the early Nineteenth Century.* M.A. dissertation University of London Institute of Education Library. (Excellent bibliography.)

Plowden Report (1967), *Children and Their Primary Schools.* A report of the Central Advisory Council for Education (England) Vol. I (London, H.M.S.O.).

Simon, B. (Ed.) (1972), *The Radical Tradition in Education in Britain* (London, Lawrence & Wishart).

Shulman, L. S. & Kreislar, E. R. (Eds.) (1966), *Learning by Discovery; a critical appraisal* (Chicago, Rand McNally & Co.).

Stewart, W. A. C. & McCann (1967), *The Educational Innovators* (London, Macmillan).

Zoldany, M. (1935), *Die Entstehungstheorie des Geistes* (Budapest, Donau).

31. Cultural Transmission in German Higher Education in the Nineteenth Century

FRITZ K. RINGER

Perhaps because, at least since the beginning of the nineteenth century, wealth has played so great a part in class differentiation in Europe, the more indirect effects of educational differences upon the status and functions of various social groups have sometimes been underestimated. In a highly industrialized society, learning does indeed rank far below wealth among the causes of social stratification. In countries which are still passing through the early stages of industrialization, however, the situation may actually be reversed, particularly where a traditional aristocracy retains some of its privileges and where membership in the administrative elite of a bureaucratic monarchy still constitutes an important route of social advancement for non-nobles. Germany is the perfect example. What might be called the "non-entrepreneurial" or "non-economic" upper middle class was perhaps the most important and influential social group in Germany until late in the nineteenth century. Higher officials and secondary school teachers, judges and lawyers, doctors and university professors, made up an elite of the highly educated or "cultivated." These people had no more in common with the new commercial and industrial classes than they had with the Junkers. Their views on politics, on technological progress, and on socio-economic change differed markedly from all those doctrines which have been thought most typical of the entrepreneurial bourgeoisie in the Anglo-American tradition. Some of the peculiarities of modern German intellectual history would certainly seem less puzzling if they were linked with the social history and the ideology of this elite of the highly educated.

The institutional history of German higher schools and universities throws much light upon the whole situation of this "cultivated" group.[1] It was of great consequence,

for example, that learning and the learned in Germany were thoroughly integrated into the administrative systems of the several states. Most high school teachers and all but the lowest ranks of university professors were government employees, and the laws covering the rights and duties of state employees were applied to them. Like other civil servants, they owed a special loyalty to their governments. They were subject to prosecution for conduct unworthy of their position in private or in public life. The universities as well as the high schools were administered directly through the *Land* ministries of culture. In this as in other fields, Prussia set many important precedents, so that it may serve as the most telling example. From the late eighteenth century until the advent of national-socialism, the General Code of 1794 was the basic source on the legal status of Prussian educational institutions. It asserted the state's rights of supervision over the universities, although it also allowed for a certain degree of academic self-government under special corporation charters. After 1816, the statutes of the University of Berlin were the most famous, influential, and representative of these academic constitutions. Beyond that, since the nineteenth century produced no fundamental innovations in educational law, a mass of administrative precedents and ministerial regulations established the pattern of ordinary procedure. Because the bureaucracy interpreted and enforced these occasional rules, it held much of the initiative in the field of education.

The universities did retain some autonomy in purely academic matters. At each institution, the full professors elected a rector and a senate every year. Neither had anything like the powers of an American college president or faculty. A curator often acted as the chief administrative representa-

From *Journal of Contemporary History* 2 (1967): 123–138. Reprinted by permission.

tive of the ministry, and an officially appointed university judge handled important legal matters at some institutions; but the rector did at least function as a general representative and spokesman for the university, and the senate ruled in matters of academic discipline. A somewhat more important role was filled by the four faculties at every university, each of which elected a dean to a more or less secretarial position for a one-year term. The faculties were responsible for providing appropriate combinations of lectures in their fields; they helped the governments to draw up the various state examinations; they gave the purely academic degrees, and they looked after the careers of their instructors. Above all, the faculties had the initiative in the field of academic appointments. Whenever a faculty felt that it could not teach all the subjects under its jurisdiction with its regular staff, it could ask the ministry to create a new position, to which the government might then appoint a professor of its own choice. On the other hand, if an already established position, recently vacated, had simply to be filled again, the faculty could suggest three scholars, in order of preference, as candidates for the vacancy. The ministry was pledged to consider these proposals, but could also overrule them. Of 1355 men appointed to German faculties of theology, law, and medicine between 1817 and 1900, no fewer than 322 were placed against or without the faculties' recommendations.[2] Since up to three proposals were ignored in each of these cases, the governments' prerogative even in this field was clearly no mere formality. The organs of academic self-government were relatively weak, especially in the executive department, and this tended to perpetuate the states' *de facto* control over higher learning and its disciples.[3]

The intimate connection with government and with the world of the higher civil service brought considerable advantages to the German academic. He stood quite high in the system of meticulously graduated ranks, titles, and salaries which played so important a role in the German bureaucracy and in German society as a whole. Much depended, of course, upon his place within the academic hierarchy, where rank also meant a great deal. There were three principal grades of faculty members at the universities: the full professor (*ordentlicher Professor, Ordinarius*), the associate professor (*ausserordentlicher Professor, Extraordinarius*), and the instructor (*Privatdozent*). Only full professors and associate professors were salaried state officials, whereas the position of instructor entailed no more, at least in theory, than a certain scholarly accreditation and the right to give "private" lectures in return for fees paid by the listeners. At most universities before 1918, moreover, the *Ordinarien* alone had seats and votes on the faculties and elected the deans, rectors, and senators. These distinctions and restrictions did not help the cause of academic self-government, especially as the disenfranchised teachers below the rank of full professor came to make up an ever larger segment of the faculty during the later nineteenth century.[4] The universities were certainly not democratic enclaves within the rigidly stratified administrative system of the bureaucratic monarchy. Indeed, professorial positions were officially related to the ranks of non-academic civil servants. Full professors were the equals of Councillors of State, Fourth or even Third Class; rectors ranked with Councillors of State, Second Class; associate professors and many secondary teachers were grouped with Councillors of State, Fifth Class. Thus the top of the academic hierarchy came fairly close to the ministerial level in the pyramid of the bureaucracy. In addition, especially distinguished scholars were often given the title of *Geheimrat*; some were actually ennobled. Needless to say, the authorities tended to reserve these special honours for men who had not been radically critical of the social and political status quo.

The income of a German university professor was derived from two sources. He had a basic salary from the ministry; in addition, students paid fees when enrolling in his "private" lectures or after passing important qualifying examinations with him, and these earnings were transmitted to him by the government. During the nineteenth century, as enrolment increased and the distinction between "private" and unremunerated "public" lectures lost much of its original meaning, men who "privately" taught basic courses in popular fields could earn huge amounts from students' fees. As a result, regular salaries declined in relative importance, and differences between the incomes of professors became disturbingly large. Towards the end of the century, instructors earned some 1500 Marks a year, while associate professors and higher-ranking secondary teachers earned around 5000, which was apparently a satisfactory income. Full professors had anywhere from 6000 to over 40,000 Marks a year, the average for 502 Prussian *Ordinarien* around 1900 being 12,000 Marks. The Prussian elementary teacher's salary was about 1500 a year. If that was a subsistence income, then the *Ordinarien* were quite wealthy, and those popular professors who earned 40,000 Marks or more were to be numbered among the very rich. In any case, it was apparently not absurd in those days to compare the financial position of German academics with that of successful lawyers, doctors, and businessmen.

Of course it is difficult to estimate the social status of any group. Information about income, ranks, and titles is only tangentially relevant, since attributed social honour is based largely upon intangibles: traditions, values, and mental habits. Fully to explain the prestige of the academic elite in nineteenth-century Germany, one must look to such imponderables as integration into the higher civil service and "nearness to the throne." It could be shown that the persistent emphasis upon personal "cultivation" (*Bildung*) in the German intellectual heritage was itself an agent of social stratifi-

cation. Study of the classics was held to be particularly productive of cultivation, and disinterested learning was thought to affect the whole person, not just the intellect, of the learner. These tenets originated in the great period of German neo-humanism and Idealism, when they reflected the genuine aspirations of a small aristocracy of the spirit. By the end of the nineteenth century they had become worn with age and constant use; but this only enhanced their efficacy as rationalizations of social privilege.

However one chooses to handle these ideological and traditional factors in German class differentiation, one cannot overlook them. There is too much evidence that to be certified as highly learned in nineteenth-century Germany was to be accorded a great deal of formal respect. In the 1840s, we are told, even teachers in the classical secondary schools married the offspring "of the most highly regarded families from within the civil service, the daughters of generals, of councillors of state, of provincial government presidents or directors."[5] The proud wife of an impoverished university instructor was still a *Frau Doktor,* and this meant something. The attitude of the cultivated towards the newly wealthy, who were sometimes portrayed as attempting to "climb" into academic circles, was reminiscent of the relationship between nobles and bourgeois financiers in eighteenth-century France.

Within the teaching profession, a sharp line of social demarcation separated primary school teachers from their colleagues at the high schools and universities. As late as 1920, an American educator was shocked by the obvious strength and importance of this barrier, which was only partly based on differences of salary and rank;[6] more important was the traditional distinction between merely practical education and "cultivation." Indeed, the very structure of the educational system reflected this distinction, for German schools were divided into two almost totally unrelated compartments. Throughout the nineteenth century, the vast majority of German children went to school for only eight years and spent all those years in the so-called *Volksschulen* (primary schools). There they were prepared for "the practical duties of everyday life" under a regime of the most rigorous discipline. They were not expected to seek the luxury of a secondary education. Some of them did go on to vocational schools or to six-year preparatory institutes or seminars for primary teachers. A very few of them might even move on to one of the less exclusive secondary institutions, but almost none of them ever reached a fully accredited secondary school or a university. Since even their teachers came from the preparatory institutes and not from the regular institutions of higher learning, the separation of popular and practical education from cultivation was quite complete.[7]

The most important German secondary school of the nineteenth century was the *Gymnasium* (grammar school).[8] It took most of its pupils from private preparatory schools at the age of nine or ten, although it also drew to some extent on the lower classes of the *Volksschulen.* Its standardized nine-year curriculum emphasized the classics. Next to the *Gymnasium,* a group of secondary schools had grown up during the nineteenth century which concentrated on mathematics, the natural sciences, and modern languages. Around 1890, the *Oberrealschulen* were the most characteristic of these modern institutions, while the more highly accredited *Realgymnasium* represented a compromise between the classicism of the *Gymnasium* and the modern curriculum of the *Oberrealschule.* Beginning in 1870, these two types of school were able gradually to improve their standing and accreditation. Until the end of the nineteenth century, however, the *Gymnasium* was the chief beneficiary of a system of official examinations and "privileges" (*Berechtigungen*) which played an immensely important role in German higher education and, indirectly, in the whole organization of German society.

A "privilege" was a right earned upon the completion of a specified curriculum. As of 1890, six years successfully spent at any secondary school brought the privilege of a shortened military obligation as a one-year volunteer, rather than as a routine conscript. Entry into the Prussian forestry department or building institute, the right to become a higher official in the postal service or to enter the provincial bureaucracy on a certain rank level—all these were privileges granted to those with a certified minimum educational background. It was a peculiarity of the system that the state, rather than the schools or universities, administered the most important examinations upon which the assigning of privileges was based. The secondary schools tested and graded their pupils regularly; but a student had only to pass the nine-year curriculum in order to be admitted to the examination for the *Abitur.* This examination was set and supervised by the authorities. In Prussia after 1832 it was possible to take a modified *Abitur* examination at one of the more highly accredited modern secondary schools, but no significant privileges were associated with the nonclassical certificate of graduation. Until late in the nineteenth century, the term *Abitur* therefore referred essentially to the *Gymnasium* examination alone, and the classically educated had a monopoly of all important privileges. Even rather minor posts in the civil service were often restricted to those who had passed the *Gymnasium Abitur.*

After 1834, the German universities gave no entrance examinations, and neither supervised their students' programmes of study, nor tested and graded their class performance. They were obliged to enrol anyone who had the classical *Abitur,* and only rarely accepted those without it. Once registered, however, a student could prepare himself in whatever way he chose for the next step along the road of examinations and privileges. Usually, his first concern was to pass one of the standard state examinations and thus to earn the official diploma in his field of study. As might be expected, admission to the state examination in a given subject was itself an important privilege. Even matriculation at a university was of little use, from a practical or professional point of view, unless it was coupled with the right to take a state examination. That right, however, was commonly reserved to those who had already earned the classical *Abitur,* who had been registered at a university for a minimum of three to five years, and who had signed up and paid fees for certain practically obligatory courses in their subject. There were two purely academic degrees: the doctorate and the *venia legendi.* With the latter and higher of these two degrees, a man was qualified (*habilitiert*) to lecture at a university, and both degrees were conferred by the university faculties alone. Although students in most fields worked for their diplomas before deciding whether or not to go on to the doctorate, there was no formal relationship at all between the academic degrees and the state examinations. The latter were established and administered by whatever ministry was concerned with the qualification to be tested, although the competent university faculties were certainly consulted.

Needless to say, *Gymnasium* graduates were freely admitted to all types of tests in all subjects. Not so the scholars of the modern secondary schools. Until 1870, they were excluded from all state examinations, even if they succeeded in matriculating at a university through special arrangements. After 1870, they could take the government tests for secondary school instructors of modern languages, mathematics, and the natural sciences; but until 1886 even this concession was limited by the further provision that they could teach these subjects only at the modern schools. It was not until 1900 that really thorough reforms were begun. In the meantime, those leaving modern secondary schools were fortunate to have an additional outlet for their talents at the so-called technical institutes (*Technische Hochschulen*). These had their earliest antecedents in the eighteenth century, but even the economic and technological advances of the 1830s and 1840s brought them only minor gains in enrolment and accreditation. By the mid-1860s, however, they were ready to begin a long and difficult battle for academic standing. Graduating from their earlier status of advanced vocational schools, they began to call themselves "polytechnical" and finally "technical" institutes, while simultaneously attempting to move towards something like equality with the universities. They fought as natural allies of the modern schools and, like the latter, met considerable opposition from the traditional champions of pure and impractical learning. Until late in the century, the technical institutes could not give doctoral degrees, and even in their areas of specialization the system of privileges was only very slowly extended in their favour. In 1878, graduates of the *Oberrealschulen* who went on to the technical institutes to study construction and machine building had been admitted to the state examinations and positions in these subjects. In 1886, however, this privilege was withdrawn, because state officials in the field of construction and machine building protested that the status of their calling would be lowered by the admission of graduates from the modern schools.[9]

It is significant that the development of the state examination system was always intimately connected with the evolution of the German bureaucracy. Indeed, the decisive decades around 1800 produced not only the Prussian General Code and the statutes of Berlin University but also the introduction of the classical *Abitur,* the consequent separation of the privileged *Gymnasium* from the existing secondary schools of a more popular and vocational stamp, the requirement of university training for secondary school teachers, the setting of state examinations for this purpose, the establishment of educational standards for various departments and ranks of the higher civil service, and the introduction of legal tenure for qualified government officials.[10] The chronological convergence of these developments was anything but accidental, and yet the requirements of the German bureaucracy alone do not suffice to account for the growing importance of the state examinations during the nineteenth century. One must remember that a student's certified training as a public forester or building inspector could be useful to him even when looking for employment outside the civil service. Governments needed not only trained lawyers, but also health officials, postal clerks, chemistry teachers, railroad engineers, and other white-collar specialists. Moreover, the authorities were naturally interested in maintaining standards in such fields as pharmacy and construction. As a result, there was hardly an area or discipline for which some sort of state examination was not eventually devised. In an economic environment in which opportunities for the self-made man without formal training were relatively scarce, the diploma offered a certain security. Thus the free and learned professions absorbed much of the available middle-class talent, and a species of private officials grew up side by side with the regular civil service. One is tempted to speak of a "social fusion" in which the administrative and higher professional classes were drawn together. The officials contributed aristocratic and bureaucratic values, but it was the academic ideology of "cultivation" which provided the most important bond between the various elements of the alliance. Institutionally, the universities were the foci of the whole system of examinations and privileges; intellectually, they took the lead in elaborating and disseminating a learned tradition which justified and maintained the elite's internal coherence.

In 1885, when the population of Germany stood near 47 million and around 7.5 million children were attending the *Volksschulen,* the total enrolment for all types of German secondary schools was only 238,000. Attendance had reached 27,000 at the universities, somewhat more than 2500 at the technical institutes, and fewer than 1950 at the academies of forestry, mining, veterinary science,

and agriculture.[11] Progress in primary education had apparently been remarkable; practically all German children were being taught to read and write.[12] For every 10,000 inhabitants, however, there were only about 50 secondary school students, and the ratio of primary to secondary school pupils was more than 30 to 1.

Differences of income undoubtedly had something to do with this abrupt narrowing of the educational pyramid. The cost of a complete higher education, not counting the customary course in a private preparatory school, was between 4000 and 8000 Marks.[13] This was a significant amount, and yet the institutional and cultural barriers between primary and secondary schools were probably more important than the financial ones; it was in fact virtually impossible to transfer from the higher classes of the *Volksschule* to a higher school. For most children, given the institution of the preparatory schools, even the road from the lowest grades of the *Volksschule* to the high schools was blocked. Moreover, a tradesman who wished to give his son a good education might naturally be inclined to begin with a modern school. But even if the youngster then showed real promise along this route, it was still almost impossible for him to get to a university. In short, parents and teachers were forced to make essentially permanent educational plans for five-year old children, and this in the absence of aptitude tests. Inevitably, a "cultivated" family background often became the actual measure of the capacity for cultivation. The *Volksschulen* were almost exclusively lower-class institutions. Primary teachers ordinarily came from the lower and lower-middle classes. The discontinuities within the educational system became rifts in the social fabric.

Of the 238,000 young people who attended German secondary schools in 1885, more than 133,000 were enrolled in Prussian schools. Of these, 84,300 were at a *Gymnasium*; 24,700 at a *Realgymnasium*; 5100 attended an *Oberrealschule,* and another 19,100 went to even less highly accredited modern schools. Of the 4173 Prussian students who passed their *Abitur* in 1885, 3567 received the cherished certificate from the *Gymnasium;* 574 from a *Realgymnasium,* and 32 from an *Oberrealschule.* Of the 3147 graduates who went on to a university, 2963 were from a *Gymnasium,* 184 from a *Realgymnasium,* and none from an *Oberrealschule.* For every 10,000 inhabitants of Prussia, 48 students attended a Prussian secondary school; 30 went to a *Gymnasium;* less than 1.5 received an *Abitur.*

These figures point up the special position of the classical *Gymnasium.* Over 85 per cent of the *Abitur* certificates went to *Gymnasium* students; about 83 per cent of those who received an *Abitur* from the *Gymnasium* chose to attend a university. An independent survey of all Prussian recipients of the *Abitur* between 1875 and 1899 showed that 83 per cent held their certificate from the *Gymnasium,* and 77 per cent of these went on to the university, whereas only 29.6 per cent of the *Realgymnasium* graduates and 20.5 per cent of the *Oberrealschule* graduates chose to continue their studies in this way.[14] Of the students at Prussian universities between 1887 and 1890, 85.2 per cent came from a *Gymnasium,* 6.7 per cent had the *Abitur* from a modern secondary school, 8.1 per cent were enrolled without an *Abitur,* under special provisions and with severely limited privileges.[15]

Given the organizational barriers which separated the *Gymnasium* from the rest of the secondary school system, one begins to appreciate how minute a proportion of the German population had access to the traditional learning and to the privileges which were its rewards. At the same time, it is not enough to say that the German school system was undemocratic or that it provided insufficient opportunities for talent from the lower classes. The obstacles to a vertical integration of society were perhaps less significant in some respects than the lines which separated industrial and commercial from professional and bureaucratic elements

within the upper as well as within the middle and lower classes. The rigid compartmentalization of higher education, the conflict between classicism and modernism, and the anachronistic predominance of the *Gymnasium,* tended to maintain such a division at all social levels. During the later nineteenth century, Germany was very rapidly becoming one of the most highly industrialized nations in the world, and yet the advance of modern subjects in secondary education was extraordinarily slow. Perhaps some of the students who left the secondary schools before the *Abitur* were willing and able to move into commerce and industry; but among the 1026 Prussian secondary school graduates in 1885 who did not plan to attend a university, only 18 per cent chose agriculture, commerce, or industry.[16] Almost all the rest opted for military careers or for the civil service. Even on this level, the close connection between higher education and government asserted itself, and learning remained relatively isolated from the private and productive sector of the economy.

Statistics on the family background of German university students suggest that the elite of the highly educated recruited itself to a remarkable extent from its own offspring.[17] Nearly 60 per cent of Württemberg *Gymnasium* graduates enrolled at the University of Tübingen in the 1840s had fathers who were educated at a university. For 1873–7, the corresponding figure was only slightly less. As the century progressed, new groups did increase their representation at the institutions of higher learning. The percentage of academically trained fathers at the University of Halle, which had been 55.4 from 1761 to 1778, fell to 33.5 by 1877–81, and the corresponding figures for all Prussian universities were down to 27 in 1899/1900 and 25.7 in 1902/03. Officials and lawyers continued to be well represented. Nearly 40 per cent of the pupils in Bavarian *Gymnasien* and *Realgymnasien* between 1869 and 1871 were the sons of officials; at the turn of the century, Prussian law students still came from more highly educated families than did university students as a whole, and 60 per cent of officials' sons chose to follow their fathers' careers. Traditionally, Protestant faculties of theology were even more closely connected with the academic classes than the lawyers. As late as 1900, about 40 per cent of students of Protestant theology at Prussian universities were sons of university men. The corresponding figure for Tübingen during the 1840s was almost 65 per cent. The field of Catholic theology, on the other hand, was one of the main channels of social mobility. The relevant indicator, the percentage of academically educated fathers, was 3 for Tübingen in the 1840s and about 4 for all Prussian universities around 1900. This may help to explain, incidentally, why German Catholicism has sometimes appeared socially more progressive and politically more democratic than German Protestantism. Finally, as might be expected, the modernizing movement in secondary education received much of its support from the non-academic classes. Statistics on the family background of Prussian secondary school graduates from 1875 to 1899 show that 21.5 per cent of the fathers were university men in the case of the *Gymnasien,* 7 per cent in the case of the *Realgymnasien,* and only 4 per cent in the case of the *Oberrealschulen.* Obviously, new social groups were rapidly increasing their rate of entry into the academic elite during the closing decades of the nineteenth century. University attendance itself grew from 13,000 in 1871 and 21,000 in 1880, to just under 34,000 in 1900. Nonetheless, as late as 1899/1900, 27 per cent of Prussian students of all faculties were still the sons of university men. This meant something in a nation which in 1895 had an academic enrolment of 28,500 for a total population of over 52 million. It was a minute fraction of the population, after all, which still supplied over a quarter of its own replacements, despite the rapidly expanding demand for academic certification.

Of the students at Prussian universities between 1887 and 1890, little more than one in a thousand were the sons of work-

ers.[18] Rather more than one in ten were the sons of high officials, judges and lawyers with full academic education, university professors, academically trained secondary school teachers, and higher army officers. Seven per cent of the fathers were clergymen and theologians; five per cent were doctors and apothecaries. Almost a quarter were middle and lower ranking state officials and teachers without full university educations; another 2 per cent were owners of large estates, and 12.7 per cent were independent farmers. That left slightly less than a third of the fathers in the remaining categories of "merchants" (17.3 per cent) and "industrialists" (15.6 per cent). Under these two labels, statisticians lumped together the whole productive sector of the middle and lower-middle classes, feeling perhaps that there was no *essential* difference between a steel manufacturer and a provincial tanner. After 1900, more careful distinctions were made, and we have the following percentage figures on the occupations of fathers of Prussian university students for the academic year 1902/3:[19]

1) Officers, military officials and
   military doctors   1.9
2) High government officials,
   judges and lawyers with
   university education   6.1
3) Teachers with university education   4.5
4) Clergy and theologians   5.8
5) Doctors, veterinarians and apothecaries   5.0
6) Teachers without university edu-
   cations, middle and lower officials
   without academic training,
   low-ranking officers (*Unter-
   offiziere*)   22.6
7) Rentiers   0.6
8) Large landowners, lessees of domain
   lands, stewards on great estates   5.2
9) Independent farmers   6.3
10) Entrepreneurs, owners, and senior
    employees in manufacturing,
    transport, commerce, finance,
    publishing, and insurance   9.7
11) Small independent merchants,

shopkeepers, innkeepers, tradesmen, and artisans 26.3
12) Middle and lower-level supervisory
and clerical personnel in industry,
commerce, transport, insurance 2.3
13) Workers and "other helpers"
(all sectors) 1.0
14) Other occupations, or none given 2.6

Categories 1, 2, 3, and 6, give a figure of 35.1 per cent for government and the government-controlled sector of education, certainly a high fraction of the total; the first five categories show 23.3 per cent for the "non-economic" upper-middle class, the academic elite in the narrow sense of the term. While the offspring of the large landed proprietors and of high government officials tended to favour the study of law as a preparation for the civil service, there was a disproportionately large number of farmers' sons in the Catholic theological faculties. The lower and working classes still added only an insignificant fraction to the university population. Above all, the business community was not well represented. The figure of 9.7 per cent in category 10 seems surprisingly low, particularly since white-collar employees, the "new middle class," made a very poor showing in category 12. Thus large-scale industry, commerce, finance, and transportation, the most progressive sectors of the economy, had relatively little contact with the universities. The older elements of the middle and lower-middle classes, the independent artisans and shopkeepers, did somewhat better; but even their 26.3 per cent was almost matched by the 22.6 per cent of the middle and lower officials and teachers. The composition of the academic elite was undoubtedly changing, absorbing elements from the lower-middle classes. But on this as on every other level of the social hierarchy, the newcomers stemmed surprisingly often from the older, "non-economic" or at least non-industrial sectors of society.

This general conclusion applies even more strongly to the entrants into the academic profession itself. Among those who were

habilitiert to lecture at German universities between 1860 and 1889, no less than 65 per cent were the sons of higher officials, professors, and academically educated professions;[20] more than 7 per cent were the sons of lower officials and teachers; 6.1 per cent of landowners and farmers. Only 5.8 per cent of the fathers were owners, managers, or senior employees in industry, commerce, transport, finance, and insurance. Given these figures, it is not difficult to imagine that the highly educated in late nineteenth-century Germany thought and acted as a unique social group and developed their own characteristic set of values. Both Max Weber and Friedrich Paulsen saw that

differences of education are one of the strongest . . . social barriers, especially in Germany, where almost all privileged positions inside and outside the civil service are tied to qualifications involving not only specialized knowledge but also "general cultivation," and where the whole school and university system has been put into the service of this [ideal of] general cultivation.[21]

The academically educated constitute a kind of intellectual and spiritual aristocracy in Germany . . . They form something like an official nobility, as indeed they all participate in the government and administration of the state . . . Together, they make up a homogeneous segment of society; they simply recognize each other as social equals on the basis of their academic cultivation . . . Conversely, anyone in Germany who has no academic education lacks something which wealth and high birth cannot fully replace. The merchant, the banker, the rich manufacturer or even the great landowner, no matter how well he stands in other respects, will occasionally be harmed by his lack of academic training. As a consequence, the acquisition of a university education has become a sort of social necessity with us, or at least the acquisition of the *Abitur,* the potential right of academic citizenship.[22]

NOTES

1. Cf. Friedrich Paulsen, *Geschichte des gelehrten Unterrichts auf den deutschen Schulen und Univer-*

sitäten, vol. II (Berlin, 1921); Wilhelm Lexis, ed., *Die deutschen Universitäten*, 2 vols. (Berlin, 1893); Wilhelm Lexis, ed., *Das Unterrichtswesen im Deutschen Reich*, 4 vols. (Berlin, 1904); Arnold Köttgen, *Deutsches Universitätsrecht* (Tübingen, 1933); Conrad Bornhak, *Die Rechtsverhältnisse der Hochschullehrer in Preussen* (Berlin, 1901); Erich Wende, *Grundlagen des preussischen Hochschulrechts* (Berlin, 1930).

2. Friedrich Paulsen, *Die deutschen Universitäten und das Universitätsstudium* (Berlin, 1902), p. 101.

3. Ludwig Bernhard, *Akademische Selbstverwaltung in Frankreich und Deutschland: Ein Beitrag zur Universitätsreform* (Berlin, 1930).

4. Franz Eulenburg, *Der 'akademische Nachwuchs': Eine Untersuchung über die Lage und die Aufgaben der Extraordinarien und Privatdozenten* (Leipzig, 1908); Alexander Busch, *Die Geschichte des Privatdozenten* (Stuttgart, 1959).

5. Paulsen, *Geschichte des Unterrichts*, vol. II, p. 390.

6. Thomas Alexander, *The Training of Elementary Teachers in Germany* (New York, 1929), pp. 10–11.

7. Lexis, *Unterrichtswesen*, vol. III; Carl H. Becker, *Secondary Education and Teacher Training in Germany* (New York, 1931), pp. 5–8; Alexander, *Training of Teachers*, pp. 6–10.

8. Lexis, *Unterrichtswesen*, vol. II; W. Lexis, ed., *Die Reform des höheren Schulwesens in Preussen* (Halle, 1902).

9. Lexis, *Reform*, p. 16.

10. Ibid., pp. 1–6; Paulsen, *Geschichte des Unterrichts*, vol. II, pp. 283–95; Franz Schnabel, *Deutsche Geschichte im neunzehnten Jahrhundert*, vol. I, 4th ed. (Freiburg, 1948), pp. 408–57, vol. II, 2nd ed. (Freiburg, 1949), pp. 198–9; Hans Rosenberg, *Bureaucracy, Aristocracy and Autocracy: The Prussian Experience 1660–1815* (Cambridge, Mass., 1958), pp. 202–28.

11. *Statistisches Jahrbuch für das Deutsche Reich*, 1903, pp. 2, 208 (figure of 7.5 million my estimate on that basis). School enrolment computed from Lexis, *Unterrichtswesen*, vol. II, pp. 178–213; Michael Doeberl, Otto Scheel, et al., *Das akademische Deutschland*, vol. III (Berlin, 1930), p. 319.

12. J. Conrad, *Das Universitätsstudium in Deutschland während der letzten 50 Jahre* (Jena, 1884), p. 181.

13. Including rough but conservative estimates of living expenses while at the university: Adolf Beier, ed., *Die höheren Schulen in Preussen und ihre Lehrer*, 3rd ed. (Halle, 1909), p. 1170; Lexis, *Universitäten*, vol. I, pp. 162–4.

14. Wilhelm Ruppel, *Über die Berufswahl der Abiturienten Preussens in den Jahren 1875–1899* (Fulda, 1904), pp. 8, 11.

15. Lexis, *Universitäten*, vol. I, p. 127.

16. Lexis, *Reform*, p. 416.

17. Conrad, *Universitätsstudium*, pp. 49–50; J. Conrad, "Einige Ergebnisse der deutschen Universitätsstatistik," *Jahrbücher für Nationalökonomie und Statistik* (Jena, 1906), p. 448; *Preussische Statistik* (Berlin, 1908), p. 147 of text; Ruppel, *Berufswahl*, p. 30; Doeberl, *Das akademische Deutschland*, vol. III, p. 319.

18. Lexis, *Universitäten*, vol. I, pp. 140–1.

19. Calculations based on *Preussische Statistik*, vol. 204, pp. 154–5 of text. Professors divided among categories 2–5.

20. Helmuth Plessner, ed., *Untersuchungen zur Lage der deutschen Hochschullehrer*, vol. III (Göttingen, 1956), p. 177.

21. Max Weber, *Gesammelte politische Schriften*, 2nd ed. (Tübingen, 1958), pp. 235–6.

22. Paulsen, *Universitäten*, pp. 149–50.

32. The Contribution of Schooling to the Learning of Norms

ROBERT DREEBEN

INDEPENDENCE

One answer to the question, "What is learned in school?" is that pupils learn to acknowledge that there are tasks they must do alone, and to do them that way. Along with this self-imposed obligation goes the idea that others have a legitimate right to expect such independent behavior under certain circumstances.[1] Independence has a widely acknowledged though not unequivocal meaning. In using it here I refer to a cluster of meanings: doing things on one's own, being self-reliant, accepting personal responsibility for one's behavior, acting self-sufficiently,[2] and handling tasks with which, *under different circumstances*, one can rightfully expect the help of others. The pupil, when in school, is separated from family members who have customarily provided help, support, and sustenance, persons on whom he has long been dependent.

This chapter first appeared as Chapter 5 (pp. 63–90) in *On What Is Learned in School* (Addison-Wesley, 1968). We have extracted pp. 66–73 for reproduction here. Reprinted by permission of the publisher.

A constellation of classroom characteristics, teacher actions, and pupil actions shape experiences in which the norm of independence is learned. In addition to the fact that school children are removed from persons with whom they have already formed strong relationships of dependency, the sheer size of a classroom assemblage limits each pupil's claim to personal contact with the teacher, and more so at the secondary levels than at the elementary. This numerical property of classrooms reduces pupils' opportunities for establishing new relationships of dependency with adults and for receiving help from them.

Parents expect their children to act independently in many situations, but teachers are more systematic in expecting pupils to adhere to standards of independence in performing academic tasks. There are at least two additional aspects of classroom operation that bear directly on learning the norm of independence: rules about cheating and formal testing. Let us consider cheating first. The word itself is condemnatory in its reference to illegal and immoral acts. Most commonly, attention turns to how much cheating occurs, who cheats, and why. But these questions, while of great importance elsewhere, are of no concern here. My interest is in a different problem: to what types of conduct is the pejorative "cheating" assigned?

In school, cheating pertains primarily to instructional activities and usually refers to acts in which two or more parties participate when the unaided action of only one is expected. Illegal or immoral acts such as stealing and vandalism, whether carried out by individuals or groups, are not considered cheating because they have no direct connection with the central academic core of school activities. Nor is joint participation categorically proscribed; joint effort is called cooperation or collusion depending on the teacher's prior definition of the task.

Cheating takes many forms, most of which involve collective effort. A parent and a child may collaborate to produce homework; two pupils can pool their wisdom (or

ignorance, as the case may be) in the interest of passing an examination. In both cases the parties join deliberately, although deliberateness is not essential to the definition; one pupil can copy from another without the latter knowing. In the case of plagiarism, of course, the second party is not a person at all, but information compiled by another. The use of crib notes, perhaps a limiting case, involves no collusion; it consists, rather, of an illegitimate form of help. These are the main forms of school cheating, but there are many variations, routine to exotic. Thus actions called cheating are those closely tied to the instructional goals of the school and usually involve assisted performance when unaided performance is expected. As one observer put it: Pupils "... *must learn to distinguish between cooperating and cheating.*"[3]

The irony of cheating *in school* is that the same kinds of acts are considered morally acceptable and even commendable in other situations. It is praiseworthy for one friend to assist another in distress, or for a parent to help a child; and if one lacks the information to do a job, the resourceful thing is to look it up. In effect, many school activities called cheating are the customary forms of support and assistance in the family and among friends.

In one obvious sense, school rules against cheating are designed to establish the content of moral standards. In another sense, the school attaches the stigma of immorality to certain types of behavior for social as distinct from ethical reasons; namely, to change the character of prevailing social relationships in which children are involved. In the case of homework, the school, in effect, attempts to redefine the relationship between parents and children by proscribing one kind of parental support, which is not a problem in other circumstances. The teacher has no direct control over parents but tries to influence them at a distance by asking their adherence to a principle clothed in moral language whose violations are punishable. The line between legitimate parental support (encouraged when it takes the form of parents stressing the importance of school and urging their children to do well) and collusion is unclear, but by morally proscribing parental intervention beyond a certain point, the teacher attempts to limit the child's dependence on family members in doing his school work. In other words, he expects the pupil to work independently. The same argument applies to pupils and their friends; the teacher attempts to eliminate those parts of friendship that make it difficult or impossible for him to discover what a pupil can do on his own. In relationships with kin and friends, the customary sources of support in times of adversity, the school intervenes by restricting solidarity and, in the process, determines what the pupil can accomplish unaided. The pupil, for his part, discovers which of his actions he is held accountable for individually within the confines of tasks set by the school.

This argument is indirectly supported by the comparison between schooling and the occupational employment for which school is intended as preparation. The question here is the sense in which school experience is preparatory. Usually workers are not restricted in seeking help on problems confronting them; on the contrary, many occupations provide resources specifically intended to be helpful: arrangements for consultation, libraries, access to more experienced colleagues, and so on. Only in rare situations are people expected not to enlist the aid of family and friends in matters pertaining to work where that aid is appropriate. In other words, activities on the job, directly analogous to school work, do not carry comparable restrictions. However, people in their occupational activities are required to accept individual responsibility and accountability for the performance of assigned and self-initiated tasks. To the extent that the school contributes to the development of independence, the preparation lies more in the development of a psychological disposition to act independently than to perform a certain range of tasks without help.

Second, as to testing, and particularly the use of achievement tests; most important for independence are the social conditions designed for the *administration* of tests, not their content or format. By and large, pupils are tested under more or less rigorously controlled conditions. At one end of the spectrum, formal standardized tests are administered most stringently; pupils are physically separated, and the testing room is patrolled by proctors whose job is to discover contraband and to guarantee that no communication occurs, these arrangements being designed so that each examination paper represents independent work. At the other end, some testing situations are more informal, less elaborately staged, although there is almost always some provision to ensure that each pupil's work represents the product of only his own efforts.

Testing represents an approach to establishing the norm of independence, which is different from the proscription against cheating even though both are designed to reduce the likelihood of joint effort. Whereas the rules against cheating are directed toward delineating the form of appropriate behavior, the restrictions built into the testing situation provide physical constraints intended to guarantee that teachers will receive samples of the work pupils do unassisted. Actually, unless they stipulate otherwise, teachers expect pupils to do most of their everyday work by themselves; daily assignments provide the opportunities for and practice in independent work. Tests, because they occur at less frequent intervals than ordinary assignments, cannot provide comparably frequent opportunities; by the elaborate trappings of their administration, particularly with college entrance exams, and the anxiety they provoke, they symbolize the magnitude of the stakes.

It may be objected that in emphasizing independence I have ignored cooperation, since an important item on the school agenda is the instruction of pupils in the skills of working with others. Teachers do assign work to groups and expect a collaborative product, and to this extent they require the subordination of individual to collective efforts, but judging the product according to collective standards is another question.

To evaluate the contribution of each member of a working team, the teacher must either judge the quality of each one's work, in effect relying on the standard of independence, or rate each contribution according to the quality of the total product. The latter procedure rests on the assumption that each member has contributed equally, an untenable assumption if one member has carried the rest or if a few members have carried a weak sister. That occurrences of this kind are usually considered "unfair" suggests the normative priority of independence and the simple fact of life in industrial societies; i.e., that institutions of higher learning and employers want to know how well each person can do and put constraints on the schools in order to find out. Thus, although the school provides opportunities for pupils to gain experience in cooperative situations, in the last analysis it is the individual assessment that counts.

ACHIEVEMENT

Pupils come to accept the premise that they should perform their tasks the best they can, and act accordingly. The concept of achievement, like independence, has several referents. It usually denotes activity and mastery, making an impact on the environment rather than fatalistically accepting it, and competing against some standard of excellence. Analytically, the concept should be distinguished from independence, since, among other differences, achievement criteria can apply to activities performed collectively.

Much of the recent literature treats achievement in the context of child-rearing within the family as if achievement motiva-tion were primarily a product of parental behavior.[4] Even though there is reason to believe that early childhood experiences in the family do contribute to its development, classroom experiences also contribute through teachers' use of resources beyond those ordinarily at the command of family members.

Classrooms are organized around a set of core activities in which a teacher assigns tasks to pupils and evaluates and compares the quality of their work. In the course of time, pupils differentiate themselves according to how well they perform a variety of tasks, most of which require the use of symbolic skills. Achievement standards are not limited in applicability to the classroom nor is their content restricted to the cognitive areas. Schools afford opportunities for participation in a variety of extra-curricular activities, most conspicuously athletics, but also music, dramatics, and a bewildering array of club and small group activities serving individual interests and talents.

The direct relevance of classroom work in providing task experience judged by achievement criteria is almost self-evident; the experience is built into the assignment-performance-evaluation sequence of the work. Less evident, however, is the fact that these activities force pupils to cope with various degrees of success and failure, both of which can be psychologically problematic. Consistently successful performance requires that pupils deal with the consequences of their own excellence in a context of peer equality in nonacademic areas. For example, they confront the dilemma inherent in having surpassed their age-mates in some respects while depending on their friendship and support in others, particularly in out-of-school social activities. The classroom provides not only the achievement experience itself but by-products of it, taking the form of the dilemma just described.

Similarly, pupils whose work is consistently poor not only must participate in achievement activities leading to their failure, they must also experience living with that failure. They adopt various modes of coping with this, most of which center around maintaining personal self-respect in the face of continuing assaults upon it. Probably a minority succeed or fail consistently; a majority, most likely, do neither one consistently, but nonetheless worry about not doing well. Schooling, then, assures most pupils the experiences of both winning and losing, and to the extent that they gain some modicum of gratification from academic activities, it teaches them to approach their work in a frame of mind conducive to achievement. At the same time they learn how to cope, in a variety of ways and more or less well, with success and failure.

Failure is perhaps the more difficult condition with which to cope because it requires acknowledgment that the premise of achievement, to which failure itself can be attributed in part, is a legitimate principle by which to govern one's actions. Yet situations that constrain people to live with personal failure are endemic to industrial societies in which many facets of public life are based on achievement principles; political defeat and occupational non-promotion being two cases in point.

As suggested earlier, the school provides a broad range of experiences other than those restricted to the classroom and academic in nature; these experiences are also based on achievement criteria but differ in several important respects. Alternatives to academic performance give the pupil a chance to succeed in achievement-oriented activities even though he may not be able to do well in the classroom.

How these alternative activities differ from those of the classroom is as important as the fact that they do so differ, as evidenced by the case of athletics. Competitive sports resemble classroom activities in that both provide participants with the chance to demonstrate individual excellence. However, the former—and this is more true of team than individual sports—permit collective responsibility for defeat, whereas the latter by and large allow only individual responsibility for failure. That is to say, the chances of receiving personal gratification for success are at least as great in sports as in the classroom, while the assault on personal self-respect for failure is potentially less intense. Athletics should not be written off as a manifestation of mere adolescent nonintellectualism, as recent writers have treated it.[5] I do not suggest that athletics has an as yet undiscovered intellectual richness; rather that its contribution should not be viewed simply in terms of intellectuality. Wilkinson, in talking about athletics in the British public schools, makes a similar argument, not so much in terms of mitigating the psychological consequences on achievement for individuals as in striking a balance between competition and social cooperation:

On the football field and on the river, the public school taught its boys to compete, not so much in personal contests, as in struggles between groups—between teams, houses, and schools. . . . They preserved middle-class morality and energy, but they adapted these to the needs of the public servant,[6]

so important, according to Wilkinson, in establishing the ethic that private privilege meant public duty.

A similar contention holds for music and dramatics; both provide the potentiality for individual accomplishment and recognition without the persistent, systematic, and potentially corrosive evaluation typical of the classroom. Finally, in various club activities based on interest and talent, a pupil can do the things he is good at in the company of others who share an appreciation for them. In all these situations, either the rigors of competition and judgment characteristic of the classroom are mitigated, or the activity in question has its own built-in source of support and personal protection, not to the same extent as in the family, but more than is available in the crucible of the classroom.

The school provides a wider variety of achievement experiences than does the family, but it also has fewer resources for supporting and protecting pupils' self-respect in the face of failure. As pupils proceed through successive school levels, the rigors of achievement increase, at least for those who continue along the main academic line. Moreover, at the secondary levels the number of activities governed according to achievement principles increases as does the variety of these activities. As preparation for adult public life in which the application of these principles is widespread, schooling contributes to personal development in assuring that the majority of pupils not only will have performed tasks according to the achievement standard, but that they will have had experience in an expanding number of situations in which activities are organized according to it.

NOTES

1. My emphasis here differs from Parsons' in that he views independence primarily as a personal resource: "... it may be said that the most important single predispositional factor with which the child enters the school is his level of *independence.*" (See Talcott Parsons, "The School Class as a Social System: Some of its Functions in American Society," *Harvard Educational Review* 29, No. 4, 297—318 (1959); p. 300.) Although independence is very likely such a predisposition—whether it is the most important single one is debatable—it is part of the school's agenda to further the development of independence to a point beyond the level at which family resources become inadequate to do so.

2. Winterbottom, for example, lumps independence and mastery together; the indices she uses to measure them, however, involve ostensibly different phenomena in that the mastery items refer to tendencies toward activity rather than to independence. Marian R. Winterbottom, "The Relation of Need for Achievement to Learning Experiences in Independence and Mastery," in John T. Atkinson (ed.), *Motives in Fantasy, Action, and Society,* pp. 453—478, Van Nostrand, Princeton (1958). As a definitional guideline for this discussion, I have followed the usage of Bernard C. Rosen and Roy D'Andrade, "The Psychosocial Origins of Achievement Motivation," *Sociometry* 22, No. 3, 186 (1959) in their discussion of independence training; and of McClelland and his colleagues in a study of independence training, David C. McClelland, A. Rindlisbacher, and Richard DeCharms, "Religious and Other Sources of Parental Attitudes toward Independence Training," in David C. McClelland (ed.), *Studies in Motivation,* pp. 389—397, Appleton-Century-Crofts, New York (1955).

3. Kaspar D. Naegele, "Clergymen, Teachers, and Psychiatrists: A Study in Roles and Socialization," *Canadian Journal of Economics and Political Science* 22, No. 1, 53 (1956).

4. See, for example, Marian R. Winterbottom, *ibid.*; Bernard C. Rosen and Roy D'Andrade, *op. cit.*, pp. 185—218; and Fred L. Strodtbeck, "Family Interaction, Values, and Achievement," in David C. McClelland *et al., Talent and Society,* pp. 135—191, Van Nostrand, Princeton (1958).

5. For one attempt to treat athletics condescendingly as non-intellectualism, see James S. Coleman, *The Adolescent Society,* Free Press of Glencoe, New York (1961).

6. Rupert Wilkinson, *Gentlemanly Power,* p. 21, Oxford University Press, London (1964).

VI

SOCIAL TRANSFORMATION AND EDUCATIONAL CHANGE

The process of educational reform during periods of revolutionary upheaval raises with particular sharpness the general problem of the relationship between educational and social change. For these are among the rare historical moments when the weight of existing institutions and practices lightens to permit radical experimentation in education. Revolutions do not merely make educational change possible, they require it. They *must* transform the educational system and bring it into harmony with a new institutional and ideological framework. Failure to do so may undermine the revolution, for it is the educational system that is responsible for the molding of future generations. Revolutionary leaders tend, therefore, to look upon change in education not only as an important indicator of the character of the new social order, but also as an active force for its development.

In order to demonstrate the complex interplay between educational and social change, we have chosen to examine educational reform in three great twentieth-century revolutions: those of Russia, Cuba, and China. Each dedicated to the attainment of the Marxist ideal of a classless society, they have nonetheless followed different roads in their efforts to establish a socialist educational system. Not infrequently, common hostility to capitalist educational institutions has given way to acrimonious internal debate. In the case of the Soviet Union and China, sharp divergence in educational theory and practice has led to mutual denunciation.

The Soviet Union, a center of radical experimentation in education in the decade after the Bolshevik Revolution, early adopted as its guiding principle the classical Marxist ideal of polytechnical education—the provision of general training in a wide range of technical and manual skills. The intention was to promote the development of many-sided individuals who would have both the inclination and the capacity to attenuate, and ultimately to abolish, the distinction between physical and intellectual labor. A wide variety of schemes attempting to link the schooling process to the performance of productive labor were established, and workers' faculties were introduced to prepare the children of peasants and workers for higher education. During this period of radical educational change, political consciousness and class background became important criteria for admission to Soviet universities.[1]

1. For a discussion of experimentation in education during the early years of the Soviet regime, see M.K. Whyte, "Educational Reform: China in the 1970s and Russia in the 1920s," *Comparative Education Review* 18 (February 1974): 112–128.

Despite the far-reaching changes that were transforming Soviet schools in the 1920s, there were nonetheless important constraints on the process of educational reform. Economic chaos, a legacy of World War I and of the Russian Civil War of 1918–1921, made reconstruction of the economy a pressing priority. Economic recovery, in turn, seemed to call for an educational system geared above all to the provision of technically trained manpower; this, in any case, was how Lenin, who had much to say about these matters, viewed the situation. Frederic Lilge, in a study of the educational policies favored by Lenin (Chapter 33), shows the great revolutionary leader to be rather conventional on cultural questions. Relegating the creation of the "new socialist man" to a distant future, Lenin stressed the teaching of existing knowledge and cognitive skills over political education. Already, during Lenin's lifetime, the main beneficiaries of the wider opportunities for higher education in the years immediately following the Revolution were not the offspring of proletarians and peasants, but the children of non-manual laborers.[2] In the 1930s, during the height of Stalin's push for industrialization and economic growth, the proportion of students from manual backgrounds declined still further as academic requirements for entry into higher education were raised.[3] Soviet schools have, of course, changed considerably since that time, but the character of contemporary Soviet education can be traced, Lilge suggests, to the actions and authority of Lenin himself.

In Cuba, unlike the Soviet Union, the creation of a "new socialist man" was, from the outset, perhaps the foremost educational objective of the revolutionary leadership. Martin Carnoy and Jorge Werthein argue in Chapter 34 that the changes that have occurred in Cuban educational strategy over the past fifteen years correspond quite closely to changes in the general economic strategy of the revolutionary regime. Marxist ideology, they argue, penetrates the content of education in terms of both *what* is studied and *how* it is studied. Yet the egalitarian ideological objectives of the regime may, they suggest, be in conflict with its economic strategy of rapid growth. This conflict is embodied in an ambiguous movement toward selectivity in the higher levels of the educational system—a movement that carries with it the possibility of the development of a technocratic elite. However, the Cuban leadership is aware of the contradictions inherent in a policy that, while advocating equality, permits the teaching of advanced technical knowledge to take precedence over political and cultural instruction. If the Cuban regime is to be successful in its effort to form a new socialist man, important features of Cuban education—most notably its heavy reliance on grades and exams as sources of student motivation and its generally authoritarian and teacher-centered method of instruction—may have to be modified.[4]

The transformation of education in China began in the Communist-dominated zones before the final fall of the regime of Chiang Kai-Shek. In these zones, particularly in the Yenan region, educational change was seen as a crucial instrument in the struggle to build socialist consciousness. By 1944, many of the features that have formed the basis of the "mass line" in Chinese education—emphasis on popular rather than elite education, decentralization, efforts to overcome the barriers between manual and intellectual labor, and the transfer of authority from professionals to peasants and workers—were already visible.[5]

But the "mass line," though consistently favored by Mao Tse-Tung, has not always been

2. From 1923–1924 statistics reported in David Lane, "The Impact of Revolution: The Case of Selection of Students for Higher Education in Soviet Russia, 1917–1928," *Sociology* 7 (May 1973): 241–253.
3. See Richard Dobson, "Social Status and Inequality of Access to Higher Education in the USSR" (Chapter 12 in this volume).
4. For a discussion of some of the dilemmas facing Cuban education, see Samuel Bowles, "Cuban Education and the Revolutionary Ideology," *Harvard Educational Review* 41 (November 1971): 472–500.
5. See Mark Selden, *The Yenan Way in Revolutionary China* (Cambridge, Mass.: Harvard University Press, 1971), pp. 267–276.

the guiding principle of Chinese policy. Under the influence of the Soviet model of economic development, a more moderate or "revisionist" tendency has frequently been prominent. Following the mixed results of the radical "Great Leap Forward" program of the late 1950s, a more academic and technocratic emphasis emerged as the dominant force in Chinese education. At Peking University during the period from 1960 to 1962, the proportion of students from peasant and worker families declined from 66.8 percent to 37.7 percent.[6] Though ostensibly meritocratic, the revisionist line, with its stress on the creation of elite schools, was not immune to ascriptive bias; the leading secondary schools, a small number of collective boarding institutions, were largely reserved for the children of Communist Party cadres. As Chinese education became more hierarchical, a new technocratic ethos developed among students in elite institutions.

The battle between the mass line and the revisionist line, a recurrent conflict, intensified during the "Great Proletarian Cultural Revolution." Rejection of the Soviet model of education and economic development, which Maoists viewed as inevitably leading to the creation of a privileged intellectual elite and the restoration of capitalist values and relations of production, grew clearer in the broader struggle against Liu Shao-Ch'i's revisionist and pro-Soviet policies. Much more even than in the early years of the Soviet regime, Chinese education during the Cultural Revolution rejected traditional curricula and pedagogy in search of a new system that would give adequate attention to political education. Yet if Mao's maxim, "politics in command," had a powerful influence on events during the Cultural Revolution, it would be erroneous to see the mass line as the expression of those who would stress ideological instruction at the expense of the inculcation of skills useful in production. Instead, as Marianne Bastid, one of the few Westerners present in China during the Cultural Revolution, argues in Chapter 35, the struggle to revitalize a lagging system of production was crucial in the transformation taking place in Chinese education. From the beginning, the objective of the mass line has been to train workers who are both "red" *and* "expert." Seen in this light, the objective of the Cultural Revolution in education was nothing less than to abolish the distinction between intellectual and manual labor while simultaneously promoting production.

Consideration of the problem of the role of educational reform in a general strategy of social change is not, of course, limited to revolutionary regimes. Charles Silberman, in *Crisis in the Classroom,* looks to open education on the British model as a means of restoring the shaken faith of the American public in the democratic and liberating character of schooling.[7] Christopher Jencks, in *Inequality,* reaches a conclusion that has been hotly debated in political and academic circles alike—that education is a "marginal institution" for those interested in greater economic equality.[8] And Ivan Illich, in his equally controversial *Deschooling Society,* argues that compulsory schooling should be disestablished altogether.[9]

Radically different visions of the educational system, often corresponding to divergent

6. See Victor Nee, *The Cultural Revolution at Peking University* (New York: Monthly Review, 1971), especially pp. 25–47, for a discussion of the growth of elitism in Chinese education prior to the Cultural Revolution.

7. Charles Silberman, *Crisis in the Classroom: The Remaking of American Education* (New York: Random House, 1970). For a critical review, see Michael B. Katz, "On *Crisis in the Classroom,*" in *Education in American History,* ed. Michael B. Katz (New York: Praeger, 1973), pp. 339–348.

8. Christopher Jencks et al., *Inequality: A Reassessment of the Effect of Family and Schooling in America* (New York: Basic Books, 1972), p. 265. See the Introduction to the present volume for a critical assessment of *Inequality.*

9. Ivan Illich, *Deschooling Society* (New York: Harper and Row, 1971). See also Herbert Gintis, "Toward a Political Economy of Education: A Radical Critique of Ivan Illich's *Deschooling Society,*" *Harvard Educational Review* 42 (February 1972): 70–96.

political ideologies, are now in competitive circulation. One vision, under increasing attack in recent years, is that of classical liberalism—the view that the social barriers that have traditionally obstructed equality must be dismantled so as to allow the most talented, whatever their origin, to rise through the hierarchies of education and class. Daniel Bell has given new life to the liberal vision in his essay "On Meritocracy and Equality" (Chapter 36). A principled defense of the meritocratic values that have supported selectivity in education and inequality of rewards in the economy, Bell's argument can be seen as a response to the populist and socialist challenges of the past decade. For Bell, openness rather than equality is the mark of the good society. This position, of course, was precisely the target of Michael Young's satire of 1958.[10] What is perhaps most striking about Bell's vision, published more than fifteen years after Young coined the term "meritocracy," is that the social ideal it upholds is not so very different from the dominant ideology of contemporary American society.

A social democratic view of the problem of education and social change is presented by Tom Schuller and Jarl Bengtsson in Chapter 37. In it they argue for a policy of recurrent education—a strategy of lifelong alternation of school and work that is expressly designed to achieve greater equity in the distribution of educational resources. A further consequence of the policy of recurrent education would, they suggest, be to impart to workers a body of technical knowledge and cognitive skills that would assist them in struggles for control over the process of production. This vision of industrial democracy gives a distinctly socialist flavor to Schuller's and Bengtsson's argument. They are aware of the numerous ways in which recurrent education may be manipulated in the interest of employers. Expanded opportunities for educational leaves of absence could, they observe, foster a mentality more oriented to individual mobility than to collective solidarity, but the general thrust of their argument points to an increase in working-class challenges to the prerogatives of management as an outcome of a policy of recurrent education. *L'éducation permanente* may lead in this direction. Or, as André Gorz has argued, it may lead to a management-oriented rationalization of the relationship between school and work.[11]

A Marxist vision of education in advanced capitalist society is put forward by the Il Manifesto group of Italy. A left-wing party born of a split with the reformism of the Italian Communist Party, Il Manifesto rejects the Russian model of socialism and draws widely upon the experience of Chinese communism in its quest for a strategy that will bring about revolutionary changes in Italian society.[12] Critical not only of the demand of Western working-class parties for equality of educational opportunity, but also of the hierarchical and selective educational policies followed by the socialist countries of Eastern Europe, Il Manifesto calls for the abolition of schooling as an instrument of selection for social positions in the class structure (see Chapter 38). The model of education they propose—which would do away with the distinction between school and society, integrate the educational and production processes, and entrust socialization to the community rather than to a body of professional experts—resembles the "mass line" in Chinese education. Like the Maoists, Il

10. Michael Young, *The Rise of the Meritocracy* (London: Thames and Hudson, 1958).
11. André Gorz, "Le programme caché de l'éducation permanente," *Les Temps Modernes,* November 1974. The political origins of recurrent education—which are to be found more in a movement from above to increase worker productivity than in a push from below to democratize education and work—would seem to suggest that the outcome predicted by Gorz may be a more likely outcome of Schuller and Bengtsson's educational strategy than their own objective of industrial democracy.
12. See Rossana Rossanda, "Mao's Marxism," in *The Socialist Register 1971,* ed. Ralph Miliband and John Saville (London: The Merlin Press, 1971), for an example of the influence Maoism and the Cultural Revolution have exerted on Il Manifesto's vision of communism.

Manifesto insists that the process of educational transformation must not wait for a distant revolutionary future, but must begin today.

These visions of and plans for possible future worlds are included here to indicate the ideological and political context of the debate. They underline the fact that the sociology of education is ultimately concerned with the passions and interests of people and societies to create or maintain men in their own or some other image through the fundamental processes of reproducing or recreating the generations. The social science of education begins and ends in values. If its distinctive task is the rational analysis of the social relations of upbringing, its final contribution is to increase understanding of the ways in which man makes himself.

SELECTIVE BIBLIOGRAPHY

Bowles, Samuel. "Cuban Education and the Revolutionary Ideology." *Harvard Educational Review* 41 (November 1971): 472–500.

Bronfenbrenner, Urie. *Two Worlds of Childhood: U.S. and U.S.S.R.* New York: Basic Books, 1970.

Fitzpatrick, Sheila. *The Commissariat of Enlightenment.* London: Oxford University Press, 1970.

Fraser, Stewart. "China: School and Society." *Comparative Education Review* 18 (October 1974): 463–481.

Freire, Paulo. "Cultural Action and Conscientization." *Harvard Educational Review* 40 (August 1970): 452–477.

Gorz, André. "Le programme caché de l'éducation permanente." *Les Temps Modernes* (November 1974).

Graubard, Allen. "The Free School Movement." *Harvard Educational Review* 42 (August 1972): 351–372.

Halsey, A.H. *Educational Priority: E.P.A. Problems and Policies.* London: Her Majesty's Stationery Office, 1972.

Hoare, Quintin. "Education: Programmes and Men." *New Left Review,* no. 32 (July–August 1965), pp. 40–54.

Illich, Ivan. "After Deschooling, what?" *Social Policy* 2 (September–October 1971): 5–13.

Markiewicz-Lagneau, Janina. *Éducation, égalité et socialisme.* Paris: Anthropos, 1969.

Tawney, R.H. *Equality.* London: Allen and Unwin, 1931. (Revised edition, 1964.)

Tomasson, Richard F. "From Elitism to Egalitarianism in Swedish Education." *Sociology of Education* 38 (Summer 1965): 203–223.

Williams, Raymond. *The Long Revolution.* London: Chatto & Windus, 1961.

Young, Michael. *The Rise of the Meritocracy.* London: Thames & Hudson, 1958.

33. Lenin and the Politics of Education

Men whom Hegel defines as world-historical figures because they shape the lives of generations by establishing systems of rule, law, or belief are sometimes called educators of their times. In such a general and figurative use of the term, the title educator is of course honorific and not bestowed for achievements specifically educational. This has happened to Lenin. When a historian attributes to him "an enormous pedagogical success,"[1] he really means that Lenin managed to impose upon his party a style of rule in which expedient action is supported by ideological justification. The educator in this case is a master political strategist and might seem to be a more suitable subject of inquiry for the political scientist than for the historian of education. The metaphor, however, conceals a part of reality. It is true that Lenin wrote no treatise on education. His ideas on the subject were few and unoriginal, and he left no master plan to guide the Soviet educational system. Yet it is also true that, as head of party and state, he participated directly in the making of educational programs and policies, often devoting astonishing attention to details. Out of his speeches, memoranda, notes, and letters that deal with pedagogical problems and set forth his recommendations and decisions, a certain conception of education emerges. There is evidence that his actions and authority helped impart to the course of Soviet education a direction basically maintained until today.

As one surveys his contribution, one soon realizes that it defies classification in terms educators customarily employ. He does not fit into any chapter of a general history of educational thought, nor can he be characterized by association with a school or movement, though his dialectical materialism might mislead one into thinking so. Rather, he takes one out into a broad territory of indistinct boundaries where a variety of claims and interests meet, mingle, conflict, and become overlaid with one another. It should be remembered in this connection that Lenin performed successively a number of historical roles. He was first a subversive political revolutionary, then a statesman, and in his very last years he became an impatient promoter of national economic development. All these roles are reflected in what he said and did about education. Following these different strands and varying emphases, one finds oneself in the midst of a dynamic complex of interdependencies.

If a label for it must be found, perhaps the politics of education comes closest to conveying what is involved. However we choose to designate it, our subject will not submit to the simple humanistic treatment in which pedagogues defend the autonomy of education against the encroachments of sociologists, political scientists, and social planners. With such preconceptions, it would be impossible to understand and do justice to the problems Lenin had to cope with. Some of these did in fact arise because he cut himself off from certain modes of educational thought that had come to be accepted in Russia as well as in the West. It is therefore appropriate to begin this study with a brief summary of two traditions that still had strong appeal to the educational profession when Lenin began to attack them and to deny them further influence.

The first of these is the secular tradition of modern public education that derives from the late phase of the Enlightenment and is inspired by its moral beliefs. Trust in the natural goodness and rationality of man is set against corrupt social institutions that have to be remade and restricted by democratic control so that eventually they may

From *Slavic Review* 27 (June 1968): 230–257. We have extracted pp. 230–244 and 251–257 for reproduction here. Reprinted by permission of author and publisher.

promote rather than obstruct the perfection of the individual. Accordingly, the more consistent *philosophes*, notably Condorcet, demanded that future national systems of education be placed under the control of autonomous bodies of intellectuals, scientists and teachers. Under their protection a rational public opinion would be formed to act as a safeguard against any future relapses into political tyranny and religious mystification. Although Lenin retained the belief in social progress of the Enlightenment, its optimism concerning the self-emancipating force of reason struck him as excessively naive. His own view of the agencies of human progress was formed by a study of Hegel, Marx, and Engels, who tied reason to certain forms of power and made its triumph contingent on society's passing through lawful stages of historical development. To entrust the rule of reason to the alleged autonomous force of education was to think abstractly, that is, unhistorically and unpolitically.

It was therefore clear to Lenin from the very start of his revolutionary career that within the workers' movement education would play a subordinate part, serving the class struggle of the adult masses by making them conscious of their economic condition and preparing them for their historical role. In short, Lenin reasserted the political domination of education that the most consistent exponents of the Enlightenment had hoped to end forever, with the consequence that in prerevolutionary Bolshevik strategy, organized political action replaced education as the primary instrument of social change. Revolution had to precede cultural reconstruction, for which it alone could lay the basis. Then, in the new society, political ideology would continue to control educational institutions in order to secure its gradual internalization and to direct common efforts toward the attainment of planned social goals. The irreconcilable conflict between this position and that of the Enlightenment became manifest imme-

diately after the October Revolution. In December 1917 the All-Russian Federation of Teachers, founded in 1905, went on a three months' strike in defense of the principles of professional autonomy and a democratic concept of education. It refused to act merely as a willing instrument but wanted to be an independent participant of educational decision-making. A year later the Federation was dissolved as counterrevolutionary.

The second educational tradition Lenin confronted in the person of Lev Tolstoi. Tolstoi revived in Russia the social and educational philosophy of Rousseau, whom he so greatly admired, but gave its anarchic and pessimistic elements an unusual emphasis. In contrast to such conservatives as Herbart and Hegel, Tolstoi—like Rousseau—did not identify education with the transmission of culture. Instead of turning the young generation into robust trustees of existing institutions, they looked to it for the regeneration of society.

Tolstoi especially cast himself in the role of the child's protector vis-à-vis society, state, and church, whose educational aims he branded corrupt and stultifying. In Russia his literary and moral authority lent a special appeal to this gospel of child-centered, free education, in which his experience of teaching peasant children at Iasnaia Poliana had confirmed him. Moreover, his educational views harmonized with his philosophy of culture and society as developed in his later writings. The suppression of children's spontaneity in state school systems had its counterpart in the extinction of human brotherhood in adults who lived by the fictitious values of society.

Lenin's condemnation of Tolstoi was tempered because he admired the artist and because he found useful elements in Tolstoi's critique of society that appealed to non-Marxists. Still, Tolstoi's philosophy remained "unpardonable": it was pacifist, anarchic, utopian, and permeated by Oriental pessimism.[2] In an overwhelmingly peasant society to which organized political action was alien, it was a dangerous influence that had to be fought. Although Lenin was familiar with Tolstoi's essays on educational theory, he made no specific reference to them. The explanation seems to be that educational ideas generally did not attract him. Despite his philosophical interests he never entered into a discussion of the antitheses at the heart of the Rousseau-Tolstoi tradition—the antitheses of nature and culture, of creativity and conformity. He acknowledged them only indirectly by taking issue with their political implications.

The Bolshevik revolution did not extinguish the Tolstoian ethos in Russia. For many, including Lenin's wife Krupskaia and some of her closest educational collaborators, Tolstoi remained a deeper source of inspiration than Marx. She repeatedly acknowledged a profound indebtedness to him. In 1923, for example, she spoke entirely out of the Rousseau-Tolstoi tradition when she said that "children and youth should not become instruments for the realization of aims that are extraneous and contrary to their interests."[3] Had that belief been allowed to determine Soviet educational practice, it might eventually have contributed to sustaining some form of humanist socialism. But both the economic conditions and the political-administrative style of the party denied any such hopes. Krupskaia never exercised any power in the party leadership, and Lenin himself realized only too late, if at all, that socialist culture supposed a quality of human relationships that authoritarian administration and organization could not create.

We have thus far described Lenin's view of education within the context of modern intellectual history by contrasting it with two major traditions of educational thought. The first of these, deriving from the Enlightenment, conflicted directly with his political ideology; the second, represented chiefly by Rousseau and Tolstoi, was rendered ineffectual by the single-party state and its totalitarianism. We turn now to a more detailed examination of Lenin's view of the uses of education in the years before the Bolshevik seizure of power.

1

At a Shrovetide party of the Petersburg Marxist circle in 1894, where Lenin first met his future wife, the conversation turned to the problem of illiteracy. Some in the group looked to education as a means of changing the social order. Lenin greeted their remarks with a cold little laugh that Krupskaia never forgot. "Well, if anyone wants to save the country through the Committee for Illiteracy," he said, "we won't hinder him."[4] He was then only twenty-four years old but remarkably sure of his convictions and strategy. Political revolution must precede cultural development. To reverse this order and to set one's hopes on the gradual reform of existing conditions was to indulge in childish fantasy. A decade later he restated this view, but this time as a party policy from which there was to be no deviation. Among other things, German revisionism had in the meantime had its divisive impact upon the Russian Marxists, and Lenin's earlier mockery of the social reformers changed to condemnation. Whoever, he wrote in 1905, would reduce the political problem to a question of education ceased to be a true Social Democrat. And should such a person take it into his head to appeal to the masses with the promise of education, thereby turning it into a slogan distinct from and opposed to the politics of the Social Democratic party, he would descend to the level of demagogy.[5] Of course, Lenin granted, the party's politics always contained an element of education: this consisted in raising the most backward stratum of the working class to a level of consciousness where it would become politically active.

This principle of the primacy of political action over education Lenin maintained with perfect consistency to the end. When, during his illness in 1923, he had time to reflect on what had gone wrong with the party and the state apparatus and how little had yet been accomplished by way of cultural construction, he still justified the course he had taken as the only right one. The political revolution had to be made first, for it alone could create the conditions for the second, or cultural, revolution that would develop the country's productive forces, including education. He granted that to establish socialism a certain level of culture was indeed necessary. But who could determine what precisely this level should be?[6] Even now he was chiding as cowards and pedants those among the Russian Marxists who had argued that the country was not ready for socialism because it was too poor, its population too passive and illiterate. Their faulty ideas of revolution were derived from German textbooks, and thus they failed to realize that the October Revolution was *sui generis* and that history outgrew all models. Soviet socialism had to be built with the corrupt human material that feudalism and capitalism had bequeathed; there was no other. It was utopian to argue that the remaking of man was a necessary prior condition to building a new social order. But once political and economic power had been seized, there was no disputing the importance of education for developing and perfecting socialism. Late in 1920, with the civil war essentially over, Lenin was able to turn his attention to this "third," neglected front.

Before we follow his efforts in this direction, certain ambiguities in his definition of the relation of politics to education must be brought to light. These ambiguities helped to fuel a pedagogical dispute that arose among Soviet educational theorists after his death and culminated at the end of the decade. What was in question was the role formal educational institutions should or could play in the cultural revolution. A group led by V.N. Shul'gin[7] revived demands advanced by radical Communists right after the revolution: schools should be replaced by an organized social environment, preferably work communes in association with farms and factories. Only communal life, they

argued, and not the school, could achieve the necessary transformation of personality. Except for a few experiments, these ideas were not put into practice, and then the NEP period cooled the enthusiasm of their proponents. In 1928 the proclamation of the First Five-Year Plan rekindled the earlier hopes. It signaled to many the beginning of the transition to the end phase of communism and provided the cultural revolution with a fresh impulse. To men like Shul'gin the vision of many millions participating in the total reconstruction of society suggested a wealth of human experience beside which the work of formal educational institutions paled to insignificance.

To these educators the schools were not only feeble but retrograde and even pernicious in their influence. During the latter part of the NEP the subject-matter curriculum had, in fact, been reestablished and polytechnical education had made no visible progress. Few students engaged in physical labor as well as in learning. This led to Shul'gin's reproach that the schools had regressed to verbalism and scholasticism. He further asserted that the ideological gap between the majority of teachers and the workers' children remained unbridged. The nine-year urban school provoked his sharpest criticism because few working-class children graduated from it. Among its students he found persistent and open anti-Semitism, pornographic literature circulated, and sexual promiscuity was not unknown. Coeducation remained ineffective in combating the degrading bourgeois relations between the sexes. Religious organizations recruited young people with impunity. Children from orphanages and national minorities suffered social discrimination, and the Young Pioneers were powerless to create comradely relations. But worst of all to him was the continued isolation of the school from life. While Soviet children read Fenimore Cooper and Harriet Beecher Stowe, they remained ignorant of the achievements of the October Revolution. In a questionnaire sent out by his institute, many students wrote that the basic accomplishment of the revolution was the abolition of serfdom.[8]

These charges helped to support Shul'gin's thesis that the traditional school had no place in a communist society and that, like the state, it was an institution destined to die out. In support of this conclusion, Shul'gin invoked the authority of Lenin with citations that placed high value upon what the masses learned directly and informally from their participation in revolutionary struggle. Thus the concept of *stikhiinost'*, the elemental and spontaneous power of the masses that was long familiar in Russian socialist thought, entered the debate over education. To Shul'gin and his followers it meant that the masses, faced with a moribund tradition of formal schooling, should take education into their own hands and by a kind of participant, grass-roots socialism accelerate the work of the cultural revolution.[9]

Now it is true that Lenin stated, both before and after the revolution, that the masses learn from their own experience, failures, and errors. He also admonished the party membership to remain, as the phrase went, "close to the people": in propagandizing and teaching the masses, party members must not resort to the book alone but should share the experience of the people. Shortly before his return from exile, he paid special tribute to the importance of spontaneity in a speech in Zurich in January 1917. Referring to the role the Russian metalworkers played in the revolution of 1905, he said: "The real education of the masses can never be separated from their own independent, and especially their revolutionary, struggle. Struggle alone educates the exploited class, reveals to it the measure of its strength, broadens its horizons, raises its capacity, clears its mind, and forges its will."[10] The meaning of these magnanimous words was not, however, to restrict the role of the party as preceptor of the proletariat. In the preceding sentence Lenin belittled the spread of free public education in Western countries, perhaps because it tended to weaken revolutionary zeal. "When the bourgeois gentlemen and their uncritical lackeys, the socialist reformers, talk so conceitedly about the 'education' of the masses, they usually mean by it something schoolish and pedantic, something that demoralizes the masses."

Such statements strongly appealed to certain radical Soviet educators, who usually ignored the context in which they were made. The idea of liquidating the schools and with them the discipline of methodical learning never entered Lenin's head. When the small minority around Shul'gin propounded the opposite view, they took the liberty of extending what Lenin had written in *The State and Revolution* to the school and revolution. They seemed to see a parallel between what Marx had described in *The Civil War in France* and the Soviet cultural revolution. Just as a standing army could be replaced by an armed populace, so the professional work of Soviet teachers could be dissolved into the processes of communal life. Factory foremen, union officials, local soviets, and social services could all initiate the young directly into economic and cultural work. The meaning of this primitive socialism was not merely that the wall between school and life had to come down. Direct, spontaneous participation in socialist construction was proclaimed a better education for life than formal and compulsory institutions could provide. Lenin's thesis of 1917 that the state and freedom are mutually exclusive was transferred to the schools with a consistency he would very likely have considered maddening. Like the state, schools were held to be compulsory institutions that obstructed a truly socialist construction, and they should be allowed to wither away. Whereas *The State and Revolution* was laid to rest because it was an embarrassment to Lenin's politics, its message was far from lost upon this group of revolutionary educators. They stubbornly defended the utopia of a self-educating proletarian democracy until all of them were silenced in 1931 and defamed as leftist deviationists bent on destroying the schools.

When Lenin came to sit in the statesman's chair, his capacity for realism, which biographers have noted, asserted itself also in education. Here, as elsewhere, the absolutes of Marxist ideology collided with the sad Russian realities. Whereas some people thought they could change the educational system from the ground up, he tempered such radicalism by a large dose of prudence. Generally speaking, he balanced the values of cultural continuity against the novel demands of a society whose shape had yet to be determined. The attempt to apply in Russian schooling the concept of polytechnical education inherited from Marx provided a first important test of his ability. Like other ideas, it could not simply be transplanted to Russian soil. Moreover, its transfer from theory to practice was beset by numerous difficulties unresolved to this day.

To understand what was at stake, it should be recognized that in the economic ruin at the end of the civil war the very principle of a general education for all was in dispute. The party had committed itself to realizing that principle in a nine-year school, called the unified labor school. This institution had jettisoned most of the scholastic burden of the gymnasium. Greek, Latin, Old Slavonic, religion, and much history were dropped from its curriculum so that, like the former *Realschule* it resembled, it appeared well adapted to the requirements of an industrial society. But, even in this revised form, a general education seemed to certain groups a social luxury. Although Lunacharskii and Krupskaia defended it valiantly, they and the entire Commissariat of Education were criticized for this by the Komsomol, by the major economic commissariats, and by the trade unions. All pressed for a diversified system of vocational and technical training, to begin at an early age, that would minister directly to acute manpower needs. In addition there was opposition from the Ukrainian Ministry of Education, which followed an independent course

under the leadership of Grinko. After either four or seven years of elementary instruction, Ukrainian students passed directly into specialized technicums. Extreme material want gave rise to such shortsighted educational utilitarianism, and concessions were inevitable. Long before the principle of the single school providing a general polytechnical education for all was abandoned under Stalin, its advocates were in fact fighting a losing battle.

Nor was the urgency of economic needs the only argument they had to counter. In 1922 all schools providing a general education beyond the first four grades enrolled only 5−6 percent of the age group twelve to seventeen.[11] Of these institutions the nine-year school enjoyed a superior reputation. It was in fact a descendant of prerevolutionary, academically oriented schools, and in it children of proletarian origins remained a minority throughout the 1920s. It was therefore not surprising that this school should become the target of social criticism as well. The Komsomol leadership, for example, charged it with being elitist, bourgeois, and indeed reactionary. The defenders of general culture, Soviet style, were thereby put in a difficult position. Under the prevailing restrictive conditions their attempt to institutionalize a high principle of social justice was bound to miscarry. All during the 1920s the nine-year general school remained, as Lunacharskii frequently acknowledged, the problem child of his commissariat. But when he and his staff reluctantly made concessions to utilitarianism by establishing special types of vocational schools, they aroused the suspicion of many teachers. Though few of them cared about Marxism and still fewer about Bolshevism, many were deeply committed to educational reforms that would abolish the traditional social discriminations resulting from a dual educational system. When a department for vocational education was established in Lunacharskii's commissariat in 1920 and special schools for peasant youth (1923) and urban factory youth (1925) were opened, the teachers' disillusionment was understandable. Such measures seemed to signal a retrogression to the tradition of a social-class system in which premature specialization excluded the children of the underprivileged from attaining full stature as men and citizens. It also seemed to many that the polytechnical principle had been routed by vocationalism pure and simple. What was Lenin's response to these strains and dilemmas?

He had himself drafted with Krupskaia's assistance those paragraphs of the party program, adopted by the Eighth Congress in March 1919, that prescribed the introduction of the general polytechnical school and deferred vocational training to after the age of seventeen. When it became all too obvious by 1921 that these objectives were unattainable, the period of general education was curtailed by two years, and the last two grades were devoted in part to various vocational courses. Lenin wanted it understood that this was a temporary retreat forced upon the party by the extreme poverty of the country. Neither the abandonment of the original program nor a surrender to the vocationalists was involved. But unless his realism deserted him this time, he must have been aware that the distinction he drew was an academic one. Secondary education of equal quality for all was not years but decades away. (The official target date today is 1970.) In the meantime vocational or monotechnical training programs built upon a four-year elementary school would have to be accepted by many young people as an inferior substitute for a general polytechnical education. And once such programs became institutionalized and relied upon by the economic commissariats to satisfy chronic manpower shortages, they would be difficult to remove. Was there after all then a real issue between monotechnical and polytechnical education? Certain participants at the first party conference on education, held in early January 1921, thought so. Among them were Grinko, the Ukrainian Commissar of Education, and Shmidt, who headed the new Department of Vocational Education in Moscow. They argued that early training for a single industry was necessary and that the general polytechnical school, because it remained a "verbal school," was of little use.[12]

Such talk was sharply rebuked by Lenin: to make an issue of monotechnical versus polytechnical education was idle chatter and vapid theorizing. The party had clearly stated that the Marxist polytechnical principle was not in jeopardy, no ideological commitment was being sacrificed in the temporary change of program, *ergo* there was no issue. Party officials were advised to turn from "abstract slogans" to the practical improvement of education in which experienced teachers stood ready to assist if only party members would take the trouble to seek them out. Lenin's irritation with pretentious Communist leadership exercised in splendid disregard of real problems was beginning to mount. Yet his steady stream of admonitions to learn from experience, to consult with the experts, and to work for concrete results could not resolve the dilemma that had been posed. He refused to be drawn into discussing its grave social and pedagogical implications. To more scrupulous Marxists his counsel to be "practical" must have sounded like a call to redouble one's efforts while the aims of socialist humanism grew dimmer and were finally lost sight of. In the light of this situation it is worth reflecting for a moment on what polytechnical education meant to Marx and what it came to mean for Lenin.

From the educator's point of view, "the fully developed individual fit for a variety of labors"[13] defines the essence of Marx's humanism. The many-sided amateur, not confined to any exclusive sphere of activity but "accomplished in any branch he wishes," was envisioned as a distinct possibility in the higher phase of communist society. Labor then ceased to be a means of life and became "life's prime want." The individual would be liberated from economic necessity as the productive forces increased and gave scope to his all-round development.

In *Capital* Marx sketched in bare outline the "technical instruction, both theoretical and practical," that would "take its proper place in the working-class schools" once the proletariat came to power. The theoretical part he defined as a knowledge of the general principles underlying all processes of production; the practical, as skill in handling elementary instruments of production.

Though Marx himself seems not to have employed the term polytechnical education,[14] it came to be regarded as representative of his ideas and carried certain meanings and messages. As interpreted in early Soviet educational thought, the concept of polytechnical education served as a warning not to relapse into narrow vocationalism, as a road sign to the industrial-collective culture of the future, and as a humanist imperative to bring up the young as masters of both nature and the man-made environment. As an educational plan, the concept was less successful. Workable ways of relating the emergent industrial culture to programs, curricula, and methods remained to be discovered.

Lenin took up the challenge in characteristically practical terms. Even if he had had the time and inclination, the very remoteness of Marx's ideal would probably have deterred him from attempts to round out the latter's sketchy notions and construct a more instrumental theory. Once again the question before him was "what could be done," what initial steps, however modest, could be taken to move the schools in the desired direction. He answered the question in some hasty notes he wrote for Krupskaia on the so-called theses she was to present at the above-mentioned party conference on education. His wife's conception of polytechnical education seemed to him too abstract, destined for a distant future but inapplicable under present conditions. Accordingly, he jotted down some practical suggestions, and these remain his fullest statement on the whole subject of polytechnical education. Their importance should not be exaggerated. They were confidential, intended for Krupskaia alone and not as policy directives. Besides, they were not published until 1929.[15] What influence they may have had was indirect, mediated by his wife. Their interest lies primarily in the insight they afford into how Lenin grappled with a difficult question.

To begin with, Lenin proposed that the upper grades of the general school (ages 12–17) be merged with, and indeed transformed into, vocational-technical schools because carpenters, joiners, locksmiths, and the like, were desperately needed. All must learn a trade. Did this mean that he was adopting the position of Grinko and Shmidt? No, because these fellows blundered into a general denial of polytechnical education—Lenin's language was a good deal stronger and more colloquial (*peresobachit' do gluposti*)—whereas he did not. For even as all students were learning some trade, their intellectual horizon would be broadened by expanding the teaching of such subjects as communism, general history, the history of revolutions, geography, and literature. They had also to master the basic concepts of electricity and agronomy, and they were to be shown the application of electrical power to the machine and chemical industries. There were to be regular visits to power stations, to state farms and factories where lectures and practical exercises would be held. For this purpose engineers, agronomists, and all graduates of university physics-mathematics departments were to be mobilized. It was the urgent task of the Commissariat of Education to draw up the necessary schedules and instructional programs; if Lunacharskii had not yet done so, Lenin half-facetiously wrote in the margin, he ought to be hanged.

This was a brave effort to adapt the Marxian principle to Russian conditions, but the difficulties were nearly insuperable. The demands made on scientific and technical personnel were already excessive without the addition of teaching responsibilities. Few schools even in cities were near enough to factories and enterprises to make visits and on-the-spot object lessons feasible; where such an opportunity existed, few enterprises were willing or sufficiently well managed to serve for demonstration purposes. Regular teachers who understood the relations of science to technology as Lenin wanted them taught were almost nonexistent, and the educational theorist able to project a coherent plan of a labor school in the context of industrial culture was a rare exception.[16] Furthermore, consumer needs were still being provided for by handicrafts, notably in the villages, so that polytechnic education was likely to be misunderstood as a return to old-fashioned apprenticeship in trades and crafts. In many instances labor education was practiced in the form of pupils' self-help and self-service, such as gathering firewood for their school, cleaning floors, repairing roofs and windows, and the like.

It hardly required exceptional foresight to perceive that the universal man in overalls must long remain a distant goal. In *The Infantile Disease of Left-Wing Communism* (1920) Lenin warned that specialization of labor would continue. The training of many-sided men able to do everything was of course the ultimate aim of communism. But to try to realize it now was like attempting to teach higher mathematics to a four-year-old. Socialism could not be built with an imaginary man created by our own fancy; it had to be done with the deformed humanity about us. The more Lenin turned to education in the concrete, the less he dwelt on the ultimate aim and its humanistic justification. As his impatience with the slowness of economic progress grew, he urged the introduction of specific educational measures to accelerate the pace.

As early as 1918 he recommended the study of the Taylor system as a means of increasing productivity by teaching labor discipline to the Russian worker. When O. A. Ermanskii published in 1922 a revised and enlarged work on the subject (*The Scientific Organization of Labor and the Taylor System*), Lenin wanted it to be required reading in all vocational and general secondary schools, provided the author would make it less verbose.[17] He was still more delighted by I. I. Stepanov's book, *The Electrification of the RSFSR,* published the same year, to which he wrote the foreword. As is well known, Lenin had extravagant hopes for what electrification of the country would do for socialism. A course on the subject had already been decreed a required subject in all higher educational institutions of the RSFSR. Now, with a book available that combined technical merit with optimistic propaganda, the resolution could be put into effect, and Lenin himself wrote detailed instructions of how to proceed.[18] Stepanov's text would be used in all schools. It would also be distributed to elementary-school teachers and engineers who were to explain the electrification plan in informal study circles, especially among peasant youth. Every power station would serve as a center for instructing and propagandizing the population. As a third illustration of Lenin's growing preoccupation with educational crash programs, there is a letter to Lunacharskii urging the publication of textbooks and propagandistic material on peat production. This, too, was to be made an obligatory subject in schools and higher educational institutions.[19]

None of these curricular innovations for achieving technical breakthroughs in the economy seems to have been carried out, and that was just as well. Precipitate changes of this kind would have further increased the instability of instructional programs, about which criticism later mounted until Stalin returned the schools to inflexible and uniform curricula. Paradoxically, Lenin was both by temperament and for reasons of cultural policy a strong advocate of systematic study. If in the examples cited above he appears to contradict himself, it is because he spoke not as an educator mindful of methodological and curricular problems but as a promoter of economic development.

In extenuation it must be said that he received little help from the Commissariat of Education. Lunacharskii was a literary man addicted to the theater and uninterested in technology. As an administrator he was a failure, and though he would spend half the night in brilliant talk or writing modernistic plays, he did not harness himself to any of the tasks Lenin considered most pressing, such as the liquidation of mass illiteracy or the drafting of instructional programs. Lenin's reprimands and appeals, his recurrent inquiries whether this or that particular request had been acted upon, went for the most part unheeded. M. N. Pokrovskii, the historian who was second in command, was more dependable and scientifically oriented. He was also better attuned to Lenin's drive for attaining specific, concrete results. Among other things he promoted the *rabfaki* (workers' faculties) to provide access for youth of proletarian origin to higher educational institutions. He fought against reducing Marxism in the schools to a catechism and insisted that "the true Marxist must above all be a good naturalist"[20] and know the natural sciences and their history. Lenin appointed him head of the State Science Council (GUS) in 1919. When his *Brief Outline of Russian History* appeared in 1920, Lenin warmly congratulated him but suggested a few improvements to make it more serviceable as a textbook. If only more Communists would follow Pokrovskii's example and write useful textbooks, especially in the social and natural sciences, socialist culture would measurably advance.

2

But what really was socialist culture? No writing of Lenin's provides an inclusive answer. He did not have a unified conception of it from which well-coordinated programs and directives could issue. But as he became involved in finding answers to specific questions, he could scarcely help deciding also matters of principle. Being a rationalist as well as a revolutionary, he did not look upon culture as spontaneous growth but as something to be organized. Given such a view, educational policies

necessarily became prime instruments for cultural construction. As we pursue Lenin's work in this field, at least piecemeal answers to the problem of socialist culture emerge. This is most evident whenever he was faced with settling conflicting claims or, more truly speaking, of having to assert his own preferences against rival notions. What importance, for example, was to be assigned to political indoctrination as compared with the spread of scientific-technological information? Was socialist culture something original, as the proponents of Proletkul't claimed, or must it ingest large parts of traditional culture? And if there was to be a blend of continuity and innovation, how could this be achieved without loss to the revolutionary *élan?* These were obviously difficult questions, and Lenin's answers were not always clear or uncontradictory. What he said, however, was more than improvisation; it carried the imprint of his whole cast of mind. To examine the problem of socialist culture, we turn first to the matter of continuity and innovation.

In Soviet texts and lectures on general pedagogy a prominent place has long been assigned to the speech Lenin delivered at the third Komsomol congress in October 1920. Between the 1930s and the 1950s it was practically regarded as his educational testament and construed to lend authority to Stalin's notion of the school as a learning institution of bookish character, from which the activity programs and project methods of the earlier experimental phase were excluded. Though this was a distortion, Lenin's speech did reject the indiscriminate condemnation of the "old school" in fashion at the time. He offered a qualified defense of traditional learning and had the courage to address it to an audience of politically excited young adults eager to perpetuate the revolution, chiefly by exterminating what they deemed bourgeois. It required considerable persuasion on his part to convince them that young Communists must now assume the prosaic burden of serious, persistent study. The backing and filling of his rheto-

ric, now making concessions to their prejudices, now assaulting them, shows that he
knew what he was up against. The following
passage illustrates his mode of argument.

It is said that the old school was a learning
school, a school of drilling and cramming.
That is true, but we must know how to
distinguish what was bad in the old school
from what is useful to us, and we must be
able to select from it what is necessary for
communism. The old school was a learning
school that forced people to master a great
bulk of useless, superfluous dead knowledge
which stuffed their heads and transformed
the younger generation into conformist
bureaucrats. But you would make a great
mistake if you draw the conclusion that it is
possible to become a Communist without
mastering the store of human knowledge. It
would be erroneous to think that it is sufficient to learn Communist slogans or the conclusions of Communist science without
mastering that sum of knowledge of which
communism itself is the result. Marxism
illustrates how communism emerged from
the sum of human knowledge.[21]

The main purpose of the speech was to
drive home the point that the task of destroying the old order had been accomplished but that the still more difficult task
of building communism lay ahead. To prepare for it, youth had to become intellectuals of a kind. They must not treat Marxism
as though it were an inert idea, "something
you have learned by heart, but rather something you have reasoned out for yourselves."
Their model was to be Marx, who combined
scholarship with criticism and innovative
thought. For a moment Lenin appeared to
be affirming the values of independent
thought. But in fact any tampering with the
dogmas of dialectical materialism made him
angry.[22] What he meant was not freedom
from, but freedom within, the system:
young people should learn to apply the
truths of Marx with some imagination to
practical problems.
The overriding consideration in this
defense of intellectual discipline and continuity was certainly pragmatic. What was

needed was know-how, and this could only
be learned from the bourgeois specialists.
They would, of course, not be on top, only
on tap. Whether they served in the army or
in industrial management, in universities or
in schools, the party would control them.
But in every sphere they were indispensable
as teachers. They would transmit and diffuse
what had been the possession of a privileged
class and so become the agency of turning
the former minority culture into a mass culture. You confront the tasks, Lenin told the
Komsomol, of reorganizing agriculture and
industry on a modern technical and scientific basis. When you have mastered the
required knowledge, Russia will emerge from
want and poverty to become "a country of
wealth."
What Lenin did not explain was how
knowledge plus organization plus wealth
would add up to a socialist culture differing
in quality from preceding cultures. Perhaps
he believed that at some point increase in
quantity would, by the law of dialectics,
become change of quality. Perhaps the previously untapped energies and talents of the
people would be developed in such range
and force as somehow to surpass anything
ever witnessed in the history of civilization.
But he was inarticulate on this question and
far too preoccupied with present problems
to scan the distant horizon. He was certain
only that those who took a different view of
socialism and how to achieve it were talking
"utter nonsense." . . .
. . . In Lenin's case the emphasis was all
on acquiring and spreading an existing culture, not on creating a new one. He took an
essentially   traditional   position,   blurred
though it occasionally was by a certain
ambivalence toward the past and to bourgeois culture in particular. On the whole, his
view that education consisted in the transmission of culture strikes one as old-
fashioned, belonging more to the nineteenth
than to the twentieth century. One is reminded, for example, of Matthew Arnold,
though Lenin would probably have resented
the comparison. But "the best that has been

said and thought in the past" is not so very different from "that store of human knowledge" that Lenin commended to the attention of young and not so young Communists.

Of course Lenin did not esteem equally all parts of that heritage: rational knowledge and useful skills clearly ranked above aesthetic and literary values. His use of tradition, moreover, was highly selective, and his approach to history entirely pragmatic. Antiquarianism, to speak in the terms Nietzsche employed in his essay on *The Use and Abuse of History,* that is, the pious regard for the roots of our being, was hardly a part of Lenin's nature. Monumental history, however, from which one could draw strength and derive models of greatness, appealed to him, and in fact he needed it. Marx for him was monumental, and so, in another sense, were Pushkin and other Russian classics of the nineteenth century. Generally speaking, philosophy, literature, and art fell into this second category. Lenin had none of Nietzsche's misgivings that the monumental use of history might have a sterilizing effect upon the present and end in the dead burying the living. For the third, the critical or surgical, approach to history, Lenin's own politics provided the most illustrious example of the century. The knife of the revolution cut out what was deemed malignant—dynasty, empire, state religion, social classification, and private property. In these respects the break with tradition was of such magnitude that it carried the threat of profound individual insecurity and social dissolution. Lenin seems to have known this intuitively: if unchecked and unlimited, the revolution would end in destroying itself. For this reason, and not merely because of his conventional tastes and upbringing, he was a cultural conservative and disciplinarian whose command, "Learn, learn, learn!" is still prominently displayed in every Soviet school.[23]

Lenin's cultural conservatism had still another side: it was nationalist. Why it took on this hue is explained partly by the con-

stellation of international powers after the First World War. The peace of Brest-Litovsk in 1918, costly though it was, had the merit of preserving the Russian state. As it had become still more obvious by 1921 that hope for revolution in Germany had to be abandoned, socialism had to survive and succeed in one country. Despite the early professions of internationalism by the Bolsheviks, an opposite trend had already been set in motion.

With respect to cultural affairs, Lenin had taken a nationalist position even earlier. In 1914 the question of cultural autonomy for national minorities within the empire was discussed in the Russian press. The liberal position was that minorities should have the right to conduct elementary schools in their own language but that, in the interest of a common national culture, Russian should continue to be taught and recognized as the official language. Lenin differed from this policy in just one respect: Russian must not be made obligatory—"We do not want to drive people into paradise with a club." Nor was it necessary. The growth of capitalism in Russia, as well as the whole trend of social life, would bring different nationalities into closer contact with each other. Hundreds of thousands of people, he predicted, would move about from one end of the country to the other, and this would create a natural need for learning Russian. As for the cultural riches to which language was the key, he needed no reminder from the liberals. "We know better than you," he remarked, "that the language of Turgenev, Tolstoi, Dobroliubov, and Chernyshevskii is a great and mighty language . . . And of course we are in favor of every inhabitant of Russia having the opportunity to learn the great Russian language."[24]

It is curious to observe how the principal differences between Lenin and Bogdanov extended right down to the question of language. Whereas Lenin found good reasons for strengthening traditional and Great-Russian cultural elements, Bogdanov staunchly remained a radical internationalist.

Socialism could only succeed by simultaneous development in many countries, and this would require a suitable means of international communication. Bogdanov dismissed synthetic products like Esperanto and suggested English: it was used in many parts of the world and was the language of the majority of the industrial proletariats; it was concise, simple, and rich in cognate words. Since nationalist feelings were deeply entrenched, he had no illusions that English could soon become the workers' international language. But he advocated that the proletarian-culture movement, which incidentally found fleeting expression also in Germany and Belgium, should take the long view in planning for the future.[25]

At about the time Bogdanov promoted the teaching of English to Russian workers, Lenin wrote repeatedly to Lunacharskii, Pokrovskii, and Litkens in the Commissariat of Education urging them to assemble a group of scholars to compile a new Russian dictionary. He was upset by the corruption of the Russian language through needless, imprecise use of foreign words, especially in the newspapers. Why say "defects," for example, when there were three good Russian words to choose from? Dal's great four-volume dictionary was obsolete and should be replaced by a shorter one for general use and for teaching purposes. This should be a dictionary of classical, "true" (*nastoiashchii*) Russian, containing both present usage and the literary language used from Pushkin to Gorki.[26]

In Bogdanov's ideas and proposals the utopian element stands out clearly enough. He idealized the workingman and exaggerated the people's capacity for sustaining the revolutionary ethos for any length of time. He underrated the power of tradition and neglected the role of force in history. Little of what civilizations achieve and of what holds societies together is, in fact, due to brotherly love and human fellowship. Refusal to accept this judgment and to try instead to enlarge the power of ethics in social life is perhaps the chief characteristic

of the true socialist. To judge by a half-century of Soviet power, it makes him as admirable as it has rendered him ineffectual. History has cast Bogdanov aside,[27] while Lenin led its victorious battalions.

Many others through whom the socialist conscience found a voice suffered the same fate as Bogdanov. Krupskaia and Shul'gin, neither of them identified with his movement, are but two examples referred to here. In different ways they all raised the painful questions that any educator-moralist was bound to face. Was the success of establishing a new power state worth the cost if a new culture—call it participant democracy, fraternal solidarity, a higher quality of human experience, or a new man—did not emerge? Were these not the promises that had fired the revolution and given ideology its all-important meaning? Without at least some realization of those hopes, ideology was bound to become a shell. It could indeed be made a compulsory subject of instruction, administered by an educational bureaucracy, and later propped up by the cult of Lenin's and Stalin's personalities. But it could not act as leavening of the body politic as Bogdanov had conceived of it. Instead of being an organic part of culture, ideology was assigned the role of controlling, manipulating, and censoring it. This posed the problem of indoctrination and propaganda, and we shall now inquire to what extent here, too, Lenin set the pattern for later developments.

3

In liberal societies the reputation of the teaching profession suffers when it is suspected of failing to distinguish between indoctrination and propaganda, on the one side, and education, on the other. There is a general awareness of the danger to intellectual and political freedom when they are confused or, worse, purposely identified. We have come to regard the educational systems of totalitarian regimes as paradigms of such identification. When examined more closely, however, propaganda and education are found to be anything but clear and distinct ideas. The difficulties political scientists have encountered in drawing a line between them cannot be discussed here. They have been apparent since the early writings of Harold Lasswell[28] and have persisted to the present, with the consequence that the problem has today largely been abandoned by political scientists and sociologists. Jacques Ellul, [29] though still maintaining the rational, responsible person to be the ideal aim of education, asserts that what technological mass society really needs is opinionated, responsive citizens, and these both propaganda and education, now declassed as subpropaganda, produce in abundance.

This pessimism was not shared by liberal American intellectuals who appraised Soviet education and society in the 1920s. Critical of laissez-faire economics and its moral concomitants at home, they were predisposed to look for the constructive consequences of the revolution. Dewey, for example, sensed a "burning public faith" behind the Soviet collective enterprise. Though this faith might be inspired by propaganda that had its obnoxious aspects, the identification of education with propaganda in the Soviet case seemed to him basically justified. "The broad effort to employ the education of the young as a means of realizing certain social purposes," he wrote, "cannot be dismissed as propaganda without relegating to that category all endeavor at deliberate social control."[30] The lack of a clear definition of propaganda, combined with contrary judgments about its political uses, should at least caution us against dismissing Lenin's views of the matter by simple references to totalitarianism and the moral condemnation that implies.

Lenin wished perhaps nothing more ardently than that the burning public faith Dewey described should be real, for it might help to solve some major problems. But the public statements of his last years show that he knew there was no such moving force. He was aware of the people's apathy and dis-

tressed by the growth of a callous, incompetent bureaucracy. The system he had introduced was already becoming autonomous. Efforts to control it failed, despite special commissions such as Rabkrin and the Central Control Commission, with their instructions to expose and correct abuses by party and state officials. With the people separated from a hierarchy of power, the prospect was hardly promising for official propaganda to be enthusiastically accepted as a gift of education.

Lenin realized that the efficacy of propaganda as a means of social control was in jeopardy. Whether he would eventually have been driven, as was his successor, to depend more heavily on the cruder means of compulsion and terror is a question which his early death relieved him of having to answer. To leave aside such speculation, it must be stated in fairness to Lenin that he distinguished between different uses of propaganda. That which was designed to mobilize youth and adults for important social and economic tasks he approved. The other, which amounted to thoughtless indoctrination, he denounced. The first was difficult to implement because it required that party propagandists should understand the country's needs and sense the people's mood. The second was easy and appealed to indolent, dogmatic minds, with which, by Lenin's admission, the party was abundantly supplied.

It cannot be said, however, that his own statements on the subject helped the membership to keep the two clearly apart. His repeated insistence on the need to politicize the schools is apposite. His often quoted phrase that "the school apart from life, apart from politics, is a lie and hypocrisy"[31] proclaimed a general principle but left its specific meaning undefined. It was a slogan of the early years, uttered in August 1918 and again in January 1919, when the party, still smarting from the "sabotage" of the Russian teachers, suppressed the old Federation of Teachers and replaced it with the Union of Internationalist Teachers. The profession was explicitly denied the luxury of ideological noncommitment. The party program adopted in March 1919 defined the school as an instrument of the class struggle. It was not only to teach the general principles of communism but "to transmit the spiritual, organizational, and educative influence of the proletariat to the half- and nonproletarian strata of the working masses."[32]

Yet to Lenin this did not mean a simple program of political indoctrination. The zealots who drew this conclusion and "clumsily implanted politics in the minds of the younger generation" (neither Russian nor Soviet usage has a simple term for indoctrination) were guilty of misinterpreting and distorting the principle of political education. It was an error, he added, which the party "would always have to fight." This seems to amount to an admission that the temptation of choosing the cruder, simpler ways of carrying out party doctrine was, so to say, built in. Moreover, the distinction between right principle and wrong application has since become a familiar device by which the party extricates itself from difficulties for which it declines to accept responsibility.

Lenin did not explicitly state his reasons for disapproving of the political indoctrination of schoolchildren, but it is fairly obvious that he thought the schools had more fundamental things to teach that could not be accomplished anywhere else. Nor can the difficulties of teaching Marxist ideology to minors have escaped him. He wrote no instructions for this subject as he did for the technical projects he was so eager to have inserted into the curriculum. The teaching of philosophy and the social sciences in universities interested him more, and he wanted those subjects placed in the care of Communists as soon as possible. Low-level indoctrination, such as the memorization and reiteration of Marxist slogans and phrases he regarded as unintelligent and unproductive. Of course, political indoctrination need not result in stupefying conformity. At its best it

may conceivably create the mental and emotional dispositions that make propaganda more effective. In Soviet usage these dispositions are described as *soznatel'nost'* and *ideinost'*, terms denoting not critical judgment and discernment but disciplined acceptance and affirmation of what has been taught. Lenin did not elaborate upon these qualities, which were later counted among the ideal civic virtues that Soviet schools attempt to inculcate.

His preference for propaganda over indoctrination must finally be viewed in the light of Soviet history. The October Revolution was itself a denial of doctrinal orthodoxy. The adulteration of Marxism by Leninism had the consequence of laying ideology open to pragmatic interpretations. As the meaning of ideology was determined by the use to which the party chose to put it, in that measure political indoctrination was deprived of a fixed and stable catechism. Propaganda was, by comparison, far more important. Lenin intended it to be a means of mobilizing people for action, and since the building of socialism was for him an immense practical task, the value of propaganda was obvious.

His pragmatism was most bluntly and emphatically stated at the beginning of the New Economic Policy. He told a congress of party propagandists and political educators in October 1921 that "the results of political education can be measured only in terms of economic improvement."[33] He confessed that he did not like the term "political educator," and he was vexed by the creation of a special organization with the high-sounding name Central Committee for Political Education (Glavpolitprosvet). Why this mania for still more bureaucracy and pretentious labels? Officially, the organization was charged with coordinating all political education outside the schools. It controlled village reading huts and libraries, adult education centers (called Communist universities), and party schools. Its personnel consisted almost exclusively of party members who were to teach and propagandize the adult, especially the peasant, population so as to bring it within the reach of politics.

Lenin was dissatisfied with their work. Instead of going among the people as ordinary citizens and setting an example by personal conduct, the political educators acted like officials, issuing a stream of directives without troubling to ascertain the local effectiveness of their work. If the good comrades would stoop to help adults learn to read, they would be more useful. They might even put the Extraordinary Commission for the Liquidation of Illiteracy out of business and thus render a double service by diminishing bureaucracy. Having done with illiteracy, the political educators might then devote themselves to stamping out the bribery of officials. As long as that existed, the political process as Lenin understood it could not even be initiated, and political education in the narrower sense of the word was futile. What he apparently meant was that bribe-taking reduced government to a system of favoritism and local boss rule.

The obvious conclusion was that the most elementary conditions of a common culture had yet to be created before a political. system that required the support of the masses could begin to function. Moreover, the establishment of a new political system would be an empty triumph unless it succeeded economically. Lunacharskii expressed the same idea in more vivid language. Glavpolitprosvet was a department of his commissariat, but since the party retained a measure of direct control over it, differences arose as to which kind of education should receive priority. The party favored political education, whereas the commissariat, while not neglecting it, felt chiefly committed to general and technical education. To give people political education without the other, Lunacharskii said, would be like feeding them salt without bread.[34]

The impression left by the sum of Lenin's educational ideas and policies is one of ordinariness and hard common sense. The revolutionary who so profoundly changed the political history of the twentieth century was never tempted to initiate a new epoch in the history of education. On the contrary, he used his power and authority to guard against adventures and high-minded schemes that aimed directly and impatiently at realizing the humanist promise of Marxist socialism. That a few such attempts were, in fact, undertaken is not surprising, for the ultimate justification of the revolutionary ideology was the realization of man's humanity, and this inevitably imparted to education a new and exceptional significance. Some who took up this challenge thought it necessary to break entirely with the scholastic tradition of learning, to dissolve the schools or replace them with models of communal life in which to fashion the new Soviet man. Although many others were less radical, they still agreed that socialist education should form the whole man and give particular attention to his emotional and social development, neglected by the old school.

Lenin stood aloof even from this moderate and widely shared conception. With all the changes he recommended or approved, the new Soviet school remained for him a school: its chief responsibility was to teach a body of received knowledge and cognitive skills useful for the internal development of the country. Schools would thus remain instruments of statecraft, as education in general was an extension of politics. This view has been familiar since the early years of the nineteenth century when Napoleon, with his reform of the French educational system, provided the first modern example. Lenin restated it, but with a consistency and rigor that were appropriate to the single-party state and its anticipated development into a highly industrialized, competitive nation.

NOTES

1. Adam Ulam, *The Bolsheviks* (New York, 1965), p. 455.
2. Lenin's five articles on Tolstoi, written between 1908 and 1911, are reprinted in *Lev Tolstoi kak zerkalo russkoi revoliutsii* (Moscow, 1965).
3. N. K. Krupskaia, *Pedagogicheskie sochineniia* (Moscow, 1958), II, 143.

4. N. K. Krupskaia, *Vospominaniia o Lenine* (Moscow, 1931), p. 5.

5. V. I. Lenin, "O smeshenii politiki s pedagogikoi," in *O vospitanii i obrazovanii* (Moscow, 1963), p. 165.

6. "O nashei revoliutsii," in *O vospitanii i obrazovanii*, p. 569.

7. Viktor Nikolaevich Shul'gin (1897–) was since 1922 director of the Institute of School Methods in Moscow, renamed in 1930 the Institute of Marxist-Leninist Pedagogy. His closest collaborator was M. V. Krupenina. For an excellent summary of Shul'gin's ideas and their significance, see Oscar Anweiler, *Geschichte der Schule und Pädagogik in Russland vom Ende des Zarenreiches bis zum Beginn der Stalin-Ära* (Berlin, 1964), pp. 414–28.

8. These indictments are found in his book *O vospitanii kommunisticheskoi morali* (Moscow, 1928). Krupenina made similar charges in some of her writings.

9. V. N. Shul'gin and M. V. Krupenina, *V bor'be za marksistkuiu pedagogiku* (Moscow, 1929), p. 18.

10. *O vospitanii i obrazovanii*, p. 301.

11. A. V. Lunacharskii, *O narodnom obrazovanii* (Moscow, 1958), p. 197. According to *Kul'turnoe stroitel'stvo* (Leningrad, 1927), Diagram 17, the social composition of the nine-year school in 1927 was: workers' children 28.2 percent, peasants' children 14 percent, others 57.8 percent.

12. Historical note in *O vospitanii i obrazovanii*, p. 646.

13. *Capital* (New York, Modern Library), p. 534.

14. The German term in *Das Kapital* is *technologischer Unterricht*, and a very similar equivalent was apparently used in an analogous passage in *Instructions to the Delegates of the Provisional Central Council*, which Marx wrote in English for the Geneva congress of the International in September 1866. The original English publication of the *Instructions* in *The International Courier* in 1867 is now rare and was not available to me. The Russian translation of the term in the relevant passage is *teknicheskoe obuchenie* (K. Marks and F. Engel's, *Sochineniia*, XVI [Moscow, 1960], 198), whereas the German translation is *polytechnische Ausbildung* (K. Marx and F. Engels, *Werke*, XVI [Berlin, 1962], 195). Hence the uncertainty.

15. Full text in *O vospitanii i obrazovanii*, pp. 482–84.

16. One whom Lenin read and admired was P. P. Blonskii. His book, *Trudovaia shkola*, appeared in 1919.

17. *O vospitanii i obrazovanii*, p. 550.

18. *Ibid.*, pp. 544–45.

19. *Ibid.*, p. 508.

20. M. N. Pokrovskii, *Marksizm v programmakh shkoly I i II stupenii* (Moscow, 1924), p. 16. For a brief summary of Pokrovskii's educational achievements, see *Pedagogicheskaia entsiklopediia* (Moscow, 1966), III, 430–31.

21. "Zadachi soiuzov molodezhi," in *O vospitanii i obrazovanii*, pp. 434–35.

22. V. I. Lenin, *O kul'ture i iskusstve* (Moscow, 1956), p. 496.

23. Lenin's tastes in art and literature are described by Louis Fischer, *The Life of Lenin* (New York, 1964), Chap. 34.

24. *O vospitanii i obrazovanii*, p. 280.

25. A. A. Bogdanov, *O proletarskoi kul'ture: Stat'i, 1904–1924* (Moscow and Leningrad, 1924), pp. 328–32.

26. *O vospitanii i obrazovanii*, pp. 404, 406, 423, 513.

27. Soviet educational historians, moreover, see to it that he should also be forgotten. Neither the two-volume *Pedagogicheskii slovar'* (Moscow, 1960) nor *Pedagogicheskaia entsiklopediia* (Moscow, 1964–66), of which three volumes have thus far been published, carries an entry for "Bogdanov," "Proletkul't," or "proletarskie universitety."

28. See especially "The Theory of Political Propaganda," *American Political Science Review*, XXI (1927), and the introduction to *Propaganda and Promotional Activities* (Minneapolis, 1935).

29. *Propaganda: The Formation of Men's Attitudes* (New York, 1965), p. 109.

30. John Dewey, *Impressions of Soviet Russia and the Revolutionary World, Mexico, China, Turkey* (New York, 1929), pp. 81–82.

31. *O vospitanii i obrazovanii*, pp. 337, 349.

32. N. I. Boldyrev, ed., *Direktivy VKP(b) i postanovleniia sovetskogo pravitel'stva o narodnom obrazovanii, 1917–1947* (Moscow and Leningrad, 1947), p. 7.

33. *O vospitanii i obrazovanii*, p. 531.

34. *O narodnom obrazovanii*, p. 235.

34. Socialist Ideology and the Transformation of Cuban Education*

MARTIN CARNOY and JORGE WERTHEIN

One educational leader at the Ministry of Education, Abel Prieto Morales, said that when he was in Italy, someone at an education conference asked him: "Is the school in Cuba an instrument of the State?" His answer was, "Yes, of course, just as it was before the triumph of the Revolution, and as it is in the present day in Italy." (Leiner, 1973, p. 6)

In Cuba the State ideology is anti-capitalist and anti-imperialist, and promotes collective action rather than individual initiative. This ideology as it is taught in the school is summarized in an official report by the Cuban government to the UNESCO Conference on Education and Economic and Social Development held in Santiago, Chile, in 1962. (For the entire document see Seers, 1964, pp. 348–351.)

The bourgeois ideology regarded education as a phenomenon isolated from its economic basis. In fact, however, education is an ideological superstructure and is closely linked with the means of production—that is to say, with the productive forces and the relationships of production.
Throughout the whole history of human society education has been a product of the social classes which dominated at each stage. The content and orientation of education are therefore determined by the social classes which are in power.
In Cuba, those in power are the workers, the peasants, the progressive intellectuals and the middle strata of the population, who are building a democratic society in which group and class privilege are disappearing and in which private ownership of the basic means

*The research reported here was carried out pursuant to a grant from the International Bank for Reconstruction and Development. However, opinions expressed do not necessarily reflect the position or policy of the International Bank for Reconstruction and Development, and no official endorsement by the International Bank should be inferred.

of production is being eliminated. If anyone wishes to know the aims of our education, they should study the interests of the workers, peasants, intellectuals and the middle strata of the population and they will find their answer. It is these which determine the purpose, the objectives, the orientation, the content and the methods of education in our country.

The document goes on to describe the development of education in Cuban society and the goals of education under the Revolution. Some of the goals stated are the following:

... Stress must also be laid on the importance of education for socialism and on the value of science in economic social cultural development.
... They (the pupils) must be brought to have a high sense of duty to work; that is to say, they must be taught to abandon the false notion of work as a punishment and they must be taught the necessity of work.
... They must be taught the value of emulative work and the difference between capitalism and socialism as being based on the difference between competition for private gain and emulation for the sake of increasing the output of the community.
... At the same time, since another of the aims of education for socialism is that of providing the necessary technical and scientific training to produce workers who are capable of directing and increasing production, and since the means of production are in the hands of the State, it is logical that, for many different ideological, practical, and pedagogic reasons, education should be linked with productive labor.
... Our plans and programmes aim at the elimination of verbalism and learning by rote and making education a living matter, in which theory is identified with practice and linked with social labor.
... Here we see two basic aims of socialist education: *the linking of education with*

productive labor as a means of *developing men in every aspect.* Educating in productive labor, making the students familiar with the details of production through practical experience, enabling them to learn its laws and organization as processes; that is, educating them in the very root of all cultural, technical and scientific progress, and giving them ideological and moral training leading to an all-around education.

The relationship between the change in ideology between 1958 and 1961 and the *content* of school curriculum under the reform could not be more obvious. In practice, the implementation of this new ideology in the schools is found in a more technical and scientific orientation, a much closer connection between schooling and work, and a greater emphasis on *collective* work in the schools rather than on individual achievement.

Specifically, ideology is reflected in a number of places in the educational system:

1) One of these is the relationship between *schools and work.* The first clear-cut effort to integrate school and work actually took place during the literacy campaign, when thousands of students went into the countryside to teach people how to read. But beginning in 1966, in part as a response to the shortage of agricultural labor, the first experiment took place: a large number of students from all over the country participated in working on farms for thirty-five days in April and May in the province of Camaguey, located 600 kilometers east of Havana in an area of large fields dedicated to sugar and livestock. The students were to carry out productive work while keeping up their studies at the same time. For this, the schools, professors, teachers, students, and employees, as well as all the necessary teaching equipment, were relocated in the countryside on various farms or recently constructed school installations. Students and teachers organized themselves in different productive units of the National Institute for Agrarian Reform. We shall discuss these schools further below, showing that

this particular form of education corresponds to important economic changes that took place in Cuba after 1964. However, the point to be made here is that the "school to the countryside" (*escuela al campo*) movement fit directly into the ideological context of the emphasis on work stated in the 1962 document.

A second manifestation of the work/school integration in addition to the university's becoming almost entirely oriented to technical subjects, was that university students after the Revolution could no longer separate themselves from the day-to-day productive activities of the economy.

The old idea of the classic university will disappear as a concept and as an institution that belongs to a superseded society. And so, production itself, the productive processes, will constitute the material base, the laboratory, where in the future all workers will receive their higher education. (Fidel Castro March 13, 1969).

The university reform of 1962 began to carry out this idea of work/study for university students. Students began to move out of the classroom: for example, medical students had to work in hospitals from the beginning of their third year of study; humanities students began to develop social work programs in agricultural development plans; civil engineering students went to the mountains and coordinated and combined their studies with agricultural production in the area.

Beginning in 1971–1972, it was decided that students must work twenty hours a week in direct production as part of their university studies. In their first two years in the university, students work in unskilled jobs. In their third year, they begin specialized work, whenever possible in workplaces that are connected with the student's speciality. Large-scale programs were also started in the early seventies to bring workers into the university for technical training.

2) In addition to the schools' moving to

the workplace, Cuba's production system has been integrated into the curriculum of the high schools. This integration was accomplished through the *circulos de interés*. An "interest circle" is a group of students led by a technical advisor who programs specialized activities in order to promote interest in science and technology, especially in those branches that are most important to economic development in Cuba. These circles are analogous in many respects to extracurricular activities in U.S. high schools, but are organized exclusively around productive activities—animal science, soil chemistry, and oceanography are typical subjects for interest circles. The circles were started in 1963–64 and have been developed extensively as a program aimed at bringing together students of similar interests. They also seem to break away from the traditional scholastic system and to use the rich experience of the community to benefit student learning. The number of these circles has grown every year since their inception: in 1966, 9,000 circles were organized; in 1967, there were 17,000; and in 1973, there were 20,000, with a total membership of 300,000 students. An important aspect of the circles is the development of a close association between the activity of future scientists and technologists and the national organizations and institutions that provide resources for their work. Students studying science lack resources such as pure breeding stock, surgical instruments, mobile weather stations, and land for agricultural experimentation, but through the sponsors they get to use these resources and have a chance to participate in the production sector.

Ideally, the interest circles are a bridge between the school curriculum and the student's later life and productive activity.

By tying the educational experience more closely to the economy the *circulos de interés* perform a very important function. A society which has foregone the use of wage incentives needs an alternative means of encouraging young people to enter occupations in short supply. Thus, the *circulos de interés* provide a means of informing young people about the content of various occupational pursuits, while at the same time stimulating student interest in careers likely to make a major contribution to national development. (Bowles, 1972, pp. 290–291.)

3) After the Revolution, students were encouraged *to study in groups rather than to study as individuals*. As a reflection of the system of socialist emulation being practiced in the productive sector, the process of expanding knowledge and competence was seen as a group effort, and elements of competition in the classroom were greatly reduced. Although under the economic strategy of the late sixties and early seventies individual study has been reemphasized (Bowles, 1972, p. 291), the monitor program continues to emphasize the collective spirit in the classroom. In the program, which draws on a type of mastery learning concept, each school class selects a student or a group of students in each subject to help the rest of the class with their studies. The role of these monitors is primarily to lead group discussions among students and to help individual students who are having difficulty; they take charge of classes being taught by educational television and perform other similar duties.

4) A crucial ingredient in utilizing the schools for propagating the new ideology was the development of a *teacher* corps with new values and skills. The elements of this development were the shift of teacher training from an urban to a rural orientation and the inculcation of socialist values into these rural cadres.

While dependent capitalist countries have great difficulties in "convincing" teachers to go into rural areas and, indeed, have a "surplus" of teachers in urban areas (although their student/teacher ratios do not decline even in urban areas), socialist countries like Cuba count on non-market incentives to move teachers into rural schools. Teachers trained to work in rural areas are depicted by the government as an *elite corps* serving the Revolution. Teaching in a rural area is not a second-class job (in which the teacher is penalized by having access neither to further education nor to promotion in the educational system); rather, teaching in a rural primary school is often required service in order to get promotion and access to university education.[1]

The Revolutionary government moved to expand teacher training greatly for both primary and secondary schools, and reduced student/teacher ratios significantly in the decade after 1959, despite a very rapid increase in the number of students enrolled. Furthermore, the new system of teacher preparation (which in this particular form remained in effect until 1968–1969) took students who had completed the sixth grade and put them in a five-year course that included a first year in the mountain school of Minas de Frio and a final two years in a training school in Havana.

This type of training program stresses two important features of the Cuban educational reform. The first is the special attention given to the particular problems and discouragements of teaching in rural areas. The second is the view of work and co-operation that we have discussed in the previous paragraphs. Teachers are trained to work alongside their pupils in the fields and to serve as examples of Revolutionary fervor.

The importance of teacher training in a society in the process of ideological transformation and simultaneously trying to increase the technical skills of its labor force is crucial to both these goals, and the Cuban leadership therefore put great emphasis on teacher training and teaching as a service to the Revolution.

5) According to Leiner,

Boarding schools are considered by educational leaders to be a key to creating the new Cuban man. First, boarding school students live together and develop attitudes and values consistent with Cuban Revolutionary goals. Secondly, they provide a full curriculum which includes physical education as well as academic subjects, for the training of the whole body and mind. Thirdly, students from rural isolated areas develop skills in arts, science, and technical areas in urban centres. Fourth, the new semi-internado (semi-boarding) schools become part of a central town development which consists of the school, a polyclinic, a social centre, and new housing for the campesinos (peasants). (Leiner, 1973, p. 6.)

Both the boarding and semi-boarding schools offer free clothing and food to the students, thereby exerting much more direct control over their health than the day schools. In 1962 the fellowship plan in the boarding schools reached more than 50,000 students in secondary education, and in 1973 it recorded 458,000 students in all levels of schooling.

Although the boarding school on a large scale is a relatively new development in Cuba, it has existed in some form since the early days of the Revolution. Boarding schools are probably much more effective in transforming the attitudes and values of young people than day schools, since a boarding school separates the student from his or her previous environment. There is also evidence, in Cuba and in at least two other countries, that boarding students perform better on tests measuring cognitive achievement. In Cuba, students attending the schools in the countryside have promotion rates (based on exam scores) considerably higher than the national average (Dahlman, 1973, p. 121). Estimates for Kenya and Tunisia show similar effects of boarding on achievement. (See Thias and Carnoy, 1972, for Kenyan data; see Carnoy, Sack, and Thias, 1976, forthcoming, for Tunisian data.)

6) Ideological socialization is also carried out in day care centers (see Table 1). Leiner stresses the ideological importance of these programs both for young children and for adults. Apparently, the first priority in organizing nurseries and kindergartens was and still is the liberation of Cuban women in order to enable them to participate in the labor force. Thus, the day care centers perform an important economic function, in

releasing women to work in the labor-short economy. But at the same time, by allowing women to work outside the home, the centers help reduce *machismo* (the Latin variety of male chauvinism), a specific aim of the Revolution since its initial period.

Further, the nursery schools are not merely day care centers to serve mothers, they also provide a structure in which children are trained toward collective consciousness even as little babies:

When a Cuban baby is placed in a playpen, he is put into no standard United States model with only room enough for himself— or at most two toddlers. The Cuban playpen—or more appropriately, "corral"—permits at least six infants to play together in a space equal to the size of a small room ... Far more rationally designed than the American playpen, it avoids the tedious efforts of adults in attendance to bend to floor level to assist children ... Group play as distinct from individual activities takes precedence. ... Encouraged to design activities to stimulate group play, *asistentes* in the *Circulos* lead children into social and play patterns to help them develop collective attitudes. *Asistentes* are to make special efforts to see to it that all children participate in the program designed for the collective. (Leiner, 1973, pp. 10–11.)[2]

EDUCATIONAL REFORM AND CHANGES IN CUBAN ECONOMIC STRATEGY

Overall, there can be little doubt that it was the change from dependent capitalism to socialism that had the greatest impact on educational institutions in Cuba. But it is important not to lose sight of the fact that many Cuban educational reforms also took (and continue to take) place within the context of the Revolutionary ideology and overall development policy *in response to changes* in particular economic strategies. One of the most fascinating aspects of Cuban educational reforms is that a number of significant changes in the educational system took place *after* the initial and over-

Table 1. Cuba: Day Care Centers (Circulos Infantiles) 1961–1970

Year	Centers
1961	37
1962	109
1963	144
1964	157
1965	166
1966	194
1967	262
1968	332
1969	381
1970[a]	430

Note: [a]Through November 1970.
Source: Marvin Leiner, 1974.

whelming commitment of incorporating the masses into economic development through adult education and the enormous expansion of primary and secondary schooling. These later changes reflected the various attempts to solve the economic growth problem within the constraints of the egalitarian and mass mobilization goals set by the Revolution. The Cuban government *continuously adapted the educational system to fit their strategies for increasing output per capita and making the socialist economy viable.* At the same time, the underlying earlier Revolutionary theme that education was a *right* to be available for everyone also continued as a foundation of educational policy.

Technical Education: Perhaps the first major change to occur in the Cuban development plan was the de-emphasis in 1963–1964 of industrial development in favor of the expansion of the agricultural sector. By that time, there had been large-scale migration to urban areas, and agricultural development had become hampered by a shortage of rural labor as well as by its low productivity.

Education responded to this emphasis on agricultural development. After 1963 there was a rapid growth of middle-level technical education in agricultural schools with a temporary decline in industrial technical school enrollment. University enrollment in agricultural sciences also increased rapidly after 1963. The emphasis on agricultural development thus had an important effect on the orientation of technical and scientific training.

With its pressing need for rural labor and the emphasis on agricultural production, the Cuban economy turned, beginning in 1966, toward moral rather than material incentives, and to the development of the new socialist man. The concept of socialist emulation had been present in the ideological basis of the economic structure since the early years of the Revolution, and it was translated in the schools into a stress on collective work rather than individual achievement. With the advent of moral incentives, a greatly *increased* emphasis was placed on the relationship of schools to work and on teaching young people in schools to behave in a collective, unselfish, and altruistic manner.

Schools to the Countryside: The educational reform that reflected the need for agricultural labor and the development of the new socialist man was "schools *to* the countryside." The first experiment of moving a school to the countryside took place in 1966. The objectives of these schools were defined around the social ideal of the formation of the "new socialist man," and they were aimed at eliminating the differences between city and country, establishing close bonds between the school and daily life, and educating the new generation in and for work. Apparently, the project had positive results in contributing to the growth of a real awareness among students of farming and related industry. Furthermore, by living together for about seven weeks in the countryside, students were introduced to the mechanics of organization and self-government based on group cooperation and work, thereby developing and understanding collective action. During the work/study period, both teachers and principals lived together with students in dormitories and worked with them in the fields. These activities—students and teachers alike working

side-by-side with peasants—probably contributed greatly to the obliteration of class lines based on the manual versus non-manual work distinction. Furthermore, as Bowles points out,

In the *escuela al campo* program, the leadership of the camp often goes to those who work well, not to the monitors or to others who excel at intellectual tasks. The occasional inversion of the hierarchy of the school's social system itself teaches an additional lesson for equality. (Bowles, 1972, p. 296.)

But the "schools to the countryside" movement also met at least part of the need for additional agricultural labor. In the 1972–1973 school year almost 200,000 students were still involved in part-year production through the program. Students did almost 20 million hours of farm work, representing about 3 million student-days. Working on 160,000 hectares of land, they harvested 2.5 million quintals of vegetables and small fruit and 800 million pounds of cane, and sowed 19,000 hectares of land. As Mesa-Lago has argued, even though the productivity of these students was much lower than the professional cane cutters', their net contribution to output (after the costs of feeding and housing them) was probably positive. Thus, the "school to the countryside" program not only was consistent with the development of the "new socialist man" but corresponded to the need for volunteer rural labor in solving significant shortages of agricultural workers.

Nevertheless, the slow growth of agriculture (in comparison with the continued growth of industry), and the dynamic role that agriculture had and has to play in Cuban development, brought out one of the fundamental economic difficulties faced by Cuban leadership: the overall achievement of equalization of incomes and the almost complete elimination of open unemployment seemed to have reduced productivity in rural areas. Even before the difficulties of the 1970 sugar harvest, Cuban leaders were beginning to reject the concept of moral incentives as a way out of the productivity dilemma and beginning to look for other solutions.

In its effort to increase economic growth the government was also faced with the diversion of large amounts of public funds into schooling. The percentage of investment going to schooling, health, and other social services declined over the decade; nevertheless, the necessary further expansion of the industrial and agricultural sectors needed not only skilled labor, but also enormous investment in machines. A way had to be found that would *reduce the cost of schooling* to the economy at the same time that it lowered dropout and repetition rates in school.

With the attempt to solve these difficulties, "schools *to* the countryside" began to be de-emphasized after 1970 for three reasons: first, it became clear that the voluntary labor system in rural areas would not solve production problems; second, students were losing an average of about forty-five days a year working in the countryside, and, although they were supposed to be studying at the same time they were working, "by nearly everyone's admission, not much serious study goes on in the work camps or other non-classroom activities" (Bowles, 1972, p. 302);[3] and third, during the rest of the year, the schools were largely traditional in their mode of operation and their cost.

Schools in the Countryside: To solve all these difficulties, the school *to* the countryside was replaced by the school *in* the countryside; the schools *in* the countryside are junior high schools (seventh, eighth, ninth, and tenth grades) catering primarily to urban students and combining work and study in the countryside on a year-round basis.

There will no longer be the school to the countryside: there is now the school in the countryside. No longer will there be five weeks, six weeks, 40 days, 50 days, in which students leave studies and do work in the countryside. No. We will combine systematically study and productive work daily. What does this permit us? It permits us to create an *economic base from this educational plan*. Because we understand that the production of these schools will cover the schools' investment costs and expenditures. If this is so, then *we will be able to construct schools of this type without limit*. If this is so, we will be able to continue expanding and developing these plans. This type of school combines two factors: First, an ideal educational type of a socialist education, a Communist education with the necessities of our own economic development. At the same time, this kind of school is not a drain on the economy but contributes to the economy and to the development of the country. Thus, we can continue to construct this type of school until we have all our students in secondary schools of this type. Because of this we consider that for the conditions of our country this is the ideal type of school. (Fidel Castro, April 25, 1971; emphasis added.)

In the 1972–1973 school year, the junior high schools in the countryside were attended by about 11 percent of the students enrolled in the first cycle of the secondary educational system. The schools have their own distinct organizational characteristics. The students, most of whom come from urban areas and board at the school, maintain contact with their families by normally spending weekends at home. Moreover, the school systematically combines study and work during the *entire school year,* producing goods that are part of the economic develpment plan.

The new program tries to raise *collective consciousness* in students through the organization of study and work; in this way, the school is similar to its predecessors. But, unlike other schooling concepts, this type of educational institution is built around plans for agricultural production (citrus, coffee, and vegetable): the group responsible in each school for productive activity is involved in the administrative council of the agricultural plan. Also, this new school is different in that it tries directly to relocate future workers from the city to rural areas, preparing urban young people to be skilled agricultural workers. Finally, the idea that schools should actually finance themselves by producing goods worth as much as the schools cost to operate is a total departure from standard educational practice and new even to Cuba.

The schools in the countryside, like secondary schools in the previous organization of education, use student monitors and have science and technology circles to promote student interest and to offer the students the opportunity to broaden their theoretical and practical studies in specified fields. Furthermore, although moral incentives have been de-emphasized in production, the schools in the countryside through the work process and heavy emphasis on Revolutionary ideology are attempting to build a level of consciousness that will make moral incentives in production more possible in the future. Despite the increased use of material incentives in factories, the schools are completely organized around socialist emulation, mass participation, and moral incentives. The schools represent a profound reform in the Cuban educational system, a reform that is a response to low productivity in the countryside in the 1960s, to the shortage of rural labor, and to the commitment of Cuban leadership to agricultural development as the lead sector in economic growth.

At the same time that the high school system is being developed along the lines of the schools in the countryside, the primary school and the university are also being transformed under this same concept. The primary school work model is based on an experiment of school gardens in Las Villas Province, where primary students began cultivating vegetables in 1971–1972. This experiment was so successful that school gardens were extended to Havana in 1972–1973, and to all of Cuba beginning in 1973–1974.

University Education: As far as the university is concerned, the new depersonalization of planning and the move to decentralize somewhat the management of production have contributed to a rapid increase in the growth of the university system. Furthermore, there has apparently been much greater commitment to a university enrollment increase now that the period of using educational expansion primarily as a means of achieving social and economic egalitarianism is over. The new emphasis on economic growth and the development of higher-level management and technical capability as a *primary* concern (it was always an important goal of the Revolutionary leadership) has been a major factor in the allocation of more resources to the university, particularly in higher technical skills.

While the overall emphasis in educational resource allocation bespeaks a strong commitment to equality, and perhaps even a desire to thwart the development of a technocratic elite, other policies seem to run against the commitment. In a society committed to rapid scientific and technological advance from a position of educational backwardness, the need to fill high level scientific positions has posed a temptation to give special educational opportunities to especially talented students. A secondary school for an intellectual elite has been established in Havana, and as of 1969, plans were under way to establish others in the remaining provinces. Students at this school are chosen primarily on the basis of their scholastic performance. (Bowles, p. 301.)[4]

Despite this tendency toward elitism through selection based on scholastic achievement for special secondary schools which then lead to university, it should be re-emphasized that students in these elite secondary schools must engage in productive work while studying and that the university student must also work concurrently with his or her studies and must be in a producing situation throughout the university stay. Furthermore, there is now increased control of the *kinds* of studies that can be undertaken at the university level, control directly related to professional manpower needs according to the development plan. Until 1969–1970, the choice of university career was up to the individual student, which produced rapid increases in prestigious occupations like medicine, but not rapid enough growth in other disciplines like the agricultural sciences. In 1970, the university began to coordinate admissions into programs with the manpower plan, limiting access to programs that historically had relatively high numbers of graduates, and attempting to expand others viewed as crucial for future economic development.[5]

Thus, while the investment patterns and selection system in Cuban education seem to reflect an increased elitism intended for increased economic growth, the curriculum at all levels, also designed to integrate schools and students into the production system, is oriented toward moral incentives, the new socialist man, and the attempt to revitalize Revolutionary ideology of love of work and the integration of manual labor and intellectual activity.

THE CONSEQUENCES AND PROBLEMS OF CUBAN EDUCATIONAL REFORMS

What have all these reforms achieved? We know that the changes in education did *not* produce more equal income distribution or lower levels of unemployment. Those economic reforms resulted from direct intervention in the economic system; indeed, the nature of educational expansion in Cuba reflected the same ideology that produced economic intervention for greater income equality and full employment. As far as growth of output is concerned, *in the short run* it probably suffered from the heavy investment in education and literacy during the early sixties; non-productive investment in 1961 was almost one-half of total investment (not including earnings foregone), and though a substantial portion of this was in adult education, most adult training in that period was for literacy and basic cognitive skills. In the longer run, the concentration on education *probably did* contribute to economic growth, particularly in the industrial sector and in those parts of the agricultural sector, like citrus growing, where other constraints did not impede increased production (sugar, for example).[6] Educational investment contributed to mass mobilization, a key element in the Cuban socialist development model.

While we can say little about the growth contribution of educational investment, we can be much more concrete about the delivery of social services: Cuba was able to replace, in a relatively short period of time, the doctors, teachers, and engineers who left after the Revolution. Education and health care are supplied in much greater quantity and in much higher quality in the 1970s for the mass of population than they were in the 1950s (see Table 2). Furthermore, almost no one is illiterate in Cuba, and reading material is available in much greater quantities now than it was before the Revolution. In part, it is through mass education that people in rural areas have been brought into the mainstream of Cuban development.

Table 2. Cuba: Estimated Educational Pyramid 20–29 Year Old Group 1953 and 1973 (Percent)

Level of schooling	1953 Educated in 1930s and 1940s	1973 Educated in 1960s
No Schooling	20	0
Primary	72	70
Secondary (Academic and Vocational)	6	20
University	2	10

Source: 1953–Jolly, in Seers, 1962, pp. 166–167.
1973–Estimated from figures in text on dropout rates for 1965–1966 cohort.

We would expect that an expansion of this magnitude would result in a decline in the "quality" of the education provided. We have no data on whether there has been a decline in the performance of students at any time during the expansion. On the one hand, however, we do know that teacher/ student ratios rose significantly after 1958 at the primary and secondary levels, decreased and then rose in the technical and professional schools, and decreased only in the teacher training colleges between 1958 and 1970 (Dahlman, 1973). Furthermore, curriculum reforms, the widespread use of new textbooks, and the introduction of new methods such as educational television and teacher training methods, particularly for rural school teachers, have probably had positive effects on student performance.[7] On the other hand, the introduction in the second half of the decade of the "school to the countryside" (discussed above), involving work in the rural areas for about forty-five days per year for primary and secondary school students, although completely consistent with the social goals of the Revolution, probably had a negative effect on student performance on achievement tests.

There was, and perhaps still is, a serious dropout problem in schools. Taking first-grade enrollment cohorts for 1958–1959 to 1965–1966, Dahlman (see Dahlman, 1973, pp. 116–121) reports (based on data provided by Nelson, 1971) that the first post-Revolutionary cohort (1958–1959) had 38.1 percent reaching the sixth grade, but thereafter the percentage fell to about 20 percent, rising with the last cohort to 32 percent. Among those who reached the sixth grade, only about 70 percent managed to graduate. Furthermore, although nationally 21.2 percent of the 1965–1966 cohort graduated in 1971, the rate for urban elementary schools was 34.2 percent while that for rural schools was just 11.7 percent. At the junior high level, of the 59,000 students who entered the seventh grade in 1966–1967, only 29 percent (or 17,000) reached the tenth grade and only 47 percent of those (or 8,000)

passed that grade. This low success rate helps explain the small enrollment in senior high schools and technological institutions. Apparently there is a serious repeater problem in Cuba, which in turn is linked to the problem of those teenagers who, because of high dropout rates, are neither in school nor working.

Castro analyzed these problems of the educational system in a speech at the Second Congress of the Young Communist League on April 4, 1972.

What factors cause these difficulties? There are quite a few. For example, the material resources: school installations, the materials available for study, the difficulties involved in going to school in the mountains, the distance, the isolated school, the poor school, the school in a hut or the school with a roof of thatched palm. There are other problems: the environment, the cultural level of the population, a persisting lack of awareness about the importance of schooling and education, of the need for discipline, regular attendance in school and parental cooperation with the school. Another important aspect is the quality and efficiency of educational personnel in the schools. Out of 79,968 teachers, only 24,265 have graduated from teacher training; in other words, 30.4% of the teachers have graduated. In the elementary schools, 61.3% of teachers are non-graduates and in the junior high schools, 73.7% are non-graduates.

The shortage of qualified personnel is greater at the junior high level because of the bulge of elementary school graduates entering junior high in the late 1960s and early 1970s. It has been estimated that between 1972 and 1976, 22,427 junior high school teachers would be needed, but in this period only 1,990 new teachers will graduate. Although 2,000 more will be available from those working as practice teachers, this will still leave a deficit of more than 18,000 qualified teachers.

Castro also pointed out that the high dropout rate in the lower levels of schooling led to low levels of enrollment in technical and professional education: in 1972, only 24,000 students were enrolled in industrial and agricultural schools.

If we consider the fact that this country must live off industry and agriculture and that every improvement in our standard of living and in our economy depends on industry and agriculture and their development, 23,960 seems like a figure for Luxembourg or Monte Carlo, but not this country. This doesn't seem to be a Cuban figure. (Castro, April 4, 1972.)

In order to solve these problems, several measures have been taken and others are in the process of implementation. One such measure, which depends on the development of new schools, is the establishment of special schools in the countryside for 13- to 15-year-old students at the elementary level. These schools are similar to the junior high schools in the countryside that we have described. The students will proceed with their elementary training, separate from the 6- to 10-year-olds. Average junior high students are sent to the polytechnical schools. The solution thus assigns students to schools according to education and age level.

The quality of teaching is to be raised through the "guerrillas of education" movement, which will try to get more young people to enroll in teacher training schools, and through refresher courses for nongraduate teachers. The number of teachers is low, especially in the junior high schools in the countryside. A movement among junior high school graduates to enroll in teacher training has been started. In 1972, 20,000 students were in the tenth grade; some of these students will be teaching under the supervision of more experienced teachers and will be enrolled in the Pedagogical Institutes. Thus they will be able to go to the junior high schools in the countryside, work with experienced teachers, and get their pedagogical training right there in the school. "At present there simply isn't any other formula except to go to our tenth-graders and recruit at least 2,000 of them this year, at least 5,000 next year, and so on" (Castro, ibid.).

These problems indicate that while the achievements of the Cuban educational efforts have been remarkable, particularly in adult education and in the rapid expansion of primary and secondary school and the extension of schooling into rural areas, such educational expansion even in a society as committed to education as Cuba is fraught with difficulty in a country where the availability of highly-trained teaching personnel is limited (for example, by the conditions of underdevelopment that preceded the Revolution). The shortage of educational personnel also reflects the overall shortage of skilled labor in the economy, and the shortage of adequate facilities in the schools reflects the overall shortages of material goods. Furthermore, as the figures indicate, one of the principal reasons that there are great difficulties in providing schooling in Cuba is the Revolution's commitment to rural areas, areas where the population is thinly spread and transportation not particularly well-developed, and where a culture of traditional values inherited from the pre-Revolutionary social and economic structure is still deeply ingrained.

Castro summarized the situation in the following way:

We face a really special situation in the coming years. Why? Because we are living through a transitional situation. We still don't have the new man and we no longer have the old one. The new man doesn't exist yet. (Castro, ibid.)

SPECULATIONS ON THE CONTRADICTIONS FOR CUBAN DEVELOPMENT CREATED BY THE EDUCATIONAL REFORMS

One of the principal political issues in post-Revolutionary Cuba, as we have described it, is whether the development of socialist consciousness can precede a high level of material production and consumption or must follow it. Cuban theoreticians have opted for socialist consciousness as part and parcel of the economic growth-process, both to create a new political culture and to increase the possibilities for material growth through mass mobilization (Fagen, 1969).

Indeed, the Cuban strategy attempts to mitigate one of the primary contradictions in socialist development: in the drive for increased production under socialism, increased consumption wants are also created among socialist workers and socialist bureaucrats. New status structures develop, particularly through the kinds of goods consumed by different parts of the socialist hierarchy. Just as schools act to reduce the contradictions in capitalist production through their socialized function (Carter, 1975), the educational system in Cuba in trying to create the New Man attempts to alter the kinds of goods and services desired by Cubans during the drive to increase production. Thus, the schools focus on teaching skills that will promote growth while at the same time putting heavy emphasis on service to others as an individual goal in place of increasing individual material consumption.

Despite this, the need for highly skilled, qualified professional-level labor has apparently led to increased selectivity for more desired, higher status work, and to the possibility of creating an elite technocratic group that might perpetuate itself from generation to generation through the educational system. Again, the possibility of contradiction arises from the goal of increased growth.

The expansion of schooling may accentuate this contradiction: with higher levels of schooling, Cuban youth may aspire to greater material welfare; at the same time, the ideals of the Revolution may begin to wane despite the socialization in the schools as the experience of the Revolution itself fades into the past. This would force the leadership to move further and further towards a technocratic State concentrating on economic growth.

On the other hand, the schools may produce a high level of socialist consciousness, creating demands for more social idealism than the economic and social structure is able to deliver. Increased levels of schooling in the population may thus lead more Cubans to demand a society beyond the centralized-planning, State-run economy. These demands might be reflected in pressure for more control over work (increased quality of working life) and more responsibility for determining how and what products are to be produced, as well as more influence in political decision. Increased education may help to dismantle the very State apparatus that developed the educational system itself.

These are speculations, but there are indications that there *is* increased pressure for *decentralization* of Cuban economic and political structures, along with undiminished idealism. We have indicated some of the changes taking place in Cuban society after 1970. First of all, there is some evidence that the schools are helping to produce a high level of socialist consciousness. Zimbalist, in a recent paper, reports that, in the case of two secondary schools he visited in 1974, when the school administration attempted to introduce prizes for the best work teams, the students objected.

These students, who were not reared and socialized in a capitalist society, see their work as promoting social welfare and not individual or group advancement. The prizes are not being used. (Zimbalist, 1975, p. 19.)

Second, Zimbalist reports that worker production assemblies are now generally meeting monthly or bi-monthly at the enterprise level to discuss production and work organization, and that there is some movement toward increased work participation.

The foregoing participation scheme is young and is still largely confined to the enterprise level. Thus, worker involvement in the setting of national priorities, investment, and foreign trade policy is as yet highly inadequate. However, a central point is that the

Party Leadership is openly calling for participation at higher levels, *thereby fanning the desires and expectations for such participation.* (Zimbalist, 1975, p. 20; emphasis added.)

Third, democratization is also taking place in local and provincial government and within the Party. "In the words of Raul Castro, the effort is to find 'the best possible combination of centralization which is indispensable for the guarantee of what is desirable for the general social interest of the country, and, at the same time, the decentralization which guarantees the particular interest of the localities and the mass of people which cannot be adequately handled from the center'" (Zimbalist, 1975, p. 23).

While this democratization at the economic and political level is still very uneven and in its infancy, and even though the central Party apparatus still sets the priorities of the plan, the movement now is in the direction of *more* participation. Increased schooling in the labor force and in the population should accelerate this movement and should contribute to dismantling the paternalistic State apparatus that has existed since the Revolution. However, we should also consider that external factors may increase demands for more material welfare, and the two goals may not be consistent with each other. Given Cuba's *geo-political situation* and the physical threat posed by the United States, the pressure for a strong central State, its military apparatus, and its ability to increase economic growth may put constraints on the move toward decentralized Communism. Schooling may therefore produce increasing demands on the central State to decentralize decision making under conditions where the state does not want to do so.

ON THE APPLICATION OF CUBAN EDUCATIONAL REFORMS TO DEPENDENT CAPITALIST ECONOMIES.

Many of the educational problems faced by developing countries have been dealt with directly by Cuban educational reforms, particularly the extension of primary and secondary schooling into rural areas and the fitting of educational output more closely to the economy's manpower needs. Furthermore, there is no unemployment of higher-trained labor despite a rapid extension in recent years of university education. Can Cuban educational reforms be applied in dependent capitalist economies? Can some of the concepts and changes we have discussed above be transferred to a society in which a radical ideological shift from capitalism to socialism has not taken place?

In theory, there is no reason why rural boarding schools at the secondary level, for example, cannot exist in a capitalist economy. Indeed, such boarding schools are common in rural East Africa, continuing the system of education imposed on those countries when they were British colonies. However, these boarding schools cater primarily to *rural* students and essentially prepare them to be incorporated into the *urban* labor market. We must consider carefully why boarding schools that bring urban students to study in the countryside could succeed in Cuba (if they do succeed), while they could not succeed in a country whose dominant elite is an urban bourgeoisie.

First, the urban bourgeoisie will not dedicate a significant fraction of its resources destined for education to the development in rural areas of a skilled labor force trained specifically to work on rural problems, primarily because one of the main objectives of education in capitalist societies run by urban bourgeoisies is to develop a skilled labor force for *urban* occupations, including manufacturing and services, thereby putting downward pressure on skilled worker wages in urban areas. We cannot expect an urban bourgeoisie to develop a labor force that is inconsistent with its self-interest.

Second, from a different perspective, it is inconceivable, in an economy where wages are much higher in urban areas than in rural areas and where all the wage incentives point people toward working in urban areas, that a government will be able to persuade either teachers to teach in the countryside, or students to stay in the countryside once given an education that will certify them to get jobs in urban labor markets.

What about other aspects of Cuban educational reform? For example, what about the relationship between work and schooling? This is, in theory, a reform that it is possible to implement in dependent capitalist societies, but again, its success in practice would depend in large part on the willingness of the urban bourgeoisie and middle class to support programs that would have their children working in manual occupations while attending secondary school and the first years of university. We suspect that it would be difficult to force such a program on the middle class. It would probably work if limited to work-study programs for working-class and rural children, with higher secondary school, private schools, and universities being exempt from any combination of work and study. Of course, there are already large numbers of university students even in low-income capitalist societies who do work and study at the same time (Carnoy, 1975), but in general their work is done to earn enough money so that they can support themselves while they advance their study to take on a different kind of work once they graduate. Thus, in capitalist societies, study and work, while occurring simultaneously, are usually separate in concept and applicability.

Finally, what are the chances of developing an independent base for research and development of technology relevant to product needs in the developing country? Again, in theory there is no reason why in a dependent capitalist economy there should not be the kind of technical education that would enable the country to develop a technology relevant to its growth needs. In practice, however, as in Cuba before the Revolution, much of the technological capability and control over goods produced is exercised by foreign companies and foreign managers with the cooperation of the local government in the low-income

country. To develop a counter-technology means at least in part to break with the kinds of goods produced by foreign companies both at home and in the foreign country, and to choose an alternative development pattern. One criterion for the success of such a program is the incorporation of the masses into the development of local technology. It is difficult to imagine, in a class-structured capitalist society, that the knowledge of technology, which is one of the bases of class division, should become universally available, as it is now in Cuba.

The correspondence principle not only tells us that educational reform in a country like Cuba corresponds directly to the economic and social changes which have taken place with the Revolution, but also suggests that there would be great difficulty in transferring these types of educational reform to societies in which similar kinds of ideological and economic transformations are not taking place. We must clearly separate the *idealistic* images of educational reforms from the realities of economic and social change. While we may formulate the theoretical transference of such educational reforms to nonsocialist societies, we can show that in practice this transference will not take place, not because of the malevolence of the parties involved, but rather because such transference is against the self-interest of dominant groups in a class-structured capitalist society.

NOTES

1. While this training program provided the means for greatly expanding rural schools, it apparently did not solve the dropout and repeater problem in rural areas. In the late sixties and early seventies, the solution to that problem was sought partly through the boarding and semi-boarding schools in rural areas.

2. Leiner reports that he tried to determine what effect the official ideology was having in the classroom by using the fairly simple technique of the open-ended question. One composition topic he offered to a number of classes in the upper grades was *If I Had Five Wishes.* He argued that in the answers to this question "the themes of commitment and sacrifice are repeatedly expressed in the composition. 'To go where the Revolution needs

me' is a most frequent expression" (Leiner, 1973, pp. 5–6).

3. In 1971, delegates representing teachers, educators, scientists, and cultural agencies and institutes participated in the First National Congress on Education and Culture. Among other recommendations, they criticized the *escuelas al campo* on the grounds that the time lost from formal schooling was having negative effects on the academic work of students and that the activities of the program had been poorly integrated into the formal school system (Dahlman, 1973, p. 79).

4. Bowles is referring to the Cento Vocational School, which was originally created in the school year 1966–1967, and which is today the Lenin Vocational School, recently built for the 1972–1973 school year. This School, the only one of this kind in Cuba, with a capacity for 4,500 high school and pre-university students, is twenty-three kilometers from the center of Havana and occupies 84,000 square meters of land. This is a school for study and industrial work, primarily in electronics. Besides annual agricultural production exceeding 500 quintals, students at the Lenin School have produced 50,000 battery-operated radios, manufactured goods and sports equipment valued at 1,000,000 pesos, and thirty electronic computers, which have been assembled for use in instruction at the center and in industrial installations elsewhere in the country. The organization cell of the Lenin Vocational School is made up of 120 science and technology circles, encompassing all fields. These circles guarantee a large university enrollment emphasizing technological, scientific, and agricultural occupations. (In the past school year, 85 percent of the graduates entered careers related to their circle.)

The work of the Lenin Vocational School is divided into agriculture, in which nearly 3,000 high school students participate, and industrial work, in which 700 pre-university students take part. The rest—students, professors, instructors, and pedagogic assistants—do community and service work.

The selection process for the Lenin School is very restrictive; only those pupils who get very high grades in the last three years of primary school are accepted. In 1972–1973, the average primary school grade average of students in the first year of the school was 85/100, and in 1973–1974, 95/100. Dropouts from the school represent only 2 percent of the cohort. (*Granma*, special issue on the Lenin School, February 1974.)

5. The selection system works in the following way: information on the high priority careers is passed on to the students in the last year of pre-university training and in the worker-peasant university. The student selects the career he or she wants to follow, and is accepted or not, on the basis of the number of places available and the student's grades in the last three years of secondary school. If a student is not selected for the career he wanted he can apply to another career where there is greater opportunity for admission. In the case of medicine, for example, the situation in 1970 was a relative saturation of the career in terms of the country's needs. Entrance to the study of medicine is now severely restricted through an examination;

as a result, enrollment in that field fell from 8,773 students in 1970 to 8,393 in 1972, while every other faculty's enrollment rose rapidly in the same period. Even so, those with the best grades may still end up in the most prestigious careers.

6. Although there was little per capita economic growth in Cuba in the 1960s (Ritter, 1974), the situation apparently changed markedly after 1970. In his staff report to the Committee on Foreign Relations of the U.S. Senate, Pat Holt said that the per capita income in Cuba in 1974 was about $1,600 (Holt, 1974). Although this seems high in terms of what Cubans can consume, Holt concluded that "the Cubans are on the verge of constructing a socialist showcase in the Western Hemisphere" (Holt, quoted in Zimbalist, 1975, p. 22).

7. The most important curriculum changes in primary schools were related to the reinforcement of self-learning, more emphasis on tying the specific objectives of the curriculum to the development of individual abilities, especially in the first, second, and third grades, and a break with the traditional pattern of purely academic class periods (Cuba, 1973).

Educational television has been used extensively in secondary and pre-university schools since 1968–1969. The system uses Havana channels 2 and 6 for broadcasting twenty-five-minute television classes to about 12,000 television sets in the schools. The television classes are supplemented by classroom activities based on guides supplied by the designers of the programs. The Ministry of Education has decided that once the teacher shortage is overcome, the number of television programs will be reduced—this number has already declined from sixty programs per week in 1969–1970 to twenty per week in 1972–1973—until television becomes just one more teaching aid among a set of technological tools available for children in school.

BIBLIOGRAPHY

Allen, Gordon. "Education in Revolutionary Cuba." *Education Digest* 40 (October 1974).

Barkin, David. "Cuban Agriculture: A Strategy of Economic Development." In *Cuba: The Logic of Revolution*, edited by David Barkin and Nita Manitzas. Andover, Mass.: Warner Modular Publications, 1973.

Bender, Lynn Darrell. *In the Politics of Hostility: Castro's Revolution and United States Policy.* Hato Rey, Puerto Rico: Inter-American University Press, 1975.

Bernardo, Robert. *The Theory of Moral Incentives in Cuba.* University, Alabama: The University of Alabama Press, 1971.

Boorstein, Edward. *The Economic Transfor-

mation of Cuba. New York: Monthly Review Press, 1968.

Bowles, Samuel. "Education and Socialist Man in Cuba." In *Schooling in a Corporate Society,* edited by Martin Carnoy. New York: David McKay, 1972.

Bowles, Samuel, and Herbert Gintis. *Schooling in Capitalist America.* New York: Basic Books, 1975.

Carnoy, Martin. *Education as Cultural Imperialism.* New York: David McKay, 1974.

Carnoy, Martin. "The Role of Education in a Strategy of Social Change." In *The Limits of Educational Reform,* edited by Martin Carnoy and Henry Levin. New York: David McKay, 1976.

Carnoy, Martin. "University Education in the Economic Development of Peru." Mimeographed. Consejo Nacional de la Universidad Peruana, 1975.

Carnoy, Martin, and Henry Levin, eds. *The Limits of Educational Reform.* New York: David McKay, 1976.

Carnoy, Martin; Richard Sack; and Hans Thias. *The Payoff to "Better" Schooling: A Case Study of Tunisian Secondary Schools.* Washington: World Bank, 1976, forthcoming.

Carter, Michael. "Contradiction and Correspondence: An Analysis of the Relation of Schooling to Work." Mimeographed. Palo Alto, Cal.: Center for Economic Studies, 1975.

Castro, Fidel. *La Educacion en Revolucion.* Havana: Instituto Cubano del Libra, 1974. (This volume contains all of Castro's speeches related to education.)

Cuba, Ministerio de Educacion. *La Educacion en Cuba.* La Habana, 1973.

Dahlman, Carl J. "The Nationwide Learning System of Cuba." Mimeographed. Princeton, N.J.: Woodrow Wilson School, Princeton University, July 1973.

Fagen, Richard. *The Transformation of Political Culture in Cuba.* Stanford, Cal.: Stanford University Press, 1969.

Fagen, Richard. In *Fidel Castro's Personal Revolution in Cuba: 1959–1973,* edited by James Nelson Goodsell. New York: Knopf, 1975.

Fagen, Richard; R.A. Brody; and T. O'Leary. *Cubans in Exile: A Demographic Analysis of Social Problems.* Stan-

ford, Cal.: Stanford University Press, 1968.

Ferrer, Raul. *Convergence* (Toronto) 6, no. 1 (1973).

Foster, Philip. "The Vocational Schooling Fallacy." In *Education and Economic Development,* edited by Mary Jean Bowman and Arnold Anderson. Chicago: Aldine Publishing Co., 1964.

Gilette, Arthur. "Cuba's Educational Revolution." Fabian Research Series, No. 302. London, June 1972.

Gintis, Herbert. "The New Working Class and Revolutionary Youth." In *Schooling in a Corporate Society,* 2nd ed., edited by Martin Carnoy. New York: David McKay, 1975.

Holt, Pat. "Cuba." Staff Report prepared for the Committee on Foreign Relations of the U.S. Senate. U.S. Government Printing Office, 1974.

Jolly, Richard. "Education." In *Cuba: The Economic and Social Revolution,* edited by Dudley Seers. Chapel Hill; University of North Carolina Press, 1964.

Jolly, Richard. "Contrasts in Cuban and African Educational Strategies." In *Education and Nation Building in the Third World,* edited by J. Lowe. New York: Barnes and Noble, 1971.

Leiner, Marvin. "Major Developments in Cuban Education." In *Cuba: The Logic of the Revolution,* edited by David Barkin and Nita Manitzas. Andover, Mass.: Warner Modular Publications, 1973.

Leiner, Marvin. *Children Are the Revolution: Day Care in Cuba.* New York: Viking, 1974.

Levin, Henry. "The Meaning of Educational Reform." In *The Limits of Educational Reform,* edited by Martin Carnoy and Henry Levin. New York: David McKay, 1976.

Manitzas, Nita. "The Setting of the Cuban Revolution." In *Cuba: The Logic of the Revolution,* edited by David Barkin and Nita Manitzas. Andover, Mass.: Warner Modular Publications, 1973.

Mesa-Lago, Carmelo. "The Labor Force, Employment, Unemployment, and Underemployment in Cuba: 1899–1970." New York: Sage Professional Paper, 1972.

Mesa-Lago, Carmelo. *Cuba in the 1970s.* Albuquerque, N.M.: University of New Mexico Press, 1974.

Mesa-Lago, Carmelo. "The Economic Significance of Unpaid Labor in Socialist Cuba."

Nelson, Lowry. "The School Dropout Problem in Cuba." *School and Society* 99 (April 1971): 234–235.

Newman, Philip. *Cuba Before Castro, An Economic Appraisal.* New York: Foreign Studies Institute, 1965.

Paulston, Rolland. "Education." In *Revolutionary Change in Cuba: Economy, Polity, and Society,* edited by Carmelo Mesa-Lago. Pittsburgh: University of Pittsburgh Press, 1971.

Ritter, Archibald. *The Economic Development of Revolutionary Cuba.* New York: Praeger, 1974.

Seers, Dudley, ed. *Cuba: The Economic and Social Revolution.* Chapel Hill: University of North Carolina Press, 1964.

Sweezy, Paul, and Leo Huberman. *Socialism in Cuba.* New York: Monthly Review Press, 1969.

Thias, Hans, and Martin Carnoy. *Cost-Benefit Analysis in Education: A Case Study of Kenya.* Washington: World Bank, 1972.

Williams, Bruce, and Michael Yates. "Moral Incentives in Cuba." *Review of Radical Political Economics* 6, no. 3 (Fall 1974): 86–90.

Yglesias, Jose. *In the Fist of the Revolution: Life in a Cuban Country Town.* New York: Vintage, 1968.

Zimbalist, Andrew. "The Development of Workers' Participation in Socialist Cuba." Paper prepared for presentation at the Second Annual Conference on Workers' Self-Management, Cornell University, June 6–8, 1975.

35. Economic Necessity and Political Ideals in Educational Reform During the Cultural Revolution

MARIANNE BASTID

Educational reform has been one of the important issues raised during the Cultural Revolution, not merely because it belongs to the realm of culture but, more important, because it bears on the question of "cultivating revolutionary successors" and on the shaping of the whole future of China. Anyone seizing power wishes to keep it for a certain length of time; it is however a special feature of people's revolutions to set their goals on the prospect of a boundless future. In this regard, gaining power in education is not simply one side of the struggle for actual total power (mastering the "superstructure" as well as the "structure") it is the guarantee of everlasting rule, on the assumption that the mind is ultimately the only thing man can rely upon and which is entirely within

his grasp. As one slogan puts it: "The earth may shake, heaven may fall, but we shall ever be faithful to Chairman Mao."

The issue of educational reform during the Cultural Revolution seems, in theoretical terms, to be mainly concerned with such political ideals as proletarian dictatorship and true socialism, together with the suppression of bourgeois or feudal attitudes and concepts. But on looking closer, these ideals appear to spring from a very stringent economic necessity. So much so that, in some reports on educational reform, political and ideological considerations are almost discarded and the reform proposals put forward on principally economic grounds. I have tried in this article to assess the respective weight of economic necessity and political

From *China Quarterly* 42 (April/June 1970): 16–45. Reprinted by permission of the author.

ideals in the educational reform in an attempt to shed some light on the nature of the new "world outlook" which the Cultural Revolution advances. The analysis follows the dialectical process through which the new order is being worked out: that is, criticism of the old system, proposals for reform and the implementation of reform.

CRITICISM AGAINST THE OLD SYSTEM OF EDUCATION

The "old" educational system under attack was essentially the system as it existed in 1965. Criticism against it was launched at the very beginning of the Great Proletarian Cultural Revolution in June 1966. Since then, the contents and main targets have not changed. They come under three headings: the inadequacy of school enrolment; the contents and methods of education; and the general orientation of the old system, dealing with who goes to school, what is taught at school and what the schools are intended for.

The main criticism against the inadequacy of school enrolment was that children from poor and lower-middle peasant families were barred from the greater part of the educational ladder. Ostracism of workers' children occurred, it seems, only at the middle school, college and university level. The direct responsibility for the exclusion of those children has been imputed first to various institutional features of the schools, such as the examination system and age limits. The entrance examination to middle schools and universities is a subject of major concern in towns. The entrance examination to primary school was a feature of well-known or special institutions in urban areas but it existed also for some schools in the countryside, and the injustice of the system has been severely attacked. But peasants were more concerned about the rules on age limits, which excluded a lot of youngsters from elementary or advanced educational opportunities, and about the promotion examinations, which eliminated a number of

"slow" children, most of them sons and daughters of the poorest. Actually it is the marks system with its corollaries of promotion and repeating that has come under the fiercest, steadiest and most united attack, as the key stratagem which excluded children of the working class. The marks system has been attacked on ideological grounds. It is pointed out that this system puts intellectual culture, self-interest and advancement above anything else, thus endangering socialism. However, the theoretical foundation of this system—the underlying assumption that it is possible to measure accurately the value of an individual and place it on a scale—has hardly been analysed and questioned. In fact, the complaints against the marks system are basically economic: the existence of tuition fees makes the matter crucial. In every report from the countryside, it is stressed that children from poor and lower-middle peasant families simply cannot afford to repeat a class, something which is almost inevitable with the marks system. This grievance is thus related to the general complaint against tuition fees and the cost of education, which are viewed by a majority of peasants as a clear discrimination against their children. While this issue is often omitted in reports from the cities, it is always raised in those from rural areas, and in a number of cases it is the first charge against the old system. A common additional charge is that the school is located too far away, so that the children cannot get there on foot, while their families cannot afford to pay boarding fees.

Though the cost of education varied from one school to another and from one locality to another, some details might be useful here. In a fashionable, well-equipped kindergarten in a Peking suburb, the fees were 25 *yuan* a month in 1965 (11 *yuan* for board, 12.4 *yuan* for tuition and 1.6 *yuan* for medical insurance). In another the fees went up to 30 *yuan*. At the same time, one of the "pilot" primary schools in Peking demanded 2.5 *yuan* tuition fees per term and 4 *yuan* per month for lunch on weekdays. A rate of

1.5 to 3 *yuan* per term was fairly common in the countryside as well as in cities. In a Liaoning brigade, in order to attend the local school, each child had to pay 12 to 13 *yuan* a year. In middle schools tuition fees could rise to 2 *yuan* per month with an average of 10 to 15 *yuan* per month for room and board. Even where no tuition fees were required, parents had to pay some 3 to 10 *yuan* a year for books and stationery, according to the grade of the pupil. Recently, a rural brigade in Szechwan complained that board and pocket money alone for a child in lower-middle school cost 100 to 200 *yuan* a year. However, tuition fees did not exist at college level. At Ts'inghua University (Peking) in 1965 the largest scholarships were of 19.5 *yuan* per month, which may be regarded as the minimum expenses of a university student. Students in Peking could hardly spend less than 15 *yuan* a month for food, and many of them, even from rural families, did not get a full scholarship and had to rely on their parents for a monthly subsidy of 5 to 15 *yuan.* Such figures may not seem excessive to a family where both husband and wife work as cadres each earning some 100 *yuan* a month. The factory worker who has three children and earns 50 *yuan* finds it more difficult, even if his wife works. But what about the commune member who may well make 400 *yuan* (payment in kind included) a year in a wealthy brigade in the suburbs of Sian but gets only 44 *yuan* (payment in kind not included) a year in an advanced Shantung brigade, and 12 *yuan* (payment in kind not included) a year in a Yunnan village? In rural areas, many children could not go to school because they had to earn their living or were needed at home while the mother went out in the fields. In June 1969 a Hunan middle-school teacher reported with concern that for such economic reasons only 8 out of 23 school-age children in the brigade where he was sent could go to school.

Criticisms of the contents and methods of education stress the length of studies, the heavy curriculum, the bookishness, and the abstruse and smothering character of the teaching with its emphasis on cramming and memorizing. The six-year primary and the six-year secondary courses are said to be excessive, especially since much of what is taught is superfluous and over-elaborate. Staggering under heavy homework, students are said to rise early and go to sleep late. They stay indoors, ruining their health or becoming short-sighted. Tied down to books, they stagger from concept to concept and lose all real power of analysis. The prominence given to academic culture leaves no time for politics and, above all, no time for the study of the thought of Mao Tsetung.

A more specific charge in rural areas is that since the schools were under the *hsien* Education and Culture Bureau and were directed in a uniform way, local needs and conditions were not taken into account. For instance, the school vacations in a Chekiang brigade were fixed according to the needs of the rice-growing areas, in spite of the fact that these particular villages were engaged in cultivating tea. The Bureaux insisted on building schools at the *hsien* seats and commune centres rather than in the brigades; and it was impossible for villagers to dismiss a bad teacher because he was a "cadre of the State." Peasants referred to the schoolmaster as one who on a beautiful summer day goes humming carelessly to fish in a pond, while everyone around him toils hard under the sun.

The defects of the old system were said to be related to its general orientation. Revisionism and feudal and bourgeois world outlook dominated the educational system owing to the lasting influence of old-type intellectuals and the treacherous policies of Liu Shao-ch'i and capitalist-roaders in the Party. Teaching was divorced from the real struggle—class struggle, a struggle for production and scientific experiment. Education, it was said, was "self-cultivation behind a closed door," turning out young people estranged from their environment, ready to become the docile tools of a capitalist restoration. Such institutions as the farm-study or work-study schools, in their time hailed as utterly revolutionary, have been criticized by city-dwellers, who did not belong to them, as creations of Liu Shao-ch'i, hateful on two counts; because they did not put politics and Mao Tse-tung's thought first; and because, as the full-time schools continued, they amounted to setting up the "double-track" system of capitalist countries. At the same time, in the countryside, many of these schools have been contrasted with the regular schools as much more reliable politically and giving a useful training, closely linked to practice.

On the key issue of the general orientation of the educational system, two different accusations are put forward. One is the charge of cultivating an elite. The system, it is claimed, fostered a promotion-conscious mentality. Liu Shao-ch'i is charged with having spread the reactionary tenet "to study in order to become a mandarin." As the Yenan middle school in Tientsin put it:

In the revisionist view . . . the aim should be to cultivate people capable of serving as cadres, engineers, *hsien* magistrates and even secretaries of provincial committees, that is to cultivate parasites and revisionist seedlings divorced from the practice of the Three Great Revolutions, class struggle, struggle for production and scientific experience.

Another report said:

Bourgeois say: if graduates just become ordinary workers, what is the use of having colleges? They declare that their purpose in running universities is to turn out highly trained "experts," such as scientists, engineers, lawyers, economists, administrators, whom they regard as the "elite" of society, superior to the working people.
The bourgeois system serves to maintain the rule of the capitalist class over the working people and make science, technology and arts its monopoly.
China is a state where the working people are the masters, it is inconceivable that the working class should run colleges to turn out

people who look down upon physical labour and the labouring people. Of course the working class requires its own intellectuals who master science, technology and other knowledge, but in the first place, schools and colleges should turn out true revolutionaries who are faithful to the cause of the working class and who always remain one with the working people. . . .
The Soviet Union provides a lesson: its universities produce a privileged stratum of bourgeois intellectuals who are the "elite" of society sitting on the backs of the working people. . . .

The issue at stake is that of producing people who gain a higher status through education and consequently feel and behave as superiors.

The other charge, which is uttered by different people, does not focus on elitism but on capacity. It could be summed up thus: the old system turns out an elite which is incompetent and useless. Peasants say: "The more they go to school, the more stupid they become." There is a whole folklore of racy anecdotes featuring the pale-faced, thin, dogmatic, dissatisfied graduate versus the quick-minded efficient, hard toiling, openhearted "local expert," who spent a short time in a less sophisticated school but grasps better the thought of Mao Tse-tung. He cannot grow Michurin apples or Caucasian maize, but he knows all about rice and wheat; he works himself instead of giving orders; he listens to the villagers and helps them.

In cities and towns, protests are mainly against the notion of "elite" itself. This accounts for the radicalism of some reform proposals which suggested nothing less than the wholesale abolition of schools. Although these proposals were dismissed later on as "anarchist," they suggest a widespread sense of guilt, even of anti-intellectualism, among young Chinese intellectuals, not unlike some recent attitudes of their western brothers.

In rural areas the issue tends to focus rather on inefficiency, incapacity, waste of time, money and talent. Education is described as an investment which does not yield interest.

The criticism against the old educational system thus mixes up economic and political motives, with, however, the latter predominant. These political motives account for the deliberate darkening of the pre-1966 education picture, which is obvious to anyone who is acquainted with Chinese schools before the Cultural Revolution. By 1965, Chinese education was very far from being a mere copy of Soviet or American bourgeois education. As will be seen below, most of the educational experiments brought in by the Cultural Revolution had been tried under various forms in Yenan or during the Great Leap Forward, and not all of them had been discontinued. It would be a travesty of the facts to regard all Chinese students, or even teachers, prior to 1966 as a host of petty mandarins with their hands in their sleeves. In education, as in other matters, there has been a long struggle between the revolutionary line and the revisionist line, and according to many reports, the latter has not always prevailed. If the general critique against the educational system holds true, it must be understood as often being directed against mere intentions or tendencies. The picture is deliberately drawn in black colours, as is frequently the case in campaigns designed to arouse powerful reactions.

REFORM PROPOSALS

The number and variety of educational reform proposals show that powerful reactions were indeed aroused. From the Chinese press it can be seen that these reform proposals fall into four stages, following directives given from the top by Chairman Mao or the Central Committee.

Before February 1967, when the call to "resume classes to make revolution" was launched, few detailed reform projects appeared. Some tentative proposals were made in early June 1966 with the decision of the Central Committee on 13 June to reform the entrance examination and postpone admission to universities. But soon after those who made them were accused of revisionism and reformism. One of the charges brought against the work teams in early August was that they tried to divert the students from politics by asking them to discuss educational reform. Only guiding principles were given, incorporated in documents dealing with other questions. Such is the paragraph relating to students in the text where Chairman Mao calls on the country to become a big school of revolution and the tenth of the Sixteen Points, which is almost identical. The two texts ruled that the control of the bourgeoisie over the schools should be ended, that the curriculum should be shortened and revolutionized, that students should also learn agriculture, industry and military science and that they should criticize the bourgeoisie. Greeted with enthusiasm, these directives helped to intensify the attack against the old system and its supporters. During this period, however, the focus was on general political issues, and no proposal for the carrying out of the new pedagogical principles received publicity.

After the great revolutionary exchanges of the summer and autumn of 1966, from 1 December, the Central Committee and the State Council repeatedly called for students and teachers to return to their schools. On 4 February 1967, the Central Committee issued a draft regulation on the resumption of courses in all primary schools after the Spring Festival, and on 19 February another document was issued for the middle schools. On 7 March 1967, three important documents were published. One was an editorial in the *People's Daily* entitled "Primary and Middle Schools Resume Classes to Make Revolution." It called for the continuation of the Cultural Revolution inside the schools, developing the criticism and struggle against reactionaries by studying Chairman Mao's Quotations and the Cultural Revolution documents, as well as some science and language courses. This summons was ascribed to the Central Committee, which also issued a circular entitled "Draft Regulations Governing The Great Proletarian Cultural Revolution Currently Under Way in Universities, Colleges and Schools—For Discussion and Trial Implementation." Everybody, it said, should be back in their unit before 20 March and should undergo short-term military and political training; leniency should be shown, except to people in authority taking the capitalist road and reactionary academic authorities; students and teachers should unite and create an organ of power to lead the Cultural Revolution; the Red Guards should be consolidated and rectified. The third document was a directive from Chairman Mao. It was published by the *People's Daily* only on 8 March 1968, although it was based on the experience of the Yenan middle school in Tientsin, an account of which appeared on 21 March 1967 in the *Tientsin jih-pao*. Its wording has similarities to that of the Draft Regulations of the Central Committee; to some it may seem only a later version of the regulations, but the directive adds a very important point: the role of the army—which had in fact intervened in the Yenan middle school experience. It reads:

... The army should give political and military training in the universities, middle schools and the higher classes of primary schools, stage by stage and group by group. It should help in reopening school classes, in strengthening the organization, in establishing a leading organ of the three-in-one alliance and in carrying out the task of struggle-criticism-transformation. It should first make experiments at selected points and acquire experience and then popularize it step by step. ...

The admonishments from the top left room for a fair amount of initiative. The only obligation of the young people was to get out of the streets and go back to school; an order which many obeyed with reluctance. During this period, until the end of October 1967, the reform proposals dealt mainly with the organization of power within the schools. Experiments and suggestions were made regarding the achievement of the Great Alliance, whether on the basis of the various militant organizations inside the school or on that of the teaching classes. Some further opinions were expressed on the setting up of school revolutionary committees with the help and participation of the People's Liberation Army.

In the heated political struggle of the spring and summer of 1967, educational change could not progress smoothly. A "black wind of anarchism" blew everywhere. On 25 October 1967, the *People's Daily* had to reiterate more earnestly the call to resume classes. This time, however, the editorial quoted the paragraph relating to students in Chairman Mao's directive of 7 May 1966:

Students, while taking studies as the main task, should learn other things as well, namely, besides learning literature they must also learn industry, agriculture and military science, and they must also criticize the bourgeoisie. The duration of the course of study must be shortened and education must be revolutionized. The situation in which bourgeois intellectuals rule our schools cannot be allowed to continue.

This instruction sets the aims of the educational reform. The editorial insisted that this reform could not be achieved without actually teaching and studying. It commented:

... In the process of resuming classes to make revolution, teachers and cadres should constantly remind themselves that the work in which they are engaged has a great bearing on the cultivation of successors to the proletarian revolution. They should have the courage and determination to thoroughly criticize the old educational system and completely break out of their own bourgeois world outlook. They should realize that they are both educators and educated and that their students are wiser than they in many respects. They must go to the students, mingle with them, establish a new socialist type of teacher-student relationship. . . .

The directive and the editorial are especially noteworthy on two points: one is the contents of education, the other one is the question of world outlook and attitude, particularly of teachers. As far as the contents are concerned, school-training should give young people several strings to their bows. In a way it amounts to a dismissal of the notion of *chuan,* usually translated as "expert." However, one should remember that *chuan* in Chinese does not mean "expert" or "skilled" so much as "specialized" in one single field. Dedication to the study of a narrow technique does not necessarily imply proficiency in its application. Peasants and workers mentioned hundreds of cases where highly trained personnel stumbled over technical problems which they themselves finally succeeded in solving by discarding the blind worship of dogmatic rules and principles. Besides, in China as elsewhere, employment planning is difficult. If young people cannot, and above all will not, do jobs which do not fall exactly within their special domain, the economic balance and progress might be endangered. Without a doubt, too many academic scientists and technicians have been trained in recent years. Not infrequently a university graduate in physics or chemistry would be found · holding some desk job in a big city administrative office. This was due not only to bureaucratic aberrations. The fact was that the massive effort started in 1958 to enrol more students in the scientific departments had not been completely discontinued, while the rate of industrialization launched by the Great Leap Forward had been much slowed, and the basic orientation of education had moved from people's science to specialists' science. The countryside was in desperate need of more, and more professional manpower, but new trainees were too learned, and equally too ignorant, to be of real use. At the same time, the already over-staffed urban industry could not absorb them all.

Versatile people were and still are needed, but versatile in concrete things. There is no idea of a reversion to the mandarin type of education—general abstract knowledge without expertise. The required study of industry, agriculture and military science, besides specialization in a particular subject, is to be understood as thoughtful work experience in those activities to familiarize the student with some of their basic principles. The value of such an education in a country where a rural economy prevails and remains largely non-differentiated, is self-evident. It meets the criticism voiced by the villagers who want the hydraulic engineer sent to them to be able to tell rice from wheat in the fields, and to lend a hand in repairing a machine.

But the question is one of moral and mental attitude even more than of variety or practicality of the students' intellectual equipment. Young people must be accustomed to adapt themselves to any situation and make the best of it. They should be open-minded, perceptive and active. Their cardinal virtue ought to be intellectual humility. All this depends on the "proletarian world-outlook" as opposed to the "bourgeois world outlook," which means serving the collective interests of the majority instead of the self-interest of an elite. The "bourgeois" scientist may show humility in front of his colleagues, in order to transcend them later on, but not in front of ordinary people. Experience in industry and agriculture at the basic level is meant to develop a proletarian world outlook in the students' minds, giving them not only a sense of reality and relativity useful to any intellectual worker, but also a personal feeling for society with its contradictions and struggles. Military instruction is intended to develop physical endurance, to teach some of the skills of the People's Liberation Army, and even more its spirit. Upon the transformation of the teacher himself lies much of the fate of revolutionary education, as it is he who sets a living example to his students and can influence them deeply. The intention is by no means to cultivate "political parrots" as spiteful critics word it—in any case Chairman Mao says that students must take studies as their main task. Neither is mystic idealism the aim, but real efficiency to achieve a rate of modernization which cannot be truly and fully brought about by revisionist bourgeois education.

The democratic basis of the educational revolution was stressed in an injunction from Mao broadcast on 2 November:

The proletarian revolution in education should be carried out by relying on the mass of revolutionary students, teachers and workers inside the schools, by relying on the activitists among them, namely those proletarian revolutionaries who are determined to carry the Great Proletarian Cultural Revolution through to the end.

The late October and early November 1967 directives stirred up new reform proposals focusing on the general organization of school work. Several tendencies appeared. One was to suggest rebuilding the school like an army with its battalions and companies, minutely scheduled periods of drill, study and productive work, military virtues and discipline. The teacher should play the role of an ordinary soldier among the pupils and, like a company cadre in the army, should make revolution and work together with the pupils. Another trend rejected compulsory methods and showed a strong reluctance to rebuild a system. As a group from Peking Normal University put it:

From the bourgeois point of view, system means authority and compulsory methods should be adopted to make pupils study. From the proletarian point of view, the human factor and politico-ideological work come first while system is secondary and auxiliary. Only by arousing people's initiative and consciousness is it possible to teach and study well.

Along these principles the practice of promotion and repeating could be abolished. Instead of an entrance examination, one could combine recommendation with selection. Spare-time school students would be

admitted to higher institutions, without age limit, and eventually in another than the first year. The curriculum should be flexible.

Others, flaunting the banner of "to rebel is justified," maintained that to resume classes to make revolution was "slave-mentality," the 7 March directive being "patchy reformism, not revolution but reaction." The great alliance they called the "big hodge-podge," and the three-in-one combination the "three-in-one conglomeration." Criticism and repudiation of the revisionist line, they said, were divorced from class struggle, disregarded state affairs and had nothing in common with the rebels. Schools, and especially universities, should be abolished; students and teachers would be distributed among communes and factories.

Judging by the relentless criticism against them, these last opinions, which were branded as anarchist, seem to have been fairly widespread. This fact partly accounts for the stress on military example and discipline, particularly from March 1968 on, as well as for the call on the workers and peasants to help reform teaching and do the ideological work. While enforcing discipline, however, a careful attempt was made to point out the difference between "proletarian discipline" and the "organization discipline" of the bourgeoisie, the former being one willingly accepted and consciously obeyed. Participation of workers and peasants in school affairs remained informal except in a few places, but the idea of unceasingly seeking their advice on educational matters, and entrusting them with the leadership of students' and teachers' manual labour and ideological transformation was put forward as a way of abiding by Chairman Mao's directives.

The fourth stage in the reform projects started in late July 1968, and soon brought to the fore the rural schools. On 22 July 1968, the *People's Daily* published a "recent" directive from Chairman Mao:

It is *still* necessary to have universities; here I refer mainly to colleges of science and engineering. However, it is essential to shorten the length of schooling, revolutionize education, put proletarian politics in command and take the road of the Shanghai machine-tools plant in training technicians from among the workers and peasants with practical experience and who should return to production after a few years of study.

This statement settled the upper level of the new fabric. It put an end to disputes on the expediency of running institutions of higher education. The Shanghai machine-tools plant experience showed that engineers and technicians directly promoted from among workers with practical experience were more efficient than university graduates. Their training was faster and therefore cost less. They were generally more progressive, more concerned with common interest, less tied down by pride and prejudice. Consequently, the plant staff suggested that, while continuing the practice of promoting technicians directly from among the workers, young workers who had graduated from lower or higher middle school and who had two to five years' experience of work should be selected to study in the universities and colleges. University graduates should never be immediately appointed as cadres but serve first as ordinary workers, to get a "certificate of ability" from the peasants and workers. Later on, according to practical needs, some might take part in technical work while still doing fixed periods of manual work, others continuing to be workers and peasants. Though stressing the shortcomings of university graduates, the Shanghai machine-tools plant report was far less harsh about formal education than many other documents. There was no suggestion that the direct promotion of workers was the best possible method for getting technicians. Light and shade was introduced into the text itself by the use of such expressions as "relatively," "rather more," "generally." The report ushered in the rehabilitation of basic theoretical studies which by this time were supported also by the first workers' propaganda teams sent to the school.

Very soon, however, attention was transferred from the upper level of the educational system to its base, as it would have been difficult to build a new system from the top down. In his article "The working class must exercise leadership in everything," published on 25 August, Yao Wen-yuan conveyed three "recent" directives from Chairman Mao, one of which applied especially to education:

In carrying out the proletarian revolution in education it is essential to have working-class leadership; it is essential for the masses of workers to take part and, in co-operation with Liberation Army fighters, bring about a revolutionary "three-in-one" combination, together with the activitists among the students, teachers and workers in the schools who are determined to carry the proletarian revolution through to the end. The workers' propaganda teams should stay permanently in the schools and take part in fulfilling all the tasks of struggle-criticism-transformation in the schools, and they will always lead the schools. In the countryside, the schools should be managed by the poor and lower-middle peasants—the most reliable ally of the working class.

Immediately an increasing number of reports came out on rural schools run by brigades. On 14 October the *Red Flag* stated:

It seems that it is quite possible that the rural areas can realize more speedily than the cities Chairman Mao's thinking on the proletarian revolution in education. This is because the superiority of the poor and lower-middle peasants can be established more easily in the schools there. It offers new proof of the pressing need to send Mao Tse-tung propaganda teams of workers, with fighters of the People's Liberation Army participating, to the schools in the cities.

The importance of these documents of the summer 1968 lies in the fact that they keep the idea of a whole system of schools as a distinct institution performing a definite task in the state, and that they suggest a new type of leadership in education. Consequently, a number of specific reform proposals sprang up, relating to every aspect of the educational system: curriculum, leadership inside the school, links of the school with the society and the state. Comparatively few of these projects relate to institutions of higher learning. There were, however, suggestions about moving the technical colleges to the places for which they were supposed to train people—agriculture institutes to the countryside, polytechnical institutes to the factories—and integrating them with *collective* production. Instead of working together in a separate workshop or field (as was generally the case previously during the manual work period), or even on the school grounds, the students would be scattered among ordinary workers and share their regular work. Others insisted, on the contrary, that the right solution was that each department or institute should establish its own factory, as in 1958. As to the departments of humanities, one finds little more than general statements that they must be integrated with society.

The bulk of the reform proposals dealt with primary and middle schools. On 14 November 1968, the *People's Daily* printed a letter from two primary school teachers of the Ma-chi brigade from Chia-hsiang district in Shantung on the convenience of having the local school directly run by the brigade with the teaching staff integrated into the brigade as ordinary members, sharing in the work-point system. The advantages were said to be both political and ideological: the school being under the direct rule of the brigade Party branch, control could be closer and tighter, especially if, as suggested, teachers were employed in their home brigade only, instead of being moved from one place to another; the school would truly become part of the village and its teaching could be linked to reality. The advantages were also economic. The brigade could benefit immediately from the help of the school in such painful tasks as accounts; later on, the new type of school graduate would meet local needs better. But, above all, the system would cost less money for more efficiency.

The sums spent by the state on salaries, building and repairs could be allocated to agricultural and industrial aid and to the defence budget. Managing their own school finances, the brigades would be free to abolish tuition fees, reduce expenditure and support schools through the source of income most suitable to them—for instance, through contributions in kind—thus enabling more children to receive education.

Reform proposals from the cities openly aimed at emulating the countryside. They varied between having the schools managed by factories, by neighbourhood organization, by suburban communes or by all together. Some wished to set up a separate administration for the school, others preferred that the school be merged with the factory as a workshop led by the factory revolutionary committee and not by a school revolutionary committee. The latter insisted that until now a school was purely a consumer unit, but once it was run by a factory, it could gradually be transformed into a semi-consumer unit, thus saving a lot of state investment. Others warned, however, that the factory could not run everything: it was not an independent unit like the brigade, and furthermore such a system would perpetuate the difference between town and country since the cities would specialize in industry. For this last reason, resourceful minds proposed that urban schools be run *jointly* by factories and communes.

Much discussion has arisen also as to the length of the curriculum, whether a through-course of seven or eight years combining primary and secondary education was advisable, or whether, if the two courses were retained, each should be three, four or five years. Very contradictory opinions have been expressed on a theme which is apparently academic, but to which much of the real bearing of the educational revolution may well be linked: should Mao Tse-tung's thought, politics and "socialist culture" (*i.e.*, language, arts and sciences) be taught as one, two or three different courses and what is the ideal ratio of time to be spent on each of them. Some believe that as Mao Tse-tung's thought is to lead all teaching and study, it is unnecessary to introduce a political language course instead of the language course. Others stress that each subject has its own points of emphasis and the students understand better if separate instruction is given.

The main suggestions relating to rural schools have been summed up in a document called "Programme for rural middle and primary school education (draft, for discussion)," published by the *People's Daily* on 12 May 1969. It had originally been drawn up by the revolutionary committee of the Lishu district in Kirin province, and was then improved by the editorial board of *People's Daily,* according to the comments of poor and lower-middle peasants, teachers and students of some communes. It placed the middle school revolutionary committee—formed by a "three-in-one" combination of poor and lower-middle peasants, commune and brigade cadres, teachers and students—under the leadership of the revolutionary committees and the Party branches of the commune and its brigades. According to this draft programme, primary schools are directly led by what is called the educational leading group of the brigade, while those members of the group employed on the school staff manage the daily school work. Regular reports and inspections ensure permanent control by the poor and lower-middle peasants, but those who are involved in school management are not, as a general rule, expected to give up productive labour. No role is mentioned for the People's Liberation Army except that, as does the militia, it should provide a few teachers if necessary. Ideological leadership is entrusted to the Party organization and the revolutionary committees, with the help of the Youth League and the Red Guards. But the actual ideological work among the students is a collective task: school education, social education and family education must be linked together. Finance comes from the brigade for the primary schools and from the

commune (or several brigades) for the middle schools with a subsidy from the state. The hiring and dismissal of teachers are first discussed by the poor and lower-middle peasants, then the brigade revolutionary committee gives its advice, and the commune revolutionary committee makes the decision and informs the district revolutionary committee, who puts it on record. The salary of primary school teachers consists of work points and an allowance drawn from state funds; middle school teachers' salaries may be paid without using work points. The new system is not intended to reduce the standards of living of the people concerned. Though the programme states that primary and secondary education are combined in a through-course of nine years, it deals also with new conditions of admission to middle schools, to be based on a combination of recommendation and selection, with priority given to children from workers', soldiers' and poor and lower-middle peasants' families. After graduation students should stay in the countryside. Age qualifications, repeating and old style examinations are abolished, but students' work and knowledge are to be checked thoroughly by practical tests or examinations with free use of books. The number of subjects taught will be reduced to five, among which politics and manual labour will fill only 30 per cent of the schedule in primary schools and 40 per cent in the middle schools. The content of "cultural courses" is flexible and may be adapted to local needs. Whenever possible, schools must establish their own place for productive labour and carry out there some scientific experiments. However, participation in brigade collective labour is expected to prevail over manual labour inside the school. Any profit from this labour is to be managed by the commune and the brigade.

Some amendments or additions to this draft programme have been suggested: "cultural courses" must take over 70 per cent of the time in primary schools; foreign languages, accounting, industrial technique, veterinary and health courses should be introduced; the study of *p'u-t'ung-hua* (Mandarin) should be compulsory. But in general this practical scheme, designed to fit peasants' needs, seems to have been approved by the rural areas.

No such charter has yet come out for urban education. The only comparable project relates to technical middle schools. It is the synthesis of inquiries held in Peking, Tientsin and T'angshan by the Peking Electricity School and was published in August 1969 for further discussion. In contrast with earlier reports, it stresses the great contribution of the graduates from technical middle schools; workers and peasants were said not to think that technical middle schools must be abolished, but that they should be more numerous. The inquirers "have felt among the masses of workers, peasants and soldiers the pressing desire to learn professional theoretical knowledge." The task of technical middle schools is to spread theoretical knowledge, while the task of technical universities is to raise the level of this knowledge. Technical middle schools will be managed by the relevant technical bureaux, they will have ties with factories and will themselves run factories. They will provide a variety of short-term courses of six months to two years for students selected from peasants and workers having at least three years of practical experience. Only in the longest course is the level of higher primary education required.

From abstract general concepts the educational reform proposals have thus developed towards very practical measures, the main features of which are to give control of the schools to those who are going to use their products, and to make these products fit for the service expected of them. It should be pointed out how far this approach is from the idea of "student power" as it appeared in the youth revolt in other countries. In China, students have certainly won through the Cultural Revolution the right to express their opinion; they are represented on the schools' revolutionary committees. But it has been felt that to substitute stu-

dent authority for the authority of teachers and cadres is nothing more than to replace an older elite by a younger elite: it runs against the very principles of socialist revolution.

Critics will not fail to point out that, from exclusive interest in political education, the reform proposals have come to lay more and more emphasis on "cultural courses." They will then go on to underline that politics and Mao Tse-tung's thought are not considered as a part of culture, since the Chinese political vocabulary itself distinguishes *cheng-chih* and *Mao Tse-t'ung ssu-hsiang* from *wen-hua*. Attention will be called also to the fact that after extolling the sole virtue of practice—often distorted to mean mere physical labour, so that one would learn agriculture by carrying water—reformers are now concerned with giving credit to theory: furthermore, from the rejection of regulations and systems they are coming to make every endeavour to discipline, unify and standardize. What is so new, the critics will ask, in the revolutionized educational system?

To this criticism the answer can be made that it is quite different to shape an ideal and to devise its concrete realization. Plans are designed and are applied by and to people who are not perfect. What is important is the prevailing spirit and the general orientation of education. The educational process has its specific requirements—for instance Chinese children must learn the ideograms, which takes a long time. It would be unrealistic to ignore them, but very different results can be achieved depending on the spirit in which these requirements are fulfilled. There is indeed a good chance that the child who has been taught characters with the constant idea that this puts him above others, and the child who is taught characters as a means to help other people by no ways inferior to him, will not behave in the same way. If the efficiency of an educational system can be appraised only after it has worked for several years, it cannot be denied that there is in China both the will and the endeavour to set up a new education. The first steps in the implementation of the reform proposals testify to this.

IMPLEMENTATION OF REFORM

The situation appears to be very different in the cities and in the countryside. Although all city schools interrupted their courses, this was not such a general phenomenon in the countryside. In the cities, army teams entered the schools in February and March 1967, and the workers' propaganda teams came in from the end of July 1968. There was no such uniformity in the villages: soldiers were stationed in an extremely limited number of schools, at very variable dates: workers scarcely came in, except in special cases, such as suburban commune schools; the seizure of power in schools by peasants took place sometimes as early as March 1967, sometimes as late as September 1969. Besides, people in the countryside know what they need. It is far less clear in the cities. It is not by accident that no draft regulations have yet come out for urban schools. Of course the urban schools can train people according to the needs of the countryside, but are these needs exactly the same as those in the cities? Should the very sophisticated schools which existed in Peking, Shanghai, Tientsin, Nanking and Canton be abolished? On the other hand, if urban schools train urban personnel and are only linked with factories or city organizations, will this not perpetuate the tendency of towns to specialize in industry, and the differences between town and country?

The implementation of educational reform displays a very wide local variety. As it was of precisely excessive standardization that the old system was accused, there has been no pre-ordained plan uniformly applied. Experiments are conducted at various points; their results are used in some of the reform proposals; interpreted and adapted, they are also the starting point of new experiments in other communities. This sensible approach is a current method in

Communist China, it bears the authority of Chairman Mao's theory of knowledge and practice, and was again advocated by him for use in education in his directive of 7 March 1967.

The experience, however, does not start *ex nihilo*: there are several reference models. One is the Resist Japan Military Academy in the Yenan period. Particular stress is placed on the fact that in K'ang-ta the students supported themselves by work; teaching was linked with practice and society; and the teacher-student relationship was a revolutionary one of equality, mutual help and confidence. The system in force during the early days of the Liberation is also set forth. The primary schools were then under the village (*ts'un*) leadership; their work was regulated by the village Party branch; teachers taught and did mass work. The "red and expert" schools of 1958 are extolled on similar grounds: they were subject to the brigade Party branch; cadres and technicians were called in to teach in addition to full-time teachers. They became spoiled, it is claimed, when the district educational bureaux took them over and put academic achievement to the fore, instead of proletarian politics. Their original name, "red and expert," was even suppressed in some cases, but was revived when peasants resumed power over them during the Cultural Revolution. Another feature from the Great Leap Forward educational pattern is often recalled by technical universities and middle schools. It is the internal organization of the schools which gives the responsibility for instruction collectively to teachers, students and technical personnel organized in specialized units, instead of entrusting it to teaching-research groups (*chiao-yen-shih*) exclusively composed of teachers. Some farm-study schools established in 1964 or 1965 under the local supervision of Party, militia and peasants are praised as saving money and fitting exactly the needs of local communities, who report that they are transforming or opening other schools along the same lines. It is worth noticing that all these models are advocated both on economic and political grounds, and that they all represent attempts to get rid of rigid systems. Except the farm-study schools—although even some of them claim to be the outcome of Chairman Mao's directives—they all go back to times when Mao's revolutionary line was supposed to be overwhelmingly victorious. They stand as paragons of the mass line in education.

Rather than describing how the few schools for which we have extensive data have carried out the Cultural Revolution, it seems better for the purpose of this discussion to pass over the details of the power struggle inside the various institutions and point out only, from a wider number of sources, the general features of the educational achievement of the Cultural Revolution.

In the administrative reorganization of the schools, no effort has been spared to do away with any independent staff specializing in educational management, and to reduce as far as possible the number of full-time teachers. A Lanchow middle school, for example, had 59 teachers before the Cultural Revolution; 24 have been retained part-time; among the new teaching staff, made up by adding soldiers, workers and peasants, only four teach full-time, all of them veteran workers. Where no such radical solution could be applied, in order to prevent the remaining full-time teachers from forming any kind of bureaucratic organization or specialized group, they are blended with other elements, namely workers, peasants and soldiers who keep a foot in another reality outside the school walls. The school Party branch is scarcely mentioned. In one case, it was put under the leadership of the Party organization of the factory which managed the school. In another, members of the workers' propaganda team have entered the school Party organization. Large schools set up a revolutionary committee in which people from outside participate in a variable ratio. In cases where the school is run by a given community—factory, commune,

neighbourhood—some of those outside members belong to the community revolutionary committee concerned, which leads the school revolutionary committee. If the school is under the joint management of several communities, there might be above the school revolutionary committee, a leading body composed of representatives of the school and of the various organizations involved. As to very large institutions, such as universities, it is not yet clear how they are to be managed above the level of their own revolutionary committee. Small schools usually do not have a revolutionary committee but are managed by given communities. Sometimes they are directly under the community revolutionary committee concerned, which can appoint some of its members to deal with daily school problems, even to form an educational leading group from people inside and outside the school, while retaining supreme control. Sometimes people from the school staff are elected to join the community revolutionary committee. Sometimes the community appoints an educational revolutionary committee or leading group which is responsible for school matters. It is composed of a majority of people who keep their regular job in the community, and a few teachers and students.

Those steps break through a rigid concept of division of work, and put forward a new praxis for the management of state affairs—the necessity of an Education Ministry has even been questioned. Bureaucracy is replaced by something called the "leading group" (*ling-tao pan-tzu*). Lin Piao is mentioned as the father of the notion, with the following quotation: "The leading group is very important because it stands for political power." The leading group is composed of a diversified personnel whose members are noted for their own dynamism and the trust put in them by others. It is still too early to know if and how the body is to be renewed. The important and new point at the moment is the idea of general initiative, responsibility and concern. Previously, initiative, responsibility and concern were in fact rather the monopoly of Party members; now they are entrusted and put forward as a duty to other people also. The change may mean a great deal for the countryside, where Party members were relatively scarce at the grass-root level.

The leading group as a general concept should be distinguished from specific applications such as the leading groups for the educational revolution—moreover the latter are usually called *hsiao-tsu* and not *pan-tzu.* Where soldiers, workers or peasants are stationed in the schools, they are included in the notion of "leading group," together with the school revolutionary committee or the educational revolution leading group, though only some of these people may be members of such formal organs; so are the factory, neighbourhood or brigade revolutionary committees. Soldiers are supposed to leave the schools as soon as the proletarian dictatorship has been firmly established, but worker and peasant control will stay permanently. Even if in the city schools those who came in as propaganda teams were, during the first months, entirely absorbed in school matters, the trend is that all should keep at least part of their former occupation. The district and provincial education bureaux turn up again—they are necessary as relays between state and local levels to co-ordinate, harmonize and distribute subsidies; but the strengthening of the leading group in each basic unit gives a real chance for a new type of administration to emerge.

As far as the enrolment of students is concerned, there is no doubt that many children from poor families in rural areas have now been given the opportunity to receive some education. All kinds of arrangements are provided by the brigades: itinerant teachers, part-time schooling, new schools, abolition or reduction of tuition fees and no age limit. In some places the children can take to school their baby sisters or brothers and even the cows. A system of recommendation is widely applied for admission to middle schools, the size of which has often

increased. Moreover, some rural schools take in educated youth for short-term training on special subjects. It seems that many of the city primary school graduates, who were unable to enter middle school, have been sent to the countryside. The same applies to middle school graduates. In July 1968 and July 1969, numerous articles praised those young people who left the cities to settle in villages. Once in the countryside, it seems that in some places these youths still get some kind of formal instruction. When they left, they knew they were going for several years; now the stress is on "being a peasant one's life long"; but it may well be that after a two- or three-year stay some of them will be selected for admission to the universities. As university courses are definitely going to be shortened to two or three years, and enrolment increased, there will probably be no fewer university graduates in 1972 than if college students had been regularly enrolled and had accomplished the five- or six-year course since 1966. As to the quality of the future graduates, it is worth pointing out that the long full-time course system has not given such outstanding results either in China or in other countries that the new system may not give better ones.

Anyway, the standards of "scholarly achievements" are altered as exemplified in the contents of the curriculum. Mao Tse-tung's thought is put first, which can account for both the diversity and common trends of the programmes set up by individual schools. Furthermore, there are interpretations according to the spirit and interpretations according to the letter, with more or less emphasis on the exclusive use of Mao's writings as the textbook. In some places, characters are learned in the *Quotations;* language courses are taught on the basis of the *Three Well-known Essays;* each chapter, each paragraph of a mathematics course is introduced by an excerpt from Mao. Elsewhere, though Mao's writings are always the basic material of instruction, the balance is different. Political education is sought through regular meetings for criticizing and repudiating the revisionist line. Workers and poor peasants are invited to give lectures on class struggle. The general knowledge courses are linked to class struggle and production struggle. In arithmetic, the questions deal with exploitation in the old times and the yield of the fields. Fundamentals of physics and chemistry are taught on the basis of the experience of pupils with machines or fertilizers. They first learn the "how" by using the implements, then the "why" through lectures by their teacher. Students receive regular military training both in drill and discipline, from the PLA and the militia. Manual labour, with emphasis on agricultural work, is integrated into the curriculum. In rural schools and some factory schools, these activities are often run in order to reap a profit. But warnings are uttered against the danger of an excessively utilitarian and mechanistic conception: to do manual work does not teach industry; students must not be used as additional unqualified manpower. Some schools organize manual labour in a very enlightened way, both to help the students in mastering skills and knowledge, and to give them social experience and political consciousness by participating in collective tasks together with ordinary workers.

However, whatever may be the goodwill and conviction of workers, teachers and students, the regulation of manual labour depends much on material conditions. In many rural schools, the schedule is equally divided between manual labour and formal teaching. Some theoretical knowledge is taught, it is true, while working, and labour is intended to keep up the revolutionary spirit of the youth, but its high ratio is an economic necessity to support the school and enable poor children to attend it. At the other end of the scale, the low ratio—often a half-day a week—of manual labour in large city schools does not inevitably mean a lack of proletarian faith. First, these institutions can afford it: their financial situation and that of their pupils is not so difficult. Second, the very organization of urban econ-omy compels these schools to reduce the proportion of manual labour: for the time being, Peking factories cannot accommodate all the city pupils and students half-time. Even when conditions are at their best—for instance, if the school is a dependency of the factory—equal division between labour and classes does not seem the ideal. Let us take the case of the Lanchow foundry middle school. It resumed courses with three days work and three days classes a week. After a period of experiment, the class-time has increased to four days, including 24 periods of class among which 12 are devoted to Mao Tse-tung's thought, four to fundamentals in industrial work, four to revolutionary litera-ture and art, two to military and physical culture, two to flexible studies.

Rural schools insist that they compile their teaching material themselves according to local needs. There is evidence, however, that this task is also carried on by commis-sions which act for a larger area.

Teaching "by enlightenment" is con-sidered to be true revolutionary pedagogy, but it is acknowledged that, at least in the primary school when pupils do not know anything, teaching "by infusion" is neces-sary. Some schools hold examinations—not "trapping" ones: the questions are given beforehand—others do not. There is no attempt to stuff the brain as during the Great Leap Forward, when for the sake of revolution the language students had to learn the dictionary by heart; on the contrary, the key phrase is "little but well." Nevertheless, educators would like to see precisely defined the political, cultural and scientific level to be reached by their students.

Education does not stop at the school door. Strenuous efforts are made to promote extra-mural activities. For instance, Mao Tse-tung's thought study-classes are run outside the schools, involving neighbours and parents as well as pre-school age children. Educational reform as it evolves from the Cultural Revolution shows deep concern about family education as an extension of school education. It is very far from the

Great Leap Forward tendency to draw children away from their families. Actually, parents and the heads of families have repeatedly been called upon to help in educating the children. Regard for the family is also emphasized by keeping country people in their village for education and work, or by sending teachers back to their native brigade.

This cannot be called a "rehabilitation," for no special values are attached to the family. As happens to many concrete realities which, at least in its practice, the Great Leap Forward wrongly ignored because they did not fit in well with its ideals, the family is now looked upon as an objective factor, like cold in winter or heat in summer, and an attempt is made to make the most of it. Cold and heat are not good or bad, they merely exist and human activities must adapt to them and in the long run they may transform them to a certain extent. The same logic may explain the paradoxical attitude of the Cultural Revolution towards the individual: fighting the "self," but extolling personal creativity, daring, awareness, consciousness. It is a fact that men are born as separate beings, different in character and abilities. Fighting "self" is designed to prevent, as in the "bourgeois conception," those differences being exalted to absolute values which must be asserted and protected at all costs. But it is recognized that a social ideal can work only if understood and applied by each of the individuals who compose the society. Hence the reaction against education as a coercive uniform mould, and the emphasis on bringing into play personal activity and consciousness.

The carrying out of educational reform is certainly not an easy task. There are numerous complaints that such sayings as "to study is of no use" and "to teach is dangerous" are widespread. Students are insolent and undisciplined in the class-room, they stay away from school as they please; they refuse to study because they do not want to become "re-education targets"; sometimes, parents themselves take them out of school for the same reason or because they think that the schools do not teach anything. The teachers' ranks have been so well "purified" that some schools are very short staffed. The remaining teachers are so much afraid of being accused by the students that they dare not enforce any kind of discipline; in order to keep safe, they mumble some excerpt from Mao Tse-tung's works all day long. They beg to be given another job. They think that if they are to be paid with work points, they would earn more by doing manual work full-time. Nobody wants to become a teacher. Peasants in charge of schools merely sweep the ground and mend the chairs. Factories get rid of sick workers and unsuccessful apprentices by sending them on the propaganda teams in the schools. Clashes of authority arise from the fact that the factory supposed to be running the school is not the one to send the workers' propaganda team. Feuds divide the students, the teachers, the workers and the army propaganda teams. There is no need to describe further academic entanglements, for which other countries are as gifted as China.

These difficulties are overcome step by step. A universally advocated remedy is to continue the "big criticism" of the revisionist line, which enables people to sift out the true from the false. At the same time, discipline, intellectual culture, educational administration receive due consideration, and the economic usefulness of education is more heavily stressed.

To many observers the originality of the current educational revolution is questionable. It is true that part of the criticism recently voiced was brought forward in 1964 and 1965, though not so harshly and radically. Pedagogy "by enlightenment," examinations with open books, "little but well," living study and living use of Mao Tse-tung's thought, opening the schools to workers', poor and lower-middle peasants' children, shortening the courses, integrating them with practice and manual labour were commonplaces—some of these principles were put into operation, but the process was slow, hampered by many psychological obstacles. As in other fields, the reform, which was sponsored by Chairman Mao, met overflowing verbal compliance and little practical support. The Cultural Revolution has not entirely removed the obstacles, but it has certainly shaken their foundation, thus opening the way to a really new education. After such a huge shock, even if people are not completely remoulded, there are certain things which they dare not do any more. It is only through revolution that the intended reform could be achieved. The Cultural Revolution type of education resumes the mass line of the Yenan period and of the Great Leap Forward. Even without going back to the *Report of an Investigation into the Peasant Movement in Hunan,* the emphasis on *min-pan* (run by the people) is a feature from the years 1943–45. When criticism of current education was developed in 1944, transfer of authority from professional educators, decentralization, integration of education with the social and economic life of the village had been implemented to cope with the failings of a too elitist system. Such have also been the trends in 1957–59. However, despite common goals and methods, the present situation is different. Realism has been learnt from past experiments. Never had the question of power over education been so thoroughly clarified. Furthermore, the average cultural level of the country is considerably higher than in 1958, not to speak of 1944, which accounts for a wider awareness of a broader range of problems, and for less shortage of spare teachers. This means that although enlightened statesmen draw up the educational directives, the official statement that it is primarily the workers and poor peasants who are behind the reforms may, this time, not become a fiction. Thus, instead of the dualistic system into which previous attempts degenerated, an education could emerge which gives equal rank to everyone by cultivating "labourers with socialist consciousness and culture."

The priority given to ideology is not a

priority to pure abstract theory. On the other hand, economic necessity has doubtless prompted a number of criticisms, proposals and measures in the educational field, though educational reform as a whole cannot merely be considered as a solution of budget difficulties. The reform meets concrete political ideals. Those ideals could be summed up through a quotation from a Liberation Army fighter, as the need to create revolutionary public opinion:

... We must create revolutionary public opinion in a big way ... To create revolutionary public opinion in a big way means spreading vigorously Marxism-Leninism and Mao Tse-tung's thought. ...

The course of the struggle in the Great Proletarian Cultural Revolution has shown us that once Chairman Mao's latest instructions and the various combat orders issued by the proletarian headquarters with Chairman Mao as its leader and Vice-Chairman Lin as its deputy are brought to the notice of the proletarian revolutionaries and the broad revolutionary masses, and translated into their conscious action, they will yield inexhaustible strength that carries all before it. ... Don't entertain the thought that to create public opinion is something intangible, and we can do with or without it, while production is something solid and it will do to grasp production alone. Actually this is not so. Theory is not anything intangible, because spirit can be translated into matter. If "solid" things are not led by "theory," they also cannot be well grasped, and would go astray in the direction of capitalism. The more we are strained in production, the greater is the need to create revolutionary public opinion in a big way and to surmount all kinds of difficulties with revolutionary drive.

The struggle for production can be successful only in a real political society, where the majority of people are concerned and are able to understand and even share in decisions related to the collective life. The advent of such a political society requires the suppression of the elite which monopolized state power, giving the illusion of the existence of a political society but actually usurping the rights and also the duties of the people below. To eradicate the roots of any established elite, the youth must be trained to be versatile, responsive to concrete challenge and unconceited. That does not pre-vent society from having leaders, but one motto of the "leading group" will be dynamism: they must "dare" to innovate not content themselves with what is already established.

36. On Meritocracy and Equality

DANIEL BELL

In 1958, the English sociologist Michael Young wrote a fable, *The Rise of the Meritocracy*.[1] It purports to be a "manu-script," written in the year 2033, which breaks off inconclusively for reasons the "narrator" failed to comprehend. The theme is the transformation of English society, by the turn of the twenty-first century, owing to the victory of the principle of achievement over that of ascription (i.e. the gaining of place by assignment or inheritance). For centuries, the elite positions in the society had been held by the children of the nobility on the hereditary principle of succession. But in the nature of modern society, "the rate of social progress depend[ed] on the degree to which power is matched with intel-ligence." Britain could no longer afford a ruling class without the necessary technical skills. Through the successive school-reform acts, the principle of merit slowly became established. Each man had his place in the society on the basis of "IQ and Effort." By 1990 or thereabouts, all adults with IQs over 125 belonged to the meritocracy.

But with that transformation came an unexpected reaction. Previously, talent had been distributed throughout the society, and each class or social group had its own natural leaders. Now all men of talent were raised into a common elite, and those below had no excuses for their failures; they bore the stigma of rejection, they were known in-feriors.

By the year 2034 the Populists had revolted. Though the majority of the rebels were members of the lower classes, the leaders were high-status women, often the wives of leading scientists. Relegated during the early married years to the household because of the need to nurture high-IQ chil-dren, the activist women had demanded equality between the sexes, a movement that was then generalized into the demand for equality for all, and for a classless society. Life was not to be ruled by "a mathematical measure" but each person would develop his own diverse capacities for leading his own life.[2] The Populists won. After little more than half a century, the Meritocracy had come to an end.

Is this, too, the fate of the post-industrial society? The post-industrial society, in its initial logic, is a meritocracy. Differential status and differential income are based on technical skills and higher education. With-out those achievements one cannot fulfill the requirements of the new social division of labor which is a feature of that society. And there are few high places open without those skills. To that extent, the post-industrial society differs from society at the turn of the twentieth century. The initial change, of course, came in the professions. Seventy years or so ago, one could still "read" law in a lawyer's office and take the bar examination without a college degree. Today, in medicine, law, accounting, and a dozen other professions, one needs a college degree and accrediting, through examina-

From *The Coming of Post-Industrial Society* (New York: Basic Books, 1973). Copyright © 1973 by Daniel Bell. Reprinted by permission.

tion, by legally sanctioned committees of the profession, before one can practice one's art. For many years, until after World War II, business was the chief route open to an ambitious and aggressive person who wanted to strike out for himself. And the rags-to-riches ascent (or, more accurately, clerk-to-capitalist, if one follows the career of a Rockefeller, Harriman, or Carnegie) required drive and ruthlessness rather than education and skills. One can still start various kinds of small businesses (unusually, now, by franchise from a larger corporation), but the expansion of such enterprises takes vastly different skills than in the past. Within the corporation, as managerial positions have become professionalized, individuals are rarely promoted from shop jobs below but are chosen from the outside, with a college degree as the passport of recognition. Only in politics, where position may be achieved through the ability to recruit a following, or through patronage, is there a relatively open ladder without formal credentials.

Technical skill, in the post-industrial society, is what the economists call "human capital." An "investment" in four years of college, according to initial estimates of Gary Becker, yields, over the average working life of the male graduate, an annual return of about 13 percent.[3] Graduation from an elite college (or elite law school or business school) gives one a further differential advantage over graduates from "mass" or state schools. Thus, the university, which once reflected the status system of the society, has now become the arbiter of class position. As the gatekeeper, it has gained a quasi-monopoly in determining the future stratification of the society.[4]

Any institution which gains a quasi-monopoly power over the fate of individuals is likely, in a free society, to be subject to quick attack. Thus, it is striking that the populist revolt, which Michael Young foresaw several decades hence, has already begun, at the very onset of the post-industrial society. One sees this in the derogation of the IQ and the denunciation of theories espousing a genetic basis of intelligence; the demand for "open admission" to universities on the part of minority groups in the large urban centers; the pressure for increased numbers of blacks, women and specific minority groups, such as Puerto Ricans and Chicanos in the faculties of universities, by quotas if necessary; and the attack on "credentials" and even schooling itself as the determinant of a man's position in the society. A post-industrial society reshapes the class structure of society by creating new technical elites. The populist reaction, which has begun in the 1970s, raises the demand for greater "equality" as a defense against being excluded from that society. Thus the issue of meritocracy versus equality.

In the nature of a meritocracy, as it has been traditionally conceived, what is central to the assessment of a person is the assumed relation of achievement to intelligence, and of intelligence to its measurement on the Intelligence Quotient scale. The first question, therefore, is what determines intelligence. In the received social science and biology opinion, the number of talented persons in a society, as measured by IQ, is a limited pool; and this is reflected in the bell-shaped curve of a normal distribution of test scores in a particular age category. By the logic of a meritocracy, these high-scoring individuals, no matter where they are in the society, should be brought to the top in order to make the best use of their talents.[5] This is the basis of the liberal theory of equality of opportunity and of Jefferson's belief in the "natural aristoi" against the ascriptive nobility.

All this makes the question of the relation of intelligence to genetic inheritance very touchy. Is intelligence largely inherited? Can one raise intelligence by nurture? How does one separate native ability and drive from improvements in skill acquired through education? The average IQ of college graduates is 120, while that of high-school graduates is only 107. As Fritz Machlup, the Princeton economist, has commented: "The greater earning capacity of college graduates, compared with high-school graduates, is, no doubt, to a large extent [the figure is about 40 percent] the result of superior native intelligence and greater ambition; it would be quite wrong to attribute all of the incremental earnings to the investment in college education."[6]

The logic of the argument has been pushed further by the Harvard psychologist Richard Herrnstein. Using data assembled by Arthur Jensen of Berkeley—that 80 percent of a person's IQ is inherited, while environmental factors account for only 20 percent—Herrnstein then proceeds to extend the implication:

1. If differences in mental abilities are inherited, and
2. if success in society requires those abilities, and
3. if the environment is "equalized,"
4. then social standing will be based to some extent on inherited differences.[7]

Herrnstein's argument mixes up two different situations: the assertion that in American society today occupational position *is* largely a function of IQ, and the model of a meritocracy, whose stratification system would *be* determined by IQ. Herrnstein concludes, however, that if all persons are given an equal start, and equality of opportunity is fully realized, then heredity will become the decisive factor, since the social environment would be the same for all. And he draws a dismal picture of the new poor:

... there will be precipitated out of the mass of humanity a low-capacity (intellectual and otherwise) residue that may be unable to master the common occupations, cannot compete for success and achievement and are most likely to be born to parents who have similarly failed.[8]

The relation of genetics to intelligence to social-class position involves five different kinds of disputed questions. The first is the question whether one can ever fix with any

exactness the proportions of genetic inheritance and environment to intelligence. (This is possible only if one assumes they are *causally* independent, i.e. that biological endowment does not influence the environment; but this is highly unlikely.) Second is the question of what the IQ tests actually measure, whether only particular skills or some more general and unified underlying intelligence. Third is the question whether IQ tests are "culture-bound," including even the self-styled "culture-*fair*" tests which do not deal with school-taught knowledge but ask the child to deduce relations and correlates within simple non-representational drawings. Fourth, the question whether the social class of the parent is more important than IQ in determining entry into college or occupational position in the society. Finally, the crucial question whether these relationships—between intelligence, social class background and other factors—have changed over time at all and, to that extent, whether the society *is* becoming more meritocratic.[9]

What the parties to these disputes mix up, however, are two very different kinds of issues. One, whether the society—because of either social-class privilege or cultural advantage (e.g. the selective biases of IQ tests) —does or does not provide genuine equality of opportunity, or a fair start for all; and two, whether a society in which genuine equality of opportunity did not prevail, but a new form of income and status inequality based on merit resulted, would be desirable? *In other words, is it a more genuine equality of opportunity that is wanted, or an equality of result?* It is the shuttling from one to another of these positions that has marked the populist argument in recent years and created a confusion in the political demands raised in its wake.

Initially, equality of opportunity was the main preoccupation. The explicit fear created by a post-industrial society is that the failure to get on the educational escalator means the exclusion from the privileged places in society. A meritocratic society is a "credentials society" in which certification of achievement—through the college degree, the professional examination, the license—becomes a condition of higher employment. Education thus becomes a defensive necessity. As Lester Thurow has observed:

As the supply of educated labor increases, individuals find that they must improve their educational level simply to defend their current income positions. If they don't, others will, and they will find their current job no longer open to them. Education becomes a good investment, not because it would raise people's incomes above what they would have been if no one had increased his education, but rather because it raises their income above what it will be if others acquire an education and they do not. *In effect, education becomes a defensive expenditure necessary to protect one's "market share."* The larger the class of educated labor and the more rapidly it grows, the more such defensive expenditures become imperative.[10]

The logical outcome of these fears on the part of disadvantaged groups is a demand for "open admissions" to universities. The underlying rationale of the demand has been the argument that social class origin of the parent was the primary factor skewing selection in the occupational system, and that open admission to colleges, despite low grades, would enable minority groups to compete more fairly in the society. To that extent, open admissions is no more than the historic American principle that everyone should have a chance to better himself, no matter where he starts. It is also the optimistic American belief that giving *any* student more education will do him more good. This was the logic behind the land-grant college acts; it was the long-standing practice of the public universities, outside the East, even before World War II.[11]

But for some, the extension of this demand has become an attack on the meritocratic principle itself. As one proponent writes: "As long as open admissions remains limited to a few institutions, it poses no threat to the meritocracy. Recruitment into the elite will be based not on *whether* one went to college, but on *where* one went to college. Universal open admissions, however, would destroy the close articulation between the meritocracy and the system of higher education; further, by the very act of abolishing hierarchy in admissions, it would cast doubt on hierarchy in the larger society."[12]

That argument, however, if pushed to its logical conclusion, would mean that admission to all higher schools in the country, from Parsons College to Harvard, should be by lot. And the further conclusion, since elite schools would still be defined by their faculty, would be to make teaching assignment in the national university system a matter of lot as well.

Open admissions is a means of widening equality of opportunity for disadvantaged students by broadening access to the university. But there is also the question of place in the university structure itself—in the faculty, staff, and administration. In their comprehensive study of the American occupational structure, Peter Blau and Otis Dudley Duncan have shown that almost all the different minority groups have been able to achieve commensurate status, power, and economic rewards—with the exception of women and blacks. Clearly, if there is discrimination—on the basis of sex, or color, or religion, or any criterion extraneous to the stated one of professional qualification—there is no genuine equality of opportunity. The second effort to widen equality has been the effort to expand the number of places of minorities in the system.

In the 1960s, the government declared it a matter of public policy that "affirmative action" had to be taken to rectify the discrimination against minorities. The policy of affirmative action was first proclaimed by President Johnson in an executive order of 1965. It stated that on all federal projects, or in any employment situation that used federal money, employers had to prove they had sought out qualified applicants from disadvantaged groups; had to provide special training where necessary, if qualified applicants could not be found immediately; and had to hire preferentially from among minority groups when their qualifications were roughly equal to those of other applicants. This program, combined with others such as Head Start and compensatory education programs, was designed to redress a historic cultural disadvantage and, quite deliberately, to give minority-group members, especially blacks, an edge in the competition for place.

In the first years of the government affirmative-action program, the efforts were directed primarily within the skilled trades—especially the building trades, where there had been a deliberate policy of racial exclusion. In the early 1970s, the Nixon administration, acting through the Department of Health, Education and Welfare (HEW), extended the program to universities, and each school with federal contracts was asked to provide data on the number of minority persons in each position, academic and non-academic, and to set specific goals for increasing the number of minority-group persons in each classification. As Edward Shils summarized the order:

Universities were informed that for each category of employee in the university it would be necessary to specify rates of remuneration and number in each category by "racial breakdown, i.e. Negro, Oriental, American Indian, Spanish-surnamed Americans. . . ." This had to be accompanied by an "Affirmative Action Program which specifically and succinctly identif[ies] problem areas by division, department location and job classification, and includes more specific recommendations and plans for overcoming them." The "Affirmative Action Program" must "include specific goals and objectives by division, department and job classification, including target completion dates on both long and short ranges as the particular case may indicate. Analytical provision should be made for evaluating recruitment methods and sources; the total number of candidates interviewed, job offers made, the numbers hired with the number of minority group persons interviewed, made job offers and hired." . . . [13]

The initial intention of the Executive Order was to eliminate *discrimination*. But discrimination is difficult to prove, especially when the qualifications required for a job are highly specific. And the government's test became: Are the members of the minority groups to be found in employment, at every level, in numbers equal to their proportion in the population? Or, if women earned 30 percent of the Ph.D.s, are 30 percent of the faculty women? What this meant, in theory, was to set "target" figures for women and blacks. In practice, this has meant, quotas, or priorities in hiring, for persons from these groups.

What is extraordinary about this change is that, without public debate, an entirely new principle of rights has been introduced into the polity. In the nature of the practice, *the principle has changed from discrimination to representation.* Women, blacks, and Chicanos are to be employed, as a matter of right, in proportion to their number, and the principle of professional qualification or individual achievement is subordinated to the new ascriptive principle of corporate identity.[14]

The implications of this new principle are far-reaching. One can, "logically," insist on quotas where the skill is homogeneous, where one person can readily substitute for another. But by focusing on group identity rather than the person, by making the mechanical equation of number of women Ph.D.s to number of positions they should hold, the government assumes that "educated labor" is "homogeneous"—that individual talent or achievement is less important than the possession of the credential. This may be true in many occupations, but not in university teaching and research, where individual merit is the singular test. Putting someone in a tenure position, which is capitalized at three-quarters of a million dollars, is very different from hiring a black rather than a white plumber; simply having the degree is not necessarily the qualification for the high position.

Furthermore, quotas and preferential hiring mean that standards are bent or broken. The inescapable assumption of the ascriptive criterion as regards tenured university positions is that minority persons are less qualified and could not compete with others, even if given a sufficient margin. What effect does this have on the self-esteem of a person hired on "second-class" grounds? And what effect does it have on the quality of a university, its teaching and research and morale, if its faculties are filled on the basis of quotas?

But quotas themselves are no simple matter. If "representation" is to be the criterion of position, then what is the logic of extending the principle only to women, blacks, Mexicans, Puerto Ricans, American Indians, Filipinos, Chinese, and Japanese—which are the categories in the HEW guideline? Why not to Irish, Italians, Poles, and other ethnic groups? And if representation is the criterion, what is the base of representation? At one California state college, as John Bunzel reports, the Mexican-Americans asked that 20 percent of the total work force be Chicanos, because the surrounding community is 20 percent Mexican-American. The black students rejected this argument and said that the proper base should be the state of California, which would provide a different mix of blacks and Chicanos. Would the University of Mississippi be expected to hire 37 percent black faculty because that is the proportion of blacks in the population of Mississippi? And would the number of Jews in most faculties of the country be reduced because the Jews are clearly over-represented in proportion to their number?

And if ethnic and minority tests, why not religious or political beliefs as the criteria of balanced representation? Governor Reagan of California has said that conservatives are highly underrepresented in the faculties of the state universities, a fact evident when the political coloration of those faculties is compared with voting results in California; should conservatives therefore be given preference in hiring? And should particular communities be asked to support the teaching of certain subjects (or the presence of certain books in school libraries) which are repugnant to the beliefs of that community?—a question first raised in the Virginia House of Burgesses in 1779 and a principle restated by the Tennessee legislature in the 1920s in barring the teaching of evolution in that Fundamentalist state.

The historic irony in the demand for representation on the basis of an ascriptive principle is its complete reversal of radical and humanist values. The liberal and radical attack on discrimination was *based on its denial of a justly earned place to a person on the basis of an unjust group attribute.* That person was not judged as an individual, but was judged—and excluded—because he was a member of a particular group. But now it is being demanded that one must have a place primarily because one possesses a particular group attribute. The person himself has disappeared. Only attributes remain. The further irony is that according to the radical critique of contemporary society, an individual is treated not as a person but as a multiple of roles that divide and fragment him and reduce him to a single dominant attribute of the major role or function he or she plays in society. Yet in the reversal of principle we now find that a person is to be given preference by virtue of a role, his group membership, and the person is once again "reduced" to a single overriding attribute as the prerequisite for a place in the society. That is the logic of the demand for quotas.

DE-SCHOOLING

From a different direction there has come another attack on the idea of meritocracy: the argument that all schooling is being subordinated to the demands of technocratic thinking and that the school is assuming a disproportionate influence in the society.

The argument is made most sharply by Ivan Illich:

The hidden curriculum teaches all children that economically valuable knowledge is the result of professional teaching and that social entitlements depend on the rank achieved in a bureaucratic process. The hidden curriculum transforms the explicit curriculum into a commodity and makes its acquisition the securest form of wealth. Knowledge certificates—unlike property rights, corporate stock or family inheritance—are free from challenge . . . school is universally accepted as the avenue to greater power, to increased legitimacy as a producer, and to further learning resources.[15]

For Illich—whose mysterious role as both Catholic heresiarch and prowler in the corridors of power has made him a figure of cultural curiosity[16]—there is a distinction between schooling and education. Schooling is an instrument that enables a person to accumulate a "knowledge stock," just as business once allowed individuals to accumulate a "capital stock."[17] Education is the "free determination by each learner of his own reason for living and learning—the part that his knowledge is to play in his life." Since schooling has become completely instrumental, and a barrier to education, one must eliminate schools and create a process whereby each person can pursue the education he wants and needs.

For Illich, schooling creates a new hierarchy in which the hierophants of knowledge maintain their position by arcane and technical knowledge that is closed off from the rest of society.[18] "Effective access" to education requires "a radical denial of the right of facts and complexity of tools on which contemporary technocracies found their privilege, which they, in turn, render immune by interpreting its use as a service to the majority."

In place of institutions—which only develop vested interests to maintain the privileges of its administrators—Illich would substitute "learning webs" made up of skill-exchanges, peer-matching and Educators-at-Large, intellectual sadhus or gurus, wandering scholars, available at call. There would be no compulsory attendance, no credentials, just education *pour le gout* in the street bazaars of learning.[19] And all of it financed by the tax money hitherto spent on the schools.

The distinction between education and schooling is a relevant one. At one time, the two were joined. We then lived, as James Coleman has put it, in an "information-poor" society.[20] The degree of direct experience on a farm or in the small town may have been large, but the range of vicarious experience—the acquaintance with the world of art, or cultures or politics outside the immediate region—was limited to books and school. School was the central organizer of experience and the codifier of values. Today the situation has changed enormously. Whether the amount of direct experience of the child has shrunk is moot; it is perhaps romantic fallacy to believe that the child today, with the increased mobility of travel and the variety of urban stimuli available to him, has fewer direct experiences than before. But the range of vicarious experience, with the spread of communication and the wider windows onto the world offered by television, diverse magazines, picture books and the like, has broadened enormously. Education takes place outside the school, in the multifarious influence of media and peer group, while schools, because of their gatekeeper roles, have become more vocational and specialized.

The question, however, is whether this changed relationship requires the de-schooling of society or a very different conception of education and schooling. Illich is a romantic Rousseauian. His picture is drawn from *Emile,* and has the same farrago of rhetoric, the emphasis on the "authenticity of being"—those cant words of modernity which can never be defined. There is the same idea that a person should not obey social convention but "make up his mind for himself," as if there are hundreds of millions of independent truths rather than multiple subgroups of socially circumscribed conventicles of thought. There is the same anti-intellectualism which regards experience alone as truth, rather than disciplined study. There is even the same manipulation by the master—the "noble lie" which Illich sells, in order to destroy institutions—to recreate the "state of nature" in order to align desires and powers. But in the end, as in *Emile,* the search is not for knowledge, or an education, but for an identity, the identity of lost innocence, the identity of the naif.[21]

The difficulty with the exoteric argument of Illich—as with so much of modernism—is that it confuses experience, in all its diversities, with knowledge. Experience has to be made conscious, and this is done, as Dewey remarked, "by means of that fusion of old meanings and new situations that transfigures both."[22] Knowledge is the selective ordering—and reordering—of experience through relevant concepts. Reality is not a bounded world, "out there," to be imprinted on the mind as from a mirror, or a flux of experience to be sampled for its novelties according to one's inclination (or its relevance for "me"), but a set of meanings organized by mind, in terms of categories, which establishes the relations between facts and infers conclusions.

Nor need there be, in principle, a contradiction between a cognitive and an aesthetic mode in which, as alleged, the technocratic orientation is concerned only with the functional and the adversary culture with sensibility—much as this may be true in sociological fact. In the very nature of knowledge, as Dewey observed, there has to be an interplay of the two: The cognitive makes the variety of experience more intelligible by its reduction to conceptual form; the aesthetic makes experience more vivid by its presentation in an expressive mode. The two reinforce each other in a singular way.

What has to be common to both is a reliance on judgment—the making of necessary distinctions and the creation of standards which allow one to sort out the meretricious from the good, the pretentious

from the enduring. Knowledge is a product of the self-conscious and renewable comparison and judging of cultural objects and ideas in order to say that something is better than something else (or more complex, or more beautiful, or whatever the standard one seeks to apply), and that something is truer. Inevitably, therefore, knowledge is a form of authority, and education is the process of refining the nature of authoritative judgments. This is the classic, and enduring, rationale of education.

But to this is added a special burden of the post-industrial society. One need not defend the technocratic dimensions of education—its emphasis on vocationalism and specialization—to argue that schooling becomes more necessary than ever before. By the very fact that there are now many more differentiated ways in which people gain information and have experiences, there is a need for the self-conscious understanding of the processes of conceptualization as the means of organizing one's information in order to gain coherent perspectives on one's experience. A conceptual scheme is a set of consistent terms which groups together diverse attributes of experience or properties of an object, in a higher order of abstraction, in order to relate them to, or distinguish them from, other attributes and properties. To see what is common and what is different about modes of experience—the theme I raised in the introduction on the need for prisms for the comparison of societies—is the function of education. And just as the resolution of an identity crisis for individuals is the amalgamation of discordant aspects of growing up into a coherent whole, so is knowledge an organization of experiences, tested against other patterns of experience, in order to create consistent standards of judgment.

The function of the university, in these circumstances, is to relate to each other the modes of conscious inquiry: historical consciousness, which is the encounter with a tradition that can be tested against the present; methodological consciousness, which makes explicit the conceptual grounds of inquiry and its philosophical presuppositions; and individual self-consciousness, which makes one aware of the sources of one's prejudgments and allows one to re-create one's values through the disciplined study of the society. Education is the "reworking" of the materials of the past, without ever wholly surrendering its truths or bending to its pieties. It is a continuing tension, "the tension between past and future, mind and sensibility, tradition and experience, [which] for all its strains and discomforts, is the only source for maintaining the independence of inquiry itself." It is the affirmation of the principle of intellectual and artistic order through the search for relatedness of discordant knowledge.[23]

II

THE REDEFINITION OF EQUALITY

The issues of schooling, of income, of status all have become matters of social policy because equality has been one of the central values of the American polity. But there has never been a clear-cut meaning to equality, and the earliest form of the idea in the seventeenth century was quite different than what it assumed in its popular form by the third decade of the nineteenth century. Those who founded the colonies—in New England, at least, beginning with the Pilgrim Fathers of the Mayflower Compact—had an image of themselves as a "community of virtuous men who understood themselves to be under sacred restraints." There was equality, but in the Puritan sense of an equality of the elect. Among the Constitutional Fathers, the idea of virtue, and election by ability (if no longer by grace), dominated their thinking. A curious blend of Roman republican imagery and the Lockean thinking—since both emphasized agrarian virtues and labor—informed their language. The central theme was independence, and the conditions whereby a man could be inde-

pendent. But in the very use of Lockean language there was an implicit commitment to a hierarchy—the hierarchy of intellect. Since thought was prized, it was assumed that some men "thought" better than others, were more able, more intelligent—and so formed the natural aristocracy.

The singular changeover was symbolized by the "Jacksonian persuasion" (to use Marvin Meyer's phrase). Thought was replaced by sentiment and feeling, and each man's sentiments were held to be as good as any others. This is what gives point to the striking observations of Tocqueville. The opening lines of Tocqueville's *Democracy in America* are:

No novelty in the United States struck me more vividly during my stay than the equality of conditions. It was easy to see the immense influence of this basic fact on the whole course of society. It gives a particular turn to public opinion and a particular twist to the laws, new maxims to those who govern and particular habits to the governed.

And, reflecting on the power of this new principle, Tocqueville concluded:

Therefore the graduate progress of equality is something fated. The main features of this progress are the following: it is universal and permanent, it is daily passing beyond human control, and every event and every man helps it along. Is it wise to suppose that a movement which has been so long in train could be halted by one generation? Does anyone imagine that democracy, which has destroyed the feudal system and vanquished kings, will fall back before the middle classes and the rich? Will it stop now, when it has grown so strong and its adversaries so weak?[24]

In nineteenth-century America, however, the notion of equality was never sharply defined. In its voiced assertions it boiled down to the sentiment that each man was as good as another and no man was better than anyone else. What it meant, in effect, was that no one should take on the airs of an aristocrat and lord it over other men. To this extent, it was a negative reaction to the highly mannered society of Europe, and travelers to this country at the time understood it in those terms. On its positive side, equality meant the chance to get ahead, regardless of one's origins—that no formal barriers or prescribed positions stood in one's way. It was this combination of attributes—the lack of deference and the emphasis on personal achievement—which gave nineteenth-century America its revolutionary appeal, so much so that when the German '48ers came here, including such members of Marx's Socialist Workers Club as Kriege and Willich, they abandoned European socialism and became Republicans instead.

What is at stake today is the redefinition of equality. A principle which was the weapon for changing a vast social system, the principle of equality of opportunity, is now seen as leading to a new hierarchy, and the current demand is that the "just precedence" of society, in Locke's phrase, requires the reduction of all inequality, or the creation of equality of result—in income, status, and power—for all men in society. This issue is the central value problem of the post-industrial society.

The principle of equality of opportunity derives from a fundamental tenet of classic liberalism: that the individual—and not the family, community, or the state—is the singular unit of society, and that the purpose of societal arrangements is to allow the individual the freedom to fulfill his own purposes—by his labor to gain property, by exchange to satisfy his wants, by upward mobility to achieve a place commensurate with his talents. It was assumed that individuals will differ—in their natural endowments, in their energy, drive, and motivation, in their conception of what is desirable—and the institutions of society should establish procedures for regulating fairly the competition and exchanges necessary to fulfill these individually diverse desires and competences.

As a principle, equality of opportunity denies the precedence of birth, of nepotism, of patronage or any other criterion which allocates place, other than fair competition open equally to talent and ambition. It asserts, in the terms of Talcott Parsons, universalism over particularism, achievement over ascription. It is an ideal derived directly from the Enlightenment as codified by Kant, the principle of individual merit generalized as a categorical imperative.

The social structure of modern society—in its bourgeois form as the universalism of money, in its romantic form as the thrust of ambition, in its intellectual form as the priority of knowledge—is based on this principle. Estate society—that of the eighteenth century and earlier—had given honorific precedence to land, the army, and the church, and only the birthright of inheritance could provide access to these institutions. Even where there was nominal mobility—the institutions of the Red and the Black—commissions in the army (as in England up to the middle of the nineteenth century) were open only by purchase, and benefices in the church available through family connection. Modernity meant the uprooting of this stratified order by the principle of openness, change, and social mobility. The capitalist and the entrepreneur replaced the landed gentry, the government administrator took power over the army, and the intellectual succeeded the priest. And, in principle, these new positions were open to all men of talent. Thus there occurred a complete social revolution: a change in the social base of status and power, and a new mode of access to place and privilege in the society.

The post-industrial society adds a new criterion to the definitions of base and access: Technical skill becomes a condition of operative power, and higher education the means of obtaining technical skill. As a result, there has been a shift in the slope of power as, in key institutions, technical competence becomes the overriding consideration. In industry, family capitalism is replaced by managerial capitalism; in government, patronage is replaced by civil service and bureaucratization; in the universities, the exclusiveness of the old social elites, particularly WASP domination of the Ivy League colleges, breaks up with the inclusion of ethnic groups, particularly the Jews. Increasingly, the newer professional occupations, particularly engineering and economics, become central to the technical decisions of the society. The post-industrial society, in this dimension of status and power, is the logical extension of the meritocracy; it is the codification of a new social order based, in principle, on the priority of educated talent.

In social fact, the meritocracy is thus the displacement of one principle of stratification by another, of achievement for ascription. In the past—and this was the progressive meaning of liberalism—this new principle was considered just. Men were to be judged—and rewarded—not by attributes of birth or primordial ties but on individual merit. Today that principle is held to be the new source of inequality and of social—if not psychological—injustice.

THE CASE AGAINST MERITOCRACY

The sociological and philosophical objections to the meritocracy are of a contradictory and overlapping nature:

1. Genetics and intelligence: If one assumes that a meritocracy is purely a selection by intelligence, and that intelligence is based on inherited genetic differences, then one obtains privilege on the basis of a genetic lottery, and this is an arbitrary basis for social justice.

2. Social class: There can never be a pure meritocracy because, invariably, high-status parents will seek to pass on their positions either through the use of influence or simply by the cultural advantages their children would possess. Thus, after one generation a meritocracy simply becomes an enclaved class.

3. The role of chance: There is considerable social mobility in the United States, but it is less related to schooling or ability or

even to family background than to intangible and random factors such as luck and competence in the particular job one falls into. Christopher Jencks and his associates, in a review of the effect of family and schooling on mobility, conclude:

Poverty is not primarily hereditary. While children born into poverty have a higher than average chance of ending up poor, there is still an enormous amount of economic mobility from one generation to the next. There is nearly as much economic inequality among brothers raised in the same homes as in the general population. . . .

. . . there is almost as much economic inequality among those who score high on standardized tests as in the general population. Equalizing everyone's reading scores would not appreciably reduce the number of economic "failures." . . .

Our work suggests, then, that many popular explanations of economic inequality are largely wrong. We cannot blame economic inequality primarily on genetic differences in men's capacity for abstract reasoning, since there is nearly as much economic inequality among men with equal test scores as among men in general. We cannot blame economic inequality primarily on the fact that parents pass along their disadvantages to their children, since there is nearly as much inequality among men whose parents hold the same economic status as among men in general. We cannot blame economic inequality on differences between schools, since differences between schools seem to have very little effect on any measurable attribute on those who attended them. Economic success seems to depend on varieties of luck and on-the-job competence that are only moderately related to family background, schooling or scores on standardized tests.[25]

Thus, a situation of inequality exists which is justified on the basis of achievement or meritocracy but does not actually derive from them, so that the rewards of mobility, or, at least, the degrees of inequality in reward, are not justified.

4. The principle—or illusion—that a meritocracy instills a competitive feeling

into society which is damaging to those who succeed and even more so to those who fail. As Jerome Karabel writes: "A meritocracy is more competitive than an overtly-based class society, and this unrelenting competition exacts a toll both from the losers, whose self-esteem is damaged, and from the winners, who may be more self-righteous about their elite status than is a more traditional ruling group. Apart from increased efficiency, it is doubtful whether a frenetically competitive inegalitarian society is much of an improvement over an ascriptive society which, at least, does not compel its poor people to internalize their failure."[26]

5. The principle of equality of opportunity, even if fully realized on the basis of talent, simply re-creates inequality anew in each generation, and thus becomes a conservative force in society.[27] In its most vulgar form, this is the argument that equality of opportunity has been the means of some (e.g. the Jews) to get "theirs" in society, and deny latecomers (e.g. blacks) a fair share of the spoils. This is the argument used in New York City, for example, where it is charged that in the school system Jews "used" the merit system to dispossess the Catholics, who had risen through patronage, but that the merit system was now a means of keeping out blacks from high place in the system. In its pristine form, this argument states that social justice should mean not equality at the start of a race, but at the finish, equality not of opportunity but of result.

This change in social temper—the distrust of meritocracy—occurred principally in the last decade. The Kennedy and Johnson administrations, as a double consequence of the civil-rights revolution and the emphasis on higher education as a gateway to better place in the society, had made equality the central theme of social policy. The focus, however, was almost completely on widening equality of opportunity, principally through the schools: on compensatory education, Head Start programs, manpower training to improve skills, school integration, bussing ghetto children to suburban schools, open admissions, and the like. It was clear that black and poor children were culturally disadvantaged, and these handicaps had to be eliminated. It was felt that these programs would do so. In justifying them, the image that President Johnson used, in proclaiming the policy of affirmative action, was that of a shackled runner:

Imagine a hundred yard dash in which one of the two runners has his legs shackled together. He has progressed 10 yards, while the unshackled runner has gone 50 yards. At that point the judges decide that the race is unfair. How do they rectify the situation? Do they merely remove the shackles and allow the race to proceed? Then they could say that "equal opportunity" now prevailed. But one of the runners would still be forty yards ahead of the other. Would it not be the better part of justice to allow the previously shackled runner to make up the forty yard gap; or to start the race all over again? That would be affirmative action towards equality.[28]

The change in attitude, however, began with the realization that schooling had little effect in raising the achievement or reducing the disparate standing of black children relative to white. In 1966, Professor James Coleman of Johns Hopkins University, carrying out a mandate of the Civil Rights Act of 1964, concluded a massive survey of 4,000 schools and 600,000 students. The Office of Education, which sponsored the research, and Coleman himself, had expected to find gross inequality of educational resources between black and white schools and to use this finding as an argument for large-scale federal spending to redress the balance. But the report—*Equality of Educational Opportunity*—found that there was little difference between black and white schools in such things as physical facilities, formal curricula, and other measurable criteria. It also found that a significant gap in the achievement scores between black and white children was already present in the first grade, and that despite the rough comparability of black and white schools, the gap between the two groups of children had widened by the end of elementary school. The only consistent variable explaining the differences in scores *within* each racial or ethnic group was the educational and economic attainment of the parents. As Coleman wrote:

First, within each racial group, the strong relation of family economic and educational background to achievement does not diminish over the period of the school, and may even increase over the elementary years. Second, *most of the variation in student achievement lies within the same school, very little of it is between schools.* The implication of these last two results is clear: family background differences account for much more variation in achievement than do school differences.

But there was no consistent variable to explain the difference between racial groups, not even measured family background—which is why some persons have fallen back on genetic explanations.

The Coleman findings dismayed the educational bureaucracy, and at first, received little attention. Issued in July 1966, the document was scarcely reported in *The New York Times* or the news weeklies. But as the explosive findings gradually became known, the Coleman Report became the center of the most extensive discussion of social policy in the history of American sociological debate, and the source of vehement public recrimination on such questions as compulsory integration, school bussing, and the like.[29]

Much of the controversy over the Coleman Report dealt with integration: some interpreted it, as did Coleman himself, in part, as a mandate to mix lower-class black schoolchildren with middle-class white to provide stronger peer-group pressures for achievement; black-power advocates saw it as justification for black control of black schools in order to strengthen the black

child's control over his own destiny; and still others felt that additional money spent on schools was a waste since schools were ineffective in reducing the achievement gaps between the races or between social classes.

But in the long run the more important aspect of the report was not its findings but its major thesis, which was the redefinition of equality of opportunity.[30] Coleman had been charged, by explicit congressional directive, to determine the extent of inequality in the educational *resources* available to black and white children, the assumption being that social policy had to equalize the "inputs" into the educational process. But what Coleman took as his criterion was achievement, or *results*. In effect, he redefined equality of opportunity from *equal access to equally well-endowed schools (inputs)* to *equal performance on standardized achievement tests (equality of outcomes)*. As he put it in the title of his *Public Interest* essay, the focus had to shift from "equal schools to equal students."

Coleman was saying that the public schools—or the process of education itself—were not the social equalizers American society imagined them to be. Children achieved more or less in relation to family background and social class, and these were the variables that would have to be changed. Equality would not be attained until an average public school in Harlem produced as many high achievers as one in Scarsdale.

The argument has been pushed one step further by Christopher Jencks. If the focus was on the "equal student," then the problem was not even the distinction between Harlem and Scarsdale. In reanalyzing the Coleman data, Jencks found that students who performed best on achievement tests "were often enrolled in the same schools as the students who performed worst," and this, he declared, was potentially the most revolutionary revelation in the report. "In the short run it remains true that our most pressing political problem is the achievement gap between Harlem and Scarsdale. But in the long run it seems that our primary problem is not the disparity between Harlem and Scarsdale but the disparity between the top and bottom of the class in both Harlem and Scarsdale."

One can carry this still another step to the disparity among children of the same family. And as Jencks argues, in fact, "There is nearly as much economic inequality among brothers raised in the same homes as in the general population. This means that inequality is recreated anew in each generation, even among people who start life in essentially identical circumstances." For Jencks, inequality is not inherited. There is no single consistent variable which explains who gets ahead and why. It is as much luck as anything else.

The logic of this argument is developed by Jencks in his book *Inequality*. Not only can one not equalize opportunity, but even if one could, equalizing opportunity does not appreciably reduce the inequality in results. He concludes quite bluntly: "Instead of trying to reduce people's capacity to gain a competitive advantage on one another, we will have to change the rules of the game so as to reduce the rewards of competitive success and the costs of failure. Instead of trying to make everybody equally lucky or equally good at his job, we will have to devise 'insurance' systems which neutralize the effects of luck, and income sharing systems which break the link between vocational success and living standards."[31] The aim of social policy, thus, has to be equality of result—by sharing and redistributive policies—rather than equality of opportunity.

If equality of result is to be the main object of social policy—and it is the heart of the populist reaction against meritocracy—it will demand an entirely new political agenda for the social systems of advanced industrial countries. But no such political demand can ultimately succeed—unless it imposed itself by brute force—without being rooted in some powerful ethical system, and for this reason the concept of equality of result has

become the Archimedean point of a major new effort to provide a philosophical foundation—a conception of justice as fairness—for a communal society.

In the nature of human consciousness, a scheme of moral equity is the necessary basis for any social order; for legitimacy to exist, power must be justified. In the end, it is moral ideas—the conception of what is desirable—that shapes history through human aspirations. Western liberal society was "designed" by Locke, Adam Smith, and Bentham on the premise of individual freedoms and the satisfaction of private utilities; these were the axioms whose consequences were to be realized through the market and later through the democratic political system. But that doctrine is crumbling, and the political system is now being geared to the realization not of individual ends but of group and communal needs. Socialism has had political appeal for a century now not so much because of its moral depiction of what the future society would be like, but because of material disparities within disadvantaged classes, the hatred of bourgeois society by many intellectuals, and the eschatological vision of a "cunning" of history. But the normative ethic was only implicit; it was never spelled out and justified.[32] The claim for "equality of result" is a socialist ethic (as equality of opportunity is the liberal ethic), and as a moral basis for society it can finally succeed in obtaining men's allegiance not by material reward but by philosophical justification. An effort in politics has to be confirmed in philosophy. And an attempt to provide that confirmation is now underway. . . .

RAWLS AND FAIRNESS

If Rousseau sought equality of result for the sake of virtue, and Mill equal representation proportionate to one's interest for the purpose of utility, the contemporary philosopher John Rawls wants to establish the priority of equality for reasons of justice. As he elegantly declares, "justice is the first virtue of social institutions, as truth is of systems of thought."[33]

What is justice? It cannot be the greatest good for the greatest number, for the price of those magnitudes may be injustice for the lesser number. It has to be a distributive principle for judging competing claims—i.e. the appropriate division of social advantages. For Rawls, this is justice as fairness,[34] and the foundation of fairness rests, initially, on two principles:

First: each person is to have an equal right to the most extensive basic liberty compatible with a similar liberty for others.
Second: social and economic inequalities are to be arranged so that they are both (a) reasonably expected to be everyone's advantage, and (b) attached to positions and offices open to all (p. 60).[35]

The first principle deals with equal liberties of citizenship—freedom of speech, vote, and assembly; eligibility for office; and so on. The second deals with social and economic inequalities—the distribution of income and wealth, differences in the degree of authority, and the like. It is with the second principle that we are concerned. The controlling terms in the propositions are the ambiguous phrases "to everyone's advantage" and "equally open to all." What do they mean?

Rawls's argument is complex, yet lucid. "Equally open" can mean either equal in the sense that careers are open to the talented, or equal in the sense of "equality of fair opportunity." The first simply means that those who have the ability and the drive are entitled to the place they have earned. This is the conventional liberal position. But Rawls notes that it does not account for the distortion by social contingencies. "In all sectors of society," Rawls writes, "there should be roughly equal prospects of culture and achievement for everyone similarly motivated and endowed.... Chances to acquire cultural knowledge and skills should

not depend upon one's class position, and so the school system, whether public or private, should be designed to even out class barriers" (p. 73).

The liberal principle accepts the elimination of social differences in order to assure an equal start, but it justifies *unequal result* on the basis of natural abilities and talents. For Rawls, however, "natural" advantages are as arbitrary or random as social ones. It is not "fair opportunity." "There is no more reason to permit the distribution of income and wealth to be settled by the distribution of natural assets than by historical and social fortune.... The extent to which natural capacities develop and reach fruition is affected by all kinds of social conditions and class attitudes. Even the willingness to make an effort, to try, and so to be deserving in the ordinary sense is itself dependent upon happy family and social circumstances. It is impossible in practice to secure equal chances of achievement and culture for those similarly endowed, and therefore we may want to adopt a principle which recognizes this fact and also mitigates the arbitrary effects of the natural lottery" (p. 74).

Therefore, Rawls concludes that one cannot equalize opportunity, one can only bend it towards another purpose—the equality of result. "No one deserves his greater natural capacity nor merits a more favorable starting place in society. But it does not follow that one should eliminate these distinctions. There is another way to deal with them. The basic structure can be arranged so that these contingencies work for the good of the least fortunate. Thus we are led to the difference principle if we wish to set up the social system so that no one gains or loses from his arbitrary place in the distribution of natural assets or his initial position in society without giving or receiving compensating advantages in return" (p. 102).[36]

The question thus turns from "equally open to all," i.e. the distribution of chances for place, to the distribution of primary social goods or values, i.e. to the meaning of "everyone's advantage." That latter phrase for Rawls, can be defined in terms of either the "principle of efficiency" or the "difference principle."

The efficiency principle is congruent with what welfare economics calls "Pareto optimality." The allocation of goods or utilities is efficient when one reaches the point where it is impossible to change an existing distribution pattern so as to make some persons (even one) better off without at the same time making some other persons (at least one) worse off. A utilitarian principle, "Pareto optimality" is interested only in a range of choices and is indifferent to actual bargains. For Rawls the difficulty with the principle of efficiency is that, as a matter of fairness, it cannot specify *who* should be better off or not worse off.

The "difference principle" simply means that if some persons are to be better off, the lesser advantaged are also to be better off, and in some circumstances even more so. If one gains, so must the others. "The intuitive idea is that the social order is not to establish and secure the more attractive prospects of those better off unless doing so is to the advantage of those less fortunate" (p. 75).[37]

This leads Rawls to his more general conception of social justice, or the social ideal:

All social primary goods—liberty and opportunity, income and wealth, and the bases of self-respect—are to be distributed equally unless an unequal distribution of any or all of these goods is to the advantage of the least favored (p. 303).[38]

For this reason, too, Rawls rejects the idea of a meritocracy. Although the meritocratic idea *is* democratic, it violates the conception of fairness:

The [meritocratic] social order follows the principle of careers open to talents and uses equality of opportunity as a way of releasing men's energies in the pursuit of economic prosperity and political domination. There exists a marked disparity between the upper and lower classes in both means of life and the rights and privileges of organizational authority. The culture of the poorer strata is impoverished while that of the governing and technocratic elite is securely based on the service of national ends of power and wealth. Equality of opportunity means an equal chance to leave the less fortunate behind in the personal quest for influence and social position. Thus a meritocratic society is a danger for the other interpretations of the principles of justice but not the democratic conception. For, as we have just seen, the difference principle transforms the aims of society in fundamental respects (p. 107).

The difference principle has two implications for social policy. One is the principle of redress for individuals:

This is the principle that undeserved inequalities call for redress, and since the inequalities of birth and natural endowment are undeserved, these inequalities are to be somehow compensated for. Thus, the principle holds that in order to treat all persons equally, to provide genuine equality of opportunity, society must give more attention to those with fewer native assets and to those born into the less favorable social position. The idea is to redress the bias of contingencies in the direction of equality. In pursuit of this principle greater resources might be spent on the education of the less rather than the more intelligent, at least over a certain time of life, say the earlier years of school (pp. 100–101).

The second is the more general principle that talent is to be regarded as a social asset, and its fruits should be available to all, especially the less fortunate:

[The difference principle] transforms the aims of the basic structure so that the total scheme of institutions no longer emphasizes social efficiency and technocratic values. We see then that the difference principle represents, in effect, an agreement to regard the distribution of natural talents as a common asset and to share in the benefits of this distribution whatever it turns out to be. Those who have been favored by nature, whoever they are, may gain from their good fortune only on terms that improve the situation of those who have lost out (p. 101).

We have here a fundamental rationale for a major shift in values: instead of the principle "from each according to his ability, to each according to his ability," we have the principle "from each according to his ability, to each according to his need." And the justification for need is fairness to those who are disadvantaged for reasons beyond their control.

With Rawls, we have the most comprehensive effort in modern philosophy to justify a socialist ethic. In this redefinition of equality as equity, we can observe the development of a political philosophy which will go far to shape the last part of the twentieth century, just as the doctrines of Locke and Smith molded the nineteenth. The liberal theory of society was framed by the twin axes of individualism and rationality. The unencumbered individual would seek to realize his own satisfactions on the basis of his work—he was to be rewarded for effort, pluck, and risk—and the exchange of products with others was calculated by each so as to maximize his own satisfactions. Society was to make no judgments between men—only to set the procedural rules—and the most efficient distribution of resources was the one that produced the greatest net balance of satisfactions.

Today we have come to the end of classic liberalism. It is not individual satisfaction which is the measure of social good but redress for the disadvantaged as a prior claim on the social conscience and on social policy.[39] Rawls's effort in *A Theory of Justice* is to establish the principle of fairness, but he pays little attention, other than using the generic term "disadvantaged," to *who* is to be helped.[40] His argument is set in social contract terms, and his "constitution of justice" is a bargain agreed to by individuals. Yet in contemporary society, inevitably, the disadvantaged are identifiable largely in group terms, and the principle of

equity has become linked with the principle of quota representation.

The claim for group rights stands in formal contradiction to the principle of individualism, with its emphasis on achievement and universalism. But in reality it is no more than the extension, to hitherto excluded social units, of the group principle which has undergirded American politics from the start. The group process—which was the vaunted discovery of the "realists" of American political science (see the discussion in Chapter 5)—consisted largely of economic bargaining between functional or pressure groups operating outside the formal structure of the party system. What we now find are ethnic and ascriptive groups claiming formal representation both in the formal political structure and in all other institutions of the society as well.

These claims are legitimated, further, by the fact that America has been a pluralist society, or has come to accept a new definition of pluralism rather than the homogeneity of Americanism. Pluralism, in its classic conceptions,[41] made a claim for the continuing cultural identity of ethnic and religious groups and for the institutional autonomy of cultural institutions (e.g. universities) from politics. Pluralism was based on the separation of realms. But what we have today is a thoroughgoing politicizing of society in which not only the market is subordinated to political decision but all institutions have to bend to the demands of a political center and politicize themselves in group representational terms. Here, too, there has been another change. In functional group politics, membership was not fixed, and one could find cross-cutting allegiances or shifting coalitions. Today the groups that claim representation—in the political parties, in the universities, in the hospitals and the community—are formed by primordial or biological ties, and one cannot erase the ascriptive nature of sex or color.

And yet, once one accepts the principle of redress and representation of the disadvantaged in the group terms that were initially formulated, it is difficult for the polity to deny those later claims. That is the logic of democracy which has always been present in the ambiguous legacy of the principle of equality.

THE REDEFINITION OF MERITOCRACY

Any principle inevitably has its ambiguities, for no moral situation is ever clear-cut, particularly in the case of equal opportunity versus equal result, since the conflict is between right versus right, rather than right versus wrong. What, then, are the difficulties and the contradictions in Rawls's principle of fairness, and are they of sufficient weight as to render it nugatory?

First, what is the meaning of disadvantage? What is the measure of fairness? Is it objective or subjective? Often a sense of unfairness depends upon expectation and the degree of deprivation. But by whose standard? One measure, Rawls writes, "is a definition solely in terms of relative income and wealth with no reference to social position. Thus, all persons with less than half the median income and wealth may be taken as the least advantaged segment. This definition depends only upon the lower half of the distribution and has the merit of focusing attention on the social distance between those who have the least and the average citizen."[42]

But for most persons the question of unfairness or deprivation is not some fixed or absolute standard but a comparison with relevant others. We know from many sociological studies that large disparities of income and status are accepted as fair if individuals feel that these are justly earned, while small differences, if arbitrary, will often seem unfair. Orderlies in a hospital compare their income with that of a nurse but not that of a doctor. Thus relative deprivation and reference group (to use the sociological jargon) at each point stipulate the degree of disparity.[43] But are we to accept the subjective evaluations of individuals as the moral norm, or an objective standard, and on what basis?[44] The point is not clear.

If disadvantage is difficult to define, there is a different kind of problem in the identification of "the least fortunate group." Rawls writes: "Here it seems impossible to avoid a certain arbitrariness. One possibility is to choose a particular social position, say that of the unskilled worker, and then to count as the least advantaged all those with the average income and wealth of this group, or less. The expectation of the lowest representative man is defined as the average taken over this whole class" (p. 98).[45]

Problems of borderlines and shadings apart—and in practical terms these are great—the identification of social position in this fashion raises a serious psychological question. One of the important considerations of moral philosophy has been to avoid labelling, or public stigmatization, of the disadvantaged. This is one of the reasons why reformers have always fought a "means test" as the criterion for public aid and tried to provide help as a right. It is one of the reasons (administrative matters aside) why proposals for the redistribution of income have suggested that a stipulated sum be given to all persons, and that money above a certain level be recouped by taxation. Yet Rawls writes: ". . . we are entitled at some point to plead practical considerations in formulating the difference principle. Sooner or later the capacity of philosophical or other arguments to make finer discriminations is bound to run out." But it is exactly at those points where principle has to be translated into rule and case that the problems of public policy and administration begin.

The question of labelling and redress leads back to a more general contradiction, the relation of equality to a principle of universalism. One of the historical gains of equality was the establishment of a principle of universalism so that a rule—as in the rule of law—applied equally to all, and thus avoided the administrative determination between persons. As in the Constitution, this meant the outlawing of bills of attainder which are aimed at one person; a law has to be written with a sufficient degree of generality so as to cover all persons within a category. In criminal law, we apply *equal punishment* to those who have violated the same law, regardless of the ability to bear punishment, and two men convicted of speeding are fined twenty-five dollars each though one is a millionaire and the other a pauper. The law does not inquire into their status differences; there is equal liability. And the court is enjoined from so prying in order to avoid the enlargement of judicial power which would enable the judge to make determinations between persons; his function is solely to find out whether they are guilty or not.

Yet, in instances where wealth and income are concerned, we have gone far in the opposite direction. Under the income-tax law, which was adopted in this century, not only do individuals not pay an equal amount (e.g. $500 each), they do not even pay equal proportions (e.g. 10 percent each, which would lead to different absolute amounts on varying incomes). In principle they pay progressively higher proportions, as incomes rise. Here ability—the ability to pay—becomes the measure. It may well be that in the area of wealth and income one wants to establish the principle "from each according to his ability to each in accordance with another's needs"; the principle of justice here applies because *marginal* amounts must be compared. (If two persons pay the same amount, in one case it comes to half his income, in the other case only a tenth, and the same principle is at work in proportionate taxes.) But, in the larger context, the wholesale adoption of the principle of fairness in all areas of social values shifts the entire slope of society from a principle of equal liability and universalism to one of unequal burden and administrative determination.

The ground of fairness, says Rawls, is a generalized social norm founded on a social contract. It is based on the theory of rational choice whereby individuals declare their own preferences, subject to the principle of redress and the principle of difference; and this rational choice would push the societal balance toward the social norm. Now, utility theory can order the preference of an individual and define the rational conduct of that individual; and in utility theory society is rightly arranged when we have a net balance of individual gains or losses on the basis of the persons' own preferences in free exchange. But here we run up against a difficulty. If rationality is the basis of the social norm, can we have a social-welfare function that amalgamates the discordant preferences of individuals into a combined choice which recapitulates the rationality of the individual choice? If one accepts the theoretical argument of the Arrow impossibility theorem (observing the conditions of democracy and majority choice), we cannot have such a social-welfare function.[46] What the social norm is to be then becomes a political question, subject to either consensus or to conflict—extortion by the most threatening, or collective bargaining in which people eventually accept some idea of trade-off. But if the decision is political, there are then no clear theoretical determinations, set by principles of rational choice, of what the social norm should be—unless, in the Rousseauian sense, the body politic is a "single" personality. We may want a social norm for reasons of fairness, but in the structure of rational choice procedures we cannot define one.

If the definition of a social norm, then, is essentially a political one, the principle of helping the least fortunate as the *prior* social obligation may mean—in a sociological as well as statistical sense—a regression toward the mean. If it is assumed that we have reached a post-scarcity stage of full abundance, this may be a desirable social policy. But if this is not so—and it is questionable whether it can ever be so—and if one defines society, as Rawls does, "as a cooperative venture for mutual advantage," why not, just as logically, allow greater incentives for those who can expand the total social output and use this larger "social pie" for the mutual (yet differential) advantage of all?

It is quite striking that the one society in modern history which consciously began with a principle of almost complete equality (including almost no wage differentials)—the Soviet Union—gradually abandoned that policy, not because it was restoring capitalism but because it found that differential wages and privileges served as incentives, and were also a more rational "rationing" of time. (If a manager's time is worth more than that of an unskilled worker, since he has to make more decisions, should he be expected to wait in line for a crowded tram or be given a car of his own to get to work?) Even those societies which have had relatively small differentials in income and incentives in the post-World War II years, such as Israel and Yugoslavia, have gradually widened these differences in order to stimulate productivity. And one of the chief pieces of advice which sympathetic economists have given to Fidel Castro to restore his stumbling economy (which has been largely organized on the basis of moral exhortation and the donation of extra labor time) is to make greater use of material incentives and wage differentials.[47] In the United States, the major period when social programs could be most easily financed was from 1960 to 1965, when the increase in the rate of economic growth, not the redistribution of income, provided a fiscal surplus for such programs.[48]

The United States today is not a meritocracy; but this does not discredit the principle. The idea of equality of opportunity is a just one, and the problem is to realize it fairly. The focus, then, has to be on the barriers to such equality. The redress of discrimination by representation introduces arbitrary, particularistic criteria which can only be destructive of universalism, the historic principle, won under great difficulty, of treating each person as a person in his own right.

The difficult and thorny question, in the end, is not just priority—who should be helped first—but the degree of disparity among persons. How much difference should there be in income between the head of a corporation and a common laborer, between a professor at the top of the scale and an instructor? The differences in pay in a business firm are on the order of 30:1, in a hospital of 10:1, and a university of 5:1. What is the rationale for these differences? What is fair? Traditionally, the market was the arbiter of differential reward, based on scarcity or on demand. But as economic decisions become politicized, and the market replaced by social decisions, what is the principle of fair reward and fair differences? Clearly this will be one of the most vexing questions in a post-industrial society.

A striking fact of Western society over the past two hundred years has been the steady decrease in the disparity among persons—not by distribution policies and judgments about fairness, but by technology, which has cheapened the cost of products and made more things available to more people.[49] The irony, of course, is that as disparities have decreased, as democracy has become more tangible, the expectations of equality have increased even faster, and people make more invidious comparisons ("people may suffer less but their sensibility is exacerbated"), a phenomenon now commonly known as the "Tocqueville effect."[50] The revolution of rising expectations is also the revolution in rising *ressentiment.*

The real social problem, however, may be not the abstract question of "fairness" but the social character of *ressentiment,* and the conditions which give rise to it. The fascinating sociological puzzle is why in democratic society, as inequality decreases, *ressentiment* increases. That, too, is part of the ambiguous legacy of democracy.

IV

A JUST MERITOCRACY

The difficulty with much of this discussion is that inequality has been considered as a unitary circumstance, and a single principle the measure of its redress, whereas in sociological fact there are different kinds of inequality. The problem is not *either/or* but what *kinds* of inequality lead to what *kinds* of social and moral differences. There are, we know, different kinds of inequality—differences in income and wealth, in status, power, opportunity (occupational or social), education, services, and the like. There is not one scale but many, and the inequalities in one scale are not coupled completely with inequality in every other.[51]

We must insist on a basic social equality in that each person is to be given respect and not humiliated on the basis of color, or sexual proclivities, or other personal attributes. This is the basis of the civil-rights legislation outlawing modes of public humiliation such as Jim Crow laws, and setting forth the principle of complete equal access to all public places. This principle also makes sexual conduct a purely private matter between consenting adults.

We should reduce invidious distinctions in work, whereby some persons are paid by the piece or the hour and others receive a salary by the month or year, or a system whereby some persons receive a fluctuating wage on the basis of hours or weeks worked and others have a steady, calculable income.

We should assert that each person is entitled to a basic set of services and income which provides him with adequate medical care, housing, and the like. These are matters of security and dignity which must necessarily be the prior concerns of a civilized society.

But one need not impose a rigid, ideological egalitarianism in all matters, if it results in conflict with other social objectives and even becomes self-defeating. Thus, on the question of wage or salary differentials, there may be good market reasons for insisting that the wages of a physician and dentist be greater than those of a nurse or dental technician, for if each cost the patient roughly the same (if one could for the same price have the services of a better qualified person) no one would want to use a nurse or

dental technician, even in small matters. The price system, in this case, is a mechanism for the efficient rationing of time. If as a result of differential wages the income spread between the occupations became exceedingly high, one could then use the tax laws to reduce the differences.

But the point is that these questions of inequality have little to do with the issue of meritocracy—if we define the meritocracy as those who have an *earned* status or have achieved positions of rational authority by competence. Sociologists have made a distinction between power and authority. Power is the ability to command, which is backed up, either implicitly or explicitly, by force. That is why power is the defining principle of politics. Authority is a competence based upon skill, learning, talent, artistry or some similar attribute. Inevitably it leads to distinctions between those who are superior and those who are not. A meritocracy is made up of those who have earned their authority. An unjust meritocracy is one which makes these distinctions invidious and demeans those below.

Contemporary populism, in its desire for wholesale egalitarianism, insists in the end on complete levelling. It is not *for fairness,* but *against elitism;* its impulse is not justice but *ressentiment.* The populists are for power ("to the people") but against authority—the authority represented in the superior competence of individuals. Since they lack authority, they want power. In the populist sociology, for example, the authority of doctors should be subject to the decisions of a community council, and that of professors to the entire collegiate body (which in the extreme versions include the janitors).

But there cannot be complete democratization in the entire range of human activities. It makes no sense, in the arts, to insist on a democracy of judgment. Which painting, which piece of music, which novel or poem is better than another cannot be subject to popular vote—unless one assumes, as was to some extent evident in the "sensibility of the sixties," that all art is reducible to experience and each person's experience is as meaningful to him as anyone else's. [52] In science and scholarship, achievement is measured and ranked on the basis of accomplishment—be it discovery, synthesis, acuity of criticism, comprehensive paradigms, statements of new relationships, and the like. And these are forms of intellectual authority.

All of this underscores a confusion between a technocracy and a meritocracy. Because the technocratic mode reduces social arrangements to the criterion of technological efficiency, it relies principally on credentials as a means of selecting individuals for place in the society. But credentials are mechanical at worst, or specify minimum achievement at best; they are an entry device into the system. Meritocracy, in the context of my usage, is an emphasis on individual achievement and earned status as confirmed by one's peers.

Rawls has said that the most fundamental good of all is self-respect. But the English sociologist W. G. Runciman has made a useful distinction between respect and praise. While all men are entitled to respect, they are not all entitled to praise.[53] The meritocracy, in the best meaning of that word, is made up of those worthy of praise. They are the men who are the best in their fields, as judged by their fellows.

And just as some individuals are worthy of praise, so are certain institutions—e.g. those engaged in the cultivation of achievement, the institutions of science and scholarship, culture and learning. The university is dedicated to the authority of scholarship and learning and to the transmission of knowledge from those who are competent to those who are capable. There is no reason why a university cannot be a meritocracy, without impairing the esteem of other institutions. There is every reason why a university has to be a meritocracy if the resources of the society—for research, for scholarship, for learning—are to be spent for "mutual advantage," and if a degree of culture is to prevail.

And there is no reason why the principle of meritocracy should not obtain in business and government as well. One wants entrepreneurs and innovators who can expand the amount of productive wealth for society. One wants men in political office who can govern well. The quality of life in any society is determined, in considerable measure, by the quality of leadership. A society that does not have its best men at the head of its leading institutions is a sociological and moral absurdity.

Nor is this in contradiction with the principle of fairness. One can acknowledge, as I would, the priority of the disadvantaged (with all its difficulty of definition) as an axiom of social policy, without diminishing the opportunity for the best to rise to the top through work and effort. The principles of merit, achievement, and universalism are, it seems to me, the necessary foundations for a productive—and cultivated—society. What is important is that the society, to the fullest extent possible, be a genuinely open one.

The question of justice arises when those at the top can convert their authority positions into large, discrepant material and social advantages over others. The sociological problem, then, is how far this convertibility is possible. In every society, there are three fundamental realms of hierarchy—wealth, power, and status. In bourgeois society, wealth could buy power and deference. In aristocratic society, status could command power and wealth (through marriage). In military and estate societies, power could command wealth and status. Today it is uncertain whether the exact relations between the three any longer hold: Income and wealth (even when combined with corporate power) rarely command prestige (who knows the names, or can recognize the faces, of the heads of Standard Oil, American Telephone, or General Motors?); political office does not make a man wealthy; high status (and professors rank among the highest in prestige rankings) does not provide wealth or power. Nor does the existence of a meritocracy preclude the use of other routes—particularly politics—to high position and power in the society.

But even within these realms, the differences can be tempered; and the politics of contemporary society makes this even more likely in the future. Wealth allows a few to enjoy what many cannot have; but this difference can—and will—be mitigated by a social minimum. Power (not authority) allows some men to exercise domination over others; but in the polity at large, and in most institutions, such unilateral power is increasingly checked. The most difficult of all disparities is the one of status, for what is at stake is the desire to be different and to *enjoy* the disparity. With his usual acuteness into the passions of the human heart, Rousseau observed: "[It is] the universal desire for reputation, honors and preferences, which devours us all, trains and compares talents and strengths . . . stimulates and multiplies passions; and making all men competitors, rivals or rather enemies, how many reverses, successes and catastrophes of all kinds it causes. . . ."[54]

Yet, if vanity—or ego—can never be erased, one can still observe the equality of respect due to all, and the differential degree of praise bestowed upon some. As Runciman puts it, "a society in which all inequalities of prestige or esteem were inequalities of praise would to this extent be just."[55] It is in this sense that we can acknowledge differences of achievement between individuals. It is to that extent that a well-tempered meritocracy can be a society if not of equals, then of the just.

NOTES

1. Michael Young, *The Rise of the Meritocracy, 1870–2033* (London, 1958).
2. A theoretician of the Technicians party, Professor Eagle, had argued that marriage partners, in the national interest, should consult the intelligence register, for a high-IQ man who mates with a low-IQ woman is wasting his genes. The activist women, on the other hand, took romance as their banner and beauty as their flag, arguing that marriage should be based on attraction. Their favorite slogan was "Beauty is achievable by all."
3. Gary S. Becker, *Human Capital* (New York, 1964), p. 112. Later writers have suggested this figure may be too high; the point remains that a college degree does provide an investment "yield."
4. For a comprehensive discussion of this major social change, see Jencks and Riesman, *The Academic Revolution* (New York, 1968). For a survey of the reaction, see Stephen Graubard and Geno Ballotti, eds., *The Embattled University* (New York, 1970).
5. As Michael Young describes the rationale in his fable:

> The proportion of people with IQs over 130 could not be raised—the task was rather to prevent a fall—but the proportion of such people in work which called upon their full capacities was steadily raised. . . . Civilization does not depend upon the stolid mass, the *homme moyen sensuel,* but upon the creative minority, the innovator who with one stroke can save the labour of 10,000, the brilliant few who cannot look without wonder, the restless elite who have made mutation a social, as well as a biological, fact. The ranks of the scientists and technologists, the artists and the teachers, have been swelled, their education shaped to their high genetic destiny, their power for good increased. Progress is their triumph; the modern world their monument. (Pelican edition, 1961, p. 15.)

6. Fritz Machlup, *Education and Economic Growth* (Lincoln, Nebraska, 1970), p. 40. Machlup cites a study by Edward Denison, which assumes that two-fifths of the income differentials of persons with more schooling was due to natural ability, while three-fifths was the result of additional schooling. Gary Becker, in *Human Capital* (New York, 1964), examined samples of persons for whom IQ and grades in primary and secondary school were available, and could be correlated with later income returns, and found that differential ability "might well have a larger effect on the estimated rate of return" than simply the effect of schooling, but that, by the college level, "education itself explains most of the unadjusted earnings differential between college and high-school graduates" (pp. 88, 124). The Denison data are in his essay, "Measuring the Contribution of Education to Economic Growth," *The Economics of Education,* ed. Robinson and Vaizey (London and New York, 1966). The figures on college and high-school IQ are from Machlup, p. 40.
   For a review of studies that question the relation of IQ to economic success, see Samuel Bowles and Herbert Gintis, "I.Q. in the U.S. Class Structure," *Social Policy,* vol. 35, nos. 4 & 5 (November/December 1972).
7. Richard Herrnstein, "I.Q.," *The Atlantic Monthly* (September 1971). Technically, one cannot say that within any single person, 80 percent of his IQ is inherited. In a large sample, 80 percent of the variance between scores would be attributed by Jensen to inheritance.
8. Ibid., p. 63. Herrnstein's arguments are paralleled by a school of ethologists who see in "the breeding process" the basis of the political struggle

in human society. Thus, anthropologists Lionel Tiger and Robin Fox write, in their book, *The Imperial Animal:*

Analogies are often drawn between human and ant societies. There are, to be sure, striking similarities—such as division of labor, caste system, and domestication of other creatures—but the analogy breaks down at one fundamental point: human societies are political, and ant societies are apolitical. The social order of an ant colony is genetically fixed. Workers are workers, drones drones, queens queens, soldiers soldiers, and so on. Workers cannot usurp power in the colony, because they are genetically programmed to be workers and nothing else. There can be no redistribution of power, of place, and, most importantly, of breeding ability, and therefore of contribution to the genetic pool. This is a crucial difference. Politics involves the possibility of changing the distribution of resources in a society—one of which is the control over the future that breeding allows. The political process—the process of redistributing control over resources among the individuals of a group—is, in evolutionary terms, a breeding process. The political system is a breeding system. When we apply the word "lust" to both power and sex, we are nearer the truth than we imagine. In the struggle for reproductive advantage, some do better than others. It is this that changes the distribution of genes in a population and affects its genetic future. This is a world of winners and losers, a world of politics—of the haves and the have-nots, of those who have made it and those who sulk on the sidelines.

[From the beginning of human time] the species has been irretrievably concerned with who can marry whom and with the relationship between position, property and productive copulation.

The result of the reproductive struggle is a social system that is profoundly hierarchical and competitive. And if human politics exhibits a constant tension between the commonly valued ideal of equality and the privately valued aim of happy inequality, then this is simply a reflection of our evolutionary history. (New York, 1971, pp. 24–25.)

What makes this formulation even more striking is the character of the "new biology," which now allows the human species control of breeding by transferring frozen sperm by "donors" to different women, the placing of the embryo in "host" *vitro,* and cloning, which allows one to reproduce the exact genetic code of an organism. For a thoughtful discussion of the disquieting social and ethical questions raised by the new biology, see Leon Kass, "Making Babies," *The Public Interest,* no. 26 (Winter 1972).

9. For a discussion of the argument that society is not becoming more meritocratic see Christopher Jencks and associates, *Inequality: A Reassessment of the Effect of Family and Schooling in America* (New York, 1972).

Jencks argues that there is no evidence that (a) the correlation between education and occupational status has changed over the past 80 years; (b) the correlation between IQ and occupational status has changed over the past 50 years; (c) the correlation between education and income has changed over the past 30 years; (d) or that the correlation between IQ and income has changed.

Equally, says Jencks, there is no evidence for a decline in the effects of family background either on occupational status or income, at least since World War I. The work of Stephan Thernstrom, *Poverty and Progress: Social Mobility in a Nineteenth-Century City* (Cambridge, Mass., 1964), suggests mobility rates as high in the nineteenth century as in the twentieth.

"In what sense, then, can we say that society is becoming more meritocratic, if the importance of family background and educational credentials is constant over time?" writes Jencks. "Why should we accept Herrnstein's thesis if (a) education is no more important, and (b) he offers not a shred of evidence that IQ is more important than it used to be, and (c) all the indirect evidence suggests no change in the importance of IQ as against other factors in determining success?" (Private communication, July 25, 1972.)

Jencks is somewhat skeptical, as well, of the argument about family background as the primary factor in determining the correlation between schooling and occupational status. "Samuel Bowles has an essay in the Spring 1972 *Journal of Political Economy* arguing that family background is a major factor in the observed relationship, although I think he greatly overstates his case. I can easily imagine that personality differences (persistence, discipline, etc.) may explain most of the differences between the educated and the uneducated, and that these may not be caused to any significant extent by schooling, but may simply affect the amount of schooling people get" (ibid).

Drawing upon the work of Jencks et al., a collaborator, David K. Cohen of the Harvard Education School, has stressed the large role of contingent factors in going to college. Cohen writes:

A comparison of IQ and social and economic status of college students reveals that being rich is nearly as big a help in increasing a student's chances of going to college as being smart. The most important fact, however, is that *ability and status combined explain somewhat less than half the actual variation in college attendance.* As in the case of curriculum placement, we must turn to other factors—motivation, luck, discrimination, chance, and family encouragement or lack of it—to find likely explanations. "Does I.Q. Matter?" *Commentary* (April 1972), p. 55 (emphasis added).

10. Lester Thurow, "Education and Social Policy," *The Public Interest,* no. 28 (Summer 1972), p. 79 (emphasis in the original).

11. But there was usually some kind of sorting device. In the midwestern systems, anyone with a C average or better in high school could enter the

state university, but a ruthless examination system would weed out the poorer students by the end of the first or second year. In the California system, any high school graduate could go on to higher education, but a grade tracking system put the top 10 to 15 percent directly into the universities (e.g. Berkeley, UCLA), the next 25 percent into the state colleges, and the remainder into junior or community colleges.

12. Jerome Karabel, "Perspectives on Open Admission," *Educational Record* (Winter 1972), pp. 42–43.

"The philosophical rationale for open admissions," Mr. Karabel writes, "is that the educational mission of the institution is not . . . to serve as a talent scout for future employers but rather to foster growth in the student." And in that light, Mr. Karabel quotes approvingly the remark of B. Alden Thresher: "There is no such thing as an unfit or unqualified seeker after education." Mr. Thresher's remark is in "Uses and Abuses of Scholastic Aptitude and Achievement Tests," *Barriers to Higher Education* (New York: College Entrance Examination Board, 1971), p. 39.

13. Edward Shils, "Editorial," *Minerva* (April 1971), p. 165.

14. In full acknowledgment of this principle, the Union Theological Seminary on June 1 voted that blacks and other minority groups would henceforth make up one-third and women one-half of all students, faculty, staff, and directors. (At the time, blacks made up 6 percent of the 566 member student body and 8 percent of the 38 member faculty; women 20 percent of the student body and 8 percent of the faculty.) "It is unrealistic," said the Seminary, "to educate people in a pluralistic society in an environment that is overwhelmingly white and male-oriented." The figure of 50 percent women was chosen to reflect their representation in society; the one-third minority as a "critical mass" to give them presence. *New York Times* (June 1, 1972).

15. Ivan Illich, "After Deschooling, What?" *Social Policy* (September/October 1971), p. 7.

16. Illich, who was a Monsignor in the Catholic Church, burst rather suddenly onto the American intellectual scene in the late 1960s with essays in the *New York Review of Books* and the *New York Times* on his theories of "de-schooling society." These essays were published as *Deschooling Society* (New York, 1970), and a second collection of essays, *Celebration of Awareness*, with an introduction by Erich Fromm, appeared a year later. Illich came to attention within the Catholic Church as the organizer of the center in Cuernavaca, Mexico, for training priests for work in South America. Though the center was set up with support from the Vatican hierarchy, after a few years it began to espouse unorthodox doctrines. A profile of Msgr. Illich—who has since resigned his church title—appeared in *The New Yorker* (April 25, 1970) by Francine DuPlessix Gray, and is reprinted in her book, *Divine Disobedience* (New York, 1971).

17. "The more learning an individual consumes, the more 'knowledge stock' he acquires. The hidden curriculum therefore defines a new class structure for society within which the large consumers of knowledge—those who have acquired large quantities of knowledge stock—enjoy special privileges, high income, and access to the more powerful tools of production. This kind of knowledge-capitalism has been accepted in all industrialized societies and establishes a rationale for the distribution of jobs and income." Ivan Illich, "The Alternative to Schooling," *Saturday Review* (June 19, 1971), reprinted in *Deschooling Society*.

18. Illich writes:

Science will be kept artificially arcane so long as its results are incorporated into technology at the service of professionals. If it were used to render possible a style of life in which each man would enjoy housing, healing, educating, moving, and entertaining himself, then scientists would try much harder to retranslate their discoveries made in a secret language into the normal language of everyday life. ("After Deschooling, What?" p. 13.)

19. As Richard Wollheim, a friendly critic, pictures the idyll:

Little vignettes of what would ensue are scattered through *Deschooling Society*. If a student wanted to learn Cantonese, he would be put on to a Chinese neighbour whose skill in his native language had been certified and whose willingness to impart it expressed. If he wanted to learn the guitar, he could rent not only a guitar but also taped guitar lessons and illustrated chord charts. If he wanted to find someone much in his own position with whom to discuss a disputed passage in Freud or Aquinas, he might go to a specially identified coffee shop, place the book by his side, and stay with whoever turned up as long a time as it took to satisfy his curiosity, or as short a time as it took to finish a cup of coffee. With the streets freed of private cars, individuals might wander freely through the city and explore the profuse teaching materials that exist not only in museums and libraries but in laboratories, storefronts, zoos, tool shops, cinemas and computer centres. And meanwhile the true teachers, the intellectual masters, would wait, presumably at home, for their self-chosen disciples to call on them.

Richard Wollheim, "Ivan Illich," *The Listener* (December 16, 1971), p. 826.

20. See James Coleman, "Education in Modern Society," in *Computers, Communications and the Public Interest,* ed. Martin Greenberger (Baltimore, 1971).

21. This is Rousseau's portrait of Emile at the end of his childhood:

He does not know the meaning of habit, routine and custom; what he did yesterday has no control over what he is doing today; he follows no rules, submits to no authority, copies no pattern, and only acts or speaks as he pleases. So do not expect set speeches or studied manners from him, but just the faithful expression of his thoughts and the conduct that springs from his inclinations. *Emile* (New York, 1911), p. 125.

22. John Dewey, *Art as Experience* (New York; Capricorn edition, 1958; original publication, 1934), p. 275.
23. I have presented these ideas, in larger historical and philosophical detail, in my book, *The Reforming of General Education* (New York, 1966). See, especially, chap. 4, "The Need for Reform: Some Philosophical Presuppositions," and chap. 6, "A New Rationale." The quotation is from the Anchor edition (1968), p. 151.
24. Alexis de Tocqueville, *Democracy in America,* ed. J. P. Mayer and Max Lerner (New York, 1966), Author's Introduction, pp. 3, 5–6.
25. Christopher Jencks et al., *Inequality*, p. 8.
26. Jerome Karabel, "Perspectives on Open Admissions," p. 42.
27. This was an argument made more than sixty years ago by W. H. Mallock, a British skeptic about democracy and perhaps the most able conservative thinker of the late nineteenth century. In *The Limits of Pure Democracy* (1917) Mallock argues that civilization proceeds only from the ability of a creative few and that complete equality would mean the end of economic progress and culture. In this respect, he writes: "The demand for equality of opportunity may, indeed, wear on the surface of it certain revolutionary aspects; but it is in reality—it is in its very nature—a symptom of moderation, or rather of an unintended conservatism, of which the masses of normal men cannot, if they would, divest themselves. . . . The desire for equality of opportunity—the desire for the right to rise—is a desire [for] some postion or condition which is not equal, but which is, on the contrary, superior to any position or condition which is achievable by the talents of all." Cited in Raymond Williams, *Culture and Society* (London, 1958), pp. 164–165.
28. Executive Order 11246, September 1965, cited in Earl Raab, "Quotas By Any Other Name," *Commentary* (January 1972), p. 41.
29. The document is formally known as "Equality of Educational Opportunity," Report of the Office of Education to the Congress and the President, U.S. Printing Office (July 1966), pp. 731.
The first discussion of the report was in *The Public Interest*, no. 4 (Summer 1966), where Coleman summarized his conclusions in an article, "Equal Schools or Equal Students." The quotation above is from p. 73 (emphasis added). As the debate widened, Coleman discussed the implications of the report in *The Public Interest*, no. 9 (Fall 1967), in the article "Toward Open Schools." He argued for the utility of integration on the following grounds:

The finding is that students do better when they are in schools where their fellow students come from backgrounds strong in educational motivation and resources. The results might be paraphrased by the statement that the educational resources provided by a child's fellow students are more important for his achievement than are the resources provided by the school board. This effect appears to be particularly great for students who themselves come

from educationally-deprived backgrounds. For example, it is about twice as great for Negroes as for whites.

But since family background is so important, Coleman warned

The task of increasing achievement of lower-class children cannot be fully implemented by school integration, even if integration were wholly achieved—and the magnitude of racial and class concentrations in large cities indicates that it is not likely to be achieved soon (pp. 21–22).

The most comprehensive discussion of the Coleman Report took place in a three-year seminar at Harvard University initiated by Daniel P. Moynihan. The various papers analyzing the report, and Coleman's reply to his critics, are in *On Equality of Educational Opportunity*, ed. Frederick Mosteller and Daniel P. Moynihan (New York, 1972).
30. I have profited here from Diane Ravitch's acute reading of the Mosteller and Moynihan book in *Change* (May 1972).
31. *Inequality*, pp. 8–9.
Jencks's key argument, to repeat, is that "economic success seems to depend on varieties of luck and on-the-job competence that are only moderately related to family background, schooling, or scores on standardized tests." And, as he concludes, "Nobody seems able to say exactly what 'competence' in this sense entails, including employers who pay huge sums for it, but it does not seem to be at all similar from one job to another. This makes it hard to imagine a strategy for equalizing such competence. A strategy for equalizing luck is even harder to conceive."
Since the factors which make for success are, for Jencks, simply wayward, there is no ethical justification for large disparities in income and status, and since one cannot equalize luck in order to create equal opportunity, one should seek to equalize results.
While Jencks's findings are important against the vulgar Marxist notion that inheritance of social class background is all-important in determining the place of the child—since there *is* social mobility in the U.S., about one-third of all children end up below their parents—and they disprove, once again, the stilted American myth that each person of ability finds a place commensurate with his merit, the inability to find a consistent set of relationships leads Jencks to emphasize "luck" as a major factor. But in his analysis, "luck" is really only a *residual factor* which is inserted because all other variables do not correlate highly. In and of itself, luck cannot be measured as a positive variable. While it may be true, as many studies show, that there is a low correlation between the career one thinks a man is educating himself for and the final outcomes, and that there is a measure of "luck" about the job one finds in relation to one's talents, the fact remains, nevertheless, that to keep that job, particularly at the professional level, a high degree of talent and hard work is required to succeed.
By emphasizing "luck" Jencks seeks to use the

randomness of a roulette occupational wheel to minimize the *earned* quality of success. And it may be that there is much more luck to the occupational system than Marxists or meritocrats would like to admit. Yet "common observation" (that other residual category of analysis) would indicate that—again on the professional level at least—hard work is a necessary condition for success, and that if a rough equality of opportunity has allowed one man to go further than another, he has *earned* the unequal reward—income, status, authority—which goes with that success. The important question of justice—as I argue later—is really "how much" unequal reward, in what dimensions, and for what.

32. Classical Marxism always eschewed the task of creating a normative ethic for socialism. Kautsky, for example, in his *Ethics and the Materialist Conception of History,* argued that socialism was a "necessary" outcome of human evolution, and did not have to be justified in moral terms. It was dissatisfaction with this view which led a number of pre-World War I socialist philosophers, principally Max Adler, to provide a neo-Kantian argument—the superior use of Reason in a socialist order—as the basis of its desirability. The victory of Bolshevism after 1917, and the spread of Marxism-Leninism, reasserted the eschatological vision as the basis of socialism.

33. John Rawls, *A Theory of Justice* (Cambridge, Mass., 1971), p. 3.

Justice, for Rawls, does not encapsulate all the energies of the society; it is a principle of distributive standards, and is itself part of a larger social ideal to which a society commits itself. He writes:

A conception of social justice, then, is to be regarded as providing in the first instance a standard whereby the distributive aspects of the basic structure of society are to be assessed. This standard, however, is not to be confused with the principles defining the other virtues, for the basic structure, and social arrangements generally may be efficient or inefficient, liberal or illiberal, and many other things, as well as just or unjust. A complete conception defining principles for all the virtues of the basic structure, together with the respective weights when they conflict, is more than a conception of justice; it is a social ideal. The principles of justice are but a part, although perhaps the most important part, of such a conception. A social ideal in turn is connected with a conception of society, a vision of the way in which the aims and purposes of social cooperation are to be understood. . . . Fully to understand a conception of justice we must make explicit the conception of social cooperation from which it derives (ibid., pp. 9–10).

(All citations in this section are from Rawls's book; page citations appear at the end of each quotation.)

34. The idea of fairness necessarily assumes a social *tabula rasa.* Rawls writes:

In justice as fairness the original position of equality corresponds to the state of nature in the traditional theory of the social contract. This original position is not, of course, thought

of as an actual historical state of affairs, much less as a primitive condition of culture. It is understood as a purely hypothetical situation characterized so as to lead to a certain conception of justice. Among the essential features of this situation is that no one knows his place in society, his class position or social status, nor does anyone know his fortune in the distribution of natural assets and abilities, his intelligence, strength and the like. I shall even assume that the parties do not know their conceptions of the good or their special psychological propensities. The principles of justice are chosen behind a veil of ignorance. This ensures that no one is advantaged or disadvantaged in the choice of principles by the outcome of natural chance or the contingency of social circumstances. Since all are similarly situated and no one is able to design principles to favor his particular condition, the principles of justice are the result of a fair agreement or bargain (p. 12).

35. A final formulation by Rawls, having to do with priority and rankings, appears on his pp. 302–303. For the purposes of our argument we can stay with the initial formulations.

36. As Rawls further notes, "The naturally advantaged are not to gain merely because they are more gifted, but only to cover the costs of training and education and for using their endowments in ways that help the less fortunate as well" (p. 101). See, too, the discussion on p. 104 about whether individuals "deserve" the advantage of natural capacities.

37. In an interesting comparison, Rawls (like Rousseau) takes the metaphor of the family as the model for this principle. "The family in its ideal conception, and often in practice, is one place where the principle of maximizing the sum of advantages is rejected. Members of a family commonly do not wish to gain unless they can do so in ways that further the interests of the rest. Now wanting to act on the difference principle has precisely this consequence" (p. 105). The difficulty with this argument—if one regards society as the family writ large—is that the family, as Freud has argued, holds together by love, which is specific. One loves one's wife and children—and tries to pass on one's advantages to them. Where love is generalized to the society, it becomes "aim-inhibited" (because one loves all) and is consequently weak and ineffective. For this reason, Freud argued that communism is impossible in the larger society. See *Civilization and Its Discontents, Standard Edition of the Complete Psychological Writings of Sigmund Freud,* vol. xxi (London, 1961), pp. 112–113.

38. An earlier, slightly variant, version by Rawls appears on p. 62. The later version, emphasizing the advantage to the least favored, is more relevant to my argument. One can say in this context that utilitarianism, which is the logic of bourgeois economics, follows the indifference principle in that each person pursues his own goods independent of the others, and the invisible hand coordinates the society.

39. The claims of the poor are, of course, among the oldest traditions in Western thought and are

central to the idea of Christian love. But Christian love—charity as *caritas*—accepted the poor as worthy in themselves and loved the poor as poor without endowing them with higher qualities than they possessed. In that sense, classic Protestant liberalism—with its sympathy and humanitarianism, rather than love—corroded the social conscience of the Catholic world. From a different source, the romanticizing of the poor, a tradition going back to Villon, also led to the erosion of *caritas* toward the poor. (For a defense of Christian love as the basis of society, and a biting attack on English moral philosophy, i.e. Hutcheson, Adam Smith, Hume, see Max Scheler, op. cit., section IV, pp. 114—137.)

40. It is striking that Rawls, like Jencks, does not discuss either "work" or "effort"—as if those who had succeeded, in the university, or in business or government, had done so largely by contingent circumstances of fortune or social background. There is a discussion of meritocracy, but not of merit. This itself is a measure of how far we have moved from nineteenth-century values.

It is equally striking that, in the "social-attention cycle," the policy concern a decade ago was with "excellence." The Stern Fund sponsored a major study on the identification of excellence; John Gardner wrote a book entitled *Excellence: Can We Be Equal and Excellent Too?* (New York, 1961). At that time, meritocracy was a positive word—so much so that Merrill Peterson, in his magisterial biography of Thomas Jefferson, said that, had Jefferson known the term, he would have used it to define his "natural aristocracy." Today the concern is almost entirely with equality and the disadvantaged. Will the "social-attention cycle" come full circle in the future?

41. See, for example, the work of R. M. MacIver, *The More Perfect Union: A Program for the Control of Inter-group Discrimination* (New York, 1948), and on the religious side, John Courtney Murray, *We Hold These Truths: Reflections on the American Proposition* (New York, 1960).

42. Rawls, op. cit., p. 98. The criterion of using half of the median was also advanced by Victor Fuchs in "Redefining Poverty," *The Public Interest*, no. 8 (Summer 1967).

43. For an elaboration of these two concepts and their application to the subjective sense of fairness, see W. G. Runciman, *Relative Deprivation and Social Justice* (London, 1966).

44. In classical ethical theory, the good is defined as independent of individual satisfaction. Aristotle distinguished between "being good" and "feeling good." A person having an adulterous affair feels good but is not being good.

45. What if the "least fortunate" are there by their own choice?" Christopher Jencks points out while "we have already eliminated virtually all economic and academic obstacles to earning a high school diploma . . . one student in five still drops out." And while one may guarantee working-class families the same educational opportunities as middle-class families, what happens if they don't want to use this opportunity. Society may have an obligation to those who are kept down or cannot advance because it is not their fault. But if individ-

uals—for cultural or psychological reasons—do not avail themselves of opportunities, is it the society's responsibility—as the prior obligation—to devote resources to them? But if not, how does one distinguish between the genuinely disadvantaged and those who are not? This is the inextricable difficulty of social policy.

46. For the previous discussion of the Arrow theorem, see chap. 5. Rawls avoids the difficulty of the Arrow impossibility theorem by rejecting the condition of majority rule. As he writes:

> It is evident from the preceding remarks that the procedure of majority rule, however it is defined and circumscribed, has a subordinate place as a procedural device. The justification for it rests squarely on the political ends that the constitution is designed to achieve, and therefore on the two principles of justice. . . . A fundamental part of the majority principle is that the procedure should satisfy the conditions of background justice. . . . When this background is absent, the first principle of justice is not satisfied; yet even when it is present, there is no assurance that just legislation will be enacted.
>
> There is nothing to the view, then, that what the majority wills is right. . . . This question is one of political judgment and does not belong to the theory of justice. It suffices to note that while citizens normally submit their conduct to democratic authority, that is, recognize the outcome of a vote as establishing a binding rule, other things equal, they do not submit their judgment to it (p. 356).

Rawls is right of course, as with most traditional conceptions of justice, that the action of a majority does not make any decision just. The tyranny of a majority has long been recognized as a source of injustice, as much as the tyranny of a despot. The procedural question, however, is whether, as a *consistent* rule there is any better method than majority vote, subject to the democratic check of a minority having the right and ability to change the decision and become a majority, in reaching consensus.

Rawls seeks to avoid the Arrow dilemma by specifying a "veil of ignorance" when the initial social contract is bargained. Since each man does not know how well he might do, it is to his interest to gain at least a minimum prize. Thus, each man would accept a set of rules that maximizes the chance of winning at least a minimum prize, and he would therefore also want to make that minimum prize as large as possible. Presumably, such veiled bargaining should move the prizes (i.e. the primary social goods, such as income, self-respect, etc.) to the mean. Yet as Lester Thurow points out:

> Although maximizing the minimum prize seems egalitarian, it need not be. . . . Rawls believes that the trickle-down effect is so large that it would be impossible to design economic activities that concentrated income gains among high income groups. As an economist I do not share this faith. There are many economic activities with marginal amounts of trickle-down. To be

really egalitarian social rules would have to state that individuals must choose those economic activities with the largest trickle-down effects ("A Search for Economic Equity," *The Public Interest,* [Spring 1973]).

Thus, some coercive device may be necessary to achieve the desired outcome of a set of rules that will maximize the minimum prize, or give priority to the disadvantaged.

47. See Wassily Leontieff, "The Trouble with Cuban Socialism," *New York Review of Books* (January 7, 1971).
48. For a review of the data, and the argument, see Otto Eckstein, "The Economics of the '60s, A Backward Look," *The Public Interest,* no. 19 (Spring 1970).
49. This is by now a commonplace argument, used tediously, often by apologetic propagandists for free enterprise. But this does not make it—as an historical fact—less true. For some striking comparisons on the exact amount of decrease of disparity, see Jean Fourastie, *The Causes of Wealth* (Glencoe, Ill. 1960), previously cited.
50. For Tocqueville's discussion of this phenomenon, see *The Old Regime and the French Revolution* (New York, 1955), part III, chaps. 4 and 5, esp. pp. 176–181, 186–187.
51. Rawls writes: "One is not allowed to justify differences in income or organizational powers on the ground that the disadvantages of those in one position are outweighed by the greater advantages of those in another. Much less can infringements of liberty be counterbalanced in this way" (op. cit., pp. 64–65).

His argument is puzzling. In any interdependent society one forgoes certain liberties—in traffic and zoning regulations—to enhance others. Nor is it clear why one has to redress inequalities in every sphere rather than allow individuals to choose which sphere represents the most nagging inequality to them.

As a political principle, it is unlikely that any single rule can dominate a polity without disruption. Aristotle distinguished between two kinds of justice, numerical equality (equality of result) and equality based on merit. As he concluded: "To lay it down that equality shall be exclusively of one kind or another is a bad thing, as is shown by what happens in practice; no constitution lasts long that is constructed on such a basis." *Aristotle's Politics,* trans. T. A. Sinclair (London, 1966), pp. 191–192.
52. For a discussion of the context of this anti-intellectualism, see Lionel Trilling, *Mind in the Modern World,* The 1972 Jefferson Lecture in the Humanities (New York. 1973).
53. W. G. Runciman, " 'Social' Equality," *Philosophical Quarterly,* XVII (1967), reprinted in his *Sociology In Its Place* (London, 1970).
54. *The Second Discourse,* pp. 174–175. In his economic lottery, Rawls would be forced to rule out the envious man. As Lester Thurow puts it: "Suppose the worst-off man were envious. In this case anything that lowers the income of better-off people faster than it lowers the income of the worst-off man maximizes the minimum prize. If envy were not ruled out, maximizing the minimum prize could lead to zero incomes for everyone."

Pareto, in his discussion of utility, argued that when income disparities are reduced, individuals seek to increase the inequalities in status and power (*The Mind and Society* [New York, 1935], vol. IV, sect. 2128–2145). For a further discussion of this question in relation to scarcity and abundance, see the next section, particularly the argument in footnote 126.
55. " 'Social' Equality," p. 211.

37. A Strategy for Equity: Recurrent Education and Industrial Democracy

TOM SCHULLER and JARL BENGTSSON

We argue in this essay for a policy of recurrent education. In doing so we follow a theory of the relation between economy (the structure of productive relations) and education (the reproduction of social relations) which begins by accepting a correspondence between class and status on the one hand, and the structure of education on the other. This relation is perceived as interactive in the sense of allowing both a modification of the relations of production through educational change and at the same time a certain responsiveness in the educational system to changes in the character of work. Educational change is held to be possible as a result of deliberate planning, the outcome of free debate, and the exercise of democratic political will. Within a theoretical framework of this kind our analysis and prescription for educational reform are put forward as a contribution to the debate.

This article appears here for the first time.

I: MORE OF THE SAME?

The extension of compulsory education, at least in the developed countries, has just about reached its limits. The same battle has been fought again and again to assure all children, rather than simply a privileged minority, the right to a basic education, and compulsion has generally been seen as the most effective way of overcoming both the hesitations of the group concerned and the obstructiveness of those whose interests lie in preserving educational exclusiveness and in disposing of an abundant supply of young, and hence cheap, manpower. Similarly, post-compulsory education has undergone an enormous expansion over the last two decades (roughly 8.5 percent per annum in higher education in OECD countries), partly as a function of deliberate measures designed to enlarge opportunity and partly in response to increased demand generated by the extension of compulsory education. Progress has been crudely measured by enrollment rates and, what is more, by enrollment rates amongst the younger generation. "We are apt to speak and think as if our problem were an extension of our present educational system to the masses whom it does not yet reach. More teachers, more schools, and bring the rest of the population into them. But it is not as simple as that."[1] Indeed not, but problems of measurement have, until recently, discouraged attempts at a comprehensive assessment of the effects of educational expenditure, and an unholy, if unwritten, alliance between institutional inertia and educational purism has inhibited discussion of any radical modification in the distribution of resources.[2]

It is often difficult adequately to judge the success of policies when the relative impact of alternative measures must remain purely hypothetical. To condemn the expansion described above as having failed, for instance, to achieve greater social equity ignores the possibility that without it such progress as has been made would have been less substantial or even negative. Yet confidence in the efficacy of education and in the value of educational reform has plummeted over the last few years, provoking a marked reluctance to maintain a continually rising investment, as research increasingly exposes education's apparent impotence in the face of prevailing social conditions.[3] Hence the claim of education to a growing share of limited resources is likely to find fewer and fewer supporters unless the resources allocated to it are more effectively deployed. Once the need to relate education to other policies has been recognized, however, a rethinking of its structures may yet help to eradicate some of its most obvious weaknesses: lack of success in meeting the changing needs of youth, especially those of the adolescent population; failure to cater adequately to its potential adult clientele; disappointing contribution to redressing inequality; inability to provide an adequate framework for integrating theory and practice; and, in particular, indifference to changes in the world of work.

One response to the perception of these weaknesses and of their causes has been the collection of a sheaf of allied measures under the heading of recurrent education.[4] The exact number and nature of the stalks which go to make up this sheaf are matters for debate, but the basic aim is to modify the educational system so that access to it is not confined to the individual's early years, but is available at intervals, in alternation with work or other activities, over his or her lifetime. For such a policy to be coherent, it must be constructed along two axes: a vertical one, along which the integration of adult education opportunities with initial schooling might be effected, breaking the current lockstep by encouraging individuals to defer the exercise of their educational rights; and a horizontal one, along which educational and training provision is coordinated with other social and employment policies which affect the work and leisure of the population. In the following pages we shall first outline, in essentially descriptive terms, the rationale for such a policy; we shall then consider some counter-arguments, and finish by referring briefly to the role recurrent education may play in supporting changes in the socio-economic structure.

Obviously the notion of recurrent education has implications for basic education, and equally obviously to argue for it is not to suggest that basic education should be left unreformed. Nonetheless, the principle of recurrence applies essentially to post-compulsory education. The case for it falls fairly neatly under two headings: effectiveness, in the sense of the degree to which certain methods of resource expenditure achieve their objectives, and equity, here understood as denoting not absolute uniformity of wealth or status but a fairer distribution of material and non-material goods.[5] Common to both is the proposition that a strong relation exists between educational and occupational distribution and reform.

Two of the most important factors determing education's effectiveness are motivation and change. The relationship between motivation and achievement has been repeatedly observed, generally via the depressing truth of its converse: the vicious circle of lack of success and absence of motivation.[6] The existing system means, perversely, that the earlier one dismounts from the educational train the more difficulty one has in clambering back on. Recognizing this, teachers often concentrate their efforts on securing for their less successful pupils at least a basic qualification, and, in spite of the fact that such minimal qualification may serve only to guide this class into a restricted occupational stratum, these efforts deserve admiration, not denigration; but there would be less heat and more light if those currently disaffected—although not only they, of course—were guaranteed the opportunity to return later, choosing for themselves when and what to study and hence appreciating more for themselves the value of education.

The argument does not at all apply only to recalcitrant learners. In most subjects, and for most people (teachers at all levels included), wider experience will help the student to define more clearly what he wants to learn, and provide him with pegs on which to hang his theoretical learning. The complex maturation of ability, with its interplay of genetic and environmental factors, will often be better served by later opportunities, provided that the teaching methods and curricula are appropriate to adult learning processes.[7] It is, moreover, a commonplace—but one comparatively unrecognized in policy terms—that capacity to learn deteriorates with lack of use, and that immense potential for general and vocational learning is currently not simply underutilized but in fact dissipated through effective lack of opportunity. In short, evidence from psychological research and common sense point in the same direction.[8]

Two side-effects of measures enabling adults to return to education should be mentioned at this point. If recurrent education develops, there will be an increase in mixed age-groups participating in education, where one can, without being too ingenuous, look for a valuable interchange between mature adults and younger students in place of the current highly homogeneous age stratification. Second, ever since the Plowden Report there has been a steadily growing awareness of the decisive effect of parental attitudes on the educational achievement of their children. The relevance of recurrent education lies not so much in the direct communication of this awareness through parent education: it is more that parents who are themselves currently involved in education are very much more likely as a result to take a positive interest in their child's educational development than someone whose last contact with educational institutions was more than twenty years earlier—and probably less than idyllic at that.[9]

The incidence of change is a platitude, its rate less easy to demonstrate but universally accepted as accelerating. The proliferation of knowledge and the obsolescence of skills have stimulated an enormous growth in expenditure on in-service training and have provided much of the impetus behind the development of schemes allowing educational leave of absence from work. In France, for instance, the 1971 law on *formation continue* allows up to 2 percent of a firm's labor force to take leave of absence at any one time, and requires a minimum proportion of the wage bill—the target is 2 percent by 1976—to be devoted to the financing of such leave; the preamble to the law proclaims as objectives individual and social fulfillment as well as vocational development, but at present it is the latter which dominates. In many other countries, increasing sums are spent on a panoply of training schemes. As usual, then, the quickest reaction has been prompted by economic imperatives, together with the demands of professional competence,[10] but the issue cannot be restricted to vocational training, however broadly conceived, and some measures—such as the agreement negotiated by the Italian Metalworkers Union allowing its members 150 hours paid leave over a period of three years—give the worker the effective right to decide on what sort of study he or she wishes to pursue whether or not it is closely related to his job.

In any event, as far as responsiveness to change is concerned, the same reasons which have led enterprises and professions to maintain their adaptability through recurrent training apply equally to society in general. However, change is not something which takes place in a vacuum and which only subsequently requires a reaction. To see it as such is to accept basic structures and trends as in some way given, a fundamentally conservative position best typified in the view of technological developments as inherently neutral. If, on the other hand, the aim is to control change so that its effects are socially beneficial, it is not a question of allowing the labor force to adapt to new techniques or of helping the population passively to comprehend what is happening in society. Many of the changes in occupational structures demand not more skill but less, in that they have reduced the job content to even more elementary and degrading opera-

tions;[11] the argument, therefore, is not so much that increased training efforts are required to meet the intrinsic demands of the job as that there must be opportunities for people to learn to assess individual and collective needs, and to inform themselves sufficiently to be able to participate actively in deciding which changes are to be supported and which rejected.

Here the ideological function of the distinction conventionally drawn between vocational and non-vocational education needs to be pointed out. It not only reflects but reinforces the division which obtains for most working people between their job and the rest of their life, by limiting the "vocational" element to the content of the job rather than allowing it to refer to the social and economic context in which the job, and the enterprise, exist. A course for managers might well include broader elements, for instance of psychology or sociology, since it is regarded as part of the management function to control the effects of social and economic movements on the operations of the enterprise. By contrast, the study of such areas by those below the management level is classified as non-vocational (and hence as falling outside many of the agreements for release from work and financial support), as though the average worker's interest in those aspects of his job were necessarily largely incidental and spare-time.

The relationship of education to the distribution of control is, as so often, symbiotic: access to learning opportunities is essential for the initial taking of decisions, and the implications of these decisions will inevitably require the further acquisition of knowledge and skills. Experience has shown, moreover, that when a reorganization of working patterns has brought training opportunities in its wake, this has in turn stimulated a vigorous demand for broader education.

We have so far described the ways in which an educational system which allows repeated alternation of education and other activities may function more effectively than the present structure. Partial recognition of this is implicit in a variety of developments, such as reformed admission policies, the growth of modular courses, and the spread of techniques which allow teaching to be carried out at a distance.[12] Although it will already be clear that this effectiveness is not a neutral, mechanistic concept but assumes the political hue of the society in which it operates, it is time to deal more explicitly with the issue of equity and the way in which recurrent education may help progress towards this objective.

There are two points to be made against the likelihood of a further extension of initial education achieving greater equity, however radically its character may be changed. The first is that in all developed countries compulsory education now continues to the age of fifteen or sixteen, and by that time the prospects for educational progress in the immediate future are basically already determined and would in relative terms be only marginally affected by an expansion of directly sequential further education.[13] There is, it is true, a small proportion of those who leave school at the minimum age who do so reluctantly, and equity demands that they should be given the financial support, lacking at present, to enable them to continue if they wish. But the great majority of this age-group have already had enough of formal schooling by this time—and the proportion would probably be greater if it weren't absolutely clear that to drop out at this point is to compromise, often irremediably, one's whole future. Attempts to reform basic education so that it caters to the needs of the whole population must continue, especially in offering a genuine choice between continuing directly and returning later to education, but it would be hugely over-optimistic to suppose that even a drastically modified system of basic education would of itself provide everyone with equal opportunities for the future—quite apart from the further inequalities between generations which would result from such a modification itself.

Let us assume, then, that it is wholly impracticable to envisage everyone's termi-nating his initial education similarly qualified (whether the qualifications are formal, in the shape of certificates, or not). Hence, the view of education as a service largely confined to the initial period of one's life implies that the egalitarian target is the broader spread of educational achievement over social classes in the hope that this will increase social mobility and reduce social inequality, presumably on at least a partially meritocratic basis. However satisfying this might be from the statistical point of view, and however much it would represent real progress compared with the current situation, it can hardly be considered as a solution to the problem of inequitable distribution. In the first place, it implicitly overestimates the independent influence of initial education. More particularly, by restricting itself to the period of initial education (however long that may be), it crucially circumscribes its application and the potential of education for achieving greater equity. The problem requires redefinition: if education is seen as recurring over the individual's lifetime, one can envisage a rolling concern for those who are, for whatever reason, worst placed—in other words, a constant commitment to rectifying social inequalities, as opposed to a once-for-all attempt to give the race a fair start.

The second argument against expanding initial education is pragmatic and simple, but nonetheless crucial: if it were carried out to any significant degree it would absorb an enormous amount of resources, which would then be available neither for other parts of the education service, nor for any other sectors of society. If we are serious about analyzing and changing the role of education in society, the conflicts between the various claimants on limited resources must be acknowledged. "Recurrent education" represents a policy proposal because it suggests not the blithe saturation of society with educational provision, but a different way of deploying existing resources.

Why should deferment of learning opportunities offer more chance for their equitable distribution? In the first place, it would prevent the distribution of post-compulsory educational resources from being determined solely by initial success which is so strongly correlated with social background.[14] Moreover, its structure is inherently more suitable for redressing the imbalances which currently place two major sectors of the population, the older generation and women, at such a disadvantage. Whatever progress has been made in reducing inequality within given age cohorts, one of its corollaries has been the widening of the intergenerational gap, which can only be reduced by a positive effort to favor the return of adults to education.[15] Inequality between the sexes is even more pervasive than that between generations. Where recurrent education has a particular contribution to make is in helping to free women from the choice which so often confronts them between the mutually exclusive alternatives of pursuing a career and having children. Obviously, the problems of equality for women cannot be solved only—or indeed chiefly—by a reform of the educational system, but a pattern of recurring opportunities for learning is better suited to their life-cycle.

The introduction of employment issues into a subject classified as educational inevitably raises several hackles, quite possibly because it raises awkward questions concerning the ugly nature of work. The most straightforward response to the defenders of education's purity is the reminder that any policy which claims to reach the majority of the population has no choice but to enter the workplace. Moreover, the process is two-way: what is suggested is a tighter relationship between the worlds of education and work, not a subjection of the former to the latter. An active manpower policy which influences as well as responds to movements in the labor market fully complements recurrent education, in that both approaches insist on the need to take demand into account as well as supply. Thus while the former involves such demand-side measures as deliberate job crea-

tion and regional development as counterparts to vocational training and guidance, the latter underlines the reciprocal relationship which obtains between education and the workplace.

This reciprocity must be given particular prominence in any analysis of the prospects for industrial democracy. The different forms which this chameleon concept may assume are likely to be faithfully reflected in the types of education which accompany it. At a minimal level—the micro-technical, as it has been called[16]—there may be wider acquisition of such skills as are called for by a policy of job enlargement, and it is this which has provided much of the thrust behind the move towards educational leave of absence, which has taken concrete form in several countries and is therefore of considerable, if limited, significance.[17] Any more comprehensive form must involve the redistribution of control; what needs to be stressed in this context is that its participants, as well as having theoretical access to relevant information, must also dispose of appropriate skills in handling that information and in relating it to their position. An informed population is a sine qua non of democracy—industrial or social.

The extension of individual choice and the improvement of adult learning opportunities are wholly unobjectionable aims, but once they are given concrete policy form, they will begin to encounter opponents who discern in them practical consequences inimical to their own interests. Initially, such opposition may come from those whose professional role and functions are defined by the existing structure, and who do not wish to see modifications in the boundaries of the subject they teach or the area they administer. An adult returning to education, for example, is likely to be interested less in pursuing an orthodox single-discipline course than in acquiring the skills necessary to solve particular problems which he has encountered, and this represents a challenge to teachers accustomed to providing the former type of education. Others may support the extension of adult opportunities only in so far as this enables existing institutions to maintain their current recruitment patterns, and would veer rapidly into opposition if it were proposed that those very institutions should be integrally involved in furnishing the new opportunities. Disagreement may occur between those who interpret recurrent education as the development of adult education and training programs into a system running parallel to formal post-compulsory provision, and those who see it as involving the unification of the youth and adult sectors and the integration of formal and non-formal provision, breaking down the administrative and psychological barriers which currently inhibit those involved in formal education from responding to external events and prevent those outside from profiting from existing facilities.

Yet even if this latter interpretation is accepted and implemented, it would be disingenuous to expect unanimity as a result. We do not subscribe to the notion that an improved flow of information will automatically induce harmonious social and labor relations—on the contrary, one consequence is likely to be the intensification of debate, as people begin to exploit their newly-developed knowledge and skills.[18] The interests of different groups may on occasion coincide, but they will certainly also conflict, and such a sharpening of differences may emanate directly from the wider diffusion of knowledge in many walks of life: the local council, the shop floor, the family, perhaps even the political parties.

At the level of macro policy, we have referred already to the integral role of manpower policies in a recurrent education approach; one should add, finally, that the imminence of substantial unemployment serves to underline the need for a purposive exploitation of education and training capacity as an immediate buffer, and, in the longer term, to draw attention to the potential of recurrent education as a counter-cyclical instrument of employment policy. The satisfactory provision of employment opportunities is, after all, an issue which is likely to arise whatever the political system may be.

II: FURTHER CONSIDERATIONS

A variety of criticisms have been leveled at the proposed policy of recurrent education, ranging from the argument that it would simply cost too much to the fundamental political charge that what is suggested would serve to subordinate the education service and its participants to the workings of the capitalist system and thereby postpone more radical changes in society. In this section, therefore, we briefly sketch out the criticisms and suggest how they might be rebutted.

The first line of attack is directed not so much at the notion of recurrent education, which may be accepted as intrinsically sensible, as at its cost, and depends basically on the following argument. A switch to enlarged opportunities for adults would entail a vast increase in opportunity costs, since the incomes foregone by them would be much greater than those foregone by younger students; moreover, investment in the education of the older age-group would be comparatively uneconomic as they are closer to retirement or death and will therefore yield a smaller overall return.[19]

This highly depersonalized approach is not only distasteful, but also methodologically fragile for a number of reasons. In the first place, the whole notion of a precise rate of return to educational investment is suspect. It is generally calculated on the differences between individuals' incomes, certain fractions of which are attributed to the respective stages of education pursued beyond the compulsory school leaving age. Yet to attribute, for example, a significant part of the superior income enjoyed by a fifty-year-old university graduate over a coeval high-school leaver directly to the spell of education which the former enjoyed some thirty years previously is grossly to overload that particular instrument of analysis. The enormous difficulty of satisfactorily isolating the impact of education on average lifetime earnings profiles, and the fact that even such differentials as are directly attributable may derive more from the selective function of education than from its intrinsic effect, drastically impair the accuracy of the rate of return approach as an estimate of the true yield to investment in education—to say nothing of the more fundamental question of how adequate income is as a measure of productivity.

As for the income foregone, it is misleading to construct individual profiles without taking into account the overall labor situation and relevant manpower policies. To argue that the productivity of an adult—valued, say, at £3,000 per annum—is wholly lost if he or she enters on full-time studies ignores the possibility of replacing that productivity, at least partly, from elsewhere through flexible labor deployment. This does not necessarily mean a simple one-for-one substitution; an active manpower policy allows the slack to be taken up, with the "vacuum effect" tending to pull underemployed workers into the situations left vacant by those taking time off for study. In general, the enormous problem of unemployment is likely to stimulate a broader approach which will embrace education and training as an instrument for preventing and countering the underutilization of labor,[20] and the coordination of education and manpower policies, at both national and local levels, is one of the major elements of a recurrent education approach.

Furthermore, the notion of incomes foregone has no application to those who were not earning in the first place, and therefore excludes not only the unemployed, as discussed in the previous paragraph, but also those who are customarily classified as outside the workforce. Housewifery is the most glaring example of an unremunerated occupation which falls outside the scope of traditional calculations.

The value of a woman's work at home (or a man's, of course) raises the whole question of externalities, which is quite separate from the difficulties involved in the direct attribution of income differentials to specific periods of education. Most rate of return calculations frankly admit the inherent problem of quantifying such benefits of education as a greater alertness among parents to their children's needs or a generally more informed populace.[21] Many of the arguments put forward earlier in support of recurrent education are at present not readily susceptible to exact quantification, but this does not make them any less valid. What we are arguing for, therefore, is not the flat rejection of cost/benefit analysis, but a refusal to make undue obeisance to narrow numerical computations, so that even in terms of restricted economic investment calculations it should be seen that the case against recurrent education is ill supported. This is especially true in view of the tendency to focus on private rather than social benefits. Of course, the overall cost of a system of recurrent education will depend on the generosity of provision, and this may be greater than at present; our point is that resources, whether great or small, would be more effectively deployed in enabling adults to pursue education in alternation with their other activities.

The cost criticism is generally made by those who declare themselves otherwise in favor of recurrent education or whose position on its intrinsic merits or demerits remains unstated. More direct opposition comes from those who argue that measures which encourage earlier termination of initial education will militate against those from lower social backgrounds and will therefore constitute a retrograde step towards greater selectivity and inequality. It is predicted that we will find ourselves reverting to the pre-expansion era where only a minute proportion, whose composition is heavily determined by social origin, proceed to further education. Moreover, the additional opportunities may themselves exacerbate the problem—one has only to look at the Open University in Britain or the system of *formation continue* in France to see that, whatever their considerable merits, they have up to now depressed still further the relative position of disadvantaged groups, especially those with least initial education.[22] The answer here is that a policy of recurrent education does not consist simply in encouraging people to terminate initial education earlier and in providing opportunities for returning later. If the goal of greater equality is seriously adopted, measures must be included of positive discrimination in favor of those least advantageously placed.

These measures would be of several kinds. Most directly, admissions policies could be weighted in favor of certain categories, to the extent of establishing quotas on their behalf—in addition to the revision of admissions policies to give greater credit to work experience, a process already particularly advanced in Sweden and the United States. In financial terms, the coordination of the financing of initial and further education would correct the regressiveness of the current system; whereas at present the average higher education student both comes from a more advantaged background and benefits far more from public funds than the average primary and secondary school pupil, financial support could be leveled out or otherwise weighted in such a way that the student who decided to continue directly with further education would not do so on the basis that this would secure for him or her—in general permanently, under the present system—access to the better occupations and greater financial benefits, but would find himself or herself at the back of the queue for later entry to study and support. Naturally, however, the effectiveness of such egalitarian discrimination will depend on the extent to which the distribution of educational opportunity and financial support for it is publicly controlled, and the probability of its implementation on the particular political context.

In addition to financial and admission arrangements, the content of the education and the way in which it is offered will affect its distribution. The first implies a substantial overhaul of current curricula and teaching methods, and comes down basically to the question of who should control the nature of the education offered.[23] But it is not only the supply which can be affected; the attitude that public responsibility extends only to the meeting of expressed demand is culpably passive. Here there is room for a whole gamut of outreach activities, both to ensure that everyone is aware of the opportunities available to him and to transmit back information on what sort of facilities and courses would be appreciated. Obvious candidates for responsibility are trade unions and those involved in social services, who can reach the population at their place of work and at home.[24] There is, in short, a battery of measures which would stimulate and meet new demands and, at the same time, include the strong element of positive discrimination which is necessary to avoid the emergence of a "second creaming," where fresh initiatives depress still further the prospects of those right at the bottom of the pile.

Nevertheless, however sharp the teeth in these measures are, it would be absurd to pretend that recurrent education can on its own eradicate the inequities of the existing social and economic system. As the inextricability of education from its broader socioeconomic context becomes increasingly apparent, changes in occupational structures are recognized as a necessary counterpart to educational reforms which aim at a more equitable distribution of opportunities. This fact is fully acknowledged in our insistence on the need to turn educational policy to face manpower policy and developments in the workplace. This implies not only recognizing the interdependence of the two worlds, but also the possibility of directly shaping educational services to support changes in the way occupations are defined and allocated.

Yet to advocate this line is to risk being caught in a crossfire. On one side are the purists who argue that education should be insulated as far as possible from unhygienic contact with the mundane goings-on of working life. Training is of course necessary for the economic life of society (which after all supports its educational institutions), but true learning is to be valued more or less in inverse proportion to its proximity to the world of the wage-packet. Here a distinction, albeit a somewhat arbitrary one, needs to be drawn between the subordination of the content of education to the economic demands of society in general and enterprises in particular, and the design of educational services so that they effectively serve the requirements of those who are involved in the process of production. The answer to the purists is twofold: if the majority of the population are to be reached more than once during their lifetimes, education must be prepared to get its hands a little dirty; and if education is to act as an effective agent for change it must adopt as its field of operation the area where the balance of socio-economic relations is determined.[25]

From the other side comes a fusillade of political arguments which accuse proponents of recurrent education of what might be called integrationism. By aligning itself more closely with the world of employment, recurrent education will sustain the present system of production by ameliorating its functioning and blunting the ideological challenge which could be better mounted by the maintenance of a clearer distinction between education and work. Obviously there is a danger that developments such as educational leave of absence will be so exploited by employers that its benefits accrue solely or predominantly to them. Already, indeed, predictable problems have emerged: for instance, if the individual has the right to leave of absence, his exercise of this right may be curtailed by obstacles placed overtly or covertly in his path, such as the virtual refusal to countenance leave for study unrelated to the enterprise's requirements or the more subtle withholding of information which the worker would

need in order to know the full extent of his rights.

Self-evidently, the value of a policy of recurrent education cannot be judged independently of the use to which it is put. If it is given the form of an expanded system of industrial training which impairs labor solidarity by encouraging workers to concentrate on their prospects for individual advancement within the current structure, then the criticism outlined above will be justified. But there are a number of forces, operating in the political domain or in the sphere of trade union activity, whose mobilization can lend recurrent education a wholly different character, in such a way that there is no suggestion that job competence should be accepted by the worker as the limit of his or her understanding of the socio-economic system. Indeed, the example of China shows how the principle of alternation can be whole-heartedly adopted in a non-capitalist system, work experience being given high priority and students interleaving their studies with spells of regular labor.[26] Attitudes toward the suggested interrelation between work and education will depend on one's view of the character of the work, but to argue that until working conditions are transformed the two should be kept as distant as possible is to ignore the dynamic nature of the relationship. Much of the education currently provided may be tightly controlled and highly functional, but the drive emanating from diverse quarters to expand it and to change its character will reinforce, and be reinforced by, complementary pressure to redistribute control over the processes of production.

Our basic point is that the sort of structure envisaged potentially allows education to play an important part in the process of change by giving it a built-in function in social and political life—a role which, after all, has an impeccable classical pedigree. The protean character of industrial democracy has already been referred to, denoting as it does anything from purely formal consultation to full-fledged workers' control. What it entails, in any of its more developed forms, is a capacity on the part of those involved to understand the processes of production and their various implications, and for this access to education will be a prerequisite.[27] Opening the company's books, for example, constitutes only a limited step towards participation if the rows of figures so exposed have no significance to anyone but a trained accountant; similarly, debate on a firm's future investment policies depends for its coherence on the level of expertise of the discussants, and expertise is here to be interpreted in the broad sense of an informed awareness, rather than the mere capacity to make technical decisions.[28]

CONCLUSION

The principle of alternation, of allowing people to interpose periods of education between their work and other activities, can be argued as a rational basis for planning, whatever one's political aims. But rational planning is not to be identified with a consensus approach; rather it consists in allowing the various sectors of society the maximum opportunity to formulate and express their interests, whether these coincide or conflict. If one is interested in the extension of democratic control over the process of production and over social developments in general, the task of the policymaker will be to ensure that this extension of control applies equally to the determination of the content of education and the use to which it is put.

We conclude by pointing schematically to three types of structures which may evolve to cater to adults who return to education. Under the first, a range of training programs is developed, designed to improve and adapt the overall skill level of the labor force and taking place in institutions which constitute a system parallel to, and more or less isolated from, the formal educational system. Control here is exercised by those whose eyes are firmly fixed on profit margins and stability, or by politicians concerned with

overall employment levels, and little response is expected either of the majority of the "managed" or of educational representatives.

The second type of structure is more influenced by trends in work organization and labor power. The content of the education offered is broadened to include both elements of *rattrapage* (the filling in of basic gaps) and subjects relating to work in its overall context ("work" perhaps being expanded to include domestic activity). More is demanded of the formal educational system in meeting the needs arising on both scores, but it continues to be organized, administered, and financed discretely. Although the distribution of control begins to emerge as a central issue for negotiation and debate, tensions arise from the uneven pace of progress in the different areas: a current example would be the incompatibility of an independent and critical spirit—generally endorsed as a part of the current orthodoxy—and the constrictive character of the role subsequently allotted in their working lives to those imbued with this spirit.

A third possibility is that if people's needs cannot be projected and met by their initial education, and if a redefinition of social and occupational roles entails concurrent availability of educational provision, then this provision will be designed both to balance the requirements of youth and adults and to complement related social and employment policies. This is not to advocate an administrative approach to political issues. The struggle for control over production processes will find its echo in the educational domain, not only in terms of content but, more importantly, as far as its relation to those processes and their evolution is concerned. The redistribution of education is one means of affecting the pace and direction of that evolution.

NOTES

1. Sir Richard Livingstone, *The Future in Education* (Cambridge: Cambridge University Press, 1941), p. 36.

2. Exceptions are Tanzania and Sweden, where there are now explicit commitments to give priority to adults in educational policy. See the *First 5 Year Plan for Economic and Social Development* (Dar-es-Salaam, 1964); *Vuxna Utbildning Studiefinansiering* (Stockholm: Ministry of Education, 1971).
3. See, for instance, J. Coleman, *Equality of Educational Opportunity* (Washington: US Department of Health, Education and Welfare, 1966); J.W.B. Douglas, J.R. Ross, and H.R. Simpson, *All our Future* (London: Peter Davies, 1968); and C. Jencks, *Inequality* (New York: Basic Books, 1972).
4. See *Recurrent Education: A Strategy for Lifelong Learning* (Paris: CERI/OECD, 1973).
5. Much of the debate on this issue has employed the term "equality," but equity seems a more accurate term in that it avoids confusing implications of quantitative standardization.
6. See, for instance, P. Freire, *Pedagogy of the Oppressed* (London: Penguin, 1970); and M.H. Seeman, "Powerlessness and Knowledge, a comparative study of alienation and learning," *Sociometry*, no. 2 (1967).
7. See E. Brunner et al., *An Overview of Adult Education Research* (Washington: Adult Education Association of the USA, 1967).
8. See, for instance, D.B. Bromley, *The Psychology of Human Ageing* (London: Penguin, 1966); and A. Heron and S. Chown, *Age and Function* (London: Churchill, 1967).
9. See, for example, A.H. Halsey, *Educational Priority*, Vol. I (London: HMSO, 1972); and the Plowden Report, *Children and their Primary Schools* (London: HMSO, 1967).
10. See, for example, on teacher training the recommendations of the James Report in the UK; in-service training is in some cases elsewhere obligatory, as for doctors in certain American states and for teachers in some Swiss cantons.
11. See Harry Braverman, *Labor and Monopoly Capital* (New York: Monthly Review Press, 1974).
12. See *Recurrent Education: Trends and Issues* (Paris: CERI/OECD, 1975).
13. See, for instance, R. Boudon, *L'Inégalité des chances,* (Paris: Armand Colin, 1973).
14. See, for instance, T. Husen, *Social Influences on Educational Attainment* (Paris: CERI/OECD, 1975), for the degree of correlation. See also W. Muller, "Social Stratification and Career Mobility," in *Social Science Information*, Vol. XI, no. 5 (Paris: International Social Science Council, 1972), for evidence that "educational success during an occupational career depends less on the conditions of social origin than does success in the school system prior to entering first occupation."
15. The recent expansion of education has led to a marked "generation gap" in terms of years of education received: in Sweden, for example, more than 80 percent of people aged 55 and over received only an elementary education, whilst roughly 70 percent of those in the 20–24 age group (1970) had at least ten years schooling. J. Bengtsson, "Intergenerational Inequality and Recurrent Education," in *Recurrent Education*, edited by Selma Mushkin (Washington: National Institute of Education, 1974).

16. See *Educational Requirements for Industrial Democracy* (Palo Alto, Cal.: Center for Economic Studies, 1974).
17. For a detailed examination of this and similar measures, see *The Implications of Educational Leave of Absence* (Paris: CERI/OECD, 1975). In addition to the instances mentioned above, there are a large number of agreements in the US, ranging from tuition refund to full-fledged paid educational leave: Sweden has recently introduced legislation granting the worker the right to such leave, and is soon to follow it up with supporting financial measures; paid leave is provided for in the Belgian law of 1973; in Yugoslavia the notion is often built into the local community structures; and the whole idea of continual alternation between work and education is integral to the current ideology in China. Paid educational leave has also been the specific subject of a recent ILO Convention.
18. "Is it not the supreme and most insidious exercise of power to prevent people from having grievances by shaping their perceptions, cognitions and preferences in such a way that they accept their role in the order of things, either because they can see or imagine no alternative to it, or because they see it as natural and unchangeable, or because they value it as divinely ordained and beneficial?" Steven Lukes, *Power* (London: Macmillan, 1974), p. 24.
19. For instance, Ken Gannicott, *Recurrent Education: A Preliminary Cost Benefit Analysis,* Australian Council of Education, Occasional Paper no. 6 (Canberra, 1973).
20. See, for example, Gösta Rehn, *Flextid och flexliv*, Ekonomisk Debätt 1/75 (Stockholm, 1975).
21. See Canadian Department of Manpower & Immigration, *A Model for the Benefit-Cost Evaluation of Canada Manpower Training Program* (Ontario, 1973), for the difficulties of assessing even a narrowly vocational training program. For a more fundamental critique of the human capital approach, see Martin Carnoy and Michael Carter, *Theories of Labor Market, Education and Income Distribution*, Institut de recherche sur l'économie de l'éducation, University of Dijon, 1975.
22. In France, in 1973, less than 10 percent of unskilled and semi-skilled workers benefited from paid educational leave compared with 30 percent of skilled and managerial employees; 3 percent of those employed in enterprises with less than fifty workers, compared with 17 percent in those with over fifty; 10 percent of the female workforce participated, compared with 16 percent of the males. *Projet de loi de finances pour 1975* (Paris: Imprimerie Nationale, 1974). In the OU the regressiveness is less marked; nevertheless 53 percent of the 1971–72 students were upper middle or middle class and a further 37 percent lower middle class, compared with 7 percent skilled working class and 1 percent straight working class (Naomi McIntosh, "The OU Student," in *The Open University Opens*, edited by Jeremy Tunstall, London: Routledge and Kegan Paul, 1974).
23. See André Gorz, "Le programme caché de l'éducation permanente," *Les Temps Modernes*

(Paris: November 1974): "Si l'éducation récurrente des adultes doit avoir un sens, son premier souci doit être de stimuler leur désir d'apprendre, ce qui veut dire: leur permettre de déterminer les buts pour la réalisation desquels ils éprouveront le besoin de nouvelles connaissances."
24. In Sweden, FOVUX (the Committee on Methods Testing in Adult Education) has stressed the role of the workplace counselor—a trade union representative—in stimulating recruitment amongst those such as shift workers with particular problems to overcome. It has also pointed to the importance of child-minding facilities being sufficiently extended so that persons with small children can participate in adult education. See *Extended Adult Education*, a summary of the Main Report presented by the Committee on Methods Testing in Adult Education, Stockholm, 1974.
25. Relevant here are the role of the school in confirming patterns of cultural dominance and the dependence of this role on the separation of the education system from the production system; see P. Bourdieu and J.C. Passeron, *Les héritiers* (Paris: Les Éditions de Minuit, 1964).
26. See, for example, Lu Ting-Yi, *Education must be combined with productive labour* (Peking: Foreign Labour Press, 1964); and *The Educational Revolution in China*, U.S. Dept. of Health, Education and Welfare (Washington, 1973).

27. For an acknowledgement of this from the side of business, see *Industrial Democracy in Europe: The Challenge and Management Responses*, Business International S.A. (Geneva, 1974), p. 17: "Since representatives of capital have a near-monopoly on information (education, experience and day-to-day operating knowledge), it is they, however much they might wish to share their role with worker representatives, who retain the genuine power."
28. It is worth reiterating at this point that supply and demand are interdependent, so that developments external to education may be supported by educational provision and at the same time will stimulate requests for study opportunities to meet recently perceived needs. It is also worth repeating, however, that opportunities for recurrent education must not be restricted to those in the active labor force. Already several unions in the United States are beginning to negotiate educational support for the worker's family as one of their fringe benefits, but responsibility cannot be left solely to the collective bargaining process. Public policy must ensure that the new right to educational leave of absence which is emerging in the world of work is effectively extended to cover all those who are not in active employment.

38. Theses on Education: A Marxist View

ROSSANA ROSSANDA, M. CINI, and L. BERLINGUER

THE SCHOOL SYSTEM IN INEGALITARIAN SOCIETY

As a public institution for the masses, the modern educational system was born with the modern bourgeoisie and carries with it the imprint of the bourgeois state. Coinciding with the development of capitalism and the ensuing necessity of cultural expansion that has accompanied those profound innovations in productive organization and technological development brought on by the Industrial Revolution, mass public education constitutes a process that has contributed to the restructuring of the social character of work. Explicitly reserved in the past to privileged social spheres for the

specific task of social management, education has become a "stock" on the labor market and the key to obtaining higher occupational positions. It is naturally accompanied by the democratic ideology of equality for all at the very time when productive development does not facilitate mass education. Hence, from the very outset, a contradiction develops between the impossibility of denying, in principle, "personal rights" to education and the impossibility of guaranteeing education on a mass scale. This explains the existence, even today, of the apparently double political "necessity" of education both for capitalist interests and for eventual conquest by the working class, and why the delays, the backwardness, and

This article first appeared as "Tesi sulla scuola" in *Il Manifesto*, February 1970. English translation by David Swartz. Reprinted by permission.

the underdevelopment imposed upon the working class by the church and the state have not yet disappeared.

Memorable battles for compulsory education have marked the founding of every modern state. It is interesting to observe, however, how the "popular" struggle for education has from the outset carried with it an unresolved and rarely perceived ambiguity between the "egalitarian" thrust (i.e., universal rights to knowledge) and the acceptance of a "promotion" model that is based not only on the technical but also on the social division of labor. In the race for material and social privileges, the working-class movement has simply demanded that there be equal *opportunity* for everyone in education. Except for certain illuminating examples that appeared during the French Revolution and the Commune, which were immediately suppressed, the idea itself of mass public education, because of this ambiguity, does not transcend the perspective of essentially accepting the social mechanisms of capitalist society and the school system as guarantors of the reproduction of social differentiation among occupational functions.

Following each great social upheaval—after the French Revolution and the Commune, or in Italy after Unification, the 1920 crisis, and finally the Liberation—the concessions granted by the bourgeoisie and the demands made by the workers' movement never transcend the demand for increased educational opportunity. In addition, the radical left parties in the working-class movement demand not only that mass public education not be *interessata* (utilitarian)—thus the demand for education for workers and artisans must be clearly distinguished from the reformist struggle that substantially coincides with productive development—but also that it be in a certain fashion autonomous and *formativa* (formative) of the person for himself and for the community instead of for an occupation. But at stake here is a separate moment that is distinct from rather than opposed to the

"selection" moment; the latter is left uncontested in that it is considered normal that vocational training at the secondary level should prepare students for lower occupational functions whereas college preparatory courses prepare students for higher occupational functions. Though limited to primary schools, "formative" education nevertheless becomes the arena for severe ideological confrontation between practicing Catholics and anti-clerical lay persons, between partisans of the "ideological" school and those of the "school of dialogue"; but for all of these the substantive issue remains one of defining a system of *valori morali di base* (basic moral values) and *educazione del cittadino* (citizen education) designed to provide at least an elementary access to a *veritable,* humanistic, and non-utilitarian culture.

Within the idea of a "formative" and "non-utilitarian" culture lies not only the ideology of the neutrality of knowledge and science (i.e., when these are freed from the contamination of productive relations and "work") but also an elitist and paternalistic conception of administering exalted and "non-utilitarian" concepts to the people. But more profoundly, this idea betrays the bad conscience of a culture, which is itself a product of the social division of labor, and which refuses to take into account this aspect of practical, applied, or professional knowledge that clearly mirrors the mark of social inequality inherent in the domain in which it operates, i.e., the productive unit. Every theory of "basic education" tries with all its force to save face by creating the notion of childhood as a separate area or moment in the life of man when there is *equality;* then comes inegalitarian society (which is assumed from the outset to be the only possible one) to resume its claims. Though decency requires that selection not be exhibited before the child reaches fourteen years of age, it in fact first begins operating through hidden mechanisms, which, when applied in similar fashion and under the cover of *equal* education to *unequals* (e.g., the son of an agricultural laborer from Calabria and a lawyer's son from Milan), will obviously lead to unequal results.

The idea of "competence" will then become a specific ideological excuse for educational selection. Competence is an objective product both of the technical division of labor and of the expansion of productive forces and knowledge that are necessarily expressed as "specialist" knowledge and as "professional profiles." Nevertheless, this double function, which is of course mediated through the school, follows a peculiar trend. On the one hand, the development of knowledge and its transmission are entirely orientated by a system of priorities set up by the mechanism of capital accumulation and by consensus manipulation through considerable superstructural mediation of class "self-consciousness" within the "democratic" state. On the other hand, this entire and contradictory process must function in relation to the social hierarchy. But, in order to satisfy this second condition, a kind of explicit "valorization" of levels of schooling becomes necessary; competence is or rather should be presented not only as "knowledge" but also as "knowledge with market value."

A veritable philosophy of prestige has accompanied this transformation of knowledge into a market commodity. The more recent theory of education as "productive investment" is linked to the thesis that the productivity of the individual's work is more or less proportional to the length of time he studies. The more one studies, the more competent one becomes; therefore, one's competence will have a higher economic value. Largely accepted by American liberalism, this thesis posits a correspondence between the range of salaries and the range of diplomas such that the expenses incurred during a given number of years of study can be viewed as an investment that will be remunerated accordingly. But this thesis also has its socialist versions that are based, on the one hand, on a school selection system that is more or less organized according to the demands of economic expansion, and on the other hand, on the collectivization of workers according to different levels of the social ladder. This way it is claimed that an *objective* base can be furnished for defining differences in labor force value; in fact, this nicely smuggles in a functional scale to accommodate the demands of any system where the labor force is characteristically reduced to a simple commodity.

In substance, this thesis, which defines technocracy, fails to recognize the *social* character of productive forces that nourish the economy of advanced capitalist societies. It attributes, on the contrary, to each individual (as if he worked in isolation, outside the context of the social relations of production) a greater or lesser portion of the social characteristics of work.

This mystifying thesis needs to be refuted by an analysis of the principal factors that have led to the breathtaking increase in labor productivity during these last decades: the extended socialization of the productive process (e.g., perfected work organization, scale factors, and industrial integration), the technological progress (e.g., automation, and introduction of new materials), the extension of markets, and as far as schools are concerned, the development of the *general* level of education. Now the efficiency of each of these factors is due to the nature of the collective process: that is to say, the process wherein the coherent and coordinated activity of all increases the potential of each one and enlarges beyond measure his sphere of action. This, therefore, concerns an efficiency that is essentially social and not one where the product can be parceled out according to the particular skills of single individuals. On the whole, "competence" plays a more important role in appropriation than it does in production; beginning with the "value" distinction between manual and intellectual work, the apparently objective standard of a social *division* of labor tends to be reproduced.

In summary, the formation of "competence" is perpetually and unjustly transferred from the level of the technical division of labor towards fulfilling a specific function of stabilization in the prevailing social organization. This function has two aspects, one economic and the other ideological.

On the one hand, the extension of parasitic and unproductive occupational positions helps reduce the danger of crises of overproduction. (This increases the consumption capacity in relation to the development of the productive capacity.) On the other hand, the increase in social differentiation provides a model of social mobility that reaches high enough so that it captures the vision of workers of the vast lower social strata.

This model appears even more convincing in that it is based upon an "objective" parameter of selection, i.e., consumption. In this manner the circle closes: the supreme social goal—i.e., the production of commodities by means of commodities—becomes the measure of all human activity and obscures, just as Marx had predicted, the substance of the social relations behind the fetish of commodities; the social relations among unequal subjects become simple, rational relations between commodities (i.e., levels of schooling) of different values. The patrimony of technical knowledge, or of "culture," invests a kind of exchange value in the mechanism of educational transmission; that is, in the selection and diploma systems, and in their liaison with social status and material advantage. Culture is produced for its exchange value and not for its use value.

Thus, by accepting as legitimate the premises of the formation of a hierarchical system of inequality and the transformation of education into a market commodity, the mass educational system of the capitalist era appears indissolubly linked to the capitalist system, and is one of the pivots, if not the fundamental instrument, of capitalist reproduction. What, therefore, has recently happened to bring into question its efficiency as an element of stabilization?

THE CRISIS OF INTEGRATION

The school system is being shaken by a crisis in its credibility. In order that schools be considered as acceptable reproducers and guarantors of social hierarchy, the society creating them must demonstrate sufficient capacity—one that is concrete and not simply ideological—to ensure the integration of the school product. Now, during the past twenty years, the expansion of mass education has taken place at speeds and according to models of needs and aspirations that do not correspond to the real productive development and social mobility of capitalist societies: schools are in an inflationary phase and are steadily losing their value. Being incapable of absorbing the educated masses by ensuring them the required "advancement," all capitalist systems tend to delay the impending collision between educational preparation and social opportunity: school life is lengthened and broadened in proportions having nothing to do with really acquiring higher knowledge; the community deducts from its budget increasingly large sums of money for the creating of ever vaster "parking zones" for youth, independent of their "productivity"; the system selects its managerial staff in relatively limited quantities, but at the same time holds hundreds of thousands of youth in schools anticipating that they will not obtain diplomas.

It is paradoxical that it is the workers and farmers, the producers of wealth, who "pay" the costs of a school system destined to educate those who will become other and more privileged than they; it is equally paradoxical that an ever vaster educational system also pays for the "semi-finished" who are finally left out by the selection process but who nevertheless require buildings, teachers, and materials for study. In order to reduce friction on the labor market, ever larger social strata of youth and retired persons are held outside of the market; social costs for them become enormous and efforts are no longer even made to render them productive. The school system becomes an end in itself, a separate body, that is essentially destined for its own self-nourishment. It produces occupational functions and itself becomes an occupational function. The process achieves scandalous proportions if one considers that more than 60 percent of university graduates end up in the public school system (the "semi-finished" go into the privately supported school system).

It is not surprising that the masses of students essentially experience this condition as a frustration. The student who continues his studies beyond the compulsory level more or less consciously accepts participation in that selection process that would ensure him, as formerly, a higher social position. But at the very moment when the doors to the university are being forced open by the thrust of masses of students, the concreteness of this prospect for social mobility, as emphasized in the preceding paragraph, fades; education becomes discredited. The student first discovers that he is the unfortunate victim of a fraud, and that it is impossible for him to become a "cadre." Next—and this occurs shortly thereafter because it concerns not an ideological acquisition but rather the crisis of a real, material situation—he experiences (as either an "irrational" or an "unjust" system) the incongruity of social stratification itself as it is proposed to him. Cultural development itself begins to enter in conflict with the fact that it is relegated to the rank of a simple commodity; a product of the system, culture becomes a critical arm and rebels against the system but finds itself handicapped by an intolerable social one-dimensionality. When an accumulation of consciousness-raising foreign political developments—e.g., the radically alternative models of Vietnam insofar as the poor achieve victory over the technological myth, the Chinese revolution as a rediscovery for today of the value of equality, and the Cuban revolution as an exaltation of subjectivism and a rediscovery of values—are added to these two processes, the student movement explodes.

Even if the explosion ebbs, the basic contradiction will nonetheless remain. Nor is it possible to imagine how mechanisms of the current social system could resolve it by creating a new equilibrium. There are, then, for the ruling class only two ways out, both of which are impracticable:

I) One could explicitly return to a type of functionality whereby schools would produce non-inflationary diplomas. This would entail that mass education be limited to lower and medium-lower levels (elementary schools and vocational training diplomas at the secondary level), and that a quota system for higher education be implemented through a brutally authoritarian selection process. This way presents two inconveniences: it would require a rigid planning of needs and a coercive system capable of imposing them. Even if one thinks that the ruling classes of the capitalist countries are capable of carrying out this process of "rationalization," such a choice would so abruptly tear the mask from the ideology of "advancement," which is based upon the rights of all to education, that it would provoke violent confrontation. It is not by chance that the Fouchet plan preceded the French "May," or that the West German S.D.S. directed its first campaign against the quota system. As a matter of fact, this solution functions only in the socialist countries. There they attribute to schools the same function of forming competence for occupational functions, and thus the functions of selection and reproduction of social stratification, but they are capable of managing their economic development and imposing its priorities through a complex system of coercion and consent.

II) One could explicitly reject the "functionality" of schools as producers of *non-inflationary* occupational credentials. This trend has appeared in Italy among certain Catholic and socialist educational experts who propose abolishing all value of academic credentials. This alternative constitutes the unacknowledged background of the "liberalization" of study programs as forseen by the "mini-reform": henceforth, the young person will study "for himself" without any guarantee that what he studies will help him out in life—as it used to do. The mystifying character of the ideology of this solution seems evident. The relation between the authoritarian study program and the professional profile is not exposed either from the viewpoint of the technical and social division of labor, on the one hand, or from the viewpoint of the use value and exchange value, on the other. Instead, a misleading dialectic is created between the authoritarian study program and the possibility for the pupil to choose his own course of study. On the basis of models borrowed from the outside, he chooses among disciplines born of the existing system of university chairs, which maintains the rigidity and meaninglessness of a classification of knowledge that no longer seems functional for any present-day cultural and social models. The choice proposed to the student is on the whole apparent; it tends to free the school system from its responsibilities of guaranteeing *directly* through academic credentials the exchange value for the schooling provided. Whether there is diploma inflation or the abolition of all academic credentials, social stratification will continue to be reproduced outside of the school system according to the exigencies of the labor market and the organization of consent. The functions and mechanisms will remain unchanged.

But if these outcomes appear difficult for the capitalists, they are no less so for any "reformist" proposal that does not challenge the very principle upon which the school system is founded. Up until now, the reformism of the Left has been founded on the fundamental hypothesis that the school system is a social service, or "good," to be more widely allocated among the underprivileged social strata; but it is not perceived that this position ends up demanding nothing more than equal opportunity for entrance into a mechanism of social selection. In a capitalist society, any extension of educational opportunity—whether through extending the instruments or means for study, or even through enlarging the student

salary system—will confront an inextricable contradiction, which is the following: we cannot deny workers and farmers ever-increasing educational opportunity, but neither can we offer to them greater educational opportunity without this transforming them into something other than they are, at their own expense, and against their own class interests; moreover, this will merely reproduce the lower social strata, which are destined to produce the wealth and to occupy the lowest occupational positions.

In short, there is no "progressive use" for an instrument designed to perpetuate a society of privileges. Even the hypothesis—derived from a choice made by Communists in 1964 who at least had enough lucidity to pose the problem—hardly appears consistent. It was originally formulated to come to grips with the "insatiable" educational growth that would consequently create explosive tensions throughout the system. But the hypothesis was set up on a misunderstanding of an implicit acceptance of social stratification and consequently its reproduction by the model of modernization; it was also based upon the mistaken prediction that one could create within the university student or graduate a revolutionary consciousness that would stem from the incapacity of the system to regulate the development of productive forces. Indeed, each policy of the reform and democratization of schools that views them as composing a separate body or a mechanism of selection cannot refrain from more or less consciously accepting one of the two outlets proposed by the capitalists; in short, they all end up being policies "within" the system and can find no other expression except in the renaissance of a "student unionism" where students demand *strong* credentials and the instruments that permit them to utilize their intellectual resources in order to obtain them. Whether we like it or not, one can even "unionize" the directives that appeared revolutionary in 1967 and 1968: participation or dual power, co-management or student assemblies, point system or final examinations are contradictory only in appearance and can just as easily become various modes of continuing the management of schools as producers and reproducers of social stratification. Bear in mind, for example, how the significance of the struggle for the final exam system was reversed: at first it began as an egalitarian demand for abolishing discriminatory evaluation criteria, but it was transformed along the way into the easiest means of obtaining academic credentials.

In brief, schools cannot be reformed unless the function for which they were created is abolished. There was keen awareness—not "ideological" but profoundly significant nonetheless—in the student protest movement that it was impossible to reform the educational institution and use it for revolutionary purposes. This, because since the beginning of the modern bourgeois state, we have never known any other type of educational system, even in the European socialist societies, where the selection process in education unfortunately continues to operate. Strip away this essential characteristic from the school system and this separate body would decompose and manifest its inability to socialize children and to transmit non-commercialized knowledge and skills. Schools, as such, must be abolished.

AN ALTERNATIVE STRATEGY

Upon what basis could an *alternative* strategy, a *political* movement for schools be built? What should be its final objective? What should be its immediate program for action?

The end objective must be nothing less than one of doing away with schools that function as instruments of selection for hierarchical social positions, and consequently also doing away with schools as a "separate body." This would require a radical reorganization of two functions, *education* and *transmission of knowledge,* which are necessary for every society, and which hitherto have been fulfilled by schools. These two

components are irreducible; they cannot be reduced to one or the other as was polemically done during the first phase of the student protest movement when the second was absorbed by the first; they are both necessary. Indeed, every society has need of a value system. Non-ideological history does not exist, and each community must define for itself a goal and "organize consensus" around it. This means evaluating the nature of the ends to determine their propensity for human oppression or emancipation. As for *knowledge,* though it is true that knowledge is always a historical product, not neutral but marked by the system that creates it, it is nonetheless equally true that knowledge— as an acquired mastery of nature and as man's self-reflective thought—represents an objective element around which there is confrontation and which is something that one cannot abolish, just as one cannot abolish the situation inherited from the development of productive forces, or from the milieu, or from bio-physiology. Neither in the destruction of history nor in his own "naturalness" can man rediscover an intrinsic and innocent positiveness. If it is true that this dream of Rousseau can be found in every popular revolution, it, itself, is nonetheless an ideological product. Similarly, immense confusion between the social and technical divisions of labor has been created by the failure to see that during the course of the different productive phases the latter constitutes a process charged with an objectivity that determines, among other things, the moment of proletarianization for those who participate in it. The earliest positions of the student movement, despite the explicit reference to the importance of the "cultural revolution," here diverge from the richest part of Mao's thinking; it is Mao who sees the "destructive" moment, intrinsic to proletarian culture, resulting from the decomposition and the highly accentuated creation of a new synthesis of concrete experience. This represents, on the whole, the dialectics of cultural "rebellion" in contrast to the exaltation of the "tabula rasa" in non-utilitarian education, which represents the terrain of the new and crudest ideological traps.

Now, returning to our first point, *education* (which tends to coincide with elementary schooling)—this process could clearly be ensured by the community as an undifferentiated body rather than by schools in a separate place for learning. In large part, education is already carried out in this manner: the process of socializing the child takes place in large measure outside of schools; it is carried out by the family, the milieu, and the mass media that surround the child. In a community capable of "education"—that is to say, a politically conscious community—this process would be carried out through an "operative" relation and in a more unified manner. The different types of job preparation would be based on the fact that the more the child lives in a system of *real* relationships, and not purely ideological ones, the more complete and the less distorted the process of socialization would be. The elementary notions furnished by schools would find direct expression in daily community activities: reading, writing, and doing math, plus an entire framework of metrical, geographical, and temporal notions would be firmly fitted into social praxis, from which, moreover, they derive and of which they constitute generalized and classified forms. If education is to be considered as "socialization" (and all existing pedagogical theories consider it as such), then it is not clear why the community should entrust education to the "expert." Delegating education in this manner is like considering the socialization of the child as a process set apart, as something different and relatively mystified (e.g., "the world of childhood" is largely an artificial construction); in like manner, the transmission of *knowledge* by means of fragmented and arbitrary notions (a little ancient history, some "science," and a little poetry) must also be reconsidered since these notions do not correspond either to the experience of the community (which rightfully ignores such notions), or to a real

level of consciousness. The apprehensiveness found in elementary students is due to the fact that the child experiences with keen awareness that the school inculcates in him a consciousness of mediocre value, if not purely fantastic or mnemonic; at the same time, it obstructs him from generalizing his world of experience "outside" of the school. And, indeed, the sole thing that will remain imprinted in the child from this "formative schooling," will be the techniques of reading, writing, and arithmetic, as well as fragments of socialization given to him by his more or less happy relationship with the mediator of the milieu and the culture, his teacher. All the rest will be forgotten— progressively erased by *real* knowledge.

Certainly, the atomized and mass-produced whole that constitutes today's social body cannot become an educative community; only a recomposed and therefore "political" community can become that. China demonstrates for us this possibility: there, not only can schools be temporarily closed, but the material impossibility of providing schooling for everyone can be anticipated, without this slowing down learning, and even with an "increase in knowledge." Moreover, even in societies such as our own, the few advanced experiments being carried out try to break down the frontiers of the "schooling site," or, as in Barbiana, to transform the school into something other than itself. All progressive pedagogical theories aim to find expression in the idea of "non-separation." They therefore try to destroy the myth of the necessity of considering the teacher-pedagogue as an expert.

Here is a point that always provokes profound indignation within the teacher corps. Rarely do we meet a professional profile so openly separatist because of its "competence"—that is, its "objective" relations—but at the same time so convinced of its irreplaceable role in society.[1] It is, however, common knowledge that schools produce teachers but do not form the teacher; this is no less the case for the teacher-training colleges, which, in spite of their objectives, are generally considered useless, or for universities, which produce university graduates who can enter teaching if they like, since university graduation meets the hiring requirement in elementary and secondary schools. Teaching itself is not an object of knowledge; it is therefore not a knowledge but rather a social status and a function, which, since the time of the reformist tradition (the schoolmaster as the heart and intelligence of the village—and his opposite, the sadistic pedagogue of Dickens), has been recognized and standardized by the state bureaucracy. Paradoxically, the most delicate of socialization processes is thus entrusted to this closed and autonomous professional category, which possesses a solid esprit de corps and maintains extraordinary differences in age, in ways of reacting, and in communication between the teacher and the student. An *invasion* of the school by the community whereby secondary school seniors and university beginners would tutor the younger students (in a non-institutional vision of the *giornata scolastica integrata*—the integrated schoolday) would succeed in breaking down the present-day rigidity of the educative relationship and would render to education a new mobility, because the educative process and a series of infinitely richer experiences of socialization would be reciprocally brought together. Moreover, almost all of the socialist countries started their experiences in this manner (but unfortunately, save China, forgot it later on): the "mass literacy" campaign launched immediately after the Revolution in Cuba represented a moment when the "school died" and "education lived," and when an extraordinary exchange of social techniques and knowledge, irreplaceable by the most modern and perfected pedagogical center, occurred.[2] In our present-day societies, this kind of occurrence can be reproduced at the initiative of a political community, student or not. But in order to avoid committing the error made by the student movement, which consisted of

horizontally separating the different levels of schooling (or of classes), we must try to remodel the educational experience vertically for the whole of schooling, and this in liaison with the "outside" avant-garde of the factory or the neighborhood. Here is a process that is immediately possible and that would represent a concrete and positive "assault on the institution" by achieving political growth and restructuring.

It is less likely, even in the long run, that we can succeed in directly managing without differentiation the elaboration and transmission of knowledge that, as an expanding body of learning, is not expected to be fully grasped by each individual; rather, it must be recomposed through the exchange of experiences from various sectors. Indeed, the current trend towards the "specialist" is of course largely arbitrary since it is expressed in the social rather than the technical division of labor. It is therefore undoubtedly correct to aim at synthetically recomposing knowledge: however, the sum of these cognitive acquisitions and their rate of growth will require separate types of formation and elaboration, not only at present, but also well beyond the end of the social division of labor. Even the "omni-dimensional man" will be replaced by a learning experience mediated by the community as a cultural experience of the "other."

But does this mean subjection to a painful and inevitable limitation? Here again it is necessary to avoid giving an ideological or crudely idealistic interpretation of egalitarianism; that would transform the political plan into a kind of undifferentiated generalization. On this point Marx makes himself perfectly clear. As a matter of fact, the reconstituting of a more advanced and articulated level of knowledge takes on a dialectically positive impetus when the linkage with material advantage and social prestige relative to the "power" of intellectuals is broken. In this sense, why not then imagine a moment for transmitting and elaborating specific skills that could also intervene at given moments and in given places? After all, it seems to us that the destruction of the school and its entire reabsorption into the social community should be carried out in a first phase that would be the moment of *education.* Afterwards, the formation that would follow would not only be carried out on a homogeneous body of students who are highly disposed towards exchanging ideas and relations; nor would it simply imply a form of labor that, being linked to work, would gradually replace the social image of the student with one of a *worker who also studies;* but by having decisively broken all traces of the authoritarian master-apprentice relationship, it would invest with significance an exchange between different levels of experience.

But above all we must consider that in a society of transition this different movement can be imprinted into the formation of knowledge as well as into its transmission. The effort towards liquidating social stratification and politically recomposing all of society through the struggle between new and old relations of production implies a radical resetting of priorities, a change in the technical division of labor, and thereby the dissolution of old professions and the creation of new competences. This consequently also implies a reclassification of culture—in the same way that the phase of the rising bourgeoisie witnessed not simply the abolition of feudal social forms, but also a total decomposition and recomposition of the framework of knowledge, which henceforth would be oriented towards different fields and would carry a "destructive" critique of those archaic models.[3]

This destructive critique is already appearing in the qualitative as well as quantitative crisis of "high culture"; it finds expression in the uncertainty of professionalism, and in the tightly paralyzing effect of present-day relations of production and types of social organization derived from cultural and scientific developments. This crisis is not expressing itself in an "evolutionary" sense—which would already be positive—as a latent potential harboring new cultural and scientific models demanding to be liberated; it is appearing as an intolerance of culture towards itself and towards the surrounding world, and as a rejection of its own one-dimensionality in "crisis" and "labor pains." The development of knowledge generates a critique of its own acquisitions and contents, and finally leads to a "sorrowful self-consciousness" without prospects.

It seems to us that it is here that the direct political liaison between the revolutionary student and worker movements is to be situated. Neither one of the two can separately confront the common goal of destroying social privilege: students cannot resolve at the university the problem of abolishing present-day professional functions, since these reflect a crisis not only in the contents and methods of knowledge, but also in the general disposition of society; workers cannot hope to accomplish a social revolution without confronting the problem that schools reproduce "capitalist" forms, roles, and relations that are permanent and inherent in the social division of labor. In this sense, it seems to us that the proposition put forth by Vittorio Foa[4] indicates a positive direction; that is, the gradual unifying of "the student in the worker." But in implementation, this proposition cannot be freed from every conceivable type of "demand for the right to study," perceived as professional or individual advancement, unless contact between the school and the factory is not confined to the level of the *person* of the student; rather, it must include a reciprocal critique and destruction of the mechanism that underpins present-day social organization of work and that is reflected not only in the selection process but also in the contents of education.

How can this take place in practice? First, by analyzing the double character of the professional profile, its *technical competence* and its *hierarchical function;* second, by analyzing the historical reality and the functionality of this competence as an objective moment of the technical division of labor; finally, by analyzing the process of the *collective organization of labor,* which itself appears riddled with authoritarian and repressive "objectivity" and "managerial functionality." If, as Garavini observes,[5] it is correct that these processes cannot be assimilated, and that the present-day organization of the capitalist process will eventually tend to attenuate the significance of the "technical" moment in favor of the "managerial" moment (in this sense, one would need an undifferentiated and functional preparation of the worker), it is equally true that this analysis must be based upon the productive unit. In other words, the social truth of the student's professional profile can become apparent to him only if he analyzes it from *outside* the school and together with the protagonists of the productive unit (or in social places where competences are put to use)—this, because it is only in the concrete that we can determine the continually changing degree of objectivity of the *technical* division of labor (as much from the angle of the individual as from that of the collective process) and the hierarchical redundancy of occupational functions and managerial organization. This analysis will show that every qualification of profession—which is more apparent in business than in other fields—is beset by the double force of interaction between the nucleus of "skills" and that of "values" (i.e., between knowledge and social function), which are always in a precarious equilibrium between equalization and differentiation, integration and reciprocal challenge.

By this analysis, the "objective" and "technical" moments of competence, and above all of its formation (by the school, the study program, etc.), will appear in a novel way. This is because the hierarchical moment is rooted not only in teaching methods but also within the contents of apprenticeship, just as the student movement had perceived. This critical work demystifies the "professor" in the eyes of the student just as in the eyes of the technician and the worker. It is a *common labor*— as our worker-student collective experiment in Bologna demonstrates—that is neither

parallel, nor rooted in solidarity, nor long-term, but nevertheless at the heart of the proletarian condition of the worker and the technical condition of the student, that requires the worker and the student to transcend the level of simply making union-type demands; it is the very natures of the factory and of the school—common participants in the formation of the same social mechanism of stratification—that must be challenged.

By this work that consists both of heightening self-consciousness and of struggle a student and worker movement can be *specifically* defined. This work can also be carried out, and more easily so, at other professional levels—from that of the medical doctor to that of the architect—even if they are more undifferentiated with respect to the exemplary character of the productive unit. Not only can it demystify these professions and restore to them their true technical dimension; it can also remodel the technical dimension by transcending the immediately projected needs as they appear *today*. In short, in the difficult struggle of exposing and destroying the multiple relations that operate and accompany the mode of capitalist production, a different organization of social necessities, and therefore of methods (not only of social groups and of the specific relations of production, but also of needs, of knowledge, and of professional profiles), must take shape. The alternative can be created only in the fire of social transformation. But this has already started in present-day struggles and in the reality of the different social levels where the project for the society of tomorrow (an alternative vision that implies the destruction of the old social relations) must be formed. Furthermore, nothing but the level of consciousness and of struggle today can determine that project; it cannot be delegated to some "after the revolution" policy without reproducing the necessity for an identical revolution.

Thus, by rejecting the reformist hypothesis we are able today to define a political line for, or rather against, schools. By rejecting the original sin of modern schools as the reproducers of social inequality, we can recreate unity between workers and students. It is not by chance that, since the development of Italian society, this unity has never been achieved on the terrain of school modernization. No one collaborates in order to tighten his own chains; at least the working class has the wisdom to avoid such folly.

NOTES

1. On this subject, see the excellent survey by Marzio Barbagli and Marcello Dei, *Le Vestali della classe media* (Bologna: Il Mulino, 1969).
2. It should be noted that the "literacy campaign" was not carried out by an ideologically unified avant-garde. The revolution had hardly been won and had not yet specified its socialist option. The preparation for the instructors and the young volunteers was improvised on the work-site itself. The campaign took place under the conditions of bitter conflict; some young persons were killed. It remains nevertheless the high point of the political *formation* of the Cuban revolution and represents, according to UNESCO, a unique date in the rapid and global defeat of illiteracy.
3. It is strange that the commentaries scandalized by the "cultural revolution" in China always overlook the length of time that accompanies all radical cultural change. The contempt of the Renaissance for the Middle Ages, or of the Enlightenment for the preceding age, the tendentious style of the Encyclopaedists—attributed by modern criticism to the absence of a historical dimension—these are "childbirth" phenomena of history, not without pain and of a new dimension. There were considerably many more Madonnas smashed to bits in the nooks of cathedrals during the French Revolution than there were Buddhas shattered by the Red Guards.
4. See the introduction by Vittorio Foa in *I lavoratori studenti* (Turin: Einaudi, 1969).
5. See the mimeographed report by Sergio Garavini for the meeting of Communist students at Ariccia on November 2, 1969.

Kautsky, 633n
Kazamias, Andreas M., 61n
Kearney, H.F., 150n
Keddie, Nell, 50n, 53, 54, 56n, 58, 60
Keech, William R., 270n
Keeves, John P., 276, 279-281
Keniston, Kenneth, 31n, 251n, 371n, 435, 442, 448n
Kennedy, John F., 618
Kenyatta, J., 150n
Kenyon, Frederic G., 472n
Kerr, Clark, 119, 336, 433
Keyfitz, Nathan, 185n
Keynes, J. M., 5
Khrushchev, Nikita, 255, 256, 270n,
Kifer, E., 298
Kilpatrick, W.H., 109, 116n
Kindleberger, C., 354n
King, E.J., 164n
King, Prudence, 25n
Kirk, G.S., 472n, 473n
Kirst, Michael W., 367, 370n, 372, 411n
Kitsuse, John I., 164n, 166n, 171, 282, 293, 294
Klein, Melanie, 529
Klönne, A., 432n
Kogan, L., 297
Kogan, Maurice, 367, 371
Kohn, Melvin, 33, 38n, 152n, 153n, 454
Kolesnikov, Iu., 272n
Kolko, Gabriel, 235, 411n
Korman, Gerd, 386n
Kossakovsky, I., 272n
Köttgen, Arnold, 544n
Kozyrev, Iu. N., 268, 272n, 274n
Kriege, 616
Krug, Edward A., 385n, 386n
Krupenina, M.V., 572n
Krupskaia, N.K. (see Lenin)
Kuhn, Thomas S., 4n, 29, 59
Kulagin, Georgi, 262, 272n
Kuzin, N.P., 270n

Labov, William, 66n
Lacey, Colin, 28, 46, 53n, 60n, 172
Ladinsky, Jack, 118, 124, 129
Lane, David, 269n, 270n, 552n
Lang, G., 297
Lapidus, Gail, 271n
Lassevell, 226
Lasswell, Harold, 569
Lauter, Paul, 232n
Lawton, Dennis, 64n
Layard, Richard, 15n, 310n
Lazarsfeld, 4
Lazerson, Marvin, 43n, 89n, 151n, 152n, 248, 251n, 368, 373, 385n, 386n
Leach, Edmund, 166n
Leacock, Eleanor Burke, 21n, 297

Learned, W.S., 122
Leavitt, Frank M., 385n
Lehrer, Leibush, 386n
Leiner, Marvin, 573, 576, 577, 586n, 587n
Lemert, E., 293, 295, 300
Lenin, Krupskaia, 558, 561-563, 568, 571n, 572n
Lenin, V.I., 272n, 552, 556-571, 572n
Leonard, 379
Leonavichius, Iu., 272n
Leontieff, Wassily, 635n
Levin, Henry, 411n
Levinson, Harold, 336
Lévi-Strauss, Claude, 471n, 472n
Levitas, Maurice, 66n
Levy, Marion J., 9n
Lévy-Bruhl, 466, 470, 472n
Lewis, H., 152n
Lewis, Oscar, 231n
Lexis, Wilhelm, 544n
Li, C.C., 214n
Lieberman, Myron, 115n
Light, Richard J., 170n, 216n
Lilge, Frederic, 269n, 552, 556
Lin Piao, 602, 606
Linton, 173, 175
Lippmann, Walter, 411n
Lipset, Seymour M., 118, 153n, 166n, 196, 232n, 235, 250n, 270n, 273n, 274n, 354n, 371n, 422n
Lisovskii, V.T., 274n
Liss, L.F., 271n
Litkens, 568
Litt, Edgar, 25n
Little, Alan, 46, 60n, 185n
Little, J. Kenneth, 214n
Litvinov, L.F., 270n
Liu Shao-ch'i, 553, 591, 592
Livingstone, Richard, 645n
Llewellyn, Catriona, 184n
Locke, John, 615, 616, 620, 623
Lockwood, David, 28, 165n
Loeb, M.B., 297
Lofland, J., 293
Lombard, George F., 123
Lombardini, S., 355n
Long, Durwood, 442, 448n
Lopate, Carol, 40
Lortic, Marie-France, 312
Lothstein, Arthur, 232n
Lowell, Abbott Lawrence, 401, 410n
Lowi, Theodore J., 411n
Lucas, Robert E.B., 309n
Luckman, Thomas, 45, 48
Lukacs, Georg, 37n
Lukes, Steven, 43n, 368n, 646n
Lunacharskii, A.V., 561, 563, 564, 568, 571, 572n
Lunt, P.S., 152n
Luria, A.R., 478

Please remember that this is a library book,
and that it belongs only temporarily to each
person who uses it. Be considerate. Do
not write in this, or any, library book.

Date Due

FE 26 02			
JE 21 '08			
ILL 10/23/09			